U.S. GO HOME

The U.S. Military in France
1945 to 1968

M. DAVID EGAN
and
JEAN EGAN

Illustrations by Charles W. Tilley

Front cover photo: French and American flags lowered for the final time on March 14, 1967, at Camp des Loges, near St.-Germain-en-Laye, France. *NDU Archives*

U.S. GO HOME: The U.S. Military in France, 1945 to 1968 / by M. David Egan and Jean Egan

Copyright © 2022 by M. David Egan and Jean Egan

Library of Congress Control Number: 2020952772

All rights reserved. No part of this work may be reproduced or used in any form or by any means—graphic, electronic, or mechanical, including photocopying or information storage and retrieval systems—without written permission from the publisher.

The scanning, uploading, and distribution of this book or any part thereof via the Internet or any other means without the permission of the publisher is illegal and punishable by law. Please purchase only authorized editions and do not participate in or encourage the electronic piracy of copyrighted materials.

"Schiffer Military" and the arrow logo are trademarks of Schiffer Publishing, Ltd.

Type set in Komu A/Garamond

ISBN: 978-0-7643-6267-5
Printed in India

Published by Schiffer Publishing, Ltd.
4880 Lower Valley Road
Atglen, PA 19310
Phone: (610) 593-1777; Fax: (610) 593-2002
E-mail: Info@schifferbooks.com
Web: www.schifferbooks.com

For our complete selection of fine books on this and related subjects, please visit our website at www.schifferbooks.com. You may also write for a free catalog.

Schiffer Publishing's titles are available at special discounts for bulk purchases for sales promotions or premiums. Special editions, including personalized covers, corporate imprints, and excerpts, can be created in large quantities for special needs. For more information, contact the publisher.

We are always looking for people to write books on new and related subjects. If you have an idea for a book, please contact us at proposals@schifferbooks.com.

CONTENTS

	Dedication, Authors, and Illustrator	iv
	Preface	v
1	Turbulent Period after World War II	1
2	NATO and SHAPE in Paris	31
3	US Military Forces Return	67
4	Construction for US Military	111
5	US European Command and Military Assistance	137
6	NATO and US Military in Fontainebleau	179
7	US Army Commands and Agencies in Orléans	211
8	Medical Care and Standby Hospitals for Wartime	255
9	Advance Section in the Northeast	275
10	Army Ports and Over the Beach Exercises	339
11	Base Section in the Southwest	423
12	Fast Withdrawal from France	489
	Chronology of US Military in France (1949–68)	520
	References / Notes	523
	Acknowledgements (Interviewees, Reviewers, Archives)	587
	Index	591

DEDICATED to THOSE WHO SERVED IN THE COLD WAR

"The oath you swore on enlistment, expires in a sense when your term is ended, but the oath you should and did take in your heart, knows no discharge, no term of service, for the man who has served his country is not as other lesser men, who have not shared our code, our job and our ideals. Good health, good luck, and a safe journey to you all."

(Goodbye message to departing troops from Lt Col John M. Stoddard, US Army, Depot Commander, St. Pryvé-St. Mesmin, France, November 1952.)

"Nous n'oublierons jamais l'aide américaine pour la liberté durant la Guerre Froide." We will never forget America's aid for freedom during the Cold War.

(Retired French Air Force Col Pierre-Alain Antoine, F-100 Super Sabre pilot at former USAF Toul-Rosières AB. Interview, Paris, France, 09 December 2015.)

THE AUTHORS

M. David Egan, graduate of Lafayette College and MIT, is Distinguished Professor of the Association of Collegiate Schools of Architecture, Professor Emeritus at Clemson University, and holds the Doctor of Laws degree (Honoris Causa). His seven architectural books are available in nine languages. From 1962 to 1964, he served with the US Army in France where he commanded the 39th Ordnance Co at Trois-Fontaines (Marne). He is a member of the Society for Military History (SMH), the US Commission on Military History, and the Cercle National des Armées, Paris, France.

D. Jean Egan, graduate of Louisiana State University, is an independent scholar. She edited five technical books for architects and engineers, published by McGraw-Hill and Wiley-Interscience. She is a member of MIT's Katharine Dexter McCormick Society, the Society for Military History (SMH), and the Council on America's Military Past (CAMP).

THE ILLUSTRATOR

Charles W. Tilley, graduate of Clemson University with a Bachelor of Science in Design and Master of Architecture, is a principal at an award-winning design firm in Richmond, Virginia. He has received the "Alice L. Sunday Prize" for excellence in graphics awarded by the AIA Richmond Chapter (VA) of the American Institute of Architects (AIA). He illustrated *Architectural Acoustics Workbook* (2000), available from the Acoustical Society of America.

PREFACE

Western leaders believed that the invasion of South Korea on 25 June 1950 was part of a Soviet plan to conquer the world. They feared the Soviet Union, which had rebuilt its troop strength to World War II levels, planned to invade Western Europe. The US had rapidly demobilized after the war and Europe was recovering from the devastation of war. To resist military aggression by the Soviets, the United States would rebuild its military, establish joint military commands with its NATO allies, and insert forces into Europe. The buildup of an enormous network of ports, depots, and air bases in France began in late 1950. On 07 January 1951, Gen Dwight D. Eisenhower arrived in Paris to become the first Supreme Commander of NATO forces. More than sixty Army Guard and Reserve units and ten Air Guard units were sent to France. By 1958, there were nearly 100,000 US military personnel and dependents in France. In the early years, troops lived in tents and worked in the mud. Families rented homes that were poorly heated and rarely had indoor toilets. Wives were advised not to use water unless it had been boiled or treated with chlorine tablets.

During the long deployment to France, the US military was a deterrent to Soviet aggression and responded to crises such as: the civil war in Lebanon, construction of the Berlin Wall, and initial buildup of forces in Vietnam. US Army depots in France processed thousands of wheeled and tracked vehicles to rearm France and other allies. A huge air depot at Châteauroux stocked parts and repaired NATO aircraft. Each month to support US Seventh Army in Germany, 70,000 tons of matériel were shipped from the US to France. From 1952 to 1962, forty-eight ship discharge exercises were held to move cargo and troops over beaches, testing a dozen locations from St.-Jean-de-Luz near Spain to Quiberon in Brittany. The US military in France also provided aid when natural disasters occurred in Europe, Africa, and the Middle East.

In March 1966, French President Charles de Gaulle asked the US military to withdraw from France by mid-1967. The US government acted surprised, portraying de Gaulle's request as a lack of gratitude by France. De Gaulle's decision was influenced by: policy differences over nuclear defense of Europe, unfavorable provisions in US basing agreements with France compared to those the US had with other NATO nations, and adverse economic impact when the US military abruptly fired thousands of French employees at bases it closed in 1963. For the French people, the communist-inspired slogan "U.S. Go Home" had become "We Want Our Jobs."

The withdrawal of nearly one million tons of supplies and equipment from France would be the largest peacetime exercise of transportation by land, sea, and air ever undertaken by US military forces. In less than a year, what had taken nearly two decades to build would be abandoned or disassembled and moved to other NATO nations. More than four-hundred US military bases, installations, and facilities on sites from Bordeaux through the Loire valley and Paris regions to Alsace-Lorraine were closed.

Fifty years after the withdrawal, the French used many of the former US military air bases, depots, hospitals, K-12 schools, and housing villages. The thousands of buildings bear witness to the American period as do the fond memories of the tens of thousands of French workers. They also served to keep the peace and freedom in Europe. After the Americans departed, the French Air Force used the former US Air Force base at Toul-Rosières for more than three decades. In the 1990s Padre Gérard Derule, French chaplain of the base, wrote a series of journal articles in *Reflets* on the history of Toul-Rosières. Derule appealed to his flock to remember the Americans "who came from the other side of the Atlantic Ocean to help us retain our liberty."

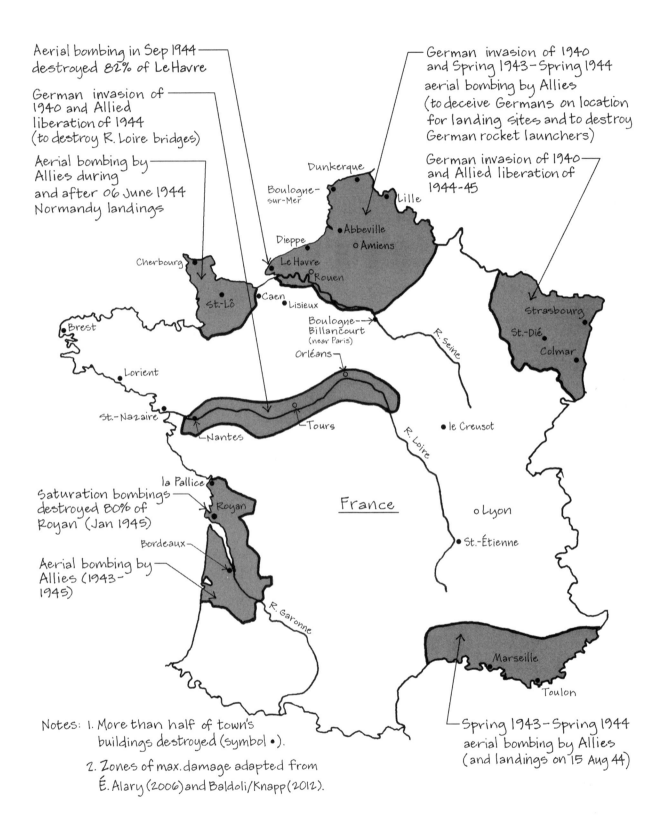

Areas of Greatest Destruction from Bombing (WWII)

ONE

Turbulent Period after World War II

"Disperse in open country…You have not a minute to lose."
(US Eighth Air Force leaflet dropped over Normandy, 06 June 1944)

France after the Liberation

On 07 May 1945, Germany signed unconditional surrender documents at a school building in Reims, France. The war in Europe had ended, but it would take years to repair the destruction from the German invasion and occupation and from the battles of liberation. Général Charles de Gaulle formed a government to replace the Vichy government which had collaborated with the Germans. Food had been rationed, Jews sent to death camps, and young Frenchmen forced to work in Germany. After liberation, matériel of war lay rusting on the former battlefields, numerous abandoned airfields were scattered along the routes of liberation, and internment camps once used to confine French Jews and political prisoners now held German prisoners of war.

Bomb destruction, St.-Lô, 1944 (US Army)

Bomb Destruction of World War II

During World War II, more than 400,000 buildings in France were completely destroyed; more than 1.3 million partially destroyed. Nearly 20% of the important works of architecture were completely destroyed or severely damaged.[1,2] In the northern French departments of the Pas de Calais and the Nord, more than 70,000 structures were destroyed or damaged. The destruction primarily was due to the German invasion of 1940 and the aerial bombing by the Allies before the D-Day landings on 06 June 1944.[3] The sustained aerial bombing of the north was intended to convince the Germans that the Allies would land in Pas de Calais. At St.-Lô, south of the actual landing beaches in Normandy, nearly eight-hundred civilians died from the bombing on D-Day. The goal in part was to destroy the town so its rubble would create a "choke point" to impede movement of German forces. More than a dozen French towns were destroyed to create choke points, which the Germans bypassed.[4]

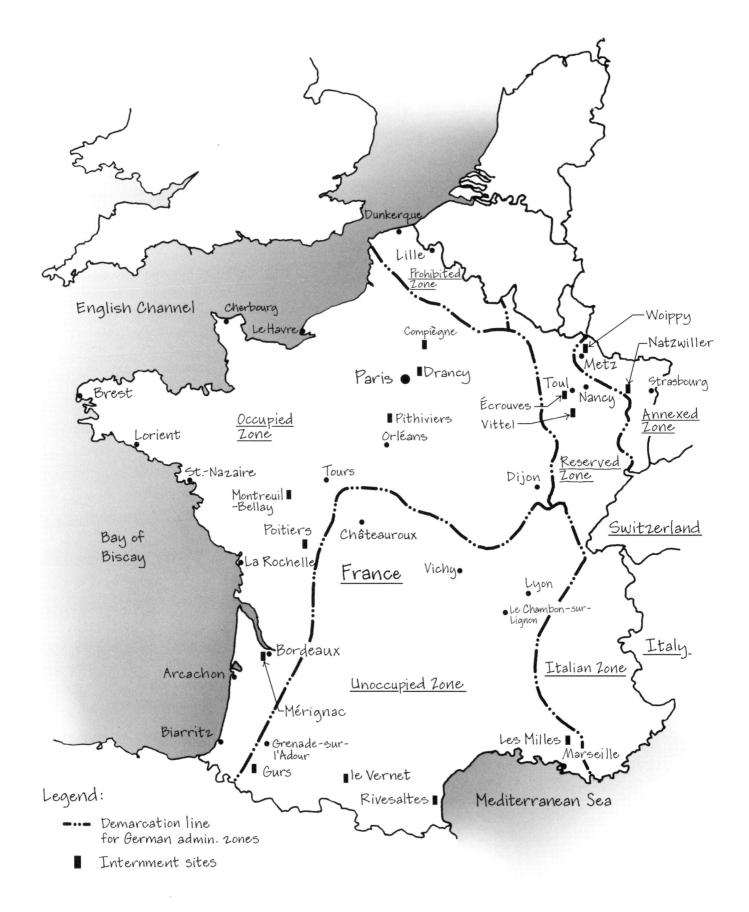

German Zones in Occupied France (1940-44)

On 06 June 1944, US Eighth Air Force bombers began dropping leaflets over numerous towns and villages in Normandy. The leaflets, written in French, urged the inhabitants to leave the danger zone of transportation centers and move to the countryside. The message on D-Day concluded: "You have not a minute to lose." [5]

The Allies targeted manufacturing plants, power plants, and transportation hubs; repeatedly bombing rail yards, bridges, and ports. The Germans repaired bomb-damaged runways, roads, and railroad tracks within days, but it took weeks to repair most of the damaged bridges. During high-altitude bombing missions, visibility often was poor and accuracy of gravity bombs always poor. The British War Cabinet estimated that only one in three bombs in 1941 landed within five miles of the target.[6] During Allied bombing raids from 1940 to 1945, more than 54,000 French civilians were killed and more than half of the buildings in numerous cities and villages were destroyed or damaged. Before D-Day, aerial bombing killed 1,262 French railroad employees.[7-10] Areas near German submarine pens at Brest, Lorient, St.-Nazaire, la Pallice, Bordeaux, and Marseille sustained massive damage.[11] In early January 1945, British bombing raids destroyed most of Royan, killing more than five-hundred civilians.[12] Three months later from 14 through 16 April, US bombers dropped napalm and other bombs on Royan, leaving the town in ruins. Although accuracy improved later in the war, the US estimated that only 40% of Allied bombs fell within 1,500 ft of the target.[13]

Vichy Government

After the defeat of France in 1940, Germany divided the country into zones. Germans governed four zones. A forbidden area for non-residents extended 5 to 12 miles inland along the coast from Dunkerque to Biarritz. A French government, located in Vichy, governed the Free Zone in the south. On 10 July 1940, the French National Assembly had voted to replace its Third Republic by a French State government. In December 1940, Germany renamed the Free Zone the Unoccupied Zone. In November 1942, the Germans occupied all of France, except the Italian Zone. It became a refuge for Jews because the Italians would not cooperate with the German roundup of Jews.[14] In September 1943, the Germans took control of the Italian Zone.

The Germans and the collaborating Vichy government confiscated Jewish property. Contents of about 30,000 homes of Jews were shipped to Germany. Before the occupation, France had been a refuge for Jews fleeing Germany. The Vichy authorities assisted in identification of Jews, but only Jews in the occupied zones were made to wear a yellow Star of David sewn on their clothing.[15] The star identified them as persons not permitted in most public places.

Deportation of Jews

Jews were deported from all occupied areas of Western Europe. The south of France was the only non-occupied area from which Jews were deported. About 76,000 Jews were deported to death camps in Germany or France. At le Struthof camp, near Natzwiller in the Annexed Zone of Alsace, prisoners were murdered during medical experiments.[16] There were more than four-hundred sites for internment in France. The Vichy government had fifteen principal internment camps; the Germans had twenty-six in the occupied zones. Drancy near Paris was the assembly camp for deportation to the death camps in Germany.

Responding to German orders to round up Jews in the summer of 1942, Vichy authorities included children to meet German quotas. René Bousquet, head of the Vichy police, deported more than 4,000 Jewish children to Auschwitz. It is believed that fewer than 5% of the Jews deported from France survived to return home after the war.[17] In 1940 there were 330,000 Jews in France, about 250,000 were saved because French men and women risked torture and execution by hiding Jews or helping them escape to Spain or Switzerland.[18] Thousands of Frenchman looked the other way when strangers, obviously Jews evading deportation, moved into their villages.[19]

Jews Deported From France to Death Camps[20]

Year	Number of Deportees	Deportees who Returned in 1945*
1942	41,951	1,248
1943	17,069	654
1944	14,833	2,041

* A. Doulut et al., *Mémorial des 3943 rescapés juifs de France*, The Beate Klarsfeld Foundation, Paris, France (2018), p. 23.

From late April to August 1945, French Général Charles de Gaulle's provisional government processed returning deportees at the renowned Hôtel Lutétia on Boulevard Raspail, Paris. After liberation, Vichy authorities claimed they had served as a shield to protect France from even greater suffering.[21] During the occupation, about 2 million French soldiers were held prisoner in Germany. The Vichy government sent about 600,000 young men to Germany for forced labor, called *Service du Travail Obligatoire*.[22] Although the anti-Semitism of the Vichy government appealed to many Frenchmen, the vast majority were between the morally courageous who opposed the Vichy government, like Charles de Gaulle, and those who supported collaboration.[23,24] During the twelve months following liberation more than 20,000 Frenchmen were executed without trials, ostensibly for collaboration. About eight-hundred were executed after a trial.[25,26] Very few Vichy government officials were punished for their role in mass murder. Maurice Papon was convicted fifty years after liberation, but served only 35 months in jail. Papon, whose work in deporting Jews was praised by the Nazis, served as a budget minister in a French government during the Cold War.

French Resisters

Resistance to the German occupation occured in twenty-two mountain villages on the Plateau Vivarais-Lignon, south of Lyon. More than eight-hundred Jewish children were saved by Christian villagers who hid the children in their homes and farms, often at remote locations inaccessible in winter. For safety the children pretended to be Christians, but the villagers did not try to convert them.[27] The leaders at le Chambon and Fay-sur-Lignon were Dr. Bernard Le Forestier and Protestant pastors André Trocmé, Edouard Theis, and Daniel Curtet. Contributing factors to saving the children were that Préfet Robert Bach and local gendarmes were discretely anti-German and the German military contingent at Le Puy was not Gestapo. Most were Wehrmacht soldiers convalescing from wounds received on the Eastern front. During this period, villagers helped an estimated 3,000 refugees escape from France, most to nearby Switzerland. In 1990, Yad Vashem Institute in Israel awarded the Medal of the Righteous to the village of le Chambon-sur-Lignon (Haute-Loire).[28]

In Grenade-sur-l'Adour (Landes), French businessman Raoul Laporterie saved more than 1,000 Jews from death camps. Laporterie, mayor of the mostly Catholic town of Bascons and owner of four clothing stores in the Landes region, gave refugees false identification papers using names from graveyards at Bascons and a nearby village. He took risks believing that neither his *réseau* (network) nor the Basconnais would betray him. To help the Allies plan the invasion of France, in early 1944 Laporterie, disguised as an ambulance driver, documented German fortifications along the Atlantic coast from Biarritz, near Spain to Arcachon, southwest of Bordeaux. Earlier his réseau had smuggled a camera into the German submarine base at St.-Nazaire to take photos for British intelligence. On 14 May 1977 at the Israeli Embassy in Paris, Laporterie accepted the Medal of the Righteous from the Yad Vashem Institute. In 1989, the French government awarded the Légion d'honneur to an elderly Laporterie.[29,30]

Army Airfields of the Liberation

To provide air support for advancing ground forces in World War II, US Army Engineer Aviation Battalions (EAB) built airfields in 50-mile increments, as close to the front lines as possible, enabling aircraft to leapfrog across France. The aircraft built for World War II were too heavy for turf runways: P-47 Thunderbolts and P-51 Mustangs weighed about 7,000 lbs; a fully loaded C-47 Skytrain weighed 29,000 lbs. It was essential to construct runways that could sustain heavy landings and braking.

In 1941, the US Army developed a pierced steel plank (PSP) that was portable and could be used to quickly construct runways on level terrain.[31] Individual 10-ft long sections of interlocking planks had three rows of 29 holes each row to reduce weight to 66 lbs, facilitate drainage, and allow vegetation to grow through the planks. Its size enabled it to be stacked for transport on Liberty ships, C-47 aircraft, or 2½-ton trucks. Although the first PSP runway, constructed during Army maneuvers near Marston, North Carolina, took eleven days to complete, engineers learned to install PSP runways in hours, not days.[32] PSP was first used in France to provide stable surfaces on the Normandy landing beaches. It later was used at depots and camps to keep supplies and GIs out of the mud.

SMT mat runway, Beuzeville, June 1944 (US Army)

Army engineers used square-mesh wire track matting (SMT, developed by the British), asphalt-impregnated burlap (PHS, known as "Hessian Mat"), and PSP to rapidly build airfields on bases liberated from the Germans and in vacant fields.[33] Captured German airfields could be cleared of mines and booby traps, bomb craters filled, and ground surfaces leveled to become operational faster than airfields built on open land. Most runways for aircraft refueling, emergency landings, and supply and evacuation were 5,000-ft long and, in the beginning, constructed of wire matt or burlap which could be delivered faster than the heavier PSP.[34] Engineers also constructed larger airfields and air depots that required main runways, taxiways, hardstands, hangars, and fuel storage sites.

On 08 June 1944, the first airfield was completed at St.-Laurent-sur-Mer (designated A-21). From June 1944 through early May 1945, sixty-seven airfields were built across France, mostly in the north. During fall rain and winter snow, numerous airfields had to be "winterized" with PSP to stabilize the landing surface. In fall 1944, air depots were located at Chartres, Beauvais/Tille, Vélizy-Villacoublay, Melun, Cambrai-Niergnies, Reims, and St.-Dizier. When Germany surrendered in May 1945, a network of two-hundred forty-one airfields had been built in France, Belgium, Luxembourg, the Netherlands, Germany, and Austria.[35] Steel needed for the PSP runways weighed nearly ½ million tons.[36] In February 1946, squadrons of the 92nd and 384th Bombardment Groups, located at Istres (Marseille), were inactivated and the 314th Troop Carrier Group returned to the US from Vélizy-Villacoublay (Paris).[37]

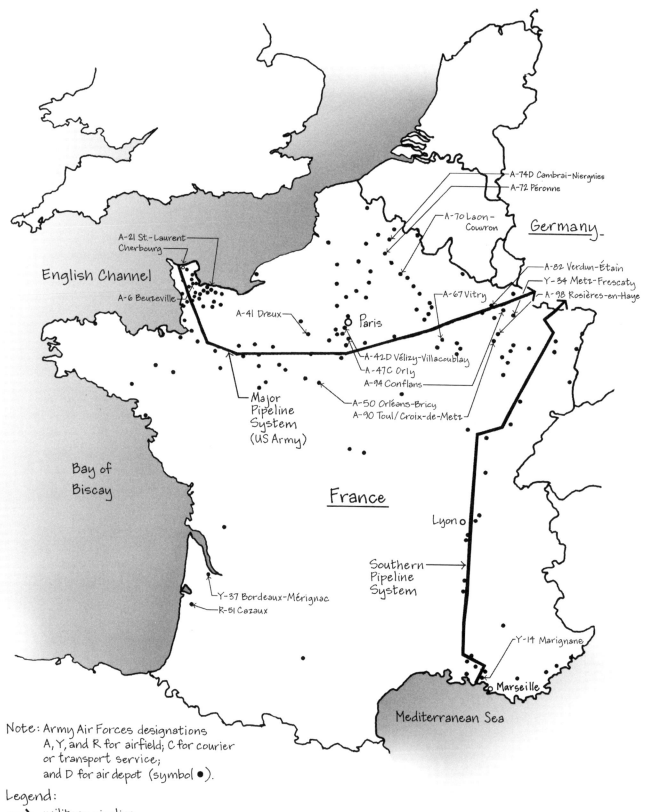

US Army Airfields and POL Pipelines (1945)

In early 1946, the airfields were closed. In late 1949, the French customs service began a crackdown on smugglers who used the deserted airfields. Most of the illegal traffic was concentrated in the Paris, Normandy, and Brittany regions. Smugglers, using small single-engine aircraft, swooped down on the abandoned airfields, quickly unloaded cargo, and took off before the authorities arrived. On some flights contraband was dropped by parachute.[38] The abandoned airfields at Verdun-Étain (A-82), Rosières-en-Haye (A-98), and Laon-Couvron (A-70) were developed by the US Air Force for wings deployed in the early 1950s to France. In Korea, takeoffs and landings of the jet aircraft had damaged the PSP runways and taxiways.[39] Consequently, NATO air bases constructed in France would require concrete runways, taxiways, and hardstands.

In France during the Cold War, PSP was used at Army depots for storage platforms and sheds and at US Air Force bases to prevent equipment, supplies, and parked aircraft from sinking into the mud. PSP also was stored to be used to build emergency runways if Allied troops retreated into France during a Soviet invasion.[40] From 1944 to 1967, enormous quantities of the planks were abandoned, misplaced, and stolen. Today in rural areas throughout France, PSP is used for cattle chutes, fencing, sheds, and other creative applications.

Prisoner of War Enclosures

During 1944 and 1945, the US Army operated prisoner of war (PW) enclosures in France. By international agreement, German prisoners were to be provided the same rations as GIs. Because most French citizens had survived four years of occupation on a Spartan diet, they became indignant when they learned that German prisoners were eating chocolate and oranges, luxuries unavailable to them. Not missing an opportunity to denigrate the United States, French communists spread the rumor that the Americans preferred Germans to the French.[41] Likely unbeknownst to communists, in November 1945 a classified Army opinion survey of US occupation soldiers in Germany found that 50% of the GIs surveyed liked Britishers best, 28% preferred Germans, and 11% the French.[42]

On 15 December 1944, MPs of the 2030th PW Overhead Detachment arrived at the abandoned Caserne Carnot in Chalon-sur-Saône to establish PW Enclosure No. 29. Buildings in the caserne were fenced in by barbed wire and wooden guard towers were quickly built. At the end of December, the 392nd MP Escort Guard Co arrived when the enclosure, eventually built to hold 20,000 prisoners, became overcrowded. The 392nd had all black enlisted personnel; the 2030th all white. The units worked, ate, and billeted together.[43]

During 1946, most of the German PWs held by the US Army were transferred to the French. Large camps for German PWs were located at Marseille, Compiègne, Troyes, Cherbourg and nearby Tourlaville, Bolbec, Ste.-Mère-Église, Châlons-sur-Marne, and Metz. At the 62nd QM Base Depot at Reims, German PWs worked as clerks, fumigators, cobblers, launderers, drivers, and mechanics.[44] Well into 1946, German PWs in France were organized into 250-man labor companies to assemble and repair US Army vehicles. In 1945-46, seven-hundred fifty German PWs worked at the Biarritz American University as laborers and in the laundry, shoe repair shop, and mess halls. At the Cigarette Camps in Normandy, hundreds of German PWs erected tents, dug drainage ditches, and worked in mess tents. According to the West German Maschke Commission, about 600,000 Germans were being held in French PW camps at the end of 1946. Most prisoners worked for the French under the labor reparations policy of the Allies.[45] The prisoners provided forced labor on farms and in quarries. In November 1946, the American Graves Registration Command (AGRC) released 4,500 German prisoners who had been used to search for and recover American war dead. By the end of 1948, all German PWs had been sent home.[46, 47]

Rapid Demobilization

After Germany's surrender, the GIs wanted immediately to return home. This was not possible. During the war, the British luxury passenger ships *Queen Mary* and *Queen Elizabeth* had been converted to troopships. In peacetime, the *Queen Mary* carried 2,500 passengers in spacious comfort; 16,000 troops when converted for war transport.[48] On the *Queen Elizabeth*, two or three GIs were assigned to each bunk, sleeping in shifts. The Queens made almost fifty trips each year carrying 750,000 troops per year. When the war ended, the Queens reverted to commercial passenger use. During June 1945, nearly 200,000 GIs sailed from Le Havre on troopships (including Victory and Liberty cargo ships adapted to carry passengers), each having far less passenger capacity than the Queens.[49]

After the sacrifices of World War II, Americans wanted to return to normalcy and demanded that politicians "bring the boys home." Thus the United States began its traditional practice of rapid demobilization, disarmament, and withdrawal from foreign commitments.[50] Within one year after Germany surrendered, the 3.5 million US troops in Europe had been reduced to about 370,000, British forces had been reduced by nearly two-thirds, and no Canadian forces remained in Europe.[51] By the end of 1946, Supreme Headquarters, Allied Expeditionary Force (SHAEF) at the Hôtel Majestic and Annex in Paris was closed. GIs nicknamed the reduction of forces in Paris "Operation Fadeout." However, drawdown operations and the AGRC continued to use office space at the Hôtel Astoria, near the Arc de Triomphe. Depots were at Caserne Lariboisière in Fontainebleau and Île St.-Germain in Paris.[52]

Who Goes Home First

A point system was adopted to determine when a GI could be sent home. Points were awarded based on length of military service between September 1940 and May 1945 (one point per month), length of service overseas (one point per month), number of combat medals and campaign ribbons (five points per award), and number of dependent children under age eighteen (twelve points per child, 36 points limit). GIs who had seen combat in both North Africa and Europe, GIs over age 42, former prisoners of war (PW), and Medal of Honor recipients were eligible to return home regardless of the number of points. Unless their specialty was needed in the Pacific, GIs with the most points went home first. GIs with fewer than 85 points remained in Europe or were sent to the US for deployment to the Pacific.[53] Although the system was designed to be fair, unmarried GIs resented the advantages given to married GIs. Surveys also found that GIs felt combat service and wounds were the most important criteria to determine who should go home first; length of service the least.[54] Many low-point GIs who had been transferred to units for deployment to the Pacific were discharged after Japan surrendered in August 1945. Ironically, they were home before high-point GIs from their former units in Europe had been processed through the Cigarette Camps near Le Havre. By 1947, the consequences of the system was a hollow US military because the most experienced soldiers had been discharged.[55, 56]

Redeployment Ports

Principal redeployment ports in France were at Cherbourg for evacuation of sick and wounded, Marseille for vehicles, and Le Havre for personnel. Headquarters for the US Army's 16th Port at Le Havre was located at Fort de Tourneville, a former French military post surrounded by a deep moat. The port could not be used when American forces arrived in late September 1944. Allied bombing raids in June 1944 and demolition by the Germans when they withdrew in July had left the port in ruins. All locks were inoperable and the entrance to the harbor had been blocked by two sunken ships and a sunken dry dock. The 16th Port, commanded by Brig Gen William M. Hoge, was assigned to repair the port. During three months in fall 1944, Army engineers removed obstacles in the harbor (mines, collapsed bridges, sunken ships and barges), repaired docks and bridges, and installed a lock gate that was essential to contain water in the inner harbor.[57, 58]

Assembly Area "City" Camps

In summer 1945, an Assembly Area Command was set up near Reims to prepare troops for redeployment from Europe. By August 1945, seventeen camps, named for US cities, were located near Mailly-le-Camp, Suippes, Sissonne, and Mourmelon-le-Grand. City camps had winterized tents to accommodate 270,000 GIs, most of whom wanted to celebrate, not wait in camps in rural areas. Medical units, nurses, and other female personnel were sent to Camp Pittsburgh near Mourmelon.[59] From assembly area camps, GIs were sent to redeployment camps near the ports of Marseille and Le Havre.

Redeployment "Cigarette" Camps

Eight redeployment camps, occupying more than 4,000 acres, were located within 30 miles of the port of Le Havre. This ensured that troops would be present to fill the ships for rapid turnaround after docking at Le Havre. Each camp had a dispensary and fixed hospital beds equal to 4% of troop capacity. To keep the GIs out of the mud, Army engineers built cobblestone walkways from the rubble of Le Havre.[60] Aerial bombing had destroyed 82% of the buildings in Le Havre.

American Red Cross tent, Camp Lucky Strike, April 1945 (US Army)

Le Havre harbor, October 1944 (US Army)

Three of the camps had been used during the war as replacement depots, dubbed "repo depots" by GIs. After arrival in France, soldiers stayed at the depots until they were deployed. As units were depleted, individual soldiers were sent to replace soldiers who had been wounded or killed. The camps, *Lucky Strike* (at a captured German airfield near St.-Sylvain), *Old Gold* (near Valmont), and *Twenty Grand* (near Duclair), had been named after American cigarettes to disguise the locations from the Germans. Headquarters for Twenty Grand was located at the impressively named, "Le Château Le Breton de Saint-Pierre-de-Varengeville." After the war, five new camps were built, *Philip Morris* (near Gainneville, east of Le Havre), *Herbert Tareyton* (at a former German ammo dump in the Forêt de Montgeon, northeast Le Havre), *Pall Mall* (near Étretat), and *Home Run* and *Wings* (both at Le Havre).[61]

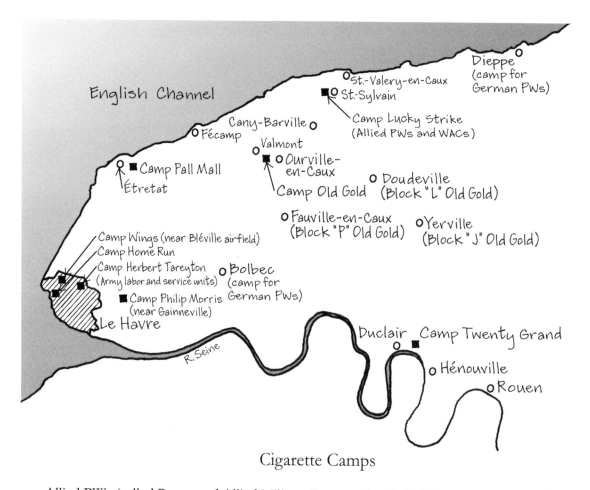

Cigarette Camps

Allied PWs (called Recovered Allied Military Personnel or RAMPs) were sent to Lucky Strike, the largest camp. The RAMPs, most of whom were emaciated and exhausted, were given penicillin to combat blood poisoning and fed a liquid, similar to eggnog, to soothe their stomachs. Almost 89,000 RAMPs passed through Lucky Strike. They were not pleased to see well-fed German PWs working in the mess tents. Women (Army nurses, Red Cross workers, GI brides) were housed in a heavily guarded fenced-in area of Lucky Strike, and those with babies had to wait for ships that could provide nursery facilities. Headquarters for the 89th Infantry Division, which administered Lucky Strike, was located at the Château Anglesqueville in St.-Sylvain. The 89th, commanded by Maj Gen Thomas D. Finley, assigned troops to the various camps and demobilized excess equipment such as jeeps, trucks, weapons, and field equipment. Engineers, who under enemy fire had built airfields and bridges and cleared minefields, now laid water pipes, wired camps for electrical services, and collected garbage.[62]

Most medical personnel also were transients, on their way home or to the Pacific. Personnel to be flown to destinations not served by the troopships were housed at Wings, near the airfield at Bléville.[63] GIs not scheduled to leave within the next forty-eight hours were free to do as they pleased, but had to be back in camp at taps each night. Army MPs, assisted by French gendarmes, provided security and maintained order. One evening, drunk GIs from Lucky Strike, behaving as if they were still in occupied Germany, evicted occupants of a nearby farmhouse. The next morning MPs, who came to arrest them, found the GIs sound asleep in the bedrooms.[64] Card games went on for hours. Most GIs spent two hours each day in line at the Red Cross tent ("Java Junction"), waiting for two doughnuts and a cup of coffee.[65] Movies were shown under circus-size tents. Camps even had mimeographed newspapers such as Old Gold's *The Goldbrick*.

Herbert Tareyton processed service and labor units, including reassigned black combat veterans who had volunteered to serve in the infantry because of severe manpower shortages in Europe. Volunteers formed 5th platoons that were attached to existing white infantry companies which normally had four platoons. NCO volunteers took reductions in rank to PFC to be able to fight as infantrymen.[66, 67] Fifty-two black 5th Platoons fought with white infantry companies from March 1945 until Germany surrendered in May 1945. When combat casualties depleted their numbers, black squads were assigned to white platoons, and eventually blacks were assigned as individuals. Blacks ate with their white infantry comrades and shared foxholes and the discomforts of the battlefields. In July 1945, two-thousand six-hundred blacks who had served in combat were sent back to their segregated labor service units. At the cigarette camps, many of the black combat veterans refused to work on tasks they considered to be demeaning service to whites. Even three-day passes to Paris did not mollify them. The blacks also felt they should be able to return to the US with the infantry units with whom they had served in combat. The white infantry GIs had welcomed them to fill depleted companies, fought alongside them, and, as confirmed by contemporaneous US Army surveys, overwhelmingly rated their performance in combat as high.[68, 69]

In August 1945, Old Gold closed; Lucky Strike and Twenty Grand were placed on reserve status. The last troopship of GIs left Le Havre on 10 July 1946; the last GI war brides on 23 July. By October 1946, engineer troops had dismantled most of the temporary structures at the five remaining camps. The Herbert Tareyton site became the largest public park in Le Havre. Until the early 1960s, French families lived in prefabs and wood-frame structures that the Army built in 1945. For several decades, the village of St.-Pierre-de-Varengeville used some buildings of Twenty Grand.

The Cigarette Camps of World War II (1945-1946)[70-72]

Name	Location	Capacity (GIs)	Size (acres)
Lucky Strike*	St.-Valery-en-Caux/St.-Sylvain	60,000	1,222
Old Gold*	Ourville-en-Caux/Valmont	32,000	546
Twenty Grand*	Duclair/Hénouville	22,000	760
Philip Morris	Le Havre (Gainneville)	35,000	860
Herbert Tareyton	Le Havre (Forêt de Montgeon)	16,400	580
Pall Mall	Étretat	7,700	20
Wings	Le Havre (Bléville airfield)	2,250	10
Home Run	Le Havre (Sanvic, near Fort de Tourneville)	2,000	8

*Part of Red Horse Staging Area camps used to deploy troops to Europe in 1944 and 1945.

Biarritz American University

Army efforts to make life interesting for GIs included establishing a university in France. Brig Gen Samuel L. McCroskey, commandant of the new university, selected Biarritz for the site. The purpose of Biarritz American University (BAU) was to offer university courses to personnel awaiting redeployment home and to help ease the transition from soldier to civilian.[73] Classes were not segregated by rank or race. The BAU library of 8,000 books was in the Casino Municipal. Capt Donald B. Engley, BAU librarian, converted the casino's huge gaming room into a reading room. Classrooms and billets were in eighty-four villas and eighty-two hotels such as: Carlton, Grand, Miramar, du Palais, and Princes. During the German occupation, some of the hotels had been used as prisons and needed extensive repairs. None had heat or hot water until Army engineers repaired them. There were one-hundred eighty-four classrooms in twenty-two buildings. One officers mess was an elegant dining room at du Palais. Instead of the tin cans and metal mess kits used during the war, GIs ate from china and silverware at tables with white linen tablecloths. Because the breakfast staff of French workers greeted each other with the traditional handshake, the mess officer required them to report to work 15 min early.[74] The 8th Field Hospital, commanded by Lt Col Horace O. Gibson, staffed a 200-bed hospital in nearby St.-Jean-de-Luz.[75] Col John W. Davis was troop commander from June 1945 until the school closed in April 1946.

Faculty numbered about 300; support staff 900. Half of the faculty were Army officers and enlisted personnel who had served in Europe; the rest were hastily recruited from over one-hundred colleges and universities in the US. On 20 August 1945, the first of three eight-week terms began with 3,900 GIs. Classes met daily to complete a semester's work in eight weeks. No reveille, no retreat, no saluting at BAU, but GIs were court-martialed if they cut class three times or did not wear their uniforms properly.[76] Walking along a sidewalk in Biarritz, Col Chauncey E. Howland was nearly knocked down by an inattentive corporal. Howland asked: "What goes on? Aren't we still in the Army?" The corporal replied: "Damn, colonel. I'm sorry! I was immersed in calculus!"[77] Honor students were permitted to attend the following term. Over 10,500 GIs attended the three terms. During the second and third terms, seventy soldier-students from France, Britain, and Canada were enrolled and during the third term, twenty-five French civilian students from Biarritz.[78]

Most of the faculty were concerned that men who had recently been in combat and were now living at a famous Atlantic Ocean resort would not do well in school. The academics were wrong. The soldier-students were eager to learn and wanted knowledge that could be applied to a purpose. Journalism students published *The BAU Banner*, a weekly newspaper. The faculty took advantage of the location. Science and engineering classes took field trips to the nearby Pyrenées. Liberal arts classes visited historic venues. Celebrity visitors, who boosted morale, included Hollywood actress Marlene Dietrich. Dietrich, elegantly dressed in sequins and furs, visited classes and ate with the soldiers in their mess. On a makeshift stage in one class she answered questions while the GIs ogled her shapely legs. At the end of her Paris shows during World War II, GIs chanted "legs" and Dietrich would lift up her skirt to reveal shoulder patches (of units being entertained) attached to her garters.[79] During the Cold War in December 1959, Dietrich invited twenty-six patients from the US Army's 34th General Hospital near Orléans to attend her performance at Théâtre de l'Étoile in Paris.[80] Today, the road in front of McCroskey's former villa is named rue McCroskey. The Hôtel du Palais, built in 1855 by Napoléon III for his wife, Eugénie, is a luxury resort hotel.

Army Depots after Liberation

By the end of April 1945, the Motor Transport Service of the US Army was delivering 15,000 tons of supplies a day through France to support US forces. The enormous depot system across northern France had been organized into a Normandy Base Section (headquartered at Deauville), Seine Section (Paris), and Oise Section (Reims).[81, 82] In 1944 and 1945, Army engineers had laid pipelines from the English Channel across northern France and from the Mediterranean Sea through the Rhône valley. Multiple pipelines extended into Germany from Cherbourg through Chartres, Verdun, and Thionville and from Marseille through Lyon, Épinal, and Sarrebourg. More than two dozen storage tank farms and one-hundred fifty pump stations were built. The pipelines delivered gasoline, diesel, and aviation fuel to US forces as they advanced across France into Germany. It took months to dismantle the pipeline systems.[83, 84] In January 1946, the Western Base Section was established to support troops in France and to liquidate World War II supplies and equipment stored at two-hundred thirty-nine installations, most of them in France. In July 1946, the US agreed to sell France all surplus ammunition in France and 52,500 tons of ammunition from Germany and Belgium.[85] By mid-1947, most supply depots had been closed or turned over to the American Graves Registration Command (AGRC), headquartered in Paris.[86, 87]

Wary of Soviet aggression, Lt Gen Curtis E. LeMay, commander of US Air Forces in Europe, used the AGRC and surplus property units as cover to establish unofficial supply installations in France.[88] In the winter of 1948, POL (petroleum, oil, and lubricants) and rations were stored at AGRC installations. The US Army also stored aviation fuel and installed pierced steel plank (PSP) at French airfields. During World War II, LeMay, known as an innovator and problem solver, was promoted from lieutenant colonel to major general in only eighteen months. In the 1960s, LeMay served as US Air Force Chief of Staff during the Kennedy administration.[89]

In 1948 at the US Army European Command (EUCOM) in Heidelberg, Germany, Col Andrew P. O'Meara directed the relocation of Army supplies from east of the Rhine River to west of the river. O'Meara, Chief of Logistics Planning at EUCOM, received permission from the French Army to store ammunition at an abandoned installation near Captieux. In the winter of 1948, ammunition surreptitiously was moved from Germany into France.[90]

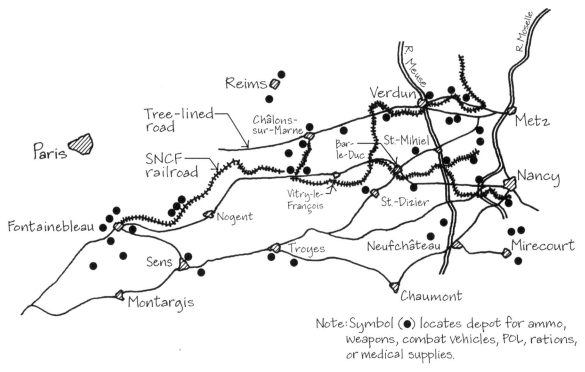

US Third Army Supply Depots (Fall 1944)

Temporary Burials of Americans

During World War II, quartermaster personnel laid out temporary burial grounds of US war dead for convenience with little thought to landscape design or historical impact. For several months during the advance of Allied forces across France into Germany, a platoon of the 611th QM Graves Registration Co, commanded by Capt Joseph J. Shomon, and a platoon from the all-black enlisted personnel 3136th Service Co worked together to care for the dead. Although segregated by unit, they were integrated by duty assignment.[91] American Graves Registration Service (AGRS) personnel remained in France until 1950 to search for and recover remains of thousands of war dead, return remains to the US if requested, and consolidate temporary burial grounds into permanent cemeteries.

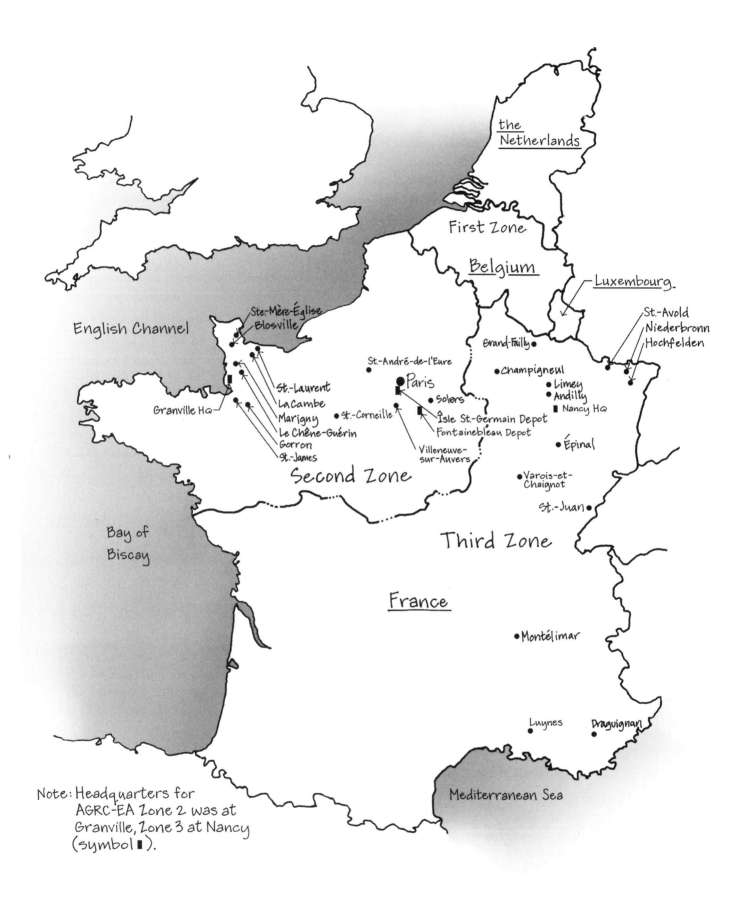

Temporary Burial Grounds in France (WW II)

Search for Remains

The immediate goal of the AGRS teams was to quickly find the remains of the missing and report the facts of death to the next of kin, including the location of the grave. To accomplish this, the AGRS established zones of responsibility in Europe: Zone 2 covered northern and northwestern France with headquarters at Granville; Zone 3 covered central, southern, and eastern France, with headquarters at Caserne Thiry in Nancy. Depots were located at Île St.-Germain near Paris and at Caserne Lariboisière in Fontainebleau. A sub-depot was located at Folembray, near Soissons. The AGRS established a Central Identification Point (CIP) in Fontainebleau and in August 1946 at Strasbourg. CIP personnel took a two-week course on how to identify remains. Identification methods included: fingerprinting, dental charts, and fluoroscopy (to reveal metal objects, healed fractures, and other hidden abnormalities).[92]

Rows of wooden crosses at burial plot, St.-James (US Army)

The task of searching battlefields for unburied remains and locating isolated graves was difficult. It took years to sweep through mine-infested areas.[93] At Malmedy, Belgium, Sgt Allan K. Okura and his AGRS team had found skeletons of two soldiers embracing each other in a foxhole. Okura, who was assigned in 1953-55 to Samec QM depot near Orléans, believed the soldiers died consoling each other.[94] Headquarters for Zones 2 and 3 remained active until 1949. Beginning in November 1947, war dead were shipped from the port of Cherbourg for reburial in the US. The remaining war dead were reinterred from twenty-four temporary burial grounds in France into five permanent cemeteries, located at St.-Laurent, St.-Avold, Épinal, St.-James, and Draguignan. These cemeteries became the final resting place for 30,386 American soldiers, about one-half of the total who were killed or had died of wounds in Europe during World War II.[95, 96] The locations were selected based on sentimental and historical interest related to the units of soldiers who fought nearby. Like the sites for America's war dead from World War I, France granted use of these burial sites in perpetuity to the United States, free of charge or taxation.[97, 98]

The 7887th AGRC Headquarters Group of the American Graves Registration Command, European Area (AGRC-EA) occupied the Hôtel Astoria on the Champs Élysées near the Arc de Triomphe in Paris. The hotel had been liberated from the Germans in August 1944. In April 1947, Brig Gen Howard L. Peckham arrived in Paris to replace Col John C. Odell as commander of the

AGRC-EA. During World War II, Peckham had planned the POL (petroleum, oil, lubricants) supply lines across Europe. Peckham lived in the Hôtel Wagram at 208, rue de Rivoli until July 1948 when he and his family moved into a three-story residence at 26, rue St.-James near the Bois de Boulogne in Neuilly-sur-Seine.[99] Bachelor officers of the AGRC were billeted at the Hôtel Celtic at 6, rue de Balzac near the Arc de Triomphe. In 1947-48, AGRC-EA had a workforce of more than 4,800 military personnel and civilians.

Commanders AGRC-EA (Hôtel Astoria, Paris)

Commanding Officer	Period of Service
Maj Gen Robert M. Littlejohn	1945-46
Col John C. Odell	1946-47
Brig Gen Howard L. Peckham	1947-49

The 7761st AGRC Depot Co was stationed at Île St.-Germain, a large island in the Seine River near Paris. The 250-acre installation had a huge motor pool that maintained AGRC jeeps and trailers, warehouses (for burial boxes, wooden crosses, and mortuary equipment), barbed-wire enclosed stockade, post exchange (PX), commissary, theater (for movies and stage shows), medical clinic, barracks, and mess facilities. Most buildings were metal prefabs. GIs who enlisted in the Army in Paris received their initial military training at the depot before being sent to their units, most to the constabulary forces in Germany.[100] Until July 1948, troops of the 523rd MP Platoon guarded the temporary burial grounds, performed routine law enforcement duties such as arresting rowdy GIs, and operated the stockade on Île St.-Germain.[101] The Army continued to use the island site until the early 1950s when new installations were built to support European Command (EUCOM) headquarters near Paris.

The 7762nd AGRC Depot Co was stationed at Caserne Lariboisière in Fontainebleau. In 1947, more than two-hundred US Army officers, enlisted men, and civilian employees attended courses at Lariboisière on how to identify the remains of GIs killed on the battlefields of Europe.[102] Warehouse buildings at the caserne were used to repair wheeled vehicles and heavy engineer equipment such as bulldozers and graders.[103]

AGRC-EA was inactivated on 01 January 1950 when the AGRC cemeteries were turned over to the American Battle Monuments Commission. On 01 December 1949, the US military presence in France became the 7966 EUCOM Detachment, commanded by Peckham. The detachment planned the buildup of the US Army supply lines across France and, when the two governments reached agreement on terms, began building the needed facilities. On 01 April 1950, US Army engineer officer Col Mason J. Young, Jr. became commander of the 7966 EUCOM Detachment.

EATS in France

Civilian airlines in Europe, devastated by years of German occupation and war, were unable to provide reliable passenger service. To meet this need, US Air Forces in Europe created the European Air Transport Service (EATS). From September 1945 until 1949, EATS used a fleet of C-47 Skytrains to fly military passengers and cargo throughout Europe. Padded seats replaced the stiff bucket seats of wartime. EATS flew sick and injured GIs to hospitals and remains of war dead to depots in France. They also served occupation forces by flying supplies to locations where German prisoners of war where being screened from displaced persons.[104] Enlisted personnel on leave could fly on a space available basis. Eventually, EATS aircraft were flown almost 40,000 air miles each day transporting VIPs, troops, and cargo.[105] Aircrews flew 10 to 12 hours each day, often for seven days without a break. Aircrews stored extra clothing at several airfields.[106]

An air terminal network was set up for occupation forces in Europe. From Paris the network extended west to London, England; east to Bucharest, Hungary; north to Bremen and Berlin, Germany; and south to Naples, Italy.[107, 108] At most of the airfields, Army engineers installed PSP to extend the length of runways. In late August 1944, the Allies had liberated the airfield at Vélizy-Villacoublay near Paris. It was briefly used by elements of the 48th Fighter Group and, from March to October 1945, by C-47s of the 27th Air Transport Group. In March 1946, EATS moved from the airfield at Villacoublay (formerly designated by US Army Engineers as A-42 Depot) to Orly Field (A-47 Courier). Orly had two new runways and better facilities. The EM Club had a soda fountain featuring ice cream sundaes, sodas, and milk shakes.[109] EATS Paris Traffic Office was located at 7, place Vendôme. EATS also flew to Nice and to Marignane near Marseille (Y-14).[110]

Note: Max. rated load of 5 tons cargo or 27 troops.

C-47 Skytrain

In August 1946, Yugoslavian fighter aircraft shot down two unarmed EATS aircraft, flying regularly scheduled legs over Yugoslavia. On 09 August, a C-47 flew off course due to bad weather and was attacked. Although the crew and passengers survived the crash landing, they were held captive for two weeks. On 19 August, a second C-47 was shot down. Five crew members were killed when the plane crashed into the side of a mountain. For several weeks, the US and Yugoslavian governments negotiated an agreement on safe procedures for EATS flights over Yugoslavia. Until the crisis was resolved in October, B-17 Flying Fortress bombers flew the endangered routes.[111]

The "Forty and Eight" Boxcars

Wooden boxcars were used in France during the two world wars to transport supplies and troops. First built during the late 1800s, these 29-ft long boxcars were designed to haul freight, but during war were converted to carry 40 soldiers or 8 horses. Because these limits, *Hommes 40—Chevaux* 8, were stenciled on the sides of the boxcars they were called 40 and 8s by the American Doughboys in World War I. The normal floor covering was trampled hay and horse manure.[112] During the German occupation of France in World War II, 40 and 8s were used to transport civilians to death camps. Early in the war, the American government learned about Nazi policy to exterminate Jews. Available evidence included: civilian eyewitnesses, captured Allied air crews who were temporarily sent to death camps by mistake, and aerial reconnaissance photographs.[113, 114] Allied war planners believed the best strategy to end the mass murders was to end the war early. So nothing was done until 1945 when the death camps were liberated as the front lines moved toward Berlin.[115]

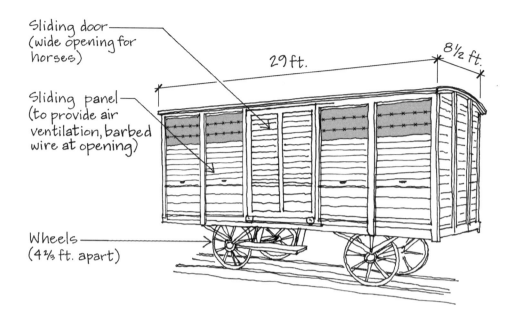

40 & 8 Wooden Boxcar of WW II

American Friendship Train

After World War II, throughout Europe buildings were in ruins, unemployment was high, and people lacked adequate shelter and food. During the occupation, Germany had requisitioned enormous quantities of agricultural products for the German forces in France and for export back to Germany, leaving little for the French to eat. Production of food grain after 1945 was less than half the production before the war.[116] Without assistance, Europe would be unable to restore its industrial base, repair transportation and municipal infrastructures, or purchase essential fertilizers and equipment for agriculture production. In 1947, the US government guided by Secretary of State George C. Marshall developed a plan to provide economic aid. In five years the Marshall Plan supplied nearly $14 billion in aid to Western Europe and helped stall the Soviet Union's attempt to destabilize France.[117-119] When newspaper columnist Drew Pearson wrote a column suggesting that individuals also could provide aid, Americans overwhelmingly responded. This voluntary effort became the American Friendship Train and provided more than seven-hundred boxcars of food and clothing for the homeless of Europe.

Merci America Train

To express their gratitude, French people responded to a suggestion by André Picard, a war veteran and SNCF railroad worker, to present America with a 40 and 8 boxcar loaded with thank you gifts from France. The idea grew to become the Merci America train that carried gifts from more than 6 million French families. Most gifts were of little dollar value but of enormous sentimental value. Among the gifts, however, were priceless souvenirs such as rare French paintings and, from the President of France, 49 vases by Cristal de Sèvres (one vase for each state and Hawaii). In late 1948, the 49 boxcars carried more than 250 tons of gifts from the port of Le Havre to the United States. Each state received a 40 and 8 boxcar with Washington, DC, and Hawaii sharing one. When Hawaii finally received its boxcar the contents were only piles of packing straw. Washington had taken everything.[120]

Occupation Forces

After Germany surrendered, the US Army in Germany became an occupation force. At first, occupation troops faced severe hazards, especially when driving at night on country roads. Germans, called "dead enders," stretched wire between trees on opposite sides of the road. The height of the wire was set to decapitate GIs on motorcycles and in jeeps if the windshield had been pivoted down onto the hood. Driving with the windshield down had been a common practice during combat because sunlight reflected off the glass was visible for miles.[121]

In January 1946, Maj Gen Ernest N. Harmon became the first commander of the US Constabulary in Germany. He picked his headquarters staff at Bamberg and established a school at Sonthofen to train constabulary troops. The constabulary would be a relatively small force of high-caliber personnel, untrained for combat.[122] Their mission was to solve crimes, make civil arrests, and help resettle displaced persons; their motto: mobility, vigilance, and justice. Constabulary regiments included a motorcycle platoon and a horse platoon. They became the Army's last mounted units, using horses to patrol rough terrain along the Soviet borders. Because their shoulder patch had a lightning bolt symbol and their vehicles had a distinctive yellow circle enclosing a "C" for constabulary, Germans referred to them as the *blitz polizei* (lightning police) or circle C cowboys.

Most road patrols had two constabulary troopers and one German policeman. If the disturbance occurred in a German home or displaced persons were outside their camp, the German officer made the arrest. If the offender was a US soldier or US civilian, the troopers made the arrest. During 1946, the constabulary uncovered 2,681 black-market transactions and one-hundred seventy-three subversive acts.[123] After 1946, crimes committed by GIs had been significantly reduced by command influence, improved policing by MPs, and policies allowing dependents to live in Germany.[124] By early 1948, ships that carried dependents to Europe returned with war dead. GIs dubbed them "coffin ships."

In November 1950, the constabulary was inactivated and the Seventh Army activated to face the Soviet threat in Europe. In 1951, Eighth Army in Korea did not receive major reinforcements because troops were sent to Europe to build up NATO. Four Army National Guard divisions were mobilized at the beginning of the Korean War. One was sent to Korea, one to Europe, and two remained in the US to augment strategic reserve forces.[125-127]

Berlin Blockade

The Potsdam agreements of July 1945 divided Germany into an Eastern sector, controlled by the Soviets, and a Western sector, overseen by Britain, France, and the US. In February 1945, diplomat Charles Bohlen served as translator for US President Franklin D. Roosevelt at the Yalta Conference which determined the final military plans for the defeat of Germany. According to Bohlen, British Prime Minister Winston Churchill was the strongest advocate for giving France a seat on the Allied Control Council and a zone of occupation, sliced out of the British and American zones.[128] Although World War II was fought in part to ensure that Poland and Czechoslovakia would be free, the Yalta agreements guaranteed that the two countries would remain under Soviet domination.[129,130]

Berlin also was divided into zones. To the Soviets, West Berlin was an embarrassment because the freedom and emerging prosperity of the West starkly contrasted with the regimentation and gloom of East Berlin.[131] On 16 June 1948, the Soviets walked out of the four-powers Allied Control Council and on 24 June 1948, they closed all highway, railway, and barge traffic to West Berlin. Even AGRC mortuary railcars were not allowed to move war dead through the Soviet zone. Many historians consider the Soviet blockade of Berlin to be the closest the US and the Soviet Union came to war in Europe.

B-29 Superfortress at RAF airfield, England, 1948 (Boeing Archives)

To deter Soviet aggression, in July 1948 sixty B-29 Superfortresses were ostentatiously deployed from the US to RAF airfields at Marham, Scampton, and Waddington in England.[132] US Army engineers were in England setting up atomic bomb assembly buildings, loading pits, and hydraulic lifts to load the bombs onto atomic-capable B-29s, originally code named "Silverplate." At RAF Stations Lakenheath and Schulthorpe, bombs would be unloaded, the fissionable cores inserted, batteries recharged, and tests run before reloading the bombs. Batteries had to be replaced after 48 hours of use. Truman's deployment of the B-29s to England was a bluff. The B-29s from the 28th and 307th Bombardment Groups had not been modified for Silverplate missions, and the US only had fissionable cores for about ten bombs, likely not enough to defeat the Soviets.[133,134] Because mass production of atomic bombs by assembly lines was not yet developed, it would take two to three days to assemble each bomb. The first Silverplated B-29s were deployed to the UK in July 1949. However, the bombs were not shipped to the UK until the next year. Non-nuclear components (atomic casings) of the atomic bombs arrived in July 1950.[135] Nuclear core components (plutonium capsules) were flown separately from the US by cargo aircraft.[136]

Although the US State and War Departments declared Berlin to be indefensible, General Lucius D. Clay, American military governor in Germany, insisted America should not budge. During the blockade, one-thousand family members of American soldiers chose to remain in Berlin to show they would not be intimidated by the Soviets. Clay initially planned to break the blockade by sending an armored convoy to Berlin.[137] However on 20 July 1948, due to determined opposition from the Joint Chiefs of Staff, President Harry Truman rejected forcible access to Berlin by ground. At a White House meeting, Clay asked for sufficient planes to sustain an airlift to Berlin. The military chiefs argued that an airlift would take most of the US military's aircraft, leaving the West vulnerable to a Russian invasion. Clay said that if Berlin fell so would Western Europe. As a dejected Clay got up to leave the meeting, Truman proclaimed "Clay, where are you going? You'll get your planes." [138] Truman chose access by air corridors that the Soviets had guaranteed in the Allied Control Council agreement signed on 30 November 1945. Robert Murphy, Clay's political advisor in Berlin, believed an airlift would show weakness to the Soviets. In his 1964 autobiography, Murphy wrote that the failure of the US to stand firm on ground access to Berlin contributed to the willingness of North Korea to invade South Korea in 1950.[139]

CHAPTER 1: *Turbulent Period after World War II*

Occupied Berlin

Berlin Airlift

Over 20% of the homes in Berlin had been destroyed during World War II and Berliners were capable of producing only a small portion of the food needed to survive. In response to the blockade, US Operation VITTLES and UK Operation PLAINFARE airlifted nearly 2.3 million tons of supplies to the 2 million people living in West Berlin during the 15 month period from June 1948 to September 1949. Col Frank Howley, commander of the US forces in Berlin, advised Clay that the first commodity flown to Berlin should be flour.[140] Essential supplies included CARE packages of food. CARE was the Cooperative for American Remittances to Europe, which packaged food and clothing to be given to needy Europeans. For every 260 tons flown into Berlin, 100 tons of manufactured goods were flown out to help the economy. The goods were flown out in crates labeled in German, "Manufactured in Blockaded Berlin." Under the leadership of Maj Gen William H. Tunner, the airlift operated like a conveyor belt to airfields in the Allied zones of Berlin: France (Tegel), Great Britain (Gatow), and US (Tempelhof). During World War II, "Tonnage Tunner" had directed the Hump airlift that delivered supplies from Dinjan, India to Kumming, China. Battling monsoons and high altitudes, pilots flew C-47s on a 500-mile route over the 3-mile high Himalayans. Many of the veteran pilots of the Hump flew in the Berlin airlift.

Tunner wanted the Berlin airlift to work with machine-like precision. He strove for maximum efficiency and paid attention to the smallest details.[141] EATS pilots, experienced in flying in European weather, formed the initial cadre for the airlift. C-47 Skytrains and C-54 Skymasters landing every three minutes at each Berlin airport meant that a plane, fully loaded with dried food, flour, potatoes, fresh milk, or coal (sacked in regulation Army duffel bags), landed every minute around the clock. For smooth flow, the aircraft were segregated by cruising speed so even intervals could be maintained between aircraft. Aircraft maintenance and repairs were performed outdoors, even in foul weather. Repair manuals were translated into German, so German mechanics could assist in the effort. At Tempelhof, Army engineers repaired the existing runway and covered it with pierced steel plank. Between landings, work crews rushed out to repair damage. Construction of a second runway began in July 1948 and was completed in sixty days.[142] The equivalent of twenty RAF squadrons from Great Britain, New Zealand, Australia, and South Africa; twenty US Air Force and two US Navy squadrons; plus civilian aviation and commercial pilots flew in the airlift. Crews flew Rhein-Main to Tempelhof two or three times a day. Pilots flew twelve to fifteen hours with six to seven hours of sleep.[143]

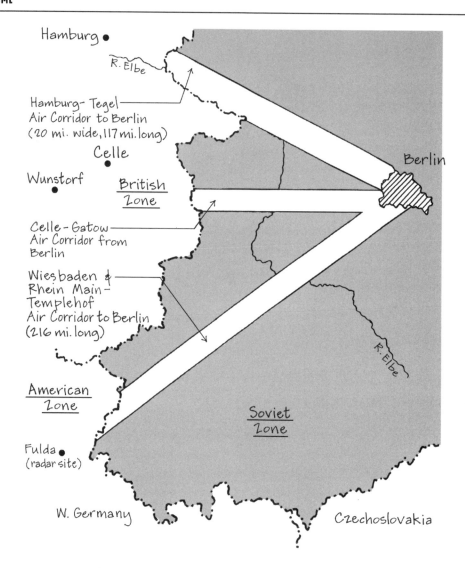

Air Corridors to West Berlin Over Soviet Zone

Aircraft at Tempelhof airport during Berlin Airlift (US Air Force)

Uncle Wiggly Wings and The Bonbon Bomber

In July 1948, US Air Force pilot 1st Lt Gail S. Halvorsen spoke with a small group of German children who were outside the security fence watching the planes land at Tempelhof. Although the children did not ask for anything, Halvorsen wanted to give them something. He only had two sticks of gum, which he split with four of the children. Seeing the disappointed looks of the others, Halvorsen promised that he would drop candy to them from his plane. So they could recognize his plane, he would wiggle the wings. The next day, Halvorsen dropped three handkerchief parachutes with candy to the children, who erupted in joy when they saw the wiggling wings. As Halvorsen taxied down a runway to depart, the three handkerchiefs were being wildly waved. The first of many drops was a success. As word of the candy drops spread, the crowd of children became enormous and Tempelhof began receiving thank you notes addressed to *Onkel Wackelflugel* (Uncle Wiggly Wings). With General Tunner's approval, Halvorsen and his squadron continued the drops, now called Operation Little Vittles. They eventually dropped several tons of candy donated by US schoolchildren and US candy manufacturers. When the crowd of children became too large, unannounced drops were made over parks, schoolyards, and playgrounds throughout Berlin. Drops in East Berlin were halted by protests from the Soviets. Because of his kindness, Halvorsen became the symbol of the Allied airlift for thousands of Germans and Americans. In 1970, Col Gail S. Halvorsen returned to Berlin to serve as commander of Tempelhof Air Base.[144, 145]

In February 1949, Capt Eugene T. Williams replaced Halvorsen on Operation Little Vittles. The operation had grown so large, Army and Air Force wives volunteered to tie handkerchief parachutes to the candy bars. After May 1949, Williams, nicknamed "The Bonbon Bomber," made drops in West Germany over displaced persons (DP) camps and orphanages. By October 1949, five months after the airlift had ended, Williams and his fellow pilots had dropped 120,000 chutes and passed out 21,000 lbs of boxed candy to German children at schools and hospitals.[146]

Lt Halvorsen with German children, Berlin, 1948 (US Air Force)

Tegel Airfield

The French made their greatest contributions to the airlift by allowing US engineers to construct an airfield at Tegel (a former Wehrmacht tank training area in the French zone of occupation) and the demonstration by French General Jean Ganeval of how to negotiate with the Soviets. Ganeval gave the Soviets a reasonable deadline to remove the 200-ft tall tower of a communist-controlled radio station. When the Soviets failed to comply, Ganeval closed nearby roads, instructed radio station personnel to evacuate the building, and ordered French engineers to dynamite the tower. The tower, which had been a serious hazard to landing operations at Tegel, crashed onto the station five minutes later. Airlift personnel cheered when AFN radio in Germany broadcast the news.[147, 148]

Blockade Ends

Soviet Premier Joseph Stalin ended the blockade on 12 May 1949, after the Allies agreed to end the counter-blockade they had imposed on all rail and waterway shipments from the Western zones into the Soviet zone. They also agreed to attend another Council of Foreign Ministers meeting on Germany.[149] The last VITTLES flight was by the C-54 nicknamed "Workhorse Harry" by aircraft maintenance workers. Harry made a total of 1,943 flights to Berlin. The airlift continued for another five months to build up a reserve in case the Soviets again blocked surface transportation. The cost of the airlift to supply Berlin was estimated to exceed $200 million. The greatest humanitarian operation in aviation history kept an isolated city of 2 million alive, fed, and warm. Seventy-six persons died in airlift operations; however, in more than 275,000 flights, only twenty-four planes crashed.[150] On the ground, Army engineers, signal, ordnance, and transportation troops had supported the airlift. Ground crews of German civilian laborers unloaded the cargo from the aircraft into Army trucks. In the 1950s, many of the Army units that had supported the Berlin airlift were stationed in France. The 55th Transportation Co deployed to Caserne Sidi Brahim at Étain, the 68th Transportation Co to Ingrandes, and the 70th Transportation Co to Châlons-sur-Marne. The 586th Ordnance Co, which had repaired vehicles in Berlin during the airlift, was sent to Saran.

Although hailed as a great victory by the West, the airlift meant the Allies had surrendered their ground and water access rights to Berlin.[151] After the blockade ended, the occupational duties of the US Air Forces in Europe changed to a mission of wartime readiness. The blockade may have been the final incentive to create NATO. By blockading Berlin, Soviet Premier Stalin had shown ruthlessness and inhumanity toward the German people. The shared hardships of the blockade and common efforts during the airlift transformed the Germans into allies of America. Berlin would remain free.

US Forces Reduced Worldwide

In the two years after Germany's surrender on 07 May 1945, active US military forces worldwide rapidly shrank from almost 12 million to 1.4 million troops. By mid-1946, the GIs who had won the war had gone home and had been replaced by young men, 18 to 22 years old. By 1950, the US had only 1.1 million troops in uniform. Due to a critical need for factory workers and farmers the Soviets also had demobilized, reaching their lowest level in 1948 of 2.8 million troops. After Soviet forces had been reduced by 75%, Stalin began preparing for war by rapidly building up Soviet forces and the arms industry. By 1950, the Soviet forces had grown to more than 4 million troops, organized into divisions of all types.[152] Gen Matthew B. Ridgway, who commanded the Eighth Army in Korea, believed the US Army was in a state of "shameful unreadiness" when North Koreans invaded South Korea on Sunday morning, 25 June 1950.[153] In Europe, US forces faced a numerically superior Soviet Army and nuclear threat because the Soviets had exploded their first atomic bomb on 29 August 1949.

Effect of Korean War on Defense of Europe

The Korean War heightened the Allies' fear of a "quick grab" of Berlin by the Soviets. Many leaders in the West believed the invasion was part of a Soviet plan to conquer the world. In response, the Allies would build up forces in Europe. Soviet armed forces in Europe were close to their enormous wartime troop levels and deployed for attack. Facing 175 Soviet divisions and 6,000 aircraft, the Allies had fewer than 14 divisions and 1,000 mostly obsolete aircraft.[154] For the defense of Europe, the US was relying on the atomic bomb, increasing the number of nuclear warheads in the US arsenal from nine in 1946 to more than 450 in 1950.[155]

During the period of 1945 to 1950, American war planners concluded that nuclear bombs alone would not defeat the Soviets. The Soviets had successfully tested a nuclear bomb and many felt that all the Soviets needed to march across Europe to the English Channel were enough pairs of shoes. In 1950, American war plans still recognized that the Allies could not stop a Soviet invasion. US occupation forces in Germany were only about 80,000 Army, 15,000 Air Force, and 2,000 Navy personnel. Logistics were based on supporting an Army of Occupation during peacetime, not a combat mission to resist an armed invasion. Consequently, plans called for a fighting retreat to French ports or over the Pyrénées into Spain.[156] Well into the late 1950s, military planners believed Soviet chances of a successful surprise attack in Europe were high.[157]

Ammo and Aircraft Diverted from Korea

In September 1950 US forces landed at Inchon, North Korea, and by late October 1950 General Douglas MacArthur's UN troops had reached the Yalu River at the Chinese border. Supplies destined for Korea now could be diverted to Europe.[158] In late November 1950, three ammunition ships bound for Korea were diverted from near the Panama Canal to the French port of Bordeaux. At the same time, US logistical forces entered France to support the buildup of combat forces in Europe. Because the defense of Europe received high priority, plans would soon become troop deployments and construction projects.[159]

At the beginning of the Korean War, the US Air Force did not have enough modern aircraft to equip Fifth Air Force for an air war.[160] Pentagon planners believed that older aircraft, such as F-51 Mustangs (designation P-51 changed to F-51 in June 1947) and F-80 Shooting Stars, were good enough to fight the North Koreans and argued that conventional aircraft were better suited for the rough PSP airfields in Korea.[161] Fifth Air Force requested modern F-84 Thunderjets because USAF pilots were fighting pilots flying Soviet MiG-15 jet fighter aircraft. The MiG's engine was a copy of the Rolls-Royce jet engine Britain had sold to the Soviets in 1947.[162] The Pentagon, believing the war would end by 01 January 1952, denied this request and sent the F-84s to Europe.

Shortages occurred in other areas. Production of B-26s had stopped at the end of World War II and had to be resumed. In early 1951, the combat-crew training center at Langley AFB, Virginia, still was not producing sufficient personnel for the bombardment wings needed in Korea. Although B-26 Invaders were needed for night bombing missions in Korea, the entire August and September 1951 production output of modified B-26s were supplied to the 126th Bombardment Wing (Light) for deployment to Bordeaux, France.[163]

Soviet-American Air War

During the Korean War, Soviet pilots flew frequent combat mission over the northwest corner of Korea (known as "MiG Alley").[164] US aircraft seldom were pursued over open waters because US Navy ships could capture downed Russians. On 25 November 1950, Communist China invaded Korea near the North Korean border where UN forces had advanced. The Soviet Union provided air cover for this invasion, operating from airfields at Shenyang, Anshan, and Antung in Manchuria.[165] Soviet Premier Stalin decided air power was needed to prevent the defeat of North Korea, but concealed Soviet participation, perhaps to avoid risking a wider war. The US had a significant lead in nuclear weapons and had dropped the A-bomb on Japan to end World War II. Until the breakup of the Soviet Union in 1989, both sides successfully covered up this Soviet-American air war which killed more than 1,000 American airmen.[166] Although North Korean pilots did not begin flying jet aircraft until early 1952, US President Harry Truman told the American public that enemy pilots were North Korean.[167] During the air war, Russian pilots flew 75 % of the combat missions against Americans.

The fuel for North Korean MiG pilots was limited to restrict their range and prevent them from defecting to South Korea.[168] The US dropped leaflets offering a $100,000 reward to any pilot who flew an MiG to an airfield in South Korea. On 21 September 1953, during the armistice, North Korean Air Force Senior Lieutenant No Kum-Sok flew a MiG-15 one-hundred five miles from Sunan Air Base, North Korea, to Kimpo AB, South Korea (near Seoul). No, who had long planned to escape communism, did not know about the bounty.[169]

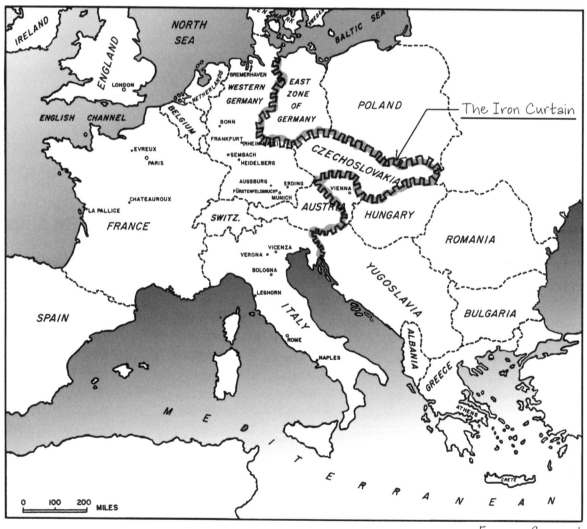

The Iron Curtain (1946)

The Iron Curtain

In March 1946, former British Prime Minister Winston Churchill and US President Harry S. Truman traveled by train from Washington, DC, to Westminster College in Fulton, Missouri. On 05 March, Churchill delivered what would become known as his Iron Curtain Speech. He spoke of his strong admiration for the valiant Russian people, but warned: "From Stettin in the Baltic to Trieste in the Adriatic, an iron curtain has descended across the Continent."[170] America and its allies were tired of war and had been complacent about the Soviet threat to values of equality under the law, due process, limited government, and free speech and assembly. Within five years after the end of World War II, the Soviets had added 580,000 sq mi of territory to their empire. During the war, the Soviets had absorbed Estonia, Latvia, and Lithuania. By military threats, Poland, East Germany, Czechoslovakia, Hungary, Bulgaria, Romania, and Albania were brought under Soviet domination. In February 1948, the Soviet-inspired coup in Czechoslovakia, the last independent nation in Eastern Europe, showed that the Soviets constituted a direct threat to Western Europe. In these ten nations, more than 113,000,000 non-Russian citizens were now behind the Iron Curtain.

In 1948, the newly chartered US Central Intelligence Agency (CIA) began training resistance forces and storing weapons for them in Western Europe. The program, dubbed Operation Rollback, was intended to sabotage a Soviet invasion.[171] Stay behind networks, CIA trainers, and locations of hidden weapons and radio equipment were kept secret. Even the existence of stay behinds was kept secret so citizens of the host country would not conclude that their military forces could not prevent a Soviet invasion.[172] To deter Soviet aggression, an organization of North Atlantic nations was formed to match the numerically superior Soviet Army.

Brussels Treaty

France, Great Britain, Belgium, the Netherlands, and Luxembourg signed the Brussels Treaty in March 1948, forming the Western European Union. Signature nations pledged to aid any pact nation attacked by an outside force. Devastated by war, these five nations collectively still could not militarily match the Soviets. In June 1948, Maj Gen Lyman L. Lemnitzer headed the US delegation to the defense committee of the newly formed Western Union. This union of five western European nations proved to be the foundation for NATO.[173] One month after the Brussels Treaty had been signed, US President Harry S. Truman's diplomatic advisors recommended that the US encourage Sweden, Norway, Denmark, Iceland, and Italy to join.[174]

NATO Established by Twelve Nations

On 04 April 1949, the North Atlantic Treaty Organization (NATO) documents were signed in Washington, DC, by the United States, Great Britain, France, Canada, Iceland, Norway, Italy, Portugal, the Netherlands, Denmark, Belgium, and Luxembourg. In February 1952, Greece and Turkey joined NATO. Each signatory pledged to regard an attack on any NATO nation as an attack on all.[175] This reciprocal agreement was intended to discourage the tactic of attacking small nations one at a time. Although Iceland had no armed forces, it did contribute use of the essential air base at Keflavík.[176] In the beginning NATO was an organization on paper only. It had few combat-ready troops, about 1,000 obsolete aircraft, and twenty operational airfields, none equipped to handle modern jet aircraft. In autumn 1950, US Secretary of State Dean Acheson, who had played a central role in shaping the Marshall Plan, proposed the establishment of a NATO integrated military force under a single commander. The NATO organization meant that the United States would defend Western Europe from the first day of war, not wait years to liberate Europe as it had in World Wars I and II.

In mid-December 1950, the North Atlantic Council of NATO adopted a strategy to deploy forces as far forward as possible to defend Western Europe against the numerically superior Soviet forces.[177] On 31 December 1950, a group of twenty-four American officers and enlisted men flew to Orly Airfield, France, to begin planning for the defense of Western Europe. The Brussels Treaty war plans, developed at Fontainebleau by a committee chaired by British Field Marshal Sir Bernard Law Montgomery, were converted to NATO plans.[178] In the early years of NATO, it was often said in jest that the Soviets now would have to struggle past committee after committee.

France Depends on NATO

From the liberation in 1944 until the mid-1950s France, still recovering from German occupation and the devastation of World War II, was militarily weak and depended on NATO and the United States for its security.[179] From 1945 to 1954, France also was fighting in Indochina, where more than 30,000 French soldiers were killed.[180] Although the Allies believed Germany should rearm to face the Soviet threat, France was not keen on the prospect of another strong German military.[181]

On 16 February 1948, US Ambassador Jefferson Caffery signed a Civil Affairs Agreement with the French government to continue the presence of American forces in France. Article 12 of the bilateral agreement provided that the present agreement would continue in force for six months from the date on which either party informed the other party in writing of its intention to terminate the agreement. During the next ten years, five other basic agreements and more than two-hundred fifty supplemental agreements on numerous subjects were signed. Some of these documents complicated exit strategies for the withdrawal of American forces in 1967. Four of the five bilateral agreements with France could be renounced only by "mutual consent." The fifth one, on operation of the communications zone (ComZ), could be renounced on one year's notice by either party to the agreement.[182] On 08 December 1958, US Ambassador Amory Houghton and French Minister for Foreign Affairs Couve de Murville signed the fifth agreement.

Soviet Threat

The immediate threat to NATO was the twenty divisions the Soviets had massed behind the Elbe River in East Germany. The 315,000 to 370,000 troops were backed by artillery and air support units. After 1948, there were numerous Soviet and satellite divisions in Eastern Europe. In an official historical study of US Army, Europe during the period of 1953 to 1963, Army historian Donald J. Hickman wrote the following.

> "By 1953, with only a limited buildup from the East and with little warning, the Soviet Union would have been able to unleash a powerful drive on the Rhine. The continued intense training of these forces and their effective modernization indicated that Soviet leaders intended to retain that capability. Moreover, Moscow's frequent announcements concerning Soviet test successes with atomic weapons indicated that the Soviet forces might soon launch a nuclear attack. Thus the NATO nations foresaw that only a powerful counterforce could deter and stop Communist expansion. Although NATO might ultimately have to defend Western Europe, its primary mission was preventive. This deterrent strategy, as termed by NATO, meant that the Western nations would have to build a collective force to deter any potential aggressor. For this purpose NATO would have to meet three requirements: it would have to maintain a defense line as far east as possible, which meant defense on German soil; its forces would have to be given a nuclear capability; and since a successful defense would be impossible without the military and political participation of the Federal Republic of German, German Army units would have to be included in the defense line."[183]

Each NATO nation had troops committed to NATO that were based within their borders. US troops were based in all NATO nations. Several other NATO nations had troops based in another NATO nation. Stationed in West Germany in 1963, France had 55,000 troops, Great Britain had 54,000, Belgium and the Netherlands each had 30,000, and Canada had 6,500.[184, 185] Canada also had 5,000 air force personnel in France. The Royal Canadian Air Force (RCAF) headquarters were located at Château du Mercy near Ars-Laquenexy, southeast of Metz.[186, 187]

US Army and US Air Force Military Personnel (1950-1967)[188-195]

Year	Army in Europe (USAREUR)	Air Force in Europe (USAFE)	Army and Air Force in France*	Local Nationals in France**
1950	79,495	16,246	2,105	1,788
1951	231,651	51,138	18,920	3,315
1952	256,557	73,204	37,843	7,886
1953	243,842	85,269	47,524	10,882
1954	251,478	79,060	47,205	12,576
1955	247,624	91,434	48,366	19,111
1956	250,277	79,410	45,342	19,455
1957	235,239	80,424	46,968	20,725
1958	227,844	66,568	41,945	19,958
1959	229,681	66,923	39,036	20,610
1960	226,513	64,330	34,895	21,790
1961	232,942	77,478	52,353	21,847
1962	277,583	62,905	42,791	22,192
1963	251,902	60,609	31,654	19,379
1964	239,753	56,982	26,060	17,670
1965	238,716	56,127	23,385	14,215
1966	208,107	58,212	13,563	12,323
1967	222,626	56,503	2,507	369

*Totals do not include US civilian employees, dependents, and personnel at US European Command (Camp des Loges) and NATO commands (Paris and Fontainebleau). From 1961-67, there were 12,000 to 16,000 at SHAPE and AFCENT.
**Totals for US Army only. French civilians hired by US military were designated local wage rate (LWR) employees.

Gaston Letraux waves at F-86 Sabre jets of 48th FBW, Chaumont, 1954 (US Air Force Academy)

SHAPE Headquarters (1950-52), Hôtel Astoria, Paris (US Army)

Main gate, SHAPE Headquarters, Marly-le-Roi, January 1959 (SHAPE)

TWO

NATO and SHAPE in Paris

"At the end of World War II, Allied troops returned home leaving their arms to rust in the battlefields of Europe." (CBS reporter Edward R. Murrow, 1951 film: *Why NATO!*)

US Supports Its European Allies

The enormous US Army logistics system and the US Air Force's forward-based, nuclear-capable jet aircraft that would be located in France were essential components of the military strength of the new North Atlantic Treaty Organization (NATO).[1] The initial cost of the buildup of the NATO infrastructure of air bases and depot facilities was $1.3 billion. NATO-funded projects, referred to as "infrastructure," included: air bases, pipelines, communications networks, and training facilities. From 1951 to 1955, the US paid 44% of the total cost, France 15%, and Britain 13%. Payments were made in yearly installments (called slices).[2] In 1954, US Secretary of State John Foster Dulles wrote that France was essential to the defense of Europe.[3] In January 1954, during a four powers conference at Berlin, French Prime Minister Georges Bidault insisted that American troops remain in France beyond 1968 when the North Atlantic Treaty expired.[4] In addition to the funds the US provided NATO, the US initially gave military equipment to its NATO allies. Later on the equipment would be purchased. As France continued to rebuild its military to meet the Soviet threat, French contracts from 1961 to 1965 with the US Department of Defense and defense industry exceeded $370 million.[5]

Truman Appoints Eisenhower to Supreme Command of NATO

During the North Atlantic Council conference in May 1950 at London, the twelve NATO nations had decided to establish a military command led by a highly respected American. US leadership and support would be essential because most European nations were still recovering from the devastation of war. In mid-December 1950, the Council asked US President Harry S. Truman to appoint General Dwight D. Eisenhower, then President of Columbia University in New York City, to be the first Supreme Allied Commander, Europe (SACEUR). He would command all military forces placed at the disposal of NATO by its member nations. The appointment of Eisenhower, nicknamed Ike, alleviated fears that America would return to isolation. The SACEUR would command troops only in times of crisis. During peacetime the SACEUR was responsible for war planning and training of NATO forces. Each NATO nation was responsible for the logistical support of its military forces.[6,7]

Temporary Headquarters for SHAPE

NATO located its military headquarters, Supreme Headquarters, Allied Powers Europe (SHAPE) in Paris. In early December 1950, Col Alfred D. Starbird was sent to Europe from the Corps of Engineers Oahe Dam project near Pierre, South Dakota, to find locations suitable for SHAPE headquarters. In France, Starbird visited the château at Fontainebleau, Caserne Limoges in Versailles, and Caserne Maginot at Verdun but chose Paris because of its central location and functioning telephone network. He recommended the Hôtel Astoria built in 1907 on the corner of rue Presbourg and ave des Champs Élysées, a block from the Arc de Triomphe.[8] The German military had used the Astoria for its general staff during the occupation of France. After the liberation of Paris, it was used by the US military and, after the armistice, by the American Graves Registration Command and Army drawdown organizations. The Astoria was close to the Blockhouse used by the Signal Corps to contact European Command in Heidelberg, Germany. From Heidelberg, secure messages could be sent to Washington, DC, and most other NATO capitals. SHAPE paid $8,000 monthly rent for the Astoria to the Société des Hôtels de l'Étoile.[9]

On 18 December 1950, an initial contingent of US officers, under the direction of Col Benjamin E. Thurston, arrived at the Astoria from European Command in Heidelberg, Germany, to establish the SHAPE Advanced Planning Group for the buildup of NATO headquarters in France.[10, 11] A group of fifteen officers and nine enlisted men joined Thurston on 01 January 1951 to set up temporary headquarters for SHAPE. The group's New Year's Eve flight to Orly Airfield, France, from National Airport in Washington, DC, was inauspicious. The plane had been diverted to Westover AFB, Massachusetts, because of engine failure. Because Truman promised Ike he could have anyone he wanted, Ike selected from the cream of the officer corps. The US contingent would include future generals: Carroll, Goodpaster, Knowlton, Rosson, Starbird, Walters, and Wood.[12, 13] These Americans were soon joined by officers and enlisted men from France and Great Britain and later from the other NATO nations. Immediately after Ike was appointed to be SACEUR, he chose Lt Gen Alfred M. Gruenther to be his Chief of Staff and summoned him to his office at Columbia University. Gruenther reported that Starbird was in Paris arranging headquarters and the basic plan for SHAPE had been written by Col Robert J. Wood's group of three lieutenant colonels: Paul T. Carroll, Andrew J. Goodpaster, Jr., and Alfred D. Starbird.[14] The group adapted the existing war plans and headquarters organization of the Western Union Defense Organization.[15, 16]

Ike Returns to Europe

On leave from Columbia, the 60-year-old Eisenhower arrived 07 January 1951 in Paris. For his arrival, the French had prepared a hero's welcome which included state dinners, parades, bands, and flag-waving crowds. Ike asked that the organized welcome be called off because he was working on serious business.[17] At Orly Airfield, French Gen Jean Le Chères greeted Ike and remarked that, after giving France its freedom in 1944, he had come again, this time to help France grow strong and keep its freedom.[18] Ike lived at the Hôtel Raphaël on ave Kléber, two blocks from temporary headquarters in the Hôtel Astoria, where his office had a view of the Arc de Triomphe.

Eisenhower, trusted and admired by Europeans, was on intimate terms with most of Europe's leaders. His first challenge was to convince the Allies and the US Congress that NATO could deter Soviet aggression. He immediately visited the capitals of NATO member nations to obtain commitments of troops and funds to NATO. Luxembourg, which had fewer than 2,000 troops, was asked to use its steel industry to help rearm the member nations. Greenland and Iceland, which had no troops, provided land for air bases. To persuade leaders to allocate troops to NATO, Ike quoted a Bible passage from St. Luke on strength keeping man's palace and goods in peace. Eisenhower completed his round of visits in only seventeen days, sleeping in eleven different beds.[19] Ike's small traveling party included Gruenther, Maj Vernon A. Walters (his interpreter), and Douglas MacArthur II (Foreign Service officer and nephew of Gen MacArthur). They did not stay at US embassies because Ike wanted to emphasize that SHAPE was international. For long flights which required sleeping berths, Ike flew from Orly Air Base near Paris in a VC-121A Constellation, his favorite which he named "The Columbine," or in the 1630th Air Base Squadron's VC-54G Skymaster, named "The Sunflower." Ike's planes were piloted by Maj William G. Draper who had a reputation in the Air Force as a perfectionist. Whenever possible, Ike allowed GIs on leave to the US to fly home on his plane.[20]

Security for Ike

Anti-American protests at the Astoria were so frequent the 16th Military Police Det (CI) was flown from the US to provide security. In February 1951, thirteen soldiers of the 450th CIC Det were sent to France. The detachment, commanded by Capt Jack B. Cameron, conducted security surveys of Ike's private quarters at the Raphaël and SHAPE offices in the Hôtel Astoria.[21] However, the principal mission of CIC detachments in France would be to foil attempts by the Soviets to turn US soldiers into traitors. The 520th Military Police Co, formed in January 1951 at Fort Meade, Maryland, provided uniformed security at SHAPE. More than one-hundred enlisted men of the 520th sailed to Bremerhaven, Germany on the USNS *Gen Stuart Heintzelman*. They arrived in Paris by rail in February 1951. The US Army leased the entire Hôtel Rochester at 92, rue de la Boétie to house the GIs. Overflow was housed at Hôtel Victor Hugo, 19, rue Copernic. The GIs ate their meals at an Army mess hall at 40, rue du Colisée, two blocks from the Rochester. To be closer to the new SHAPE headquarters being built at Marly-le-Roi, the 520th moved on 04 July 1951 from the two hotels in Paris to abandoned French barracks at Camp des Loges.[22]

Buildup at Hôtel Astoria

Initially, WACs on temporary duty from Germany operated communications facilities in the Astoria. The cryptographic equipment was installed on the top floor.[23] By mid-January, officers from other nations began to arrive. The first French language classes for Britishers and Americans met three evenings a week in January in the snack bar of the Astoria. The offices in the Astoria quickly became so overcrowded that classified documents had to be stored in bathrooms. Ike's Chief of Staff, Lt Gen Gruenther, used a conference room adjacent to a noisy movie theater. Occupying a corner of the ground floor was the bar of former world-champion, professional boxer Georges Carpentier. Because Carpentier had been evicted during the occupation, an eviction during peacetime likely would have created adverse publicity.[24]

During the organization phase of SHAPE, all personnel were allowed to purchase supplies in the small US Army PX in the Astoria. In June 1951, the PX Shopping Center at 24, ave de la Grande Armée moved to the leased Blériot Aircraft Factory in Suresnes so it could serve the growing American community. Allegedly, an American sent to SHAPE from European Command in Germany became trapped in the inter-most ring of traffic circling the Arc de Triomphe. Streams of traffic from twelve streets entered the circle, forming several concentric rings of geometric mayhem. Believing he would have been forced to circle until he ran out of gas, he abandoned his car at the Arc.[25] By the end of summer 1951, a new facility for SHAPE would be built near Versailles. Construction, under the supervision of French Army engineers, began in March 1951.

In 1958 an American-style drugstore, with a pharmacy and soda fountain that served milkshakes 24-hours a day, occupied the ground floor of the Astoria, which had been sold to a French advertising firm. To the chagrin of traditional Parisians, it was named Le Drugstore.[26]

Women at SHAPE

WACs, WAFs, and WAVEs worked at SHAPE offices and at 82, ave Marceau, typing reports and correspondence, answering phone calls, and taking messages for various staffs. Women were restricted from combat and jobs that exceeded their physical capabilities. WACs worked in the Signal Section on classified communications, others in the Photo Section. In March 1951, the US Air Force sent a small group of Women in the Air Force (WAF) to work as stenographers at the Astoria. Until barracks were built at the new facility for SHAPE, women lived in the Hôtel Queen Elizabeth on 41, ave Pierre 1ᵉʳ de Serbie and Hôtel Balmoral on 6, rue Général Lanrezac. At 11 pm each evening, WAC sergeants held bed checks at the hotels by determining if room keys were hanging from hooks behind the front desk. In France, it was mandatory for guests to turn in room keys when they left a hotel, even for a brief time. If they did not see keys, the sergeants assumed the women were in their rooms. However to enjoy Paris nightlife past bed check, the young women learned that male desk clerks could be persuaded to hide their room keys until they returned.[27]

When SHAPE moved to new facilities, one-hundred thirty-eight women moved into three barracks, living two to a room, that were furnished like college dorms. A large sign on the barracks warned: "Off Limits to Male Personnel." Enlisted men and NCOs where housed in barracks at nearby Camp Voluceau and at Caserne Limoges in Versailles, sleeping ninety-six to a barracks in double-decker beds.[28] The Voluceau barracks were divided into twelve-man rooms. In 1952, some SHAPE support units were billeted at Camp des Loges while Camp Voluceau was being built.

In 1951, WACs at the SHAPE Photo Section worked for US Army 1ˢᵗ Lt Samuel J. Goldwyn, Jr, the son of the famous Hollywood producer. Goldwyn had served in the Army during the occupation of Germany in 1946 and had been recalled to active duty for the Korean War buildup.[29] At SHAPE, he produced documentary films such as *Alliance for Peace*, that had its grand opening for SHAPE staff and guests at a Paris theater. The film won first prize at the Edinburgh (UK) Film Festival. After his service at SHAPE, Goldwyn returned to Hollywood where he had a successful career producing and distributing films. His father was known for his successful films and for malapropos, called "Goldwynisms," such as "Anyone who would go to a psychiatrist ought to have his head examined!"

Ike's Second Crusade in Europe

Most Western Europeans felt reassured by the broad smile of Eisenhower and his legacy as commander of the victorious Allied forces in World War II. However, even he faced anti-American sentiment. Communists posted signs throughout Paris: "*Eisenhower rentrez chez vous et restez-y!*" (Ike go back home and stay there!) They scheduled an anti-Ike rally to coincide with Gen Eisenhower's return to Paris on 23 January 1951 from his visit to European Command forces in Germany. The rally fizzled because nearly 10,000 French police, wearing riot gear, sealed off the area around the Hôtel Astoria. More than 2,000 people were arrested, most even before they could form small groups.[30] The next month, the French atomic energy commission fired six employees who had participated in the anti-Ike rally.

Ike gave an interview in October 1951 to *Paris-Match* magazine lamenting that France "seemed to lack the old virtues of Verdun." However, citing the fighting spirit of the Battle of Verdun in 1916, where 300,000 Frenchmen had died, did not arouse the enthusiasm of most Frenchmen.[31] The bitter experiences of war had created a hopeless attitude in France and French communists vigorously fought rearmament. According to Harvard University President James B. Conant, French intellectuals were not writing anything that could be held against them if communists took over France.[32] Responding to the "U.S. Go Home" sentiments, Ike said the French people should understand that US forces were in Europe to protect France and would gladly go home when they were no longer needed.[33] Morale was more important to Ike than weapons. In speeches, correspondence, and private meetings, he stressed America's role in improving the self-confidence of the NATO Allies. On 10 October 1951, Ike wrote in his diary that the NATO political leaders must start a crusade in their own countries to explain that NATO's purpose was to resist aggression and provide freedom for its citizens.[34] At a farewell press conference in April 1952, Ike emphasized that two years of military training were required "to teach a man to take care of himself."

Ike Issues First General Orders

Ike formally assumed command of SHAPE on the morning of 02 April 1951 by signing General Orders No. 1 (drafted by Lt Col Goodpaster). He also signed General Orders No. 2 which named French Admiral André-Georges Lemonnier to be his Naval Deputy. Eisenhower believed it was prudent to divide responsibilities so all NATO member nations were satisfied that they would fulfill an important role. That afternoon he held a press conference, attended by two-hundred reporters, and answered questions on a wide variety of topics, including his command structure and NATO war plans. Answers to questions on war plans were purposefully vague.[35] Ike referred to the size of his staff at SHAPE as "meager." In August 1951 it would number only two-hundred twenty-five, but by 1966 there would be more than 2,700 personnel at SHAPE. Although SHAPE initially allocated sixty positions to France, only fifteen were filled. One was French Lt Col Charles Ailleret, hero of the French resistance and survivor of Buchenwald concentration camp. In the 1960s, Ailleret became France's top general. French officers, who did not speak English, were reluctant to serve on an American-dominated staff. Most also wanted to avoid the humiliation of working in an organization where a US lieutenant received pay equal to a French general.[36]

Gen Dwight D. Eisenhower, Hôtel Astoria, Paris, 02 April 1951 (SHAPE)

NATO Commands

Eisenhower insisted that the loyalty of his staff be to NATO, not to the soldier's own nation. As had been his goal with the Allied armies during World War II, Ike wanted to mold the different interests and viewpoints of the officers from the NATO nations into one.[37] At Supreme Headquarters, Allied Expeditionary Force (SHAEF) in England, Ike had banned liaison officers between the Allied nations and insisted that soldiers of all nations work in the same offices. At SHAPE in Paris, each division's chief would have a deputy of another nationality. Although nine languages were spoken at SHAPE, the official languages were English and French.

Under Eisenhower there were three regional commands for continental Europe: Northern (at Oslo, Sweden), Central (Fontainebleau, France), and Southern (Naples, Italy). Land forces of Allied Forces Central Europe (AFCENT) were commanded by French General Alphonse-Pierre Juin, Allied Air Forces Central Europe (AAFCE) were commanded by American Lt Gen Lauris Norstad, and Allied naval forces (small gunboats on the Rhine and port facilities at Bremerhaven, Germany, and in France, Belgium, and the Netherlands) were commanded by French Vice Admiral Robert Jaujard.[38] The chief of the Budget and Fiscal Division was Guillaume C. LeBigot from the French Navy. During a political rally on 01 May 1951 in a Paris suburb, Général Charles de Gaulle, leader of the political party *Rassemblement du Peuple Français* (RPF), challenged Ike to give a French general officer command of NATO land, sea, and air forces in Central Europe and the Mediterranean.

Ike's Deputy Supreme Commander was the famous British general, Field Marshal Bernard Law Montgomery. During World War II, Montgomery had planned the D-Day landings in Normandy and, under Allied Supreme Commander Eisenhower, had commanded the American and British invasion ground forces. Ike sent Monty on numerous inspection tours to strengthen military forces of NATO nations, but also to keep the prickly Monty away from headquarters where Ike's Chief of Staff Lt Gen Gruenther was organizing a multi-national operation.[39] Monty did not permit smoking in his presence and, during World War II, even had made Ike, his superior, put out his cigarette. Gruenther's seven key deputies would include French Lt Gen Marcel Maurice Carpentier and other senior officers from Britain (three officers), France (one), Italy (one), and America (one). Early each morning, Gruenther gave his staff Dictaphone cylinders containing assignments recorded the previous night. The messages, called "Gruenthergrams," were to be answered promptly. Behind his back, Gruenther's American staff officers called the demanding, diminutive general "Little Al." [40]

NATO War Plans

During the early 1950s, the Allies could not prevent the numerically superior Soviet forces from overrunning Western Europe. Initial NATO war plans, based on Montgomery's Western Union Defense Organization plans, were to fall back to the Rhine River. In January 1950, the US Joint Chiefs of Staff (JCS) approved war plan OFFTACKLE which committed the US to defend Western Europe, but assumed the Soviets would drive US military forces from the continent.[41] According to the plan, after regrouping and dropping atomic bombs on more than one-hundred strategic targets in the Soviet Union, eventually the Allies would build up forces for an invasion through the Rhône valley of France.[42] War plans were highly classified and not to be shared with foreign nationals. By early 1952, Ike was assigned eighty atomic bombs.[43]

The JCS successor war plan IRONBARK included provisions for withdrawal through French ports. If the Soviets invaded, US occupation ground forces were to withdraw from Germany, destroying bridges, rail yards, and infrastructure as they fought their way out by a "scorched earth" retreat. All railroad equipment would be evacuated to France.[44-46] In June 1950, German communists claimed in the event of war with the Soviets the Allies planned to blast the Lorelei cliffs into the Rhine River.[47] According to German legend, a golden-haired maiden sat on top of the Lorelei. Lured by her beauty, river pilots crashed on the rocks. In 1950, French newspapers astonished their readers by reporting that Rhine River bridges had compartments for explosives. Maj Gen Daniel C. Noce, Chief of Staff to Gen Handy at US European Command, dismissed the report as a "lot of nonsense" in a telephone conversation with John J. McCloy, the US High Commissioner for Germany.[48] Although the Lorelei story was false, according to secret annual reports of US Army, Europe, by the end of August 1954 demolition chambers had been installed on almost three-hundred railway and roadway bridges in Germany. On 08 March 1951, Brig Gen Joseph J. "Red" O'Hare, the US Army Attaché in Paris, asked the French government to provide engineering information on all bridges along twenty-seven Route Nationale (RN) roads that would be used by the American line of communications. O'Hare asked for span length, number of piers, clearances, load capacity, and the like.[49] No doubt the French deduced that this was useful for engineers ordered to destroy bridges to impede the Soviets during an invasion.

Ike had the difficult task of coordinating the US war plans with those of NATO and, to keep morale high, forbade any discussions at SHAPE about possible troop withdrawals from the Rhine. During Ike's seventeen months at SHAPE, Gen Thomas T. Handy commanded US forces in Europe and kept his headquarters in Germany. During his 1953-55 tour as commander of US Army, Europe, Gen William M. Hoge tried to change the "scorched earth" policy. He believed it would make enemies of the Germans and do little to slow an invasion by the Soviets. Hoge's plans evolved to be a mobile defense between the border and a final stand along the Rhine.[50, 51]

At three month intervals during the 1960s, Army Engineers practiced extending eight "swing bridges" across the Rhine River. Riverboat traffic was halted during the exercises. Swing bridges were heavy-load capacity Bailey Bridge sections attached to lashed together pontoon cubes. Under US Army control, the swing bridges would ensure reliable routes for logistical supplies from France to combat forces in Germany. Unlike fixed bridges, the spans could be rapidly repaired or replaced if damaged or destroyed. The bridges also could be used if troops were ordered to fall back to the west bank of the Rhine.[52]

Seventh Army "swing bridge" on Rhine River (US Army)

Security Classifications

Although Ike wanted all members of his international staff at SHAPE to believe they filled important roles, it was difficult for officers from other NATO nations not to feel second class to Americans because many documents were stamped AEO (American eyes only).[53] Access to documents also was limited by SHAPE security classifications higher than Top Secret, named Metric and Cosmic. Only NATO officers who had been carefully screened, dubbed "cosmicized," could see NATO war plans. Metric was a classification from the Western European Union Defense Organization in Fontainebleau. Sensitive US European Command documents not to be released to foreign nationals were stamped NOFORN (no foreign nationals). Because of the grave damage to national security if information regarding the handling and use of nuclear weapons was leaked, US European Command had a security classification higher than Cosmic, so secret that even the classification name (Atomal) was classified. To view any classified document, an individual even if cosmicized had to have an official "need to know." When Col Andrew J. Goodpaster, Jr. left SHAPE in 1953 to be District Engineer in San Francisco, he had to account for a missing classified file on nuclear weapons that was recorded as being in his custody. In the 1950s, if enlisted personnel assigned to burn discarded classified material dumped too many documents into the brick oven at Marly-le-Roi, partially burned paper would float into the air to land who knew where.[54]

US Combat Troops Return to Europe

In late January 1951, Eisenhower returned to the US to persuade the US Congress to appropriate needed funds and troops for NATO. He gave a speech to a joint session of Congress, answered questions from Congressional committees, and gave a radio and TV address to the nation. Ike's prominent public supporters included retired Gen Lucius D. Clay, New York Republican Gov Thomas E. Dewey, and Republican US Senator Joseph R. McCarthy of Wisconsin. In France, Général Charles de Gaulle warned that Europe would be condemned to an invasion unless the United States sent troops. Prominent opponents to sending US troops to Europe included former US Ambassador Joseph P. Kennedy, former US President Herbert Hoover, and Republican US Senator Robert A. Taft of Ohio. The opponents claimed that troops sent to Europe would stay there for at least two decades, eighteen, not four, Army divisions would be sent, and the US could be defended best by air and sea, not by troops in Europe.

On 04 April, after three months of debate, the US Senate by a vote of 69 to 21 approved sending four Army divisions to Europe. President Truman immediately ordered the divisions plus supporting naval forces and air wings be deployed.[55] On 27 May, Ike's AFCENT commander French Général Juin and US General Handy went to the port of Bremerhaven, Germany to review the first contingent of US Army troops to arrive in Europe. They stood in the rain to welcome 1,500 troops of the 4th Infantry Division disembarking from the USNS *Gen Alexander M. Patch*. By 05 June, more than 8,000 troops had arrived at Bremerhaven. In late June, an agreement was signed in London on the status of armed forces of NATO nations who sent troops to another NATO nation. Ike now could deploy forces among NATO nations without political interference.

NATO Standardization Program

The US aid program of weapons and equipment accounted for the initial standardization among NATO nations, even though aid at first was based primarily on whatever was available. The long-range goal among member nations was to standardize weapons (so all would fire same ammo), equipment (aircraft engines, combat tank components, medical kits), spare parts, and petroleum, oil, and lubricants (POL); and to conduct joint training exercises under simulated wartime conditions.[56] France would support standardization if it did not interfere with weapons production in France based on national goals. Most land exercises would be held in the fall, after crops had been harvested. In May 1951, Brig Gen John H. Michaelis was assigned to Ike's staff to concentrate on training NATO forces. Michaelis, who in 1948 had been Ike's aide in the Pentagon, received two battlefield promotions in Korea for leading his troops in routs of Chinese communist forces.

In 1959, NATO began using the symbol of a four-leaf clover to identify ammunition and explosives that were interchangeable among weapons of the fourteen member nations. By the early 1960s, US troops in France were issued M-14 rifles and M-60 machine guns, both fired the 7.62 mm ammo that had been adopted by NATO. NATO Planning Boards endeavored to standardize transportation infrastructure such as: track gauge and roadbed of railroads, markings on vehicles for wide loads, and characteristics of roadways.[57] Although member nations were responsible for their own logistics, by the early 1960s agreements were in place to provide mutual logistical support.[58]

SHAPE Relocates Near Versailles

Initially, a horse-breeding farm near Versailles was recommended as the site for the new SHAPE headquarters but the owner Marcel Boussac, a wealthy French industrialist, refused to lease the land to NATO.[59] Three other sites were eliminated because of owner's objection or difficulty in construction of utilities (water supply, sewage removal, electricity). Gen Eisenhower's staff then recommended another site near Versailles, in government-owned hunting grounds used by the French president. The site was away from the distractions of Paris, had access to communications facilities in Paris, was near a national highway, and the airports at Vélizy-Villacoublay and Orly could be reached without driving through Paris. Unlike most of France, Paris and Versailles had automatic rotary-type switchboard telephone equipment. Orly Air Base, on the east end of the airport, was expanded so US Air Force facilities could support the air transport needs of SHAPE.

SHAPE Headquarters, Marly-le-Roi, 1953 (SHAPE)

On 24 January 1951, French Defense Minister Jules Moch told Ike that elements of the French public were bitterly protesting the location of SHAPE near the Château de Versailles. Moch assured Ike that the French government would ignore the complaints.[60] In February 1951, the French approved use of the 67-acre site in the forest of Marly-le-Roi. The French name for the land was *le Trou d'Enfer* (the Hell hole). Some of the land at the edge of the forest was cultivated by Marcel Hertault. In 1951, Hertault had seeded the land with rye; on 02 April 1952, the first anniversary of SHAPE, he was proud that SHAPE had taken his land and told reporters, "Last year there was talk of war. It was war, war, war. Today there is less fear."[61] Compensation had to be paid to the French *Eau et Forêts* to replace the pheasants that disappeared when the site was cleared.

A sprawling complex of prefabricated buildings, similar in layout to the cantonment military hospitals built during World War II in the United States, was quickly constructed at a cost of about $2 million. In six months, French military engineers had surveyed the site, designed the buildings, selected contractors, and supervised construction of the headquarters.[62] During construction, French transportation workers were on strike for nineteen days. Eighteen wings, containing nearly four acres of single-story office space, were connected by 600-ft long Corridor A, nine wings on each side.[63,64] Each office wing had security rooms to store classified documents. Walls were concrete block, ceilings concrete slab, and the wood doors were covered on both sides by metal plate. Although Ike's office in Wing A-4 had a separate side entrance, he preferred to arrive at the front entrance so he could greet the staff and be seen. By the end of 1951, Ike had received visitors from all twelve NATO nations, averaging one every 15 minutes during his workdays at SHAPE.[65]

During two weeks in mid-July, Ike's "meager" staff of two-hundred officers moved from the Hôtel Astoria to Marly-le-Roi. The first official event was a briefing by Ike for visiting members of the US Senate Foreign Relations Committee on 22 July 1951. At the dedication ceremonies the next day, French President Vincent Auriol reiterated the French government's pledge to place ten divisions at the disposal of NATO. By December 1951, France was to provide NATO with five combat-ready divisions and another five divisions subject to a three-day mobilization order.[66] At the time, France had twelve divisions in Indochina and North Africa, but only five divisions at full strength in Europe.[67,68] An American division and a French division each had about 18,000 combat troops. To test the readiness of the reserves, in September 1951 the French Army mobilized a reserve division based at Nancy. Within thirty-six hours all units had assembled, drawn equipment, and begun movement to a training area in Germany.[69]

Language classes for officers and enlisted men were given at SHAPE for beginning, intermediate, and advanced students. Because NATO officers were assigned work that took long hours, it was difficult to attend the five hours of language instruction scheduled each week. Nevertheless, most English-speaking officers did learn useful French phrases which put their French-speaking colleagues at ease.[70] Maj Gen Francis H. Lanahan, chief signal officer, attended the beginners class. Ike's liaison officer Brig Gen Anthony J. Drexel Biddle, Jr., a veteran diplomat in civilian life, took the advanced class to refresh his already fluent French.[71] Biddle was Executive for National Military Representatives, whose members were to express their nation's points of view to the Supreme Commander. All staff officers, regardless of nationality, were to represent SHAPE. By mid-1952, there were sixteen US general and flag officers assigned to SHAPE. Thirty-seven officers of equivalent rank were from the other NATO nations.[72]

Due to the sensitive nature of work at SHAPE, all parts of the building except the cafeteria were considered restricted areas. The cafeteria was run by the British Navy, Army, and Air Force Institute (NAAFI), roughly equivalent to the American USO organization. French officers complained that

NAAFI imported canned goods and meat from the UK rather than purchase fresh produce from France. French cafeteria employees complained they were badly fed and badly paid because the English prepared the cuisine and the French managed the budget. Most meals cost $1.50, including a glass of wine and cup of bland coffee.[73, 74]

In a spoof guide to SHAPE headquarters, called "The Anglo-Saxons Guide to SHAPE By Day," the anonymous French authors wrote that in the modern SHAPE buildings heat came up from the floor and rain down through the roof. Parking, for vehicles displaying SF license plates, was divided into two categories called large vehicles (meaning American cars) and small vehicles (European). The guide advised owners of medium size cars not to worry about the categories, they would be ticketed by MPs wherever they parked. The newsstand, located in Corridor A, sold daily papers from capital cities of member nations. Ambitious officers read *Le Monde* (French), *The New York Herald Tribune* (US), and *The Manchester Guardian* (British).

In 1965, French military engineers directed by Brig Gen Michel Laferrerrie submitted architectural plans for a new $8 million SHAPE headquarters. The design, modeled after the Hôtel des Invalides in Paris, was approved by NATO Supreme Commander Gen Lyman Lemnitzer in May, but President de Gaulle opposed its construction.[75]

For many years after SHAPE moved in 1967 to Belgium, the buildings were used by BULL (a French government supported computer company). French contractors had guaranteed Ike that the structures would last ten years.[76] In 2008, the SHAPE buildings were bulldozed to the ground—they had lasted nearly sixty years.

Villas at Marnes-la-Coquette

The French government, pleased that Ike had returned to France, gave NATO the choice of several villas for use as the official residence of the Supreme Commander. By tradition, the residence of the highest-ranking officer of an American command is referred to as Quarters One. Mamie Eisenhower selected the Villa Saint-Pierre at Marnes-la-Coquette to be Quarters One, although it was the least elaborate of the villas she was shown. After living for six months in a four room, two bathroom suite at the Hôtel Trianon Palace in Versailles, Ike and Mamie moved into the villa on 22 August 1951. The entire second floor of the Trianon had been leased by SHAPE for Ike and high-ranking officers. During World War II, from September 1944 to February 1945, Ike's SHAEF headquarters had been located at the Trianon.

Villa Saint-Pierre, once used by Napoléon III, had fourteen rooms and a dining room that could seat twenty-two. Although the dining room and two salons were large, the upstairs bedrooms were very small. To furnish the villa, the French government assigned several interior designers to help Mamie select antique furniture from French warehouses. Even Napoléon's bed from Fontainebleau was loaned for use in one guest bedroom.[77] (See photo on page 56.)

For leisure, Ike enjoyed golf, fishing, poker, and bridge. The six-acre property, within a compound of four villas, included a small pond stocked with trout, enough land for Ike's vegetable garden, and nine holes for putting. Tall bushes discretely concealed a large statue of a nude female. The Villa La Chênaie next door was used by Ike's Chief of Staff, General Alfred M. Gruenther, for Quarters Two. Ike and Gruenther, his best friend in the Army, had adjoining offices at SHAPE. The next door neighbors, both avid card players, often played poker or bridge in the evenings.[78] They were joined by Ike's physician Maj Gen Howard McCleary Snyder, the senior medical officer at SHAPE and an evening kibitzer, who looked on and offered unwanted card-playing advice. Snyder lived in the third villa in the compound. The fourth was used by Lt Col Robert L. Schulz, Ike's aide, and M/Sgt Leonard D. Dry, Ike's driver. During his first term as US President, Ike occasionally summoned Gruenther to Washington for advice, bridge, and a round of golf.[79]

Security for the compound, surrounded by a high wall, was provided by US and British MPs and French gendarmes. MPs, armed with M2 carbines, secured the perimeter of the compound at night. According to PFC Joseph T. Miller of the 520th MP Co, on cold nights Mamie sent coffee to the soldiers guarding the perimeter. Signal corpsmen from the 7th Signal Bn operated the switchboard in the guardhouse at the compound. One cold night in 1951, PFC Francis J. Bentz answered a call from a Quarters One bedroom. A female voice (Mamie) asked if the GIs were warm.[80]

In 1953, Maurice Chevalier purchased a large villa located on the edge of the compound from a millionaire philanthropist. The villa at 4, rue de Réservoir was named La Louque in honor of his mother. Chevalier, an internationally popular actor and singer, starred in the musical *Gigi,* winner of the 1958 Academy Award for Best Picture.[81] His SACEUR neighbor would be a series of four-star generals: Gruenther, Norstad, and Lemnitzer. During a birthday party for Chevalier hosted by Gruenther at Villa St.-Pierre, Col Edward L. Rowny overheard an awe-struck US Army wife ask "Monsieur Chevalier have you lived in Paris all of your life?" Chevalier quipped in English "Not yet, Madame."[82] In December 1967, Chevalier, recently retired from show business, sent his best wishes for 1968 to Gen Lyman L. Lemnitzer at the new SHAPE headquarters in Belgium. In his handwritten note, Chevalier said that he missed his former neighbor's amiable nature.[83] Today the former NATO villas are occupied by private citizens and rue de Réservoir has been renamed rue Maurice Chevalier. For many years after the Americans departed, Johnny Hallyday (the "French Elvis Presley") lived nearby.

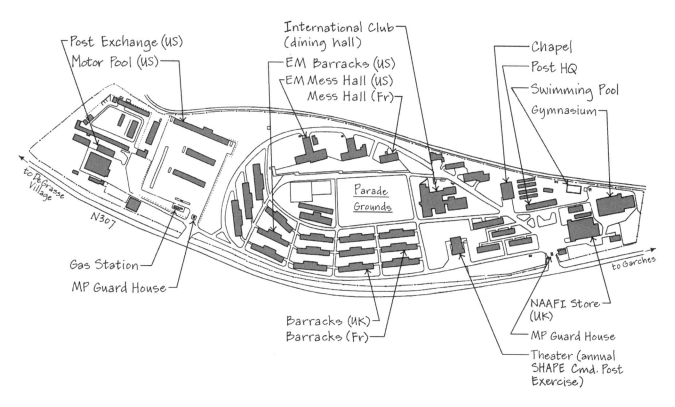

Camp Voluceau

Camp Voluceau at Rocquencourt

In November 1952, SHAPE Support Group troops from the 520th Military Police Co (Service), 7th Signal Bn (Service), and 22nd Transportation Co (Car) moved to new buildings at Camp Voluceau in Rocquencourt, near SHAPE. Troops of 7th Signal Bn had been billeted at Caserne Limoges in Versailles, where rooms were heated by coal-burning, pot belly stoves. The 520th MP Co, commanded by Capt Roy W. Lundquist, had been billeted in dilapidated buildings at Camp des Loges. The 22nd Trans Co had been billeted at the leased Blériot Aircraft Factory along the Seine River in Suresnes. Camp Voluceau had an International Club, theater, gymnasium, post exchange, and two outdoor swimming pools (adults and children). There were separate modern mess halls and barracks for American, French, and British troops. Although they ate nationally, according to a French gendarme, "we think in SHAPE." [84] Gen Gruenther believed it was essential to have a chapel at Voluceau. American, French, and British doctors held sick call each day at international infirmaries at Camp Voluceau and nearby SHAPE headquarters.

The 520th MP Co was responsible for the security of SHAPE Headquarters, Camp Voluceau, and SHAPE Village. Before the move of headquarters, they had provided security at the Hôtel Astoria. GIs of the 520th MP Co had to be dependable, meet high standards of appearance, called "military bearing," and have working knowledge of laws and military regulations. Each newcomer went through a two-week orientation period to determine if he met the high standards. Those who did not measure up were sent to other posts in France. Six foot tall MPs in well-starched uniforms, brass polished, and shoes shined, were the front gate face of the US military in France.[85] MPs of the 520th MP Co controlled crowds of civilians who, inspired by the French communist party, frequently gathered outside the front gate of SHAPE to protest the US, including Ike. French gendarmes accompanied American MPs on motor patrols outside military installations.[86] MPs were trained to identify suspicious behavior and to mark the scene of a vehicle accident. Four GIs of the 520th had a Cosmic security clearance. One of the four stood guard outside the Supreme Commander's door to the corridor when the SACEUR was at headquarters. Armed with a .45 cal automatic pistol, loaded with a 7-round magazine, the guard was the last line of defense.[87]

One MP assigned to the 520th in 1952-53 was Private Edward M. Kennedy. His father had been US Ambassador to Great Britain; his older brother was US Senator from Massachusetts who would become president in 1960. Kennedy enlisted after being expelled from Harvard University for academic dishonesty.[88] Although the 520th prohibited unmarried, low-ranking GIs from owning a car, Kennedy drove a Hillman Minx, which he parked at Camp des Loges. Most privates in the 520th did not object to this favoritism, they were glad someone in the barracks had a car.[89]

The 7th Signal Battalion, commanded by Lt Col Charles E. Burner, arrived in France in May 1951. A WAC company joined the battalion at the end of 1951.[90] The battalion installed and maintained about 2,000 telephones and teletype machines linking SHAPE by commercial landlines to subordinate commands and the capitals of the fifteen NATO nations. During construction of SHAPE headquarters at Marly, 7th Signal Bn personnel dug trenches and installed twenty-five underground trunk phone lines. The battalion worked closely with the French signal detachment and the British signal squadron. Signal personnel operated cryptographic equipment to code and decode classified messages.[91]

Personnel of the 22nd Transportation Co drove high-ranking officials throughout the Paris area. Most drivers held Secret security clearances; a few had Cosmic clearances. The GIs were armed with guide books, street maps, and lists of military installations and facilities. Beginning in March 1953, the annual NATO command post exercise (CPX) was held in the theater at Camp Voluceau. During NATO conferences and command post exercises, it was essential that the drivers knew the quickest route from hotels to Voluceau, SHAPE headquarters, and Palais de Chaillot.[92] Drivers also learned how to evade Parisian drivers, who raced wildly from one intersection to the next. Adding to the confusion were the small cars and motorbikes that darted into gaps in traffic without warning. In December 1959, the Western Big Four, US President Eisenhower, French President de Gaulle, British Prime Minister Harold Macmillan, and West German Chancellor Konrad Adenauer, met in Paris. Fifty-three US Army sedans were kept busy transporting diplomats and military personnel to and from various functions. Drivers from the 82nd Transportation Co (Light Truck) at Caserne Sidi Brahim, Étain, were sent on temporary duty to Camp des Loges to assist the Paris-based drivers.[93]

In the early 1960s, the fleet of American-made sedans at Camp Voluceau were replaced by French Peugeot 404s. The SACEUR used a Mercedes-Benz 300-SE leased to SHAPE by the German manufacturer for $1 a year. A modified 5-ton signal communications van, normally parked at the Camp Voluceau motor pool, was used as the SACEURs mobile command post. Each year, the van was deployed to a remote location to test the ability of SHAPE to operate in the field.[94] Buildings at the former Camp Voluceau installation are now used by INRIA (French government organization for research in computer science) and as a training center by the fire department of Paris.

Gen Lemnitzer at SHAPE Command Post Exercise, Camp Voluceau, Rocquencourt, 1964 (SHAPE)

Multi-national military police patrol, SHAPE, Marly-le-Roi, 1966 (SHAPE)

Command Posts for War

In time of war, key personnel of SHAPE and European Command were to take refuge in the underground atomic blast-resistant SHAPE command post built in the Forêt de St.-Germain-en-Laye on the outskirts of Le Mesnil-le-Roi and at the renovated Rochonvillers Maginot Line fort in the Lorraine region. SHAPE command post was 3 miles north of St.-Germain-en-Laye; Rochonvillers fort was 7 miles northwest of Thionville. By the 1960s, the SHAPE command post, nicknamed "The Nightclub," continuously monitored a network of radar sites from Norway to Turkey to provide early warning of a Soviet attack.[95] Staff from SHAPE at Marly-le-Roi rode to the command post in buses marked "Nightclub." Ad hoc groups of NATO engineering experts studied how to reduce vulnerability of war headquarters to sabotage, nuclear blast and radiation effects, and chemical attack. Tunnels were designed to divert blast away from interior entry doors, walls were lined to reduce concrete spalling, and charcoal filters were installed in ventilation systems.

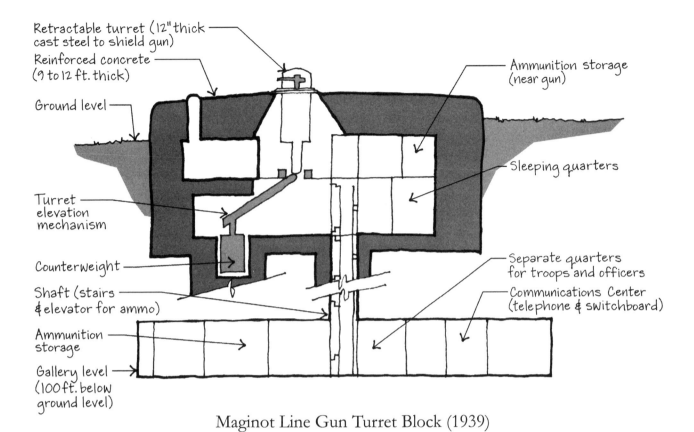

Maginot Line Gun Turret Block (1939)

The Maginot Line forts, constructed during the period of 1930 to 1938, were believed to be sufficiently hardened to resist nuclear attack. At forts designed by French engineers to have the highest degree of protection, roof slabs and exterior walls were 12 ft thick reinforced concrete. The forts also had an extensive network of tunnels about 100 ft below ground level.[96] In the late 1940s, France restored electrical power to the Maginot Line forts and assigned a small maintenance staff to work the entire 150-mile-long line of defense. However, communication between forts and anti-gas, air-pressure systems remained in disrepair until funds for renovations were provided by NATO.[97]

During the Cold War, Block 5 at Rochonvillers, the largest firing block in northeastern France, was closed because it was not conveniently located for storage. It also was believed that firing blocks would not be needed to defend the NATO command centers. In the 1950s, three underground structures in the garrison area at Rochonvillers were renovated: *magasin* (originally ammo storage), *caserne* (living quarters), and *usine* (power plant). The NATO command center was located in the main magazine. For security, the entrance was protected by a diamond-shaped moat (called *fossé diamant*) and an armored door.[98] Water was pumped out of the underground chambers, the narrow-gage railroad was repaired, and modern communications equipment was installed. In 1955, the 175th Signal Co (Service) was sent to France to maintain and operate communications equipment at Maginot Line installations. The 175th and 208th Signal Companies were billeted at Camp Angevillers, a French caserne built in 1933 near Rochonvillers and Molvange. The caserne had been built so French troops on the Maginot Line could live above ground until it was believed an invasion was imminent.

When SHAPE moved to Belgium in 1967, a new NATO underground command post was built under a huge earth-covered berm at the side of SHAPE headquarters building at Casteau. The Pentagon approved $2.9 million to build a communications center in Germany for European Command, relocated from Camp des Loges. For its nuclear strike force, France used command posts at Taverny, built 190 ft under a hill near Paris; at Mont Verdun, near Lyon; and at Drachenbronn, a Maginot Line fort near Lambach. At Drachenbronn, French units assigned to NATOs 4th Allied Tactical Air Force had provided control of NATO aircraft and plotted all aircraft movements observed on radar within their area of responsibility. This enabled them to issue warning of a Soviet air attack.[99, 100]

Paris Blockhouse

The US Army Signal Communications Center was located at 27-29, rue La Pérouse, a few blocks from the Astoria.[101] The six-floor building, which the French called the *Blockhaus*, had been built by the Germans during World War II on private property. It was an incredibly ugly, massive reinforced concrete structure designed to withstand Allied bombing. The walls and roof were similar to the blast-resistant submarine pens built along the Atlantic Coast of France. A tunnel from the basement led to a nearby hotel where German officers were billeted during the occupation. In September 1944, it was requisitioned by the US Army and used rent free until November 1949 when the owner and the French government signed a lease. The US paid rent until December 1957 when the French government acquired the property and leased it to the US Army rent free.

In 1957, the Center had eighty-nine long distance lines operated by twenty-four French female employees. The "red-line" operators gave instant attention to the top eight military and civilian chiefs. Communications staff included two officers, eight enlisted men, and thirty-five French civilian operators and supervisors.[102] The SHAPE switchboard was located at the Blockhouse from January until July 1951 when SHAPE moved to Marly-le-Roi. The White House Communications Agency also had a small detachment at the Blockhouse. In December 1957, the detachment was augmented by signal specialists when President Eisenhower attended NATO meetings in Paris. During his six-day visit to Paris, Ike spoke at the North Atlantic Council meeting, visited his former headquarters at SHAPE, and met privately with heads of NATO nations to assure them that US troops would remain in Europe as long as the Soviet threat persisted.[103] In September 1959, when Ike attended the Four Powers Summit Meeting in Paris, the Agency provided communications links between the President's traveling party, the US Embassy, and hotels where the VIPs were housed. Among the VIPs was popular radio/TV personality Arthur Godfrey.[104] Godfrey, a US Navy reserve commander, had volunteered in 1951 to serve on Ike's staff at SHAPE.

From 1955-67 headquarters for US European Command's unconventional warfare planning task force, called Support Operations Task Force, Europe (SOTFE), was located on the second floor of the Blockhouse. SOTFE staff consisted of personnel from the uniformed armed services and the Central Intelligence Agency. In wartime, SOTFE would control the US Army 10th Special Forces Group (SFG), which had been formed in June 1952 at Fort

Signal Corps Blockhouse, Paris (US Army)

Bragg, North Carolina. The 10th SFG, with detachments stationed at Bad Tölz in Germany and St.-André-de-l'Eure in France, recruited volunteers fluent in Central European languages.[105] An Army Special Forces unit of six teams (cover name Det A) was stationed in Berlin. The special forces trained with unconventional forces of several NATO nations. Training emphasized combat fitness, map reading, advanced first aid, and survival techniques.[106] In the event of a Soviet invasion, teams would be dropped by parachute behind enemy lines to link up with partisans in the Soviet bloc. Plans also included using teams trained to swim underwater into East Germany on missions to disable command and control centers.[107] SOTFE coordinated plans for the secret stay-behind NATO resistance forces which had been organized outside the normal armies. The "stay-behinds" were to engage in guerrilla warfare and sabotage, and assist the escape and evasion of Allied military. In France these forces, code named *Rose des Vents*, trained in the Forêt d'Orléans near Cercottes and Fort Montlouis near Spain.[108, 109] From 1958 to 1960, SOTFE was commanded by Col Howard B. St. Clair, who had received medals for valor in combat in World War II and the Korean War. There were about a dozen field grade officers assigned to SOTFE.

Although its demolition was difficult, French construction workers destroyed the Blockhouse in the early 1970s so a modern office building could be built on the valuable property. Due to stringent safety measures, it took almost a year to demolish the building. A temporary enclosure was built to contain flying debris and explosives were carefully sized to lessen the impact of vibrations.[110] Similar attempts in Berlin and Hamburg, Germany to demolish 130-ft high reinforced-concrete towers, designed by Albert Speer for use as anti-aircraft gun emplacements, were halted because the demolition explosions damaged nearby buildings.[111]

NATO Communications Systems

To transmit sensitive information, NATO installed radio-relay links and funded cable projects to augment landline telephone and telegraph networks of member nations.[112] In France the *Postes, télégraphes et téléphones* (PTT) integrated NATO's landline circuits into its civil systems for use during peacetime. However, the time it took PTT to convert these circuits to exclusive military use would take more than one hour, rendering the system useless to respond to a surprise attack by the Soviets.[113] In addition, landline circuits were vulnerable to sabotage and attack; radio links were vulnerable to jamming techniques NATO believed the Soviets had developed.[114] For nuclear retaliation to be credible, it was essential that "go codes" could be transmitted rapidly and securely.

In 1955, SHAPE submitted a plan to the North Atlantic Council, NATO's political directorate, to install an exclusive military network to transmit reliable and secure messages instantaneously between SHAPE at Marly and key NATO commands. The plan, approved for the Allied Command Europe (ACE) in 1956, would be called project ACE HIGH. Voice and telegraph circuits would be converted to very-high frequency (VHF) signals. Amplified VHF signals were beamed upward where they would scatter downward through the tropospheric layer, which extends from the ground to 6 to 10 miles above the earth. The ACE HIGH tropospheric scatter system transmitted the VHF signals between 65-ft diameter dish-shaped antennas at forty-nine sites, located about 200 miles apart. Each site "captured" scattered signals and relayed them on to the next. Five two-man military teams of technicians were assigned to each intermediate station. The system also incorporated line-of-sight microwave towers at forty sites, located on high ground about 25 miles apart. The routes of the microwave systems were called "tails."

ACE HIGH antennas, Norway, 1959 (SHAPE)

The routes of ACE HIGH extended over 9,000 miles through nine NATO nations. One route extended from northern Norway through central Europe and France to eastern Turkey; one from Norway through Great Britain to France. The master system control center, located about 40 miles north of Paris at Auneuil, was called "Paris North." Paris North had equipment to convert two-hundred fifty voice circuits and one-hundred eighty telegraph circuits to VHF signals and transmit them. It also received VHF signals and converted them back to voice.[115] When completed during 1963, ACE HIGH instantly could transmit early warning, alert, and authorized retaliation messages.

SHAPE Village at St.-Germain-en-Laye

In the 1950s, housing was difficult to find in France and expensive. In Paris, more than 70% of dwellings were rated substandard by Paris housing authorities.[116] It was impossible for some SHAPE personnel to find affordable housing because pay among NATO nations differed widely. US Army master sergeants received greater pay than French lieutenant colonels.[117] Concerned about the difference in pay, Ike convinced the French to build a residential complex for SHAPE personnel. The project, called SHAPE Village, was designed by French architects Félix Dumail and Jean Dubuisson and funded with French government appropriations and Marshall Plan counterpart funds (monies held in European banks for use on projects in Europe).[118] Because structural components were prefabricated off-site, ten apartment buildings were completed in only five months on the grounds of Château d'Hennemont in St.-Germain-en-Laye. The château had been camouflaged during the German occupation to reduce its visibility to Allied bomber pilots. Initially, a Bachelor Officers Quarters, Officer's Club, and NCO Club were located in the château. On 14 September 1951, Ike visited SHAPE Village as the buildings neared completion. Afterwards, he wrote to French Prime Minister René Pleven that construction progress was splendid and his Allied officers were looking forward to completion of the village. In his letter, Ike also asked for funds from France to build a village for AFCENT personnel at Fontainebleau.[119]

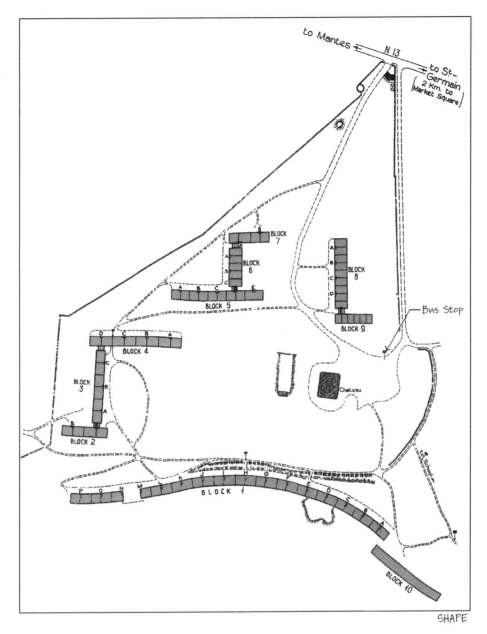

SHAPE Village at St.-Germain-en-Laye (1952)

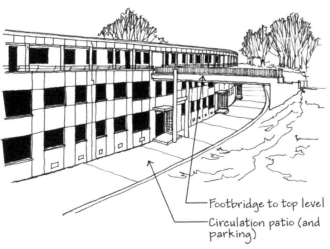

SHAPE Village Apartment Block No. 1

During the grand opening of SHAPE Village on 31 October 1951, Ike presented the first keys to an NCO family.[120] The three-hundred three apartments would house more than one-thousand in a 55-acre park like setting. The unusual "S"-shape of Apartment Building No. 1 provided daylight and natural ventilation to all its units. Regulations for occupants included: chimneys to be swept once a year, no bonfires on park grounds, carpets not to be shaken or beaten at windows (except between 8 and 10 am), and rubbish not to be thrown from windows or dumped on lawns or nearby wooded areas.[121] Because apartments were assigned based on rank and number of family members not nationality, officers and dependents from many nations became friendly neighbors.[122] However, largely due to differences in pay and language, occupants tended to socialize primarily with fellow countrymen.[123]

On 18 January 1952, the SHAPE dependents school (grades 1 to 8) opened with only eighteen pupils and two teachers using one classroom in the former stables of the château. By 1965, more than 1,600 students attended grades 1 to 12 at the modern SHAPE International School annex built across the road.[124] René Taillard was director of the school from 1952 until 1965, when he was succeeded by Edgar Scherer. From 1952 to 1967, more than 6,000 students from fourteen nations had attended the SHAPE International School. Today, SHAPE Village, now called Village d'Hennemont, provides housing for Paris area French military personnel and civilians who teach at the Lycée International.

Château d'Hennemont, St.-Germain-en-Laye, 1964
(SHAPE)

Gen Lyman L. Lemnitzer visits SHAPE School, 1965
(NDU Archives)

American Hospital at Neuilly

In 1906, the American Hospital at Neuilly-sur-Seine opened to serve Americans living in Paris. It was given a federal charter by the US Congress in 1913. During World War II, the hospital was administered by the French Red Cross. Retired French General Aldebert de Chambrun, a descendent of Lafayette, served as interim director. Chief physician Dr. Sumner W. Jackson, an American, remained at the hospital during the German occupation. He worked long hours and aided the French resistance. Allied airmen were hidden in the hospital and in his apartment until false papers could be obtained for them so they could be taken to neutral Spain. His apartment on 11, avenue Foch also was a mail drop for the resistance. In May 1944, Dr. Jackson, his wife Charlotte, and teenage son Phillip were arrested by the Milice (Vichy's Gestapo) and taken to internment camps. Charlotte and Phillip survived. Dr. Jackson was killed in May 1945 when the Allies bombed German prison ships on the Baltic Sea, just days before the Germans surrendered.[125]

In September 1944 shortly after Paris was liberated, the French ministry of health requisitioned the American Hospital for the US Army's 350th Station Hospital.[126] The Army used the buildings until they were returned to the American Hospital in February 1946. In 1947, the US Army signed an agreement with the American Hospital to allocate forty beds to serve personnel of the American Graves Registration Command and other Army units still in France.[127] By the late 1940s, the civilian hospital had 160 beds, a staff of eighty doctors, and one-hundred thirty-six nurses and technicians.[128]

In April 1951, the US Army leased two floors of the American Hospital for a dispensary. In 1953, the annual rent was $237,552. Initially, the 61st General Dispensary had 52 beds (including one psychiatric closed room) on the first floor of the east wing, a staff of eight doctors, seven dentists, three Army nurses, sixteen civilian nurses, and seventy-six enlisted men. Administration offices were on the second floor and mess facilities on the ground floor. Barracks for the enlisted personnel were at Camp des Loges.

American Hospital, Neuilly (US Army)

The 61st Gen Disp was a SHAPE support unit serving American and Canadian military personnel and their dependents. The other NATO nations had their own medical service arrangements. The dispensary treated 3,500 patients each month; dentists 1,500. In July 1951 at the Neuilly maternity ward, Jennifer Goldwyn, wife of 1st Lt Samuel Goldwyn, Jr., gave birth to a girl, nicknamed Cricket.[129] Patients needing more than one to two weeks hospitalization were transported to Germany. For some complicated surgeries, experienced specialists from the civilian wings at the hospital aided the Army doctors. Labs, X-ray unit, and operating rooms were shared with the civilian hospital staff.

So many general and flag officers were treated at Neuilly that Maj Thomas L. Robbins, commander of the 61st Gen Disp in 1953, told a reporter that he could not remember all their names. The dispensary also treated celebrity USO entertainers and Pentagon officials in France on Army business.[130] In 1955, the 196th Station Hospital replaced the 61st Gen Disp. In 1958, the 196th Sta Hosp was authorized seventeen officers and one-hundred seventy-four nurses and enlisted personnel. When the US military forces departed from France in 1967, the 196th Sta Hosp moved to Casteau near Mons, Belgium. The American Hospital purchased the US Army's abandoned modern medical equipment (X-ray machines, operation tables) for about 25% of its estimated value.[131, 132]

Artillery wing of École Militaire, Paris, 1952 (SHAPE)

NATO Defense College

The NATO Defense College was established in Paris to train senior officers (lieutenant colonel, colonel, or equivalent grade) and civilians on military, political, economic, and social problems faced by the alliance. During the period of occupation and war, Allied officers had not attended staff colleges. As envisioned by Gen Eisenhower, the purpose of the college was to imbue NATO officers with a spirit of cooperation and collaboration. In 1931-32, Ike had taught at the Industrial College of the Armed Forces in Washington, DC, one of the senior military education colleges in the US. Attendance not only broadened knowledge, but also fostered lifelong friendships among fellow students. Retired Lt Gen Edward L. Rowny, who served as secretary of the general staff at SHAPE under the demanding Gruenther and the low-key Norstad, believed that "next to fighting side-by-side in combat," the colleges were one of the best places to make friends.[133]

The NATO College used part of the artillery wing of the École Militaire (French Military Academy), across the Champ de Mars from the Eiffel Tower. Graduates of the famous school, built during the reign of Louis IX, include the great marshals of France. Napoléon, who was admitted in 1784, graduated as a lieutenant of artillery. For several decades, the rooms utilized by the College had stored French military records. Because the ceilings were extremely high, the rooms were renovated to provide two levels of modern classrooms, offices, and a library.[134, 135]

Forty-five students representing ten nations attended the first course which began on 19 November 1951 under the supervision of the commandant, French Admiral André-Georges Lemonnier. Lemonnier had been serving as Ike's Naval deputy at SHAPE and in 1944 had participated in the Normandy invasion to liberate France.[136] Initially, NATO agreed that the commandant should be an officer from the US, France, or Great Britain, the three nations that formed the NATO Standing Group of chiefs of staff responsible for military doctrine. US Army Brig Gen Paul W. Caraway became the first coordinator of instruction. Caraway was believed to be destined for higher rank due to his strategic planning prowess and tact with allies. The College had a faculty of six officers of general or flag rank and eleven colonels, ten part-time language instructors, and an administrative staff of one-hundred twenty-five. It had a far lower student-faculty ratio than the senior military colleges in the US. Students were to learn the art of compromise, overcome language barriers, and understand how national viewpoints affected NATO.

The courses, lasting just over five months, were held twice each year. Each course had sixty slots allotted among the fifteen member nations, but fifty-four was the maximum accepted because of space limitations. The US, France, Great Britain, and Italy each had seven slots, the other nations fewer. Iceland and Luxembourg each had one. During the years in Paris, Luxembourg sent a representative to one course, Iceland none. By 1955, the normal enrollment of the College had students representing thirteen countries and speaking ten different languages. The official languages were French and English and lectures were given in one with simultaneous translation into the other. Although basic proficiency in French or English was a requirement for admission, two of the five months had to be devoted to language training. Regardless, most students from Germany, Greece, and Turkey still had difficulty understanding lectures.

Because students were responsible for finding living accommodations, which in Paris were scarce and expensive, they were dispersed throughout the city. This and the language barrier made socializing after class difficult. Students seldom were invited into French homes because French social life revolved around family. Closer relationships were developed during the month when students toured other member nations. The host countries entertained students in groups and by individual visits to homes, enabling them to observe other cultures.[137]

Unlike military colleges that define problems from a national viewpoint, the NATO Defense College strove to create an international outlook through its lectures, seminar discussions, and tours to member nations. From the beginning in 1951, Ike intended that the graduates would form a cadre of officers and civilians, which would contribute to the success of NATO. About one-hundred students graduated each year; more than 1,500 students graduated during the fifteen years the College was in Paris. The twenty-ninth course ended on 23 July 1966 and preparations began to move the College from Paris to Rome, Italy.[138]

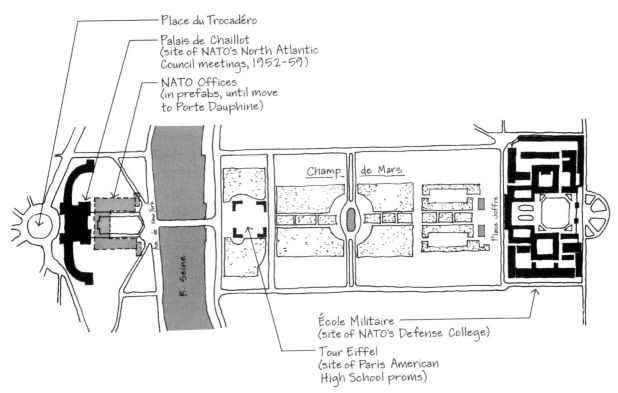

NATO at Palais de Chaillot & École Militaire

Palais de Chaillot

Palais de Chaillot at Place du Trocadéro, across the Seine from École Militaire and the Eiffel Tower, was built for the 1937 International Exposition of Modern Art. Designed by French architect Jacques Carlu, the Art Deco style building has two prominent curved wings on a bluff overlooking the Seine.[139] For several years, Carlu had been an architectural educator at Fontainebleau, France, and the Massachusetts Institute of Technology, Cambridge, Massachusetts. In 1951, temporary structures were hastily erected in the gardens between the Palais and the Seine for use by the sixth annual session of the General Assembly of the United Nations. The prefabricated buildings of inexpensive panels were designed by Carlu to be compatible with the Palais and were scheduled to be demolished within six months. Before demolition began, the French government invited the North Atlantic Council (NAC), consisting of top cabinet officers from each NATO nation, to install its permanent headquarters in the buildings. In April 1952, the NAC held its formal meetings at the Palais annex. By the 1960s, the NAC met two or three times a year. Permanent NAC civilian representatives, holding rank of ambassador, met one or two times each week.[140]

In December 1957 for the first time in NATO history, heads of government attended the NAC meeting. At this historic meeting, the NATO nations agreed in principle to President Eisenhower's offer to place US intermediate-range ballistic missiles in Europe to counter the Soviet missile threat. On the morning of 17 December, during a lull in the meetings, Ike made a nostalgic visit to SHAPE headquarters at Marly-le-Roi. After seeing his old office, now occupied by Gen Norstad, he stopped on the front steps to address a crowd of SHAPE personnel and their family members. It was the first time Ike had spoken extemporaneously in public since his stroke in late November.[141]

Porte Dauphine

Parisians considered the prefabricated buildings at Chaillot to be an eyesore. The buildings were demolished after NATO headquarters moved in 1959 to a newly constructed building, designed by Carlu at Porte Dauphine, on the edge of the Bois de Boulogne. Excavation for the basement uncovered buried walls of the 1840s fortifications of Paris. NATO member nations contributed to the project. France built the stone-clad, concrete and steel-frame structure. The US provided the air-conditioning system; Great Britain kitchen equipment for two restaurants and the cafeteria. Belgium installed the aluminum-frame windows; Italy the marble floors and patios; West Germany the telephone system. Denmark sent furniture for the council chamber, library, and offices. There were two underground garages for five-hundred vehicles and one-hundred scooters and motorbikes. About 1,400 civilians from the fifteen member nations worked in the modern, seven-story A-shaped building. Staff no longer worked in cramped rooms. There were thirteen conference rooms and the new council chamber had: a press gallery that seated one-hundred seventy, glass-enclosed radio and TV booths, and workrooms along the perimeter for the press.[142-144] Today the Porte Dauphine building is the Université de Paris IX, adjacent to the *Périphérique*, the highway which encircles Paris.

When France withdrew from NATO's integrated military commands in 1966, President Charles de Gaulle did not ask the NAC to leave Paris. Most political leaders, however, believed that civilian control of military at SHAPE in Belgium would be diluted if NAC remained in France. Consequently, NATO headquarters moved in 1968 to Evere on the outskirts of Brussels, Belgium, to be close to the relocated SHAPE headquarters at Casteau near Mons. NATO headquarters were built on the site of the 1958 Brussels World's Fair, ironically at the former location of the French pavilion.[145]

CHAPTER 2: *NATO and SHAPE in Paris*

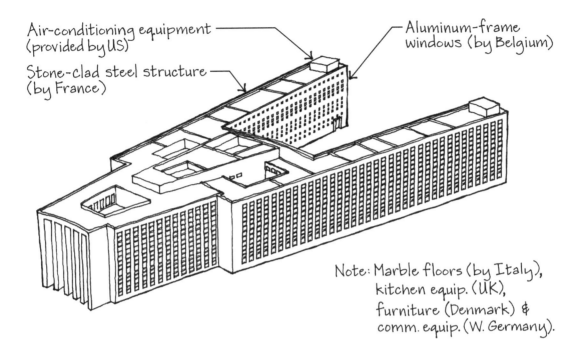

NATO Headquarters at Porte Dauphine

Ike's Farewell to France

In 1951, it was believed that the Soviets had 175 to 200 divisions. Ike had to convince NATO nations to rearm to meet this threat. During meetings held from 20 to 25 February 1952 in Lisbon, Portugal, NATO ministers finally approved the rearming of West Germany and set goals for NATO forces that included having twenty-five active army divisions with twenty-five in reserve and 4,000 aircraft by the end of 1952.[146] France, Belgium, and the Netherlands were not keen on rearming the Germans. There would be about fifty NATO air bases in France. The Europeans called this emerging NATO force the "Eisenhower Army." During his tenure at SHAPE, Ike also persuaded the NATO nations to increase their defense budgets, expand the size of their armed forces, and lengthen time of service for their conscripts. Denmark and France increased length of service to eighteen months, the Netherlands to twenty, and Belgium to twenty-four. Ike's farewell tour from 16 April to 20 May 1952 included visits to heads of state of Belgium, Luxembourg, Germany, Italy, Denmark, Norway, Great Britain, and the Netherlands. On 21 May, Ike received the *Medialle Militaire* from Prime Minister René Pleven at Les Invalides in Paris and afterwards lunched with French President Vincent Auriol.

On 23 May, he gave a farewell speech to NATO units assembled in formation at the Henri IV courtyard of the château in Fontainebleau. At the brief ceremony, French Gen Alphonse-Pierre Juin, commander of land forces in Central Europe, introduced Ike. Juin told the general that "wherever you may go in the future, you will always be in our hearts our supreme commander—our general." As professional soldiers, Juin noted that Ike's subordinates could not express any wishes of good luck in the future (because Eisenhower would be campaigning to be the Republican candidate for US president), but it was correct to "express gratitude for the leadership and guidance you have given us." With gendarme motorcycle escorts, Ike sped back to Paris for meetings with Auriol and Pleven.[147, 148]

Ike speaks to NATO troops at Cour Henry IV, Château de Fontainebleau, 23 May 1952 (US Air Force)

On 30 May, a boys choir sang "Auld Lang Syne" as Ike and Mamie left their villa in Marnes-la-Coquette. The next day, Ike returned to the US to run for president. His seventeen months at SHAPE were hectic, with daily briefings, numerous meetings with VIP visitors, and frequent travel to inspect troops and installations of the twelve allied countries. However, he did play golf. About three afternoons a month, Ike golfed at St.-Germain-en-Laye, Morfontaine at Senlis, or Fontainebleau, but did not play during five of his months in France.[149]

Boys choir at Villa St.-Pierre, Marnes-la-Coquette, 30 May 1952 (SHAPE)

Ike's Successors at SHAPE

General Matthew B. Ridgway (1952-53)

General Ridgway, a battle-tested leader, became the second Supreme Commander. To assure the NATO political leaders of continuity, Gen Gruenther continued to serve as Chief of Staff at SHAPE. On D-Day, Ridgway, then commanding officer of the 82nd Airborne Division, jumped behind German lines in Normandy. He was the first American general to land in France. In less than four months in Korea, Ridgway transformed a dispirited Eighth Army into a determined fighting force. He always wore his .45 cal M1911 automatic pistol in a hip holster, ready for action. GIs called him "Old Iron Tits" because he wore a grenade and a medical kit on his chest, attached to his paratrooper harness. This not too subtle message was that Ridgway always was ready to fight and his GIs also should be ready.[150] Because of his frequent and lengthy visits to troops at the front lines, senior leaders at the Pentagon feared Ridgway would become a casualty. Consequently, during Ridgway's command of Eighth Army, Lt Gen James A. Van Fleet was kept on alert to be his replacement. During Operation KILLER in Korea, Ridgway rallied UN forces to turn the tide of battle, but was falsely alleged to have used biological weapons against the invading communists.[151-154] Thus French communists referred to Gen Ridgway as "Le Général Microbe" or "Ridgway-la-peste," as if his name ended in *peste* (plague).

L to R at center: Lt Gen Norstad, Gen Ridgway, and Fr Gen Juin at Fontainebleau, 1952 (US Air Force)

The Chinese communists had initiated a worldwide disinformation campaign to blame the US for epidemics suffered by its conscripts in Korea. The devastating spread of diseases primarily was due to unsanitary living conditions and inadequate medical care.[155, 156] To prove the US dropped "germ bombs" in Korea, the communist press worldwide published photos of a sheet of paper covered with dead flies and an empty bomb casing used to drop leaflets.[157] In French communist newspapers, Ridgway was called the *tueur microbien* or *germ assassine*, which to most GIs sounded like a compliment as who could oppose killing germs.[158] Communist propaganda efforts also included painting slogans on walls in Paris such as "Ridgway Go Home" and "Ridgway- à la porte!" (- to the door!).

More than seven-hundred French protestors were arrested during a riot at the Place de la République in Paris, timed to protest Ridgway's arrival on 29 May 1952. SHAPE staff officer Lt Col William A.

Knowlton took his two young sons, Bill and Davis, to witness the protest, but prudently withdrew when protestors began attacking the police with poles, clubs, and cobblestones. The violence lasted five hours. The riot was organized and directed by French Communist National Assemblyman Jacques Duclos.[159] Duclos, a former pastry chef from Toulouse, had led rallies against Coca-Cola, claiming its big red trucks and bright neon signs stained the soul of French culture. The French communists also claimed Coke was not a healthy drink like wine. In response, a prominent Coca-Cola executive was quoted saying that Coke had not injured the health of the GIs who had liberated France.[160] A group of American expatriates (including some GI Bill of Rights students in Paris) planned to establish a "coke-easy" if the French National Assembly prohibited the sale of Coca-Cola in France.[161] On 09 October 1952, to counteract the communist protests, two Frenchmen presented Ridgway with a medal they had designed. The medal had the seal of Paris on one side and an American eagle, with an "R" for Ridgway on the obverse. The artisans, veterans of both world wars, believed that they represented many Frenchmen who believed that only through NATO would France be secure.[162]

Ridgway became the first SACEUR who also would command US European Command (EUCOM). This dual role clearly demonstrated the commitment of the US to NATO. The US would be involved in a war in Europe from day one, not years later as had occurred in both world wars. Eventually EUCOM headquarters would be moved from Germany to Paris. Near the end of his tenure, Ridgway placed French Gen Juin in control of land, coastal sea, and air forces in Central Europe. Previously, the SACEUR was to command AFCENT in time of war. Ridgway's tenure as SACEUR was short, in part because he lacked the advantage of being an Eisenhower protégé like Gruenther and Norstad. Unlike Ike, he also had to deal with the newly-formed permanent North Atlantic Council of political leaders who set goals and budgets for NATOs military forces. To prevent waste and duplication during the NATO buildup of infrastructure, Ridgway created a unified construction agency, called the Joint Construction Agency (JCA), that would be responsible for all US military construction in Western Europe, except Germany.[163] During his 14 months, Ridgway also solved several organizational problems involving command of Greek and Turkish forces, Mediterranean naval forces, and NATO air forces.[164] By the end of 1952, NATO exercises would include planning for the use of American nuclear weapons.[165]

Ridgway placed Greece and Turkey, who had joined NATO in February 1952, under a separate NATO command because they were not keen to be under a British officer. Ridgway located headquarters of Allied Land Forces Southeast Europe at Izmir, Turkey and, in the event of war, an advance command post at Salonika, Greece.[166] He assigned US Army Lt Gen Willard G. Wyman to be its commander. Wyman, a West Point classmate of Gruenther, would have control of ground forces of Greece and Turkey during war with the Soviets. During several visits to Greece and Turkey, Ridgway persuaded military leaders to drop their historic territorial disputes. On an inspection visit to the Southeast Command, Ridgway took with him the commanding general of Turkish land forces and his Greek counterpart. The traditional enemies were together for two days and the generals believed it was the first time Greek and Turkish officers dined together as allies.[167]

On his June 1953 farewell tour of installations in France, Ridgway stayed overnight with US Army troops in one of the "winterized" tents at Camp Bersol, rather than at a hotel in Bordeaux. The tents, built by Company A of the 83rd Engineer Construction Battalion, had plywood on the floors and sides.[168] Near the end of Ridgway's tenure as SACEUR, French newspapers covered the ceremony where French President Auriol presented the Legion of Honor to Ridgway. An accompanying photo revealed an uncomfortable Ridgway—his expression that of a soldier unaccustomed to being kissed on the cheeks by a man.

General Alfred M. Gruenther (1953 - 56)

In July 1953, the ebullient General Gruenther succeeded the more restrained Ridgway. Gruenther, who had served as Chief of Staff at SHAPE for Eisenhower and Ridgway, was well liked by the political leadership of the NATO nations. He placed greater trust in NATO officers than Ridgway who had restricted access to most NATO war plans to Americans. On inspection trips to NATO nations, Gruenther demonstrated his confidence in the Allies by taking with him officers of the country he visited. Gruenther believed his job was to raise morale of NATO and he incorporated more Allied officers at SHAPE than had Ridgway. Gruenther sent handwritten notes acknowledging births, anniversaries, promotions, and bereavements affecting any of his staff of four-hundred Allied officers at SHAPE. All departing officers were expected to drop by his office to say good bye.[169] Gruenther, a devout Roman Catholic, attended mass at the Caserne Limoges chapel with GIs of the 7th Signal Battalion and 520th MPs rather than services in Versailles with prominent French citizens.[170]

British Gen Montgomery, Gen Gruenther, Gen Norstad, and French Admiral Léon Antoine Sala at Marly-le-Roi, 20 November 1956 (SHAPE)

In 1954, Gen Gruenther opined that the strategic location of France was even more essential for the defense of Western Europe than a rearmed Germany.[171] In the 1954 Command Post Exercise (CPX) held at the theater at Camp Voluceau, Gruenther's Deputy Supreme Commander Field Marshal Montgomery used a whistle to call the generals and admirals to order. Two-hundred military chiefs responded to Monty's scenarios and pondered how atomic weapons would be used against an aggressor. One of the generals was Gen Curtis E. LeMay, chief of Strategic Air Command, America's atomic striking force of bombers.[172] During a November 1955 trip to Washington, Gruenther asked Ike's Secretary of Defense Charles E. Wilson to provide new air defense systems to NATO nations. Gruenther described existing systems as effective, if the Soviets attacked on weekdays from 8 am to 4 pm and the bombers flew no higher than 20,000 ft.[173] Although Norstad, his successor, was called the "nuclear SACEUR" by the press, Gruenther also had advocated the use of atomic weapons to support ground troops and to attack industrial and other targets in the Soviet Union. Until the mid-1950s, NATO nations were unable to assemble sufficient ground forces and relied on the threat of massive nuclear attack to deter Soviet aggression. In December 1950, NATO had an inadequate number of aircraft, including four-hundred obsolete piston-engine aircraft relics from World War II based on deteriorating airstrips. By the late 1950s, the Allied Air Forces Central Europe (AAFCE) had grown to more than 2,000 modern combat jet aircraft from seven nations: US, France, Great Britain, Canada, Belgium, the Netherlands, and West Germany.

The first 280-mm atomic cannons, called "Atomic Annie," were deployed in 1953 to Europe amid widespread publicity. The cannons could fire a W-9 atomic artillery shell at a target 18 miles away. Atomic Annie was moved by two engine-cab transporters connected at front and rear ends of the gun's long transport carriage. Overall length was 84 ft. The driver in the front transporter controlled the speed and brakes, the driver in the rear transporter just steered. They communicated by phone. Occasionally Atomic Annie would tip over in transit due to inadequate communication between drivers.[174] Atomic Annie, with a published weight of 85 tons, was limited to paved roads. Low bridges and narrow streets in some villages were impassable.

When set up in a field, the cannon was so heavy that the carrier would sink into the soil, making it impossible to "shoot and scoot." On maneuvers, an infantry platoon guarded Atomic Annie. By 1954, five-hundred twenty-five 280-mm rounds for spotting and practice were stored in the open at the US Army's Trois Fontaines Ordnance Depot, near Robert-Espagne. Spotting rounds were fired to adjust aim so atomic round would be on target. The atomic inserts did not arrive until the next year. In 1954 during Exercise INDIAN SUMMER maneuvers in Germany, it took four hours to set up and fire a practice round on target. With repetition the time was reduced to less than thirty minutes. Conventional artillery normally could deliver a round on target in four minutes.[175] Farmers living near the Army's training area at Grafenwoehr, Germany, complained that shock waves from the 280-mm practice rounds damaged their homes.

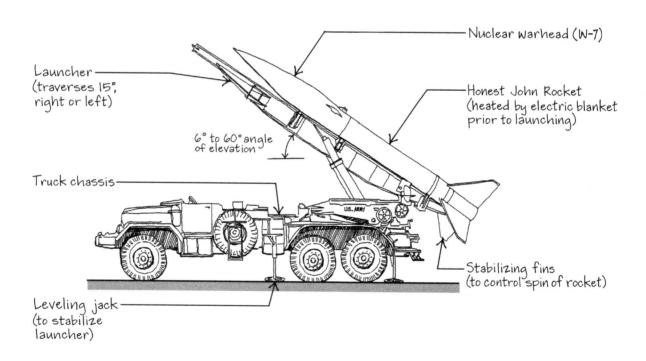

Honest John Rocket System

By 1955, NATO nations formally agreed to rely on nuclear weapons rather than the costly conventional defenses needed to deter the Soviets.[176] Defense now would rely less on numbers of troops on the ground and more on nuclear retaliation to attack invading forces and supply lines in Warsaw bloc nations. It was hoped that atomic artillery in Germany would be sufficient to repel a Soviet attack without igniting a nuclear exchange targeting US and Soviet cities. In July 1955, Gen Lauris Norstad, the youthful-looking air deputy to Gruenther, asked that Col Edward L. Rowny be assigned to SHAPE to work on nuclear policy. Norstad was developing a strategy to deploy ground troops closer to the Soviet borders and to have an incremental not massive nuclear response to Soviet aggression. Atomic artillery and rockets would be used to destroy large concentrations of invading forces and to block enemy advances through valleys and at river crossings.[177] Unbeknownst to Rowny, in June 1954 Col Goodpaster had been impressed by a recent paper Rowny had written on the influence of atomic weapons on tactics and had recommend that Rowny be assigned to SHAPE.[178]

The new administration of President Eisenhower, keen not to bankrupt the US economy, wanted a military force that would provide "a bigger bang for the buck" as some pundits wrote.[179] By US law, the use of nuclear warheads allocated to NATO was under the exclusive control of the Supreme Commander. Ironically, because a limited nuclear war would require more supporting units than a conventional war, USAREUR manpower was not reduced.[180]

In 1953, GIs at most installations received only a one-hour lecture on how to get along with the French. Army orientation pamphlets for France did not reach many of the GIs. In 1954, Gen Gruenther issued a pamphlet for US troops serving in Europe, reminding them of the importance of personal behavior because they represented the US.[181] The troops must act as guests in the homelands of friendly allies, not as conquerors. If the troops were discourteous, boastful, or dishonest, Europeans would believe a majority of Americans were the same. The pamphlet stressed that Americans should exhibit characteristics of fairness, honesty, and tolerance. Like good sportsmanship learned on the athletic field, troops were to see that everyone got a fair break. GIs were reminded that their pay was far greater than compensation for similar work in Europe. Tips on conduct included: "Don't brag.", "Don't drink more liquor than you can handle.", and "Show respect for an ally's women and old people." When in doubt, Gruenther advised following the Golden Rule: Treat others as you would like them to treat you. The 1953 "Welcome to Fontainebleau" booklet stressed that US military personnel in uniform passing the Tomb of the Unknown Soldier at the Arc de Triomphe in Paris should stop, come to attention, and render the hand salute. In spite of these good will efforts, most French men felt like poor relations to the American GIs, who wore handsome uniforms and drove big cars.[182]

On his last day at SHAPE in November 1956, Gruenther gave toys to the four-hundred children of SHAPE personnel who were not American. The toys, donated to Gruenther by Louis Marx, a wealthy American toy manufacturer, had been stored in the attic at Villa Saint-Pierre. Gruenther's wife, Grace, considered that the toys belonged to her so Col Rowny, who had been assigned the "good bye gift" project, had to negotiate a division of ownership.[183]

General Lauris Norstad (1956 - 62)

At a press conference in May 1956, Gen Gruenther announced the appointment of US Air Force General Norstad as Supreme Commander. When asked if the appointment of an Air Force officer meant a change in policy by SHAPE, Gruenther replied that in the event of another war, if the air battle were lost, the war would be lost.[184] Therefore, it was essential that NATO have a well coordinated air-ground shield in Europe. In his final press conference at SHAPE, Gruenther predicted that if the

Gen Norstad, Queen Elizabeth, Prince Philip, Mrs. Isabelle Norstad at Marnes-le-Coquette, 08 April 1957 (SHAPE)

Soviets attacked the Allies, the Soviets "would be destroyed…as sure as day follows night."[185] The taciturn, 49-year-old Norstad, who became SACEUR in November 1956, believed his primary job was to develop strategies to defend Europe. Unlike Gruenther, who preferred speeches before large audiences, Norstad preferred one-on-one contacts or talking to small groups. He excelled at the cerebral tasks of developing strategy, letting his staff take care of the details. Norstad expected his staff to be prompt, thorough, and ethical. He set a highly-visible example for integrity by not allowing his wife, Isabelle, to ride in government vehicles unless he was accompanying her. At home in Villa St.-Pierre, he preferred to read books or listen to music. Unlike Ike and Gruenther, he considered playing cards a waste of time.[186]

To compensate for the lack of sufficient ground forces, Norstad in 1960 organized the Allied Mobile Force (AMF). The AMF, which grew to be a 5,000 man force with nuclear capability, could be rapidly deployed to any NATO area from Norway to Turkey that was threatened by Soviet invasion. Because the AMF had troops from seven NATO nations, its deployment would demonstrate that an attack on one NATO nation would be an attack against all.[187]

NATOs Military Committee's 1957 nuclear strategy plan MC 14/2 unambiguously provided for a nuclear response to any intrusion by the Soviets into a member nation.[188] During war game HOSTAGE BLEU in November 1958, senior commanders evaluated using atomic weapons to blunt a Soviet attack. In his combat effectiveness report for 1958, Norstad criticized US land forces for having insufficient trucks, ammunition handling units, and CBR (chemical, biological, radiological) defensive units. This meant Norstad was criticizing himself because as SACEUR, Norstad was also US Commander-in-Chief, Europe.[189] However, his deputy, Gen Williston B. Palmer took the blame and worked to correct the cited deficiencies.

Exercise SIDE STEP, held during 17 to 23 September 1959, was a NATO-wide logistics command post exercise (CPX) designed to evaluate: movement of refugees, liaison between NATO commands (and in France between military districts), and use of local civilian labor to sustain the line of communications to combat forces. During the exercise, 8 million refugees were estimated to be on the roads of Germany and France. In addition to revealing significant liaison and labor problems, the CPX concluded that, had there been a real war with the Soviets, roads clogged with refugees would have seriously impeded military operations unless brutal measures were used on civilians.[190]

In the fall of 1961, Norstad had four-hundred eighty-nine nuclear weapons in US European Command. One-third of these weapons were part of the "Alert Forces" that could be released upon warning that the Soviets had attacked.[191] To reduce the danger of nuclear war, Norstad advocated the concept of a pause after a Soviet attack. The "Norstad Pause" before unleashing a full nuclear response was intended to permit the Soviets to withdraw if they had made a mistake. To prevent French military forces in Germany from being overrun, the French government wanted assurances from the United States that any pause would be brief.[192] If the troops were overrun, it would be impossible to target only the Soviet forces. In the early 1960s, Norstad advocated increasing stockpiles of NATO weapons and supplies in Europe. In an emergency, troops could be airlifted rapidly from the US to Europe using chartered commercial aircraft. However, it would take at least three months to move their weapons and supplies. Later in his tenure, Norstad advocated giving NATO greater control over the US nuclear arsenal in Europe, called the "Norstad Plan." Under the Plan, nuclear warheads would be in the custody of American officers who were responsible only to NATO, not to any national authority including the US.[193] US Secretary of Defense Robert S. McNamara did not agree and the US maintained its control of the nuclear weapons.[194]

General Lyman L. Lemnitzer (1963 - 69)

In November 1962, General Lemnitzer was selected by President Kennedy to succeed Norstad, who had served for twelve consecutive years in Europe. While assigned to the Pentagon in 1948, Lemnitzer helped draft NATO legislation and worked on "super top secret" plans to supply military equipment to European Allies before the NATO treaty was ratified. In accordance with bilateral agreements signed in January 1950, the largest share of US weapons would be sent to France. Initial shipments were reconditioned surplus and reserve equipment. When appointed SACEUR years later, the 63-year-old Lemnitzer was known by most political leaders of the Allies, but only French President Charles de Gaulle exercised his prerogative to interview Lemnitzer before approving the appointment. The meeting with de Gaulle was not really an interview as the old friends exchanged views for three hours at the Élysée Palace.[195, 196]

The good-natured Lemnitzer served as SACEUR for nearly seven years during which SHAPE was moved in 1967 to Belgium after France withdrew from SHAPE. Lemnitzer personally reviewed NATO war plans and cajoled Allies to build up their military forces. Lemnitzer prohibited the use of the Kennedy administration's public rhetorical term "flexible response" at SHAPE because he believed the appropriate response to the Soviets should not be limited to predetermined gradual escalation. Instead, Lemnitzer advocated an appropriate defense that could be strictly conventional weapons, a combination of conventional and tactical nuclear weapons, or full nuclear response.[197]

In January and June of 1964, Lemnitzer persuaded Turkey not to invade Cyprus. Tensions rose again in August because a Greek majority of 78% ruled a Turkish minority of 18% on Cyprus. Turkey and Greece withdrew forces from NATO and Greek staff officers moved from Izmir, Turkey, to Salonika, Greece. Lemnitzer appealed to the Turks and Greeks to return their forces to NATO control. Their land and air forces were essential to the defense of NATOs southern flank. Headquarters for Allied Forces Southern Europe (AFSOUTH) at Izmir was directed by a triad of a US, Greek, and Turkish officer under the command of American Lt Gen John H. Michaelis who had been Ike's training officer in 1952 at SHAPE. By the end of August, Greece and Turkey had returned the withdrawn forces to NATO control. Lemnitzer again had fourteen Turkish and nine Greek army divisions and more than 1,000 Greek, Turkish, and Italian planes to defend NATOs southern flank.[198, 199]

In 1967, after the withdrawal from France, Lemnitzer initiated contingency planning with his French counterpart, Gen Charles Ailleret, for use of French forces if the Soviets invaded.[200] Lemnitzer and de Gaulle had conferred often in Paris and socialized together at hunts held each year in the Forêt de Rambouillet. Unlike de Gaulle whose poor eyesight prevented hunting, Lemnitzer was a superb marksman and shot numerous birds. De Gaulle normally stood behind the shooters commenting on each pheasant that was missed.[201]

De Gaulle also invited Lemnitzer to attend official functions such as the celebrations for the 20th anniversary of the Allied landings on 15 August 1944 in southern France. During frequent stops along the coast between Cannes and Toulon, de Gaulle unveiled plaques, made extemporaneous remarks, and shook hands with hundreds of French, some in bathing suits. Lemnitzer was impressed by the 74-year-old's vigor throughout the long day. To reach the site of the 1964 ceremony at Mont Faron near Toulon, de Gaulle climbed a steep hill. During the ceremony, Lemnitzer, US Air Force Gen Jacob E. Smart, US Ambassador Charles Bohlen, and de Gaulle stood in front of an ornamental flower stand. The jardinière contained a remote-controlled bomb, the seventh attempt on de Gaulle's life during his political career. The bomb, which failed to detonate because heavy rains had filled the jardinière with water, was discovered two weeks later.[202] French police who examined the unexploded bomb believed it would have killed fifty people, including de Gaulle and his American guests. When Jacques Foccart, de Gaulle's personal intelligence chief, informed him about this latest attempt on his life, de Gaulle looked up from his writing and said *"et alors?"* (so what?).[203]

When SHAPE moved to Belgium, de Gaulle gave Lemnitzer the ten place setting of hand painted Limoges china that had been used by all the SACEURs at Villa St.-Pierre since Ike and Mamie arrived in August 1951. Although Lemnitzer was invited by de Gaulle to continue using the villa, on 01 April 1967 he moved into the BOQ at the new SHAPE complex in Belgium. His family stayed at Marnes-la-Coquette until August 1967.

Gen Lemnitzer (second from left) at Arc de Triomphe, Paris, July 1963 (SHAPE)

Supreme Allied Commanders, Europe (SACEUR)[204-208]

Supreme Commander	Period of Service	Prominent Achievements and Events
GEN Dwight D. Eisenhower	Dec 50-May 52	Raised morale of war-weary NATO nations. Structured SHAPE so twelve allied members would act jointly. Persuaded Allies to rearm West Germany. Greece and Turkey joined NATO.
GEN Matthew B. Ridgway	May 52-July 53	US European Command established under single chain-of-command. Solved command problem between Greek and Turkish forces. Advocated concept of Joint Construction Agency (to accelerate buildup of airfields and logistics infrastructure).
GEN Alfred M. Gruenther	July 53-Nov 56	Reduced excessive use of security classifications. Initiated buildup of modern air defenses for NATO nations. Advocated use of atomic weapons to support ground forces (because Allies were far below agreed upon troop levels). West Germany (FRG) joined NATO and began forming army (Nov 1955).
GEN Lauris Norstad, USAF	Nov 56-Dec 62	Oversaw widespread buildup of nuclear weapons (to counter Soviet threat by "massive retaliation" defense). Completed buildup of NATO air forces (including pipeline network and more than 200 airfields). LIVE OAK group formed at Camp des Loges (to plan defense of Berlin). Organized Allied Mobile Force (AMF). Advocated pre-positioning of equipment and supplies in Europe for US based combat units.
GEN Lyman L. Lemnitzer	Jan 63-May 69	Deployed more NATO forces forward along East-West border to delay Soviet attack. Persuaded Greece and Turkey to return forces to NATO control (Cyprus dispute of 1964). Moved SHAPE from Marly-le-Roi, France to Casteau, Belgium. Strengthened SHAPE's "appropriate response" defense after withdrawal of France in 1966. Initiated contingency planning for use of French military forces if Soviets invaded.
GEN Andrew J. Goodpaster	May 69-Nov 74	Resisted political movements in US Congress to reduce US forces in Europe. Maintained close relations with French liaison staff at SHAPE.[209, 210]

NOTE: All above SACEURs were graduates of United States Military Academy, West Point, New York. Eisenhower held General of The Army rank (5-stars); the others held General rank (4-stars).

U.S. GO HOME

European Command

US Army Supply Lines Through Germany (1950)

THREE

US Military Forces Return

"L'occupation américaine c'est La Guerre." The American occupation means war. (PCF slogan, 1950)

France Becomes the Hub for Defense of Europe

By 1950 in France, the US Army Cigarette Camps near Le Havre had been closed, most wartime surplus property disposed of or abandoned, nearly 83,000 war dead returned to the US, and twenty-four temporary cemeteries consolidated into five permanent cemeteries. The Berlin Blockade in 1948 followed by the Korean War in 1950 energized the Allies to form a military structure for coordinated rearming to meet the Soviet threat. For the third time in the 20th Century, the US military would be deployed in large numbers to France. This time they stayed for nearly two decades. France would become the operational headquarters and logistical hub for the defense of the West. In the 1950s, US Army logistics headquarters at Orléans grew to oversee the largest US military supply system, with supply lines for more than 250,000 troops extending across France into Germany. In France, ports had to be rehabilitated; and depots, air bases, barracks, and hospitals had to be built. Thousands of troops and their dependents needed housing, schools, commissaries, chapels, and recreation facilities. French government officials believed that the presence of the US military in France should be portrayed as a triumph of diplomacy.[1]

Achilles' Heel in Europe

The existing US Army supply lines from the German port of Bremerhaven to American and French occupation forces in southwestern Germany had become the Achilles' heel of the American forces in Europe. The supply lines were on the wrong side of the Rhine River, ran parallel to the Soviet zone only 50 miles away, and would not be difficult for the Soviets to sever. Although Bremerhaven was an excellent port, the surrounding terrain was flat without natural barriers to impede an invading Soviet force. In addition, most depots in the American zone were concentrated within a small area, creating a bull's-eye target for the Soviets.

The US Air Force bases in Germany were crowded into forward areas near Soviet occupied East Germany and Czechoslovakia. Erding Air Depot and key fighter air bases at Fürstenfeldbruck and Neubiberg were closer to the Soviets than the American ground troops that would have to defend them. It would be essential to base aircraft in the French Zone of Occupation. After the 1950-51 exchange of facilities in Germany between US and France, US air bases were built in the French Zone at Bitburg, Hahn, Landstuhl (Ramstein), Sembach, and Spangdahlem.[2]

In France, there were several ports along the Atlantic coast that could be used to establish a network of widely separated US Army supply routes to Germany. A line of communications across France had been planned since October 1948 when Gen Lucius D. Clay asked the Joint Chiefs of Staff in Washington, DC, for authority to supply troops in Germany from Atlantic ports in France. Clay, the US military governor in Germany, was directed to prepare plans, but negotiations with the French were delayed until after the North Atlantic Treaty became effective in late 1949.[3] France also would be asked to provide land for NATO air bases.

Communist Party in France

The return of the US military did not receive universal acclaim. At first there was uncertainty about how long the troops would remain, but by 1953, most French believed the US military would remain in France for an indefinite period. Postwar poverty and hunger had facilitated the growth of the Parti Communiste Français (PCF) which vigorously protested the presence of US soldiers. One argument was that the buildup for supply lines merely disguised an occupation. The slogan of the PCF was *l'occupation américaine c'est La Guerre* (the American occupation means war). In Orléans, it was *les américains en amérique* (the Americans in America); in Bordeaux, *Amerloo go Home*.[4] After World War II, France was considered a key battleground for the communist movement, supported by poets and intellectuals. It was generously funded by the Soviet KGB. In May 1946, US President Harry S. Truman had granted authority to the US military commander in Europe to move troops from Germany to France if the PCF staged an insurrection.[5]

In the 1950s, the PCF obstructed port operations at Bordeaux, la Pallice, and St.-Nazaire by blocking roads used to transport supplies from the docks. To aid the US forces, French riot police quickly dispersed the protestors. Unlucky communists were pummeled to the ground and arrested.[6] At night, communists painted anti-American signs, slashed tires, broke windows, and committed other acts of vandalism on cars and homes of Americans. On 20 October 1951 in Paris, French President Vincent Auriol gave a speech to honor the one-hundredth anniversary of the birth of Marshal Ferdinand Foch, French hero of World War I. Auriol condemned anti-American propaganda, handbills, and posters which were "directed against a great and noble friendly people…who twice aided us in our struggle for liberation."[7] However during 1952, twenty incidents of vandalism were reported each month.[8] French journalists like Marcel Valtat of the PCF newspaper *L'Humanité* seemed delighted to report that cafes near US installations had signs in their windows announcing that American troops were not welcome.[9-11] Many French did welcome the Americans, especially those in the northeast who had suffered during two wars under German occupation. Likely motivated by a desire to share in the economic benefits from the buildup, the Brest Municipal Council adopted a resolution on 28 November 1950 that requested the US military to build a supply base in Brest, similar to the base being established at Bordeaux. The resolution passed 19 to 17, with socialists and communists opposed.[12]

Initial Agreements for Buildup in France

In November 1949, Col Mason J. Young arrived in Paris to meet with his logistics counterparts on the French General Staff to determine which installations and facilities would be available to the US Army. Hoping to look like a tourist, Young, accompanied by his wife, Mary, wore civilian clothing on his first visit to evaluate port facilities at La Rochelle. Because his assignment to negotiate the buildup in France was politically sensitive, cover orders were cut assigning Young to the American Battle Monuments Commission in Paris. At first even his family had believed he was sent to France to supervise work on the World War II cemeteries and memorials.[13] Young, like Gen Dwight D. Eisenhower, was a West Point graduate of the class of 1915. He proved to be ideal for this assignment because he spoke fluent French and had many French friends from his year teaching at the French Military Engineer School in Angers. After thirty-five years of military service, including combat in France during both world wars, Young was promoted to brigadier general on 23 September 1950 by Army Chief of Staff Gen J. Lawton Collins.

On 24 January 1950, the US European Command and French General Staff reached agreement on installations, facilities, and other requirements for the buildup of the US Army in France. Land and

French caserne buildings for the line of communications (LOC) were provided "rent free." Twenty-five sites were to be used by the US Army for a peacetime rail and road LOC across France. Along the Atlantic Coast, most sites were at La Rochelle, Rochefort, and Bordeaux. A large depot was at Fontainebleau. In the Advance Section, several sites were at Verdun and Metz. It was believed that more than 3,000 French employees would be needed during the first year.

However, it took nearly a year for diplomats to agree on: judicial status of American troops in France, use of displaced persons to guard American installations, and financial contribution by the French government toward cost of an LOC. Shortly after the North Koreans invaded South Korea on 25 June 1950, the US stopped insisting that France pay most of the cost for the LOC and, to get the LOC underway, was willing to accept any reasonable proposal.[14] Finally, agreement was reached which included acceptance by the French to pay 20% of the estimated cost of the LOC. It was later discovered that French taxes on LOC related expenditures (production tax, national transaction tax, local transaction tax, contract registration tax, reforestation tax) would exceed 20%, thus yielding a profit to France during the first year. In March 1952, the US Embassy and French Foreign Ministry exchanged letters of agreement on tax relief.[15] By June 1952, after persistent complaints from the Americans, the French government agreed "in the interest of common defense" to waive all taxes related to the LOC.[16]

Inexplicably, the French government did not grant permission for the US Armed Forces Network (AFN) to broadcast in France until 23 May 1958.[17] The AFN network had studios at Orléans, Verdun, and Poitiers. Transmitters, at three-dozen widely separated locations, carried news, sports, and entertainment programs to all Army and Air Force installations in France. Local music request shows included "ComZ Jamboree" and "Beaucoup de Musique." AFN Orléans broadcast "First Aid" French lessons on Tuesday and Thursday evenings in cooperation with *Radio Diffusion TV Française*. Because AFN was broadcast on FM wavelengths, troops had to purchase an FM radio at the PX. Comparison shoppers discovered the Canadian PX at RCAF Station Marville, north of Verdun, had the best selection of reasonably priced European radios.

Logistics for Defense of Europe

Logistics is the procurement, maintenance, and transportation of matériel (equipment and supplies), facilities, and personnel. Failure to provide sufficient logistical support to combat troops is an "almost certain recipe for defeat." [18] In the 20th Century, there were numerous examples of logistical power contributing to over-whelming superiority over the enemy, such as St.-Mihiel and Meuse-Argonne offensives in World War I; Operation OVERLORD, the Normandy landings in World War II; and to a degree, Operation DESERT STORM to liberate Kuwait in the Gulf War.[19-22] In World War I, the Quartermaster Corps Doughboys delivered nearly 50 million gallons of motor gasoline and 5 million gallons of aviation gasoline to the front lines in France. In World War II, logistics considerations had determined the time and place of the D-Day invasion to liberate Europe and limited the pace of Patton's advance across France.[23] Each day, US supply lines were stretched farther as Germany supply lines became shorter. In fall 1944, the logistics supply distribution system proved to be the weak link in the advance toward Germany. According to Carl von Clausewitz, author of the classic 19th Century Prussian treatise *On War*, the army with the shortest line of communications has the advantage.

During the Cold War, self-sufficiency of troops in combat for more than a few days would have been nearly impossible. Logistical capabilities determined combat strength and, in the event of war with the Soviets, units in France would provide the essential lifeline to US forces in Germany. The supply lines in France extended more than 500 miles, from the ports of Bordeaux (Bassens), La

Rochelle (la Pallice), and St.-Nazaire (Donges) on the Atlantic coast through the Loire valley (Chinon, Saumur, Orléans) to the ancient military triangle formed by the fortified towns of Metz, Verdun, and Toul. By scattering the depots across France, it was unlikely supplies would be decimated by a single bombing attack. By 1963, more than 70% of supplies and all gasoline for US forces in Europe would flow across the lifeline in France. Each day, the Seventh Army in Germany required more than 500 tons of food, 225 tons of equipment (such as spare parts), 800 tons of fuel, and 125 tons of ammunition.[24] The Army also furnished about 80% of the supplies and materials used by US Air Forces in Europe.[25]

Troops Arrive from Germany

Shortly before noon on 06 November 1950, US Ambassador David K. E. Bruce and Alexandre Parodi, French Secretary General of the Ministry of Foreign Affairs, signed the document to establish a line of communications (LOC) in France. The LOC Agreement was to remain in effect for 5 years, to be renewed automatically unless terminated by notice given 6 months in advance by either party. Five days later, the unprecedented peacetime insertion of military forces into a friendly nation began. About one-thousand US technical service troops, including the 571st Ordnance Co (Ammo) and 595th Transportation Truck Co, entered France. Three-hundred trucks and trailers loaded with ammunition, supplies, and equipment were moved from Germany to Captieux so they could not be captured during the early stages of a Soviet invasion.[26] By mid-November, ships were unloaded at Bordeaux by troops who had to live in tents or abandoned French barracks severely damaged by the war. The lifeline for vital supplies and strategic storage was underway.[27] At first, French railroads were the primary means of transport across France to Germany. Although the buildup would mean jobs for French civilians, it would compete with the reconstruction of France.

To expedite establishing the LOC, French General Staff recommended using only government-owned land and buildings. It was believed that appropriating private property, usually owned for many generations by the same family, would delay progress and be unpopular with French citizens.[28] However, to meet initial deployment goals, some of the installations used by Americans before 31 December 1951 were obtained through lease or rental agreements with French civilian owners. In most cases, the French government chose areas where unemployment was high. These areas would benefit economically from the American presence. Hundreds of French citizens would be employed at smaller installations; thousands at larger installations.

The rapid buildup aroused curiosity of nearby villagers and on occasion a French tourist. In September 1951, a Frenchman on vacation in the Charente-Maritime asked the guard at the front gate of US Army Camp Bussac if he could visit. The GI asked the duty officer who called Lt Col Thomas A. Weadock, the commanding officer. Weadock asked the Frenchman why he wanted to visit the base. He replied: "Just because I'm a tourist." After a moment of silence, Weadock said: "OK sir! Here is your authorization. You can visit the whole base, but don't tell anyone. I'm not afraid of spies, but of tour operators. We could very quickly be invaded by tourists!" [29]

Young Moves from Paris to Orléans

On 01 December 1949, the 7966 EUCOM Detachment, authorized eight-hundred sixty officers and enlisted men, officially was organized and eventually would command the LOC. A year later, the detachment also was directed to provide logistical and administrative support to Supreme Headquarters, Allied Powers Europe (SHAPE) during its initial buildup in Paris.[30] Brig Gen Howard L. Peckham, who had commanded the American Graves Registration Command in Paris, was named commander of the 7966; Col Mason J. Young was assigned to head the engineer section. Peckham established the first headquarters for his 7966 EUCOM Detachment in Paris at the Hôtel Astoria and at 17, rue La Pérouse. Troops were billeted at the leased Blériot Factory in Suresnes and in 1951 also at Camp des Loges in St.-Germain-en-Laye. In April 1950, Young succeeded Peckham and was promoted to brigadier general shortly thereafter. On 29 December 1950, Young moved from the cramped quarters at the Astoria to establish LOC headquarters at Caserne Coligny in Orléans. Before the caserne could be used, significant restoration was required. Army engineers, who assessed the war damage to Caserne Coligny, found most of the buildings partially or totally demolished. A rehabilitated three-story building being used by French troops did not have hot running water, central heating, or indoor toilets.

Although the major elements of Young's detachment went directly to Orléans, the move from Paris took three months. A small element remained in Paris and a temporary base was established at Fontainebleau until Caserne Coligny was sufficiently rehabilitated.[31] Young lived with his wife and five dogs in a château in Orléans. The château had an impressive exterior, but the interior was somewhat dilapidated and very cold in winter. The Youngs' rental agreement stipulated that the owner could use the château's only bathtub once a week.[32]

Young followed World War II practices and Army doctrine to organize his growing command into two sections: a base section (BASEC) of ports, storage depots, and maintenance depots in the southwest and an advance section (ADSEC) of depots in the northeast to store items that could be rapidly delivered to troops in Germany.[33] BASEC, commanded by Brig Gen Charles C. Blanchard, had its headquarters at La Rochelle.[34] ADSEC, commanded by Col John F. Cassidy, had its headquarters at Verdun. Like Young, both section commanders were graduates of West Point. Col Le Count H. Slocum, Young's Chief of Staff, ran the day-to-day operations of the command at Orléans. Nicknamed "The Count," Slocum had served as a brigadier general commanding artillery of the 89th Infantry Division during World War II. During three days in 1945, the 89th Inf Div advanced 50 miles under enemy fire to the Moselle River. In the early 1950s, most of the senior officers and NCOs in France were veterans of World War II.

Main gate, Caserne Coligny, Orléans, December 1951 (US Army)

According to a December 1952 press interview given by Maj Gen Samuel D. Sturgis, Jr., who had succeeded Young at Orléans, depots would not be located in Paris. In the event of a war with the Soviets, he hoped that Paris could be declared an "open city" to prevent its destruction. To be open, as it theoretically had been during World War II, Paris would not be defended and would have no legitimate military targets.[35] In 1961, the peak year of the deployment, there were more than 100,000 US military and civilian personnel and their dependents in France.[36] By agreement, all construction projects for the US were built by French firms using materials purchased in France. Under the guise of "training," Young stretched his authority to speed construction, using Army engineers to build roads and temporary housing for troops.[37]

Rapid Buildup of Supplies and Troops

By December 1950, there were 1,300 American troops at Bordeaux and Captieux, 175 at La Rochelle, 25 at Rochefort, and 605 at Verdun. Six months later, the total number of troops reported by the US Army to the French government had grown from 2,105 to 5,627. At the end of 1951 there were more than 13,000 troops. In addition, the Army employed 1,438 Polish displaced persons to guard the depots.

The Bruce-Parodi agreement of 06 November 1950 stipulated that only Polish personnel recruited in West Germany would be permitted to work for US forces in France. Organized as military units, the Polish guards wore gray uniforms and held ranks similar to US officers and enlisted men. Although they were legally civilians, the guards were subject to military discipline. Counter Intelligence Corps (CIC) agents monitored suspicious activities of the Polish personnel. Because many of the displaced persons had family members and friends living behind the Iron Curtain, they were believed to be vulnerable to reprisals from the Soviets. CIC agents worked closely with the French *Direction de la surveillance du territoire* (DST) which monitored foreigners.[38]

For the first deployments, supplies literally poured into France. Stocks would be built up so combat troops in Germany would not run out of supplies and equipment if the Soviets invaded.[39]

Initial Supplies to France (1950-51)

Technical Service	Supplies and Equipment
Engineer	Bulldozers, graders, bridge sections, pipe sections
Medical	Beds, medicine, hospital equipment, tents
Ordnance	Ammunition, small arms and field artillery, tracked armored vehicles, wheeled vehicles
Quartermaster	Rations, clothing, POL in jerry cans and drums
Signal	Switchboards, cable, batteries, radio sets
Transportation	Tractor trucks, semitrailers, tires

Draftee Soldiers

The Universal Military Training and Service Act, passed by the US Congress in 1951, extended selective service until 1955, lowered the draft age to 18, and lengthened the period of service to 24 months active duty followed by six years in the reserves. In the 1950s, draftee soldiers represented a geographic, economic, and ethnic cross-section of America. Draftees had an active duty service obligation of two years, but enlistees served longer because they could select their job training for a Military Occupational Specialty (MOS). The pay for recruits who had served less than four months was $78 per month. Their GI haircut was extremely short for hygiene and so gas masks would seal properly. The "high and tight" haircut cost 25¢ on posts in France. Recruits were issued two 1-inch by 2-inch oblong metal tags called "dog tags" because they were to be worn around the neck. The tags were stamped with the GI's name (last name first, first name, middle initial), blood type, Army serial number, and religious preference. In combat the tags would be used to identify the dead: one to stay with the body, the other given to graves registration personnel.

Basic Training

During stateside basic training, teenage recruits endured taunts from their Drill Sergeants, became physically fit, and learned basic military skills such as map reading, marksmanship, and first aid to save lives by prompt action. Recruits learned how to salute, whom to salute, and when to salute. In a well-executed salute, the right upper arm was held parallel to the ground and fingers formed a flat surface extending the lower arm in a straight line at an angle to the upper arm. The head was held erect with finger tips touching the uniform cap, helmet, or forehead when indoors. They learned how to march in formation and the difference between a preparatory command ("Forward") and the command of execution ("March").[40] By marching and frequent formations, recruits learned teamwork and to obey orders without hesitation, which would be essential for success in battle.[41] Each day during physical training (PT), Drill Sergeants required the recruits, wearing leather combat boots, to run in formation and do exercises (called "the daily dozen") such as push-ups, leg lifts, jumping jacks, sit-ups, and squats. Mistakes incurred their wrath. "Drop and give me ten" meant the Drill Sergeant was displeased and the recruit paid with push-ups.

Recruits learned how to fire weapons at targets 300 yards away, how to throw hand grenades, and how to crawl on their bellies or inch on their backs under barbed wire through mud at night. In live fire exercises, live rounds were fired overhead and demolition charges were set off nearby to simulate battle conditions. Repetition was essential because, in battle, soldiers must overcome their fear by acting automatically. They were required to learn the name of each part of their weapon, to disassemble it (called "field stripping"), clean it, and put it back together. In combat, the M1 rifles would jam from dirt and grime, so it was essential for soldiers to know how to keep their weapons clean. If a recruit missed the entire target on the firing range, a red flag called "Maggie's drawers" was waved from the pit. Recruits who were poor shots were designated "Bolo" and received special attention from Drill Sergeants to improve their scores.

Phonetic Alphabet

Recruits were required to memorize their chain-of-command and the phonetic alphabet, a list of words from A to Z designed to prevent misunderstanding similar sounding letters such as M and N. In 1956, the US Army changed the list which had been used since World War II. Only four letters were unchanged: Charlie, Mike, Victor, and X-ray.[42] ComZ became "Charlie, Oscar, Mike, Zulu."

A	Alpha	H	Hotel	O	Oscar	V	Victor
B	Bravo	I	India	P	Papa	W	Whiskey
C	Charlie	J	Juliett	Q	Quebec	X	X-ray
D	Delta	K	Kilo	R	Romeo	Y	Yankee
E	Echo	L	Lima	S	Sierra	Z	Zulu
F	Foxtrot	M	Mike	T	Tango		
G	Golf	N	November	U	Uniform		

Kitchen Police

Recruits also learned the Army tradition of "hurry up and wait" and that "policing the area" meant picking up cigarette butts and trash, not crime prevention. During combat in Korea, units that did not police their areas after meals were exposed to enemy gunfire when metal trash glittered in the sun.[43] GIs, who naively had volunteered to prepare mess hall meals (called kitchen police, KP), learned from the backbreaking work never again to volunteer for anything. KPs peeled potatoes, washed pots and pans, scrubbed tables, and mopped floors. Although exhaustion not additives likely dampened libidos during basic training, most recruits believed that saltpeter (sodium nitrate) was added to their food.

Inspections

Each soldier had a small bunk bed, wall locker, and footlocker in which to store his uniforms and personal items. His toothbrush, toothpaste, razor, shaving cream, comb, and cigarettes had a designated location and orientation in the footlocker. For field equipment inspections, his steel pot (helmet), bayonet, canteen, entrenching tool (small shovel), shelter half (tent), and other equipment were to be displayed on the bed according to military precision. GIs called this "junk on the bunk." Soldiers learned how to shower regularly, shine shoes, keep the bunk area neat and clean, and make a bed properly. Blankets were tucked in tightly, with "hospital corners" creased at 45 degree angle, so a coin thrown at the bed would bounce. Uniforms were worn so the edges of shirt opening, belt buckle, and trouser fold were aligned (called the "gig line"). Gigs were assessed for a variety of inspection infractions. Too many gigs meant no weekend pass, or worse. The night before a "white glove" inspection, GIs cleaned their barracks until the windows sparkled and the sinks, toilets, urinals, and floors shined. This event sarcastically was called a "GI Party." During a GI Party at St.-Baussant, PFC Carter J. Doering and his fellow GIs used carbon tetrachloride, from the laboratory at Metz Quartermaster Tank Farm B, to clean the ceramic tile floors of their barracks. Fortunately, open windows provided sufficient airflow to dilute the poisonous fumes.[44]

MOS Training

Specialized training to qualify for a Military Occupational Specialty (MOS) followed basic training. GIs who scored high on the military's IQ test, called the Armed Forces Qualification Test, were assigned to technical service schools or other mentally demanding specialty schools. When a unit lacked sufficient trained personnel, on-the-job training (OJT) was an expedient used by commanders to train GIs for technical tasks. GIs learned by performing the job under the guidance of experienced technicians. Beginning in 1954, specialist ranks were created for GIs trained to perform technical jobs that paralleled NCO leadership ranks. The rank Specialist Fourth Class (Sp4) corresponded to Corporal (pay grade E-4) and Sp7 to Sergeant First Class (E-7). Even soon to be discharged GIs (called "short-timers") usually worked hard if they believed their MOS training and Army experience would be an asset to finding a desirable civilian job.[45]

Officer candidate schools (OCS) were located at the US Army Infantry School, Fort Benning, Georgia; US Army Artillery and Missile School, Fort Sill, Oklahoma; and the Woman's Army Corps School, Fort McClellan, Alabama. To be accepted, civilians and enlisted personnel had to be between 18½ and 28-years-old. GIs referred to Fort Benning as "Fort Benning School for Boys."

Technical Service Schools in US (1958)

Technical Service	Location
Chemical Corps	Fort McClellan, Alabama
Corps of Engineers	Fort Belvoir, Virginia
	Fort Leonard Wood, Missouri
Medical Service Corps	Fort Sam Houston, Texas
Ordnance Corps	Aberdeen Proving Ground, Maryland
Quartermaster Corps	Fort Lee, Virginia
Signal Corps	Fort Gordon, Georgia
	Fort Monmouth, New Jersey
Transportation Corps	Fort Eustis, Virginia

Reserve and National Guard Units to France

Manpower for the US Army was built up during the Korean War period by ordering into federal service individuals and units of the Organized Reserve Corps (name changed to Army Reserve in January 1953) and units of the National Guard. Fifty-eight Army Reserve and National Guard units, mobilized for service during the Korean War, were sent to France. The guardsmen went home as individuals when their mobilization tours were completed, but the units remained in France for longer time periods. Most of the Federalized Guard units, filled by draftees and Regular Army personnel, served for more than four years until their release from active duty status in late 1954.[46] Most of the reserve units were released by mid-1955.[47]

Army National Guard (ARNG) Units Federalized for Korean War[48-50]

Location in France	Unit	State ARNG	Release Date*
Billy-le-Grand	289th Petroleum Supply Co (Mobile)	New York (NYC)	03 Dec 1954
Braconne	961st Ordnance Park Co	Tennessee (Knoxville)	03 Dec 1954
Bussac	480th Trans Truck Co**	West Virginia (Welch)	09 Feb 1955
Metz	102nd QM Group, Hq and Hq Co	New York (Brooklyn)	24 Jan 1955
Nancy	109th Ordnance Medium Maintenance Co	Alabama (Phenix City)	01 Dec 1954
	112th Ordnance Medium Maintenance Co	Ohio (Cleveland)	01 Dec 1954
Toul	109th Trans Truck Bn, Hq and Hq Co	Minnesota (Camp Ripley)	18 Sept 1954
Trois-Fontaines	37th Ordnance Bn (Ammo Depot), Hq and Hq Co	Ohio (Cleveland)	03 Dec 1954
Vassincourt	213th Medical Bn, Hq and Hq Det	Mississippi (Drew)	21 Feb 1955
Verdun	109th Engineer Const Bn***	South Dakota (Rapid City)	17 Dec 1954

*Units deployed to Billy-le-Grand, Braconne, Metz, and Trois-Fontaines entered active service on 19 August 1950. The other units entered on 11 September 1950.
**All enlisted personnel were black. Official date of racial integration was 02 January 1954.
***Assigned temporarily (TDY) in late 1952 to Advance Section from Mannheim, Germany to build roads and install prefabs at Nancy (Co C), Trois-Fontaines (Co A), Frescaty (Co B), and Verdun (Co B).

Army Reserve (USAR) Units Mobilized for Korean War[51-53]

Location in France	Unit	Location in US	Release Date
Billy-le-Grand	877th QM Co (Petro Depot)	Ahoski, NC	03 Dec 1954
Bordeaux AB	469th Engineer Bn (Aviation)	Hackensack, NJ	25 Sep 1955
	359th Engineer Co (Aviation Support)	Philadelphia, PA	28 Mar 1955
Braconne	998th Construction Bn (Co C)	Menomonie, WI	20 June 1955
Bussac	806th Trans Bn (Trk), HHC	Little Rock, AR	18 Mar 1955
Châteauroux AD	866th Engineer Bn (Aviation)	Andalusia, AL	25 Sep 1955
Chinon	998th Construction Bn (Co A)	Menomonie, WI	20 June 1955
	986th Engineer Co (Pipeline)	Monroeville, AL	03 Dec 1954
	646th Trans Co (Light Trk)*	Birmingham, AL	03 Dec 1954
	395th Engineer Det (Gas Gen)	Portland, OR	01 Feb 1955
Croix-Chapeau	406th Construction Bn*	Birmingham, AL	21 Feb 1955
	432nd Engr Const Bn, HHC**	Houston, TX	09 Feb 1955
	478th Engr Co (Dump Trk)	Denver, CO	15 Nov 1954
	343rd Medical Det (Prev Con)	Bartow, FL	10 Mar 1953
Dreux AB	821st Engineer Bn (Aviation)	Trenton, NJ	25 Sep 1955
Fontainebleau	306th Field Hospital	Greenville, SC	09 Feb 1955
	833rd Signal Co (Service)	Minneapolis, MN	10 Mar 1955
Ingrandes	699th QM Co (Rclm & Maint)	Baltimore, MD	03 Dec 1954
	853rd QM Co (Service)*	Baltimore, MD	01 Feb 1955
	978th QM Co (Service)*	Petersburg, VA	05 Jan 1955
	998th Construction Bn (Co B)	Menomonie, WI	20 June 1955
Metz	240th QM Co (Supply Depot)	Atlanta, GA	24 Feb 1955
	465th QM Co (Service)*	Raleigh, NC	05 Jan 1955
Nancy	343rd Ordnance Bn	Tampa, FL	01 Dec 1954
	651st Trans Co (Hvy Trk)	Hot Springs, AR	10 Mar 1955
Orléans	982nd Construction Bn	Duluth, MN	15 Nov 1954
	302nd Field Hospital	Chicago, IL	03 Dec 1954
	432nd QM Co (Salvage)	Jay, OK	10 Sep 1954
	469th QM Co (Laundry)	Grenada, MS	20 Sep 1954
	609th QM Co (Graves Reg)	St. Louis, MO	10 Mar 1955
	497th Signal Co (Photo)	Binghamton, NY	24 Feb 1955
	655th Trans Co (Med Trk)	Opp, AL	03 Dec 1954
Rochefort	646th Trans Co (Light Trk)*	Birmingham, AL	03 Dec 1954
La Rochelle	889th QM Co (Petro Depot)	San Francisco, CA	03 Dec 1954
St.-Nazaire AD	472nd Engineer Bn (Aviation)	Buffalo, NY	25 Sep 1955
Sampigny	330th Chemical Co (Maint)	Scranton, PA	01 Nov 1954
	337th Chemical Co (Depot)	Los Angeles, CA	01 Nov 1954
Toul	322nd Engr Gp (Avn), HHC	New York, NY	25 Sep 1955
	998th Construction Bn	Menomonie, WI	20 June 1955
	420th Engr Co (Dump Trk)	Towanda, PA	17 Dec 1954
	747th Engr Co (Hvy Equip)	Albuquerque, NM	09 Feb 1955
	947th Engr Det (Avn Topo)	Chicago, IL	25 May 1954
Toul-Rosières AB	843rd Engineer Bn (Aviation)	Indianapolis, IN	25 Sep 1955
	885th Engineer Co, FM (Avn)	Dunkirk, NY	25 Sep 1955

Trois-Fontaines	421st Ordnance Co (Ammo)	Norfolk, VA	03 Dec 1954
	450th Ordnance Co (Ammo)	Columbia, SC	15 Nov 1954
Vassincourt	309th Field Hospital	Springfield, MA	03 Dec 1954
Verdun	313th Engr Gp (Const), HHC	St. Louis, MO	28 Mar 1955
	315th Signal Bn (Const)	Atlanta, GA	18 Mar 1955
	432nd QM Co (Salvage)	Jay, OK	10 Sep 1954
	698th Engineer Co (FM)	Dodge Center, MN	17 Jan 1955
	894th QM Co (Service)	Jackson, MS	10 Sep 1953
	901st Medical Det (Food Insp)	Kansas City, KS	17 Dec 1954

*All enlisted personnel deployed were black.
**Assigned TDY in late 1952 to Base Section from Kaiserslautern, Germany to build "winterized" tent cities at Braconne and Ingrandes (Co A), and at Bordeaux, Crois-Chapeau, Fontenet, Rochefort, and St.-Jean d'Angély (Co C).

Abbreviations

AB	Air Base	FM	Field Maintenance	Petro	Petroleum
AD	Air Depot	Gen	Generator	Prev	Preventive
Ammo	Ammunition	Gp	Group	QM	Quartermaster
Avn	Aviation	HHC	Headquarters &	Rclm	Reclamation
Bn	Battalion		Headquarters Co	Reg	Registration
Co	Company	Hq	Headquarters	TDY	Temporary duty
Const	Construction	Hvy	Heavy	Topo	Topographic
Con	Control	Insp	Inspection	Trahs	Transportation
Det	Detachment	Maint	Maintenance	Trk	Truck
Equip	Equipment	Med	Medium		

Crossing the Atlantic Ocean

During the US military buildup in France, airmen and Army troops traveled by cramped troopships, dubbed "floating barracks." Depending on weather and time of year, the typical Atlantic crossing took ten to fourteen days by troopship; five to seven days by luxury liner. The Atlantic Ocean in winter months was especially rough. Violent waves pitched troopships up and down as they rolled from side to side. GIs had to endure dizzy spells, loss of appetite, and malaise from seasickness.

Boarding USNS Eltinge, Houston, TX, 29 November 1954 (US Air Force)

Troopship USNS Gen Alexander M. Patch (US Army)

In the early 1950s, combat aircraft were flown along the World War II polar route from Maine to Labrador to Greenland to Iceland to Europe. The short range of most of the aircraft made this island hopping method necessary. The longest leg over water was about 800 miles. Due to bad weather during December 1954 and January 1955, it took the 21st Fighter-Bomber Wing thirty-one days to fly its seventy-eight F-86F Sabre jets from George AFB, California, to France.[54]

Travel by Troopship

On 05 June 1951, three troopships transported 3,872 troops of the 4th Infantry Division to join the burgeoning "Eisenhower Army" in Germany. The upper bunks were not used because USNS *Gen R. E. Callan* carried 1,100 troops, USNS *Gen S. D. Sturgis* 2,050, and USNS *Henry Gibbons* 722. The three ships arrived on the same day at Bremerhaven, Germany. The USS *Gen H. W. Butner*, the first ship manned by a US Navy crew to enter the French harbor of la Pallice since 1940, docked during the last week of November 1952. The *Butner* carried Army troops, bound for installations in France, on a three week voyage from Fort Mason, California, through the Panama Canal.[55] On 29 November 1954, airmen from the 21st and 388th Fighter-Bomber Wings sailed from Houston, Texas, on the troopship USNS *Gen LeRoy Eltinge*. The ship arrived at la Pallice on 12 December 1954. The *Eltinge*, built in 1945 by Kaiser Shipbuilding Co at Richmond, California, carried about 3,500 men in extremely cramped troop compartments and a crew of one-hundred fifty-nine civilian merchant marines and twenty-one Navy personnel.[56]

Metal Dungeons

There was no space on the *Eltinge* to hang clothing, no laundry service, and too many meals featured hot dogs or mystery stew served by cooks who wore the same dirty clothing the entire voyage.[57] GIs slept on bunks in compartments that they described as "metal dungeons." In summer months, the compartments were extremely hot and humid. Bunks typically were stacked three to five high in rows with little space between. Life preservers were stored on the top bunk. The standard bunk was a metal pipe frame with canvas stretched between. GIs, warned by veterans who had endured crossings in World War II, chose upper bunks because seasick GIs vomited on bunks below them. Turbulent seas made passages rough. Veteran merchant mariners advised sick GIs to keep their stomachs full. GIs who reported to sick bay were given pills for motion sickness by the ship's doctor. However, neither pills nor eating galley food settled their stomachs.[58]

Each day troops were allowed on open decks to get some fresh air. In cold weather, a few lucky GIs huddled near exhaust stacks for warmth. With nothing to do, in good weather GIs walked. From bow to stern was almost the length of two football fields. When asked how they got to France, some GIs could say "I walked." When it was not raining or snowing, GIs also played cards or rolled dice on metal decks, although Army troopship rules forbade gambling. During a February 1964 voyage from Brooklyn Army Terminal to Bremerhaven on the USNS *Gen Simon B. Buckner*, a lucky GI won more than $1,000 playing poker all night near the bunk of seasick PFC James R. Lewis. Someone stole the GI's winnings the next day. On land GIs could lock valuables in lockers; at sea they did not have secure locations.[59]

Below deck, GIs hosed down the foul-smelling compartments. GIs slipped and fell off ladders and lost their balance on the wet decks.[60] In the mess, seasick GIs vomited on their food trays which, when the ship rocked violently, slid in front of nearby GIs. US Army 2nd Lt Richard K. Neeld, a chemical engineer in civilian life, recalled that on his voyage in 1955 from New York to Germany, the

Eltinge seemed to cover more distance up-and-down than forward.[61] Prisoners and guards in the brig (stockade), which was located near the bow, experienced the greatest motion.

Duty Assignments

The senior military passenger acted as commanding officer during the voyage. He had a small staff of officers assigned to help him. A duty roster, completed according to Army Regulation (AR) 220-45, was kept by NCOs to assign GIs to KP, clean the heads and holds, fire watch, and other work details. Head duty meant a six-hour tour cleaning foul-smelling surfaces and mopping contaminated water which sloshed back-and-forth. Some GIs were given Brasso to polish the metal pipes and sinks. Twice each day, GIs assigned to fire watch duty walked two-hour tours through troop compartments looking for fires and preventing GIs from smoking. Smoking was not permitted in bunks, even in cabin class. Savvy GIs knew that KP on a troopship was better duty than KP on land. Usually more GIs were assigned to the galley (kitchen) than were needed so most tasks had a worker and a watcher, taking turns. Tasks included cleaning stainless steel cookware, lugging frozen food to the galley, and hosing down the galley with hot water. GIs carried garbage cans from the galley to the stern and dumped the contents into the ocean. On the USNS *Upshur*, color coded cards were distributed to each troop compartment. The color sequence to report for chow was announced over the ship's loudspeakers, so there would be a steady flow during the two hours it usually took to feed two-thousand troops. In November 1964, Sp5 Michael A. Stone volunteered for KP on the *Upshur*. Between meals he played cards on the mess (dining room) tables and had access to snacks between meals.[62] Choice assignments included working in the ship's newspaper office, cabin class library, and theater. Theater seats were folding metal chairs. Theater audiences were segregated with separate showings for ship's crew, passenger officers, and troops. Cpl Frank Souza, assigned to be a projectionist on a December 1956 voyage from Germany to New York, showed the film *Three Coins in the Fountain* three times each day. It seemed to Souza that it took forever to erase the theme song from his mind.[63]

In September 1951, Pvt Lyle A. Ross sailed to Bremerhaven in cramped quarters with more than two-thousand GIs on the USS *Gen Harry Taylor*. Ross was assigned to the mop cleaning detail which sounded undesirable because mops were used to clean heads and holds filled with seasick GIs. When the mop cleaning detail reported to the open deck, a crewman showed them how to tie a rope to the mop handle, tie the other end of the rope to the ship's rail, and throw the smelly mop over the *Taylor's* stern. The mops were then cleaned as they were dragged through the turbulent saltwater, churned by the ship's screws (propellers). The GIs retrieved the mops by pulling in the ropes like fisherman. Each morning the detail got to breathe fresh sea air while cleaning mops.[64]

However, because it was difficult to find work assignments for thousands of GIs, the primary daily activity was waiting in line for chow. On a September 1951 voyage from New York to Bremerhaven, the USNS *Gen S. D. Sturgis* carried two-thousand one-hundred men and five women. In the 21 September 1951 issue of the troopship's newspaper *The Sturgis Barnacle*, GIs were implored to keep their bunk areas clean and to keep the chow line moving rapidly.

Troopship Newspapers

Troopships had a daily edition four-page newspaper prepared by GIs who had experience in journalism or could type with all fingers. The newspapers were printed from stencils by hand-crank mimeograph machine on both sides of 8 in by 13 in standard government size paper. For news of the world, the GI editor selected items from commercial wire services. Regular contents included tips for living in Europe, GI humor (jokes and stories), sports results from the US, and a map showing the ship's position crossing the Atlantic. Some newspapers changed names in the 1950s.[65]

Troopship	Newspaper	Troopship	Newspaper
USNS Aultman*	Trade Winds	USNS Hodges	Sea Foam
USNS Ballou	Ballyhoo	USNS Muir	Daily Muirer
USNS Brewster*	The Brewster Newster	USNS Patch	Dis Patch
USNS Callan	The Callan Courier	USNS E. D. Patrick*	The Patrick Press
USNS Darby	Darby Daily	USNS Rose	Daily Herald/The Rose Report
USNS Eltinge	The Eltinge Crier	USNS Stewart	The Trooper/Topsides
USNS Gaffey*	Gaffey Gazette	USNS Sturgis	Sturgis News/The Sturgis Barnacle
USNS Gibbons	The Gibbons Express	USNS Upshur	Unicorn
USNS Gordon	Gordon News	USNS Walker	Spotlight/The Walker Report
USNS Greely	Greely Gazette	USS Butner	Butner Bulletin
USNS Hase*	The Hasette	USS Pope*	Pope Scope
USNS Hersey	Sea Rover	USS Taylor	Taylor Times

*Home port at Army terminal on West Coast.

The Eltinge Crier

In a 1954 souvenir issue of the *Eltinge's* newspaper *The Eltinge Crier*, Air Force Col Harold J. Whiteman warned the troops that they likely would be greeted by anti-US demonstrations in France. Whiteman wrote that communist-inspired actions did not represent "the sentiment of the French people." [66] In June 1953, Army Cpl Allen J. Kolons experienced the paradox expressed by Whiteman. On a weekend pass, his civilian vehicle broke down in Meaux, outside Paris. A gendarme helped Kolons, who was wearing his Army uniform, push it to the nearby gendarmerie. Although it was Saturday night, the gendarmerie's civilian mechanic was summoned from home, but he did not have the part needed to repair the American-made vehicle. Kolons was invited to spend the night at the gendarmerie, sleeping on a wooden bench. The next morning, after the mechanic had attended Catholic mass, he reappeared with a part which miraculously fit the distributor. Neither the mechanic nor the gendarme

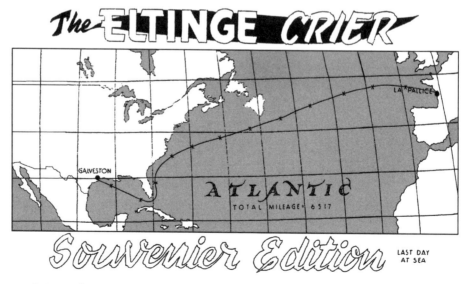

Map of USNS Eltinge's Altlantic crossing (29 Nov-12 Dec 54)

Anti-American sign near Meaux, 1953 (A. J. Kolons)

would accept payment for their services. As Kolons, who was grateful for the hospitality and aid of the French, drove from Meaux, he passed a huge message painted on a wall along the road: "Ridgway Go Home." [67]

Cabin Class Passengers

Cabin class passengers had access to lounges (for bingo, cards, and movies), barber shop, children's playrooms, small exchange (which sold toothpaste, soap, and cigarettes), and dispensary-hospital (staffed by Army doctors and nurses). The dining room (mess) had several sittings for each meal, with choices from a menu.[68] Class A uniforms were mandatory for evening meals. Fraternization was discouraged between cabin class passengers and enlisted men traveling in the lower deck troop compartments. Cabin class passengers were instructed not to violate the boundaries between deck areas set aside for troops and not to visit troop compartments unless on official duty. GIs were assigned security duty to enforce separation of the decks. Cabins were segregated by gender so wives bunked together.[69] Enlisted men bunked in cramped troop compartments while wives and children were assigned to upper deck cabins.[70] Instructions to parents advised them to put children in lower bunks, where they "won't have so far to fall" if the ship rolled badly. When on open decks, children had to be attached to a leash.[71] Starting on 01 July 1956, GIs in top three pay grades (and E-4s with more than four years service) were authorized to travel on troopships in cabin class with their dependents.[72]

In late September 1957, Mrs. William Preblud and her two children sailed from New York on the USNS *Gen Maurice Rose* to join SFC Preblud at Nancy Ordnance Depot. Sixteen-year-old Arlan befriended crew members assigned to the "off limits" radio shack, where messages were sent and received. Arlan discovered that the ship's broadcast of the Milwaukee Braves-New York Yankees World Series baseball games were delayed an hour, but wire service scores were received live after each inning. Arlan visited the radio shack for scores before placing $1 bets with fellow dependents. The Braves beat the Yankees 4 games to 3 in a series of seven exciting games. Arlan won his bets.[73]

In late December 1959, the USNS *Gen Maurice Rose* sailed from New York to Bremerhaven, Germany, on extremely rough seas. Pvt John B. Robert, who was assigned to the Special Weapons Supply Control Agency at Maison-Fort, near Orléans, witnessed difficulties in the head located in the ship's stern. If a GI forgot to grab on to the sides of the commode, rough seas would propel him in an upward trajectory. Women on the *Rose* were advised to stay in their cabins, except to eat meals or use the head. There were six women per small cabin. Dogs, kept in cages in a heated cabin near the women, barked constantly throughout the rough voyage.[74] Pets, such as dogs, cats, and certain birds, but not horses or monkeys, were authorized to be shipped. If the pets were sent by Military Sea Transportation Service (MSTS) "pet ship," owners paid a fee to cover cost of feeding the pet. GIs volunteered to take care of the pets. Each volunteer fed, cleaned, and exercised four or five dogs during the voyage. If the owner was on the same ship, he took care of his dog or, if an officer, paid an enlisted man to care for the dog.[75]

Troopships Making Atlantic Crossings

Troopships listed below sailed between US ports (Brooklyn, NY; Hampton Roads, VA; Charleston, SC; New Orleans, LA; and Houston, TX) and European ports (Bremerhaven, Germany, and la Pallice, Cherbourg, and Le Havre in France). In the early 1950s, the ships returned to the US with refugees from the war. In 1957-58, ships returned with refugees from the Hungarian Revolution. In 1959, the primary ships on the Atlantic run were the *Butner, Darby, Geiger, Patch, Rose,* and *Upshur*.[76] By early 1960, due to the increased use of air transportation and commercial passenger liners, only ten troopships were operating out of Brooklyn. Regularly scheduled runs to Europe ended in 1966.

Troopships Making Atlantic Crossings[77-79]

USNS Gen C. C. Ballou (4,179)*	USNS Gen W. C. Langfitt (3,699)
USNS Barrett (2,164)**	USNS Gen J. H. McRae (3,699)
USNS Gen R. M. Blatchford (4,179)	USNS Gen C. H. Muir (4,179)
USNS Gen Simon B. Buckner (5,047)	USNS Gen Alexander M. Patch (5,047)
USNS Gen R. E. Callan (4,272)	USNS Gen Maurice Rose (5,047)
USNS Gen William O. Darby (4,988)	USNS Gen M. B. Stewart (3,951)
USNS Gen LeRoy Eltinge (4,179)	USNS Gen S. D. Sturgis (3,699)
USNS Geiger (2,164)**	USNS Upshur (2,164)**
USNS Henry Gibbons (1,976)	USNS Gen Nelson M. Walker (5,047)
USNS George W. Goethals (1,976)	USS Gen H. W. Butner (5,766)
USNS Gen W. H. Gordon (4,777)	USS Gen W. A. Mann (5,607)
USNS Gen A. W. Greely (4,179)	USS Gen William Mitchell (5,741)
USNS Gen W. G. Haan (4,179)	USS Gen George M. Randall (5,796)
USNS Gen Stuart Heintzelman (4,179)	USS Gen Harry Taylor (3,580)
USNS Gen M. L. Hersey (4,179)	USNS Pvt Elden H. Johnson (1,626)
USNS Gen H. F. Hodges (4,179)	USNS Pvt William H. Thomas (1,626)

*Nominal capacity (total) for crew, officers, enlisted men, and dependents in parentheses. Large ships accommodated 450 cabin-class passengers; the smaller ships, 300.

**Converted from American President Line passenger ships so cabins accommodated 400 officers and dependents, and more than 1,500 troops in bunks. Air-conditioning made them the favorite of officers, dependents, and crews.

NOTE: USNS (United States Naval Ship) ships were manned by civilian crews, USS (United States Ship) ships by US Navy crews.

Travel by Ocean Liner and Turboprop Aircraft

Later in the 1950s, troops and their family members came to France by commercial passenger ship to Le Havre or Military Air Transport Service (MATS) flight by turboprop aircraft to Orly Airport near Paris. Turboprop planes, with a refueling stop in Iceland or Ireland, took fourteen hours from McGuire AFB, New Jersey, to Orly. In the early 1950s, MATS flights from Westover AFB, Massachusetts, to Orly had taken seventeen hours. It usually took seven days or less to cross the Atlantic Ocean by commercial passenger ships SS *America* and SS *United States*. The SS *United States*, known as "The Big U," was the largest American-built passenger ship and had been designed so it could be converted into a troopship during war. It operated on the Atlantic Ocean from 1952 until 1969, when commercial jet air travel ended the era of ocean liners.

By the late 1950s, military personnel traveling on commercial passenger ships were assigned to first class cabins. As part of an Army-wide effort to enhance prestige of NCOs, starting in January 1959 the top five enlisted grades were eligible to cross the Atlantic on a luxury liner. The MSTS arranged with American Banner Lines to send GI families on its one-class luxury liner the SS *Atlantic*. The ship, which sailed between New York and Rotterdam, the Netherlands, had accommodations for 900 passengers in air-conditioned comfort.[80] In January 1959, M/Sgt Leon Lewis, who was assigned to the 70th Engineer Co at Metz, and his family sailed to Rotterdam on the *Atlantic*. Lewis and his wife had breakfast in bed, won a daily dancing contest, and attended two parties hosted by the ship's captain.[81] This space-available benefit ended in November 1959, when a new owner discontinued service from New York to Rotterdam. Once in France, troops and dependents traveled by train to their assigned installation. At their units, GIs were supposed to receive orientation which included an hour on how to get along with the French. Some installations also gave GIs a pamphlet on life in France.[82]

Commercial Passenger Ships (1959)

SS America (9,000)*	SS Constitution (5,000)	SS United States (15,000)
SS Atlantic	SS Independence (5,000)	

*Nominal capacity, when converted to carry troops, given in parentheses.

Paris Air Passenger Center

The US Air Force opened the Paris Air Passenger Center in the mid-1950s, when air transportation replaced the troopship as the common carrier for US Air Force personnel assigned to France. The 7415th Air Base Group operated the center at the leased Hôtel Littré on 9, rue Littré. The hotel had one-hundred twenty rooms with bath, American-style bar, and a large restaurant a few steps below entry level with a stage platform at one end. Airmen and Army troops traveling on permanent change of station (PCS) orders or temporary duty (TDY) orders for Paris could stay at the Littré or around the block at the Hôtel Victoria Palace, 6, rue Blaise-Desgoffe. Both hotels were owned by the Schmitt family. Army personnel were processed at the Littré by the 524th QM Company (Replacement). On 08 May 1958, two-hundred thirty-four military personnel and dependents arrived at Gare de l'Est. It took all day to process the passengers. GIs determined if immunization certificates, passports, tickets, and hand-carried baggage were in order. In the late afternoon, the group was driven by bus to Gare St.-Lazare where they boarded the train for Le Havre. Three Paris area MPs accompanied them to Le Havre where the group boarded the SS *United States*.[83]

Segregated Units in France

Thirty-eight segregated units were active in France from 1950 to 1954. The first segregated units assigned to France were the 571st Ordnance Co (Ammo) and the 595th Truck Co. Black officers commanded only blacks and were not assigned to units where they would give orders to whites. Several all-black enlisted personnel units were moved after their missions were completed or when there was a greater need elsewhere. The 661st Truck Co (Heavy) moved from Captieux to Bussac; the 39th Ordnance Co (MAM) from Captieux to Verdun; the 571st Ordnance Co (Ammo) from Trois-Fontaines to Captieux; the 75th, 77th, and 543rd Truck Companies moved from Trois-Fontaines to Toul; and the 33rd Medical Holding Co moved from Croix-Chapeau to la Chapelle (Orléans). Engineer battalions had companies stationed at other installations. The 94th Construction Bn had Co B at Ingrandes and Co C at Braconne; the 97th had Co A at Toul and Co B at Trois-Fontaines; and the 406th had Co A at Orléans, Co B at Verdun, and Co C at Poitiers. Quartermaster service companies operated mobile laundries and bakeries; stored, issued, and repaired clothing; and stored and issued rations. By February 1955, the four QM companies had been inactivated. During period of segregation, non-white US Army units were officially designated as "Colored" (or "Negro") and "Puerto Rican."[84]

Segregated Units in France (1950-54)

Unit	Location	Unit	Location
Engineer		82nd Truck Co	Metz
94th Construction Bn	Chinon*	480th Truck Co	Bussac*
97th Construction Bn	Verdun	543rd Truck Co	St.-Eulien
406th Construction Bn	Croix-Chapeau*	595th Truck Co	Bussac
40th Pipeline Co	Braconne	646th Truck Co	Chinon*
515th Firefighting Plat	Laleu	661st Truck Co (Heavy)	Captieux**
519th Firefighting Plat	TFOD	**Ordnance**	
520th Firefighting Plat	Verdun	39th MAM Co	Captieux
521st Firefighting Plat	Bussac	550th Ordnance Co (DS)	Fontenet
522nd Firefighting Plat	Toul	551st MAM Co	Verdun
523rd Firefighting Plat	Bordeaux	571st Ordnance Co (Ammo)	St.-Eulien*
Medical		583rd Ordnance Co (Ammo)	Captieux*
33rd Holding Co	Croix-Chapeau	**Quartermaster**	
36th Holding Co	Bussac*	465th Service Co	Metz*
550th Ambulance Co	Bussac	574th Service Co	Metz*
591st Ambulance Co	Toul	853rd Service Co	Ingrandes*
Transportation		978th Service Co	Ingrandes*
41st Truck Co	TFOD	**Special Services**	
55th Heavy Truck Co (Petroleum)	Bussac	17th Special Services Co	Laleu
72nd Truck Co	Bussac	**Band**	
75th Truck Co	TFOD	118th Army Band	Verdun
77th Truck Co (Light)	St.-Eulien	**Military Police**	
78th Truck Co (Heavy)	Bussac	382nd MP Bn (Co D)	Verdun

*units inactivated during period of November 1954 to July 1955.
**stationed at Bussac in 1952.

Abbreviations
DS   Direct Support   Plat Platoon
MAM Medium Automotive Maintenance TFOD Trois Fontaines Ordnance Depot

Army Desegregation

In 1948, A. Philip Randolph, labor leader of the Brotherhood of Sleeping Car Porters, threatened to lead a boycott of selective service and acts of civil disobedience until the military was integrated.[85] Republican presidential candidate New York Governor Thomas E. Dewey promised to end segregation in the armed forces if elected. In response, President Harry S. Truman issued Executive Order 9981 on 26 July 1948. The order stipulated equal treatment and opportunity for all within the armed services, without regard to race, color, religion, or national origin. However, Truman's order did not give a deadline for ending racial segregation.[86]

Because no reference to desegregation was included in the order, the Army implemented 9981 as a doctrine of equal treatment and opportunity. Retired Lt Gen Julius W. Becton, Jr. remembers his post commander announcing in 1949 that there still would be separate officers clubs, swimming pools, and NCO clubs at Aberdeen Proving Ground, Maryland.[87] Although in 1949 the Army had dropped its 10% limit on number of blacks in the total force, in January 1950 Truman's Army Secretary Gordon Gray affirmed that existing racial segregation would continue for a long time.[88] The Army continued to be segregated until demands of the Korean War forced some integration at training posts such as Fort Ord, California, and Fort Jackson, South Carolina.[89] In July 1951, Lt Gen Matthew B. Ridgway initiated a program to integrate combat units in Korea over a period of six months.[90] Ridgway believed that racial segregation was wrong.

In Europe, the Army's goal for integrated units was to be 10% black. During fall 1952, the Base Section touch-football champion Bersol Goatherders at Bordeaux fielded a racially integrated team before the athletes' Army units had begun to integrate.[91] By 1953, the 97th Engineer Battalion at Verdun had reduced to fifty-nine blacks among its 729 troops. By 1954, the 39th Ordnance Company at Verdun had reduced to eighteen blacks among its 179 troops.[92, 93] Racial integration in Europe, initiated in April 1952 by Gen Thomas T. Handy, was completed by November 1954 without publicity. By September 1955, President Eisenhower had integrated the armed forces, VA hospitals, and dependents schools.[94-96]

Line of Communications Becomes Communications Zone

The US Army line of communications (LOC), a major subordinate command of the US European Command (EUCOM), oversaw the Base Section, headquartered at La Rochelle, and the Advance Section, headquartered at Verdun. Detachments were stationed at Fontainebleau, Paris, and the port of Cherbourg.[97] To support an evacuation to England if the Soviets overran France, the Army stored supplies in leased warehouse space at Cherbourg.

By mid-1951, defense requirements had changed from a plan to store about 100,000 tons of matériel (two-thirds at forward areas of Verdun, Metz, and Nancy) to more than 700,000 tons in France. The Army needed a more extensive communications zone (ComZ), with a network of depots for ammunition, weapons, gasoline, food, medical supplies, wire and radio communications equipment, and combat vehicles.[98] In February 1951, French Defense Minister Jules Moch gave permission for the US Army to begin searching for additional sites and installations, if visits had a French observer and were conducted according to existing diplomatic agreements.[99]

Although a ComZ buildup meant numerous construction projects and jobs for the struggling French economy, the presence of foreign troops was particularly sensitive because memories of the German occupation were still vivid. French communists, who held the biggest voting bloc in the French Chamber of Deputies, criticized any foreign military presence in France.[100] The Communist

Party tried to convince the French people that US forces were a "thinly disguised occupation army." Although the US military presence in Paris became substantial, the communists exaggerated its size. The December 1951 issue of the French communist monthly magazine *Démocratie Nouvelle* contained a map of Paris with hundreds of black dots, triangles, and squares to show the "occupation" of buildings by Americans, even including those of private businesses.[101]

Maj Gen Ralph J. Canine, EUCOM Director of Logistics, was reluctant to call the buildup a ComZ, a designation used by the Allies during World War II. He believed French communists would cite a ComZ as proof the US was "preparing for war" by establishing permanent military bases on French soil, which of course it was, albeit a defensive one. After communist representation in the French Chamber of Deputies was considerably reduced (from 183 seats to 100 seats) by the June 1951 national elections, EUCOM publicly announced on 13 July 1951 the establishment of the ComZ in France.[102] With the new alignment of French political power, the French Minister of the Interior Henri Queuille was determined to eliminate any opposition to the buildup of the US military in France. During 1952, the French government of President Auriol now urged mayors of towns near US bases to work with commanders to lessen friction. French radio broadcasts and films explained American customs to the French and French customs to US soldiers.[103]

Sites Offered to US Army

Many of the thirty-nine sites the French government offered "rent-free" in 1951 to the US Army dated back to the time of the old Services of Supply of World War I.[104, 105] The Quartermaster depot site at Ingrandes was the abandoned French St.-Ustre ammo depot. The Engineer depot at Toul was the abandoned Croix de Metz airdrome where Capt Eddie Rickenbacker's famous "Hat-in-the-Ring" 94th Aero Squadron had been based. Army depots at Vassincourt, Buzy (near Étain), Bussac, and Fontenet also were abandoned airdromes.[106-108] Several of the sites were in national forests.

Advanced Section (ADSEC):

Brion-sur-Ource
Chevillon
Condé-sur-Suippe
Étain
Mailly-le-Camp
Metz
Nancy (Forêt de Haye)
St.-Dizier (Forêt de Trois-Fontaines)
Sampigny
Sommesous
Toul (Aérodrome Croix de Metz)
Vassincourt (Aérodrome de Bar-le-Duc)
Verdun

Base Section (BASEC):

Agen
Angoulême (Forêt de la Braconne)
Bordeaux
Bussac (Aérodrome de Bedenac)
Captieux (le Poteau)
Châtellerault (Ingrandes)
Cherbourg
Chinon (Forêt de Chinon)
Cosne-sur-Loire
Fontainebleau
La Rochelle
Mignières
Montargis
Montereau-Fault-Yonne
Montluçon (Depot de Quainssaines)
Nantes
Orléans
Paris
Pauillac
Périgueux
Poitiers
Rochefort
St.-Jean-d'Angély (Aérodrome de Fontenet)
St.-Sulpice-et-Cameyrac
Saumur
Sens

US Army Installations (1954)

US Army Installations in France (1952-53)[109-112]

Depots	Advance Section	Intermediate*	Base Section
Chemical	Sampigny		Bussac
Engineer	Étain Toul	St.-Ay	Bordeaux Chinon Croix-Chapeau Poitiers
Medical	Vassincourt	Fontainebleau	La Roche-sur-Yon (Usine Transocéanic)
Ordnance	Nancy St.-Hubert Trois-Fontaines		Braconne Captieux Fontenet Rochefort (Arsenal)
Quartermaster	Billy-le-Grand Metz Woippy	Paris (Île St.-Germain)	Bussac Ingrandes La Rochelle (Usine Jeumont) Périgueux (Chamiers)
Signal	Verdun		Cherbourg St.-Jean-d'Angély Saumur
Transportation	Étain Metz (Frescaty) Sommesous	Maison-Fort	Bussac
Hospitals	Verdun	Fontainebleau Orléans (la Chapelle) Paris (Neuilly)	Bordeaux (Gradignan) Captieux La Rochelle
Ports			Bordeaux (Bassens) La Rochelle (la Pallice)
Airfields	Metz (Frescaty) Verdun (Fromeréville)	Fontainebleau (Melun) Orléans (Saran)	La Rochelle (Laleu)

*Orleans Area Command (OAC) headquarters at Caserne Coligny, Orléans; Seine Area Command, Communications Zone (SACCZ) at 2, rue de la Faisanderie, Paris.

French Casernes

Military installations in the United States normally are located on vast acreage away from population centers. They are virtually self-contained cities with offices, housing, post exchanges (department stores), commissaries (supermarkets), hospitals, chapels, schools, training grounds, and recreational facilities. Early Army forts in America were located near towns and trails to be protected.[113] French military barracks (*casernes*) traditionally were located in towns and villages. Verdun, Metz, and Toul, like many French cities, are encircled by walled fortifications. During the second half of the 20th Century, hundreds of French towns still had active military casernes. To French citizens, the routine sight of French Army vehicles and uniformed troops symbolized the importance of military service and preparedness to defend France. Several French Army casernes were offered rent free to the US military as part of the 1950 Bruce-Parodi agreement.[114] Most buildings required significant repairs and modernization. They primarily would be used for troop barracks, troop support, and administrative functions. In the Base Section, Binot, Daumesnil, Haxo, and Renaudin were only briefly occupied.

Most of the casernes used by the US Air Force, Army, and Navy are still used by French government agencies, local governments, and French military (including the *Gendarmerie nationale*).[115] Harville, Voyer, and Senarmont have been abandoned. Limoges and Joinville have been converted to private housing.

French Casernes Used by US Military

Location	Caserne	Location	Caserne
Advance Section		Orléans	Coligny
Ebersviller	Ising		Salbris
Étain	Sidi Brahim	St.-Germain-en-Laye	des Loges
Metz	Colin	Versailles	Limoges
	Tournebride	Base Section	
Nancy	Donop	Bordeaux	Crespy
	Thiry		Xaintrailles
Pont-à-Mousson	Duroc	Cosne	Binot
Sampigny	Harville	Moulins	Villars
St.-Mihiel	Senarmont	Périgueux	Daumesnil
Thionville	Angevillers	Poitiers	Aboville (des Dunes)
Toul	Jeanne d'Arc*	Rochefort	Joinville
	Lamarche		La Touché-Tréville
	Luxembourg	La Rochelle	Aufrédi
Verdun	Estienne		Renaudin
	Gribeauval	La Roche-sur-Yon	Haxo
	Maginot	St.-Jean-d'Angély	Voyer
	Villars	St.-Nazaire	Beauregard
Intermediate Sections**		Saintes	Bremont d'Ars
Châteauroux	la Martinerie	Mediterranean Coast	
Fontainebleau	Lariboisière	Villefranche (Nice)	Nicolas

*Completely destroyed during World War II.
**US Army Orleans Area Command (OAC) and Seine Area Command, Communications Zone (SACCZ).

Air Power in France

On 14 June 1951, Gen Dwight D. Eisenhower, in his capacity as Supreme Commander of NATO military forces, wrote to French Minister of Defense Jules Moch to urge release of land needed for air bases in France. Negotiations between the US and France had been so slow it appeared that agreement would not be reached before the US Air Force sent reinforcements to Europe in Summer 1951.[116] Finally on 31 October 1951, a temporary air basing agreement was signed with the French government. It was believed air power would be essential should the "balloon go up." The expression, military jargon for the start of a war, was used frequently during the Cold War. It originated in World War I when balloons went up for surveillance immediately before an attack. To deter a Soviet invasion, overwhelming air power was needed to deliver atomic bombs on military and industrial targets in the Soviet Union (called strategic bombing) and to control the air above ground forces (called tactical air support). If the Soviet air forces were neutralized, NATO ground forces could proceed into battle unhindered by air attacks. Since Germany attacked Poland in 1939, no country has won a conventional war without controlling the air.[117, 118] The standard NATO airfields were main operating bases (MOB) for a permanent deployment of an air wing, dispersed operating bases (DOB) for quick relocation of an air squadron in emergencies, and alternate air bases to be used if an air base became unusable in time of war.[119]

French Airfields

On 01 October 1951, the French Air Force proposed twenty-one locations to the US Air Forces in Europe (USAFE) for use as NATO bases. The proposed airfields near Étain and Toul had been built during World War II by engineers of US Ninth Air Force for P-47 Thunderbolt and P-51 Mustang aircraft. They had unpaved runways, parking aprons, and open areas for tent camps. Laon, a German airfield during World War II, had two concrete runways. The first Cold War deployments to France of US Air Force combat aircraft were to: Chaumont, Chambley, Étain, Laon, and Toul. The civilian airport near Bordeaux at Mérignac also was used. The US Army had constructed the original aerodrome at Mérignac during World War I.[120] After liberation from the German occupation of World War II, the airfield was used by US Army Air Forces medium bombers from December 1944 to July 1945. After the war, Mérignac reverted to civilian control. The US Air Force would share the base with the French. By the end of 1951, the US Air Force had 5,920 personnel in France.[121] For liaison and training, the French government also authorized the USAFE to use runways and limited facilities at French Air Force bases (abbreviated BA for *Base Aérienne*): Cazaux, Metz-Frescaty, Orléans-Bricy, Reims-Champagne, and Tours-St.-Symphorien.

Airfields Offered to US Air Force in 1951[122]

Bordeaux/Mérignac (C)*	Lorient (C)
Brienne-le-Château/Lassicourt (FAF)**	Lunéville (FAF)
Chambley-Bussières site	Lyon (C)
Chaumont/Semoutiers (FAF)	Melun/Fourches (C)
Cherbourg/Maupertus-sur-Mer (C)	Metz/Frescaty (FAF)
Cognac/Châteaubernard (FAF)	Nantes (C)
Dreux/Senonches (C)	Neufchâteau/Damblain site
Étain/Rouvres (FAF)	Phalsbourg/Bourscheid site
Évreux/Fauville (C)	Sézanne/Marigny-le-Grand site
Istres (FAF)	St.-Dizier (FAF)
Laon/Couvron (FAF)	St.-Simon/Clastres (FAF)**
	Toul/Rosières (FAF)

*The first name is the largest town near the airfield; the second name usually is the closest small village. Designation C means under civil jurisdiction, designation FAF means French Air Force control.
**FAF offered Brienne and St.-Simon as substitute for airfield at St.-Dizier.

Air National Guard Units

During 1951-52, Air National Guard (ANG) units federalized for the Korean War were sent to France. The 126th Bomb Wing (Light) was deployed in December 1951 from Illinois and Missouri to Bordeaux; the 137th Fighter-Bomber Wing in May 1952 from Georgia, Kansas, and Oklahoma to Chaumont; and the 117th Tactical Reconnaissance Wing in June 1952 from Alabama, Ohio, and South Carolina to Toul. Flying by instrument flight rules (IFR) became routine at Chaumont and Toul because visibility in northeastern France was bad. The first ANG unit to deploy to France was the 126th Bomb Wing, commanded by Brig Gen Frank Allen. Its mission was to protect the new supply routes across France. Aircraft arrived by 26 November 1951; airmen and officers sailed from New York on the USNS *Gen H. F. Hodges*, which docked on 07 December at la Pallice.

Airmen lived and worked in tents pitched in muddy fields until permanent structures could be built. A public road ran through the base at Bordeaux-Mérignac and sheep, which were used to cut grass, grazed between runways. Before landing, pilots had to make low passes over the runway to disperse the sheep. Ironically, "cutting the grass" was Air Force slang for flying low. Due to limited ramp space, some of the B-26 Invader bombers had to be parked on turf. Because an empty B-26 weighed over 11 tons, the propeller tips would sink into the mud overnight.[123, 124] In May 1952, the 126th Bomb Wing, commanded by Allen's successor Col William L. Kennedy, moved to Laon-Couvron. To fly all forty-eight B-26s from Bordeaux to Laon, parts had to be removed from three aircraft at Laon, flown back to Bordeaux, and installed in aircraft needing parts.[125]

Beginning in April 1952, USAFE aircrews were sent to Korea to obtain combat experience. Crews from Bordeaux, Chaumont, and Toul were assigned for 60 days temporary duty (TDY) as part of training plan Project 7019. The US Air Force believed this combat experience would prove invaluable should there be an air war with the Soviets in Europe. After completing the TDY in Korea, the aircrews were given fifteen-day leave in the US. On their return, pilots reported it appeared that Russian pilots were flying the North Korean MiGs. They also lamented that air bases in France were in worse condition than those in the Korean war zone.[126]

The 126th Bomb Wing trained French Air Force B-26 crews that were urgently needed for operations in Indochina. On one training flight, a French pilot demonstrated how to shorten the return flight from Istres-le-Tubé to Laon AB. As the plane neared Paris, to the amazement of his American instructor, he shut off the radio so he could head straight to Laon at 4,000 ft without interference from French air traffic controllers.[127] In 1953, the 38th Bomber Wing (Light) succeeded the 126th Bomb Wing at Laon. In 1955, it became the first overseas wing to receive B-57B Canberra aircraft, licensed by Great Britain for manufacture in the US by the Glenn Martin Company.[128] The sixty Canberras, painted black and shaped like a "bat," were equipped with low-altitude bombing systems and short-range navigation radar, enabling them to fly nuclear bombing missions at night or in bad weather. The aircraft also were used for secret overflights of the Soviet Union.

B-57B Canberra at Laon AB, 1957 (A. L. Christensen)

B-26 aircraft near bomb-damaged hangar, Bordeaux AB, 1951 (US Air Force)

Air Force Combat Wings Deployed to France during 1951-1955[129-132]				
Organization*	**Location in US**	**Aircraft**	**Personnel**	**Location in France**
126th Bomb Wing (Light) (38th BW (L) on 01 Jan 53)	Chicago, IL St. Joseph, MO (ANG)**	B-26B B-26C	1,376	Bordeaux-Mérignac (moved to Laon-Couvron in May 1952)
21st Fighter-Bomber Wing	Victorville, CA (George AFB)	F-86F	1,510	Chambley-Bussières
137th Fighter-Bomber Wing (48th FBW on 10 July 52)	Oklahoma City & Tulsa, OK Wichita, KS Marietta, GA (ANG)	F-84G	1,452	Chaumont-Semoutiers
388th Fighter-Bomber Wing	Clovis, NM (Cannon AFB)	F-86F	1,391	Étain-Rouvres
117th Tactical Reconnaissance Wing (10th TRW on 10 July 52)	Birmingham, AL Toledo, OH Congaree, SC (ANG)	RB-26C RF-80A	1,506	Toul-Rosières
465th Troop Carrier Wing	Greenville, SC (Donaldson AFB)	C-119C***	1,205	Toul-Rosières (moved to Évreux-Fauville in April 1955)

*Fighter wings had 72 fighters. Light bombardment wings had 48 bombers.
**ANG indicates Air National Guard organization mobilized by the US Congress in June 1950 for 21 months during Korean War (extended to 24 months in 1951).
***C-119 Flying Boxcar had more cargo space (16 tons or 62 troops) than a railroad boxcar.

Gate house, Chaumont AB (US Air Force)

Air Force Installations

The Air Force developed main operating bases (MOB) for combat and troop carrier wings, Châteauroux Air Depot (CHAD), and a sector at Orly. Main operating bases had more than eighty permanent and temporary buildings, hangars (37,000 sq ft each for jet fighter aircraft), underground fuel storage tanks, and weapons storage sites. Parking aprons were dispersed on each base. Viewed from overhead, they looked like a *marguerite* (daisy). To deceive Soviet attackers, in the early years inflatable rubber decoy aircraft were parked on marguerites. Airmen called the decoys "Goodyear fighter jets." [133] Paved roads on bases varied from 5 miles at Phalsbourg AB to more than 24 miles at Laon AB. The USAFE Confinement Facility for France and Spain was located at Étain AB. At Orly, 350 acres were developed to include Quonset hut barracks for four-hundred fifty airmen. Runways were under French control.

In 1956 at nearby Grigny, two-hundred thirty-two guaranteed rental income (GRI) housing units were built for Air Force families. In February 1958, the name Orly AB was changed to Orly Airport.

Base commanders were expected to have good relations with nearby communities. On 04 July 1954 to recognize friendship between America and France, USAFE designated the 48th Fighter-Bomber Wing at Chaumont AB to be the "Statue of Liberty Wing." In 1886, France had given the Statue of Liberty, sculpted by Frédéric-Auguste Bartholdi, to the United States. Lt Col Wayne Wills of the 48th located the original molds for Bartholdi's 9-ft tall second-stage model of the statue at a foundry in Sommervoire near St.-Dizier. The base raffled a Ford Versailles automobile to raise $1,752 for a statue from the molds. The Statue, installed on a pedestal in front of wing headquarters, was dedicated on 04 July 1956. It became the focal point for outdoor ceremonies. A plaque on the pedestal was inscribed: "This Statue is Dedicated to The Friendship Uniting France and The United States." [134, 135]

F-86F Sabre jets over Chaumont AB, 1956
(US Air Force Academy)

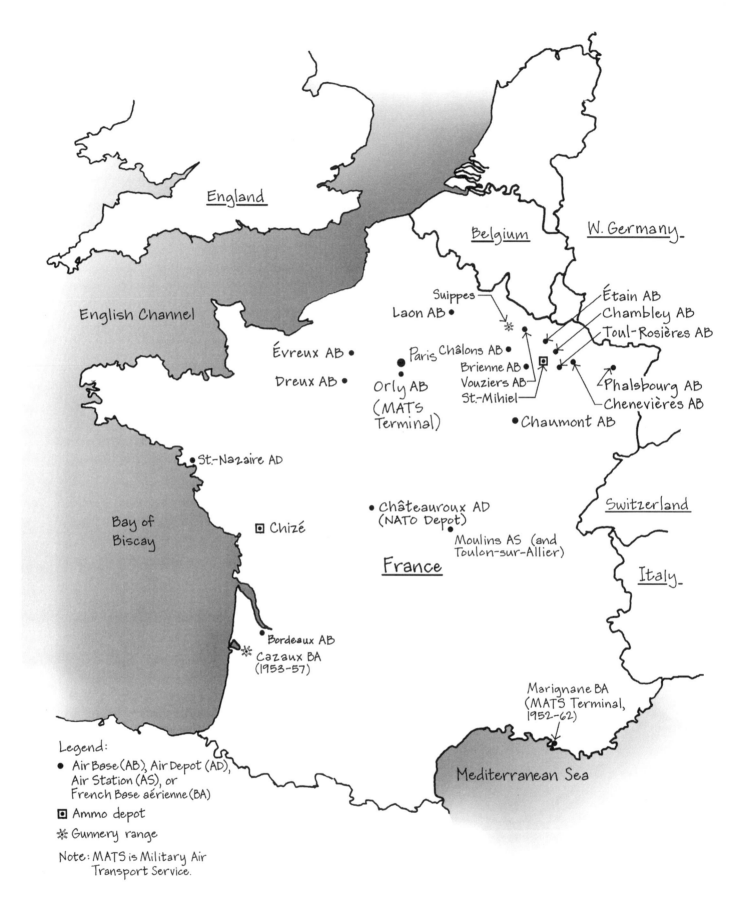

US Air Force Installations (1955)

When the 48th FBW received its F-86 Sabre jet aircraft in late 1953, Wing Commander Col Chesley G. Peterson warned his pilots not to accelerate in steep dives which would produce sonic booms. Booming would disrupt the French countryside and crack windows and plaster.[136] Pilots who ignored the warning were called "boomers." Experienced boomers pulled up sharply so time over target would be brief, making it difficult to identify their tail numbers. In 1956, the 48th FBW was the first wing in Twelfth Air Force to be equipped with F-100D Super Sabres. To control noise, flight paths avoided the town of Chaumont and jet afterburners (mixture of exhaust and fuel re-fired for added thrust) were turned off seconds after wheels up.[137]

The commander of Phalsbourg AB, Col Albert J. McChristy dubbed his base "The Friendliest Base in France." Each December, base personnel and French villagers joined together in the evenings to sing carols at a large Christmas tree in the center of Phalsbourg. During 1961-62, Brig Gen Charles W. Sweeney commanded the 102nd Tactical Fighter Wing deployed from the US to Phalsbourg AB during the Berlin Wall Crisis. The communist press called Sweeney, who had dropped the atomic bomb on Nagasaki ending World War II, "uncaring about Japanese people."[138] Sweeney was not a good choice for a villain because he was a devout Catholic in a predominately Catholic country and he supported Japanese orphans. The protests fizzled.

Size of Air Force Installations[139, 140]

Real Estate	Bordeaux	Chambley	CHAD	Chaumont	Dreux
Land Use (acres)	>150	1,912	1,588	2,223	2,278
Runway Length (ft)	9,900 & 7,800	7,800	12,000	9,900	7,900
Hangars	2	3	2	3	5
Ammo Storage (acres)	0	41	0	52	0
Trailers	0	263	74	128*	242
Family Housing (GRI & CCH units)	132	0	1,023	408	424

*Before 1967, 128 trailers were transferred from Chaumont AB to other bases.

Real Estate	Étain*	Évreux	Laon	Phalsbourg	TRAB
Land Use (acres)	1,932	2,144	1,297	1,853	2,112
Runway Length (ft)	7,900	7,900	7,900 & 3,800	9,900	8,000
Hangars	3	5	3	4	3
Ammo Storage (acres)	40	43**	>50	52	>40
Trailers	179	318	218	71	289
Family Housing (GRI & CCH units)	492	496	200	276	320

*In the 1960s, 350 tons of aluminum foil strips (called chaff) were stored at Étain AB for aircraft at Chambley AB, Étain AB, and Toul-Rosières AB (TRAB). Aircraft dropped chaff to confuse enemy radar.
**US Army Ammunition Storage Site at Sassey.

US Air Force Dispersed Bases

In 1957, NATO approved a plan to build fourteen dispersed operating bases (DOB) in France. Aircraft would be dispersed during periods of crises to make it difficult for the Soviets to destroy aircraft of an entire wing. A wing would be dispersed on its main operating base and on at least two dispersed operating bases. Each DOB would consist of one runway, parking areas for the dispersed aircraft, one hangar, a few small buildings, and connections to the NATO pipeline system for fuel. There were no runway lights. During a crisis, for example at Laon one squadron would remain at Laon, a second squadron would be dispersed to the abandoned aerodrome at Laon-Athies, and a third squadron would be dispersed to a seldom used airfield at St.-Simon/Clastres, which had some old French barracks available for use. During training exercises, a squadron would fly to its DOB where flight operations would take place to test readiness. Aircraft maintenance sections would set up shop operations in the field. In addition to the ten DOBs listed below, six other abandoned airfields were available to US and Canadian forces for use in emergencies.[141-143] From September to December 1958, entire wings were deployed to Brienne-le-Château/Lassicourt and Châlons-sur-Marne/Vatry while runways at Chaumont and Étain ABs were being repaired.

Brienne-le-Château/Lassicourt*	Chenevières*	Péronne/Mons-en-Chaussée
Cambrai-Epinoy	Laon-Athies	St.-Simon/Clastres
Cambrai-Niergnies	Merville/Calonne-sur-la-Lys	Vouziers-Séchault*
Châlons-sur-Marne/Vatry*		

*Originally to be MOB, but converted to DOB due to budget cuts by US Congress. Construction was by French firms, supervised by Joint Construction Agency (JCA). In 1960s, they were transferred to the US Army.

US Air Force Depots in France[144-147]

Location	Land Use (acres)	Function	LWRs*	Period of Use
Aircraft				
Châteauroux-Déols	1,588	Repair and cargo terminal	3,750	1951-67
La Martinerie	953	Parts storage and supply		1951-68
St.-Nazaire (Montoir Airfield)	47	De-cocooning of deliveries by ship	**	1951-61
Vehicles				
Moulins-sur-Allier	10	Parts (and communications equip.)	512	1951-58
Toulon-sur-Allier	30	Park and parts		1951-61
Metz-Frescaty***	French control	Park (and SAC matériel for Project SEAWEED)	0	1951-59
Munitions				
Chizé	6,533	Storage, renovation, and supply	216	1952-61
St.-Mihiel#	900	Storage, renovation, and supply	189	1951-67
Supplies				
Bordeaux-Bacalan	18	Clothing and medical supplies	289	1951-61
Villefrance-d'Allier	15	Aircraft parts		1952-57

*French civilian employee designation, local wage rate (LWR). Combined totals given for Châteauroux-Déols and la Martinerie and for Moulins and Toulon.
**French labor was hired by contract for specific projects at St.-Nazaire.
***Vehicles stored at Metz-Frescaty until 1954 when they were relocated to Toulon-sur-Allier.
#St.-Mihiel was built to store 16,000 tons of conventional munitions and "classified" number of atomic weapons (Mk-7) for five air bases in northeastern France.

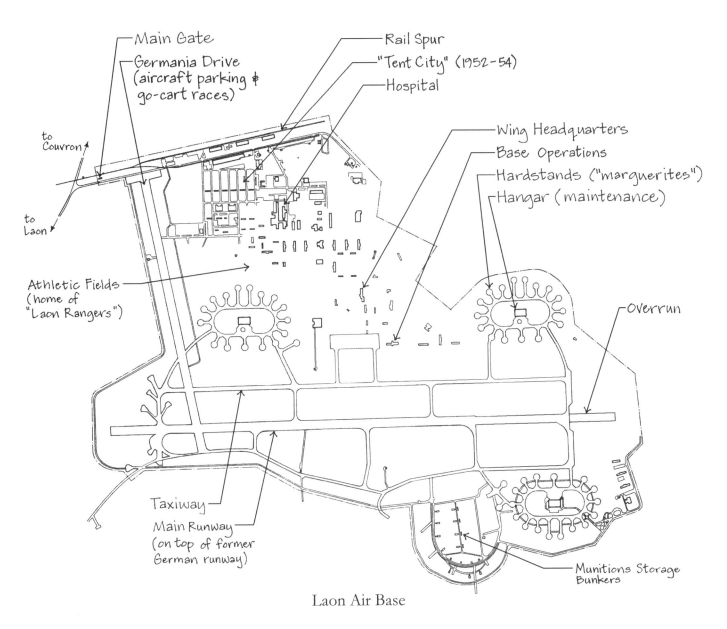

Laon Air Base

Hangar and parking areas (marguerites), Chambley AB, 1956 (A. L. Christensen)

Air Force Units and Aircraft in France (1951-1967)[148-151]

Air Base	Location (Department)	Primary Units	Primary Aircraft
Bordeaux (1951-58)	Mérignac (Gironde)	126th BW (L) (ANG)	B-26B/C (1951-52)
		12th ARG	C-47B (1952-53) SA-16A (1952-53) H-19B (1952-55)
Chambley (1954-67)	Bussières (Meurthe-et-Moselle)	21st FBW 7122nd TFW (ANG) 25th TRW	F-86F (1954-58) F-84F (1961-62) RB-66B/C (1965-66)
Châteauroux (1951-67)	Déols (Indre)	73rd ADW	C-47 (1951-67) C-54 (1951-67) EC-118 (1961-66)
Chaumont (1952-67)	Semoutiers (Haute-Marne)	137th FBW (ANG)	F-84G (1952)
		48th FBW	F-86F (1953-56) F-100D (1956-60)
		7108th TFW (ANG) 366th TFW	F-84F (1961-62) F-84F (1962-63)
Dreux (1955-67)	Louvilliers-lès-Perche (Eure-et-Loir)	60th TCW 309th TCG (Assault) 322nd AD 7117th TRW (ANG)	C-119G (1955-58) C-123B (1956-58) C-119G (1958-61) RF-84F (1961-62)
Étain (1954-67)	Rouvres-en-Woëvre (Meuse)	388th FBW	F-86F (1954-56) F-100D (1956-57)
		49th TFW 7121st TFW (ANG) 366th TFW	F-100D (1957-59) F-84F (1961-62) F-84F (1962-63)
Évreux (1955-67)	Fauville (Eure)	465th TCW 322nd AD	C-119C (1955-57) C-130A (1955-64)
		317th TCW	C-119F/G (1956-58) C-130A (1958-64)
		513th TCW	C-130 (1966)
Laon (1952-67)	Couvron (Aisne)	126th BW (L) (ANG)	B-26B/C (1952)
		38th BW (T)	B-26B/C (1953-55) B-57B/C (1955-58)
		66th TRW	RF-84F (1958-59) RF-101C (1958-66)
Phalsbourg (1956-67)	Bourscheid (Moselle)	23rd HS 86th TFW 66th TRW 7102nd TFW (ANG) 366th TFW	H-21B (1956-58) F-86D (1958-61) RF-101C (1958-59) F-86H (1961-62) F-84F (1962-63)
Toul (1952-67)	Rosières-en-Haye (Meurthe-et-Moselle)	117th TRW (ANG) 10th TRW 465th TCW 10th TRW (Det. 1)	RB-26C (1952) RF-80A (1952-53) C-119C (1954-55) RB-66 B/C (1959-65)
		50th FBW	F-86H (1956-58) F-100D (1957-59)
		7131st TFW (ANG) 26th TRW	F-84F (1961-62) RF-4C (1965-66)

Abbreviations

AD	Air Division	FBW	Fighter-Bomber Wing
ADW	Air Depot Wing	H	Helicopter aircraft
ANG	Air National Guard	HS	Helicopter Squadron
ARG	Air Rescue Group	RB	Reconnaissance aircraft
B	Bomber aircraft	RF	Reconnaissance aircraft
BW (L)	Bomb Wing (Light)	SA	Search and rescue aircraft (Albatross)
BW (T)	Bomb Wing (Tactical)	TCG (A)	Troop Carrier Group (Assault)
C	Cargo aircraft	TCW	Troop Carrier Wing
EC	Electronic-laden aircraft	TFW	Tactical Fighter Wing
F	Fighter aircraft	TRW	Tactical Reconnaissance Wing

NOTE: Most wings had two or more squadrons of same or related function. In 1962-63, the 366th TFW, headquartered at Chaumont AB, assigned squadrons to Chaumont, Étain, and Phalsbourg ABs. The 86th TFW, headquartered at Ramstein AB in West Germany, assigned its 513th Squadron to Phalsbourg from 25 April 1958 to 08 January 1961.

Rail Transportation for GIs

The US Army's 594th Transportation Traffic Regulation Group (commanded by Col Edwin J. Herrington in 1951-52) manned Rail Transportation Office (RTO) facilities at six of the main train stations (*gares*) in Paris. Most unmarried RTO military personnel lived in the Hôtel Des Voyagers, across the street from Gare de l'Est.[152]

Paris Train Stations*

Gare d'Austerlitz (southwestern France)	Gare Montparnasse (western France)
Gare de l'Est (northeastern France and Germany)	Gare du Nord (Germany and Belgium)
Gare de Lyon (Italy)	Gare St.-Lazare (Le Havre)

*Destinations for passengers, baggage, and freight in parentheses.

The RTO operated a 20-passenger bus to transport soldiers between the Paris train stations. The GI's first ride in Paris was memorable. Parisians drove like maniacs, weaving at high speeds between vehicles, racing between traffic lights, passing on sidewalks, and vigorously cursing other drivers and pedestrians. One GI, surprised by the sight of so many churches in Paris, reasoned that they were needed so pedestrians could pray before crossing the street.

Smaller RTOs were located at French railroad stations near US installations, such as La Rochelle and Bordeaux in the southwest and Verdun, Metz, and Bar-le-Duc in the northeast. The structural engineer for the railroad station in Verdun was A. Gustave Eiffel, designer of the famous Eiffel Tower in Paris. During a twelve month period in 1955-56, the RTO at La Rochelle moved more than 11,000 troops and dependents to and from installations in the Base Section. Each day, five trains arrived from Paris and two from Bordeaux.[153]

Traveling to his duty station at Braconne in 1957, PFC M. Brian Hackett used his World War II-era French Phrase Book, issued at the Troop Assignment Center in Germany, to converse with French passengers in his compartment on the SNCF train from Paris to La Rochelle. The passengers, one of whom spoke some English, were amused by the phrases read aloud by Hackett, especially: *Sont-ils nos ennemis?* (Are they our enemies?) and *Allez chercher quelque chose pour servir de bandge.* (Get something to use as a bandage.)[154, 155]

RTO Robert-Espagne

In the early 1950s, the initial RTO for Trois Fontaines Ordnance Depot was at the railway station in nearby Robert-Espagne. On 29 August 1944, this small station had been the site of a massacre. During the German retreat, Panzergrenadier-regiment 29 and Schutzstaffel (SS) officers ordered their soldiers to round up all males in Robert-Espagne and three nearby villages of Beurey-sur-Saulx, Couvonges, and Mognéville. Nearly one-hundred defenseless civilians (mostly boys and old men) were taken to the railway station and executed. In the villages, the soldiers raped women and girls, looted homes, and set buildings on fire.[156-159] The next day, GIs from Patton's Third Army arrived. They set up mess tents to feed the homeless villagers and provided clothing and blankets. More importantly they brought freedom and hope. The liberation of these Saulx River valley villages and the kindness of the Americans have never been forgotten. During the Cold War, villagers in the region were proud to work for the US military in depots at Trois-Fontaines, Vassincourt, and Vitry-le-François. After the war, villagers received reparations from the French government to rebuild their homes. Many American families became neighbors by renting apartments, rooms, and houses from them.

Cargo Transportation

In the early 1950s, France had extensive systems of roads and railways. Major rail terminals were at Tours, Orléans, Metz, and Sommesous (109-acre marshalling yard near Châlons-sur-Marne). More than 100,000 railcars were available to move supplies across France. By the late 1950s, France had more than 55,000 miles of railways and more than 85,000 miles of two-lane roads.[160] Buses of the Military Express Passenger Service provided transportation between La Rochelle, Orléans, and Verdun. All military personnel and dependents were authorized to use the buses.[161]

Maneuvering Army truck and trailer rigs through France was an incredible challenge for the Transportation Corps drivers trained at Fort Eustis, Virginia. Most French national highways (designated N) and departmental roads (D) were high-crowned, tree-lined, narrow, winding, and poorly maintained. In addition, the drivers had to contend with the hazards of foul winter weather from December through February and the seemingly suicidal French drivers who drove like madmen (*conduire comme un fou*). Although it was difficult to change stateside driving habits, drivers had to adapt to the French rule of *priorité à droite* which meant the vehicle approaching on the driver's right from roads of equal importance had the right-of-way. The rule was broadly interpreted by French drivers who would pop out from side streets without concern for traffic on the main road.[162] To be prudent, GIs were instructed to always give priority to vehicles entering an intersection on the right. Headlights for all vehicles in France were yellow. The yellow lights provided better visibility in fog than white lights, but at night they cast a gloom in villages.

The two-lane roads passed through the center of every city and small village along the route. To drive the nearly 240 miles from Orléans to Toul could take between eight and nine hours. In the cities, the French raced between traffic lights; fast starts and screeching stops were common. It was not unusual for bicycle and moped riders to hang on to the sides of Army trailers as they were driven slowly through towns.[163] In the countryside, drivers had to avoid slow-moving farm equipment, farm animals being paraded to or from pastures, and the unpredictable French drivers who routinely would pass another car that was passing a slow-moving truck that was passing a bicycle.[164] The GIs had to be alert to avoid head-on collisions. To further challenge GI drivers, a new French Traffic Law (*Code de la route*) in 1954 gave bicyclists the same rights of way as cars and trucks.[165]

Mature poplar trees, spaced 20 ft apart, lined both sides of most roads. The trees provided a canopy that shaded the roads in hot summer months, prompting some GIs to quip that they had been planted because the German Army preferred to march in the shade. Hundreds of GIs were killed in vehicular accidents when driving under the picturesque, but difficult conditions. In 1952, American vehicles were involved in more than six-hundred reported accidents that killed more than forty French citizens. Most accidents involved alcohol and excessive speed. In the early 1950s, the greatest number of accidents occurred on French national roads between Camp Bussac and Bordeaux, Toul and Nancy, and La Rochelle and Rochefort.[166] From 01 May to 31 July 1963, twenty-eight Americans died in automobile accidents on French roads.[167] To remind troops to drive safely, wrecked vehicles were displayed at main gates of installations. Despite efforts by US military commanders to reduce the number of accidents, the hazards of driving in France remained during the entire Cold War period. In December 1966, there were seven fatalities from automobile accidents, most due to excessive speed on icy roads. The majority of multi-vehicle accidents were the fault of US drivers.[168]

Narrow Road in France

Another Red Ball Express?

Movement of supplies across France from the Atlantic ports to Germany was reminiscent of the famous Red Ball Express of World War II. However, French liaison officers advised US public information officers that memories of the reckless Red Ball drivers were not happy ones. The large 2½-ton cargo trucks had roared through French villages day and night at excessive speeds.[169, 170]

For eighty-one days of combat in the fall of 1944, a 1,000-mile route was established to move supplies on roads from the beachheads in Normandy to the advancing front lines. Rail lines had been badly damaged. The route was called Red Ball, the designation US railroads used for a priority shipment. Because the roads in Normandy were too narrow to allow continuous heavy two-way traffic, a circular one-way route was used. The northern roads were restricted to loaded military vehicles carrying essential supplies (food, ammunition, and gasoline) and the southern roads for returning empty vehicles. Bivouac areas were established 60 miles apart for refueling, emergency repairs by ordnance troops, and brief rest periods and snacks. Two weeks after Red Ball began, the St.-Lô to La Loupe-Dreux-Chartres delivery area was extended beyond Versailles. Headquarters for the Red Ball convoy's Motor Transport Brigade moved into a small requisitioned compound in Versailles.[171] To support Patton's Third Army as the front line shifted eastward, some truck companies operated as far east as Verdun and Metz. On 29 August, nearly 6,000 Red Ball trucks hauled more than 12,000 tons of supplies to forward depots.[172] Seventy-three percent of truck company personnel in the Motor Transport Service in the European Theater of Operations (ETO) were black.[173]

The cost of Red Ball was high. Nearly ½ million tons of supplies were moved forward by overworking personnel and vehicles. Vehicles were used day and night without proper maintenance. C-ration and jerry cans littering the roads caused severe tire damage. Excessive speed and fatigue contributed to numerous accidents.[174] Because accountability for trucks and cargo was lax, it was easy for GIs to succumb to temptations of the black market and the lure of females. A pack of cigarettes that sold for 5¢ at the PX sold for $2.40 on the black market. Numerous deliveries were delayed due to unauthorized detours for sexual encounters. For the most part after Red Ball, truckers had less stressful schedules and fewer temptations.[175, 176]

Army truck convoy, La Rochelle, July 1955 (US Army)

Convoy Traffic Control

The 9th Transportation Highway Transport (THT) Group, headquartered at Saran near Orléans, had served in the Red Ball during World War II. Unlike Red Ball, the ComZ transportation network supervised by the 9th THT Group did not seek to set speed or tonnage records. Its objective was to regulate a smooth-flowing, disciplined network of truck convoys across France. The emphasis was on safety. The experienced drivers would form a nucleus that could be rapidly enlarged during emergencies.[177] Before deploying in 1951 from Fort Eustis, Virginia, to France, personnel of the 9th THT Group participated in the filming of the Hollywood movie *Red Ball Express*. In France, they watched themselves driving in World War II convoys on the silver screen. The movie, released in 1952, starred Jeff Chandler, Hugh O'Brian, and Sidney Poitier.[178]

9th Transportation Group (1954)*

1st Trans Co (Med Trk) at Saran	651st Trans Co (Med Trk) at Nancy
78th Trans Co (Med Trk) at Bussac	655th Trans Co (Hvy Trk) at Saran

*The 1st Trans Co drove tractor trucks towing 7½-ton refrigeration vans, the other companies towed cargo semitrailers.

The drivers competed among themselves by comparing their records of miles driven without an accident or traffic violation. The awards given in recognition of safe driving were highly prized. Drivers who recorded 100,000 miles without an accident or incident received a gold-plated wristwatch.[179]

The 594th Transportation Traffic Regulation Group, which regulated military road and rail traffic in France, was headquartered at Maison-Fort near Orléans. Teams from the group, commanded by Lt Col Frederick G. Ward in 1953, set up highway checkpoints to be sure vehicles in Army convoys had the required transit documents; were properly maintained; and had safety items in good working order (such as yellow headlights, windshields, vision mirrors, and fire extinguishers). The inspection teams consisted of MPs, Ordnance Corps maintenance personnel, and French police.[180] During 1952, most accidents in Base Section that involved US military vehicles were due to excessive speed, reckless passing of another vehicle, or failure to negotiate sharp bends in the road. Some GI drivers claimed the greatest hazard to safe driving was the distraction of French girls riding bicycles.[181] In May 1954, the US Army installed custom-designed silencers to reduce the noise from the exhaust pipes of the heavy trucks. French villagers had been annoyed by the noisy trucks.[182]

On 26 January 1953, three railcars filled with ammunition destined for Trois Fontaines Ordnance Depot exploded at nearby Châlons-sur-Marne. Georges Girard, an SNCF employee, ran to the burning railcars, uncoupled the cars on each side of the burning railcars, and directed movement away from the danger. Girard's bravery prevented greater destruction and loss of life. On 09 April 1953 during a ceremony at the US Embassy in Paris, US Ambassador C. Douglas Dillon presented Girard with the Medal of Freedom with Bronze Palm for his life-saving actions at Châlons, taken without regard for his own safety. Maj Gen Lemuel Mathewson, Commanding General of ComZ, and French Général André Navereau attended the ceremony.[183] After the accident at Châlons, French authorities became adamant that all US Army truck convoys carrying explosives would be escorted by gendarmes. The front of vehicles carrying explosives was to have a highly visible sign labeled "*explosifs*." By agreement, all ammunition in transit was to be guarded at all times by American personnel.

Jerry Cans

In World War II the British, and later the Americans, copied the 20-liter container Germans used for gasoline, dubbing them jerry cans.[184, 185] "Jerry" was slang for Germans. Gasoline was shipped from French ports by tank railcars, tank trucks, and pipeline to depots. In World War II, the major pipeline system ran from Cherbourg to Thionville, north of Metz. Jerry cans were needed to deliver the gasoline from the depots to troops in the field. Before D-Day, the Allies had built up a stock of

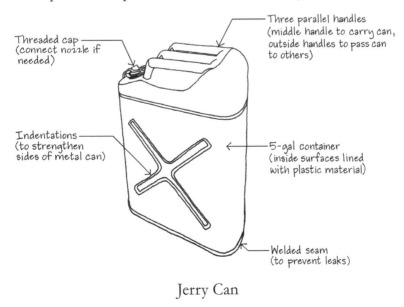

Jerry Can

12 million jerry cans. By mid-October 1944, 3.5 million cans were missing. Hundreds of thousands of cans had been stolen or abandoned; thousands more had been used to build walkways in the mud or to serve as chairs.[186] To help recover the cans, the French Ministry of Education offered prizes to school children who collected the most cans. The children also received a certificate (*Certificat de Mérite*) signed by General Eisenhower. A photograph of the famous general was on the certificate. On the side of roads in France, the Army used rhyming sign messages similar to the advertising signs for Burma Shave along roads and highways in the US. The first sign read, "When you find a jerry can, bud." A second sign farther down the road read, "Don't leave it in the mud." Another sign combination was: "Be a Bright Joe," followed by "Pick up and drop at this depot." About 1 million cans were recovered by the campaign.[187]

Initial Supplies of POL

In a war with the Soviets, petroleum products would be essential for everything from heating food for soldiers in the field to fuel for combat vehicles and jet aircraft. Tanker ships delivered vital supplies of POL (petroleum, oil, and lubricants) to port storage tanks at la Pallice, Pauillac, and St.-Sulpice-et-Cameyrac. Until a pipeline was completed across France in 1956, tank railcars and truck companies moved the POL to depot locations in open fields at Lagord, Fontainebleau, Sommesous, Billy-le-Grand, Buzy, and Pouilly. These "temporary" storage installations were acres of 55-gal drums and 5-gal jerry cans stacked in fields near tent villages for the troops. Typically, drums and jerry cans were stacked in three to five layers to form huge truncated pyramids. The security of these temporary POL depots was very poor.

At the Avon rail station near Caserne Lariboisière in Fontainebleau, troops from the 877th QM Co (Petro Depot), an Army Reserve unit from Ahoski, North Carolina, pumped gasoline from tank railcars into 55-gal drums. Drivers from the 55th Heavy Truck Co (Petroleum) delivered drums to storage fields at the Polygone d'Artillerie in Fontainebleau and a French Army storage site at Montereau.[188] In 1951, nine French Army installations and five leased civilian property sites also were used to store POL for the US Army. Normally, products shipped out were from containers that had been stored the longest (first-in, first-out concept). Today cows graze on lush green pastures that show no ill effects from the numerous oil spills and other pollution from the US Army POL storage sites.

POL drum storage area, Camp Bussac, 1963 (US Army)

During 1955-56, tank truck drivers, transporting POL from the Bouy railhead to the Billy-le-Grand POL Depot, passed through the villages of Livry-sur-Vesle and Bouy. French children waved and shouted greetings to the drivers and the GIs smiled and waved back. For Easter 1956, the depot, commanded by Capt David D. Rutledge, Jr., invited fifty French children from the villages to an Easter party. The children were transported to the depot in Army trucks. At the party, for the first time they drank milk dispensed from a machine, which fascinated them.[189] In early December 1956, fifty underprivileged children from the villages were driven to the depot. Santa arrived by Army helicopter carrying a sack of gifts for the children. On Christmas Eve, GIs from the depot visited the Épernay Orphanage bearing gifts and a decorated Christmas tree.[190]

Storage Locations for POL (December 1953)[191, 192]

Contracted Sites*	US Army Depots and Sub-Depots
Agen [FA]	<u>Base Section</u> (BASEC):
Ambès (north of Bassens)	Bussac
Amilly (near Montargis) [FA]	Donges
Castelsarrasin	Fontainebleau (Polygone d'Artillerie)
Cherbourg [FA]	Lagord (near La Rochelle)
Honfleur	Montmorillon
Montereau [FA]	la Pallice (Usine Bertrand)
Nantes [FA]	Pauillac
Quinssaines (near Montluçon) [FA]	St.-Sulpice-et-Cameyrac (east of Bassens)
St.-Herblain (near Nantes) [FA]	
St.-Malo	<u>Advance Section</u> (ADSEC):
Saumur [FA]	Billy-le-Grand (Livry-sur-Vesle)
Sens [FA]	Buzy (Aérodrome de Étain)
la Souterraine	Châteauneuf
	Pouilly (near Metz)
	Sommesous

*French Army control [FA] and leased civilian property.

US Troops Aid French

French villages and towns near US Army and US Air Force installations benefited from enhanced emergency services. The US military had vast supplies (C-rations, blankets, tents), equipment (ambulances, firefighting apparatus, heavy-lift cranes, helicopters), and well-trained men who could provide emergency assistance and disaster relief. At first, base commanders were reluctant to acknowledge that aid had been given to the French. It was believed that US military equipment was to be used only for military purposes. However, when higher headquarters recognized the value that assistance meant to community relations, commanders were encouraged to aid the French. By mid-1953, aid became common and was routinely cited in French newspapers. There was precedence for community service in France. After the Armistice of World War I, US Army engineers stationed near Dijon practiced construction skills by working in French villages. They repaired windows, doors, and wired homes for electricity which was unheard of at the time in rural France.[193]

At large installations, formal agreements were signed with nearby French fire departments (*sapeurs-pompiers*) establishing that US firefighters had command on US bases and French had command off base, the procedures for requesting emergency assistance, and immunity from damage claims. Adapters had to be fabricated so American-made fire hoses could connect to French fire hydrants. In November 1955 at the Loiret Préfecture in Orléans, Robert Hoveck (Préfet of the Loiret) and

Col Henry C. Britt (commander of US Army Orleans Installation) signed an agreement for mutual fire-fighting assistance. The agreement involved three US fire stations (at Saran, Maison-Fort, and la Chapelle) and eight French fire departments (at Orléans, Saran, Olivet, la Chapelle, Ardon, Fleury-les-Aubrais, Chevillly, and Artenay). In addition, the US Army agreed to provide special equipment such as bulldozers, cranes, and ambulances when requested by French authorities for rescue operations.[194]

American sirens were changed from a shrill, piercing whine to the European "ee-ah" "ee-ah" repetitive warning signal. French authorities believed the unfamiliar whine of the siren would be confusing to the French. Blue flashing lights on MP vehicles also were prohibited because the strange color might frighten French drivers. MPs called the rotating light the "Gumball machine."

Responses to Emergencies

During the winter of 1954, heavy rains in southwestern France caused a levee along the Garonne River to break near Barie. Homes in the small farming village were flooded to a depth of over 10 ft. Because the village did not have the equipment needed to repair the levee, personnel from the 83rd Engineers at Bussac, commanded by Lt Col Hobert H. Hoover, repaired the levee and homes.[195]

During the extremely cold February of 1956, iced-over water isolated the Île de Ré from the mainland, near La Rochelle. More than four-hundred inhabitants were without food and fuel to heat their homes. Brig Gen James K. Woolnough, BASEC commander, directed his troops to provide assistance. More than 1,000 C-rations from Périgueux QM Depot and firewood donated by GIs from La Rochelle Installation were loaded onto Army trucks and delivered by landing craft to the stricken island.[196] Well known to millions of GIs from World War II and Korea, the US Army's primary combat meal still was "Field Ration C" (C for combat). The rations were packed in steel cans that could be opened with an enclosed P-38 pocket can opener, nicknamed "The John Wayne." A complete C-ration provided 3,800 calories in three meals and, to the delight of the French islanders, included cigarettes, matches, chewing gum, and soft toilet paper (a rarity in France). On the mainland, six-hundred families in La Rochelle also needed aid. The La Rochelle Installation, commanded by Col Verle D. Miller, provided C-rations and powdered milk for the children.

On 26 July 1957, the yacht *ALOMA* capsized in rough seas at the entrance to the Bay of Arcachon. A US Air Force H-19B air rescue helicopter from the 83rd Air Rescue Squadron at Cazaux BA, commanded by Maj Richard K. Broesamle, responded to the emergency by dropping a rescue harness attached to a cable to pluck the yacht's passengers from their dingy.[197] Cazaux BA, 6 miles south of Arcachon, was used as a gunnery range by the French and US air forces.

Even cows were rescued by Americans. In August 1959, Madame Adrien Ratinaud's cow, named Lunette, fell into a well at Puy de Nanteuil, near Braconne. Neighbors unsuccessfully pulled on a rope attached to Lunette, but the weight was too great. By nightfall hope had dimmed when one of the Frenchmen decided to go to the front gate at the Braconne Ordnance Depot to ask for help. The duty officer dispatched Sp4 Lee Hamilton's M62 wrecker truck to the scene. Hamilton lifted the "half-drowned" cow out of the well by attaching his crane to Ratinaud's rope. After the rescue, the French gave Lunette a liter of wine and Mme Ratinaud said: "I think Americans are wonderful."[198,199]

On 18 June 1961, the Strasbourg-Paris SNCF express train derailed at Blacy near Vitry-le-François, killing twenty-eight passengers and injuring more than one-hundred seventy. The high-speed derailment was caused by explosives placed under the rails by terrorists of the French OAS (*Organisation de l'Armée Secrète*).[200] Personnel from the nearby US Army 77th Medical Depot cared for the injured and drivers of the 591st Ambulance Co from Vitry transported the injured to hospitals. A military M43 ambulance could carry four patients on litters or eight seated patients. From Robert-

Espagne, personnel of the 39th Ordnance Co brought wreckers to hoist damaged railcars and MPs of the 61st Military Police Co assisted French gendarmes. Two H-34 Choctaw helicopters from the 26th Transportation Co (Light Helicopter), commanded by Maj Steve Bosan at Rozelier Air Field, flew critically-injured passengers to hospitals. The next day, GIs donated more than 200 pints of blood.[201, 202]

When canals in northeastern France froze in January 1963, barge traffic could not carry coal, the primary source for heat. Water pipes froze and burst in residences in Verdun and nearby villages. Engineers of the 97th Engineer Battalion at Caserne Maginot, commanded by Lt Col Robert H. Montjoy, trucked water to housing areas and loaned water pumps to French communities. The emergency lasted six weeks.[203] During the harsh winter of 1965, Laon AB personnel, commanded by Col Frank C. Malone, responded to an emergency request from the Préfet du Aisne. For five days the US Air Force tanker trucks traveled thousands of miles over dangerous icy roads to deliver fuel oil to French hospitals and schools in the region.[204]

French Liaison Officers

In 1958, there were eleven French Army officers assigned as liaison to US Army installations. Four were assigned to Verdun, three to Poitiers, and two each to Paris and Bordeaux. One French Navy officer was assigned to la Pallice. The liaison officers had no authority on the installations, but assisted the US Army with employment of French civilians and relations with nearby communities. They reported US Army activities that they observed to their chain-of-command in Paris.[205]

The French Air Force assigned a liaison officer to each US Air Force base. Liaison officers normally were fluent in English and were expected to participate in the social life of the base. Their children were encouraged to have contact with American children so they would learn English. The officers found their own lodging off base, but could eat at officers clubs, shop at base exchanges, and use recreation facilities. They had no operational control at the bases and only monthly totals of air operations were reported to them.[206] However, like US military attachés, they gathered intelligence for their government. They observed and reported on activities such as unauthorized aircraft on base, movement of nuclear weapons, and any suspicious activities. In March 1963, the liaison officer at Évreux AB, commanded by Col Archie R. Lewis, discovered an Iranian C-47 Skytrain parked at the base. The failure of the US to ask for permission prior to a visit by the Iranian military upset French authorities, especially since Iran was not a member of NATO.[207]

Flag Negotiations

Initially, only the American flag was flown at Army and Air Force installations. Early in 1952, US Army Gen Thomas T. Handy objected to the provision in a proposed US-French Air Forces agreement that required flying the French flag over US installations in France. Handy withdrew his objection when the agreement was modified so the flag provision unequivocally applied only to USAFE bases.[208] Handy believed that if the French flag was flown on US installations the French then would ask to inspect and supervise the installations. Therefore, US European Command had insisted that the "rights, privileges, and dignity" of US forces be protected by invoking Article 10 in the Civil Affairs Agreement of 1948. This Franco-American agreement, to cover US forces in France to support the occupation of Austria and Germany, had been signed on 16 February 1948. It gave US forces the right "to police all the installations, camps and other establishments which they might use or maintain in France," but did not mention an LOC across France.[209]

After lengthy negotiations, it was announced on 03 January 1954 that by mutual agreement both French and American flags were to be flown on all US installations in France. This resulted in two flagpoles side-by-side in front of US Army and US Air Force headquarters buildings. Prior to the agreement, the French flag was flown only on French holidays or when a French dignitary visited the installation. Public information officers told the French the two flags symbolized that France and America were allies for the common defense of France and NATO.

Flags were important symbols to the French. During World War II, French businessman Raoul Laporterie, who risked death numerous times to save Jews, also risked death to retrieve a French Army flag that had been inadvertently left behind at a hotel in German-occupied Arcachon. When asked why, the astonished Raoul replied, *"Le drapeau, c'est sacré."* (The flag is sacred.)[210]

Army troops from Ingrandes Depot parade at Châtellerault, 1961 (US Army)

Flag Ceremonies

To initiate the two-flag policy, most installations had elaborate French flag raising ceremonies which featured honor guard platoons, bands, and remarks by high-ranking officers. French military and civilian officials, such as préfets of the local département, were invited to attend. Préfets, appointed to represent the French government, also controlled the gendarmes stationed in their départements.

In May 1954, a typical flag raising ceremony was held at Braconne Ordnance Depot. Maj Gen Oliver P. Newman, BASEC commander, and René Coldefy, Préfet of the Charente, along with several hundred French and American guests, attended the ceremony. The US flag was raised while the 279th Army Band from La Rochelle played the "Star Spangled Banner" and the French flag was raised while "La Marseillaise" was played. US and French troops marched past a reviewing stand. After the ceremony a reception was held in the office of depot commander, Lt Col Abner C. Hutcherson.[211] In the Advance Section, the French flag raising ceremony was held in April 1954 at Caserne Maginot, Verdun; in October 1954 at Trois Fontaines Ordnance Depot; and in May 1955 at Billy-le-Grand.[212]

Flags at Orléans

In 1957, Company C of the 553rd Engineer Battalion, commanded by Capt John E. Hurst, Jr., was assigned to install a new steel flagpole at the parade grounds of Caserne Coligny in Orléans. To the great surprise of the construction engineers, the flagpole sank into the ground during placement by a mobile crane. The base for the pole ruptured and the heavy steel pole slowly sank to a depth of about 15 ft below ground level. Hurst consulted drawings at the local office of *Ponts et Chausées* and discovered that numerous tunnels, dug centuries ago to mine limestone, crisscrossed under the city. To support the flagpole, the 553rd Engineers worked two weeks dumping numerous 5-ton M51 dump truck loads of gravel and soil each day into the "sinkhole." Eventually, the ground was sufficiently firm to support ComZ's new flagpole for its garrison flag.[213]

In late 1958, two flagpoles were installed on the parade grounds, near the front gate. When Brig Gen Mason J. Young moved his headquarters from Paris in December 1950, the French flag was flown on a wooden pole in front of a memorial to the French 131ème Régiment d'Infantrie, that occupied Coligny until World War II. For eight years the American flag had flown on a 23-ft high steel pole at the center of the parade grounds and the French flag had flown on the shorter wooden pole, just inside the front gate. Because Charles de Gaulle had returned to power, it was prudent that this flagpole height inequity be corrected and the French and American flags fly side-by-side at the same height.

Flagpoles at Caserne Coligny, Orléans, 1957 (US Army)

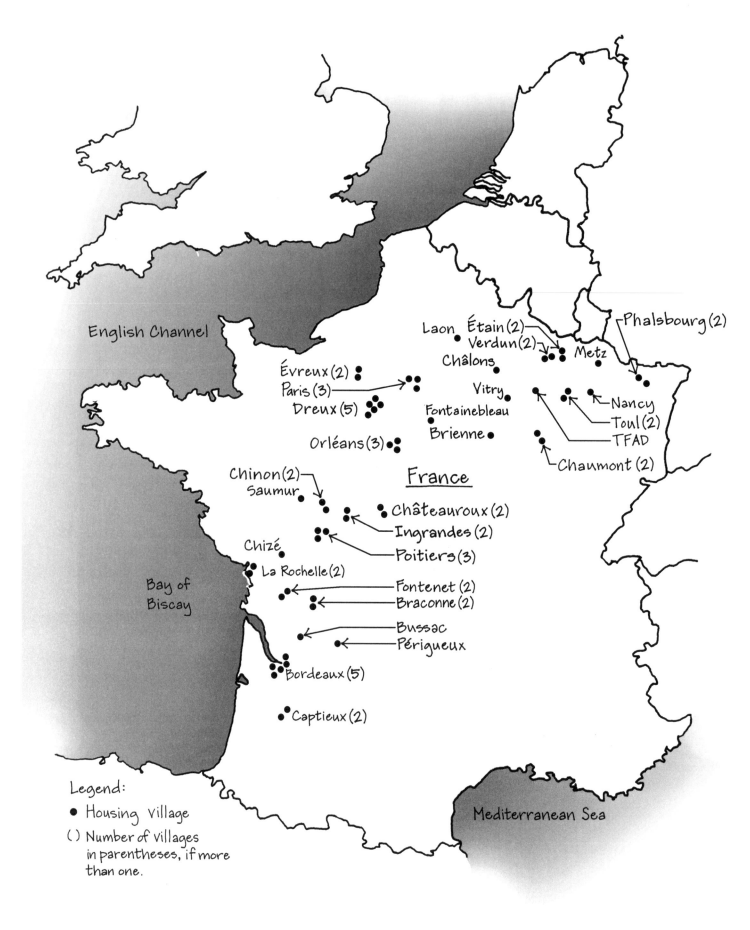

US Military Housing Villages (1959)

FOUR

Construction for US Military

"Facilities there [in France] are as bad as some of the worst I saw last year in Korea."
(Episcopal Bishop Austin Pardue, Laon AB, 25 December 1953)

Living in Tents

In the early 1950s in France, soldiers lived in austere conditions. Troops were crammed ten to a tent. To save construction funds for operational facilities, such as depots, ports, and pipelines, dilapidated French casernes were rehabilitated and prefabs were built to house troops. It was several years before modern barracks buildings would be built at most installations. US installations in France were in acres of mud. During rainy months, Army troops had to work at sites where the mud was so deep they would sink to above their ankles. The troops dubbed their living and working conditions Operation MUDBALL. Draftee soldiers deployed to Europe learned the Army acronym for continental United States was CONUS (pronounced "cone-us"). Most would count the days until they would rotate back to CONUS, dubbed "land of the round doorknobs" by GIs. Doors in France had lever door handles that were easy to use, but seemed strange to the Americans.

Winterized Tents

By 1952, most tents had wooden floors. Tents with wooden flooring and 4-ft high plywood sides covered by tarpaper were designated "winterized." By 1953, more than 12,000 troops still lived in winterized tents that were sized for ten Army beds, ten wall lockers, and ten footlockers.[1] In winter months, cold air blew through cracks between boards in the floor and walls, and the canvas roof provided little thermal insulation. Heat was provided by small coal-burning stoves at both ends of the tent. Each night a GI, assigned as barracks orderly, was required to stay awake all night on fire watch. The next day orderlies were allowed to sleep late and miss morning formation.

General Handy Rejects Prefabs

To provide adequate shelter for the troops at the US air bases under construction in 1952 at Chaumont, Laon, and Toul-Rosières, the USAFE proposed using the high-quality, German-built insulated prefabs used by US forces stationed in Germany. Initially the French government rejected this proposal, citing the adverse effect on employment in France. Desperate, the USAFE tried subterfuge by painting some of the German prefabs olive drab and labeling them "Property of US Air Force." The French were not fooled. After intensive negotiations, the French agreed to allow one-hundred sixty German prefabs to be imported for Châteauroux AD, and twenty-two each for Chaumont, Laon, and Toul-Rosières ABs. However, US Army Gen Thomas T. Handy, Commander-in-Chief of EUCOM, intervened. The German prefabs had been purchased by German funds intended to support the Allied occupation of Germany. Handy felt that prefabs for France should be purchased separately by US funds.[2,3] The airmen were forced to spend another bitterly cold winter in winterized tents that they sarcastically called "canvas castles." Handy lived in comfort in Quarters One in Heidelberg, Germany. Although EUCOM headquarters were in the IG Farben Building in Frankfurt, Handy commuted from Heidelberg. His Quarters One was a huge requisitioned castle that was very expensive to staff and maintain. Because Mrs. Handy refused to move, EUCOM headquarters remained in Germany until Handy retired.[4]

Austerity Program

To not exceed the $300 million budget to build a line of communications, which was now an even larger ComZ, it was decided to build enlisted men's barracks of lesser quality than those in the US and Germany. Bureaucrats called the original tent cities and cheaply-built depot buildings the "austerity program." The troops called it a lousy assignment. In 1952, French contractors still were unable to deliver prefabricated buildings needed to replace tents. To expedite construction of winterized tents, the 406th Construction Battalion (reserve unit from Birmingham, Alabama) was sent to Croix-Chapeau, the 982nd (from Duluth, Minnesota) to Orléans, and the 998th (from Menomonie, Wisconsin) to Toul. The 12-month overseas tour for these two-thousand engineer troops was extended several months before the reserve battalions were inactivated.[5] In late 1952, elements of two construction battalions were sent on temporary duty from Germany to winterize tents, install prefabs, and build roads in France. The 109th Engineer Construction Battalion (National Guard unit from Rapid City, South Dakota, stationed at Mannheim, Germany) was sent to Verdun and the 432nd Engineer Construction Battalion (reserve unit from Houston, Texas, stationed at Kaiserslautern, Germany) to several locations in the Base Section.

Hutments, Chaumont AB, 1953 (US Air Force Academy)

Initial Construction Projects

Throughout 1951, supplies poured into France from Germany and the US while construction of structures to store them lagged far behind schedule. The buildup was so rapid that crates, ammo, pipe sections, and tires had to be dumped on the ground or stored in caves. Trucks, combat tanks, and engineer heavy equipment were parked in forests. Supplies and equipment stored in the open were exposed to rain and snow, and had no protection from sabotage and theft. Eventually rusted metal and cracked hoses would have to be repaired or replaced.[6] By April 1952, numerous construction projects were several months behind schedule. After a three month freeze on new construction in early 1953 by the new Eisenhower administration, the delays would be 3 to 6 months longer.[7]

Stacks of prefabricated construction panels, Saran Army Airfield, January 1952 (US Army)

Construction of the US installations during the period of 1951 to 1954 was considerably slower than experienced on similar work in the US. Few French construction firms had heavy equipment and power-driven tools that were common in the US. Most ditches and trenches were dug by shovel. Skilled labor was scarce because, during the German occupation, draft-age Frenchmen had been conscripted to work in German factories or held in POW camps.[8] Bureaucratic red tape, language difficulties, and the normal leisurely pace of French construction contributed to long delays.[9] During summer months, decisions were slow or nonexistent. By French custom, government ministries shut down from Bastille Day on 14 July to mid-September. French workers traditionally took vacations in August, a sunny month suited for rapid construction. In August, Paris looked uninhabited. Shops, banks, bakeries, and laundries displayed the notice *fermeture annuelle* (annual closing).

By summer 1952, 40% of the required tonnage of supplies had been shipped to France, but less than 10% of the new construction had been completed.[10] The ComZ Engineer Division Construction Branch was located in twenty-eight leased rooms at the Hôtel West End on 7, rue Clement Marot, Paris. The sixty-five engineer officers and civilians assigned to design and oversee construction of the vast ComZ infrastructure were fewer than the number needed and authorized by the Department of the Army.[11] Because pay and allowances were low, it was difficult to lure Department of Army Civilians (DAC, pronounced "dax") to work in France.[12]

Joint Construction Agency (JCA)

In July 1952, the US Air Force hired an association of three US architectural-engineering firms to manage its air base construction projects in France. Unlike the ComZ engineers, commanded by Maj Gen Samuel D. Sturgis, Jr. who insisted on strict adherence to plans and specifications, the Air Force encouraged French bidders to submit alternate designs. The Air Force method was faster than the Army's design and bidding procedures, but the quality of Air Force construction was lower. Although Sturgis had argued that US Army engineers should control all construction in France, NATO Supreme Commander Gen Matthew B. Ridgway advocated a joint effort. To expedite construction, a Joint Construction Agency (JCA) was created in December 1952 to oversee all US Army, US Air Force, and US Navy construction in France. Previously, the US Army and US Air Force programs had overlapped and competed for scarce French labor and materials.[13, 14] After JCA began operations in 1953, the ComZ Construction Office closed its Paris office at Hôtel West End. ComZ refurnished the rooms at West End to provide billets for single enlisted men.

Directors, Joint Construction Agency (JCA)

Commanding Officer	Period of Service
Brig Gen Orville E. Walsh	Jan-Feb 1953
Maj Gen George J. Nold	Feb 1953-July 1955
Maj Gen Bernard L. Robinson	July 1955-July 1957

The JCA reported that the construction cost for the early period exceeded $400 million.[15] By 1954, the JCA would be authorized 1,010 military and civilian personnel, and it awarded $93 million for projects that year. The main office was located at 94, rue Escudier, Boulogne-sur-Seine (a suburb of Paris) in several buildings within the 3-acre walled compound of the leased Partner Factory. The owner, a clothing manufacturer, had moved his factory operations to accommodate the US military. The interiors of the buildings were subdivided for offices, drafting rooms, print shop for drawings and specifications, and storage for records.[16] Initially, JCA District Offices were located at Bordeaux, to oversee port construction, and at Verdun.

Construction of concrete runway, Déols, April 1952 (US Air Force)

Air Base Construction

Air base construction took up to five years because of diplomatic, economic, and political problems. Many French politicians, who believed US air bases would turn France into a target for Soviet bombs, did little to expedite construction. At Bordeaux-Mérignac, the French contractors charged the Americans high prices to rehabilitate runways and buildings for the NATO buildup, but paid low wages to the French construction workers. The French, expecting to be treated like workers in the US, blamed the Americans for their 19¢ per hour wages.[17]

US Air Forces in Europe (USAFE) air bases for modern jet aircraft took longer to build and cost more than the austere, standard NATO air base. US airmen required more latrines, took more showers, washed more vehicles, and watered more grass than their French counterparts. The grass caused problems. In 1954, farmers working land near USAFE air bases complained to the French government that wild grass on the bases had not been cut. The grass had gone to seed which caused their farm lands to be covered with weeds. The USAFE promised to alleviate the conditions by frequent mowing and allowing sheep herders to graze their flocks on the bases.

Sheep "cutting the grass," Rozelier Army Airfield, 1959 (G. S. Bosan)

Funds had to be appropriated by the US Congress to build additional facilities for airmen dormitories, clubs, recreation, and base exchanges (shopping), and to provide utilities for electrical and water needs. The additional cost to the US for construction of eight NATO main operating bases for USAFE in France exceeded $170 million.[18] Main runways, taxiways, and parking aprons were built for NATO by French contractors. The basing agreements, negotiated without engineer representation, did not give the US Air Force the right to inspect construction.

PSP sections at construction site, Chaumont AB, November 1953 (US Air Force)

Engineer Aviation Battalions (EAB)

The US Air Force funded Engineer Aviation Battalions (EAB), but personnel were recruited and trained by the US Army. These heavy construction units were known as Special Category Army Personnel with Air Force (SCARWAF). An EAB had about 30 officers and 750 enlisted men. GIs called EAB troops "Army orphans." In France, EABs built tent camps and trailer parks (called Project Caravan), graded roads, surfaced runways, and repaired poorly constructed NATO-funded buildings.[19] Five of the EABs deployed to France were Army Reserve units mobilized for the Korean War. Most of the units arrived in France in early 1953. On 16 April 1953, troops of the 472nd, 821st, and 843rd EABs made a dramatic entry at la Pallice by climbing down six nets on the side of the troopship USNS *Gen W. G. Haan* into Army DUKWs which took them to shore.

EAB troops climb down net of USNS Haan into DUKW, la Pallice, April 1953 (US Army)

EAB units worked at more than one location. The 843rd EAB from Indianapolis, Indiana, had companies at Chaumont, Laon, and Toul-Rosières ABs. The 469th EAB from Hackensack, New Jersey, assigned companies to Bordeaux AB and St.-Nazaire AD. The 472nd EAB from Buffalo, New York, primarily worked at Châteauroux AD, and the 821st EAB from Trenton, New Jersey, at Châteauroux AD and Dreux AB. In March 1955, the 821st, commanded by Lt Col Raymond W. Welch, rapidly built a concrete nose deck taxiway at Orly AB. The 866th EAB from Andalusia, Alabama, commanded by Lt Col Albert H. Taylor, built hardstands and roads, and erected forty-seven prefab Quonset huts to replace two-hundred forty tents at Châteauroux AD. The new housing area at la Martinerie, dubbed "Quontown," was completed before winter 1953-54.[20] These EAB units, which entered active duty during March to June 1951, were released from active duty on 25 September 1955. All SCARWAF personnel remaining in France were transferred from US Air Forces in Europe to US Army, Europe.

St.-Nazaire Air Depot was a supply and maintenance base for Air Force fighter aircraft. A French Air Force base was on the opposite side of a long perimeter road. During construction of the depot, French motorists stopped along the roadside to watch the huge American bulldozers, rock crushers, and asphalt plant in action.[21] In February 1954, Lt Col Joseph G. Elliott, commander of the 472nd EAB, assigned two platoons to help the French build a 5-mile long macadam road between St.-Nazaire and Montoir, site of the EAB camp. The battalion had the earth-moving equipment at

Montoir needed to cut and fill the base layer of the road. The new road rerouted National route 771 to bypass several small villages and improved vehicle access to St.-Nazaire and La Baule. Most US military traffic would continue to use the old road. In summer months, the population of the resort area of La Baule grew from 20,000 to 200,000. Gen Thomas T. Handy approved this unusual US Air Force project if the work would be considered a training exercise, have lower priority than military construction, and not set a precedent for other EAB work in France.[22] In April 1954, the 850th EAB built concrete apron parking areas at Bordeaux AB. Earlier they built runways at Cazaux for USAFE units deployed for annual aerial-gunnery exercises.[23]

Poor Construction

Air Force personnel in France wondered if some of the poor construction was due to sabotage. During this time period, a US Army counter intelligence unit discovered that underground fuel storage tanks and piping at SAC air bases in French Morocco had been designed to fail by a civilian engineer who was a communist.[24] The Right Reverend Austin Pardue, an Episcopal bishop from Pittsburg, Pennsylvania, touring US military installations in Europe, believed living conditions in December 1953 at Laon AB were as bad as the worst he had seen in Korea. Pardue told a United Press reporter that although the morale of 38th Bomber Wing was high, the base was a disgrace. Airmen at Laon believed French bureaucratic red tape slowed construction progress.[25] Deficiencies in runway construction were common. At Toul-Rosières AB, the concrete surface spalled; at Laon AB, a steep drop-off at both ends of the runway made aircraft overruns unsafe; at Chaumont AB, the surface of the runway was so slippery that aircraft would slide off; and at Chambley AB, underground natural springs caused

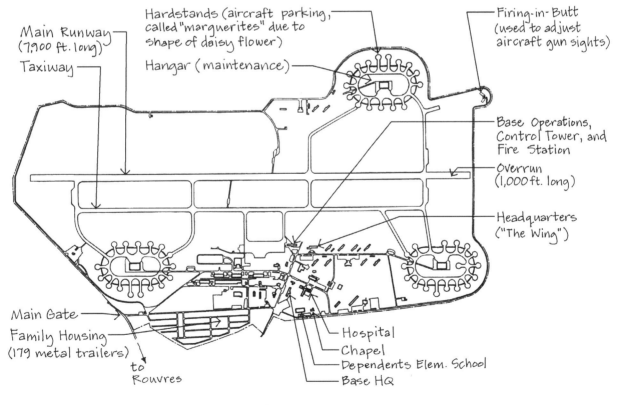

Étain Air Base

erosion beneath the runway. In 1952 at Toul-Rosières AB, 55-gal drums of burning gasoline had to be placed along both sides of the runway to serve as landing lights. The gasoline frequently had to be relit because turbulence from flight operations extinguished the flames.[26]

Construction was so poor and so far behind schedule at Étain AB, that when the 388th Fighter-Bomber Wing arrived in December 1954 its seventy-seven F-86F Sabre jet aircraft had to be based in Germany. The support elements of the wing worked and lived at Étain in a sea of mud. On Christmas Eve 1954, one-thousand men sat in barracks without heat and light. Some wrote complaint letters by candlelight to their US Congressman. Wing Commander Brig Gen James E. Whisenand was so vexed by the inept French contractors he wrote to his boss, Maj Gen Robert M. Lee at Twelfth Air Force, urging an investigation.[27] It took most of 1955 to complete the base. The aircraft returned from Germany in November.

Air bases at Chambley, Dreux, and Évreux were not completed until 1955; Phalsbourg AB did not have full operations until 1957. Construction at Phalsbourg was delayed because the remains of an underground bunker, built by the Germans during World War II, had to be demolished by dynamite.[28] Once the bases became operational, noise from jet engines disturbed nearby inhabitants and farm animals. Base commanders improved community relations by routing takeoffs and landings to avoid built-up areas and scheduling flying hours at times less objectionable to locals.[29]

Impediments to Rapid Construction

Most of the existing buildings released for US use required major rehabilitation and most of the land for depots in the Base Section of southwestern France was marshy. Initially, the French government was reluctant to permit drainage of surface water.[30] To US Army engineers, this policy to conserve marshlands was an inexplicable obstacle to construction programs for the defense of the West. Other JCA problems included misunderstandings due to language barriers, improper use of Form 101 (the request form for supply or services that required ten copies for each action), and disagreements on who would inspect construction work and maintain roads on and near the US bases. All construction was by French firms. France had agreed to furnish supplies, services, and facilities at cost, but the French government would control all construction.

Agreements placed all US construction work under three French-government agencies: *Génie Militaire* (French Army engineers), *Ponts et Chausées* (bridges and roads), and *Service de l'Infrastructure* (NATO work). French construction agencies doubted that JCA projects could be urgent if they were changed so frequently and work delayed by Pentagon imposed freezes of 60 to 90 days on construction. A second freeze by the Eisenhower administration lasted from 28 September 1954 to early January 1955.[31] French-government agencies did not have national engineering standards to guide their builders. As a consequence, local representatives made their own decisions. A request by the JCA might be accepted in Verdun, but an identical request rejected at Chinon.[32] French contractors and material suppliers were paid by the French-American Fiscal Liaison Office (FAFLO) in Paris, which received its funds from the US forces. Form 102, which also required ten copies for each action, was used to certify that the French contractor should be paid. In 1954, CBS News broadcaster Edward R. Murrow visited the Advance Section to film Army activities for his *See It Now* TV program. During his five-day visit, he reported on construction progress at Verdun and Metz area installations.[33]

Agreements on US construction in France stipulated that the US have funds available before asking the French to advertize bids for the work. In 1954, the French Liaison Mission in Paris agreed to make an exception for the proposed Paris Area Hospital at Melun, if funds would be available after routine clearance by Department of The Army. Bids were opened in early October 1954, but funds still had not been approved by the end of the year. This breach of faith adversely affected relations of the JCA with French contractors and, after additional delays by the JCA, the project was cancelled in 1956.[34]

Many misunderstandings during construction were due to the differences in terminology. In negotiations, the French word *demande* seemed to Americans to be a strident "demand" until they understood that it only meant a request or desire. In 1956, the JCA, now commanded by Army Maj Gen Bernard L. Robinson, translated important French construction measures and specification documents into English. Earlier in Base Section, the technical services had begun to translate unclassified maintenance and repair manuals into French.[35] Army engineers discovered unfamiliar, but not very useful, terms such as *jetu de pelle* for shovelful and *dos d'âne* for a donkey load.[36]

In 1955 at Verdun, a GI in the 97th Engineer Battalion was dumping a truck load of 100-lb sacks of "acquajel" in the town's landfill. The diatomaceous silica, which looked like cement but had none of its strength, was used as drilling mud when the engineers drilled water wells. Because most installations now had reliable sources of water, the drilling rig at Jardin Fontaine was seldom used and the silica was surplus. At the landfill, a Frenchman asked if the sacks were *béton* (concrete). The GI, not knowing what béton was but wanting to be helpful, replied *oui* (yes) and the Frenchman took most of the sacks. The GI had been directed by his Supply Officer, 1st Lt Lloyd A. Leffers, to dispose of excess material but, in his eagerness to be a good guest, he may have unintentionally sabotaged civilian construction work in Verdun.[37]

Franco-American Engineer Relations

At Verdun, Brig Gen William W. Ford assisted the French Army Engineers who were assigned to oversee work of the JCA in the Advance Section. In November 1953, French Général de Brigade Marie-Joseph Kauffeisen told Ford that there were not enough engineers at Metz to handle the workload and believed his request to Paris for additional personnel would benefit from outside support. Kauffeisen asked Ford to contact Maj Gen Lemuel Mathewson, Commanding General of ComZ at Orléans. Mathewson passed Ford's request to Maj Gen George J. Nold at JCA who contacted his counterpart on the French General Staff. Nold, without mentioning Kauffeisen, wrote that the JCA District Engineer at Verdun had observed that the small French staff in Metz likely would be overwhelmed by the $28 million of US construction scheduled for 1954. Kauffeisen got his engineers.[38, 39]

In 1956, Maj Gen Bernard L. Robinson, who succeeded Nold, and Col Lynn C. Barnes, JCA North District Engineer, organized a Paris chapter of The Society of American Military Engineers. The chapter, officially named the "Paris Post," quickly grew to two-hundred American and French members. Robinson's goal was to enhance Franco-American relations by monthly meetings and field trips.[40] By 1960, there also were active chapters at Orléans and Toul.

JCA Criteria for the Building Program

In mid-1953, most of the 23,000 US Army troops still lived in substandard barracks, used rudimentary latrines, and had few recreational facilities. Many GIs believed facilities were better even in Korea and, if given the option, they would transfer to Germany.[41] To boost troop morale, stimulate US Air Force re-enlistments, and reduce maintenance costs for structures in France, the JCA was directed in 1954 to build more suitable facilities. The JCA concluded that common French construction using concrete block would be the least expensive and most durable. Masons were plentiful and less costly than carpenters. Concrete block construction cost less than two of the five types of prefab structures available to ComZ and required less maintenance than all five. The concrete block walls and lightweight structural steel roof trusses were expected to last at least 20 years. The concrete floor slabs, aircraft runways, hardstands, water towers, and fence posts could last more than 100 years.

Multipurpose facilities, consisting of chapel, theater, craft shop, service club, and library, were authorized for installations with less than 300 troops. Separate buildings for chapels, officers clubs, service clubs, gymnasiums, libraries, craft shops, and NCO clubs were authorized for larger installations with 300 to 1,000 troops. The number of persons on the base determined the square footage permitted for each building. For recreation, two-lane bowling alleys were authorized for installations with less than 600 troops; gymnasiums for installations with 500 to 3,000 troops; and service clubs (to include theater, craft shop, library) for the larger installations. For smaller installations, a minimum of one of each type of athletic facility was authorized where justified by the commanding officer. Educational facilities, exchange gas stations, and outdoor facilities for athletic and recreational use could be authorized for air bases and large Army installations.[42]

Basing agreements stipulated that US forces could repair existing buildings, but could not construct permanent buildings. To overcome this obstacle, the JCA established an ingenious definition for US buildings in France. Buildings were designated "permanent" for leased or rent-free existing French-owned structures, "semipermanent" for masonry and metal-frame structures built by the US, and "temporary" for most metal prefabs and wood-frame structures that could be easily disassembled when the US departed. Although temporary (T) structures were the cheapest to build, the maintenance and operating costs proved to be high. The French government accepted construction of permanent buildings if they were designated semipermanent (abbreviated S). More than half a century after they were built, thousands of semipermanent buildings still stand, many with a faded yellow painted S followed by two or three numbers still visible near a corner.

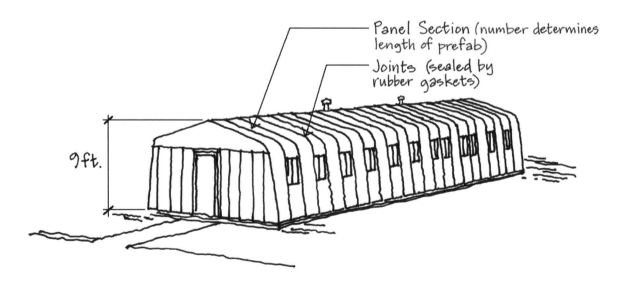

Metal Prefab Structure

Prefab Barracks

Because barracks were desperately needed, the JCA evaluated proposals from French companies to supply prefabs. Constructions Métalliques Fillod was selected to manufacture metal prefabs at their Florange plant near Thionville. In 1953, Fillod installed several "company size" prefabricated metal building units, each serving 200 troops. Requiring about 4 acres, a nine building cluster consisted of: six troop barracks, one kitchen-mess hall, one orderly-supply room, and one dayroom-latrine.[43] The metal prefabs, installed on concrete slabs, had a similar bunk-locker layout to barracks in the caserne buildings, but less troop capacity. Latrines and showers were in a nearby prefab—an arrangement the troops disliked, especially during cold winters. GIs called the Fillod barracks "metal mansions."

On smaller installations, Fillods also were used for chapels, theaters, and shops. Because gaskets were used to seal joints between the metal panel sections, Fillods were leak resistant. They could be disassembled, moved, and reassembled on concrete slabs at another location. This was an advantage during the rapid withdrawal in 1967.

By 1954, two-thirds of the Army troops were sheltered in prefabs or renovated French barracks, instead of tents. The rehabilitated, war-damaged French caserne buildings used to house troops had huge undivided rooms where 20 or more men lived together without any privacy.[44] One shower head and one 2-ft long urinal trough was provided per 20 men; one toilet per 15 to 20 men.

Because Caserne Maginot in Verdun was surrounded by high concrete walls, newly arrived GIs thought it was a large prison. Late one evening in 1959, Private Harry F. Puncec arrived at the caserne after a long train ride from Germany. Reporting to the 97th Engineer Battalion, he was issued bedding and taken to an upper-floor squad room. Anxious to make a good first impression on his fellow soldiers, he quickly made his bed while pondering what to say. From a distant bunk came his welcome to France, "Turn off the lights, asshole!"[45]

In August 1956, fifty-seven Quonset huts arrived at St.-Nazaire on the SS *America*. The huts replaced plywood-tar paper hutments at Sampigny, Vassincourt, and Verdun (Jardin Fontaine).[46] At Saran, the 553rd Engineer Battalion installed ten Quonset huts for use as barracks. Each of the 20-ft by 48-ft long huts housed fourteen men.[47] The straight-sided Quonset hut provided more useable floor space than the arch-shaped Quonset hut of World War II.

Prefab Temporary (T) Structures Installed in France

Manufacturer	Country of Manufacture	Primary Use
Acomal	Belgium (Mechelen)	Storage, barracks, classrooms
Butler MB*	US (Kansas City, MO)	Maintenance hangars, warehouses
Fillod, Constructions Métalliques (CMF)	France (Florange near Metz)	Troop barracks, mess halls, chapels, classrooms, offices, ammo storage
Polynorm	the Netherlands	Storage, barracks, chapels, classrooms
Quonset huts (Stran-Steel)	US (Detroit, MI)	Troop barracks, family housing at Châteauroux AD, storage
Taylor-Woodrow	England	Warehouses

* Rigid-frame, straight-sided structures installed at air bases during Berlin Wall crisis in 1961.

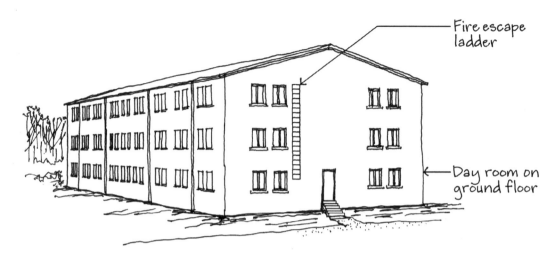

Masonry Barracks

Masonry Barracks

The JCA designed a standard two or three-story masonry barracks to house more than 200 men in 10 and 20-man squad rooms, four rooms or bays each floor. The ground floor had a large day room and each floor had a common shower and latrine. In May 1954, the first three-story barracks in the Orléans area was occupied by GIs at St.-Pryvé-St.-Mesmin (SAMEC). In August 1954, Saumur was the first Base Section installation to move its troops into modern barracks. Signal troops occupied two new three-story barracks at Château des Ifs. Enlisted men of the Polish Labor Service were assigned to one of the barracks.[48] Verdun's first modern two-story barracks at Jardin Fontaine was occupied by troops of the 23rd Engineer Co (FM). Compared to prefabs, the new quarters were luxurious, but the GIs complained that they were constantly being inspected. Most VIPs who visited Advance Section in 1956 were paraded by senior officers through the new barracks to show evidence of progress in improving troop housing.[49]

Alcoholic beverages were not allowed in ComZ barracks. However, some NCOs did not enforce the ban. They believed it was better to have GIs drunk in the barracks rather than in French cafés where fights with locals were likely and POV accidents could occur when driving back to post under the influence of alcohol.

Living on the Economy

Troops and their dependents were unenthusiastic about service in France. There was a lack of rental housing and support services such as schools, hospitals, and post exchanges.[50] In the rebuilding Germany, occupation forces had priority for available rental units. Officer and NCO families could live in clean rental spaces among pleasant villagers. The Federal Republic of Germany provided deutsche mark (DM) funds to partially support the cost of occupation. The DM program financed new construction for US Army, Europe (USAREUR) that eventually would revert to Germany. The German government built thousands of family housing units near US installations in exchange for the return of war requisitioned properties.[51]

Army policy was to provide family quarters or a monthly rental allowance for married officers and NCOs of the top grades (Staff Sgt and above).[52] In France, the average wait for government housing was one year. Therefore, military and Department of Army Civilians (DAC) personnel with families often rented houses in nearby villages, called "living on the economy." The average size of American families in France was four. In rural France, the scarce housing available generally was substandard, and many houses did not have hot water, central heat, or indoor toilet facilities.[53] Many villages had public bathhouses. At remote posts, DACs received a supplement to their monthly housing allowance from USAREUR to compensate for "notably unhealthy conditions" of the French housing.[54] In 1952 at Orleans Area Command, eighty-seven families lived in Paris even though the commute was 4 hours round trip. In 1952 at Metz, there were only forty French housing units that could be rented by Americans. However, by 1955 the number of units had increased to four hundred. A joint Army-Air Force housing board at Metz listed available rentals so Army personnel at Metz and Air Force personnel at Chambley AB and Étain AB would have an equal chance to rent on the economy.[55]

The villagers at first seemed indifferent toward their new neighbors. However by the mid-1950s, French landlords welcomed US military tenants because they would pay higher rent than the French and often improved the rental property by installing heating and plumbing. Major commands maintained an approved list of available housing to discourage bidding, which would drive up rents, or paying "under the table" bonuses to French owners, which would give an unfair advantage to those who had more money. In 1955, ComZ rated French rental houses based on size of rooms, heating method and cost, kitchen features, location of bath and toilet, and water supply. Houses in Advance Section rated adequate were 24%, in Base Section 40%, and in Orléans area 55%. The highest rated location was Paris at 70%, the lowest Captieux at 9%.[56] In addition to rent and rental taxes, Americans paid taxes to municipalities and departments, road taxes, and radio/TV taxes. In 1959, only 60% of French homes had indoor plumbing, 10% had a shower or bathtub.

Telephones

It was difficult to have telephone lines installed and telephones were so expensive that most French households did not have one. It cost about $100 to have a phone installed in a home. In the early 1950s, a telephone call to the US cost $4 per minute.[57] Most draftee GIs, who earned about $90 per month, could not afford to call home. In July 1954, the first dial telephone system in the Advance Section became operational. The fifty-line automatic system serving Caserne Tournebride troop housing area near Metz replaced three military operators needed for the previous switchboard system.[58] By the late 1950s if willing to wait, GIs could contact most Army installations by civilian telephone. For emergency calls, the code P-C-V (using the French pronunciation, pay-say-vay) was used so female LWR switchboard operators would reverse the charges.

Civilian phone service in the Seine valley was so bad that it took 10 min to an hour to connect a call. The French believed that, in the event of a fire, it was faster to drive to the fire station than report a fire by telephone. If a caller picked up a phone when no circuits were open, operators would not know a call was being attempted. Repeated attempts could go on seemingly forever. Due to the persistence of Mayor Alain Peyrefitte of Provins, the *Postes, Télégraphes et Téléphones* (PTT) began to improve service. It took about ten years to upgrade the system in the Seine valley.[59]

The sole telephone line to the American housing village at Cenon, near Bordeaux, was installed in one of the homes. The phone was to be used only for emergencies, but its availability depended on an occupant being home. In March 1962, when the father-in-law of Army Capt Burnett H. Radosh broke his hip in a fall from a bicycle, Mrs. Radosh had to drive to the nearest café to use a phone. Fortunately, she was able to reach personnel at the 319th Station Hospital who told her to bring her father, now in considerable pain, to the hospital. The drive to Bussac Depot, with her father cramped in the back seat of her small car, took Katherine Radosh almost a hour.[60]

Trailer Parks

Lt Gen William H. Tunner, commander of USAFE from 1953 to 1957, testified before the US Congress on the urgent need for housing in France. After Air Force approval in 1954 of a construction program called Project Caravan, engineers began installing trailer parks at eight bases (75 units for each base, to expand to 150 units if additional funds were approved).[61] The engineers poured concrete slabs, installed water and sewer pipes, and built roads at the parks. The 843rd EAB completed the first on-base trailer park in early 1955 at Toul-Rosières AB. The dependents school teachers at Toul-Rosières AB lived in trailers and used hutments for classrooms. In 1955, half of the young female faculty members moved to a hotel in Nancy to escape the mud.[62] The Évreux AB trailer park opened in fall 1955. It was named Boenderville in honor of PFC Roger J. Boender, 821st EAB, who died in an accident during construction of the 318-unit park. During the first winter, water pipes froze and power lines snapped during record cold temperatures. Boenderville families spent numerous days without water and electricity.

From a distance, the trailers looked like tin cans on a grocery store shelf. Occupants dubbed their trailer homes "Spam Can Alley." Because the trailers normally were surrounded by ankle-deep, gooey mud, the children were called mud babies.[63] A 40-ft long by 8-ft wide metal trailer had cramped living space to accommodate two adults and up to four children. There was a double bed, bunk bed, divan, and small bathroom with tub and shower. In 1965, Lt Col William P. Riddling, commander of Dreux AB, considered the two-hundred forty-two on-base trailers to be substandard housing. They were occupied anyway. Riddling lived in two trailers connected by a living area that base engineers had built.[64] Although the Air Force had designated the trailer parks as "interim family housing," they were occupied until 1967 when US troops were withdrawn from France.

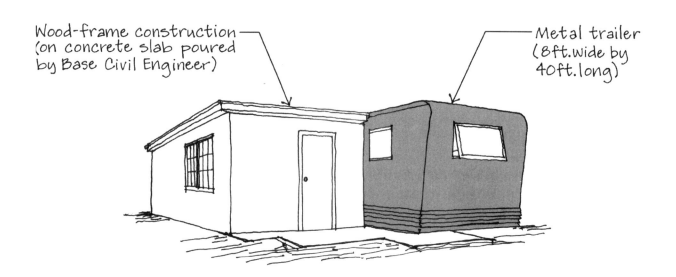

Trailer Housing at Dreux Air Base

Trailer park, Chambley AB (J. J. McAuliffe)

Family Housing Projects

In the mid-1950s, due in part to pressure from the American public, the US Congress appropriated funds to build needed family housing.⁶⁵ Because Americans were outbidding French families for scarce rentals, the French government agreed it was essential to build houses for Americans. The housing villages were to be located at least 5 miles from the military installations so, in theory, American families would spend money on the French economy rather that at post exchanges and commissaries. The housing projects introduced the French to the concept of single-family housing neighborhoods, similar to the famous post-World War II Levittowns in the US.⁶⁶

Depending on how the housing was funded, the single-family units were called rental guarantee housing (RGH) or surplus commodity housing (SCH).⁶⁷ More than 7,300 single-family, duplex, triplex, and apartment housing units were built at fifty-seven locations. The developments consisted of as few as 20 units at Coulounieix-Chamiers near Périgueux to 615 units at Déols near Châteauroux. Most developments had small parks for recreation and cul-de-sac street layouts that prevented through traffic. Some had a nearby dependents elementary school. School playgrounds had swings, see-saws, and slides. Patrols of French police with American MPs or Air Police drove through the housing villages to provide security and enforce curfews for school children (midnight on weekdays). It took two years to build the SCH houses due to the traditional August shutdown for French vacations, shoddy workmanship, and French bureaucratic obstructions such as delays in granting construction permits.

The French were astounded to see villages of identical single-story houses surrounded by green lawns and trees, not walls for privacy. Americans even had tiny houses for their pets. It seemed to the Chinonais, like young Jean Ruaud, that the main street at Rochambeau Village was at least three times wider than streets in a French village. Everything from America seemed big.⁶⁸ For recreation, many housing villages had a softball diamond, tennis court, and volleyball court.

The RGH program, called guaranteed rental income (GRI) by the Air Force, guaranteed an occupancy rate of 95% for 5 to 7 years to French developers who built, operated, and maintained the housing. Occupancy guarantees by the US were longer for the remote locations. One, two, and three bedroom units varied from 550 sq ft to 950 sq ft.⁶⁹ Monthly rents were not to exceed $125 per unit. Military personnel living in RGH housing paid rent from their monthly housing allowance. In the beginning, French investors were reluctant to build housing villages in rural areas because they believed it would be extremely difficult to rent or sell the houses after the Americans left.

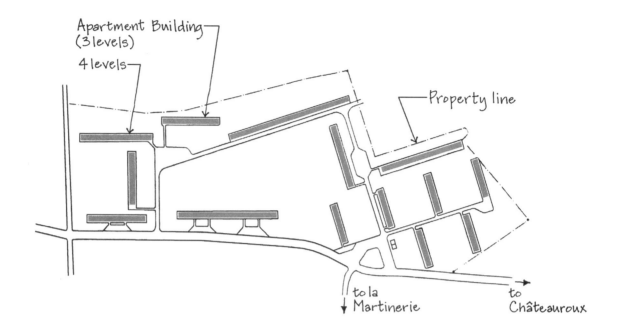

Cité Touvent Apartments near Châteauroux (1953)

RGH pilot projects in 1954 included a 300-unit apartment complex at St.-Jean-de-Braye (Orléans), a 300-unit apartment complex near Rocquencourt (Paris), and a 410-unit apartment complex at Touvent (Châteauroux). US Air Force families dubbed the Touvent apartments "the four ten."

RGH apartment buildings, St.-Jean-de-Braye, 1961 (US Army)

SCH, called commodity credit housing (CCH) by the Air Force, was funded by a complicated $50 million barter program, devised by US Congress, to pay French developers from sales of surplus agricultural commodities, including tobacco. The Army or Air Force reimbursed US Department of Agriculture from projected military housing allowance funds. SCH housing units (unofficially called "Tobacco Houses") were to be used by Americans for twenty years.[70] JCA Director Maj Gen Bernard L. Robinson, believing payments to French developers of SCH housing were extraordinarily high, asked the General Accounting Office (GAO) in Paris to monitor the program. The GAO assured Robinson that the convoluted payment arrangement was legal.[71] Each SCH unit had shrubbery, two shade trees, and two fruit trees. The units were furnished with gas stove, refrigerator, clothes washer, and hot water heater. Unlike most housing in France, SCH houses had radiant heating from hot water pipes in the concrete floor slabs. During cold winters, radiant heat provided warmth, but did not prevent drafts from cold windows. Because SCH was considered government housing, occupants did not pay rent nor receive a rental allowance.

Surplus Commodity Housing unit, Étain, 1959 (G. S. Bosan)

The family units were assigned so that officers and NCOs would not be next door neighbors. In August 1961, US Army SFC Edmond R. York received a direct commission to first lieutenant. At the time, York was living with his wife, Betty, and their young sons David and Douglas in an NCO unit in Lafayette Village, near the Ingrandes Depot. Because all units for officers were occupied, the Yorks were unable to move. Aware that York would be living amongst NCOs, the executive officer at Ingrandes told York he could no longer associate with his neighbors. York did not faithfully comply.[72]

Like most of the American housing villages, Cité Maréchal Foch housing village in Olivet had only one telephone line.[73] During periods of crisis, the hand-crank phone, installed on a telephone pole, was manned twenty-four hours a day by an American soldier. One rainy August night in 1961, Col Henry A. Miley, Jr. was called to the phone and asked if the Berlin Brigade had the expertise to install dozer blades on their tanks. When Miley replied that they did, he was told to send dozer blades, 105 mm howitzers, and ammunition loaded with rock salt to Berlin. If Washington approved the plan, the tanks would be used to bulldoze down the recently built Berlin Wall and rock salt pellets used as a "non-lethal" weapon to disperse crowds.[74]

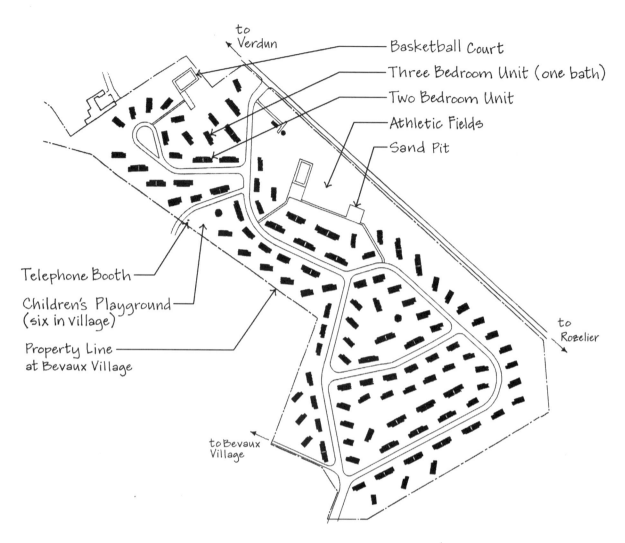

Louis Best Village near Verdun (1959)

In June 1955, the JCA signed contracts for the construction of GRI housing units at several locations for the Air Force.[75] Phalsbourg AB had a 236-unit village near Sarrebourg, named Cité Perkins, and a 40-unit village in Phalsbourg, named Cité Clark. Perkins and Clark were USAF officers who had died when their T-33 T-Bird jet trainer crashed on 31 March 1958 near the base.[76] Chaumont AB had a 300-unit village, named Lafayette Village, on 42 acres for NCO families, and a 108-unit village, named Pershing Village, for officer families. Seven of the Lafayette units had a telephone to be used only to report emergencies.[77] By 1961, more than four-thousand housing units had been built near ten large Air Force installations. In addition, the dispersed operating bases at Brienne-le-Château and Châlons-sur-Marne each had 40-unit housing villages near the base. The Air Force ammunition depot at Chizé had a 32-unit village at Niort.

After the 48th Fighter-Bomber Wing was redeployed from Chaumont AB to England in 1959, the French owner of Lafayette Village offered his housing units to the public. The monthly rents were reduced from $125 to $40 so the French could afford them.[78] The housing villages built for the US military still exist. Most homes now are surrounded by high walls or thick hedges for privacy. Garages have been added and many duplex units converted into one large house.[79] In rural areas they often are second homes.

Army Fraternization Policy

Although officers and enlisted men worked and trained together, officers were not to "fraternize" with enlisted personnel. The Army believed fraternization gave the appearance of partiality. Housing, clubs, and dining facilities were separate, and officers and enlisted men rarely attended the same off-duty social event. This Army custom was taken seriously because Article 134 of the Uniform Code of Military Justice, enacted by US Congress in 1951, allowed commanders to punish those who violated "a custom of the service."

Bachelor Officers Quarters (BOQ) were "off limits" to all enlisted personnel unless they had assigned duties there or were visiting in an official capacity. At Fontenet, 2nd Lt Ross A. Gagliano took annual leave in 1962 to drive to Italy with two enlisted men with whom he played on the post basketball team. Upon his return he was summoned to the post commander's office and warned by fellow West Point graduate, Lt Col Thomas E. Griess, that such associations were not appropriate and would harm his career.[80]

Bachelor Officers Quarters

Although a program had been started to build BOQs for bachelor officers and married officers waiting arrival of their dependents, USAREUR reported in December 1952 that 1,148 BOQ rooms were needed in France, but none were available.[81] During 1955, more than eighteen BOQ were constructed.[82] BOQs now were available at most posts in ComZ for officers, Special Services women, and Department of Army Civilians (DAC). DACs included male and female school teachers. Company-grade officers (2nd Lt, 1st Lt, and Capt) were authorized one room with a bed, bureau, small desk, and chair. They shared a small bathroom (two sinks, one toilet, and one shower) located between two adjacent rooms. Occasionally, officers improvised by putting both beds in one room and using the other room as a living room. Field-grade officers (Maj, Lt Col, and Col) were authorized two rooms, separated by a bathroom. BOQ residents were to silence all radios and phonographs by 10 pm, not to use heating appliances, and not to smoke in bed.[83]

At large posts, like Orléans and Verdun, there were separate buildings for females. The Orleans Area Command had BOQs for females at Château de La Mothe (two-story building for 34 females) and la Chapelle (two buildings, occupied mostly by Army nurses). Smaller installations divided buildings by gender. At Trois-Fontaines, females were assigned to the second floor of the BOQ; males to the first floor. USAREUR considered BOQ facilities to be equal to those provided by dormitory accommodations at a typical stateside college.[84] At Verdun, three sets of adjacent BOQ rooms were furnished to be VIP Guest Quarters. Two GIs at the Billeting Office were sent to live and work at the BOQ. The enlisted men assigned rooms, supervised maid services, submitted repair orders to post engineer, and stocked the liquor cabinet in the VIP suites.[85]

During the extremely cold winter of 1955-56, water pipes froze and toilet bowls cracked in the poorly-heated French homes rented by Americans. To survive the cold, Americans used kerosene space heaters to provide some warmth at night. Because the heating plant at Chaumont AB was unaffected, numerous officers living at the BOQ each "adopted" an American family living on the economy. Washing machines were installed in the BOQ bathrooms so wives could do the family laundry during duty hours when the bachelors were away.[86]

Mess Halls

Mess halls were in rehabilitated French caserne buildings, metal prefabs, and JCA constructed masonry buildings. The Army motto posted in most mess halls was "Take all you want, but eat all you take." Quartermaster personnel supplied food so mess halls could prepare meals based on the Army's Master Menus which were published six months in advance.[87] In the early 1960s, the best liked food by GIs included grilled steak, southern fried chicken, strawberry shortcake, and ice cream sundaes. Least liked were broccoli, cabbage, asparagus, and parsnips.[88] To avoid KP, GIs at most ComZ installations chipped in to pay French local wage rate (LWR) employees to work in the kitchens.

Mess halls in France improved dramatically in 1954 after a new rating system was implemented in the Base Section. The rating system, devised by CWO George W. Kiefer, awarded "star" recognition similar to ratings used for European restaurants. Previously, mess halls receiving recognition had been rated as "Best Mess" and lumped together without distinction. Kiefer's system awarded five, four, or three stars to the best mess halls, nothing to the unsatisfactory ones. The system was intended to improve food preparation, cooking, and service. Raters evaluated sanitation and cleanliness, storage of food and equipment, attractiveness of food and dining room, and appearance of cooks and servers. The system was strict. Five-stars were awarded only after a mess hall received four-stars for three consecutive months. Maj Gen Philip E. Gallagher, Commanding General of ComZ, implemented it throughout ComZ because he liked the system and its results.[89] In late 1954 Sgt Edward E. Porter, first cook of the Army's Consolidated Mess Hall at Fontainebleau, was selected to learn French cooking. For two months, Porter worked in the kitchen of the Hôtel Claridge in Paris, learning how to prepare culinary delights such as rich sauces, French pastries, and soups not likely to be served in EM mess halls. Porter's unit the 833rd Signal Co, a reserve unit from Minneapolis, Minnesota, was released from active duty in March 1955.[90]

In early December 1954, more than nine-hundred LWRs were hired to work in Army mess halls in France, relieving GIs from KP duties. Two LWRs worked where 50 GIs were fed, one more LWR for each additional 50 GIs. However, Army personnel would continue to serve as cooks and bakers. In the Base Section, four-hundred twenty-five French civilian KPs, paid by funds appropriated by the US Congress, were authorized to work in forty-seven mess halls.[91] In late 1955, the Army ended the use of appropriated funds to pay French KPs. As a consequence, in January 1956 most installations in the Base Section reverted to using enlisted personnel to work in mess halls. However, the enlisted men at Bordeaux and Captieux each paid $3 per month to retain the French KPs.[92] In 1956, Chinon Engineer Depot reverted to using French KPs. PFC James L. Lepant of the 581st Engineer Co (FM) transported two daily shifts of a dozen LWRs from their homes to the consolidated mess hall at the depot. Driving an Army ¾-ton van, Lepant's first run began at 4 am to pick up the first shift; his last run at 7 pm to return the second shift. It took longer to take the French KPs home because each LWR invited Lepant and the remaining passengers into his residence to have a glass of wine. As a result, Lepant often didn't return to the depot until after 11 pm. The first week Lepant, who rarely drank alcoholic beverages, arrived back at Chinon in a dizzy condition.[93]

Each Thanksgiving and Christmas, mess halls throughout France prepared special meals featuring roast turkey and baked ham. The menu read like a French meal of several courses, but at most installations was served "cafeteria-style" on standard segmented metal trays that prevented the giblet gravy from floating into the buttered, fresh green beans. Meals were free for enlisted troops. The cost of meals for officers eating at mess halls was 25¢ for breakfast, 55¢ for lunch, and 65¢ for dinner.

Thanksgiving Menu (1960)

Chapels

All US Army installations and US Air Force bases with more than three-hundred troops had a chapel. A standard chapel design, with pews seating about one-hundred fifty persons, was used at numerous installations. Because signals from the electronic bell in the chapel at Toul-Rosières AB interfered with base radar and communications, it was replaced with a real bell.[94] Trois-Fontaines depot used a Fillod metal prefab. There were two chapels at Laon AB and four in the Orleans Area Command, at Caserne Coligny, Maison-Fort, Harbord Barracks, and la Chapelle-St.-Mesmin. At la Chapelle, the Army used the historic church that was integral to a building housing hospital facilities. There were five chapels in the Verdun area, at Jardin Fontaine, Rozelier Ammo Depot, Sidi Brahim, Étain AB, and in the hospital at Désandrouins Barracks. At Army and Air Force installations, religious services were regularly held for: Protestant, Catholic, Episcopal, Jewish, Lutheran, Latter Day Saints, 7th Day Adventist, and Christian Science. In the 1950s, USAREUR estimated that, throughout Europe, 25% of Army personnel regularly attended church services.

Post chapel, Camp Bussac, 1963 (US Army)

During fall 1954, US Army personnel stationed in the La Rochelle area donated a statue of Our Lady of Fatima to St.-Louis Cathedral, next door to Caserne Aufrédi in La Rochelle. The statue was placed in the nave of the 18th Century church. Chaplain (Maj) Kenny E. Lynch, representing Base Section, spoke at the dedication ceremony.[95]

Chaplains were to preserve the role of religion in the US military and were selected because of their devotion to God and Country. Army chaplains were dubbed "sky pilots," their assistants "amen clerks." In France, chaplains counseled GIs, performed wedding ceremonies, and wrote weekly columns for the command newspapers. They also led training sessions on character guidance, covering subjects such as Plato's cardinal virtues of courage and justice.[96] Thousands of US soldiers and airmen married French women. There were four-hundred fifty-two Franco-American marriages at Châteauroux, more than two hundred at Toul-Rosières, and three-hundred sixty at Laon.[97-99] French law required a civil ceremony be held at the *mairie* (city hall). An additional wedding ceremony could be held at the base chapel or a French church.

American Churches in Paris

Early in 1952, the American Church in Paris, located on the west bank of the River Seine at 65, Quai d'Orsay, installed fifty, double-decker beds in their theater. The beds were on loan from the US Air Force and three airmen were assigned to the facility. The ground-floor theater was used as a hotel for GIs on leave or in transit through Paris. Showers and a gymnasium were located down the hall. The charge of 85¢ for two nights included use of bunk bed, toilets, and showers. Curfew was 1:30 am. The church also sponsored weekend dances where many GIs met their future wives.[100, 101]

The American Cathedral (Episcopal) at 23, avenue George V also sponsored social events during the 1950s and 1960s where GIs could meet American female students who were members of the Cathedral College Club. To the surprise and delight of GIs of different religious faiths, alcoholic beverages were available during the mixers held in the Parish Hall. The church was founded in 1857. Its cloisters, dedicated on Memorial Day 1933 in the presence of US Gen John J. Pershing and Marshal Ferdinand Foch of France, are a memorial to Americans who fought in World War I. The flags of all US states were hung in the nave. General Matthey B. Ridgway presented a SHAPE flag to the cathedral during his tenure as Supreme Commander of NATO.[102] For several decades, actress Olivia de Havilland served as a lay reader on Sundays.

Recreation Facilities

In the early 1950s, GIs who had served in Korea griped that recreation facilities were better in Korea than in France.[103] It was difficult for the French to understand the American requirements for: bowling alleys, baseball diamonds, tennis courts, golf courses, snack bars, theaters, gymnasiums, service clubs (book and record libraries, game rooms), and the like. Certainly these morale, welfare, and recreation services were not available to French soldiers. To expedite mobilization of reserves in an emergency, French draftees were normally assigned to military units near their homes. They could go home on *le week-end*, whereas American GIs were far from home.

Senior leaders believed that athletics and recreation activities would keep off-duty GIs entertained and out of trouble. The JCA construction program to build permanent recreation facilities throughout ComZ also made the statement to NATO allies and the Soviets that the US was in France to stay. For example, by 1957 the US Army had built five theaters in the Orléans area at Caserne Coligny, Harbord Barracks, Saran, la Chapelle, and Maison-Fort. There were four theaters in the Verdun area. The

JCA standard-design theater, Camp Bussac, 1963 (US Army)

latest American films and newsreels were shown two or three times nightly, with afternoon matinees on weekends. In the early 1960s, matinee admission was 25¢, a bag of popcorn 10¢. Rules were strictly enforced. At Coligny, attendees were to wear appropriate military or civilian clothing, not smoke within theater at any time (except in lobby), and stay away from areas designated "off limits."[104] Females were not to have curlers in their hair. Bowling alleys were at Caserne Coligny, Harbord Barracks, and Maison-Fort; crafts shops at Caserne Coligny, Saran, and la Chapelle. Photo shops were maintained by Special Services at Caserne Coligny, Harbord Barracks, and Saran.[105] A large banner was hung at most gymnasiums reminding troops that "The price of admission is good sportsmanship."

Golf Courses

Although the first golf course on continental Europe was built in 1856 at Pau, golf was not a popular sport in France. Because land was scarce in France, courses were short and narrow. The US military played on French courses at Fontainebleau and Tours, at negotiated fees, or on newly built courses near US installations. Golf courses were first built at US military bases around the time of World War I. Peak construction occurred worldwide during the 1950s when Dwight D. Eisenhower, America's best known golfer, was president.[106] During July 1953, American golf legend Ben Hogan and Tony Longo gave an exhibition for US military personnel at the Fontainebleau Golf Club. In 1953, Hogan won three major professional championships: The Masters, US Open, and British Open.

By the 1960s, the US military had built a dozen golf courses, about one of every five golf courses in France at the time. Air bases had a nine-hole course; several Army installations shared the five courses approved by USAREUR. Châteauroux AD had an eighteen-hole course at la Martinerie. Because Air Force golf courses often were near runways, it took great concentration to putt during jet aircraft operations. Exceptions were courses at St.-Mihiel and Phalsbourg. The US Air Force 7372nd Ammo Supply Squadron built a six-hole golf course in 1957 at St.-Mihiel Ammunition Depot storage area and Phalsbourg AB had a 9-hole course on leased land outside the town of Phalsbourg.

Col Henry C. Britt, Orleans Installation commander, and 1st Lt Robert Greendale designed the Orleans Golf Course built by 553rd Engineers at Château de la Touche near Donnery. For reference, Britt borrowed a book on golf courses from the Special Services Library at Caserne Coligny. Army engineers removed trees and shaped fairways. When the course officially opened in August 1956, greens fees were $1 on weekdays, $2 on weekends and holidays.[107, 108] US Army engineers also built courses at Verdun (Désandrouins Hospital), Trois-Fontaines (Combles-en-Barrois), Nancy (Aingeray), and Poitiers (Camp de Chalon). Although not authorized a golf course, in August 1962 Bussac used non-appropriated funds to build a fifteen tee driving range. The range was open every day.

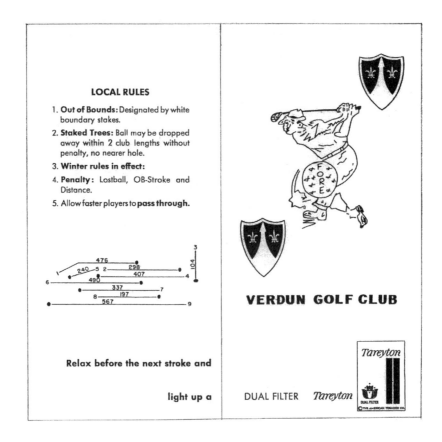

Verdun Golf Course Scorecard

US Army Construction Agency, France

The JCA was abolished on 01 August 1957 after significant construction progress had finally been achieved in France. Completed or nearing completion by the end of 1957 were more than two dozen depot and port installations, more than a dozen main and dispersed air bases, thirty-nine rental guarantee housing villages, schools, network of microwave communication towers, Donges-Metz POL pipeline, and chain of nine standby hospitals. Responsibility for military construction passed to the newly formed US Army Construction Agency, France (USACAF). Its first director, Col Lynn C. Barnes, supervised a staff of five-hundred thirty military and civilian personnel. From 1957 to 1961, major programs of USACAF were the completion of the surplus commodity housing program of 2,700 housing units and the design and construction of three depots to store atomic weapons. Earth-covered, atomic blast-resistant (ABREST) storage structures for atomic weapons were located at Rozelier near Verdun, Vatry southwest of Châlons-sur-Marne, and Aboncourt near Metz. In 1958, Col Edwin A. Bedell succeeded Barnes; in July 1959, Col Warren S. Everett succeeded Bedell. In 1961, engineers at Orléans assumed the workload of USACAF.[109]

US Construction Agencies in France (1951-67)

Agency	Period	Location
US Army ComZ Construction Office	1951-1953	Paris (7, rue Clement Marot)
US Air Force Construction Office (USAFE)	1952-1953	Paris (22, rue de la Trémoille)
Joint Construction Agency (JCA)	1953-1957	Boulogne-sur-Seine (94, rue Escudier)
US Army Construction Agency, France (USACAF)	1957-1961	Boulogne-sur-Seine (94, rue Escudier) Paris (36, rue Laperouse)
US Army Field Engineer Office, France	1961-1967	Orléans (Caserne Coligny)

Top Ten Reasons Construction Was Slow in France[110-114]

Due to the French
1. Construction industry was depleted by war. Equipment was antiquated, skilled labor scarce, and available labor force paid low wages.
2. Communist party (PCF) pressured French government to oppose buildup by US military and organized strikes to impede progress.
3. Complicated legal process to acquire private real estate and slow release of government land.
4. Traditional consecutive construction process in France was slower than concurrent process in US where different trades worked at the same time.
5. Work shut down during numerous holidays and traditional August vacation, when weather was most favorable for construction. From mid-July to mid-September, decisions by French ministries and agencies were long-delayed or nonexistent.

Due to the Americans
6. Competition between US Army and USAFE for scarce labor and construction materials prior to formation of JCA to coordinate all construction by US military in France.
7. Construction freezes by the Pentagon during the 1950s resulted in a total delay of 2½ years. Typically, construction halts were for 60 to 90 days to study ways to reduce defense spending or for political reasons when the US State Department placed an embargo on oil shipments to France in 1956 during the Suez Crisis.
8. Changes, such as function, size, and location of buildings, requested by depot commanders resulted in design delays. Nearly half of the projects in 1955 were delayed due to change orders.
9. Budget cuts by US Congress and diversion of funds. Seven million dollars allocated to USAFE projects were diverted in June 1956 to the B-52 bomber program in the US.

Due to Both
10. Red tape obstacles such as refusal by French to advertise bids for work (Form 100) until US allocated funds, but by law the US military could not release funds until contracts were awarded to low bidder. This Catch-22 impasse was resolved by the US allowing JCA to move funds between projects. Funds the JCA received from the Army and Air Force were deposited into a special account from which the French could withdraw funds to pay contractors.

U.S. GO HOME

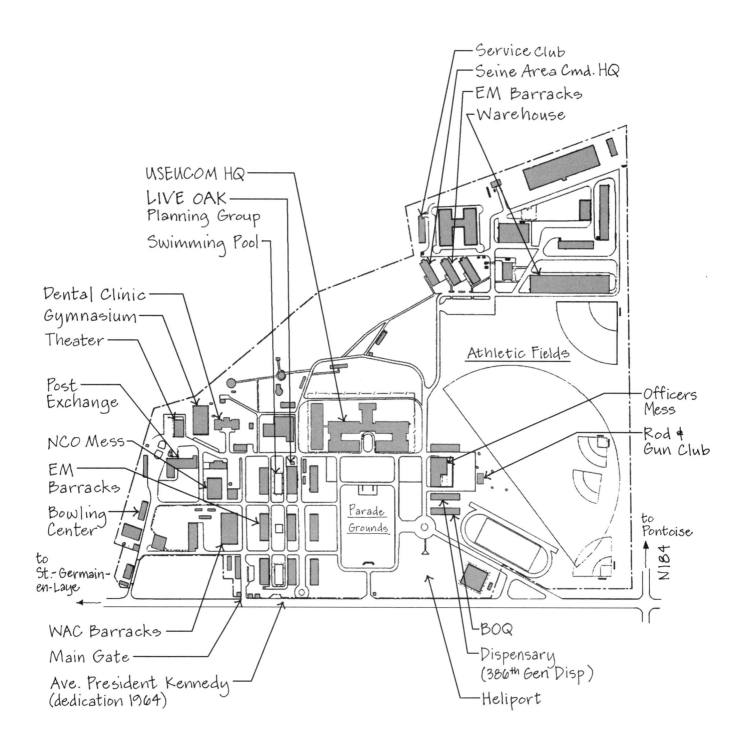

Camp des Loges (1961)

FIVE

US European Command and Military Assistance

"Properly balanced strength will promote the probability of avoiding war."
(NATO Supreme Commander Gen Dwight D. Eisenhower, diary entry, 16 November 1951)

US European Command

NATO and the US agreed that the American general officer appointed Supreme Commander (SACEUR) also would serve as Commander-in-Chief of US European Command (EUCOM). EUCOM was responsible for the operations of all US military forces in Europe and Military Assistance Advisory Groups. To handle the demands of this dual position, the SACEUR would delegate broad authority to his deputy commander at EUCOM (abbreviated USEUCOM after 01 August 1952). In June 1952, Gen Matthew B. Ridgway became the first SACEUR also to be designated Commander-in-Chief of US European Command. His deputy, Army Gen Thomas T. Handy, became responsible for day-to-day operations of EUCOM and oversaw its three major subordinate commands of the US Army, Air Force, and Navy. US Army, Europe (USAREUR), the senior US Army headquarters in Europe, was located in Heidelberg, Germany. US Air Forces in Europe (USAFE) was located in Wiesbaden, Germany. US Naval Forces in the Eastern Atlantic and Mediterranean was located in London, England.[1]

Camp des Loges

In November 1952 Maj Gen Samuel D. Sturgis, Jr., ComZ commander, asked the French government to propose 100-acre sites in the Paris area that could be used for US European Command headquarters. The sites were to be beyond six miles from SHAPE headquarters at Marly-le-Roi (or the château in Fontainebleau) and within nineteen miles from Notre Dame Cathedral in Paris (or the obelisk in Fontainebleau). It was believed that locating headquarters close together would facilitate coordination between the staffs.[2, 3]

Camp des Loges, a 131-acre site near St.-Germain-en-Laye, was chosen for the headquarters. The historic site, once used by Napoléon's armies, was a seven mile drive from SHAPE. The site, which had been occupied by the Germans during World War II, had been abandoned by a French infantry battalion in August 1951.[4, 5] Thirty of the dilapidated French buildings were rehabilitated at a cost of $1.1 million Fifty-nine new buildings were constructed at a cost of $6.6 million. Seventeen Acomal prefab structures were installed at a cost of $500,000. In April 1953, US Army engineer troops built roads and hardstands, and completed other work to expedite new construction.[6, 7] In May 1954 after Gen Handy retired, US European Command headquarters moved from the IG Farben Building in Frankfurt, Germany, to Camp des Loges. US Air Force Gen Orval R. Cook, who had replaced Handy at Frankfurt, served at Camp des Loges until June 1956.[8] A memorable feature of the IG Farben Building was its unique conveyor-belt elevators, dubbed "Pater Nosters" by GIs. They believed it was prudent to pray before stepping onto the door-less contraption, a series of open plywood cabs that continuously moved up or down at a relatively slow speed. Users were required to time their jump on or off the moving elevator, hoping that they would not stumble.[9]

Entrance to Camp des Loges, June 1953 (US Army)

Because headquarters buildings were given highest priority, the plumbing in most of the barracks at Camp des Loges was not completed until several months after the troops had moved in. Each Friday in early 1954, Chief Petty Officer Earl L. Corbin borrowed a staff car to drive his supply section GIs to Marly-le-Roi where sympathetic MPs allowed them to use showers in the SHAPE male barracks.[10] The Women's Army Corps (WAC) Joint Enlisted Women's Detachment lived in separate barracks at Camp des Loges. Most of the WACs performed clerical jobs in administration, communications, and finance.[11]

In April 1956, electronic "bugs" were discovered in conference rooms and offices at Camp des Loges. During this time period, it was believed that Soviets also had stolen NATO war plans from SHAPE headquarters.[12] The stolen plans gave the Soviets details of how NATO would respond to an attack. When USEUCOM moved to Germany in 1967, there were 700 military personnel and 100 civilians at Camp des Loges.

Seine Area Command

In 1956, Seine Area Command (SACCZ) moved from 2, rue de la Faisanderie, not far from the Arc de Triomphe, to new headquarters at Camp des Loges. The command supported European Command headquarters and US elements of SHAPE. Initially, logistical and administrative support included providing motor pool vehicles, signal communications, dependents schools (which would require three dozen buses), and PX and commissary services for all US military elements in Paris and Fontainebleau areas.[13] Offices and barracks for SACCZ were located at the north end of the post. The first dependents school in Paris was located in a residential building at 3, rue Cimarosa.

Seine Area Command MPs had their offices at the leased Blériot Aircraft Factory, 3, quai Galliéne in Suresnes. The US Army's Paris Motor Transport Services operated more than four-hundred motor vehicles at six motor pools located throughout the Paris area. The first auto park was on Île St.-Germain.[14] At the Blériot Factory, the 514th Ordnance Company (MAM) repaired vehicles for units assigned to the Paris area.[15] In the late 1950s, the 553rd Engineer Battalion stationed "B" Company's second platoon at Camp des Loges for construction work in the Seine Area.

US European Command Headquarters, Camp des Loges, 1961 (US Army)

Seine Area Command (SACCZ) Commanders*

Commanding Officer	Period of Service	Commanding Officer	Period of Service
Col Alexander G. Kirby	1952-53	Col Donald A. Phelan	1959-61
Col Edward M. Fickett	1953-54	Col Paul R. Jeffrey	1961-64
Col Richard H. Lawson	1954-57	Col Robert Besson	1964-66
Col Chester T. Barton	1957-59	Col John J. Farren, Jr.	1966-67

*Command name changed to US Army Post, Paris on 01 January 1965.

LIVE OAK at Camp des Loges

In February 1959, SACEUR Gen Lauris Norstad ordered the establishment of a small "top secret" group to coordinate Allied planning for the Berlin Crisis initiated by Soviet Premier Khrushchev's threats and Soviet harassment of Allied convoys to and from Berlin. The group at Camp des Loges grew to include American, British, and French officers operating under the code name LIVE OAK. Norstad's Deputy Commander-in-Chief Gen Williston B. Palmer supervised LIVE OAK until October 1959, when he was succeeded by his brother Gen Charles D. Palmer. LIVE OAK contingency plans included providing fighter escorts for cargo aircraft, dropping five nuclear bombs to demonstrate resolve, and massive ground attacks through East Germany toward Berlin.[16] At the time, Georges Paques, a former official in the French Ministry of Defense, served as deputy press secretary for NATO. Paques, who had a Cosmic security clearance, was a spy for the Soviets. Before the French *Direction de la surveillance du territoire* (DST) caught him in 1963, he passed on numerous war plans to his Soviet handlers.[17] From his disloyalty, the Soviets not only learned that the Allies would fight over access to Berlin, but also how the Allies planned to do it. The Soviets also learned that the Allies would not use force to stop them if they sealed off East Berlin.[18, 19]

During periods between crises, like the summer of 1960, LIVE OAK staff spent their afternoons swimming in the outdoor pool next to their building.[20] Eleven underground air raid shelters, that had outdoor entrances, were nearby. The Deputy Commander-in-Chief, who would be in charge of all US Forces in Europe during wartime, had an Airstream trailer outfitted as a mobile command post. The

Airstream was parked on PSP behind the headquarters building. In August 1961, LIVE OAK moved from Camp des Loges to SHAPE at Marly-le-Roi so plans could be closely coordinated with NATO.[21]

Berlin Wall Crisis

In 1960, more than 152,000 East Germans escaped to West Berlin. Between 1949 and 1961, more than 2.5 million refugees left East Germany through Berlin. In 1959, the rate was about 10,000 per month, peaking at 30,000 in July 1961, the month before the wall went up.[22] On 13 August 1961, under cover of early morning darkness, East German soldiers erected a barbed-wire barrier along the entire border between East and West Berlin. Within days a second barrier of concrete block was built. A 29-mile long wall of barbed wire and concrete now divided East from West. The Wall closed seventy-six streets, five railroad lines, and four subway lines.[23, 24] It cut off more than 53,000 East Berliners from their jobs and 5,000 students from their classes at the Free University in West Berlin. An additional 75 miles of barrier encircled West Berlin to isolate it from the East German countryside. Eventually the Wall had watchtowers spaced at 3,000-ft intervals and open killing zones to prevent escapes.[25]

After attending a 15 August meeting of President John F. Kennedy's advisors on Berlin, Chairman of the Joint Chiefs of Staff Gen Lyman L. Lemnitzer believed "everyone appeared to be hopeless, helpless, and harmless." [26] In September, Kennedy recalled Gen Lucius D. Clay from retirement to be his envoy to West Berlin. Clay was known to Germans as "the Father of the Berlin Airlift." The commander of US forces in Berlin reported to Gen Norstad, Gen Bruce C. Clarke (Commander-in-Chief, USAREUR), and US Ambassador in Bonn. Clay, who held the rank of ambassador, reported to Kennedy.

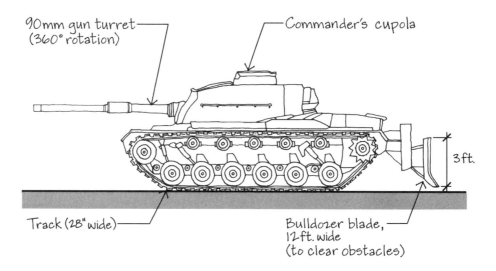

M-48 Patton III Combat Tank

Clay, who did not fear the Soviets, flew by helicopter over East German territory to the small isolated enclave at Steinstuecken. He also ordered the Berlin forces to run patrols on the Autobahn in the Soviet zone of Germany and insisted that rights of free passage to East Berlin not be diluted. He was determined not to cede any Allied rights to the Soviets and to expose that the Soviets controlled the East German government. Clay ordered Army engineers in Berlin to build replica sections of the Wall. M-48 Patton tanks mounted with bulldozer blades were used to field test how to penetrate the Wall. When Gen Clarke found out, he shut down the wall-smashing operations.[27, 28]

In October, more than 148,000 Reserve and National Guard soldiers were called to active duty for a year. To the chagrin of baseball fans, many major league players, such as New York Yankee all-star shortstop Tony Kubek, were called to duty.[29] Unlike the mobilization for the Korean War, Army Reserve and National Guard units were used as replacement units in the US and not deployed overseas. For example, the 231st Trans Co (Float Craft Maint), a reserve unit from St. Petersburg, Florida, was sent to Fort Eustis, Virginia, to replace the 73rd Trans Co (Float Craft Maint) which was deployed to Bassens, France.[30] From late August 1961 until early 1964, three nuclear artillery battalions were stationed at Chenevières, between Lunéville and Baccarat. Two of the battalions had 155-mm towed guns and one had shorter range 8-inch howitzers. The howitzers fired at higher angles so they could drop projectiles down onto targets. The 155-mm guns could fire a nuclear weapon more than 14 miles.

During Operation ROUNDOUT in fall 1961, US Army personnel in Europe were increased by 40,000 troops. The Army used the ports of Cherbourg and Le Havre to supply the buildup. The French government also gave the US Army permission to develop nearly one-thousand acres at twenty-seven sites to house troops and store supplies. Clay returned to the US in early May 1962 after Soviet pressure on Berlin had abated.[31] However, the Wall between East and West Berlin remained until 1989 when the Soviet empire began to disintegrate.

Deputy Commanders-in-Chief (DCINC), US European Command (USEUCOM)

Deputy CINC	Period of Service	Prominent Events
GEN Thomas T. Handy, USA	Aug 1952-Apr 1954	Troop deployments to France continue. Austere living conditions. Joint Construction Agency (JCA) formed to oversee all construction in France.
GEN Orval R. Cook, USAF	Apr 1954-Jun 1956	Headquarters moves from Frankfurt, Germany to Camp des Loges. Buildup of permanent ComZ infrastructure.
GEN George H. Decker, USA	Jun 1956-Jun 1957	Suez Crisis (France and UK attempt to retake Egypt's Suez Canal). Hungarian Revolution.
GEN Williston B. Palmer, USA	Jun 1957-Oct 1959	Berlin Crisis (Khrushchev threatens Allies). Operation SAFE HAVEN. JCA succeeded by US Army Construction Agency, France (USACAF).
GEN Charles D. Palmer, USA	Oct 1959-Mar 1962	LIVE OAK planning continues. Berlin Wall Crisis. Operation ROUNDOUT. USACAF inactivated.
GEN Earle G. Wheeler, USA	Mar 1962-Oct 1962	Cuban Missile Crisis.
GEN John P. McConnell, USAF	Oct 1962-Aug 1964	McNamara drawdown begins. Operation BIG LIFT.
GEN Jacob E. Smart, USAF	Aug 1964-July 1966	McNamara drawdown continues. USAFE Voodoo overflies French atomic energy facility at Pierrelatte (16 July 65).
GEN David A. Burchinal, USAF	July 1966-Apr 1973	Operation FRELOC begins. Withdrawal from France complete (01 Apr 67).

NOTE: Handy was graduate of VMI, Decker of Lafayette College, and Burchinal of Brown University. All other DCINCs were graduates of United States Military Academy, West Point, New York.

Army Units Deployed to France During Operation ROUNDOUT (Fall 1961)[32-34]

Location in France	Unit	Auth Strength Officer	Auth Strength EM	Home Station
Bassens	73rd Trans Co (Float Craft Maint)[1]	20	147	Fort Eustis, VA
	264th Trans Co (Terminal Service)	6	323	Fort Eustis, VA
Braconne	574th Engineer Co (Depot)	6	195	Granite City Engr Depot, IL
Bussac	552nd Military Police Co[2]	5	152	Activated in France
	62nd Trans Co (Med Trk)	5	176	Fort Eustis, VA
Châlons DOB	150th Trans Co (Med Trk)	5	176	Fort Campbell, KY
Chenevières DOB	16th Arty Brigade, 3rd Howitzer Bn (155 mm)	30	545	Fort Bragg, NC
	30th Arty Brigade, 1st Howitzer Bn (155 mm)	30	545	Fort Lewis, WA
	36th Arty Brigade, 2nd Howitzer Bn (8")	33	545	Fort Sill, OK
	19th Engineer Bn (Combat)	33	586	Fort Meade, MD
	35th Engineer Bn (Combat)	33	586	Fort Lewis, WA
Chinon	84th Engineer Bn (Const)[3]	41	850	Fort Ord, CA
	63rd Engineer Co (Parts Depot)	5	131	Columbus Gen Depot, OH
	185th Engineer Co (Hvy Maint)	8	144	Granite City Engr Depot, IL
	554th Ordnance Co (DAS)	9	114	Fort Leonard Wood, MO
Chizé	611th Ordnance Co (Ammo)	8	255	Fort Bliss, TX
Dreux AB	84th Engineer Bn (Const)	41	850	Fort Ord, CA
Fontainebleau	3rd Ordnance Co (DAS)[4]	9	114	Fort Campbell, KY
Fontenet	228th Signal Co (Radio Relay)	12	154	Fort Gordon, GA
Ingrandes	54th QM Co (Equip Maint)	8	221	Fort Lee, VA
	598th Trans Co (Med Trk)	5	176	Fort Eustis, VA
Metz	11th Ordnance Co (DAS)	9	114	Fort Devens, MA
	34th QM Bn (GS), Co A	13	184	Fort Lee, VA
	84th Trans Co (Med Cargo)	4	132	Manheim, Germany
Orléans	586th Signal Co (Support)	11	266	Fort Sheridan, IL
	76th Chemical Det (RADLCEN)	1	4	Fort Meade, MD
Paris (Camp des Loges)	29th Signal Bn (THQ)[5]	24	660	Karlsruhe, Germany
	3rd Ordnance Co (DAS)	9	114	Fort Campbell, KY
Périgueux	29th Signal Bn (THQ)	24	660	Karlsruhe, Germany
Poitiers	1st Logistical Command	100	168	Fort Bragg, NC
	202nd Military Police Co[6]	5	152	Activated in France
	529th Signal Co (Combat Area)	6	166	Fort Sill, OK
La Rochelle	504th Military Police Bn, Co A[7]	27	631	Fort Gordon, GA
	188th Military Police Co	5	152	Activated in France
	54th Signal Co (Fwd Sup & Maint)[8]	10	136	Fort Hood, TX
Rozelier	820th Ordnance Co (Ammo)	8	255	Fort Benning, GA
St.-Baussant	643rd Engineer Co (Pipeline)	5	173	Fort Leonard Wood, MO
Saumur	221st Signal Co (Base Depot)	8	111	Sacramento Sig Depot, CA
	510th Signal Co (Base Maint)	10	276	Tobyhanna Sig Depot, PA

St.-Nazaire	105th Trans Co (Terminal Service)	6	323	Fort Eustis, VA
Toul	62nd Engineer Bn (Const)	41	850	Fort Leonard Wood, MO
Trois-Fontaines	820th Ordnance Co (Ammo)	8	255	Fort Benning, GA
Vassincourt	69th Signal Bn	14	634	Fort Meade, MD
Verdun	132nd Ordnance Det (EOD)	1	9	Fort Tilden, NY
	525th Signal Co (Combat Area)	6	166	Fort Sill, OK
	73rd Chemical Det (RADLCEN)	1	7	Fort McClellan, AL

Notes
1. Detachments at La Pallice, Rochefort, and St.-Nazaire.
2. Platoons at Bordeaux (1st), Braconne (2nd), Captieux (4th), Fontenet (5th), and Périgueux (3rd).
3. Company C at Dreux Air Base.
4. Two platoons transferred from Fontainebleau to Paris (Camp des Loges).
5. Companies at Fontainebleau (B) and Périgueux (C).
6. Platoons at Chinon (2nd), Ingrandes (1st), and Saumur (3rd).
7. Units at Orléans (3rd Platoon) and Metz (Co B).
8. Detachments at Fontenet, Orléans, Paris (Camp des Loges), Poitiers, and Verdun.

Abbreviations

AB	Air Base	Fwd Sup	Forward Supply
Arty	Artillery	Gen	General
DAS	Direct Automotive Support	GS	General Support
DOB	Dispersed Operating Base	RADLCEN	Radiological Center
EOD	Explosive Ordnance Disposal	THQ	Theater Headquarters

Operation STAIR STEP

During Operation STAIR STEP in fall 1961, Air National Guard (ANG) units from seven states were deployed to France. To indicate a partial wing during the deployment, the prefix "7" was added to ANG unit designations. On flights from the US to France, several ANG pilots flew dangerously off course.[35] False course alteration messages likely had been received from Soviet trawlers who sent messages in English on US Navy Ocean Station Vessel radio frequencies. Pilots who regularly flew across the Atlantic were harder to fool. A code, changed daily, was required to authenticate transmissions. If the correct response was not given, pilots knew it came from Soviet trawlers or surfaced submarines. The normal American sign off would be: "Nice try Ivan."[36]

By 02 November 1961, more than 1,000 airmen of the 106th Tactical Reconnaissance Squadron of the Alabama ANG 7117th Tactical Reconnaissance Wing, commanded by Brig Gen George "Poppa" Doster, had arrived at Dreux AB. Six months earlier, Doster had recruited pilots from the wing to volunteer to fly B-26 bombing sorties for the failed invasion in April 1961 by Cuban exiles at the Bay of Pigs in Cuba. Four air guardsmen died during the sorties, two in a shootout after surviving the crash of their B-26.[37] Because the air base at Dreux had been on standby status, buildings needed repair, essential equipment for communications was missing, and the runways and aprons needed renovation. After several days, the squadron's twenty RF-84F Thunderstreaks, the only reconnaissance aircraft sent to Europe during the Berlin Wall Crisis, were ready to fly.

To the Americans' surprise, the French air traffic controllers refused permission for flight operations at Dreux. The French claimed that, due to heavy civilian traffic at nearby Le Bourget and Orly airports, they had insufficient air traffic controllers to handle the additional military traffic. Back home in Birmingham, the local newspapers reported that Alabama boys had been deployed to Europe just to sit idle in France.[38] Family members of the Alabama air guardsmen complained to their US Congressman who in turn asked US Secretary of Defense Robert S. McNamara to investigate the complaints. The question most often asked was: "If the unit cannot fly, what purpose do they serve in France?"[39] At the end of November, the squadron moved to Chaumont AB to share facilities with the 7108th Tactical Wing of the New Jersey ANG.

Because the ANG tactical fighter squadrons had been trained for toss-bombing nuclear missions, most of the F-84F Thunderstreak and F-86H Sabre pilots had to be retrained for conventional missions such as ground target attacks, dogfighting, and close air support for ground troops. However, pilots still practiced toss bombing. Each tactical fighter squadron had four aircraft on quick reaction alert status. These aircraft, armed with conventional weapons, were ready to fly within fifteen minutes after the alarm was heard. During simulated alerts, aircraft flew toward real targets in the Soviet bloc, but always were recalled before they crossed the border. For example, in Operation GRAND SLAM exercises in April 1962, hundreds of US jet aircraft were scrambled toward East Germany.

By the end of 1962, most of the ANG troops, mobilized for one year, had returned to the US.[40] Due to the Cuban Missile Crisis of October 1962, seventy-five ANG F-84F aircraft were kept in France and assigned to the 366th TFW, headquartered at Chaumont AB.

ANG Mobilization for Berlin Crisis (Fall 1961)[41]

Organization*	Location in US	Aircraft	Personnel	AB in France
163rd TFS (of 122nd TFW)	Ft. Wayne, IN	F-84F	888	Chambley-Bussières
141st TFS (of 108th TFW)	Wrightstown, NJ	F-84F	764	Chaumont-Semoutiers
106th TRS (of 117th TRW)	Birmingham, AL	RF-84F	1,003	Dreux-Louvilliers
166th TFS (of 121st TFW)	Columbus, OH	F-84F	1,185	Étain-Rouvres
131st TFS	Westfield, MA	F-86H	267	Phalsbourg-Bourscheid
138th TFS**	Syracuse, NY	F-86H	606	Phalsbourg-Bourscheid
101st TFS (of 102nd TFW)***	Boston, MA	F-86H	1,217	Phalsbourg-Bourscheid
110th TFS (of 131st TFW)	St. Louis, MO	F-84F	827	Toul-Rosières

*TFW is tactical fighter wing, TFS tactical fighter squadron, TRW tactical reconnaissance wing, and TRS tactical reconnaissance squadron.

**This ANG squadron was called *The Boys from Syracuse*.

***The 102nd TFW was commanded by Brig Gen Charles Sweeney, the pilot of the B-29 that dropped the atomic bomb on Nagasaki, Japan. F-86H aircraft were flown from US to France with refueling stops at Labrador, Greenland, Iceland, and Scotland.

Airborne Command Post

In November 1961, the 7120th Support Squadron was activated at Châteauroux Air Station to operate five C-118 Liftmasters being used as airborne command posts. The airborne command post was equipped to provide a survivable operations center in the event that Camp des Loges (code name Strong Hold) and the mobile ground alternate command post (code name Greyhound) were destroyed or disabled by a surprise Soviet nuclear attack. The official, unclassified nickname for the mission was SILK PURSE. To maintain UHF radio contact with Paris, three preselected orbits (called alpha, bravo, and charlie) could be flown, all within 150 miles of Camp de Loges. During an alert, one of the C-118s, which could fly at altitudes of 17,000 ft, was airborne at all times. The mobile communications ground station uplink to SILK PURSE was called the Paladin Van. Paladin was the lead character in the popular American TV series *Have Gun, Will Travel*.

EC-135 "Silk Purse" aircraft of 513th Troop Carrier Wing, 15 April to 01 July 1966 at Évreux AB (US Air Force)

The crews used the BOQ at Déols as alert quarters so planes could be airborne within 15 to 30 minutes from "scramble" notification. Because most personnel who lived off base did not have home phones, an alert system, called "Paul Revere," was devised. Drivers alerted personnel in person or placed alert cards on their front doors if they were not at home. The card read: "This is an Alert, Report Immediately to Your Duty Station." Aircrews were forbidden to drink alcoholic beverages 12 hours prior to a mission or when on alert status.[42]

In 1966, the squadron transitioned from C-118s to EC-135 Stratolifter aircraft. Five EC-135s were assigned to the squadron. The EC-135, able to fly at altitudes of 31,000 to 37,000 ft, had a Boeing 707 airframe that had been converted to store fuel in the lower half of its fuselage and have communications equipment in the upper half. The only windows were in the flight deck. Normally, each mission, called a sortie, was nine hours in the air. There were three sorties each day beginning at 1:30 am, 9:30 am, and 5:30 pm. A general officer was always on board to authenticate nuclear go codes.[43] On several occasions, fighter aircraft of the French Air Force flew extremely close identification intercepts. The US crews filed "Near Collision Reports" after every dangerous intercept, and the French government was asked to stop the intercepts.

Secure Communications

The 29th Signal Corps Battalion (Theater Headquarters) was sent to Camp des Loges to operate sensitive communications equipment during Operation ROUNDOUT in fall 1961. It was vital for Camp des Loges to maintain secure communications with SILK PURSE. One-time use code pads were used to manually encrypt the messages. Signal personnel had sheets of paper containing 240 digits randomly arranged in rows. Each sheet was duplicated only by its mate in the airborne command post. The 29th Sig Bn (THQ) also had 2½-ton vans and 5-ton tractor trailers configured for microwave radio equipment to provide secure mobile communications in the field. Microwave radio signals had a range of about 40 miles.[44] The 257th Signal Co (Service) installed and maintained secure communications lines for the deputy commander at his office in Camp des Loges, official residence in Garches, and military sedan. The automatic secure voice communications system, called AUTOSEVOCOM, scrambled voice impulses before transmission. By Army tradition, profane language was not permitted on military networks. Even during combat in Korea, GIs were reprimanded if they used profane language over military networks. Deputy commander Gen John P. McConnell, who rarely spoke without cursing, severely taxed the secure system.[45]

Field Exercises

By the early 1960s, more than eight-hundred American military personnel were assigned to Camp des Loges, nicknamed "Little Pentagon." There were more than a dozen generals and two-hundred colonels and lieutenant colonels. Exercises were held each year to practice moving the Deputy Commander-in-Chief's headquarters to the field. It usually took two weeks to move equipment, set up a concealed tent camp, complete communications links to SHAPE and subordinate commands, and break down and load up for the return to Camp des Loges. Field headquarters consisted of command tents, administration tents, mess tents, a medical dispensary tent, and tents for sleeping. The tents were pitched in a wooded area and barricaded by barbed-wire entanglement. Cables were run from Signal Corps vans to command tents and documents were stored in classified security containers (safes) in the administration tents. During an exercise in 1965 at Mont Morillon near Fontainebleau, Gen Jacob E. Smart arrived for a brief site visit to verify that his field headquarters had been set up satisfactorily. After several days at the camp, some married GIs who were accustomed to daily showers snuck into nearby Caserne Lariboisière to shower in the evening.[46]

Disruptions at Camp des Loges

In early 1963, shortly after leaving Camp des Loges by Army sedan, MP Sgt LaMar E. Hummel received an urgent voice message on his two-way radio: "Sarge we're under attack!" Frenchmen in an old black Citroën *Traction Avant* (called a "gangster car" by GIs) had sped by number 2 gate, firing automatic weapons at the MPs. No one was wounded; however, the guard house was riddled with bullet holes. The shooters likely were members of the OAS (*Organisation de l'Armée Secrète*).[47]

In spring 1963, the Little Pentagon was given an unusual task. During a layover at nearby Évreux AB, Vice President Lyndon B. Johnson planned to visit Gen McConnell at Camp des Loges. Headquarters staff were ordered to report to their workstations at midnight and act as if it were normal working hours.

Recreation

The southeast corner of Camp des Loges had diamonds for baseball, softball, and little league; football and track fields; and a large area for skeet shooting (when no one was using the baseball diamonds). The Rod and Gun Club managed the skeet range for its dues paying members and guests. In the 1960s, American civilian James Jones, who lived in Paris, frequently shot skeet at the club. Jones, the author of *From Here to Eternity*, also took advantage of the low-priced alcoholic beverages at US military clubs in the Paris area. A bottle of beer was 15¢ during Happy Hour.

One weekend in 1963, the Enlisted Men's Club hired "Bill Haley and His Comets" to perform. In the 1950s, Haley recorded the iconic hit "Rock Around the Clock" and briefly had received top billing over a young Elvis Presley. Haley's loudspeakers were too robust for the small EM Club so the roof literally shook as the Comets rocked for an audience of a hundred GIs and guests. The group's fee, alleged to be $2,000, was paid from the club's profits from slot machines, alcoholic beverage sales, and meal services.[48] The US military designated these kinds of funds as "non-appropriated" and restricted use to support morale of troops.

Staff at Camp des Loges could lounge by the pools in summer months, but due to severe reductions in the 1966 physical plant budget, some had to wear overcoats, ear muffs, and gloves indoors during the cold winter.[49]

Villa Valençay in Garches

The Villa Valençay, at 68, rue du 19 Janvier (Garches), was Quarters One of European Command. The residence staff included the general's enlisted orderlies, cook, security, and driver. The Deputy Commander-in-Chief could walk out the backyard gate of his villa onto the St.-Cloud Golf Course. When US forces left France in 1967, there were more than a dozen leased residences in the Paris area for general officers. The American Battle Monuments Commission (ABMC) moved its Paris office into the villa, after Gen David A. Burchinal relocated headquarters to the former Kurmaerker Kaserne at Stuttgart-Vaihingen, Germany, in March 1967. The villa, which had accommodated bachelor Gen Jacob E. Smart from August 1964 to July 1966, was large enough to provide office space for more than two dozen ABMC employees. For nineteen years, the ABMC had used a building at 20, rue Quentin-Bauchard, near the Arc de Triomphe. The new location in Garches did not have access to public transportation.[50]

Villa Valençay, Garches, 1967 (ABMC)

Paris Area Housing

The only US Army Bachelor Officers Quarters (BOQ) in the Paris area was a two-story building built in 1953 at Camp des Loges to house thirty-four officers. Consequently, most single male and female officers had to find private housing. In the fall of 1956, a GRI housing village for two-hundred thirty-two US Air Force families opened at Grigny, near Orly AB. The one-hundred thirty-six units were a mix of single-family and duplex houses. In 1959, seventy-eight residences for US Army families were completed on 28 acres of flat farmland at Feucherolles, near St.-Nom la-Bretèche golf course where the 1963 Canada Cup Tournament was held. The land, 14 miles from Camp des Loges, was purchased for $192,000. Each dwelling unit cost the US government $20,600 (more than 2.5 times the cost of a Levittown house in the US).[51, 52] Most of the ranch-style houses were duplexes, each family having three small bedrooms. A few units were single-family houses with four bedrooms. Seine Area Command managed the SCH development at Feucherolles, called De Grasse Village in honor of French naval officer, Admiral François Joseph Paul de Grasse. In 1781, Comte de Grasse fought the British Navy to a standstill off the Virginia Capes and delivered 3,000 French troops near Yorktown to help America win independence from Britain.[53] One telephone line from Camp des Loges exchange served De Grasse Village.

Many European Command personnel at Camp des Loges lived at Petit Beauregard, an RGH complex of mid-rise apartment buildings in le Chesnay, near Versailles. There were two-hundred four three-bedroom and ninety-six two-bedroom apartments for three-hundred families. Officers had to wait 3 to 5 months for vacancies at Petit Beauregard; NCOs, 6 to 8 months. Most hotels charged $3 to $7 a day, but from April to October provided no heat regardless of outside temperature. Private toilets were rare. Department of Defense civilian employees assigned to Camp des Loges received a supplemental allowance to compensate for the high cost of living in Paris.[54] By a quirk of planning, Petit Beauregard was close to SHAPE headquarters and SHAPE Village was close to Camp des Loges. Many wished they could swap apartments or assignments to eliminate their long commutes. When President Charles de Gaulle announced in 1966 that France would withdraw from SHAPE, there were more than 4,000 dependents living in the Paris area and more than 2,500 military, civilian, and French employees working at SHAPE and USEUCOM.[55]

Bel Manoir Shopping Center

The US Army acquired Château du Manoir de Bel Air from the French government in June 1955. The property had a château and two smaller buildings on an 18-acre site located in le Chesnay, across the street from Petit Beauregard housing area. The château was renovated for offices and a nursery for dependent children. By Spring 1963, an average of 1,500 children were cared for each month at the

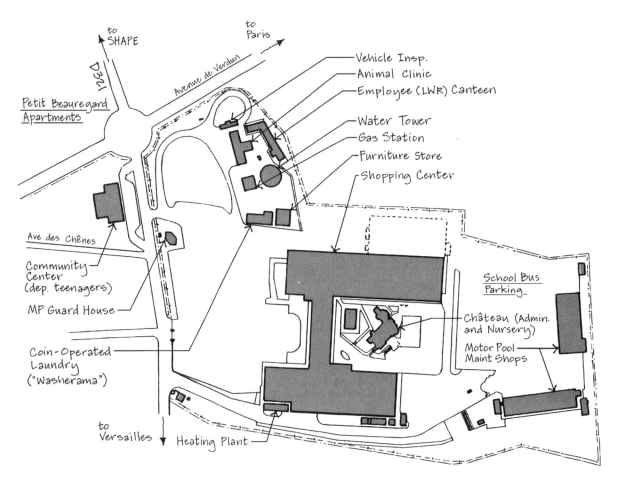

Bel Manoir Shopping Center

nursery which included a baby room with fourteen cribs, toddlers' room for thirty to forty youngsters, and playroom for older children. The permanent staff included a registered nurse. The nursery was managed by volunteers from military women's clubs in the Paris area and was open from Tuesday through Saturday.[56]

The remainder of the site was developed for a US military shopping center, called "Bel Manoir," the first modern *supermarché* in France. Built by Magnard-Moinon of Versailles at a cost of $2.8 million, it had more than 140,000 sq ft of indoor shopping space. The shopping center, operated by the US Army's European Exchange System (EES), was open Tuesday through Saturday. From 10 am until 6:30 pm, a US military bus made nine roundtrips between the Arc de Triomphe and le Chesnay. The post exchange and commissary were self-service with a central checkout. The post exchange grossed about $11 million a year; the commissary $3.3 million.[57] A cheeseburger at the snack bar cost 30¢; frozen T-bone steaks at the commissary were $1.25 per pound. By US Army, Europe directives, dependent females were required to wear dresses when shopping in the post exchanges and commissaries. Even in cold weather they were not permitted to wear slacks.[58]

On many Saturdays, Gen Lyman Lemnitzer would stand near the entrance to the shopping center, like a modern day Wal-Mart greeter, to shake hands with GIs and their family members. Lemnitzer, who was greatly admired by his SHAPE staff and European leaders, asked shoppers how they were adapting to France and if they had any problems he could fix.[59] At SHAPE headquarters, Lemnitzer was well-informed about his personnel and their families, insisting the he be told about any illnesses and personal concerns.

Veterinarian personnel of the 76th Medical Detachment (Vet Food Insp), who were responsible for the safety of meat, dairy products, fresh vegetables, and fruits purchased in bulk to feed troops in the Paris area, were stationed in the Carriage House at le Chesnay. Tainted meat products could spread trichinosis, tuberculosis, anthrax, and tapeworm. Refrigerated foods were inspected frequently, perishable foods monthly, and non-perishables every three months. Refrigerated food also was inspected after power outages. A list of food suppliers that had been inspected and approved by 76th Med Det personnel was provided to quartermaster purchasing agents. In 1955, the only dairy plant in France given an Army contract was at Le Mans in Brittany. All milk for US military installations was processed separately at the dairy, tested for bacteria by Army personnel, and loaded into separate sealed boxcars and trucks. Veterinarians inspected the dairy for a high degree of cleanliness and tested herds within 10 miles of Le Mans to be sure the cows were free of TB and brucellosis. To be rated TB-free, fewer than 0.5% of the cattle could test positive.[60-62]

When Charles de Gaulle returned to head the French government in 1958, there were only eight *supermarchés* in France. By 1962, de Gaulle could brag that there were more than two hundred.[63] Growth was primarily due to Brittany grocer Edouard LeClerc (1926-2012) who by 1959 had a chain of sixty self-service grocery stores located from Brest to Grenoble.[64] After 1967, the Bel Manoir Shopping Center site became a motor pool for the French Ministère de l'Interieur.

32, rue Marbeuf

In 1955, the US Army leased a six-story building at 32-34, rue Marbeuf, just off the avenue des Champs Élysées. The Marbeuf building had an officers open mess, snack bar, small PX, medical clinic staffed by Army personnel from the 386th General Dispensary, and indoor parking on four levels for one-hundred vehicles. The annual rent paid to the private owner was $531,800. The 513th Intelligence Group, located at Camp King in Oberursel near Frankfurt, Germany, had a field office in the building. In spring 1959, undercover agents of the 513th occupied unmarked offices and sought to gather information on subversive groups in Paris. Their mission product was called clandestine human intelligence. Young agents infiltrated left-wing student groups.

On weekends, the Paris Officers Club hired a violinist who roamed throughout the dining room, stopping to play at each table. (Punsters said he often played "over chewers.") Evenings and weekends, US military personnel usually could find a parking space in the garage, a rarity in Paris. Most motorists searched for parking spaces that did not exist. Traffic jams were so bad that some Parisians suggested that the Tuileries Gardens should be converted into a huge parking lot.[65] The US Air Forces in Europe liaison office in Paris was located at 22, rue de la Trémoille, adjacent to the Hôtel West End. The facility included a barbershop, Air Forces Europe Exchange (AFEX), laundry, and officers club. On 30 June 1966, the liaison office moved to the Marbeuf building.

USO on Champs Élysées

GIs on leave or weekend pass to Paris could visit the USO Paris Lounge and Information Center at 93, ave des Champs Élysées (initial location at no. 15) and American Legion Post No. 1 (Pershing Hall) at 49, rue Pierre Charron. The USO had showers, game room, and television room and was open from 9 am to 10 pm daily (midnight on Saturdays). Games included ping-pong, checkers, and chess. A French combo played at weekend dances. Volunteer junior hostesses, mainly college girls and US State Department employees, entertained the GIs. TV reception was limited. In the early 1950s, France had one government controlled channel. By 1963, there were two French channels and one from Luxembourg. The USO also provided tour information, hotel reservations, reduced prices on tickets to shows at the Lido and Moulin Rouge, and arranged babysitters for children of married personnel. Paris museums had reduced admission fees for US military personnel in uniform. Pershing Hall had a snack bar and currency exchange.[66-68]

American Dependents Schools at St.-Cloud

When the American Dependents School opened in September 1954 at 41, rue Pasteur in St.-Cloud, it was the most modern high school in France. The fifteen buildings, which cost $2.2 million, included high school and elementary school classroom buildings, an auditorium, cafeteria, and gymnasium. Lunch in the cafeteria cost 50¢. Two dormitories housed students who lived beyond commuting distance. Parents paid about $1.50 per day, including meals, for each dormitory student.

The 18-acre site bordered SNCF railroad tracks. Former students, like Douglass Donnell, recall that loud passing trains were a welcome distraction when class was boring.[69] Teachers, newly arrived from public schools in the US, were astonished at the discipline of the students. They behaved even when the teacher left the room! According to former varsity players, the Paris American High School (PAHS) Pirates basketball team had an outstanding season in 1962 and almost won the USAREUR championship. For many years the PAHS prom was held at the dining room of the Eiffel Tower restaurant.

Each day more than sixty school buses, operated by Seine Area Command, logged over 4,000 miles delivering students to and from school. The buses were assigned to the Bel Manoir motor pool. In 1965, mufflers were installed on new GM diesel school buses after the mayors of St.-Germain-en-Laye and St.-Cloud complained about the noise.[70] Complaints were based on who was making the noise. French trucks and motorbikes were much louder than the American buses.

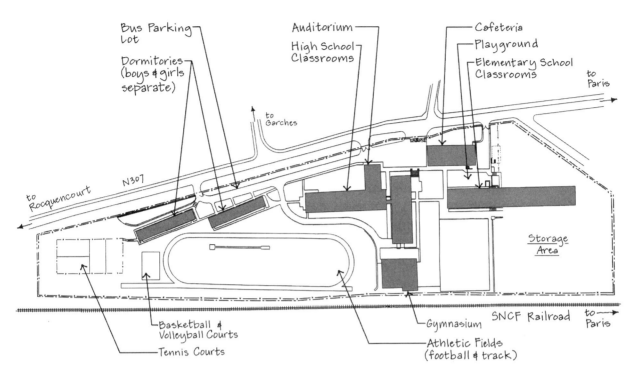

St.-Cloud Dependents Schools

After US forces withdrew from France in 1967, the American School of Paris (ASP), a private school, purchased most of the campus. Negotiations to acquire the property were complicated because, although the address was St.-Cloud, part of the site was in Garches. Eventually, the Lycée Santos-Dumont acquired the former cafeteria and elementary school buildings in Garches; ASP the buildings in St.-Cloud. Most of the original buildings are still in use. Commencement speakers at ASP have included journalist Art Buchwald and Hollywood actress Olivia de Havilland, a two-time Oscar winner, who were longtime American residents of Paris.[71] In 1954, Buchwald wrote an article on his "hair raising" ride in an F-86 jet of the USAFE Skyblazers acrobatic team at Chaumont AB.

Counter Intelligence in Europe

During World War II, the US Army Counter Intelligence Corps (CIC) captured spies and collaborators. CIC agents helped gather combat intelligence, evaluated enemy documents and equipment, and recruited civilian sources. After the war ended, they cracked down on black marketers, exposed plots to damage US installations, and foiled a half-baked conspiracy to reestablish Nazi influence in Germany. The conspiracy was dubbed the Axmann Conspiracy for its organizer Arthur Axmann, the former leader of the Hitler Youth.[72] Agents also sanitized records (most at behest of US State Department) of dozens of Germans recruited to spy on the Soviets and hundreds of German scientists brought to the US to continue their work, including developing chemical weapons.[73] The Army recruited German scientists, regardless of their despicable deeds during the war, because Germany was far ahead in the development of rockets, jet engines, sweptback wings, and synthetic fuels.[74]

The CIC sponsored the Gehlen Group, an intelligence organization that employed former Nazis and German war criminals as informants. During 1947-51, former Gestapo officer Klaus Barbie, known as the "Butcher of Lyon" because of his atrocities, was in the group.[75, 76] The group was named for its leader, German general Reinhard Gehlen, the intelligence chief of the Eastern front during World War II.[77] When Gehlen surrendered to the US Army he offered access to his files, anticipating they would be coveted by the Americans. The files had been buried in steel boxes or hidden under floorboards in remote forester's lodges.[78] Well into the late 1940s, the CIC apprehended Nazi war criminals and identified communists who had penetrated the emerging German democratic institutions. The secret intelligence program named PAPERCLIP, authorized in September 1946 by President Truman, exempted numerous war criminals from prosecution.[79-81]

Training at The Bird

The Army's CIC school was located at Fort Holabird, Maryland (called "The Bird"). Because special agents could be commissioned officers, warrant officers, or enlisted men, all ranks in the CIC were trained to perform tasks such as conducting investigations, interrogations, and surveillance. Numerous classroom hours were devoted to learning how to type and write reports. Specialty training included methods of entry ("pick locks" and "crack safes"), operation of polygraph equipment (called the "brown box"), and sound equipment used to plant and detect hidden electronic transmitters and microphones ("bugs").

At The Bird, students learned how to follow suspects without being observed and to tell if they were being followed, called "fox and hare" exercises. To expose a tail, they learned to simulate lengthy window shopping to observe images reflected in the glass, take abnormally short taxi or bus rides, and aimlessly walk around the block (four right or left turns in a row). To follow someone, the future agents practiced in teams of three, alternating en route who would be the follower. Urban area exercises were held in Baltimore, Maryland.[82]

The course on how to open mail without leaving indications of tampering was called "flaps and seals."[83, 84] In the "French opening" method, one short end of the envelope was slit and the cut carefully sealed after the contents had been read. Students also were shown how to "roll out" contents of an envelope without opening it. Knitting needles or paper clips were inserted at both ends of the flap's crease to grasp and roll the sheet of paper.[85]

The course on surreptitious entry, called "picks and locks," included how to use modeling clay to make impressions of keys and lock-aid devices to vibrate tumblers (supposedly available only to locksmiths). Lock tool kits contained more than a dozen steel picks with handles. The course had the official CIC acronym DAME (defense against methods of entry). The name was somewhat misleading because by learning the defenses, students learned the course objective of how to enter locked buildings, desks, safes, and vaults. At the factory, locks for safes and vaults were set with a standard sequence of numbers. Because many users did not bother to change the combination, surreptitious entry was sometimes relatively easy.[86] To open locks with unknown combinations, students learned to use their fingers to feel turn resistance when each drop lever fell into its open position. Training on planting and detecting "bugs" had the acronym DASE (defense against sound equipment). The defense training also included instruction on where and how to tap into a telephone line without leaving evidence, and how to wear a hidden microphone to record conversations. In Driver Qualification instruction, students learned how to disable vehicles, evade a trailing vehicle, and drive unobtrusively during surveillance missions.

In addition to the usual military recreational facilities (bowling alley, outdoor athletic fields), Fort Holabird had an Army T-Boat (68 ft long). Students could contact Special Services to reserve it for fishing or drinking excursions. The post swimming pool, located behind the Officers Club, was used by enlisted men on odd numbered days; by officers on even numbered days.[87]

CIC Buildup in France

In late 1950, thirty-six CIC personnel from the 66th CIC Group in Germany were sent to France. The unit stayed in France until October 1954 when the 766th CIC Detachment was activated. Their mission was to protect US forces against espionage, sabotage, and subversion. Because local wage rate (LWR) French employees initially hired to work for the US Army had not been thoroughly screened, one of the first tasks was to identify security risks within the work force. LWRs suspected to have communist sympathies were discharged or given jobs away from sensitive materials. By the end of 1951, more than sixty CIC personnel, commanded by Lt Col David H. Huntoon, were working in France; by 1953, one-hundred twenty.[88, 89] Huntoon's agents investigated suspicious, potential lapses of security of Army documents reported to them, tapped into electronic communications to catch security violators, intercepted mail from or to East bloc countries, and screened foreign national employees. Members of the Polish Labor Service, who guarded most of the US installations in France, were a potential source of intelligence for the Soviets. Most had family and relatives living behind the Iron Curtain who could be threatened with reprisals. Consequently, their mail would be opened and contacts with officials of the Polish Embassy in Paris and Polish Consulate at Toulouse were monitored. Postal clerks at Army Post Offices helped agents intercept mail prior to delivery to subjects being investigated.

GIs who had homosexual relationships, financial problems such as large debts, or extramarital affairs were susceptible to blackmail by Soviet agents. If discovered, homosexuals quickly received a general discharge "for good of the service." In mid-1963, CIC agents discovered a ring of homosexuals at the US Army's 77th Medical Depot located at Vitry-le-François. A dozen enlisted men were discharged from military service, most had been assigned to the 591st Ambulance Co.[90]

By 1955, the 766th CIC Det at Orléans had moved from St.-Jean-de-Braye to the larger Château de la Touche at nearby Donnery. The château was leased from the Heuzé family. In August 1956, the US Army's nine-hole golf course opened on the château property to the delight of avid golfers like 766th commander Lt Col Willard N. Thompson. In the 1960s, the detachment also had Resident Agencies at Maison-Fort in Ardon and at 1, rue du Commandant Arago in Orléans. At smaller installations, like Saumur in Base Section and Trois-Fontaines in Advance Section, normally only one special agent was assigned from the 766th. Resident agents were given use of a car, apartment, .38 cal lightweight revolver, and told to send their reports to the field office: Poitiers for Saumur, Verdun for Trois-Fontaines. Field offices were designated "Field Service Detachments" to disguise their function. If an agent married a foreign national without a waiver, his service with the CIC would be terminated. Once a week in 1964 at Fontainebleau, Resident Agent Hugh Roy Thompson visited Capt Patrick J. Browne at the 67th Military Police Co, Caserne Lariboisière to read the 3x5 arrest record cards. Thompson used the information to identify trouble-prone GIs.[91]

In February 1951, the 450th CIC Detachment was sent to Paris to serve Gen Eisenhower's NATO command. The detachment acquired a building on rue Montfleury in Versailles rent free from the French government. The two-story structure had thirty-nine rooms and a basement. The 450th protected the secret documents at SHAPE in Marly-le-Roi and performed liaison with civil and military intelligence agencies of other NATO nations. Because French intelligence agencies had been widely infiltrated by pro-Soviet communists, the CIC had to be extremely careful when dealing with them. By 1960, the 450th had fifteen officers and ten enlisted men at Versailles.

Locations of Army CIC Offices (1953)

Bordeaux (Pessac)	Hôtel du Vallon (37, ave du Vallon)
Metz (le Ban St.-Martin)	Maison Legris
Orléans (St.-Jean-de-Braye)	Château Le Petit Cormier (65, ave de Verdun)
Paris	32-34, rue Marbeuf
Versailles (SHAPE Unit)	6, rue Montfleury

Background Investigations

The French Interior Ministry helped the CIC by investigating French nationals seeking employment at US installations. Information was entered on ComZ Form No. 12 regarding membership in the Communist Party in France (PCF), travel to Germany during period of 1939 to 1945, and drinking habits (*sobriété*). Like investigations for US military security clearances, called "Personnel Security Investigations," the *Sûreté Nationale* tried to determine attitudes toward French and American governments and evaluated the applicant's moral conduct, temperament, and reliability. The French applicant's past affiliations and police record were checked and inquiries were made with former employers, school teachers, and neighbors. Americans holding security clearances were expected to be discrete and loyal. During "Complaint Investigations," Americans being investigated were given polygraph exams to help ensure the accuracy of the information. The polygraph was based on the principle that, for most persons, lying causes a physiological response that can be measured. The box man evaluated the subject's truthfulness by recording breathing, sweating, and blood pressure during responses to questions. Polygraph exams were given regularly to CIC agents.

Anonymity

To protect their identity and keep records and documents secure, if feasible CIC personnel were billeted and fed separately from other military personnel. In the early 1950s at Château Le Petit Cormier near Orléans, special agents of the 66th CIC Group Det ate their meals in a dining room. Wine was served with the meals which were prepared by a French chef and his wife.[92] To disguise their military rank, CIC agents normally wore civilian clothing, for which they received a cash allowance. Rank was not to be mentioned away from the office. Agents were to be addressed as "Mister," not by rank. This deception was necessary in part because officers did not socialize with enlisted men and would be reluctant to answer questions from a CIC agent holding a lower rank. If an agent was asked to reveal his rank, the usual response was: "My rank is confidential." In the event of war, CIC enlisted men in France were to be issued the uniform of a Warrant Officer. (Coincidentally, Army warrant officers were addressed as Mister.) Enlisted agents were given a bogus civilian government service (GS) rank of GS-9 on their Armed Forces Identification Card (ID). The CIC official ID card identified all ranks as "Special Agent" as did the official gold-plated badge. To look more like civilians, agents were permitted to grow their hair longer than the standard GI "high and tight" haircut.

In 1953, personnel of the 66th CIC Group formed a team to compete in the Orleans Area Command (OAC) company-level touch football league. Fourteen, nine-man teams competed in games played in the evenings at Saran and Maison-Fort. The 66th CIC Gp team won the season title to represent OAC at the ComZ championship tournament held at Camp Bussac. Game summaries in the sports pages of the *ComZ Cadence* weekly troop information newspaper did not reveal the names of the CIC team members. Win or lose the agents, dubbed the "Sleuths," were anonymous. Although touchdowns and interceptions by players on other teams were reported by name, those of the Sleuths were not.[93]

CIC agents used unmarked civilian vehicles for routine duties. Initially, the civilian vehicle fleet in France contained Chevrolet, Ford, and Plymouth sedans painted Army green. On clandestine missions, the huge sedans were conspicuous among the much smaller European vehicles. In June 1956, the US Army purchased four-hundred eleven French-made Renault sedans, at $1,217 each, for ComZ. The smaller, less conspicuous Renaults were more compatible with narrow French roads and could be repaired by French garages.[94] The 766th purchased a few used old black Citroëns. In the early 1960s at Braconne Ordnance Depot, bachelor CIC agents assigned to the field office lived on post in the BOQ. One agent inexplicably owned a Facel-Vega, a conspicuous, exotic sports car.[95]

When CIC agents were hospitalized in the 34th General Hospital at la Chapelle, they were admitted under a false name. If surgery was required, another agent was present while the agent was under anesthesia. French interns and foreign doctors were not allowed to treat agents.[96]

Classified Documents

Units in ComZ secured their classified documents in locked file cabinets or safes (officially called classified security containers) located within locked rooms called "the cage." GIs, who were assigned to classified documents clerk duty, had to ensure that only personnel holding proper security clearances could see the documents. Authorized users signed a receipt to remove the documents and signed the receipt when the documents were returned.[97] Special agents at Orléans conducted annual security inspections of nearby installations. Installations were given thirty days to correct deficiencies and were re-inspected before the CIC report was sent to higher headquarters.

On surreptitious missions to observe how well an installation secured classified documents during duty hours, CIC agents, who were not commissioned officers, dressed in a uniform of a field-grade officer and wore a fake name tag. Officers on "CIC special duty assignment" were also used for surveillance and as informants. They normally performed the duties of their "cover" branch of service but, unbeknownst to fellow officers, also performed their confidential duties.

Using master keys borrowed from the post engineer or relying on their training to pick locks, agents also conducted investigations to uncover mishandling of classified documents. Locked desks were opened to see if they contained classified documents that should have been stored in safes. At most post headquarters, MPs conducted security checks during off-duty hours to be sure classified documents were properly secured and all safes, desks, and file cabinets were locked. Contents of wastebaskets, which could contain worksheets and notes used to prepare or review classified documents, were supposed to be burned each day.[98]

Penetration Tests

In July 1965, the 766th CIC Det was asked to test security at US European Command, Camp des Loges (CDL). Special agents from Orléans and Braconne were assigned to the "penetration test." During their first evening at the CDL Officers Club, the three agents found the command telephone directory which listed name, rank, assignment, and office location for key personnel. They targeted a J-2 Division (Intelligence) officer. While the officer ate dinner, an agent visited the cloakroom to insert a simulated electronic bug (wire and duct tape) in the officer's service cap. Learning the name of another intelligence officer, who was on vacation, the agents asked a civilian secretary to place a large envelope on the officer's desk which was behind steel doors of the Intelligence Watch Center. Upon his return, the officer would discover the envelope on his desk in a secure area. The envelope contained a crumpled paper on which was written "This is a bomb." During the three-day test, agents also planted simulated bugs under several office phones in the headquarters building and behind curtains in Gen Jacob E. Smart's DCINC conference room. Although CDL formally thanked the 766th CIC Det for the test, Smart was not pleased by how easily CDL was penetrated. The Supreme Commander's counter intelligence advisor Lt Col Samuel B. Sinai of the 450th CIC Det was ordered to tighten security.

Surveillance Missions

Old timers in the CIC believed if they were not violating restrictive provisions of the Status of Forces Agreement (SOFA) with France they were not doing their job to protect ComZ. Officially, off-post surveillance missions, such as unauthorized entry, occurred only when authorized by the French. Unauthorized entry was called a "second-story job" because second-story windows normally were not locked.

CIC agents also gathered intelligence on ships from Poland, Yugoslavia, and the Soviet Union which arrived every two or three weeks at the port of la Pallice.[99] The agents photographed the ships and used informants to obtain a list of personnel on board and details on the cargo. The standard French *Sûreté Nationale* form provided date of birth, nationality, duty on ship, and passport number of crew members. At la Pallice, informants who worked at the port provided CIC agents the names of those who did not appear to be seamen.

In 1956, Brig Gen James K. Woolnough, BASEC commander, directed the CIC field office at Caserne Aufrédi to investigate a married lieutenant colonel who was suspected of fraternization with enlisted men. CIC agents monitored his movements away from the port of la Pallice and installed bugs to record his conversations. It was discovered that the officer was having homosexual relationships with his NCO driver and other enlisted men. Brig Gen William Whipple, who succeeded Woolnough, relieved the officer from port command and gave him two choices: resign from the US Army or be court-martialed. He resigned.[100]

Deputy port commander Maj Charles Miguel Duncan, Jr. assumed command on 01 May 1956. Duncan commanded the port until 30 June 1958 and received outstanding efficiency reports from his superiors at the 11th Trans Port Command B. Officers assigned to la Pallice had to be discrete because secret shipments of US weapons and ammo were sent from la Pallice to North Africa and the Middle East. In October 1957, Duncan supervised a confidential delivery of weapons to the Arab Army of Jordan. The cargo, which included numerous combat tanks, dragon wagons, jeeps, and ammunition, was shipped from la Pallice to Aqaba, Jordan.[101]

Jeep offloaded from USNS Marine Fiddler, Jordan, October 1957 (C. M. Duncan, Jr.)

USNS Marine Fiddler cargo ship in Gulf of Aqaba, Jordan, October 1957 (C. M. Duncan, Jr.)

Social Contacts and Informants

Because valuable information could be obtained from social contacts, CIC detachments had a "black" fund (meaning off the books) to pay for alcohol, tobacco, and gifts. Sources were more likely to reveal information after consuming alcohol. To maintain the advantage of clear thought, it was common for agents to drink less alcohol than their sources. Special agents cultivated a network of informants on base by giving money or gifts in exchange for information and, in violation of SOFA, also cultivated informants off base. Contacts in the towns and villages near Army installations were a source of advance notice of communist-organized protests and strikes.[102]

In 1958, Special Agent Ronald D. Flack was sent to France after CIC training at Fort Holabird and six months French language training at Presidio of Monterey, California. Assigned to Saumur, Flack developed valuable off-base contacts through a Frenchman who worked as an engineer at the huge Montreuil-Bellay US Army Signal Depot. The Frenchman lived at the nearby Château de la Fessardière at Turquant which was used as a retreat for French Ministry of Justice officials. The chateau director's brother was a general officer on President Charles de Gaulle's staff in Paris. Flack socialized with the director's family, who likely were aware that he was in the CIC. During the period of turbulence in Algeria, information from Flack's secondary source at the Élysée Palace, French Général Guy Marie Henri Grout de Beaufort, was highly prized.[103]

Troop Briefings

CIC agents also briefed newly arrived troops, stressing the importance of their assignments to defend Europe. During basic training, GIs were instructed to deny information to the enemy by camouflage, concealment, and secure handling of classified documents. US Army, Europe Circular 380-20 described typical espionage attempts toward US military and dependents. It urged that similar situations, even if apparently insignificant, be reported promptly to the CIC. In 1959, Special Agent Robert F. Elliott held a monthly briefing in the post chapel for troops newly assigned to Toul Engineer Depot. He explained the mission of his CIC detachment and asked the troops to report to him any attempts by unknown persons to obtain information that they would not have the need to know, foreign nationals who cultivated friendships that appeared to have purpose of securing obligations, or anyone who acted suspiciously. Of course, any blackmail attempts to obtain military information were to be reported. Elliot advised the troops not to drink alcohol to excess, but if they had to get drunk to do so only on post. He encouraged the troops to behave like guests of France, to learn the French language, and to visit historic sites such as the nearby battlefields of World War I.[104]

Ironically in the mid-1950s at Évreux AB, readers of the biweekly base newspaper *Skyliner* were encouraged to answer questions about the Air Force from curious civilians. The US Air Force believed it was good public relations for airmen to explain their jobs, if the information was not "detrimental to US security." However, the article did not define what information would be detrimental.[105] During the Cuban Missile Crisis in fall 1962, troops at Base Section depots were asked to report suspicious vehicles displaying green diplomatic license plates. The Soviets would be keen to observe depot activities such as unusual movement of war reserve stocks.

Private Thornwell

In 1961, PFC James R. Thornwell was suspected of stealing a file folder of Top Secret documents from the ComZ Staff Message Center at Caserne Coligny in Orléans. During March to June 1961, the 766th CIC Det confined Thornwell in Orléans and, for a period of enhanced threats, in a former watermill on rue du Bac in Olivet. The historic mill was on a small island in the Loiret River, not far from the Army BOQs at Château de La Mothe in Olivet. The four bachelor Army officers, who were renting the mill, were asked to move into a hotel for one night.[106]

Thornwell was harshly interrogated; denied food, sleep, and latrine visits; hypnotized; and on 26 May given sodium pentothal by an Army doctor from the 34th General Hospital. Between 08 and 12 June, as part of a nonconsensual human behavior experiment, a Special Purpose Team of three personnel from Fort Holabird and Edgewood Arsenal surreptitiously gave Thornwell EA 1729 in a glass of water when he was confined at the mill.[107] EA 1729 was the Army code name for d-lysergic acid diethylamide (LSD) known to cause irrational behavior, depression, and paranoia.[108,109] Beginning in the 1950s, numerous volunteers were given LSD under "informed consent" conditions at the US Army Chemical Research & Development Center, Edgewood Arsenal, Maryland.[110]

Prior to being given LSD, Thornwell was subjected to dramatized threats to his life. While he was under duress from LSD, the team threatened to extend its mind-altering effects unless he cooperated. The CIC agents were determined to recover the missing highly sensitive classified documents, but Thornwell had given multiple false stories of where he had dumped the documents. During interrogation at the mill, Thornwell finally admitted he had thrown the documents into the Loire River. In the summer of 1961, a CIC agent told one of the officers living in the mill that some of the missing documents had been retrieved downstream along the riverbanks. Thornwell was not a traitor. He was a rebel who did not like his very strict lieutenant at Coligny. He was not charged with theft and, based on a medical diagnosis of schizophrenic paranoia, received a general discharge on 23 October 1961.[111] Because his discharge was less than honorable, employment opportunities in civilian life were diminished and the lasting effects of LSD precluded stable personal relationships. An Army Inspector General report on psychochemical field testing euphemistically referred to the prolonged confinement of Thornwell as "voluntary protective custody."[112]

Seventeen years later in 1978, Thornwell's attorney, Harvey M. Kletz of Oakland, California, sued the government for $10 million. Kletz could not overcome the Feres Doctrine, a 1950 Supreme Court decision which shielded the Army from litigation for death or injury "incident to military service." However, Kletz's allegation that Thornwell was harmed during his subsequent civilian life by not knowing what drugs he had been given without his consent was upheld by the US District Court in Washington, DC. To avoid a court ruling against the US government, the US Congress paid

Thornwell $625,000 by means of a private relief bill as compensation for his treatment by the Army. In 1979, a Pentagon spokesman told reporters the treatment of Thornwell was "unconscionable."[113, 114]

Ironically unbeknownst to the 766th, during November 1959 to May 1961, Sgt Robert Lee Johnson, who worked at the Ordnance Supply Control Agency at nearby Maison-Fort, was providing classified documents to Russian agents.[115, 116] From late 1961 until September 1963, Johnson worked at the Armed Forces Courier Center at Orly Airport. Up-to-date defense plans of NATO and US European Command passed through the Center. At night he removed top secret documents from the vault, gave them to his KGB handlers to copy, and returned the documents before morning. The haul was so important that samples were shown to Soviet Premier Nikita Khrushchev. Johnson was arrested in November 1964 while AWOL in Reno, Nevada. After he pled guilty to conspiracy charges in July 1965, Johnson was sentenced to serve twenty-five years in prison.[117, 118]

French Interior Ministry

The French Interior Ministry provided CIC agents with information on activities of the Communist Party in France (PCF). For security, it was essential that installation commanders identify PCF members who were prone to violence or working undercover. The CIC resident agent was considered to be an advisor to the installation commander and attended commander's conferences. The PCF organized protests when locations of US installations were announced in the 1950s. To avoid incidents, installations normally were located where the PCF influence was weak. The Paris Préfet de Police did not approve an American request to use warehouse buildings at 144, avenue Wilson in the suburb of St.-Denis because the potential for protests was high.

The French bureaucracy kept very extensive records on its citizens, including where each person spent the night. At hotels, guests filled out a comprehensive registration form and foreigners were required to surrender their passports at the front desk. GIs showed their military ID-card to the front desk clerk who copied name, rank, and other information from both sides of the card. American dependents (wives and children) and civilian employees were required to surrender their French government-issued identification document (*Carte de Séjour Temporaire*), which was to be carried at all times. The French collected the information each evening and gave a courtesy copy of the report the next morning to nearby US Army MP units. AWOL soldiers from Germany were shocked to be arrested so quickly by MPs in France. The report also revealed when married soldiers shared a room with a female other than their spouse.[119] (Prescribed by US President Harry S. Truman in 1951, the "Manual for Courts-Martial" prohibited adultery by military personnel.) The French police believed that the hotel registration law helped them each day to locate dozens of criminals and missing persons.

In 1963 at Trois Fontaines Ammunition Depot (TFAD), a young PFC asked his commanding officer for permission to marry a French national who was considerably older than the GI. Within a few days, *Sûreté Nationale* documents on the prospective bride arrived at the 39th Ordnance Det. Sent by the CIC resident agent, the documents alleged numerous sexual liaisons with Germans during the occupation. The French called this "horizontal collaboration." The commanding officer requested assistance from Chaplain (Maj) Elwyn C. Edwards who discouraged the GI from marrying the woman.

French authorities temporarily imprisoned all Frenchmen believed to be a threat to President Charles de Gaulle's safety during his visit on 24 April 1963 to St.-Dizier, near TFAD. Standing in the town square, de Gaulle gave a speech on France's emerging nuclear striking force. He ended his speech by singing "La Marseillaise." The large crowd at St.-Dizier sang along with their president and many shook de Gaulle's hand when he walked to his Citroën. De Gaulle often traveled throughout France because he believed it was important to have close contact with ordinary citizens.[120, 121]

766th CIC Det Commanders*

Commanding Officer	Period of Service	Commanding Officer	Period of Service
Lt Col David H. Huntoon	1950-52	Lt Col Willard N. Thompson**	1959-61
Col Edwin J. Barry	1952-55	Lt Col Albert F. Rutledge	1961-64
Lt Col George B. Collins	1955-56	Lt Col Nestor J. Dourlet	1964-65
Unknown	1957-59	Lt Col Emmett M. Chandler	1965-67

*66th CIC Group, Det A (Dec 50-Oct 54).
**Thompson commanded Naples, Italy subordinate element of 450th CIC Det (1958-59).

450th CIC Det (SHAPE Unit) Commanders[122]

Commanding Officer	Period of Service	Commanding Officer	Period of Service
Capt Jack B. Cameron	Jan 51-Feb 51	Lt Col John W. Downie	Nov 58-Jun 60
Col George R. Eckman	Feb 51-Mar 51	Lt Col Thomas V. Mullen	Jun 60-Feb 64
Lt Col Jack B. Cameron	Mar 51-Mar 55	Lt Col Samuel B. Sinai	Feb 64-Feb 67
Lt Col Gordon Flaherty	Mar 55-Nov 58	Lt Col Joseph Knittle	Feb 67-Dec 69

Criminal Investigations

CIC special agents worked closely with the Army's plainclothes investigators from the Military Police Corps. Unofficially called CID agents, these investigators were assigned to most installations and their duty assignments were listed as confidential. Most troops were unaware of their presence. MP Criminal Investigators (CI agents) investigated crimes ranging from theft to murder. In ComZ, typical investigations involved robberies, break-ins, hit-and-run vehicle accidents, and physical assaults. In late January 1951, the 16th Military Police Detachment (CI) arrived at the Hôtel Astoria in Paris to support the rapid buildup of SHAPE. The detachment investigated crimes in the Paris area until March 1967 when it moved to Mons, Belgium.

Office of Special Investigations (OSI)

Office of Special Investigations (OSI) agents stationed in Paris and at air bases in France conducted criminal investigations and intelligence work for the US Air Force. Agents investigated aircraft accidents, oversaw security of classified documents that were to be locked up at night, and made background checks on French civilian employees at the bases. Agents from the OSI Paris office at 9, rue Weber investigated a murder at the Hôtel Littré in 1958.[123]

Aerial photos taken by 66th Tactical Reconnaissance Wing from Laon AB were published in the 14 July 1959 issue of *The Stars and Stripes*. In the two page article, Airman Second Class Leon T. Moon explained how he identified objects in the photos by their shape, shadow patterns, and context as observed through magnifying glass. OSI personnel believed this kind of information should have been restricted. When the base newspaper *Laon Sentinel* printed an aerial photo of the base taken in 1964, the OSI agent-in-charge at Laon became apoplectic, challenging the editor to not publish target information for the Soviets. The agent declared that Laon should "Make the Russians work for their intelligence, don't give it to them."[124, 125]

US Embassy Paris

The US Ambassador to France not only managed US State Department employees, he nominally headed Defense Attachés, Military Assistance Advisory Group (MAAG) mission, US Information Service (USIS) staff, and the CIA station. These diverse elements were part of his "country team." Personnel in the US Embassy on 2, ave Gabriel were so numerous that two nearby mansions also were used. In 1948, the State Department had purchased a 34,000 sq ft mansion on 41, rue du Faubourg Saint-Honoré for $2 million from Baron Henri Rothschild. In late 1953, US Congressman John J. Phillips from California revealed that the State Department failed to prevent the Baron from removing oak paneling and a marble staircase after he sold the mansion to the US.[126] In 1951, the State Department purchased the Talleyrand mansion on 2, rue St.-Florentin from the Rothschilds. During the occupation, the Germans had used the basement of the Talleyrand to confine prisoners. From 1948 to 1951, European headquarters of the Marshall Plan was granted rent free use of the Talleyrand. Restoration began in 1966 to convert the mansion on Faubourg Saint-Honoré into the residence of the US Ambassador. In January 1972, the Ambassador moved from 2, ave d'Iéna into the mansion, adjacent to the Embassy.[127, 128]

US Ambassadors to France

US Ambassador	Period	Bilateral Agreements/Achievements
Jefferson Caffery	1944-49	Facilities for US military forces in France to support occupation army in Austria and Germany (16 Feb 48). Six American doctors authorized to practice medicine in France.
David K. E. Bruce	1949-52	Establishment and operation of US line of communications (06 Nov 50). Establishment of USAFE air depot at Déols-la Martinerie (27 Feb 51).
James C. Dunn	1952-53	Offshore discharge exercises along Atlantic coast of France (05 May 52). Evacuation of US noncombatants (NEO) across France (14 Feb 53).
C. Douglas Dillon	1953-57	Construction of Donges-Metz petroleum pipeline (30 June 53). Restrictions for storage of nuclear weapons in France (08 Apr 54). Enhanced French civilian-American troop relations.
Amory Houghton	1957-61	Operation of ComZ in France (08 Dec 58).
Gen James M. Gavin	1961-62	Advocated nuclear aid to France. Requested use of Sites "X" for storage of US nuclear weapons in France.
Charles E. Bohlen	1962-68	President de Gaulle invokes *rebus sic stantibus* to withdraw France from SHAPE (Mar 66).

NOTE: Sources for overview of bilateral agreements include J. R. Moenk (1955) and G.S Prugh (1976).

Military Attachés and Intelligence Gathering

Military attachés and assistant attachés were accredited to the French Ministry of Defense. The attachés were issued diplomatic passports and conducted their duties under protection of diplomatic immunity. Diplomatic privileges included immunity from arrest or detention, personal documents were inviolable, and words spoken and acts committed in an official capacity were not subject to French jurisdiction. Attachés had offices at 58, rue de la Boétie, a fifteen minute walk from the Embassy. In 1960, there were seventy-five US military personnel at Boétie.

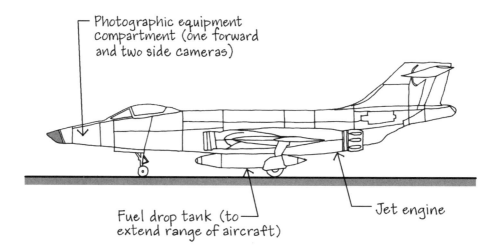

RF-101C Voodoo

Although denied publicly, intelligence was the principal occupation of military attachés. By long established tradition, intelligence gathering had the unspoken approval of the nations exchanging attachés.[129] Traditionally attachés overtly collected information about the host nation, such as military force structure, weapons deployed (tanks, aircraft, and ships), and, beginning in the 1950s, nuclear weapons programs. To determine progress of the French nuclear weapons program, soil samples to be analyzed for radioactivity were collected surreptitiously near nuclear facilities at Pierrelatte and Marcoule. Attachés also took photos at ground level that CIA photo interpreters in Washington, DC, used to evaluate aerial images.[130]

French President Charles de Gaulle was irritated to learn that on 16 July 1965 a USAFE RF-101 Voodoo reconnaissance aircraft flew over the French atomic energy facility at Pierrelatte, north of Avignon. He considered the overflights to be a serious violation of French sovereignty. The facility produced the enriched uranium required to trigger an H-bomb. The initial response by USAFE to French complaints was to profess ignorance of why there were four flyovers. The next official response was that the overflights by the Voodoo, which took one-hundred seventy-five photos, were accidental.[131] The Pentagon claimed the aircraft may have been blown off course by high winds, although it was a clear, calm day. In response to formal protests by the French government on 19 July 1965, USAFE "cancelled" all photo reconnaissance flights in France. Aircraft would still fly standard low-level routes, but under orders not to expose any film. To the French, it appeared that the Americans could not get their story straight.[132, 133] Gen Jacob E. Smart, Deputy CINC, US European Command, told friends that he could have provided a more believable story.

Gathering physical intelligence was required primarily because the Soviet bloc nations were closed to outsiders; its citizens controlled by vast network of security forces and informants.[134] Therefore, when Soviet bloc aircraft landed at airports in France, attachés wearing clothing borrowed from French ground crews would approach the aircraft to take fuel samples from the sediment drain and cut off a small piece of a tire. The samples would help scientists at Wright-Patterson AFB in Ohio to determine the quality of products produced by Soviet manufacturers. Normally, collected information was sent to the Pentagon until 1961, when attaché offices reported to the newly organized Defense Intelligence Agency (DIA) at Arlington Hall Station in Arlington, Virginia. A month before he left office, Eisenhower's Joint Study Group recommended that all Department of Defense intelligence be integrated into a single DIA. Although the attachés worked for the Ambassador, they were under operational control of the DIA. However, ambassadors normally were asked if the nominee was acceptable before the attaché was assigned.

Spying efforts seem adventuresome in novels and movies, but in reality most sources were in the open: French-government pronouncements, newspaper and magazine articles, military journals, radio broadcasts, speeches by active and retired military officers, visits to military bases, and social contacts. Reading government reports and technical journals was necessary drudgery. In the spirit of reciprocity, French military attachés in the US were accorded visiting privileges to military bases.

US Air Force Defense Attachés

In fall 1956, Capt Joaquin A. Saavedra arrived in Paris to serve as air technical intelligence liaison officer in the US Air Force Defense Attaché office which occupied a secure floor at rue de la Boétie. Attachés normally moved into housing vacated by the officer they replaced. Most lived in US State Department owned residences in Neuilly-sur-Seine. Saavedra, his wife Margot, and their son Michael lived in a rented home at 21, ave des Sycomores near Bois de Boulogne. There were four technical liaison officers among the twelve Air Force officers in Paris. In 1956, all officers were designated Assistant Air Attachés so they could be issued diplomatic passports.

Air Force Attachés in Paris

Air Attaché	Period of Service	Air Attaché	Period of Service
Brig Gen Monro MacCloskey	1949-52	Col Frank B. Chappell	1959-62
Col Hollingsworth F. Gregory	1952-56	Col Vernon P. Martin	1962-66
Col Raleigh H. Macklin	1956-59	Col William B. Bailey	1966-70

Attachés were driven in black, four door sedans that did not have the conspicuous white star that was painted on the doors of SHAPE and EUCOM vehicles. For long trips they used a VC-47 Skytrain, normally parked at Orly AB. In November and December 1955, the French civilian control tower operators and radar personnel at Orly walked out on strike. Consequently, most US military air traffic was diverted to Évreux AB, 45 miles from SHAPE headquarters.[135] By the late 1950s, a fleet of Skytrains were maintained at Évreux AB by the 7317th Operations Squadron (CRT) for use by SHAPE and US Embassy personnel.

To prepare for the assignment, Saavedra, known as Bill to his classmates, attended training in Washington, DC. From 04 November 1955 to 31 August 1956, he completed a four-month attaché course run by the Army's Strategic Intelligence School and six-month French Language Course at the Institute of Languages and Linguistics, Georgetown University. The attaché course included instruction on intelligence tools such as a camera disguised as binoculars and the Leica camera and lenses that Saavedra would be issued to take hundreds of photos during the biannual Paris Air Show at le Bourget Airfield.[136] The photos, taken in 1957 and 1959, documented worldwide advances in aeronautical engineering, with emphasis on East bloc countries. Valuable photographic images were interior of cockpit, control panels, electronic gear, and propulsion system.[137] At the 12 to 21 June 1959 air show, the Russian Tupolev Tu-104, the world's first successful jet passenger airplane, was demonstrated in flight. The USAF Boeing V137 (military version of Boeing 707) was parked next to the Tu-104. The Tupolev Tu-114, a long range passenger airplane, was shown only parked on the ground (called "static display").[138] Saavedra's film was processed at the secure Photo Lab at Boétie.

Saavedra's reports on aircraft development and other intelligence information were sent contemporaneously to the Air Technical Intelligence Center (ATIC) at Wright-Patterson AFB, Dayton,

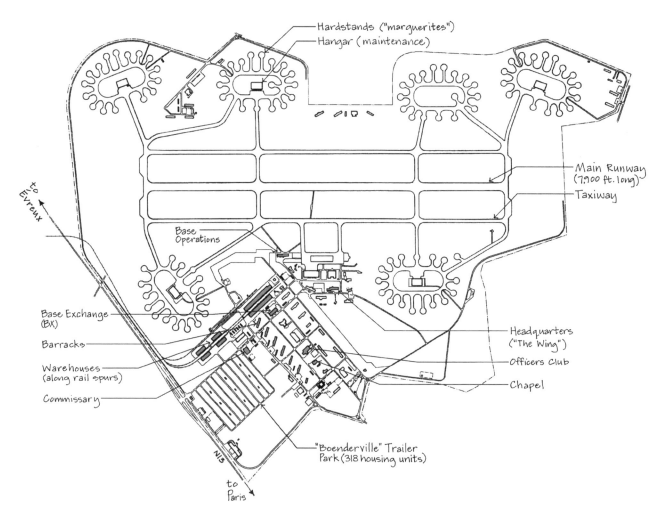

Évreux Air Base

Ohio, and to Headquarters, US Air Force at the Pentagon. The ATIC evaluated Soviet technology so the Air Force could counter Soviet developments. Saavedra also worked closely with AGARD (Advisory Group, Aeronautical Research and Development) at NATO headquarters, Palais de Chaillot in Paris. AGARD was the NATO organization that supported military aircraft development (speed, maneuverability, weapons accuracy) to offset the numerical superiority of Warsaw Pact forces. He coordinated meetings between leaders of the aircraft manufacturing industry in the US and their counterparts in France. Each Christmas he took advantage of the low prices at the small PX in the American Embassy to buy expensive whiskey at only $2.50 a bottle for gifts to his French contacts.

When his tour in Paris ended in summer 1960, Saavedra believed he had visited nearly every French aircraft manufacturer and French Air Force test facility.[139] Assistant Air Attachés monitored developments such as Breguet Aviation's short-takeoff and landing (STOL) aircraft that had its four propellers linked. If one engine failed, the other three engines could turn all four propellers. Visits to Melun-Villaroche Airfield were important because most of France's military prototype aircraft were tested there. In 1959, France acknowledged that its new Mirage IV, built by Dassault, flew 940 mph with a range of 2,000 miles. The Mirage IV was developed to deliver atomic bombs for France's emerging *force de frappe* (nuclear striking force).

The Defense Attaché (DATT)

In July 1965, Brig Gen Charles H. Hollis became the first Defense Attaché (DATT) in Paris who would supervise all the attachés. Previously there was wasteful duplication and coordination problems because the Army, Navy, and Air Force each managed their own intelligence programs.[140] It was considered highly desirable that an attaché be married (Maj Gen Vernon A. Walters would be an exception) and speak French (Clemson College graduate Hollis did not). According to Army Regulation 611-60, Army officers selected for attaché duty were to be at least a captain and proficient in French. He, his wife, and children should "present a good appearance and be free of embarrassing physical handicaps." Before leaving for France, officers and their wives normally attended language training in Washington, DC. The wife was to "possess essential social graces" because relationships with counterparts in the French military were deemed to be very important.[141] French citizens would see more of the officer's family than the officer, and therefore their impressions of American ways would be more influenced by the family's behavior.[142]

Defense attachés represented the United States at official functions and organized numerous world war memorial ceremonies on behalf of the US Ambassador. Each year, the DATT obtained permission from the French government for the US Army to conduct annual unit training exercises, use French Army firing ranges, and motor march over French roads. Permission also had to be obtained for airdrops at Normandy to commemorate D-Day on 06 June and for US military units (bands and honor guards) to visit the eleven American Military Cemeteries on Memorial Day. On 06 June 1951, Army Attaché Brig Gen Joseph J. O'Hare accompanied NATO Supreme Commander Gen Eisenhower to Omaha Beach. Ike and Mrs. Eisenhower laid a wreath at the grave of an unknown soldier in the American Military Cemetery which overlooks Omaha Beach. Ike also spoke at Bayeux and Ste.-Mére-Église, the site of airborne drops on D-Day. In his speech at Bayeux, Ike castigated the Soviet Union for the brutal treatment of its citizens and its aggression in Korea.[143]

Army and Defense Attachés in Paris

Army Attaché	Period of Service	Events
Brig Gen Joseph J. O'Hare	1948-53	Soviet takeover of Czechoslovakia. Korean War.
Brig Gen Frederick P. Munson	1953-56	Algerian War begins. Anglo-French Suez intervention.
Brig Gen Frank W. Moorman	1956-58	Hungarian Revolution. Lebanon Civil War.
Brig Gen Charles Coburn Smith, Jr	1958-61	Revolt of top French generals in Algeria. Berlin Wall erected.
Brig Gen Charles R. Bymroski	1961-64	Algerian War ends. Soviet missiles in Cuba.
Defense Attaché (DATT)	**Period of Service**	**Events**
Brig Gen Charles H. Hollis	1964-67	France withdraws from SHAPE. Operation FRELOC.
Maj Gen Vernon A. Walters	1967-72	Vietnam War peace negotiations in Paris. Secret meetings with Chinese to arrange President Nixon's visit to China.[144]

Memorial Day

In 1959, Memorial Day ceremonies started at 10 am in front of the American Cathedral, Paris. Inside the cathedral to honor war dead were Amory Houghton (US Ambassador to France), Gen Lauris Norstad (SACEUR), and Gen Cortlandt Van R. Schuyler (Chief of Staff, SHAPE). After services, the 76th Army Band from Orléans, led by WO Howard W. Vivian, and ComZ Honor Guard followed the French *Compagnie républicaine de sécurité* (CRS) band marching down ave George V and up the Champs Élysées to the Arc de Triomphe, where the US Ambassador laid a wreath on the tomb of the Unknown Soldier of France. At the Arc, the 76th Army Band played "La Marseillaise" and the CRS band played the "Star Spangled Banner." The next ceremony was held at Neuilly cemetery where American dead are buried under an American Legion Monument, followed by a ceremony at the American Military Cemetery in Suresnes. The final Memorial Day ceremony was held at the Lafayette Escadrille monument at Marnes-le-Coquette.[145]

Fourth of July

Each year on 04 July, America's Independence Day, a solemn ceremony is held in Paris at the grave of the Marquis de Lafayette in Cimetière de Picpus at 35, rue de Picpus. At the ceremony, the US Ambassador pays tribute to Lafayette, cites the enduring friendship between America and France, and replaces the American flag which flies above Lafayette's grave with a new one. During the Revolutionary War, Lafayette raised and led an army to help America gain its independence from Britain. In gratitude, the General Assembly of Maryland in 1784 granted US citizenship in perpetuity to Lafayette and all his male descendants. Its validity was upheld by New York State's highest court in 1933.

US Army troops at Arc de Triomphe, Paris, 04 July 1957 (US Army)

CHAPTER 5: *US European Command and Military Assistance*

US Army troops at George Washington Monument, Paris, 04 July 1957 (US Army)

US officers of general or flag rank attended the ceremony at Picpus with French officers of equivalent rank and other dignitaries. On 04 July 1955, the 76th Army Band and ComZ Honor Guard, commanded by Capt John T. Monaghan, also participated in ceremonies at the George Washington Monument, place d'Iéna, Paris. After wreaths were placed by French and US officials, the 76th Army Band, led by CWO Eugene D. Vacher, and a French Army band gave a concert at the monument.[146] In 1957, NATO Supreme Commander Gen Lauris Norstad and Gen Williston B. Palmer, Deputy CINC of USEUCOM attended the ceremony at Picpus. To celebrate the 200th Anniversary of Lafayette's birth, French President René Coty gave a speech and several descendents of Lafayette attended. The Honor Guard from ComZ Headquarters at Orléans, commanded by Capt James D. Currie, represented US military forces. According to Palmer, the platoon's lightweight summer uniforms, polished boots, and gleaming chrome helmets appeared sharp especially when contrasted with the French troops who were sweating in their dark wool uniforms. The temperature was 97°F.[147, 148]

The Cimetière de Picpus adjoins the mass grave of 1,300 French, many from noble families, guillotined during the last six months of the French Revolution. Their relatives purchased adjoining acres to build a convent, garden, and a cemetery so family members would be buried nearby. The grandmother, mother, and older sister of Lafayette's wife, Adrienne, were among the nobility who were executed. Adrienne requested burial at Picpus and Lafayette wanted to be buried next to her. Soil from Bunker Hill in Boston, Massachusetts, was brought to cover Lafayette's coffin.[149] The cemetery is still within the walls of the Convent of the Perpetual Adoration and two sisters of the Sacred Heart continuously kneel at the altar of the chapel, praying for the 1,300 souls. In the 1950s, it was difficult for the GIs to find the small cemetery behind the high stone walls and unmarked entrance door of the convent.[150] It still is.

VIP Visits

The attachés also escorted VIPs. During a Paris junket in 1964 by US Congressman Olin E. Teague of Texas, Army Capt Roswell E. Round, who spoke fluent French, was assigned to escort the VIP. The congressman only had two requests. He wanted to meet with President Charles de Gaulle and wanted to go to the top of the Eiffel Tower. The first request was easy to arrange but the second was not, because the observation platform was closed for security. During the courtesy call on de Gaulle the next day at the Élysée Palace, the French president asked the Texan if he was enjoying his stay in Paris. Teague emphatically answered no, because he always had wanted to go to the top of the Eiffel Tower. De Gaulle asked his translator, a French Army colonel, to explain and was told that French security had determined that a rocket could be aimed at de Gaulle's office from the tower. After a momentary pause, de Gaulle turned back to his translator and gave his instructions. "Open the tower, but observe all visitors. If anyone has a rocket, arrest him. You are also to take the congressman to the top after this meeting has concluded." [151]

Military Assistance to France

The Military Defense Assistance Program (MDAP), which followed the Marshall Plan in 1949, was designed to rebuild the military strength of Western Europe. It was organized by a small working group that included Maj Gen Lyman L. Lemnitzer who had returned to Washington, DC, from representing the Joint Chiefs of Staff at meetings of the Western Union.[152] Rearmament in Europe was slow, primarily due to a lack of precision machine tools. In France, row-upon-row of American-built trucks and tanks could not be used due to lack of spare parts and proper maintenance. The MDAP program would provide obsolescent US military equipment to the Allies and offer advice on training methods. The US, however, insisted that NATO allies have units ready to use the equipment and that maintenance and storage conditions would conform to US standards.[153-155] At the December 1955 ministerial meeting of the North Atlantic Council (NAC), the US announced that new weapons would be provided to NATO nations able to maintain and use them effectively. The assistance program would no longer just be a dumping ground for old US weapons.[156] As the economies of NATO nations recovered, the aid from the US shifted from grants to sales. From 1949 to 1963, the US provided more than $4.1 trillion in grants and sales of military equipment to France. This aid included 1,600 fighter aircraft, 100 cargo aircraft, 4,000 combat tanks, and 35,000 trucks.[157]

Military Assistance Advisory Groups (MAAG)

In 1949, the size of the military mission to oversee the transfer and use of US equipment provided to France had to be small. French officials worried that the communists would allege that America was acting as a conqueror if its officers roamed through Paris in uniform, occupying lavish quarters and eating at the best restaurants. Consequently, the US mission personnel wore civilian clothes. France also believed that its bilateral agreement on US aid, which restricted use of arms and military equipment, would be cited by the communists as evidence that France was in bondage to the US.[158] Military Assistance Advisory Groups (MAAG) in the NATO nations were assigned to EUCOM. The MAAG for France, located at 58, rue de la Boétie, was commanded by a US Army major general. His duties included attending numerous social functions where he was observed by politicians, private citizens, and molders of French public opinion. MAAG officers were expected to represent the United States with tact and dignity. Prior to assignment to Paris, officers and wives attended a four-week training course which included lectures on the history and culture of France. Because MAAG personnel operated as part of the US Embassy, they had the same privileges given diplomats of comparable rank.[159]

During the 1950s, about three dozen US officers and enlisted personnel were assigned to MAAG, France. France sent a *Groupe d'liaison du MAAG* to Boétie. The liaison group, headed by a French general, had ten members. From 1949 to 1953, France received one-half of the military aid to NATO. In return, France was expected to furnish most of the troops for the defense of Western Europe.[160] Initially, the French Army received combat vehicles, machine guns, and radio communications equipment that were scheduled to be replaced with newer models by the US Army. During the Algerian War, US Army officers from MAAG, France made periodic visits to Algeria to discretely verify that the US military equipment was not being used to fight the rebels.[161]

MAAG, France used the Villa Majestic at 34-36, rue La Pérouse in Paris for a low-profile liaison facility, where in 1952-54 aid to the French forces in Indochina was coordinated. From May 1950 to June 1954, US shipments to Indochina totaled about 1,800 combat vehicles, 362,000 rifles and machine guns, and 500 aircraft. In April 1954, Maj Gen Jacob E. Smart at US Far East Air Forces in Japan sent five-hundred cluster bombs to support France in the battle at Dien Bien Phu.[162]

The Military Assistance Program (MAP) succeeded the MDAP in 1951. The Mutual Weapons Development Program (MWDP), authorized by the US Congress in 1953, was part of MAP and had offices at the Talleyrand in Paris. The MWDP teams evaluated projects proposed by NATO member nations. Projects to develop new weapons were supported by substantial US funds. In theory, Pentagon resources would not be wasted on problems already solved by Allies.[163]

Chiefs of MAAG, France

Officer	Period	Officer	Period
Maj Gen George J. Richards	1950-53	Maj Gen C. Stanton Babcock	1957-59
Maj Gen Thomas E. de Shazo	1953-56	Maj Gen Philip C. Wehle	1959-62
Maj Gen Cornelius E. Ryan	1956-57	Maj Gen Herbert G. Sparrow	1962-64*

*Military assistance programs were terminated in France in 1964.

US Army Depot Support

Combat vehicles were rebuilt in France at US Army Ordnance depots at Braconne, Fontenet, and Nancy. From 1951 to 1955, more than 5,000 wheeled and tracked vehicles were processed at Fontenet Ordnance Depot for delivery to NATO.[164] At Braconne, GIs of the 601st Ordnance Battalion (Armament Rebuild) removed gun barrels and engines of M-47 Patton II and M-48 Patton III combat tanks. The engines were rebuilt and gun barrels were replaced if X-rays detected cracks. By 1958, the MAP program had provided eight-hundred fifty-six M-47 combat tanks to France.[165] US Army, Europe enrolled French military personnel in courses, funded by MAP, at the Seventh Army Tank Training Center in Germany and at supply and maintenance schools of the technical services such as the Ordnance School at Fuessen in the Bavarian Alps. In 1956, to improve the technical skills of the new German Army, experienced GIs were selected from Base Section in France to serve 4 to 5 months temporary duty in Germany teaching their specialties to German soldiers. Signal training included radar and VHF radio operations and maintenance; Quartermaster included storage and supply methods; and Ordnance included supply and maintenance of tracked combat vehicles, artillery, and small arms. In 1959, military and civilian personnel from six NATO nations attended 8-week courses on pipeline operations conducted by the Petroleum District Command at Fontainebleau. Military aid to France ended when France withdrew its military forces from NATO in 1966.[166-169]

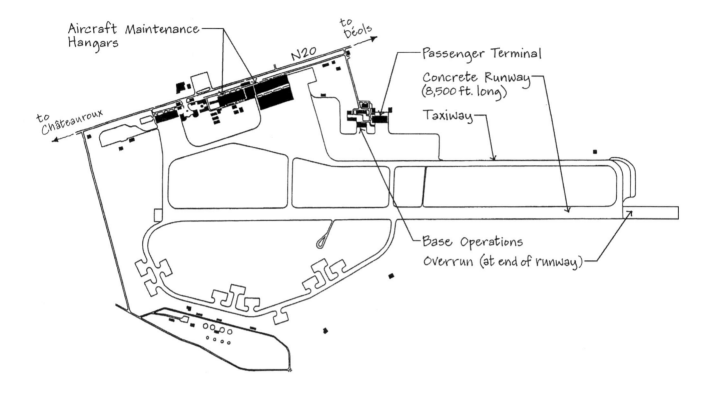

Châteauroux Air Depot at Déols (1956)

MDAP at Châteauroux

On 27 February 1951, US Ambassador David K. E. Bruce signed an agreement with France, called the Parodi-Bruce Agreement, to establish an air depot and maintenance facility at Châteauroux, France. The 73rd Air Depot Wing (ADW), commanded by Brig Gen Joseph H. Hicks, was deployed from Kelly AFB, San Antonio, Texas, to Châteauroux. Personnel of the 73rd ADW were Air Force reservists called to active duty during the Korean War. Hicks established his first headquarters at the Hôtel de France in downtown Châteauroux. By the end of August, more than 2,300 officers and airmen had arrived at Châteauroux (pronounced "Shatoo Rocks" by airmen). The local communist press claimed that Americans were "occupying" Châteauroux, crowding the narrow streets with their huge automobiles.[170] The 73rd ADW developed two installations, one at la Martinerie, 4 miles northeast of Châteauroux; the other at Déols, 3 miles north of Châteauroux and 5 miles west of la Martinerie. At la Martinerie, a huge depot complex for MDAP supplies was built on the 500-acre site of a former French Air Force base. It had a sod airstrip, fourteen small dilapidated hangars, ten warehouse buildings, and sufficient open acreage for new buildings. The depot at la Martinerie was officially dedicated on 29 March 1952. French General Maurice Challe attended the ceremonies. Challe became well-known in 1961 for his participation in a plot to overthrow President de Gaulle. At Déols, the former Société Nationale de Construction Aéronautique de Sud-Ouest (SNCASO) aircraft factory was renovated and used to overhaul aircraft, engines, and components required for NATO air forces. An 8,500 ft long concrete runway, completed in early 1953, replaced the sod runway at Déols.[171] In 1957, it was lengthened to 12,000 ft.

In 1952 at la Martinerie, Capt George N. Stokes briefed Marshal Josip Broz Tito, Prime Minister of Yugoslavia, on the supply system because Yugoslavia received military aid from the US. Yugoslavian F-84 jet pilots were trained at Chaumont AB. Although Yugoslavia was a communist country, Soviet Dictator Joseph Stalin had ejected it from the international communist movement in 1948.[172, 173]

Equipment and supplies were moved so rapidly to Châteauroux from Germany and the United States that many supplies had to be stored in the mud under tarpaulins. During the spring of 1951, airmen worked long days unloading supplies and equipment which had to be stacked on wooden pallets or pierced steel plank (PSP) to prevent its sinking in the mud. Offices had water buckets near doors so airmen could wash the mud off their boots. Low priority was given to precise inventory records. Because the Supply Division did not know where everything was stored at la Martinerie, it was difficult to fill some requests.[174]

US Air Force supplies under tarps, la Martinerie, 1953 (NARA)

Airmen lived in tents, dubbed "Mud City," until 1953 when metal prefabs were installed. Cooks used field-kitchen equipment to set up mess facilities in one of the old hangars. The layout of Quonset huts was called "Quontown." Eventually, three-story masonry buildings were built for airmen dormitories. Nine dormitories, each housing 200 airmen, and two mess halls were completed in 1954.[175, 176]

In 1952, Air Force personnel discovered that fifty-two French government-owned houses at Châteauneuf-sur-Cher had been abandoned. The structures built after World War II required extensive repairs. Numerous airmen wanted to live there because it was only 30 minutes from Déols, where only 43% of housing had running water and 22% had an indoor toilet. Because of the demand, the houses were renovated by the French *Intendant Militaire*. The Americans paid $58 rent. The French-style houses, called "The Project," had masonry walls and red tile roofs, although some of the front doors had round doorknobs. In the small front yards, surrounded by white picket fences, were children's red wagons. Large American cars were parked nearby.[177] The 73rd ADW leased the three-story Hôtel Sainte-Catherine in Châteauroux to use as family housing until the apartments at Touvent were completed in fall 1954.

By 1955, more than 28 acres of new warehouse space had been built at la Martinerie. Two-hundred cargo carts, propelled by motor-driven moving cables installed in concrete floor slabs, were used to move supplies in and out of storage. The cargo system was dubbed "Towveyer." During 1956-57, Maj Gen George F. Smith rode a bicycle to observe activities throughout the vast complex of warehouses for Central Air Materiel Area, Europe, which succeeded the 73rd ADW.[178]

"Towveyer" cable trench, la Martinerie, 1955 (NARA)

The 7300th Material Control Group had technical experts who advised the emerging air forces of NATO nations and personnel who monitored the use of MDAP and MAP funded aircraft and repair parts. The military assistance programs provided 4,789 jet aircraft to air forces of NATO nations. The total included two-hundred twenty-five Mystere IV-A fighter-bombers built at the Dassault aircraft factory at Mérignac, near Bordeaux. The US purchased the Mysteres from Dassault for the French Air Force at a cost of about $50 million.[179]

The number of French civilians employed at Châteauroux rapidly grew from six-hundred thirty in 1951 to more than 2,000 in 1953. The program to replace US officers and airmen with French workers was called Project Native Son. By 1959, more than 3,900 French were employed at Châteauroux and eight-hundred were employed by AEMCO-Bréguet (a joint American-French contracting firm) to work at Déols.[180, 181] AEMCO of Oakland, California, had devised a "moving" overhaul line which saved man-hours on inspect and repair as necessary (IRAN) contracts.

U.S. Go Home

One evening in 1953 at Châteauroux, a young Frenchman was trying to paint YANKE GO HOME! on a wall. A stranger stopped to lend a helping hand. He held the can of paint, pointed out that Yankee was spelled with two e's, offered a cigarette, and went on his way when the job was finished. Thirteen years later, the letters had faded but it was obvious that they had been painted with a trembling hand. In 1966, the Frenchman related his story to a journalist. His helper had been a huge US Air Force sergeant and the Frenchman did not understand why the American, "two heads taller than I," had helped him. The answer was obvious, the sergeant was only following orders. General Hicks had admonished his troops at Châteauroux AD to: "Do nothing that could displease the local population. Be friendly and helpful, do not contradict them in their opinions, and try to make yourself useful as often as possible. Do not forget that we are here as guests." [182]

By the late 1950s, the "U.S. Go Home" signs became less prevalent. Consequently in June 1959, Paris police were surprised to discover "U.S. Go Home" chalk-marked in large letters on fashionable apartment buildings in the Passy district near the Bois de Boulogne. The police erased the signs, gave statements to the French press that anti-American propaganda must stop, and finally captured the perpetrators. The slogans had been written by homesick, young Americans attending a school in Passy.[183]

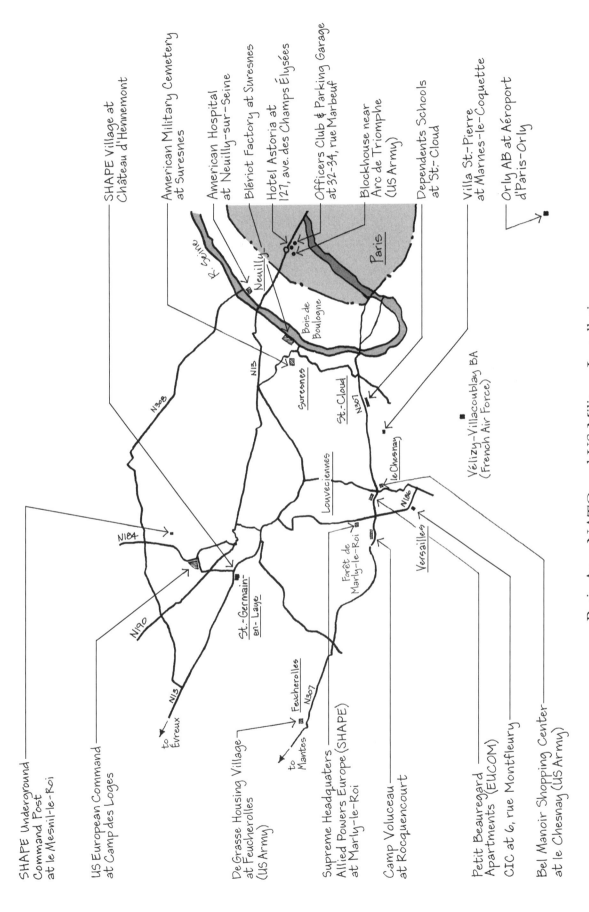

Paris Area NATO and US Military Installations

Paris Area NATO and US Military Installations

Installation	Location	Activity and Units
Headquarters	Marly-le-Roi (67 acres)	Supreme Headquarters Allied Powers Europe (SHAPE)
	St.-Germain-en-Laye (Camp des Loges, CDL, 131 acres)	US European Command (USEUCOM) Seine Area Command (SACCZ) LIVE OAK Planning Group
	Paris (Porte Dauphine)	US Representative to NATO Advisory Group, Aeronautical Research and Development (AGARD)
	Paris (58, rue de la Boétie)	Military Assistance Advisory Group, France (MAAG) Office of Military Attaché US Claims Office, France
	Paris (Hôtel de Talleyrand, 2, rue St.-Florentin)	Mutual Weapons Development Program (MWDP) Military Liquidation Section (MLS)
	Paris (7, rue Ancelle)	NATO Maintenance and Supply Agency (NAMSA)
	Paris (22, rue de la Trémoille)	USAFE Liaison Office
	Rueil-Malmaison (20, rue Gallieni)	HAWK Missile Liaison Office
	Versailles (11, rue du Général Pershing)	Central Europe Pipeline System (CEPS)
Support	Rocquencourt (Camp Voluceau, 45 acres)	SHAPE Support Group
	Aubervillers	SACCZ Ordnance Plant
	Boulogne-sur-Seine (94, rue Escudier)	Joint Construction Agency (JCA)
	Buc (near Versailles)	Motor pool
	Gennevillers (near St.-Denis)	European Exchange System (EES) Warehouse
	Orly (Aéroport d'Orly)	Armed Forces Courier Service
	Paris (82, ave Marceau and 3, rue de la Tasse)	SHAPE offices
	Paris (25, rue de Murille and 17, rue La Pérouse)	US Army offices
	Paris (US Embassy, 2, ave Gabriel)	Central Intelligence Agency (CIA) Paris Station, restaurant (open to US military personnel)
	Paris (Blockhouse, 27-29, rue La Pérouse)	Support Operations Task Force, Europe (SOTFE) USAREUR Paris office
	Paris (Villa Majestic, 34-36, rue La Pérouse)	US Army Liaison Office for MAAG
	Paris (53-55, rue François 1er)	USAFE office
	Paris (41, rue d'Alleray)	Main Post Office (USAFE)
	Paris (32-34, rue Marbeuf)	Counter Intelligence Corps (CIC) office, Finance office, AAFES snack bar and deli, medical clinic, and Officers Mess
	Paris (Hôtel Rothschild, 41, rue du Faubourg St.-Honoré)	General Accounting Office (GAO) US Information Services (USIS)
	Paris (15, rue Vernet)	ComZ Civilian Personnel Office

Support	Paris (7, rue Clement Marot)	ComZ Construction Office
	Paris (51, Blvd de LaTour-Maubourg)	Mission Centrale de Liaison Pour L'Assistance aux Armées Alliées (MCLAAA), French-American Fiscal Liaison Office (FAFLO), and European Communications Security Agency (ECSA)
	Paris (20, rue Quentin-Bouchart)	American Battle Monuments Commission (ABMC)
	Paris (9, rue Weber)	USAFE Office of Special Investigations (OSI)
	St.-André-de-l'Eure	US Army Aerial Support Center (USAASC)
	Suresnes (3, quai Gallieni)	Blériot Factory (6 acres), 514th Ord Co
	Versailles (6, rue Montfleury)	450th CIC Det (SHAPE Unit)
Welfare	Paris (53, rue François 1er)	US Armed Forces Visitors Bureau
	Paris (127, ave des Champs Élysées)	Allied Armed Forces Information Center
	Paris (129, ave des Champs Élysées)	American Library (USIS)
	Paris (93, ave des Champs Élysées)	USO Information Center
	Paris (Pershing Hall, 49, rue Pierre Charron)	American Legion Post (snack bar, currency exchange, barber shop)
	Paris (12, Blvd Haussmann)	Service Club
Communications	Paris (Blockhouse, 27-29, rue La Pérouse)	US Army Signal Communications Center
	Paris (72, ave Marceau)	USAREUR Communications Center
	Le Mesnil-le-Roi (Forêt de St.-Germain-en-Laye)	SHAPE Command Post (underground, called the "Nightclub")
Hospital/Medical Dispensaries	Neuilly-sur-Seine (63, Blvd Victor Hugo)	196th Station Hospital (200 beds)
	St.-Germain-en-Laye (CDL) and Paris (32-34, rue Marbeuf)	386th General Dispensary
Schools	Bougival (Marymount School)	Private international school (girls)
	Boulogne (45, Blvd d'Auteuil)	American Community School (private, grades 1 to 12)
	St.-Cloud (41, rue Pasteur)	Dependents elementary and high schools (18 acres)
	Paris (École Militaire, 21, Place Joffre)	NATO Defense College
	St.-Germain-en-Laye (Château d'Hennemont)	SHAPE International School (dependents)
General Officer Quarters	Marnes-la-Coquette (6 acres)	Villa St.-Pierre (NATO Supreme Commander) Villa La Chênaie (NATO Chief of Staff) Villa de Marnes (NATO Deputy Supreme Commander)
	Garches (68, rue du 19 Janvier)	Villa Valençay (DCINC, USEUCOM)
	St.-Germain-en-Laye (16, rue Jeanne d'Arc)	USEUCOM Chief of Staff
	Paris (25, rue Boissière)	Director, MAAG, France
	Paris (58, rue Singer; 2, ave de Ségur; and 179, rue de l'Université)	USEUCOM
	Chatou (8, rue de Sahune)	USEUCOM

General Officers Quarters	Boulogne-sur-Seine (7 bis, Blvd Anatol France)	USEUCOM
Bachelor Officers Quarters (BOQ)	St.-Germain-en-Laye (CDL)	Two-story building (34 men), Officers Mess
	Marly-le-Roi	SHAPE BOQ (32 rooms)
Housing (families)	le Chesnay (Petit Beauregard)	300 RGH units
	Feucherolles (DeGrasse Village)	78 SCH units (28 acres)
	St.-Germain-en-Laye (Château d'Hennemont)	303 apartments at SHAPE Village (55 acres)
	Grigny (near Orly Air Base)	136 GRI units (USAFE)
Troop Barracks	Rocquencourt (Camp Voluceau)	520th Military Police Company 16th MP Detachment (CI) 7th Signal Bn (Service) 22nd Transportation Co (Car)
	St.-Germain-en-Laye (CDL)	67th Military Police Company 106th Signal Group 246th Signal Company 275th Signal Company (Service) 594th Trans Group Det (Mov Con) 553rd Engineer Bn Detachment 386th General Dispensary 1141st Special Activities Squadron (USAFE) Det 7 Women's Army Corps (WAC) Det
	Suresnes (Blériot Factory)	552nd QM Co (Refrig) 175th Military Police Det
	Orly Air Base (750 acres)	7415th Air Base Group (USAFE) 18th Weather Squadron (MATS) 12th Air Postal Squadron Det
	Marly-le-Roi	WAC, WAVE, and WAF Dets 7th Signal Bn (Service) Headquarters Command Det
	Versailles (Caserne Limoges)	7th Signal Bn (Service) 520th Military Police Company
Post Exchange	le Chesnay (Château du Manoir de Bel Air)	Bel Manoir Shopping Center (18 acres) 76th Medical Det (Veterinary Food Inspection), nursery at Château
Recreation	Marly-le-Roi	Football and soccer fields, baseball diamond
	Rocquencourt (Camp Voluceau)	Gymnasium, two swimming pools
	St.-Germain-en-Laye (CDL)	Gymnasium, two swimming pools, tennis courts, skeet range
	Suresnes (Blériot Factory)	Gymnasium, bowling alley, EM Club

Transient Quarters	Paris (9, rue Littré)	Hôtel Littré (Paris Air Passenger Center and TDY billets)
	Paris (6, rue Blaise-Desgoffe)	Hôtel Victoria Palace (TDY billets)
	Paris (52, rue François 1er)	Hôtel Powers (TDY billets)
	Paris (25, ave Pierre 1er de Serbie)	Hôtel Pierre Premier de Serbie (USAFE VIPs)
	Paris (8, Blvd de la Madeleine)	Hôtel de Paris (US Army VIPs)
	Paris (28, ave d'Iéna)	Hôtel d'Iéna (EUCOM VIPs)
	Paris (15, Place Vendôme)	Hôtel Ritz (EUCOM VIPs)
	Paris (8, Place Saint-Augustin)	Cercle National des Armées (French)
	Paris (7, rue Clement Marot)	Hôtel West-End (EM billets)
	Paris (65, Quai d'Orsay)	American Church (cots for EM)
	Paris (37-39, ave Hoche)	Hôtel Royal Monceau (SHAPE VIPs)
	Paris (17, ave Kléber)	Hôtel Raphaël (SHAPE VIPs)
	Paris (16, rue de Berri)	Hôtel California (SHAPE VIPs)
	Versailles (1, Blvd Reine)	Hôtel Trianon Palace (SHAPE Distinguished Visitors)
Air Fields	Orly (Aéroport d'Orly)	7415th Air Base Group (USAFE)
	Évreux Air Base (USAFE)	7317th Operations Squadron (CRT)
	Villacoublay-Vélizy (Base Aérienne 107)	French Air Force control
Training Sites	St.-Germain-en-Laye (67 acres)	Bois d'Arcy (small arms weapons)
	Versailles (at Mail)	Stand de Tir (rifle range)
	Orly (Aéroport d'Orly) and Évreux Air Base	Aircraft available to USAF officers to maintain flying proficiency
Newspapers	Camp des Loges	Command Summary
	Orly	Orly Diplomat, Orly Oracle
	Paris	The Pariscope

Abbreviations

AAFES	Army and Air Force Exchange Service (1964 merger of AFEX and EES)	RGH	Rental Guarantee Housing (US Army)
		SCH	Surplus Commodity Housing (US Army)
AFEX	Air Forces Europe Exchange	TDY	Temporary duty
CDL	Camp des Loges	USAFE	US Air Forces in Europe
CI	Criminal Investigation	USAREUR	US Army, Europe
ComZ, CZ	Communications Zone	USEUCOM	US European Command
CRT	Combat Readiness Training (USAFE)	USO	United Service Organizations
DCINC	Deputy Commander-in-Chief	WAC	Women's Army Corps
EES	European Exchange System (US Army)	WAF	Women in the Air Force
GRI	Guaranteed Rental Income (USAFE)	WAVE	Women Accepted for Volunteer Emergency Service (US Navy)
MATS	Military Air Transport Service		
Mov Con	Movement Control		

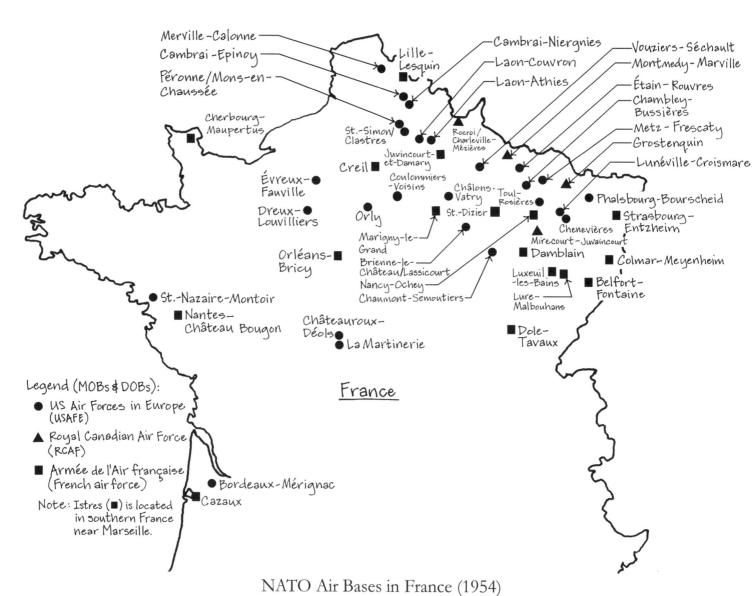

NATO Air Bases in France (1954)

Allied Air Forces Central Europe (AAFCE) Headquarters, Camp Guynemer, Avon, 1958 (SHAPE)

SIX

NATO and US Military in Fontainebleau

"Aerial dogfights were necessary' to keep NATO's air forces from 'getting fat and useless."
(Air Chief Marshal Sir Basil Embry, Fontainebleau, 31 July 1953)

Allied Air Forces Headquarters

On 02 April 1951, US Air Forces in Europe (USAFE) assumed NATO responsibilities. The USAFE Commander, Lt Gen Lauris Norstad, also became Commander-in-Chief, Allied Air Forces Central Europe (AAFCE). During World War II, Norstad had served as Ike's director of plans and operations and was a close friend. AAFCE initially consisted of US Twelfth Air Force, the British Air Force of Occupation, and the 1st French Air Division. On 07 June 1951, the air commanders of forces from US, Great Britain, France, and Canada met in Paris to plan the air power needed to defend Europe, agreeing to collectively provide more than 9,000 aircraft by 1955.[1] In time of war, the role of AAFCE air forces, together with NATO ground forces, was to hold Soviet invaders as far east of the Rhine River as possible. Then, if needed, the US Air Force Strategic Air Command (SAC) long-range bombers based in the US, England, and North Africa would drop atomic bombs on key Soviet targets. By the early 1950s, fighter-bombers based in Europe also could drop atomic bombs on Soviet targets.[2,3] In a December 1952 report to new NATO Supreme Commander Gen Matthew B. Ridgway, Norstad reiterated that only atomic bombs could offset the Soviet's superior number of land and air forces.[4] AAFCE's first large-scale air exercise in April 1951 involved 500 aircraft operating from ten airfields. In the air exercise in June 1952, there were 1,400 aircraft from forty-five air bases.[5]

Temporary Headquarters

In May 1951, temporary headquarters for AAFCE was established in leased rooms at the Hôtel Cadran Bleu at 9, rue Grande in Fontainebleau. Headquarters soon moved down the street to the Henri IV wing of the 500-year-old château which 5th Infantry Div of Lt Gen George S. Patton's Third Army had liberated on 23 August 1944.[6] From 26 February until 09 August 1945, administrative offices of a US Army Ground Force Training Center, commanded by Col Harold E. Potter, and an Adjutant General School used thirty-two rooms in the Louis XV wing of the château. Classrooms were at the Lycée Carnot. The last class of officers graduated on 14 July 1945. Officer instructors were housed across the street from the château at the Hôtel Aigle Noir; enlisted men in the Princes wing of the château; and WACs at a residence expropriated from a German collaborator. From 01 October until 31 December 1945, the US Army used the same facilities for Infantry Basic Training and Administration (clerk-typists, stenographers, file clerks) schools. More than 9,000 officers and enlisted men from the US, France, and Luxembourg attended the center and schools.[7]

Camp Guynemer

In July 1952, Norstad was promoted to four-star general and his AAFCE headquarters moved from the château to a complex of two-story buildings hastily built on 100 acres of the Avon forest. Instigated by the French communists in 1951, several citizens of Fontainebleau wrote to the French government to protest the loss of forest land in Avon. The forty buildings, which cost $10 million to build, were designed to accommodate 2,000 military and civilian personnel.[8] During dedication ceremonies, which included remarks by French Minister of Defense René Pleven, twenty-one jet aircraft flew overhead, rattling windows. The complex was named Camp Guynemer in honor of Capitaine Georges Guynemer, the famous French aviator from World War I who shot down fifty-four German planes and survived being shot down seven times.[9] In December 1952, AAFCE set up a weather forecasting service in cooperation with the French meteorological service to give pilots advance warning of storms. In 1959, radar with a range of 300 miles, which covered most of northern France, was installed at Châteauroux.[10] The military police contingent at Camp Guynemer was staffed by personnel from air forces of seven nations. English and French were the official languages. MPs served as gate guards and checked identity cards at the SHAPE Shop. Routine work included registration of vehicles, traffic control duties, and crowd control at events for VIPs. Discipline at headquarters was not a problem so the holding cells at Guynemer were used for storage.[11] Norstad's Chief of Staff was French Général de Corps Aerien Pierre J. Fay, Deputy Chief of Staff for Operations was British Air Vice Marshal Thomas G. Pike, and Deputy Chief of Staff for Administration was USAF Brig Gen William T. Thurman.

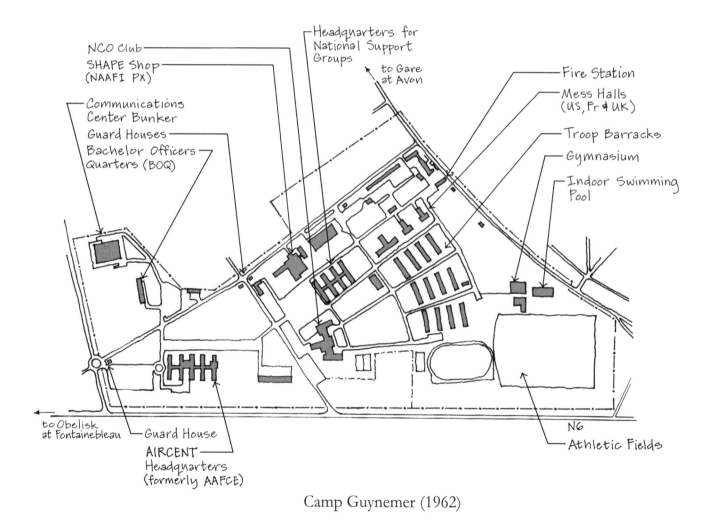

Camp Guynemer (1962)

Training Exercises

The original four air forces of AAFCE were joined by Belgium, Luxembourg, and the Netherlands. Personnel from all seven nations were intermingled, from guards at the front gate to senior officers. To merge the tactical air forces (meaning no large bombers) of the seven nations, Norstad worked to standardize equipment, build infrastructure (air bases, pipelines, radar warning sites), and improve communications networks. Each week, some type of exercise was held to test the multi-national staff and diverse air forces under his command.[12] AAFCE held several exercises each year, dubbed CO-OP. Aircraft from 2nd and 4th Allied Tactical Air Forces (ATAF) participated by flying sorties to test early warning and missile defense systems of NATO. In the late 1950s, AAFCE was changed to the easier to pronounce AIRCENT.

In August 1953, Norstad moved to Marly-le-Roi to become NATO Supreme Commander Gen Gruenther's Air Deputy at SHAPE. Norstad would control all Allied air power in Europe and co-ordinate these forces with "external" forces such as SAC nuclear bombers of Gen Curtis E. LeMay, British Bomber Command, and US Navy air power from aircraft carriers. SAC alert bombers were deployed on a rotational basis to air bases in England and North Africa. Air Chief Marshal Sir Basil Embry from Great Britain replaced Norstad as Commander-in-Chief of AAFCE.[13]

Operation GRAND SLAM

From 27 February to 05 March 1952, nineteen B-26 Invaders and one C-47 Skytrain aircraft from the 126th Bombardment Wing (Light) at Bordeaux AB were deployed to the French Air Force base at Istres near Marseille to support NATOs air exercise, Operation GRAND SLAM. The 126th Wing was the aggressor force that simulated aerial attacks on aircraft carriers to test the defenses of the NATO Mediterranean Fleet. Two thirds of the two-hundred fifty-two sorties, flown by the crews of the 126th under radio silence, were successful. US Navy aircraft carriers, USS *Midway* and USS *Tarawa*, and a French aircraft carrier were attacked. The B-26s, originally developed as attack bombers during World War II, made simulated bombing runs over the ships. Although the bomb bays were empty, one B-26 accidentally dropped a clothing bag on a ship. Caught by surprise, the carriers did not resist, but in retaliation launched four F4U Corsair fighter aircraft to chase the B-26s. These exercises were important because the US Navy believed that control of the Mediterranean was essential for NATO.[14] The only US Navy installation in France at Villefranche-sur-Mer, near Nice, was homeport for the flagship cruiser of the Sixth Fleet. NATO controlled choke points into the Mediterranean Sea at Gibraltar and at the Turkish Straits.[15]

Exercise CORONET

During NATO Exercise CORONET held 22 to 31 July 1953, the 4th Allied Tactical Air Force (units of US, France, and Canada) fought a simulated air war against 2nd ATAF (units of the Netherlands, Belgium, and Great Britain). The exercise over central Europe simulated hostilities between imaginary countries (US was "Fantasia"). Pilots of the 48th Fighter-Bomber Wing at Chaumont AB flew six-hundred thirty sorties. The two sides took turns "attacking" each other's airfields, often pitting entire squadrons of jet aircraft in dangerous dogfights (aerial combat maneuvers). Seven NATO airmen were killed and several planes crashed. British Air Chief Marshal Sir Basil Embry, Norstad's successor at AAFCE, supervised the exercise, which he believed was necessary to keep NATO air forces from "getting fat and useless."[16]

Exercise CARTE BLANCHE

NATO Exercise CARTE BLANCHE in June 1955 simulated dropping more than three-hundred atomic bombs on military targets in northeastern France, West Germany, and Benelux countries. More than 3,000 aircraft, training under simulated atomic war conditions, participated in the exercise. NATO air forces were divided into two opposing forces. The exercise was designed to test dispersal concepts, aerial combat, and electronic countermeasures. Two squadrons of the 48th Fighter-Bomber Wing were dispersed: one to Brienne-le-Château and one to Vouziers-Séchault. At the end of the exercise, each side claimed more kills than its opponent had aircraft. During the exercise, USAFE air traffic controllers could not identify 42% of the aircraft flying in the zone of responsibility of US Army's 34th Antiaircraft Artillery Brigade.[17] SHAPE war planners believed that 1.7 million civilians would be killed and another 3.5 million injured had real weapons been used. Rather than assure Europeans that NATO had the capacity to repel a Soviet invasion, the press reports on CARTE BLANCHE frightened most Europeans.[18]

Training in North Africa

Because thick clouds, heavy rains, and frequent fog made flying difficult in France, pilots also trained at bases in North Africa where the weather usually was sunny. During winter months, the Suippes Gunnery Range near Reims rarely was used. Every ninety days, pilots spent two weeks in French Morocco or Libya where training included firing live ammo and rockets. They practiced shooting at fixed targets on the ground and at towed targets in the air over the Mediterranean Sea near Libya. Occasionally the towing aircraft was hit by gunfire. USAFE fighter-bomber squadrons rotated twice a year to Wheelus Air Base, Libya.

F-86 Sabre jet aircraft flyby, Chambley AB, 1956
(A. L. Christensen)

F-86 Sabre jet aircraft, Chaumont AB, 1955
(US Air Force Academy)

Toss Bombing

Pilots of F-84 Thunderstreak and F-100 Super Sabre aircraft practiced tossing dummy bombs upward during low altitude bombing so they would gain time to escape a nuclear explosion in wartime. The T-63 concrete-filled dummy bomb had the same weight, size, and shape as the Mk-7 atomic bomb. Low altitude bombing tactics were devised so pilots would fly below Soviet radar and toss the bomb forward or climb abruptly over the target tossing the bomb upward. The roll and downward loop escape maneuver was nicknamed "the idiot loop" because pilots did not believe it would work.[19] Weather permitting, toss bombing was practiced at Suippes.[20]

According to NATO war plans, the arming system for the Mk-7 was to be set so the bomb would explode in the air above targets in Poland, East Germany, and the other Warsaw Pact Nations. Romania was not targeted after 1963. Ground bursts, which would produce greater nuclear radiation fallout, were only to be used on targets within the Soviet Union.[21] In spite of these orders, most pilots agreed among themselves that they would use ground bursts on all targets to give themselves additional time to escape before the blast.

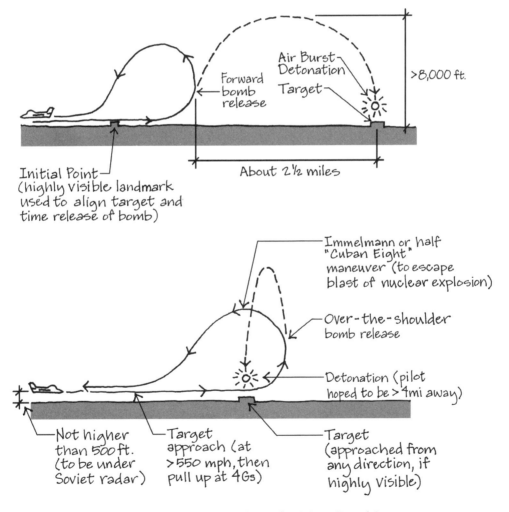

Forward and Over-the-Shoulder Toss Bombing

Aerial photo of Chaumont Viaduct taken by 106th Tactical Reconnaissance Squadron, 1962 (US Air Force)

Exercise ROYAL FLUSH

Beginning in 1956, reconnaissance teams from the two allied tactical air forces of AAFCE competed in NATO Exercise ROYAL FLUSH. Each year the 5-day exercise tested reconnaissance capabilities from high-altitude flights. Competing teams flew short, medium, and long-range day sorties and, beginning in 1960, night sorties. The score for a ground and air crew team was based on rapid and accurate gathering of photographic images, processing of film, and photo interpretation. In 1962, the American team from Toul-Rosières AB (TRAB) flew RB-66 Destroyers for night sorties; the team from Laon AB flew RF-101 Voodoos for long-range day sorties.[22] From 1959-65, the 10th TRW at RAF Alconbury (UK) deployed Detachment 1 of twenty-four B-66 Destroyer aircraft to TRAB. On 10 March 1964, a Soviet MiG-19 shot down an RB-66C from TRAB flying 30 miles inside East Germany. The reconnaissance aircraft was en route to the site of a Soviet air-defense exercise. The crew of three parachuted to earth, were captured, and held prisoners by the East Germans for three weeks. USAFE declared that the overflight was due to a faulty compass.

Guynemer Trophy Competition

Beginning in the mid-1950s, teams of pilots from the NATO nations each year competed in live fire at targets and dogfights at the Atlantic Ocean gunnery range of the French Air Force base at Cazaux near Bordeaux. In the early 1950s, US Army SCARWAF engineers had repaired the war-damaged runway and built hardstands at Cazaux. Pilots fired live rounds at a 6-ft by 30-ft wire-mesh target towed on a 1,200-ft long cable by a T-33 T-Bird jet aircraft. Scores were based on numbers of holes in the mesh. Victory in simulated combat between jet aircraft was based on film recorded by gun-cameras. The winning team received the Guynemer Trophy. Canadian teams won the trophy from 1958 to 1960. According to RCAF veterans of France, new rules in 1961 may have awarded points for "high and tight" haircuts and polished boots, thereby unfairly penalizing Canadian pilots.[23, 24]

Canadian Deployment to France

Canadian air wings were deployed to RCAF Station Grostenquin, near Metz and RCAF Station Marville, near Verdun. RCAF Headquarters were at Château du Mercy near Ars-Laquenexy, southeast of Metz. The Canadian combat operations center was in a concrete World War I-era bunker at Ars-

Laquenexy. In September 1952, the RCAF No. Two Fighter Wing was rushed to Grostenquin (GT) so their Canadian-built Sabre jets would help NATO counter the threat posed by the Soviet bloc's high performance MiG-15s.[25] For Canadian airmen, their first winter at GT in Lorraine was miserable: insufficient heat, no water for bathing, no sun just constant rain, cold, and lots of mud. Canadians believed the English translation for Grostenquin should be big swamp and their catch phrase was: "Someday we'll laugh about this." Many airmen called GT "Gross Tin Can." The US Army supplied food in the early days at Grostenquin because mess facilities had not been built. Canadians suspected that the American mess sergeant who unloaded the most lima beans on the Canadians would receive a promotion. USAFE billed the Canadian government for these Army food services.[26, 27]

In June 1955, RCAF No. One Fighter Wing arrived at Station Marville. Married airmen lived in 4-story apartment buildings built at Longuyon (for Marville) and at Wenheck in St.-Avold (for Grostenquin).[28] Off-base housing villages were designated PMQs (Permanent Married Quarters). In Canada, children and aviation enthusiasts followed the comic strip adventures of Dan Cooper, heroic fighter pilot of 441st Squadron ("Stalk and Kill") of RCAF No. One Fighter Wing.[29]

Canadian fighter pilots often attacked US Air Force fighter jets on routine flight operations from air bases in France. Any allied aircraft was fair game to the Canadians who wanted to sharpen their aerial combat skills in case of attack by Soviet MiGs. Aerial combat tactics, unchanged since World War I, were to get as high as possible with the sun at your back, then swoop down on an unsuspecting target before he was aware of your presence. Because they could not shoot down an ally, the Canadians just recorded the kill on gun-camera film.[30]

Survival, Escape, and Evasion Exercises

In a US Air Force escape and evasion exercise in mid-1954, flight crews from the 38th Bombardment Wing at Laon AB were trucked to locations fifty miles from Laon. Because the French Army, Gendarmerie Nationale, and local villagers were alerted to capture *les américains*, nearly everyone hiking back to the base was captured. Local rat-infested jails became overloaded. After three days, all prisoners had been transferred to equally squalid conditions in the French prison at Laon. American survival experts from the US simulated enemy interrogations, using physical and psychological methods to break the will of prisoners to resist. The exercise ended when one overcrowded cellblock attacked their guards and led a breakout. The escaped prisoners ran around like madmen to free the other prisoners. Real bullets were fired over the heads of the escapees. As he scaled the prison roof, Maj James Farrell of the 822nd Squadron, heard an air policeman shout to the armed French guards, "Shoot em, Shoot em!" During the exercise, an Air Force officer died from a heart attack.[31]

Every six months, pilots from the fighter-bomber wings at Chambley, Chaumont, and Toul-Rosières ABs practiced water survival in the large indoor swimming pool at RCAF Station Grostenquin. USAFE did not authorize construction of indoor swimming pools at any air base in France. At Grostenquin, pilots learned how to wear waterproof, anti-exposure suits (nicknamed "poopy suits" because there were no provisions to eliminate body waste) and getting into an air-inflated raft. To survive the frigid North Atlantic Ocean, it was essential to quickly get into a raft.[32]

Nuclear Quick Reaction Alerts

In October 1958, in response to the Eisenhower administration's drive for economy, selected USAFE wings kept twelve aircraft on nuclear quick reaction alert status (called "Victor Alert"). Victor Alert (VA) meant that nuclear weapons were attached to the aircraft and pilots were quartered nearby so aircraft could be launched within 15 minutes from the moment orders were received.[33] Maintaining dispersed operating bases was costly, but VA was a relatively inexpensive way to have a near immediate reaction to a Soviet attack. Pilots, nicknamed "Victor Dogs," and ground crews served 72-hour alert periods on base, most waiting in an alert shack. The base dining hall, many of which were open 24 hours, delivered meals to the VA personnel. Some pilots stayed at their aircraft which were fueled, armed, and connected to power carts. These planes could be streaking toward their targets in the Soviet Union within 3 minutes. The exercises looked like an athletic contest with sirens blaring to signal a race by foot and jeep toward nuclear-armed aircraft ready for takeoff.[34] VA pilots wore a black patch over one eye to shield it from the blinding flash of a nuclear explosion (called "flashblindness"). However, the patch made it difficult for pilots to read the target folder while flying the aircraft.[35] Unbeknownst to VA pilots, early nuclear war plans did not coordinate VA targets with SAC targets. Consequently, they risked tossing a nuclear bomb at the same target at the same time a SAC bomber dropped its nuclear bomb, blowing both aircraft out of the sky. A plan to coordinate targets, designated the Single Integrated Operational Plan (SIOP), was completed in late 1960. Ordered by the Eisenhower administration, SIOP was America's first integrated nuclear war plan.[36]

Operation RED RICHARD

In April 1959, the French government asked the US to withdraw its atomic-capable tactical fighter wings (TFW) from air bases at Chaumont, Étain, and Toul-Rosières, and to remove USAFE nuclear weapons, euphemistically called "special deliveries." [37, 38] Official US policy was not to acknowledge the presence of nuclear weapons in France. Therefore, during Operation RED RICHARD, the USAFE removed weapons that officially were not there. The 50th TFW's emblem had an atomic mushroom cloud in the background.

While on guard duty in July 1959 at Toul-Rosières AB, Airman Second Class Orlandus Bell reported an intruder near the hangar of 417th Tactical Fighter Squadron. The intruder darted into the woods, ignoring the standard commands of "Halt" and "Advance to be recognized!" Around midnight, the base provost marshal, Capt John E. Stacey roused the air police (AP) for a manhunt. Searching the base, APs saw a fleeing shadow. The intruder darted toward the perimeter fence and cleared the fence on the second leap. It was believed to be the first deer sighted on the base.[39]

Beginning on 10 July 1959, more than 5,300 military personnel and two-hundred twenty-five F-100D Super Sabre aircraft from three TFWs were moved to bases in Germany and Great Britain at a cost of more than $11 million. More than one-thousand French civilians lost their jobs.[40, 41]

Organization*	Location in France	Redeployed Location
48th TFW	Chaumont AB	RAF Lakenheath (UK)
49th TFW	Étain AB	Spangdahlem AB (Germany)
50th TFW	Toul-Rosières AB	Hahn AB (Germany)

*On 08 July 1958, the Fighter-Bomber Wing (FBW) designation changed to Tactical Fighter Wing (TFW).

The British government authorized USAFE to control all air operations at RAF Lakenheath, but a British station commander was nominally in charge of the former SAC base. The 48th TFW completed its relocation to Lakenheath on 15 January 1960. In France, Chaumont, Étain, and Toul-Rosières ABs were placed on standby status. Each base was to be maintained by a small contingent of Air Force personnel and French employees. The USAFE designated the evacuated bases as "standby operating bases." Due to its acronym SOB, the designation did not last long.

Exercise SPEAR HEAD

In November 1959, the Tactical Air Command's 19th Air Force, headquartered at Seymour Johnson AFB, North Carolina, deployed one-hundred aircraft to France. The training exercise, called SPEAR HEAD, was initiated without advance warning from the Pentagon. Within 24 hours, the command element had set up at Chaumont AB. F-100 Super Sabres were sent from three bases in the US (including Myrtle Beach AFB, South Carolina) to Chaumont AB, RF-101 Voodoos were sent from Shaw AFB, South Carolina, to Laon AB. C-130 Hercules cargo aircraft and KB-50J aerial tankers also were deployed. Military Air Transport Service (MATS) provided additional cargo aircraft support. In France, the fighters and reconnaissance aircraft participated in mock air strikes. The exercise, lasting one week, demonstrated the capability of the Air Force to respond rapidly to an emergency in Europe.[42]

F-100D Super Sabre, Chaumont AB, May 1957
(A. L. Christensen)

Operation BIG LIFT

The purpose of Operation BIG LIFT was to demonstrate US Secretary of Defense Robert S. McNamara's desire to reduce US forces in Europe without reducing NATOs strength to respond to crises.[43] From 22 to 24 October 1963, in just over 63 hours, the US Air Force airlifted personnel of the entire 2nd Armored Division from Fort Hood, Texas to two air bases in France and three in Germany. On land, the 16,000 troops used weapons and equipment left behind in Europe from the buildup for the Berlin Wall Crisis in 1961. Three months before the exercise, USAREUR ordnance troops began inspecting and correcting deficiencies in the vehicles the division used in Europe. Without pre-positioned equipment, the lift would have taken months not hours.[44, 45] After the troops were "married-up" to M-48 Patton combat tanks, M-113 armored personnel carriers, and self-propelled guns, the 2nd Armored Division joined NATO forces in Germany for maneuvers conducted by French General Pierre-Élie Jacquot, AFCENT commander from Fontainebleau. Four squadrons of tactical fighter and reconnaissance aircraft also deployed to France: F-100 Super Sabres to Phalsbourg AB and Étain AB, F-105 Thunderchiefs to Chaumont AB, and RB-66 Destroyers to Toul-Rosières AB. BIG LIFT, costing over $20 million, was the largest transatlantic deployment ever made by air.[46]

Many European leaders believed McNamara's BIG LIFT was a signal for American withdrawal. They believed the peace in Europe depended on a commitment of US ground forces integrated with NATO armies to deter a Soviet attack, not US troops based 5,600 miles away at Fort Hood, Texas.[47] It would take one-hundred forty sorties just to airlift troops of one division from the US to France. In a war, the Soviets would have attacked the air and sea deployments of troops to Europe and Soviet special forces would have sabotaged French ports.[48] The conversion from a doctrine of massive nuclear retaliation to reliance on conventional military forces also was seen by Europeans to be a prelude to disengagement by the US. In 1963, McNamara closed most of the installations in Base Section.

Commanders, US Air Forces in Europe (USAFE), 1947-1968[49]

Commander	Period of Service	Prominent Events
Lt Gen Curtis E. LeMay	Oct 47-Oct 48	Berlin Airlift begins (June 48).
Lt Gen John K. Cannon	Oct 48-Jan 51	Berlin Airlift ends (Sep 49). Korean War begins (June 50).
GEN Lauris Norstad	Jan 51-July 53	USAFE assumes NATO duties (Apr 51). Aircrews sent TDY from France to Korea (1952).
Lt Gen William H. Tunner	July 53-June 57	NATO air base construction completed in France. Dual-based squadrons (US and France at Chaumont AB and Évreux AB). Airlift of Hungarian refugees (Op SAFE HAVEN).
GEN Frank F. Everest	July 57-July 59	Berlin Crisis (Khrushchev threatens Allies). Victor Alerts begin (Oct 58).
GEN Frederic H. Smith, Jr.	Aug 59-June 61	Operation RED RICHARD completed.
GEN Truman H. Landon	July 61-July 63	Berlin Wall Crisis. Operation STAIR STEP (Fall 61). Cuban Missile Crisis (Oct 62).
GEN Gabriel P. Disosway	Aug 63-July 65	McNamara Drawdown begins. Operation BIG LIFT (Oct 63).
GEN Bruce K. Holloway	Aug 65-July 66	Dual-based squadrons (US and France at Étain AB and Toul-Rosières AB). Operation FRELOC begins (Mar 66).
GEN Maurice A. Preston	Aug 66-July 68	Withdrawal from France declared complete (01 Apr 67).

Communications Center

An underground Communications Center was built at Camp Guynemer to house signal equipment. GIs described it as a "dark windowless hole in the ground." At ground level the facility had a large, single-story building and the perimeter of the site was enclosed by a thick 12-ft high concrete, ribbed-panel wall. Entry to the site was guarded by military police. The underground bunker had space for seventy-five teleprinters, microwave terminals, and maintenance shops. French engineers installed modern signal equipment, costing $9 million, designed to control a network of radar, radio, and telecommunications for Allied fighter wings. The transmitter site was on a hill at Vernou-la-Celle, 8 miles east of Fontainebleau. In the 1960s, personnel from the 2172nd Communications Squadron at Évreux AB operated the long-line switching center at Vernou. During training exercises in Europe and North Africa, the network linked fighter wings based in six NATO nations and US Air Force Strategic Air Command (SAC) bombers from the US. Radar along the Soviet border monitored hostile aircraft.[50]

In 1955, the US Air Force built sixteen radio-relay sites to link Camp Guynemer with its two major subordinate commands, the 2nd Allied Tactical Air Force and 4th Allied Tactical Air Force. The sites were staffed by airmen from several NATO nations.[51] Sites were located on high ground about 30 miles apart. Antenna towers were 80-ft high and had small parabolic antennas and flat, rectangular-shaped reflector antennas, called "fly swatters." Each site had an emergency diesel generator to supply electricity twenty-four hours a day, seven days a week.[52]

During the Cuban Missile Crisis in October 1962, anxious British personnel in the Communications Center at Guynemer hacked into signal transmissions of the Associated Press, Tass (Soviet Union), and other news services. The Britishers feared the US and Soviets were close to nuclear war. To keep informed, they read what the US and Soviet adversaries were telling their citizens. They illicitly collected so many transmissions that the detachment nearly ran out of paper.[53] At Camp des Loges, NCOs were issued flares and 5-gal jerry cans of gasoline. In the event of wartime evacuation, NCOs were to pour bags of concrete mix into toilets and set buildings on fire.[54]

Recreation at Guynemer

In 1954, work began on a 10-acre sports complex at Guynemer to be used by personnel from the seven nations of AAFCE. Huge granite boulders were shattered by dynamite before the ground was cleared and leveled. A large stadium, fields for several sports, roads, and parking areas were built. Personnel of the 553rd Engineer Battalion from Orléans operated the heavy construction equipment. It took two years to complete the complex. A gymnasium and large indoor swimming pool, which could be used by dependents, also were constructed.[55, 56] The swimming pool, which cost $150,000 to build, opened in August 1959. After the US Army gave medical approval in 1958, US military personnel also could use the Fontainebleau municipal swimming pool. An eighteen-hole miniature golf course was built near the NCO Club. On Friday evenings in winter months, the theater at Guynemer was used for Bingo. After Allied forces departed from France in 1967, *École Interarmées des Sports* (EIS) occupied Guynemer, consolidating military schools from Joinville and Antibes.[57]

Main gate, Cour Henri IV, Château de Fontainebleau (AFCENT)

Allied Land Forces Headquarters

The mission of central European land forces of NATO, designated Allied Forces Central Europe (AFCENT), was to defend Europe between Switzerland and the Baltic Sea. Headquarters were set up in the Henri IV and Princes wings of the château in Fontainebleau. From April 1951 until May 1952, Gen Eisenhower controlled all NATO forces in Central Europe. Under Ike, French Gen Alphonse-Pierre Juin controlled the land forces and US Gen Norstad the air forces. Until 1966, when France withdrew from the integrated NATO commands, the top general officer at AFCENT was French. In mid-July 1953, Juin assumed responsibility for combat readiness, logistics arrangements, and training of all Allied land, air, and sea forces in the central sector of Europe. Juin had graduated at the top of his 1912 class at the French Military Academy at St.-Cyr. During World War II, Juin commanded a Free French army corps fighting with the Allies in Italy. At St.-Cyr, his classmate Charles de Gaulle was described by one exasperated instructor as "average in everything, except height." De Gaulle's nickname at St.-Cyr, given to him by the commanding officer of his basic training company, was the Constable (*le Connétable*). The nickname alluded to his lack of humility because the Constable was the highest rank of the ancient French army.[58, 59]

NATO Exercise LION NOIR, held from 21 to 27 March 1957, tested AFCENT's ability to repel a hypothetical Soviet invasion. LION NOIR included staff officers from armies of nine NATO nations including, for the first time, West Germany, Luxembourg, and Portugal. The air-land exercise was commanded by Juin's successor, Gen Jean-Étienne Valluy.[60, 61] During NATO Operation COUNTER PUNCH in September 1957, more than 1,500 aircraft tested the national air-defense systems of Britain, France, Belgium, and the Netherlands. It was the largest maneuver since World War II. Valluy's commander of land forces was German Gen Hans Speidel, whose assignment to AFCENT on 01 April 1957 was controversial. From 1940 to 1942, Speidel had served on the German military command staff at the Hôtel Majestic in Paris. Most French were not keen to have Field Marshal Rommel's Chief of Staff back in uniform in France. Ironically in 1952, most of Gen Lauris Norstad's AAFCE multi-national staff believed German military forces would be welcome to join the defense of Western Europe.[62] If the Soviets attacked, all of Valluy's logistics staffs were to set up joint operations in the forest of la Madeleine, north of Fontainebleau.

Valluy was replaced in 1960 by Gen Maurice Challe. Challe's tenure was brief because of his involvement in OAS activities. The OAS (*Organisation de l'Armée Secrète*), a secret organization of French soldiers who opposed Algerian independence, made several attempts to kill President Charles de Gaulle. An ambush occurred on 12 August 1962 on the road from Paris to the French military airfield at Vélizy-Villacoublay. Two groups of OAS assassins fired 150 rounds at de Gaulle's Citroën. Miraculously no one was hit, although the windows were shattered and one round barely missed de Gaulle and his wife.[63] At Villacoublay, de Gaulle brushed shards of glass off his clothes and said to his driver Francis Marroux, "This is getting to be dangerous. Fortunately those gentlemen are poor shots."[64] Challe, who was replaced in 1961 by Gen Pierre-Élie Jacquot, was tried by the High Military Tribunal and sentenced to fifteen years confinement for his part in a coup to seize power in Algeria. After Challe had served five and one-half years of his sentence, he was pardoned by de Gaulle and released from prison on Christmas Eve 1966.[65] Gen Lyman L. Lemnitzer, NATO Supreme Commander, assigned Jacquot to plan and conduct LONG THRUST exercises, a series of exercises that tested methods of reinforcing NATO defenses by airlifting combat forces from the US to Europe.

Gen Jacquot was replaced in 1963 by Gen Jean Albert Émile Crépin, an officer loyal to de Gaulle. Crépin, who disliked political soldiers, was the last French AFCENT commander. In the fall, Crépin's command conducted NATO exercises FALLEX which set up field command posts to practice communications for land and air forces of AFCENT. In November 1966, Crépin was replaced by German Army General Johann-Adolf Graf von Kielmansegg, who supervised the move of AFCENT headquarters in 1967 from Fontainebleau to Maastricht, the Netherlands.[66]

Thirty-five years after the departure of AFCENT, an abandoned apartment in the Henri IV wing still had a lockable map-display wall cabinet in the huge bathroom. An AFCENT staff officer could sit on the toilet contemplating how to defend Central Europe. The Henri IV wing has been restored to accommodate civic and cultural activities.

Commanders of AFCENT at Fontainebleau

Commander	Nationality	Period of Service
Gen Alphonse-Pierre Juin*	French	Aug 53-Sep 56
Gen Jean-Étienne Valluy	French	Oct 56-May 60
Gen Maurice Challe	French	May 60-Feb 61
Gen Pierre-Élie Jacquot	French	Mar 61-Dec 63
Gen Jean Albert Émile Crépin	French	Dec 63-June 66
Gen Johann-Adolf Graf von Kielmansegg	West German	Nov 66-Apr 68

*French abbreviation for general is Gal.

Wolfsschlucht 2 at Margival

German Chancellor and Führer Adolf Hitler's former headquarters, Wolfsschlucht 2 (Wolf's Gorge), became an underground command center facility for NATO. Although construction of the German Führerhauptquartiere (Führer's headquarters) was scheduled to begin in 1940, it was suspended after France surrendered to Germany. The site, at the south end of a 2,100-ft long railroad tunnel near Margival, 6 miles northeast of Soissons, was chosen because it was near airfields at Laon, and the tunnel could be used to conceal Hitler's armored train.[67] Construction on the fortified headquarters, designed and supervised by the German Organization Todt, resumed in September 1942. A workforce of 13,000 completed the complex in two years. The tunnel was fitted with armored sliding doors at each end. Shafts were installed to exhaust fumes and supply fresh air.[68] Six large bunkers with 12-ft thick concrete walls and ceilings were built into the slope of a hill. Eight bunkers with 2½-ft thick concrete walls were built primarily for offices. A security fence enclosed the complex that was defended by machine gun nests, anti-aircraft gun emplacements, and searchlight batteries. Two additional fortified headquarters for Hitler were built in France. In 1942, Wolfsschlucht 3 was constructed at St.-Rimay near Vendôme (10 miles northeast of Blois), using an existing railroad tunnel. In 1944, construction of Anlage Brunhilde began near Thionville, utilizing existing Maginot Line tunnels at Hackenberg.[69]

Hitler used Wolfsschlucht 2 only one time, when he met with Generals Erwin Rommel and Gerd von Rundstedt on 17 June 1944, eleven days after the D-Day landings in Normandy. Hitler flew from Salzburg to Metz-Frescaty and was driven through Reims to Margival, accompanied by fighter aircraft flying overhead.[70] Unlike other command headquarters for Hitler in Europe, the Wolfsschlucht 2 buildings were not destroyed. On 28 August 1944, German troops abandoned the site. The next day, the complex was occupied by elements of US 1st Infantry Division of VII Corps.[71] After the war, the French Army used Margival as a school for female personnel.

In early 1951, an advance party of seventy American troops from Fontainebleau arrived at Margival to prepare the former German headquarters for use by AFCENT. New bunkers and concrete buildings were added and a communications tower was built on a hill. A new mess hall building had a huge bar and changing rooms for the nearby German-built outdoor swimming pool. In 1969, after AFCENT returned the bunker facility to France, it was used as a training area for the French 6th Commando unit.

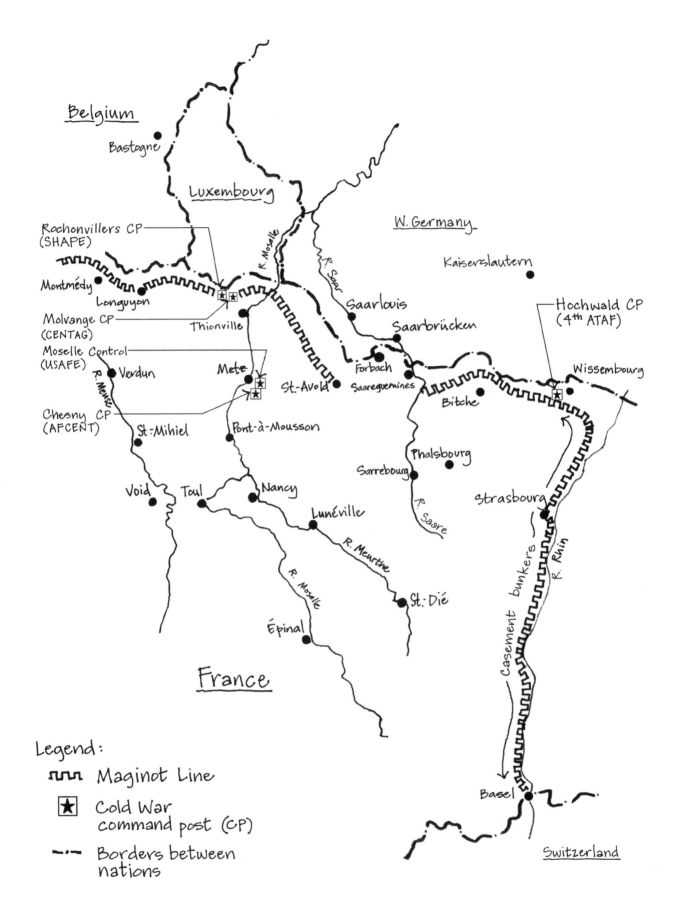

Maginot Line Command Posts (1951-67)

Wartime Command Posts in France

During a war with the Soviets, US and NATO military commands would use blast-resistant shelters. Four command posts would be located in renovated Maginot Line forts, two in structures built by the Germans during the 1940-44 occupation (Paris and Margival), and three built during the 1950s (near Fontainebleau, Paris, and Orléans).

The Maginot Line fort Rochonvillers was the forward command post for SHAPE, designated Project R by NATO. The rear command post for NATOs Central Army Group (CENTAG) was at Maginot Line fort Molvange, designated Project M.[72] From 1952 to 1961, CENTAG was headquartered at Heidelberg, Germany (at Seckenheim, 1961-80). In wartime, CENTAG would consist of US Army V and VII Corps, two German Army corps, and the French forces in southern Germany. Chesny, a Maginot fort near Metz, was not rehabilitated. It was used only by AFCENT for yearly training exercises which lasted a few days. The French government also made available for NATO exercises: Fort de Jussy (near Mécleuves), Fort d'Yser (Orny), and Fort d'Aisne (Verny).

The 4th Allied Tactical Air Force (ATAF) used Maginot Line fort Hochwald, which was part of the former Lauter Maginot Line Complex, designated Project H. Fort Jeanne d'Arc near Metz was a World War I-era fort restored by the Germans during the World War II occupation. Designated "Moselle Control," it was used for military air traffic control, staffed by personnel from the air forces of the US, France, and Canada.[73]

Command Post Bunkers

Advance Section	Orléans Area
Margival, near Soissons (AFCENT)	Maison-Fort, near Orléans (USAREUR)
Rochonvillers (SHAPE)	**Seine Area**
Molvange (CENTAG)	Paris Blockhouse, near Étoile (SOTFE)
Chesny north, near Metz (AFCENT)	Le Mesnil-le-Roi, near St.-Germain-en-Laye (SHAPE and USEUCOM)
Hochwald (4th ATAF)	
Fort Jeanne d'Arc, near Metz (USAFE)	Camp Guynemer at Avon (AAFCE, AIRCENT)

Caserne Lariboisière

Caserne Lariboisière, built in 1875 in Fontainebleau, was named for Général Jean Ambrose Baston de Lariboisière who commanded French artillery during the Napoleonic Wars. His family founded the Hôpital Lariboisière, in Paris. From 1871 to 1939, the French Army's artillery school *École d'application d'Artillerie* was located at Fontainebleau. Students fired rounds from cannons at the nearby Polygone d'Artillerie toward the Champ de Tir, a 203-acre site adjacent to the Hippodrome du Grand Parquet on the road to Ury. Rounds flew over public roads and hikers in the forests. After World War II, the 38-acre caserne served as a depot for the 7762nd American Graves Registration Command Depot Company. The US Army used Caserne Lariboisière from 04 November 1944 until 01 June 1967.

In May 1950, Major General Henri Coudreaux of the French Ministry of War helped the 7966 EUCOM Detachment engineers, commanded by Col Hubert E. Klemp at 17, rue Lapérouse in Paris, obtain bids from contractors to rehabilitate several buildings at Caserne Lariboisière. By June, Kemp's engineers were working 6 hours of overtime per working day. Most of the work involved construction projects in Fontainebleau, repairs at the Hôtel Astoria in Paris, and field surveys needed for the anticipated LOC across France.[74] By the late 1950s, ninety-five original buildings at the caserne had been renovated at a cost of nearly $1 million. Because the chapel occupied a former stable, the walls still had the metal rings to tether horses. In December 1951, the French assigned Coudreaux to Ike's staff.

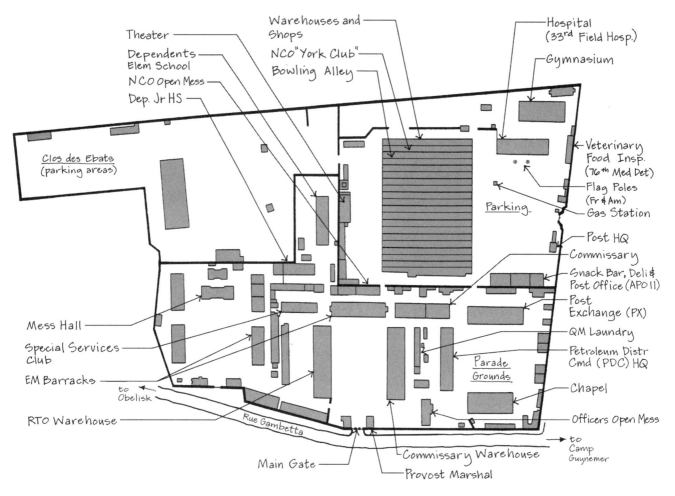

Caserne Lariboisière (1959)

Initial Occupants

The USAFE 7495th Headquarters Support Group was stationed at the caserne in September 1951 to support US military units in the Fontainebleau area. The Air Force group was inactivated when the US Army took over the logistics and administrative responsibilities in September 1953. During the initial buildup in France, part of Lariboisière became the 504th Medical Base Depot. Medical supplies and equipment were moved from Rhein Medical Depot in Germany to warehouses at Lariboisière. SHAPE planners decided it was unwise to locate depots close to NATO headquarters in Fontainebleau because they would be a key target if the Soviets invaded France. Therefore in 1953, most medical supplies at Lariboisière were relocated to leased warehouses at La Roche-sur-Yon.[75] In August 1952, French police solved a series of thefts of sheets, blankets, and surgical equipment from the warehouses at Lariboisière and arrested a gang of three US Army enlisted men, six French civilians, and one Polish Labor Service member. The smallest member of the gang had been hoisted through a high window to gain entry at night.[76]

In May 1953 the 33rd Medical Depot, commanded by Lt Col Roy E. Brooks, was sent from Germany to Lariboisière to stock the warehouses with slow-moving medical supplies and equipment. The depot supplied Army hospitals at la Chapelle and La Rochelle. Work in the warehouses could be dangerous. In September 1953, a forklift driver turned a blind corner too quickly and ran into Maj Robert M. Anderson from behind. The impact of the prongs of the forklift caused numerous fractures in Anderson's lower back.[77] The 503rd Medical Detachment manufactured eyeglasses at the caserne for ComZ and Air Force personnel in France.[78] In 1957, medical supplies at Lariboisière again were relocated, this time to modern warehouses at Vitry-le-François. In early January, Lt Col Arthur

CHAPTER 6: *NATO and US Military in Fontainebleau*

European Command gate, Caserne Lariboisière, Fontainebleau, 1951 (US Army)

F. Maeser was sent from Fontainebleau to Vitry with two Medical Service Corps officers and forty enlisted men to stock the new warehouses.

Fontainebleau Garrison

The Fontainebleau Garrison provided administrative and logistical support to the Petroleum Distribution Command (PDC) and US elements of AFCENT and AIRCENT. Administrative support services included finance, personnel records, and postal. Logistical support services included medical, construction, vehicle maintenance, and rations for mess halls. In 1960, more than six-hundred fifty French employees worked at the caserne, over half at the bakery.[79]

Fontainebleau US Army Garrison Commanders

Commanding Officer	Period of Service	Commanding Officer	Period of Service
Col Vincent M. Hidalgo	1953-56	Lt Col Delbert O. Carpenter	1961-62
Col Noble J. Wiley, Jr.	1956	Lt Col Robert J. McDonough	1962-63
Col William I. Russell	1956-58	Lt Col Frederick J. Young	1963-64
Lt Col John B. McKean	1959-61	Lt Col Robert X. Sheffield	1964-66
		Maj Frederick C. Becker	1966-67

Field Hospital

In 1955, the 33rd Field Hospital, commanded by Maj Willard R. Warren, replaced the 34th Station Hospital at Fontainebleau. The 33rd, a 400-bed mobile medical unit, operated a 42-bed fixed hospital at the caserne to serve US military personnel and dependents. Pharmacy and exam rooms were on the ground floor; two surgery rooms, female patient rooms, and a large ward were on the second; and enlisted medical personnel lived on the third floor of the building built in 1876. The X-ray technicians took annual chest X-rays of GIs and French employees. During sick call and emergencies such as vehicle accidents, they X-rayed broken bones and, on rare occasions, gun-shot wounds from MPs who accidently shot themselves while practicing quick-draws with their .45 cal pistols. When deployed to the field, each platoon of the 33rd was to set up a 100-bed hospital in tents. In the spring of 1958, 1st Platoon of the 33rd was ordered to deploy to Lebanon as part of Operation BLUE BAT. However,

US Army Hospital, Caserne Lariboisière, Fontainebleau, 1966 (F. G. Quinn)

US Army, Europe sent a hospital unit from Germany instead, because it took too long for the Fontainebleau platoon's equipment to be readied for movement to the airhead.[80] After the 33rd Field Hospital was inactivated in 1962, the 6th General Dispensary moved into the building to provide medical care.

Col William I. Russell, an infantry officer, believed Army doctors and medics did not salute properly, avoided retreat, and lacked military bearing. Traditionally, retreat is held at 5 pm each day on American military posts. To show respect, all outdoor activity stops and everyone stands at attention, facing the US flag if visible. Even persons driving are to stop, get out of their vehicle, and stand at attention. Retreat is sounded by an Army bugler or over loudspeakers from a recording, followed by the national anthem as the flag is lowered. Standing at his upper-floor office window, Russell used field binoculars to catch egregious offenders. Russell reprimanded doctors and medics who casually observed retreat without standing at attention.[81]

Communications Support

Three signal companies were billeted at Lariboisière: 275th Signal Co (Service), 293rd Signal Co, and 507th Signal Co (Support). Personnel maintained communications systems, operated cryptographic equipment, and deployed to the field to practice operating microwave radio equipment vans. There were more than two-hundred vans and vehicles at Fontainebleau that could be deployed to the field to set up emergency communications networks from NATO headquarters to subordinate commands (called the "Greyhound" mission). Personnel from the 275th Signal Co maintained and operated communications equipment at the AFCENT bunker at Margival. A British Signal Squadron, assigned to support AFCENT, also was billeted at Lariboisière.

Petroleum Distribution Command

The Petroleum Distribution Command, Europe (PDC), activated on 15 November 1954 at Orléans, moved to Caserne Lariboisière in September 1955. By the late 1950s, the PDC oversaw about 2,000 personnel. Units of the PDC delivered petroleum products in bulk (by pipeline, tank railcars, and tank trucks) and in containers (by 5-gal jerry cans and 55-gal drums). The PDC operated four large distribution-storage installations (called tank farms), eight pump stations, and storage depots at Niort and Pauillac. Subordinate units were the 55th Transportation Truck Co (Petroleum) at Étain and the 543rd Engineer Co (Pipeline) located near Chinon.[82] In 1959 at Lariboisière, the PDC presented courses on pipeline operations to personnel from several NATO nations. The PDC also staffed a petroleum products laboratory at Zweibrücken, Germany. The lab tested the quality of aviation and motor gasoline. In 1959, the lab processed between 1,000 and 1,500 samples a month.[83]

Donges-Metz Pipeline

The US needed a pipeline in France to rapidly transport POL for US military forces in Europe.[84, 85] After more than a year of negotiations, progress finally was made in April 1953, when US Secretary of Defense Charles E. Wilson met in Paris with French Minister of National Defense René Pleven. The French agreed to pay for the acquisition of land and rights-of-way. On 30 June 1953, US Ambassador C. Douglas Dillon and French Foreign Minister Georges Bidault signed an agreement for a pipeline from the port of St.-Nazaire to Metz.[86] Because of greatly improved cooperation between the French and the Joint Construction Agency in Paris, dredging of the mooring basin at Donges had begun and more than 35 miles of pipe had been laid before the agreement was signed.[87] The pipeline, buried 3 ft underground, was 12 inches in diameter to Châlons-sur-Marne; 10 inches in diameter from Châlons to Metz. Construction of the 391-mile long pipeline was completed and the system tested by 30 June 1956. The first product pumped from Donges to Melun was motor gasoline in January 1957. The tank farms mostly were completed by 30 November 1957 when the pipeline was considered operational. The pipeline and facilities, designed and constructed by the French government-controlled *Société des Transports Petroliers par Pipeline* (TRAPIL), cost $55 million.

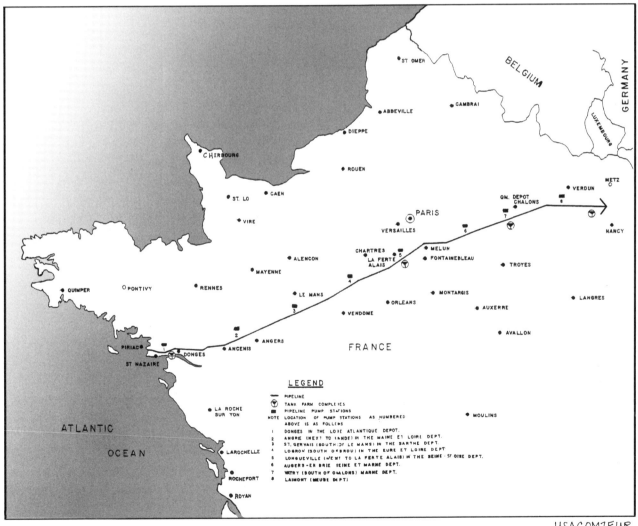

US Army Donges-Metz Pipeline

Pipeline Inspections

TRAPIL hired civilian aircraft to visually inspect the pipeline. Flights normally were thirty hours per month. By agreement with the French government, the US Army had the right to inspect the entire length of the pipeline four times each year. Telltale signs of a leak included: rainbow sheen on nearby body of water, spots of dead vegetation, and unusual noises or odors. Visual inspections were conducted from low-flying Army helicopters stationed at Poitiers and Verdun. Occasionally, French Air Force fighter-jets would "buzz" the helicopters to remind the Americans that they were in France. In 1959, an illegal tap was placed on a NATO pipeline buried 2 ft underground near Charleroi, Belgium. The tap was hidden under a fence, likely so farmers would not uncover it by plowing. The tap was discovered when a farmer reported that grass was dying and he could smell gasoline.[88]

Products Delivered by Pipeline

The pipeline primarily transported motor gasoline (Mogas), aviation gasoline (Avgas), jet fuel (JP-4), and diesel fuel. Gasoline traveled from Donges to Metz at about 5 mph.[89] The pipe, specified by Army engineers, was manufactured in France. Where buried pipe passed under roads and railway track, it was encased by larger diameter pipe to protect it from heavy loads. The delivery capacity of the pipeline, in 24 hours, from Donges to Germany was equivalent to several hundred tank railcars. From November 1958 to July 1959, ComZ released five-hundred seventy-three leased French and German tank railcars which had been standing idle. The Army still had an inventory of six-hundred fifty Army-owned tank railcars available to use in an emergency.[90]

Because aviation and motor gasoline contained lead that could contaminate jet fuel, each fuel had to be pumped separately. To prevent contamination, the commingled portion between fuels moving through the pipeline was diverted to a separate tank at the tank farms. Metal scrapers, shaped like huge bullets, were inserted to clean the pipeline. The scrapers were called "pigs" because they squealed like a pig as they moved through the pipe.[91, 92] About 40% of the fuel delivered by pipeline was used by the US Air Force. Jet fuel was delivered by 8 inches in diameter NATO branch pipelines to underground storage tanks located on the air bases. In the early 1950s, the Air Force stored jet fuel in tank railcars at air bases until the underground storage was installed. By agreement, the French military could use up to 5% of pipeline capacity each month.

The Tank Farms

High-pressure pumping stations with nearby storage tanks, called tank farms, were located at four districts: Donges, Melun, Châlons-sur-Marne, and Metz.[93] Four additional blast-resistant pump houses, with 16-inch thick reinforced-concrete walls, were located along the pipeline. The four terminal districts had fourteen tank farms located on more than 1,400 acres. There were more than eight-hundred fifty French employees at the terminal districts. The farms had storage tanks, pumps, warehouses, and laboratories which daily tested the fuel. During one 8-hour shift, Donges Terminal could fill 80 tank railcars; Melun and Metz, 60 each; and Châlons, 54. The Metz tank farm at Thiaucourt had nine semi-buried storage tanks to resist blast from an attack. Personnel at St.-Baussant transferred fuel from the pipeline to tanker trucks and 55-gal drums. The drum fill header at St.-Baussant could fill twelve 55-gal drums at the same time. Trucks from the 55th Transportation Co delivered fuel to units in the Metz, Nancy, and Toul areas.[94]

The tank farms in each district were separated so an attack on one would not affect the use of others. In September 1959, construction began on nineteen 10,000-barrel bolted steel tanks to store

Scraper trap manifold at Longueville Pump Station near la Ferté-Alais (US Army)

Demo of "hot tap" connection for Gen A. P. O'Meara and Maj Gen R. C. Kyser, Melun, 1965 (US Army)

diesel fuel used to heat military installations in France. Army troops erected six tanks at Châlons, ten at Donges, and three at Metz.[95] After erection, tanks were filled with water to test for leaks at seams or in the base. Camp Ising, an abandoned French Army caserne at Ebersviller, 10 miles northeast of Metz, was obtained in 1962 for use as an off-depot storage facility. In early 1960 at Donges, one of the six 84,000-barrel floating roof tanks at "B" farm exploded while being filled with JP-4 jet fuel. Although the GIs applied foam to smother the fire, it continued to burn because the local French civilian fire department sprayed water on the blaze, scattering the foam until the GIs were able to persuade the French firemen to stop.

Terminal District Tank Farms[96, 97]

District	Tank Farm	Size (acres)	Number of Tanks	Total Storage (barrels)	US Army Personnel*	LWRs**
Donges	La Fernais (A) Dorieux (B) Savenay (C) Piriac-sur-Mer (D)	355	31	1,617,000	91	147
Melun	la Ferté-Alais (A & B) Bouville (C) Orgemont (D)	454	41	1,723,000	226	350
Châlons-sur-Marne	Vatry (A) Cheniers (B) Coupetz (C) Dommartin-Lettrée (D)	337	33	1,678,000	45	300
Metz	St.-Baussant (A) Thiaucourt (B)	276	27	1,018,000	57	59

*Totals from US Army report to French government, dated 31 July 1964.
**French civilian employees, 1966.

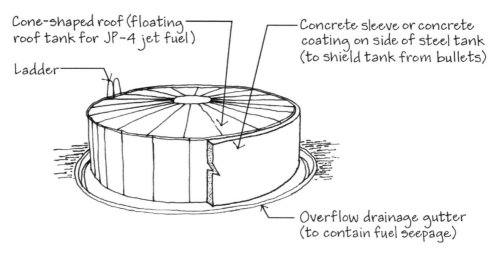

Storage Tank

Melun Terminal District

The Melun Terminal District had four tank farms. Two tank farms were at la Ferté-Alais, one at Bouville, and one at Orgemont. At Bouville and Orgemont, 5-gal jerry cans and 55-gal drums were piled high in warehouses and stored in fields behind security fences. Personnel at the farms transferred fuel from the pipeline to tank railcars and tank trucks. There were thirty 5,000-gal tank semitrailers and one-hundred forty 16,000-gal tank railcars at Melun. Tank trucks and tank railcars were labeled to only transport Mogas or JP-4. Twelve 5,000-gal tank semitrailers could be filled at the la Ferté-Alais "A" farm truck rack at one time; thirty-two 16,000-gal tank railcars at the rail rack. A 60-ton diesel locomotive was used to switch railcars from rack to marshalling yard.[98] Trucks delivered fuel to units in the Fontainebleau, Orléans, and Paris areas. A platoon of the 55th Trans Co, stationed at la Ferté-Alais, lived in metal prefab barracks. The 524th Quartermaster Co was billeted at Orgemont. Each year troops from the Melun Terminal District used Mont Merle Rifle Range near Fontainebleau to qualify with their small-arms weapons. First Lt Billy J. Stalcup served from 1958 to 1961 at Melun, where he met his wife, Nicole. Twenty-five years later in 1986, Brig Gen Stalcup headed a logistics command at Zweibrücken, Germany. One of his duties was to oversee the Donges-Metz pipeline, still operated for the US Army by TRAPIL.[99]

Petroleum Distribution Command Commanders

Commanding Officer	Period of Service	Commanding Officer	Period of Service
Maj Lester C. McGoldrick	1955-56	Col Francis P. Sweeney	1962-65
Col Merton Singer	1956-60	Col Robert C. Borman	1965-66
Col Charles D. Peterson	1960-62	Col Elmer J. Neary	1966-67

Emergency Pipe and Collapsible Tanks

Depots at Bussac and Chinon each stored 750 miles of 6-inch diameter flexible military pipe to be used in the event of war for an emergency pipeline and to quickly replace sections of damaged pipe. Depots also stored collapsible fuel storage tanks made of nylon cloth coated with synthetic rubber. Collapsible tanks could be installed in about one-tenth the time it took to erect an equal capacity steel tank. Six 10,000-gal collapsible rubber tanks, linked to a pump, could provide fuel supply to a combat division in the field. Smaller 600-gal collapsible rubber tanks could be used to convert 2½-ton cargo trucks to tank trucks.[100, 101] GIs called the rubber tanks "pillow tanks."

Open House

Each May on Armed Forces Day, Caserne Lariboisière held an open house for civilians and military personnel in the Fontainebleau area. The Army displays in 1961 included a Nike Hercules missile, 10,000-gal collapsible rubber fuel tank, medical tents and ambulances, and mobile communications equipment. The Signal Corps displayed two radio-relay vans, a manual switchboard with 200 lines, and a teletypewriter which printed the latest worldwide news. Visitors could talk to each other using battery field phones set up on tables. The French Army displayed anti-tank missiles and radar, and French gendarmes displayed motorcycles and a helicopter. The program booklet listing displays and demonstrations was in French and English. Visitors could enter the bowling alley, mess hall, and service club.[102]

Dependents Schools

After a brief period using two rooms on the floor over the service club at Caserne Lariboisière, the dependents school moved to Villa Lavaurs at 88, rue St.-Honoré. By the end of the 1951-52 school year, five teachers and one-hundred forty-five students in grades 1 to 8 filled the villa. A hot lunch costing 30¢ was provided to the students. To lessen overcrowding at the villa, Schools Officer 2nd Lt Irving J. Linden found empty rooms in a former French barracks at Lariboisière that could be rehabilitated for school use. Repairs were slow, but by September 1952 three classrooms were completed. By mid-school year 1952-53, there were ten teachers and more than two-hundred students at the two locations. Buses picked up children in the mornings and returned them to their homes at the end of the school day. After the hospital at Lariboisière closed in 1962, a nurse from Bel Manoir (Paris) visited the dependents school at least once a week.[103-105] For many years, the Villa Lavaurs, once the home of a French Count, housed the third largest Napoléon museum in France.

In Spring 1966, *Compagnie républicaine de sécurité* (CRS) personnel arranged red and white striped traffic cones to form a large figure-eight driving circuit behind the warehouse and hospital buildings at Lariboisière. Peugeot, a prominent French automobile manufacturer, sponsored the event. Peugeot provided three sedans that had automatic transmissions for the American junior high school students to drive. The 13 and 14-year-old drivers maneuvered the cars around the circuit, trying not to hit the cones. CRS driving instructors sat in the front passenger seat and two or three students, awaiting their turn to drive, sat in the back. Instructors rated the first-time drivers as *trés bien* (very good), *bien* (good), or *honorable,* depending on the number of cones knocked over. Each student who completed the circuit received a *Certificat d'Aptitude au Pilotage* signed by representatives of the CRS and Peugeot.[106]

Lycée Carnot

In September 1954, an international school for children of NATO personnel opened in Lycée Carnot at 11, rue Victor Hugo. The school was authorized by SHAPE and the *Ministère de l'education national français.*[107] In 1959, Jean Dupré was head of Lycée Carnot and the faculty had fifty-one teachers from France, Great Britain, Canada, Germany, and the Netherlands. Because the US had a dependents school, there were no American teachers. The nine-hundred students, age 8 to 18, were from nine nations that were part of NATO commands in the Fontainebleau area. Among the student body were fifty Americans. One American student won first prize in a French language competition even though some of her fellow competitors were French.[108] Americans also could send their children to French schools where they would be immersed in another culture.

French CRS-Peugeot sponsored "student driving course" at Caserne Lariboisière, Fontainebleau, 1966 (F. G. Quinn)

Dependents elementary school, Villa Lavaurs, Fontainebleau, 1952 (US Air Force)

Village Faisanderie

To ease the housing shortage in Fontainebleau, NATO built an apartment complex to house three-hundred twenty families. Half of the units were allocated for enlisted personnel; half for officers. The apartments for officers had a maid's room. After debating the impact on the skyline of four, 7-story buildings versus five, 5-story buildings, construction began in 1952. Prefabricated concrete panels, designed by French engineer Raymond Camus, were used to rapidly construct four, 7-story apartment buildings on the outskirts of Fontainebleau.[109] To minimize the adverse impact on tourism from traffic congestion and construction noise, the modular panels were fabricated and stored at a concrete factory in nearby Melun. The concrete structural elements (floor-ceilings and walls) were carefully marked to indicate placement, trucked to Fontainebleau, and rapidly assembled at the construction site. Eight large cranes (two per building) were used to join the components together like a giant jigsaw puzzle. Construction took eleven months rather than the nearly two years normally required for a project of this size. Fontainebleau residents, called Bellifontains, recall that the buildings "grew like mushrooms."

The apartment complex was designed by French architect Marcel Lods, a professor at the *École nationale supérieure des beaux-arts* in Paris. The buildings were supported by free-standing, reinforced-concrete columns so the ground level was open for pedestrian circulation under the first level of apartments. The complex resembled the famous *Unité d'Habitation*, a modern "machine for living" design concept of world-renowned architect Le Corbusier, built in 1947 at Marseille and in 1952 at Nantes. Although the buildings mimicked many of the design elements Le Corbusier believed indispensible, roof gardens were not provided, likely due to military thrift.[110] The prefab system worked well, but conventional French construction methods were used for most buildings at US installations. Forty families of Americans assigned to NATO units were eligible to live in Village Faisanderie. By the late 1950s, newly assigned personnel had to spend months on the official wait list before an apartment became available. As in many French buildings, heat was turned off from 15 April to 15 October regardless of the outdoor temperature.

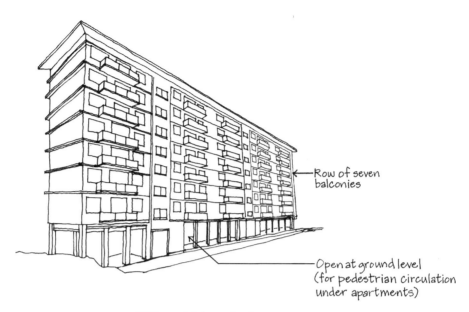

Village Faisanderie

De Fontaine Village

In 1959, seventy-eight ranch style residences for officer and NCO families of American support units were completed at Achères-la-Forêt, 8 miles from Fontainebleau. During construction, GIs from Caserne Lariboisière were assigned to patrol the site at night. However, the security did not prevent vandals from starting a fire in one of the units.

The mayor of Achères suggested the name of De Fontaine for the village. During World War II, the father and son team of Eugene and Julien De Fontaine were active in the French resistance against the Germans.[111] Even after these residences were available, most American families had to live on the economy, which in 1964 typically cost about $160 a month for an apartment large enough for three to five persons. Most of the apartments and houses for rent were old, expensive to heat in winter, and the plumbing, heating, and electricity were unpredictable.[112] In 1964, a road in Cité De Fontaine was named rue Marquis de La Fayette and another rue President Kennedy.

Officer Housing

Senior officers, including the commander of AFCENT ground forces, lived in the Hôtel d'Aube at 11, rue Royale, which had only one outside phone line to the MP desk on the ground floor.[113] The Aube had one toilet per floor, an electric elevator, and a large garden and orangerie behind the building. Norstad lived at Villa Bellune at 4, rue St.-Honoré, another AIRCENT general officer lived at 4, rue Le Primatice, and NATO leased the Château de la Madeleine in nearby Samois-sur-Seine for additional officer housing.[114] BOQs were built at Camp Guynemer for AIRCENT officers and on Blvd Circular for Allied Land Forces Central Europe (LANDCENT) officers. The LANDCENT BOQ, located behind the International Officers Club, had a squash court used by the *Club Interallié de Squash*.

Recreation

For recreation, GIs visited the Special Services Club which was located in a two-story building next to barracks at Caserne Lariboisière. The club, established in 1951, was the first service club to open in France.[115] Crafts shops, music listening room, and game room were on the ground floor; a library with more than 3,000 books was on the second floor. The club was staffed by French employees and Special Services women, affectionately called "Doughnut Dollies" by the GIs.[116] On Thursday evenings in the late 1950s, the club organized dinner-dances for GIs. Female students from the Alliance français and the Sorbonne in Paris were invited to the dances, and Army buses were used to transport them from Place de la Concorde in Paris to the caserne.[117] Family members of NATO personnel could use the indoor swimming pool at Camp Guynemer and, without charge, ride French Army horses at the Quartier du Carrousel, located behind the château.

Monty at Courances

Ike's flamboyant Deputy Commander at SHAPE, British General Bernard L. Montgomery, lived at Château de Courances, a moat-surrounded mansion located in Courances, 10 mi west of Fontainebleau. The 17th Century château, owned since 1872 by the de Ganay family, was much more elaborate than Ike's villa at Marnes-la-Coquette.[118, 119] The grounds of the château, built on the foundation of a medieval castle, had numerous fountains and cascades, and a tree-lined canal.[120] Security at Courances was provided by 520th MP Co, French gendarmes, and British MPs. Montgomery had been ensconced at Fontainebleau since 1948 when the Western European Union was formed. Monty was to plan for the common defense of the five Brussels Treaty nations. At Fontainebleau, Monty often clashed on defense strategy with his commander of land forces, French Gen Jean de Lattre de Tasigny.[121]

In March 1951, Ike assigned Monty to organize and train NATO forces. Monty critiqued NATO joint training exercises like a schoolmaster. Generals and colonels were seated on benches like schoolboys, facing Monty who was seated at a table in front. To begin "class," he rang a handbell and, if anyone coughed, an aide would deliver a cough drop to the perpetrator.[122] Monty also did not permit smoking in his presence, a quirk that had irked the "chain smoking" Ike during their World War II encounters.[123]

NATOs Command Post Exercises

For four days in early April 1952, two-hundred twenty officers attended SHAPE's first command post exercise (CPX) in the Arts et Métiers building at 9 bis, avenue d'Iéna, Paris. Prior to the exercise, personnel from the 450th CIC Detachment searched the building for explosives and "bugs" (hidden electronic transmitters and microphones). French security screened the fifty-six employees who worked in the building. CPX One, which included all of Ike's senior commanders, was organized by Monty and focused on how the Allies would counter a Soviet invasion. Monty encouraged all participants, including junior officers, to critique responses to invasion scenarios posed by Monty or his deputy. To the chagrin of US senior officers, ideas deemed weak were heckled in the tradition of British military schools. Monty did not permit smoking in the building. During breaks, hoards of NATO officers smoked on the sidewalk in front of Arts et Métiers.[124-126]

In his final address on 11 April to the participants, Monty bluntly stated that even though SHAPE had included some imaginary West Germany armed forces in the exercise, it would not have been possible to even temporarily stop a Russian invasion on the east side of the Rhine River. To defend the West, Monty believed that more NATO forces were essential and that success also would depend on: sound plans for battle, leaders who inspired loyalty, coordination of air-land forces, and effective logistical support. Although there still was much work to do, Monty told the participants that the exercise had been of immense value.[127]

Gen Eisenhower and French Gen Juin arrive at Arts et Métiers, Paris, April 1952 (F. J. Bentz)

At the end of CPX One, Ike congratulated Monty and the senior commanders for their flexibility in considering use of atomic weapons. His remarks were based on notes prepared by Lt Col Goodpaster before the exercise. Goodpaster suggested that Ike avoid controversial issues such as whether the Army or the Air Force should control tactical air forces. Monty, who rarely avoided controversy, spoke in public and wrote articles within two years of the first CPX "to make it absolutely clear" that SHAPE planned to use atomic weapons if the Soviets attacked.[128]

CPX Four, directed by Monty for NATO Supreme Commander Gen Alfred M. Gruenther, was held from 26 to 30 April 1954 at Camp Voluceau. Prior to the exercise, SHAPE signal personnel installed a maze of cables throughout the auditorium. Simultaneous translations into five languages were fed into individual headphones. Before speaking, participants stated name and language to be spoken. The CPX Administrative Instructions booklet asked participants to "please be kind to headphone and microphone orderlies" who scurried from general to general. The exercise included using Atomic Annie and SAC nuclear bombers.

NATO Withdrawal

In March 1966, President Charles de Gaulle notified the Allies that France would withdraw from SHAPE. US and Canadian bases and all NATO military headquarters in France would close. The departure in 1967 of AIRCENT from Avon and AFCENT from Fontainebleau involved more than 3,000 military personnel and dependents. About four-hundred fifty French civilians worked at these headquarters and another 1,100 worked in the region for the US Army. Fontainebleau's Deputy Mayor Paul Séramy anticipated that the adverse economic impact from the loss of these jobs would be devastating to the town of 20,000. He predicted high unemployment and higher taxes for residents.[129, 130] Séramy wrote to businesses in the region asking them to hire French workers who had been employed by NATO and the US Army. On 22 June 1966, he spoke at the National Assembly in Paris, asking the French government to support workers who had lost their jobs when France withdrew from SHAPE.[131]

U.S. GO HOME

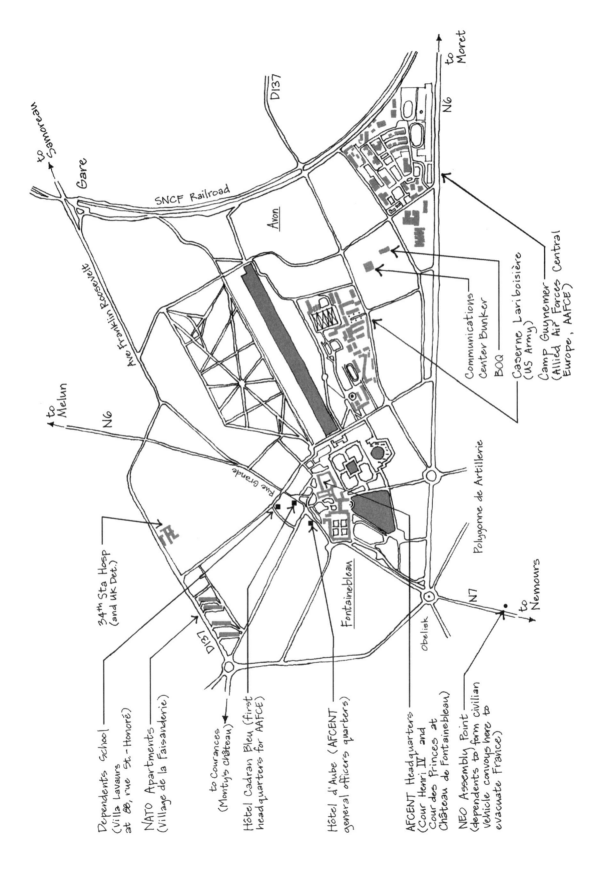

Fontainebleau Area NATO and US Military Installations

Fontainebleau Area NATO and US Military Installations

Installation	Location	Activity and Units
Headquarters	Fontainebleau (Cour Henri IV at Château)	Allied Forces Central Europe (AFCENT)
	Fontainebleau (Aile des Princes at Château)	Allied Land Forces Central Europe (LANDCENT)
	Avon (Camp Guynemer, 200 acres)	Allied Air Forces Central Europe (AAFCE, AIRCENT)
	Fontainebleau (Caserne Lariboisière, 38 acres)	US Army Garrison, Seine Area US Army Petroleum Distribution Command, Europe (PDC)
	La Ferté-Alais	US Army Terminal District (POL)
Support	Avon (Château des Fougères)	AFCENT Military Police
	Fontainebleau (Hôtel de France et d'Angleterre, 43, Blvd de Magenta)	AFCENT Housing Office, AFCENT Budget and Finance Office, NCO Club (Cercle Interallié des Sous Officiers)
	Fontainebleau (Caserne Lariboisière)	USEUCOM Detachment
	Fontainebleau (Camp du Breau, 20 acres)	AFCENT warehouses and NCO barracks
	Fontainebleau (Caserne Damesme)	French Army QG RAF Detachment (Great Britain)
	Fontainebleau (Quartier Châtaux)	British Army Detachment
	Fontainebleau (Caserne Boufflers, Caserne Raoult, and Quartier Héronnières)	French Army
	Fontainebleau (Camp des Gliéres)	German Army
Depots	Fontainebleau (Clos des Ébats, 10 acres)	Secondary storage
	La Ferté-Alais (454 acres, A to D total)	Melun Tank Farms A & B
	Bouville	Melun Tank Farm C
	Orgemont	Melun Tank Farm D
Communications	Avon	AAFCE Communications Center
	Le Chenoy and Vernou-la-Celle	Two microwave & radio relay sites (US Army-USAF joint control)
	Fontainebleau (Polygone d'Artillerie)	Radio relay sites (AAFCE)
	Fremont and le Plessis-aux-Tournelles	Microwave sites (US Army)
Hospital/Medical Dispensary	Fontainebleau (Caserne Lariboisière)	33rd Field Hospital (42 beds)
	Fontainebleau (rue des Bois)	34th Station Hospital (US Army) and Medical Det (Great Britain)
Schools	Fontainebleau (88, rue St.-Honoré)	Villa Lavaurs (1½ acres)
	Fontainebleau (Caserne Lariboisière)	Elementary and junior high school
	Fontainebleau (11, rue Victor Hugo)	Lycée François 1er and Lycée Carnot (international school)

General Officers Quarters	Avon (Les Bruyères, 29, ave du Général de Gaulle)	LANDCENT
	Courances (Château de Courances, 190 acres)	NATO Deputy Supreme Commander
	Fontainebleau (Villa Bellune, 4, rue St.-Honoré)	Commander-in-Chief AAFCE
	Fontainebleau (4, rue le Primatice)	AIRCENT
	Fontainebleau (80, rue St.-Honoré)	AFCENT
	Fontainebleau (Hôtel de Aube, 11, rue Royale)	Four-story apartment building
Bachelor Officers Quarters (BOQ) and Mess Halls	Avon (Camp Guynemer)	AIRCENT BOQ (2 stories), 3 mess halls (US, UK, and Fr)
	Fontainebleau (Blvd Circular)	LANDCENT BOQ (29 units)
	Fontainebleau (Villa Stücken, 43, rue Royale)	Officers Club (Cercle Interallié des Officers)
	Fontainebleau (17-19, Blvd. de Magenta)	Mess Magenta (French Army)
	Samois-sur-Seine (5 acres)	Château de la Madeleine (NATO)
Housing (families)	Achères-la-Forêt (Cité De Fontaine)	78 SCH units (30 acres)
	Fontainebleau (La Faisanderie Village, rue de la Faisanderie)	4 seven-story NATO apartment buildings (320 units)
Troop Barracks	Avon (Camp Guynemer)	1141st Special Activities Sq Det 7th Radio Relay Squadron
	Fontainebleau (Caserne Lariboisière)	33rd Field Hospital 76th Medical Det (Veterinary Food Inspection) 67th Military Police Company 3rd Ordnance Co (Direct Automotive Support) 595th Army Postal Unit 275th Signal Co (Service) 293rd Signal Co (Service) 298th Signal Co (Microwave) 507th Signal Co (Support) 227th Signal Squadron (UK) 4505th Labor Service Platoon
	Fontainebleau (Château)	7470th HQ Support Sq (USAFE) 12th Air Postal Sq Det
	La Ferté-Alais (Farm B)	543rd Engineer Co (Pipeline) 55th Trans Co (Med Truck)
	Orgemont	524th QM Co (Petroleum Depot)
	Vernou-sur-Seine	102nd Signal Battalion (Co D)
Post Exchanges	Avon (Camp Guynemer)	SHAPE Shop (NAAFI)
	Fontainebleau (Caserne Lariboisière)	Clothing sales store, barber shop, beauty shops, washerette, snack bar

Recreation	Avon (Camp Guynemer)	Indoor swimming pool, tennis courts gymnasium, soccer field, baseball diamond, miniature golf (18 holes)
	Fontainebleau (Blvd Circular)	Squash court
	Fontainebleau (Caserne Lariboisière)	Bowling alley (8 lanes), gymnasium
	Fontainebleau (Quartier du Carrousel)	Horseback riding (French Army)
	Fontainebleau (Quartier Châtaux)	Cinema (Great Britain)
Transient Quarters	Fontainebleau (27, place Napoléon)	Hôtel Aigle Noir (26 rooms)
	Fontainebleau (9, rue Grande)	Hôtel Cadran Bleu (50 rooms)
	Fontainebleau (16, rue du Château)	Hôtel Moret et Armagnac (40 rooms)
Air Field	Limoges (near Melun)	French civilian control
Training Sites	Polygone d'Artillerie (Fontainebleau)	Firing range (SHAPE)
	Étampes-Champmotteux and Petit Mont Chauvet	Maneuver areas (US Army)
	la Bertrand (Melun)	Camp Leger de Boissie (French Army)
	Mont Merle and Le Mont Pierreux	Firing ranges (French Army)
Newspapers	Fontainebleau	The Font Parade, Revue d'AFCENT

Abbreviations

AAFCE	Allied Air Forces Central Europe	QG	Quartier Général (French HQ)
AIRCENT	Formerly AAFCE	RAF	Royal Air Force (Great Britain)
CINC	Commander-in-Chief	SCH	Surplus Commodity Housing
NAAFI	Navy, Army, Air Force Institute (UK)	Sq	Squadron
NCO	Noncommissioned Officer (US)	USAFE	US Air Forces in Europe
POL	Petroleum, oils & lubricants	USEUCOM	US European Command

Allied Forces Central Europe Headquarters, Château de Fontainebleau, 1958 (SHAPE)

U.S. GO HOME

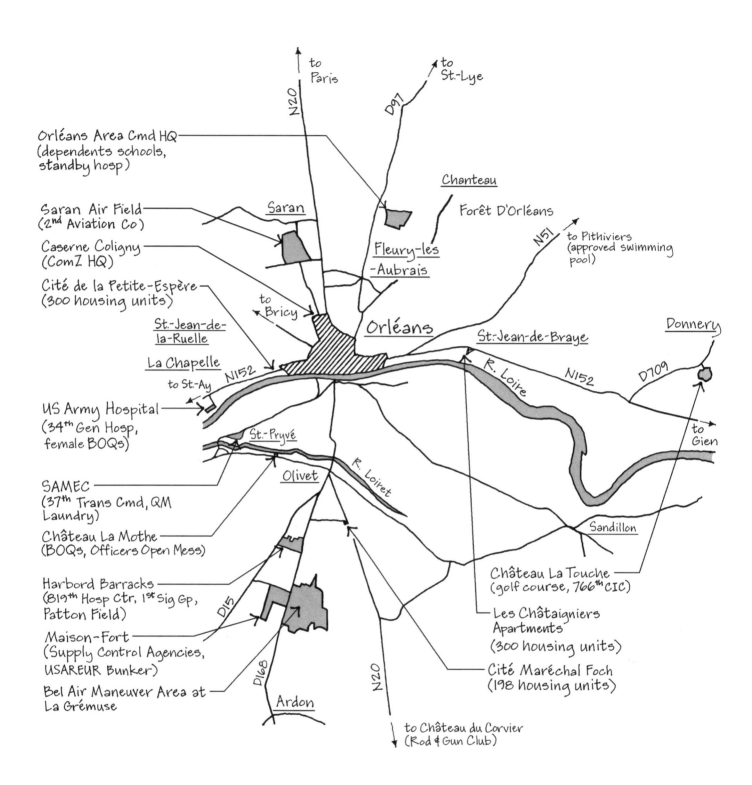

Orléans Area US Army Installations (1960)

SEVEN

US Army Commands and Agencies in Orléans

"Welcome to Our American Liberators. Orléans is delivered."
(Bulletin d'Information du Commissariat de la République, Orléans, 17 août 1944)

Seventh Army

During peacetime, Seventh Army was responsible for the security of the 300-mile border separating West Germany from Czechoslovakia and the Soviet Zone of Germany. The Soviets could move an armored division to Germany in three or four days, whereas it would take the US Army two months to move an armored division from the US by sea.[1] Two Seventh Army armored cavalry regiments patrolled nearly 200 miles of border facing more than 200,000 Czechoslovakian soldiers and security forces. To keep their own people from defecting to the West, the Czechs cleared a wide swath of border, installed a series of three electrified barbed-wire fences, and mined another wide clear strip parallel to the border. In part to deter defections by Czech sentries, watch towers were spaced so each tower could be observed by the adjacent towers.[2] US Army troops in France would be the lifeline to the combat forces of US Army, Europe (USAREUR).

Logistics Buildup

In 1950, ammunition and supplies poured into France. Stocks were moved from concentrated areas in Germany to widely scattered depots in France.[3] Later, to further disperse matériel, specialized depots were converted to general depots, each handling a balanced inventory of chemical, engineer, medical, ordnance, quartermaster, and signal supplies. About 75% of the inventory in France was earmarked for wartime use; 25% for current operations. Stocks were rotated, especially weapons which lose accuracy with age. The early use of facsimile transmission (FAX) to alert depots when supplies and equipment had arrived in France and the use of the latest IBM and UNIVAC computers to process 50,000 supply requests per week streamlined service to the combat forces. Ship-discharge exercises were held along the Atlantic coast of France to develop methods to move supplies from ship to shore in the event the Soviets destroyed the ports.[4]

By the late 1950s, to broaden their military experience, combat arms officers (infantry, armor, artillery) were assigned to command depots and to serve on logistics staffs in France. Infantry officers such as Maj Julius W. Becton, Jr. who served at Verdun (1961-63), Maj Edward C. "Shy" Meyer at Orléans (1960-61), and Brig Gen Frederick C. Weyand at Orléans (1960-61) later held senior leadership positions. In 1978, Becton became a three-star general, assigned to command more than 85,000 troops of VII Corps in Germany. Weyand (1974-76) and Meyer (1979-83) became four-star generals, both serving as Chief of Staff, the Army's top leadership position.

War Damaged Orléans

During the 1940 invasion of France, German air raids targeted Orléans and other cities along the Loire River. During liberation in 1944, retreating Germans and advancing Allies launched bombing attacks against the same cities and villages. Allied air forces dropped bombs on Orléans and nearby villages an average of five raids a day, four raids each night. By 13 June 1944, only four bridges were standing

GIs at Statue of Jeanne d'Arc, Orléans, 16 Aug 1944 (US Army)

over the Loire River between Nantes and Gien.[5] US bombers, targeting the centrally located Les Aubrais railroad station in Orléans, destroyed most of the city. Accuracy was so low on bombing missions during frequent cloud cover in Europe, normally only 40% of Allied bombs fell within 1,500 ft of the target.[6] Civilian casualties were high. Like many French cities after World War II, parts of Orléans were a sea of rubble. More than 1,200 buildings were totally destroyed; more than 3,500 partially destroyed.[7] Stores were open only a few hours each day. At night, citizens hid in basements or fled to the countryside.

During the German retreat, French civilian vehicles were commandeered, stores set on fire, and electric power plants blown up. French firemen who fought the fires were shot by the Germans. American forces, commanded by Col Bruce C. Clarke, arrived at the Hôtel de Ville of Orléans at 2:30 pm on 16 August 1944. Thousands of liberated French citizens sang "La Marseillaise" for the first time since the occupation began. French and American flags, hidden for four years, were hung from buildings.[8] Rebuilding of Orléans would continue well into the 1960s.

On 16 August 1952, the eighth anniversary of the liberation of Orléans by the 4th Armored Division of Patton's Third Army, a torchlight parade and public dances were held, with US military personnel invited to be guests of honor. That evening a ComZ engineer officer, who rented a room in the *maison* (home) of a French family, arrived from Caserne Coligny to find the entire family waiting at the front door. A bottle of champagne was opened and toasts given to commemorate the occasion. In his room, the officer found a bouquet of flowers with a note in English attached. It read: "Eight years ago, on August 16, 1944 General Patton delivered Orléans. We have not forgotten. And today, a French family of Orléans asks its friend to renew its warmest thanks to the United States and to the U.S. Army." [9]

ComZ Headquarters

Col Mason J. Young, sent to France in December 1949 to negotiate on the line of communications (LOC), became its first commander. Promoted to brigadier general in September 1950, Young faced an almost impossible task. It took the French government seemingly forever to release land to the Americans, the repair of the dilapidated French casernes and construction of new facilities lagged months behind schedule, and deplorable living conditions motivated experienced officers and NCOs to avoid service in France. Headquarters of the LOC shared space with the Advanced Planning Group of SHAPE in the crowded Hôtel Astoria in Paris.

CHAPTER 7: US Army Commands and Agencies in Orléans

In December 1950, LOC headquarters moved from Paris to Caserne Coligny in Orléans. The caserne, named in 1897 for Admiral Gaspard de Coligny, the 16th Century French Huguenot leader, had been severely damaged during the war. More than one-third of the French employees working for Young in Paris resigned rather than move to Orléans. In July 1951, the LOC was changed to a communications zone (ComZ). By Army doctrine a ComZ was an area or zone of logistical installations organized to support forward-based combat troops. ComZ headquarters at Caserne Coligny rapidly grew to command a network of more than two dozen major installations in France to support the more than 250,000 troops in Germany. There were four major commands under US European Command: ComZ, Seventh Army, Twelfth Air Force, and US Naval Forces, Germany.

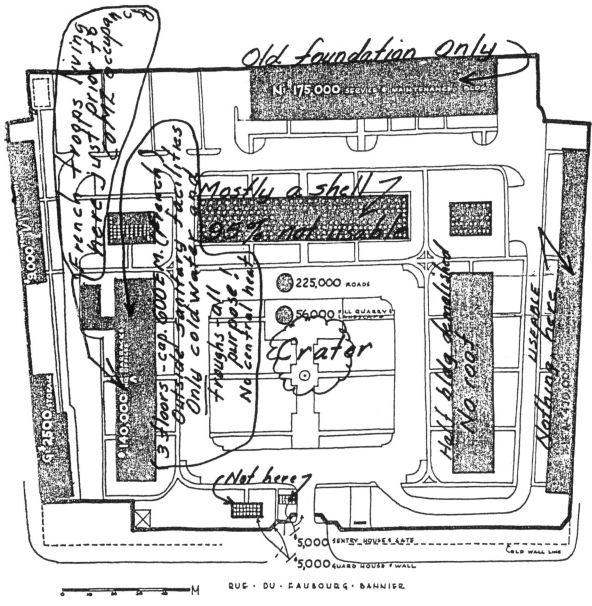

Bomb Damage Notations by US Army Engineers (Dec 1950)

Sturgis Replaces Young

After doing the best he could by cajoling the French and stretching the Status of Forces Agreement (SOFA) in favor of the United States, Young was replaced by Maj Gen Samuel D. Sturgis, Jr. in March 1952. Sturgis, a highly regarded engineer officer, was believed to be the man needed to accelerate construction in France. Sturgis had extensive experience on large public works projects and had recently commanded the 6th Armored Division at Fort Leonard Wood, Missouri.

To persuade senior officers to join his staff in Orléans, Sturgis emphasized that, despite the adversities of living in agrarian France, wives would be pleased to be only two hours from Paris and the Loire valley inhabitants were friendly toward Americans.[10] Sturgis described occupied Germany as "a very unnatural place to live." [11] (Sturgis likely meant that the defeated Germans were too eager to please.) The ComZ, which initially cost the US more than $350 million to build, had installations from Atlantic ports at St.-Nazaire, La Rochelle, and Bordeaux to Verdun, Nancy, and Metz.[12]

EUCOM Controls Depots

US Army Technical Service units were deployed to France to build the huge logistics infrastructure. Most of the depots were located in national forests, on abandoned airfields, or in dilapidated casernes. One was located in an insect infested swamp near Captieux. After ComZ had acquired the land, supplies were rapidly moved by truck and rail from Germany and by ship from the US. Supplies piled up without adequate cover because depot construction could not keep up with deliveries. It took days to deliver supplies from ports, years to construct sufficient warehouses.

Inventory control was provided by the technical service chiefs at US European Command (EUCOM) in Heidelberg, Germany. At first, EUCOM believed the chiefs would devote full support to the buildup of depots in France if primary responsibility remained with them. In practice, the separation of responsibility between EUCOM in Germany and ComZ at Orléans proved to be confusing, and the distance from Heidelberg to the depots prevented close supervision. Sturgis was irked by the arrangement and let his superior officers know it.[13] In France, Sturgis was responsible for the training and discipline of the troops, but the depot commanders reported to the EUCOM chiefs, who controlled stocks, supply, and maintenance functions at the depots. In hindsight this arrangement was a mistake, because Sturgis' staff in France could best solve local problems involving troops, real estate acquisitions, and construction by French firms.[14] Finally, by early 1953, control reverted to ComZ after the depots had been declared fully operational.[15]

Stockpiles in France were to provide USAREUR with supplies to support 120 days of combat with the Soviets. More than 320,000 different items of matériel, from small nuts and bolts to giant machines, were stored at Army depots across France. Most items were rotated to prevent deterioration and would no longer be stored if yearly demand fell to eight or fewer requisitions.[16]

Tent Villages and Mud

Army troops in France worked in the mud and lived in tents and prefabs along unpaved roads. In spite of these hardships, by the late 1950s, they had built a line of modern installations across France. To prevent troops assigned to France from observing the better living conditions in Germany, Sturgis wanted GIs to arrive at the port of la Pallice, France, not at Bremerhaven, Germany. Sturgis himself was experiencing austere living conditions. His rented room in a home nine miles from Caserne Coligny was tiny, without a private bathroom, but cost an exorbitant $154 per month.[17] During 1952, many officers assigned to ComZ headquarters in Orléans still lived in tents at nearby Saran. At the US Army Troop Classification and Assignment Center, Zweibrücken, Germany, a sergeant extolled the virtues of assignments in Germany and then derided the conditions in 1953 in France. After reading the names of the young GIs assigned to France, he concluded with "God help you." [18]

Commanding Generals, US Army Communications Zone, Europe

Commanding General	Period	Prominent Events
BG Mason J. Young	Apr 50-Mar 52	Korean War begins. France and US sign LOC agreement (06 Nov 50). Troops deploy from Germany to France (Nov 50).
MG Samuel D. Sturgis, Jr.	Mar 52-Jan 53	Most troops live in "winterized" tents. First supply over the beach exercise (June 52). Thirty-five installations and activities assigned from USAREUR to ComZ control.
MG Lemuel Mathewson	Jan 53-Feb 54	Joint Construction Agency (JCA) oversees construction. Ambulance train makes initial run (July 53). Racial integration of ComZ troops completed.
MG Philip E. Gallagher	Feb 54-Mar 56	Buildup of permanent ComZ infrastructure continues. ComZ to provide staging area camps for NEOs. Donges-Metz pipeline begins operations (1956).
MG Robert W. Colglazier, Jr.	Apr 56-Nov 57	Suez Crisis slows construction (1956). Airlift of Hungarian refugees (Operation SAFE HAVEN). First RORO ship docks at St.-Nazaire (Feb 57).
MG Edward J. O'Neill	Nov 57-Sep 59	Logistics troops to Lebanon (Operation BLUE BAT). ComZ depot stocks of Tech Services dispersed (1958). Offshore discharge exercises halted, twenty-one sites selected for use in wartime. Nine standby hospitals and 7,300 housing units built.
MG Henry R. Westphalinger	Sep 59-Oct 62	Commanding General, ComZ serves as Deputy Commander, USAREUR (1960). Offshore discharge exercises resume due to Berlin Crisis. Revolt of top French generals in Algeria (Apr 61). Berlin Wall erected (Aug 61). Atomic blast-resistant storage structures built at Vatry, Rozelier, and Aboncourt (1961). USAREUR combat units augmented (Operation ROUNDOUT).
MG Webster Anderson	Oct 62-Mar 65	McNamara orders drawdown of Base Section, fires 6,200 LWRs (1963). Supply and Maintenance Agency (S&MA) formed at Orléans. MOBIDIC computer arrives at Maison-Fort (Mar 63). 2nd Armored Div airlifted from Texas to Europe (Operation BIG LIFT). S&MA data processing center opens at Verdun (Dec 64).
BG Joseph M. Heiser, Jr.	Apr 65-June 65	McNamara drawdown of ComZ continues.
MG Robert C. Kyser	June 65-Feb 69	Fast withdrawal of troops and base closures begin (Operation FRELOC). Withdrawal from France declared completed (01 Apr 67).

NOTE: Heiser was commissioned by Officer Candidate School (OCS), Colglazier was graduate of Texas A&M College, O'Neill of University of Vermont. All others were graduates of United States Military Academy.

Army Technical Services

In peacetime, technical service troops would support combat troops in Germany by operating the lifeline across France. In wartime, some technical service units would operate the reinforced lifeline and over the beach supply operations, others would accompany combat forces into battle (called "direct support"). The technical services of the US Army were: Chemical, Engineer, Medical, Ordnance, Quartermaster, Signal, and Transportation.

Chemical units trained personnel on use of gas masks and decontamination procedures. They maintained supplies of flame throwers, smoke generators, and nerve gas as a deterrent to use by the Soviets.[19] Senior Army leaders believed that the Soviets might attack the West with chemical rather than atomic weapons so buildings and infrastructure would survive. Chemical agents could be used to disable workers, but most could rejoin the workforce after they recovered.[20] At the end of World War II, the Soviets had transported to Russia the chemical workers who had made nerve gas and the entire IG Farben chemical factory from Dyhernfurth, near Wroclaw, Poland.[21]

Engineer units built hardstands and roads at the depots and repaired runways at air bases. They practiced installing floating bridges on nearby rivers and trained to erect Bailey bridges.[22] The Bailey bridge, first used by the US Army during World War II, was a portable metal bridge designed to carry heavy loads. Each section had continuous trusses on both sides of the roadway and multiple sections could be connected to span wide rivers.[23] During offshore discharge exercises, engineers repaired ports, stabilized beaches, and installed floating piers, DeLong piers, and aerial tramways.

Medical Service units administered hospitals and ambulance trains, deployed hospital personnel to the field for training, and maintained supply depots to support medical care for the sick and wounded in peace and war.[24] Hospitals and medical depots were assigned ambulance companies, whose personnel drove ¾-ton truck ambulances that could carry four litters and military buses that could be converted to carry eighteen litters in two rows of three tiers each. In the early 1950s, railcars of the 80th Ambulance Train Company (Rail) were located at St.-Jean-de-Braye; the personnel at Maison-Fort.[25]

Ordnance units provided spare parts and repaired weapons and vehicles; stored, reworked, and delivered ammunition to Army and Air Force combat units; and disposed of unexploded bombs from both world wars. Ordnance maintenance units stocked repair parts so more than 85% of requisitions would be filled from items on hand.[26] Ordnance wreckers retrieved disabled vehicles. Their job was to "keep 'em moving and shooting." In 1955, for wartime use by Seventh Army, a thirty days supply of ammunition was stored in the Advance Section and another thirty days supply in the Base Section.[27]

Quartermaster units operated mobile bakeries and laundries and supplied food, petroleum, and clothing to the troops.[28] From Fontainebleau, the US Army Petroleum Distribution Command oversaw a pipeline from Donges, near St.-Nazaire, across France to St.-Baussant, near Metz. The pipeline supplied the POL needs of US forces in Europe. The US Army Aerial Support Center at St.-André-de-l'Eure, near Évreux, prepackaged supplies for airdrops to combat forces.

Signal units installed and maintained communication networks, such as the cryptographic circuits to the US and the microwave relay system across France. They trained in the field to install wire circuits and operate tactical radio circuits. A reliable telephone network was essential to direct troops in the field. Until 1954, tactical switchboards were used at nearly all ComZ installations.[29] In 1956, supply communications between the United States and Maison-Fort included sending punch card data by landlines and radio signals. A large antenna array was installed at Saran, near Orléans.[30]

Transportation units moved supplies and equipment from French ports to Seventh Army in Germany. Using the line-haul method, they relayed loaded trailers from truck terminal to truck terminal throughout France.³¹ In 1960, GIs of the 37th Transportation Command, headquartered at St.-Pryvé near Orléans, drove their 2½-ton trucks (the famous "deuce and a half" from World War II) and huge tractor-trailer rigs more than 28 million miles to deliver 1 million tons of cargo.³²

ComZ Depots (1958)

Army Technical Services in France

Technical Service	Primary Tasks	Principal Locations (1958)
Chemical Corps	Store chemicals, gas masks and related protective equipment. Conduct courses on countermeasures to CBR attack. Monitor and decontaminate contaminated areas. Train personnel to use flame throwers and smoke generators. Oversee storage of chemical munitions at ordnance depots.	Bussac, Sampigny
Corps of Engineers	Build depot roads, air base hardstands and runways. Support offshore discharge exercises (repair ports, prepare beaches, remove underwater obstacles and mines). Train for combat support (bridge, pipeline, and storage tank construction; mine warfare). Print, store, and issue maps for USEUCOM. Evaluate French roads, bridges, caves, and beaches. Install metal prefab buildings, rehab barracks and mess halls, and construct recreation areas.	Bordeaux, Chinon, St.-Ay, Toul
Medical Service Corps	Store medical supplies at depots for USEUCOM and in caves for NEO evacuees. Administer hospitals and ambulance trains. Operate dental and optical labs for USEUCOM. Provide preventive medical services for troops and dependents. Deploy hospital units to field for training (erect tents, set up equipment). Inspect mess halls, barracks, and recreation facilities. Spray DDT to kill mosquitoes.	Croix-Chapeau, Vassincourt, Vitry-le-François
Ordnance Corps	Repair weapons and vehicles. Recondition combat vehicles for MAP. Store, maintain, and issue conventional ammo and advance weapons. Store war reserves and pre-position combat equipment for USAREUR. Dispose of unexploded munitions (EOD).	Braconne, Captieux, Fontenet, Nancy, Trois-Fontaines
Quartermaster Corps	Operate mobile bakery, shower, and laundry units. Store and issue rations, clothing, bed rolls, furniture, and POL. Repair clothing, refrigeration units, and office equipment. Manage commissary system. Operate Donges-Metz POL pipeline. Provide airdrop delivery of supplies for SOTFE and humanitarian operations.	Ingrandes, Metz, Périgueux, St.-André-de-l'Eure

Signal Corps	Store, repair, and issue field telephones, radar equipment, cable, batteries, and Geiger counters. Take photographs and provide training films. Install and maintain microwave transmitter stations. Train to deploy mobile communication networks in field. Support Silk Purse airborne command post. Operate emergency underground command posts.	Camp Angevillers, Maison-Fort, Poitiers, Saumur, Verdun
Transportation Corps	Move supplies and equipment from ports to depots. Conduct offshore discharge exercises. Store and operate US Army marine fleet. Transport personnel by helicopters and fixed-wing aircraft. Operate and maintain diesel locomotives at tank farms and depots.	Maison-Fort, Poitiers, Rochefort, La Rochelle, Rozelier, Sommesous, Toul, le Verdon-sur-Mer

Abbreviations

CBR	Chemical, biological & radiological	POL	Petroleum, oil & lubricants
EOD	Explosive Ordnance Disposal	SOTFE	Support Operations Task Force, Europe
MAP	Military Assistance Program	USAREUR	US Army, Europe
NEO	Noncombatant Evacuation Order	USEUCOM	US European Command

Supply and Maintenance Depots

By the end of 1953, twenty depots for the Army technical services were operational in France. Each depot handled the stocks of a single technical service. The Ordnance Corps had the most depots, five; the Transportation Corps, one. Each of the seven technical services had a staff at Orléans to manage its own supply and maintenance system. By the late 1950s, staffs of three technical services had moved to Poitiers; one to Ingrandes.

War planners decided the best way to survive an atomic attack was to disperse stocks. Combat essential items of each technical service were to be stored in at least two separate locations in the Advance Section and two separate locations in the Base Section.[33, 34] To disperse supplies at each depot, at least two separate locations were used to store the same type of supplies.[35] War plans included moving 1,400 military vehicles and 20,000 tons of critical supplies of weapons and ammunition from depots in Germany to France. Twelve-thousand, non-tactical troops were to be relocated to France to support logistical operations (acronym RONTU). In the event of a Soviet invasion, stocks that could not be moved from highly-vulnerable depots in Germany were to be demolished on order of the Commanding General, Seventh Army.[36]

In 1957, ComZ asked permission from the French to evaluate caves for underground storage that could withstand atomic attack. Signal equipment and POL had been stored in caves near Saumur, NEO supplies in a cave near Montuçon, and tires in caves near St.-Dizier. ComZ evaluated several caves including sites near Pont-à-Mousson and north of Metz before USAREUR cancelled the proposed cave storage program. USAREUR planners believed that supplies stored underground in confined spaces could not be delivered to Seventh Army as rapidly as supplies stored aboveground. Ordnance personnel believed ammunition stored aboveground in widely dispersed igloo structures would best survive atomic attack. Quartermaster personnel believed stocks of POL, stored above ground in containers, had been sufficiently dispersed throughout France.

By 1958, technical service depots at Braconne, Chinon, Saumur, Ingrandes, Nancy, and Verdun had been converted to general depots to store a balanced stock of combat-essential items from all the technical services. This reduced the risk of a Soviet attack destroying the entire supplies of a technical service. General depots were staffed with a cadre of personnel from each technical service.[37] Most stocks were rotated on a "first in, first out" basis so about 25% of stock would be items received that year. If the item was needed to support combat troops, it would be brand new or in well-preserved condition. War plans in 1958 were contingent on sufficient stocks in ComZ to sustain operations of Seventh Army for at least forty days of combat.[38]

Secondary sites were designated to allow further dispersion of stocks in the event of hostilities. In the northeast, secondary depot sites were the old Aérodrome d'Azelot (southeast of Nancy General Depot), Aérodrome de Doncourt-lès-Conflans (off route N3, midway between Étain and Metz), and Aérodrome Rouceaux (near Neufchâteau). During the Berlin Wall Crisis in 1961, Army engineers built ten additional off-depot storage sites to disperse supplies and equipment from depots at Verdun, Nancy, and Toul in the northeast; Chinon and Saumur in the southwest. Each of these 100-acre storage sites had one warehouse building, numerous hardstands, and perimeter security fencing.

US Army Supply Classifications (1958)

Class	Commodity
I	Subsistence items (rations*, health, and comfort items)
II	Clothing, individual equipment (e.g., weapons), and vehicles
III	Petroleum, oil, and lubricants (POL)
IV	Construction materials
V	Ammunition

*A ration is the food for one man for one day, consisting of three nutritionally adequate and balanced meals. USAREUR stored three days of rations per soldier.

In 1959, the General Accounting Office (GAO) submitted a report to US Congress that acknowledged improvements in the ComZ supply system had been observed since its recent investigations. However, the GAO reported they found large surpluses in some items, but serious shortages in others. The report cited examples of uneconomical shipping practices and suggested items that the Army could buy locally rather than purchase at higher prices in the US.[39]

Radio Relay Sites

Because the French telephone system was unreliable, the US military planned to install radio relay sites across France. Believing that tall towers would be vulnerable to air attack by the Soviets, the French initially wanted to limit the height of the towers to 130 ft. In 1952, after a long period of negotiations, twelve radio relay sites were approved; seven with 230-ft high towers, five with 165-ft high towers.[40] In 1953, the 102nd Signal Battalion operated and maintained the twelve sites, located from Saran through Fontainebleau and Verdun to Metz. Microwave relay towers had to be located less than 40 miles apart with line-of-sight between towers.[41] Most sites had two or three masonry buildings to house the reserve power generator, receiver/relay equipment, and enlisted men (EM) billets-mess.

GIs from Company D of the 102nd Signal Battalion manned the site at Clermont-en-Argonne. In 1958, site commander SFC Gordon R. Molina and four EM technicians operated microwave equipment round-the-clock to relay wireless voice and teletype communications. Voice communication was to be clear and concise, and to use the phonetic alphabet for letters when necessary. For numerals, the Army prescribed pronunciation: zero not oh (o), niner not nine, thuh-ree (3), and so on. Radio technicians were assigned to 12-hour shifts. If civilian electric power was interrupted, the technicians immediately started the reserve power generator. The GIs worked and lived at the site. They chipped-in to hire a French cook and, to supplement rations from Verdun, purchased spices and pastries on the local economy. Twice each week, a GI made the mail and food run to Verdun. For recreation, the site had a basketball net and backboard, pool table, and motion-picture projector.[42]

US Army Microwave Sites (1955)

Orléans to Fontainebleau	Fontainebleau to Metz
Saran (Loiret)*	le Plessis-aux-Tournelles (Seine & Marne)
St.-Lyé-la-Forêt (Loiret)	les Essarts-les Sézanne (Marne)
Nibelle at Bois de Beaumont (Loiret)	Soulières (Marne)
Fromont (Seine & Marne)	Tilloy-Bellay (Marne)
Vernou-la Celle near Fontainebleau (Seine & Marne)	Clermont-en-Argonne (Meuse)
	Moulainville (Meuse)
	Camp Angevillers near Metz (Moselle)

*Name given site was closest village. French department in parentheses.

In 1961, the 228th Signal Co (RR-VHF), commanded by Capt Franklyn W. Gross, was sent from Fort Gordon, Georgia to Fontenet, France during Operation ROUNDOUT. The specialized unit practiced their mission to deploy to the field with tactical radio relay (RR) vans, 8-ft tower sections and guy wire, and cable to be used to establish communications if the fixed relay sites were destroyed by the Soviets.[43] During alerts, Signal units were to rapidly set up communications in the field.

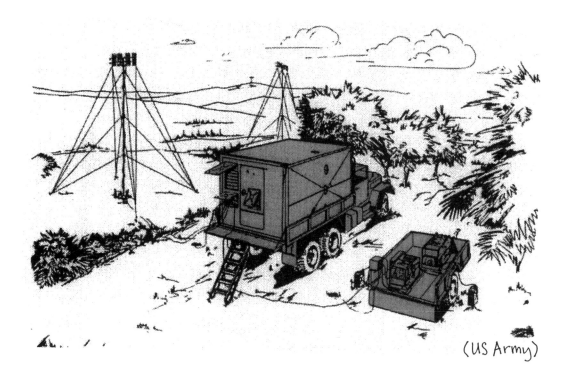

Signal Corps Mobile Communications Station

Supply Control Agencies

Supply Control Agencies (SCA) managed the supplies of the technical services in France. It was important to form a permanent civilian work force at SCAs because GIs completed their tours of duty soon after they became proficient at their jobs. Consequently in 1955, the 7962nd Army Unit at Orléans organized eight-week long courses to train French LWRs on the operation of modern IBM computer equipment. IBM personnel from Paris served as faculty, lecturing in French.[44] In 1957, the Engineer SCA at Maison-Fort assumed responsibility for all engineer supplies to ComZ and Seventh Army. In June 1958, the Quartermaster SCA at Maison-Fort moved to Ingrandes Depot.

The 269th Sig Co operated the European Data Gateway Station (EDGS) at Maison-Fort. Established in 1958, the EDGS was the data link between depots in Europe and the US. Each month, operating twenty-four-hours a day, seven days a week, EDGS traffic to and from the US averaged 825,000 IBM punched cards. Punched cards were converted to electrical impulses to travel by transmission lines over the trans-Atlantic cable at Cherbourg, or by radio waves, from Maison-Fort to Fort Detrick, Maryland. In 1964, forty-seven personnel worked at EDGS.[45]

In 1958, the Army established the Electric Accounting Machine School at Maison-Fort. The first director was M/Sgt Christian Soares. In two years, 1,021 personnel enrolled in the daytime on-duty courses. Students called the IBM electric accounting machine "The Monster."[46] In 1964, the Unit Data Processing Equipment School at Maison-Fort taught operation of key punch machines, sorters, collators, punched card interpreting, as well as calculators (IBM 604) and accounting (IBM 407) machines. The general course was seven hours per day for five weeks.[47]

In 1961, the SCAs at Maison-Fort installed electronic manifest systems to expedite delivery of supplies. At French ports, a ship's manifest could be transmitted by FAX to the appropriate SCA. This provided almost instantaneous tracking and accounting of military supplies. Under normal operations, SCAs ordered and distributed supplies throughout Europe. Under direct requisitioning, requests from the using unit went directly to the depot. Paperwork was sent to SCAs after the transaction occurred. To drastically reduce the number of requisitions by the depots, SCAs ordered up to a twelve months supply of low cost items. To ensure fast delivery to Seventh Army, special attention was given to high cost items, such as tank engines and missile components.

During the Berlin Wall Crisis, Pentagon war planners, called "McNamara's Whiz Kids" by the US press, developed a contingency plan (designated USAREUR OPLAN 704-61) to seize Albania if the Soviets attacked West Berlin. Essential war reserves were moved from ComZ depots in France to Germany and northern Italy in case the order to invade Albania was given. Most military contingency plans are drafted to be used when the implemented plan does not succeed, because hastily improvised plans also likely would not succeed. Although planners at Orléans followed orders of the Whiz Kids, they believed the contingency plan for Albania was irrational.[48]

In 1962, Maj Gen Webster Anderson, ComZ commander, directed Col Joseph M. Heiser, Jr., ComZ Chief of Staff, to streamline logistics operations in France. Previously, the technical services independently managed their own matériel. The Engineer, Ordnance, and Transportation SCAs were at Maison-Fort; Chemical, Medical, and Signal at Poitiers; and Quartermaster at Ingrandes. Now modern IBM computers would be used at the consolidated SCA to control supply, movement, and maintenance of one large logistics system rather than seven separate systems.[49] The consolidated SCA used the new Military Standard Requisition and Issue Procedures (called MILSTRIP), which had been established by the Pentagon in July 1962 to be the military-wide streamlined language of codes (stock/part number, quantity) and standard forms for requisition and issue transactions. However in the rush to complete punch cards to meet Heiser's deadlines, the task force at Maison-Fort based some of its data on guesswork.[50, 51]

Moby Dick Computers

In March 1963, the 37th Transportation Command delivered a huge mobile digital computer system from St.-Nazaire to the newly organized Supply and Maintenance Agency (S&MA), successor to the SCAs. The manufacturer Sylvania Electronics chose the acronym MOBIDIC ("Moby Dick") to emphasize the enormous size of the computer. The $4 million computer system was housed in four 6-ton, 30-ft long vans so it would not present a fixed target to the Soviets.[52] Although also installed in mobile vans, computers of 8th Infantry Division headquarters in Germany were not deployed to the field in the late 1960s. In an earlier exercise, the computers failed, likely due to temperature swings and impacts from driving on rough terrain.[53] The S&MA at Maison-Fort used MOBIDIC to enhance inventory control and to increase speed of delivery of supplies to Seventh Army. It also served as backup to the MOBIDIC at Zweibrücken, Germany, delivered to Seventh Army in 1961.[54] In 1965, the satellite S&MA computer center at Caserne Maginot, Verdun was merged with the Maison-Fort data center, controlling millions of items of supplies in depots throughout France. The Verdun computers primarily were used to process supply and equipment requests and record status of stocks. Maison-Fort computers primarily were used for supply studies and planning for future requirements.[55]

Headquarters of Logistical Commands

The greatest bulk of supplies were handled by: Ordnance, Quartermaster, and Engineers. Lesser amounts by: Signal, Medical, Transportation, and Chemical.[56] For most of the US deployment to France, headquarters for ports and depots in the southwest were at La Rochelle or Poitiers; for depots in the northeast at Verdun. From 1951 to 1958, installations in the northeast were designated the Advance Section (ADSEC); in the southwest the Base Section (BASEC). The bulk of war reserves of all technical services were located at BASEC depots and were not to be used for current operations. The ADSEC depots provided most of the supplies for the on-going operational needs of all US forces in Europe. In 1958, the sections were redesignated as numbered logistical commands.

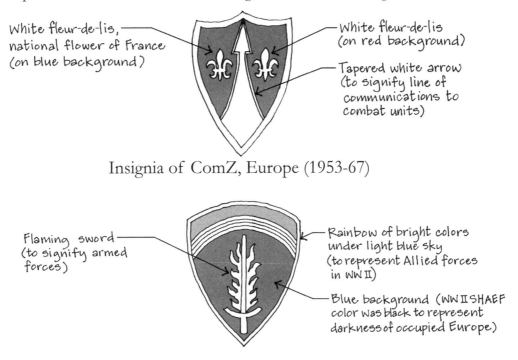

Insignia of ComZ, Europe (1953-67)

Insignia of US Army, Europe (EUCOM patch, 1947-52)

ComZ Insignia

In 1953, the Department of the Army approved an insignia design for the shoulder sleeve patch of ComZ troops. Until January 1954, troops in ComZ and in Germany wore the US Army, Europe (USAREUR) patch, Gen Eisenhower's flaming sword patch from World War II, but with a dark blue, not black, background. The ComZ patch was shaped like a shield and incorporated the red, white, and blue of the French and American flags. A tapered white arrow, representing the flow of supplies across France, divided the shield. The left portion was blue, the right red, with a white *fleur-de-lis*, the national flower of France, centered on both. ComZ troops in France wore the new insignia from January 1954 until April 1967. In 1955, a ComZ patch cost 4¢. For a few months in 1960, when the Commanding General of ComZ also served as Deputy Commander of USAREUR, ComZ troops again wore the USAREUR patch.[57]

Chiefs Move Back and Forth

USAREUR leadership believed that control of all wartime logistics should be under the ComZ commanding general. Therefore by mid-1957, the logistics command of USAREUR was reorganized by shifting all Technical Service Chiefs from Heidelberg, Germany, to Orléans.[58] After a 1959 study showed it would save money, the Technical Service staffs at Caserne Coligny in Orléans were moved back to Heidelberg, Germany, and consolidated with the logistics staff of USAREUR. The study had been prepared to please Maj Gen Edward J. O'Neill, the new USAREUR Chief of Staff, who wanted the Technical Service staffs in Germany. Shortly after the move, another study showed that money could be saved if Technical Service staffs were in Orléans where Maj Gen Henry R. Westphalinger, O'Neill's successor in Orléans, wanted them. In 1960, they moved back to Caserne Coligny where they remained until the withdrawal from France in 1967.[59] The building they vacated at Campbell Barracks in Heidelberg became headquarters of NATO's Central Army Group (CENTAG), with a staff of one-hundred US, French, and German officers. CENTAG combat troops maintained a vigil along the borders of East Germany and Czechoslovakia.[60]

Logistical Commands Merge

To streamline commands, in 1960 the 4th Logistical Command at Caserne Maginot, Verdun and the 5th Logistical Command at Caserne Aboville, Poitiers merged to become the Theater Army Support Command (TASCOM) at Verdun. TASCOM, commanded by Brig Gen Robert J. Fleming, Jr., had the largest geographic responsibility of the subordinate commands in Europe.[61] To help supervise the buildup of forces in 1961 during the Berlin Wall Crisis, 1st Logistical Command, commanded by Brig Gen William N. Redling, was deployed from Fort Bragg, North Carolina, to Poitiers. The 4th Log Command was reactivated at Verdun and TASCOM was inactivated. More than 15,000 troops were sent to ComZ during Operation ROUNDOUT. After the crisis abated in 1962, the 1st Log Command, authorized three-hundred thirty-five officers and enlisted men, returned to the US.

Drawdown of Logistical Commands

In 1963, the 3rd Logistical Command at Caserne Coligny, authorized two-hundred twenty-eight officers and enlisted men, oversaw the drawdown of logistical operations in southwestern France. In 1965, it was commanded by Brig Gen Robert C. Kyser. The 4th Log Command at Verdun continued to have responsibility for logistical operations in northeastern France until November 1963 when it returned to the United States. Beginning in January 1964, depot complex headquarters for the northeast at Nancy and southwest at Ingrandes reported to 3rd Log Command at Orléans. By 1966, when the Army began to withdraw all military forces from France, the US Army Logistical Command at Orléans, commanded by Kyser, had responsibility for all depots in France.[62]

Major Subordinate Commands in France (HQ location)

Period	Northeast Installations	Southwest Installations
1950-51	7965 Area Command (Verdun)	7964 Area Command (La Rochelle)
1951-58	Advance Section, ADSEC (Verdun)	Base Section, BASEC (La Rochelle)
1958-60	4th Logistical Command (Verdun)	5th Logistical Command (Poitiers)
1960-61	Theater Army Support Command, TASCOM (Verdun)	Theater Army Support Command, TASCOM (Verdun)
1961-62	4th Logistical Command (Verdun)	1st Logistical Command (Poitiers)
1962-63	4th Logistical Command (Verdun)	4th Logistical Command (Verdun)
1964-65	3rd Logistical Command (Orléans)	3rd Logistical Command (Orléans)
1966-67	US Army Logistical Command (Orléans)	US Army Logistical Command (Orléans)

NOTE: On 05 November 1958, ComZ was officially designated Headquarters Co, 3rd Logistical Command for personnel who operated ComZ headquarters. 3rd Log was reorganized several times in France.

Highway Transportation Command

The 37th Transportation Command (TC), successor in 1956 to the 9th Trans Highway Trans Group at St.-Pryvé-St.-Mesmin, operated the military highway line of communications, hauling matériel throughout Western Europe. In France, the 37th TC had three battalions equipped with 5-ton tractor trucks that could tow a trailer load of 7½ tons, consuming fuel at 2.7 miles per gallon.[63] The young GI drivers were responsible for loads from C-rations to missile parts worth more than $1 million. They drove from French ports to Germany, primarily on routes N10, N152, and N4. In June 1953, the 37th TC in Germany had participated in Exercise LONG HAUL, which simulated transporting cargo over routes in France that normally were not used. Trucks of the 37th TC, commanded by Col Gerald Peterson, were driven more than 200,000 miles during the exercise. Helicopters flew overhead to control convoy movements by radio contact and visual signals using colored cards.[64]

Convoy tractor truck being fueled, Camp Bussac (US Army)

In the late 1950s, truck transfer terminals in France were at Bussac, Croix-Chapeau, St.-Nazaire, Ingrandes, Maison-Fort, Châlons-sur-Marne (Vatry), and Toul. Each terminal was a self-contained trucking community equipped to refuel and maintain trucks and to provide meals and sleeping quarters for drivers. Mess halls provided drivers with box lunches. Terminals were located about 100 miles apart so drivers did not travel farther than one-day from their home terminal.[65, 66] To develop "pride-of-ownership," each driver was assigned a tractor truck and was responsible for its maintenance. Company and battalion awards were given each month for the best-maintained vehicle, mechanic of the month, and driver of the month. Safety incentive awards programs rewarded drivers for miles driven without an accident. Drivers compared mileage charts and number of safe-driving certificates awarded for each 5,000 miles of accident and violation free driving. Companies tried to achieve one million accident-free miles. Members of the US military in uniform could ride as passengers along the trucking routes. They received a free ride and, it was believed, drivers would be more alert if they had a companion.

French officials, worried about large tractor-trailers barreling down their narrow roads, frequently were reassured by 37th TC public information officers that safety was paramount. Army drivers were given courtesy cards to use if they encountered French civilians who appeared to be having vehicle problems. The card, printed in French and English, asked the "fellow driver" (*camarade de route*) to check the appropriate box next to eight situations, such as "I am out of gas" and "I need an ambulance." In the 1960s, 37th TC drivers received engraved gold plated wristwatches for achieving 100,000 accident-free miles.[67]

During trips to Germany, some ComZ drivers "borrowed" outside rearview mirrors from Seventh Army vehicles because the mirrors were larger than the standard size on Army tractor trucks in France. It appeared that units in Germany had priority for new equipment, so ComZ drivers tried to correct the inequity. Especially prized, were the outside rear view mirrors of Army Faegol buses. When no one was looking, "truck jockeys" from France removed the mirrors to install on their vehicles. Savvy drivers removed their mirrors if they had to leave their trucks unattended while on the road and hid spare mirrors in their trucks.[68, 69]

Line Haul Relays

Unlike the "Red Ball" of World War II, semitrailers carried more cargo. Truck terminals along the routes from ports to Germany allowed the cargo to keep moving because trucks were driven by locally-stationed drivers in well-maintained tractor-trailers. Loaded trailers were not permitted to stand more than one night at any truck terminal, called the "one night stand" policy. To maintain an even distribution of trailers along the line, terminals coordinated the movement of trailers, empty or loaded with US-bound goods, from Germany back to the ports.[70] Trailers were connected to tractors by "quick-connect" cable fittings. To return without a trailer was called "bobtailing." In the 1960s drivers of the 106th Trans Bn (Truck), based at Croix-Chapeau, hooked their tractor trucks to fully-loaded vans that had rolled off ships at St.-Nazaire. They delivered the cargo to Ingrandes and returned home. In the first of many leap-frog exchanges, drivers of the 28th Trans Bn (Truck), headquartered at Poitiers, hooked their tractor trucks to the vans and delivered the cargo to Maison-Fort. At the terminal, engines were allowed to cool and trucks refueled and hooked to another trailer for the return trip to Ingrandes. Drivers rested and ate at the snack bar. Another 28th Trans Bn driver and his tractor truck delivered the cargo from Maison-Fort to Vatry, near Châlons-sur-Marne, one of the longest legs of the route. Near Fontainebleau, drivers took a break at the 28th Trans Bn roadside coffee stop before continuing on to Vatry.[71] GIs called coffee break vans "sugar vans." The 70th Trans Co (Medium Truck) used the abandoned US Air Force hangars at Vatry for maintenance shops. Drivers of the 2nd Trans Bn (Truck), based at Toul, moved the cargo from Vatry to depots at Verdun, Nancy, and Metz or drove to depots in Germany. Drivers of the 72nd Trans Co (Light Truck), based at Nancy, used 2½-ton cargo trucks to deliver supplies throughout the region. These trips had many stops and could take several days.[72]

In February 1953, the first refrigerated truck company in the US Army was assigned to France. Commanded by Capt Maurice K. Wilgus and stationed at Saran near Orléans, the 1st Trans Truck Co (Refrig) transported perishable subsistence cargo throughout ComZ. The "reefer" trailer trucks could keep perishable cargo frozen for indefinite periods.[73] In March 1956, the 1st Trans Co had sixty 7½-ton reefers (called "rolling ice boxes" by GIs). The longest weekly haul was from Paris to Bordeaux. If a reefer broke down on the road, an emergency maintenance team was dispatched from Saran.[74]

Traffic Problems

In the early 1950s, most GI drivers had a difficult time finding US Army installations in France. In June 1952, Lt Col V. G. Paul, who served on ComZ engineering staff, claimed that it took his driver two hours to find the Nancy Ordnance Depot.[75] In October 1953, the Orleans Area Command (OAC) asked the Préfet du Loiret to authorize the posting of directional traffic signs in English to help relieve the traffic congestion caused by US military vehicles. The OAC believed that signage in English would assist drivers from Germany and other posts in France to locate the many US Army installations in the Orléans area. Drivers frequently became lost and used streets too narrow for the 2½- and 5-ton cargo trucks. The standard 5-ton cargo truck, over 8-ft wide, would totally block the street. Unfortunately, the French did not like to be reminded of the presence of the US military and the yellow and blue directional signs in English quickly disappeared. The posting of signs in English did not respect the principle that signage in France should be in French. Eventually, better road maps and way-finding briefings by NCOs lessened the problem.

To verify the length of convoys, provided in advance by the US military, French national police posted plainclothesmen on street corners to count the number of military vehicles in convoys entering Orléans. Because the convoys could be long, standing at the same location counting vehicles was an extremely boring assignment.

In January 1960, to prevent injury to pedestrians and cyclists, France outlawed "lethal" hood and radiator ornaments on vehicles. At Orléans, ComZ provost marshal Col Patrick H. Devine ordered owners of privately owned vehicles (POV) to remove animal, rocket, torpedo, and other stylized hood ornaments which American car manufacturers used to identify make of vehicle. He also suggested owners remove metal curb feelers, headlight visors, and insect deflectors.[76] Starting in June 1952, POVs displayed black license plates with white numerals preceded by the letters CF. License plates for Constabulary forces in Germany had a C. An F was added for the plates in France. By early 1954, there were 12,000 POVs registered in ComZ.[77] GIs purchased gasoline ration coupons at the post exchange to use on base and at QM-approved civilian ESSO stations. Monthly allowance of gasoline depended on size of the vehicle. In the late 1950s, a gallon of gas using coupons cost 25¢, much less than highly-taxed French gasoline.

Roadeos

Each year competitions, called "roadeos," were held to test a military driver's skills. To test parking ability, drivers of 5-ton tractor trucks had to back a trailer between closely spaced wooden barriers up to a simulated loading dock. Points were awarded for not touching a barrier and for how close the trailer was to the loading dock. Drivers of 2½-ton trucks had to parallel park without bumping wooden barriers or barrels simulating curbs. Drivers of ¼-ton jeeps drove through an "offset alley" which represented village streets. Wooden barriers were placed parallel and straight for 15 ft, then offset to the left and back to the right, with only 2-inch clearance for the jeep.[78, 79]

During the winter of 1963, the coldest of the century, canals in France froze. Coal, which most French used to heat their homes, could not be transported by commercial barges. In January and February, the 37th TC hauled coal from Mannheim, Germany, to Orléans and Ingrandes.[80] One convoy of twenty trucks from the 69th Trans Co departed with 300 tons of coal at midnight from Rhineau, Germany. Driving in the dark on icy roads, they arrived by mid-afternoon the next day at Orléans.[81]

37th Transportation Command (TC) Commanders (USAREUR)*

Commanding Officer	Period of Service	Commanding Officer	Period of Service
Col Gerald Peterson	1953	Col Erman M. Newman	1958-61
Col Burton E. Miles	1953-54	Col Floyd H. Buch	1961-63
Col Luis Greenfield	1954-56	Col Jack C. Knox	1963-65
Col John A. Martin	1956-57	Col John E. Murray	1965-67
Col George R. Russell	1957-58		

*In November 1956, headquarters moved from Mannheim, Germany to Saran. In March 1958, it moved to SAMAC at St.-Pryvé-St.-Mesmin.

French Employees

French nationals were hired in great numbers to work at US installations, but not directly by the US. Article 9 of the NATO Status of Forces Agreement stipulated that conditions of employment of nationals would be determined by the host nation. The US requested personnel and the French recruited, screened, and hired workers through government labor offices. The French added an administration surcharge of 2½% of the gross payroll. The workers were called local wage rate (LWR) employees because their wages were based on prevailing wages for similar work on the French economy. At the end of 1952, ComZ employed 5,892 French nationals. Two years later the total had more than doubled to 13,201. However, recruitment was difficult because skilled workers were hard to find, most installations were at remote locations, and nearby housing was scarce. Bonuses were offered for passing English-language tests and suggesting work improvements. Pay increased after 6 months or a year, and per diem was paid for work-related travel.[82] Each year wages were raised by 5 to 10% to compete with civilian jobs in the growing economy. LWRs employed at post exchanges and clubs could be paid higher than comparable jobs on the economy because the funds came from sales (food, beverage, slot machines) and dues, not funds appropriated by US Congress. In rural areas, LWRs were trained to be automobile mechanics, typists, and forklift operators.[83] This training by the US military increased the skill level of the French civilian workforce. In 1957, qualified French personnel at ComZ installations were given more responsible jobs. The program, called the "Nancy Staffing Plan," began in late 1955 at Nancy Ordnance Depot. The goal was to increase career opportunities for LWRs. The better jobs now open to LWRs would normally have been held by Department of Army Civilians (DACs) or military personnel.[84]

Like the GIs, who dreaded being sent from Germany to France, most of the initial French workforce hired in 1950-51 in Paris resigned rather than move to depots in rural areas. Although the pay scale was set by the French government, Americans could offer substantial performance and

Christmas bonuses and travel allowances to lure workers to undesirable posts.[85] At larger installations, like Orléans, the US Army provided free bus transportation to outlying villages where LWRs lived. In January 1954, the Intendance Militaire, a French Army element attached to the French Quartermaster, assumed administration of the LWRs. Annual leave was reduced to less than equivalent jobs in the private sector and paid sick leave was eliminated, making hiring more difficult.[86] Nevertheless by 1962, the Orléans area installations employed about 3,000 French LWRs, although ongoing unrest in Algeria from 1954 to 1962 and the Suez Crisis in 1956 had significantly reduced the labor pool. In 1956, the French government agreed to the US plan to hire qualified Hungarian refugees to work for ComZ in France. Refugees were to be hired in accordance with normal LWR employment procedures.[87, 88]

Awards to LWRs

Workers were offered awards for suggestions to improve workplace production at US military installations. In 1952 at La Rochelle, Robert Lesbazeilles, an LWR employed at the 319th Station Hospital in Caserne Aufrédi, invented a method to painlessly remove plaster casts from patients. Previously surgical shears or vibrating saws were used. By the Lesbazeilles method, a wool sock and two strips of piano wire were placed lengthwise on the patient's broken arm or leg before a cast was applied. Using an H-shaped key, the wires were pulled to slice the cast in half. Brig Gen Ernest A. Bixby, BASEC commander, presented Lesbazeilles with a 3,500 franc award (about $10) and certificate for his submission to the Army Suggestion Program.[89]

By the late 1950s, LWRs could earn up to 3% of their annual pay for accepted suggestions. It was hoped that every LWR would submit a suggestion each quarter.[90] In early 1958, M. Lallement, an enterprising LWR at the Verdun General Depot, suggested the reward for a good suggestion should be a ride in a helicopter. Lallement had watched Army helicopters from Rozelier flying over the depot. The awards committee accepted his suggestion, and the depot commander arranged a ride for Lallement. In a newspaper interview, Lallement thanked the US Army for helping him realize his dream and said: "My next suggestion is going to be a trip to the moon."[91]

Col Joseph I. Gurfein with French employees, Chinon Depot, 1962 (US Army)

French Customs in Workplace

Americans were frequently reminded that they were in France as guests subject to its laws and culture.[92] Base newspapers stressed the importance of being a well-behaved guest. Troops were told to respect traditions such as the mandated two-hour lunch break for LWRs. Each morning upon arrival at work, LWRs shook hands and greeted each of their colleagues. At the end of the workday, they shook hands and bid them farewell. At first, this French custom seemed odd to the Americans who only shook hands when introduced to strangers or with a friend after a long absence. GIs who worked closely with the French soon became proficient at rendering the correct handshake, one pump up and down, not the vigorous American shake of two or three ups and downs. In 1961 at Fontenet, 1st Lt John A. Nark, who supervised fifty LWRs at the US European Command Property Account Office, arrived at least fifteen minutes early to allow time to shake hands before beginning work. When Nark was late, he sneaked in a side door.[93] Strong odors were another difference. Many workers rarely bathed and often wore the same clothing for many days, masking body odors with strong perfume. Cigarettes had a strong "skunk-like" odor. Frenchmen smoked pungent Gauloises or Gitanes cigarettes, which dangling from their lower lips seemed to defy gravity.

Relations with the French

At the end of 1951, a Troop Relations Committee was sponsored by the French Ministry of Defense to study how to improve Franco-American relations. To explain what the US military was doing in France, most installations arranged tours for French journalists and invited private citizens to visit during "open house" each year on Armed Forces Day and Memorial Day.

In January 1953, ComZ began distributing an orientation handbook to newly arrived military and civilian personnel. The 45-page "Handbook on France" (written by Harry Mann of ComZ Information Div) explained why the US Army was in France, stressed the importance of good relations with the French, and provided examples of French customs and traditions.[94] The same month at a Base Section commander's conference in La Rochelle, Brig Gen Ernest A. Bixby, BASEC commander, ordered the seventy senior officers in attendance to "conform to French customs and not expect the French to conform [to yours]."[95]

In 1956, Maj Gen Robert W. Colglazier, Jr., ComZ commander, hired a young French woman to be his community relations advisor. Believing that children made friends faster than adults, she suggested that students in home economics classes at French and American schools exchange places one day each week. French children were fascinated by drinking fountains at the dependents schools. Due to the student exchanges, French families invited Americans to their homes and American families reciprocated.[96] By 1959, fourteen Army installations had hired French civilians to advise the post commanders on community relations.[97] Post commanders also had an LWR, who served as an interpreter, accompany them to French functions.

On 17 March 1955, Maj Arthur G. Petrich, Adjutant of the Orleans Installation, endorsed a letter request from the Orléans Police Commissioner. Military and privately owned vehicles (POV) were not to use loud horns within city limits, and POVs parked on city streets at night should be illuminated by parking lights. Because parking lights drained the battery if left on all night, most Americans installed special French-made warning lights on their cars. Commanders were to take measures to curtail drunken GIs from shouting and singing on the streets late at night.

Each Christmas, the OAC and ComZ Headquarters held parties for hundreds of French orphans. The parties featured entertainment, refreshments, and presents for the children.[98] In December 1953, off-duty carpenters of the 982nd Engineer Construction Battalion built twenty-five wooden "Hobby

Horses" for French orphans.[99] Every summer, the MPs at Harbord Barracks hosted a picnic for the children of the French gendarmes. In 1960, to thank the French for use of the Loire River for a pontoon bridge building exercise, the 553rd Engineer Battalion from Maison-Fort leveled ground for a playground at Beaugency. On their off-duty time, 553rd Engineer troops used sand and gravel from the nearby Sandillion quarry to build an athletic field for handicapped children of the Institut des Sourds-Muets in Orléans.[100]

In fall 1953, WACs from 7962nd Army Unit Det C at Maison-Fort, at the urging of SFC Alice E. Flynn, adopted the Ste.-Marie's Orphanage in Olivet. The orphanage, run by Catholic nuns of the Order of St. Vincent de Paul, had fifty girls aged 2½ to 14 years old. That Christmas, the orphans had their first Christmas tree. A French speaking GI, dressed as Santa Claus (*Père Noël*), distributed toys and clothing to the girls. Funds were raised at the EM Club at Maison-Fort and the Ordnance Supply Control Agency where Flynn worked. In 1954, the WACs donated a large refrigerator and food mixer for the orphanage kitchen and a sewing machine because the nuns had been repairing girl's clothing by hand. They also gave the girls leather suitcases to carry their clothing to summer camp. Previously, the girls had used paper bags.[101]

On 26 June 1954, the only water pump at la Ferté-St.-Aubin near Olivet broke. The 982nd Engineers, commanded by Lt Col Hobert H. Hoover, responded to the mayor's request for help. Until the pump was repaired, the battalion's 1,500-gal tanker delivered potable water to the 4,000 villagers. Each day, housewives of la Ferté arrived with buckets when they heard the horn of the tanker arriving at one of nine distribution locations. Painted on rear of the tanker was: "eau potable USA-gratuit." [102, 103]

In October 1962, the *Gazette d'Orléans*, a monthly news bulletin in English, printed an anonymous letter regarding aid to the French by US Army engineers. The letter cited construction projects such as sports fields built for several small villages around Orléans. Perhaps tongue-in-cheek, the Frenchman wrote that no one would blame the GI if in the evening he visited a bar to drink alcohol for antiseptic purposes and sang loudly to clear his throat that had been "ill-treated" during his dusty construction work to benefit French citizens.[104] Jean Autran, an Orléans businessman, published the bulletin because of his affection for GIs who had liberated Orléans in August 1944. Autran, who operated the Klenix dry cleaners at 15, rue du Faubourg-Bannier near Caserne Coligny, was called "Johnny" by his American customers. His 10-page bulletin was distributed free to Americans. It included tips on living in France, travel, peculiarities of Orléans citizens, and local food and entertainment. The number of copies printed increased from 700 per issue in 1957 to 3,000 in 1959.[105] Autran also led the group which donated a bronze bell to the Maison-Fort chapel. The 20-inch diameter bell, cast at Bollée Fonderie de Orléans, weighed 175 pounds. In 1957, the bell was mounted in an Alpine-type belfry built by the 553rd Engineers. Inscribed on the bell was: "Dedicated to a Better Understanding Between Peoples of All Faith." [106]

In 1964, Sp5 Robert M. Hanson, tractor operator with the 553rd Engineers, received a medal for bravery from Orléans Mayor Roger Secrétan. Shortly after 6 pm on 02 April 1964, Hanson rescued a young woman from the flood swollen Loire River. After parking his POV in front of the American Red Cross Center on Quai Barentin, Hanson saw Mlle Nicole Le Follic being carried downstream by the swift current. French bystanders watched Hanson dive into the icy river and bring the pregnant woman to safety on the riverbank. The modest Hanson left the scene after medical personnel arrived.[107, 108] In March 1965, Maj Gen Webster Anderson, ComZ commander, presented the Soldier's Medal to Hanson for saving Le Follic's life.[109]

Mail Service for the Troops

Mail was important for troop morale, especially young men far away from home for the first time. GIs relied on the Army Post Office (APO) system to keep in touch with family and friends. Shipment of alcoholic beverages was forbidden, and mail from the US to France could not contain sugar or tobacco. Airmail from the US took about one week; surface mail, including newspapers and packages, took four to six weeks. Airmail for the Advance Section installations became two days faster in the summer of 1954, when the 29th Base Post Office at Metz started using commercial airlines at Orly. Previously, airmail had been delivered to Rhein-Main AB near Frankfurt, Germany, and flown by Military Air Transport Service (MATS) when sufficient mail had accumulated.[110] The cost for mail by APO was equal to rates for equivalent class of mail within the US. In the 1950s, an airmail letter cost 7¢; a regular first-class letter 4¢. Rates increased by 1¢ in early January 1963.[111]

Army Postal Units (APU) received, sorted, and delivered mail to the troops and secured large sums of money for monthly payrolls and from sales of money orders and stamps. In the 1950s, APU commanders had to be alert to prevent theft of funds from money order and Military Payment Certificate transactions. Dishonest postal clerks could record the correct amount of money on the original copy of the purchase form, but alter the carbon copies retained for postal records to show a lesser amount. The clerk then pocketed the difference. Eventually auditing of disbursed funds compared to payments received would reveal the theft, which could then be traced to the clerk. Normally, the thief would be court-martialed.[112]

In 1962, 1st Lt Ollie P. Anderson, Jr. was sent to France from Fort Dix, New Jersey, to command the 17th APU at Bussac although he had not received training on how to operate a postal unit. Like most young Army officers, he quickly learned to rely on his top sergeant. SFC Charles A. Travenia, an experienced chief postal clerk, showed Anderson the basics of postal operations and how to provide service to troops scattered over a vast area of southwestern France. Small detachments of the 17th APU were stationed at Braconne, Fontenet, Bordeaux, and Captieux. APUs in France had 2½-ton vans configured as mobile post offices to be deployed to the field during war.[113]

SFC Charles A. Travenia, 17th APU, in mobile post office, May 1962 (US Army)

Military Post Offices

Most Army Post Offices (APOs) were full service post offices, but at smaller installations they were only addresses that had regular mail runs to the nearest full service APO. Troops received mail during the traditional "mail call" formation, where sergeants shouted out names of individuals who had mail.[114] If a GI had a long name that was difficult to pronounce, usually he was given the moniker Private Alphabet. In the beginning, there were three APOs for the US Army in France: Paris was APO 58; Advance Section, APO 122; and Base Section, APO 21. When ComZ Headquarters moved from Paris to Orléans, they kept APO 58. By the mid-1950s, installations in the Paris and Orléans areas were so widespread that numerous APOs were required. To correspond to the five digit ZIP code used in the US, by 1965 the prefix 09 or 090 had been added to existing APOs in Europe (Trois-Fontaines became 09287, Poitiers 09044).

US Army APO Addresses in France*

Advance Section	Bussac 215	**Intermediate** (OAC and SACCZ)
Aboncourt 42	Captieux 213	Ardon (Maison Fort) 52
Angevillers 216	Chinon 256	Camp des Loges (EUCOM) 128, 163
Billy-le-Grand 122	Chizé 219, 44	La Chapelle-St.-Mesmin 58
Brienne-le-Château 325	Croix-Chapeau 219	Fontainebleau 11
Châlons-sur-Marne 325, 757	Fontenet 259	Marly-le-Roi or Louveciennes
Étain 122	Gradignan 255	(SHAPE) 55
Metz 216	Le Havre 253	Melun 11
Nancy 204, 679	Ingrandes 258	Neuilly (Hospital) 230
Rozelier 122	Laleu 21	Olivet 41
St.-Baussant 288	la Pallice 21	Orléans 58
Sampigny 122	le Pellerin 681	Paris 58, 161
Toul 288	Périgueux 215, 257	Paris (Bel Manoir) 163, 181
Trois-Fontaines 287	Poitiers 44	Paris (JCA) 230
Vassincourt 287	Pornichet 203	Paris (Embassy, MAAG) 777
Vatry 325	La Roche-sur-Yon 21	Paris (32-34, rue Marbeuf) 686
Verdun 122	Rochefort 217	Paris (SACCZ) 62
Vitry-le-François 325	La Rochelle 21	St.-André-de-l'Eure 253
Woippy 110	St.-Jean d'Angély 21, 259	St.-Cloud (Dependents School) 670
Base Section	St.-Nazaire 681	
Bassens 255, 682	Saumur 322	
Bordeaux 16, 255	Soulac-sur-Mer 78	
Braconne 211	Le Verdon 78	

*OAC is abbreviation for Orleans Area Command, SACCZ for Seine Area Command, JCA for Joint Construction Agency (Paris), and MAAG for Military Assistance Advisory Group.

The Air Post Office (APO) system served the USAFE air bases and depots. In July 1953, USAFE activated the 12th Air Postal Squadron (APS) at 8, ave Kléber in Paris to operate six APOs. The squadron grew from ninety-six officers and airmen in 1953 to one-hundred ninety-four in 1955. A two-story facility at 41, rue d'Alleray was acquired to process the large volume of mail for the numerous air bases and depots now in France.[115] Mail from the United States arrived by ship at Bremerhaven, Germany, or by airlift to Orly. At the Alleray facility, mail was sorted for delivery to APOs where unit mail clerks then distributed it at "mail call."

The 12th APS also delivered monthly payrolls by train from Paris to the air bases and depots. Payroll couriers were required to carry loaded .45 cal automatic pistols, but were instructed to fire weapons only when all other means of defense had failed. Responding to French complaints in 1952 about "trigger happy" depot guards who had fired at civilians, Maj Gen Samuel D. Sturgis, Jr. assured the French that GIs would not fire warning shots or even point loaded weapons as a threat.[116] In August 1955, Airman Second Class Melvin B. Magin of the 12th APS accidentally shot himself while serving as postal guard on a train to La Rochelle. Magin was seriously injured when his .45 cal pistol discharged when he inserted a clip of seven rounds.[117]

US Air Force APO Addresses in France

Air Base		Air Depot
Bordeaux 16	Évreux 253	Châteauroux 10, 656
Cazaux 16	Évreux (St.-Michel Hosp) 62	Chizé 131
Chambley 247	Laon 17	Metz-Frescaty 83
Chaumont 119	Paris (Orly) 230	Moulins 10, 290
Dreux 84	Phalsbourg 115	St.-Mihiel 188
Étain 87	Toul-Rosières 83	St.-Nazaire 203

Troop Newspapers

The first weekly Army troop information newspaper in France was the *ComZ Cadence*. The first issue, edited by M/Sgt Albert W. Spratley, was printed on 05 October 1951 in Orléans. The Army had to purchase type with dollar symbol and quotation marks for the French printers.[118] Spratley set the standard for newspapers in France and was known for clever headlines such as "The Yanks are Coming" for a story on mobile dental service for troops in remote areas and a review of training film that was "reely good."[119]

In 1953, the ComZ became so vast that newspapers were inaugurated at Verdun to cover the northeast (*The Advance*) and at La Rochelle to cover the southwest (*Basec Mission*).[120] The *ComZ Cadence*, which for two years had served troops throughout France, transitioned to primarily serve troops in the Orléans area. In June 1955, it was renamed the *Orleans Item*. In addition to the three weekly newspapers, there were twelve mimeographed newspapers in the command. In March 1957, editor M/Sgt Raymond L. Parsons launched *The Pariscope* to serve troops in the Seine area.[121] The troop newspapers were free, but GIs were asked to share their copy. *The Stars and Stripes*, an "unofficial" newspaper published in Germany for US forces in Europe, was sold on installations in France and was delivered to government housing for 6½¢ per issue.

By tradition, established by *The Stars and Stripes* during the World Wars, commanders were not to interfere with content of troop newspapers, although sometimes they did. Troop newspapers generally did not slant the news and advertisers had no influence—there were no advertisements.[122] Many units had monthly newspapers printed on standard size government paper. GI editors tried to include stories and photos that pleased their commanding officer. In 1964, Nancy Depot's *Nancy Times* was cited by the Department of Defense as top overseas publication in direct image offset multilith. Braconne Depot's *La Foret* was tops in mimeograph class.[123]

Army Troop Newspapers (Orléans Area)

Name	Period	Name	Unit
The Orleans EM Report	1951	The Communicator	1st Signal Group*
ComZ Cadence	1951-55	The Constructioneer	982nd Engineer Bn
Orleans Item	1955-64	Journal de L'Hopital	34th General Hospital
Panorama (for LWRs)	1957-66	The Signal Scene	Sig Agency Maison-Fort
ComZ Cadence	1964-67	The Transporter	37th Trans Group**
		The Transeair	ComZ Trans Command

*In 1960s, the 1st Signal Group included: 269th Signal Co (Svc) and 275th Signal Co (Svc) at Orléans, 313th Signal Co (Svc) at Poitiers, 256th Signal Co (Spt) at Verdun, and 532nd Signal Co (Svc) at Toul.
**37th Transportation Group included: 106th Trans Bn at Croix-Chapeau, 28th Trans Bn at Poitiers, and 2nd Trans Bn at Toul.

To keep servicemen busy and out of trouble, newspapers included schedules of Special Services Club activities (dances, language classes), religious worship services, Rod and Gun Club and other sports activities, and travel hints. Like hometown news, reports were on births, vehicle accidents, fires, deaths, personnel transfers, and promotions in rank. Extensive coverage was given to sporting events in France and professional sports in the US. Most issues had articles on service to others (such as troops supporting French orphanages, Gray Lady volunteers at hospitals), opportunities for education (University of Maryland Overseas, US Armed Forces Institute courses), and value of experiencing travel and French culture. Consistent themes of the newspapers were importance of education, family, service to others, and to drive safely and be good guests in France. The first US Air Force newspapers were at Bordeaux (*Bordeaux Traveler*) and Châteauroux (*CHAD News*). In 1961-62, the *Toul Tiger* published "Conversation with a Mouse," a biweekly column written by Capt Arnold Porter, chaplain at Toul-Rosières AB. Randolph Mouse, an opinionated church mouse, offered spiritual and ethical advice. Randolph allegedly had flown from Randolph AFB, Texas, by hiding in Porter's footlocker.[124]

GI Santa Claus, Poitiers, December 1962 (US Army)

Air Force Newspapers in France

Installation	Newspaper	Installation	Newspaper
Bordeaux	Bordeaux Traveler Bordeaux News	Étain	Vapor Trails
Chambley	Chambley Sabre Recon-Recount (1962-63) Air Strike Sentinel (1966)	Évreux	Skyliner Normandy Wings Combat Cargo (1960-64) Evreux Image (1964-65)
Châteauroux (CHAD)	CHAD News (1952-54) CAMA News (1954-58) AMFEA News (1958-62) Sabre Blade (1962-66)	Laon	Laon Sentinel
		Moulins	Depot Digest
		Orly	Orly Diplomat (1953-55) Orly Oracle (1955-58)
Chaumont	Jet-Gram (1952-53) Jet-48 (1953-59) Wing Tips (1961-62) Bold Defender (1962-63) Chaumont Gazette	Phalsbourg	Phalsbourg Falcon Phalsbourg Flyer
		Toul-Rosières (TRAB)	Skyliner (1954-55) Toul Tiger (1956-62) The Photogram (1965-66)
Dreux	Dreux Review		

Abbreviations

AMFEA   Air Materials Force, European Area   CAMA   Central Air Material Area

Troops and the Law

Many draftee soldiers were not enthusiastic to serve in the Army. Some, who had been convicted of crimes in civilian life, were given the option of going to jail or into the Army. An option the Army called a "judicial referral." It was hoped that long work hours, sports activities, and Special Services Clubs would keep GIs so busy that drinking, fighting, and general delinquency would be low. In 1952, USAREUR issued a curfew to keep GIs off the streets at night, from midnight to 6 am during weekdays, 1 am to 6 am on Saturday nights. Officers and upper three grades of NCOs with dependents were exempted.[125] Cafés would be declared off limits to Americans if prostitution was prevalent or brawls were frequent.

According to the NATO Status of Forces Agreement (SOFA), US troops and their dependents were subject to French civil and criminal laws while in France.[126] When off duty, on leave, or absent without official leave (AWOL), troops could be arrested by French police for violations of French laws. In the US, a person could not be tried for a criminal offense unless present during trial proceedings. In France, defendants could be convicted whether or not they were present in court. During the 1950s, about two-thirds of US troops, who were tried in French courts, did not attend proceedings. Most of these troops received fines and could not leave France without paying them.[127]

Criminal Jurisdiction Provisions of SOFA (1953)

Primary Jurisdiction	Offenses by US Forces or Civilian Employees
US Forces (military courts-martial)	Violate US law, but not French law Committed on duty Committed off duty, if solely against US forces or civilian employees, or against US property
French Government (local courts)	Violate French law, but not US law Committed off duty Committed on leave or when AWOL

In 1957, the French Ministry of Justice agreed to waive jurisdiction on all offenses by Americans against French nationals, including serious offenses, unless there was considerable public interest or political importance involving the case.[128] By the mid-1960s, each year about 4,000 criminal cases were subject to French jurisdiction, but more than 80% involved relatively minor traffic offenses. Because waivers of jurisdiction were granted for most of the cases involving serious offenses, each year only about sixty US prisoners were held in French jails, pending trial. By agreement with the French government, each month Army MP officers visited the soldiers in French jails to assess their treatment compared to US prison standards. Common complaints about freezing cells during winter in northeastern France were noted by the MPs, but usually nothing was done.[129] A stockade opened in September 1954 at Châteauroux AD for prisoners of the US Air Force. Each of its twenty cells had a shower, unlike the Spartan conditions at the Army's 44th MP Det stockade at Verdun and 51st MP Det stockade at Laleu. When US forces withdrew from France in 1967, ten US prisoners remained in French jails.

Military Police in France

From 1951 to 1953, the 529th MP Battalion provided military law enforcement for the Base Section; the 382nd MP Battalion for the Advance Section. In 1953, the 524th MP Battalion, headquartered at La Rochelle, became the sole provider of military law enforcement for ComZ. In December 1955 after occupation service in Austria, the 61st and 64th MP Companies were reactivated in France to replace the 524th MP Battalion. Because the two companies did not have sufficient personnel to police the entire ComZ, numbered detachments were created to provide port security at Bassens, la Pallice, and St.-Nazaire. Detachments also were assigned to depot security at Bussac, Captieux, and Chinon and to small stockades at Braconne, Fontenet, Ingrandes, and Poitiers. Most of the detachments served from 1956 to 1961.[130] To check depot security, MP vehicle patrols drove along security fences. At night, MPs "tested the perimeter" of the depots to be sure guards were posted and alert.

In May 1952, personnel from Company D of the 382nd MP Battalion at Caserne Maginot conducted a course on military policing for handpicked GIs from the Advance Section. The future MPs learned how to respond to reported incidents and how to mark an accident scene. For vehicle searches, they learned which perfectly innocent household tools were used by burglars. After graduation, the new MPs were stationed at Nancy, Metz, Verdun, and Bar-le-Duc.[131, 132]

During 1955 to 1966, the 61st MP Co had platoons at Verdun, Trois-Fontaines, Vitry-le-François, Châlons-sur-Marne, and Brienne-le-Château. During 1955 to 1967, the 64th MP Co had platoons at Toul and Metz. In 1961-62 during the Berlin Wall Crisis, the 504th MP Battalion had elements of Co A at La Rochelle and Chizé, and Co B at Metz, Brienne-le-Château, and Toul. The 202nd MP Co had platoons at Poitiers, Braconne, Chinon, and Ingrandes.

At Orléans, routine work in 1959 for ninety-two enlisted MPs involved security checks of government property and investigation of reported incidents. They also escorted convoys, checked vehicle registration, and staffed guard posts at main gates. A roving patrol worked along with French police. The Provost Marshal duties were similar to a civilian chief-of-police. Charts recorded incidents by location and frequency so patrols could be sent to incident-prone areas.[133] At most posts, the vehicle "courtesy patrols" handled civilians and military personnel and normally were one American MP, one French CRS, and one French gendarme.[134]

Relationships with Females

A pamphlet given to troops assigned to France warned troops to keep out of trouble and not to act on false assumptions of French morals. It noted that parents would "size you up" before allowing their daughter on a date, and many girls would not go out without a chaperon. Troops were advised that they would be disappointed "if you have the idea that you'll find a nation of pretty girls with you on their minds." Troops were to stay away from places where "tarts" congregated. They also were to avoid women who were sitting alone in cafés "for obvious business reasons."[135] Troops who contacted sexually transmitted diseases were treated with penicillin and sent to their commanding officers, who could administer non-judicial punishment such as forfeiture of pay and/or confinement to barracks. Commanders had discipline authority under Article 15 of the Uniform Code of Military Justice.[136] At some Army hospitals in France, enlisted medics ran illicit "VD Clinics" for their fellow GIs.

Troops and the Courts

On 02 July 1953, two GIs while AWOL assaulted an Orléans taxi driver and drove the stolen taxi to Paris. French police arrested them four days later and charged them with "highway robbery." If convicted of violent theft under the French Penal Code, they faced a mandatory life sentence at hard labor in a French penal colony. Fortunately for the GIs, the French court was lenient. The convicted GIs were sentenced to five years in French prison without hard labor and to pay court costs of $76.[137, 138] In 1955, the sentences were reduced to 4½ years. A few months later, they were paroled to the US Army with the proviso that they immediately would be removed from France.[139]

US troops would be arrested if they were caught emulating the urination habits of French males who relieved themselves facing away from traffic alongside roads and on the walls of buildings. Unfortunately, some US troops took this as a license to urinate anywhere. In the late 1950s, a drunk, off-duty GI was arrested by French police in La Rochelle for urinating on a parked taxi with the driver and a passenger inside. To the amusement of Raymond Carter, LWR interpreter for the US Army Port Area Command who accompanied him to trial, the GI said he had learned his lesson and promised his commanding officer: "Sir, the only way I'll ever get into trouble again is by singing too loudly in church!" The French court fined the GI.[140] In Paris, major streets had metal cylindrical enclosures called *pissoirs*. The size of phone booths, they provided semi-privacy for urination into the storm sewer. Because enclosures were open at the bottom, a user's legs and urine stream were exposed to public view.[141] During the presidency of Charles de Gaulle, the smelly *pissoirs* were removed from the streets of Paris.

In 1962, US Army Maj Samuel Desist was assigned to Caserne Coligny in Orléans as the OAC information officer. Desist, well liked by the Orléanais, received numerous honors from the French for his efforts in promoting Franco-American relations. In 1964, Desist retired from the Army and settled with his French wife and children in a 14-room villa in St.-Jean-Le-Blanc. In December 1965, the French equivalent of the US Bureau of Narcotics, called the *Brigade des Stupéfiants*, arrested Desist for his part in smuggling more than 200 lbs of pure heroin into the US. One of Desist's associates, CWO Herman Conder of the 553rd Engineers, was charged with shipping the drugs in his household goods from Orléans to Fort Benning, Georgia. The value of the narcotics, hidden in Conder's refrigerator, was estimated to exceed $100 million after cutting and diluting. At the time, it was the biggest single haul of heroin ever captured in the US. Desist was held in the Orléans jail until his extradition to the US. Conder was the chief witness for the prosecution at the trial, where Desist was found guilty and sentenced to 18 years imprisonment.[142, 143]

Firing range near Metz, 1966 (US Army)

Combat Training for ComZ Troops

From 1945 to 1950, all Army live-fire training exercises had been suspended. However, twelve days after US troops entered combat in Korea, the exercises were reinstated. The goal was to familiarize GIs with the sight and sound of all types of live ammo.[144] By the early 1960s, many of the Army's best officers and NCOs were assigned to Europe.[145] In spite of the troop buildup in Vietnam, in 1966 there still were more than 210,000 troops deployed in Europe; five combat divisions were based in Germany[146] USAREUR wanted male soldiers, except chaplains, to be combat ready. Even "desk jockeys" of Headquarters Co, 4th Logistical Command at Verdun spent Saturday mornings climbing ropes, shinnying up poles, and scaling vertical walls at confidence courses.[147] Every other Saturday morning in 1957, officers at ADSEC headquarters were required to march 4 miles.

In September 1956, WACs of the 7962nd Army Unit Det C at Olivet, led by Capt Mary Ann Rice, marched two miles from Harbord Barracks to Bel Air Maneuver Area at La Grémuse. The WACs pitched tents, posted security guards, and went to sleep. The overnight exercise was intended to determine how quickly the barracks could be evacuated and tents set up in the field. After reveille at 6 am, the WACs were subjected to a full field inspection before breakfast. After eating, they rolled up their tents, put on field packs, and marched back to Olivet.[148]

For the ComZ mission to support combat forces in the field and to resist enemy airdrops or infiltration in France, field training exercises stressed night operations under conditions as realistic as possible. However, GIs were to avoid damaging French land and property and to report any damage to their commanders. ComZ troops were to complete a minimum of two field training exercises per year.[149] In the field, GIs pitched tents, dug foxholes with entrenching tools, and ate from metal mess kits. The blade of the entrenching tool (dubbed "Army banjo") was attached to a wooden handle by a hinge with a locking nut. GIs could unfold the blade to be a shovel or set the blade at 90-degree angle to be a pick. They used their M-1 steel helmet (dubbed "steel pot") to shave and wash. The helmet had two parts: steel pot and plastic helmet-shaped liner. GIs learned that canned food from C-rations could be warmed up by placing them on hot vehicle engines. However, if holes were not punched in the cans to release steam, the cans would explode.

French firefighters, Bussac-Forêt, September 1962 (US Army)

Advance Section troops trained at the 7,000-acre Camp de Moronvilliers near Reims. Base Section troops trained at the 4,000-acre Montmorillon maneuver area, about 30 miles southeast of Poitiers. During a "live fire" qualification exercise in 1963 at Montmorillon, an errant round set the dry grass on fire. It took French firefighters hours to control the blaze. They were aided by the 547th Ordnance Co (FM) whose troops accidently had started the fire. GIs hauled fire hoses, carried French fire equipment, and dug fire breaks.[150]

Engineers were expected to train at least 8 hours per week. Engineers trained bridging the Vienne River at Île-Bouchard near Chinon; the Loire River at Beaugency near Orléans; and the Moselle River at Metz. Powerboat training took place on the north bank of the Loire River, about 1,500 ft east of the George V Bridge in Orléans. Combat engineers called "sappers," such as the 19th and 35th Engineer Battalions sent in 1961 to Chenevières AB during the Berlin Wall Crisis, trained to set demolitions and to build trails, bridges, and fortifications. In March 1959, the 553rd Engineers motor marched to a bivouac area for three days of construction work while being continually harassed by "aggressors." When the engineers reached the bivouac area, the aggressors began hurling tear gas at them. Aggressor tactics included a simulated CBR attack by air and nighttime infiltration raids. To deter the aggressors, the engineers placed concertina barbed-wire around the battalion's perimeter and covered equipment with camouflage tarps. Infantry officers graded performance of the engineers.[151]

The Army also scheduled small unit training at Petit Mont Chauvet near Fontainebleau; at Bois d'Arcy near Versailles; and at La Grémuse near Orléans. At Verdun, ordnance and signal troops trained for weapons proficiency at the French Army firing range at nearby Fort de la Chaume. At Metz, QM troops used the range at Bois des Ognons near Ars-sur-Moselle. By local French ordinance, a bugler was required to sound an alarm warning farmers and hunters prior to commencement of firing.[152] The M1 Garand (the famous weapon of World War II and Korea) was the standard rifle issued to ComZ troops until it was replaced by the M14 in the early 1960s. Troops who were skilled shooters received marksmanship badges. The expert badge was the highest, sharpshooter second. Troops who shot poorly were called "Bolos" and required to return to the range until qualified.

During a field training exercise in summer of 1955, two companies of the 524th Military Police Battalion used the Jeanne d'Arc maneuver area near Metz for eight days of training for their platoons assigned to Metz, Toul, Nancy, and Trois-Fontaines. The training included a daylight motor march under simulated combat conditions and night attacks by aggressors using simulated artillery barrages. The MPs also practiced how to escort convoys, route stragglers, detain POWs, and process refugees. According to Army manuals, training was to stress that POWs must be treated humanely, protected against reprisals, and not coerced in any way. During the night attack, Company D, headquartered at Toul, captured the commanding officer of the aggressor forces.[153]

Alerts

Practice alerts were held randomly every 30 to 90 days in Europe to test how quickly US troops could assume their wartime readiness. The goal of the European Command was to have at least 85% of each unit's personnel ready to roll within two hours of alert notification. Alarms could sound any time of day or night, although most were in the early morning hours. Married GIs who lived off-post stored their alert field gear in metal wall lockers on-post. At large installations, hundreds of married GIs lived in government housing villages that did not have telephone service. In Verdun and Étain, GIs drove 5-ton tractor trucks through the villages using the loud air horns to sound an alert. The shrill sound could awaken even deep sleepers.[154] Although the day and time of alerts were highly classified, wives of senior officers and GIs who worked in crypto centers knew in advance. Without verbally revealing classified information that an alert was imminent, some GIs devised methods to signal fellow squad members, such as moving their field pack from top of wall locker to foot locker.[155] During alerts, troops reported to their duty station or emergency assembly location. Usually they did nothing until higher headquarters sent word that the alert was over.

During 1961-62, 1st Lt James C. Conwell, commander of the Engineer Map Depot at St.-Ay, lived about 10 miles from the depot. Like most Americans living on the economy, he did not have a telephone. When notice of an alert was received at the depot, Conwell's driver was sent to notify him. During early stages of an alert, hundreds of Army vehicles were driven in all directions to notify personnel living throughout the Orléans area. It took an hour for Conwell to receive the notice from his driver, dress, and arrive at St.-Ay. He sometimes arrived after the alert had ended.[156]

For a former NCO, alerts at Trois-Fontaines triggered flashbacks to his combat experiences in Korea, causing stress which the soldier self-medicated with whiskey. If he reported drunk for normal duties at the 39th Ordnance Co, his fellow GIs could hide him in a metal wall locker during his commanding officer's daily rounds to observe shop activities. However, it was difficult to hide him during alerts.[157] By the end of his tour in France, the decorated Korean War veteran had been reduced to private ("slick sleeve"). Because doctors are more willing to diagnose mental illness, today this condition likely would be treated as post-traumatic stress disorder (PTSD).[158]

ComZ Headquarters, Caserne Coligny, Orléans, 1961 (R. A. Atkins)

Orléans Area Installations

The buildup of the US Army had an enormous impact on the Orléans region. Orientation pamphlets, given to newly assigned personnel, stressed the economic hardships of the French and asked American soldiers not to boast about their pay nor spend money ostentatiously.[159] Orleans Area Command (OAC), activated in 1952 at Caserne Coligny, was similar to a post headquarters in the US. Trumpeters from the 76th Army Band played reveille at 6 am, retreat at 5 pm, and taps at 11 pm (lights out in barracks was 10 pm). The OAC supported military units and activities located at twelve geographic areas within the French department of the Loiret. Support included providing housing, repairs and utilities, commissaries, clubs and mess halls, and contracting. In October 1957, the OAC moved to Harbord Barracks in Olivet and in 1960 to Forêt d'Orléans near Chanteau.

Orleans Area Command (OAC) Commanders*

Commanding Officer	Period of Service	Commanding Officer	Period of Service
Col John W. Mott	1952	Col Silas B. Dishman	1958-60
Col James H. Howe	1952-53	Col John C. Cougill	1960-61
Col Chester M. Willingham	1953-54	Col Roy E. Goode	1961-63
Col Stephen D. Slaughter, Jr.	1954	Col Lund F. Hood	1963-64
Col Chester T. Barton	1954-55	Lt Col Thomas R. Rodgers	1964
Col Henry C. Britt	1955-57	Col Franklin H. Hartline	1964-65
Lt Col Hurley W. Chase	1957	Col Joseph R. Boisvert	1965-66
Col James O'Hara	1957-58		

*From January 1952 to September 1954 this sub-command of ComZ was the OAC; from September 1954 to July 1957 it became the Orleans Installation (ORIN); from July 1957 to 1964 it again was designated OAC; in 1964 it became US Army Post Orleans (USAPORL).

Caserne Coligny

At Caserne Coligny, the OAC supported ComZ Headquarters and subordinate units such as the 269th Signal Co, 63rd Finance Disbursing Section, 103rd US Army Security Agency Det, 541st Engineer Det, and 76th Army Band. The pictorial section of 269th Sig Co operated photo facilities at Caserne Coligny and Maison-Fort. They produced 4,500 black and white prints each month and had 1,500 motion pictures in stock.[160] The first signal troops at Coligny developed film in latrine washbasins. The 63rd Finance Section paid military and civilian personnel monthly salaries, travel reimbursements, and invoices for contracted services. The section kept meticulous paper records and periodically microfilmed the records. In the 1950s, finance personnel secured and disbursed monies in US dollars, French francs, and Military Payment Certificates.

The 103rd ASA Det provided communications security for ComZ. ASA detachments, which reported to the National Security Agency at Fort Meade, Maryland, had equipment to monitor radio and landline transmissions. From the top floor of Building A at Caserne Coligny, GIs of the 103rd ASA Det monitored transmissions of the communications center located on the ground floor of Building B. The 103rd used mobile vans to monitor transmissions of headquarters at Paris (Camp des Loges), Verdun, and Poitiers. Personnel caught discussing classified information on the telephone were reported to the intelligence staff (G-2) at ComZ.[161] The few GIs who deduced that the mission of the ASA was communications security called the eavesdroppers "Buddy F**kers." However, the only thing most GIs knew about the detachment was that they were not supposed to know anything about it.

CHAPTER 7: *US Army Commands and Agencies in Orléans*

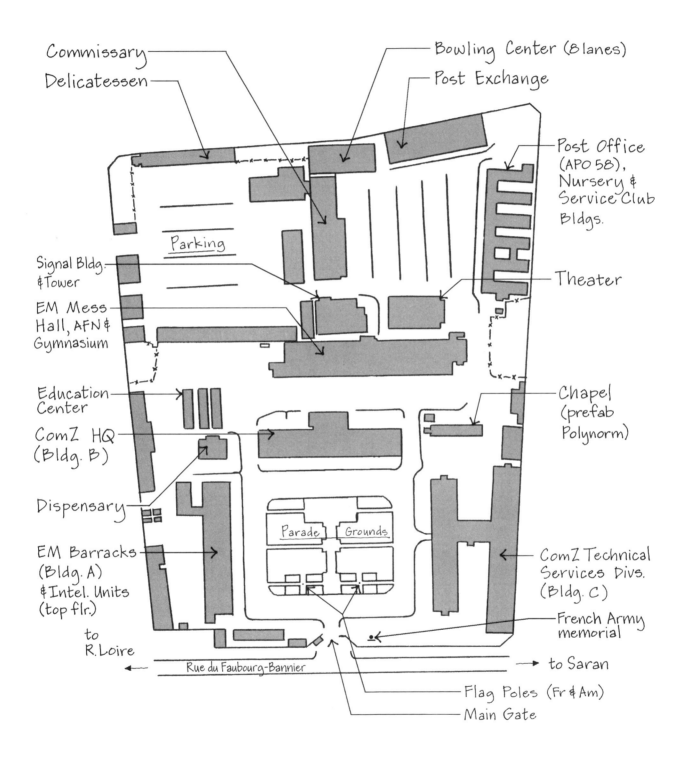

Caserne Coligny (1961)

Engineer Terrain Analysis

According to an agreement with the French, the US could assist *Ponts et Chaussées* to survey war damage to the French transportation infrastructure. The agreement allowed the US Army to rate load-bearing capacity of bridges and measure roads, but mostly unbeknownst to the French, the 541st Engineer Det (Terrain) at Caserne Coligny stretched the agreement to include photographing and mapping potential landing beaches, French military facilities, and nuclear plants.[162] Using aerial photos taken by US Air Force and US Navy aircraft, they produced new maps and revised existing maps. To map conditions for off-road movement, engineers evaluated ground slopes, soil stability, and obstructions by trees and vegetation. Excessive slopes (greater than 50% was impassable), soft soil, and dense forests were obstacles to military vehicles. Engineers graded soil by sifting samples through a series of screens of different size mesh. They also tested the load-bearing strength of a sample, and dug holes to observe how quickly water drained through the soil.

In 1955, the 541st Engineers, commanded by Capt George Stukhart, Jr., was assigned to evaluate more than one-hundred bridges along five routes to be used to evacuate noncombatants from Germany and France, if it appeared that a Soviet invasion was imminent. The 541st Det determined load capacity, clearance width, and clearance height for each of the bridges.[163] The evacuation routes would use secondary roads because primary roads would be clogged with military vehicles of the 37th Trans Command delivering troop reinforcements and supplies from the ports to Seventh Army in Germany. Caves along the routes would be needed to store rations and tents for the evacuees. To find conveniently located caves, 1st Lt Gaston C. Jost, who was fluent in French, and three GIs visited the bibliothèque of the Sorbonne in Paris. Publications of French associations of mushroom growers (who grew mushrooms in caves) and reports on speleology (study of caves) revealed location of caves the 541st would evaluate by surreptitious visits. Reports from the visits, which included cave dimensions, accessibility, and photographs, were sent to Brig Gen Frederick P. Munson, Defense Attaché in Paris.

Although they wore civilian clothes, GIs of the 541st Det were easy to spot on clandestine missions because they had short haircuts and drove olive green Chevy sedans. To photograph bridges over the Seine River in Paris, they tried to act like tourists, but the French usually were not fooled. In 1955, when PFC Keith E. Dyas and Sp3 Maury Bornstein traveled to Royan to survey landing beaches, the next morning a nearby door had a freshly painted message: "U.S. Go Home."[164] If challenged by French authorities, GIs of the 541st Det were to show military ID and claim they were on NATO business. It did not always work. On a trip to evaluate caves, 1st Lt Gaston C. Jost, PFC William A. Drapeau, and three other GIs of the 541st Det were challenged at their hotel by French authorities. The French did not believe the cover story that the GIs were spelunkers on vacation and sent a formal complaint of trespass on private land to ComZ.

PAL Detachment

In 1958, Seventh Army command post exercises and field maneuvers in Germany revealed that procedures to authenticate release of nuclear weapons took too long.[165] Instead of streamlining procedures, the Kennedy administration implemented complicated rules and permissive action link (PAL) devices, which implied a lack of trust in the Army's command of nuclear weapons.[166] In the 1960s, teams from the PAL Detachment at Caserne Coligny traveled to Army depots and to other NATO nations to install and verify operability of permissive action links on nuclear weapons. The links were designed to prevent weapons from being armed until the US President authorized release of a numerical emergency action message, called the "go-code" by the troops. Without the code, nuclear weapons could not be armed. Another control was known as the "two-man rule," which meant nuclear weapons could be fired only by joint action of at least two persons. It was believed the rule would prevent irrational action by an individual.[167]

Saran, Chanteau, and Donnery

Other installations north of the Loire River were at Saran, Chanteau (Forêt d'Orléans), and Donnery. In 1952 at Saran, the 2nd Aviation Co (Fixed Wing) shared a 2,000-ft long sod airstrip with the French. The following year, the US Army extended its length to 2,500 ft, paved the airstrip with asphalt, and installed landing lights. On weekends, the airstrip had to accommodate heavy traffic from civilian aircraft.[168] In 1959, the 2nd Aviation Co, commanded by Maj Ned B. Baker, had twelve pilots and twenty-four enlisted men. The 2nd Avn Co fleet of Army aircraft included L-20 Beaver and L-23 Twin Bonanza aircraft. The unit's nickname was TWA for "Tinny Weenie Airline." Pilots were on call twenty-four hours a day and flew an average of fifty-five hours each month. Routine duties were to evacuate personnel in medical emergencies, transport commanders throughout ComZ, and perform courier deliveries. From January 1955 to May 1959, pilots flew 12,574 hours without any accidents. "All-weather" flights transported critically-ill patients from remote areas in France to Army hospitals.[169, 170] The US military also shared the runway of the French Air Force base at Bricy (Base aérienne 123). The Saran installation also housed the 586th Ordnance Co (FM), a Signal Service Battalion, and the morgue of the 5th QM Mortuary Det. In January 1952, the mud was so bad at Saran that GIs from the 586th Ord Co voluntarily chipped in to buy cinders from the local French gas company. The GIs spread the cinders throughout the tent camp area in an attempt to control the mud until Army engineers could pave roads and sidewalks.[171]

French generals in Algeria revolted in April 1961, after it became clear that French President Charles de Gaulle intended to grant self-determination to Algeria. The French Army parked military vehicles on the runway at the Saran Air Field to obstruct landings of French aircraft carrying paratroopers loyal to the generals.[172] At Périgueux, Sgt Lloyd D. Rowell was issued an M2 carbine, given only two rounds of ammo, and told to guard the main gate from a window on the top floor of his barracks.[173] In Paris, de Gaulle broadcast an appeal to all French citizens for help in preventing a coup (*"Françaises, Français, aidez-moi!"*). The unarmed citizen volunteers, mostly veterans of the world wars, believed it would be impossible to stop the paratroopers. Some French suggested, tongue-in-cheek, that they go to Le Bourget and Orly airfields with champagne for the rebels. While the rebels drank, the veterans could hit them on the head with empty bottles. De Gaulle's appeal was successful. French conscripts in Algeria obeyed de Gaulle, not the generals.[174, 175]

At Chanteau, the Joint Construction Agency (JCA) built a 1,000-bed standby hospital which was used as an elementary school and a regional high school for dependents. For use in time of war, the hospital had an underground surgery with adjacent space for holding wards. The schools, which opened in 1960, used five of the hospital's two-story wings for classrooms to accommodate 1,500 students.[176] School bus service was provided to families living within 15 miles.

At Donnery, the Army leased the Château de La Touche for the 766th CIC Det. So they would be separated from other troops, CIC personnel had quarters and mess at the château. The property was so large that part of the wooded area was cleared for a nine-hole, par 36 golf course built during off-duty hours by troops of the 553rd Engineers, led by Capt John E. Hurst, Jr. The first six holes opened in 1955, the remaining three holes were completed in July 1956. It was the first golf course built in France for the US Army.[177, 178]

Olivet and Maison-Fort

Installations south of the Loire River were at Olivet, Ardon (Bois de Maison-Fort), and St.-Pryvé-St.-Mesmin. In 1954, the JCA built four BOQ buildings and Officers Mess on the leased property of Château de La Mothe in Olivet. Quarters One, the residence of the ComZ commander, was Villa Les Charmes at 60, rue du Général de Gaulle in Olivet. The 2½ acre site faced the Loiret River and was enclosed by walls for security. Quarters Two was the Villa La Tourelle at 32, route d'Olivet, that had been leased for an Officers Club from 1951-54.

The installation at Olivet was named Harbord Barracks in honor of Maj Gen James G. Harbord, who commanded the Services of Supply (SOS) of the American Expeditionary Forces during World War I. The SOS, the Army's first ComZ in France, was established in February 1918. The JCA built a 1,000-bed standby hospital at Harbord Barracks to be used as a troop barracks until needed for wartime. From 1962 to 1966, the 819th Hospital Center was located in wings of the hospital. The Center administered five active hospitals, thirty dispensaries, thirty dental clinics, and seven veterinary food inspection detachments.[179]

819th Hospital Center (1964)

Location	Hospital Unit	Authorized Active Beds
Chinon	60th Station Hospital	35
Orléans (La Chapelle)	34th General Hospital	125
Paris	196th Station Hospital	35
Verdun	319th Station Hospital	100
Bremerhaven, Germany	33rd Station Hospital	50

Maison-Fort had barracks, offices, and shops for the 553rd Engineer Battalion, 1st Signal Group, and 594th Transportation Group. In 1952, prefab barracks were installed at Maison-Fort which could house up to five-hundred enlisted women (Women's Army Corps, WAC). GIs called the barracks "WAC Shacks." In 1954, the first enlisted WACs arrived at Orléans. They primarily were assigned to administrative tasks.[180] WACs were assigned to the Stock Control Center at Maison-Fort, staffs at Caserne Coligny, and 34th General Hospital. In August 1956, WAC Detachment C commanded by Capt Mary Ann Rice, moved from barracks at Maison-Fort to Harbord Barracks. It was the largest WAC Det in Europe.

In the 1960s, the 1st Signal Group included five signal companies stationed at Olivet, Poitiers, Toul, and Verdun. In 1964, the 1st Signal Group, commanded by Col Lawrence R. Klar, also supported NATO activities in Paris and Fontainebleau. Signal photographers took ID photos, photos of vehicle accidents, and photos to record Army activities. Negatives were processed in the darkroom, and prints developed in the "soup" room.[181]

In 1956, the 594th Trans Gp inaugurated "port call train" service to Bremerhaven. The train originated at Bordeaux, rolled through La Rochelle, Poitiers, Orléans, and Metz to Bremerhaven. The first train left Bordeaux on 06 December 1956 with homeward-bound GIs and their families. They arrived at Bremerhaven on the morning of 08 December and boarded the USNS *Upshur* which sailed for the US that afternoon.[182]

The technical services located their supply control agencies at Maison-Fort. In 1958, ComZ established a school to provide basic and advanced training on electronic accounting machines for Army and Air Force supply personnel in Europe. Students were required to hold a high school diploma or equivalent and have an IQ of at least 100.[183] A secret underground command post was built at Maison-Fort for USAREUR to use in case the Soviets forced Seventh Army to retreat into France.

553rd Engineer Battalion

After post-World War II service in the Philippine Islands and Guam, the 553rd Engineer Battalion was inactivated in January 1950. On 15 November 1954, the 553rd was reactivated at Orléans, absorbing the troops and equipment of the inactivated 982nd Engineer Construction Battalion. The 982nd, an Army Reserve unit from Duluth, Minnesota, had been mobilized in September 1950 for the Korean War. The 553rd had an authorized troop strength of twenty-eight officers and six-hundred eighty enlisted men. In the early 1950s, engineer enlisted troops lived in 8-man wood and tarpaper hutments at Maison-Fort. Huts were heated by potbellied stoves in the center of the huts. Coal was delivered by a chute from an outside bin. Encouraged by Lt Col Fred W. Aron, commander of the 553rd, troops laid linoleum floors, hung curtains on windows, and added enclosed screened front porches.[184] In 1956, Company C of the 553rd erected "Polynorm" metal prefabricated classroom buildings for the dependents elementary school at Maison-Fort. The company, commanded by Capt John E. Hurst, Jr., completed the project in thirty-two working days.[185]

The 553rd constructed roads and facilities for the Orleans Area Command and the Seine Area Command (Paris). They also trained to lay landmines, build bridges, and place pipelines over rough terrain. Technical training normally was held between mid-December and late March, when weather was not favorable for construction work. In a war with the Soviets, the battalion would help evacuate noncombatants through the Orléans area.[186]

Typical construction projects in 1961 were a sewage treatment plant at Chinon, a sheltered grandstand for Patton Athletic Field at Harbord Barracks, and paved parking lots at Forêt d' Orléans and Maison-Fort. During the Berlin Wall Crisis in fall 1961, the 553rd poured concrete slabs to support wood-frame walls and roof trusses of tent housing for the buildup of troops. The battalion was fulfilling the promise of Maj Gen Henry R. Westphalinger to keep troops out of the mud.[187, 188]

The 553rd Engineers conducted powerboat training for troops of the 97th Engineers from Verdun and the 83rd Engineers from Fontenet. The 27-ft long by 8-ft wide powerboats were used to push sections of floating bridges. During the two-week course, boat operations were on the Loire River and classroom work at Maison-Fort.[189, 190]

In 1956, at the request of Seine Area Command, Company B troops, led by 1st Lt Kenneth Patterson, built a floating stage in the Basin de Neptune on the grounds of Château de Versailles. The 3,600 sq ft wooden stage, supported by M-4 Floating Bridge components, was used for a pageant performed by French children. French onlookers were amazed that the troops were able to erect the unique stage in thirteen hours and dismantle it in less than eight.[191] In 1960, the 553rd built a sports complex for the Orléans Institute des Sourds-Muets. Three-hundred deaf boys between the ages of 6 to 17 were trained to read lips and use sign language. One American dependent attended the school. Troops, led by 1st Lt Sven Jorgenson, built two terraced sports fields for soccer, five paved courts for basketball and volleyball, and a 1,250-ft long track.[192]

At Christmas and Easter, GIs hosted parties for French orphans. Between holidays, GIs helped orphanages by repairing plumbing and electrical wiring, and fixing doors and windows. In summer months, they raised funds to sponsor orphans to attend summer camps organized for dependents of US military. Their good deeds earned them the nickname "Dozers with a heart."

In 1958, Capt Lieto "Pete" DiPrieto, commanding officer of Headquarters & Service Co of the 553rd Engineers, rented a watermill at 759, rue du Bac from a French count who lived in Paris. The 600-year-old Moulin des Bechets had not functioned as a mill since 1915. To provide lodging for his wife and two sons, DiPrieto rehabilitated five rooms, improved plumbing and wiring, and cleared the overgrown grounds. He even restored the waterwheel so it would rotate. The mill attracted many sightseers, even postcards of the mill were sold in Orléans. Because the mill's first occupants had been Catholic nuns, DiPrieto believed he should be courteous to the uninvited sightseers who wandered about the property.[193]

Moulin des Béchets watermill, Olivet, 1961 (J. C. Conwell)

553rd Engineer Battalion (Const) Commanders

Commanding Officer	Period of Service	Commanding Officer	Period of Service
Lt Col Hobert H. Hoover	1954	Lt Col Edward G. Anderson, Jr.	1960-61
Lt Col John L. Parsons	1954-55	Lt Col Robert R. Wessels	1961-62
Lt Col Fred W. Aron	1955-56	Lt Col Tom L. Peyton, Jr.	1963-64
Lt Col Robert W. Fritz	1956-58	Lt Col Charles P. Towsend	1964-65
Lt Col Harold A. Gould	1958-59	Lt Col Harold L. Myron	1965-66
Lt Col Arthur B. Grace, Jr.	1959-60		

St.-Pryvé-St.-Mesmin

The 982nd Engineers renovated factory buildings of SAMEC (*Société d'application mécaniques et chimiques*) in St.-Pryvé-St.-Mesmin. From 1940 to 1943, the Germany Army had used the SAMEC facility for a gas mask factory. The QM Laundry and Dry Cleaning Plant, operated by the 469th QM Laundry Co, opened in February 1953. The 469th, commanded by 1st Lt Billy J. Bristol, had mobile washing and dry-cleaning equipment that could process 4,000 garments every 48 hours. The rehabbed equipment was built in Germany from salvaged parts and mounted on three trailers. Trailer units were: washer and extractor, steam presses, and boiler/generators.[194] Troops were charged 35¢ for trousers, 20¢ for shirts. By the late 1950s, a fixed plant at SAMEC had been built, with pickup points at SAMEC, Caserne Coligny, and Maison-Fort. Another renovated building housed the QM bakery. Two-thousand loaves a day were baked for Fontainebleau, Châteauroux AD, Évreux AB, Dreux AB, and OAC. The Field Maintenance Shop repaired wooden items, such as desks, chairs, and bookcases.[195] The 223rd QM Co (Reclamation & Maintenance) operated shoe repair machinery at Château de La Mothe. The specialists repaired 300 to 600 pairs of shoes each day for the troops.[196] The QM Mortuary Det was responsible for handling the remains of ComZ troops and dependents who died in France. The detachment also conducted search and recovery operations for missing dead from the world wars.

La Chapelle and St.-Ay

Installations west of the Loire River were at la Chapelle-St.-Mesmin and St.-Ay. In 1952, the JCA began renovating a historic building at la Chapelle for use as a 250-bed hospital to serve the medical needs of troops and dependents in the Orléans area. Located 4 miles west of Orléans, it would become the first comprehensive Army hospital in France. The main building had been completed in 1846 for use as a school for Catholic priests. The school closed in 1905. During World War I, the French Army occupied the building, establishing a school for orthopedic surgeons and hospital for war wounded. After the war, it became a French government tuberculosis sanitarium. During 1939-40, it was used as a French military hospital and, during the occupation, as headquarters for a German Engineer Corps. In 1953, the 34th General Hospital moved to la Chapelle.[197] On 06 June 1954, the tenth anniversary of D-Day, sixteen French families from Olivet sent flowers to the 34th General Hospital. The card with the flowers read: "We cannot let this day pass without paying tribute to the American forces which landed on the Normandy beachhead."[198]

In 1956, the la Chapelle dependents elementary school, built by the 982nd Engineers, had four-hundred seventy-two pupils. All pupils were required to study French. Three young French women helped with instructions. According to one of the women, Mlle Françoise Boyer, the children spoke French at home when they did not want their parents to know what they were saying.[199] When the cafeteria opened in September, parents could purchase twenty meal tickets for $7.

The Engineer Map Depot, staffed by the 23rd Engineer Platoon (Map), was located at St.-Ay, a small village along the Loire River halfway between Beaugency and Orléans. The depot previously had been the SEFA (*Société d'épuration, filtration et air*).[200] In the early 1960s, the depot stored 2½ million maps in 3-ft deep wooden boxes, stacked in 8-ft high rows. In the event of evacuation in wartime, thermite grenades would be used to destroy the rows of maps.[201]

Warehouse, Engineer Map Depot, St.-Ay, 1961 (J. C. Conwell)

Schools and Recreation

The first dependents school opened in 1952 at the École de Chevilly and the post exchange (PX) was at École l'Ermitage in Chevilly, about 7 miles north of Orléans. By the mid-1950s, elementary schools had opened at Maison-Fort, la Chapelle, and adjacent to the new housing village at St.-Jean-de-la-Ruelle. When the standby hospital at Chanteau was completed in 1960, the high school relocated from Maison-Fort. Five wings of the hospital were used for school activities. Because hospital wards were long and narrow, teachers had to adapt to classrooms that placed many students far away from the teacher and chalkboard. The high school had an exchange program with Lycée Jules Ferry in Orléans. One day each week students traded places; American teachers taught French students and French teachers taught American students.[202] Students who attended dependents schools at Orléans included future Speaker of the US House of Representatives Newt Gingrich and future Army Brig Gen Frank A. Partlow, Jr.

The NCO Club leased space in the Hôtel Sébastopol at 25, rue de Patay, near Place Gambetta in Orléans. Called "The Oasis," the club had dining rooms and bar on the first floor; nursery and game room on the second. In 1957, the club leased space in the Hôtel du Gai-Logis in Fleury-les-Aubrais. Opening night entertainers were the popular US vocal group "The Platters."[203]

The first Officers Club was in the Villa La Tourelle. In 1951, the French communist press ridiculed the use of this château as an example of the American "menace" to France.[204] The first motion picture theater was the leased Loigny Theater. The American Red Cross had an office at Caserne Coligny and a center located at 2, quai Barentin. In January 1951, the Special Services Library opened in Building "B" at Caserne Coligny. It had 1,300 books and eight easy chairs. In 1955, there were 6,600 books and by 1959 more than 11,500.[205]

Family Housing

Satisfactory rental units were difficult to find in the Orléans area. In 1953, several Army families lived in the leased Château Villefallier near Cléry-St.-André, 12 miles southwest of Orléans. The 84-room château was leased jointly by the families, who divided expenses for its upkeep and food, including hiring a French cook. Capt and Mrs. W. B. Park served as volunteer leaders of the enterprise. The wooded grounds were so large they were used by hunters.[206] In 1956 in Orléans, officer and NCO families moved into three-hundred housing units built by French contractors for Americans at St.-Jean-de-la-Ruelle (named la Petite-Espère), and into three-hundred units in three-story apartment buildings at St.-Jean-de-Braye (named Châtaigniere). Only one telephone was installed to serve the entire apartment complex. In 1959, a one-hundred ninety-eight unit housing village was constructed at Olivet (briefly named Quatre-Vents). The official opening on 02 July was attended by Louis Maury, Mayor of Olivet, and other French dignitaries. Maj Gen Edward J. O'Neill, ComZ commander, was in Germany so he sent his chief of staff to the ceremony. In November, the mayor and dignitaries returned to witness Maj Gen Henry R. Westphalinger, the new ComZ commander, unveil a large sign renaming the village "Cité Maréchal Foch" to honor the French hero of World War I.[207] Although these three new housing villages did not provide nearly the number of homes needed by the Americans, they did alleviate somewhat the scarcity of housing in the Orléans area. In 1962, almost 3,000 American families lived on the economy in the Orléans area in rented apartments or homes in fifteen villages within 3 miles from Caserne Coligny, thirty-two villages 3 to 12 miles away, and fifteen villages more than 12 miles away.[208]

CHAPTER 7: *US Army Commands and Agencies in Orléans*

Orléans Area US Army Installations

Installation	Location	Activity and Units
Headquarters	Orléans (Caserne Coligny, 131, rue du Faubourg-Bannier, 16 acres)	ComZ Command HQ US Army Permissive Action Link (PAL) Det Armed Forces Network (AFN) 1st Military Censorship Det 103rd US Army Security Agency (ASA) Det
	Orléans (296, rue du Faubourg-Bannier)	Provost Marshal Division
	Ardon (Bois de Maison-Fort)	Supply Control Agencies (SCA)
	Donnery (Château de La Touche)	766th CIC Detachment HQ
	Olivet (Harbord Barracks)	1st Signal Group HQ
	St.-Pryvé-St.-Mesmin	37th Motor Transportation Cmd
	Chanteau (Forêt d'Orléans)	Orleans Area Command (OAC)
Depots	Ardon (Bois de Maison-Fort, 195 acres)	553rd Engineer Battalion 594th Transportation Group
	Fleury-les-Aubrais (4 acres)	QM warehouse
	Orléans (177, rue des Murlins)	QM warehouses
	St.-Ay (3 acres)	Engineer Map Depot
	St.-Pryvé-St.-Mesmin (9 acres)	QM Laundry and Bakery (SAMEC)
Communications	Ardon (Bois de Maison-Fort)	USAREUR underground command post
	Saran	Major Signal Relay Center
Hospitals	La Chapelle-St.-Mesmin (35 acres)	34th General Hospital (250-beds, expandable to 500-beds)
	Olivet (Harbord Barracks, 70 acres)	819th Hospital Center (1,000-bed standby hospital)
Schools (dependents)	Ardon (Bois de Maison-Fort)	Elementary school
	Chanteau (Forêt d'Orléans, 205 acres)	Elementary and high schools (1,000-bed standby hospital)
	La Chapelle-St.-Mesmin	Elementary (Les Mouettes)
	St.-Jean-de-la-Ruelle	Elementary school
Bachelor Officers Quarters (BOQ)	Olivet (Château de La Mothe, 12 acres)	Four 2-story buildings, Officers Mess
	La Chapelle-St.-Mesmin	Two 2-story buildings (females)
Housing (families)	Olivet (Cité Maréchal Foch)	198 SCH units (62 acres)
	St.-Jean-de-Braye (Les Châtaigniers and Clos Moulin)	Five 3-story RGH apartment buildings (300 units)
	St.-Jean-de-la-Ruelle (Cité de la Petite-Espère)	300 RGH units
General Officer Quarters	Olivet (Villa Les Charmes, 60, rue du Général de Gaulle)	Commanding General, ComZ (Quarters One)
	Olivet (Villa La Tourelle, 32, rue d'Olivet)	Deputy Commanding General, ComZ (Quarters Two)
	Olivet (rue Travers-Baudelin)	Chief of Staff, ComZ

Troop Barracks	Caserne Coligny	HQ Company, ComZ 5th Replacement Bn, HQ Det 76th Chem Det (RADLCEN) 103rd ASA Det 541st Engineer Det (Terrain) 63rd Finance Disbursing Sect 76th Army Band
	Ardon (Bois de Maison-Fort and Bel Air)	553rd Engineer Battalion 275th Signal Co (Service) 1st Transportation Co (Med Trk) 76th Trans Co (Med Trk)
	Olivet (Harbord Barracks)	33rd Medical Co (Holding) 586th Signal Co (Support) 269th Signal Co (Service) 63rd Army Postal Unit US Army WAC Det C
	La Chapelle-St.-Mesmin	163rd Medical Battalion 550th Ambulance Co Det US Army WAC Det 3335th Labor Service Med Det
	Chanteau (Forêt d'Orléans)	5th QM Mortuary Det 544th Military Police Platoon HQ Company, US Army Garrison
	St.-Ay	23rd Engineer Platoon (Map)
	St.-Pryvé-St.-Mesmin (SAMEC)	37th Transportation Command
	Saran	2nd Aviation Co (Fixed Wing) 586th Ordnance Co (FM) Signal Service Battalion, Europe 4082nd Labor Service Co
	Donnery (Château de La Touche)	766th CIC Detachment
Post Exchanges	Chevilly (1951-59)	Dry goods sales
	Orléans, 293, rue du Faubourg-Bannier (1953-55) Orléans, Caserne Coligny (1955-67)	Dry goods sales
Recreation	Ardon (Bois de Maison-Fort)	Skeet range at Bel Air, Riley Fields
	Donnery (104 acres)	Golf course (9 holes, 3,174 yds)
	Fleury-les-Aubrais (Hôtel du Gai-Logis)	NCO Club (15 transient billets)
	Lamotte-Beuvron (Château du Corvier)	Rod and Gun Club
	Lorris (Etang du Que l'Éveque)	Lake (fishing and duck hunting)
	Olivet (Harbord Barracks)	Patton Athletic Field, photo lab, craft shop, gymnasium
	Orléans (Caserne Coligny)	Bowling alley (8 lanes), photo lab, craft shop
	Saran	Athletic field, photo lab
Air Fields	Saran (41 acres)	2nd Aviation Co (Fixed Wing) 56th Aviation Detachment
	Bricy (Base Aérienne 123)	French Air Force control

Training Sites	Blois	Firing range area
	La Grémuse (736 acres)	Bel Air Maneuver Area
	Orléans (Les Grouses)	Pistol range
	Saran (Camp de Cercottes)	Weapons range (including 3.5 inch rocket)
	Ardelles, Thimert, and Le Tremblay-le-Vicomte (near Dreux AB)	Dispersed sites

Abbreviations

CIC	Counter Intelligence Corps	SAMEC	Société d'application mécaniques et chimiques (French factory site)
FM	Field Maintenance		
RADLCEN	Radiological Center	SCH	Surplus Commodity Housing (US Army)
RGH	Rental Guarantee Housing (US Army)	USAREUR	US Army, Europe
		WAC	Women's Army Corps

Maison-Fort, April 1962 (US Army)

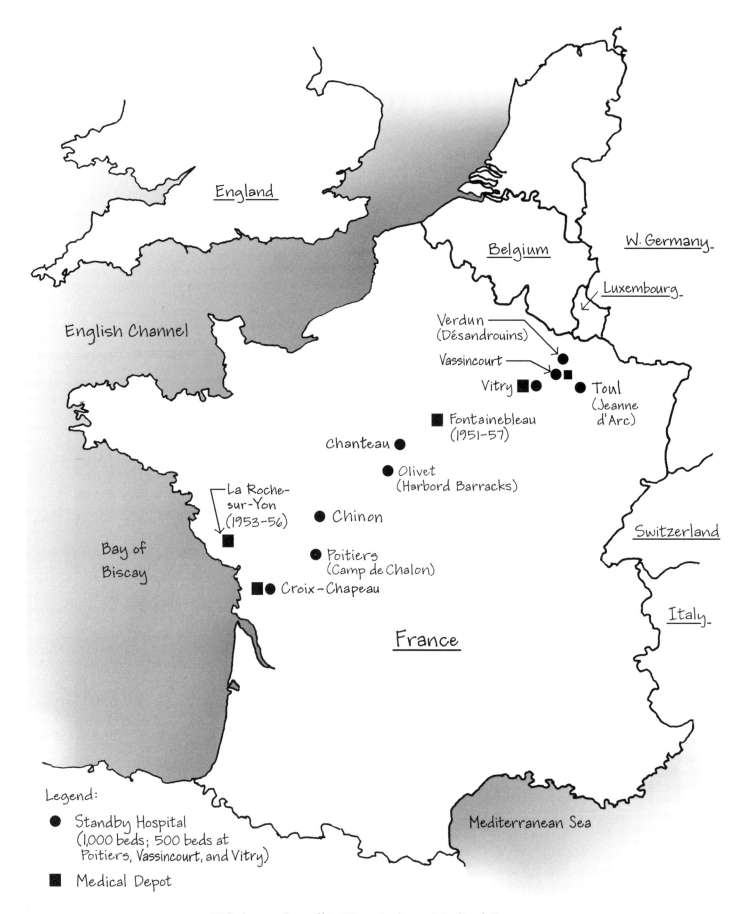

US Army Standby Hospitals & Medical Depots

EIGHT

Medical Care and Standby Hospitals for Wartime

"Everyone takes them [dirty mess trays] to the kitchen, don't they?"
(Hollywood actress Olivia de Havilland, 34th General Hospital, la Chapelle, 02 February 1955)

Medical Care for the Buildup

During 1951, the US Army made arrangements to use French civilian hospitals, but this proved to be impractical due to the rapid increase in the number of troops. By 1952, the Army had established 25-bed hospitals at Gradignan near Bordeaux (33rd Station Hospital), Fontainebleau (34th Station Hospital), and Verdun (32nd Station Hospital).[1] Hospitals at Fontainebleau and Verdun were in dilapidated French caserne buildings. Broken windows were replaced, potbellied stoves installed, and Army generators used to provide electricity. At La Rochelle, two floors in the war-damaged *Hôpital Aufrédi* were rehabilitated for the 319th Station Hospital. In 1952, there were 74 active beds at Aufrédi. These small hospitals could handle cases from births to emergency appendectomies; patients who needed specialized care were transported to hospitals in Germany. In 1952 at Camp Bussac, personnel of the 302nd Field Hospital, an Army reserve unit from Chicago, Illinois, set up in temporary wood-frame structures covered by canvas. The 302nd staffed a dispensary and patient wards. By the mid-1950s, Army hospitals in France would be needed to provide about 700 beds for peacetime.[2]

302nd Field Hospital, Camp Bussac, April 1952 (US Army)

The US Air Force built hospitals at the NATO air bases and at Orly Field near Paris.[3] The air base hospitals were modern masonry structures staffed by nearly thirty officers and more than seventy NCOs and airmen.[4] For example in 1960-61, the 608th Tactical Hospital at Toul-Rosières AB was authorized 50 active beds. Its one-hundred fifty personnel staffed medical and dental clinics for Air Force personnel and their dependents.[5] Larger hospitals were at Évreux (115 active beds) and at la

Martinerie near Châteauroux (125 active beds). The 7373rd US Air Force Hospital at la Martinerie renovated buildings of the former French Air Force pilots school and became the USAFE hospital center for France.[6,7] In 1957 the 7373rd, commanded by Lt Col Gerrit L. Hekhuis, had a staff that included fourteen medical officers and thirty-five nurses.[8]

The hospitals were to treat dependents as well as military personnel. Medical care for dependents included dental, obstetrical, gynecological, and pediatric care. Under the Dependents' Medical Care Act, passed by US Congress in 1956, dependents paid $1.75 per day for hospitalization in military facilities, a minimum of $25 per hospital admission in civilian facilities.[9] The US Army leased part of the civilian American Hospital at Neuilly, a suburb of Paris, to treat personnel and dependents in the Paris area.

Medical Dispensaries

By the mid-1950s, most Army installations and air bases had a medical dispensary for physicians to examine and treat patients who did not require hospitalization. Dispensary personnel kept immunization records up-to-date and maintained a small pharmacy. Sick call was held each morning at 8 am. A sick slip (DD Form 689) was used to send military personnel to the dispensary. Doctors listened to patients describe cold symptoms, hangovers, and other maladies—some concocted by GIs to avoid "Return to Duty" diagnosis. The APC pill (dubbed the "all purpose capsule") was dispensed for numerous symptoms.[10] Coughing patients received a bottle of coveted "GI gin" (cough syrup containing the opiate codeine). A patient could be returned to duty or authorized to rest in the barracks or at home, called assigned to "Quarters Status." It was essential that the dispensary send a copy of the authorization to the patient's commander or the patient likely would be listed as absent without official leave (AWOL) in the morning report.[11] Although dispensaries were open twenty-four hours a day, seven days a week, only one doctor and one or two enlisted men were on duty during off-duty hours. Dependents and Department of Army Civilians (DAC) were advised to schedule routine visits during weekday afternoons to avoid the morning patient load due to military sick call.[12]

Transport of Patients to Germany

In June 1952 a medical service train, commanded by 1st Lt Robert F. Haas, began to transport patients once a week from the 32nd Station Hospital in Verdun to Landstuhl, Germany. The hydro-diesel powered train (called a "doodlebug") was similar in exterior appearance to a European commuter train. Its main compartment could accommodate twelve litter patients; a private compartment another three. Because only SNCF engineers could operate the train in France and only German engineers in Germany, the train stopped at the French-German border to exchange engineers.[13] By September, the 32nd Station Hospital began using buses to transport patients because the trip by bus was faster and cost less than by train. An Army Twin-City bus could carry two attendants and thirty-six ambulatory patients or, with its seats removed, eighteen patients on litters. Dispensary equipment and a cabinet for medical supplies were installed on the bus.[14] In wartime, casualties also could be carried by jeep (two litters), 2½-ton truck (sixteen litters, loaded on three levels), and even amphibious DUKW (twelve litters, tied securely to withstand motion on water).[15,16]

American Red Cross

Best known for its first aid and safety courses, the American Red Cross overseas was the principal resource for troubled servicemen in France. Red Cross staffs were available at most posts to help solve personal and family problems. They worked closely with unit commanders and installation chaplains. The Red Cross also helped GIs place telephone calls to their families in the US. In financial emergencies, a Red Cross field office could provide grants or loans to GIs and dependents. GIs, authorized emergency leave to return home because of the death or serious illness of a family member, were provided with interest free loans or grants to cover travel expenses in the US.[17,18] On 16 March 1956, the Red Cross representative at Verdun contacted the commanding officer of PFC Roy E. Anderson at Trois Fontaines Ordnance Depot to obtain permission for emergency leave and made arrangements for Anderson to return home to Ohio after his father suffered a heart attack. Because Anderson's enlistment ended in thirty days, he had been scheduled to return home the next week by troopship. Instead, three hours after notification by the Red Cross, Anderson was driven by jeep to Paris and later that evening flew home from Orly AB.[19] In the 1960s, the Red Cross had a representative at Vitry-le-François during mornings from Monday to Thursday and all day on Friday. The representative also was available two afternoons each week at Trois-Fontaines and one afternoon each week at Brienne-le-Château and Châlons-sur-Marne. In 1963, the Red Cross began offering first aid and CBR survival courses to dependents.

American Red Cross Centers near Army Posts*

Installation	Location
Metz	16, rempart Saint-Thiebault
Nancy	109, rue de Metz (near Champigneulles)
Orléans	2, quai Barentin
La Rochelle	40, quai Duperré (over arcade)
Verdun	21, ave de Douaumont (across street from Hôtel Bellevue)

*Centers were near Châteauroux AD (rue Molière), Chaumont AB (1, rue Bartholdi), and Évreux AB.

Off-post centers offered travel advice and a place where GIs could interact with local citizens. Most were open every day; 1 to 11 pm on weekdays, 10 am to 11 pm on weekends.[20] Wives of officers and enlisted men volunteered to serve as aides; high school students could enroll as Junior Red Cross members. The Red Cross Center at Orléans, which welcomed GIs and French citizens, offered free German language lessons on Monday evenings, English lessons on Tuesday evenings, and on other evenings had activities such as square dancing and art classes. Free coffee and card games always were available.

In 1956, the Red Cross Center at Nancy leased a château, owned by the Michel family, north of town. During the occupation, the German Army had requisitioned the château. After liberation the US Army had used it for a hospital in 1944-45. On most days, the center served busloads of GIs from Nancy Ordnance Depot, Toul Engineer Depot, and Toul-Rosières AB. The high-ceilinged rooms were used for ping pong, music, dancing, and socializing over coffee and donuts. The gardens provided space for archery and badminton. The staff of five women organized travel tours, recreation, and educational events such as language classes: English classes for the French and French classes for Americans.[21]

Gray Lady at Cité Clemenceau housing village, Bussac-Forêt, 1962 (US Army)

Gray Ladies

Military wives in Europe formed the volunteer Gray Lady service to be an adjunct to the American Red Cross. At hospitals, the Red Cross trained the Gray Ladies (named for their gray uniform) who visited patients, wrote letters for them, and shopped and ran errands for bedridden patients. Gray Ladies also taught courses in home nursing, pre-natal, and baby care.[22] On 07 April 1959 at the 34th General Hospital near Orléans, sixteen women graduated from classes to become Gray Ladies. Among the sixteen receiving Red Cross volunteer caps and pins were two French citizens, Dominique Brabant and Marie de Kerjegu. The 34th Gen Hosp now had thirty-five Gray Ladies.[23] In 1957, T/Sgt Martin J. Hynes, Jr. became the only "Gray Gentleman" to volunteer at a hospital in France. His wife was one of thirty-two Gray Ladies at the 7373rd US Air Force Hospital at la Martinerie.[24] During summer months in the 1960s, Army and Air Force hospitals in Europe hired high school students to fill vacancies of regular employees on vacation. The students worked in dental clinics, laboratories, pharmacies, and supply rooms. They also assisted Gray Ladies by working in hospital libraries and at dispensaries.[25] GIs who were ambulatory patients at Army hospitals also helped. They were required to clean floors by their beds and to perform other chores such as pushing wheelchairs.

Types of US Army Hospitals

During wartime, field hospitals were set up to treat and return patients to duty and keep patients alive for evacuation to station or general hospitals. Field hospitals were mobile; station and general hospitals were at fixed locations. More than one-hundred fifty personnel were authorized for 400-bed field hospitals; more than two-hundred fifty personnel for 750-bed station hospitals.[26, 27] The 1st Medical Group, stationed at Verdun from 1954 to 1962, was responsible for hospitals, dispensaries, dental clinics, and veterinary services. In France, the three hospital types were used interchangeably to staff active bed hospitals.

Army Hospitals

Hospital Type	Wartime Bed Capacity	Purpose	Normal Location
Field	400	Serve as temporary station hospital set up in tents.	Not fixed
	300	Serve as three separate temporary station hospitals set up in tents.	
Station	200 to 750	Treat patients for return to duty within prescribed time limit (during World War II, normally 30 days). or Evacuate patients to general hospital, if longer care is needed.	Fixed
General	1,000	Treat patients evacuated from field and station hospitals.	Fixed

La Chapelle Army Hospital

The former St.-Mesmin tuberculosis clinic at la Chapelle near Orléans was renovated at a cost of $125,000 for use as a hospital, staffed by the 34th General Hospital. In May 1953, it replaced the 302nd Field Hospital which had 75 beds housed in prefabs. The 34th Gen Hosp provided 250 active beds and had dental, X-ray, and emergency clinics. The staff had twenty-one doctors, thirty-three nurses, and fifty French civilian employees. In 1964, the 3335th Labor Service Medical Det had thirty-two Polish doctors and medical specialists at la Chapelle and Harbord Barracks. The mess hall at la Chapelle could seat five hundred. Until the late 1950s, the 34th Gen Hosp was the only comprehensive Army hospital in France.[28, 29]

La Chapelle US Army Hospital near Orléans

In February 1955, Hollywood actress Olivia de Havilland and Paris-based American writer Art Buchwald appeared at an Army variety show in Orléans to benefit the March of Dimes polio fund. Olivia de Havilland lunched with the enlisted men at la Chapelle. After lunch at the 34th Gen Hosp mess hall, she was told not to bother with her food tray. As she returned her tray, she replied "Everyone takes them to the kitchen, don't they?" In the afternoon, she spoke to every patient in every ward.[30]

In August 1960, a $1 million addition opened at the 34th Gen Hosp. It took French contractors two years to build the three-story wing. It added twenty-four beds to the hospital and housed all out-patient services, ob-gyn clinic (two delivery rooms, four labor rooms), ENT clinic, and pharmacy. The roof had a garden and glass enclosed sundeck where patients could relax and enjoy a view of the Loire River.[31] The hospital had the only Army orthopedic shop in France. In the late 1950s, Sp5 Stanley C. Faulkender fabricated braces and artificial limbs for injured GIs and dependents.[32]

As part of May Day 1966 activities in Orléans, a crowd of French communists decided to protest that weekend at the 34th Gen Hosp. The duty officer at the hospital, 1st Lt LaCosta, rounded up a dozen off-duty enlisted men who were scattered throughout the installation. The GIs were directed to quickly put on their fatigue uniforms and steel helmets, draw M-14 rifles from the arms room, and report to the main gate. At the gate, the protesters yelled anti-American slogans and some began climbing the closed metal gate to enter the grounds. LaCosta, who had aligned pharmacist Sp5 Johst A. Burk and his fellow "volunteers" at parade rest facing the protesters, loudly ordered the GIs to lock and load one round in their rifles. Unbeknownst to the communists, the GIs did not have ammo for their weapons. However, the noise of chambering phantom rounds frightened the climbers to drop off the gate. Within minutes, *Compagnie républicaine de sécurité* (CRS) vans arrived. The CRS, a civilian police force of the *Sûreté Nationale*, was organized as a military unit. It was disliked by most French. The CRS riot squad personnel used clubs to pummel the protesters to the ground before dragging them to vans (called "salad baskets" by the French). Some of the GIs, shocked by the brutality, booed the CRS personnel.[33]

French Intern Program

In 1959, the 34th Gen Hosp began a one-year medical intern-training program for French doctors. Four French interns were invited each year to learn American medical techniques. The interns had to obtain approval from their deans to participate in the program, which was identical to the American Medical Association (AMA) internships at hospitals in the US. The first to approve the program for his students was the Dean of the University of Paris Medical School. It was believed the program would help promote Franco-American understanding in the public health field.[34] Dr. Claude Emil Duperier, the first intern in the program, previously had studied medicine at the University of Paris and Yale University in New Haven, Connecticut. He was 29-years-old and had a wife and two children. Each day he worked in the patient wards and at night studied medical texts for at least three hours.[35, 36]

At la Chapelle, the French interns worked long hours, received training during daily rounds with US Army medical officers, attended numerous conferences, and took part in the field exercises which simulated providing treatment to patients in a hospital set up in tents.[37] In 1965-66 Dr. Harald Sontag, a French intern from the University of Strasbourg, delivered one-hundred fifty American babies, performed routine operations, and evaluated psychiatric-care patients.[38] Interns learned up-to-date techniques and trained with modern equipment that was not yet available in French hospitals. They were paid more than interns at French hospitals and the quarters were better. Interns lived at the hospital in a private room furnished with a hospital bed, sharing a bathroom between the rooms. The bathroom had a toilet, shower, and sink. At French hospitals, French interns normally had roommates sharing a drafty room in very old buildings, with one bathroom per floor.[39] Because interns at la Chapelle were given the status of a commissioned officer, they were authorized to use the Officers Club at Olivet.

34th General Hospital Commanders

Commanding Officer	Period of Service	Commanding Officer	Period of Service
Col William A. D. Woolgar	1953	Col Frank J. Vita	1962-64
Col Hobart D. Belknap	1953-56	Col Louis S. Leland	1964-65
Col William B. Stryker	1956-59	Col Paul E. Sieber	1965-67
Col Karl D. MacMillan	1959-62		

Station Hospitals

In 1957, station hospitals were located at Bussac, Chinon, and Paris. The 60th Station Hospital at Chinon (which had moved from Croix-Chapeau) and the 319th Station Hospital at Bussac each were designated 750 beds; the 196th Station Hospital at Paris (Neuilly), 200. The 750-bed station hospitals served troop concentrations of 20,000 to 30,000; the 200-bed station hospitals served 4,000 to 8,000. The 196th at Neuilly was authorized thirty officers and ninety-five enlisted personnel.

Brig Gen Ferdinand J. Chesarek (2nd from R), 60th Station Hospital, Chinon, 1961 (US Army)

Chain of Army Standby Hospitals

Hospital requirements for the sick and wounded from a war in Europe would overwhelm peacetime capabilities. To prepare for war casualties from a Soviet invasion and to be far to the rear of the expected attack, the Army planned to construct a chain of eleven standby hospital facilities across France.[40, 41] According to Army doctrine for general hospitals, the 1,000-bed capacity could be increased to 1,500 beds for a short duration. Ideally in wartime, patients would be moved by ambulance trucks and trains at a continuous flow from field to station to general hospitals (the standby hospitals in France).

To gain funding from the US Congress for the estimated cost of $60 million, these standby hospitals had to be "dual-purpose," utilized as barracks or dependents schools during peacetime. Because the hospitals could be used for barracks, the US Congress reduced the budget for barracks. To be used as barracks, the hospitals needed to be located where most of the troops would be within three miles of their normal work areas.[42] However some of the hospitals, such as Vitry and Vassincourt, were located too far away from the troops. Consequently, throughout the long deployment to France, thousands of troops remained in prefab barracks to be near their duty stations.

The French government preferred that the US build many small hospitals, but this would have substantially increased construction and operating costs. In 1952, Maj Gen Samuel D. Sturgis, Jr., ComZ commander, assured the French government that the American hospitals would be located as far away as possible from military targets.[43] However, the actual locations were close to railroad stations and airfields, which would be targeted by the Soviets. To avoid adversely affecting staffs of nearby French civilian and military hospitals, the US assured the French government that only Americans would staff the hospitals. Nevertheless in 1957, several French nurses worked in patient wards of the 34th General Hospital at la Chapelle.[44] In 1958, the 34th Gen Hosp nursing staff consisted of: twenty-eight Army nurses, five DACs, and ten French civilian nurses.[45] By the 1960s, Polish and French contract doctors were employed at some of the hospitals.

American architect Edward Durell Stone, who designed the Stanford University Medical Center in Palo Alto, California, was hired to consult on the design of Army standby hospitals in France.[46] In 1925-26 at MIT, Stone had studied under French architect Jacques Carlu. At age 60, Stone became prominent as the designer of the Kennedy Center for the Performing Arts in Washington, DC. Only nine of the eleven proposed hospitals were built because projects at St.-Nazaire and Bordeaux were cancelled. Six almost identical 1,000-bed hospitals were built in the late 1950s at Chinon, Croix-Chapeau, Forêt d'Orléans (Chanteau), Olivet, Toul, and Verdun.[47] Using the same architectural plans, but building only half of the wings, three almost identical 500-bed hospitals were built at Poitiers, Vassincourt, and Vitry-le-François. In April 1956, the 1,000-bed hospital at Chinon was the first of the standby hospitals to be completed. During peacetime, it would be used as troop housing, dependents school classrooms, and a 50-bed hospital to serve troops and dependents in the northern part of Base Section. To help visitors and ambulatory patients navigate the maze of corridors, colored stripes placed on corridor floors led to key destinations. The hospital, staffed by the 60th Station Hospital from 1956 to 1965, was the nucleus for emergency expansion during wartime.[48]

Standard Design Features

The design of the two-story masonry buildings was similar in layout to the Type A wood-frame cantonment military hospitals built during World War II in the United States.[49] The hospitals had a central core for operating rooms, doctor's offices, dining rooms, and kitchen. Copper mesh was installed under the ceramic tile floors to ground operating rooms, preventing sparks which could ignite gases used for anesthesia. To reduce the possibility that an air attack would disable an entire hospital, the hospitals were designed to have multiple two-story parallel wings protruding along both sides of a wide central corridor. In an emergency, the wide corridors could be filled with beds. During the years following the withdrawal of US forces, French civilian doctors at Chinon and Toul cited the benefits that separate wings provide by limiting the spread of infectious diseases.[50]

Vassincourt Medical Installation

From October 1939 to April 1940, flat terrain near Vassincourt was an airfield for the British RAF. During the subsequent German occupation, the land was farmed. In January 1952, the US Army acquired the property for use as an interim medical depot.[51] The first medical troops, the 306th Field Hospital from Greenville, South Carolina, and 309th Field Hospital (commanded by Lt Col Richard S. Fraser) from Springfield, Massachusetts, arrived in March 1952. Both were Army Reserve units mobilized for the Korean War. Although the medical equipment stored at Vassincourt was valued at $1 million, the troops did not have weapons. To secure the installation at night, Lt Col Norman Lepper issued a pistol to the duty officer.[52] Conditions were so primitive during summer 1952 that medical service troops, directed by WO John W. Lamb, dug a storage cellar for perishable food. Scrounged wood was used for shelves, 18 inches of sawdust for thermal insulation of walls and ceiling, and an ice bin for cooling.[53] In April 1953, the dependents elementary school moved from leased rooms at Hôtel de la Source in Sermaize-les-Bains to a prefab at Vassincourt. On 27 January 1954, a fire which started in a storage tent destroyed nine tents. Five GIs were treated for burns.[54]

In 1960, the US Army Construction Agency, France built a 500-bed standby hospital at Vassincourt at a cost of $1.2 million. Wings of the modern hospital were used by the 97th Engineer Battalion, 69th Signal Battalion, and dependents elementary school. French language classes for GIs were taught in the evenings in the new classrooms. Troops still lived in metal prefabs. During Operation ROUNDOUT in 1961, the 69th Signal Bn, commanded by Lt Col Rufus Z. Johnston, was sent from Fort Meade, Maryland, to Vassincourt. On 12 April 1963, six-hundred fifty officers and enlisted men of the 69th departed from la Pallice for the US on the USNS *General R. M. Blatchford*. In November 1965, the 69th was sent to Vietnam.[55]

Vassincourt Medical Depot, January 1953 (US Army)

42nd Field Hospital

On 10 June 1944 during the Normandy landings, the 42nd Field Hospital treated hundreds of wounded GIs at Utah Beach. After the war the unit was inactivated. On 03 December 1954, the 42nd Field Hospital was activated at Verdun to replace the inactivated 309th Field Hospital which had transferred in June from Vassincourt to Verdun. The 309th, an Army Reserve unit, was released from active duty. Its personnel remained in France to form the 42nd Field Hospital at Caserne Maginot. The 42nd, commanded by Lt Col Norman Lepper, was authorized one-hundred seventy personnel.

Désandrouins Barracks, a 1,000-bed standby hospital built near Verdun, was dedicated on 18 October 1958. It took French contractors 2½ years to complete the network of interconnected two-story buildings. The hospital wing was authorized 50 active beds to serve personnel and dependents in the Verdun area. The dependents elementary and high schools used wings to accommodate more than eight-hundred students and GIs lived in the barracks wings. From 1954 to 1962, the 42nd Field Hospital, a mobile medical unit, operated the fixed 50-bed hospital. The hospital staff, directed by

42nd Field Hospital, Verdun, 1962 (US Army)

Maj (Dr) Albert W. Stratton in 1958, included ten Army doctors, eight dentists, and two Polish Labor Service doctors. The hospital had a whirlpool for patient therapy and an "Iron Lung." Patients needing specialized care were sent to hospitals in Germany.[56] Royal Canadian Air Force (RCAF) personnel, stationed at Metz and at NATO air bases at Marville and Grostenquin, received medical care at Verdun and Toul (Jeanne d'Arc) for procedures not available at the Canadian installations.[57]

The hospital was named in memory of Maréchal Jean Nicolas Désandrouins, who was born in Verdun and served with Rochambeau in the fight for American independence. It was built on a plateau near Verdun which had been the site of the 27th Aero Squadron's forward airfield in September and October 1918. On 29 September, legendary "balloon buster" 2nd Lt Frank Luke, Jr. took off from the airfield on his final flight. Luke shot down his thirteenth and fourteenth balloons before he was hit by ground fire.[58] Luke's total was incredible. Tethered to a motorized winch, balloons were used to suspend observers high above the front lines. They were dangerous targets that most pilots avoided because they were heavily guarded by anti-aircraft guns and enemy aircraft.

Conversion to Wartime Hospitals

Most of the Army's two-story wings at standby hospitals were dual purpose. They could be used for troop barracks, classrooms, or school dormitories until needed as hospital wards during wartime. Electrical conduit, fluid piping, and other services were installed, but blanked off. A large warehouse building contained all the equipment for conversion to wartime mission as a hospital. In event of hostilities, time for conversion to medical service was estimated to be 48 to 72 hours.[59]

The wartime goal of US Army, Europe (USAREUR) was to provide more than 18,400 beds in France. More than 5,200 medical personnel would relocate from Germany to staff the nine standby hospitals.[60] In 1960, the nine had an emergency capacity of 11,250 beds. Hospital facilities at Camp Bussac, la Chapelle (Orléans), and Neuilly (Paris) would provide an additional 1,450 beds. At la Chapelle, emergency capacity was 500 beds. In 1962, the 42nd Field Hospital (1st Det) at Poitiers had equipment and tents for an additional 500 beds.

US Air Force hospitals near Évreux AB and Châteauroux AD each had an emergency capacity of 600 beds. Smaller hospitals on the other air bases each had an emergency capacity of 100 beds.[61] Deployed to the field in an emergency, the 608th Tactical Hospital at Toul-Rosières AB could be enlarged to 400 beds in tents. Medical equipment and tents were stored in vans at the air base, ready to roll on short notice.[62]

Army Medical Depots

Medical supplies initially were stored at Fontainebleau, La Roche-sur-Yon, and Vassincourt. In 1951, the 504th Medical Base Depot Co, commanded by Capt Russell S. Kribs, arrived at Fontainebleau. After months of hard labor by troops of the 504th to set up a huge depot at Caserne Lariboisière, war planners decided that depots should not be located in Fontainebleau. They feared that the nearby NATO military headquarters would be key targets during a Soviet invasion.[63] Until depots could be constructed at Vitry-le-François and Croix-Chapeau, medical supplies stored at Lariboisière were moved to leased warehouses at Aérodrome des Ajones near La Roche-sur-Yon. The Army signed a five-year lease for the 19-acre aérodrome.[64] The *Parti Communiste Français* protested use of the Ajones property, describing Americans as "champions de la bombe atomique." The protest was ineffective because the depot would provide jobs for hundreds of French workers.

On 07 May 1953, volunteer Medical Service Corps troops from Germany arrived at La Roche-sur-Yon. Lt Col Donald D. Fisher, depot commander, used a tent for temporary headquarters. Existing masonry buildings were converted to a dispensary, EM barracks, and a mess hall. In September 1953, a two-room schoolhouse for grades 1 to 8 opened on the depot. The airfield was repaired and five hangars were rehabilitated to provide covered storage for the medical supplies.[65] In an emergency, war planners believed that cargo aircraft could use the airfield to deliver supplies rapidly to Seventh Army in Germany. The 7788th Army Unit (AU) managed the depot. In 1953, the 36th Medical Holding Co was reassigned from Camp Bussac to La Roche-sur-Yon.

The 492nd Medical Maintenance & Equipment Co, which repaired medical equipment at hospitals and clinics throughout the Base Section, stored spare parts at La-Roche-sur-Yon. Because medical equipment was purchased from various American and European manufacturers, many spare parts were similar, but not interchangeable.[66]

In 1954, construction work began on medical depots at Vitry-le-François and Croix-Chapeau. At Vitry, the Joint Construction Agency (JCA) monitored construction progress of the Entreprise Bollard et Cie of Paris; at Croix-Chapeau, progress of Société Industrielle Foncière et Routière of Paris. These depots, each authorized nearly one-hundred military personnel, would store more than 75% of all medical supplies in Europe. The La Roche-sur-Yon Medical Depot, commanded by Maj Edward J. Meyer, closed in early 1956. It took three months to move the medical supplies and hospital equipment to the huge new warehouses at Croix-Chapeau. Enough equipment would be stored at Croix-Chapeau to set up several hospitals.[67]

Croix-Chapeau Medical Depot

The 70th Medical Depot was located between Croix-Chapeau and Aigrefeuille d'Aunis, 10 miles east of La Rochelle. The JCA also built a 1,000-bed standby hospital adjacent to the depot buildings. The 28th General Hospital was assigned to Croix-Chapeau from 1952 to 1964; the 60th Station Hospital during 1955 and 1956.

All prescription eyeglasses and dental crowns for US European Command were made at Croix-Chapeau. The 70th Medical Depot's Optical Division manufactured 3,829 pairs of eye glasses

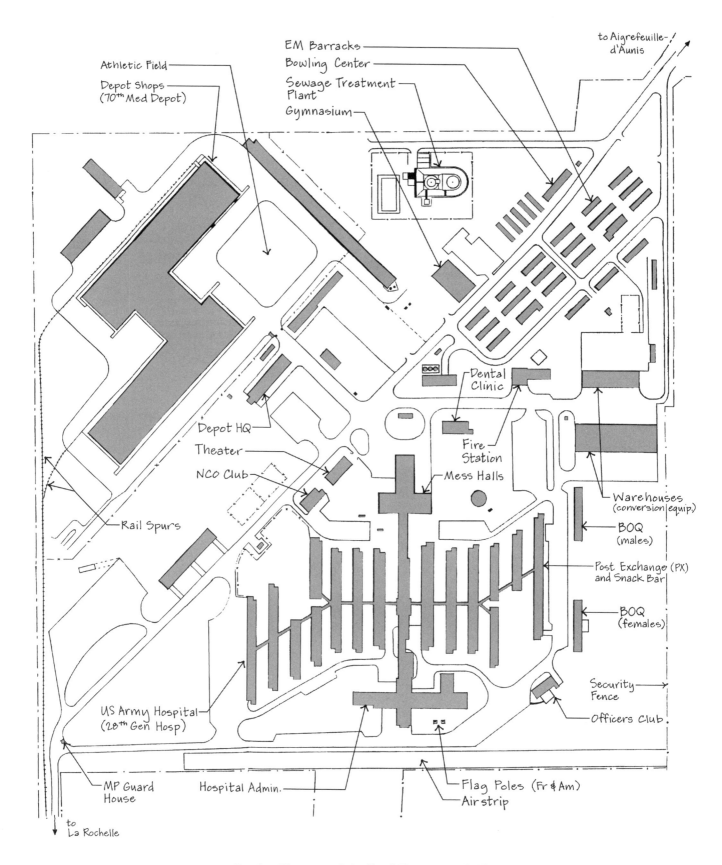

Croix-Chapeau Medical Depot (1960)

each month. Nine types of frames were stocked, including two for protective masks and one for aviation helmets.[68] This medical work provided good wages for hundreds of French nationals in the La Rochelle region. The US Army provided bus transportation from La Rochelle to the Croix-Chapeau depot for most of these skilled workers.[69]

PFCs John D. Chambers and James M. Greenwood, who had received basic medical training at Fort Sam Houston, Texas, were assigned in 1954 to Croix-Chapeau before the depot buildings were completed. Their platoon sergeant kept his men busy with creative assignments such as moving heavy boxes of supplies to a new location on post one day and back to the original location the next day. To avoid these tasks, the young GIs had a competition to see who could disappear for the longest period during duty hours without being discovered. Chambers found that pews in the empty chapel were an excellent hiding place. Assigned work at the hospital in Caserne Aufrédi at La Rochelle, Chambers learned to put casts on broken arms, take blood pressure, and other medical tasks. Chambers and Greenwood also were unsupervised medics at summer camps for dependent children. Their Army experience inspired them to attend medical schools when they returned home. Both had long, distinguished careers. Chambers as an ophthalmologist in Anacortes, Washington; Greenwood as a family practice physician in Bay City, Michigan.[70]

70th Medical Depot Commanders

Commanding Officer	Period of Service	Commanding Officer	Period of Service
Col Richard W. Pullen	1955-58	Col Volney H. Rattan	1959-61
Lt Col Robert C. Stokes	1958	Col Walter F. Dunn, Jr.	1961-62
Col Frederic B. Westervelt	1958-59	Col Robert N. Read	1962-63
Col Gerard A. Belanger	1959	Maj Marion Rutkowski	1964

Vitry Medical Depot

The 77th Medical Depot was located along Nancy-Paris route N4 at the outskirts of Vitry-le-François on property acquired in January 1953. The JCA also built a 500-bed standby hospital adjacent to depot buildings. In January 1957, troops from Fontainebleau arrived at Vitry to establish the 77th Medical Depot. Vitry was stocked with medical equipment (such as dental chairs, surgical lamps, steam sterilizers, X-ray units) which had been relocated from the 33rd Medical Depot at Fontainebleau.[71] There were stacks of refrigeration units for blood, boxes of spare parts to repair medical equipment, and piles of oxygen bottles. In 1959, a metal-frame shelving system (called Dexion) was installed in the warehouses at Vitry to compartmentalize storage of boxed items. Previously, access to boxes had been difficult because they were stacked on top of each other from floor to ceiling.[72] Field hospital kits were kept ready for delivery to units who were required to set up a hospital in the field within 72 hours of alert.[73]

In December 1957, nearly one-fifth of all personnel at Vitry enrolled in the French I language course offered by the University of Maryland Overseas. Because many depot personnel lived in distant villages and drove to the depot on narrow tree-lined roads, depot commander Lt Col Arthur F. Maeser believed it would be prudent to avoid long commutes at night. Therefore, the language class met for 6 hours each week at the depot during duty hours, although most University of Maryland courses in France were scheduled in the evenings.[74]

In February 1962, North Sea tidal waves and hurricane-force winds pounded the coast of Germany, leaving hundreds dead and over 400,000 homeless. Army depots in France provided blankets, winter clothing, mattresses, rations, and medicine. Depot commander, Col Louis J. Molli

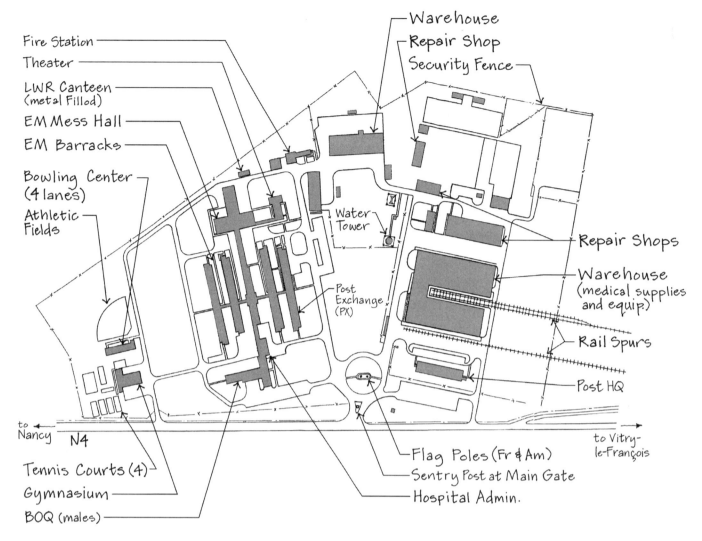

Vitry Medical Depot (1963)

sent several troops from Vitry to deliver blankets and medicine to the victims in Germany. Air Force C-130 Hercules aircraft from Évreux AB airlifted troops and disaster relief supplies to Germany.[75, 76] In May 1963, PFC Michael Richter was sent TDY from Vitry to Paris to drive senior officers during a US European Command medical conference at Camp des Loges. Among the drivers, one stood out because he did not salute his general. Richter discovered that he was the driver of NATO Supreme Commander Gen Lyman L. Lemnitzer. The nonsaluter explained that Lemnitzer did not want his driver saluting all day long. A "Good morning sir" salute each day was sufficient.[77]

77th Medical Depot Commanders

Commanding Officer	Period of Service	Commanding Officer	Period of Service
Lt Col Arthur F. Maeser	1957-58	Col Henry D. Roth	1962-63
Lt Col Carrol C. Barrick	1958-59	Lt Col Layton O. Burris	1963-64
Lt Col Charles B. Gault	1959	Lt Col Charles R. Kinney	1964-65
Col Louis J. Molli	1959-62	Maj Albert L. Hayes, Jr.	1965-66

At the time of withdrawal from France in 1966-67, the Army depots contained medical supplies valued at more than $19 million. Moving the delicate and expensive hospital equipment, such as X-ray machines and dental chairs, would be a challenge to rapid withdrawal. During the withdrawal, more than 10,600 hospital beds were moved to depots in Germany and England. Due to lack of covered storage in the UK, temporary storage was sought in hotels and churches.[78]

Training Exercises for Medics

Each year hospitals conducted training exercises in the field to test readiness to operate under combat conditions. During exercises, troops endured smoke bomb and simulated gas attacks. In the 1950s, simulated atomic attacks were held to test responses and methods of treatment provided patients. In early April 1956, the 60th Station Hospital at Croix-Chapeau deployed to the field. The three-day training exercise tested the ability of medics to manage a 50-bed hospital in huge canvas tents, similar to circus tents. Upon arrival in the field, tents were erected, medical equipment set up, and guards posted in case "aggressor" forces attacked. Hospital sections set up to handle simulated combat injuries included admission and disposition, X-ray, surgery, and ward tents for patients. Ward tents, arranged in groups of four to form a cross, allowed one nurse in the center to care for four wards. If lined up side-by-side, each tent would require a nurse.[79] Stretcher bearers delivered simulated casualties tagged with their simulated injuries (called "wound tags"). Enlisted personnel checked pulse rates of patients; surgeons performed simulated operations. The hospital also had a neuro-psychiatric section to treat combat fatigue. Security and bivouac techniques were rated by an infantry officer.[80]

In summer 1957, personnel of the 42nd Field Hospital at Verdun were assigned to one of three cycles of three-week training sessions. They set up tents near Fort du Channa at Fromeréville, 8 miles from Verdun. Hospital sections included X-ray, surgery, pharmacy, and ward tents for patients. Each morning, sick call patients were delivered from Verdun to the site by ¾-ton truck ambulance or H-13 Sioux helicopter. Healthy GIs were assigned to play roles of wounded patients. Staff not in training maintained the permanent hospital and dispensary at Caserne Maginot.[81]

During an exercise in October 1962, it took one week to set up the tent hospital at La Grémuse for the 34th General Hospital. Setting up large tents, 54-ft long by 18-ft wide by 14-ft high, took more than two dozen GIs to hold poles and pull ropes. GIs from the 34th Gen Hosp support group from la Chapelle-St.-Mesmin and the 553rd Engineer Battalion from Ardon pitched tents, dug latrines, and set up electric generators and water trailers. Pierced steel plank covered by canvas was used for flooring in the tents. The doctors arrived on site after everything was in place.[82]

Nuclear and Biological Survival

In a nuclear war with the Soviets, GIs believed they would be safer at the front lines in Germany than in France. They reasoned that the Soviets would target logistical installations in the rear rather than expose their own troops to radiation. Throughout the Cold War, each installation in France had sealed boxes of nuclear survival kits that contained medicine, such as aspirin, penicillin, and Phenobarbital tablets. The US Army called the kits "Phase I Medical Kits." The Verdun area had seventy-five large cardboard boxes containing kits. The 249th Engineer Battalion, which redeployed in March 1960 from Kaiserslautern, Germany, to Étain AB, had nine; Caserne Gribeauval, twelve; Caserne Maginot, eleven; and Désandrouins Hospital, twenty-nine.[83] The US Air Force called the kits "Medical Material for the Prevention of Nuclear Casualty."

Air Force dispensary personnel trained to respond to accidents involving nuclear weapons where radioactive materials might be dispersed (code-named "Broken Arrow"), such as jettisoning a weapon or aircraft crashes. Medical teams were warned not to enter areas where radiation exceeded 50 roentgens per hour.[84] In April 1957, SHAPE at Marly-le-Roi (Paris) hosted a Surgeons General Conference that included a dramatic presentation on "Medical Management of Mass Casualties in Nuclear Warfare." Actors, pretending to be victims, added realism to the presentation.[85]

Although the troops trained for a nuclear war with the Soviets, their first aid kits were designed for additional threats such as chemical weapons. Because the Soviets had produced vast quantities of Sarin nerve gas which could be used during an invasion, Army personnel were issued an atropine Syrette to be used as an antidote. The Syrette was a small, collapsible metal tube filled with an atropine solution. Atropine neutralized the effects of nerve agents in the body, but had to be injected immediately after exposure to be effective. Dosage had been determined by tests on laboratory mice and on human volunteers at Fort Detrick, Maryland. If exposed to nerve gas, a GI was to jab the needle, at the end of the Syrette, into his thigh and inject the atropine by squeezing the tube. By 1959, an improved cigar-shaped Syrette had a recessed, spring-loaded needle because GIs were reluctant to stab themselves.[86] GIs were trained to self-inject, but sometimes were not warned that in most cases artificial respiration also would be required.[87] A major effect of nerve agent was acute lung constriction.

Students at the CBR School (chemical, biological, and radiological), established in 1954 at Camp Bussac, received more than eighty hours of instruction. Topics included: detection and identification of chemical agents, maintenance of chemical munitions, decontamination and protection against CBR attack, and tactical use of CBR agents. For safety on the battlefield, it was essential that the M17 Protective Mask was donned properly within nine seconds. On the last day of the basic course, students had three drops of liquid "mustard" agent, which smelled like garlic, placed on a forearm. One drop was placed on a dab of protective ointment, which had been applied to the skin. The other two drops were applied directly to the skin. One was treated with ointment, the other left to burn and permanently scar the skin. The procedure was intended to emphasize the importance of the protective ointment, which had to be applied within 5 minutes of exposure.[88, 89] Students, who had been tipped off by CBR School graduates, applied ointment to their forearms prior to class. In March 1954, forty-nine GIs graduated from the Advance Section's first CBR course at Sampigny. The two-week course was directed by Lt Col Richard N. Borgfeldt.[90]

Chemical Agent	Odor	Chemical Agent	Odor
Hydrogen cyanide	Bitter almonds	Phosgene	Newly mowed hay
Lewisite	Geraniums	Sarin	None
Mustard	Garlic, Horseradish	VX	None

Radiation Survey Teams

During the mid-1950s, radiation survey teams were formed at Army installations in France. At the Nancy Ordnance Depot, PFC Doran A. Ditlow volunteered to serve on the survey team. Ditlow, who had trained at Aberdeen Proving Ground, Maryland, as a Fuel and Electrical Systems Repairman, wanted relief from the monotony of his work at the maintenance shop of the 109th Ordnance Co (Park). His three-man survey team was issued a jeep, maps of the depot, Geiger counter, and two-way radio set. The first field test was to find a small radioactive test sample hidden on the 2,500-acre depot in the Forêt de Haye. The team was told the sample had been buried in a wooden box at Armstrong Athletic Field. Without the hint, the exercise likely would have taken days due to the limited range of radiation detectors.[91] In 1954, the Chemical Depot at Camp Bussac held 10-day courses for personnel assigned to radiation survey teams. Students learned how to use Geiger counters, plot fallout from atomic explosions, and decontaminate troops and equipment. More than four-hundred GIs from ComZ installations completed the course, directed by Maj Roy D'Amore.[92] In March 1956, personnel from Metz, Nancy, Trois-Fontaines, and Verdun completed a sixty-five hour course at the Radiological Defense Survey Team School at Sampigny. The course was supervised by Maj Edward J. Odachowski.[93]

Ambulance Trains

US European Command maintained ambulance trains designed to serve as rolling hospitals. During transit, patients were given necessary care. The eleven car train of the 80th Ambulance Train Company (Rail) at Orléans could carry one-hundred sixteen patients on stretchers or three-hundred ambulatory patients.[94,95] Ambulance trains normally consisted of: six to eight ward cars (each having eight, two-tier bunks), pharmacy/office car, kitchen-dining car, and sleeping car for train personnel. The kitchen-dining car could feed one-hundred fifty. Meals of meat, fruit, and coffee normally were served on metal trays to patients in the ward cars.[96] In older ward cars, litter patients had to be lifted through windows. Newer model ward cars had a large sliding door on each side to load and unload litters and could carry up to thirty-six litter patients. Litters could be stacked in six triple tiers of bunks on each side of the aisle, like GIs on troopships. However, it was difficult to treat patients on the upper tier. During World War II, nurses in the Malinta Tunnel at Corregidor (Philippines) found it almost impossible to nurse patients in the upper level of triple-tier bunks.[97] Upper bunks on ward cars were hinged to fold out of the way; lower bunks could be converted to seating for four ambulatory patients. All cars had electric lighting, water, ventilation by blower, and heaters. Only ward cars had air-conditioning.[98-100]

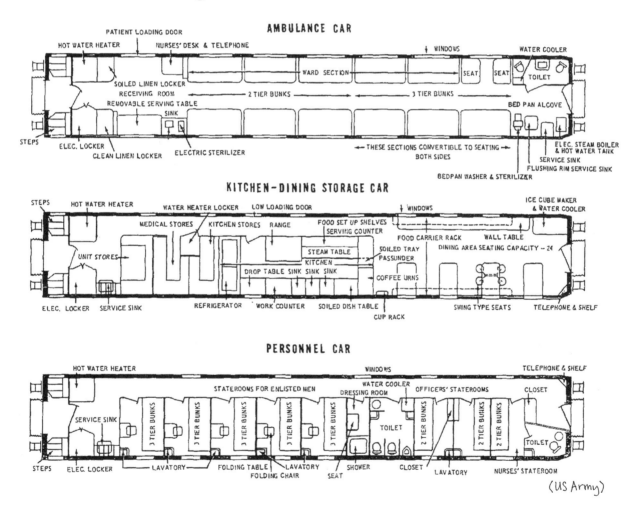

Cars of US Army Ambulance Train

Trains initially were located at St.-Jean-de-Braye near Orléans, then at Chinon and Tours, and in the 1960s at Toul. The 80th Amb Train Co (Rail) made its initial run in July 1953, commanded by Maj Gerard A. Bertrand. The train was staffed by two Medical Service Corps officers, two nurses, and thirty-six medics and cooks. The medics were billeted at Maison-Fort. In December 1953, the 80th received new ward cars that increased train capacity to two-hundred fifty-two patients on stretchers or three-hundred thirty-six ambulatory patients.[101] The train traveled to La Rochelle, Bussac, and Bordeaux twice a month to transport Base Section patients to the 34th General Hospital at la Chapelle.[102, 103] Training exercises to Germany were held once a month in the 1950s. It took forty-five minutes for the train staff to conclude their hospital tasks, load, and board the train.[104] Trains traveled from Bordeaux, through Orléans and Nancy, to Landstuhl, Germany. At Landstuhl, patients were transported by ambulance vehicle to the 320th General Hospital. By the 1960s, exercises were less frequent. In early January 1963, a 5-day exercise was held to provide experience for train staff and crew. The exercise simulated the movement of patients between Landstuhl and the standby hospital at Forêt d'Orléans. The six-car train from Landstuhl stopped at Toul, Vitry-le-François, Fontainebleau, and Orléans.[105] Three additional trains, parked at Pirmasens, Germany, were ready to move casualties to hospitals in France if the Soviets invaded. However by 1970, only two trains were operational, the other two were in storage.[106, 107]

Except during emergencies, ambulance trains traveled on French railroad lines (SNCF) far slower than passenger or freight trains. In summer 1956, Gen Henry I. Hodes, Commander-in-Chief of USAREUR, encouraged Maj Gen Robert W. Colglazier, Jr., ComZ commander, to use a ComZ ambulance train railcar to speed his inspection visits to installations throughout France. Hodes used the official USAREUR train, pulled by a locomotive nicknamed "The General," on trips throughout Germany. Unfortunately on his first trip, Colglazier's railcar was diverted to sidings to allow higher priority rail traffic to roll by. Upon his return to Orléans, Colglazier received an enormous bill from SNCF. It was the only time he used the train.[108] As a civilian, Colglazier, an Army reserve officer, owned a construction firm in San Antonio, Texas and was adamant to not waste money. In 1956, he was the only reserve general officer on active-duty in the Regular Army.

US Army, Europe ambulance train ward car (US Army)

Sales of Army Standby Hospitals

At the time the US military withdrew from France in 1967, most of the US Army standby hospitals were too large to be used by nearby communities and therefore were difficult for the US to sell. ComZ reported that $3,749,800 had been spent for the construction and improvements at the US Army Hospital near Chinon. During negotiations with the French government for the return of this property, the US asked $627,468, the French countered with an offer of $70,260. Agreement was reached after three more rounds of offers and counteroffers. The accepted sale price was $320,000. At Poitiers, $3,873,000 had been spent on the US Army Hospital. The US asked $453,400, the French offered $60,000. After four more rounds of offers and counteroffers, agreement was reached at $220,000.[109] At Toul, $5,368,000 had been spent on Jeanne d'Arc US Army Hospital. Agreement on the sale was reached at $461,600. However, this sale was controversial in France because the hospital was not used for several years until it became part of the Université de Nancy regional hospital system.[110]

Army Hospital Units in France (1951-67)[111, 112]

Location	Hospital Unit	Wartime Beds*	Period
Bordeaux	33rd Station	200	1952-54
Bussac	302nd Field (Unit II)	400	1951-52
	319th Station	750	1953-62
	42nd Field	400	1962-65
Captieux	60th Station	750	1952-53
Chinon	60th Station	750	1956-65
	130th General	1,000	1965-67
Croix-Chapeau	28th General	1,000	1952-64
	319th Station	750	1953
	60th Station	750	1955-56
Fontainebleau	34th Station	200	1952-55
	33rd Field	400	1955-62
Orléans	302nd Field	400	1952-53
	34th General	1,000	1953-67
Paris	196th Station	200	1955-67
Poitiers	60th Station	750	1953-55
	42nd Field (Det 1)	400	1962-64
La Rochelle	319th Station	750	1952-53
Toul	57th Field	400	1952-62
	60th Station	750	1965-66
Vassincourt	306th Field	400	1952-55
	309th Field	400	1952-54
Verdun	32nd Station	200	1951-54
	309th Field	400	1954
	42nd Field	400	1954-62
	319th Station	750	1962-64
	56th General	1,000	1965-67
Vitry-le-François	16th Field	400	1957-65

*Initially, the 32nd, 33rd, and 34th Station Hospitals each had twenty-five active beds.

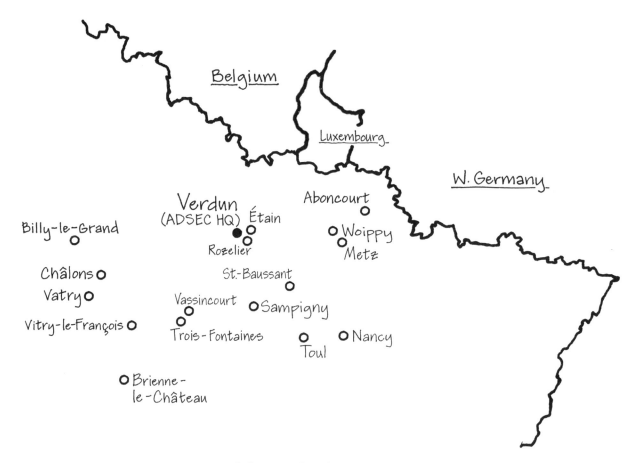

Advance Section in France

Main gate, Caserne Maginot, Verdun, 1952 (US Army)

NINE

Advance Section in the Northeast

"Let the bugles blare! When you need support, ADSEC's there!" (1956 song: *Lifeline*)

Advance Section Buildup

In November 1950, six-hundred Army troops commanded by Col John F. Cassidy arrived at Verdun to establish the Advance Section (ADSEC) headquarters and a signal depot.[1] The Advance Section grew to have a dozen major depots extending eastward from Vitry-le-François and Châlons-sur-Marne to Nancy, Toul, and Metz. Three huge ordnance depots, totaling more than 18,000 acres, were built in the French national forests of Trois-Fontaines (near Bar-le-Duc), Haye (Nancy), and Sommedieue (Verdun). By 1957, seven depots in Germany also were assigned to ADSEC.

By the mid-1950s, the depots rotated their stocks to better support the day-to-day operations of ComZ and Seventh Army. Drivers of the 37th Transportation Command delivered weapons, ammunition, POL, and medical supplies to troops scattered throughout Germany. In the 1960s, strategic reserve supplies were pre-positioned in the Advance Section for combat troops who would be airlifted to Europe in an emergency. Combat tanks and trucks were stored at Nancy, engineer equipment at Toul, and ammunition at Rozelier near Verdun.

Caserne Maginot

Headquarters of ADSEC was established at Caserne Maginot in Thierville-sur-Meuse. The caserne, built in 1880, was named for French Sergeant André Maginot (1877-1932) who fought bravely near Verdun in World War I. Later, as a civilian, Maginot served French veterans as Minister of Pensions. Due to his government work on defense, Maginot is forever linked to the myth of impenetrable fortifications, known as the "Maginot Line." The fortifications were designed to defend Alsace and Lorraine regions until reserve forces could be mobilized.[2] However in 1939, the German Army invaded France through Belgium, bypassing the fortifications. In the early 1950s, ADSEC used some of the Maginot Line fortifications for storage and shops. The thick concrete structures were believed to be atomic blast-resistant.[3]

Dilapidated buildings in the caserne were rehabilitated for offices, troop barracks, 25-bed hospital, elementary school, PX, and commissary. A staff of twenty French women, supervised by Mlle Françoise Moulet, operated the telephone switchboards. The staff processed ten-thousand local and three-hundred long-distance calls each day.[4] On 30 October 1954, a telephone dial system became operational, replacing the tactical switchboard equipment that had been used since November 1950. The new 600-line dial system equipment was manufactured in France under specifications of the US Army and French PT&T.[5] In 1958 at the communications center, thirty-five enlisted men worked 8-hour shifts operating several teletype machines twenty-four hours a day, seven days a week.

The 2nd Platoon of the 102nd Quartermaster Co (Bakery), commanded by 1st Lt Thurston A. Blakely, baked 9,600 lbs of bread each day at Maginot. Personnel of the 901st Medical Det (Vet Food Insp), an Army Reserve unit from Kansas City, Kansas, commanded by Capt Richard E. Hineman, inspected railcars containing refrigerated cartons of milk. The temperature of the milk, delivered three times each week from the Netherlands, was not to exceed 50° F. A random sample of cartons

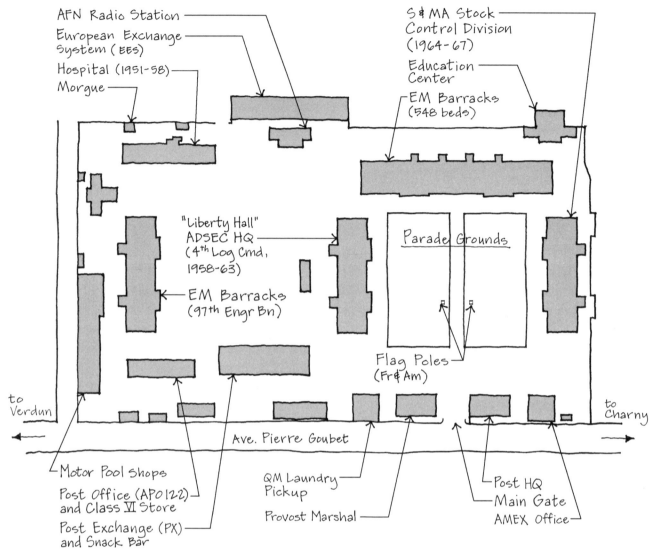

Caserne Maginot

was opened to determine bacteria count. The only local food inspected by the 901st Med Det was horse meat purchased to feed guard dogs.[6] On 17 December 1954, the detachment was released from active duty. Its personnel remained in France to form the 105th Med Detachment.

In May 1952, fifteen dentists of the 767th Dental Service Detachment provided dental care at Maginot. At remote installations, such as Billy-le-Grand and Sampigny, mobile dental equipment was set up in tents. Normally, two dental chairs would be in operation within an hour of arrival. Mobile units could treat 15 to 20 men per day.[7]

In 1952, personnel from the all-black 31st Army Band at Würzburg, Germany, were sent to Maginot to form the 118th Army Band. The band, commanded by CWO Peter L. Crawford, performed ceremonial, show, and dance music. The bandsmen enhanced Franco-American relations by playing in villages and towns throughout the northeast. Because bandsmen served as security guards during alerts, one day each week was devoted to military training.[8, 9]

Advance Section Honor Guard, commanded by 1st Lt Sherman Weldon,
Caserne Maginot, Verdun, July 1953 (US Army)

The American Village

US Army installations became so numerous that locals called Verdun *le village américain*. In the beginning, German firms provided architectural engineering services for the buildup. The arrangements angered the Verdunois because Germans were being paid to rehabilitate the same buildings that only a few years earlier they had forcibly occupied and damaged when they retreated.[10]

In December 1950, Caserne Gribeauval was acquired by the US military primarily for use as troop barracks. Patton's Third Army had used Gribeauval in 1944-45, after liberating it from the Germans. The caserne, built in 1913, was named for Jean Baptiste Vaquette de Gribeauval (1715-89). As French Inspector General, Gribeauval had implemented innovations in French artillery that enhanced mobility (by reducing the length and weight of howitzer barrels) and accuracy (by adding an elevating screw to raise and lower the breech for more precise ranging).[11] One large upper-level barracks room served as an auditorium to show movies and hold training classes. For recreation a 4-lane bowling alley, called "Gribeauval Lanes," was installed in a former warehouse.

In 1952, part of the 17th Century Citadelle was leased from the French government. Although the buildings were dilapidated, they were used for a communications center. The Northeast District Office of the Joint Construction Agency (JCA) in Paris was located in cramped, cold quarters at the Citadelle. After numerous pleas to the French, the JCA engineers moved to Nancy. The 7768th ADSEC Signal Depot Det used a five-acre site at Fort de Regret to park sixteen 2½-ton vans, equipped with high-frequency radio sets. The vans provided communications in the field.[12]

Army single-engine L-19 Bird Dog fixed-wing aircraft, called "jeeps with wings," used an airstrip at Fromeréville. The 432nd Quartermaster Co (Salvage), commanded by 1st Lt Howard N. Keithley, operated a salvage point to dispose of scrap and discarded items from the buildup. The 432nd was an Army Reserve unit from Jay, Oklahoma. The Army leased the Blanchisserie Herbelin building on rue des Minimes in downtown Verdun. The 469th Quartermaster Co (Laundry) installed laundry and dry-cleaning equipment sized to serve 10,000 troops.[13]

In early 1952, Franco-American traffic patrols in ADSEC consisted of three men: an MP from Company D of the 382nd Military Police Battalion to control US military vehicles, a French CRS policeman to control civilian vehicles, and a French gendarme to control French military vehicles.[14] The 382nd MP Bn stationed detachments at Bar-le-Duc, Metz, Nancy, and Toul. In fall 1951 at Sandhofen Troop Assignment Center in Germany, Pvt Lyle A. Ross volunteered to serve as an MP in France. Based on his basic training experiences at Fort Dix, New Jersey, he believed that MP duties would be better than infantry. Ross received on-the-job MP training from the 382nd before being assigned to Laleu in Base Section.[15]

Commanding Generals at Verdun

In February 1952, Cassidy was succeeded by Brig Gen William W. "Wally" Ford. In April 1953, after SFC John Reed, a surgical technician at the 309th Field Hospital at Vassincourt, saluted Col Francis H. Barnes near the parade grounds at Maginot, he was asked to accompany Barnes to the office of the commanding general. Perplexed, Reed apprehensively followed but relaxed when, before entering the general's office, Barnes told him "it makes me proud to be in the Army with a soldier who can appear like one while wearing fatigues." After Reed met Ford, the general praised him for his shined boots, polished belt buckle, straight gig line, and soldierly bearing.[16]

Ford allowed elementary school pupils to eat hot lunches in the mess hall at Caserne Maginot. Reasoning that children eat less than soldiers, Ford charged only 25¢. The standard price for lunch in the mess hall was 45¢. When Maj Gen Samuel D. Sturgis, Jr., ComZ commander, learned that children were eating in the mess, he directed Ford to end this irregular use of an Army mess. Sturgis boasted that he had carried cold lunches to school for eight years without ill effects.[17] Ford oversaw the tent "winterization" program to move his troops into warm shelter before the cold winter. All troops finally moved into prefabs and permanent buildings during the tenure of his successor, Brig Gen Raymond W. Curtis.

In February 1956, Brig Gen William R. "Lifeline" Woodward became commander. Woodward adopted his nickname "Lifeline" from the ComZ motto: "Lifeline to the Frontline." The motto had been suggested in December 1954 by PFC James R. Batt.[18] Woodward's St. Bernard dog, named "Lifeline 1," accompanied him each day to work at Maginot from the general officer quarters on rue du Général de Gaulle, Verdun. In 1956, when the band played "Strike up the Band" most troops recognized it as "Lifeline," the Advance Section's song inspired by Woodward to boost morale. "Lifeline" ended "Let the bugles blare! When you need support, ADSEC's there!"

Normally ceremonies were held on the parade grounds at Caserne Maginot. However, on Friday afternoons in spring 1956, Woodward had his troops assemble in formation near the construction site for the new standby hospital, located outside Verdun along the road to Étain. Troops marched to the site behind the 118th Army Band, led by bandleader CWO Emilio Rodriquez and Woodward's dog. Instead of walking in front of the formation to review the troops (called "trooping the line"), Woodward hovered overhead, seated in an H-13 Sioux helicopter. The H-13 had a distinctive bubble canopy and could carry one passenger. The pilot, Capt William V. Goodwin, kept the H-13 at an angle so the troops could see Woodward return their salute. Hats were blown off, clouds of dust and dirt enveloped the troops, and formation decorum was disrupted by downwash of the rotor blade.[19]

Lifeline The Dog

Lifeline 1, who was assigned dog-handler Sp3 William Croce, became well known through weekly photos and stories in Advance Section's newspaper, *The Advance*. At the official opening of the Donges-Metz POL pipeline in January 1957, Lifeline 1 was photographed with his paws on the wheel of a large valve at the QM tank farm at St.-Baussant.[20] He also witnessed reenlistment oaths taken by NCOs, greeted visiting dignitaries, and made inspection visits to installations with Woodward. The dog's newspaper column, "Lifeline 1 Looks at Life," reported on travels with his master and gave advice to the troops. The columns urged readers to serve others, not to drink alcohol and drive, and not to waste food. Woodward reasoned that morale would be boosted if the dog belonged to ADSEC. At a commander's conference on 08 November 1956, he floated the idea of selling his troops 5¢ shares in the dog. In April 1957, Woodward was succeeded by Brig Gen Robert J. Fleming, Jr. During the change-of-command ceremonies at Caserne Maginot, the flamboyant Woodward presented Lifeline 1's leash to Fleming.[21] On 15 June 1958, the 4th Logistical Command was activated at Maginot to replace ADSEC. Authorized more than one-hundred seventy officers and enlisted men, 4th Log oversaw depots and installations in northeastern France and Germany. It employed 6,000 French civilians, Department of Army Civilians, and Continental Wage Scale (mostly Britishers) personnel.[22]

Commanding Generals, Advance Section (Verdun)

Commanding General	Period	Events
Col John F. Cassidy	1950-52	Initial buildup of depots. Troops live in tents and dilapidated casernes.
BG William W. Ford	1952-54	Dependents elementary schools open. Troops move into prefabs.
BG Raymond W. Curtis	1954-55	Construction of housing villages and standby hospitals begins. French and American flags flown at US installations.
BG Harry W. Johnson	1955-56	Building construction projects continue.
BG William R. Woodward	1956-57	Donges-Metz pipeline begins initial operations (Nov 57). Rhine Engineer Depot (Kaiserslautern), Pirmasens Signal Depot, and 53rd Chemical Laboratory (Hanau) assigned to ADSEC.[23] Security enhanced at Trois Fontaines Ammunition Depot.
BG Robert J. Fleming, Jr.	1957-60	Advance Section becomes 4th Log Command. 4th Log Command (Verdun) and 5th Log Command (Poitiers) merge (Apr 60). Theater Army Support Command (TASCOM) at Verdun controls all logistics for USAREUR (Apr 60-Aug 61).
MG William C. Baker, Jr.	1960-61	Revolt of top French generals in Algeria (Apr 61).
BG Ferdinand J. Chesarek	1961-62	TASCOM inactivated. 4th Log Command reactivated (Aug 61).
BG Donald G. Grothaus	1962-64	Operation BIG LIFT (Oct 63). 4th Log Comd to US during McNamara drawdown (Dec 63).

NOTE: All commanding generals were graduates of United States Military Academy, West Point, New York.

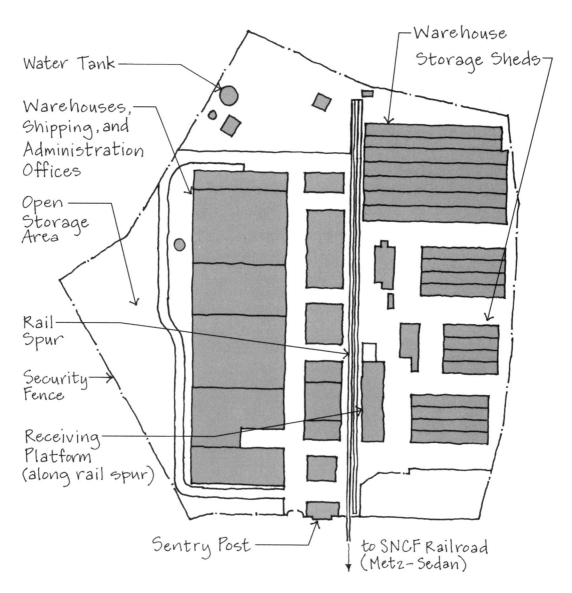

Verdun Signal Depot (1956)

Verdun Signal Depot

In 1951, the 27th Signal Base Depot Detachment, commanded by Col Walter J. Rosengren, was the first Army unit to occupy Usine de la Viscose, an abandoned textile factory built in 1925 in Thierville. The buildings, which had been used as a prison during the German occupation, were renovated for use as the Signal Corps Depot. GIs at the depot stored and repaired communications equipment such as microwave radio-telephones, spiral cable, field telephones, and switchboards.

In February 1955, a production line was set up at the depot to manufacture and insert metal clips in 3,000 field telephones needed by Seventh Army. The 29¢ clips would not be available through Army supply channels for several months. The cost to manufacture the clips at Verdun was less than 1¢ each. LWRs had the field phones ready to ship in one week.[24]

In 1958, the depot installed electronic equipment needed to repair spiral "four-cable" wire used for multi-channel communications. By November 1959, the Cable Shop had repaired over 2,500 miles of wire. Defective wire first was cleaned, tested for breaks using the depot's custom-designed equipment, and spliced where necessary. After splicing, electrical conductivity (flow of current) and tensile strength (resistance to pull) were tested. The repaired wire was wound on wooden reels that each held ¼ mile of wire and shipped to signal units throughout US Army, Europe. The shop employed twenty-six French civilians.[25] At the nearby Plating Shop, parts from radios, microwave sets, and teletype machines were cleaned and "plated" with a thin coating of metal such as silver, nickel, or chromium.

For depot security at night, GI guards were issued 30 cal, M2 carbines loaded with 15-round or 30-round magazines. In February 1959, an Army private fatally shot another private while they were horseplaying. The senior gate guard, PFC Charles Green, had told them to stop pointing their carbines at each other, but they continued to horseplay when no one was watching.[26]

Verdun Signal Depot Commanders*

Commanding Officer	Period of Service	Commanding Officer	Period of Service
Col Walter J. Rosengren	1951-52	Col Herman B. Boyle	1962-63
Col Lawrence E. Fouchs	1953-56	Lt Col George T. Gabelia	1963
Lt Col Joseph Griffith	1956-58	Col Lester K. Olson	1964-65
Lt Col Randolph H. Vinding	1958-60	Col Daniel W. Rachal	1965-66
Lt Col Beverly Risque	1961-62		

*Converted to General Depot in August 1957.

72nd Ordnance Battalion

In early 1954, the 72nd Ordnance Battalion Headquarters Det, authorized seven officers and twenty-one enlisted men, arrived at Caserne Maginot. It assumed command of 39th Ordnance Co (FM) at Verdun and 565th Ordnance Co (FM) at Nancy.[27] In late 1960, the 72nd Ord Bn was reorganized and given a nuclear support mission. It was no longer responsible for automotive maintenance support. It now operated depots storing nuclear warheads for the US Army Advance Weapons Support Command (AWSCOM), located in Pirmasens, Germany. The 72nd Ord Bn stationed three nuclear weapons supply and maintenance companies in Germany, two at Miesau (NATO Site 104) and one at Kriegsfeld (NATO Site 107). These depots were two of the seven heavily guarded depots that stockpiled nuclear weapons in Germany. After France had given permission in 1957 for the US to store nuclear weapons in France, the 72nd likely would have been responsible for supply and maintenance of nuclear weapons to be located at Rozelier, Aboncourt, and Vatry.[28] However, early in his tenure as President of France, Charles de Gaulle asked the NATO Allies to remove nuclear weapons from France. In the 1960s, ComZ stored 45,000 tons of combat essential items for Seventh Army in the massive structures originally built to store nuclear weapons.

The Fake Depot

To avoid disrupting depot operations, a fake depot for VIP visitors was set up in caves at Massweiler, Germany. The four-level caves had been abandoned in 1957 due to moisture problems.[29] The only matériel in the caves were training weapons and parts of weapons. However, all elements of a real depot, except real weapons, were there: redundant security barriers, guard dogs, troops wearing special clothing with face shields, and observance of "two-man" rule.[30] The two-man rule for nuclear weapons meant that all maintenance, storage, and transport operations had to be carried out by at least two individuals. The Hollywood-like set at Massweiler not only impressed VIPs, it allowed ComZ troops at real depots to work without disruptions.[31]

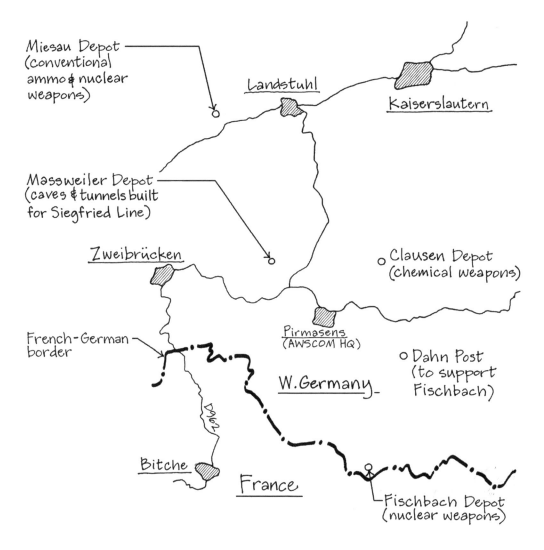

Advance Weapons Support Command Depots

Désandrouins Barracks

On 26 September 1958, the 42nd Field Hospital moved from Caserne Maginot to wings of the new 1,000-bed standby hospital built along the road to Étain. New medical equipment had been installed in wings of the 50-active bed hospital so the move could be completed in one day. On moving day, the staff moved emergency equipment and patient records. Ambulatory patients were transferred by bus and litter patients by ¾-ton truck ambulances of the 591st Ambulance Co.[32]

The new complex, named Désandrouins Barracks, also housed hundreds of troops and commuting high school students. Commuting students arrived at Verdun by bus on Sunday afternoon and returned home after the last class on Friday. Dorms were segregated by gender, two students per room. Adult dorm counselors enforced rules such as in-room study hours and lights out at 10 pm.[33] The elementary and high schools at Désandrouins had more than nine-hundred students in school year 1958-59. Previously, high school students had boarded at Kaiserslautern, Germany, and elementary school students attended classes at Caserne Maginot. During lunch hour, high school students danced to music from a jukebox. For recreation, the site had a gymnasium, baseball diamond, football field, and a nine-hole golf course.[34, 35] Doctors could play golf within minutes of leaving the hospital.

256th Signal Company

For two weeks in May 1958, the Signal Det of 4th Log Command at Caserne Maginot provided two 2½-ton mobile vans to support the ceremony to select the unknown soldier from the European Theater of Operations in World War II. The vans had voice and Morse code radio-wave equipment. One van was parked on the grounds of the American Military Cemetery at Épinal; the other at a small French airfield near Dogneville.[36] On 01 May 1960, the detachment was succeeded at Maginot by the 256th Signal Co (Combat Support), authorized eight officers and two-hundred forty-six enlisted men. The 256th operated the Verdun photo lab for IDs, official photographs, and *The Advance* newspaper. The company maintained a library of more than 1,350 training films and instructed projectionists from units throughout 4th Log Command. Small detachments were assigned to Metz, Nancy, Trois-Fontaines, and Vitry-le-François.[37]

ComZ Stock Control

In December 1964, the Stock Control Division of the ComZ Supply and Maintenance Agency (S&MA) opened at Caserne Maginot. A detachment of the Systems Engineering Division operated the data processing system. Each day, detachment personnel and LWRs processed thousands of records, using codes of the Military Standard Requisition and Issue Procedures (MILSTRIP) system. Data was transmitted by magnetic tape, transceiver, and 80-column punched cards. Magnetic tape files were exchanged each day between Verdun and S&MA in Orléans.

The key-punch card machines and IBM data-processing equipment were installed in a basement at Maginot. The IBM 7010 and IBM 1460 computers were on the first floor. The IBM 1403 printer could print 1,200 lines of type per minute.[38] The division processed supply and equipment receipts at depots (quantity on hand), requisitions from Army units throughout Europe (customer request), and records of items sent to the receiving unit (confirmation of shipment). During the hectic withdrawal from France in 1967, a box of 2,000 punched cards was lost.[39, 40] Inaccurate records meant supplies already on hand might be ordered from the US, supplies and equipment might be shipped to the wrong depot, or similar mishaps.

Jardin Fontaine

Jardin Fontaine, a former French Army training area behind Maginot, was developed for troop support functions. Headquarters of 32nd Engineer Construction Group and Company C of the 97th Engineers were at Jardin Fontaine. In the 1960s, the engineers moved to Désandrouins Barracks.

In August 1952, Maj Gen William H. "Red" Middleswat, Chief of USAREUR Quartermaster Division, complained to Maj Gen Samuel D. Sturgis, Jr., ComZ commander, that quartermaster troops were still living in tents at Verdun. Sturgis explained that new prefabs at Jardin Fontaine were occupied by troops of 4128th Labor Service Co and 6954th Labor Service Center because the Polish LS personnel had lived in tents the longest. He added that they were doing important work for the Army and therefore it would not be right to treat them "as a lower caste" by giving priority to Army troops.[41] The QM troops waited their turn. In 1955, several masonry buildings were completed at Jardin Fontaine, including a 3-story EM barracks, chapel, gymnasium, theater, indoor pistol range, and stockade. Cpl Antonio Virduzzo painted the windows in the chapel. Virduzzo, who had been born in New York City and educated in Italy, was an accomplished artist and art critic in civilian life.

In October 1958, Olivia de Havilland, best known for her role as Melanie Wilkes in the classic movie *Gone With the Wind*, attended opening night of a play at the theater in Jardin Fontaine. De Havilland also visited the new facilities of the 42nd Field Hospital at Désandrouins and was the courtly Fleming's guest for dinner at the Officers Club.[42] They ate at the general's table which had been permanently so designated by Woodward whose less formal predecessor, Brig Gen Harry W. Johnson, had eaten at any table. By tradition, clubs did not close until the commanding general had departed. Johnson, an infantry officer, would stay beyond closing time when his officers were merrymaking.

Bulge Deserter

In March 1958, Sp4 Anthony J. Zuvich, an M-60 wrecker truck operator from the 23rd Engineer Co (FM), was assigned to 30-day prison-watch duties at the stockade at Jardin Fontaine. Some GIs on prison watch conspicuously loaded their weapon in front of the prisoners and then unloaded it out of sight. On most days, Zuvich took a work detail of four or five prisoners outdoors to paint curbs, cut grass, or fill pot holes. Although Zuvich was off-duty on 28 March, he was told to grab his M12 shotgun and guard a prisoner who had deserted from the US Army during the Battle of the Bulge in World War II.[43] By Army tradition, guards were told that if their prisoner escaped, they would serve the sentence. Therefore, Zuvich was especially vigilant because deserters in time of war could be executed. He escorted his prisoner, Pvt Wayne Powers, from the stockade to a nearby building so Powers could visit his French common-law wife and meet with members of the press.

For fourteen years, Powers had been hiding in the home of Mlle Yvette Beleuse in the village of Mont-d'Origny, near St.-Quentin. The couple had five children aged two to twelve. Powers was discovered when he went outside to witness an automobile accident. Because he could not produce identity papers, French police arrested him. He was turned over to the US Army when it was discovered that he was a deserter. In August 1958, Powers was sentenced by general court-martial at Caserne Maginot to 10-years confinement.[44] Three days later, perhaps influenced by overwhelming support for Powers from French newspapers and citizens, Fleming reduced the sentence to six months. Ten weeks later Powers was set free.[45]

After the US withdrew from France in 1967, the French Army occupied Caserne Maginot and Jardin Fontaine. The stockade at Jardin Fontaine, sized to confine sixty-two prisoners, was used to store POL containers behind bars in the abandoned, windowless cells. French officers of the 4e division aéromobile were puzzled by the bigness of the stockade, which they called "Sing Sing."[46]

Porte Chaussée, Verdun

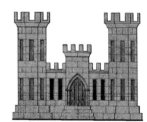

Corps of Engineers Insignia

Insignia Story

The twin towers of the 17th Century Porte Chaussée, on the Meuse River near the Hôtel Coq Hardi, resemble the castle insignia of the US Army Corps of Engineers.[47] In the spirit of camaraderie, US military leaders told the French the insignia was based on the Chaussée. This imaginative story appears on the dedication plaque at the former Désandrouins Barracks. Even newly arrived personnel received a welcome pamphlet that reinforced the myth by declaring that US Army Corps of Engineers personnel "wear a replica of this tower as their insignia." However, historical documents at the US Military Academy, West Point, New York, indicate that the 1839 design of the triple-turreted castle insignia likely was based on Atlantic Coast fortifications, the earliest important construction work of the Corps in the United States.[48]

97th Engineer Battalion

During World War II, the 97th Engineers, commanded by Col Stephen C. Whipple, helped construct the Alaskan highway. The highway would be an overland route to Alaska if Japanese forces blocked shipping lanes along the Pacific coast. Officers of the 97th were white, except Chaplain (Capt) Albert L. Smith, a graduate of Howard University in Washington, DC. Working twelve-hour shifts, seven days a week, the 97th built bridges and more than 194 miles of highway, most through unexplored Alaskan territory.[49] Because few members of the all-black regiment had lived in a cold climate, their work efficiency was low in the bitter cold. In December 1943, the temperature dropped to 40° F below zero, freezing water and fuel supplies. After Alaska, the 97th served in the Pacific Theater of Operations until it was inactivated on 15 March 1948 in the Philippine Islands.[50, 51]

In November 1951, the 97th was reactivated as a battalion. Commanded by Lt Col John A. Crawford, the 97th was deployed from Fort Leonard Wood, Missouri, to France. After a 14-day ocean voyage on the USNS *General A. W. Greely* from New Orleans, Louisiana, to Bremerhaven, Germany, the 97th traveled by train to France. Company A was stationed at Toul Engineer Depot, Company B at Trois Fontaines Ordnance Depot, and Headquarters Company at Caserne Maginot in Verdun. The battalion, authorized forty-one officers and eight-hundred forty-four enlisted men, rehabilitated dilapidated buildings, "winterized" tents for troops, and built warehouses.

Engineer bridge training on River Moselle, 1966 (US Army)

Enlisted men of the 97th discovered that blacks were not barred from restaurants and cafés in Bar-le-Duc, Toul, and Verdun, and there apparently was no racial barrier to dating French women. However, the 97th had discipline problems. After a huge brawl in a café at Toul, Brig Gen William W. Ford relieved Crawford from command.[52] The battalion began to integrate on 25 August 1952. By the end of the year, the percentage of black enlisted personnel in the 97th had been reduced from 100% to 20%. In October 1954, Chaplain (Lt Col) Albert L. Smith completed his assignment as chaplain of Verdun Installation. His integrated flock at Caserne Maginot had included the 97th, his unit from World War II.[53]

During the 1950s, the 97th Engineers installed railroad track, surfaced depot roads, placed fuel and water pipes underground, and repaired buildings throughout northeast France. Two months each year, the battalion trained to sharpen its combat readiness. In the 1960s, pipeline training was conducted at Vassincourt, panel bridge construction at Jeanne d'Arc maneuver area near Metz, and fixed bridge construction on the Moselle River.[54] In 1965, Company B, led by Capt Homer Johnstone, erected a huge, prefabricated aircraft hangar at Brienne-le-Château. The 197-ft wide by 190-ft long hangar, supported by 48-ft high arches, was the largest troop construction project in Europe since the end of World War II. Heavy equipment brought to the site to erect the hangar included: a 40-ton crane, D8 tractors, scrapers, 10-ton rollers, 50-ton compactors, and 5-ton dump trucks. Electricity in Neufchâteau was turned off for an hour so the 40-ton crane could be moved safely under power lines. The twelve bolted steel arches had to be sandblasted and painted because they had rusted during six years of outdoor storage at Dreux AB. Troops assigned to install the interior shops and support facilities were given unfamiliar tasks to broaden their skills. Tractor operators worked as electricians; truck drivers as plumbers.[55, 56]

97th Engineer Battalion (Const) Commanders

Commanding Officer	Period of Service	Commanding Officer	Period of Service
Lt Col John A. Crawford	1951-52	Lt Col William F. Crise	1959-61
Maj John D. Wieben	1952	Lt Col John H. Carlson	1961-62
Lt Col James B. McNally	1952-55	Lt Col Robert H. Montjoy	1962-63
Maj Robert A. Atkins	1955-56	Lt Col Fernand M. Achée, Jr.	1963-65
Lt Col Chester D. Brewer	1956-58	Lt Col William P. Gardiner	1965-66
Lt Col Dale E. O'Brien	1958-59	Lt Col Harold L. Myron	1966-67
Lt Col Frank Gaines	1959		

Chicago Area Depot

In February 1953, the Army formally acquired the Champ de manoeuvres de la gare, an abandoned French Army training area near the Verdun rail terminal. The 36-acre site was renamed the Chicago Area. In August-September 1952, troops of the 109th Engineer Construction Battalion, an Army National Guard unit from Rapid City, South Dakota, worked 16 hours a day to build "winterized" tents for troops at Advance Section installations. Wood for floors and walls, and frames for tent roofs were cut at Chicago Area for delivery by trailer truck to nine installations. Before production started, the engineers, led by 1st Lt Richard B. Kenehan, built a model structure to evaluate construction methods and to show to Brig Gen William W. Ford. Working two shifts, the "wood butchers" at the depot were able to complete twenty to thirty-five tent frames each day.[57]

In 1954, the Joint Construction Agency in Paris constructed six masonry warehouses and maintenance shops at the depot. GIs and LWRs at the Signal Maintenance Shop repaired radios, telephones, teletype machines, and other electronic equipment. The radio receiver/transmitter (designated SCR-536), that was hand held, was called a "handi-talkie." The larger unit (AN/PRC-6), that was carried on a GIs back, was called a "walkie-talkie." The QM Field Maintenance and Repair Shop repaired a variety of QM-issue items from forklifts and refrigeration equipment to tents, furniture, and shoes. One of the warehouses had three 4,000 cu ft prefabricated cold storage rooms.

In summer of 1957, modern baking equipment was installed at Chicago. The QM bakery, which employed twelve LWRs, could produce 4,500 pounds of bread per eight-hour shift. Products included sliced white bread (wrapped for commissary sales), rye, whole wheat, and raisin.[58] In 1958, the bakery had a staff of thirty GIs and LWRs.

During an inspection of Chicago in 1961, Capt Milton S. Killen, Commanding Officer of 39th Ordnance Co, was surprised that Brig Gen Ferdinand J. Chesarek, Commanding General of 4th Logistical Command, did not ask about the mission or maintenance procedures of the company. Instead, the aloof Chesarek hurried through the shop areas, stopping only to closely inspect the latrines.[59]

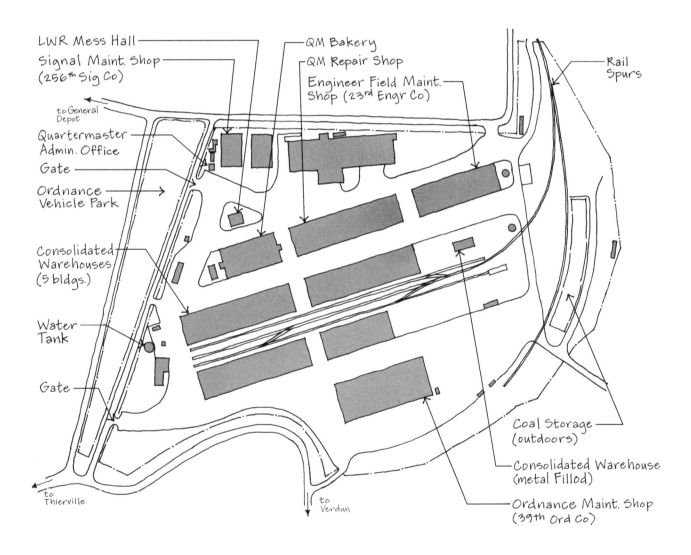

Chicago Area Depot

39th Ordnance Company

On a typical day in the 39th Ordnance Co (FM) maintenance shop, about sixty vehicles, from jeeps to 5-ton wrecker trucks, were undergoing various stages of repair by forty mechanics. Repairs varied from routine bodywork, such as straightening bent fenders, to complete overhaul of engines. Parts that were not readily available were cannibalized from vehicles that could not be repaired. This was valuable training because vehicles damaged during wartime would need to be cannibalized for spare parts.[60] The Army in World War II learned that lack of spare parts was a serious problem. During combat operations, vehicle parts such as spark plugs, battery acid, tire patches, and filters, were quickly expended.[61] If repairs were not completed within ten days at Chicago, a replacement vehicle was sent to the owning unit. The shop also repaired small arms, from pistols and rifles to machine guns and rocket launchers.

Although the 39th normally worked at the Chicago Area, their field maintenance (FM) mission included relocating to dispersed sites if a Soviet invasion appeared imminent.[62-64] At least once a year, the 39th moved out to the field where they resisted simulated attacks by "aggressor" forces. Training in the field included repairing vehicles and small arms.

Three platoons of the 39th Ordnance Co, authorized more than one-hundred fifty troops, were billeted at Caserne Gribeauval. During 1954 and 1955, the 2nd Direct Support Platoon was stationed at Metz. In 1957, the 1st Direct Support Platoon was permanently stationed at Trois-Fontaines. Each month during 1961-62, the 39th Ordnance Co completed about 350 major vehicle repairs: 200 at Chicago, 150 at Trois-Fontaines.[65]

39th Ordnance Company (FM) Commanders

Commanding Officer	Period of Service	Commanding Officer	Period of Service
Capt Archie Nelson	1951-53	Capt William E. Crosland	1958-61
Capt Frank T. Walton	1953-54	Capt Milton S. Killen, Jr.	1961-62
Capt Frank A. DuBois	1954-56	Maj John K. Hillman	1962-64
Capt John B. Spruiell	1956-57	Capt Niles B. Winter, Jr.	1964

French Employees

ComZ established Efficiency Awards Programs to raise employee morale and increase production. For accepted suggestions, civilian employees could receive cash awards and salary increases.[66] Nineteen skilled French employees worked for the 39th Ordnance Co at Chicago Area as mechanics, machinists, warehousemen, bookkeepers, and inspectors. From 1960-63, LWR employee Antoine Seng submitted a record twenty-two suggestions to improve efficiency. The US Army accepted nineteen of his suggested improvements, estimated to save the US government 92,000 francs ($18,400). Seng, a machinist who previously had worked for the French national railroad SNCF, was awarded 4,500 francs (about $900), almost half of his annual salary.[67] The US Army was always anxious to receive suggestions to legally improve work production. However, experienced NCOs taught younger troops the art of "moonlight requisitions," where parts and supplies, that were unavailable through normal channels, were relocated from other Army units without authorization. During World War II, Patton's Third Army allegedly was able to procure badly needed supplies by using fake orders, verbal deception, and "theft" by moonlight requisition.

CHAPTER 9: *Advance Section in the Northeast*

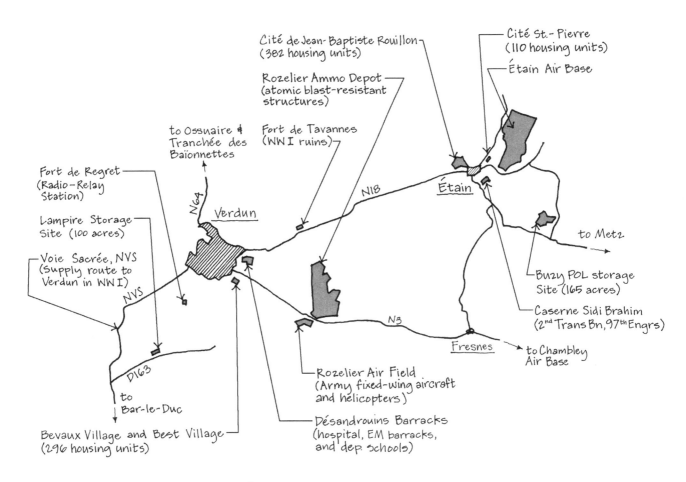

Verdun-Étain Area Installations (1962)

Main gate, Caserne Sidi Brahim, Étain, 1965 (US Army)

Caserne Sidi Brahim

Caserne Sidi Brahim, built in 1913 in Étain, had been used by the French Army between the World Wars. Occupied by the Germans during World War II, it was liberated in September 1944 by Patton's Third Army. For two months, the Hôtel de la Sirène at Étain was headquarters for Lt Gen George S. Patton's battle command post, code named "Lucky Forward."[68] In January 1951, the 7825th Engineer Depot Det, commanded by Maj William F. Jenike, arrived at Sidi Brahim to establish an engineer depot. On 30 September 1952, the Toul Engineer Depot assumed the engineer functions of Étain. By the mid-1950s, twenty-one of the existing buildings at Sidi Brahim had been renovated and eleven small structures and metal prefabs had been installed. About half of the permanent structures were used for troop housing.

The caserne also was used for truck terminal operations. From September 1951 to September 1954, elements of the 109th Trans Truck Battalion, an Army National Guard unit from Camp Ripley, Minnesota, were stationed at Étain. In 1954, the 109th was replaced by the 2nd Transportation Battalion. In 1957, the 2nd Trans Bn stationed the 82nd and 543rd Trans Cos at Étain, the 520th Trans Co at Vassincourt, and the 574th Trans Co at Toul.

In 1959, the 2nd Trans Bn started a program of roving safety patrols in jeeps. Two-man teams of an NCO and driver were assigned from each company in the battalion to serve for one month. Each day, SFC Roland D. Douglas briefed the patrols on scheduled movements, anticipated locations of heavy traffic, and dangerous locations. Patrols were to be sure battalion drivers did not speed, especially on curves or steep grades. Violators were flagged down and counseled by the NCO on the dangers observed. Because the NCOs did not "chew out" or punish the violators, GIs called them "Smile Patrols." The safety patrol program reduced accidents.[69]

2nd Transportation Battalion Commanders*

Commanding Officer	Period of Service	Commanding Officer	Period of Service
Lt Col Charles R. Glass	1952-53	Lt Col Arthur W. Delaney	1957-58
Maj Artie Jines	1953	Lt Col Robert J. Keefer	1958-59
Lt Col Seaborn H. Mosely	1953-54	Lt Col Charles H. Dickey	1959-61
Maj Joseph W. Enright	1954-55	Lt Col William J. Daly	1962-63
Lt Col Hiram L. Lawyer	1955-56	Lt Col Glen E. Petrie	1963-64

*Headquarters located at Camp Bussac 1951-52, Poitiers 1953-54, Nancy 1958-60, and Toul 1960-64. Battalion was inactivated in Dec. 1964.

In the 1960s, Company C of the 97th Engineer Battalion was billeted at the caserne. One member of the 97th, SSgt Benjamin F. Miller, was believed to have been at Sidi Brahim during WW II. GIs were told that in 1944, while serving with all-black support troops, Miller had been captured by the Germans and held prisoner for several days at the caserne. Fifteen years later he worked in the same building as an engineer NCO supervising troops in the integrated 97th Engineers. It was a fantastic story about the highly respected Miller, but there are no official records that he was held prisoner.[70]

Buzy POL Depot

In 1954, Buzy POL Depot, the site of the former Aérodrome de Étain near the Buzy railhead, stored 6 million gallons of gasoline and 2 million gallons of JP-4 jet aviation fuel. In an emergency, POL supplies stored at Buzy were to be transported by cargo trucks and railcars to combat units in Germany.[71] On a typical day in 1958, GIs poured fuel from 5-gal jerry cans into a deep trough. Fuel was pumped from the trough into 5,000-gal tank semitrailers of the 55th Transportation Truck Co. GIs could fill four semitrailers a day.⁷² In the early years, loaded cargo trucks often sank in the mud.

The QM troops lived in tents and worked in mud. GIs used the portable QM shower units, which consisted of tents, truck-mounted pumps, and heaters. GIs piled their clothes in the first tent and then walked through tents fitted with multiple shower heads, like a drive-thru car wash. As more space became habitable, troops were moved from Buzy into barracks at Caserne Sidi Brahim. Although at first the commodes at Sidi Brahim had no seats, indoor latrines were an upgrade from primitive slit latrine conditions at Buzy.⁷³,⁷⁴

Rozelier Ammunition Depot

In 1959, the Army began building a large ammunition depot at Fort du Rozelier in the Forêt de Sommedieue. Debris from World War I was scattered throughout the forest. Common artifacts of war were trenches, rusted barbed wire, helmets, and unexploded chemical munitions. GIs dug up unexploded shells and mines even when landscaping areas near depot buildings.

Three atomic blast-resistant (ABREST) structures were built to store and maintain nuclear weapons. Walls and roof were thick reinforced concrete with closely spaced steel-reinforcing bars. Side and rear walls were built into sloped earth; the roof was earth-covered. Entry was secured by massive 16-inch thick steel doors. At first, the depot was to store nuclear warheads for Atomic Annie (W9 weapon) and the portable special atomic demolition munitions, abbreviated SADM (W54). Army engineers would use SADMs to destroy fixed bridges and block roadways at mountain passes.

The depot also had eighty-eight Stradley storage huts for conventional ammo, 10 miles of roads, and 9 miles of railroad track. The Army estimated that railcars and trucks could move 80 tons of conventional ammunition in and 80 tons out of the depot each day in peacetime; 375 tons in and out in time of war.⁷⁵ Nearby French villagers were annoyed by the constant roar of engines, thick clouds of dust and dirt, and exhaust fumes from the heavy traffic during buildup of the depot. During the Berlin Wall Crisis, so many railcars of ammo were shipped to Rozelier, the crates had to be stacked haphazardly until sufficient ammo handler personnel arrived from the US. In September 1961, troops from units in Verdun were borrowed to move ammunition into storage huts. For a period of four weeks, the 39th Ordnance Co at Chicago Area sent thirty GIs to Rozelier.⁷⁶

Ordnance Corps Capt Henry W. Stupakewicz was the first commander of the depot. His security officer was former CIC Special Agent Capt Arthur M. Fell. In June 1961, Fell was transferred from the 766th CIC Det to the depot after his marriage to Teri, a French citizen from La Rochelle. Fell was trained at Fort Holabird, Maryland, and his cover branch in the Counter Intelligence Corps was Artillery. At Rozelier, he continued to wear Artillery branch insignia on his Class A uniform. This proved to be awkward when real "cannon cocker" officers, trained at Fort Sill, Oklahoma, wanted to talk to Fell about the good old days at Fort Sill.⁷⁷

A detachment of the 4507th Labor Service Co, commanded by Maj Teodor P. Kroja-Kopec, guarded the depot at night. The 132nd Explosive Ordnance Disposal Det, commanded by 1st Lt Charles R. Spinner, Jr., also was assigned to the depot. Because Rozelier was a sub-depot of Trois-Fontaines, the post engineer at nearby Verdun gave low priority to requests for repairs and ignored most requests for small construction projects at the depot. Fell discovered that many of the Polish guards had construction experience in carpentry, plumbing, and welding. Using materials bartered from nearby Army units and items borrowed by "moonlight requisitions," LS personnel were able to repair fences and maintain buildings on the depot.

The security fence surrounding the depot had only four strands of barbed wire supported by shoulder high concrete posts. It was not difficult to cut the wire or climb over the fence. The depot perimeter road was patrolled by MPs in a jeep, but they could not stray far from the road due to the danger of unexploded munitions from World War I. In the fall of 1961, a MP discovered a group of French soldiers marching through the depot. The soldiers were told to leave. They retraced their steps to the opening in the fence where they had entered. Repairing the fence was a weekly chore.[78]

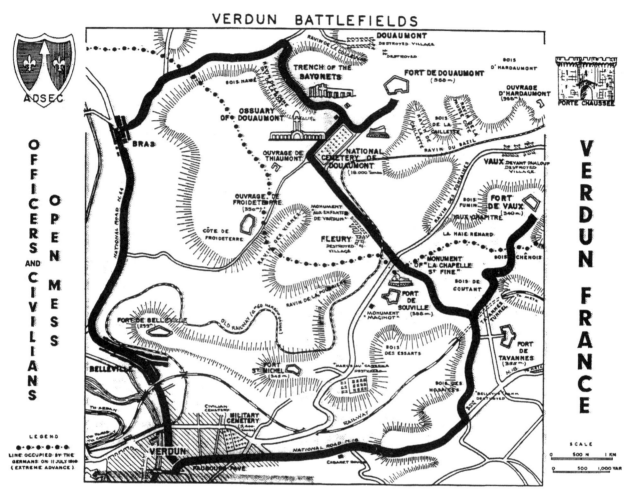

Officers Club Paper Placemat

Hazards of Verdun Battlefields

A century after World War I, land near Verdun cannot be farmed due to poisoned soil and unexploded ammunition. An estimated 12 million unexploded shells and mines are still in the ground and two million acres of land in France remain closed, designated *terrain interdit* (forbidden ground). Due to deterioration from age, unexploded ammunition becomes sensitive to movement. Blasting caps can be detonated by impact, friction, or even changes in temperature. GIs assigned to Verdun were warned not to handle ammo discovered on the former battlefields and not to enter underground fortifications without an experienced guide. Rotting timbers supporting walls could collapse when touched and boards covering deep vertical shafts could break if stepped on.

Paper placemats at the Verdun Officers Club featured a drawing of the Verdun battlefields to remind diners about these dangers. Army troops and their dependents were warned not to touch anything resembling a bomb: "Do not pick up duds for a souvenir." An official French poster with photos of duds was more explicit: *Touche Pas. Ça Tue!* (Don't touch. These kill.) The warning was essential. In July 1957, two soldiers were killed at the Bricy French Air Force base near Orléans when a souvenir World War II dud hand-grenade, used as a paperweight, exploded in an office.[79]

In 1954, a ComZ explosive ordnance disposal (EOD) squad, led by CWO Fred Hartkop, Jr., traveled throughout northern France to remove or destroy dud artillery and aerial bombs from the two world wars. During an 18-month period, the five GIs of the EOD squad deactivated or destroyed more than 20 tons of dangerous explosives.[80] Since 1946, more than seven-hundred employees of *Département du Déminage* have died in the effort to remove unexploded munitions. These French *démineurs* (de-miners) have destroyed millions of artillery shells, grenades, and aerial bombs.[81] Despite their work, farmers die each year from accidental detonations.

On a weekend in April 1956, Sp2 Gerald H. Dunnigan and his wife, Barbara, were exploring the site of Fort de Tavannes, an underground fortress built in 1745 near Verdun. Stones and bricks that lined the numerous tunnels had fallen onto floors and many of the tunnels were filled with water. Dunnigan, assigned to the 32nd Engineer Group at Jardin Fontaine, disappeared after entering a concrete bunker, one of many entrances to the old fort. When his wife could not find him, she returned to Verdun to report his disappearance. The Chicago Area fire station sent a response team to the fort. The smallest member, PFC Gordon W. Murray (nicknamed Mouse), volunteered to be lowered into a shaft but found nothing. The next day, Verdun Garrison asked for volunteers who had coal mining experience. Several volunteers were trucked to the fort, issued gas masks, and sent into the tunnels to find Dunnigan. Frenchman Victor Pont, who had hidden in the tunnels during World War II, volunteered to help. Maj Robert A. Atkins, commander of 97th Engineers, directed rescue operations at the site for 48 hours without sleep. GIs from the 97th, who were moving rubble and bracing weakened tunnel walls with boards, found Dunnigan's body at the bottom of an 80-ft deep shaft. Two French soldiers, who had aided in the search of the area, were killed when they stepped on World War I munitions.[82, 83]

On 16 February 1957 in a ceremony at Caserne Maginot, Brig Gen William R. Woodward presented the Soldier's Medal to PFC Murray for risking his life to find Dunnigan. Sp3 Orville Mortimore, Jr., Pvt2 Russell D. Furlong, and Pvt2 Richard C. Young, from the 97th Engineers, received Army Commendation Medals for their hazardous work in the tunnels. French Général de corps André Demetz, commander of the French Sixth Military Region, pinned medals on the three GIs and kissed them on both cheeks. As ADSEC troops marched by in review, Woodward, Demetz, and the four medal recipients stood on an elevated platform and returned the salutes.[84]

249th Engineer Battalion

In March 1960, the 249th Engineer Battalion (Construction), commanded by Lt Col Felix R. Garrett, was assigned from Kaiserslautern, Germany, to Étain AB. The troops were billeted in vacant airmen dormitories. Their first big project was to build 9 miles of railroad line, siding, and spurs to serve the new Rozelier Ammunition Depot.

The railroad construction project, which began on 15 March 1960, crossed over World War I trenches, bunkers, and tunnels. Engineers filled the trenches with soil and rubble, and compacted the fill to be level at grade. During excavation work, remains of five French and German soldiers were uncovered. One of the human remains was draped over a rusted machine gun, his helmet nearby.[85] The 12 tons of explosives uncovered during the project were destroyed by the 132nd Explosive Ordnance Det.

The ballast under the rails settled excessively in November 1961 because heavy loads had been shipped to the depot before the railroad project was completed. To gain experience on railroad construction, the 97th Engineers replaced the 249th Engineers in December 1961. The 97th Engineers repaired the sunken ballast and realigned track. The remaining track and extensive drainage system needed to prevent erosion of adjacent private land was completed in January 1963.[86]

In 1962, the 249th Engineers supported the aftermath of Operation STAIR STEP by repairing runways and building hangars, firing-in butts, and storage facilities at air bases in France. During STAIR STEP in October 1961, eight Air National Guard tactical fighter squadrons were sent from the US to air bases at Chambley, Dreux, Étain, Phalsbourg, and Toul-Rosières.[87] After the Cuban Missile Crisis had abated, the more than 6,750 air guardsmen were sent home in 1963. From 1963 to 1966, the 249th Engineers primarily worked at air bases, Suippes Gunnery Range near Reims, Châteauroux Air Depot, and Nancy General Depot.[88] At Nancy, Company A stabilized the sides of a steep gorge along the railroad that connected the depot to the Paris-Strasbourg SNCF railroad line.[89]

Rozelier Air Field

In November 1953, the Army acquired from the French government gently sloped land for use as an airfield at Rozelier, 6 miles southeast of Verdun. In 1956, two large maintenance hangars were constructed and a 5,000-ft long by 100-ft wide airstrip paved with asphalt. In 1959, Army engineers built a 2,000-ft long taxiway and six concrete helipads (each 80 ft by 50 ft).[90] Communications networks linked Army airfields at Rozelier, Saran, and Poitiers and were used to warn pilots of hazardous flying conditions.[91] Enlisted men of the aviation units at Rozelier lived in barracks of the Désandrouins hospital.

Pocket Patch of 2nd Aviation Co   Pocket Patch of 26th Trans Co

2nd Aviation Co (Fixed Wing)

The three platoons of 2nd Aviation Co (Fixed Wing) were stationed at Rozelier, Poitiers, and Saran. At Rozelier Air Field, fifteen fixed-wing aviators of the 2nd platoon flew L-20 Beavers and, in the 1960s, U-1 Otters. The Otter, with a pilot and copilot, could carry 2,000 lbs of cargo or six litter patients. In 1962, the Army redesignated the L-20 Beaver ("L" for liaison) to be the U-6 Beaver ("U" for utility). Beavers could land on short, unpaved runways and carry six passengers.

The 2nd Aviation Co transported nuclear weapon components to and from depots of the Advance Weapons Support Command. In Germany, pilots of the 2nd flew airborne surveillance for truck convoys moving nuclear weapons on autobahns. They orbited overhead to watch the convoy below. Because Otters generally were not flown above 12,000 ft, pilots overflew France to avoid tall mountains when transporting weapons from Germany to Italy. The French government was not told that the Otter cargo was nuclear.[92]

US Army, Europe allocated three L-23 Twin Bonanzas to ComZ, one for use by the Commanding General of 4th Log Command. Pilots of the 2nd flew VIPs in and out of the Advance Section and medical evacuations at any time of day or night. The 2nd Aviation pocket patch insignia featured "Orville the Otter." Orville, wearing a French béret, held the ComZ insignia as his shield and grasped the Eiffel Tower in his left paw.

Army Fixed-Wing Aircraft (1956)

Designation	Name	Passenger Load	Cruising Speed (mph)	Range (miles)
L-19	Bird Dog	One	100	400
L-20	Beaver	Six (or four litters)	125	900
L-23	Twin Bonanza*	Five	200	1,200

*Required 2,500-ft long, hard-surfaced landing strip.

In February 1963, four U-1A Otters from 2nd Aviation Co were sent to Finthen, Germany, for an 8th Infantry Division airdrop exercise. The parachutists, grounded for two months due to bad weather, boarded the Otters in five man sticks (line of troops that jump one after another). During the exercise, 4,000 parachutists completed the four jumps needed annually to maintain jump pay.[93]

On weekends, if "the Brass" were away, pilots could give rides to wives or girlfriends. If caught, they risked being grounded for flying unauthorized passengers. Grounded pilots did not receive monthly flight pay (for captains, equal to one-fourth of basic pay). In summer months, many young pilots flew low over rivers and lakes hoping to see French women sun bathing in the nude. Occasionally, some rambunctious Otter pilots buzzed French vehicles on country roads.[94]

U-1A Otter fixed-wing aircraft (US Army)

H-34 Choctaw helicopters on PSP, le Verdon, 1957 (US Army)

26th Transportation Co (Light Helicopter)

A detachment of seventeen rotary wing aviators of the 26th Transportation Co (Light Helicopter) was stationed at Rozelier to support the Advance Section. Another detachment at Poitiers supported Base Section. The 2nd Platoon was stationed in Pirmasens, Germany, to support the Advance Weapons Support Command by transporting nuclear weapons components to and from the depots. Ground convoys did not transport entire nuclear weapons; helicopters carried the inserts. The 26th Trans Co had two H-13 Sioux and twenty H-34 Choctaw helicopters.[95] Two Choctaws of the 26th Trans Co were at Camp des Loges near Paris for US European Command.

Helicopters were not used to transport troops in France. They hauled cargo when rapid delivery was required, overflew NEO convoys, supported offshore discharge exercises along the Atlantic coast, and evacuated medical emergencies to hospitals. The Choctaw could carry sixteen ambulatory patients or one medic and eight patients on litters. During discharge exercises, the Choctaw could carry a load of more than 2 tons from the deck of a cargo ship to the beach or to an inland depot within a range of 200 miles. Pilots also practiced air-sea rescues.

During 1957-58, Chaplain (1st Lt) Rufus B. Sprayberry of the 97th Engineer Battalion was flown in an H-13 Sioux helicopter from the Jardin Fontaine helipad to remote installations. Each week, Sprayberry, nicknamed the "flying chaplain," visited installations east of Verdun at Étain, Metz, and Angevilliers and west at Billy-le-Grand and Châlons-sur-Marne.[96] Returning from Billy-le-Grand to Verdun in mid-August 1957, Chaplain Sprayberry spotted a four car accident on the Châlons-Verdun road. Capt William R. Lynn landed the H-13 in a field so Sprayberry could aid the victims. Sprayberry and a French motorist loaded a victim onto the H-13. Lynn flew 82-year-old Madame Husson to Caserne Maginot where she was treated at the 42nd Field Hospital for shock, lacerations, and a broken arm. When Sprayberry visited Mme Husson the following week in a French hospital, she could not recall details of her first helicopter ride. She had believed the helicopter "was taking me to heaven."[97]

For flights to Paris, Army helicopters landed on the Champ de manoeuvre et d'aviation along the Seine River at Issy-les-Moulineaux. During President John F. Kennedy's visit in May 1961, the US Embassy requested helicopter support from Rozelier to fly President and Mrs Kennedy and Président and Mme de Gaulle from Paris to de Gaulle's country home for lunch. Three Choctaws, configured for the VIP mission, were flown from Rozelier to Paris. Because de Gaulle refused to fly in an American helicopter, they rode in French Citröen DS 19s to Colombey-les-Deux-Églises.[98, 99]

In 1962, fifty-five enlisted men of the 87th Transportation Det (Cargo Hel FM) at Rozelier repaired or completely overhauled electrical equipment of US Army, Europe aircraft. In 1963, this avionics repair mission was transferred to Brienne (commanded by Lt Col Roland V. Jager, 1962-64).

Recreation

In 1952, an enlisted men's club, called the REX Club, opened in downtown Verdun. In December, the Army also leased the 700-seat Vox Cinéma on rue Louis Couten. Movies were shown at 7:30 pm each evening; 2:30 pm matinees on Saturdays and Sundays. Matinees cost 15¢ for children under twelve, 25¢ for everyone else. Previously movies had been shown in barracks rooms at Casernes Maginot and Gribeauval.[100] The lease on Vox expired in 1955 when the new theater opened at Jardin Fontaine.

In April 1953, a golf driving range opened near Bevaux. The charge for a bucket of balls was 25¢. In 1958-59, the 97th Engineers built a 9-hole golf course on level terrain near the new 1,000-bed standby hospital. The par 37 course had fifty-seven sand traps. During construction, shrapnel and unexploded munitions from World War I were discovered on the site. Engineer work details placed the dangerous munitions into piles for disposal each day by ordnance personnel.[101]

In 1957, more than $1.2 million in construction began on gymnasiums, enlisted men's clubs, libraries, and community centers throughout Advance Section. Community centers provided a facility for youth activities and Franco-American gatherings. GIs, organized into company leagues, competed in basketball at the gymnasiums at Jardin Fontaine, Désandrouins Barracks, and Caserne Sidi Brahim in Étain. Bowling alleys were located at Caserne Gribeauval and Caserne Sidi Brahim.[102]

The Verdun Cardinals football team practiced on the field at Désandrouins and played big games at the stadium in Verdun's Parc de Londres. After a poor performance by the Cardinals in a fall 1961 football game against a USAREUR team from Germany, spectators jeered the players. Because the spectators were mostly black and the players mostly white, the yelling, pushing, and shoving almost created a race riot. Dressed in civilian clothes like most of the spectators, Col Joseph M. Heiser, Jr., Chief of Staff of 4th Logistical Command, intervened. Assisting Heiser, who was white, were two blacks, Maj Julius W. Becton, Jr. and Sgt Isaiah Gray. Becton, who was known by most of the GIs, shielded Heiser from harm; Gray, an all-Army athlete, escorted the angry ringleader from the field. The next day at the morning staff meeting, Heiser berated officers who were at the game for not acting like Becton.[103, 104] Heiser's intensity in meetings earned him the nickname "Screaming Joe."

In 1957, the US Army leased 1,400 acres of hunting grounds near Les Éparges for recreation use of the Verdun Rod and Gun Club. Members hunted wild boar, deer, rabbit, and fox, and fished on three spring-fed lakes. According to the "Welcome to Verdun" pamphlet, the membership fee was $4 per "sport-filled year" of hunting, fishing, and camping.[105] Part of the annual fee and monthly user fee of $1 was to restock the lakes with fish and the woods with animals.

Temporary Lodgings

Upon arrival, most officers and NCOs traveling with dependents were billeted at hotels in Verdun. Room rents, including tax, ranged from $2.05 per day for a single room without bath at the Terminus to $8.70 per day for a double room with bath at the Bellevue. GIs called the manager of the Bellevue "Big John" because he was taller than the typical Frenchman. At the Hôtel Coq Hardi, Dorothy Davis, wife of Lt Col William V. Davis, medical service administrator at the 42nd Field Hospital, filled her bidet with ice to chill bottles of soda for her three young daughters.[106] In the late 1950s, the temporary lodging allowance for officers or enlisted men with three or more dependents was $15 per day to cover quarters on the economy for sixty days. Subsistence allowance for officers was $1.57 per day for meals; for enlisted men, $1.15.[107, 108]

Housing

By 1961, new construction at Verdun included five large two-story BOQs and Officers Open Mess at the Champ de manoeuvers de Bevaux, and two villages of single-family houses near the Désandrouins hospital. In the 1960s, US Army installations in the Verdun area had more than 2,000 troops, eight-hundred with family members.[109] About five-hundred units of housing available on the French economy were on an approved list controlled by the Billeting Office at Maginot. Thirty privately-owned trailers at the Bevaux Trailer Court, across the street from the BOQs, were passed from one family to the next.[110] Two-hundred ninety-six families lived in rental guarantee housing (RGH) at Bevaux, which opened in October 1956, and the adjacent surplus commodity housing (SCH), which opened in July 1959. On 10 May 1962, Brig Gen Ferdinand J. Chesarek and French dignitaries participated in a ceremony to name the SCH housing village in memory of Adjudant-chef Louis Best, French hero of World War I battles of Verdun and the Somme.[111, 112] In 1964, the City of Verdun named the Bevaux RGH housing village, Cité Kennedy, in memory of President Kennedy.

In August 1959, Étain AB was put on standby status after the 49th Tactical Fighter Wing departed for Spangdalhem AB in Germany. Two housing areas built for Air Force personnel became available to Army personnel. One-hundred ten families lived in guaranteed rental income (GRI) housing at Étain. After the withdrawal of US military in 1967, the GRI village named Cité St.-Pierre was renamed Cité Patton in memory of Lt Gen George S. Patton. Three-hundred eighty-two families lived in surplus community housing (SCH) at Foameix, near Étain. In May 1964, the US military named the housing village Cité de Jean-Baptiste Rouillon in memory of the mayor of Étain during the German occupation. In 1944, the Germans arrested Rouillon and deported him to Dachau concentration camp. In 1969, the French owner of the village changed its name to Les Clairs Chênes, but local authorities demanded that the memorial stèle to Rouillon, dedicated by the Americans in 1964, remain on the site in perpetuity.

During the extremely cold winter of 1963, canals in northeastern France froze, halting barge deliveries of coal. Military housing villages were heated by oil that was transported through pipelines, but most French houses were heated by coal. Supplies of coal were so low that European Exchange System (EES) outlets only had coke briquettes for sale to families living on the economy.[113] Water pipes froze and burst in Louis Best Village, leaving residents without water. The 97th Engineers used 400-gal tank trailers to deliver potable water to the homes.[114]

Soviet Premier Khrushchev Visits Verdun

In spring 1960, President Charles de Gaulle hosted a state visit to France by Soviet Premier Nikita Khrushchev. Members of the French Communist Party came from throughout France to see Khrushchev visit the Verdun battlefields. They unfurled a red banner to greet Khrushchev at the National Cemetery of Douaumont, but did not shout slogans to embarrass the French Minister of State Louis Jacquinot, de Gaulle's representative for the Verdun visit.[115] To avoid provoking an incident, US troops were confined to their barracks. Unfortunately, the 97th Engineers platoon based at Étain received an emergency request to fix a serious water leak at Caserne Maginot. Although the engineer plumbers took back roads to avoid the communist crowds, they encountered protestors who threw rocks at their US Army vehicle.[116] Franco-American relations returned to normal the day after Khrushchev and the imported French communists departed. In the winter of 1950, French communists organized their first protests against the NATO presence. US officers with the military planning group working at the Hôtel Astoria in Paris were spit on.[117] Even Ike had faced protests in Paris.

Président De Gaulle Visits Verdun

On Armistice Day, 11 November 1961, President Charles de Gaulle scheduled an official visit to speak at Verdun. Georges Krieger, Sous Préfet du Meuse, lamented to his friend Brig Gen Ferdinand J. Chesarek that there were not enough place settings of china for the dinner honoring de Gaulle. Jane Chesarek responded to the Verdun china shortage by loaning forty-eight place settings of her Limoges china. Although President de Gaulle did not visit any American installations, his meal was served on American-owned china. Krieger, the local administrative representative of the French government, prudently did not mention the unofficial American support.[118] In early 1964, de Gaulle suffered prostate problems just prior to a state visit to Mexico. To enable him to make the trip, a temporary drain was inserted by a medical team at Hôpital Cochin in Paris. When de Gaulle learned that the inventor of the drain was an American, he proclaimed: "Good God, isn't there a French drain?" The surgeon, trying to sooth him, said the drain was technically French. It had been manufactured in France, although under an American license. De Gaulle said this was good, but not quite good enough. France should have its own design. The surgeon was sworn to secrecy: "Doctor, I do not wish it known that I have an American drain in me. You will regard this as a secret of state."[119]

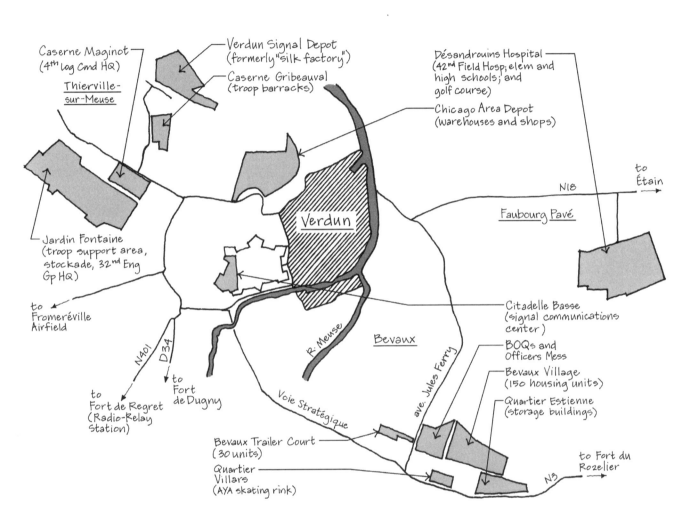

Verdun Area US Army Installations (1958)

Verdun Area US Army Installations

Installation	Location	Activity and Units
Headquarters	Thierville-sur-Meuse (Caserne Maginot, 14 acres)	4th Logistical Command 32nd Engineer Group 1st Medical Group 72nd Ordnance Battalion 766th CIC Field Office European Exchange System, France Area (FRAX)
	Thierville-sur-Meuse (Caserne Gribeauval)	39th Ordnance Company (FM) 61st Military Police Company
	Étain (Caserne Sidi Brahim)	2nd Transportation Battalion
Depots	Rozelier (1,200 acres)	US Army Ammunition Depot
	Thierville-sur-Meuse (23 acres)	US Army Signal Depot, Verdun
	Thierville-sur-Meuse (36 acres)	Chicago Area Depot
	Billy-le-Grand (Livry-Louverey)	US Army POL depot (135 acres)
	Fort de Dugny	Ammo storage site (20 acres)
	Fort de Troyon Lempire Buzy (Aérodrome d'Étain)	Three off-depot storage sites (365 acres total)
	Verdun (Quartier Estienne and Quartier Villars)	Warehouses (15 acres)
	Doncourt-lès-Conflans (Aérodrome)	Secondary depot site
Communications	Fort de Regret (7 acres)	Radio-relay station
	Verdun (Citadelle Basse)	Communications center
Hospital	Verdun (Désandrouins Hospital, 63 acres)	42nd Field Hospital, 1,000-bed standby hospital
Schools (dependents)	Verdun (Désandrouins)	Elementary and high schools
Bachelor Officers Quarters (BOQ)	Bevaux	Five 2-story buildings, Officers Mess (17 acres)
	Étain	One building
Housing (families)	Bevaux (Cité Kennedy)	150 RGH units
	Bevaux (Adjudant Louis Best Village)	146 SCH units (49 acres)
	Étain (Cité de Jean-Baptiste Rouillon at Foameix)	382 SCH units (105 acres)
	Étain (Cité St.-Pierre)	110 GRI units (30 acres)
General Officer Quarters	Verdun (19, rue du Général de Gaulle)	Commanding General
Troop Barracks	Billy-le-Grand	289th QM Company 877th QM Co (Petro Depot) 6941st Labor Service Platoon
	Étain (Caserne Sidi Brahim, 20 acres)	97th Engineer Battalion 55th Trans Co (Med Trk) 82nd Trans Co (Lt Trk) 543rd Trans Co (Lt Trk)
	Étain Air Base	249th Engineer Battalion
	Rozelier	132nd Ordnance Det (ED) 4507th Labor Service Co
	Thierville-sur-Meuse (Caserne Gribeauval, 12 acres)	39th Ordnance Company (FM) 61st Military Police Company

Troop Barracks	Thierville-sur-Meuse (Caserne Maginot and Jardin Fontaine, 80 acres total)	4th Log Command Hq Co 256th Signal Company 97th Engineer Battalion 23rd Engineer Co (FM) 24th Army Postal Unit 118th Army Band 4128th Labor Service Co 6954th Labor Service Center
	Verdun (Désandrouins Barracks)	2nd Aviation Co (Fixed Wing) 26th Transportation Co (Lt Hel) 87th Transportation Det (FM) 42nd Field Hospital 105th Med Det (Vet Food Insp) 485th Med Co (Prev Med)
Confinement Facility	Jardin Fontaine (62 prisoners)	44th MP Detachment
Commissary	Bevaux	Grocery items sales
Laundry	Verdun (rue des Minimes)	QM Herbelin Laundry
Recreation	Bevaux	AYA indoor roller skating rink
	Les Éparges	Rod and Gun Club (1,400 acres)
	Marville (RCAF Station)	Swimming pool, Arrowhead Hockey Rink
	Rozelier (Air Field)	Skeet range
	Verdun (Désandrouins)	Golf course (9 holes, 3,116 yds)
	Verdun (ave de Douaumont)	REX Club (enlisted men)
	Thierville-sur-Meuse (Jardin Fontaine and Caserne Gribeauval)	Bowling alleys
	Étain (Caserne Sidi Brahim)	Bowling alley
	Thierville-sur-Meuse (Mechanics Field)	Football field, baseball diamond
	Thierville-sur-Meuse (Caserne Niel)	Indoor tennis court (French Army)
Transient Quarters	Verdun (Rond-Point de Lattre de Tassigny)	Hôtel Bellevue (80 rooms)
	Verdun (8, ave de la Victoire)	Hôtel Coq Hardi (60 rooms)
	Verdun (9, rue Edmond-Robin)	Hôtel Continental (42 rooms)
	Verdun (8, rue Edmond-Robin)	Hôtel Metz (30 rooms)
	Verdun (place de la Gare)	Hôtel Terminus (36 rooms)
Air Field	Rozelier (93 acres)	2nd Aviation Company (Fixed Wing) 26th Transportation Co (Lt Hel) 87th Transportation Detachment (Cargo Helicopter FM)
Training Sites	Blancharderie at Fort de la Chaume	Dispersed site shared with French
	Camp de Moronvilliers (near Reims)	Maneuver area (6,667 acres)
	Fort de Regret (near Verdun)	Firing range (small arms and rocket launchers)

Army Troop Newspapers (Verdun Area)

Name	Period	Name	Unit
The ADSEC Advance	1953-58	The Castle News	32nd Engineer Gp
The Advance (4th Log)	1958-59	The Builder	32nd Engineer Gp*
The TASCOM Times	1960-61	Chez Nous	97th Engineer Bn
The Lifeline Times (4th Log)	1961	The Falcon	1st Medical Gp**
The Advance (4th Log)	1961-63	Roundup	Verdun Garrison
Maginot Line	1965-67	The Verdun Support	Verdun Garrison
		The Observer	Verdun Post

*In the 1960s, the 32nd Engineer Group included: 83rd Engineer Bn at Chinon, 97th Eng Bn at Verdun, and 28th Water Supply Det at Fontenet.

**In 1962, the 1st Medical Group included: 16th Field Hosp at Vitry-le-François, 42nd Field Hosp at Verdun, 57th Field Hosp at Toul, and 80th Ambulance Train at Toul.

Abbreviations

AYA	American Youth Activities	POL	Petroleum, oil & lubricants
ED	Explosive Disposal	Prev Med	Preventive Medicine
FM	Field Maitenance	RCAF	Royal Canadian Air Force
GRI	Guaranteed Rental Income (USAF)	RGH	Rental Guarantee Housing (Army)
Lt Hel	Light Helicopter	SCH	Surplus Commodity Housing (Army)

The Sacred Way

During the Battle of Verdun in 1916, a continuous line of supplies was maintained along the muddy road from Bar-le-Duc to Verdun. Using French General Henri Philippe Pétain's concept to supply front lines by motor convoys, 3,000 trucks moved more than 27,000 tons of ammunition and supplies to beleaguered Verdun. After World War I, the road from Bar-le-Duc to Verdun was designated the *Voie Sacrée* (Sacred Way). To honor the sacrifices of World War I, kilometer markers along the road are short concrete pylons, painted white and red, capped by French Army helmets.[120-122] GIs called the markers "tombstones."

During the Cold War, the Sacred Way was the main route from installations near Bar-le-Duc to Verdun. The narrow, high-crowned road had several sharp curves and was especially dangerous during winter. Winter weather in northeastern France usually was very cold with thick fog and black ice. The closely spaced poplar trees on both sides of the road often proved fatal to drivers who lost control of their vehicles. In 1963, one-third of traffic accidents of US military and civilian employees in the Verdun-Nancy area involved only one vehicle. Alcohol was a contributing factor in nearly one-fourth of the accidents.[123]

Trois Fontaines Ordnance Depot

On 21 March 1951, a 14,000-acre sector in the Forêt de Trois-Fontaines, near Bar-le-Duc, was acquired from the French government for an ammunition depot. Permission had to be obtained from French foresters before any trees could be cut down, and numerous unexploded munitions from World War II had to be removed. During July and August 1944, the rail yards at nearby Revigny had been a major target for Allied bombers. Off-duty during the 1950s, GIs could wander throughout the huge depot to collect souvenirs from World War II aircraft wrecks. Although Trois Fontaines Ordnance Depot (TFOD) was in the French department of the Marne, headquarters and troop barracks were located near Robert-Espagne in the Meuse.

St.-Eulien to Robert Espagne

The headquarters company at TFOD was from the 37th Ordnance Battalion (Ammo Depot), an Army National Guard unit from Cleveland, Ohio. In March 1951, troops of the 7863rd Ordnance Ammunition Depot Det, commanded by Lt Col Gordon B. Borin, pitched their tents at St.-Eulien northwest of St.-Dizier. Each 16-ft wide by 32-ft long tent, equipped with two stoves for heat, could sleep twelve men. In July 1951, troops of the 571st Ordnance Co (Ammo) and 543rd Trans Co (Truck) moved their tents from St.-Eulien to a hilly site near Robert-Espagne. The enlisted personnel of both companies were black; the officers white.

The same month, troops of the 421st Ordnance Co (Ammo) an all-white reserve unit from Norfolk, Virginia, commanded by Capt Arthur G. Nenno, arrived from Germany. Until prefab barracks were built, each week troops were driven by 2½-ton trucks to Bar-le-Duc to use the public bathhouse. For entertainment, troops were shown motion pictures set up under a circus-size tent.[124]

To continue the buildup of ammo handler personnel at TFOD, in April 1952 two-hundred fifty troops of the 450th Ordnance Co (Ammo), a reserve unit from Columbia, South Carolina, were sent from Germany to TFOD. That year, troops moved into prefabricated metal barracks. On 15 November 1954, the 450th Ord Co was released from active duty. Its personnel remained in France to form a regular army unit, designated 609th Ordnance Co (Ammo).[125]

Depot Buildup

As areas in the depot were cleared, piles of ammunition sprouted under trees like mushrooms. Troops worked seven-day weeks, many days from 7 am to 6 pm, unloading shipments of ammo from Germany and the French port of Bassens. Shipments were received at a rail siding at Robert-Espagne and loaded onto trucks. At the depot, the ammunition was removed by hand and stacked in widely separated piles.[126] During May 1952, more than 1,000 tons of ammo were received each day from French ports. Troops reverted to 12-hour work days, but normally did not work on Sundays.[127] In June 1953, twenty airmen from the 85th Ammo Supply Squadron at St.-Mihiel Air Force Depot helped diffuse German landmines at Trois-Fontaines.[128]

During rainy months, the depot was so muddy that personnel became stuck in the mud, sometimes falling down. GIs risked getting caught carrying bayonets onto the depot to dig their boots out of the sticky mud. To pull 2½-ton cargo trucks out of the mud, GIs attached cable from the truck front end winch to a nearby tree. Sometimes the tree toppled over, but the truck remained stuck. Depot personnel had to carry ammunition to roller-conveyors and from the end of the conveyors to trucks that were parked 50 to 300 ft away on the nearest road. ComZ planners worried that it would take far too long to load trucks during an emergency.

During the early years at TFOD, live rounds were not issued to GIs who guarded the depot at night. For protection against the wild boars which roamed the forest, most GIs brought a bayonet or long knife. An unloaded M1 rifle was no protection against the dangerous marauders that weighed more than most GIs. The boars attacked without warning and could kill a man with their sharp tusks.

The 519th Engineer Firefighting Platoon, in which all personnel were black, was stationed at TFOD. If asked by the French the 519th Engineers, equipped with two trucks and a 750-gal pumper, responded to fires in nearby villages. To reduce costs in the mid-1950s, the US European Command replaced many GIs in service jobs with French nationals, freeing the soldiers for other work. In 1954, Trois-Fontaines was authorized to employ 1,365 French nationals (called LWRs). Laborers at the depot were transported to and from their villages by Army buses. In 1957, the fire department had twenty-eight enlisted men and forty-five French nationals to staff three fire stations: one at Robert-Espagne and two in the depot.[129]

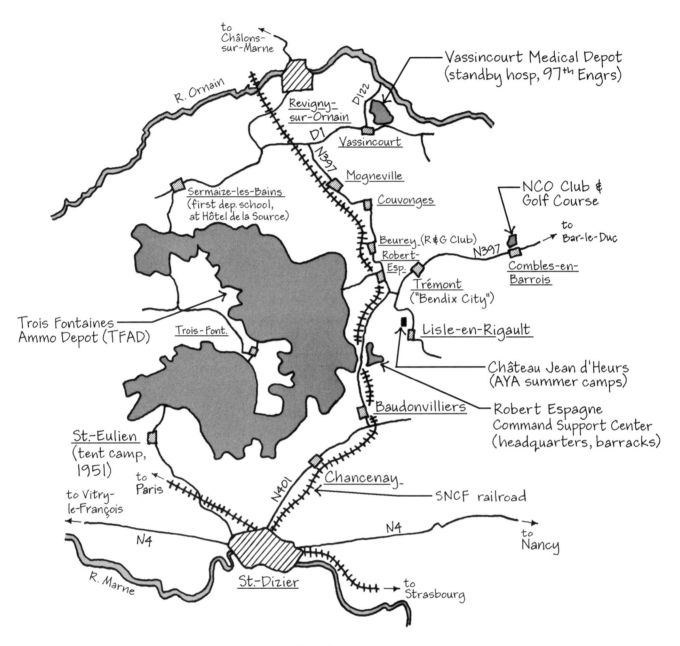

Trois-Fontaines Area Installations (1959)

Ammo Storage

For safety, ammunition depots required enormous space so munitions could be dispersed to prevent chain reactions that cause large explosions.[130, 131] Army ammunition depots in France were located far away from populated areas. When entering an ammo depot, GI drivers and passengers were required to surrender all smoking materials (cigarettes, matches, and lighters) to the guards. Despite safety precautions, accidents occurred. Three railcars loaded with ammunition for TFOD exploded on 26 November 1952 at Châlons-sur-Marne.[132]

In 1953, US Army, Europe estimated that ammunition stored at TFOD had a value of $500 million. It was discovered in 1954 that, due to long exposure to high humidity, rain, and mud, 51,000 tons of ammunition at Trois-Fontaines had become unusable. An investigation concluded that most of the ammo received the first year had been stored in a haphazard manner, and construction of hutments, roads, and security fencing was far behind schedule. Howitzer projectiles should have been stored upright, not on their sides.[133]

In 1955, more than five-thousand hutments were erected at Trois-Fontaines to shelter ammo from the weather. The hutments (called "igloos") were constructed from materials that were not prone to form dangerous missiles or firebrands in the event of an explosion. Acomal hutments were cement asbestos board; Fillod were metal. Igloos, each storing 10 to 20 tons of ammo, were widely separated throughout the forest. Eighty-five miles of asphalt-paved roads and a rail spur were constructed at the depot. Because the igloos were set back from the roads to conform to French forestry restrictions, all ammunition had to be moved in and out of storage by hand.

During the December 1955 offshore discharge exercise at le Verdon-sur-Mer, 684 tons of ammunition were discharged from ships to lighterage, transported to the beach, and shipped by rail to Robert-Espagne. Trois Fontaines "ammo humpers" carried the ammo from the railcars to trucks of the 82nd and 520th Transportation Truck Cos. The truckers drove the ammo to the depot, where it was unloaded and stacked in shelters by hand. It took three weeks to properly store the ammo.[134]

Ammo Maintenance

The stock of conventional munitions at Trois-Fontaines normally included: gun and mortar cartridges, landmines, hand grenades, howitzer projectiles (155 mm, 8 inch, and 105 mm), rockets, and various fuses. Some of the rockets, landmines, and howitzer shells were loaded with chemical nerve agents. In the early 1960s, mustard agent and VX, which was more toxic and persistent than Sarin, were stored in one-ton containers. Maintenance shop personnel cleaned rusty shells and restored the standard color-coded markings or applied camouflage coatings. Shells loaded with chemicals had three parallel stripes.

In the 1950s, conventional ammunition had a life span of about eight years, but had to be "worked over" every three years.[135] By the mid-1950s, TFOD had acquired equipment to restore deteriorated ammunition. The final step was painting the shells. In the new paint shop, arrays of infrared lamps were used to dry paint rapidly. Artillery shells were painted for identification of contents and to protect from rust and corrosion.[136] Ammo that could not be restored was taken to the French Army Camp Militaire de Maily near Vitry-la-François. It was destroyed by explosion in a deep pit that directed the blast upward.

Labor Service Guards

Labor Service (LS) personnel were employed in military units to guard installations throughout France. Most were displaced persons, refugees, or liberated prisoners-of-war from Eastern European countries. The French government permitted only Poles recruited in West Germany to serve in LS units in France. These former citizens of Poland were displaced from their homeland by the aftermath of World War II and depended upon NATO for employment. Because they had supported the Allies and were not communists, they could not return home.[137] Polish LS personnel were considered "stateless persons," however, under provisions of the NATO Status of Forces Agreement, they were given protection of the US Constitution.[138] As part of their compensation, they were housed, fed, and given uniforms. Their uniforms initially were US Army enlisted men's uniforms dyed blue.[139] The average annual salary of a LS guard was $1,600. LS guard companies, authorized about 200 men, were organized like an infantry unit. LS centers, authorized about 100 men, were organized like a battalion headquarters to command a group of LS companies. The guards normally worked 48 hours per week, subject to call day or night.

In April 1952, a LS guard at Trois-Fontaines shot at the mayor of a nearby village who apparently did not know the road he was using had been closed to the public. Fortunately, the guard was a poor shot. To prevent further incidents, Lt Col Borin assigned US Army MPs to guard the front gates, LS personnel to guard the interior of the depot. Brig Gen William W. Ford, ADSEC commander, reported on the incident of the trigger-happy LS guard to Maj Gen Samuel D. Sturgis at Orléans. Ford lamented to Sturgis that off-duty LS personnel "get drunk and raise the devil."[140]

Authorized levels for LS personnel were never reached in France because most Poles preferred to work in Germany where living conditions were better. Unlike Germany, the French required LS personnel to register with the police, did not provide social insurance and hospitalization benefits, and initially did not allow family members to join them in France. Medical care was provided by LS medical units. The cost was paid by deductions from their salaries. To compensate, ComZ offered higher pay and PX privileges. The LS personnel already in France welcomed the changes, but they had little effect on recruiting personnel from Germany. When forced transfers to France became necessary in 1954 to provide a minimum LS force of about 2,400 personnel, about half of those transferred refused to move and were discharged.[141] The US Army asked the French government to permit wives of LS personnel to live in France. The US reasoned that wives would be a good influence on the men, families would spend money in France, and French-Polish relations would improve. Starting in 1954, LS families could live in France.

Labor Service Units in France (1964)

Labor Service Unit	Location	Labor Service Unit	Location
Advance Section		Base Section	
4095th LS Company	Toul	4006th LS Company	Saumur
4128th LS Company	Verdun	4011th LS Company	Captieux
4506th LS Company	Nancy	4013th LS Company	Braconne
4507th LS Company	Robert-Espagne	4085th LS Company	Fontenet
6954th LS Center	Verdun	4086th LS Company	Croix-Chapeau
8584th LS Company	Metz	4088th LS Company	Bussac
Orleans Area Command		4096th LS Platoon	Poitiers
3335th LS Med Det	la Chapelle	4158th LS Company	Ingrandes
4082nd LS Company	Maison-Fort	4230th LS Company	Chinon
Seine Area Command		6953rd LS Center	Poitiers
4505th LS Platoon	Fontainebleau		

Algerian War

France's war in Indochina ended in June 1954 at Dien Bien Phu. Four months later war broke out in Algeria. Both sides used US weapons. In August 1955, National Liberation Front (FLN) Muslim terrorists massacred one-hundred twenty-three unarmed men, women, and children at Phillipeville, Algeria.[142] The thousands of tons of ammunition, casually stored at the huge depots in France, were an inviting target for supporters of the Algerian terrorists. The depots in rural areas were not heavily guarded because the number of personnel needed was never achieved. In addition to ammunition from TFOD, more than 3,000 field jackets from Woippy Quartermaster Depot were stolen for the rebels. Because of security concerns, in 1954 Brig Gen William W. Ford discouraged the French government from establishing an Algerian migrant workers camp near Trois-Fontaines.[143]

Ammo Aids Algerian Rebels

Although publicly denied by the US Army, theft of ammunition was a serious problem at TFOD. Polish LS personnel of the 4092nd LS Company provided security at night, but the depot was too vast. French citizens, sympathetic to the Algerian rebels, and a few corrupt LS guards, after easy money, could load without detection stolen ammo into civilian vehicles. The French police called the thieves the "green car gang" because they used green American-made vehicles, previously owned by GIs or civilian employees of the US government. Some of the vehicles had CF license plates, issued by the French, which were not subject to the usual search by French customs agents at border crossings. The ammo was transported by boat from Fréjus, France, to Morocco or from Genoa, Italy, to Tunisia, then overland to Algeria where it would be used by the rebels against French soldiers.[144]

On 04 March 1956, Pierre Rezard, a French reporter for the Reims *Union* newspaper, surreptitiously entered the depot. For two hours, Rezard roamed throughout the depot looking into unlocked storage huts and lifting up tarpaulins covering piles of explosives stacked on pierced steel plank (PSP). To prove how easily he could steal ammo, he took a case of "four deuce" ammo (4.2-inch M30 mortar shells) and delivered it to the office of the Préfet of the Meuse in Bar-le-Duc. After Rezard's story was published, the US Army denied that any ammo had been stolen. At a press conference, Brig Gen William R. Woodward, ADSEC commander, reasoned that this was not really a theft because Rezard had given the mortar shells to French authorities. Subsequent statements by the US military also downplayed any problems: "at Trois-Fontaines, the 4.2-inch mortars are stored separately from the fuses" and "dissidents in Algeria do not have 4.2-inch mortar launchers."[145]

Newspapers throughout France carried stories about stolen US ammo being used to kill French soldiers in Algeria. In 1953, US Army, Europe intelligence personnel had evaluated the security of depots in ComZ. A top secret report, issued in January 1954, described TFOD as susceptible to theft and sabotage at any time.[146] The French Sûreté estimated that 13,000 tons of ammo had been stolen from Trois-Fontaines since 1951. After numerous protests by the French government, the US Army finally agreed to improve security. For an immediate and ostentatious show of force, Woodward ordered armored weapons carriers and helicopters from Verdun to patrol the depot. At night, an H-19D Chickasaw helicopter used rotating searchlights to discourage intruders.

Enhanced Depot Security

At the end of summer 1956, Woodward announced a $1 million project to enclose the 45-mile perimeter of the wooded depot with 7-ft concrete posts topped with three to five strands of barbed wire. Security patrols would be increased and, to verify that guards made their rounds at night,

Watchman's Time Clocks would be located at depot buildings, railheads, gates, and along the depot perimeter. There now would be more than four-hundred LS guards and more than two-hundred guard dogs available for security.[147] Igloos would be secured by at least two locks, and only MPs would have access to the keys. By the fall of 1957, drivers entering the depot had to obtain a pass at the main gate. The storage areas were beyond a second gate. Before entry, drivers had to show a pass proving they had authorized access. In addition to enhanced entry security measures, GIs armed with M12 shotguns patrolled nearly 100 miles of depot roads in jeeps. The patrols had radio contact with security headquarters and were reinforced at night by French civilian guards and LS personnel with guard dogs.[148]

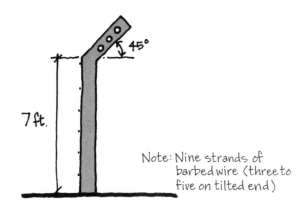

Concrete Security Fence Post

Labor Service guard dog scaling barrier (US Army)

Guard Dogs

The Army used German shepherds as guard dogs because of their size, firm bite, temperament, keen sense of smell, and stamina. The only friend of a guard dog was his handler; everyone else was an enemy. The handler fed, groomed, and trained his dog. The dog was restrained by a choke chain when off duty and by a leather collar when on duty patrolling the depot at night. During the day, dogs trained by crawling under and jumping over obstacles, walking on narrow boards, and attacking padded simulated intruders. Dogs were an excellent deterrent to trespassing because they could detect motion at greater distance than humans and could subdue an intruder by gripping an arm or leg firmly in its teeth until the handler gave the release command.[149, 150] Guard dogs at air bases which stocked nuclear weapons worked six hour shifts. One shift worked from 6 pm to midnight, the next until 6 am.

Kennels were built at nearby Vassincourt. At the kennels, dogs barked furiously and leapt at anyone who walked by the cages. Brig Gen William Whipple described kennel inspections in ComZ as a nerve-wracking experience because "having forty large German shepherds intent on killing you is a bad feeling."[151] The Air Force cautioned airmen not to run from a loose guard dog, because dogs could easily catch someone running away. It was best to stand still and shield your throat with your hands until the dog's handler arrived[152] In 1964, there were more than five-hundred guard dogs in Europe; three-hundred were in France.[153]

CHAPTER 9: *Advance Section in the Northeast*

May Day Protests

The resident agent of the 766th CIC Det at Robert-Espagne learned that communist-organized protests might occur outside the depot on May Day 1956. Col Fred J. Gosiger, depot commander, was an experienced officer who had been transferred from Fontenet Ordnance Depot to oversee improvements to security. Gosiger replaced Col Sumner E. Smith, who had been relieved of command by Woodward. Smith was to be the scapegoat for the lack of security fences at Trois-Fontaines.[154] Worried that the protestors might try to enter the depot storage areas, Gosiger had light machine guns issued to headquarters personnel and posted GIs at strategic locations along the perimeter of the depot. His driver, Cpl Frank Souza, was surprised that Gosiger did not issue ammunition. Regardless, wearing their steel helmets, Souza and his fellow GIs looked menacing crouched behind their unloaded machine guns. Unauthorized personnel did not enter the depot.[155] During protests earlier in 1956, similar security arrangements kept protestors out of the depot. However, at the Robert-Espagne railhead a protester hurled a Molotov cocktail at a railcar loaded with ammo. The famous Molotov cocktail is a glass bottle filled with gasoline, plugged with a saturated rag that is ignited before hurling. At Robert-Espagne, the burning rag fell out of the bottle before it hit the railcar. Fortunately no damage occurred.[156]

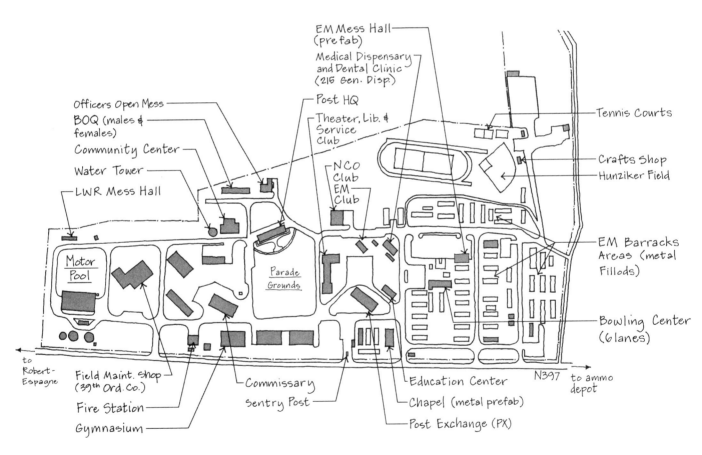

Robert-Espagne Command Support Center (1963)

Robert-Espagne Command Center

In June 1956, construction began on a permanent Command Support Center at the existing site of tents and prefabs near Robert-Espagne. New buildings included post headquarters, BOQ, officers mess, NCO Club, theater, gymnasium, commissary, motor pool, fire station, medical dispensary, and education center.[157, 158] Two-hundred fifty Frenchmen from the local area were hired to work on the construction. During the transition from old to new buildings, post headquarters temporarily moved into the service club building. The fifteen buildings, completed in November 1957 by Entreprise Ossude of Paris, had concrete block walls and corrugated steel roofs. To provide natural light, the roofs of the gymnasium and motor pool had reinforced corrugated glass panels. The new buildings were luxurious compared to tarpaper shacks and tents.[159] Prior to 1956, the Army had leased Château Jean d'Heurs for a BOQ, the NCO Club had been in Revigny, and the EM Club in Bar-le-Duc.

The Officers Club moved from a leased building in Bar-le-Duc into a masonry building behind the new two-story post headquarters building. At the new officers open mess, a hamburger, salad, dessert, and beverage cost $1.50; a steak dinner $4. A slot machine provided entertainment. Membership in the Officers Club was strongly encouraged. In June 1963, Capt Harold D. Harris, Jr., mess officer at TFAD, warned junior officers to eat at the club not at the EM mess hall. The EM mess had a raised floor area at one end for two reserved tables: one for officers and one for NCOs. Troops ate together at tables on the lower level. Harris conceded that once in awhile it was permissible to eat with the troops, but normally officers should eat at the club. Some junior officers believed that the meals SFC E. Schweider prepared at his EM mess were better value than meals at the officers mess.

The commissary received meat from the Giessen QM Depot, Germany; vegetables from Nahbollenbach General Depot, Germany; and milk from Le Mans, France. Any loss of electrical power was reported to the 158th Medical Det (Vet Food Inspection) at Metz. The 158th Med Det sent personnel to determine if the refrigerated food was safe to eat or should be destroyed.[160]

215th General Dispensary

The 215th General Dispensary at the Command Support Center provided medical service to GIs and dependents who did not require hospitalization. Expectant mothers normally delivered their babies at the US Army Hospital in Verdun. However, on 29 May 1962 a birth occurred at the 215th Gen Disp. As 1st Lt Richard A. Grim drove his wife, Mary, from their home in Beurey-sur-Saulx to Verdun, she went into labor near Bar-le-Duc. Grim immediately turned around and drove to the Command Support Center. Before her son Randy was born, Mary heard GIs, outside her improvised birthing room at the dispensary, taking bets on her child's gender.[161]

In 1964, the 215th Gen Disp had two Army doctors, one Polish LS doctor, three dentists, and thirty-six enlisted personnel to staff three clinics. The dispensary building at the Command Support Center had three doctor's offices and one large exam room. GIs and dependents needing surgery could be sent to Verdun by ambulances of the 591st Ambulance Co. In an emergency, helicopters from the 26th Trans Co at Rozelier Air Field or from Brienne Avionics Center could transport patients. The 215th Gen Disp also staffed a clinic within the depot and a clinic, mainly to serve LS personnel, at Vassincourt.[162]

The PhD at TFAD

In April 1957, Col George W. Taylor succeeded Gosiger as Commanding Officer of the depot, which would be renamed Trois Fontaines Ammunition Depot (TFAD). Taylor, who had been a professor at Washington University (St. Louis) for eight years, may have been the most highly educated officer in the Advance Section. He held a Bachelors degree from the University of Richmond, a Masters and PhD in Physics from Princeton University, and had two years post-doctorate studies at Princeton. Prior to TFAD, he served for two years at Los Alamos Scientific Laboratory and four years as the Chief of Ordnance representative on Joint Atomic Energy Commission (AEC)-Army programs.[163] At the time of Taylor's assignment to TFAD, plans were underway to build atomic blast-resistant structures to store Army nuclear warheads at three dispersed sites in northeastern France. Taylor oversaw the completion of the permanent buildings at Robert-Espagne, which greatly enhanced morale of the troops. He also encouraged his men to take continuing education courses. In the evenings, high-school level classes were taught at the new education center.

Depot in the 1960s

In 1960, the 97th Engineer Battalion built four-hundred rabbit hooches for the depot. Until reliable, portable detection devices became available, rabbits were used to detect chemical leaks, similar to canaries used to detect gas in coal mines. Rabbits were more sensitive to nerve agents than humans. Low concentrations of nerve agents caused the pupils of a rabbit's eyes to shrink to pinhead size, a condition called myosis or "small eye." If a rabbit was exposed to very low levels of the odorless Sarin, the constricted pinpoint pupils of its large pink eyes would be easy to see.[164] Hooches were placed just beyond the four corners of each igloo that stored chemical munitions. The small wire-cage hooches had sheet metal roofs and were installed on posts 4 ft above the ground to prevent wild animals from eating "Thumper" the leak detector.[165] When chemical munitions were loaded on railcars at the depot, caged rabbits were placed nearby.

More than 65,000 tons of conventional ammunition was stored at TFAD. Only Captieux in southwestern France was larger. TFAD became so large it had its own 42-ton diesel locomotive. The locomotive, manufactured in the US, was modified to operate on the narrow gage European rails. A rail spur connected to the Paris-Strasbourg SNCF railroad line at the "Big Cut" near the depot entrance.[166] In 1957, Army engineers cut down trees and blasted rock to lay more than six miles of railroad track. About 10 million cubic feet of earth was hauled away or shifted. Five sidings were paved with asphalt so trucks would have easy access to railcars.[167] Previously, the rail siding at Robert-Espagne had been used and ammo was moved to and from the depot by truck. In 1963, the depot name was changed to US Army Ammunition Depot Activity, Trois-Fontaines. More than nine-hundred troops were stationed at the depot; more than five-hundred French were employed at the depot and Robert-Espagne.

Transportation Corps diesel locomotive (US Army)

Soldier of The Month ceremony,
39th Ord Co, TFAD, June 1963 (US Army)

The 820th Ordnance Co (Ammo), commanded by Capt Roger A. Hoisington, was deployed from Fort Benning, Georgia to Trois-Fontaines in October 1961 during the Berlin Wall Crisis buildup, called Operation ROUNDOUT. These troops received, stored, maintained, and shipped ammunition stored throughout the vast depot and at the new depot at Vatry. The 820th Ord Co returned to the US in September 1962 on the troopship USNS *Gen Maurice Rose*. In September 1965, the 820th was sent to Vietnam.

Ordnance Field Maintenance (FM) Shop

The 1st Direct Support Platoon of the 39th Ordnance Co (FM) operated the Ordnance Field Maintenance Shop at Trois-Fontaines. It had been increased to more than sixty troops during the Berlin Wall Crisis. The platoon was responsible for the maintenance of more than 750 wheeled vehicles from units stationed at TFAD, Châlons, Vatry, Vitry-le-François, Brienne-le-Château, and Vassincourt.[168] Repair parts that were used at least three times in 180 days were stocked at the shop. Infrequently used parts were requisitioned from warehouses at Nancy. The platoon worked and trained six days each week. During field exercises and operations such as BIG LIFT in October 1963, the men worked continuously until the mission was completed.

39th Ordnance Co (FM) Det Commanders

Commanding Officer	Period of Service	Commanding Officer	Period of Service
1st Lt Edgar C. Garrison	1957-58	Capt Richard A. Grim	1960-63
Capt Edward Strater	1958-59	1st Lt Martin D. Egan	1963-64
1st Lt Barney "Bubba" Dillard	1959-60	WO 2 James B. McMullen	1964

Trois-Fontaines Area Installations

In 1961, the depot commander at Trois-Fontaines had responsibility for installations at Châlons-sur-Marne, Rozelier, Vassincourt, and Vatry. Support was provided to Rozelier although it was closer to Verdun. Limited support was to be provided to Brienne-le-Château and Vitry-le-François.[169] Support included post engineer construction and maintenance services, repair of vehicles and small arms, and provision of rations for mess halls. Post engineers cut the grass, hired janitors, repaired plumbing, and paved roads. Installations west of Trois-Fontaines were at Châlons, Vatry, and Vitry. At Châlons, the Petroleum Distribution Command operated tank farms at Vatry, Cheniers, Coupetz, and Dommartin-Lettrée. Barracks for the QM troops were at the former US Air Force dispersed operating base near Vatry. Hangars were used as a truck terminal of the 37th Trans Command. In 1961, the Vatry ammunition depot was built near Sommesous at a cost of $10 million. It contained one-hundred earth-covered, storage igloos for conventional and chemical munitions and three atomic blast-resistant (ABREST) storage facilities for nuclear weapons. Five of the 2,500 sq ft igloos stored chemical munitions.

Brienne-le-Château

South of Trois-Fontaines at Brienne-le-Château, the Army converted the former US Air Force dispersed operating base to an aviation maintenance center. The US Army Aircraft Field Maintenance & Avionics Center repaired and retrofitted aircraft from the US Army, Europe fleet of more than 750 helicopter and fixed-wing aircraft. By 1963, more than four-hundred GIs and French employees worked at the Center. GIs of the 582nd Transportation Co (Aircraft Maint) repaired engines, power trains, hydraulic systems, airframe skin, and radar components.[170] Mechanics tore down and rebuilt aircraft engines and used sheet metal to repair damaged airframes. When aircraft could not be flown to Brienne for repairs, teams of aircraft mechanics were sent to the aircraft. Retrofit programs could be extensive. It took fifty working days to convert a CH-34A Choctaw to a CH-34C model.[171]

Madame John

Until they could find housing, officers assigned to Trois-Fontaines were billeted at Madame Ensminger's Hôtel de Metz et du Commerce at 17, Blvd Rochelle in nearby Bar-le-Duc. During the Battle of France in 1939-40, Madame Ensminger's daughter-in-law, affectionately known as "Madame John," was an honorary member of British RAF No. 1 Squadron based at the airdrome in nearby Vassincourt.[172] In the late 1950s, rent for a month at the Metz was $50. Breakfast, served by Madame John, consisted of coffee and a roll. Each of the fifty rooms had a small sink and a *bidet*, a plumbing fixture for pelvic area hygiene that looked like a low sink. Americans used it to wash their socks or, for the more daring, as a punch bowl for parties. Each floor had a common toilet (labeled *WC* for water closet), but no bathtub. Public baths were located across the street from the hotel. Most homes in Bar-le-Duc and nearby villages did not have indoor plumbing.

Rural Economy Housing

Most officer and NCO families lived on the economy. In rural France, farmers kept their cows in barns attached to their houses. Each morning, cows were paraded through village streets to pastures outside the village. GIs driving to the depots had to join the rear of the parade unless they could quickly circle around the block to beat the cows to the next intersection. Streets were decorated with steaming piles of cow manure. The status of a villager allegedly was measured by the height of the manure pile (called a *fumier*) in front of his doorstep. The higher the pile, the larger the herd the farmer owned.[173] The fumier aroma inspired the troops at Toul-Rosières AB to call nearby Rosières "Fragrant Rosie" or "Perfume City." Near Verdun, the dozen small village names ending in "sur-Meuse" were pronounced "sewer mouse," as in "I live on the economy at Charny Sewer Mouse." [174] Today, the formerly smelly villages compete to earn the prestigious designation *ville fleurie* (village of flowers). Manure piles have been replaced by flower boxes and paved sidewalks.

GIs called the small village of Tremont-sur-Saulx "Bendix City." Bendix was a US manufacturer of washing machines; an appliance taken for granted by Americans, but rare in rural France. It was common to see village women washing clothes in the stream that flowed through Tremont along the road from the depot to Bar-le-Duc. After the clothes were scrubbed on stones in the water, they were solar dried on flat rocks beside the road. The owner of Garage Warnant, a single-pump ESSO gas station at Robert-Espagne, was called "Pops" by the GIs.

Government Housing

In 1955-56, Aaron-Bertrand et Cie of Paris built seventy-two RGH units at Pilviteuil on a hillside overlooking Bar-le-Duc, a 10-minute drive from the depot.[175] Completion of the housing units had been delayed by a few months due to shortage in France of pipe for water and sewer lines. Because factory production of pipe could not meet demand, the French government allocated supplies on a priority basis.[176] The Army named the housing area Yorktown Village to be a reminder that France was America's oldest ally. During the Revolutionary War, France had aided the decisive American victory at Yorktown, Virginia. Many of the single-story two and three bedroom homes had washing machines; all had green lawns. Late one evening in May 1964 after a party at the nearby French school,

French students ran through Yorktown Village knocking on windows. Because the noise awoke his baby which he finally had gotten to sleep, an angry Maj Donn R. Adrian quickly dressed, grabbed his 5-iron golf club, and gave chase down the hill toward Bar-le-Duc. According to Joan Adrian, within days rumors had spread at the Officers Club that her husband had been seen chasing French students while brandishing his sword.[177]

Château Jean d'Heurs and Youth Activities

After liberation from the Germans in August 1944, the 18th Century Château Jean d'Heurs served as a recuperation facility in 1944-45 for American GIs treated at hospitals in Verdun. In the early 1950s, the château was leased for a Bachelor Officer Quarters. In 1962, three lieutenants from TFAD rented a second floor room at the château. During the bitterly cold winter, their kerosene space heater was inadequate for the high-ceilinged room. To stay warm, they set up a tent in the middle of the room, moved the space heater into the tent, and slept under several Army blankets.[178]

The Boy Scouts of America used the grounds of Château Jean d'Heurs for outdoor sports activities. An Army Advance Section summer camp for children opened in July 1953 on the grounds of the château. Parents paid $9 per participant. For the one-week program, boys and girls were organized into age groups of 7-9, 10-11, and 12-13 years old to participate in recreational activities such as baseball, badminton, horseshoes, swimming, and hiking.[179, 180] The camp, located near the Saulx River, had a "Pow-Wow Tent" and tents for mess, medical aid, showers, and sleeping. The tents had wood floors and walls, and were connected by gravel paths. Seventy-two underprivileged French children, mostly orphans, attended the camp as guests of the Army. Donations from GIs in the Advance Section paid their camp fees.[181]

By 1959, American Youth Activities (AYA) summer camp week for dependent children in the Advance Section included days devoted to instruction in bowling, golf (at Combles-en-Barrois), horseback riding, baseball, swimming (at RCAF Station Marville), and firing rifles and pistols (at a range near Bar-le-Duc).[182] The last AYA summer camp in France was held from 21 June to 09 August 1966 at the recently vacated depot grounds of TFAD. Most of the ammo had been removed. The camp offered activities in swimming, handicrafts, team sports, and camping skills.[183]

Recreation

Basketball teams of GIs competed at the gymnasium; bowling teams at the bowling center. The northeast corner of the Command Support Center was graded so troops could play baseball and football. The 97th Engineer Battalion built a 9-hole, par 33 golf course in front of the NCO Club at Combles-en-Barrois. Five holes were completed when it opened on 18 July 1958.[184] The greens fees were a bargain at only 75¢ on weekdays; $1 on weekends and holidays. A Rod and Gun Club was built on the banks of the Saulx River at the end of rue des Pressoirs in Beurey-sur-Saulx.

Community Relations

In December 1952, troops from TFOD donated six truckloads of scrap wood for use in stoves at the home for the aged poor operated by *les Petites Soeurs des Pauvres* (the Little Sisters of the Poor) at St.-Dizier.[185] In May 1953, cooks of the 421st Ordnance Co (Ammo) built a meeting house for French Boy Scouts. The original house had been destroyed during World War II. In December 1953, troops at Trois-Fontaines donated a washing machine to an orphanage at Bar-le-Duc and money to an orphanage at St.-Dizier. On Christmas morning, eighty children from the two orphanages were transported to Robert-Espagne where they ate dinner at the mess hall with the troops. In the afternoon, the children were taken to the EM Club in Bar-le-Duc where live entertainment, candy, and toys were provided.[186] The tradition of service by GIs at TFAD to orphanages continued until the depot closed in 1966.

In 1959, the TFAD Officer's Wives Club awarded a $300 scholarship to Mlle Marie Madeleine Bertrand, a 17-year-old French orphan, who wanted to become a teacher. She and her two sisters lived with their widowed grandmother in Trois-Fontaines. The girls' father had died in 1945 in a German concentration camp; their mother had died in 1946. The scholarship enabled Marie Madeleine to continue her education.[187]

Trois Fontaines Ammunition Depot Commanders

Commanding Officer	Period of Service	Commanding Officer	Period of Service
Lt Col Gordon B. Borin	1951-52	Col George W. Taylor	1957-60
Lt Col Louis J. Poudre	1952-53	Col Edward H. Hilsman	1960-62
Lt Col George J. Holly, Jr.	1953-54	Col William W. Bell	1962-63
Col Oliver G. Kinney	1954	Lt Col William L. Latta	1963-64
Col Sumner E. Smith	1954-55	Lt Col Martin A. Shadday	1964-65
Col Fred Joe Gosiger	1955-57	Lt Col Hubert R. Jones	1965-66

Winterized tents, TFOD, Robert-Espagne, 1952 (US Army)

Trois-Fontaines Area US Army Installations

Installation	Location	Activity and Units
Headquarters	Robert-Espagne	TFAD Command Support Center (88 acres)
	Brienne-le-Château	US Army Aircraft FM & Avionics Center (939 acres)
Depots	Forêt de Trois-Fontaines (13,933 acres)	US Army Ammunition Depot
	Vassincourt (216 acres)	US Army Medical Depot, 500-bed standby hospital
	Vatry (552 acres)	US Army Ammunition Depot
	Vatry (337 acres, A to D total)	Chalons Tank Farm A
	Cheniers	Chalons Tank Farm B
	Coupetz	Chalons Tank Farm C
	Dommartin-Lettrée	Chalons Tank Farm D
	Vitry-le-François (106 acres)	77th Medical Depot, 500-bed standby hospital
	Châlons-sur-Marne (former US Air Force DOB)	Transportation Truck Terminal, Vatry
	Sommesous (110 acres)	Railroad consignment point
Medical Dispensary, Dental Clinic	Robert-Espagne	215th General Dispensary 767th Medical Detachment
Schools (dependents)	Brienne-le-Château	Elementary school
	Vassincourt and Vitry-le-François	Elementary school (K to 8)
Bachelor Officers Quarters (BOQ)	Châlons-sur-Marne (Vatry) and Brienne-le-Château	Two-story buildings at former US Air Force DOBs
	Robert-Espagne	Two-story building, Officers Mess
	Vitry-le-François	Wing of hospital
Housing (families)	Bar-le-Duc, at Pilviteuil (Yorktown Village)	72 RGH units
	Châlons-sur-Marne, at Sarry (Cité Américaine)	40 GRI units
	Brienne-le-Château (Cité Américaine)	40 GRI units
	Vitry-le-François (Marolles)	30 SCH units (12 acres)
Troop Barracks	Robert-Espagne (metal prefabs)	39th Ordnance Company (FM) 609th Ordnance Company 820th Ordnance Company 61st Military Police Company 256th Signal Company 24th Army Postal Unit
	Vassincourt	97th Engineer Battalion 69th Signal Battalion 520th Transportation Co (Lt Trk) 4507th Labor Service Co
	Brienne-le-Château	582nd Transportation Company 256th Signal Company
	Vitry-le-François	16th Field Hospital 505th Medical Co (Holding) 591st Ambulance Company 61st Military Police Company

Troop Barracks	Châlons-sur-Marne	70th Trans Co (Med Trk) 543rd Engineer Co (Pipeline)
Recreation	Beurey-sur-Saulx	Rod and Gun Club
	Combles-en-Barrois	Golf course (9 holes, 2,668 yards), NCO Club
	Robert-Espagne	Gymnasium, Hunziker Athletic Field, bowling alley (6 lanes)
	Vassincourt	Bowling alley
	Vitry-le-François	Athletic fields, bowling alley (4 lanes)
Air Field	Brienne-le-Château (former US Air Force DOB)	US Army Airfield Detachment 582nd Transportation Company (Aircraft Maintenance)
Training Site	Champ de Tir du Haut Juré (near Bar-le-Duc)	Firing range (shared with French Army)
Newspaper	Robert-Espagne	The Fountainhead

Abbreviations

DOB	Dispersed Operating Base (USAF)	RGH	Rental Guarantee Housing (Army)
FM	Field Maintenance	SCH	Surplus Commodity Housing (Army)
GRI	Guaranteed Rental Income (USAF)	TFAD	Trois Fontaines Ammunition Depot

Toul Buildup

In July 1951, the US Army began constructing an engineer depot on a flat site, called la Croix-de-Metz, at the outskirts of Toul. When the first GIs of the 83rd Engineer Co (Depot) arrived in September 1951, only skeletons of World War I-era hangars remained. However, a faded aero squadron emblem was still visible on one of the smaller buildings.[188] For two years, the troops worked in mud and lived in "winterized" tents. Supplies poured in from the US, but most had to be dumped in the mud.[189] The temporary storage area at the south end of the depot was piled high with 40,000 tons of bridging and other engineer supplies. The 698th Engineer Co (FM), an Army Reserve unit from Dodge Center, Minnesota, arrived in November 1952. The troops, commanded by Capt Elmer E. Buegler, waded through ankle deep mud to reach their tents that were full of holes. For six months, they endured primitive latrine and shower facilities. Because pipes were clogged with lime, water flow was a trickle. The 698th Engineers repaired all the engineer equipment in the Advance Section.[190]

The 998th Engineer Battalion, an Army Reserve unit from Menomonie, Wisconsin, also arrived at Toul in November 1952. The 998th Engineers, commanded by Lt Col Charles L. Badger, were responsible for most of the construction at Toul and Nancy. In early 1954, Gen William M. Hoge, Commander-in-Chief of US Army, Europe, made a surprise inspection visit from Heidelberg, Germany, to Toul. Hoge believed that living conditions for the troops were substandard, and that the 998th Engineers were not performing well. After the visit, Maj Robert A. Atkins was sent from Verdun to command the 998th. Although Atkins was able to improve morale and performance, as an outsider he was not accepted by the Wisconsinites. In January 1955, the battalion moved to Base Section. Personnel with less than sixty days until separation from the Army (called "short timers") stayed at Toul. The remaining GIs formed the three companies sent to Base Section. Co A was stationed at Chinon, Co B at Ingrandes, and Co C at Braconne. The battalion was inactivated on 20 June 1955. Atkins returned to Verdun to command the 97th Engineer Battalion.[191, 192]

Croix-de-Metz in the World Wars

During World War I, the American air service used an airdrome at Croix-de-Metz. On 21 March 1916, the French air service established the Escadrille Américaine for American volunteers who served as pilots for France before the US entered the war. Renamed the Lafayette Escadrille, the squadron flew French-built Nieuport 17 fighters, and its aviators provided valuable experience when the US entered the war.[193] On 18 February 1918, the escadrille became the 103rd Aero Squadron of the American air service. The most famous aviator of the Lafayette Escadrille was French-born, American Raoul Lufbery, an ace who shot down seventeen German planes. In 1918, he was transferred to the 94th Aero Squadron. Known as the "Hat-in-the-Ring" squadron, the 94th achieved the highest total of aerial victories for an American unit. One of the airman trained by Lufbery at Croix-de-Metz was Capt Edward V. "Eddie" Rickenbacker, America's ace of aces.[194, 195] Older than most pilots, the 28-year-old Rickenbacker had twenty-six confirmed kills: 22 German planes and 4 German balloons. Rickenbacker was awarded the Medal of Honor for heroism in aerial combat. Between the world wars, the site was used as a civilian airfield and French Army training area.

During the German occupation of 1940-44, the Luftwaffe used Croix-de-Metz for fighter aircraft. It was liberated by Patton's Third Army in August 1944. From 14 September 1944 until 22 May 1945, it served as an airfield for the US Army Air Forces 358th Fighter Group. The 2nd Engineer Aviation Brigade covered the flat site, designated airfield A-90, with pierced steel plank (PSP) to provide stable runways for fighter aircraft.[196] From airfield A-98 at nearby Rosières-en-Haye, US Army Air Forces P-47 Thunderbolts and P-51 Mustangs of the 354th Fighter Group also supported the advance of Patton's Third Army toward Germany.[197] Until the US Army returned in 1951, Croix-de-Metz was used by local farmers and a civilian flying club.

Toul Engineer Depot

The Toul Engineer Depot stored, maintained, and supplied the heavy construction equipment needed to build bridges, roads, and airfields. Equipment, such as bulldozers, cranes, and generators, were repaired and rebuilt at the depot. Each year, tons of supplies and equipment were processed through the depot. Pontoon bridges were stored north of the depot at Fort du Vieux Canton, near Villey-St.-Etienne. The 747th Engineer Co (Heavy Equipment), an Army Reserve unit from Albuquerque, New Mexico, arrived at Toul on 15 May 1952. The 747th Engineers, commanded by Capt William A. Cardwell, set up quarry operations at nearby Nancy Ordnance Depot to support construction of roads and railheads at Advance Section depots. Crushed rock was used in concrete for buildings, roads, and parking lots. Army engineers used explosives to blast rock loose at quarries so it could be crushed for delivery by dump trucks to construction sites.[198]

In 1955, the 40th Antiaircraft Artillery Battalion was temporarily stationed at Toul. Its 90-mm guns were to protect the depot and nearby air bases from air attack. By the end of 1955, several masonry buildings had been constructed, including warehouses, maintenance shops, barracks, BOQs, chapel, gymnasium, and PX. A modern theater replaced the World War I-era Cinéma Pathé the US Army had leased on rue du Général Gengoult in downtown Toul. Films had been shown five evenings each week at the Pathé. Regularly scheduled Army bus service was provided from the depot to Toul and Nancy.[199]

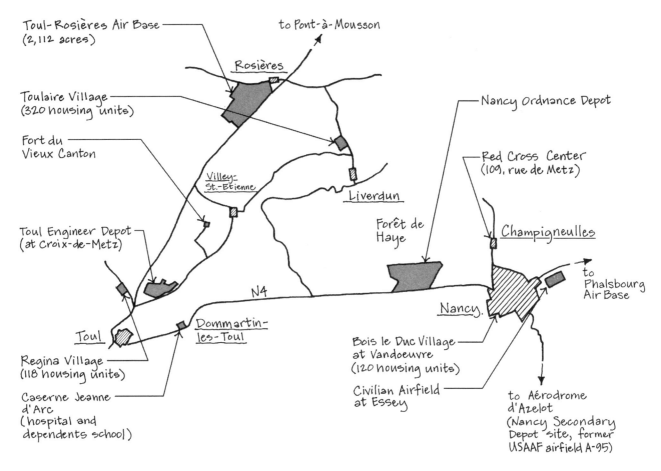

Toul-Nancy Area Installations (1959)

109th Trans Truck Battalion

Headquarters company of 109th Transportation Truck Battalion, an Army National Guard unit from Camp Ripley, Minnesota, arrived at Toul in September 1951. To form the battalion, the 75th, 77th, and 543rd Truck Companies (Light) were transferred from Robert-Espagne to Toul. The 109th moved cargo throughout Advance Section in 2½-ton trucks.

To qualify for a military driver's license, Army truck drivers had to pass a difficult test. Drivers had to identify French road signs, take a reaction test on a drive simulator, check a vehicle for leaks and safety features, park in a tight space, and drive through a marked serpentine course.[200]

In November 1951, Lt Col Carl F. Vonder Haar, commanding officer of the 109th Trans Truck Bn, presented "Safe Driver" award certificates to eighteen drivers of the 543rd Truck Co. The presentation ceremony at Toul recognized six months driving without an accident for thirteen GIs; three months for five GIs.[201] Contests to challenge Army truck drivers at the July 1952 Verdun Roadeo included: braking vehicle traveling at 20 mph within 40 ft without spilling milk bottle of water sitting on floorboard, driving vehicle 175 feet without wandering more than four inches off a straight line, and backing up vehicle 20 feet to stop with rear wheels touching an 8-ft long 2 x 4 wood board. During 1953, vehicles of the 109th Trans Bn, commanded by Lt Col George H. Davies, were driven over 2 million miles.[202, 203]

Hobart Baker Field

In 1957, the football field at Toul Engineer Depot was named Hobart Baker Field in memory of "Hobey" Baker, an All-American athlete who led the hockey and football teams at Princeton University to national championships. During World War I, Baker was a pilot with the 103rd Aero Squadron and shot down three German planes in aerial combat. In December 1918, one month after the armistice had been signed, Capt Hobart A. Baker was killed when his recently repaired airplane crashed landed at Croix-de-Metz.[204]

62nd Engineer Battalion

During Operation ROUNDOUT in 1961, the 62nd Engineer Battalion deployed for one year from Fort Leonard Wood, Missouri, to Toul. At Laon AB and Chaumont AB the battalion, commanded by Lt Col Darwyn Robins, erected prefab aircraft maintenance hangars, paved aircraft parking areas (called *marguerites*), and built reinforced-concrete firing-in butts. The butt, a 48-ft high, 40-ft deep shed-like structure, was open on one long side. Aircraft fired .50 cal guns into the butt to align their sights. The interior was filled with soil to absorb impact of the rounds.[205, 206]

Caserne Luxembourg

In 1951-52, Caserne Luxembourg in Toul was used by the US Air Force for barracks while the air base was under construction at Toul-Rosières. Because World War II damage had not been repaired, conditions were Spartan. The buildings were not heated, windows were broken, and the plumbing did not work. Once a week, the airmen were trucked to Toul to use the public baths.[207] In 1952, truckers of the 109th Trans Truck Bn were billeted at the caserne. In 1953, the US Army 57th Field Hospital, authorized one-hundred seventy personnel, also billeted their enlisted men at the caserne. The 57th staffed medical dispensaries at the caserne and at Toul Engineer Depot and Nancy Ordnance Depot. In 1957, the 57th Field Hospital and 591st Ambulance Co moved into barracks at the new Jeanne d'Arc Hospital.

Jeanne d'Arc Hospital

A 1,000-bed standby hospital was constructed at Caserne Jeanne d'Arc at Dommartin-les-Toul. Jeanne d'Arc Hospital, built by Compagnie Parisienne d'Entreprise of Neuilly, was completed in 1957 at a cost of $3.4 million. Wings of the hospital were used for troop barracks and dependents school. The school cafeteria could seat 150 children. Patients at the hospital could be taken by Army ambulance train from Toul to Landstuhl, Germany. Previously to board the train, patients from Toul were taken by ¾-ton ambulance to Verdun.

School buses transported children between the dependents school at Jeanne d'Arc and their homes, some in villages more than 20 miles away. During the winter of 1958-59, a school bus carrying two children slid off the road into a snow bank near the village of Dolcourt. The bus guard, Sp4 Robert D. Kelley, did not abandon his two passengers. He carried the 7-year-old boy on his shoulders and led the boy's 9-year-old sister two miles through the snow to the nearest village to phone the depot. A French villager at Dolcourt took the children into her home. She gave them dry clothing and shelter until Army transportation arrived from Toul.[208]

In 1959, the French government asked the US to remove its nuclear weapons from France. During the withdrawal operation, code-named RED RICHARD, the Air Force relocated more than two-hundred nuclear-capable aircraft to Germany and Great Britain.[209] The 574th Transportation Co

(Medium Truck), stationed at Jeanne d'Arc, made 120 five-day roundtrips hauling 1,100 tons of cargo from nearby Toul-Rosières AB to Hahn AB in Germany.[210] It was US policy to not acknowledge the presence of nuclear weapons in France, so RED RICHARD removed weapons that officially had not existed. In 1967 at Jeanne d'Arc, the Army dug a huge pit to bury supplies abandoned during withdrawal. The Universitaire de Nancy renovated the empty buildings to be a center for othropedic surgery.[211]

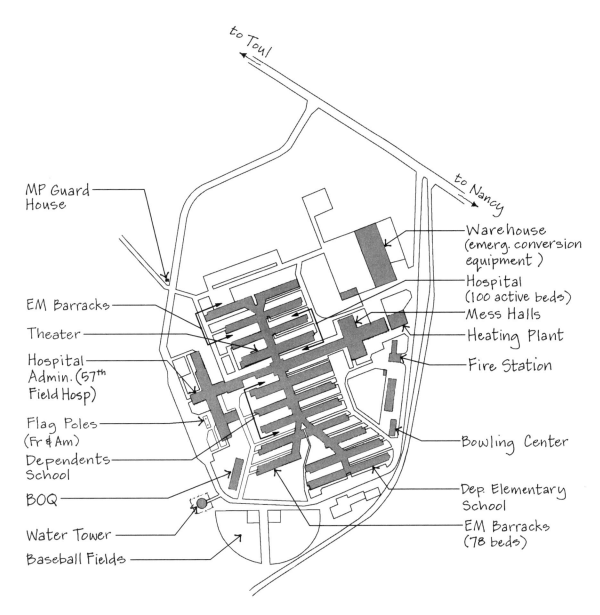

Jeanne d'Arc US Army Hospital

Regina Village

By 1960, there were more than 1,500 troops at Toul. Officer and NCO families lived on the economy or at Regina Village, located on a hilly site two miles north of Toul. The housing village had one-hundred eighteen single-family units, built at a cost of $18,500 per unit. Col Willard Roper, depot commander, dedicated the village on 11 December 1959. The village was named in memory of Mme Suzanne Regina, a heroine of the French resistance who had been born in 1900 in Toul. Known to the underground as "Madame Kricq," she helped hundreds of downed Allied airmen to escape from the Germans. Her last mission was to take information to the Allies. She was captured and shot by the Germans on 03 June 1944.[212]

Toul Engineer Depot Commanders

Commanding Officer	Period of Service	Commanding Officer	Period of Service
Lt Col William J. Brown	1951-52	Col Willard Roper	1959-60
Lt Col Thomas T. Smith	1953-54	Col James O. Younts, Jr.	1960-61
Col Jay A. Abercrombie	1954-55	Col Herbert W. Radcliffe	1961-62
Col Helmer A. Holmstrom	1955-57	Lt Col William J. Daily	1962
Col Herbert B. Murnan	1957-58	Lt Col Glen E. Petrie	1963-64
Col Paul H. Lanphier	1958-59	Lt Col Wilbert D. Fisher, Jr.	1965-66
Lt Col Jay W. Doverspike	1959		

Forêt de Haye

During World War II, the Forêt de Haye, located between Toul and Nancy, had been a battleground for Gen Patton's advancing Third Army. To slow down Third Army in early September 1944, the Germans hastily regrouped to form a defensive position, anchored on Pont-à-Mousson and Forêt de Haye. Minefields were placed throughout the forest. By 14 September 1944, the forward position of the 3rd Battalion of the 319th Infantry Regiment was between Croix-de-Metz and Nancy.[213] It would take months of hard fighting to advance into Germany. In late September, the Germans counterattacked at Lunéville, and in November 1944 the battle for Metz was underway.[214] Seven years later the US Army returned to Forêt de Haye.

Prefabricated barracks, Nancy Ordnance Depot, 1953 (US Army)

CHAPTER 9: *Advance Section in the Northeast*

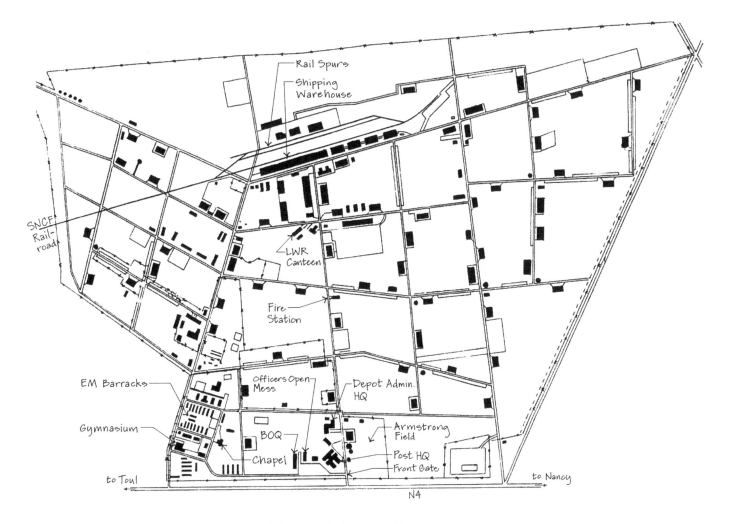

Nancy Ordnance Depot

Nancy Buildup

In September 1951, the US Army began construction of an ordnance depot on a heavily forested site in the Forêt de Haye.[215] Until it was replaced in 1956, the guardhouse at the front gate was the rear end of an old panel truck.[216] The 343rd Ordnance Bn, an Army Reserve unit from Tampa, Florida, was assigned to European Command in December 1951. Troops of the 343rd, commanded by Lt Col Homer J. Victory, originally lived in tents in the Forêt de Haye. In 1951, the 109th Medium Maintenance Co (Park) from Phenix City, Alabama, and the 112th Ordnance Medium Maintenance Co from Cleveland, Ohio, were sent to Nancy. Both Army National Guard units were released from active service in December 1954, but the troops stayed at Nancy. By 1955, there were more than 1,300 troops at Nancy.

Nancy Ordnance Depot

The Nancy Ordnance Depot stored, maintained, and supplied wheeled and tracked combat vehicles. Over 20 miles of roads were required for the vast 2,500-acre site. During construction of depot roads, a bulldozer uncovered an unexploded 100-lb bomb from World War II.[217] In 1953, most equipment had to be stored in the forest, and roads were not paved. A major construction program began to build one-hundred sixty-six permanent masonry buildings to house repair shops, warehouses, and command support facilities such as EM barracks, BOQ, two gymnasiums, and a fire station. Inside, the new warehouses looked like gigantic hardware stores. Open bins were stacked from floor to roof. The first three warehouses to be opened had a total capacity of 70,000 storage bins.[218] In July 1953, eight miles of rail spurs were completed to connect the depot to the Paris-Strasbourg SNCF railroad line. About one-hundred railcars could be moved into the depot each day. Previously, only ten or twelve railcars could enter the depot.[219]

In early 1954, troops at Nancy worked six and seven days per week, ten and twelve hours per day, to prepare Army vehicles for turn over to Air Force units, dubbed "Project SWAPPO." More than 2,000 jeeps and ¾-ton vehicles were taken from storage in the depot and shipped by SNCF flatcars to air bases or turned over to airmen drivers from nearby bases. The Army vehicles replaced the Air Force's World War II-era vehicles in France.[220]

By the end of 1954, prefabs or permanent structures replaced most of the tents. Most roads were paved and equipment was moved into sheds, protected under tarpaulins, or stored in large hangars which were open on the sides. Cranes, used to unload semitrailers, fit under the high roof structures. When full, the hangars were closed on the sides by canvas. Many of the modern structures were built by Entreprise A. Puifferat of Paris. By late 1955, masonry buildings were completed for assembly-line warehouses along railroad spurs and for the stock control center, which had modern electric accounting machines. A diesel locomotive replaced Army trucks which had been fitted with railroad wheels.[221] The 565th Ordnance Co (FM), which had moved platoons from Toul and Metz to Nancy in 1955, was responsible for the maintenance of more than 1,500 wheeled vehicles from motor pools and Army units stationed at Buzy, Metz, Nancy, Sampigny, and Toul.[222]

In April 1957, Nancy became the first Advance Section depot to have a dial telephone system. It had taken nearly a year for the *Compagnie Général de Construction Téléphoniques* to install the 400-line system. The new automated system, which replaced three manual switchboard operators, provided faster connections throughout the depot.[223]

Labor Service guards used thirty-two dogs to patrol the depot perimeter at night. The dogs had been trained for six months at the US Army, Europe Quartermaster School, Lenggries, Germany. On patrol, when released from its leash, the dog would charge an intruder, leap to knock him down, and grab the intruder's arm or throat firmly in its teeth.[224]

To celebrate the tenth anniversary of the liberation of Nancy on 12 September 1944, an American convoy of five tanks and three jeeps drove from the "Monument of the Resistance" on the outskirts of Nancy to Place Stanislaus in the center of town. Depot commander Col Robert F. Peters rode in the lead jeep with three Frenchmen who had ridden into Nancy during the liberation. At Place Stanislaus, the national anthems of France and the United States were played, followed by a reception at City Hall.[225] In April 1955, Peters instituted "French only conversation hour." For one hour on Tuesdays and Thursdays, only French was to be spoken at the depot. Peter's goal was to overcome the language barrier between LWR employees and GIs. Americans who lapsed into English had to contribute 10¢ for each offense to the American Red Cross fund.[226, 227]

The Cinéma Caméo in Nancy was leased to show movies to the troops. In the early years, wives rode in the back of Army 2½-ton trucks to the commissary at Toul-Rosières AB. A truck departed the depot in the early morning for the 46-mile round trip, returning in mid-afternoon. Nancy opened its own commissary in 1955.[228]

Volunteer Projects

In spring 1952, off-duty ordnance troops converted a Quonset hut to serve as a chapel, called the "chapel in the woods." They painted the outside gleaming white and built a small steeple at the entrance.[229] In 1957, a new chapel was built which could seat one-hundred sixty-eight worshipers. The troops donated more than $2,500 to purchase stained glass windows and mahogany doors. In fall 1953, off-duty troops worked on Saturday and Sunday afternoons in Dommartemont. The "pick and shovel" crew of volunteers leveled a site for an enlarged classroom of a French school.[230]

Sedan Staff Cars

During his August 1952 inspection visit to Nancy, Lt Gen Maxwell D. Taylor raised a fuss when he noticed three new Chevrolet sedan staff cars stored in the open at the depot. Taylor, Army Assistant Chief of Staff for Operations, reasoned that visiting US Congressmen likely would question the need for sedans in the war reserve.[231] By mid-1953 more than 8,000 combat vehicles, such as M47 Patton tanks and half tracks, were lined up in parallel rows at the depot.[232] No sedans were visible. In June 1955, Taylor succeeded Gen Matthew B. Ridgway as Army Chief of Staff.

Amphibious DUKWs

Amphibious DUKWs, which could be driven on land or water, also were stored at Nancy. The depot equipped two DUKWs with water pumps to fight fires along riverbanks and at locations inaccessible by road. Seven DUKWs were used to rescue people stranded by floods in February 1958. Within two hours after the call for help, DUKWs were taken from storage, inspected, and readied for use. CWO Charles H. Morgan supervised seven GI drivers. Rescue efforts were coordinated by French fire department.[233]

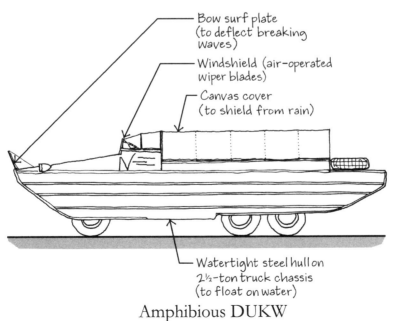

Amphibious DUKW

Safety Patrols

In 1959, the 72nd Trans Co (Light Truck) safety patrols from Nancy were sent to locations along route N4, a high-crowned, two-lane highway from Nancy to Paris. Patrols, consisting of an NCO and driver, were located at hazardous intersections, dangerous curves, and steep hills. They stopped drivers who were driving too fast and discussed the dangers observed. If warranted, the NCO issued a notice of traffic violation and sent a copy to the driver's commanding officer.[234]

The General Depot

In 1958, Nancy was converted from a specialized depot to a general depot which stored supplies for all of the technical services. More than 1,700 French employees worked at the depot. In the summer of 1958, Company A of the 801st Engineer Battalion was sent on TDY from Germany to Nancy. The construction company completed projects throughout the depot. In the summer of 1959, the 94th Engineer Battalion, commanded by Lt Col Earl B. Fauber, was sent on TDY from Germany. They rehabilitated 11 miles of roadway, installed twelve prefab buildings, and poured 2,000 cubic yards of concrete at Toul, Nancy, and TFAD.[235] In 1960 to further disperse supplies in the Advance Section, the 97th Engineer Battalion built off-depot storage sites at Graux, Lempire, Neufchâteau, and Void. Each of these 100-acre sites had one warehouse, numerous concrete hardstands, and perimeter security fencing. To serve Nancy by air, US Army fixed-wing aircraft used the civilian airfield at Essey. For rapid pickup and drop-off, single-engine aircraft used a sod landing strip adjacent to the front gate along the Nancy-Paris route N4.

Recreation

In the mid-1950s, Special Services rented an indoor swimming pool at 45, rue Sergeant in Nancy. The 50-meter long pool was open to US military personnel on Friday, Saturday, and Sunday afternoons.[236] At the depot there were fields for baseball and football, two gymnasiums, skeet range, and bowling center. In 1955, the athletic field for baseball and football was named Armstrong Field in memory of Sgt Orland L. Armstrong, who had been killed in an accident at the depot. Before the 1955 football season, GI volunteers worked on weekends to grade the surface of the gridiron.[237, 238]

Housing and Community Service

Officers and NCOs with dependents lived on the economy or in the Bois le Duc housing village of one-hundred twenty ranch-style units in Vandoeuvre, south of Nancy. Wives of officers and NCOs volunteered to assist nurses at Army hospitals as Gray Ladies and to serve in scout programs as Den Mothers. Wives clubs and depot personnel supported homes for the elderly and French orphanages in the Nancy-Toul area. In 1958, they supported five French orphanages.

Nancy Ordnance Depot Commanders*

Commanding Officer	Period of Service	Commanding Officer	Period of Service
Lt Col Homer J. Victory	1951-54	Lt Col Glen E. Shaw	1959
Col Thomas L. Gaines	1954	Col Martin Cunningham	1959-62
Col Robert E. Peters	1954-57	Col Selmer J. Espelund	1962-64
Col Edward J. Ormiston	1957	Col Oscar C. Tonetti	1964-65
Col Thomas J. Raber	1957-58	Col Walter W. Hogrefe	1965-67
Lt Col Harold E. Cone	1958-59		

*Converted to General Depot in 1958. In December 1966, during the withdrawal of forces from France, the US Army Depot Complex, Eastern France headquarters was activated at Nancy. The complex consisted of depots at Nancy, Toul, Aboncourt, Rozelier, Vatry, and Vitry-le-François.

Nancy-Toul Area US Army Installations

Installation	Location	Activity and Units
Headquarters	Forêt de Haye (Nancy)	US Army Garrison NATO pipeline Central European Operating Agency (CEOA)
	Croix-de-Metz (Toul)	US Army Garrison
Depots	Forêt de Haye (2,500 acres)	US Army Ordnance Depot, Nancy
	Neufchâteau, Chenevières, and Fresne-St.-Mamès	Three off-depot storage sites, Nancy (more than 1,000 acres total)
	Azelot (Aérodrome)	Secondary depot site, Nancy
	Croix-de-Metz (567 acres)	US Army Engineer Depot, Toul
	Caserne Jeanne d'Arc (66 acres)	US Army Sub-depot, Toul
	Caserne Lamarch Graux (100 acres) Void (100 acres) Villey-St.-Etienne (Fort du Vieux Canton)	Four off-depot storage sites, Toul (more than 350 acres total)
	Rouceux (Aérodrome)	Secondary depot site, Toul
Hospital	Dommartin-les-Toul	57th Field Hospital, 1,000-bed standby hospital (102 acres)
Schools (dependents)	Dommartin-les-Toul	Elementary school, at hospital (K to 9)
Bachelor Officers Quarters (BOQ)	Forêt de Haye (Nancy)	Two-story building, Officers Mess
	Croix-de-Metz (Toul)	Three 2-story buildings, Officers Mess
	Dommartin-les-Toul	Two-story building
Housing (families)	Liverdun (Toulaire)	320 CCH units (USAF control)
	Toul (Regina Village)	118 SCH units (37 acres)
	Vandoeuvre (Bois le Duc)	120 RGH units
Troop Barracks	Forêt de Haye (Nancy)	197th Ordnance Battalion 565th Ordnance Company (FM) 256th Signal Company 72nd Transportation Company 539th Army Postal Unit 4506th Labor Service Co
	Croix-de-Metz (Toul)	97th Engineer Battalion 52nd Engineer Co (Parts Depot) 507th Engineer Co (Depot Maint) 510th Engineer Co (Heavy Eqp) 525th Engineer Co (Dump Truck) 64th Military Police Company 2nd Transportation Battalion (Truck) 4095th Labor Service Co
	Dommartin-les-Toul	57th Field Hospital 591st Ambulance Company 574th Transportation Co (Med Trk)
Recreation	Forêt de Haye (Nancy)	Armstrong Athletic Field, skeet range, bowling alley, gymnasiums
	la Flye	Golf course (9 holes)
	Croix-de-Metz (Toul)	Hobart Baker Field, Tullum Gymnasium, bowling alley (6 lanes), theater
	Dommartin-les-Toul	Bowling alley (4 lanes), skeet range

Recreation	Nancy (57, ave Foch)	5-6-7 Club (Army-Air Force NCO Club)
Air Fields	Essey	French civilian control
	Nancy	Airstrip at depot (along N4)
Training Sites	Pierre-la-Treiche (Bois l'Evêque)	Rifle Range (French Army)
	Toul (Ste.-Anne)	Maneuver area (French Army)
	Toul (Jeanne d'Arc)	Engineer bridge construction
Newspapers	Nancy	The Mudlark (1953), The Arrowhead (1954), Nancy Times, The 565 Bomb (565th Ordnance Co)
	Toul	The Toulois, Toul Post

Abbreviations

CCH	Commodity Credit Housing (USAF)	Maint	Maintenance
Eqp	Equipment	NCO	Noncommissioned Officer
FM	Field Maintenance	RGH	Rental Guarantee Housing (Army)
LWR	Local Wage Rate (French employees)	SCH	Surplus Commodity Housing (Army)

Metz Buildup

During the November-December 1944 battles to liberate Metz, Germans retreating from Patton's forces destroyed twenty bridges over the Moselle River and adjacent canal. Only three were undamaged. Six years later, the US Army returned to war-damaged Metz.[239] In November 1950, Caserne Colin was first occupied by the 465th, 574th, and 978th Service Companies. The caserne, built in the 1870s, was one of five French casernes located on rue du Général Franiatte near the SNCF rail yards in Metz. To support the rapid buildup of depots in the Advance Section, railheads were repaired and improved to receive quartermaster supplies at Woippy and ammo in the Forêt de Villers. The 514th QM Co operated leased cold storage plants at Homécourt near Metz, Maxéville near Nancy, and near Gare de l'Est in Paris. Warehouse storage also was leased at Uckange.[240] The Metz depot installations were developed to supply the US military in France with meat, fish, dairy and egg products, fresh fruit, and vegetables. Clothing, tents, and bedding were stored, repaired, and distributed at Woippy. In 1951, supplies were stacked so rapidly at Woippy that tall stacks of tents partially sank into the mud. Large fuel storage sites at Billy-le-Grand, Buzy, and Pouilly supplied gasoline and oil to Army installations in the Advance Section and aviation fuel to US and Canadian air bases in northeastern France. By 1955, there were more than 1,400 troops at the Metz area installations.[241]

Plan HEADRACE

During 1951, more than 4 miles of railroad were improved in the Forêt de Villers near St.-Hubert, a sub-depot of Trois Fontaines Ordnance Depot (TFOD), to store conventional ammunition for a mobile reserve, called Plan HEADRACE. The mobile reserve had a balanced stock of ammunition ready to be rapidly delivered by rail to Seventh Army combat troops in Germany.

The St.-Hubert site had been used during the world wars as a railhead for ammunition in turn by the French, German, and American forces. In September 1953, Army M/Sgt Arthur J. Noakes, Jr. discovered a 2,500-pound dud from a World War I French naval railroad gun. The dud, buried close to the railroad tracks, finally was removed in April 1954.[242]

During 1952-53, there were two-hundred twenty-four loaded railcars, divided into four trains on sidings at St.-Hubert.[243] Most of the railcars had been hurriedly loaded without securing the ammo in place. In 1954, Lt Col Louis J. Poudre, TFOD commander, sent thirty-five men from 450th Ordnance Co (Ammo), an Army Reserve unit from Columbia, South Carolina, on temporary duty from Trois-Fontaines to St.-Hubert to properly crate and secure the ammo for transport. The ordnance troops pitched tents and "humped" ammo. They removed crated ammo from railcars, and repaired and banded the wooden crates with ¾"-wide metal straps. After the crates were reloaded onto the railcars, scrap wood and dunnage lumber were used to brace the crates to prevent shifting during transport.[244] A mess truck from Metz provided meals. By the late 1950s, the railcars had been removed from St.-Hubert and the installation placed on reserve status.

Caserne Colin

In early 1951, the 7867th QM Depot Group, commanded by Col Leonard E. Engeman, arrived at Metz. During World War II, Engeman's Combat Command B of the 9th Armored Division captured the Remagen Bridge which allowed four divisions to cross the Rhine River. Two months later in May 1945 Germany surrendered.[245] The depot group renovated Caserne Colin for troop barracks and warehouse functions. Ten warehouses at Colin were filled with QM supplies. Sack goods, like flour and beans, had to be stored indoors to prevent deterioration. Canned goods, like meat and vegetables, could be stored under canvas tarps until warehouse space became available. Eighteen special purpose vehicles, including a mobile laundry and six mobile bakeries, that would be needed to feed combat troops in the field, were stored in the open at Colin. In 1951, the 64th QM Battalion, commanded by Lt Col Hurlbert R. Pilburn, served as troop administration detachment until July 1952 when it was replaced by the 95th QM Battalion, transferred from Germany. By the end of 1952, the caserne had a barbershop, commissary, PX, and small theater.

Franco-American Relations

In 1955, the former stable at Colin was converted into the Sergeant's Club. The German Army had used the stable during both world wars. The troughs filled with plants not water, tethering rings, and old lanterns hung from horseshoes reminded troops and their guests that horses had been the first occupants. Every other week French guests were invited to use the club.[246] French citizens in Metz organized a "Franklin Club" to offer social and cultural activities for American soldiers. Located on 63, rue de Pont des Loges, the club opened at 8 pm each evening.[247] In 1958, Col Fred E. Gerber, depot commander, initiated a program to permit French employees to use recreation facilities at Caserne Colin. His first step was to open the post library to French employees.[248]

Excess Property

The Metz QM Property Disposal Section had monthly sales of excess or obsolete US government property which would be too costly to ship back to the US. Businesses in NATO nations could bid on numerous items, even large equipment such as forklifts. Army personnel and dependents could shop at the QM Retail Sales Outlet at Caserne Colin. Popular purchases at bargain prices included: rifles, bedding, china, clothing, light fixtures, tools, and cameras. Bargain hunters could furnish their homes from sales at the outlet. For example, footlockers could be used as benches or low tables.[249]

Woippy Depot

The Woippy Depot was acquired from the French in June 1951. It consisted mostly of war-damaged buildings. Two years later the French government expropriated adjacent land from several private owners. Because the land was taken for disposition of the French military, the land owners' legal objections did not succeed.[250] The US Army developed the depot to provide more than ½ million sq ft of warehouse storage space. For incoming and outgoing rail shipments, a one-mile rail spur on the depot connected to the Metz-Thionville SNCF railroad line. In 1956, Woippy began receiving supplies by rail from the port of Rotterdam, the Netherlands. At the port, cranes transferred cargo directly to barges or railcars. This provided an additional supply route for ComZ.[251]

During the command of Col John T. Lynch, the third officer to command Metz QM Depot during 1951-52, pilferage of cartons of combat boots and fatigue uniforms was discovered at Woippy. Lynch believed that Labor Service guards of the "green car gang" were involved in the theft.[252] During World War II, Lynch had commanded the 14th Tank Battalion of the 9th Armored Division that liberated Metz.

On 05 June 1955, while on authorized leave to Germany from his unit at Woippy Depot, Sgt Walter S. Winter inadvertently crossed the Czechoslovakian border and was observed taking photographs. Even though the crossing was due to poor signage on a nearby road, Czech border guards arrested him at gunpoint.[253] Initially, the local Czech authorities indicated that the sergeant would be released within a few hours, but the Czech Foreign Ministry intervened. Unfortunately, Winter became a pawn in an attempt by the Czechs to obtain extradition of a Czech border guard who had sought asylum in the West and to pressure US Army, Europe (USAREUR) to inactivate two Labor Service units of Czech refugees in Germany. Both efforts failed. After being held in prison for 13 months, Winter was released on 15 July 1956.[254]

McNamara Drawdown

In 1963, during the McNamara drawdown of US forces in France, numerous installations were closed in the Base Section and some in the Metz area. In 1964 the Woippy Depot closed when the 552nd Quartermaster Co, commanded by Capt John W. Renn, moved to Croix-de-Metz at Toul.[255] Nevertheless in 1964, more than seven-hundred French nationals still were employed in the Metz area. In 1965, USAREUR approved a plan to pre-position equipment at Woippy, Toul, and Nancy to support one US Army combat division. Nearby air bases at Chambley, Étain, and Toul-Rosières would be used to receive the one-hundred forty troop transport sorties needed to airlift personnel of one division from the US to France.[256]

Camp Tournebride

In early 1953, troop housing for 1,000 enlisted men was to be built at Camp Tournebride near Ars-sur-Moselle. However in 1954, the Chief of USAREUR Quartermaster Division asked the Joint Construction Agency in Paris to provide housing for 1,500 men, then in spring 1954 reduced the request back to 1,000, and by the end of the year to 600.[257] The fluctuating demands delayed completing the final design of the troop housing area. By 1957, Camp Tournebride had masonry buildings for EM barracks, mess hall, PX, gymnasium, and chapel.[258] Army engineers also cleared level areas for baseball, softball, basketball, and volleyball. Tournebride was closed in August 1964.

Aboncourt Depot

In 1959, eight 21,000 sq ft ammunition shelters were built into the sloped terrain at Aboncourt. Engineers used the excavated soil to cover the 2-ft thick reinforced-concrete vaulted roofs of the shelters, a method called "cut and cover." The atomic blast-resistant (ABREST) structures were secured by locked 16-inch thick steel doors.[259] The year they were built, French President Charles de Gaulle asked the US to remove its nuclear weapons from France. In the mid-1960s, the eight ABREST structures at Aboncourt were used to warehouse hundreds of jeeps.

Frescaty Air Field

From 25 December 1944 to 01 October 1945, four US Army Air Forces (USAAF) fighter groups were stationed at Metz-Frescaty, designated airfield Y-34. On New Years Day 1945, during the German Ardennes offensive, the Luftwaffe attacked the airfield destroying dozens of 365th and 368th Fighter Group aircraft. From April to September 1945, the 442nd Troop Carrier Group used the airfield.[260]

In 1951, the 7962nd Ordnance Light Aircraft Maintenance (OLAM) Det, commanded by 1st Lt Ned J. McCord, Jr., was sent to Frescaty Air Field. In late 1952, when the US Army transferred responsibility for all aviation support worldwide from the Ordnance Corps to the Transportation Corps, the 45th Transportation Army Aviation Maintenance Co replaced the OLAM Det.[261,262] The 45th, commanded by Capt Daniel B. Wilson, was the only Army helicopter and fixed-wing aircraft supply and repair unit in Europe. Frescaty had one paved runway. Two hangars, built by the Germans during the occupation, were used to

H-13 Sioux bubble-nose helicopter (US Army)

repair aircraft. The unheated hangars were extremely cold during winter. GIs assembled the Bell H-13 Sioux, a two-seat bubble-nose helicopter used in the 1950s by Mobile Army Surgical Hospital (MASH) units in Korea. The H-13 flying ambulance became famous due to the opening of each episode of M*A*S*H, a popular TV series. In 1952, the US Air Force 73rd Warehouse Squadron stored more than two-hundred fifty vehicles at Frescaty. Some were on loan to support NATO air base construction operations at Chambley, Chaumont, Étain, and Toul-Rosières. In 1954, the Air Force vehicles were relocated to Toulon-sur-Allier.[263]

Training

To qualify on small arms each year, units at Metz used the French firing range at Bois des Ognons, near Ars-sur-Moselle. In 1958, personnel of the 70th Engineer Co (Const) rehabilitated the range. The work officially was designated engineer training. The engineers repaired roads, renovated firing lines, repaired target frames and pits (trenches from which targets were raised), and repainted signage. Before the troops could fire weapons, a French bugler sounded an alarm to warn hunters in the forest.[264]

Housing

In the early 1950s, officers and NCOs with dependents lived on the economy. In 1954, thirty families lived in trailers on 40 ft by 30 ft lots in an area along the Luxembourg Road on the outskirts of Metz. Most of the GIs purchased a British-manufactured "Governor-General" trailer, which sold for $2,500. It had a bathroom and kitchen, and could sleep up to six people.[265, 266] The Woippy housing village of one-hundred single-family units opened in 1956. In fall 1957, depot personnel built a children's playground at the Woippy housing village. The playground, surrounded by a wire-mesh fence, contained a merry-go-round, jungle gym, teeter-totters, and swings. Bachelor officers lived in the BOQ at Camp Tournebride or on the economy.

Metz Depot Commanders

Commanding Officer	Period of Service	Commanding Officer	Period of Service
Lt Col John M. Stoddard	1950-51	Col Carl W. Kohls	1957
Col Leonard E. Engeman	1951-52	Col Clyde C. Simkus	1957
Col John T. Lynch	1952	Col Fred E. Gerber	1958-59
Col Carmon A. Rogers	1952-53	Col Raymond Van Fleet	1959-61
Col George L. Darley	1953-54	Lt Col Christopher L. Stahler	1961-62
Col John W. McDonald	1955-56	Col Paul E. Bruehl	1962-64
Col James E. Butler	1956-57		

Sampigny Chemical Depot

War planners believed the US Army needed sufficient chemical weapons in Europe to deter the Soviets from using their vast supply. Consequently during the early 1950s, more than 8,000 tons of chemical munitions would be stored in France for Seventh Army. Initially, the 15th Chemical Group oversaw the chemical munitions segregated by type at Camp Bussac in the Base Section. To indicate shell contents, chemical munitions were color-coded.[267, 268]

Two Army Reserve units, mobilized for the Korean War, were assigned to the 13th Chemical Service Battalion and deployed to Sampigny. The 330th Chemical Co (Maintenance) from Scranton, Pennsylvania, and the 337th Chemical Depot Co from Los Angeles, California, moved into Caserne Harville at Sampigny. The abandoned caserne, built in 1833 for French Army cavalry units, occupied a flat site between the St.-Mihiel-Commercy road and the SNCF railroad tracks behind the caserne. For barracks, the troops used dilapidated horse stables. After three months in the smelly stables, troops moved into tents where they spent two cold winters until wooden hutments were built. Dilapidated warehouses were used to store: gas masks, decontamination apparatus, detection devices, flame throwers, and smoke generators.[269] To improve morale of the troops, the depot ran shuttle buses from Sampigny to the larger towns of Commercy, Nancy, and Toul.[270] In June 1953, a six-bed dispensary and dental clinic opened at Sampigny.

Flame Throwers and Smoke Generators

Chemical personnel repaired flame throwers and mechanical smoke generators used by units of Seventh Army in Germany. The M2 portable flame thrower, fueled by napalm, was a "fear-provoking" weapon to be used against unprotected enemy troops and flammable targets.[271] GIs called it "The Zippo," a popular brand of cigarette lighters. Smoke generators were to be used to conceal troop movements such as river crossings, which otherwise would expose troops to enemy fire. Fog-oil generators produced thick white smoke that could be an effective visual barrier if winds did not disperse the smoke screen.

CBR Training

In March and April 1954, one-hundred sixteen officers and NCOs completed two-week courses on CBR (chemical, biological, and radiological) training at Sampigny. The courses, designed to train students to be instructors at their home installations, included defenses against chemical weapons, and hands-on training for use of flame throwers, landmines, chemical grenades, smoke generators, and napalm. Students also learned how to use a Radiac Set (Geiger counter) to measure the strength of an atomic bomb blast. Students measured the strength of radio signals (not radiation) at intervals as they drove their jeeps toward a simulated blast.[272, 273]

Self-Help Construction

During the summer of 1952, chemical troops volunteered to help a GI carpenter build a 150-seat movie theater using scrounged lumber from wood crates. The temporary roof was canvas on wood framing and the walls were scrap boards.[274] During off-duty hours in 1953, GIs also scrounged lumber to build dayrooms at the caserne. In the summer of 1953, the French Army let Sampigny use an indoor firing range at Commercy. Because the range had not been used since World War I, the US Army built new target frames and provided flags to signal shooters at the firing line.[275]

In late August 1954, troops volunteered to work from sunrise to sunset converting tents to forty-three hutments. Some of the lumber came from abandoned temporary structures at Toul-Rosières AB.[276] However, higher authorities at Verdun directed Lt Col Colin C. Campbell, depot commander, to permit construction work only during off-duty hours. Campbell negotiated a compromise with Brig Gen Raymond W. Curtis, ADSEC commander. Day work would continue using a small permanent detail and off-duty crews would rotate each night and weekend so work could be completed by mid-October, before cold weather began.[277] In May 1955, troops moved from the hutments they had built from scrap lumber into metal prefab barracks which were dubbed "metal mansions." Prefabs also were erected for depot headquarters and a mess hall.[278]

Recreation and Dependents School

Troops entertained themselves by forming vocal, instrumental, and comedy groups. In 1953-54, Sgt Jerome Keresey was master of ceremonies for "The Harville Players."[279] Troops also built a four-lane bowling alley, the first in Advance Section. Lt Col Frederick A. Jacobs, whose family owned bowling alleys in the US, used his contacts to spearhead the project. The alley attracted bowlers from posts as far away as Vitry-le-François.[280] In 1955, Sampigny organized an eight team bowling league with teams from Sampigny, Toul (Caserne Luxembourg), and St.-Mihiel Ammo Depot.[281]

In the early years, the Sampigny Dependents School met in one room at the motor pool maintenance building. The school had an outdoor latrine built by the troops, 55-gal drums for wash water, and used the motor pool parking area for a playground.[282] At noon, students walked to the Snack Bar for lunch. In May 1955, a metal prefab was erected for additional classroom space.

Community Relations

In the fall of 1952, a wrecker truck from the depot lifted a new bell into the belfry of the village church at Sampigny. Depot personnel also supported the nearby orphanage. During off-duty hours in 1957, personnel built a playground for the orphanage which occupied the summer home of former French President Raymond Poincaré. By 1957, one-hundred ninety military and Army civilian personnel were assigned to the depot. Sampigny employed one-hundred eighty LWRs.

Palmer Closes Sampigny

After his inspection of the depot in 1954, Lt Gen Williston B. Palmer, head of the Department of Army Logistics Division, decided that the site was unsatisfactory due to cramped space and poor security.[283] By the late 1950s, all chemical munitions in France had been moved to Trois Fontaines Ammunition Depot; gas masks and other chemical supplies were stored at the general depots. In July 1957, Sampigny Chemical Depot became a secondary storage site for the Verdun General Depot.[284] When the depot was closed in fall 1958, Sampigny Mayor Mme Georges Vautrin hosted a dinner attended by ADSEC commander Brig Gen Robert J. Fleming, Jr. and former Sampigny Depot commander Lt Col Cecil D. Miller. Vautrin thanked the US Army for aiding her village when there were fires and accidents, organizing events for the youth of Sampigny, and supporting the orphanage. In November 1958, during Palmer's tenure as Deputy Commander-in-Chief, US European Command at Camp des Loges, Caserne Harville was returned to the French government. Sixteen wood-frame buildings built by the GIs were donated to the village of Sampigny.[285]

Sampigny Chemical Depot Commanders

Commanding Officer	Period of Service	Commanding Officer	Period of Service
Lt Col Marvin A. Middlebrooks	1951-52	Maj Edward J. Odachowski	1956
Lt Col Frederick A. Jacobs	1952-53	Lt Col Cecil D. Miller	1956-57
Lt Col Colin C. Campbell	1953-56	Maj Robert W. Lane	1957-58

Collapsible rubber POL tanks at Open House,
Caserne Colin, Metz, May 1962 (L. W. Howell)

CHAPTER 9: *Advance Section in the Northeast*

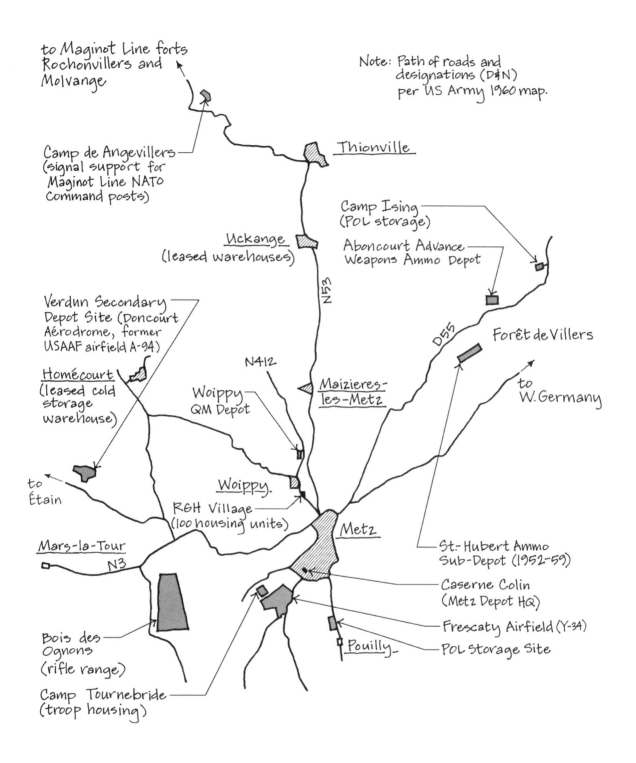

Metz Area Installations (1951-64)

Metz Area US Army Installations

Installation	Location	Activity and Units
Headquarters	Metz (Caserne Colin)	US Army Garrison, Metz
	St.-Baussant	US Army Terminal District, Metz
Depots	Metz (Caserne Colin)	US Army Depot, Metz
	Aboncourt (81 acres)	Advance Weapons Ammunition Depot
	Woippy (48 acres)	US Army Quartermaster Depot
	St.-Hubert (Forêt de Villers, 82 acres)	US Army Ammunition Sub-Depot of Trois-Fontaines
	Angevillers (Camp de Angevillers, 22 acres)	Signal facility (support for underground command posts)
	Angevillers	Off-depot storage site, Metz
	Ebersviller (Camp Ising, 15 acres)	Off-depot POL storage site
	Pouilly (16 acres)	US Army POL Depot
	St.-Baussant	Metz Tank Farm A
	Pont-à-Mousson (Thiaucourt)	Metz Tank Farm B (A&B total 276 acres)
	Sampigny (Caserne Harville)	US Army Chemical Depot (34 acres)
Medical Dispensary	Metz (Caserne Colin)	332nd General Dispensary
Schools (dependents)	Metz (Caserne Colin)	Elementary school (K to 8)
	Sampigny (Caserne Harville)	Elementary school
Bachelor Officers Quarters (BOQ)	Ars-sur-Moselle (Camp Tournebride)	Two-story building (47 units)
Housing (families)	Woippy	100 RGH units
Troop Barracks	Metz (Caserne Colin, 27 acres) and Ars-sur-Moselle (Camp Tournebride, 69 acres)	34th QM Battalion 70th Engineer Co (Const) 643rd Engineer Co (Pipeline) 84th Transportation Co (Med Truck) 504th Military Police Battalion 11th Ordnance Company (DAS) 552nd QM Company (Supply Depot) 256th Signal Company (Support) 158th Medical Det (Vet Food Insp) 29th Base Post Office 8584th Labor Service Co
	Angevillers (Camp de Angevillers)	175th Signal Company 208th Signal Company
	Sampigny	330th Chemical Co (Maint) 337th Chemical Depot Company
Recreation	Angevillers (Camp de Angevillers)	Athletic fields
	Ars-sur-Moselle (Camp Tournebride)	Gymnasium, theater (300 seats), baseball field, football stadium (bleachers seating 1,000), cinder track, skeet range
	Lessy	Rod and Gun Club (25 acres)
	Metz (Caserne Colin)	Bowling alley (6 lanes), gymnasium, theater (700 seats)
	Sampigny (Caserne Harville)	Bowling alley (4 lanes)

Transient Quarters	Metz (23, ave Foch)	Hôtel Royal (100 rooms)
	Metz (3, place de la Gare)	Hôtel National-Le Globe (100 rooms)
	Metz (4, rue Charlemagne)	Hôtel Regina (60 rooms)
Air Field	Frescaty (two hangars)	45th Transportation Army Aviation Maintenance Company
Training Sites	Bois des Ognons (near Gravelotte)	Rifle range (shared with French Army)
	Commercy	Indoor firing range (French Army)
	Metz (Camp Jeanne d'Arc)	Jeanne d'Arc Maneuver Area
Newspapers	Metz	The Sword and Key
	Sampigny	Sampigny Spotlight

Abbreviations

DAS Direct Automotive Support   RGH Rental Guarantee Housing

Size of ADSEC Installations[286]

The US Army had twelve major depot installations in the Advance Section. The table below presents the data for six installations at the peak of deployment. Toul was equal in size to Central Park in New York City; Verdun to Fort Story, Virginia; Nancy twice the size of The Presidio of Monterey, California; and Trois-Fontaines twice the size of Fairmont Park in Philadelphia, Pennsylvania. The acreage of the four tank farms at Vatry was equal to Hyde Park in London, England.

Real Estate	TFAD	Vassincourt	Vitry-le-François	Verdun	Toul	Nancy
Land use (acres)	14,021	216	106	1,814	935	2,700
Permanent buildings (masonry)	112	13	32	317	180	166
Temporary buildings (prefab)	5,287	79	4	64	58	55
Family housing (RGH & SCH units)	152	0	30	788	118	120
Roads (miles)	107	2	4	23	11	20

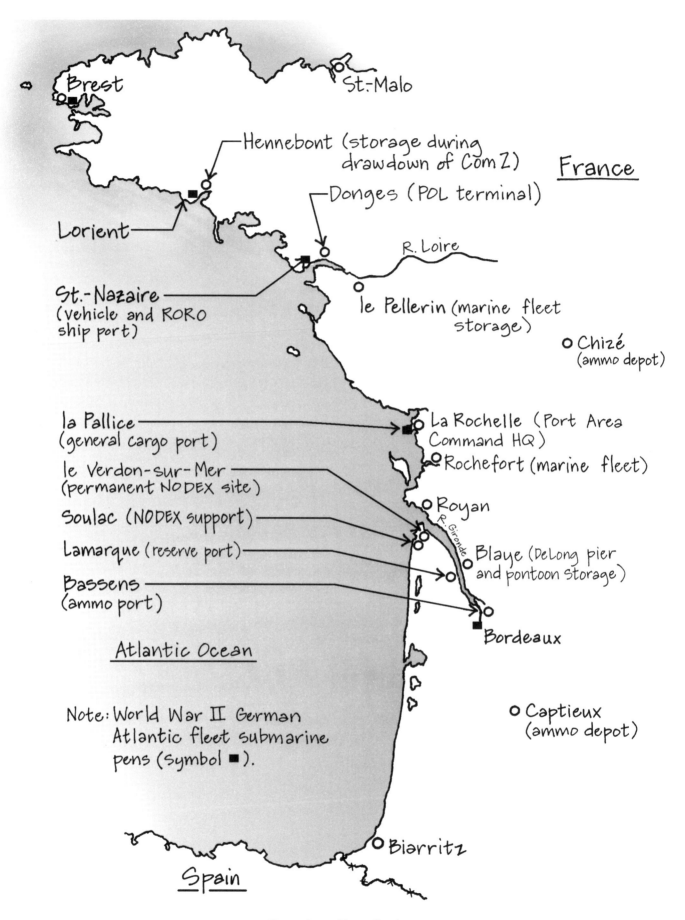

Port Area Installations

TEN

Army Ports and Over the Beach Exercises

"It was a tricky business to unload ships without a port."
(SFC Irvin Wilson, 81st Transportation Co, Rochefort, 03 March 1955)

Fixed and Emergency Ports

French ports were needed to receive weapons and ammunition; petroleum products; tracked and wheeled vehicles; and other supplies and equipment shipped from depots, factories, and refineries in the US.[1-3] Ports offered to the US by France had been heavily damaged during World War II. The port at Bassens (Bordeaux) would be rehabilitated primarily to receive ammunition, the port at la Pallice (La Rochelle) to receive general cargo and troops, and the port at St.-Nazaire to receive petroleum products and vehicles. It was believed that the ports of Nantes, Cherbourg, Brest, and Lorient also would be needed during wartime.[4]

In 1953, planners at the Pentagon intended to supply Seventh Army during wartime by moving supplies through the Gironde Estuary. Four ships would berth at Bassens and twenty additional ships would anchor far apart near improvised jetties so attack by the Soviets would be complicated.[5] Exercises in the 1950s and early 1960s over beaches at more than a dozen locations, from St.-Jean-de-Luz near Spain to Quiberon in Brittany, revealed better methods to discharge supplies.

Forty-eight offshore discharge exercises were conducted using innovative methods such as aerial tramways and DeLong piers. Planners concluded that during a war, ships anchored offshore or in midstream, unloaded by amphibious vehicles and landing craft, would be best. Ideally, emergency operations would be "discharge and run" so the Soviets would not have fixed targets.[6,7]

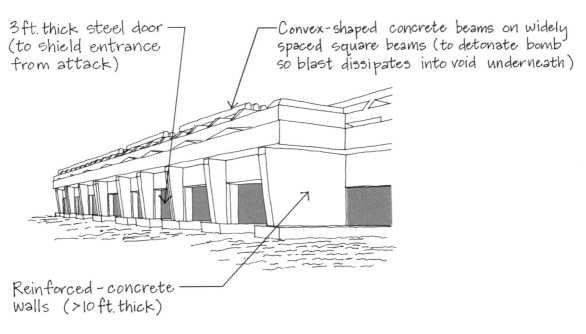

German Submarine Pens at Bordeaux

German Submarine Pens

From 1940 to 1943, the Germans built massive, blast-resistant submarine pens at Brest, Lorient, St.-Nazaire, la Pallice, Bordeaux, and Marseille. The pens were sheltered docks for servicing and repairing the U-boat Atlantic fleet. Reinforced-concrete walls more than 10-ft thick and roofs more than 20-ft thick were constructed in layers to provide blast-absorbing chambers. The top surface was covered with convex-shaped concrete ribs to detonate bombs before they could penetrate the roof. The complex at la Pallice was built in 1941 by 1,800 forced laborers.[8, 9] Blast-resistant pens for minesweepers and torpedo boats were built at Cherbourg, Le Havre, Boulogne, and Dunkerque.

British RAF bombing raids in January and February 1943 at Lorient and St.-Nazaire caused little damage to the pens, but flattened the centers of both towns.[10] The pens were so strongly fortified that Lorient, St.-Nazaire, and la Pallice held out until the end of the war. Allied bombing raids in August 1944 at la Pallice and Brest also caused little damage to the pens, but damaged the surrounding areas. Targets were seldom hit because pilots maneuvered every few seconds over the target, hoping to avoid anti-aircraft fire from the ground. US Army bombing accuracy did not improve until Col Curtis E. LeMay ordered his pilots to stop zigzagging over the target. LeMay, a civil engineering graduate from Ohio State University, reasoned that the less time the bombers spent over the target, the less time the Germans would have to shoot them down. LeMay's "straight-and-level" bombing method also significantly reduced civilian casualties from errant bombs.[11]

During the Cold War, the US Army used port facilities near the abandoned pens at St.-Nazaire, la Pallice, and Bordeaux. At la Pallice, Army barges and the 97th Transportation Co (Port) fireboat were berthed at the pens. Each December, Santa Claus (*Père Noël*) sailed into La Rochelle harbor on the fireboat, carrying gifts for French and American children. In the late 1960s, the US government built an enormous in-earth structure at Mount Pony near Culpeper, Virginia, to store $3 billion in coins and currency believed necessary to reprime the economy after a nuclear attack by the Soviets.[12] For similar purposes, in 1961 the US Army evaluated the abandoned 60-ft high U-boat command bunker at la Pallice for use as secure storage for large amounts of foreign currency.[13] Resistance forces could use the currency to fund unconventional warfare operations if the Soviets invaded. In the 1980s, several scenes for the German movie *Das Boot* were filmed at the pens at la Pallice. On the face of the reinforced-concrete shelter over the nearby lock, the film crew repainted the faded German motto, *Wir banen für den Sieg!* (We are working for victory!)

Bordeaux

In December 1950, more than 1,000 GIs arrived at Bordeaux to establish temporary port operations at Blaye, Lamarque, and Bassens, and a large ammunition depot at Captieux. Initially, the troops lived west of Bordeaux in tents at Camp Sougé, which had been built during World War I for Gen John J. Pershing's Doughboys. Army engineers also had built a 10-berth wooden dock at Bassens. During the Cold War, Army installations were scattered throughout the Bordeaux area due to the lack of sufficient land or buildings available at one location. Brig Gen Charles C. Blanchard, BASEC commander, believed the French Army liaison officer at Bordeaux did little to assist the US Army.[14] Initially, Bordeaux Detachment headquarters, commanded by Col Cornelius A. Lichiria, were at the Hôtel Bon Repas; MPs were at 1, rue Rolland. Officers were billeted in several rooms leased at the Hôtel des 7 Frères on rue Porte Dijeaux. Because US Army, Europe (USAREUR) estimated that more than 47 million maps would be required during a war with the Soviets, a map printing and storage center was established by Army engineers in the leased Pillot shoe factory in Bordeaux.[15] Engineer personnel prepared most maps of Europe by using aerial photographs that were coordinated with clearly identifiable surveyed points on the ground. Topographic maps for military operations were prepared at a scale of 1:25,000; for beach operations at a scale of 1:10,000 or larger.[16] Until it moved in 1959 to Orléans, the USAREUR Adjutant General Publications and Records Center leased space at the former Tannerie Tainturier factory in Bordeaux.

Communist Protests

Initially, troops endured violent protests and vandalism, usually instigated by communists. During his address to the Anglo-American Press Club on 03 December 1952 in Paris, Maj Gen Samuel D. Sturgis, Jr., ComZ commander, cited the courage of SSgt Morris A. Garrett. Garrett, alone and unarmed on a Sunday evening, was stabbed and beaten unconscious by a communist mob as he tried to defend an Army warehouse in Bacalan. Before the MPs arrived, almost two-hundred vandals broke windows, battered down locked doors, and tried to set fire to the warehouse.[17] The seriously wounded sergeant was hospitalized for three months. When asked about the effectiveness of communist propaganda, Sturgis said vandalism, such as slashed tires, broken windows, and snapped-off radio antennas of American cars, was on the decline. Troops also had learned to laugh at slogans, such as "U.S. Go Home," *les américains en Amérique*, and *Bordeaux restera français*, painted on walls.[18]

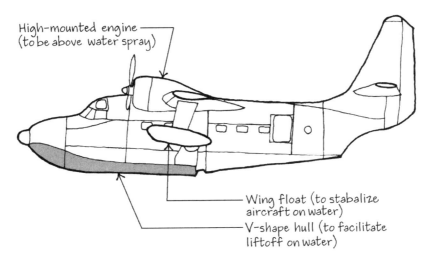

SA-16A Albatross Amphibious Aircraft

Twelfth Air Rescue Group

In May 1952, the 126th Bomb Wing (Light) moved to Laon AB and the 12th Air Rescue Group (ARG) became the primary tenant at Bordeaux AB. From 1952 to 1955, the 12th ARG flew three SA-16A Albatross (amphibious, fixed-wing aircraft, dubbed the "ugly duck") and eight H-19B Chickasaw search and rescue helicopters. When they jumped, para-rescue airmen of the 81st Air Rescue Squadron, commanded by Maj Rufus R. Hessleberg, wore wire mesh masks and canvas suits to deflect tree branches, which could stab them like spears when they landed. The 35th Crash Rescue Boat Flight operated four rescue boats that were docked at Bacalan near the World War II German submarine pens. Two boats, each operated by a crew of ten airmen, were 63-ft long; two were 24-ft long. The forty airmen of the 35th, commanded by Capt John B. White, trained to rescue survivors of boat accidents and air crashes in the ocean.[19, 20]

In 1954, the 12th ARG assigned three H-19B Chickasaw helicopters and two rescue boats to the French Air Force base at Cazaux, near Arcachon. On 01 July 1955, a formal agreement for US Air Force tenant use of Cazaux BA was signed by the US and France. The US was authorized use of barracks, mess hall, motor pool, and portions of two hangars, and space was allocated for parking more than thirty US fighter aircraft.[21] The US was granted one-third of air-to-air firing ranges at Biscarrosse and one-half of air-to-ground firing ranges at Cazaux. Each year, fighter aircraft squadrons from US air bases in France, Germany, and the Netherlands were sent to Cazaux for two to four weeks of gunnery training. Squadrons primarily flew F-86 Sabre and F-100D Super Sabre jet fighter aircraft. Rescue operations were practiced on Lake Cazaux until 1957 when the US Air Force stopped used Cazaux gunnery ranges on a regular basis.[22] From 1958 to 1960, air forces from six NATO nations participated at Cazaux in an annual two-week-long, air-to-air gunnery competition in live fire at aerial targets and dogfighting armed with gun cameras.

Bassens

The port at Bassens was in ruins when the US Army arrived in 1950. The initial tasks at Bassens were to clear the port for inbound cargo ships and to hire French stevedores (*dockers*) to unload ammunition. Because American port operations had to compete with commercial companies for scarce facilities and skilled labor, Americans paid wages well above union scale during the buildup. French communists tried to discourage dockers from unloading American ships. Although the dockers union called for strikes and other forms of protest, operations in December 1950 were disrupted for only one day. French workers traditionally would strike for higher wages or better working conditions, but not for political reasons which only meant they would lose wages. Because there were no sorting areas on the docks, cargo had to be rapidly cleared from the port.

In August 1953, troops at Bassens finally moved into metal prefabs installed on a tract of pastureland near the port. When grading the site for the prefabs, dozer operators of the 83rd Engineers learned to avoid the chickens, ducks, and geese wandering in the pasture. Brig Gen Ernest A. Bixby called the new quarters the best troop housing in France and described the old site, only a mile away, as the worst "hellhole" he had seen in his long Army career.[23] At the old site, departing Germans had demolished a nearby chemical factory and poured huge vats of sulfuric acid into the soil. Tents for the GIs were pitched on the contaminated soil. When it rained, the US Army worked in a yellow, mustard-like soup.[24] In May 1964, the property used for troop housing was returned to the French government. Three months later, the land was reacquired for use as a storage site for engineer port construction equipment relocated from Rochefort.

Gradignan

In 1952, troops moved from Camp Sougé to winterized tents at Gradignan and at Domaine de Bersol in Pessac. Engineers cleared an area at Gradignan to dispose of live ammunition dug up during construction. A 5-ft deep trench, almost a mile long, encircled the demolition area to serve as a fire break. The main building at Gradignan had been a tuberculosis sanatorium for French children so GIs had to stoop to wash or shave.[25] In spring 1953, Company A of 83rd Engineers, led by 1st Lt John D. Flanagan, assembled prefabs for a PX and commissary. A nearby château was remodeled to serve as a dispensary and dependents school for one-hundred fifty children of troops in Bordeaux.[26] The PX was formally opened on 16 June 1953 by SHAPE Supreme Commander Gen Matthew B. Ridgway during his farewell tour, before returning to Washington, DC to become US Army Chief of Staff.

Ridgway asked Cpl Darland Heaps of the 687th Engineer Co (Water Supply) at Bersol about Army food. When Heaps said that it was not very good, Ridgway told an aide to be sure the men, especially those who were living in tents, received better food. Heaps gained respect from his fellow GIs for speaking up to a four-star general. The PX, operated in cooperation with the US Air Force, stocked hundreds of German cuckoo clocks, which were a popular gift for GIs to send home.

Initially, drinking water at Gradignan was supplied by tankers of the 687th Engineers. Lister bags were suspended from wood-frame tripods set up in shaded areas throughout the installation. Evaporation from the canvas bags cooled the water. The Enlisted Men's Club billed itself as "Base Section's smallest EM Club." In 1955, it featured steaks at 50¢ each. In 1957, the commissary at Gradignan moved to the Air Force Supply Depot at Bacalan.

Camp Crespy and Caserne Xaintrailles

The US Army shared Camp Crespy in Talence with French troops of the 4th Military Region. US troops set up a small tent city, rehabilitated seven existing buildings, and installed prefabs at Crespy.[27] The French Army's band room was used for court-martial proceedings.

Although the French Army occupied Caserne Xaintrailles, a small part was used by the Signal Corps for a communications center. Like the American "Hello Girls" working in France for AT&T during World War I, French women were hired to operate the US Army telephone system. Most of the operators were reasonably bilingual. On 22 February 1956, during the worst winter storm to hit Bordeaux in the 20th Century, all transportation shut down. Throughout the blizzard, fifteen operators manned their teletype machines and the telephone switchboard in the communications center. To reach the caserne, some of the women had to walk more than six miles in the bitter cold through 3-ft high drifts of snow.[28]

The Bordeaux Rail Transportation Office also used office space at the caserne. Sgt Robert H. Campbell, at 62 the Army's oldest enlisted man, worked in the office during 1952-53. Campbell was no stranger to the region. He had worked with the 71st Engineer Construction Regiment in 1920-21 on the Môle d'Escale at la Pallice.[29]

Housing

At first, most married officers and NCOs lived in hotels or rented apartments in the Bordeaux area. In 1954, one-hundred thirty-two housing units were built at Pessac for the US Air Force. The French developer was guaranteed five years rental income by the US government housing program, called guaranteed rental income (GRI) by USAF and rental guarantee housing (RGH) by the Army. Another sixteen housing units of identical design were added at Pessac and fifty-two units at Cenon. By 1956, the Air Force presence in the Bordeaux area had been significantly reduced. The more than 1,700 officers and airmen of the 126th Light Bomb Wing at Mérignac had moved to Laon AB and the 12th Air Rescue Group had departed. Because the Army also reduced its presence, the need for government housing diminished. In 1958, one-hundred ten of the one-hundred forty-eight housing units at Pessac were unoccupied. The French were appalled that Americans would abandon new homes in a region where housing was scarce, and wanted the homes to be rented or sold to the public. However, the US believed it would be prudent to keep its housing stock because of the variability of personnel requirements. Until withdrawal in 1967, troop levels in France would rise or fall depending on periods of crisis or tranquility.

USO Centers

Because of the buildup of troops in southwestern France during the Berlin Wall Crisis, a USO Center was opened in 1962 at 4, place Jean-Jaurès in Bordeaux. Like the USO in Paris, it had game and television rooms, tour information, and refreshments for GIs and their families. The USO provided counseling services, operated snack bars, arranged dances, and sponsored "live" shows.

United Service Organizations (USO) Centers

City	Location	City	Location
Bordeaux	4, place Jean-Jaurès	Nice	14, ave Felix Faure
Cannes	8, rue Émile Negrin	Paris	93, ave des Champs Élysées

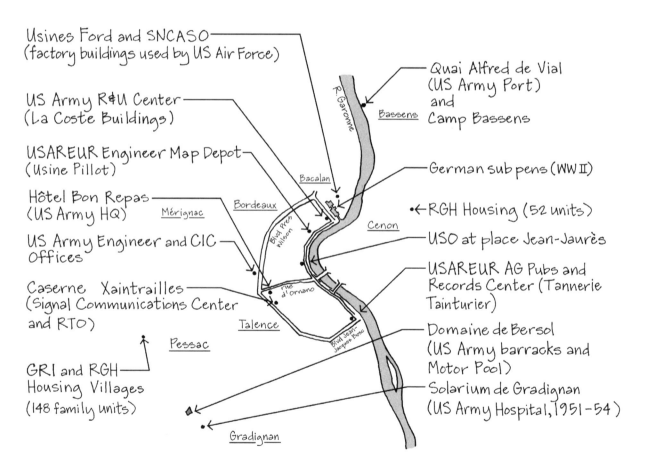

Bordeaux Area Installations

Bordeaux Area US Army Installations (1952-55)

Installation	Location	Activity and Units
Headquarters	Bordeaux (Hôtel Bon Repas, 191, rue d'Ornano)	Bordeaux District Command
	Bassens (Château de Lagarde)	Sub-depot at Camp Bassens
	Gradignan	Southern District Command of Base Section
Depots and Support	Bacalan (Usine Pillot, 56-62, cours Balguerie-Stuttenberg)	USAREUR Engineer Base Reproduction Plant (map depot, 1 acre)
	Bordeaux (Tannerie Tainturier, 53, Blvd Jean-Jacques Bosc)	USAREUR Adjutant General (AG) Publications and Records Center (4 acres)
	Bacalan (La Coste Buildings, 69-75, cours Édouard Vaillant)	US Army Repairs & Utilities (R&U) Center (1 acre)
	Bacalan (91, rue Blanqui)	Warehouses
	Bordeaux (55, Blvd Wilson)	66th CIC Field Office
	Bordeaux (39, rue Bouffard)	Provost Marshal
	Bordeaux (Caserne Xaintrailles)	US Army Signal Communications Center Rail Transportation Office (RTO)
	Cestas	Off-depot storage site (205 acres)
	Pessac (Domain de Bersol)	Motor pool, photo lab, joint USAFE-Army billeting office
	St.-Sulpice-et-Cameyrac	POL storage site (68 acres)
Ports	Bassens (Quai Alfred de Vial)	US Army Port Facility (7703rd Trans Major Port), cold storage plant
	Blaye (Port Basalan)	81st Transportation Co (Boat)
Dispensary	Gradignan (Solarium de Gradignan)	33rd Station Hospital (9 acres)
School (dependents)	Pessac	Elementary school (3 acres)
Housing (families)	Cenon (Cité Américaine)	52 Rental Guarantee Housing (RGH) units
	Pessac (at Pape Clément)	132 Guaranteed Rental Income (GRI) units 16 RGH units
Troop Barracks	Gradignan (40 acres) and Domaine de Bersol (82 acres)	83rd Engineer Battalion 7th Engineer Brigade (SCARWAF) 40th Engr Co (Pipeline) 687th Engr Co (Water Supply) 116th Med Det (Veterinary Food Insp) 594th Trans Gp (Traffic Regulating)
	Talence (Camp Crespy)	33rd Station Hospital 529th Military Police Co (Service) 343rd Medical Co (Preventive Medicine)
	Bassens (15 acres)	73rd Trans Co (Float Craft Maint) 81st Transportation Co (Boat) 98th Transportation Co (Port) 513th QM Co (Bath) 566th Army Postal Unit
	St.-Sulpice-et-Cameyrac (Izon)	889th QM Co (Petroleum) 4230th Labor Service Co
Commissary and Post Exchange	Gradignan	Operated in cooperation with USAFE

Recreation	Bordeaux (Café La Fayette, 19-21, rue Mably)	Special Services Club
	Bordeaux (6, cours de l'Intendance)	Officers Club
	Gradignan	Baseball field, EM Club
	Mérignac (US Air Base)	Bowling alley (USAFE)
	Pessac (Château de Bersol)	NCO Club
Training Site	Mérignac (Camp Luchey-Halde)	French Army firing range

Abbreviations

CIC	Counter Intelligence Corps	SCARWAF	Special Category Army with Air Force
NCO	Noncommissioned Officer	USAFE	US Air Forces in Europe
POL	Petroleum, oil & lubricants	USAREUR	US Army, Europe

Cherbourg

Prior to World War II, Cherbourg had been a passenger port where large ocean liners could berth. In June 1944, the German occupiers sank ships in the harbors, mined three large basins, and destroyed piers, cranes, and terminal buildings. After D-Day, US Army engineers removed booby traps and rehabilitated the port. By September 1944 it could handle 14,000 tons of cargo per day.[30] After Germany surrendered in May 1945, Cherbourg was used by the US military to evacuate the sick and wounded. In 1947, the American Graves Registration Command (AGRC) began using a terminal to send remains of war dead home. By 1949, most of the AGRC primary mission to locate remains and to establish permanent cemeteries had been completed, and its personnel had been greatly reduced. A fifty-man detachment, commanded by Maj William S. Terrell, was retained at Cherbourg to carry out administration and logistical functions of the European Command units in France that had previously been handled by AGRC. Redesignated the 7805th Area Command Det, it was stationed at the Nacqueville Cablehead.[31] The trans-Atlantic cablehead connection at Cherbourg was essential for military communications with Washington, DC. Because telephone lines were rare at the locations of US installations, radio relay stations had to be built across France.

During the buildup of US forces in 1950, military equipment and supplies were unloaded at Cherbourg. If the Soviets invaded Western Europe in the early 1950s, the port would be used to support an emergency withdrawal of US forces to England. After the buildup of ComZ, the port rarely was used. In the late 1950s, a platoon from the 553rd Engineer Battalion was stationed at Cherbourg for construction work. In 1958, the plywood-tar paper hutments (called "channel shanties") were replaced by metal prefabs.

During the Berlin Wall Crisis in 1961, five ships discharged 4,570 US Army troops at Cherbourg and cargo was shipped to the port.[32] The USNS *Gen Simon B. Buckner* was the first ship to discharge US troops at Cherbourg in fifteen years. On 11 October 1961, five-hundred troops debarked at Cherbourg, one-thousand sailed on to Bremerhaven, Germany. At the dock, Maj Gen Henry R. Westphalinger, ComZ commander, greeted the troops assigned to France. Using a bullhorn, he told the troops: "Some of you will have to live in tents for a time—but I promise you, you won't be living in the mud." Consequently, at the temporary tent camps, Army engineers poured concrete floor slabs and built walkways and roads surfaced with gravel.[33] Westphalinger's staff at Orléans called the portly general, "Fat Henry."[34] On 17 October, the USNS *Gen Alexander M. Patch* discharged two-thousand troops at Cherbourg.

In 1961-62, drivers of the 37th Transportation Command hauled cargo from Cherbourg, a greater distance from their home installations than the ports at Bordeaux, La Rochelle, and St.-Nazaire. Somewhat inexplicably, planners at ComZ in Orléans had overlooked the advantages of using existing Army port facilities for the emergency buildup ordered by President Kennedy.[35] However, la Pallice at La Rochelle was used when the Berlin Wall Crisis abated. On 11 and 12 August 1962, more than two-thousand US Army officers and enlisted men boarded the USNS *Gen W. H. Gordon* to sail to the US. During the embarkation at la Pallice, civilian vehicle and pedestrian traffic had to be restricted by gendarmes due to limited space on the dock.[36]

Le Havre
Prior to World War II, Le Havre had been a principal passenger port and commercial harbor, containing eleven major docks. Many Americans, including Gold Star Mothers of World War I, got their first glimpse of France at Le Havre. During the liberation of France, the Allies damaged the port by air raids that sank about twenty German ships. The Germans demolished the rest of the port when they retreated. Between 05 and 11 September 1944, Allied bombers destroyed most of Le Havre, killing more than 2,000 civilians.[37] In late September 1944, US Army engineers began rehabilitating the port so troops, ammunition, and supplies could flow into France. By summer 1945, the flow of troops was reversed. Troops and supplies now were needed for the war with Japan.[38]

The US Army used Le Havre in the early 1950s to receive shipments of POL prior to completion of the Donges-Metz pipeline in 1956. On 17 February 1953, the first ComZ dependents to sail to France by commercial ship arrived at Le Havre on the SS *America*. Personnel from the 594th Transportation Traffic Regulation Group gave welcome packages to the one-hundred eighty-two dependents and put them on the "boat train" to Paris.[39] Although dependents were sent by commercial ship to Le Havre,

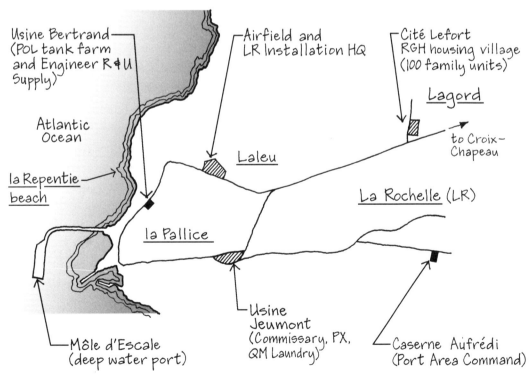

La Rochelle Area Installations (1958)

most GIs who sailed by troopship to France arrived at la Pallice. After a lull of almost five years, American ships docked at Le Havre in 1961 during the Berlin Wall Crisis.[40]

In late 1963, ships began discharging mail at Le Havre for delivery to APOs in France. Previously mail had been discharged at Bremerhaven, Germany. Using Le Havre reduced delivery times by seven to ten days.[41] Starting in May 1966, privately owned vehicles (POVs) were shipped from the port of Le Havre to the US. Previously POVs had been shipped from the port of St.-Nazaire. It took about three to five weeks in transit from drop-off to pick-up at US ports.[42]

La Rochelle

On 10 August 1950, Col Hubert E. Klemp led an eight-man site evaluation team from 7966 EUCOM Detachment in Paris to La Rochelle. Although the LOC Agreement was still being negotiated, the team surveyed facilities at the port of la Pallice, Usine Jeumont, and Caserne Aufrédi. The team also inspected the 100-ton floating crane which the US Army had sent to la Pallice from Hamburg, Germany. Floating cranes were used for heavy lifts during engineer port construction operations and to speed discharge of a ship. Cranes could be positioned on the offshore side so cargo could be unloaded from both sides of a ship.[43] In addition to the crane, train loads of ammunition from Germany were arriving at Captieux and Rochefort. The French Army attempted to keep secret the shipments of US military supplies and equipment, but the communist *Les Nouvelles de Bordeaux et du Sud-Ouest* published the serial numbers and contents of the railcars. The LOC Agreement signed on 06 November 1950, sanctioned what was already underway. In December 1950, one-hundred seventy-five GIs, commanded by Lt Col Paul E. Haines, arrived at La Rochelle to establish headquarters at Caserne Aufrédi, a QM depot at Usine Jeumont, and port operations at la Pallice. By the end of the month, the first American ship since World War II, the USNS *Private Francis A. McGraw*, docked at la Pallice.

Army Terminal at Port of La Pallice

The wharf (*Môle d'Escale*) at la Pallice, originally built in 1917 for Pershing's Doughboys, had been damaged by the Germans at the end of World War II. Rebuilding the deep-water port and extending the dock area were top priorities for the Army. The terminal did not have defined berths for ships and, because there was insufficient area to sort cargo, initially it took seven to eight days to unload ships. Stevedoring was provided by the *Société Navale Delmas-Vieljeux* under contact to the US Army. The terminal operated on French time, including two-hour lunch breaks for the dockers. The Army operated the 100-ton floating crane in addition to using the six huge French dockside lift cranes at the repaired môle. Four warehouses were leased for storage. Most cargo was rapidly cleared from the port by Army trucks or shipped on SNCF railcars. After rehabilitation, the five rail spurs at the môle could park one-hundred fifty-four railcars.[44, 45] The rail spur behind the former German submarine pens at la Pallice was used to store oversized cargo until it could be loaded onto special railcars or routed by SNCF to avoid low bridges and narrow tunnels.

Port Area Command

The US Army Port Area Command received cargo from the US, prepared and stored cargo for distribution to US forces in Europe, and supervised exercises to discharge cargo over the beaches. In December 1950, the *McGraw* delivered 6,000 tons of gasoline, shipped in thousands of 55-gal drums

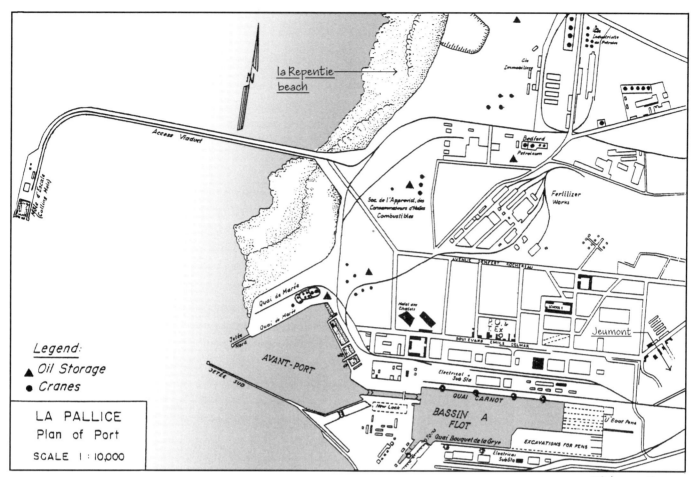

Port at la Pallice

and jerry cans.[46] Most of the dock workers were communists whose union, the *Confédération générale du travail* (CGT), opposed the US buildup. Early in 1950 after communist unions at Bassens announced they would not unload ships carrying NATO armaments, two ships were diverted to Antwerp, Belgium.[47] A 25 December strike called to protest the American presence fizzled out because the lure of jobs that paid good wages trumped union loyalty. However, devoted French communists sarcastically referred to the stevedores who worked for the Americans at la Pallice as *valets des américains*. Communist newspapers mocked them such as the 28 December 1951 article "*Le Silence des Valets!*" in *Les Nouvelles de Bordeaux et du Sud-Ouest*.

During 1951, French communists painted "Americans Assassins—Go Home" on walls throughout La Rochelle. French youngsters on bicycles got into the anti-American spirit by knocking hats off GIs in uniform. The cyclists pedaling stealthily approached GIs from behind, swatted at hats, and then sped off, knowing GIs on foot could not catch them.[48] In August 1951, a more serious incident occurred in Châtelaillon-Plage when Frenchman Henri de Buffon attacked the car of US Army nurse Capt Dale A. Hawkins, who was accompanied by four nurses from the 319th Station Hospital at Caserne Aufrédi. Hawkins had stopped her Chevy because a large crowd leaving a circus performance blocked the road. De Buffon became enraged after his Simca bumped Hawkins' fender as he pulled out of a parking space. De Buffon first broke the radio antenna, and then he and his female companion pounded on Hawkins' car, using clenched fists and a long metal bar which shattered the front windshield. The unprovoked attack terrified the nurses. Hawkins required medical treatment for cuts to her face from the flying glass. De Buffon attempted to incite anti-American sentiment by claiming Hawkins had repeatedly honked her car horn, pushed people aside with her fender as she tried to drive through the crowd, and hurled insults at the bystanders. Based solely on the preposterous statement de Buffon made to the French police, Préfet Robert Holveck of the Charente-Maritime blamed the nurses, claiming that their aggressive behavior disturbed the tranquility of the village. However, according to Brig Gen Charles C. Blanchard's investigation, de Buffon had willfully injured Hawkins without provocation and terrorized the nurses, none of whom spoke French.[49]

Port Activities

On 09 December 1951, more than 1,300 US Air Force troops of the 126th Bomb Wing (Light), commanded by Col Wilson V. Newhall and assigned to Bordeaux AB, debarked from the USNS *Gen H. F. Hodge*s at la Pallice in just over two hours. It was the first large troop debarkation in southern France since World War II.[50] In August 1952, the 7703rd Transportation Major Port transported two-hundred fifty enlisted men to Bremerhaven, Germany, on the USNS *Gen Stuart Heintzelman*, which was scheduled to continue on to Bremerhaven after discharging passengers at la Pallice. Major Lyle W. Edgar, Assistant Adjutant General at Base Section headquarters, suggested taking advantage of the empty bunks on the troopship. Transporting the GIs by ship to Germany rather than by train saved $8,000.[51] During the second half of 1952, the port processed more than 1,000 POVs shipped from the US. By the late 1950s, the American presence had become so large that more than 1,200 French employees worked at US installations throughout the La Rochelle area. On 12 August 1962, during the end of the Berlin Wall Crisis, two-thousand GIs sailed home from la Pallice on the USNS *Gen W. H. Gordon*. On 09 December 1963, after most of the Base Section shut down, the SS *Jean Lafitte* became the last American ship to dock at la Pallice.

WAC Lieutenants Margaret C. Crawford, Harriet A. Simons, and Thelma A. Payne, La Rochelle, July 1952 (US Army)

Army vehicle park at former German submarine pen, la Pallice, September 1952 (US Army)

Usine Jeumont

Usine Jeumont, located near the abandoned German submarine pens in la Pallice, was a former civilian enterprise that imported exotic wood. During the German occupation, one of the buildings had been used to manufacture torpedoes. The 102nd QM Bakery Co (Mobile), headquartered at Jeumont, had detached platoons at Bussac, Orléans, and Verdun. Each platoon used mobile equipment to produce baked bread for mess halls and commissaries. Forty-nine new and rehabilitated buildings were completed by 1958. The new structures provided nearly ¼ million sq ft of covered storage and maintenance space. Also completed were troop barracks, dependents nursery school, bowling alley, gymnasium, laundry, commissary, PX, post office, and EES gas station. Only authorized Americans could use the PX; the French were limited to browsing. The PX shelves and countertops were stacked high with so many dry goods, rarely available in French stores, that the Rochelais called Jeumont the *caverns d'Ali-Baba*.[52] The new laundry, which had a capacity of 10,000 lbs of clothes per day, employed one-hundred twenty French civilians. Initially the laundry served troops at installations along the coast from Rochefort to St.-Nazaire and inland to Fontenet and St.-Jean d'Angély.[53] Rates were $1 to launder twenty-five pieces of clothing and $1 to dry clean four pieces.

Veterinarians at Jeumont

In 1955-57, 1st Lt Frank A. Ramsey, a licensed veterinarian, commanded fourteen enlisted men of the 73rd Medical Detachment (Vet Food Insp). Immediately after a ship docked, 73rd Med Det personnel inspected the cargo in the holds to be sure the cartons of food were dry and had not been damaged in transit. During rough seas, salt water could flood the hatches. The detachment was stationed at Jeumont because most of the food shipped to Europe for US forces was unloaded at la Pallice. Ramsey's GIs learned how to inspect food at the US Army Medical Services Meat and Dairy Hygiene School, Chicago, Illinois. It was important that food and beverages, served in mess halls and clubs or on sale at commissaries, were safe. Personnel had to determine that food products were properly wrapped, transported, and stored. Detachment personnel also were responsible for food purchased in Europe. They inspected food suppliers throughout Base Section to be sure they met Army sanitation standards. For example, doors and windows were to have screens to keep out insects, employees were to wear hair nets and frequently wash their hands, and meat-cutting knives were to be sterilized between cutting carcasses. These sanitation procedures were unheard of in postwar rural France. In the French dairy industry, employers did not supply toilet paper, soap, hot water, or towels for their employees.[54] First Sgt Andrew Gibson assigned personnel to their food inspection tasks. Before ships could be unloaded during offshore discharge exercises, personnel boarded the ships to inspect the subsistence cargo.

Personnel of the 73rd Med Det also took care of pets of US military personnel and the aggressive German shepherd guard dogs used at Army installations in Base Section and Air Force installations at Chizé and Bordeaux. Guard dog were trained so everyone except its master was an enemy, therefore even a routine teeth cleaning was a challenge.[55] Three Polish Labor Service guards were required to hold the dog so Ramsey could scrape its teeth without being bitten. At Bordeaux AB, Ramsey had to improvise during surgery on a guard dog that had been hit by a 2½-ton truck. Ramsey used a large stainless-steel soup spoon, with the handle cut off, to cover the crushed portion of the dog's skull. The dog survived and, after it recuperated, returned to duty.[56]

Caserne Aufrédi

Base Section headquarters was established at Caserne Aufrédi, located on Place de Verdun in downtown La Rochelle. The caserne was named for Alexandré Aufrédi, a wealthy 13th Century French merchant who invested his entire fortune in a fleet of trading ships. When the fleet did not return, Aufrédi was abandoned by his friends and became a homeless beggar. According to local legend, the fleet unexpectedly returned seven years later and Aufrédi's wealth was restored. His former friends reappeared, teaching him the true meaning of hypocrisy. Moved by this experience, Aufrédi devoted his life to supporting the poor of La Rochelle.[57]

Caserne Aufrédi entrance on rue Aufrédy, La Rochelle, January 1952 (US Army)

When GIs of the 7964 Area Command arrived at Caserne Aufrédi on 07 November 1950, they found their new home in ruins. The crumbling buildings, many with barnyard animals living in the corridors, needed extensive structural repairs. One bunk fell through the floor with a GI in it. The buildings were not heated, had no electricity, and there was only one latrine. Once a week troops were driven to Laleu for a cold shower.[58] Some of the underground network of tunnels in La Rochelle led into basements of buildings at the caserne. The Army blocked off the tunnels for security and to hold back sea water. To protest the use of the caserne by Americans, French communists staged demonstrations in Place de Verdun. Prior to the demonstrations, MPs removed American-owned vehicles from the area and troops were ordered to stay indoors.

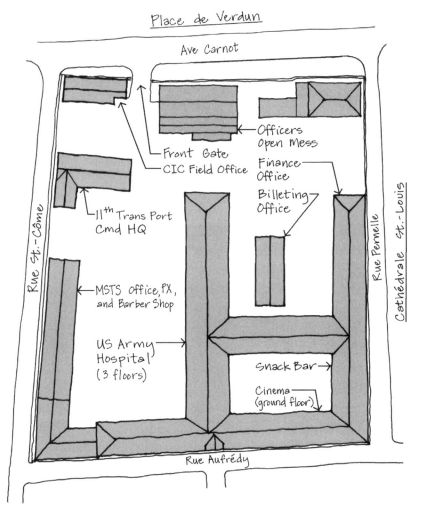

Caserne Aufrédi (1957)

Two upper floors of Hôpital M. d'Auffredy buildings at the caserne were used by the 319th Station Hospital for clinics, pharmacy, and hospital ward. In early 1953, the ward was enlarged to one-hundred fourteen beds and an officer's ward, pediatrics ward, and delivery room. In June 1953, when the 319th Station Hospital was transferred to Camp Bussac, the 28th General Hospital, commanded by Col Fred J. Fielding, took over operations at La Rochelle. Enlisted personnel assigned to Aufrédi lived at the site of a medical depot being built near Croix-Chapeau. Army buses shuttled them between La Rochelle and Croix-Chapeau. From August 1951 to October 1954, the hospital at Aufrédi averaged two-hundred sixty admissions a month. In 1956, after Base Section headquarters moved to Poitiers, the 11th Transportation Terminal Command moved from Gradignan to Caserne Aufrédi.

Commanding Generals, Base Section (La Rochelle)

Commanding General	Period	Events
Col John W. Mott	1950-51	Initial occupation of ports and depots. Troops live in tents and dilapidated casernes.
BG Charles C. Blanchard	1951-52	Buildup of ports and depots. First supply over the beach exercise (SOB).
BG Ernest A. Bixby	1953 (Jan-Sep)	SOBs continue. Troops move into metal prefabs at Bassens (Aug 53). Dependents elementary schools open.
MG Philip E. Gallagher	1953-54	Troops continue move into prefabs.
MG Oliver P. Newman	1954 (Feb-Oct)	First new offshore discharge exercise (NODEX). French and American flags flown at US installations.
BG Bogardus S. Cairns	1954-55	Seven NODEXs conducted. Construction of housing villages and standby hospitals.
BG James K. Woolnough	1955-57	Aerial tramway tested (April-June 56). Base Section headquarters moves from La Rochelle to Poitiers, becomes 5th Log Command.

Recreation and Training

Space for an Officers Club at the Restaurant Hollywood and the Cinéma Trianon in La Rochelle were leased for five years so personnel could relax after long workdays in mud and rubble. Wood-surfaced tennis courts in La Rochelle's municipal gymnasium on rue des Gentilshommes could be reserved for 60¢ per hour. On 24 December 1953, an NCO Club opened at the leased Petite Casino in Châtelaillon-Plage, a twenty minute drive south of La Rochelle. In the fall of 1955, the club moved into a nearby 35-room 17th Century château which had been used in World War II as a hospital for German soldiers. The facility had bedrooms for GIs on temporary duty (TDY), a nursery for dependent children, and a restaurant. For training, GIs used the Pointe de Roux firing range on the beach at Aytré. The range could not be used on Thursday, Saturday, or Sunday when oyster farmers were working in the nearby oyster beds.[59]

Croix-Chapeau

The site of the Croix-Chapeau medical depot had been used as a coal storage depot by the US Army in World War I. Troops at first lived in tents. In late September 1952, hurricane winds blew away most of the tents at Croix-Chapeau. Several GIs, who tried to hold their tents against the 80 to 105 mph gusts, were carried 12 ft up into the air by the flying canvas.[60] The repaired tents were soon "winterized" by Company C of the 432nd Engineer Construction Battalion. GIs called the new structures "tarpaper shacks" because they had canvas roofs and wood panel sides covered by tarpaper. During the winter months, the winterized tents were so cold that GIs slept wearing their field jackets. Finally, in 1955, metal prefab barracks were installed. Stray dogs roamed throughout the site, biting some GIs. To be a good neighbor, US officials sought advice from French authorities and permission to put down aggressive dogs.[61] In August 1955, Croix-Chapeau headquarters ordered GI dog owners to properly supervise their pets and keep them under control so they did not disrupt Army formations. Dogs were required to have annual rabies shots and wear dog tags. Stray dogs would be turned over to French authorities for disposal.[62]

Detachments of the 687th Engineer Co (Water Supply), which arrived at Croix-Chapeau in April 1952, supplied drinking water to installations throughout Base Section. Commanded by Capt Robert V. Chambers, the company borrowed a drilling rig from Usine Bertrand to drill fresh water wells at Ingrandes, Chinon, and La Roche-sur-Yon. To haul water from Croix-Chapeau to distant posts, the company had four 1,500-gal semitrailers and twelve 1,000-gal 2½-ton water tankers.[63] In 1955 at Soulac, the third platoon installed a 3,000-gal rubber-coated collapsible storage tank and mounted 6,000-gal reservoirs on towers. During offshore discharge exercises at nearby le Verdon, troops used almost 14,000 gallons of treated water each day. Under the command of Capt Gregory J. Kuehl, who succeeded Chambers in July 1954, the 687th Engineers trained to provide potable water to troops in the field and continued to serve installations in Base Section until post engineers took responsibility for their own water supplies.

In 1955, the 60th Station Hospital moved from Poitiers to Croix-Chapeau. For three days in April 1956, GIs of the 60th Station Hospital pitched huge tents so medical staff could practice operating a 50-bed hospital in the field. The around-the-clock exercise divided personnel into sections that included: admission, X-ray, surgery, and patient wards. The medics diagnosed GIs who had simulated injuries, including battle fatigue. Bivouac techniques and security measures were evaluated by an infantry officer.[64]

In summer 1955, 1st Lt Robert A. Hedeen of the 485th Medical Co (Prev Med) discovered mosquito-infested areas surrounding La Rochelle, Rochefort, Bordeaux, Poitiers, and La Roche-sur-Yon. To reduce the risk of malaria, the preventative medicine company sprayed DDT on stagnant water, where mosquitoes breed, in the ditches and ponds near the Army installations.[65] In addition to insect control, the 485th inspected mess halls, troop barracks, and recreation facilities to be sure that conditions were hygienic.

In July 1958, an overnight readiness exercise was held at Croix-Chapeau. GIs from the 64th Medical Group set up tents, posted guards along the depot perimeter, and, wearing gas masks, resisted simulated attacks.[66]

By the late 1950s, the hospital at Caserne Aufrédi had closed. In May 1959, the 28th General Hospital moved into new buildings at the huge 70th Medical Depot complex at Croix-Chapeau, using wings of the 1,000-bed standby hospital. The depot, which employed nearly three-hundred French civilians, fabricated prescription eyeglasses and dental crowns for US European Command. When needed, supplies of rare blood types were flown from Germany to Châteauroux AD and transported by ambulance to Croix-Chapeau.[67, 68]

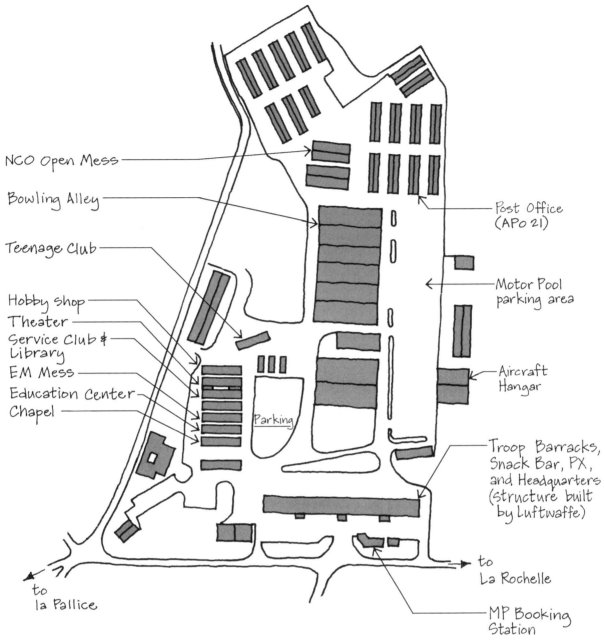

La Rochelle Installation at Laleu (1960)

Laleu

Laleu Installation was located at the site of an airfield adjacent to the ocean. In 1951, two transportation companies and a military police company were assigned to Laleu. GIs from the 529th Military Police Co slept in sleeping bags (dubbed "fart sacks") on metal cots in the abandoned airfield operations building. Because glass was missing from the windows, it was very cold.[69] Eventually, troops moved into a renovated 3-story, masonry building at Laleu that had been home to the German Luftwaffe during the occupation.

The 529th MP Co provided safety patrols for the La Rochelle area. Patrols normally consisted of two MPs and a French policeman. Before dawn on 26 June 1952, a patrol jeep was hit by rocks dropped from a railway bridge. The French policeman and one of the MPs were seriously injured.[70]

In 1953, the 529th MP Co was transferred to Germany. It was replaced by the 524th MP Battalion, commanded by Lt Col Robert T. Lisk. The 524th MP Bn, headquartered at Laleu, was divided into platoons and detachments assigned to posts from Bordeaux to Metz.[71] In 1955, the 524th MP Bn operated a training school at Laleu to teach new MPs French traffic regulations and signage, and how to work with French police. To patrol the 45,000 sq mi Base Section, the battalion only had sixty-two jeeps and sedans. On night patrols, MPs broke up fights in bars, picked up passed-out drunks, investigated robberies, and aided victims of vehicle accidents.[72]

After a fire in May 1952 destroyed several homes in the town of Laleu, forty French families temporarily were housed in tents at the Army installation.[73] Ever alert to highlight so-called "imperialist aggression," communist newspapers printed pictures of the tents at Laleu, alleging that the French were being forced out of their homes by Americans. This communist propaganda was met with widespread ridicule because most residents of the Charente-Maritime knew Brig Gen Charles C. Blanchard had instructed his troops to aid the homeless.[74] Four years later, GIs cleared rubble from a bomb damaged three-acre site in Laleu to be developed by a French Catholic charity for low-cost housing.[75]

In 1953 at Laleu, the Army had four small fixed-wing aircraft and two H-13 Sioux helicopters. The landing strip was not paved and aircraft parked in the motor pool area. The small aviation unit, commanded by Maj Hubert C. Beauchamp, was nicknamed "Air Petite ComZ." In addition to flying senior personnel, the aircraft flew search and rescue missions and reconnaissance to support offshore discharge exercises. During exercises, helicopters were stationed nearby, ready to fly injured troops to hospitals.[76]

In July 1954, Laleu Installation became La Rochelle Installation, commanded by Lt Col Robert M. Lantz. Lantz's responsibilities included activities at Laleu, and sub-installations at Usine Bertrand, Usine Jeumont, and Môle d'Escale.[77] La Rochelle Installation grew to include a chapel, theater, bowling alley, stockade, and swimming pool. Built next to the NCO Open Mess in 1960, the pool was 50-ft wide by 40-ft long, with a graded water depth of 2 ft to 12 ft.[78] Funds for the swimming pool were approved because engineer deep-water divers could use it for training.

Former US Army buildings at Laleu have been adapted for use as a school for French customs agents (*École Nationale des Douanes*). The school has mock-ups of air-terminal baggage claim areas and apartments so students can practice detecting custom violations. Its museum displays numerous ingenious methods used to smuggle illegal drugs and currency. The complex includes a roadway where students learn how to ride motorcycles and an indoor firing range. Also trained at Laleu are the dogs used to detect concealed illegal drugs (*stupéfiants*).

Lagord and Usine Bertrand

Until the pipeline from St.-Nazaire to Metz was completed, a fenced-in site at Lagord was used as a petroleum depot. The 889th Quartermaster Co, a reserve unit from San Francisco, California, stored POL products in huge stacks of jerry cans and 55-gal drums. Beginning in 1953, each morning Madame Simone Guyau herded more than fifty sheep through the main gate of the depot for grass-cutting duties. At dusk she herded the flock back to her nearby farm.[79]

At Usine Bertrand, engineers repaired graders, tractors, electric generators, cranes (such as the 90-ton cranes used during offshore discharge exercises), and stored a 35-ft high drilling rig that had been used to drill fresh water wells at Captieux and Rochefort.[80] A POL tank farm was developed at Usine Bertrand so acres of jerry cans and 55-gal drums no longer would be stacked in the open at Lagord and Dompierre.

Housing

In the beginning, all officer and NCO families lived on the economy. In 1951, three-hundred sixty-four Americans lived in homes and apartments in Châtelaillon-Plage and five-hundred twenty-six in Fouras, seaside resorts south of La Rochelle.[81] Because most of the homes were built for summer use and rented only during the summer, they did not have heating and many did not have indoor toilets. Although the Americans rented the homes year-round, landlords asked for higher rent during the summer months. Brig Gen Charles C. Blanchard intervened on behalf of his men. He wrote to local officials arguing that higher rents should not be charged because the rent from the yearly rentals significantly exceeded that of the exclusively summer rentals.

In September 1952, Préfet Robert Holveck of the Charente-Maritime wrote to Brig Gen Charles C. Blanchard asking him to report the amount of rent Americans paid to French home owners. Army billeting offices in France kept card files of rental information for each occupied and available residence approved by the command.[82] Blanchard declined to provide this information and responded that the French government now was receiving taxes on rentals year-round, not just in summer months. Blanchard also surmised that owners of summer homes in villages like Fouras and Châtelaillon-Plage were reluctant to report as rent the reimbursement received from Americans for installation of indoor toilets and heating systems.[83] The persistent Holveck sent an identical request to Blanchard's successors. Brig Gen Ernest A. Bixby in April 1953 and Maj Gen Oliver P. Newman in July 1954 also declined to provide records of rent paid by GIs.

Children of US Army personnel living in Fouras contributed to strained Franco-American relations. Risking reprimand or worse for their Army parent, American boys used BB guns (*carabines à air comprimé*) to shatter streetlights throughout the small town—breaking twenty-seven in December 1952. In his letter to French higher authority, the mayor of Fouras described the vandalism as a "*veritable massacre de lamps electriques*." Brig Gen Ernest A. Bixby promised the French that he would take corrective action.[84] By 1958, two-hundred new RGH housing units at Cité Lefort in Lagord and Cité Lafayette in Aytré helped ease the housing shortage and gave commanding officers more control over off-post activities. MPs enforced curfews for American teenagers.

In September 1959, Sp5 Gerald D. Campbell found two German antipersonnel mines (World War II "bouncing betty") near an abandoned bunker at Châtelaillon-Plage. US Army ordnance personnel defused the mines.[85]

AYA Summer Camps

On 15 June 1953, an American Youth Activities (AYA) Camp for dependent children age 8 to 17 was held at Boyardville on Ile d'Oléron. The two-week camp cost $1.20 per day per camper.[86] In July, the camp moved to the Forêt de la Coubre near La Tremblade, 56 miles south of La Rochelle. There were four two-week sessions with seventy-five campers each session. A fee of $10 covered cost of food and materials for arts and crafts.[87] Two AYA camps were held in 1955, one on the grounds of Château Jean d'Heurs near Bar-le-Duc, and one at Bois des Combots in the Forêt de la Palmyre near Royan.[88] At la Palmyre, enlisted men from the La Rochelle area served as camp counselors, cooks, drivers, and medics. During the two-week sessions for dependents of different age groups, activities included: swimming, hiking, volleyball, and singing around the campfire. Campers slept nine to a tent, in Army cots on wooden floors.

In 1959, the Base Section AYA camp at la Palmyre was to be relocated near Biscarrosse. However, in June two DUKWs from Rochefort capsized while placing buoys to mark the swimming area. Eleven GIs, were dumped into the ocean and had to swim to shore. Because the severe undertow made it unsafe to swim at the rented beach, Brig Gen Richard J. Meyer, BASEC commander, moved the camp to Lake Cazaux, near Arcachon.[89]

The Longest Day

Landing scenes for the classic war movie *The Longest Day* were filmed in 1961 on the Île de Ré, an 18-mile long island off the coast of La Rochelle. The movie, based on Cornelius Ryan's 1959 best-selling book on D-Day, told the story from the point of view of the soldiers who fought in the invasion.[90] Because producer Darryl F. Zanuck had the cooperation of the American and French governments, US Army, Europe promised over one-thousand US Army airborne troops from Germany and off-duty ComZ soldiers to participate as extras in the movie.[91] Due to congressional criticism, the number of troops from Germany was reduced from 700 to 250. Eighth Infantry Division soldiers from Baumholder, commanded by Col Joseph M. Conway, took part in the filming of amphibious landings. Conway reported that the experience of storming the beach from LCMs was excellent training. Sgt Charles Pace, a veteran of the actual D-Day landings on 06 June 1944, believed the movie scenes were realistic, but "a lot more fun." [92]

The Hollywood stars included John Wayne, Henry Fonda, Richard Burton, Robert Mitchum, a young Sean Connery (whose next role was James Bond), and Curt Jurgens (who played a German general). Off-duty French employees of the US Army Port Area Command at La Rochelle served as translators for media events. The 26th Trans Co (Light Helicopter) from Verdun, commanded by Maj Steve Bosan, provided two H-34 Choctaws to drop French parachutists and dummies during filming at Ste.-Mère-Église. French parachutists, dressed as GIs, were dropped from an elevation of 2,000 ft; the 3-ft tall dummies at 1,000 ft. To fool the Germans during the actual invasion, the Allies dropped hundreds of sand-filled, sack dummies dressed as parachutists.[93, 94]

Several GIs contacted their congressmen with complaints that they had been trained for military duties, not to be Hollywood extras. Three GIs stationed at Rochefort wrote to US Senator Sam J. Ervin, Chairman of the Senate's Constitutional Rights subcommittee, complaining that they were pressured to volunteer to participate in the landing scenes. Ervin then wrote to Secretary of Defense Robert S. McNamara requesting an inquiry, because "Congress did not raise armies to take part in private commercial ventures." [95, 96] For several months, USEUCOM Public Affairs Office at Camp des Loges answered congressional inquiries and arranged trips for congressmen who were eager to visit Paris while investigating complaints of their GI constituents.

Chizé Ammunition Depot

The US Air Force built a large ammunition depot in the Forêt de Chizé near Niort, 40 miles from La Rochelle. The storage capacity of the depot was to be 40 days combat supply of ammunition for five fighter-bomber wings, one bomber wing, and two tactical reconnaissance wings. Completed by the JCA in 1953, the depot had a headquarters building, single-story barracks for about two-hundred airmen, maintenance shops, and storage shelters for munitions. Concrete hardstands, each designed to support 130 tons of ammunition, and more than two-hundred concrete shelters for ammunition were spaced 600 ft apart for safety throughout the forest. Shelter roofs were corrugated metal so explosions would be directed upward, not laterally toward adjacent shelters.

CHAPTER 10: *Army Ports and Over the Beach Exercises*

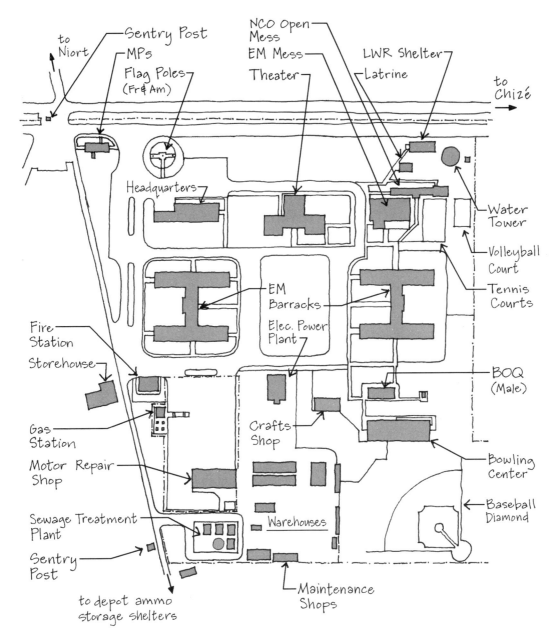

US Army Chizé Ammunition Depot (1963)

After US Air Force nuclear-capable aircraft were withdrawn from France in 1959 during Operation RED RICHARD, the depot was transferred to the US Army. In October 1961, the 611th Ordnance Co (Ammo), commanded by Capt George D. Gates, Jr., arrived at Chizé from Fort Bliss, Texas, during the Berlin Wall Crisis. The 611th Ord Co, authorized two hundred sixty-three officers and enlisted men, maintained more than 20,000 tons of conventional ammo stored at the depot. Officer and NCO families lived on the economy or in the thirty-two unit GRI housing village built for the US Air Force in 1956 at Niort, 15 miles from the depot.

Today the 20-acre command support area of the depot is the *Centre d'Études Biologiques de Chizé* (CEBC), which studies the reproductive habits of snakes, birds, deer, and other mammals.[97] In 2002, CEBC renovated the theater to serve as a modern learning facility, a big change over its former use showing John Wayne movies to GIs.[98] "Chizé Lanes" bowling center now contains animal cages, laboratory refrigerators, and supplies of dry food for animals. On the wall of the former machine shop next door, the slogan "A clean shop is a safe shop. Clean your area." in yellow paint was still legible. The two flagpoles, used for the French and American flags, provided the framework for scientific equipment that records outdoor air quality. The Office National des Forêts, the French forestry service, manages the Forêt de Chizé, where hundreds of hardstands remain. The foresters exchange wild animals with Forêt de Trois-Fontaines, the former site of US Army Trois Fontaines Ammunition Depot.

Rochefort

In November 1950, twenty-five GIs of the 7703rd Transportation Major Port Detachment, commanded by Col Sydney F. Hyde, arrived at Rochefort, 20 miles south of La Rochelle. In the beginning, living and working conditions were so Spartan that each day troops were trucked to the nearby French Air Force base for their physical training (PT), and each week to the French Polygon de Marate Rifle Range to fire their weapons. Post Headquarters, commanded by Lt Col William A. Evans, was located at Caserne Joinville. The 15th Transportation Battalion (Terminal) headquarters, dispensary, chapel, and troop barracks were located at Caserne La Touche-Tréville. The dilapidated caserne, built in 1728, allegedly had been condemned by Napoléon and required major rehabilitation work.[99] It was named for Amiral Levassor de La Touche-Tréville, the first captain of the frigate *l'Hermione* and later commander of the port of Rochefort. On 10 March 1780, *l'Hermione* sailed on a 38-day voyage to America with Marquis de Lafayette on board. In the Revolutionary War, Lafayette commanded troops who fought against the British. In 1956, the casernes were returned to the French government.

Elements of the 15th Trans Bn and three transportation companies were stationed at Soulac, near le Verdon-sur-Mer. By 1953, US European Command considered the beaches at le Verdon to be a semipermanent site for the offshore discharge exercises. In March 1955, the French officially designated the beaches as a permanent site. The tent camp grew to have hutments for troop barracks, PX, library, and dependents elementary school. Engineers also cleared a wooded area for an airstrip.

Porte du Soleil, Rochefort Arsenal, May 1961 (US Army)

The Arsenal

The 7703rd Trans Det established port support operations at the abandoned 17th Century Arsenal de Rochefort. Arsenal buildings had been badly damaged by the Germans when they retreated in 1944.[100] During 1952, three-hundred seventy GIs still lived in austere conditions. One challenge was the five showerheads (only one per 74 men). According to Army engineer standards at the time, new barracks in ComZ should provide one showerhead per 18 men, one toilet per 12 men. Quarters housing WACs should provide one showerhead per 14 women, one toilet per 8 women.

By the late 1950s, two French-owned buildings had been renovated at the Arsenal and fifty-six masonry buildings had been built. The installation now had modern maintenance shops (for LCMs, DUKWs, and other Army watercraft), dependents schools, 3-story EM barracks, theater, snack bar, fire station, warehouses, offices, bowling alley, commissary, and a small MP detention facility near the historic main entrance Porte du Soleil. Buildings of a French Navy installation bordered the Arsenal. When a new post theater was built in 1958, the Army located the building away from the river so it would not block the French Admiral's view of the Charente River.[101]

On 01 October 1953, the 7703rd Trans Det at Rochefort was redesignated the 11th Trans Port Command B. It relocated to La Rochelle where it continued to command the 15th Trans Bn and oversee offshore discharge exercises.

11th Transportation Port Command B Commanders

Commanding Officer	Period of Service	Commanding Officer	Period of Service
Col Sydney F. Hyde	1950-51	Col Harry C. Dodenhoff	1955-56
Col Ruel R. Neiger	1951-53	Col Charles D. Penniman	1956-59
Col August H. Schroeder	1953-54	Col Arnold A. Berglund	1959-61
Lt Col Gordan A. Jordan	1954	Col Robert A. Smoak	1961-64
Col Charles B. Claypool	1954-55		

Diving Team

The 89th Engineer Co (Port Construction) arrived at la Pallice on 14 April 1951 after eight days at sea on the USNS *Gen William O. Darby*. The 89th Engineers, commanded by Capt James T. White, Jr., had been activated at Fort Worden, Washington, during mobilization for the Korean War. The Army HB (Helmet Breathing) Diving Team of the 89th Engineers at Rochefort, headed in 1963 by Sp7 Henry Waskevitch, regularly inspected and repaired the deep-water pipe extensions at St.-Nazaire and la Pallice.[102] Diving equipment was tested under controlled conditions in a diving tank located at the south end of the Arsenal. During offshore discharge exercises, Army divers removed sunken ships and other underwater obstacles, repaired piers, and recovered sunken DUKWs and cargo accidentally dropped overboard.[103] Pier construction work under water was physically and mentally more demanding than similar work on land. Using cutting tools in low visibility could be dangerous. If a diver dropped an unattached tool, it could fall to the bottom of the ocean where it would not be visible in the inky darkness. A diver's equipment included copper helmet and breastplate weighing 54 lbs, rubberized-canvas diving suit at 18 lbs, and lead-weighted belt at 96 lbs.[104]

Dry Docks

The Army was able to use three old dry docks along the Charente River. Two of the dry docks, built in 1671, were located within the Arsenal. In May 1957, the Army acquired a large basin on a tract of 5 acres, one-mile north of the Arsenal. The property, designated basin no. 3, was used to store barges,

U.S. GO HOME

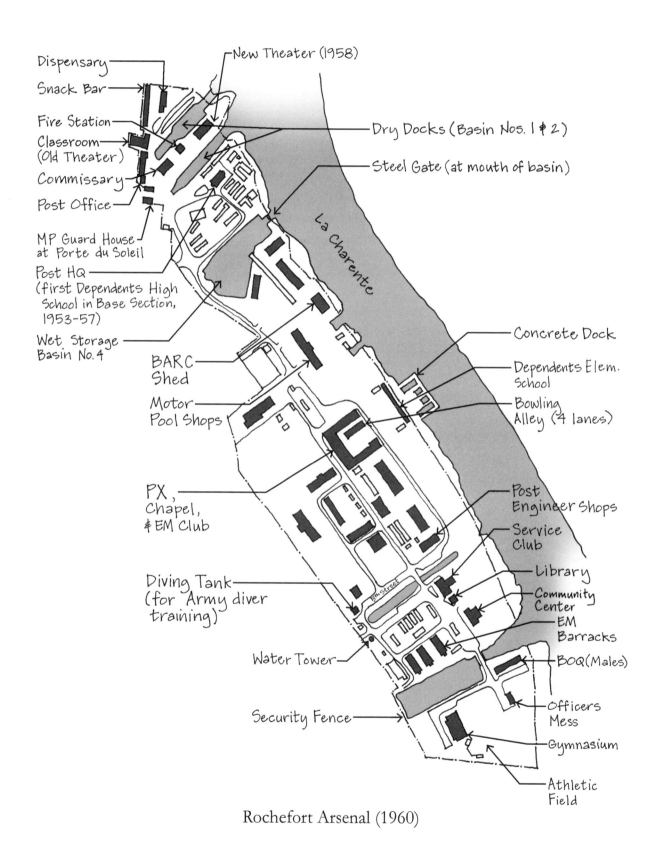

Rochefort Arsenal (1960)

tugboats, landing craft, and a floating machine shop. About two-thirds of the Army's marine fleet was stored in the basin. It was shared with the French military, and the lock between the basin and the Charente River was operated by the *Ponts et Chaussées Maritimes*. Two miles of rail spurs, connected to the Bordeaux-Saintes SNCF railroad line, were used for shipping. Three miles of old two-lane roads had to be resurfaced in the Arsenal. Three decades after the depot closed, abandoned dry docks were repaired to build a full-scale replica of the frigate *l'Hermione*, on which Lafayette had sailed to American during the Revolutionary War. In 2015, the replica of *l'Hermione* sailed to America.[105, 106]

Wet Storage Basin

The 81st Transportation Co (Boat), activated in December 1951 at Fort Worden, was based at the Arsenal. Originally designated the 81st Engineer Boat Co, more than one-hundred officers and enlisted men arrived at la Pallice on 28 February 1952 after ten days at sea on the USNS *Gen S. D. Sturgis*. Coincidentally, the *Sturgis* was named for the grandfather of Maj Gen Samuel D. Sturgis, Jr., ComZ commander, who had advocated that troops be sent directly from the US to France. At full strength, the boat company was authorized forty-three LCMs.

In September 1960, after two years of construction at a cost of $2 million, basin no. 4 was completed as a wet storage basin for the marine fleet of the 81st Trans Co. The new basin, constructed at the site of an old basin used during the Napoléonic era, was 300-ft wide by 470-ft long and about 11-ft deep. Portions of the sides were formed by hundreds of 50-ft long steel sheet pilings. Entry to the basin, nicknamed an "aqua-garage," was through a 45-ft wide mouth at the Charente River. A 9-ft thick hollow-steel "floating" gate, V-shaped like a ship's hull, was designed to slide into grooved slots on each side of the basin's mouth.

To close the basin, the gate was maneuvered into place and filled with water so it would sink into perimeter slots. To raise the gate, water was pumped out and the now buoyant gate would rise. Normally, it took just a few minutes to open or close the gate. The gate, which extended about five feet above the high tide water level, separated the basin from the tidal effects of the Charente. Sluices on the bottom of the gate controlled water flow in and out of the basin. The empty basin could be filled at high tide or emptied at low tide within 45 minutes.[107] If the water level was slightly higher on the basin side of the gate during opening operations, the gate tended to pop up like a cork and float out into the Charente. Fortunately, the gate would become stuck on a nearby sandbar where it could be recovered during high tide.[108]

The new basin had space for watercraft awaiting maintenance and had access to shops and the railhead. It could store three LCMs (56-ft and 74-ft long diesel-powered landing craft), four 119-ft long LCUs, and one 65-ft long tugboat. Army tugboats, designated ST for small tugboat, were used to move barges, recover disabled lighterage, and position floating cranes. The 81st Trans Co could transport more than 1,400 tons of cargo daily from ship-to-shore. GIs of the 81st hoped the tide would be high if the "balloon went up."

Returning to Rochefort from le Verdon-sur-Mer on 17 January 1963, engines of an LCU from the 81st Trans Co failed near Fouras. The LCU, without a radio to contact help, drifted 60 miles out to sea. The twelve-man crew and their mascot dog bobbed up and down on the stormy Atlantic Ocean. After two days adrift the LCU skipper, SSgt Wallace Kimball, used flares to signal a passing ship. The Soviet tanker *Aladir* responded and towed the LCU to St.-Nazaire. Col Robert A. Smoak, commander of Port Area Command, told newsmen at La Rochelle that if the Soviets sent a bill for towing, the US State Department could handle it.[109]

Dependents Schools

In 1950, the US Army acquired the Travaux Maritime building near the main gate of the Arsenal. The modern building, which later became post headquarters, had convex-shaped ends and "Travaux Maritime" in huge embossed letters over the entrance. In September 1953, a dependents high school began using the two-story masonry building. Sixty-four students attended the first year. Initially, ¾-ton ambulance trucks were used to transport dependents to and from school. In 1957, there were one-hundred fifty high school students and two-hundred fifteen elementary school students. From 1953 to 1957, Rochefort High was the only Army high school in Base Section. Students were bused from installations as far away as St.-Nazaire in the north to Captieux in the south. Students arrived by Army buses on Sunday and returned home on Friday afternoon. Dorms were in metal prefabs divided into four person cubicles. The Rochefort Rockets fielded teams in football, baseball, basketball, and soccer. In 1956, eight students from the graduating class of sixteen were accepted to attend colleges and universities.[110]

Adaptive Reuse of Casernes

After the US departed, the Travaux Maritime building was used for offices. Caserne Joinville was converted to civilian residences and Caserne La Touche-Tréville renovated for city government functions.[111] During the McNamara drawdown in 1963, the Arsenal area south of Fifth Street was returned to the French government. The French Navy converted the modern three-story barracks, BOQ, and gymnasium buildings into facilities for a French Navy quartermaster school (*École des Fourriers*) that trained cooks and naval orderlies. In 2004, the school moved to Brest and the site has been developed for use as a modern office park.

Caserne Joinville, Rochefort, 1953 (US Army)

La Rochelle-Rochefort Area US Army Installations

Installation	Location	Activity and Units
Headquarters	La Rochelle (Caserne Aufrédi, 2 acres)	11th Transportation Terminal Command US Army Garrison 766th CIC Field Office
	Rochefort (Caserne Joinville)	11th Transportation Terminal Command "B" 15th Transportation Battalion
	Laleu	La Rochelle Installation HQ
	Croix-Chapeau	20th Engineer Brigade 106th Trans Battalion (Truck)
Depots/Ports	Croix-Chapeau (128 acres)	70th Medical Depot Central Dental Lab (3rd Medical Det)
	Lagord (44 acres)	889th QM Petroleum Depot
	La Pallice (Usine Bertrand, 16 acres)	US Army POL Tank Farm Engineer R&U Supply warehouses
	La Pallice (Môle d'Escale)	Deep-water port., Military Sea Transportation Service (MSTS) Det
	La Pallice (Usine Jeumont)	US Army QM activities (35 acres)
	Rochefort (Arsenal, 90 acres)	US Army Marine Fleet Depot
	Forêt de Chizé (6,533 acres)	US Army Ammo Depot, Chizé
NODEX Support	Le Verdon	Dry storage site (8 acres)
	Soulac	15th Transportation Bn Det 81st Transportation Co (Boat) 98th Transportation Co (Port) 570th Trans Co (Terminal Service) 687th Engineer Co (Water Supply)
Hospital/Dispensaries	Croix-Chapeau	28th General Hospital (1,000-bed standby hospital)
	Rochefort (Arsenal)	61st General Dispensary
	Chizé	218th General Dispensary
Schools (dependents)	La Rochelle (Caserne Aufrédi)	Elementary school
	La Pallice (Usine Jeumont)	Nursery and elementary school
	Rochefort (Arsenal)	Elementary and high schools
General Officer Quarters	La Rochelle (150, ave Carnot)	Commanding General, BASEC
Bachelor Officers Quarters (BOQ)	Chizé	One-story building, Officers Mess
	Croix-Chapeau	Two 2-story buildings (one for men, one for women)
	Rochefort (Arsenal)	Two-story building, Officers Mess
Housing (families)	Aytré (Cité Lafayette)	100 Rental Guarantee Housing (RGH) units
	Lagord (Cité Lefort)	100 RGH units
	Niort (Cité Américaine)	32 Guaranteed Rental Income (GRI) units

Troop Barracks	Chizé	611th Ordnance Company (Ammo) 504th Military Police Battalion Det
	Croix-Chapeau (Aigrefeuille-d'Aunis)	106th Trans Battalion (Truck) 78th Transportation Company 188th Military Police Company 64th Medical Group 485th Medical Co (Preventive Medicine) 555th Ambulance Company 4086th Labor Service Company
	Laleu	97th Transportation Co (Port) 460th Trans Co (Amphi Trk) 581st Engineer Company (DS) 165th Military Police Det (CI)
	Jeumont	102nd QM Bakery Company 77th Transportation Co (Lt Trk) 73rd Medical Det (Veterinary Food Insp)
	Rochefort (Arsenal)	15th Transportation Battalion 81st Transportation Co (Boat) 570th Trans Co (Terminal Service) 595th Trans Co (Hvy Trk) 522nd Trans Platoon (BARC) 89th Engineer Co (Port Constr) 547th Ordnance Company (FM)
Post Exchange	La Pallice (Usine Jeumont)	Dry goods sales
Recreation	Chizé	Baseball diamond, volleyball court, "Chizé Lanes" bowling alley (4 lanes)
	Croix-Chapeau	Gymnasium, athletic field, bowling alley, golf driving range (ten tees)
	Fouras	NCO Club
	Lagord	Skeet range
	Laleu	Swimming pool, volleyball courts, bowling alley
	Jeumont	Gymnasium, bowling alley
	Rochefort (Arsenal)	Gymnasium, athletic fields, bowling alley (4 lanes)
	La Tremblade (Forêt de la Palmyre)	AYA Summer Camp (20 acres, 200-yd sandy beach front)
Air Field	Laleu (17 acres)	Three hangars, airstrip
Training Sites	Aytré (Pointe de Roux)	Firing range (small arms)
	Les Sables-d'Olonne	Firing range (.50-cal weapons)
Newspapers	Croix-Chapeau	Pick and Pill (1953-55), The Medic
	Laleu	News Patrol (524th MP Bn)
	La Rochelle	Basec Mission (1953-56), The Sea Sider, Le Caneton (for LWRs)
	Rochefort	Rochefort Wheel

Abbreviations

Amphi Trk	Amphibious truck	DS	Direct Support
AYA	American Youth Activities	FM	Field Maintenance
BARC	Barge, amphibious, resupply, cargo	POL	Petroleum, oil & lubricants
CI	Criminal Investigation	R&U	Repairs & Utilities

Landing on the Beaches

The role of the US Navy was to move cargo across the ocean; the Army to discharge cargo at fixed ports or over the beach. From June 1952 to February 1954, sixteen exercises unloading supplies over the beach were held along the Atlantic coast of France. The purpose of the monthly training exercises was to develop techniques to move cargo from ship to shore if the ports became inoperable. Without using port facilities, cargo was to be rapidly discharged and transported across water to a beach, where it was sorted, documented, and shipped by railcars or trucks to depots. To load and unload ships by conventional crane-lift methods, called lift-on lift-off (LOLO), took far longer than the time it took for ships to cross the Atlantic Ocean. During a war with the Soviets, reducing the time it took to unload ships would be more important than increasing cruising speed.[112] US Army, Europe wanted the exercises to develop the capability to handle 8,000 tons of supplies a month in peacetime and at least 100,000 tons per month during wartime.[113, 114] Although the early exercises in mid-1952 were redesignated over the beach (OTB), the troops continued to call them by the first official designation of supply over the beach so they could use the acronym SOB.

Beaches south of Pointe de Grave, 1952 (US Army)

Proposed Landing Beaches

Initial beach surveys in 1951 identified five sites for SOB exercises: les Sables-d'Olonne, la Repentie (rocky beach north of port at la Pallice), Fouras (beaches near Rochefort), le Verdon (two useable beaches south of Pointe de Grave), and St.-Jean-de-Luz (sandy beaches faced by high dunes). The sites were considered suitable by Army engineers, who had evaluated soil conditions, beach gradients, and access to nearby road and rail networks. Offshore conditions were approved by the Navy. However, because the beach at les Sables-d'Olonne was along the central business district, conflicts with civilians during the exercises would be unavoidable. Rochefort presented similar conflicts with ground transportation rights-of-way. Therefore, the early exercises were held at Pointe de Grave and la Pallice. Brig Gen Charles C. Blanchard, BASEC commander, advised EUCOM that the 45-acre la Repentie beach only should be used in emergencies. There would be a high risk of damage to landing craft using the rocky beach, and a reef 50 yards offshore was only 1 ft below the waterline at low tide. Nevertheless, Maj Gen Samuel D. Sturgis, Jr., ComZ commander, approved the site for SOBs.[115]

Permission to Hold Exercises

US diplomats feared that the French government might object to SOBs because the exercises would deprive dockers of jobs. The French did not raise this objection, but negotiations were deadlocked until the US offered a satisfactory plan to settle claims for damages. To the chagrin of Sturgis, the French delayed the first SOB from 15 May until 04 June 1952 so it would not conflict with the five-day Pentecost (*Pentecôte*) holidays. Before each exercise, numerous French authorities had to grant permission. Sturgis wrote to François Leduc, *Chef de la Mission Centrale de Liaison pour l'Assistance aux Armées Alliées* in Paris, who reported directly to the Prime Minister of France. Leduc, on behalf of the US Army, then sought permission from the commanding general of the French military region and préfets of departments affected by the exercise. The French military and the préfets, who also notified mayors of affected towns, sent their approval or disapproval to the French Interior Ministry in Paris. The Minister then sent his decision to Leduc. Authorization to move cargo from ships had to be granted by the *Base de Transit Militaire Inter-Armées* and, if railheads were beyond its jurisdiction, permission had to be granted by the *Direction Régionale des Transports*. After each exercise, préfets sent a list of damages caused by the exercise to Sturgis for reimbursement. Most claims for damages under $500 were settled at the site of the exercise.

Landing Site Preparation

The European Command beach operation plan, dubbed "Operation Sand," was the first over the beach operation in France since World War II. A month before the ship arrived, Army engineers began preparing the site, a sandy beach south of Pointe de Grave near le Verdon. The 81st Trans Co (Boat) used its LCMs to ferry military vehicles and equipment between Royan and Pointe de Grave. Explosive ordnance demolition personnel from Orléans, led by CWO Fred Hartkop, Jr., removed landmines from the beach.[116] Bulldozers moved almost 20,000 cubic yards of sand from a large dune to construct roadways and a flat area for sorting supplies. Then the sorting area was covered with pierced steel plank (PSP) to create a stable, hard surface. Engineers pitched tents, dug latrines (one 8-hole box latrine per 200 men), and installed perimeter fencing. To be with his men, Brig Gen Charles C. Blanchard lived in the troop "tent city." [117] For security, MPs from the 529th MP Co worked with French *Compagnie républicaine de sécurité* (CRS) and gendarmes to set up fixed sentry posts and roving patrols. During the exercise, Chaplain (Capt) Henry F. Speck found a herd of cows, which had slipped past the guards, grazing in the tent city.[118] In addition to site security and traffic control, MPs tried to keep GIs away from the huge encampment of prostitutes who had moved to nearby Soulac from Bordeaux.[119]

Quartermaster troops set up portable shower units and repaired field kitchen equipment. Troops from the 469th QM Laundry Det from Laleu washed clothes. For fire safety, tent areas had one water-filled 55-gal drum per four tents. "For Fire Only" was stenciled on the drums. GI helmets served as emergency water buckets. The beach and ship were illuminated at night so troops could work around the clock on 10-hour shifts. Because the exercise was conducted under simulated combat conditions, troops were supposed to be armed at all times, from the beach to the chow-line. The rule was waived when the GIs were engaged in manual labor. Troops of the 15th Trans Port Battalion set up .50 cal anti-aircraft gun emplacements on the beach to simulate defense against air attacks.[120] To boost morale of the troops, movies were shown each night on the beach. Medical care was available and an ambulance was kept at the site. After the ship departed and the beach was cleared of cargo, the troops began cleanup, including burning all human waste. The latter detail, called "honey dipper duty" by GIs, usually was given to troops as punishment. Gasoline was poured into metal drums, which had been used as latrines, and then ignited.

CHAPTER 10: *Army Ports and Over the Beach Exercises*

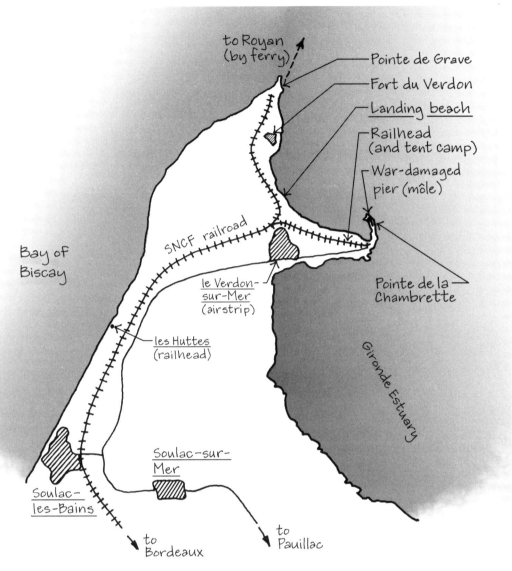

Supply Over the Beach Discharge Site (1952)

The First SOB

The first SOB in June 1952 near Pointe de Grave unloaded 6,726 tons of cargo from the SS *Nevadan*, anchored a mile offshore. Col Sydney F. Hyde, 7703rd Trans Major Port commander at Rochefort, supervised the discharge operations.[121] Most of the cargo were supplies, such as canned fruits and vegetables, and small-arms ammunition. Four-hundred tons of ammunition was shipped to Trois-Fontaines, the rest to Germany. French Navy patrol boats escorted convoys of US Army landing craft from Rochefort and la Pallice to Pointe de Grave. To avoid German mines, the convoys had to sail far out to sea. The Army's marine fleet in France had 56-ft and 74-ft long flat-bottom landing craft mechanized (LCM), called "mike boats" by the GIs. Most of the LCM landing craft were built by Higgins Industries of New Orleans, Louisiana. Higgins was the foremost designer and builder of flat-bottom boats for the US military.[122] The 460th Transportation Amphibious Truck Co drove their thirty-eight DUKWs from Rochefort to St.-Georges-de-Didonne, across the Gironde Estuary from Pointe de Grave. It took an hour for the DUKWs to cross the estuary. (During World War II, the 460th was the first DUKW company to cross the Rhine River.)

369

During the exercise, the LCMs were beached perpendicular to the shoreline to be unloaded. Crawler cranes were used to transfer cargo from the LCMs to 2½-ton trucks which moved the cargo to the sorting area. Although a DUKW carried less cargo than an LCM, it could transport the cargo from ship to shore and over the beach to the sorting area in less time than the LCM. On the first day, it was discovered that Army forklifts were too high to use on the *Nevadan*, so US Air Force forklifts had to be borrowed from Bordeaux AB. In the ship's holds, boxes of various sizes were scattered about. At shipside, the DUKWs and LCMs "bobbed" gently up-and-down during calm seas; violently during rough seas.

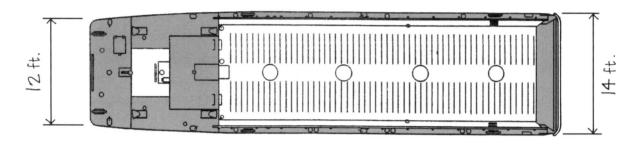

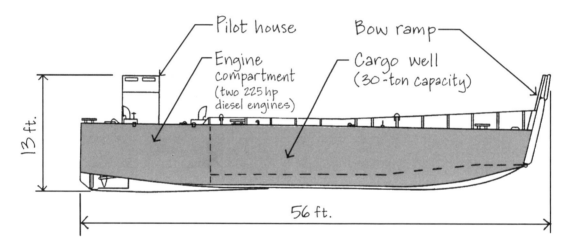

Landing Craft, Mechanized (LCM)

On 06 June 1952, a crew member of the *Nevadan* fell overboard, landing in the midst of churning propellers of DUKWs and LCMs. Cpl Robert R. Masuret, a "jumper" with the 460th Trans Amphibious Co, dove off his DUKW to rescue the seaman. Jumpers were soldiers, who after loading a DUKW alongside a ship, jumped onto the next empty DUKW. For his heroism, Masuret received the Soldier's Medal during a March 1953 ceremony at Camp Bussac.[123]

The five-day exercise required 1,539 officers and enlisted personnel, but Sturgis believed this was too many. Sturgis renamed the second exercise over the beach (OTB) to eliminate the awkward SOB designation. The exercise, also held near Pointe de Grave, unloaded 4,005 tons of cargo from the SS *Oshkosh Victory*. Like the first exercise, it had been delayed because of a holiday. This time due to Bastille Day on 14 July. Sturgis was not pleased. The exercise required 814 troops, but it was believed that this was too few. The third was conducted with 857 troops; the fourth with 938.

Cargo from SS Nevadan loaded onto LCMs and DUKWs, Pointe de Grave, 04 June 1952 (US Army)

Offshore Discharge Exercises

Although the exercises were not called offshore discharge exercises (ODEX) until February 1953, all previous SOB and OTB exercises eventually would be redesignated as ODEX. In the seven ODEX exercises in 1952, the Army learned how cargo should be sized (some engineer bridge components were too long), stacked (uneven stacks of medical supplies were not stable), and rapidly unloaded (practice would reduce unloading and sorting time). Thin metal packing straps easily broke, cardboard containers sustained water damage, and pallets were difficult to maneuver without handles (called "ears"). Wooden pallets were constructed so prongs of forklifts could enter any side to lift the "palletized" load. By the end of the first SOB, it was obvious that Army personnel needed training as winch operators and stevedores. If palletized loads were dropped onto a DUKW from too great a height and not centered over the cargo well, the impact could sink the DUKW. At sorting areas on the beach, Army veterinarians inspected broken packing cases to determine if rations could be delivered or should be destroyed.

ODEX 3 in August 1952 at la Pallice discharged 3,851 tons of cargo from the SS *East Point Victory*. Before the exercise began, divers from the 89th Engineer Co (Port Construction) removed a scuttled ship by cutting it into 1-ton chunks. The engineers also removed huge slabs of concrete and twisted cable that had been part of a German harbor barricade.[124] DUKWs carried cargo over a ramp engineers built on the rough stone beach of la Repentie. Without ramps, the DUKWs could land cargo only during high tide. Although not strictly following rules for an OTB exercise, LCMs used leased commercial docks which significantly reduced damage to the hulls and propellers. Dust clouds from trucks at the sorting area were a problem. Before future exercises, a thin coating of oil would be sprayed over the runways and sorting areas. For the first time during an exercise, Army vehicles (2½-ton trucks) were offloaded into LCMs. Cargo was sent to depots by SNCF railcars, which were difficult to load because they were smaller than US railcars.

Discharging cargo from SS Nevadan, Pointe de Grave, 04 June 1952 (US Army)

Discharging cargo from USNS Lt James E. Robinson, in background ocean liner Champlain sunk during WW II, la Pallice, September 1952 (US Army)

ODEX 4 in September 1952 at la Pallice was conducted using the same discharge techniques as the previous exercise. More than 2,700 tons of cargo were removed from the USNS *Lieutenant James E. Robinson*, using the ship's gear and Army forklifts. The five hatches of the *Robinson*, a Victory-class ship, had been enlarged to transport jet aircraft.[125] To reduce time at sorting areas, the cargo had been palletized for the receiving depots. This also reduced onshore pilferage because the pallets did not need to be broken down for sorting and could be loaded directly into railcars. Slack space between palletized loads was filled with loose packages. DUKWs could carry three pallets; LCMs could carry twenty-four pallets, loaded in two layers. Only one pallet, containing ammo, fell into the sea. A radio-equipped DUKW was positioned shipside to direct other DUKWs. The 458th Trans Amphibious Truck Co from Laleu, commanded by Capt Charles C. Brown, and 460th Trans Amphibious Truck Co from Rochefort moved cargo to the rugged stone beach, where cranes were used to remove the cargo. The 40th Engineer Co (Pipeline) from Bussac and 986th Engineer Co (Pipeline) from Croix-Chapeau sent personnel to work as stevedores. Eleven huge Caterpillar bulldozers, each weighing 23 tons, were unloaded into LCMs. DUKWs were used to hold the LCMs against the side of the ship during rough seas. A 100-ton floating crane at la Pallice unloaded the bulldozers. Because of the difficulty in maneuvering heavy loads, it was recommended that future items should not exceed 10 tons.

ODEX 5 in October 1952 near Pointe de Grave attempted to reduce the time cargo would remain on shore. However, unlike the previous four around-the-clock exercises, only a day shift was used. Empty tractor-trailer rigs were backed onto LCMs, taken to the USNS *Robinson*, loaded, and returned to shore. This innovation reduced the time needed to unload each LCM from one-hour to 5 minutes. Because of dangerous rough seas near the end of the exercise, Brig Gen Charles C. Blanchard, BASEC commander, sent the *Robinson* to la Pallice. The final 200 tons of the 3,654 tons discharged during the exercise were unloaded onto the Môle d'Escale. Sturgis, who believed combat engineers would not quit during hazardous conditions, and expected his directives to be obeyed without deviation, relieved Blanchard from command effective on 01 December 1952.[126]

ODEX 6 in early December 1952 near Pointe de Grave discharged more than 2,300 tons of cargo over the beach from the USS *Oberon*. **ODEX 7**, the following week at the same beach, discharged more than 2,500 tons from the USNS *Robinson*. One-third of the cargo was discharged by the trailer-in-LCM method. Heavy fog slowed both discharge operations and deliveries to Camp Bassens. Deliveries also were interrupted when SNCF railroad tracks washed out at the outskirts of Bordeaux. High winds on 13 December destroyed twenty tents at le Verdon. A DUKW from the 458th Trans Amphibious Truck Co sank in the rough sea at the *Robinson*. The driver PFC Martin O. Shanor and PFC Jacob Ricco were rescued by another DUKW.[127] After eleven days of bad weather, the *Robinson* was sent to Bordeaux where the rest of its cargo was unloaded. In late December, Sturgis lamented that DUKWs were not being used when swells exceeded 2 ft. Sturgis cited his recollection of wartime amphibious operations in the Pacific when Army engineers drove DUKWs through 7-ft swells. Sturgis wanted ships aggressively discharged regardless of surf conditions.[128]

In the eight ODEX exercises in 1953, the 15th Trans Port Battalion, commanded by Lt Col Murray E. Manley, tested new techniques and equipment. With experience, troops had become more efficient, especially those operating winches on ships and forklift equipment on the beach. To further increase efficiency, courses to train troops prior to the exercises were initiated. In April, for the first time since World War II, US troops made a beach landing in France. During the exercise, designated personnel over the beach (POB), more than one-thousand six-hundred Special Category Army with Air Force (SCARWAF) engineers climbed down nets over the side of USNS *Gen W. G. Haan* into DUKWs. The DUKWs transported the SCARWAFs to the railhead at la Pallice where they boarded trains to travel to Air Force installations under construction at Dreux, St.-Mihiel, St.-Nazaire, and Toul.[129] LCMs were not used. At low tide, troops would have to be dropped into water 600 ft from shore.

ODEX 8 in January 1953 near Pointe de Grave discharged more than 3,600 tons of cargo from the USNS *Greenville Victory*. Pounding waves and heavy surf unearthed German Teller mines (flat mine filled with 11 lbs of TNT). First Lt Victor E. Gibson from the 81st Engineer Co (Boat) supervised the marking of the mines for removal by a French Army bomb-disposal unit.[130] The exercise tested six rough-terrain forklifts, a four-wheel vehicle with a heavy-lift frame in front, recently developed by the Quartermaster Corps. The new forklifts could lift 3 tons, drive up a slope of 45%, and work in water up to 5-ft deep. In the 1960s, improved models became the workhorse of ammunition companies in Vietnam. A pontoon cube barge, powered by two 165 horsepower Murray & Tregurtha outboard motors (called "sea mules"), was tested. Because Army crews had no experience in navigating barges, operations were restricted to calm seas. Barge loads averaged 50 tons per trip, well below the rated load capacity of more than 100 tons.[131]

ODEX 9 in March 1953 at Quiberon Bay discharged 3,651 tons of cargo. Prior to the exercise, the 7703rd Trans Major Port conducted extensive technical training at Rochefort. The 7703rd, authorized thirty-six officers and sixty-four enlisted men, controlled activities at the port areas of Bordeaux and la Pallice. Over a six week period, ODEX troops attended classes on: rigging cargo, discharge operations, beach operations, safety, security, and stevedoring. French dockers were hired to teach stevedoring. Unlike the French, GIs were not authorized a two-hour lunch break and a liter of wine per day. At Quiberon, five barges were lashed together to form a finger pier for LCMs. Cargo from the SS *Laredo Victory*, anchored offshore from Port-Haliguen, was moved to the beach by barges and lighterage and then directly to the railhead at Auray by trucks. One-half the cargo on the beach was stacked on PSP. The 82nd Trans Truck Co from Metz used its fifty-seven vehicles to move 280 tons of cargo from Quiberon to Mannheim, Germany. On the long trip, convoys from the 82nd made overnight stops at French Army casernes at Auxerre and Angers. Two helicopters were onsite to airlift medical emergencies to the airstrip at Vannes.[132]

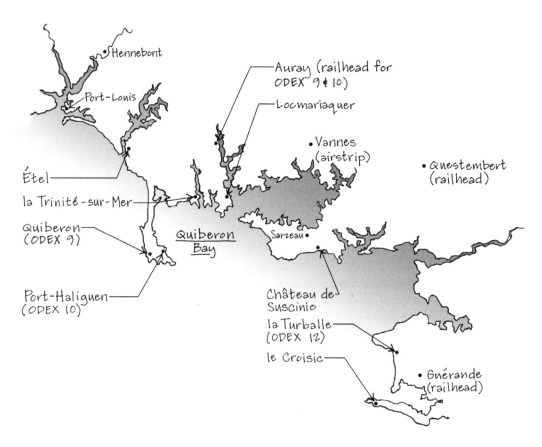

Offshore Discharge Sites (March & June 1953)

ODEX 10 in late March 1953 at Port-Haliguen set a record by unloading 916 tons of cargo from the USNS *Kingsport Victory* in a single day. The seven-day exercise discharged 2,973 tons on two beaches during calm seas and sunny skies. At one beach, personnel of the 89th Engineer Co (Port Construction) installed a 365-ft long pontoon-barge "finger" pier. Mobile cranes on the pier loaded cargo onto trucks for delivery to the railhead at Auray, 21 miles away.[133] On the other beach, troops of the 15th Trans Port Battalion were aided by a French Army transportation unit which brought twenty-eight tractor-trailers. The French trailers were backed into LCMs, moved to shipside, and loaded for return to shore. On land, tractors pulled the trailers to the railhead at Auray. MPs and French gendarmes controlled traffic. US Army personnel continued testing rough-terrain forklifts.[134] The *Kingsport Victory* was unloaded by nine-man Army crews in 83 hours of working time. It had been loaded at New York by sixteen-man civilian crews in 86 hours.

ODEX 11 in late April 1953 at le Verdon unloaded more than 4,500 tons of cargo from the SS *Laredo Victory* in hazardous weather. Strong winds and high waves broke a pier constructed for the exercise. After several LCMs of the 81st Engineer Co (Boat) were beached during the storm, only DUKWs were used to transport cargo. Brig Gen Ernest A. Bixby, Blanchard's replacement at Base Section, did not divert the ship to la Pallice. The exercise took longer than planned because the cargo load carried by a DUKW, which was far less than that of an LCM, had to be further reduced due to the rough seas.[135] However, on 23 April the troops unloaded a record 1,024 tons of cargo, winning Bixby a bottle of Coca-Cola. Navy Capt William N. Mansfield, Director of the MSTS office at la Pallice, had bet Bixby that Army troops could not unload more than 1,000 tons in a day.[136]

ODEX 12 in June 1953 at la Turballe unloaded 3,925 tons of cargo from the USNS *Private Francis X. McGraw*. Strong winds and rough seas delayed discharge operations for 24 hours. DUKWs towed plastic-coated "cocooned" cargo to shore and a Farrell deck was tested on the ship. The Farrell rolling-wing deck was a movable shelf, six inches above the deck of the hold, which increased effective size of hatch opening by rolling cargo into the wing recesses. Engineer heavy-lift cranes, secured on barges, were used as floating cranes. One of the seven experimental cocooned pallets broke up, scattering 48 cartons of C-rations along the shore. A storm destroyed a pier, and the tide washed sand from under the PSP used by engineers to surface roads and sorting areas. Due to road congestion from sightseers in the resort areas, 2½-ton trucks were substituted for 10-ton semitrailer trucks to deliver cargo from beach to railhead, 4 miles away at Guérande.[137]

ODEX 13 in August 1953 at la Pallice unloaded more than 5,000 tons of mostly palletized cargo from the USNS *McGraw*. Two hatch gangs from British Army Port Operating Squadrons participated in the exercise. The French government denied permission to use the beaches because, in August, all beaches would be covered with sun-bathing French vacationers. LCMs and DUKWs moved cargo from the *McGraw* to the Môle d'Escale and the former German submarine pens at la Pallice. Because SNCF railroad workers were on strike during the exercise, all cargo was hauled by Army truck companies, in convoys of five vehicles, to Ingrandes, Saumur, and Chinon. Ingrandes QM Depot received mostly Class I supplies such as 6,900 sacks of flour and 2,452 cartons of toilet paper. Army drivers were ordered not to exceed 15 mph in towns; 30 mph on the open road.[138]

On 01 October 1953, the 7703rd Trans Major Port at Rochefort was redesignated the 11th Trans Command "B" and was responsible for US Army ports along the Atlantic coast of France. Commanded by Col August H. Schroeder, the 11th was authorized three-hundred eighty-three officers and enlisted men. Headquarters was moved to La Rochelle. A mobile sub-port, operated by 15th Trans Port Bn, was responsible for ODEX operations.[139]

ODEX 14 in late October 1953 at le Verdon unloaded more than 3,500 tons of cargo from the SS *Greece Victory*. The 15th Trans Bn devised flat, steel cargo sleds to slide cargo off the well deck of the LCMs onto the beach. The sleds worked well on hard sand and could be pushed and pulled by several men. On soft sand two bulldozers, one to push one to pull, were required to move the sled over the beach. The sorting area, camouflaged by nets draped over stacks of cargo, looked like a traveling circus lot. Although the operation appeared to be disorganized, cargo was arranged by category and destination.[140] Sturgis emphasized to Bixby that if beach operations were widely dispersed the unloading time would increase, but losses from air attacks in wartime likely would be reduced.[141]

ODEX 15 in early November 1953 at le Verdon unloaded more than 4,100 tons from the SS *East Point Victory*. Radar-equipped T-Boats of the 81st Trans Co (Boat), commanded by Capt William J. Jenkins, were used to lead lighterage through dense fog. The fog was so thick that flares, ship's bells, and loudspeakers were ineffective. The 65-ft long freight supply boats (crew of six) also led convoys of DUKWs and LCMs to and from the ship anchored about one mile off shore.[142, 143] During the exercise, the T-Boats were diverted to guide a French fireboat to a French oil tanker that was on fire. Doctors from the 28th General Hospital at Croix-Chapeau were on site during the week-long exercise. To test response to an emergency, a DUKW delivered a GI with a simulated broken leg from shipside to land in thirty minutes.[144] In November 1953, the 646th Trans Co (Light Truck), an Army Reserve unit from Birmingham, Alabama, was transferred from Chinon to Rochefort to support offshore discharge exercises. During World War II, the 646th was part of the "Red Ball Express."

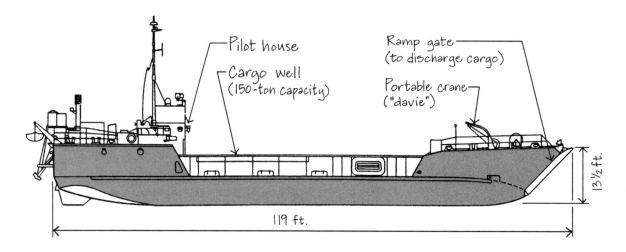

Landing Craft, Utility (LCU-1466)

ODEX 16 in February 1954 at le Verdon tested the experimental amphibious barge "BARC-3X," which could travel on land and water and carry fifteen times the cargo load of a DUKW.[145] The BARC arrived at Bassens aboard the USNS *Greenville Victory* on 23 January. (See photo on p. 422.) From there, it sailed under its own power up the Gironde River to le Verdon. The exercise also tested the LCU, a 119-ft long flat bottom landing craft operated by a crew of eleven. An LCU could carry more than three times the load of an LCM. Night shifts of the 15th Trans Port Bn consisted of three "bull gangs" to work in the holds. The gangs cleared small and loose cargo so the day shifts could concentrate on the large, water-sealed wooden crates.[146]

Bad weather, which shut down operations a few times, made life miserable for the troops on the beach. Only 80% of requested support troops had been provided for the exercise and the 15th Trans Port Bn was ordered by Maj Gen Oliver P. Newman, BASEC commander, to form an honor guard for the visit of French Generals Jean Humbert and Roger Le Coq. More than 1,320 man-hours were lost during the first three days of the exercise when forty-four personnel (truck drivers, stevedores, and crewmen of DUKWs and LCMs) had to be used for the honor guard. Although Newman sent the 279th Army Band, he declined to release any troops from his headquarters at La Rochelle. Due to rough seas, VIP visitors, and mechanical problems, the BARC only made four cargo runs. On a day with good weather and calm seas, the BARC gave rides to French VIPs or stood idle for film and TV camera crews.

To complete the exercise, DUKWs and LCMs moved most of the more than 3,600 tons of cargo from the USNS *Kingsport Victory*, anchored about one mile offshore. LCMs could carry five of the experimental steel shipping containers (acronym CONEX) in rough seas, nine in calm water. DUKWs could carry one; the BARC could carry sixteen.[147, 148] Because operators of crawler cranes were unable to see over the 14-ft high sides of the BARC, engineers improvised a special 5-ft deep "BARC pit" with ramps on each side. The sloped sides of the pit were formed by sand bags. To support heavy-lift cranes, the ramps were strengthened with layers of timber beams, sand, and PSP. The boom of a crawler crane collapsed while hoisting an overweight container. No one was injured, the contents of the container sustained little damage, but the crane had to be salvaged.[149]

CHAPTER 10: *Army Ports and Over the Beach Exercises*

Rated Load Capacity (1965)[150]

Lighterage*	Tons**	Lighterage*	Tons**
DUKW	2½	LCM-8	60
LARC-5	5	BARC	60
LCM-6	34	LCU	150

* Lighters are watercraft and barges used to carry cargo from ships anchored offshore.
** Actual loads carried during exercises normally were far below the "official' rated loads.

CONEX containers from USNS Kingsport Victory loaded onto LCU, le Verdon, February 1954 (US Army)

Cargo stacked on PSP, Pointe de Grave, 1953 (US Army)

Loading railcars, le Verdon, February 1954 (US Army)

Snow during offshore discharge exercise, le Verdon, February 1956 (US Army)

Lessons Learned from SOBs

According to SFC Irvin Wilson of the 81st Trans Co (Boat), it was "a tricky business to unload ships without a port." Wilson, who participated in all of the offshore-discharge exercises, believed GIs learned something new from each exercise.[151] The early exercises confirmed the difficulties in moving heavy equipment and supplies over beaches and tidal flats. Tracked vehicles generally could climb steep slopes even on soft sands, but wheeled vehicles became immobilized on slopes. Rocky beaches damaged the bottoms and propellers of LCMs and tires of the DUKWs. Ideally, landing beaches should be wide, sheltered from high winds and rough surf, near flat areas for airstrip construction, and near roads or railheads for inland movement of supplies.[152] Ten of the sixteen exercises were held near Pointe de Grave-le Verdon because of the flat sandy beach at high tide, shallow gradient at the shoreline, and natural shielding from high winds. SNCF railroad connections to Bordeaux were excellent after extensive rehabilitation.

Engineers found that pierced steel plank (PSP) worked well on beaches only when the sea was calm. Pounding surf washed away the sand from underneath the PSP. After each tide, PSP on soft, sandy beaches had to be taken up, the beach surface leveled, and bent sections replaced. By the late 1950s, PSP had been tested on mud flats at Pauillac, round pebble gravel at Suscinio, medium coarse sand at le Verdon, and coarse sand at la Turballe. By trial and error, it was learned that steel treadway sections from bridges, although cumbersome to install, could provide stable runways on most soft beaches regardless of surf conditions.[153, 154] The most important engineer equipment on the beach was the bulldozer, which could rescue beached landing craft and move earth as needed. Most of the exercises could have used more bulldozers. LCM operators learned to steer at water's edge so that they did not beach the boat. When crawler cranes operated on soft beaches, they were prone to tip over because surf washed sand from under their tracks. To prevent corrosion from salt water, cranes had to be washed frequently with fresh water and all lubrication points had to be greased. Veterans of amphibious operations in World War II believed that Jeehemys should have been used. The Jeehemy, a portable crane pulled by an Army tractor, could lift a disabled landing craft and haul it over the beach. Each summer the US Atlantic Fleet conducted landing operations at Little Creek, Virginia, to train joint forces. Jeehemys were used to pick up landing craft.[155]

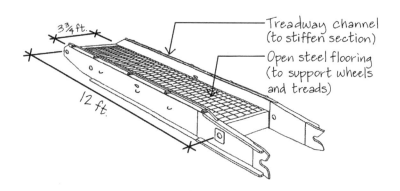

Engineer Treadway Section

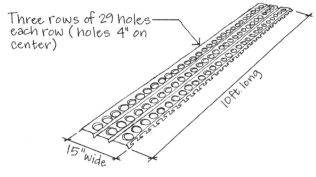

Pierced Steel Plank (PSP)

Palletized Cargo

To speed movement of cargo at Army depots in the United States, small packages were strapped together on pallets, called "palletized." Small packages had to be moved one at a time by hand, but palletized cargo could be moved by forklift.[156] Initially, all cargo for SOBs was to be on pallets, but early exercises revealed problems. Metal straps became loose when cargo settled during transit and the packages easily could be damaged or pilfered en route. Handling palletized cargo required heavy-lift equipment that was not easy to maneuver on soft beaches. Space in ships and railcars would be wasted unless about 40% of the pallets were broken down to utilize all available space.[157] Cargo on ships had to be braced with filler cargo or dunnage lumber to prevent damage from shifting. Because transportation would be scarce in time of war, it would be essential to fully load all wheeled vehicles and railcars. After several exercises, the 40" by 48" pallet proved to be the best fit for cargo wells of DUKWs and LCMs. It was obvious in the first exercise that metal straps needed to be wider (1¼" not ¾") and thicker (0.035" not 0.023").[158, 159] The most efficient beach operations occurred when cargo could be properly segregated and palletized in the US or in hatches of ships. To prevent crushing, GIs limited the height of stacked supplies on the beach and placed heavy items at the bottom.

Shipping Containers

By the end of the fourth exercise, terminal service personnel in France were convinced most cargo should be shipped in lightweight, reusable containers. Commercial items packed in cardboard boxes and fragile subsistence items were definitely not suitable for an ODEX. Rapidly forming rain showers damaged cardboard cartons being sorted on beaches, because it took GIs too long to cover them with tarps. Wooden crates, sealed by plastic film, were used to ship cargo in the sixteenth exercise. Army stevedores quickly learned it was essential to balance the weight of side-by-side crates on DUKWs so they would not capsize.[160] The experimental metal container (called CONEX), which the Army began using in 1952, dramatically reduced pilferage and could be unloaded in far less time than pallets.[161, 162] During the final ODEX, it took only five minutes to place a CONEX container on a railcar. The same load on pallets took about twenty-five minutes. Cargo in CONEX containers could be lifted from LCMs into trucks or trailers in less than 10 minutes, whereas an equal weight in pallets took more than an hour. Troops of the 15th Trans Port Bn improvised a "bridle frame" to facilitate lifting of the containers at shipside and on shore. A frame of wood 2x4s was sized so lifting cables would hang precisely above the four corners of the containers. The design became the prototype for a metal "scissors frame."

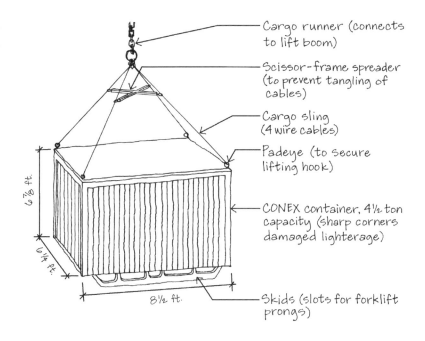

Sling Lift for CONEX Container

Disasters Yield "Excellent Results"

Many of the officers participating in the discharge operations believed the early exercises were a disaster. Before an exercise could begin, war damaged piers had to be rehabilitated, sunken ships removed, and sea and landmines cleared. It took weeks to prepare sites, heavy supplies and equipment got stuck on the beaches, and combat tanks and engineer equipment were too wide for narrow SNCF railroad tunnels.[163] It took several exercises and many innovations to overcome most of the obstacles to rapid delivery of supplies over the beach. Because amphibious landings in World War II had been conducted by combat engineers, Maj Gen Sturgis felt confident running the early SOB and OTB exercises. BASEC commander, fellow West Point graduate Brig Gen Blanchard, was given onsite authority. After the early exercises, it became obvious to Pentagon observers that Transportation Corps personnel should be in charge. They had extensive experience in port operations and knew how to rapidly deliver supplies and equipment. It also was revealed that training between exercises was essential due to the normal turnover of enlisted personnel. Experienced winch operators always seemed to be in short supply. By the mid-1950s, GI stevedores received training at the Fort Eustis, Virginia, "winch farm." However, according to the US Army, Europe official history of the LOC in France, written in 1955, the "First ODEX at Pointe de Grave yielded excellent results." [164]

Offshore Discharge Exercises (ODEX), 1952-54[165]

ODEX*	Location**	Date	Exercise Personnel	Supplies Discharged (tons)
1	Pointe de Grave	04-08 Jun 52	1,539	6,726
2	Pointe de Grave	26 Jul to 02 Aug 52	814	4,005
3	La Pallice	24-28 Aug 52	857	3,851
4	La Pallice	22-25 Sep 52	938	2,715
5	Pointe de Grave	20-30 Oct 52	711	3,654
6	Pointe de Grave	01-07 Dec 52	577	2,312
7	Pointe de Grave	12-23 Dec 52	617	2,508
8	Pointe de Grave	21-31 Jan 53	599	3,638
9	Quiberon Bay	07-14 Mar 53	824	3,651
10	Port-Haliguen	19-25 Mar 53	750	2,973
11	Le Verdon	19-29 Apr 53	672	4,556
12	La Turballe	15-25 Jun 53	725	3,925
13	La Pallice	17-29 Aug 53	879	5,033
14	Le Verdon	26 Oct to 05 Nov 53	953	3,564
15	Le Verdon	12-19 Nov 53	950	4,158
16	Le Verdon	09-19 Feb 54	1,008	3,655

*The first exercise was designated supply over the beach (SOB), the next seven designated over the beach (OTB). In Feb 1953, the official designation became ODEX for all sixteen exercises.
**The port of Le Verdon was near the beach at Pointe de Grave and names were often interchanged in after-action reports.

Personnel Over the Beach Exercises (POB)[166, 167]

POB	Location	Date	Exercise Personnel	Troops Discharged
1	La Pallice	15-16 Apr 53	336	1,643*
2	Quiberon Bay	05 Oct 57	323	513**

* Troops of the 472nd, 821st, and 843rd Engineer Battalions (Aviation) and 885th Engineer Co, FM (Aviation) climbed down nets over the side of the USNS *Gen W. G. Haan* into DUKWs.
** Troops of the 532nd Artillery Battalion climbed down nets over the side of the USNS *Upshur* into LCUs of the 81st Transportation Co (Boat) from Rochefort.

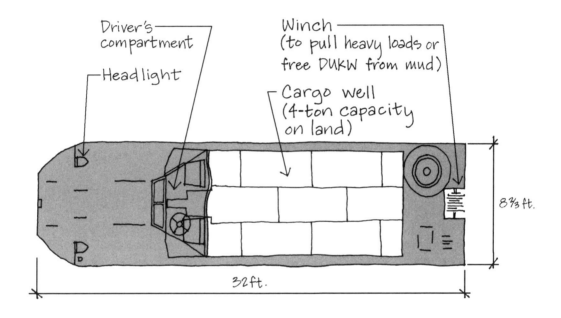

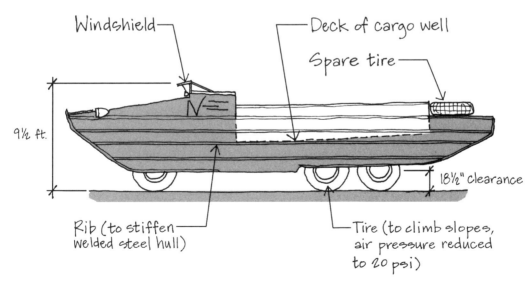

Amphibious Vehicle (DUKW)

The DUKWs

To support offshore discharge exercises, the 460th Trans Co at Rochefort had thirty-six DUKWs. GIs in World War II called the 2½-ton amphibious vehicle "the Duck" because its General Motors Corp (GMC) designation was Model DUKW-353. D stood for the year 1942, U for utility vehicle, K for four-wheel drive, and W for two rear-driving axles.[168] Its watertight hull fit on the Army's standard 2½-ton truck chassis and used the same GMC engine. The DUKW, designed for short runs between ship and shore, was famous for its use during the Normandy invasion.[169] Two-thousand DUKWs delivered troops and supplies to the beaches and returned to ships with the wounded. Later in the war, nearly four-hundred DUKWs crossed the Rhine into Germany.[170]

During the offshore exercises, DUKWs from the 460th Trans Co could transport more than 700 tons of cargo per day from ship to shore. At shipside, DUKWs formed a row to be loaded one at a time. When a DUKW was fully loaded, GIs would jump onto the next empty DUKW to repeat the process. Because turbulence from a ship's propellers could flip over a DUKW, drivers kept their DUKW at least 100 ft away from the ship's stern.

DUKWs had not been manufactured since 1945 and most had been scrapped or sold to private enterprises. During the Suez Crisis in 1956, the British had to conscript DUKWs that were being used at seaside resorts in the UK.[171] By the early 1960s, it was not unusual for a DUKW to sink near the end of an exercise. A DUKW sank rapidly if the bilge pumps were shut down and hull drain plugs were removed. It seemed suspicious to troops of the 547th Ordnance Co (FM), who maintained the DUKWs at Rochefort, that DUKWs that sank were those most often needing repairs. During the offshore discharge exercises, one DUKW was designated for rescue and control purposes. It also served as a water taxi, called the "VIP DUKW." GIs installed varnished wood benches so VIPs could sit during their trips between ship and shore. On land, the nemesis of the DUKW was mud.

The BARCs

Although the DUKW served well in World War II, its limited cargo capacity made it essential to develop an enhanced amphibious cargo vehicle. In 1953, at a cost of $2.4 million, Pacific Car & Foundry, Renton, Washington, built four prototype BARCs (acronym for: barge, amphibious, resupply, cargo) for evaluation by the Army. The first BARC tests by the manufacturer, witnessed by Brig Gen Frank S. Besson, Jr., were at Renton and at Monterey, California, where beach landings were made in 15-ft high swells.[172] Designated BARC-1X to BARC-4X, the four were then tested by the Transportation Corps primarily at Virginia (Fort Story), Canada, and France. The hulls were fabricated by Le Tourneau-Westinghouse at Davenport, Iowa. The BARC, which weighed 60 tons, was rated at 60-ton load capacity, more than 20 times the load carried by a DUKW.[173] On calm seas or land, the BARC could carry far more than 60 tons of cargo. Speed on water was 7½ mph; on land 10 mph.[174] BARCs could be dropped into water from the deck of a cargo ship if the bow end was covered by honeycomb cardboard to cushion impact.[175] BARCs could pick up cargo from the side of a ship, transport the cargo ashore over a soft beach, and unload the cargo well inland. A crew of three was assigned to each BARC (called "Besson's Ark" by the GIs).

Low-pressure tires reduced bearing pressure to facilitate mobility of the BARC on soft beaches. The giant wheels, over 9 ft in diameter, were developed by the R. G. Le Tourneau Co, Longview, Texas, a leading manufacturer of earth-moving construction equipment. Each wheel was powered by an individual 165-horsepower diesel engine. On water, the wheels could be used to steer the BARC if the rudder failed. To move sideways on land, front and rear wheels could be turned in the same direction.

CHAPTER 10: *Army Ports and Over the Beach Exercises*

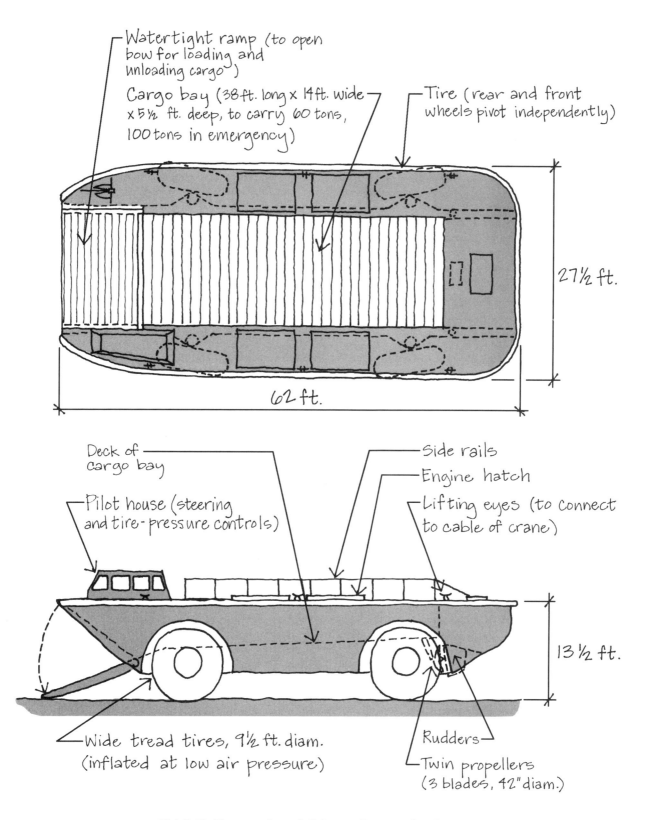

BARC (Barge, Amphibious, Resupply, Cargo)

To lower angle of an extended ramp on soft beaches, BARC operators learned to lock one front and two rear wheels and spin the other front wheel to dig the tire into the ground. The front end of the BARC could be lowered almost level with the ground after the opposite front wheel was released to spin.

Many features of the BARC were similar to the "Snow Cruiser" designed in 1939 by Thomas C. Poulter for the Admiral Byrd expedition to Antarctica. Like the BARC, the Snow Cruiser had four huge wheels powered by diesel engines, a pilot house at its front end, and a 56-ft long by 22-ft wide by 14-ft high hull. Unlike the BARC, the Snow Cruiser was not amphibious, and its hull contained living-sleeping quarters, galley, and engine room. As the Snow Cruiser was driven across the frozen continent, members of the expedition lived and worked inside.

In February 1954, BARC-3X was sent from Fort Story, Virginia, to France to be evaluated during ODEX 16 at le Verdon. During the exercise it only made four cargo runs, primarily due to rough seas and its frequent use for VIP rides. The following year, the four experimental BARCs were sent by US Navy landing ship dock (LSD) to Frobisher Bay, Northwest Territories of Canada. The LSD could lower its ramp to fill its dock with water. After the BARCs sailed into the dock, the ramp was lifted and the water pumped out. At Frobisher Bay, the BARCs discharged cargo from ships supporting the construction of Project Pinetree and Distant Early Warning (DEW) Line radar stations. After field testing of the X models, the design was changed so the pilot house would be at the rear. It was higher than the original to enable the operator to see forward over the ramp. Fourteen BARCs were manufactured in 1955 by Treadwell Construction Co of Midland, Pennsylvania, at a unit cost of $254,900. In 1960, four were assigned to France, eight were on loan to Formosa (now called Taiwan), four went to Fort Story, Virginia, and six more were being built.[176] At Rochefort, the 522nd Trans Platoon (BARC), assigned two warrant officers and forty-five enlisted men, operated and maintained the four BARCs. During the Vietnam War buildup, BARCs (renamed LARC-LX, Roman numeral 60 for load capacity) were used for ship-to-shore operations. After deep draft ports were built, they were used for discharge operations where no ports existed.[177]

BARC in pit on beach, Pointe de Grave, February 1954 (US Army)

BARC on display during Open House, Rochefort Arsenal, May 1961 (US Army)

The LARCs

In 1959, the US Army tested the LARC (acronym for: lighter, amphibious, resupply, cargo), an amphibious vehicle designed to carry a greater load and require less maintenance than a DUKW. The LARC was manufactured by Le Tourneau-Westinghouse, Peoria, Illinois. In the 1960s, it was designated LARC-5, for its load capacity of 5 tons. Unlike the DUKW, which had been designed, built, and tested by a General Motors team in only six weeks in 1942, the LARC had a long period of development and testing. The DUKW was a 2½-ton truck with amphibious capabilities; the LARC had a welded aluminum-alloy hull shaped like a boat. The LARCs hull was 25 inches above the ground. Its engine was an "off-the-shelf" V-8, 270-horsepower gasoline engine, so repair parts were easy to find. The LARC was only 3 ft longer than the DUKW, but could carry twice the cargo load and was almost twice as fast on water. Speed on water was 10 mph; on land, 35 mph. During tests at Fort Ord, California, the LARC-5 climbed loose sand slopes slightly better than an experimental "Superduck" built by General Motors Corp, Detroit, Michigan.[178, 179] In mid-1962, the Army awarded a contract to Consolidated Diesel Electric Corp of Stamford, Connecticut, to build two-hundred ninety LARC-5s. LARCs arrived in France just in time for the McNamara drawdown of Base Section. After offshore discharge exercises were terminated in 1963, LARCs at Rochefort were shipped by rail to Germany or moved to storage at le Pellerin.

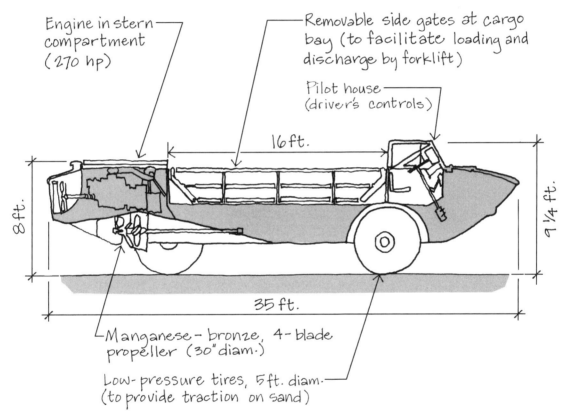

LARC (Lighter, Amphibious, Resupply, Cargo)

New Offshore Discharge Exercises (NODEX)

After a pause of eight months in 1954, the offshore discharge exercises resumed under yet another official designation. They now were called NODEX for new offshore discharge exercise. The primary purposes of NODEXs were to: develop methods to discharge cargo over improvised piers or beaches and to test new concepts (such as DeLong pier, aerial tramway, and RORO ship) and new equipment (such as MV *Page* beach discharge lighter and Ranger MR-60 rough-terrain forklift). Prior to an exercise, the 541st Engineer Det (Terrain) from Orléans compiled data on hazards to navigation (location of sunken ships, rocks, sand bars) and weather records (wind force and direction, tidal extremes, currents). To determine how many ships could be simultaneously discharged, terminal port personnel and engineers evaluated the exercise site (dimensions, soil conditions, and gradients), flow capacity of nearby roads and railways, and suitability for innovations such as DeLong piers and aerial tramways.

Until mid-1957, NODEXs were held at bimonthly intervals, usually unloading two or three cargo ships. Landing sites were tested from St.-Jean-de-Luz, near Spain, to Quiberon in Brittany. In Normandy, frequent bad weather and tides that rose and fell by more than 30 ft would have made landing operations too difficult. (In September 1950, the tidal range was 32 ft at Inchon Harbor, Korea.) Crawler cranes, forklifts, and trucks could not operate when the tide was in, and landing craft would be stranded when the tide went out. The French government suggested five sites be considered for a permanent NODEX site: Bénedat, Fouesnant, Quiberon, la Pallice, and le Verdon. In March 1955, Brig Gen Bogardus S. Cairns, BASEC commander, selected le Verdon.[180] Six of the first seven NODEXs, conducted in 1954 and 1955, were at le Verdon; NODEX 4 in June 1955 was at la Pallice.

Troops were stationed at le Verdon to support the frequent offshore discharge exercises. Volunteers built a small building at nearby Soulac-sur-Mer to use as an elementary school.[181] The school closed in 1956 and the students were bused to the new elementary school at Rochefort.

The first seven NODEXs discharged more than 63,000 tons of cargo. Before each exercise, the 594th Trans Group (Movement Control) detachment at La Rochelle obtained permission from French authorities for convoys of more than five vehicles and to move oversize vehicles, such as engineer cranes. The first vehicle in convoys with oversize vehicles was marked *convoi exceptionnel* (often misspelled). Speed limits for Army vehicles were stenciled prominently on the dashboard.

After most exercises, there were damage claims to be resolved. Army trucks dented parked vehicles and damaged walls and corners of buildings while maneuvering through narrow streets. Lighterage damaged piers if camels (marine fenders) were not positioned over the sides. Owners of oyster beds complained that fuel spills harmed their oysters. Army JAG officers were on site to be sure claims were legitimate.[182] From 1955 to 1967, the US Claims Office, France was headed by JAG officer Reginald E. Ivory. Ivory retired as a lieutenant colonel in 1962, but continued to be Chief of the Claims Office, Paris as a civilian because he liked living in France. During the withdrawal from France, Ivory worked from 1966 to 1970 in the Legal/Claims Office of the Military Liquidation Section (MLS) located in the Talleyrand Building, Paris.[183]

In late September 1954, Col James E. Holley, Base Section Chief of Staff, wrote to the French liaison mission at la Pallice requesting support for NODEX 1. Holley asked for: CRS security forces to guard the exercise sites, use of airfield at Royan for medical evacuations, French Navy escorts for convoy of Army landing craft from Rochefort, and use of harbor at Mortagne-la-Rive to shelter the landing craft on the northeast side of the Gironde.[184]

NODEX 1 in November 1954 at le Verdon simultaneously discharged nearly 8,000 tons of cargo from the USNS *Lieutenant James E. Robinson* and SS *Greece Victory*. LCMs moved 340 tons of cargo from the *Robinson* to a partially rehabilitated war-damaged pier at Pointe de la Chambrette, south of Pointe de Grave. The exercise, conducted with eight-hundred eighty-five troops, took nearly one month because most of the cargo arrived in small cardboard containers that had to be palletized in the holds of the ships. To cover the containers stacked on the beach, hundreds of tarpaulins had to be requisitioned on short-notice from depots in France. Before cargo could be moved inland, time was wasted because thousands of containers had to be repacked and repaired (called "re-coopering").[185] More than 43,000 drums of oil were discharged by net to DUKWs. In spite of rough handling, only

CHAPTER 10: *Army Ports and Over the Beach Exercises*

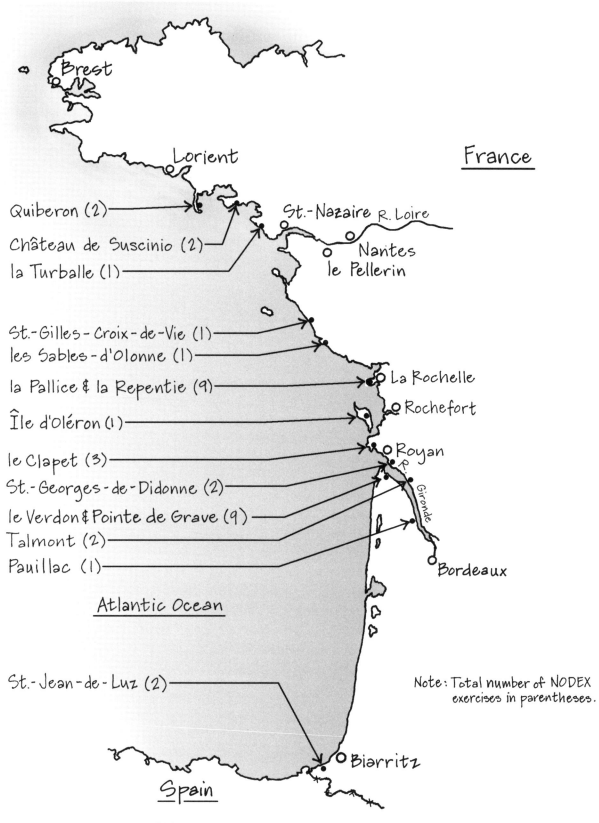

Offshore Discharge Exercise Sites (1954-62)

sixty drums developed leaks. Unloading operations on the beach would have been faster if LCMs had landed near the 10-ton crawler cranes rather than moving the cranes to the LCMs. Due to shortage of crawler cranes, most heavy crates were pulled out of LCMs by bulldozers. The 30-ton cranes in the sorting area were too heavy to use safely near the surf. The exercise showed that the enlarged, provisional 1st Trans Bn (Terminal) unit, commanded by Lt Col Alexander R. Krupsky, needed more personnel. During NODEX 1, LCMs could make about three trips during the load-to-discharge time of an LCU. However, it took an LCM six trips to deliver the load that could be carried by an LCU.

Performance of Lighterage at NODEX 1

Lighterage	Average tons (per trip)	Loading Time (minutes)	Transit Time (minutes)	Discharge Time (minutes)
LCM-6	10	57	52	43
LCM-8	12	78	69	54
LCU	62	309	44	161

NODEX 2 in February 1955 at le Verdon discharged more than 7,800 tons of cargo from the USNS *Private Francis X. McGraw* and the USNS *Lieutenant James E. Robinson*. Cargo included more than 124,000 boxes, cartons, and crates from the *McGraw*; more than 3,000 bundles of PSP weighing 13 tons from the *Robinson*. On 09 February the USS *Lindenwald*, a US Navy Landing Ship Dock, delivered two LCUs to the site at le Verdon.[186] Four anti-aircraft guns, each weighing about 10 tons, were discharged onto the LCUs. Troops devised a detachable counterweight for the rear end of conventional forklifts to balance lifting heavy loads on the beach. To stabilize crawler cranes on the sandy beach, Army engineers fabricated heavy timber platforms which were placed under the crane's narrow tracks. This field expedient, called the "floating platform," kept surf from washing sand from under the tracks, but rendered the cranes immobile. When currents moved an unbeached landing craft, the cranes could not continue unloading cargo. During preparations for the exercise, Pvts Ernest J. Register, Clifford B. Johnson, and Jerome J. Cirner, Jr. of the 81st Trans Co (Boat) drowned when their LCM was battered against rocks during fog and rough seas. Because of the severe weather, several LCMs in the convoy of thirty-two watercraft from la Pallice had to beach near Royan.[187] On the third day of the exercise another storm damaged more LCMs. An LCU sank in 80 mph winds and rough seas, but all fifteen crew members were rescued by an H-19B helicopter from the 12th Air Rescue Group. DUKWs and LCUs were used to carry most of the cargo from the *Robinson* to the partially-rebuilt concrete pier. More than 1,050 officers and enlisted men participated in the exercise. A fourth enlisted man, Sgt Thomas M. Payne from the 460th Trans Co (Amphi Truck), died during the exercise. Memorial services for the four soldiers, conducted by chaplains Lt Col Theodore E. Curtis, Jr. and Maj Robert J. Saunders, were held on the landing beach.[188]

NODEX 3 in April 1955 at le Verdon discharged nearly 9,000 tons of cargo from the SS *Enid Victory* and SS *Greece Victory*. Salvaged tires were spread on the rocky pier to prevent damage to the hulls of the landing craft. Cargo included howitzers and other ordnance equipment; POL and other quartermaster supplies. The exercise was supervised by Lt Col Charles E. Davis of the 15th Trans Bn (Terminal Service). Lift cables were positioned by an experimental "scissor spreader" metal sling frame. An Army L-19 Bird Dog aircraft from Laleu guided a small convoy of watercraft from la Pallice to le Verdon. By radio contact, the Bird Dog gave periodic chart readings and bearings.[189] The LCU (designated 1466 Class) was tested during the exercise. The LCU-1466 carried more than twice the cargo of the LCM-8, was seaworthy for coastal and inland waterway operations, and its twelve man crew could be fed and billeted on board. Yellow-painted 10-gal drums were attached to the winch cable of DUKWs. When a DUKW sank, the drum marked its location so engineer divers could retrieve it. In an experiment to protect cranes from pounding surf, a bulldozer blade, called a "surf deflector," was suspended in front of a wide track crawler crane. At water's edge the surf was deflected around the ends of the blade, but formed a small sand dune behind it. To back up, the crane operator had to raise the blade above the mound of sand.

In early April on a four-day visit to Base Section, Gen Anthony C. McAuliffe, the new commander of US Army, Europe, inspected the troops at le Verdon standing at attention on PSP by their rough-terrain forklifts and on soft sand by their DUKWs. During the Battle of the Bulge in World War II, McAuliffe had made the now legendary, but likely euphemistic reply, "Nuts" to a German request to surrender Bastogne, Belgium.[190]

While exploring a nearby German bunker during his off-duty time, crane operator Pvt Edward L. Sutphin was injured when he accidently set off a chemical grenade, left in 1945 by departing Germans.[191] A fire, ignited by a field-stove malfunction, destroyed the dispensary tent at le Verdon. During the blaze, SFC Joseph Sink risked his life to recover medical equipment which could have exploded due to the intense heat.[192]

NODEX 4 in late June and early July 1955 at la Repentie beach and nearby la Pallice pier discharged more than 8,100 tons of cargo from the SS *Greece Victory* and SS *Rayvah Liberty*. Cargo was colorcoded to identify the receiving depot. Because landing craft could be used only at high tide, DUKWs moved most of the cargo to la Repentie. Four DUKWs were fitted with A-frames. Roller conveyors were used to transfer cargo from DUKWs to trucks. Trucks of the 28th Trans Bn (Truck) moved cargo from a 150-ft section of rocky beach and the pier. More than 3,100 tons of cargo was delivered to Bussac, more than 1,100 tons to Fontenet and Ingrandes, and more than 600 tons to Braconne and Croix-Chapeau. Nearly 12,000 drums of POL were moved by suspended cable harnesses in lifts of 4 to 6 drums each. Because the 55-gal drums hung in a circular arc, the load was called a "chime." More than 1,770 officers and enlisted men participated in the exercise.

NODEX 5 in October 1955 at le Verdon discharged more than 10,000 tons of cargo from the SS *Mormacpine*, SS *American Eagle*, and SS *Northwestern Victory*. The *Victory* anchored offshore; the *Mormacpine* and *Eagle* docked at two DeLong piers, installed in tandem.[193] The piers had been towed to France from Charleston, South Carolina. Between exercises they were berthed at the port of Blaye on the Gironde River.[194] The piers were towed from Blaye to the exercise site and, as required by French authorities, aligned with the flow of current of the Gironde. The piers were connected to land by Bailey bridging from Chinon Engineer Depot. The 89th Engineer Co (Port Construction), commanded by Capt Robert G. Croad, installed the piers and bridging. The 300-ft long Bailey Bridge, which connected the DeLong pier to the war-damaged môle, had two intermediate "sea island" supports. The sea islands were 45-ft wide by 56-ft long component piers that were designed to support towers of the aerial tramway.[195] For the first time, troops of the 15th Trans Bn (Terminal Service) lived in semipermanent hutments instead of squad tents. Three-hundred troops of the 570th Trans Co (Terminal Service) from Soulac were organized into two "ship" platoons to work inside hatches of ships, and two "shore" platoons to work on the beaches or piers. Discharge of the ships, conducted with 1,187 troops, took two weeks.

The 81st Engineer Boat Co, permanently assigned to NODEX support, had a platoon stationed at Blaye. In April 1953, it was reorganized as the 81st Transportation Co (Boat) so its engineer personnel could be replaced by transportation personnel. Most of its LCMs, LCUs, and tugboats were docked at Rochefort. At Blaye, the company stored three-hundred fourteen pontoon "cubes" which could be lashed together to form two 100-ton capacity barges. Equipped with ramps, these self-propelled barges could be used during calm seas to discharge cargo from ships anchored offshore. At high tide, the barges could be unloaded by DUKWs; at low tide, the beached barges could be unloaded by crawler cranes.[196]

DeLong Piers

Fixed piers normally took several months to construct, but portable DeLong piers could be erected in a few days. Retired US Army Col Leon B. "Slim" DeLong, president of DeLong Engineering & Construction Co, New York City, developed the pier and its self-elevating jacking mechanism. The standard DeLong pier was a 90-ft wide by 300-ft long barge, supported by twenty-two 6-ft diameter tubular caissons in collars along the perimeter. The 13-ft deep hull was divided into watertight compartments which could be used to store fuel or spare parts. In 1951, DeLong rapidly installed a 1,000-ft long portable pier at Thule, Greenland, for the US Air Force and, in 1953, a 677-ft long pier at Whittier, Alaska, for the US Army.[197]

In France, the portable piers were used during several discharge exercises. Before a pier was towed from the storage site at Blaye to an exercise site, cranes were used to insert the ¾-in thick steel caissons through the hull, called "lacing the pier." Lacing, which consumed most of the time it took to erect a pier, was completed when the caissons were secured so they would not protrude more than 10 ft below the bottom of the hull. After the pier had been moved to the site by tugboats, air was

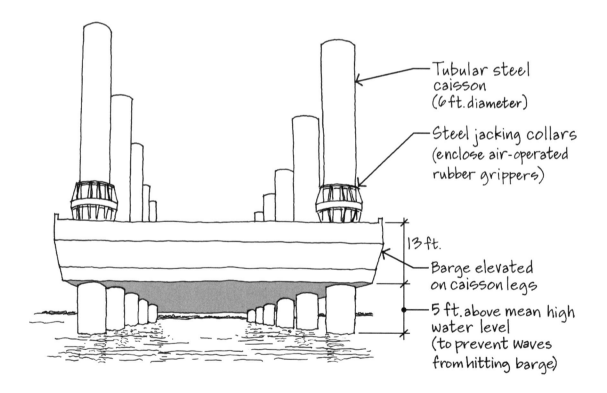

DeLong Pier

bled from the rubber tubes between the two barrel-shaped steel jacking collars and the caisson. This released the caisson, which then dropped to the ocean floor. Pile hammers were used to drive the 100-ft long caissons into the ocean shelf. The pier was raised above the water by applying compressed air to alternately expand and deflate rubber tubes in the steel jacking collars. The bellows action pushed the collars apart, producing a "shinnying" action. At the desired elevation, the pier was supported by an array of twenty-two caissons forming rigid legs gripped firmly by the jacking mechanism.[198, 199]

Army engineers could rapidly create ports by installing the piers alone or in tandem. Each pier section could provide berthing capacity for at least two ships. DeLong piers were tested during NODEXs 5 to 7 at le Verdon, 8 and 9 at Talmont, and 17 at Batz. A violent storm seriously damaged the pier at Batz before an aerial tramway was erected, so cargo was not discharged at the site. When DeLong piers were installed in late 1965 in Vietnam, they doubled the port capacity of Cam Ranh Bay.[200]

Tugboats maneuvering DeLong piers,
le Verdon, October 1955 (US Army)

Discharging vehicles from USNS Pvt John R. Towle
at DeLong pier, le Verdon, February 1956 (US Army)

NODEX 6 in December 1955 at le Verdon, conducted by 1,253 troops, discharged more than 8,600 tons of cargo from three ships. The SS *John C.* and USNS *Sergeant Morris E. Crain* were unloaded simultaneously onto DeLong piers; the SS *Jefferson City Victory* over the beach by landing craft and DUKWs. Lighterage moved empty 2½-ton trucks from the beach to the *Jefferson City* and back loaded with cargo. The LCM-6 was less prone than the 18 ft longer LCM-8 to broach on the beach during rough surf. Due to hazardous weather, the *Jefferson City* was diverted to Pauillac. Because the nearby les Huttes railhead was unavailable, Camp Bussac was used as the in-transit area for cargo from the *John C.* and *Crain*. Traffic from le Verdon to Bussac, 96 miles away, was routed through Bordeaux and could not exceed one-hundred vehicles each way during a 24 hour period. From Bussac, cargo was sent by SNCF railcars or Army trucks to USAFE depots in France and Seventh Army in Germany.[201] The *John C.*, whose cargo gear extended over the pier, pulled away when rough seas began to batter it against the pier. Lighterage was used to finish discharging the ship. Five US Army generals, including Lt Gen Carter B. Magruder, the Army's top logistical officer at the Pentagon, and French Admiral André-Georges Lemonnier from SHAPE in Paris spent a day at the exercise.

NODEX 7 in February 1956 at le Verdon, conducted by 1,149 troops, discharged nearly 12,000 tons of cargo from three ships. Cargo from the USNS *Haiti Victory* was off-loaded to lighterage which discharged the cargo at the DeLong pier or on the beach. All cargo from the USNS *Private John R. Towle* was discharged at the pier during foul weather. To test rapid discharge, all cargo had been placed on pallets or in containers at the Hampton Roads Army Terminal, Virginia. No loose filler cargo was placed in the hatches. The cargo was cleared so rapidly it exceeded the loading capacity at the Les Arros railhead, creating a bottleneck. Instead of lift booms, troops worked the pier using a cable and sheave unloading method (called "House Falls"). The marine cargo rigging system used shipboard lift gear connected by cable to hoists at the pier.[202, 203] During the exercise, the 570th Trans Co (Terminal Service), commanded by Capt Harold J. Lloyd, set the discharge record of over 3,500 tons in 24 hours. The record, about five-times the normal tonnage for two 10-hour shifts, was achieved despite freezing temperatures and high winds and waves that buffeted the *Towle*.[204] After the *Towle* departed, the USNS *Lieutenant James E. Robinson*, loaded with more than 4,200 tons of ammunition, docked at the pier. Cargo included three-hundred fifty-two rocket motors to be shipped on gondola railcars to Germany. Canvas tarps were used to hide the rockets from view and shield them from inclement weather. The rockets were guarded by six unarmed enlisted men and three armed French gendarmes, riding in a 3rd class coach car. Although without weapons, the Americans were issued flashlights and authorized to

DeLong pier sections,
Talmont, April 1956 (US Army)

Aerial tramway, fishermen carrelets in foreground,
Talmont, April 1956 (US Army)

Aerial tramway cables from DeLong piers to land,
Talmont, April 1956 (US Army)

Cargo sorting area and troop tents, Ste.-Radegonde church
in background, Talmont, April 1956 (US Army)

place a "collect" call to ComZ headquarters at Orléans if there was an incident.[205] On 22 February, the worst winter storm in the 20th Century hit the Gironde region, dumping snow on le Verdon beach. On 23 February, the master of the *Robinson* moved the ship into the Gironde River. He feared that high waves buffeting the *Robinson* against the sharp edges of the DeLong pier would damage his ship. Conventional piers had floating shock absorbers (called "camels") between ship and pier. Lighterage was used to offload the remaining ammo after old tires were hung along the sides of the DeLong pier.

NODEX 8 and **NODEX 9** from April through June 1956 at Talmont, a small village along the Gironde River, tested the aerial tramway system. In mid-March, five French Navy ships swept the Gironde River for German mines. Two DeLong piers were towed from Blaye to Talmont and installed in tandem about a ½ mile from shore. Tires were hung along the fenders of the piers to cushion impacts. In previous exercises, sharp edges of the steel piers had damaged mooring lines and caused ship's masters to back off in rough seas. Caissons for two tubular towers between the piers and shore were driven into the river bottom. Cables were then suspended between the towers. One end of each cable was connected to a steel-frame tower on a pier, and the other end to a huge steel frame anchored in the ground. The two 300-ft long pier sections and the two 45-ft x 56-ft tower platforms were called "sea islands." It took the 89th Engineer Co (Port Construction), authorized six officers and two-hundred three enlisted men, nineteen days to erect the tramway, which looked like a giant ski lift. To transport the cargo from ship to shore, self-propelled skycars, each operated by a GI, moved along the cable at 30 mph. To compensate for tidal extremes, an improvised block-and-tackle hoist was rigged between two caissons on a pier.[206]

At the exercise site, a French Army camp during World War II, Army troops laid out roads of crushed gravel, sprayed liquid asphalt coating to control dust, installed PSP for storage areas and walkways, and built a tent city for 1,500 men.[207] More than one-hundred squad tents were pitched in military precision, even tent pegs were lined up. Twenty-four of the tents were used by the 577th Trans Co (Aerial Tramway) from Fort Eustis, Virginia, commanded by Capt Robert E. Erbe. NODEX 8 in April 1956 discharged 15,396 tons of cargo from the SS *Black Dragon*, SS *North Pilot*, and SS *Northwestern Victory* onto the DeLong piers. The cargo was transported to land by the aerial tramway and driven to the railhead at Saujon. During NODEX 9 in May-June 1956, 1,661 troops and French stevedores discharged more than 6,600 tons of cargo from the SS *Black Dragon* and SS *Heywood Broun*. Seven M-48 combat tanks were offloaded over the side of the *Dragon* into LCUs of the 81st Trans Co (Boat) from Rochefort. The *Broun*, a World War II Liberty ship, discharged one-hundred twelve vehicles, one-hundred ten CONEX containers, and nearly 500 tons of 24-inch diameter steel pipe. Some pipe lengths extended well beyond the 26-ft semitrailer beds, testing the maneuvering skills of Army drivers who hauled the cargo to the railhead. Loads of 35-ft long pipe were moved by dolly trailers. For the first time, unskilled French laborers were hired as stevedores, but were not always reliable. Half of the laborers hired for the night shift during NODEX 9 had to be fired because they arrived at Talmont drunk. Their bus from Royan broke down near a café, and the men, who had been paid the previous day, spent their wages on booze. The tramway was so efficient, even sober stevedores could not lift cargo out of the hold fast enough to keep up with the men loading the skycars.

Aerial Tramway

The aerial tramway system was designed to transport cargo over rough terrain (such as cliffs, forests, and marshes), unimproved beaches, and inadequate ports. Maj Gen Frank S. Beeson, Jr., commander of Fort Eustis, Virginia, likely got the idea of a tramway from a similar system Arabian-American Oil Co

(ARAMCO) used in Saudi Arabia to unload cargo from ships anchored three miles offshore.[208] John A. Roebling's Sons, Trenton, New Jersey, built three tramway systems for the Army at a cost of $12 million each.[209] During March to June 1955 at Camp Wallace near Williamsburg, Virginia, the Transportation Corps tested the aerial tramway over shallow water, uneven terrain, and a 100-ft bluff. One tramway, set up to demonstrate discharging cargo from an LST, collapsed because of faulty anchorage in the James River. Fortunately, no GIs were seriously injured and the West Point cadets, who were to witness the demonstration, did not arrive until the following day. The next test was held in summer 1955 under simulated wartime conditions at the Amphibious Naval Base, Little Creek, Virginia. In twenty-seven working days, the 497th Engineer Co (Port Construction) installed the 5,000-ft long tramway from a land anchor structure to a DeLong pier.[210] The M2 light tramway, developed by the Corps of Engineers during World War II, was limited to 3,000-ft length and load capacity of one ton per hour.[211]

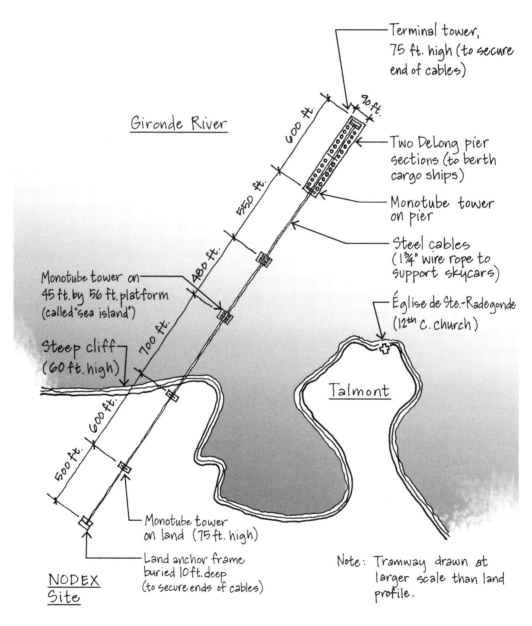

Aerial Tramway Site at Talmont

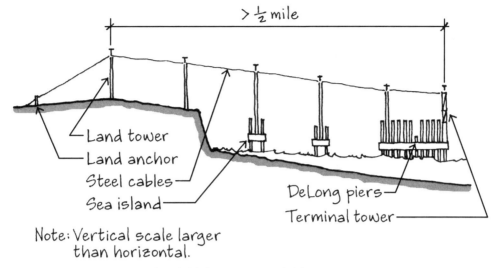

Aerial Tramway at Talmont

At Talmont, the tramway was field tested to move cargo from DeLong piers to shore. A self-propelled skycar moving along a cable strung from the piers to shore could lift up to 10 tons of cargo. Because the aerial tramway could not be rapidly installed and dismantled, the system was not suitable for "discharge and run" operations. However, it did work well at the Talmont site.

The tramway resembled the Rochefort *transbordeur*, an aerial ferry suspended by cables that carries vehicles and pedestrians across the Charente River. The transbordeur, built in the late 1890s, is one of few historic cable bridges remaining in Europe. It remains in working order because the soldier assigned to blow it up when the Germans retreated in 1944 did not follow his orders.[212] In 1976, a civilian aerial tramway began service in New York between Manhattan and Roosevelt Island. It was the first aerial tramway in the United States to be used as part of a transportation network.[213] In the 2002 movie *Spider-Man*, the superhero rescues passengers from a dangling tramway cab of the New York system.

Les Demoiselles de Rochefort

In the 1950s, American movie studios shot many films on location in France because the US dollar was strong compared to the French franc.[214] In the 1951 Oscar Award-winning film *An American in Paris*, American film star Gene Kelly danced on the Pont-Neuf in Paris. In 1966, the 54-year-old Kelly and youthful French actresses, Catherine Deneuve and her sister Françoise Dorléac, were in Rochefort to film a musical, written and directed by Jacques Demy. Michel Legrand wrote the musical score, which was nominated for an Academy Award. Key scenes for the love story, *Les Demoiselles de Rochefort*, were shot at Place Colbert, a few blocks from the entrance to the US Army Depot. In the movie, Kelly (dubbed in French) woos the considerably younger Dorléac. Kelly was enthusiastic to star in a musical written especially for film by Demy, the director of the successful 1963 classic, *The Umbrellas of Cherbourg*.[215] *Les Demoiselles* was not a box office success.

The Real Demoiselle de Rochefort

Unbeknownst to Kelly, a real Demoiselle de Rochefort had worked at the Arsenal depot. Henriette Bibaud, a stylish petite blond, was the only female chief of French personnel (*Chef d'Antenne*) at a US Army installation. The 30-year-old Bibaud was hired before 1954, when the French government

Self-propelled skycar of aerial tramway
Talmont, April 1956 (US Army)

assumed authority to hire and administer French employees (LWR). At Rochefort Installation, Bibaud was responsible for four-hundred fifty LWRs. She handled complaints and approved paperwork for payment of their salaries. At Talmont, her duties included hiring two-hundred sixteen temporary laborers, mostly unemployed fisherman and farmers, to unload ships participating in the offshore discharge exercises.[216] The French dockers, hired by Bibaud to unload the cargo at NODEX 9, revolted when they saw the aerial tramway. Bibaud's tent soon was filled with angry men. There were only two ships to unload, not three as promised, and they were not going to ride on such an unsafe looking apparatus. As a compromise the dockers agreed to unload the cargo, but only if the Demoiselle rode with them on the first trip. Even though she was wearing a skirt and high heels, as was customary for female civilian employees, Bibaud bravely agreed. Like the cartoon character Mighty Mouse: "On the sea or on the land. Here I come to save the day." Off she rode with about twenty Frenchmen whom she had shamed into taking the first ride, which ended safely at the ship about a ½ mile from shore. The men had an amusing ride because, on the skycar, the wind blew Bibaud's skirt upward like the iconic image of Marilyn Monroe standing on the subway grate in the movie *The Seven Year Itch*.[217]

Each day of the exercise brought new problems for Bibaud. US Army buses transporting the Frenchmen broke down. Fishermen, who found work, or farmers, who were needed in their fields, did not show up for their shift. French workers, unlike US military personnel, were permitted to consume one liter of wine during their shift at Talmont. This proved difficult to monitor. Bibaud fired those who reported for work drunk. Through her dedication, the exercise was successfully completed. Bibaud faithfully continued to work for the Americans until they departed from Rochefort in 1963.[218]

NODEX 10 was cancelled by the French government because it coincided with the peak resort and tourist season of August.

NODEX 11 in October 1956 at St.-Jean-de-Luz, near Bayonne, differed greatly from the five previous exercises. It was initiated with only 30 days advance notice, only DUKWs could be used the first 24 hours, and only LCUs and LCMs the next 24 hours. Before the exercise began, the USNS *Macalester Victory* sailed from Bassens to St.-Jean-de-Luz carrying more than 80 tons of equipment, which included DUKWs, forklifts, cranes, and PSP. Two Army H-19 Chickasaw helicopters were stationed at Biarritz Airport for use in air-sea rescues and medical evacuations. Exercise cargo was discharged from the USNS *Lieutenant Robert Craig*, USNS *Haiti Victory*, and USNS *Duke Victory*. Troops of the 460th Trans Co (Amphibious Truck), commanded by Capt Harold E. Lewis, and 81st Trans Co (Boat) moved more than 12,000 tons of cargo over Socoa and Bidart beaches. The rocky, flat-gradient beaches damaged the screws and shafts of lighterage. A shuttle system of stake and platform semitrailers (called S&P) moved cargo from lighterage at the beach to an inland transfer point where the cargo was loaded onto 2½-ton trucks. The exercise used 1,566 officers and enlisted men. During the exercise, two-hundred eleven crates of ammunition fell into the sea, most at shipside during rough seas, which caused the *Duke Victory* to list by as much as 24 degrees. Eighty crates were recovered shortly after they were dropped. Divers from the 89th Engineer Co (Port Construction) at Rochefort recovered an additional eighteen crates. Brig Gen James K. Woolnaugh, BASEC commander, promised the French government that the Army would conduct weekly air and ground searches for ammo crates that might wash ashore. The search was discontinued on 31 December 1956.

NODEX 12 in December 1956 at le Verdon discharged more than 12,500 tons of cargo from the USNS *Lieutenant Robert Craig*, USNS *Lieutenant James E. Robinson*, and USNS *Lieutenant George W. G. Boyce*. Most cargo from the first two ships consisted of CONEX containers, palletized cargo, and UNITEX (unitized cargo, experimental) boxes. The exercise tested a mobile port unit, augmented by additional troops, and tested a provisional railhead company. The 15th Trans Bn borrowed a ramp from the French Army Transportation School at Tours to load vehicles onto railcars at Les Arros railhead. Troops worked twenty-four hours a day (two 12-hour shifts, instead of the normal two 10-hour shifts). Based on this exercise, it was believed that working men this long for an extended period during wartime would cause a higher rate of accidents, mainly from fatigue. A helicopter detachment based at the Soulac airstrip stood by for medical evacuations and air-sea rescues. Three GIs in a DUKW on the Gironde River simulated an air-sea rescue by climbing up a rope ladder dropped from a hovering H-19 Chickasaw. More than 1,520 officers and enlisted men participated in the exercise.

NODEX 13 in February 1957 discharged more than 8,800 tons of cargo from three ships, the USNS *Haiti Victory* and USNS *Lieutenant Robert Craig* over the beach at le Verdon and USNS *Lieutenant George W. G. Boyce* over mud flats at Pauillac. For the first time, helicopters were used to move cargo. Seven Army H-34 Choctaw helicopters of the 110th Trans Co (Light Helicopter) delivered 42 tons of cargo to Camp Bussac from a PSP airstrip constructed on the beach. During the night of 14 February, a severe wind storm bent and scattered PSP all over the beach at le Verdon. An LCM was tossed onto a sandbar by violent waves and winds that exceeded 60 knots. The three man crew was returning five civilian crewmembers to the *Craig*. The eight were rescued by an Army helicopter the next day.[219] To avoid delaying the exercise, DUKWs bypassed the damaged areas and delivered cargo to a new truck transfer point of hastily laid PSP. At Pauillac, a BC barge was anchored offshore to be used as a lighterage transfer point. An engineer treadway bridge was used over the tidal mudflats to connect the 30-ft by 120-ft floating barge pier to land. The treadway floated on pontoons at high tide and lay on soft mud at low tide, enabling traffic to proceed normally during all tidal conditions.[220] However, the bridge could handle only one-way traffic and the freeboard of the barge (distance between waterline and deck) was too high. Strong currents at Pauillac slowed DUKW operations. Unlike most exercises, which avoided conflicts with business districts, the treadway bridge discharged in front of commercial buildings facing the Gironde River. More than 1,650 personnel participated in the exercise. The 520th Truck Co, commanded by Capt Walter F. Shaw, was sent TDY from Vassincourt.

NODEX 14 in April 1957 discharged cargo from the USNS *Sergeant Morris E. Crain*, anchored 2 miles offshore near Château de Suscinio and the USNS *Private Francis X. McGraw* at la Turballe, 48 miles south of Suscinio. The arrival date of the *McGraw* was kept secret to evaluate the movement of equipment and personnel to a second site on short notice. Because DUKWs were not used during the exercise, runways had to be constructed on the sandy beaches. At Suscinio, PSP proved to be unsatisfactory because it had to be taken up after each tide, bent sections replaced, and put down on

Treadway pier, Pauillac,
February 1957 (US Army)

BC barges at quay, Port-Haliguen,
October 1957 (US Army)

Crawler crane discharging cargo from BC barge,
la Turballe, April 1957 (US Army)

Army troops climb down nets over side of USNS Upshur
onto LCU, Quiberon Bay, 05 October 1957 (US Army)

regraded surfaces. At la Turballe, the steel treadway bridge sections from Camp Bussac provided stable runways regardless of surf conditions. More than 380 tons of ammunition were moved over the beach at la Turballe. The USNS *Kingsport Victory* was diverted to port at St.-Nazaire because SNCF railroad workers were scheduled to strike the next day.[221] At the St.-Nazaire airfield, two C-123B Provider aircraft from Dreux AB were loaded with CONEX containers. A Provider could carry 8 tons of cargo and take off or land on airstrips only 3,000 ft long. BC barges were used, but did not speed discharge as much as anticipated. When beached, their height required long-reach booms, which reduced lift capacity of the cranes. Because bulldozers were unable to move the heavy barges until the tide came in, barges were stuck on the beach for 6 to 10 hours, depending on interval between tides. It was concluded that barges would only be beneficial if loaded with more than 200 tons of cargo. More than 1,220 troops participated in the two-week exercise. In addition, more than two-hundred fifty LWR personnel were hired to work at the Guérande and St.-Nazaire railheads. Most of the LWRs complained that they were transported to work by Army 2½-ton trucks, not by buses. The Mayor of Sarzeau, M. Bouillard, welcomed Col William Whipple, the new BASEC commander, and his official party to Brittany. Bouillard remarked that not too long ago he also welcomed Americans who had liberated his country.[222] Bouillard may not have known that the modest, cerebral Whipple had been Gen Eisenhower's logistical plans chief for the Normandy landings in June 1944.

NODEX 15 in early June 1957 at St.-Gilles-Croix-de-Vie was intended to test the ability of Army engineer troops to work as longshoremen unloading cargo and to evaluate the use of DUKWs to move cargo directly to a railhead. During the nine-day exercise, troops of the 89th Engineer Co, commanded by 1st Lt Peter D. Starnes, and the 570th Trans Co (Terminal Service) moved nearly 6,200 tons of cargo from the USNS *Dalton Victory* and USNS *Private Francis X. McGraw* directly onto a small quay instead of over the beach. The average tidal range was 12 ft. A BK barge pier worked well for the LCMs, which navigated in shallow depths of water. After a DUKW overturned in the Vie River due to a strong current at ebb tide, DUKWs were not used within 1½ hours before and after low tide. Large rocks exposed in the channel bed at low tide made navigation difficult. Army lighters and barges respected the "rules-of-the-road" so the local fishing fleet could use the channel during the exercise. However, the channel was so narrow that all traffic had to be stopped at high tide if French tugs were moving barges. More than 1,110 troops participated in the exercise.

NODEX 16 was cancelled by US Army, Europe so more cargo would be delivered during the large-scale September 1957 exercise, planned to be at three landing sites.

NODEX 17 in late September-early October 1957 tested beach gradients in Brittany. A record of nearly 30,000 tons of cargo was discharged from seven ships. Although conceived as a three site exercise, only sites at Château de Suscinio and Port-Haliguen were used. On 22 and 23 September, an Atlantic storm with hurricane force winds damaged a DeLong Pier installed offshore at Batz, near La Baule.[223] Violent ocean waves broke the steel caisson legs of the pier and washed it ashore. The broken tubular caissons were recovered by a French Navy minesweeper, but the pier required extensive repairs before it could be returned to service.[224] Because the pier could not be used as the terminal island for the aerial tramway system, Brig Gen William Whipple cancelled the Batz phase of the exercise. The aerial tramway was to have been installed by 83rd Engineer Battalion personnel from Bussac and Ingrandes. Incoming ships, scheduled to be discharged at the DeLong Pier, were diverted to Port-Haliguen and Château de Suscinio. Some of the cargo was flown from Vannes by C-119G Flying Boxcar and C-123B Provider aircraft based at Dreux AB.

Most exercises used troops from Base Section, reinforced on occasion by specialized units on TDY from the United States. Because NODEX 17 was so large, troops were requested from Germany. The 37th Ordnance Co (Park), deployed to Fontenet from 1951 to 1955 and now stationed at Germersheim, Germany, was ordered to support the exercise. The 37th Ord Co, authorized one-hundred sixty-six officers and enlisted men, made a three-day, 680-mile trip by motor convoy from Germersheim to Suscinio. Upon arrival, the 37th Ord Co, commanded by 1st Lt Theodore L. Schleiffer, were told they were not needed because of the storm. After a one-day bivouac near the beach, the troops headed back to Germany. The two-day return trip on the narrow French roads took 29½ hours driving time, with an overnight at Maison-Fort.[225]

At the Quiberon sites, three ships discharged more than 11,000 tons of cargo. Two of the ships discharged simultaneously at Plage de Porrigo, near Port-Haliguen. LCMs pushed loaded BC barges into the small quay at Port-Haliguen. The 98th Trans Co (Port) from Soulac handled cargo at the Auray railhead, 19 miles from the beach site. To speed loading of railcars, pallet jacks were in great demand. Of the six sent to the railhead, one arrived in inoperable condition. In subsequent exercises, more pallet jacks, including spare parts and hydraulic fluid, would be provided. The Suscinio beach site extended from the town of Château de Suscinio eastward to Pointe de Penvins. Four ships discharged more than 17,000 tons of cargo at Suscinio. Rations were shipped in large cardboard boxes with "one-time use" metal cups bonded to the bottom of each box. The shipping method was designated UNITEX (unitized cargo, experimental). Because most of the boxes and cups were badly damaged, it was believed that UNITEX was not suitable for over-the-beach operations. For the first time, French and American amphibious truck companies worked together. Four new M-60 Ranger rough-terrain forklifts, which had forks that could be tilted left or right and shifted 2 ft to either side of center, were sent to France to be tested. A "security train" of sixteen railcars was loaded with 187 tons of ammunition at Questembert (Morbihan) railhead, thirty miles from Suscinio. More than 2,930 troops participated in the exercise. SNCF personnel at Vannes and Rennes did not work on Sundays and SNCF was unable to provide sufficient flat railcars needed for large loads, such as M-59 Armored Personnel Carriers. Therefore, it took over two weeks from the first discharge on the beach until the last flatcar was loaded.

Exercise Ships

Suscinio Sites	Quiberon Sites
SS Massillon Victory	SS Flying Foam
USNS Private John R. Towle	USNS Haiti Victory
SS President Arthur	USNS Upshur*
SS Mormactern	SS William Patterson

*USNS *Upshur* debarked only troops. All other ships discharged cargo.

The second personnel over the beach (POB) exercise in France was held on 05 October. More than five-hundred troops of the 532nd Artillery Battalion climbed down "scramble nets" over the side of the USNS *Upshur* into LCUs which took them to the beach. The *Upshur* then sailed on to Bremerhaven, Germany, where the rest of its passengers disembarked. From the beach at Quiberon, troops were trucked 8 miles inland to a bivouac area at Plouharnel, where they pitched tents. The next day, the troops were divided into two groups. In the morning one group was taken by trucks to the airstrip at Vannes. In the late afternoon, the second group marched about ¼ mile to the SNCF railroad line where ten passenger cars awaited. (See map on p. 374.)

NODEX 18 in early October 1958 at Île d'Oléron was the only exercise held in 1958. It was believed that all suitable coastal areas had been identified and a sufficient variety of unloading techniques had been tested. The SS *Santa Mercedes*, SS *Mormacelm*, and SS *Cape Ann* were scheduled to arrive at four day intervals from 01 to 09 October and the exercise was to last a month. By the third ship, the mostly untrained stevedores and winch operators of the 97th Trans Co had improved their skills so that discharge rates had doubled. The French 311ème Compagnie de Transbordement discharged cargo by DUKWs and LCMs. At concrete pads along the La Saurine canal, Army cranes lifted cargo from LCMs. During the exercise, more than 8,600 tons of cargo was discharged. To move cargo to the mainland, trucks from the 37th Trans Highway Transport Command used the commercial ferry from Le Château d'Oléron to le Chapus, although it shut down from midnight to 4 am.[226] Due to size limitations of the ferry, all oversize and heavy equipment was taken by LCU to la Pallice. The 594th Trans Group, commanded by Col George W. Barry, had control of movement to final destination.[227] French CRS and gendarmes controlled all military traffic on the island. More than 1,480 officers and enlisted men participated in the exercise.

Exercises resumed in response to Soviet Premier Nikita Khrushchev's threats during the Berlin Crisis in 1959. Four or five exercises were held each year until the last exercise in 1962.[228] The primary purpose now was to demonstrate to the Soviets that logistics forces in France were trained and ready to support the defense of Western Europe. During May and June 1959, Army engineers tested combinations of three prefabricated membranes and three metal landing mats on beaches at la Turballe and Suscinio. Loaded 5-ton dump trucks and DUKWs were driven back and forth over 30-ft strips of different combinations of mats and membranes. M8 steel landing mat (perforated steel plate similar to PSP) installed over a neoprene-coated nylon membrane worked best.[229]

NODEX 19 in May 1959 was a small-scale exercise at la Pallice that discharged more than 2,600 tons of cargo from one ship.

NODEX 20 in July 1959 discharged more than 4,800 tons of cargo from the USNS *Kingsport Victory*. DUKWs and landing craft moved cargo to la Repentie beach where trucks delivered it to the nearby railhead at la Pallice.[230]

Cargo transferred from DUKW to truck, les Sables-d'Olonne, October 1959 (US Army)

Rough-terrain forklift loading cargo onto truck on beach, les Sables-d'Olonne, October 1959 (US Army)

Crated ammo discharged by roller conveyor from BARC onto truck, les Sables-d'Olonne, October 1959 (US Army)

Mobile cranes discharge cargo from LCMs and LCUs at quay, les Sables-d'Olonne, October 1959 (US Army)

NODEX 21 in October 1959 at les Sables-d'Olonne, southwest of La Roche-sur-Yon, tested the cargo discharge ability of the four BARCs assigned to the 522nd Trans Platoon at Rochefort. Due to rough seas throughout the exercise, only BARCs delivered cargo to transfer points on the beach. Nearly 5,200 tons of high explosives, shipped on pallets, were unloaded from the USNS *Sergeant Morris E. Crain*. Because French authorities would not permit the ammunition to be placed on the beach, the cargo was moved from lighterage to trucks to railcars at the les Sables-d'Olonne railhead. Gendarmes controlled all traffic during the exercise. Half of the cargo discharged from the USNS *Greenville Victory* was shipped in UNITEX boxes and CONEX containers. The cargo was offloaded into LCMs of the US and French Army boat companies.

The MV *John U. D. Page*, the Army's new beach discharge lighter ship, and the *Comet*, a roll-on roll-off (RORO) transport ship configured so vehicles and trailers rapidly could be loaded and discharged, were used during the exercise. Due to rough seas with 8 to 12-ft swells, the *Comet* and *Page* sought sheltered anchorage off the Île d'Aix, 42 miles from les Sables d'Olonne. Finding smoother waters, the *Page's* master was able to link with the *Comet* (called "vessel marriage") for roll-on roll-off operations. The *Comet* carried more than three hundred-fifty jeeps, seventy cargo trailers, and twenty-four CONEX containers. On the second of three vessel marriages, LCUs laid their ramps on the ramp of the *Page* so vehicles could roll off the *Comet* through the *Page* onto the LCUs. More than 1,580 officers and enlisted men participated in the exercise.

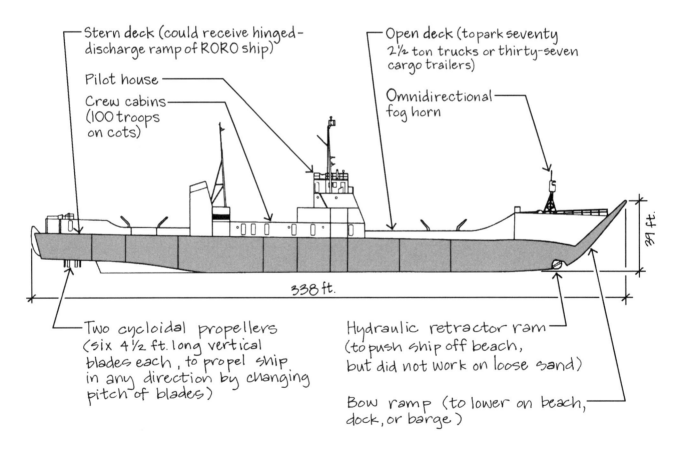

MV John U.D. Page

Beach Discharge Lighter

The MV *John U. D. Page*, a beach discharge lighter (designated: BDL-1X), was built in 1957-58 by National Steel and Shipbuilding Co, San Diego, California, at a cost of almost $2½ million. The *Page* was named to honor US Army Lt Col John Upshur Dennis Page, who was posthumously awarded the Medal of Honor for his courageous actions in combat during the Korean War. In April 1959, the *Page* completed its shakedown voyage from San Francisco, California, through the Panama Canal, to its home port at Fort Eustis, Virginia. The 338-ft long shallow-draft ship, operated by a twenty-seven man crew of the 469th Trans Detachment, could deliver cargo from deep-draft ships to the shore. Its deck could hold seventy 2½-ton trucks or thirty-seven large cargo trailers. Vehicles could be offloaded from the stern ramp of a RORO ship onto the deck. In three trips the *Page* could deliver the entire load of the RORO ship to the beach.[231]

After the *Page* beached and discharged its cargo, two built-in hydraulic "retractor rams" at the ship's stern were supposed to push it back into the water.[232] Unfortunately during NODEX 21, this design feature did not work on the sandy beach at les Sables-d'Olonne. The mushroom-shaped pad at the end of the ram merely punched a hole in the beach. CWO Ethelbert "Bert" S. West, master of the *Page*, relied on his two cycloidal propellers to wiggle free. Each propeller had six 4½-ft long vertical axis blades, which could propel the *Page* in any direction. Each blade, which rotated around its vertical axis, could change pitch to provide thrust in the desired direction. Unlike other lighterage, the *Page* could move forward, reverse, or from side-to-side.

Beach discharge lighter MV John U.D. Page at quay,
les Sables-d'Olonne, October 1959 (US Army)

During the buildup of US forces in Vietnam, the *Page* discharged numerous deep-draft ships to overcome the shortage of LCMs and LCUs. In 1966, to include maintenance personnel, the authorized crew was increased to forty-four. The *Page* carried spare propellers, bearings, and other parts for engines so repairs could be made by the crew without downtime in dry dock.[233] After extensive service in Vietnam, the beach discharge lighter *Page* now serves as an artificial reef at the bottom of the Atlantic Ocean off the coast of Charleston, South Carolina.

NODEX 22 in May 1960 at St.-Georges-de-Didonne used a barge ramp to discharge vehicles and vans from the USNS *Comet*, anchored in mid-stream of the Gironde Estuary. A barge was floated to the stern of the *Comet*, secured, and partially flooded to lower the far end. One-hundred forty-nine vehicles were driven off the ship, across the barge, and onto landing craft. The 311ème Compagnie de Transbordement, a French Army amphibious truck company, participated in the exercise. The unit had participated in four previous exercises also under the operational control of the 15th Trans Bn (Terminal). The 311ème had twenty DUKWs and four LCMs, which enabled it to equal the discharge capacity of the 460th Trans Co (Amphibious Truck) from Laleu.[234] Lighterage from French and American units discharged more than 3,000 tons of cargo from the USNS *Sergeant Morris E. Crain*. More than 1,520 personnel participated in the exercise.

NODEX 23 in late July 1960 at la Pallice harbor rapidly discharged 2,641 tons of cargo from the USNS *Comet*. Engineers of the 89th Engineer Co (Port Construction) from Rochefort built a floating causeway to connect the *Comet* to the sea wall. Prior to the exercise, the French dredged the area so the *Comet*, which needed 30 ft of water depth, could anchor 325 ft from shore. A pontoon cube barge, built by engineers to move with the tide, connected the stern ramp of the *Comet* to the steel treadway bridging on land.[235] Walter Tractors were used for the first time in an exercise because Army M-52 tractor trucks had difficulty maneuvering in the decks of the *Comet*. The compact Walter Tractor had four-wheel steering and could maneuver around deck stanchions with ease. Vans and trailers on the *Comet* were supported by aluminum struts rather than heavy, bulky wooden supports. The new struts were lightweight and did not shift during the Atlantic voyage. Only six-hundred fifty-one troops participated in the exercise.

CONEX Load (number of containers)

Lighterage	Calm Sea	Rough Sea	Lighterage	Calm Sea	Rough Sea
DUKW*	1	1	LCU	28	25
LCM-6	9	5	BARC	16	14

*load to be under 8,000 lbs.

NODEX 24 in early September 1960 at la Repentie beach discharged more than 2,100 tons of cargo from the USNS *Lieutenant Robert Craig*. DUKWs and BARCs hauled cargo, mostly loaded in CONEX containers, from the ship over the beach to trucks. LCMs and LCUs hauled cargo to the Mole d'Escale at la Pallice. At nearby Bertrand, rough-terrain forklifts of the 97th Trans Co (Port) loaded the containers onto SNCF railcars. Troops who were not from La Rochelle Installation were housed at Usine Jeumont and Laleu. More than 650 personnel were onsite during the exercise. Unlike previous around-the-clock exercises, NODEX 24 had only one 10-hour shift each day.

NODEX 25 in late October 1960 on the Crach River near la Trinité-sur-Mer demonstrated the capabilities of a U-type pontoon "floating pier" to discharge a cargo vessel in bad weather. The 50-ft by 285-ft pier was formed by more than 330 pontoon cubes, which could move up and down in the 18-ft tidal range. Bailey bridging was used to extend two 700-ft long causeways from the pier to shore.[236] Ten cluster piles of wood telephone poles were driven into the ocean shelf to hold the pier in place in 25-ft deep water. Engineers used an improvised floating pile driver assembled from pontoons to drive the piles.[237] It took three weeks to install the pier. The USNS *Comet* was unloaded within 40 hours of its arrival. Nearly 20,000 tons of cargo was discharged from the *Comet*, USNS *Greenville Victory*, and USNS *Private John R. Towle* before a major Atlantic storm, with hurricane force winds greater than 100 mph, destroyed the pier. Col Arnold A. Berglund, commander of the Port

U-type floating pier, Crach River near la Trinité-sur-Mer, October 1960 (US Army)

Area Command, ordered Capt Wayne F. Alch, commanding officer of the 89th Engineers, to have his men dismantle the pier during dangerous 20-ft waves. Alch ignored the order because he believed his men would be put at unacceptable risk. Several pontoon barges broke loose and were tossed on the beach which looked like Omaha Beach after D-Day. First Lt James W. Creech, who had signed the property book for pontoon equipment from Rochefort and bridge treadway components from depots in Germany, worried that he would be liable for the cost of the damaged equipment.[238] More than 1,740 personnel participated in the exercise. Before the next exercise, Alch was replaced by Capt James R. Knox from ComZ headquarters at Orléans.

NODEX 26 in early April 1961 at la Repentie discharged more than 4,200 tons of cargo from the USNS *Greenville Victory*. The cargo was mostly loaded in 146,000 boxes and crates of various sizes and 14,118 drums of POL. Army personnel working hatches were rotated to give hands-on experience to as many GIs as possible. Winch operators handled more than 5,000 drafts. To smoothly discharge such a large amount of loose cargo, it was determined that there should have been at least 1,000 pallets, not 700, on site when the exercise began. At the sorting areas, roller conveyors were used to unload cargo from BARCs. All BARCs and DUKWs maintained radio contact with the shore. The rocky beach proved to be rough on the flat bottom landing craft.

NODEX 27 in May 1961 at St.-Georges-de-Didonne discharged CONEX containers, vehicles, and RORO trailers from the USNS *Comet*, anchored in midstream of the Gironde Estuary. Cargo rolled out the stern port over a wide steel treadway bridge, mounted on a barge, onto a LCU or LCM. The lighterage moved cargo to an improvised dry ramp on the beach. The 89th Engineers used 16,000 sand bags to construct the ramp and covered the top surface with pierced aluminum plank (PAP). Eight-hundred bundles of PAP also were used to cover operating areas and roadways on the beach. Because the ramp was too narrow and the sloped face was not long enough, most lighterage discharged cargo directly onto nearby flat areas of firm sandy beach.[239]

NODEX 28 in late July 1961 at la Repentie discharged more than two-hundred fifty CONEX containers, thirteen 5-ton tractor trucks, and five combat tanks from the USNS *Sergeant Morris E. Crain*. Two of the M-60 full-tracked combat tanks were moved by BARCs from the ship to the railhead. One BARC, loaded with a tank, drove up a 43% grade over rough terrain. (A slope of 43% is 23½ degrees above ground level, 90 degrees would be straight up.) When the other BARC hit land its tank cargo, which had not been securely blocked, rolled forward. The tank broke through the watertight ramp of the BARC and dropped into 4 ft of water. Gen Bruce C. Clarke, Commander-in-Chief of US Army, Europe, who visited the exercise, was pleased by the climbing ability of the BARC, but not by the dropped M-60 tank. The tanks, each weighing more than 50 tons, were loaded onto flatbed railcars using an improvised steel treadway ramp and winch apparatus. One tank was driven off the BARC directly onto a railcar.

NODEX 29 in October 1961 at Boucau near Bayonne and the Golfe de Gascogne near St.-Jean-de-Luz discharged more than 9,200 tons of cargo from three ships. Railheads were used at St.-Jean-de-Luz and La Negresse, about 10 miles from the beach. It took the 89th Engineers three weeks to prepare the site at Boucau. Piles were driven by a pile driver mounted on a barge formed from pontoon cubes. The barge had been assembled at Rochefort under the supervision of Sgt Greuling and floated down the Atlantic coast to Bayonne. The exercise tested a U-type pontoon wharf with dual causeways to discharge RORO ship USNS *Comet* through two side ports, and general cargo ship USNS *Private John R. Towle*. Before the exercise began, the French dredged the Adour River to allow the pier to float, but the 89th Engineers dredged deeper so there would be sufficient depth for the *Comet*. Divers had to use explosives to blast a layer of rock that impeded the dredging. During blasting, stunned fish floated to the surface, delighting local fishermen.

The USNS *Sergeant Morris E. Crain*, anchored in the bay at St.-Jean-de-Luz, was unloaded by landing craft, BARCs, and DUKWs. For the sixth time, the French amphibious truck company 311ème Campagnie de Transbordement (Amphibie) participated in a NODEX. Twenty-seven rough-terrain forklifts were used and a QM experimental rough-terrain forklift (called a "telefork") was tested lifting CONEX containers. The telefork had a lift frame, attached to the front end boom, which could grab CONEX containers. It worked well with trucks and railcars, but had difficulty unloading DUKWs. The three ships delivered a total of four-hundred fifty-six CONEX containers. During off-duty hours, many troops of the 15th Trans Bn (Terminal Port) took a 30-minute train ride to Hendaye, near the border. By showing their military ID, GIs could cross into Spain, where food, drink, and entertainment cost far less than in France.[240, 241]

At the end of the exercise, the seven barges used to form the pontoon wharf were disconnected and lashed to piles in the Adour River for storage. Engineer truck driver Sp4 James W. Reed delivered fuel to the beach to assist GIs assigned to burn the human waste ("honey dipper duty"). Gasoline was poured into the metal drums containing human waste and ignited. Reed topped off one of the drums with diesel fuel, inadvertently creating an explosive mixture. (One gallon of diesel fuel per 100-lb sack of fertilizer-grade ammonium nitrate is highly explosive.) When the drum was ignited, the mixture blasted upward and poop rained down on the beach.[242]

NODEX 30 in early February 1962 at la Repentie discharged more than 2,300 tons of cargo over a soft, muddy beach. The exercise primarily was intended to train inexperienced personnel, not to test innovations. Due to rough seas, crews of DUKWs, BARCs, and lighterage gained valuable experience operating under difficult conditions. Cargo, which included more than 17,000 footlockers, was unloaded from the USNS *Towle* by the LOLO method, using cargo nets over the side of the ship. Troops of the 264th Trans Co (Terminal Service) laid a wide strip of PAP for a roadway to the railhead, ¼ mile from the beach.[243] The 264th Trans Co was deployed to Bassens from Fort Eustis, Virginia, during Operation ROUNDOUT. Troops were bivouacked 5 miles away at the Lagord QM Salvage Depot, which had a grassed area for the tents. Two months of rain and a NATO pipeline construction project had deepened the ubiquitous French mud at the la Repentie bivouac site.

NODEX 31 in late February-early March 1962 at la Repentie discharged more than 3,400 tons of cargo from the USNS *Greenville Victory*. The exercise was held on the same soft, muddy beach as the previous NODEX.[244]

NODEX 32 in late March-early April 1962 at le Clapet, near Royan, discharged more than 3,800 tons of cargo from the USNS *Greenville Victory* during high winds, swells up to 15 ft, and flooding conditions. The mixed cargo of CONEX containers and pallets included more than 51,000 cases of C-rations. To avoid congestion on the beach, DUKWs and BARCs moved cargo over the sandy beach to inland sorting areas. Two BARCs sustained hull damage because it was difficult to avoid the numerous sunken shipwrecks off the beach. Access to the railhead at La Tremblade, 10 miles from le Clapet, was through a narrow city street.

NODEX 33 in April 1962 at le Clapet discharged nearly 4,000 tons of cargo from the USNS *Lieutenant George W. G. Boyce*. Working two 10-hour shifts, DUKWs and BARCs moved cargo from the *Boyce* to the sorting area 1½ mile from the beach. Each day more than two dozen 2½-ton trucks moved cargo from the sorting area at le Clapet to the railhead at La Tremblade. The exercise was planned for amphibians only. Two of the four BARCs assigned to the 522nd Trans Platoon (BARC) broke down and a third could not be used until repair parts arrived, confirming the importance of on-site backup lighterage. LCMs were used to finish the exercise, although the le Clapet beach had a shallow gradient which made it difficult for LCMs to reach shore.

NODEX 34 in May 1962 at le Verdon and le Clapet tested the discharge of a RORO transport ship anchored at mid-stream in the Gironde Estuary. The ability of rough-terrain forklifts, using a modified lifting device, to move trailers on the RORO ship was compared to Walter Tractors, which could maneuver easily in tight spaces. Vehicles were driven off the USNS *Comet* over a barge onto landing craft that delivered the vehicles to shore. At le Verdon, Army personnel rapidly discharged more than 1,700 tons of cargo from the USNS *Towle* and 1,500 tons from the USNS *McGraw*. More than nine-hundred CONEX containers were discharged from the two ships. The exercise confirmed that CONEX containers: consolidated loads, streamlined handling of loads aboard ship and on shore, protected contents from damage, and the locked containers discouraged pilferage. Twenty DUKWs were in operation each 10-hour shift. To avoid overloading the civilian ferry service between Royan and le Verdon, Army lighterage carried personnel and wheeled vehicles between St.-Georges-de-Didonne and le Verdon. The exercise used railheads at Les Arros and les Huttes, north of Soulac, where a French Army 25-ton switch engine was used to move railcars between railheads and holding spurs. French and British troops participated at le Verdon. During the exercise, the 11th Transportation Terminal Command "B" from La Rochelle moved to a remote field near Pisany to test its ability to control port units under simulated emergency conditions. Voice communication was provided by the 529th Signal Co (Combat Area) from Croix-Chapeau.

End of Exercises

Beginning in 1962, the Department of the Army (DA) vacillated over who would assume responsibility and cost for discharge exercises in France. At first, US Continental Army Command (CONARC), headquartered at Fort Monroe, Virginia, was to assume responsibility and US Army, Europe (USAREUR) would maintain the equipment. Late in 1962, it was decided that CONARC would not be responsible and ComZ would conduct NODEX 35 in September 1963. In January 1963, ComZ asked DA to hold future exercises in the United States. However, DA believed that the experience gained from the exercises along the coast of France, using the personnel who would discharge ships in wartime, could not be duplicated elsewhere. Consequently, ComZ was allowed to delay NODEX 35 until late 1964.[245] When the McNamara drawdown in 1963 reduced the ability of ComZ to conduct exercises, NODEXs became impractical. Most depots and port activities in the Base Section were closed, reducing force levels by 5,400 troops. More than 6,200 French employees at Army installations lost their jobs.[246]

Although NODEX 34 was the official end of the series, a discharge exercise was scheduled for Spring 1965. The exercise was cancelled when US President Lyndon B. Johnson ordered Operation POWER PACK in late April 1965 to prevent a communist takeover of the Dominican Republic. Troops from Fort Eustis, Virginia, scheduled to be sent TDY to La Rochelle for the exercise, were sent to the Dominican Republic to support the 82nd Airborne Division from Fort Bragg, North Carolina. Consequently, the advance party of the 1099th Trans Co (Med Boat) spent nearly a month in France, without much to do, before joining their unit in the Dominican Republic.[247]

Lessons Learned from NODEX

The NODEX series of thirty-two completed exercises from 1954 to 1962 tested numerous offshore discharge innovations and equipment such as DeLong piers, aerial tramway, rough-terrain forklifts, helicopter airlift of cargo, BARCs, and the beach lighter MV *John U. D. Page*. Starting in 1955, before being sent to France troops learned how to operate winches on a full-size mockup of a ship, named the USS *Neversail*, at Fort Eustis, Virginia. The skills of Army stevedores in France were tested by purposefully shipping cargo in different packaging and by the oversize equipment which had to be maneuvered under difficult conditions. Loose general cargo provided better training for personnel during exercises, but required winch operators to handle ten times the loads needed to offload the same cargo weight packed in CONEX containers. Transportation personnel learned to overcome language differences and work with French gendarmes, and with French Army amphibious and land transportation units. Engineers improvised floating piers for RORO ships and found the best way to place plank and treadway bridge components on a variety of beach conditions. The many innovations enabled far fewer troops to unload more ships (two or three per exercise) at a faster discharge rate than the earlier SOB, OTB, and ODEX exercises. Most after-action reports recommended that DUKWs be replaced by BARCs and LARCs. The reports also affirmed the importance of using CONEX containers and RORO ships.

Exercises, usually lasting three weeks, had been held regularly at more than a dozen sites, often during foul weather conditions. It became obvious that prior knowledge of surf conditions and accurate weather forecasts would be essential to ensure rapid and safe discharge operations. In bad weather, short time lapses between successive wave crests did not allow lighterage to recover from the impact of the previous breaker. The innovations and training had improved significantly the efficiency of the ComZ engineers, stevedores, and transporters. US Army, Europe now had an organization and experienced cadre ready to move cargo rapidly from ship to shore if the Soviets destroyed the Atlantic ports. The skills developed during the NODEX series also would enable Forward Floating Depot (FFD) ships to be rapidly discharged over the beach. In 1962, the Army began converting Victory-class ships to carry ready-to-use vehicles, weapons, ammunition, POL, and other combat gear. The ships, operated by MSTS, could be prepositioned along the coast of France. Each ship carried an Army maintenance detachment.[248]

New Offshore Discharge Exercises (NODEX), 1954-1962[249]

NODEX	Discharge Location	Date	Cargo Ships	Cargo (tons)	Innovations and Equipment Tested
1	Le Verdon	01-27 Nov 54	2	7,882	Simultaneous discharge of two ships. Performance of LCM-8 compared to LCM-6. Personnel strength for terminal battalion evaluated.
2	Le Verdon	01-25 Feb 55	2	7,866	Digital code marked on cargo to expedite flow. Detachable counterweight for conventional forklifts. Floatation platform under tracks of crawler cranes. Portable dental equipment used on beach.
3	Le Verdon	11-25 Apr 55	2	8,956	L-19 Bird Dog aircraft guides convoy of vessels. Performance of LCU (1466 Class) compared to LCM. Marker buoy (10 gal drum) mounted on DUKWs. Surf deflectors attached to crawler cranes.
4	La Repentie	27 Jun 55 to 12 Jul 55	2	8,142	All trucks, no SNCF railcars. Performance of LCM-6 compared to LCU. Roller conveyor to transfer DUKW cargo to truck. POL drums (4 to 6) discharged by "chime" harness.
5	Le Verdon	03-17 Oct 55	3	10,477	DeLong pier for simultaneous discharge of two ships. Bailey bridging connected DeLong pier to land. Cargo shipped in UNITEX boxes.
6	Le Verdon	06-21 Dec 55	3	8,693	Ship discharge to trucks on lighterage. Remote in-transit area and railhead at Camp Bussac.
7	Le Verdon	05-29 Feb 56	3	11,871	All cargo of one ship on pallets or in containers. House Falls cable rigging used on DeLong pier.
8	Talmont	11-25 Apr 56	3	15,396	Aerial tramway. Liquid asphalt used to seal ground at operations area. Tire fenders hung along sides of DeLong pier.
9	Talmont	27 May 56 to 08 Jun 56	2	6,607	Aerial tramway. Unskilled locals hired to be stevedores. Dolly trailers used to haul long pipe.
10	Cancelled by French government.				
11	St.-Jean-de-Luz	02-19 Oct 56	3	12,043	Short notice exercise.
12	Le Verdon	01-18 Dec 56	3	12,504	Railcar loading ramp (borrowed from French Army). Personnel transfer from DUKW to H-19 helicopter. Troops work 12-hour shifts. Augmented mobile port unit evaluated.
13	Le Verdon & Pauillac	01-20 Feb 57	3	8,878	Treadway bridge and PSP on mud flats. Helicopters move cargo to depots. Floating BC barge discharge point.
14	Suscinio & La Turballe	01-16 Apr 57	3	7,862	Shift to second landing site on short notice. Cargo not moved by DUKWs. Treadway bridge components laid on sandy beach. French commercial tugs tow BC barges.

15	St.-Gilles-Croix-de-Vie	31 May 57 to 08 Jun 57	2	6,189	Engineer troops unload cargo. DUKWs move cargo to railhead. BC barges transport cargo in narrow tidal channel. LCMs anchor alongside BK barge pier.
16	Cancelled by US Army, Europe (USAREUR).				
17	Suscinio & Quiberon	30 Sep 57 to 18 Oct 57	7	28,969	Simultaneous operations at widely-separated sites. BC barge maneuvered by two LCMs. MR-60 Ranger rough-terrain forklift. Metal cups on pallet bases (prone to damage). POB exercise discharges troops at Quiberon Bay.
18	Île d'Oléron	01-14 Oct 58	3	8,639	Commercial ferry used to move cargo from island.
19	La Pallice	08-14 May 59	1	2,639	No new methods tested.
20	La Pallice	09-14 Jul 59	1	4,845	No new methods tested.
21	Les Sables-d'Olonne	19-27 Oct 59	3	7,081	Beach discharge lighter MV *John U. D. Page*. Platoon of BARCs.
22	St.-Georges-de-Didonne	02-14 May 60	2	5,616	Barge ramp for RORO ship anchored offshore.
23	La Pallice	26-29 Jul 60	1	2,641	Floating causeway built from pontoon cubes. Aluminum struts support RORO vans and trailers. Walter tractor used to discharge RORO ship.
24	La Pallice & La Repentie	01-05 Sep 60	1	2,192	Lighterage moves CONEX cargo.
25	Quiberon Bay	26-31 Oct 60	3	19,793	Pile driver mounted on pontoon floating barge. U-shaped pontoon floating pier. Simultaneous discharge of three cargo ships.
26	La Pallice & La Repentie	03-10 Apr 61	1	4,244	All loose cargo. Roller conveyors used on BARCs.
27	St.-Georges-de-Didonne	21-24 May 61	1	2,528	Dry ramp built with 16,000 sand bags and PAP. Barge deck modified to connect RORO to LCUs.
28	La Repentie	25-31 Jul 61	1	2,881	BARC moves M-60 combat tank up 43% grade.
29	St.-Jean-de-Luz & Boucau	05-14 Oct 61	3	9,233	RORO ship discharge to U-shaped floating pier. Experimental "telefork" rough-terrain forklift.
30	La Repentie	04-09 Feb 62	1	2,311	LOLO discharge using nets.
31	La Repentie	28 Feb to 01 Mar 62	1	3,413	No new methods tested.
32	Le Clapet	26 Mar to 06 Apr 62	1	3,899	Amphibians move cargo to inland sorting areas. Restricted access to railhead.
33	Le Clapet	08-13 Apr 62	1	3,983	Cargo moved only by amphibious vehicles.
34	Le Verdon & Le Clapet	08-17 May 62	3	5,596	Command of operations from remote location. Ships anchored on opposite sides of estuary. RORO ship discharges to barge in midstream. Modified forklift used to clear RORO ship.
35	Cancelled by ComZ due to drawdown of Base Section.				

Abbreviations (including US Army and US Navy designations)

BARC	Barge, amphibious, resupply, cargo	LSD	Landing ship dock
BC	Barge, dry cargo (non-propelled)	MSTS	Military Sea Transportation Service (US agency responsible for ocean shipping)
BD	Crane, floating		
BDL	Beach discharge lighter	MV	Motor vessel
BK	Barge, dry cargo, knockdown (non-propelled)	PAP	Pierced aluminum plank
		POB	Personnel Over the Beach exercise
BSP	Barge, self-propelled	PSP	Pierced steel plank
CDS	Container delivery system	RORO	Roll-on roll-off
CONEX	Experimental shipping container (later called "Container Express")	RTF	Rough-terrain forklift
		SNCF	*Société nationale des chemins de fer français* (French national railroad)
DUKW	Amphibious 2½-ton truck (Ordnance Corps vehicle)		
		S&P	Stake and platform trailer
F	Fireboat	SS	Merchant marine steamship
FFD	Forward floating depot	ST	Small tug, harbor
J	Boat, utility patrol	T	Transport boat (passenger or cargo)
JCCA	Joint CONEX Control Agency	UNITEX	Unitized cargo, experimental
LARC	Lighter, amphibious, resupply, cargo	USNS	United States Naval Ship (manned by civilian crew)
LCM	Landing craft, mechanized		
LCU	Landing craft, utility	USS	United States Ship (manned by US Navy crew)
LOLO	Lift-on lift-off	WST	Wide steel treadway

Victory Ships Participating in Exercises

More than five-hundred 455-ft long Victory ships were built during World War II. The ships could carry more than 7,600 tons of cargo at a cruising speed of 17 knots, 6 knots faster than Liberty ships.* Most Victory ships were named for American cities and education institutions. Thirty-three were named for Allied nations.[250] On 17 June 1948, the *Greenville Victory* sailed from Cherbourg to Brooklyn, New York, carrying the remains of 3,754 GIs who had died during the war.[251] From 1952 to 1962, twenty Victory ships participated in offshore-discharge exercises. The USNS *Greenville Victory* and USNS *Lt James E. Robinson* each participated in seven. During the Cold War, Victory ships also delivered military cargo to ports in France.

Victory ship USNS Pvt Francis X. McGraw, la Turballe, June 1953 (US Army)

Victory Ship	US Maritime Hull Number	Type VC2-S-AP	ODEX (1952-54)	NODEX (1954-62)
USNS Lt George W. G. Boyce	852	2/AK 251		12, 13, 33
USNS Lt Robert Craig	811	2/AK 252		11, 12, 13, 24
USNS Sgt Morris E. Crain	741	2/AK 244		6, 14, 21, 22, 28, 29
USNS Dalton Victory**	21	3/AK 256		15
USNS Duke Victory	731	2		11
SS East Point Victory	645	2	3, 15	
SS Enid Victory	712	2		3
SS Greece Victory	2	3	14	1, 3, 4
USNS Greenville Victory	18	3/AK 237	8, 16	21, 25, 26, 31, 32
USNS Haiti Victory**	532	3/AK 238		7, 11, 13, 17
SS Jefferson City Victory	165	3		6
USNS Kingsport Victory***	20	3/AK 239	10, 16	14, 20
SS Laredo Victory	723	2	9, 11	
USNS Macalester Victory	188	3		11
SS Massillon Victory	578	2		17
USNS Pvt Francis X. McGraw	796	2/AK 241	12, 13	2, 14, 15, 34
SS Northwestern Victory	173	3		5, 8
SS Oshkosh Victory	808	2	2	
USNS Lt James E. Robinson	86	3/AK 274	4, 5, 7	1, 2, 7, 12
USNS Pvt John R. Towle	162	3/AK 240		17, 25, 30, 34

*Multiply knots by 1.15 to convert to miles per hour (mph). Two Liberty ships participated in the offshore discharge exercises: SS *Heywood Broun* in NODEX 9 and SS *William Patterson* in NODEX 17. GIs called Liberty ships "Ugly Ducklings."

**In 1960, *Dalton Victory* and *Haiti Victory* were converted to missile range instrumentation ships for the US space program. On 11 August 1960, the *Haiti Victory* (renamed *Longview*) became the first ship to recover the nose cone of a missile from orbit in outer space.

***In 1962, *Kingsport Victory* became a satellite communications ship.

Abbreviations (including Maritime Commission designations)

V	Victory (ship)	AP	Transport
C	Cargo	AP2	Steam turbine of 6,000 horsepower (hp)
C1	Waterline length less than 400 ft	AP3	Steam turbine of 8,500 hp
C2	Waterline length of 400 to 449 ft	AK	Cargo ship classification (US Army ships transferred to US Navy in 1950)
C3	Waterline length 450 ft or greater		
S	Steam propulsion		

US Army Cargo Ships

In 1946, twenty Victory ships (Type C2) were loaned to the US Army and renamed for Army war heroes who had been recognized for extraordinary valor in World War II. The six ships listed in the table were named for soldiers who posthumously received the Medal of Honor. By 1951, most of the twenty ships had been transferred back to the US Navy and the six ships were used in offshore discharge exercises, operated by civilian crews.

Ships Named for Medal of Honor Recipients

Army Name	Previous Name
USNS Pvt John R. Towle	Appleton Victory
USNS Lt Robert Craig	Bowling Green Victory
USNS Lt James E. Robinson	Czechoslovakia Victory
USNS Sgt Morris E. Crain*	Mills Victory
USNS Pvt Francis X. McGraw	Wabash Victory
USNS Lt George W. G. Boyce	Waterville Victory

*On 13 March 1945 at Haguenau, France, Tech/Sgt Morris E. Crain gave his life when he held off a numerically superior German force so five of his men could withdraw to safety.

War Plans

The offshore discharge exercises helped demonstrate to the Soviets that the US military was determined to defend Europe. They showed how a peacetime Army could be expanded in wartime to operate at less favorable sites if fixed ports and good beaches were destroyed in a surprise atomic attack. Rapid discharge methods using RORO ships and beach discharge lighter ships, such as the MV *Page*, would reduce time that ships were targets in the discharge area. After rapidly discharging cargo and transporting it inland, Army personnel would move to another site.[252, 253]

Discharge and Run

To test the "discharge and run" concept, NODEX 11 in October 1956 was a short notice exercise held at St.-Jean-de-Luz. During NODEX 14 in April 1957, troops were shifted on short notice from Suscinio to la Turballe. NODEX 17 in September-October 1957 evaluated simultaneous cargo discharge operations at widely separated sites and simulated wartime staging of personnel disembarked from a troopship anchored offshore. The exercise command post for NODEX 34 in May 1962 at le Clapet was located near Pisany, far from the beach. Army war planners learned from the exercises that the best method of discharge during combat would be to anchor ships offshore or in mid-stream. Cargo immediately could be unloaded onto landing craft and amphibious vehicles. There would be no long delays needed to set up DeLong piers, pontoon piers, or aerial tramways. Novel methods could be effective in peacetime, but were vulnerable to storms and aerial attack during war. They did not follow von Hindenburg's maxim that, in war, only the simple succeeds.[254]

Watercraft Fleet in France (1959)[255, 256]

DUKW*	LCM**	LCU	BARC	Floating Crane***	Harbor Tug (ST)	Cargo Barge	Freight and Supply Vessel
245	53	16	4	7	10	19	9

*All built in 1945 or earlier.
**Landing craft, mechanized (LCM-6) had overall length of 56 ft, LCM-8 length of 74 ft.
***60-ton and 100-ton capacity cranes mounted on steel barge.

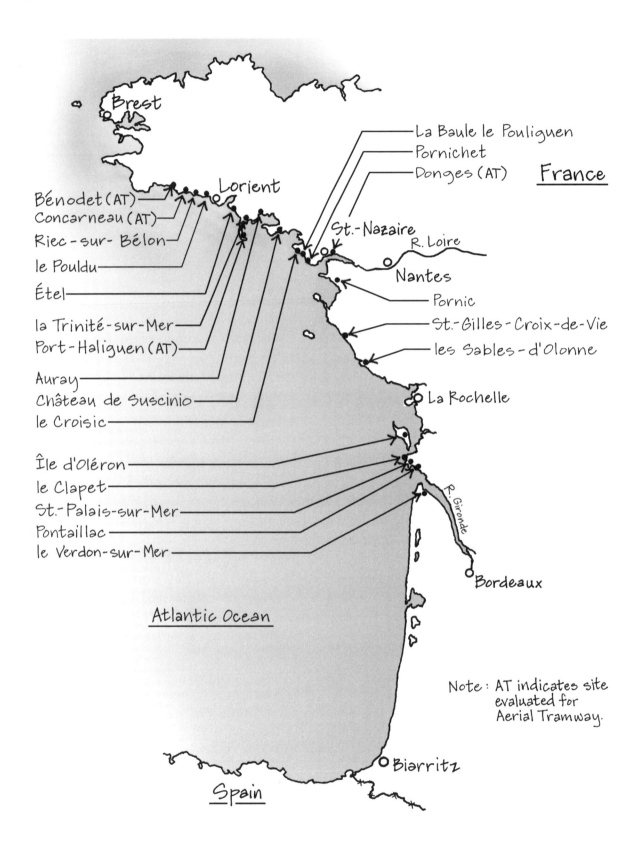

Locations for Emergency Ports & Beaches (1958)

Emergency Ports and Beaches

During war with the Soviets, numerous landing sites would be needed to avoid concentrations of ships and accumulations of supplies on beaches. For the exercises, engineers prepared charts showing rise and fall of tides, data on tidal currents, and profiles of sea bottom and beach (to locate sand bars and other obstacles).[257] By 1958, secret plans for wartime use of ports and beaches listed twenty-one locations along the coast of France that initially would be used to simultaneously discharge thirty-seven ships at an estimated monthly rate exceeding 1 million tons of cargo. Each site was to be at least 5 miles away from adjacent sites.[258] Two-thirds of the emergency sites, selected by Army planners on ComZ staff at Orléans, had not been tested in exercises. Experienced Army cadre at the port areas believed it would be difficult to discharge supplies rapidly at some of the untested sites. They had learned that productive sites should have: natural protection against violent weather, anchorage for deep-draft ships, low range of tides, beaches that were not too soft or rocky, and access to roads and railways so supplies could be moved rapidly inland. Bénodet and Donges were selected to be emergency sites for the aerial tramway, although NODEXs 8 and 9 in April through June 1956 at Talmont had revealed that the innovative contraption could not be installed rapidly. The emergency site at Île d'Oléron was tested during NODEX 18 in October 1958. Trucks used the commercial ferry to haul cargo to the mainland.

Auray Landing Site

The war plan site at Auray had been studied in World War II for port reconstruction after D-Day. The secret plan, code named CHASTITY, called for mooring thirty deep-draft ships in a 80-ft deep sheltered channel of the Auray River, near Locmariaquer. Ships were to discharge over a floating "landing stage" and a floating pontoon pier.[259] Initially Quiberon Bay beaches were considered, but the wide tidal range of 30 ft would have complicated operations and gentle slope of the sea bottom near shore would have required construction of extremely long piers. In winter months, bad weather would preclude the use of lighters in the bay, but not at the sheltered river site. Although approved for development, the port was not needed because of the Allies unexpected, rapid capture of the virtually undamaged port at Antwerp, Belgium.[260] During war with the Soviets, ships would anchor along the Auray River at Locmariaquer.

Marine Fleet Relocates

In 1963, most of the US Army marine fleet was moved to le Pellerin, 15 miles west of Nantes, where Jules Verne, author of *20,000 Leagues Under the Sea*, grew up. The remainder of the fleet of two-hundred forty-two landing craft, barges, and tugboats was located at Rochefort and le Verdon.[261] DUKWs, under Ordnance Corps jurisdiction in the Army supply system, were stored at Braconne.

The le Pellerin Depot, which opened in 1957, had a 12-acre wet storage basin on the Canal de la Martinère, west of le Pellerin along the Loire River. Facilities at le Pellerin were austere—two small masonry gatehouses and twenty prefabs for storage and troop housing. The French *Ponts et Chaussées* operated the lock system that controlled the water level of the canal. The Army also used part of a nearby canal east of le Pellerin at la Telindière, called "Bikini." In 1965, four enlisted men and twenty-one French employees chipped, brushed, primed, and painted hulls of the marine fleet. One harbor tug was kept in working condition to move watercraft. Engine and compartments of landing craft and tugboats were sealed airtight to keep metal parts dry.[262]

In September 1966, US Secretary of Defense Robert S. McNamara ordered all landing craft to be withdrawn from the marine fleet in Europe. Fifty-three LCMs and sixteen LCUs were shipped to the US for eventual use in Vietnam.[263] The former depot site at le Pellerin became a public recreation area for fishing and camping. Only a small masonry US Army gatehouse remains.

Wet storage basin, le Pellerin, 1962 (US Army)

St.-Nazaire

In March 1953, the first US Army troops arrived at St.-Nazaire. On 10 April 1953, the USNS *Waltham Victory* became the first US Naval ship, since the end of World War II, to unload cargo at St.-Nazaire. Army troops, commanded by Maj Mark P. Hughes, sorted cargo on the dock and loaded it onto railcars. The cargo was discharged two weeks before the French government gave official permission to use the port.[264, 265] St.-Nazaire would be developed primarily to handle tanker shipments of POL. A marine reception installation at Donges had berths for an ocean tanker at l'Arceau jetty, five miles east of St.-Nazaire. It took two to three days to pump fuel from a tanker anchored at the jetty. More than 200,000 barrels of fuel was pumped through large diameter rubber hose connections to an underwater pipeline to the tank farms. In April 1953, the US Army acquired Camp de Gron, a 25-acre tract near Bellevue, for troop housing and support facilities. Most of the buildings, including troop barracks and the chapel, were metal prefabs. French Padre Felix Monot served as Catholic priest for the American troops.[266] The first school for dependents used leased space at La Baule. In 1953, an NCO Club, called "Parley Vous," opened at La Baule. Troops of the 188th Trans Co (Terminal Service) supported port operations at the Quai des Grand Puits dock at St.-Nazaire. A huge warehouse was rented for $13,750 per year.

On a food inspection visit to the port of St.-Nazaire in 1956, 1st Lt Frank A. Ramsey of the 73rd Medical Det at La Rochelle drove his POV between warehouse buildings toward his next stop. His blind turn at the wharf end of the road abruptly ended at the fringe of a protest rally by hundreds of stevedores. Ramsey's Studebaker, which displayed ComZ black and white 1CF plates, exposed him to be an American. Ramsey knew French dockers were members of the communist-controlled dockers union and a common practice of communist mobs was to overturn American cars. Fortunately, on the way to St.-Nazaire, he had purchased a jug of cider, sliced meat, and a baguette for lunch. Quickly surrounded by the stevedores, Ramsey was asked if he was American and what was that jug on the front passenger seat. Ramsey replied "oui" (yes) and asked if his inquisitor would like to taste his cider. The Frenchman accepted, took a swig, and passed it around the ring of stevedores surrounding the Studebaker. After the jug had been emptied, the leader loudly proclaimed in French that "The American likes our cider!" and waved "allez, allez," meaning go on. Ramsey was relieved that he had not been tossed into the Loire River.[267]

Deep Water Pipeline Extensions

The deep sea anchorage at Piriac-sur-Mer had five mooring buoys, each secured by a 10-ton anchor. Large super tankers could discharge POL while at sea by an underwater pipeline extension. The extension on the seabed was ½-inch thick, 2-ft diameter pipe sections welded together and encased by 2½-inch thick concrete coating.[268] Connected to the extension were 200-ft long, 10-inch diameter rubber hoses. Chains connected to the undersea hoses were marked by buoys. After tankers moored, winches on the ship lifted the hoses to the open deck. Then Army divers opened valves of the submerged pipe so POL could be pumped from the tankers through the hoses and pipe to Donges. On land at "D" farm, it took three GIs about 30 minutes to open the 24-inch gate valve by slowly turning a huge wheel. Although discharge operations had to be cancelled frequently due to rough seas, more than sixty tankers were able to unload each year. La Pallice also had a pipeline extension from the Môle d'Escale. Both extensions were serviced by US Army divers. The Donges Terminal District leased a French-owned fishing boat to serve as its T-boat to ferry GIs and French employees from shore to the tankers and buoys.

Periodically, buoys required painting to prevent corrosion and be highly visible to shipping. It took GIs several hours to paint the 7-ft diameter buoys. Because PFC Thomas L. Simons could not swim, his sergeant tied a rope around Simons' waist and secured the other end to a pad eye at the top of the buoy. Simons safely bobbed up-and-down as he painted the buoy.[269]

Donges Tank Farms

Drivers from Detachment 1 of the 37th Highway Trans Command hauled jerry cans and 55-gal drums of grease and other lubricants from the four Donges Terminal District tank farms near La Fernais, Dorieux, Savenay, and Piriac-sur-Mer. "A" farm at La Fernais had filling points for thirty tank railcars and twelve tank semitrailers. The drum plant had a capacity to fill 5,000 drums per day. "B" farm near Dorieux, the heart of the Donges complex, had the main pipeline pump station, offices for the district, laboratory, warehouses, and metal prefab barracks for sixty GIs. Three times each day, seven days a week, troops were driven by Army bus from the tank farms to the mess hall at Camp de Gron. Most of the GIs had to ride 7 miles each way. More than two-hundred local wage rate (LWR) employees worked at Donges Terminal District.

Each year, about one-hundred personnel from the Donges Terminal District bivouacked at Camp de Coëtquidan-St.-Cyr, near Beignon. For one week, the GIs practiced small unit infantry maneuver tactics and qualified with the M-14 rifle, .45 cal pistol, and shotgun. US military attachés at the Paris Embassy coordinated use of training areas with the French.[270]

ComZ Replacement Center

From late 1955 to mid-1957, individual replacements for Army troops in France were processed at the St.-Nazaire ComZ replacement center, commanded by Lt Col Byron B. Bradford. In 1957, the replacement center was relocated to Rochefort; in 1958 to Orléans. Individual replacements were assigned to fill vacancies by matching rank and skills, identified by the military occupational specialty (MOS) code, to the needs of the units in France. By the late 1950s, most replacements were given their assignment before being sent overseas. Transceiver machines at Fort Dix, New Jersey, transmitted personnel data from punched cards over telephone lines to machines at Orléans. Direct assignment reduced transportation costs in Europe and time wasted in replacement depots.[271, 272]

Pornichet Hotel

From 1953 to 1955, the Army leased a resort hotel at Pornichet near St.-Nazaire for use as a ComZ recreation center. Personnel could stay up to 10 days (extensions on space-available basis). Rooms cost $1.50 per person per night, breakfast 50¢, lunch 75¢, and dinner $1. Meals for children were half price. The hotel was intended to serve enlisted personnel and their families, although officers could use the facility on a space-available basis. Hotel guests could use a nearby 18-hole golf course for a greens fee of $2.[273]

Ocean Shipping Innovations

The demobilization after World War II reduced the US Army ports in the US from thirteen to four. Established in 1949, the Military Sea Transportation Service (MSTS) assumed responsibility for ocean shipping of all US Army cargo. To meet the needs of the Korean War and buildup of forces in Europe, the Transportation Corps had to rely heavily on commercial ports and innovations such as experimental loaded semitrailers (called VANEX), experimental shipping containers (called CONEX), and roll-on roll-off transport ships (called RORO).[274] By the early 1960s, surveys showed that 42% of Army cargo consisted of packaging which could be shipped by CONEX containers.[275]

RORO Concept

The roll-on roll-off (RORO) concept was developed to enable cargo to be rapidly discharged. At the French ports, vehicles were driven off the ship onto the dock, eliminating the costly and time-consuming crane-hoist operations. Harbor locks at St.-Nazaire closed to create a self-contained water basin when the water level had aligned a RORO ship to the dock. A French fabricator built a metal ramp and bridge to connect RORO ships to the dock. The ramp was constructed in five sections that could be disassembled and stored when not in use. During discharge operations, RORO semitrailers were maneuvered in the ship and towed over the ramp by Walter Tractors.

Initially, the Army acquired nearly six hundred RORO semitrailers to fit RORO ships and be suitable for roads in Europe. However, half of the trailers were too tall to maneuver in low-clearance holds of RORO ships.[276] The top priority of cargo shipped by RORO to France in 1959 included: ordnance spare parts to Nancy, QM supplies to Metz, and signal equipment to Verdun and Nancy. RORO trailers were carefully tracked to ensure they would be returned to the system.[277]

SS Carib Queen Becomes USNS Taurus

The SS *Carib Queen*, a 475-ft long converted US Navy landing ship dock (LSD), was the first RORO ship to discharge cargo in France. A Navy LSD could submerge its well deck to allow watercraft through its stern door and then pump out the water. The first trans-Atlantic trip of the *Queen*, chartered by the Military Sea Transportation Service (MSTS), took nine days. On 02 February 1957 at St.-Nazaire, the *Queen* discharged: seventy-five semitrailers, twenty-two refrigeration vans, nine DUKWs, sixty sedans, and twenty jeeps. The semitrailers were loaded with medicine, food, tires, and electronic equipment. Army drivers in ComZ trucks hauled the trailers and vans from the port to depots. Sixteen drivers from the Orléans area picked up Army sedans.[278, 279] In 1955, the *Queen* was sold by MSTS to Gulf Transportation Corp, who sold it to TMT Trailer Service, which operated it between US and Caribbean ports. In 1959, the MSTS reacquired the *Queen* and renamed the ship the USNS *Taurus*.

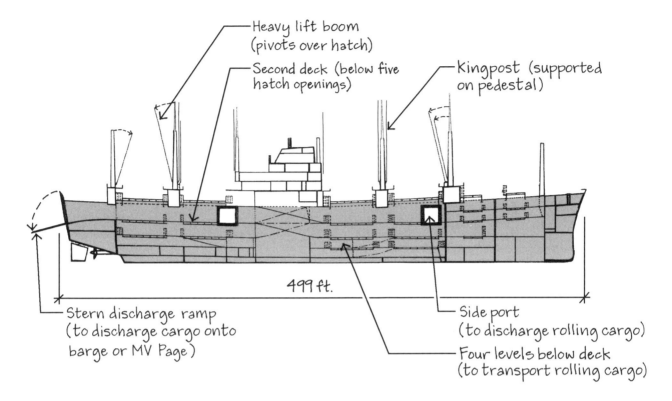

USNS Comet RORO Ship

USNS Comet

In late January 1958, the USNS *Comet*, a 499-ft long transport ship designed to be a RORO vehicle cargo ship, sailed at 18 knots from New York to St.-Nazaire with seventeen officers and a crew of forty-three. It would take more than four World War II Liberty ships to hold as much cargo as the *Comet*. It could transport one-sixth of the equipment of an armored division. To load and discharge rolling cargo rapidly, the *Comet* had five loading ports leading to the second deck. Described as a "floating garage" by GIs, the ship could hold more than four-hundred military vehicles. On her maiden voyage to St.-Nazaire it took only eight hours to discharge four-hundred nine vehicles.

During the Lebanon deployment in 1958, the *Comet* moved equipment of a tank battalion from Europe to Lebanon in considerably less time than it would have taken by conventional loading methods. However, there were delays because the US Army port troops in Germany did not properly load the 10,700 tons of combat cargo. After rapidly discharging the armored vehicles in Lebanon, the *Comet* sailed to Israel where large dockside cranes were used to rearrange the remaining cargo so it could be rapidly discharged when the ship returned to Lebanon.[280]

RORO semi-trailer maneuvered by Walter Tractor on ramp for USNS Comet, St.-Nazaire, 1959 (US Army)

RORO semi-trailer discharged from USNS Comet, la Pallice, July 1960 (US Army)

RORO Atlantic Fleet

By 1959, RORO ships USNS *Comet* and USNS *Taurus* shuttled between the US and Europe every 15 days.[281] The Army estimated that 25% of its cargo shipped to Europe rolled on wheels or treads. During 1959, truckers from the 106th Trans Bn supported eighteen RORO operations at St.-Nazaire. In 1962, the 520-ft long USNS *Transglobe* joined the Atlantic Ocean roll-on roll-off fleet. Most shipments from the ports of New York and New Orleans were combat vehicles; most shipments back to the US from St.-Nazaire were privately owned vehicles (POV). War-risk cargo, such as ammunition, military vehicles, and aircraft were shipped to French ports. Household goods, PX merchandise, refrigerated cargo, and other administrative cargo were shipped to Germany. In April 1965 at Seattle, Washington, the US Navy launched another RORO ship. The USNS *Sea Lift* entered MSTS service in May 1967, one month after US forces departed from France.

RORO Ships to Support Invasion

In August 1962, U-2 Dragon Lady aircraft photographed Soviet missile sites which had secretly been constructed in Cuba. The nuclear missiles could reach most of the continental United States. In October 1962, the USNS *Comet* and USNS *Taurus* were diverted to the port of Savannah, Georgia, to transport equipment of the 1st Armored Division should orders be given to invade Cuba. If the sea was calm off the coast of Cuba, the MV *John U. D. Page* would transfer the equipment from ship to shore. Ordnance personnel removed the commander's cupola from M-48A2 Patton III combat tanks so the tanks would fit into the two lower levels of the *Comet*.[282] RORO ships were not used in an invasion because US President John F. Kennedy chose a naval blockade of Cuba. In exchange for Soviet removal of their missiles from Cuba, Kennedy pledged to not invade Cuba and to remove NATO's forty-five Jupiter nuclear missiles from Turkey.[283-285]

St.-Nazaire Area US Army Installations

Installation	Location	Activity and Units
Headquarters	St.-Nazaire (Camp de Gron, 25 acres)	St.-Nazaire Support Activity
	Doriex (Tank Farm B)	US Army Terminal District, Donges
Depots/Ports	St.-Nazaire (Quai des Grand Puits)	Deep water port (11th Transportation Terminal Command "B")
	St.-Nazaire (Blvd Leferme)	POV parking facility (7 acres)
	La Fernais (355 acres, A to D)	Donges Tank Farm A
	Dorieux	Donges Tank Farm B
	Savenay	Donges Tank Farm C
	Piriac-sur-Mer	Donges Tank Farm D
	le Pellerin (La Martinère), La Telindière (Bikini)	US Army Depot Activity, le Pellerin, off-depot wet basin storage sites (60 acres)
	Hennebont	Warehouses
	Cherbourg (Nacqueville)	Signal Corps Cablehead (4 acres)
Medical Dispensary	St.-Nazaire	218th General Dispensary
School (dependents)	St.-Nazaire (Camp de Gron)	Elementary school (K to 8)
Bachelor Officers Quarters (BOQ)	St.-Nazaire	Two metal prefabs (21 men each)
Troop Barracks	St.-Nazaire (Camp de Gron, near Bellevue)	67th Trans Company (Med Truck) 188th Trans Co (Terminal Service) 547th Ordnance Company (FM) 313th Signal Company (Service) 153rd Army Postal Unit 165th Military Police Det (CI)
	Donges (at Dorieux)	543rd Engineer Co (Pipeline)
	La Martinère	US Army Depot Activity, le Pellerin
Deep-Water Pipeline Connections	Piriac-sur-Mer (1½ mi offshore)	Atlantic Ocean extension
	l'Arceau jetty (5 mi east of St.-Nazaire)	Loire River extension
	la Pallice (Môle d'Éscale)	Atlantic Ocean extension
Recreation	Pornichet (52 rooms)	Leased hotel for enlisted personnel and their families (1953-55)
	St.-Nazaire (Camp de Gron)	Bowling alley (2 lanes)
Training Site	Beignon (Camp de Coëtquidan-St.-Cyr)	Maneuver area and firing ranges (French Army)

Abbreviations

CI　Criminal Investigation　　　FM　Field Maintenance　　　POV　Privately-owned vehicle

Base Section in France

Floating crane lifts BARC, Bassens, 25 January 1954 (US Army)

ELEVEN

Base Section in the Southwest

"I promise you, you won't be living in the mud."
(Maj Gen Henry R. Westphalinger, Port of Cherbourg, 11 October 1961)

Base Section Buildup

Base Section (BASEC) grew from a detachment of 1,500 troops stationed at Bordeaux, Captieux, and La Rochelle to twenty-one installations from the ports of Bordeaux, La Rochelle, and St.-Nazaire to depots at Chinon, Saumur, and Ingrandes. Troops and supplies arrived well before barracks and warehouses could be rehabilitated or constructed. Army engineers built roads and hardstands so trucks and supplies would not sink in the mud and they "winterized" tents for the troops. Until the installations matured in the mid-1950s, Base Section was divided into three area commands: Bordeaux, La Rochelle, and Poitiers. Each had a colonel in command who reported to headquarters. Initially headquarters, commanded by Col John W. Mott in 1950-51, was located at Caserne Aufrédi in La Rochelle. By 1957, it had moved to Caserne Aboville in Poitiers. Huge ordnance and engineer depots were built in the French national forests of la Braconne and Chinon.[1]

Base Section installations stocked the war reserves needed by Seventh Army. The goal of the Modern Army Supply System (MASS), first tested in 1956 in Europe, was to stock fast-moving items at forward depots, with less frequently needed parts stocked in the rear depots. Anything requested three or more times in 180 days was considered fast moving.[2] Repair parts outnumbered the equipment BASEC supported by more than 20 to 1. The mature BASEC of the late 1950s extended over an operating area of 45,000 sq miles.[3-5]

On short notice in July 1961, Army engineers installed prefab barracks throughout Base Section for the significant buildup of troops during Operation ROUNDOUT. US forces in Europe were reinforced by 40,000 troops and from October through December 1961 more than 475,000 tons of supplies and equipment were delivered to ComZ.[6]

Commanding Generals at Base Section

By December 1951, the Base Section was commanded by a general officer, Brig Gen Charles C. Blanchard. Just prior to his December 1952 departure from France, Blanchard wrote to Maj Gen Samuel D. Sturgis, Jr., ComZ commander, summarizing the problems that slowed the growth of Base Section. Major obstacles were: lengthy negotiations to acquire land from private owners, bureaucratic delays to acquire government property, lack of skilled civilian labor, and reluctance of US Army, Europe to send their best officers to Base Section. In December 1952, BASEC was short two-hundred seventy officers.[7, 8]

Blanchard's replacement, Brig Gen Ernest A. Bixby, had served in Patton's Third Army during World War II and commanded 90th Division Artillery at the battle to liberate Metz. By early 1953, Bixby commanded more than 10,000 troops. More than 4,600 French nationals and 1,500 Polish Labor Service personnel were employed at the ports and depots. During the nine months Bixby commanded Base Section most troops moved into prefab barracks, PX and snack bars opened at all installations, and roads were paved. Roads had been mud in rainy seasons and clouds of dust and dirt in dry weather. Bixby was admired by his troops due to his efforts to improve living conditions and his fatherly demeanor which put enlisted men at ease. On his way to Caserne Aufrédi in the morning, Bixby normally asked his driver to stop and give a ride to GI pedestrians.[9]

Bixby was succeeded by Brig Gen Philip E. Gallagher, who had served as commanding general of US Army Airlift Support Command during the Berlin Airlift. Gallagher's tenure at Base Section was only five months. After promotion to major general in February 1954, he moved to Orléans and assumed command of ComZ. At Orléans he earned a reputation as a stickler for military courtesy. He once bounded into the EM Club at Caserne Coligny to "chew out" a GI who had inadvertently flicked a cigarette butt at Gallagher's official sedan. Gallagher demanded that the culprit confess to this act of disrespect, but silence prevailed.[10]

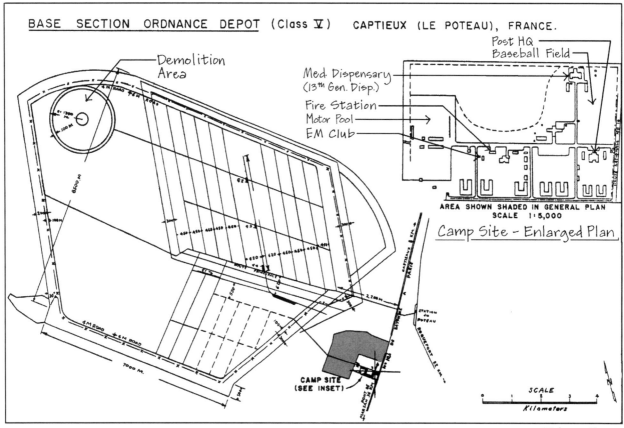

Captieux Ordnance Depot (1951)

Captieux Ordnance Depot

In the winter of 1948 during the Berlin Airlift, Col Andrew P. O'Meara, Chief of Plans Branch, Logistics Division at European Command in Germany, arranged with the French Army to store ammunition near Bordeaux. Ammunition was moved by rail from US Army depots in Germany to the former French Camp de Captieux le Poteau. The railcars purposefully were sent by circuitous routes to not attract attention. The existing fenced site would be guarded by the French Army.[11] The German army had occupied the site after France surrendered in June 1940. The camp was austere because the Germans removed the steel roof trusses and stripped interiors from all buildings before their departure. Following the war, the French Air Force had used the camp to practice bombing. However by 1948, most of Captieux le Poteau was abandoned.[12]

424

In November 1950, the 7862nd Ordnance Ammo Depot Det, commanded by Lt Col James K. Osterman, officially established the US Army Captieux Ordnance Depot at le Poteau. When the first troops arrived in November 1950 from Germany, they pitched tents on marshland that was bordered by pine forests. GIs believed Captieux was in the middle of nowhere. In Germany, they had lived in heated barracks surrounded by grass, not mud. The occupation Army had provided recreation facilities and there were nearby German cities to visit. At Captieux, Bordeaux was more than an hour away. The 25,000-acre site was a sandy, hot desert infested by insects in summer, and a swamp whipped by cold winds in winter. GIs called it the "Siberia of France" and believed that if you screwed-up elsewhere in Europe you would be sent to Captieux.[13] (Ironically in the early years, officers who did not perform well at US European Command were sent to Verdun.) Security at night was provided by the 4011th and 4230th Labor Service Companies.

The first year at Captieux was so windy that a latrine was blown over with a GI inside. Extra long tent pegs were fabricated to be driven deep into the mud to prevent tents from blowing away. Nevertheless, each year the high winds destroyed several tents. It was a poor location for a depot, but land to store vast quantities of ammunition was urgently needed.[14] The front page of the 24 November 1950 issue of Bordeaux's newspaper *Les Nouvelles* featured two photos of the new US Army ammunition depot. The caption of one photo stated that white soldiers were resting comfortably in tents while blacks shoveled trash outside in the rain.[15] It was unlikely any whites were in the tents. All enlisted personnel were black in the 39th Ordnance Co (MAM), 583rd Ordnance Co (Ammo), and 661st Truck Co (Hvy). There were few white enlisted troops, most of whom were Polish Labor Service guards.

"Canvas Castles," Captieux Ordnance Depot, 1952 (US Army)

Lodge Act Soldiers

In June 1950, five days after North Korea invaded the South, the US Congress authorized the enlistment of 2,500 foreign nationals in the US Army. It was called the Lodge Act because Senator Henry Cabot Lodge, Jr., Republican from Massachusetts, had been the primary advocate of the plan. Lodge hoped that eventually large numbers of foreigners would volunteer to fight alongside US forces to defend Europe. After the war ended in 1945, the US Army of Occupation in Germany and Austria had organized displaced persons by nationality into paramilitary guard, transportation, and engineer labor service units. Most displaced persons were from the Soviet-occupied nations of Albania, Bulgaria, Czechoslovakia, Estonia, Latvia, Lithuania, and Poland, and they could not return home.[16] Only labor service units of Poles recruited in Germany were permitted to work in France. Assigned to the 4011th Labor Service Company at Captieux, Henry M. Kwiatowski volunteered to join the US Army as a Lodge Act recruit. After training in Germany, Kwiatowski was sent to the United States to begin a long career in Special Forces.[17,18] About one-hundred "Lodge Boys" volunteered for Special Forces training. Although supported by US President Dwight D. Eisenhower, Lodge's proposed volunteer army of displaced persons was not wanted by West European governments. They objected to combat units of ethnic identity stationed within their borders, but tolerated covert military roles for elements of the European labor service.

Ammunition Storage

In November 1950, immediately after the LOC Agreement was signed, three Liberty ships nearing the Panama Canal were diverted to Bordeaux. The ships were loaded with ammunition originally destined for Korea. During the first six months of 1951, more than sixty railcars of ammunition arrived each day at Captieux. There were no structures in which to store the ammunition, only acres of mud.[19,20] Most of the 1,430 prefabricated, wood-frame hutments, hastily manufactured by a Belgium firm, could not be used because they were poorly designed and the cement asbestos panels for the walls and roofs were damaged in shipment. The US Army, Europe Inspector General recommended that two engineer colonels at Orléans be officially reprimanded for the hutment fiasco. Subsequent requests for proposals to build prefab hutments were based on an improved design.[21,22] It seemed to take forever to move ammunition by hand and improvised mud-sleds through the acres of deep mud.

In the early evening of 05 August 1952, lightning struck an ammunition storage area. Although the depot fire department responded within 10 minutes, the fire burned violently for almost three hours, destroying 200 tons of ammunition (mostly .50 cal cartridges and aircraft rockets) and injuring fourteen GIs. The injured were treated at the 13th General Dispensary; most for cuts, abrasions, and concusions.[23] During dry seasons the fire department often aided French firefighters by clearing firebreaks to contain fires which destroyed pine trees and threatened the depot.

In May 1953 during their off-duty hours, troops from Company C of the 83rd Engineer Construction Battalion helped depot ammo humpers unload large shipments of ammunition. Company C troops also cleared a one-mile diameter demolition area. An engineer GI modified a dozer blade to dig a deep trench around the perimeter.[24]

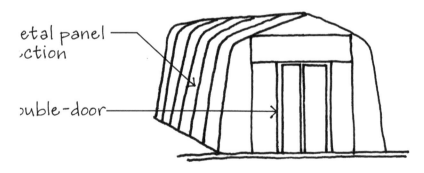

Metal Prefab Ammo Hutment (1961)

A seven-mile rail spur to the Bordeaux-Pau SNCF railroad line opened in December 1953. Eventually, more than 75,000 tons of ammunition was stored in 4,608 prefabs. On 16 and 17 January 1955 hurricane force storms battered Captieux, causing nearly ½ million dollars in damages. One-hundred fifty storage huts were destroyed; another two-hundred twenty-six were damaged. Most of the supplies and equipment stored under tarpaulins sustained water damage.[25]

In the mid-1950s, wood plank floors of Fillod ammo huts were seriously damaged by wood worms. To replace the wood plank, clever GIs devised a worm-proof ammo support from three sections of pierced steel plank (PSP). Each section was 15-inches wide by 10-ft long. The bottom section was laid flat on the ground. The other two sections were attached to the long ends of the bottom section and tilted to join at the top. Ammo boxes and pallets were placed on top of the triangular-shaped PSP supports so they would be 13 inches above the ground.[26]

In extreme freezing weather in February 1956, nearly six-hundred troops and French LWR employees loaded over 10,000 tons of ammunition onto SNCF boxcars. The outmoded ammo was sent to Bassens, where it was loaded onto cargo ships for shipment to the US. Ordnance depots in Kentucky and Nebraska renovated the shells and filled them with new powder.[27] In 1961, ammunition was stored in metal prefabs and the surviving wood-frame huts erected ten years earlier. An additional seventy-two canvas covered A-frames had been erected to replace original huts destroyed each year by high winds.[28]

In 1957 after complaints from French bird lovers, depot commander Col Harvey Bower agreed to close the small-arms ammunition "popping pit" at Captieux for six weeks each year during nesting season. Nesting hens had been disturbed by the exploding ammo.[29]

Draining the Big Swamp

In many areas of the depot, the water table was only 18 inches below ground surface. During the rainy winter months of 1950, depot roads were flooded with 1 to 2 feet of water that could not drain through the impermeable subsoil. Pranksters placed "No Fishing" signs nearby. Areas rarely dried out where the sandy soil was covered by sod. In September 1951, troops of the 83rd Engineers, commanded by Lt Col Earle B. Butler, began improving roads and digging 8 miles of drainage ditches. More than six-hundred French construction workers were hired to work on the drainage project. In 1953, gravel and topsoil for 27 miles of depot roads were hauled from a gravel pit located 30 miles away near Langon. The 83rd Engineers, now commanded by Lt Col Howard F. McKeown, assigned four hundred twenty-five men to the project. Dozens of Army dump trucks hauled about 250 loads of gravel each 20-hour workday. By the fifth week, drivers had exceeded 500,000 miles to and from the gravel pit. The project was nicknamed the "Big Haul." Initially, the gravel sank into the mud, but gradually some of the roads became high enough to shed water.[30, 31]

Drainage problems persisted throughout the 1950s because the ditches filled with mud. A three-year project to drain the depot began in May 1961. Army engineers dug several 12-ft wide canals, 3 to 6 ft deep, to drain rain water to the perimeter of the depot. Canals had to be laid out so privately owned land outside the depot would not be flooded. Crawler tractors of the 83rd Engineers towed graders to form ditches and canals in the mud. When a tractor became stuck in the mud, another tractor pulled it out, although sometimes the second tractor also became stuck. Work was halted at Captieux from September 1961 to May 1962, because the engineers were assigned tasks related to the troop buildup during Operation ROUNDOUT for the Berlin Wall Crisis.[32]

Construction of permanent structures, Captieux Ordnance Depot, 1952 (US Army)

Operation MUDLARK II

In October 1952, troops at Captieux grabbed their alert gear and moved to remote locations of the pine-forested depot, where they bivouacked and set up ammo supply points. There the troops withstood simulated gas attacks by ground forces and simulated air attacks. The week-long exercise was designed to test the ability of ordnance units to defend themselves.[33] Dubbed Operation MUDLARK II, the exercise was observed by Lt Gen Manton S. Eddy, Commander-in-Chief of US Army, Europe (USAREUR). In November 1950, Eddy had activated Seventh Army in Germany to discourage Soviet aggression. Eddy served in France during World War I and commanded the 9th Infantry Division which liberated Cherbourg during World War II.

Sturgis and Army Uniforms

Maj Gen Samuel D. Sturgis, Jr., ComZ commander, was frustrated with the slow progress at the depots. He had no authority over depot commanders because they reported to technical service chiefs in Germany, not to Sturgis. Sturgis and Eddy were determined that troops wear their uniforms properly at all times, even when stuck in the mud. In August 1952, Eddy wrote to Sturgis demanding that prompt disciplinary action be taken against soldiers who improperly wore their uniforms.[34] Sturgis inspired senior leaders in his chain-of-command to be vigilant, even when off-duty. One weekend in Paris, Brig Gen William W. Ford noticed GIs wearing T-shirts and civilian khaki trousers with the cuffs rolled up. Ford gave chase down the Champs Élysées, stopping the GIs to reprimand them and ask for their names and Army units.[35] In USAREUR, the wearing of T-shirts, sweatshirts, blue jeans, shorts, or similar "teenage costumes" was considered to be inappropriate for Army personnel. Wearing parts of military uniform with civilian clothing was expressly forbidden. Lt Col James K. Osterman, depot commander at Captieux, particularly irked Sturgis because he removed the front stiffener and grommet of his regulation cap so it would sag Air Force style, creased ear-to-ear.[36] During World War II, the crease was called "The Fifty-Mission Crush" because when officers repeatedly wore aircraft headphones over their caps during flight, it caused a permanent dent. Osterman commanded the Captieux Depot during the first two years, when rutted muddy roads became paved, troops moved from tents into rehabilitated masonry barracks, and recreation facilities were built at the isolated installation.[37] In June 1952, Osterman was replaced by Lt Col William F. Kaiser, who wore his hat properly.

Elevated Firing Range

Building a firing range in 1953 at Captieux was a challenge for Company C of the 83rd Engineers. The unusual project was supervised by 1st Lt William R. Hamby. Because the ground usually was saturated with water, a pit could not be dug for the target butts. Instead, bulldozers formed a long 10-ft high berm to shield the GIs who raised and lowered the targets. Carpenters then built elevated firing line platforms at the same elevation as the top of the berm. The platforms were located at 100 and 200 yards away from the targets.[38]

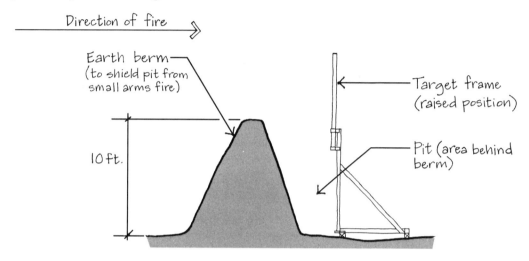

Target Butt at Captieux

Igloos Cancelled

In 1962, ammunition was still being stored in the metal prefabs and wood-frame hutments. In springtime, temperatures inside metal Fillods varied from below freezing at night to a roasting 90° F in the afternoon. Ammo deteriorated rapidly at Captieux due to condensation on ammo stored in the metal prefabs. The wide variation in temperature and high humidity resulted in nearly constant moisture on the ammo. Depot personnel had to carry ammunition from huts to roller-conveyors and from the end of the conveyors to trucks, parked 50 to 300 ft away along the nearest road. It took six separate operations to move a round of ammo to a railcar. During an emergency, this would be far too slow. To improve delivery conditions, a $11 million project was underway in the mid-1960s to install modern Stradley earth-covered, storage igloos and concrete hardstands connecting the igloos to existing roads.[39] The project was cancelled in 1966 when France withdrew from SHAPE.

Recreation and Housing

On weekends in 1951, GIs and Polish LS personnel were driven by 2½-ton trucks to Bordeaux and Mont-de-Marson. The GIs referred to Bordeaux as "Milleville" because they believed it would cost at least 50 mille francs (about two months pay) to visit. Because the depot was in the middle of nowhere, it was essential that recreation facilities be provided on the depot. A movie theater, snack bar, service club, photo shop, and miniature golf course opened at Captieux well before similar facilities were built at other installations in France. At the grand opening of the bowling alley on 27 April 1954, Lt Col William F. Kaiser thanked the personnel who had worked on the six-lane facility, named "Kingpin Alley." [40, 41]

By the end of 1951, living conditions at Captieux had been improved. More than three-hundred, heated "canvas castles" were arranged in military precision along elevated boardwalks and drainage ditches dug to keep the troops out of the mud. Drinking water, which had been trucked from Rochefort, now was provided by a deep well. It had taken the French contractor more than eight months to dig the 700-ft deep well because his drilling equipment was antiquated and silt plugged the pipes. One of the 1939-era buildings the Germans had stripped was rehabilitated for the post theater. Used cushioned seats were purchased from the Alhambra Theater in Bordeaux. In late April 1952, troops moved into permanent masonry buildings restored by French contractors at a cost of $1.8 million. Until the mid-1950s, families had to live cramped 3 to 4 persons in small hotel rooms in Bazas, 19 miles from the depot, and Langon, 25 miles away. Until the commissary opened in early 1953, wives had to buy groceries in Bordeaux, a 100-mile roundtrip by bus.[42] After 1959, officer and NCO families lived in forty RGH housing units, called Cité Pradère, built at Bazas, and in twenty-four SCH housing units, called Cité Brémontier, built at Captieux, 8 miles northeast of the depot. Rental housing on the economy still was scarce. In 1963, there were twenty officers and more than four-hundred enlisted men stationed at the depot, and more than seven-hundred French employees.

Off-duty in the early 1950s, the men of Captieux participated in sports and musical groups, studied to obtain eighth-grade education certificates, and took weekend tours to Bordeaux and Spain, 70 miles to the south. In 1952, fewer than half of ComZ troops had completed high school.[43] Men of the 571st Ordnance Co (Ammo) and 503rd Fire Fighting Co formed the Captieux Choral Group, led by M/Sgt Joseph E. Hodges. On 15 August 1952, sponsored by the US Embassy, the 25-man group gave a concert of "Negro spirituals" at Château de la Napoule near Cannes. Gian-Carlo Menotti, well-known Italian-born American composer and librettist, also was featured on the festival program. Back at Captieux the group gave numerous concerts at French towns in the southwest and were broadcast by a Bordeaux radio station.[44] The Captieux Bombers basketball team played exhibition games against French teams throughout the region. Like the famous Harlem Globetrotters, the team won nearly all of their games. According to the team manager and high-scorer Cpl A. C. Owens, the French were good sports, wanting to play the Bombers again even after being outscored by wide margins.[45] When the village of Captieux was flooded in February 1952, troops shoveled mud and contributed 53,000 francs to help in the recovery.[46]

PCF Propaganda

In the 1960s, the French communist press claimed that Captieux was a secret CIA training center (allegedly "Base USA 312") guarded by Polish sentries and German dogs. At most Army posts in France, the Labor Service sentries were Polish and the dogs German; however, the non-communist newspaper *Sud-Ouest* pointed out on 06 February 1966: "Captieux was a huge ammunition depot in a vast game reserve teeming with wild life, but James Bond was not to be found there." Perhaps CIA Director of Central Intelligence Allen Dulles could have been found there in the 1950s, because Captieux was a remote location where personnel of the CIA's Operation Rollback could train. During a Soviet invasion, displaced persons and émigés from the Communist bloc were to harass Soviet forces as they rolled through Western Europe.[47] In 1951, the Parti Communiste Français (PCF) in Bordeaux had insisted that the US Army stored atomic bombs at Captieux. The US military authorities dismissed the allegation because it was false. Army tactical nuclear weapon delivery systems, such as the 280-mm cannon dubbed "Atomic Annie," were not sent to Germany until late 1953.[48] Atomic ammo for Annie arrived a year later. From 1953 to 1959, the fighter-bomber jet aircraft needed to drop atomic bombs on targets in the Soviet bloc were deployed to NATO air bases in northeastern France. Nuclear warheads at Captieux would have been too far from the US Army artillery units in Germany and the nuclear capable US Air Force wings in France. It was ironic that after the US military left Captieux in 1967, the French Air Force used this secure, remote area to test precision bombing methods for its emerging nuclear strike force (called *force de frappe*).[49]

Captieux Ordnance Depot Commanders

Commanding Officer	Period of Service	Commanding Officer	Period of Service
Lt Col James K. Osterman	1950-52	Col Francis B. Goodwin	1958-60
Lt Col William F. Kaiser	1952-54	Col Ray A. Pillivant	1960-63
Maj Edward G. Heider	1954	Col William L. Clay	1963-64
Col Don M. Hoffman	1954-55	Lt Col Spurgeon C. Boyd	1964
Col Harvey Bower	1955-57	Maj G. R. Daugherty	1965-66
Col Addison V. Dishman	1957-58	Capt Ronald L. Gambolati	1967

Ammunition Depots

During the long deployment to France, the Army stored more than 75,000 tons of conventional ammunition at Captieux, more than 66,500 tons at Trois-Fontaines. During the 1950s, the Air Force stored more than 30,000 tons of rockets, flares, napalm tanks, and aircraft gun ammunition at Chizé near Niort. In October 1961, the depot was transferred to the Army. In 1959, three depots were built at Aboncourt near Metz, Rozelier near Verdun, and Vatry near Vitry-le-François to store nuclear munitions in earth-covered, reinforced-concrete magazines. Class V supplies (ammunition and explosives) were stored at Sassey for air delivery by cargo aircraft of the 322nd Air Division based at nearby Évreux AB. All chemical munitions in Europe were stored in France. In the early 1950s, chemical munitions were stored at Bussac; in the 1960s, at Trois-Fontaines and Vatry. In 1966, they were moved to Clausen, Germany. The US Army maintained more than 27 miles of rail spurs in the Class V depots. SNCF unsuccessfully urged various French government agencies to obtain permission for SNCF to control use of rail spurs in the depots.

Size of US Army Ammunition Depots (1962)[50]

Depot	Storage Huts	Land Use (acres)	Roads (miles)	Rails (miles)
Captieux	5,732	24,907	156	7
Trois-Fontaines	5,266	13,933	107	7
Aboncourt (Metz)	8	81	4	0
Rozelier (Verdun)	88	1,199	10	9
Vatry	100	552	8	0
Chizé	272	6,533	51	4
Sassey	20	43	1	0

Camp Bussac

The US Army acquired 2,146 acres from the French government for use as a depot named Camp Bussac. Initially, the vast depot was used to store supplies of three Technical Services: Transportation, Chemical, and Quartermaster. Part of the relatively flat site had been used by the French Army for an airfield, called Aérodrome de Bedenac-Bussac. Two small rivers, the Saye and Coudrelle, crossed the property. Before World War II, the site was an emergency landing field. The airfield was enlarged during the German occupation, but most of the buildings and hangars built for the Luftwaffe were stripped and burned when the Germans retreated in 1944. Piles of live bombs and minefields were abandoned. Antipersonnel "Schü" mines and the more powerful antitank "Teller" mines, which the weight of any military vehicle could detonate, had to be removed. During a wind storm in May 1951, a dilapidated former German hangar collapsed into a mass of twisted iron.[51] Several 2½-ton cargo trucks, parked for the night in the hangar, were badly damaged.

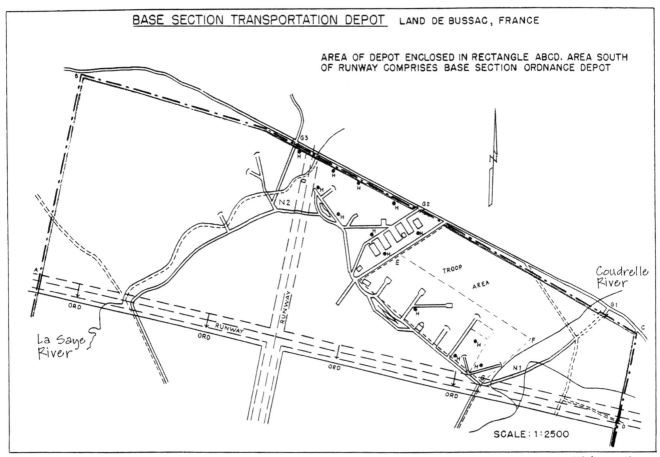

Camp Bussac (1951)

Bussac Buildup

In March 1951, Lt Col Thomas A. Weadock arrived with troops of the 661st Heavy Truck Co from Captieux as his advance party to establish the Transportation Depot at Bussac. During World War II, the 661st was part of the "Red Ball Express." The transportation troops, commanded by Capt Richard P. Castles, pitched their tents on an open muddy plain near damaged buildings, surrounded by the uncleared minefields. Under Weadock's leadership, transportation troops used scrap lumber to build tent frames, floors, walls, and even furniture.[52] Like other officers who had served with Patton's Third Army in World War II, Weadock believed saluting properly was an indication of troop morale and alertness. A stickler for saluting, Weadock on occasion would look away from NCOs to trick them into not saluting. NCOs who did not salute would be severely reprimanded (GIs called this "being chewed out").[53]

GIs lived "under canvas" in tents and hutments at the depot site. When GIs of Headquarters Company, 2nd Transportation Truck Battalion arrived in April 1951 from Germany, they scrounged sheet metal to place on tent tops. Exhaust pipes from stoves penetrated the tent tops, and the metal shielded the canvas from hot embers which could ignite the canvas.[54] Eleven original French-owned buildings were renovated for $350,000. The former control tower became the post commander's office, giving him a bird's-eye view of the depot.[55] In January and February 1953, Col William E. Hicks commanded Camp Bussac. During World War II, Hicks had worked on the famous Ledo Road to China from India through northern Burma. Working night and day during the torrential rains of monsoon season, Hick's engineers built a two-mile long causeway through the jungle.

To control flooding at Bussac, in July 1953 the 83rd Engineers diverted the Saye River into a mile long channel dug west of its natural course through the depot. The 319th Station Hospital moved from Croix-Chapeau to staff a hospital at Bussac from 1953 to 1962. By late 1953, the hospital, commanded by Maj (Dr) Roy A. Highsmith, had one large ward, pharmacy, X-ray room, and pathology laboratory. The 550th Ambulance Co provided service throughout the region. In August 1955, an additional 1,500 acres of land adjacent to Camp Bussac was obtained from the French.[56] From 1954 to 1957, sixty-seven new permanent buildings were built by Pitel-Cochery of Paris, enabling the troops to work and live out of the mud. In 1955, the bakery at Camp Bussac used mobile equipment to bake 50,000 lbs of bread a month for the troops at Bassens, Braconne, Bussac, Gradignan, Périgueux, and St.-Sulpice. The bakery also supplied US Air Force units at Cazaux, Chizé, and Mérignac.[57]

Transportation Depot

In early 1951, all supplies for transportation units in Europe were stored at Bussac and organized by the 529th Transportation Base Depot Co, commanded by Maj Vincent Bellucci. Truck drivers at Bussac supported the rapid buildup of Base Section. Supplies and equipment, which arrived at the ports of Bassens near Bordeaux and la Pallice near La Rochelle, had to be quickly cleared from the docks. In March 1951, six all-black enlisted personnel truck companies were assigned to Bussac, forming the 2nd Trans Truck Battalion.

In September 1951, the motor vehicle accident rate for the 72nd Truck Co was nearly five times the rate for all units in ComZ. The ComZ Safety Office presented the 72nd with a porcelain mule, dubbed the "Jackass Award," which was to be displayed for one month on the desk of the company commander.[58] Conversely in early January 1952, drivers of the 595th Truck Co were given safe-driver awards by Maj Robert E. Dittmer. Cited for three years of driving without an accident were: PFC Henry Varner, Pvt Henry McKeithen, and Pvt Louis C. Tillman. Eight GIs drove two years without an accident; fifteen drove for one year without an accident.[59] In early 1952, the 806th Trans Truck Bn, an Army Reserve unit from Little Rock, Arkansas, replaced the 2nd Trans Truck Bn at Bussac.

Transportation Truck Companies at Bussac (1952)

55th Heavy Truck Co (Petroleum)	480th Truck Co*
72nd Truck Co	595th Truck Co
78th Heavy Truck Co	661st Heavy Truck Co

*Army National Guard unit from Welch, West Virginia.

In the mid-1950s, drivers of the 78th Trans Truck Co moved cargo from Bassens and Captieux to Bussac for an overnight stop. Early the next morning, the drivers continued on to Maison-Fort, stopping to rest and refuel at Ingrandes or Châteauroux. Arriving at Maison-Fort in the early evening, they dropped off their loaded trailers and picked-up another for the return trip to Bussac the next morning.[60] In July 1955, the delivery time for hauls from Bassens and la Pallice to Verdun was reduced by three days because thirty 10-ton vans ran on a regular schedule. Five truck terminals between Bussac and Verdun received cargo for delivery to nearby installations.[61]

106th Transportation Battalion

The 106th Transportation Battalion issued a "Drivers Code" of Do's and Don'ts to its GIs. The code's "I wills" included: perform all preventive maintenance on any vehicle required to be driven, obey all speed limits (both military and civilian), yield right-of-way to vehicles approaching from the right, and aid disabled military vehicles. Especially difficult for some GIs to obey were: "I will not smoke while driving" and "I will not drink alcohol while driving or within eight hours before dispatch." For example, when alerts were called during early mornings after an evening of happy hour drinking, GIs drove under the influence of alcohol. The 106th Trans Bn, which succeeded the 806th Trans Truck Bn, was headquartered at Bussac from March 1955 until August 1958 when it moved to Croix-Chapeau. Drivers of the 106th cleared the ports of Bassens, la Pallice, and St.-Nazaire. Cargo from the ports was driven to the truck terminal hub at Ingrandes. The terminal controlled a pool of ninety-two semitrailers and had three 5-ton trucks to make deliveries to nearby depots.[62] In November 1963, the 106th Trans Bn moved from Croix-Chapeau to Germany.

In 1959, the 583rd Trans Co (Light Truck), commanded by 1st Lt Melvin I. Feldman, parked its "Coffee Stop Truck" near Ruffec, between Angoulême and Poitiers. The Army truck provided coffee and snacks to GI drivers to help relieve the monotony of long hauls. There was no charge, but GIs were asked to sign a logbook.[63] In support of Operation ROUNDOUT in 1961, the 583rd Trans Co, commanded by 1st Lt Donald L. Woodhouse, logged more than 280,000 miles. It was the highest operation mileage total ever recorded in the 106th Trans Bn.[64]

On 18 August 1962, the 62nd Trans Co (Medium Truck) departed Bussac for la Pallice. The 62nd Trans Co had been deployed from Fort Eustis, Virginia, during Operation ROUNDOUT. One-hundred twenty-five officers and enlisted men of the 62nd sailed home on the USNS *Gen W. H. Gordon*. During Operation FRELOC from 1966 to 1967, trucks of the 106th Trans Bn, commanded by Lt Col Robert F. Wanek, moved supplies and equipment from France.

106th Transportation Battalion Commanders[65]

Commanding Officer	Period	Commanding Officer	Period
Lt Col Herbert N. Reed	1955-56	Lt Col Edwin B. Owen	1960-61
Maj John R. Powell	1956	Lt Col Lawrence A. L. Scheftel	1961-62
Maj Randall P. Smith	1957	Lt Col Virgil G. Brown	1962-63
Lt Col Marcus A. Petterson	1958-59	Lt Col Henry R. Del Mar	1963-64
Lt Col Thomas L. Lyons	1959-60		

Chemical Depot

The US Army stored chemical munitions in France to deter the use of chemical weapons by the Soviets. In October 1951, the 15th Chemical Group established a chemical depot at Bussac. The depot, commanded by Lt Col Ralph B. Cummings, stored and maintained gas masks, decontamination apparatus, detection devices, and chemical munitions. In October 1953, headquarters moved from tents into a new masonry building. At the depot, chemical munitions were renovated, crated, and stored. The depot also stored components (TNT, napalm, white phosphorus grenades) of the Atomic Bomb Simulator used for training purposes. The simulator exploded with a vivid flash, loud roar, ball of fire rising upward, and plume of thick smoke that formed a distinctive mushroom-cloud shape at the top. The explosion had the characteristics of the real bomb, but without intense heat, nuclear radiation, and physical destruction.[66] At open house on Armed Forces Day 16 May 1953, the simulated atomic bomb explosion was a spectacular sight.

In May 1953, depot commander Maj Edward R. Harper organized the first course at Bussac on CBR (chemical, biological, and radiological) for officers and enlisted men throughout Base Section.[67] Graduates in turn would train troops at their own units. Lessons learned during the 35-hour course included detecting chemical agents, use of protective masks and clothing, decontamination and protection against attack, and tactical uses of CBR agents.[68] In 1954, Maj Roy D'Amore organized ten-day courses for ComZ radiological survey teams so personnel would learn to detect and measure levels of radiation from nuclear explosions. During the year, several hundred ComZ troops attended the 85-hour course, which ended with a simulated atomic attack kicked off by a mushroom-cloud explosion.[69, 70]

Quartermaster POL Depot

In September 1953 the Quartermaster POL Depot, commanded by Col Bennett D. Farnham, began operations. Petroleum products were delivered from the ports to Bussac by rail tank cars. At the depot, the product was unloaded, tested, and stored in jerry cans and drums, or shipped to Army and Air Force units in Base Section. Until a pipeline could be built across France, acres of jerry cans and 55-gal drums were stacked in the open at Bussac.[71] Gasoline in the POL reserve was rotated to prevent the settling of impurities (called gumming) caused by long-term storage. The 562nd QM Co (Petroleum Supply) shipped the older gasoline to other Base Section installations and replaced it with motor gas received from Bassens.[72] The 55th Heavy Truck Co (Petroleum) had more than sixty trucks and tankers to haul POL throughout Base Section.[73]

During his 30 September 1953 inspection of Bussac, Brig Gen Philip E. Gallagher, BASEC commander, lifted a clerk's typewriter to see if the underside was clean. After finding dust, Gallagher hurled the typewriter through an open window. While inspecting outdoor QM storage areas, Gallagher repeatedly asked if he could be of any help. After the sixth "No Sir," the lieutenant briefing Gallagher started to ask for help. Gallagher immediately began cursing the lieutenant and yelling: "I want results, not excuses!"[74]

83rd Engineer Battalion

The 83rd Engineer Construction Battalion, deployed to France from Fort Sill, Oklahoma, arrived at la Pallice on 20 May 1951. On their first day at sea on the USNS *Gen M. B. Stewart*, GIs gulped Dramamine pills to control seasickness. In France the battalion, commanded by Lt Col Earle B. Butler, worked at more than twenty locations clearing roads, drilling wells, digging drainage ditches, pouring concrete hardstands, and erecting tents. The mud was so deep at some depots that dozers had to be replaced with old-fashioned "pick and shovel" work. Graders, dozers, and cranes had to be transported by truck and tractor rig that was 60-ft long by 10 ft wide. It was difficult to maneuver the huge engineer construction equipment through the narrow, crooked streets of French villages.[75] Headquarters and B Companies were at Bussac; A and C Companies at Poitiers. In 1951, Company A was temporarily stationed at Cosne-sur-Loire, 70 miles southeast of Orléans, to rehabilitate Caserne Binot for use as a POL depot. In November 1951, the 83rd Engineers assisted the US Air Force at Bordeaux to clear more than fifty railcar loads of pierced steel plank (PSP) and telephone poles at the Mérignac rail spur.[76] For the US Air Force, they poured concrete slabs, reinforced walls, and hung doors at the war-damaged Ford-SNCASO plant in Bacalan. The 83rd Engineers completed 185 projects in 1951, 109 projects in 1952, and 126 projects in 1953. Initially most of the projects were rehabilitating casernes and building tent camps, hardstands, and roads. Later construction projects included prefab barracks, dependents schools, hospitals, rifle ranges, and other projects needed to establish the Base Section. Because projects often were 300 miles or more apart, during its first 2½ years in France the battalion logged more than 4 million miles with few accidents on a variety of road conditions.[77]

Asphalt paving crew of 83rd Engineer Battalion, Ingrandes Depot, 1962 (US Army)

83rd Engineer Battalion (Const) Commanders*

Commanding Officer	Period of Service	Commanding Officer	Period of Service
Lt Col Earle B. Butler	1950-52	Lt Col Eldridge H. Cockrell	1960-61
Lt Col John E. Bowman	1952-53	Lt Col Thomas E. Griess	1961-62
Lt Col Howard F. McKeown	1953-54	Lt Col James A. Bowden	1962-63
Lt Col Hobert H. Hoover	1954-55	Lt Col Rudolph W. Staffa	1963-64
Lt Col Daniel R. Clark	1955-56	Lt Col Walter H. Johnson	1964-66
Maj Rolland E. Broadwell	1956-57	Lt Col William F. Halley	1966
Lt Col William Johnstone	1957-60		

*In 1960, battalion headquarters was relocated from Bussac to Fontenet. From 1960 to 1963, the commanding officer of the 83rd Eng Bn also served as commander of Fontenet Depot.

Tour de France

The Tour de France is the biggest annual sports event in France. During three weeks in July, nine-man teams of cyclists compete to win a 2,000-mile race across France. The course changes each year, but always ends at the Arc de Triomphe in Paris. Normal procedure for all roads selected for the Tour was to close them to military and civilian traffic from 1½ hours prior to passage of the cyclists until ½ hour after the last race vehicle had passed. In July 1952, a convoy of 83rd Engineers driving from Bussac to build a hardstand at Périgueux was delayed by the Tour. French gendarmes forced the drivers to detour 37 miles out of their way and just before reaching Périgueux, the convoy was halted for an hour to allow the cyclists to pass by.[78]

Community Relations

Each July the village of Montlieu-la-Garde invited US Army units from Bussac to a memorial ceremony honoring US airmen killed when their B-24 Liberator bomber was shot down on 31 December 1943 near the village. A French army veteran of World War I was the first person to reach the downed plane. In memory of the airmen, he erected a stone monument with the names of nine dead crew members inscribed on the stone. One crew member safely parachuted to the ground, but was captured by the Germans. The official dedication ceremony in 1951 was attended by Lt Col Thomas A. Weadock, Lt Col Earle B. Butler, and Maj Vincent Bellucci from Bussac and Capt James T. White, Jr. from Rochefort.[79]

Monument to US airmen, Montlieu-la-Garde, December 1958 (US Army)

In November 1953, officers and enlisted men at Camp Bussac adopted the Jean Bost Home for orphans and the disabled, located at la Force, southeast of the camp near Bergerac. During the first year, GIs raised more than $1,800 to purchase clothing, bedding, and food for the home. The children were dinner guests at Christmas, receiving a gift, and at Easter, receiving a candy basket and gift.[80] In 1953, the 597th Engineer Co (Heavy Maintenance) built a firing range for the French Army at Biard near Poitiers. In April 1955, the 597th Engineers were sent to fight a nearby forest fire. The engineers used a bulldozer and grader to form a berm firebreak that halted the spread of the fire.[81] In early 1956, the 83rd Engineers cleared land for an athletic field in the village of Brantôme. Villagers used the field for soccer, basketball, and track.[82]

Housing

Families of officers and NCOs lived on the economy or in one-hundred sixty-eight RGH housing units at Blaye, Cenon, Pessac, and St.-André-de-Cubzac. Authorized personnel from Bassens and Bordeaux also could live in the units. In 1959, an additional fifty-two housing units were built at Commune de Bussac-Forêt, two miles from the depot. The SCH housing village was named Cité Clemenceau to honor French Prime Minister Georges Clemenceau. Clemenceau, known as "The Tiger," had led France to victory in World War I. In 1962, the French forestry service donated 1,000 pine trees to Camp Bussac. Three hundred of the saplings were planted at Cité Clemenceau. After the drawdown of Base Section in 1963, Bussac still had more than five-hundred troops. Today, part of former Camp Bussac is a French prison enclosed by high walls.

Camp Bussac Commanders

Commanding Officer	Period of Service	Commanding Officer	Period of Service
Lt Col Thomas A. Weadock	1951-52	Col Andrew V. Inge	1957-58
Lt Col Bryan C. Arnold	1952-53	Col Frank C. Quinlin	1958-61
Col William E. Hicks	1953	Col Lund F. Hood	1961-62
Col Ralph W. Hansen	1953-54	Lt Col Charles I. Balcer	1962-63
Col Eugene G. Bennett	1954-55	Lt Col George H. Bourcher	1963-64
Col Chester T. Barton	1955-56	Col John J. Kiely, Jr.	1964
Col Robert L. Rhea	1956		

Military Police tents in foreground, Camp Bussac, 1952 (US Army)

Périgueux Quartermaster Depot

On 03 October 1951, Lt Col Paul E. Haines and two-hundred men from Giessen QM Depot, Germany, opened a depot at Coulouniex-Chamiers near Périgueux. Half the population of the farming and railroad town was believed to be supporters of the French Communist Party. At first, vandals slashed tires of American vehicles and painted "U.S. Go Home" on walls.[83] The depot used the former Usine Forclum which had fabricated concrete poles. Quartermaster supplies were relocated from Usine Jeumont in la Pallice where they had been stored for three months. To provide 60,000 sq ft of covered warehouse space, ComZ purchased six prefabricated structures from Taylor-Woodrow, a British manufacturer. Components for the 50 ft by 200 ft structures were delivered in January 1952, but only three had been erected and occupied by July because original construction contracts did not include concrete floors. The other three prefabs had been damaged in shipment or during erection because French workers were not familiar with the British prefab system. Replacement parts were not available in France, and negotiations to determine responsibility for damage took weeks.[84] All structures finally were erected by early 1953, allowing GIs from the 541st QM Company (Clothing & General Supplies Depot) to move supplies from outdoor storage under tarps into the prefabs.

Initially the 78th QM Co (Base Depot) stored and issued clothing and subsistence items such as C-rations and canned food. To reduce spoilage, C-rations and canned food were replaced after a set time. The old rations were sent to mess halls, where Army cooks disguised canned meat in pot pies and mixed C-rations with fresh rations.[85] The depot also stored graves registration supplies such as body bags, wooden grave markers, and lumber for coffins. The Garage Gonthier was leased for additional storage space. Military truck traffic significantly was reduced in April 1955 when an SNCF rail spur was completed. The ¾-mile long track held more than two dozen railcars.[86]

Troop Barracks, Family Housing, and Schools

At first, GIs lived in tents. The rows of squad tents at Périgueux were distinctive because the wood siding was painted white. GIs lived in the hutments until a three-story masonry barracks building was built in 1955. The depot did not have enough open space for single-story barracks. Two upper floors accommodated two-hundred sixteen men; the ground floor had a day room and supply rooms.[87]

Married officers and NCOs lived on the economy or in twenty RGH housing units built at Chamiers. In 1953, dependents from Périgueux attended high school at Rochefort. Dependents from Braconne, Bussac, Captieux, La Rochelle, St.-Jean d'Angély, and St.-Nazaire also attended Rochefort High School. The students lived in dormitories during the week and were driven home in Army buses on Fridays.

Franco-American Relations

In 1952, Frenchmen Lucien Barriere and Dr. André Rebeyroi formed the France-US Friendship Association. WAC Capt Normandie N. Rioux, who spoke French, and depot commander Lt Col Paul E. Haines encouraged the association, believing that the GIs should take part in the social and cultural life of Périgueux. Although the association had meager financial support, its first major project was to establish a France-United States library in downtown Périgueux. The association grew to sponsor movies, live concerts, and children's shows intended to encourage interaction between locals and GIs.[88, 89] In 1953, the wife of depot commander Lt Col Harold W. Sax, initiated activities to reach out to the French community. Serving as president of the Périgueux Officers Wives Club, Mrs. Sax invited wives of French officers from nearby French military casernes to become associate members. The club provided aid to French orphans and to children patients at the Périgueux hospital.[90]

Périgueux Post Chapel

Worship and Recreation

Using wood-frame construction, depot personnel built a modern chapel that had an open-frame, shed-roof steeple. In March 1955, Lt Col Theodore E. Curtis, Jr, Base Section chaplain, conducted the first Sunday services.[91] In the early years, the depot did not have an EM Club or formal recreation program. GIs used salvaged lumber to build a library in the attic space above the Service Club.[92] Units organized teams for weekend sports competitions; individuals toured nearby historic sites on off-duty time. In early 1955, buildings for offices, EM Club, and library with 2,000 books and listening room for music were completed, and the mess hall was remodeled. In the late 1950s, depot activities were reduced, but briefly were revived during the Berlin Wall Crisis of 1961.

29th Signal Battalion (THQ)

During Operation ROUNDOUT in 1961, Company C of the 29th Signal Battalion (THQ) from Pirmasens, Germany, was stationed at the depot. The one-hundred fifty officers and enlisted men of Company C, commanded by 1st Lt Freemont E. Reif, provided communications support to nearby US Army and US Air Force installations. In the field, they operated communications networks from vans. They also operated from secret communications centers, called Theater Headquarters (THQ), located in underground bunkers at the Maginot Line and Maison-Fort. Company A was stationed at Dreux AB.[93] After the Berlin Crisis abated, the 29th Signal Bn departed and depot activity again was reduced to caretaker status. In 1962, there were one officer, eighteen enlisted men, and one-hundred French employees at the depot. Early the next year, Garage Gonthier was returned to the French government.

Périgueux Quartermaster Depot Commanders

Commanding Officer	Period of Service	Commanding Officer	Period of Service
Lt Col Paul E. Haines	1951-52	Lt Col Harold W. Sax*	1953-55
Col David C. Alexander	1952-53	Lt Col Robert H. Souder	1955-56
Col Oswaldo de la Rosa	1953	Col Kenneth O. Schellberg	1957-58

*From February to August 1953, Sax commanded Ingrandes QM Depot.

Bussac-Captieux-Périgueux Area Installations

Installation	Location	Activity and Units
Headquarters	Bussac-Forêt	US Army Garrison, Bussac
	le Poteau (Captieux)	Captieux Command Support Center
	Coulouniex-Chamiers (Périgueux)	US Army Sub-Depot
Depots	Bussac-Forêt (3,646 acres)	US Army Transportation Depot, Bussac 1st QM Petroleum Products Lab
	le Poteau (24,907 acres)	US Army Ammunition Depot and NEO warehouses, Captieux
	Coulouniex-Chamiers (166 acres)	US Army QM Depot, Périgueux
Hospital/Dispensary	Bussac-Forêt	319th Station Hospital
	le Poteau (Captieux)	13th General Dispensary (31 beds)
Schools (dependents)	Bussac-Forêt	Elementary school
	Périgueux	Elementary school
	le Poteau (Captieux)	Elementary school
Bachelor Officers Quarters (BOQ)	Bussac-Forêt	One-story building, Officers Mess
	le Poteau (Captieux)	One-story building (8 men), Officers Mess
Housing (families)	Bussac-Forêt (Cité Clemenceau)	52 SCH units (16 acres)
	Bazas (Cité Pradère)	40 RGH units
	le Poteau (Cité Brémontier)	24 SCH units (7½ acres)
	Périgueux (Cité Américaine)	20 RGH units
	Blaye (Cité Patton), Cenon, Pessac, and St.-André-de-Cubzac	168 RGH units (four sites near Bordeaux)
Troop Barracks	Bussac-Forêt	55th Chemical Processing Co 83rd Engineer Construction Battalion 597th Engineer Co (Hvy Maint) 574th Ordnance Company (FM) 552nd Military Police Company 562nd QM Co (Petroleum Supply) 55th Transportation Co (Petroleum) 78th Transportation Co (Med Trk) 583rd Transportation Co (Lgt Trk) 555th Ambulance Company 4088th Labor Service Company
	le Poteau (Captieux)	583rd Ordnance Co (Ammo Depot) 552nd Military Police Detachment 17th Army Postal Unit 4011th Labor Service Co 4243rd Labor Service Co
	Coulouniex-Chamiers (Périgueux)	313th Signal Co (Service) 541st QM Co (Clothing & General Supplies Depot) 520th Medical Detachment 552nd Military Police Detachment 29th Signal Bn (THQ)

Recreation	Biscarrosse (Étang de Cazaux)	American Youth Activities (AYA) Camp
	Bussac-Forêt	Golf course (9 holes), driving range, bowling alley (6 lanes)
	Bussac-Forêt (15 mi from depot)	Rod and Gun Club (2,500 acres)
	le Poteau (Captieux)	Gymnasium, miniature golf course, baseball and football fields, "Kingpin Alley" bowling center (6 lanes)
	Périgueux	Bowling alley (4 lanes)
Air Fields	Bussac and Captieux	Airstrip at depots
	Mérignac (Base Aérienne 106)	French Air Force control
Training Site	Camp Sougé (near Bordeaux)	Maneuver area and firing range (French Army control)
Newspapers	Bussac	Votre Bussac, Le Chateau (83rd Engr Bn)
	Captieux	The Captieux Chronicle, Broadway-des-Landes (for LWRs)
	Périgueux	The Green and White

Abbreviations

FM	Field Maintenance		RGH	Rental Guarantee Housing
LWR	Local Wage Rate (French employee)		SCH	Surplus Commodity Housing
NEO	Noncombatant Evacuation Order		THQ	Theater Headquarters

Braconne Ordnance Depot

Land for the Braconne Ordnance Depot (BROD) was acquired from the French government in September 1951. The depot, built on about 10% of a 1,795-acre site in the Forêt de la Braconne, northeast of Angoulême, was developed to have more than ½ million sq ft of warehouses and maintenance shops. Permission had to be obtained from the *Eaux et Forêts* before trees could be removed and land cleared for buildings. Ordnance personnel constructed the first maintenance shops in 1951.[94] Because a layer of rock near ground surface impeded digging, flexible "invasion" pipe was laid on the ground for temporary waterlines. Depot personnel built the mess hall and PX from corrugated metal. Until fall 1952, most enlisted men lived in tents and had to walk a mile to the showers. Off-duty personnel from Tennessee played banjos and sang hillbilly songs.[95]

In 1954, a new "tilt-up" wall construction method was tried at Braconne to rapidly build twenty-five warehouses and three shop buildings. Concrete blocks were cast on the floor slab of each building. The 15-ft high panels were tilted up into place by a crane after the grout, mortar coating, and frame of reinforced concrete had cured. The assembly-line method, devised by French engineer Jacques Meffroy, significantly reduced labor costs.[96]

Braconne Buildup

In 1951, GIs of the 83rd Engineer Construction Battalion found deposits of "chert", a fine-grained, dense rock, on the depot site. The chert, which proved to be a better ground cover than gravel, was used to build roads.[97] Eventually, 25 miles of the depot roads were paved. In May 1953, the bottom of the chert quarry was leveled and used for a below-grade firing range. The 961st Ordnance Park Co, an Army National Guard unit from Knoxville, Tennessee, set up assembly lines in maintenance shops to rehab wheeled vehicle engines, drivetrains, and bodies. Vehicles could be rebuilt for about 25%

Retreat ceremony, Braconne Depot, 1965 (US Army)

the cost of a new vehicle.[98] The 961st, released from active duty in December 1954, was replaced by the 601st Ordnance Battalion (Armament Rebuild). GIs of the 601st removed gun barrels and engines of M47 Patton II and M48 Patton III combat tanks. The engines were rebuilt and gun barrels were replaced if X-rays revealed cracks.[99] After the rebuilt tanks passed final inspection, they were delivered to Allied forces. In the early 1960s, more than one-thousand French worked at the depot.

DUKW Pit

Amphibious vehicles (DUWKs), which had not been manufactured for the Army since the end of World War II, were stored under camouflaged netting in the forest of Braconne. The 574th Ordnance Co (FM) overhauled DUWKs that were used during the offshore discharge exercises along the French coast. An 8-ft deep, concrete lined pit was constructed in 1960 so ordnance troops could determine if the hull of a DUKW was watertight. The pit was one-third the size of an Olympic swimming pool. Soon after the pit was completed and filled with water, heavy rains saturated the ground. The slab bulged upward and cracked due to pressure from groundwater under the pit. When a hole was drilled in the slab, water gushed upward creating a 4-ft high geyser because the pit had created a dam for underground water flow. The 83rd Engineers, commanded by Lt Col Eldridge H. Cockrell, repaired the pit by installing a check valve in the center of the slab. The one-way flow valve allowed groundwater to flow upward into the pit, reducing pressure on the slab, but prevented water in the pit from flowing out.[100] During a summer drought in 1959, water from the underground source was transported by Army tank trucks to nearby farmers.

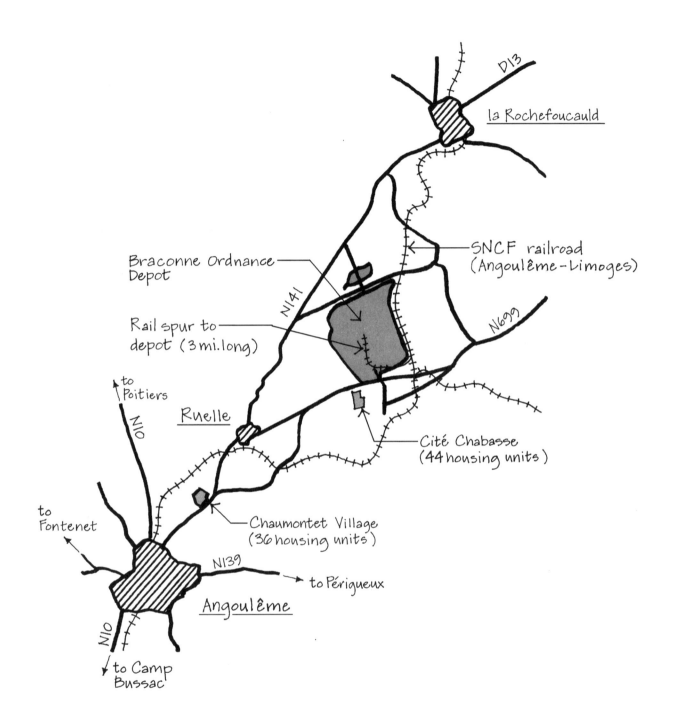

Braconne Area Installations (1960)

Dragon Wagons

In November 1954, the mission of the 595th Trans Co, previously stationed at Bussac, was converted to heavy lift at Braconne. Commanded by Capt James H. Kendrick in 1955-56, the 595th Trans Co (Heavy Lift) became the only unit in ComZ to operate a fleet of M25 tractor-trailers. Because the 12-ton tractor belched flames from the exhaust pipe when driven in low gear, and the eight huge wheels of the 50-ton semitrailer it pulled resembled a monster's legs, the M25s were called "dragon wagons." A crew of five (four drivers, one mechanic) operated the 12½-ft wide by 60-ft long wagons, which could transport M48 combat tanks, buses, engineer mobile cranes, and even mike boats (LCMs). The drivers rotated, each limited to a stressful one-hour shift. The others served as lookouts as the huge tractor-trailer slowly passed over narrow bridges and negotiated sharp turns in small villages. Nevertheless, often corners of buildings were crushed, masonry walls gouged, and parked cars dented. Upon return to Braconne, NCOs in charge submitted damage reports to Army lawyers to evaluate so the US Claims Office in Paris could reimburse the owners for property damage. Because the M25 consumed 1 gal of fuel every two miles it traveled, a gasoline tank truck usually followed each wagon.[101]

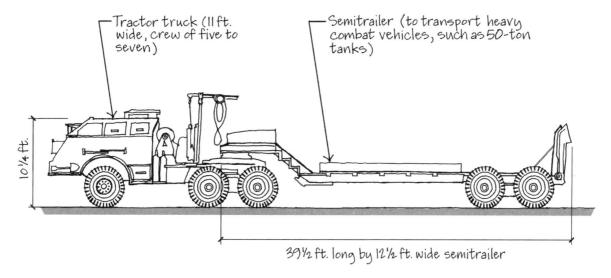

Dragon Wagon

De Gaulle Visits Angoulême

A 3-mile rail spur, which opened in November 1953, connected the depot to the Angoulême-Limoges SNCF railroad line that bordered the eastern side of the depot. The spur allowed direct rail service to the depot, reducing the need to transfer cargo from railcars to Army trucks at Angoulême and eliminating most convoy traffic through Ruelle to Braconne.[102] The French government used the spur to park the railcar of President Charles de Gaulle while he spoke at a political rally on 13 June 1963 in nearby Angoulême. MPs of the 552nd Military Police Co guarded de Gaulle's railcar while French helicopters hovered overhead. Because many communists lived in the nearby village of Ruelle, it was "locked down" during de Gaulle's visit. The gendarmes did not allow anyone to enter or leave the village until de Gaulle's train had departed for Paris. Security measures near the Angoulême préfecture at Place Bouillaud, the site of de Gaulle's speech, also were strict. Because the third floor apartment of 1st Lt Harry F. Irwin, Jr. and his wife, Judy, was opposite the préfecture, their window shutters had to remain closed during de Gaulle's visit. The Irwins' landlord, who spoke little English, pantomimed that French security forces would shoot the Irwins if they looked out the windows during de Gaulle's speech.[103]

Jerry Cans

In 1963, 1st Lt B. Lamar Thomas found several jerry cans hidden in the woods behind the 81st Trans Co motor pool. Thomas and his shop foreman used an unconventional method to discourage theft of gasoline. Rather than retrieve the cans, the sergeant poured sugar from the EM mess hall into the cans. The contaminated gasoline, likely to be sold on the black market, would damage car engines and hopefully reduce the demand for gasoline stolen from the depot.[104]

In another sector of the depot, the Petroleum Distribution Command (PDC) stored thousands of jerry cans filled with gasoline that would be used to support the evacuation of noncombatants. In late 1965 as part of the continuing drawdown of Base Section, this emergency supply of gasoline was to be moved from Braconne to Germany. Sp4 James R. Lewis, assigned to Headquarters Co message center, volunteered to work on the "decant project" with a dozen other GIs and LWRs. During four weeks, they emptied jerry cans into tank trucks of the 55th Trans Truck Co, which transported the gasoline to Germany. Workers had to be careful not to pour out the sediment at the bottom of the cans. Because sparks could ignite the fuel, it was dangerous to bang the metal cans on metal surfaces or hit stuck screw caps with a hammer. Ironically, the greatest safety hazard may have been the cigarettes dangling from the lips of LWRs.[105]

Jerry can "decant project," Braconne Depot, 1965 (US Army)

Recreation

On 29 March 1954, the first bowling alley in Base Section officially opened at Braconne when Lt Col Abner C. Hutcherson rolled the first ball down one of the four lanes at "BROD Lanes" recreation facility. Each game cost 25¢ with a limit of three games per person per day.[106] In 1961, BROD Lanes moved into the Bowling Center, a masonry building constructed for $24,900 from non-appropriated funds. Theaters at Braconne, Fontenet, Ingrandes, Chinon, and Croix-Chapeau were built using architectural plans and specifications for the theater at Dreux AB. The 345-seat theater at Braconne was completed in 1956.[107]

Franco-American Relations

In 1964, US Army personnel from Braconne joined local Frenchmen on the 20th anniversary of a German ambush of members of the French resistance. They paid homage to the war heroes who died on 22 March 1944 at St.-Laurent-de-Céris. Thirty-seven members of the French resistance and one Army Air Forces sergeant, whose plane had been shot down, were ambushed as they exited a farmhouse for the nearby woods. Thirty-two of the Frenchmen were killed by the Germans. It was the first time Americans had participated in the annual ceremony since the end of the war.[108]

Housing

Officer and NCO families lived on the economy or in government housing. Thirty-six RGH houses were located at Chaumontet near Angoulême, 10 miles southwest of the depot. A housing village of forty-four SCH houses, built in 1959 at the outskirts of the depot along the road to Mornac, was named Cité Chabasse in memory of René and Pierre Chabasse, brothers who were heroes of the French resistance. At the entrance to the village, a memorial plaque was attached to a large boulder in the front lawn of the depot commander's residence. In 1964, the family of newly promoted WO 1 Douglas A. Brown occupied the coveted 3-bedroom unit. It was rumored that the depot commander's wife did not want a boulder in her front lawn.[109]

A 40-ft long steel truss arched over the main gate to the depot. A huge sign, attached to the depot side, reminded drivers leaving the depot: "Courtesy Prevents Accidents—Be Vigilant, Be Alert, Be Alive." By the 1960s, there were more than 1,000 troops stationed at Braconne. More than seven-hundred French were employed at the depot; more than 1,500 during the Military Assistance Program (MAP) years.[110] After the depot was returned to the French government in 1967, part of the property became a technical school. Students and staff reside in the former BOQ. Many of the former warehouses are occupied by commercial enterprises.

Braconne Ordnance Depot Commanders*

Commanding Officer	Period of Service	Commanding Officer	Period of Service
Col Herbert B. Quinn	1952-53	Col Elwyn N. Kirsten	1958-60
Lt Col Abner C. Hutcherson	1953-54	Col Paul H. Raftery	1961-62
Lt Col Albert N. Bray	1955	Col John J. Kiely, Jr.	1963-64
Lt Col Charles D. Austin	1955-56	Col Harvey S. Holt	1964-66
Col Ernest R. Gillespie	1956-57	Capt Charles E. Brown	1966-67
Col Miles B. Chatfield	1957-58		

*Converted to General Depot in 1958.

Fontenet Ordnance Depot

In early 1951, enlisted troops of the 37th Ordnance Artillery and Vehicle Park Co, commanded by Maj Frank B. Greer, lived in rundown barracks at Caserne Voyer at St.-Jean d'Angély. The abandoned buildings had cracked floors overgrown with shrubs and weeds. At night, bats dove around the high-ceilinged, musty rooms. Nevertheless, GIs believed that any barracks would be better than tents. The morale of the troops greatly improved when they moved into prefabs constructed on the site of an abandoned French airdrome at Fontenet, 4 miles southeast of St.-Jean d'Angély.[111] The 37th stored trucks, jeeps, ambulances, and vehicle parts at Fontenet.

U.S. GO HOME

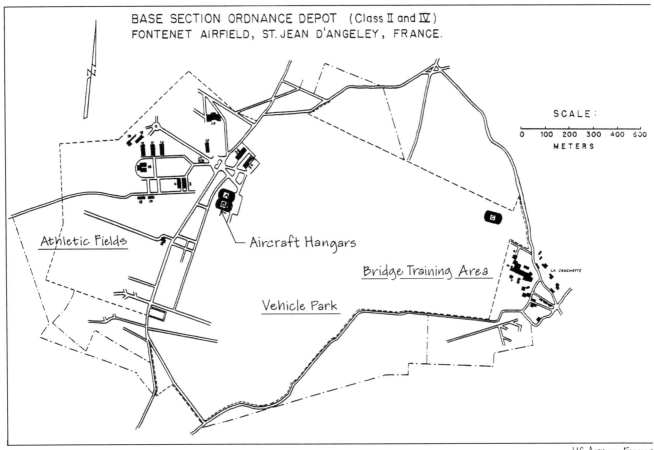

Fontenet Ordnance Depot (1951)

Caserne Voyer

In the summer of 1951, the 7775th Army Unit (AU), the Signal Service Co of Base Section, began renovating Caserne Voyer. By necessity, the signal troops, supervised by SFC James C. Throckmorton, became carpenters, painters, laborers, and gardeners. The men, spending their own money, bought plants and whitewashed the bases of trees to landscape the courtyards. Army engineers installed latrines and repaired water pipes.[112] The signal troops, now living in clean, bat-free barracks, stored and issued parts and equipment to seventeen installations in Base Section.[113] Soldiers from Caserne Voyer and Fontenet Depot shared the EM Club at St-Jean d'Angély and the chapel at Fontenet. In June 1955, the 7775th AU was inactivated at St-Jean d'Angély and replaced by Company B of the 29th Signal Battalion (Construction). Caserne Voyer was closed in 1956 when a modern Signal Depot opened at Montreuil-Bellay. The property was returned to the French in September 1957.

Fontenet Depot Buildup

By the mid-1950s, forty-nine existing buildings at Fontenet had been renovated, nearly two-hundred masonry and prefab buildings constructed, 7 miles of railroad track laid, and 15 miles of roads paved. Two of the three aircraft hangars, built earlier in the century for the French Air Force, were used for vehicle repair shops. In 1954, GIs begin using Hangar A, which had a concrete floor, as a basketball court in the evenings. In June 1955, an ordnance supply school opened for Base Section personnel and French employees. Subjects in the two-week course included: use of supply manuals; how to identify parts; and receipt, storage, and issue procedures.[114] In August 1955, Col Fred J. Gosiger, Depot Commanding Officer, and Henri Brisset, Mayor of Fontenet, signed an agreement authorizing French emergency vehicles unlimited access to drive through the depot on the main road between Fontenet and La Combe. Private citizens could use the road if they showed MPs a pass from the Mayor.[115]

Mini-Industrial Detroit

Fontenet set up production lines to repair general purpose, special equipment, and combat vehicles by rebuilding chassis and other subassembly parts. Vehicles were to roll off the production line like a "mini-Detroit."[116] Company D of the 601st Ordnance Battalion (Armament Rebuild) rebuilt vehicle power trains. GIs and French employees tore down jeep assemblies, replaced the defective parts, and shipped the repaired assemblies to ordnance shops in ComZ.[117] Vehicles to be completely rebuilt were entirely disassembled. Worn out pistons, sleeves, gears, and other parts were replaced. Chassis and frames were thoroughly cleaned and painted. Rebuilt vehicles were given a test ride and, if they passed inspection, were stored for shipment to NATO Allies. Nearly half of shop personnel were French.

Military Assistance Program (MAP)

The purpose of the Military Assistance Program (MAP) was to rebuild the military strength of the NATO Allies. In 1953, the MAP stockpile at Fontenet included 5,000 vehicles for use by US forces in Austria (called "Stockpile A"). In December, during Project GEORGE, stocks were moved to Italy to be closer to Austria. More than sixty 2½-ton trucks a day, with jeeps strapped in the cargo beds, were shipped from St.-Jean d'Angély railhead. By May 1954, most of the Stockpile A vehicles had been moved to Army depots in Italy.[118, 119] In May 1955, several general purpose vehicles (jeeps and 2½-ton trucks) were given to the Yugoslavian Army.[120] By mid-1955, most MAP projects had been completed.

Former French hangars A and B,
Fontenet Depot, 1963 (H. F. Irwin, Jr.)

Vehicle park, Fontenet Ordnance Depot,
1954 (US Army)

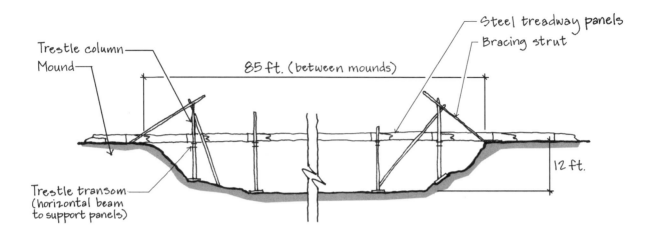

Steel-Treadway Fixed Bridge

Bridge-Building Exercises

At the southeast end of the depot, a large open area was used by engineer troops on temporary duty to practice bridge-building skills From 1959 to 1962, the 83rd Engineer Battalion was headquartered at Fontenet. During the December 1960 to March 1961 rainy season, troops of the 83rd Engineers piled dirt into two 12-ft high mounds spaced 85 ft apart. The 83rd Engineers practiced erecting Bailey bridges, fixed bridges, and pipeline suspension bridges to span the gap between the mounds.[121] Bailey bridges, which had been used by the US Army since World War II, could be installed on piers or pontoons. The bridge had 10-ft long by 5-ft high metal truss panels, the heaviest of which weighed 600 lbs. To increase load-carrying capacity, the trusses could be stacked two or three high and placed side-by-side.[122] The nomenclature of the many combinations, such as single-double (stacked trusses) and double-single (side-by-side trusses), could be confusing.

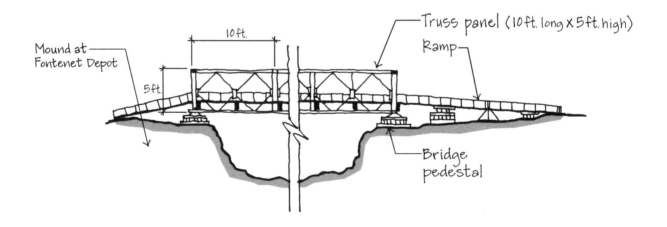

Bailey Bridge

450

Activities of Technical Services

In the 1960s, the 28th Water Supply Det of the 32nd Engineer Group, which had deployed to Verdun from Korea in March 1955, was stationed at Fontenet. The 28th Water Supply drilled wells, laid pipe, and operated mobile water purification units (chlorine injection). Potable water could be stored in 3,000-gal rubber-coated, collapsible tanks or delivered by water tank trailers. Purification units had a cone-shaped basin to remove mud and suspended matter from the water.

The 547th Ordnance Co (FM), authorized nine officers and two-hundred forty-seven enlisted men, repaired wheeled vehicles and rebuilt automotive parts at Fontenet. Damaged vehicles were stripped down and rebuilt. Maintenance platoons of the 547th Ord Co also were stationed at Rochefort and St.-Nazaire, where they repaired vehicles and supported offshore discharge exercises.

The 313th Signal Co (Service) repaired switchboards, microwave radio-telephones, field telephones, and other electronic equipment. In wartime, teams from service companies were to disperse throughout the combat zone, maintaining signal equipment on the spot.[123]

Housing

Officer and NCO families lived on the economy or in government housing. In 1956, twenty-eight RGH houses were built at St.-Jean d'Angély. In 1959, fifty ranch-style SCH houses, called Cité Château Gaillard, were built near the depot on farm land along road D939. The only telephone at Gaillard was attached to a telephone pole.

Because government housing was full in 1961, 1st Lt John A. Nark and his family lived in Brizambourg, a small village 10 miles southeast of the depot. The Narks rented a second floor apartment on a dairy farm owned by Jean Giraud. During the day Giraud's cows were pastured on the outskirts of the village, but at night they were sheltered in a barn attached to the farmer's home. Because Nark's apartment was over the barn, the pungent aroma meant windows seldom could be opened. During the summer of 1961, agricultural riots broke out throughout central and southwestern France. The riots started in Brittany when farmers protested cuts in government subsidies by dumping potatoes on roads to disrupt traffic.[124] Giraud, a leader of the local farmers union, gave Nark advance warning of upcoming strikes. Without the tips, Nark would have been unable to drive to Fontenet because French farmers normally blocked roads with tractors.[125]

In 1961-62, bachelor Capt Edwin J. Rennell, Jr., Army dentist at 349th General Dispensary, rented a small apartment near Aujac, 9 miles from Fontenet Depot. The monthly rent was $40, about half Rennell's housing allowance from the US Army. Because the village did not have telephone service, when alerts were called at night a GI from the dispensary drove to Aujac and threw pebbles at Rennell's window. The GI yelled "Alert," Rennell quickly put on his fatigue uniform and drove to the depot to report for duty. At Fontenet, Rennell was issued a steel helmet, web belt, holster, and a .45 caliber automatic pistol, but was not given bullets.[126]

Fontenet Ordnance Depot Commanders

Commanding Officer	Period of Service	Commanding Officer	Period of Service
Maj Frank B. Greer	1951-53	Lt Col Bernard H. Schimmel	1958-60
Lt Col Warren B. Steele	1953-54	Lt Col Eldridge H. Cockrell	1960-61
Lt Col Eugene F. Utley	1954	Lt Col Thomas E. Griess	1961-62
Col Fred Joe Gosinger	1954-55	Lt Col James A. Bowden	1962-63
Lt Col Eugene F. Shook	1956-58		

Braconne-Fontenet Area Installations

Installation	Location	Activity and Units
Headquarters	Forêt de la Braconne	US Army Garrison, Braconne
	St.-Jean d'Angély (Caserne Voyer)	117th Labor Service Center
	Fontenet	US Army Garrison, Fontenet US European Command Property Office, Fontenet
Depots	Braconne (1,795 acres)	US Army General Depot, Braconne
	Fontenet (397 acres)	US Army Ordnance Depot, Fontenet
Medical Dispensaries	Braconne	11th General Dispensary
	Fontenet	349th General Dispensary
Schools (dependents)	Braconne	Elementary school
	Fontenet	Elementary school (grades K to 8)
Bachelor Officers Quarters (BOQ)	Braconne	Two-story building, Open Mess
	Fontenet	Combination BOQ-Open Mess
Housing (families)	Mornac (Cité Chabasse)	44 SCH units (13 acres)
	Angoulême (Chaumontet)	36 Rental Guarantee Housing (RGH) units
	St.-Julien de l'Escap (Cité Château Gaillard)	50 Surplus Commodity Housing (SCH) units (15 acres)
	St.-Jean d'Angély	28 RGH units
Troop Barracks	Braconne	83rd Engineer Construction Battalion 574th Engineer Company (Depot) 552nd Military Police Company 554th Ordnance Company 313th Signal Company (Service) 595th Transportation Co (Heavy Lift) 17th Army Postal Unit 4013th Labor Service Co
	Fontenet	28th Water Supply Det 83rd Engineer Construction Battalion 548th Engineer Co (Dump Truck) 597th Engineer Co (Constr Support) 552nd Military Police Company 547th Ordnance Company (FM) 313th Signal Company (Service) 4085th Labor Service Co
Recreation	Braconne	Gymnasium, athletic fields, "BROD Lanes" bowling alley (5 lanes), DUKW pit (3,900 sq ft pool)
	Fontenet	Gymnasium, athletic fields, bowling alley (4 lanes), skeet range
Confinement Facility	Braconne	51st MP Detachment
Training Sites	Camp de la Braconne	Firing range (French Army)
	Saintes	Indoor firing range, 300 yds (French Air Force)
	Fontenet	Engineer bridge building site at depot
Newspapers	Braconne	Caserne Crier (601st Ordnance Bn), The BROD View, La Foret
	Fontenet	Fontenet Review

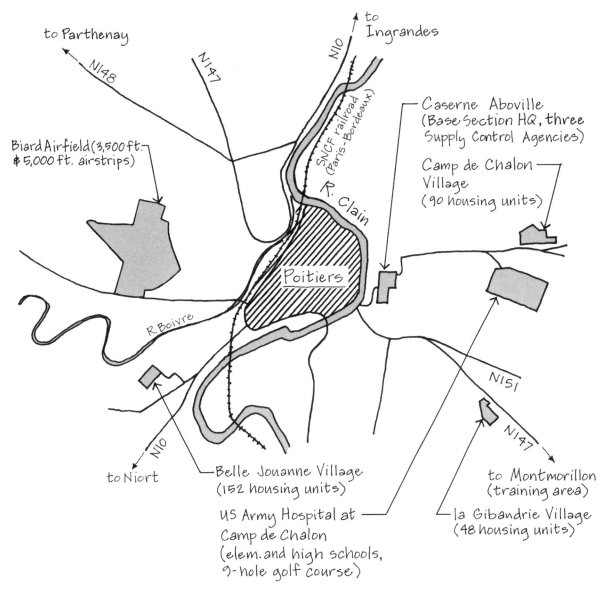

Poitiers Area Installations (1960)

Poitiers

The city of Poitiers, préfecture of the Vienne, overlooks the River Clain. In October 1951, the US Army acquired from the French government the Napoleonic-era Caserne Aboville, located across the river from the city. Like many buildings in the city, the former French Army caserne had been severely damaged by Allied bombers during the German occupation. A 2½-acre contiguous site, bisected by rue du Père Delacroix, also was acquired rent free. The Joint Construction Agency in Paris hired French contractors to renovate existing buildings for offices and troop barracks, and to build new buildings for support activities such as chapel, theater, bowling alley, and gymnasium. Twenty-two permanent structures were renovated for $1.7 million. Horse stables were converted to modern office buildings. Because underground water pipes and other utilities were uncharted, the 29th Signal Bn (Constr) very carefully dug trenches for cables.[127] It took four years to renovate the caserne. Aboville provided space for Base Section headquarters, three supply control agencies, and a transportation battalion.

Base Section Headquarters

In 1957 Base Section headquarters, which oversaw depots, installations, and ports in southwestern France, moved from La Rochelle to the larger Caserne Aboville. Brig Gen James K. Woolnough, BASEC commander, lived at Château de la Roche. Woolnough was succeeded by Brig Gen William Whipple, who had served as a colonel at ComZ in Orléans. Whipple, a former Rhodes Scholar who ranked third in the West Point Class of 1930, commanded the most complicated offshore discharge exercise. During two weeks in October 1957, seven ships were discharged rapidly over beaches at three locations. While serving as ComZ Chief of Staff, the widowed Whipple met Paola, a young French director of a girl's school. After their marriage, the Franco-American couple was very popular in the Poitiers community. Because of his cordial relations with the French military and the people of the Vienne, when his tour ended in May 1958 the French government awarded Whipple the rank of *Officier de la Légion d'Honneur*.[128]

In April 1960, all logistics installations in France were assigned to the Theater Army Support Command (TASCOM) at Verdun. For sixteen months, TASCOM controlled twenty-seven depots in France and Germany. The three commanders during this period were Fleming, Baker, and Chesarek. There was no general officer at Poitiers until the Berlin Wall Crisis in 1961, when Brig Gen William N. Redling arrived from Fort Bragg, North Carolina. Redling, a civil engineering graduate of the University of Washington, Seattle, was the first general officer to command Base Section who had not graduated from West Point.

Commanding Generals, Base Section (Poitiers)

Commanding General	Period	Events
BG James K. Woolnough	1955-57	Base Section headquarters moves from La Rochelle to Poitiers, becomes 5th Log Command. Donges-Metz pipeline begins initial operations (Nov 57).
BG William Whipple	1957-58	Locations selected for beach landings during wartime. Seven ship NODEX held (Sep-Oct 57). NODEX exercises halted. Standby hospitals built.
BG Richard J. Meyer	1958-59	NODEX exercises resume due to Berlin Crisis.
BG Robert J. Fleming, Jr.	1959-60	5th Log Command (Poitiers) and 4th Log Command (Verdun) merge (Apr 60).
MG William C. Baker, Jr. BG Ferdinand J. Chesarek	1960-61 1961	Theater Army Support Command (TASCOM) at Verdun controls all logistics for USAREUR (Apr 60-Aug 61). Revolt of top French generals in Algeria (Apr 61).
BG William N. Redling	1961-62	1st Log Command deploys from US to Poitiers during Operation ROUNDOUT (Oct 61).

Logistical Commands

During most of 1958 to 1967, depots, installations, and ports in Base Section were overseen by a general officer commanding a numbered logistical command. In 1958, the Base Section designation was changed to 5th Logistical Command. From 1958 to 1960, 5th Log Command, authorized more than two-hundred eighty officers and enlisted men, was headquartered at Caserne Aboville. In April 1960, it merged with the 4th Logistical Command, headquartered at Caserne Maginot in Verdun, to become the Theater Army Support Command (TASCOM).[129]

CHAPTER 11: *Base Section in the Southwest*

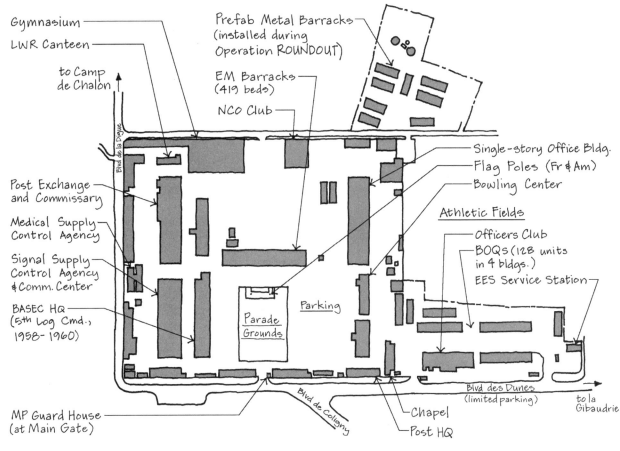

Caserne Aboville (1961)

During the Berlin Wall Crisis, the 1st Logistical Command was deployed to Caserne Aboville to oversee logistics in the Base Section and 4th Log Command was reactivated at Verdun. In July 1958, 1st Log Command, based in Fort Bragg, North Carolina, had been designated a Strategic Army Corps (STRAC) unit. The command trained to deploy on short notice to trouble spots. The 1st Log Command troops sailed on the USNS *Gen W. H. Gordon* from Hampton Roads, Virginia, to Cherbourg, France, arriving at Caserne Aboville on 19 October 1961. In 1961-62, all depots and installations in southwestern France were assigned to 1st Log Command. The troops wore the 1st Log Command shoulder patch, a circular patch with a white arrow penetrating a blue bull's-eye centered within a red band border.[130] On 11 August 1962, after the crisis had abated, the STRAC unit was sent to Fort Hood, Texas.

In 1960, Supply Control Agencies for chemical, medical, and signal technical services, staffed to oversee elements of the vast logistical infrastructure in Europe, moved from Orléans to Caserne Aboville. In 1963, there were more than eight-hundred troops stationed at Poitiers. More than three-hundred French employees worked at Caserne Aboville and the 42nd Field Hospital at Camp de Chalon.

Base Section Aviation

The US Army used one hangar and shared two asphalt-paved runways with civilian aircraft at Biard airfield, two miles from Caserne Aboville. The airfield did not have a control tower or fire department. The Base Section Aviation Det had five fixed-wing aircraft: two L-19 Bird Dogs, two L-20 Beavers, and the general's L-23 Twin Bonanza; and two helicopters: one H-13 Sioux and one H-19 Chickasaw. In the 1960s, a platoon of 2nd Aviation Co (Fixed Wing) flew U-1A Otters at Biard.

Early one morning in May 1957, Capt George R. Cockle was flying an L-20 Beaver from Biard to Camp Bussac. The engine shut down near Cognac. Sighting a flat area, Cockle glided his single-engine aircraft to a safe landing between rows of grapevines in a vineyard. Mechanics of the 19th Aviation Det (Maint) arrived by helicopter later that day to repair the Beaver's engine. After the carburetor was replaced, Cockle flew the plane from the vineyard back to Biard. Unfortunately, the landing and takeoff of the Beaver damaged trellises and vines. After investigation by Army JAGs, the owner received 800,000 francs (about $2,300) from the US Claims Office in Paris.[131]

Award for one-million miles of accident-free driving presented to 598th Trans Co of 28th Trans Battalion, Ingrandes Depot, February 1963 (US Army)

28th Transportation Battalion

In 1962, Lt Col Richard C. Rantz, who in the late 1940s had commanded a segregated transportation unit, was sent to Poitiers to command the 28th Trans Bn. Half of the enlisted men in the battalion, but only two of the twenty-eight officers, were black. Rantz mentored Capt Edward Honor, a black ROTC graduate of Southern University in Baton Rouge, Louisiana. To expedite the line-haul method of transportation, where loaded trailers were relayed across France, Honor used a color-coded control board that displayed the location of each truck and type of load being carried (red discs for ammunition, blue for rations).[132] Rantz encouraged Honor, a bachelor, to participate in battalion social events. In 1989, Honor retired as a lieutenant general. Maj Samuel M. Gottry, a planner at the Medical Supply Control Agency at Poitiers during 1961-1963, understood discrimination. On a previous assignment, his wife, Kay, had organized a bridge club social for wives of Medical Service Corps officers. The wife of the post commander informed Mrs Gottry that she would not attend the function if a black attended. Mrs Gottry, supported by her husband, refused to rescind the invitation and the ranking wife did not attend.[133] Until the late 1950s, the US Army annual officer efficiency report, upon which promotions were based, included evaluation of wives.

28ᵗʰ Transportation Battalion Commanders*

Commanding Officer	Period of Service	Commanding Officer	Period of Service
Lt Col Howard F. Schlitz	1957-59	Lt Col John J. Policastro	1963-64
Lt Col Dan K. Dukes, Jr.	1959-61	Lt Col Ernest A. Hinojosa, Jr.	1964-65
Lt Col Donald M. Davis	1961-62	Lt Col Carl R. Breining	1966-67**
Lt Col Richard C. Rantz	1962-63		

*In March 1959, 28ᵗʰ Trans Bn headquarters arrived in France from Germany. In June 1964, the battalion departed Poitiers for reassignment to Germany.
**Served as commander during Operation FRELOC.

42ⁿᵈ Field Hospital

In 1958, a 500-bed standby hospital was built at Camp de Chalon by Genie Civil et Bâtiment of Neuilly-sur-Seine (Paris) at a cost of $3.9 million. From 1962 to 1964, the 42ⁿᵈ Field Hospital (1ˢᵗ Det), authorized more than one-hundred officers and enlisted men, staffed the hospital. Buildings of the facility also were used as dependents elementary and high schools, dormitories (girls on first floor; boys on second), and dispensary. Because the French contractor did not seal the openings around pipe penetrations through the floor, the students slipped notes between floors through the openings. In September 1952, the Poitiers American School (grades 1 to 7) had opened in a leased building in Poitiers that had been a French bakery.

Dealing with the French bureaucracy was a challenge. The body of an American soldier, burnt beyond recognition in an automobile accident, was brought to the 42ⁿᵈ Field Hospital one evening in 1963. After the paperwork was processed, the body was to be transported by ambulance to the QM Mortuary at Chanteau, near Orléans. The French Army liaison officer advised Capt (Dr) Donald J. Logan, the medical duty officer, to indicate on the paperwork that the GI was still alive when the ambulance left Poitiers. If a dead body was transported to Orléans, each French administrative jurisdiction along the route would have to give permission for passage, increasing the time it took to transport the body from hours to weeks.[134]

202ⁿᵈ Military Police Company

In 1961, during Operation ROUNDOUT, the 202ⁿᵈ Military Police Co, authorized five officers and one-hundred forty enlisted men, was activated at Poitiers. The 202ⁿᵈ MP Co (called "deuce-oh-deuce") provided security at depots in Base Section and would control motor convoys of civilians being evacuated from Germany and France during a noncombatant evacuation order. Platoons of the 202ⁿᵈ were stationed at Ingrandes, Chinon, and Saumur. One unusual mission of the 202ⁿᵈ was providing security for President Charles de Gaulle during his visit to Poitiers on 16 June 1963. At the insistence of the French, Capt Ferdinand C. Meyer issued live ammunition to his MPs.[135]

Evacuation of Noncombatants

In the event of impending war with the Soviets, all noncombatants (American female employees, wives, and children) were to be evacuated from Europe. In planning for a noncombatant evacuation order (NEO) during the early 1950s, officers in France were assigned to deliver convoys of noncombatants to safe haven in Spain. Privately owned vehicles (POV) would be commandeered for the NEO, but instructions on what to do with the evacuees after arrival in Spain were not included in the early briefings.[136] Subsequent plans became more complete, including evacuation from safe havens to US by air and sea. On 08 February 1955, agreement was reached with the Portuguese government to evacuate 70,000 noncombatants to Portugal if the US also would evacuate 2,400 Portuguese nationals from the Bordeaux staging area. Accommodations and subsistence in Portugal would be provided to the American evacuees for up to 120 days.[137] By 1962, there were 270,000 noncombatants to be evacuated from Europe. It was believed that more than half of ComZ troops in France would be tied down for the first 15 days of an actual NEO. This would seriously reduce the ability of ComZ to fulfill its primary mission to support combat forces.[138] Many officers in ComZ doubted the feasibility of NEOs as well as the devastation to troop morale if the Soviet air force attacked convoys.

NEO Kits

Married US military personnel were required to register all dependents at the NEO office. Emergency supplies necessary for the journey were to be kept at home. This included packaged food, canned milk for children, two blankets per person, clothing, and medicine. The slogan for NEO blankets was: "Do not leave home without them."[139] The US Army's 1957 NEO booklet, "Instructions to US Sponsors and Noncombatants," contained advice on how to maintain a NEO kit to survive for three to five days on the road, a strip map showing route to first service area, and 5x7 inch identification card to be taped to the windshield.[140] The card had an American flag under the "USA" oval international vehicle sign. (See p. 586.) MPs made yearly visits to off-post housing to confirm that every ComZ family had a complete NEO kit at home. GIs called the kits "bug out bags."

Assembly Points

When a NEO alert was given (called Order for Reinforced Alert), dependents were to immediately drive to assembly points to form convoys. At Fontainebleau, the assembly point was near the Obelisk in a field along the road to Nemours. At Orléans, Mrs. Robert B. Gingrich, mother of future Speaker of the US House of Representatives, Newt Gingrich, worried that she would not find "Newtie" if a NEO started while he was at school.[141] At assembly points, the evacuees would be provided with food, a jerry can of gasoline, and additional oil for each POV. The POVs would then move in convoys under the control of armed military personnel. Red Cross volunteers, trained in first aid, were assigned one volunteer for eight to ten POVs.[142] MPs were responsible for reconnoitering and marking the routes, maintaining traffic flow, and security at staging areas. Movement of convoys was not to exceed 35 mph and all refugee traffic was to be removed from the evacuation routes, using force if necessary. In the mid-1950s, the primary NEO routes through France were named: Axle, Brake, Choke, Dynamo, and Engine. Near Bordeaux, the five routes were merged into two; in the 1960s another route ended at Perpignan. If the Soviets attacked without warning, noncombatants in Germany were to drive on their own to staging areas in France. The goal was to evacuate Germany within 72 hours.

Before West Germany was granted sovereignty in May 1955, NEOs also would evacuate German scientists who were on a secret list called the "King List." The 66th CIC Intelligence Group kept the master list at Camp King, near Frankfurt. The 66th gathered intelligence on the Soviets by debriefing refugees from Soviet bloc nations. During a NEO, CIC agents were to deliver the foreign scientists to vehicle assembly points. If a scientist objected, he was to be moved forcibly.[143]

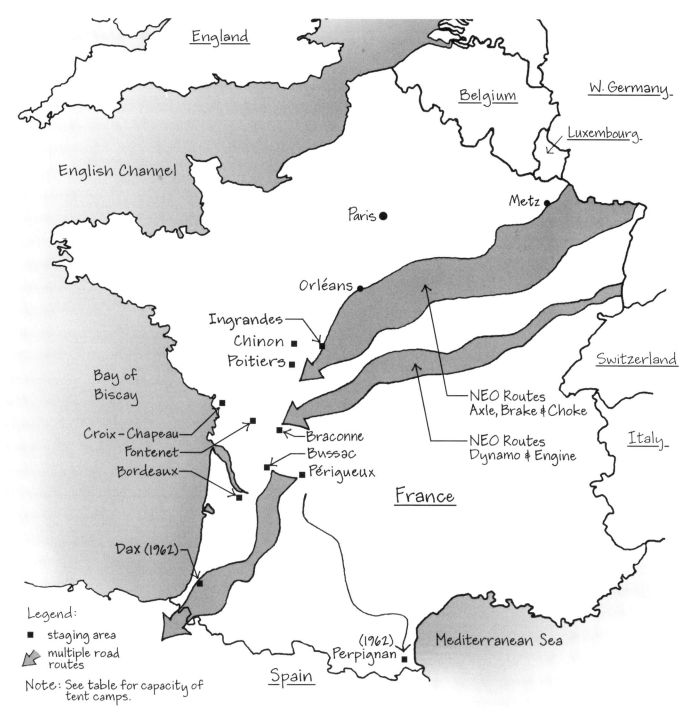

NEO Evacuation Routes and Staging Areas (1957)

Service Areas

Engineer, ordnance, and quartermaster troops annually practiced setting up service areas to provide gasoline and food to NEO convoys en route to staging areas. Several depots stored 3,000 to 5,000 jerry cans of gasoline for use in NEOs.[144] Depots also stored 2,000 cases of disposable diapers and sufficient sanitary napkins for 200,000 female evacuees. There would be thirteen main service areas and fifteen emergency service areas in France.[145, 146] In 1963, Capt (Dr) Donald J. Logan was assigned an additional duty to inventory NEO medical supplies stored in a cave near Montluçon. Logan reported that most of the NEO supplies, including hundreds of cases of disposable diapers and sanitary napkins, were floating in deep puddles of water.[147] An underground NEO depot also was located at Villemandeur, near Orléans.

Staging Areas

Beginning in 1954, ComZ troops were to set up tent camp staging areas at nine locations in the Base Section and provide support along the NEO routes. Later on, tent camps at Bordeaux, Croix-Chapeau, and Périgueux were replaced by camps at Dax and Perpignan. Each tent camp was to be stocked with a 30-day supply of food, medical supplies, fuel, sanitary supplies, and infant-care items. ComZ staffing was to include security by MPs, medical services, chaplains, postal service units, and even some European Exchange System (EES) services.[148,149]

Capacity of Tent Camps (persons)

Location	1954	1962	Location	1954	1962
Bordeaux	10,000	0	Fontenet	10,000	15,000
Braconne	10,000	20,000	Ingrandes	20,000	10,000
Bussac	25,000	30,000	Périgueux	10,000	0
Chinon	10,000	25,000	Perpignan	0	5,000
Croix-Chapeau	20,000	0	Poitiers	10,000	10,000
Dax	0	15,000	**Total** (all camps)	125,000	130,000

NEO Exercises

Periodic exercises were held to test NEO plans. Exercise ROADBOUND in November 1953, tested the first NEO plan. Five-hundred vehicles departed Germany for staging area camps near Bordeaux. Subdivided convoys, called serials, had at least thirty vehicles, one bus configured as an ambulance, and one wrecker. Wrong turns were common in France due to poor signage and lack of accurate maps issued to drivers. It took 72 hours for all the vehicles to reach Bordeaux. If it had been a real NEO, more than 25,000 vehicles would have entered France, compounding the confusion.[150]

A practice exercise in 1958 evacuated several housing areas in Germany to staging areas in France. Some convoys got lost in France due to lack of road markers and confusing road signs.[151] By the late 1950s, NEO plans were revised to allow free flow of evacuee vehicles at the beginning of a NEO, rather than wait for additional vehicles to form convoys. Vehicles were to be routed through France to safe haven in Spain and Portugal or through Switzerland to Italy. Army helicopters would fly overhead to help MPs control flow of traffic.[152]

SNCF Train Service

Because the train from Paris to Bordeaux normally was nonstop, a very brief stop at Poitiers was arranged for US military personnel. GIs usually were detailed to meet and assist newly assigned personnel at the station. In June 1957, as the four young children of Capt Thomas E. Peters were hustled off the train, they were astounded to see the family luggage being hurled out the windows.[153] In June 1962, Sergeant Major Willie Johnson organized a 28th Trans Bn greeting party for the new commander, Lt Col Richard C. Rantz, and his family. The GIs quickly passed twelve suitcases through the windows of the train and rushed the Rantz family to the platform as the train began to roll on to Bordeaux.[154] The Logans departure in 1963 from Poitiers almost separated the newlyweds. As Capt Logan turned to retrieve the last suitcase from the platform, the train started to roll. Logan, young and physically fit, ran along side of the train until he could leap onto a passenger car to join his wife, Judy, for the ride to Paris.[155]

The PGA

On 14 June 1959, a nine-hole golf course officially opened on land adjacent to the US Army's Camp de Chalon Hospital near Poitiers. It had taken a year for the 83rd Engineers to build the 2,542 yard, par 35 course and a clubhouse. Like the golf course at Verdun, it was located so close to the hospital that Army doctors could tee off minutes after leaving their offices.

Membership in the Poitiers Golf Association (called the PGA) was $4 a month for an individual, $5 for a family. The greens fees were $1 on weekdays, $2 on weekends. The course was open to the public and French citizens were welcome to join the PGA.[156] In 1964, the PGA stopped charging membership and greens fees. A complete set of clubs could be rented for 25¢ per day. The Snack Bar offered hamburgers and hot dogs at reasonable prices. In the evenings, a steak dinner cost $1.50. The French Golf Association, with a membership of twenty-five families, participated in Franco-American events at the club.[157]

Housing

In the early 1950s, officer and NCO families lived on the economy. Shortly after assuming command of Base Section at Poitiers, Brig Gen William Whipple received an unusual petition from the mayor of a nearby village. All the villagers had signed the request that an American sergeant living in the village not be reassigned to the US. It was likely that the villagers did want to lose their American, who may have owned the only vehicle in the village.[158]

In summer 1956, two-hundred RGH housing units were completed at Belle Jouanne and la Gibaudrie, on the outskirts of Poitiers.[159] In 1959, ninety SCH housing units were built near the hospital. The SCH housing village, called Camp de Chalon by the Americans, is currently named "le Petit Breuil." The French referred to it by its ancient name Vallée des Crapaud.

Today, all housing units built for the Americans are owned by French private citizens. The Camp de Chalon hospital buildings are used for the care of mental patients, and the adjacent former Army nine-hole golf course is operated by the Université de Poitiers.

Ingrandes Quartermaster Depot

On 28 February 1952, US Army troops of the 566th Quartermaster Co (Base Depot) pitched their tents on a weedy tract of relatively flat land near Ingrandes, midway between Poitiers and Tours, to establish the Ingrandes Quartermaster Depot. The depot received, stored, and issued: rations, clothing, tents, weapons, and construction materials. The site had been the French Army St.-Ustre ammunition depot. During the occupation, the Germans had used it as a supply depot and demolished most of the buildings when they retreated. The initial task of the 1st Quartermaster Group, commanded by Capt Henry E. Wooddall, was to clear away dud explosives, some of which had been in the mud since World War I. Even during construction work in the 1960s, unexploded munitions were uncovered buried in the ground. The 83rd Engineers renovated damaged buildings by putting glass in windows, hanging doors, and patching floors and ceilings; and cleared areas for new construction.[160]

Ingrandes Buildup

The depot, bordered on the west by route N10 and on the east by the Paris-Bordeaux railroad line, had a spur to the storage areas. The spur was repaired so fifteen railcars could be switched into the depot. The depot needed more land, but the French owner of the adjacent property did not want

Americans on his land and refused to rent or sell. It took the French government until August 1952 to expropriate 133 acres of his land by eminent domain for military purposes.[161] Adding to the initial delays was the refusal of French national railroad (SNCF) to deliver rail shipments consigned to Ingrandes Depot. The very strict SNCF bureaucrats insisted the correct name was St.-Ustre, the nearest village. Shipping documents were changed to satisfy the SNCF.

By the end of 1953, the three original French buildings had been renovated and were surrounded by prefabs, hutments, and warehouses. Outdoor storage was necessary until sufficient warehouse space could be built. By December 1954, most supplies were finally moved out of the mud by the 853rd Quartermaster Co from Baltimore, Maryland, and the 978th Quartermaster Co from Petersburg, Virginia. Both were Army Reserve units that had been mobilized for the Korean War. It took three years for the French EDF to provide sufficient electricity to the depot. In 1954, most warehouses still had to use diesel generators for electricity.[162] Troops moved into hutments and the depot had a commissary, PX, service club, and snack bar. GIs believed the depot had more boardwalk than Atlantic City, New Jersey. The walks were built to keep the men out of the mud when it rained and out of the dust when the sun shined.[163] An EM Club opened in leased space at Châtellerault. The three-story building had a restaurant that served American-style food, dance hall, two bars, and a lounge. By May 1955, Ingrandes had five miles of railroad track and a nearby marshalling yard which could handle 300 railcars. The depot warehoused $40 million in supplies: 50,000 tons of rations and 5,000 tons of clothing, tents, weapons, and construction materials. Another 4,000 tons of supplies were stored in the open. Over eighty powered material-handlers were used to move supplies about the depot.[164] Ingrandes also was the bakery, shoe repair, laundry, and dry cleaners for nearby installations, such as Chinon, Saumur, and Rochefort. In November 1954, the laundry charged enlisted men $3 per month to clean one 30-piece bundle each week.[165]

Temporary tent camp, Operation ROUNDOUT, Ingrandes Depot, 1961 (US Army)

Maintenance Division personnel steam clean rough terrain forklift, Ingrandes Depot, 1962 (US Army)

CHAPTER 11: *Base Section in the Southwest*

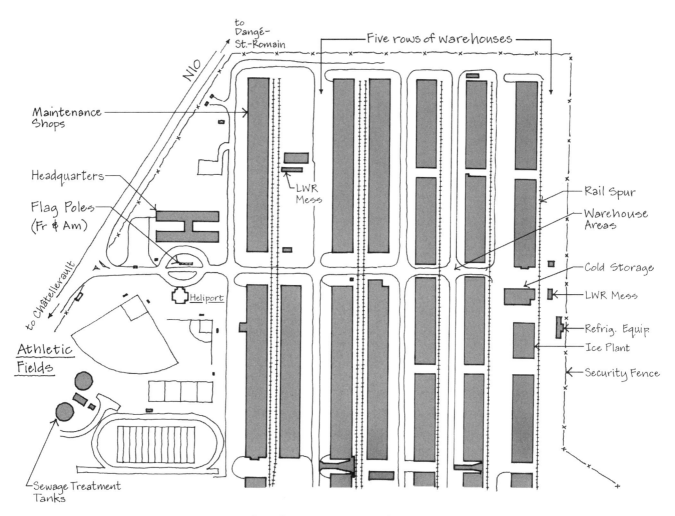

Ingrandes Quartermaster Depot

By the early 1960s, Ingrandes had more than one-hundred masonry buildings, constructed at a cost of $7.5 million by Robin et Cie of Angoulême. The depot had 1.2 million sq ft of indoor storage; 11 miles of two-lane paved roads; and 7 miles of railroad track. The depot served troops throughout France and Germany with rations and supplied QM spare parts from its inventory of more than 40,000 items.[166] In 1963, more than 1,200 troops were stationed at Ingrandes and more than 1,300 French were employed. Ingrandes Depot was organized into three divisions.

Depot Divisions

The *Maintenance Division* repaired equipment, primarily forklifts, electric motors, office machines, refrigeration equipment, and field heaters. About 1,500 items were repaired each month. Repair work required skilled personnel such as mechanics, welders, millwrights, and parts experts. It took a week to rebuild a field laundry unit; two and a half days for a tractor; and less than an hour for a carburetor. Mobile teams repaired kitchen refrigeration equipment, stoves, and field heaters throughout ComZ.[167]

The *Storage Division* stored clothing, bedding, tents, and rations (canned food, C-rations). Damaged cans were sold for animal consumption or fertilizer. Clothing had to meet requirements of season and climate (from cold Norway to sweltering hot Persian Gulf). Nearly 6,000 tons of supplies were received and stored each month; another 6,000 tons shipped out. In mid-1955, the depot, commanded by Col Chauncey E. Howland, received a new 42-ton diesel locomotive to operate on the depot track. The locomotive moved railcars to warehouse areas, where GIs used forklifts and cranes to unload the cargo. In early November 1960, the division provided 19,400 blankets for survivors of cyclones in East Pakistan. The blankets were delivered to Évreux AB, where they were loaded onto C-130 Hercules cargo aircraft.[168]

The storage process reversed when the *Stock Control Division* received requests from US military forces in Europe. The orders were drawn from the huge stacks in warehouses, placed on railcars, and shipped to the unit. High-priority requisitions were given color codes to ensure rapid shipment out of the depot, such as "Blue Streak" for immediate shipment.[169] A detachment of the 7856th QM Supply Control Office in Germany was stationed at Orléans to oversee supplies in France. Electric accounting machines were used to maintain accountability records. To ensure that stocks were kept at proper levels, Ingrandes personnel followed a routine schedule of inventories and sent reports to Orléans. Excess stocks were disposed of to make room for necessary items; insufficient stocks were replenished from the US or by local purchases.[170-172]

In 1961, the Société Européenne de Teleguidage plant near the depot began manufacturing Hawk ground-to-air guided missiles for NATO. The Hawk could be fitted to carry a nuclear warhead to attack enemy bomber formations.[173]

Education Activities

In 1952, the Mayor of Châtellerault offered classrooms rent free for use as a dependents elementary school until prefabs were installed at the depot.[174] The new school, located in Quonset huts, opened in 1954. The curriculum included French history and culture. Students in grades 10 to 12 from Ingrandes, Orléans, Poitiers, Chinon, and Saumur attended the high school operated by the US Air Force at Châteauroux AD. The students lived in dormitory rooms during the week and returned home by Army bus on Fridays. Their days were structured like most military life: wake-up bell at 7:15 am, breakfast 7:45 to 8:15 am, school hours 8:45 am to 3:45 pm, report back to dorm for free time 4 to 6 pm, dinner 6 to 7 pm, study hall 7 to 9 pm, and lights out at 10 pm.[175]

During lunch hour at Ingrandes, GI instructors taught English to LWR personnel. The French employees could volunteer to take beginning or advanced English classes. GIs also studied French. In 1955, more than 1,300 GIs throughout Base Section took courses in conversational French. The Ingrandes service club library had more than 3,000 books and numerous language tapes. GIs could earn extra income by working in the library during their off-duty hours. The pay was $1 per hour.[176]

French Orphanages

Beginning in 1952, personnel at Ingrandes supported nearby French orphanages by contributing gifts of clothing, food, and funds. In July 1955, troops working in the Storage Division, led by Capt Paul V. Gee and SFC George McCallum, collected funds to send forty girls from St. Joseph's Orphanage in Châtellerault on a holiday vacation. The girls, age two to eighteen, received their academic and religious training at St. Joseph's. The Officers Wives Club raised funds to support the French orphanage at Mirebeau. The women donated dolls and toys to the home.[177]

During the 1955 Christmas season, all Base Section installations hosted Christmas dinners for French orphans and tried to answer their requests to Santa Claus (*Père Nöel*). Funds were raised by "voluntary" collections on payday and by raffles at EM Clubs and bake sales at Wives Clubs.[178]

Housing

In 1956, a twenty-eight unit RGH village opened in Châtellerault. The homes were assigned to the families of twenty enlisted men, one Department of Army civilian, and seven officers.[179] Lafayette Village, 1½ miles north of the depot, had eighty-eight SCH units for officers and NCOs with dependents. The road into Lafayette Village was named Foch Drive and connected to Franklin Boulevard and Descartes Square. When the depot closed in 1967, the adverse effect on the local economy was overwhelming. For many years after US withdrawal, warehouse buildings were used as a distribution facility for a chain of grocery stores.[180]

Ingrandes Quartermaster Depot Commanders*

Commanding Officer	Period of Service	Commanding Officer	Period of Service
Capt Henry E. Wooddall	1952-53	Col Carl W. Kohls	1957-60
Lt Col Harold W. Sax	1953	Col Harold F. "Joe" Jenks	1961-62
Col Jack H. Weske	1953	Col James S. Griffin	1962-64
Lt Col Homer E. Long	1953-54	Lt Col Otis B. Palmer	1964
Col Robinson Biard Rider	1954	Col George C. Blackwell	1964-65
Col Chauncey E. Howland	1954	Maj Robert L. Price	1966
Lt Col Lawrence B. Curtis	1954-55	Capt William J. Edwards	1966-67
Col Russell K. Kuhns	1955-56		

*Converted to General Depot in 1958. During the 1966-67 withdrawal from France, the US Army Depot Complex, Western France headquarters was at Ingrandes. The complex consisted of depots at Ingrandes, Braconne, Chinon, and Saumur.

Review of troops, Ingrandes Depot, 1962 (US Army)

Poitiers-Ingrandes Area Installations

Installation	Location	Activity and Units
Headquarters	Poitiers (Caserne Aboville)	5th Logistical Command US Army Chemical, Medical, and Signal Supply Control Agencies US Army Garrison (26 acres)
Depots	St.-Ustre (222 acres)	US Army Depot Activity, Ingrandes US Army QM Equip and Parts Center
Hospital/Dispensaries	Poitiers (Camp de Chalon)	42nd Field Hospital, 500-bed standby hospital (115 acres) 6th General Dispensary
	Ingrandes	385th General Dispensary
Schools (dependents)	Poitiers (Camp de Chalon)	Elementary and high schools (at hospital)
	Ingrandes	Nursery and elementary school
Bachelor Officers Quarters (BOQ)	Poitiers (Caserne Aboville)	Four 2-story buildings, Officers Mess
	Ingrandes	Two-story building, Officers Mess
Housing (families)	Poitiers (Camp de Chalon)	90 SCH units (29 acres)
	Poitiers (Belle Jouanne)	152 RGH units
	Poitiers (la Gibaudrie)	48 RGH units
	Dangé-St.-Romain (Lafayette Village)	88 Surplus Commodity Housing (SCH) units (30 acres)
	Châtellerault (plateau des Minimes)	28 Rental Guarantee Housing (RGH) units
Troop Barracks	Poitiers (Caserne Aboville)	28th Transportation Bn (Truck) 202nd Military Police Company 54th Signal Co (Forward Support) 599th Army Postal Unit 279th Army Band 4096th Labor Service Platoon 6953rd Labor Service Center
	Ingrandes	54th QM Co (Equip Maint) 514th Ordnance Company (FM) 202nd Military Police Company 68th Transportation Co 598th Transportation Co (Med Truck) 81st Medical Det (Vet Food Insp) 4158th Labor Service Co
General Officer Quarters	Poitiers	Château de la Roche
Recreation	Montmorillon	Rod and Gun Club (two lakes)
	Poitiers	Golf course (9 holes, 2,542 yds), club house, gymnasium, bowling center
	Ingrandes	Gymnasium, baseball and football fields, bowling alley (6 lanes)
Transient Quarters	Poitiers (28, rue Carnot)	Hôtel France
	Poitiers (215, ave de Paris)	Hôtel Royal-Poitou
Air Field	Poitiers (2 airstrips at Biard, 6 acres)	2nd Aviation Co (Fixed Wing) 19th Aviation Det (Maint)
Training Site	Montmorillon	US Army Training Facility (3,915 acres)

Newspapers	Ingrandes	The Ingrandes Ration (1952-54), Ingrandes Boardwalk
	Poitiers	Basec Mission (1956-60), The BALOG Banner (1961-62), The Transportation Wheel (2nd Trans Bn)

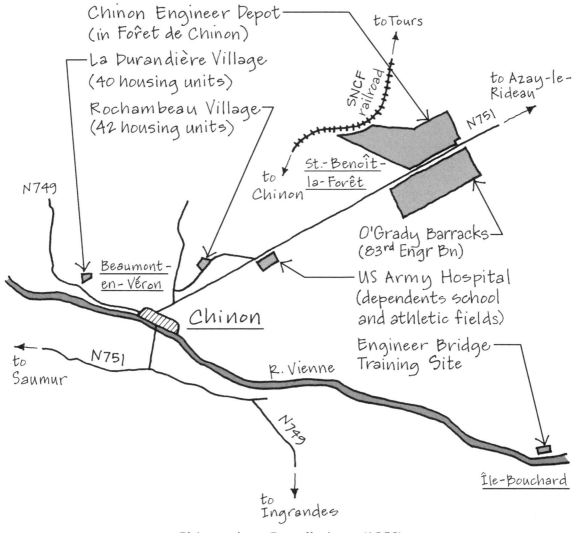

Chinon Area Installations (1959)

Chinon Engineer Depot

In October 1951, a tract of flat land in the Forêt de Chinon was acquired from the French government. Located 7 miles east of Chinon, the Chinon Engineer Depot was bisected by route N751. The agreement for use of the land stipulated that the US could not build on a substantial amount of the forest, which was to remain a tree nursery.[181] In the early years, conditions were Spartan. In December 1951, GIs commanded by 1st Lt John L. Duggan worked in the mud and lived in tents. In 1952, engineers built a 10-ft high water tower to supply potable water through pipes laid across the depot.

During an inspection visit on 08 April 1952, Maj Gen Samuel D. Sturgis, Jr. observed 4-ton dump trucks sunk in mud up to their beds. Four months later, Sturgis was displeased that the same dump trucks were still immobile, although they had been chucked up on logs. Sturgis believed it was essential that crushed rock be used on the shoulders of roads, and directed his ComZ staff to expedite road work.[182] Crews from the 83rd Engineers formed road beds by digging along each side of the cleared path of a road and using the excavated soil to build up the road bed.

A spur at St.-Benoît-la-Forêt connected the depot's railroad track, which included a 1.2-mile marshalling yard, to the Tours-Chinon SNCF railroad line that bordered the northwest corner of the depot. In March 1952, one-hundred seven railcars arrived in a 24-hour period, but the depot only had storage space for the tonnage from thirty cars. In 1953, one-thousand Army personnel worked seven days a week, including holidays, to overcome storage and maintenance backlogs. Working long hours, GIs often unloaded late afternoon arrivals of twenty or more railcars.

The depot received, stored, maintained, and distributed engineer supplies and equipment. It primarily stored wheeled vehicles and heavy construction equipment used to build roads and bridges. The shops rebuilt trucks, cranes, electric generators, and earth-moving equipment such as dozers, loaders, and graders.[183] By 1958, the depot also stored steel bridge sections, port rehabilitation supplies, and more than 6,000 tons of pierced-steel plank (PSP). The bridge sections were to be used to repair war-damaged bridges; the PSP for beach stabilization and airfields.[184]

Engineer Heavy Equipment Maintenance Shop, Chinon Depot, 1961 (US Army)

Chinon Buildup

The Joint Construction Agency in Paris contracted with French firms to build ninety-two masonry buildings and one-hundred fifty-five metal prefabs. During construction, huge clouds of dust and dirt hovered over the depot and could be seen for miles.[185] Construction progress was slow in part due to strikes by French workers. However by 1956, the depot had a headquarters building, PX, theater, troop housing area, and more than ¾ million sq ft of warehouse storage and maintenance shops. A 2,300-ft long earthen runway was cleared for light aircraft. Permission from the French government was required before any trees could be removed. Because of the restriction on tree removal, a commissary and a pipeline school had to be located along N751, two miles from the depot.

During the extreme drought of July 1959, personnel from Chinon battled two widely-separated forest fires. One-hundred enlisted men from Chinon volunteered to fight the fires. They worked 14 hours alongside French soldiers and local farmers. The 522nd MP Det provided communications between the teams. Engineer bulldozers cut a 40-ft wide mile long fire break. The fire destroyed 620 acres of forest and farmland.[186]

In 1961, to disperse selected supplies and equipment, four off-depot storage sites were built at Linières-Bouton, Pont-de-Ruan, Neuil, and St.-Michel. Each site had one semipermanent structure and was enclosed by perimeter security fencing. Most stocks had to be stored on hardstands.

French Language Day

Because education centers offered free French language courses, Lt Col Joseph I. Gurfein, Post Engineer in 1960 at Orléans, insisted that his troops speak French when dealing with the French employees (LWRs).[187] After promotion to colonel, Gurfein became post commander at Chinon General Depot from 1961 to 1963. Col Gurfein designated one day each week as French language day, during which everyone was required to speak French. Although not a popular directive with his troops, it was welcomed by the LWRs. The Gurfeins attended dinners and fêtes in the nearby villages. Because the Loire valley produces excellent wine, the wine flowed freely. Gurfein, who normally did not drink alcohol, would politely nurse one glass, which sometimes made him dizzy.[188]

Construction of 10,000-barrel bolted steel tank, Donges Tank Farm, Dorieux, 1959 (US Army)

Pipeline School

In December 1954, the 986th Engineer Co (Pipeline), an Army Reserve unit from Monroeville, Alabama, was released from active duty at Chinon. The 986th Engineers were replaced by the 543rd Engineer Co (Pipeline), commanded by Capt Robert J. Collins. The 543rd Engineers staffed a pipeline school for ComZ. Twenty-one instructors taught students how to lay, operate, and maintain a military pipeline. A seven-week basic course, which stressed hands-on learning, required students to build storage tanks, lay 6 miles of pipe, and set up pump station manifolds. Practical classwork included using a suspension cable to lay pipe across a quarry filled with water.[189] The 10,000-barrel bolted-steel, storage tank had more than 6,500 bolts. Engineer companies, who had graduated from the school, returned every two years for a thirty-day refresher course on pipeline hydraulics, construction, and safety. For the final five-day field problem, each company built, operated, and dismantled an entire pipeline system. During 1957, engineer troops from Great Britain, Turkey, and West Germany attended the school.[190] Pipe was stored at Chinon in "pipeline supply packages" consisting of 6-inch diameter flexible pipe and quick couplings for a 700-mile pipeline. In 1961, personnel from the 543rd Engineers were stationed at Donges, Melun, and Châlons.

543rd Engineer Co (Pipeline) Commanders

Commanding Officer	Period of Service	Commanding Officer	Period of Service
Capt Robert J. Collins	1954-56	Maj James C. Tice	1960-63
1st Lt Odell Nails	1956	Capt Charles R. Sprague	1963-65
Capt Joseph A. Kemp	1956-58	Capt Milton D. Sullivan	1965-67
Capt William R. Fulton	1958-60		

60th Station Hospital

In spring 1956, the 60th Station Hospital buildings were completed by Société Genie Civil et Bâtiment of Paris at a cost of $2.5 million.[191] A baseball diamond, football field, and volleyball courts also were constructed on the hilly, hospital site four miles west of the depot. Buildings of the 1,000-bed standby hospital also were used as a BOQ, dependents elementary school, chapel, theater, officers club, library, and other support activities.[192] The hospital, commanded by Lt Col Maurice K. Wright, was authorized two-hundred thirty officers, nurses, and enlisted personnel. Because sheets were available in abundance at Army hospitals, occasionally a GI or LWR employee would raid the laundry supply room, knowing that French hotels would buy the sheets without asking questions.[193] The 550th Medical Co (Ambulance) and the 80th Ambulance Train Co (Rail) were located at the hospital. In 1960, the ambulance railcars were relocated to Toul. After the US military forces withdrew from France in 1967, a French regional hospital occupied the site. The original US Army buildings have been renovated and enlarged several times.

Engineer Battalions

From 1963 to 1967, the 83rd Engineer Battalion (Construction) was headquartered at the depot. Engineers practiced installing floating bridges on the Vienne River near Chinon and on the Loire River between Orléans and Blois. For NEO exercises each year, engineers pitched tents to simulate a staging area for 25,000 evacuees. The staging area, along the road from Chinon to Tours, was at the site of the original depot tent camp in 1952. MPs from the 202nd MP Co controlled traffic flow.

From mid-January through 28 February 1963, units of the 83rd and 553rd Engineer Battalions built fixed bridges and laid pipe over frozen ground at the bridge-training area at Fontenet Depot. They also constructed a floating bridge across the ice-packed Vienne River near Île-Bouchard.[194] In fall 1963, more than 12 miles of depot railroad needed repair. The 83rd Engineers replaced ties, laid ballast, and aligned the track.[195] In April 1964, the 83rd Engineers moved two French-owned bridge ramps from Monts to Chinon, passing slowly through tight clearances in small villages. The 51-ft long ramps were installed over the Vienne River to make a small island accessible to the public.[196]

In October 1961, during Operation ROUNDOUT, the 84th Engineer Battalion (Construction) arrived at Chinon from the United States. Company C was assigned to Camp des Loges in Paris. During the Korean War, the 84th Engineers built two bridges over the flood-prone Imjim River. The bridges were urgently needed to supply combat forces.[197] Originally scheduled to live in tents, the battalion lived in metal prefabs on concrete slabs because Maj Gen Henry R. Westphalinger had intervened. Westphalinger, ComZ commander in 1960-62, persuaded Army Chief, Gen George H. Decker to supplement the ComZ budget for the buildup. After the Berlin Wall Crisis had abated, the 84th Engineers were rotated back to Fort Ord, California. On 09 September 1962, eight-hundred fifty officers and enlisted men of the 84th departed from la Pallice on the USNS *Gen W. H. Gordon*.

During the early 1960s, more than eight-hundred fifty troops were stationed at Chinon. More than 1,000 French were employed at the depot and hospital. In 1961, the payroll for French employees at the depot exceeded $2 million, according to Chinon's "Quarterly Statistical Reviews." The 4230th Labor Service Company provided depot security.

Family Life

In the early 1950s, some wives purchased groceries at local stores, but most purchased canned goods and other items that did not require refrigeration at the large commissary in Orléans. Once a week an Army bus transported wives 180 miles roundtrip to buy groceries. A small PX, built at the depot from scrounged lumber, was called "Uncle Tom's Cabin" because of its rustic appearance.[198] Newly married PFC Larry Randall arrived at Chinon in May 1955. Randall had just completed automotive maintenance school at Fort Leonard Wood, Missouri. During the day he worked at the depot motor pool, during the evening he worked as a "shade tree mechanic" in Chinon to earn extra income. On occasion, a local garage asked him to consult on American cars that French mechanics were unable to repair. In November 1955, his wife, Jean, and two children arrived from Michigan. The Randalls adapted to the hardships of living on the economy at 84, rue Voltaire in Chinon, enjoyed their neighbors, and traveled as much as their budget allowed. Randall re-enlisted in France so his young family could experience European living for another three years. Their third child, Connie, was born in November 1958 at the 60th Station Hospital. Bachelor GIs who worked hard at the motor pool could earn rewards such as being assigned "night duty driver." The choice assignment for the young GIs included driving the young female, French librarian to her home in the evening.[199]

Dependents School Students

Six Army buses were used to deliver children to the dependents elementary school at Chinon depot, stopping at each location where children lived in French villages. Until the Army standby hospital was built at Poitiers, high school students at Chinon attended the school at Châteauroux AD. In September 1955, PFC James L. Lepant became a school bus driver after only one day to practice driving a Ford-built Army school bus in the motor pool parking lot. On Friday afternoons, he picked up twenty high school students at the dormitory and drove them back to Chinon, usually arriving home at 7 pm. On Sundays, Lepant left the EM Club parking lot pickup point in Chinon at 4 pm to return the students for their week of classes. Lepant's teenage passengers generally were well behaved. On rare occasions when they became too exuberant, they calmed down when asked. Although Lepant was not much older than his passengers, he was the authority figure on the bus.[200]

Recreation

In 1953, sports competition was limited to basketball games played with French teams because trees had not been cleared for outdoor athletic fields. The Officers Club was in a rented château between Chinon and Tours; an NCO Club had been built on the depot from funds chipped in by the NCOs. Movies were shown in a circus-size tent. The town of Azay-le-Rideau offered its cinema to the depot, and Chinon offered its town hall for a soldier talent show and dance.

Housing

Married officers and NCOs lived on the economy until government housing was built. In 1953, most rentals lacked adequate heating, refrigeration, or even running water. The depot provided daily bus service for families who lived in Chinon and in Tours, 25 miles away. The 30-seat Faegol-manufactured buses had to bypass the center of Azay-le-Rideau on the route to Tours because the streets were too narrow to allow turns. In an emergency, the buses could be converted to huge ambulances by removing the seats. RGH housing was built in 1956 near Beaumont-en-Véron; SCH housing in 1959 near St.-Benoît-la-Forêt. The SCH housing village, conveniently located a mile west of the hospital, had forty-two ranch style units. It was named Rochambeau Village to honor French General Jean Baptiste de Rochambeau. During the Revolutionary War, Rochambeau had helped America gain its independence by commanding the French Army at the siege of Yorktown.

Chinon Engineer Depot Commanders*

Commanding Officer	Period of Service	Commanding Officer	Period of Service
1st Lt John L. Duggan	1951	Col Philip J. Galanti	1958-60
Col David L. Jarrett	1952-53	Col Donald J. Miller	1960-61
Lt Col Odell D. Williams	1953	Col Joseph I. Gurfein	1961-63
Col Frederick B. Hall, Jr.	1953-56	Col Russell J. Wilson	1963-64
Col Andrew V. Inge	1956	Lt Col Charles E. Jett	1964
Col Robert J. Kasper	1956-57	Col James H. Clark, Jr.	1964-66
Col John U. Allen	1957-58	Lt Col Jerry A. Irvin	1966-67

*Converted to General Depot in 1958.

Saumur Signal Depot

In May 1952, the US Army leased the Château des Ifs property at Varrains and the nearby caves of La Perrière Carrières. The 7794th Signal Depot Det, twenty officers and enlisted men from Hanau, Germany, pitched tents and rehabilitated the caves to store signal supplies and equipment. In July 1952, elements of the 552nd Signal Co arrived at Saumur from the US. Rubble, cleared from the site, was used to build a rail spur to the depot. Headquarters were in the Château des Ifs, built in the 17th Century.[201] The first post chapel was a large tent with a wood-frame façade similar to a Hollywood set. In summer 1953, enlisted personnel volunteered to build an indoor firing range in the abandoned wine cellar under the château. Supervised by M/Sgt Wendel B. Kender, the men used salvaged lumber to construct a 50-ft long rifle range. Sand-filled bags, stacked behind the targets, stopped the .22 cal bullets.[202]

The first dependents school opened in January 1953 in the leased Château de Salvert at Neuillé, 12 miles from Saumur. In 1954, the elementary school moved into a metal prefab building at Château des Ifs. On 14 August 1954, troops moved from wood hutments into two modern three-story masonry buildings, the first permanent barracks built in Base Section. Polish guards of the 4230th Labor Service Co were the first to move in.[203] The barracks, built by Bringer and Tondut of Paris, had a capacity of

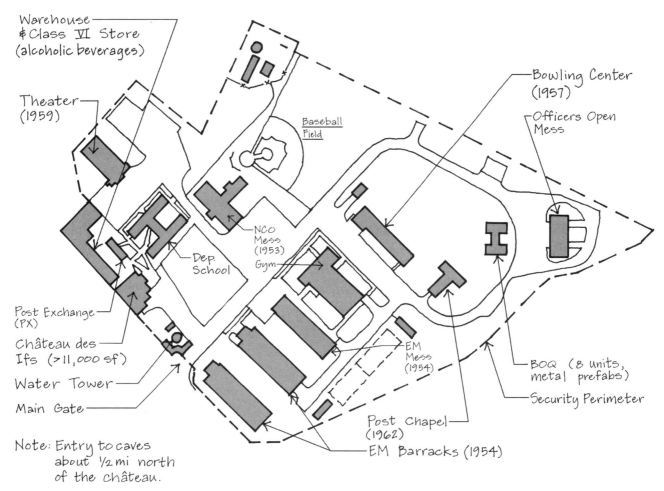

Varrains Troop Support Center (1962)

three-hundred enlisted men, housed in ten and twenty-man squad rooms. Although the men still had no privacy, they preferred living in the barracks, with two shower rooms per floor, to sleeping under canvas and trekking outdoors in foul weather to the slit latrine. The gymnasium, dedicated in October 1955, also had indoor showers.[204] By May 1956, the depot had an EM Club that featured a $1,000 juke box, hobby shop which had five photo enlargers, baseball field, gymnasium, PX, and snack bar.[205] The EM Club held slide-show nights for "shutter-bugs" to project their 35-mm color slides.

Col Rolla D. Pollock, depot commander from 1955 to 1957, wrote to the wives of newly assigned GIs, emphasizing that their husband's job was important. He assured them that the post had an excellent elementary school and chapel and, for off-duty time, the men had wholesome recreation and athletic facilities such as EM Club, hobby shop, and modern gymnasium. Pollock concluded by noting that GIs were asked to serve far from home, and nothing meant more to them than letters from home. He asked the wives to write often to their husbands and to write to him if they ever had questions or worries about their husband's welfare.[206]

Polish Labor Service personnel provided security at night. It took guards five minutes to walk the perimeter of des Ifs. At noon each day during the 1954 Traffic Safety Week, the depot public address system broadcast a live 10 minute safety skit complete with hair-raising sound effects provided by SFC Vernon C. "Ike" Eisenhardt.[207] More than half of the depot workers were French.

Château des Ifs, Saumur Signal Depot, Varrains, 1954 (NARA)

The Caves

GIs tried to avoid being assigned to the caves because the tedious work consisted of cleaning green fungus and mildew off tons of signal equipment. The caves, originally mined for limestone to build *châteaux*, had been used for centuries to grow mushrooms. Before the German invasion in 1940, the French used the caves for a factory to manufacture hydraulic-landing gear for military aircraft. During the occupation, the Germans used the caves to manufacture, repair, and store parts for their Atlantic Ocean U-boat fleet. They attempted to destroy the caves in 1944 when they retreated, but only created piles of rubble at the entrances.

In the 1950s, the caves provided the Signal Corps with ¾ million sq ft of storage space that had stable cool temperature at 55° F, but high relative humidity of 95%. Thirty-five miles of tunnels, 15 to 20 ft wide, fanned out 50 ft below acres of vineyards. The easily secured tunnels were widened to accommodate 2½-ton vehicles. Unused tunnels were sealed off. Electrical wiring was installed to illuminate about 8 miles of tunnel, which contained 40,000 metal storage bins. Spools of field wire were stacked from floor to ceiling. Unfortunately, moisture and residual parasites from the mushrooms damaged cardboard boxes and electronic equipment. Use of the caves was discontinued until the discovery that equipment could be sealed in plastic film.[208] It was one of the earliest extensive use of thin plastic film as a vapor barrier to protect electronic equipment. Depot personnel unwrapped walkie-talkies, microwave radio-telephones, switchboards, and other electronic equipment every two years to verify working condition and then resealed the equipment.[209] Worried about Soviet air superiority, in December 1955 the Army searched for additional underground sites in France. Ironically, by 1958 most supplies at Saumur had been moved aboveground.

La Perrière Quarry caves, Varrains, 1955 (US Army)

Weekend Pass to Paris

Some GIs were intimidated by living in a foreign land and learning a foreign language. Others, like two young draftees stationed at Saumur in 1953, were eager to explore. On their first weekend pass to Paris, Privates Louis D. Sisk and Patrick Kelleher took a taxi from the Champs-Élysées back to their hotel near Place Pigalle ("Pig Alley" to the GIs). Their elderly taxi driver, who spoke some English, recognized that they were Americans by their haircuts, clothing, and GI French. He told them he was very proud that his son was serving with the French Army in Indochina, but wished he was home in France. When the GIs got off the hotel elevator at their floor, Sisk realized he had left his wallet on the back seat of the taxi. Running down the stairs, without much hope of finding the taxi or his wallet, Sisk was shocked to see the driver talking with the night clerk. The old man gave Sisk a pat on the head and pointed to his own head, indicating that Sisk should be more careful. The driver had told the night clerk he was thinking of his own son and could not keep the wallet. After *mercies* (thank yous) from Sisk, the driver departed. The night clerk, surprised at what he had witnessed, commented that the man must be the most honest taxi driver in Paris.[210, 211]

Depot at Montreuil-Bellay

In May 1956, Camp Méron, a former French Army ammunition depot near Montreuil-Bellay, was acquired from the French government. The war-damaged site was developed by the US Army to have ½ million sq ft of warehouses and maintenance shops and 3½ miles of railroad track. Most of the masonry buildings were built by Entreprise Billiard of Paris. The new depot was modeled after the modern Tobyhanna Signal Depot in the Pocono Mountains of Pennsylvania. Troops moved equipment to the new depot from: Caserne Voyer at St.-Jean d'Angély, Pirmasens Signal Depot in Germany, and the caves near Château des Ifs.[212] Signal personnel repaired, stored, and issued: radio, radar, and wire equipment. The Signal Corps mobile counter-mortar radar system, developed by Sperry Gyroscope Co during the Korean War, had a dish-shaped antenna which tracked the path of enemy shells in flight, and a separate radar scope console which pinpointed the position of the enemy's mortar launcher.

The depot had electronic equipment test-repair shops, machine shops, and coil-winding shops. Teams were assigned repair vans to work on communications equipment at other depots and in the field. Unserviceable equipment, which had been exchanged for new equipment, was repaired for return to stock. It was estimated that millions of dollars were saved by repairing and rebuilding signal equipment.[213, 214] A single-story masonry building was used to house equipment to calibrate Radiac Sets. The sets, issued to radiation survey teams and CIC detachments, measured the level of radiation from atomic explosions. During World War II, the Signal Corps maintained and repaired Geiger counters that were issued to personnel of the Chemical Warfare Service.[215] A secondary security fence enclosed the Radiac building. After Saumur was designated a general depot in 1958, a balanced supply of matériel from all the technical services was stored in the warehouses.

In 1961 during Operation ROUNDOUT, the 221st Signal Co (Base Depot) from Sacramento Signal Depot, California, and the 510th Signal Co (Base Maintenance) from Tobyhanna Signal Depot, Pennsylvania, were sent to Saumur. These Regular Army units were authorized a total of eighteen officers and three-hundred eighty-seven enlisted men. After the Berlin Wall Crisis had abated, both companies returned to the US in 1962, and the military population of the depot, commanded by Col William Schwartz, was drastically reduced. In 1964, only three-hundred fifty troops were stationed at Saumur, but more than 1,200 French worked at the depot.

Due to the drawdown the photography lab, where three GIs and six French employees had worked, was closed. Photographic equipment repairman Sp4 Donald G. Walker was still assigned to the depot although he had no duties. Anxious to appear busy and in charge of something, he carried his clipboard as a symbol of authority when he walked around the depot each day. After six weeks of pretending to work, Walker was approached by an officer who asked if Walker was doing what the officer surmised he was doing. Walker explained that he had no job. The officer, apparently admiring Walker's initiative and military bearing, told him to keep looking sharp and, if he got bored during his "workdays," to visit the EM Club, which might need some help. Walker was due to rotate home to the US in sixty days.[216]

Housing

Officer and NCO families lived on the economy or, after 1959, in thirty SCH housing units at St.-Cyr-en-Bourg, about six miles from the depot. The housing village was named Dulles Heights in honor of John Foster Dulles, consultant to President Truman's State Department and President Eisenhower's first Secretary of State. It was a small American oasis of red tile roofed ranch houses and green lawns surrounded by acres of vineyards. After the depot closed, Château des Ifs was divided into apartments and the former barracks were leased by the French to commercial enterprises.

Saumur Signal Depot Commanders*

Commanding Officer	Period of Service	Commanding Officer	Period of Service
Maj Edward I. Melton	1952-53	Col William Schwartz	1960-62
Lt Col Honzie L. Rogers	1953	Lt Col Wyatt B. Peterson	1962-63
Lt Col Oscar W. Akerstrom`	1953-54	Lt Col Harry F. Yuill	1963-64
Lt Col Robert A. Starr	1954-55	Col Edward J. Dougherty	1964-65
Col Rolla D. Pollock	1955-58	Maj Charles F. Hudson, Jr.	1966-67
Col Paul A. Feyereisen	1958-59		

*Converted to General Depot in 1958.

CHAPTER 11: *Base Section in the Southwest*

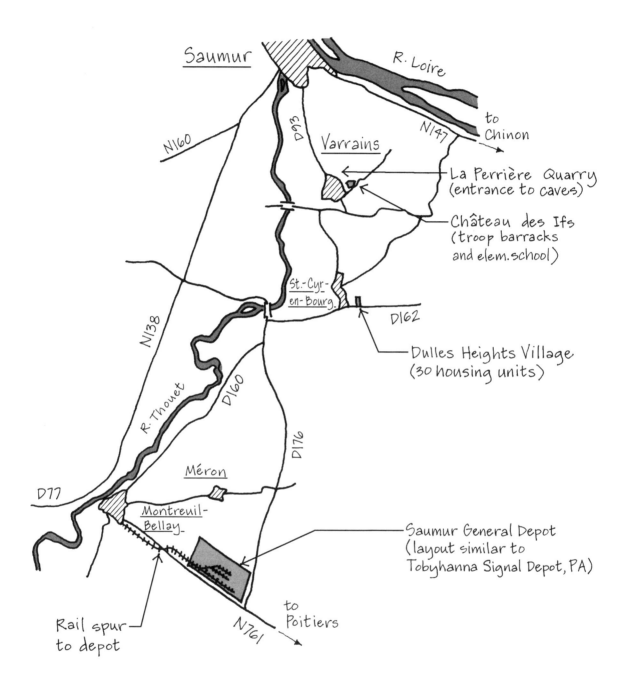

Saumur Area Installations (1959)

Chinon-Saumur Area Installations

Installation	Location	Activity and Units
Headquarters	Forêt de Chinon (JFK Loop)	US Army Engineer Depot, Chinon
	Varrains (Château des Ifs)	Saumur Troop Support Area (13 acres)
Depots	Forêt de Chinon (2,267 acres)	US Army Engineer Depot, Chinon
	Montreuil-Bellay (517 acres)	US Army General Depot, Saumur
	Varrains (La Perrière Quarry)	US Army Signal Depot (caves, 8½ miles long)
	Linières-Bouton, St.-Michel, Pont-de-Ruan, and Neuil	Off-depot storage sites, Chinon (400 acres total)
	Louresse and St.-Macaire-du-Bois	Off-depot storage sites, Saumur (200 total acres)
Hospital	Forêt de Chinon (near St.-Benoît-la-Forêt)	60th Station Hospital, 1,000-bed standby hospital (123 acres)
Schools (dependents)	Forêt de Chinon (at hospital)	Elementary school
	Varrains (at Château des Ifs)	Elementary school
Bachelor Officers Quarters (BOQ)	Forêt de Chinon	Two-story wing of hospital and a building at depot
	Montreuil-Bellay	Two-story building, Officers Mess
	Varrains	Metal prefabs (8 units)
Housing (families)	Beaumont-en-Véron (La Durandière)	40 Rental Guarantee Housing (RGH) units
	St.-Benoît-la-Forêt (Rochambeau Village)	42 Surplus Commodity Housing (SCH) units (15 acres)
	St.-Cyr-en-Bourg (Dulles Heights)	30 SCH units (9 acres)
Troop Barracks	Forêt de Chinon (including O'Grady Barracks)	83rd Engineer Battalion 63rd Engineer Company (Parts Depot) 185th Engineer Co (Heavy Maint) 543rd Engineer Company (Pipeline) 581st Engineer Maint Co (DS) 202nd Military Police Company 4230th Labor Service Co
	Montreuil-Bellay	221st Signal Company (Base Depot) 510th Signal Company (Base Maint) 532nd Signal Company (Wire Constr)
	Varrains	313th Signal Company (Service) 202nd Military Police Company 4006th Labor Service Co
Recreation	Bouillé-Lorets	Rod and Gun Club (skeet range)
	Forêt de Chinon	Gymnasium, baseball field, bowling alley (6 lanes)
	Varrains	Gymnasium, baseball field, bowling alley (4 lanes)
Training Sites	Camp de Fontevraud	Maneuver area (French Army control)
	Crouzilles and Camp du Bouchard	Firing ranges (French Army control)
	Île-Bouchard (near Chinon)	Bridge construction
Newspapers	Chinon	The Depot Echo, The Chinon Guidon
	Saumur	Saumur Sounds Off, Saumur Mission, A Tous les Vents (for LWRs)

Size of BASEC Installations[217]

The US Army had twelve major depot installations in Base Section. The table presents data for six of the installations at the peak of deployment. Saumur was equal in size to the Reagan Ranch, Santa Barbara, California; Chinon to Fort Sam Houston, San Antonio, Texas; Captieux to Walt Disney World, Orlando, Florida; and Périgueux to Disneyland, Anaheim, California (when the park opened in 1955).

Real Estate	Chinon	Saumur	Ingrandes	Bussac	Captieux	Rochefort
Land use (acres)	3,052	730	222	3,646	24,907	90
Permanent buildings (masonry)	119	45	122	87	104	58
Temporary buildings (prefab)	165	40	78	79	4,608	42
Family housing (RGH & SCH units)	82	30	116	220	64	0
Roads (miles)	39	12	11	13	156	3

St.-André Quartermaster Aerial Support Center

In 1953, the US Army acquired land for an Aerial Support Center at St.-André-de-l'Eure, 10 miles south of Évreux AB and 20 miles northeast of Dreux AB. During World War II, the Germans had occupied the 93-acre site. From liberation in 1944 until August 1945, the airfield was used by the 442nd Troop Carrier Group. The site had a concrete runway installed by the Luftwaffe, and a 3-mile double-track rail spur to the Dreux-Évreux SNCF railroad line. Two-dozen masonry buildings were constructed by Entreprise Rangeard et Fils of Rouen at a cost of $1.6 million. At the end of July 1955, an advance party of twenty men from Périgueux, headed by Capt Howard J. Durell, arrived at St.-André to help set up a resupply depot. The 7868th Army Unit, commanded by Lt Col Benjamin J. Sekowski, arrived in February 1956. The unit, activated on 01 February 1955, temporarily had been stationed at Périgueux QM Depot.[218] During Operation ROUNDOUT in 1961, ten prefabs were hastily erected at the depot.

557th Quartermaster Company

The 557th Quartermaster Co (Aerial Support), authorized five officers and one-hundred fifty-two enlisted men, was stationed at the Center. The Center provided storage for all classes of supplies for aerial delivery to combat forces. Stocks that were stored in the 100,000 sq ft of warehouse space at St.-André had been prerigged for airdrops. Many GIs in the 557th had completed advanced airborne training at Ft. Benning, Georgia.[219] At Ft. Lee, Virginia, they learned how to pack supplies to absorb and distribute forces of impact with the ground. It also was essential to load aircraft so weight of cargo would be properly distributed and cargo securely lashed. In February 1953 while stationed at Stuttgart, Germany, troops of the 557th had packed supplies for aerial drops to Dutch civilians stranded when the North Sea broke through dikes and flooded a wide area of the Netherlands. Flood waters had breached sixty-seven dikes, and more than 1,800 drowned. Several thousand C-rations were packed for airlift from Echterdingen US Army Air Field in Germany to feed the flood victims.[220] In addition to airdrop missions, the 577th at St-André transported combat vehicles and equipment from railheads to cargo aircraft at Évreux AB. In 1964, more than two-hundred French employees worked at St.-André.

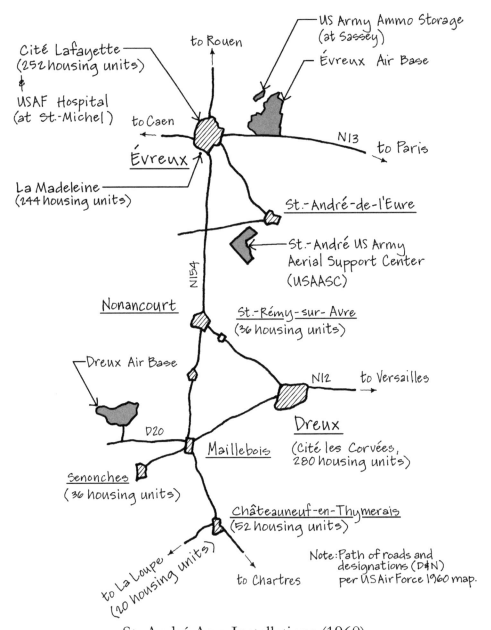

St.-André Area Installations (1960)

While driving back to St.-André in February 1964, Sp4 Robert K. Dewey saw a helicopter crash into an open field and burst into flames. Dewey drove onto the plowed field, parked in the mud, and ran to the wreckage. Dewey was able to pull the pilot, copilot, and one of the two passengers from the crash before the helicopter was engulfed by flames. Dewey drove the three survivors to the US Air Force hospital at St.-Michel.[221]

10th Special Forces Group

Elements of the 10th Special Forces Group trained at St.-André for unconventional logistical operations. Covert operations were planned and directed by the "super-secret" Support Operations Task Force, Europe (SOTFE), headquartered at the Signal Corps Blockhouse in Paris. At the height of the Berlin Crisis in 1958, the 10th Special Forces Group sent a cadre of communications specialists from Bad Tölz, Germany, to St.-André. The cadre conducted training exercises for long-range communication behind enemy lines.[222] Pre-packaged bundles of weapons, ammunition, and C-rations were stored at St.-André, ready to be dropped behind enemy lines.

Sassey Storage Site

Supplies also were stored at the US Army Ammunition Storage Site at Sassey, near Évreux AB. Sassey had twenty ammo storage huts and one mile of paved roads. The site had 20,300 sq ft of storage in canvas covered wood-frame huts and metal prefabs. In 1965, several earth-covered igloos were built. The Army stored ammunition for airdrops to special forces behind enemy lines, and the Air Force stored munitions to be delivered to fighter-bomber wings.[223] Security at Sassey and St.-André was provided by the 525th Military Police Detachment. To enhance security at Sassey in 1964, twelve volunteer dog handlers from the 557th at St.-André were assigned by company commander Capt Charles J. Williford to patrol the perimeter of Sassey. Each handler worked with his own dog. The handlers, supervised by SSgt John W. Lebo, were the first Army dog handlers in France. Dogs normally were handled by Polish Labor Service personnel. At St.-André, a few dogs had been trained to prowl warehouses at night without a handler. The dogs would bark ferociously to discourage intruders.[224, 225]

Pocket Patch of 322nd Air Div (Combat Cargo)

Airdrops

Airdrops were practiced three to five days each week during daylight hours and twice a month during nighttime. After each use, parachutes were hung in a "shakeout" tower so moisture could evaporate and dirt could be shaken out before riggers repacked them on long, flat tables. The shakeout tower at St.-André was taller than similar towers built at NATO air bases.[226] After a rigger packed a parachute for use by personnel, he signed a form indicating that the chute was in serviceable condition. If a chute failed, a board of inquiry determined the cause of failure. More than a dozen French women were hired to repair parachutes at the Center.[227]

In April 1959, the first joint airborne exercise was conducted with the French Army airborne school at Pau. C-130 Hercules transport aircraft of the US Air Force 322nd Air Division, based at Évreux AB, moved US Army troops and supplies from St.-André to a departure airfield, near Tarbes in southern France. US Army rigging teams and supply troops of the 557th QM Co worked around the clock to improve reaction time loading the C-130s.[228] At Pau, the 322nd airdropped a 2½-ton truck, using four 100-ft diameter G-11A parachutes. The 2½-ton truck landed within 35 ft of the target.[229] The 322nd routinely dropped jeeps, howitzers, and ¼-ton trailers.

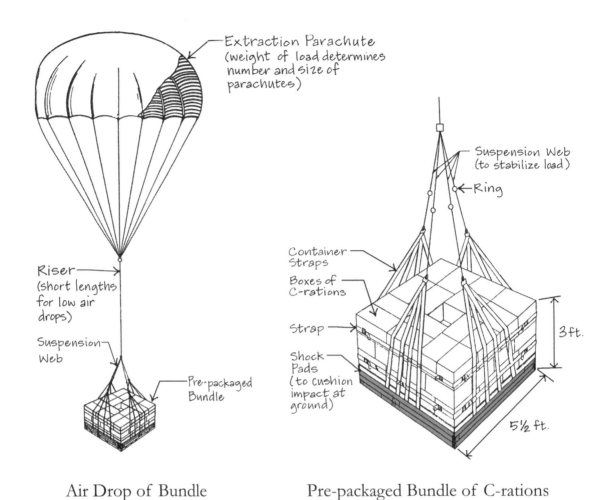

Air Drop of Bundle   Pre-packaged Bundle of C-rations

C-123 Provider, from Dreux AB, loading troops at Chaumont AB, 1957 (A.L. Christensen)

CHAPTER 11: Base Section in the Southwest

In January 1964 at the French airborne test center near Toulouse, French and American military personnel tested their ability to airdrop equipment from each other's aircraft. The two-week exercise was the first NATO bilateral airborne experiment in France. SFC Brigham B. Wilson headed the Army contingent from the 557th. French troops and equipment were airdropped from C-130 aircraft from Évreux AB. After the exercise, work began on writing a bilingual technical manual to be used in future operations.[230]

The main runway at nearby Dreux AB was used to practice low-level airdrops of jeeps. Jeeps, strapped to layers of honeycomb cardboard, were released from C-130s about 5 ft above the runway. Although extraction was slowed by a drag chute, these drops were difficult.[231] Low-level airdrops used the para-extraction method. When a C-130 reached the drop point, loadmasters released fasteners that held the cargo in place. A 22-ft diameter ribbon parachute was deployed through the open cargo ramp. The chute yanked the load clear of the aircraft.

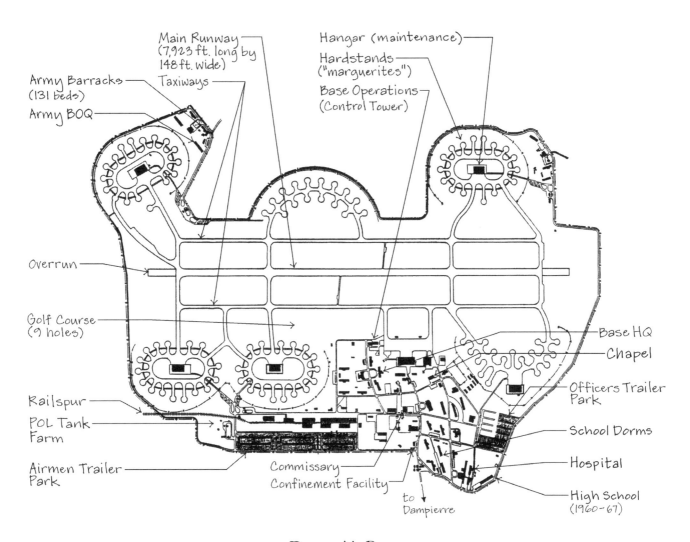

Dreux Air Base

New Methods for Airdrops

The 577th tested new methods, including roller conveyors in cargo aircraft, modified parachutes for supplies and equipment, and use of "shock pads" to cushion ground impact. Rollers enabled loadmasters to move cargo without manhandling equipment. The 3-inch thick shock pad layer consisted of honeycombed paperboard bonded between two 1/8 inch thick sheets of cardboard. The numbers of layers used was matched to the weight of the load.[232, 233] To cushion impact forces for heavy loads, such as trucks and engineer bulldozers, felt-filled pads were placed between the equipment and drop platform. Four 100-ft diameter parachutes were attached to the drop platform to deliver the load to the ground. One extraction parachute and one pilot parachute were used to pull the load from the aircraft.[234] Two-sack packaging was developed for humanitarian operations. Tightly tied sacks of commodities, such as corn or lima beans, were placed in oversized sacks. When the packages hit the ground the inner sacks ruptured, but the outer sacks remained intact.

In 1963, the C-130s at Évreux AB were fitted with the new Air Force mechanical loading and airdrop equipment. Parallel steel rails ran along the length of the cargo compartment and loading ramp. Cargo was loaded on platforms that fit the rails and could be locked in position, eliminating time-consuming tie downs.[235]

Housing, Schools, and Community Relations

Married officers and NCOs lived on the economy or in government housing built for the US Air Force. There were four-hundred twenty-four housing units near Dreux AB at five housing villages: Châteauneuf-en-Thymerais, Dreux, La Loupe, St.-Rémy-sur-Avre, and Senonches. Another four-hundred ninety-six housing units were built near Évreux AB. Cité Lafayette was a commodity credit housing (CCH) village of two, three, and four bedroom homes near the Air Force hospital at St.-Michel. The St.-Michel dependents elementary school was built near this park-like housing area.[236] La Madeleine was a guaranteed rental income (GRI) housing village, five miles west of Évreux AB.

Due to the proximity of St.-André to Dreux and Évreux ABs, the Army also benefitted from Air Force medical services, schools, commissary, and non-appropriated fund recreation activities. Sick call for St.-André troops was held from 8 to 9:45 am at Évreux AB. Those needing hospitalization were sent to the Air Force hospital at St.-Michel. The dependent children attended schools on the Air Force bases.

During 1958-59, in the spirit of Franco-American cooperation, the commander of St.-André Center allowed PFC Calvin W. "Bobby" Clinkscales to play basketball for the Évreux city team. The 6-ft 4-in tall Clinkscales, a supply clerk at the Center, was noted for his high vertical jump. He could dunk the ball with ease and was the top rebounder for the Évreux team.[237]

Tribute to Liberators of France

On 19 November 1964, five paratroopers from St.-André jumped at Ste.-Mere-Église from an Army U-1A Otter. On land, the troopers were greeted by the mayor and Lt Col Henry L. Corkill, Jr., commanding officer of the Aerial Support Center. Corkill's 19-year-old brother PFC Roger S. Corkill was one of the jumpers. After lunch at city hall to commemorate the liberation in June 1944, the St.-André troops walked 150 miles back to Évreux AB following the route of liberation used by Allied troops in August 1944.[238]

St.-André Area Installations

Installation	Location	Activity and Units
Headquarters	St.-André-de-l'Eure	US Army Aerial Support Center (USAASC)
Depots	Sassey (43 acres)	US Army Ammo Storage Site (19 igloos)
	St.-André (93 acres)	Warehouses (supplies pre-rigged for airdrops)
	Évreux AB (2,144 acres)	Three US Army warehouses
Hospitals	Dreux AB	US Air Force hospital (100 beds)
	St.-Michel (near Évreux)	US Air Force hospital (115 beds)
Schools (dependents)	Dreux AB	Elementary school (1 to 6)
		High school (7 to 12)
	St.-Michel	Elementary school (1 to 6)
Bachelor Officers Quarters (BOQ)	Dreux AB	One building (adjacent to marguerite)
Housing (families)	Chateauneuf-en-Thymerais	52 Guaranteed Rental Income (GRI) units
	Dreux (Cité les Corvées)	280 GRI units
	La Loupe	20 GRI units
	St.-Rémy-sur-Avre	36 GRI units
	Senonches	36 GRI units
	Évreux (La Madeleine)	244 GRI units
	St.-Michel (Cité Lafayette)	252 Commodity Credit Housing (CCH) units
Troop Barracks	St.-André (2), Évreux AB (1), and Dreux AB (1)	557th QM Company (Aerial Support)
		525th Military Police Company
		275th Signal Company (Service)
		10th Special Forces Group Detachment
Recreation	Dreux AB	Bowling alley (6 lanes), gymnasium, theater, wood and photo hobby shops, golf course (9 holes), skeet range
	Évreux AB	Bowling alley, gymnasium, baseball and football fields, theater
	St.-André	Bowling center, baseball field, theater
Training Sites	Dreux AB (2,278 acres)	Runway for airdrops
	Pau	French Army Airborne School
Newspaper	St.-André	The Aerial Review

St.-André Aerial Support Center (USAASC) Commanders

Commanding Officer	Period of Service	Commanding Officer	Period of Service
Lt Col Benjamin J. Sekowski	1956-58	Lt Col Edward J. Downing	1959-61
Maj Howard A. Greenawalt	1958	Lt Col Kenneth Shipman	1961-62
Lt Col William Pencak	1958-59	Lt Col Henry L. Corkill, Jr.	1963-66

Lebanon Deployment

On 14 July 1958, President Camille Chamoun of Lebanon, whose pro-Western government was under threat from armed bands of rebels and infiltrators, asked the US to deploy troops to his nation. The deployment of US forces, commanded by Maj Gen Paul D. Adams, was designated Operation BLUE BAT. In July 1958, more than 6,500 combat troops sailed from German and French ports to Lebanon on the troopships USNS *Geiger*, USNS *Upshur*, and USS *Gen George M. Randall*. Starting on 19 July, US airborne troops from West Germany were flown to Lebanon by 322nd Air Division C-130 Hercules from Évreux AB and C-119 Flying Boxcars from Dreux AB; and by MATS C-124 Globemasters from Donaldson AFB, Greenville, South Carolina. The airborne troops were to secure the Beirut Airport and the port at Beirut.[239, 240] It was the first US airborne-amphibious operation in peacetime.

Units Deployed from France to Lebanon (1958)[241, 242]

Location	Unit	Authorized Strength*	
		Officer	Enlisted
Bussac	78th Trans Co (Med Truck)**	5	176
	583rd Trans Co (Light Truck)	4	126
Chinon	687th Water Supply Co	1	32
Croix-Chapeau	570th Trans Co (Terminal Service)	6	325
Orléans	1st Trans Co (Med Truck Refrig)	4	160
	594th Trans Group (Movement Control)	32	132
La Rochelle	11th Trans Terminal Command B	53	223
St.-André-de-l'Eure	557th QM Aerial Supply Co	5	152

*Officer total includes commissioned and warrant officers. Not every platoon of a company or all personnel of a group or command were deployed.
**Redeployed to Adena, Turkey for three months. In Oct 1958, the 78th Trans Co moved from Turkey to Croix-Chapeau.

During the sealift to Lebanon, more than 72,000 tons of supplies and equipment from the ports of la Pallice and St.-Nazaire were moved by three troopships and thirteen cargo ships. At la Pallice, stevedores employed by the French contractor Delmas-Vieljeux refused to load US military cargo bound for Lebanon. However, port operations representative, Frenchman Jacques André Rivière (known to GIs as "Old Man River"), persuaded the stevedores to load the ships by appealing to them as a Frenchman who had been loyal to his stevedores. ComZ delivered supplies to the beach at Beirut before there were enough combat troops to use them.[243, 244]

Most of the ComZ troops were from transportation units in the Base Section. To bring these units up to authorized strength, GIs in France who were not working in their primary MOS were assigned as "fillers." On 17 July, a US Army bus left Caserne Coligny to take a contingent of logistics experts to Châteauroux AD for a flight to Lebanon to join the 201st Logistics Command. Four American soldiers and one Frenchman were killed and twenty-one Americans were injured when the bus collided with a French truck at 4:15 am in Olivet. Military Police SSgt Claude F. Maynard, the first American to arrive at the accident scene, organized the rescue efforts of French bystanders. It took six hours to free all of the passengers trapped in the bus. That afternoon, a replacement contingent of thirty personnel was assembled at Caserne Coligny and flown on 19 July from Châteauroux AD to Lebanon. In February 1959, Maj Gen Edward J. O'Neill presented the Army Commendation Medal to Maynard for his rescue efforts and care of the injured.[245]

US Army bus accident, 17 July 1958, Olivet (US Army)

By late September 1958, order had been restored to Lebanon and US forces began their departure.[246] During the withdrawal of logistics supplies, the Army dumped into the sea 26 tons of unserviceable ammunition.[247] In October, the USNS *Gen LeRoy Eltinge* made two voyages to Lebanon to return troops to France and Germany.

Lt Gen Paul D. Adams reviews troops, Orléans, 1959 (US Army)

U.S. GO HOME

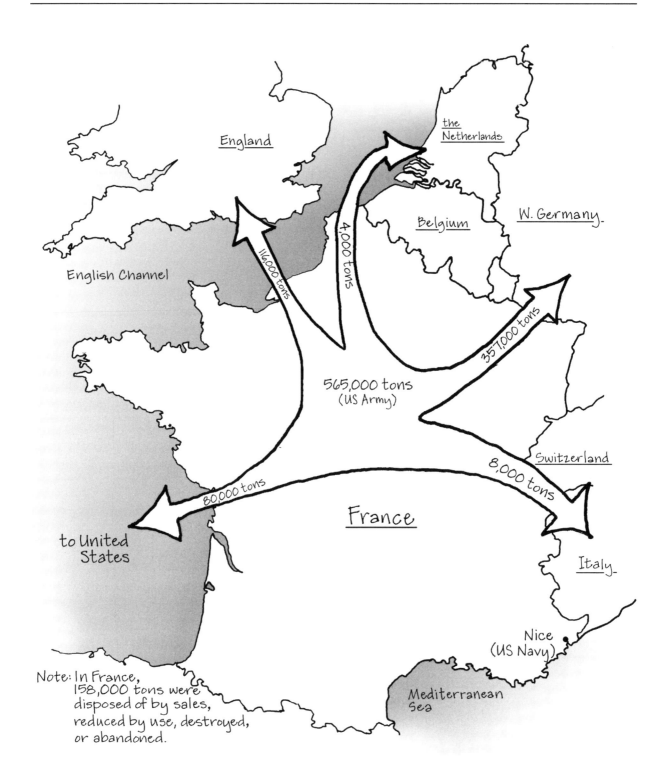

Relocation of US Army Matériel (1966-67)

TWELVE

Fast Withdrawal from France

"Treaties are like young girls and roses; they last as long as they last."
(French President Charles de Gaulle, Paris, July 1963)

Lifeline across France

The vast infrastructure, built across France from ports along the Atlantic coast to installations near the German border, included huge storage and maintenance depots, air bases, modern hospitals, K-12 schools, and housing villages. Each year, one million tons of matériel were transported across France to support Seventh Army in Germany. This transportation network used the roll-on roll-off method (where loaded trailers were driven onto ships at Brooklyn, New York, and driven off at St.-Nazaire or la Pallice, France) and the line-haul relay method (where trailers, loaded at French ports, were relayed across France).[1] Facilities that had been built during nearly two decades were emptied and abandoned in 1967 when more than 70,000 US troops and their families left France. In addition to their regular duties, troops in France had provided humanitarian aid to victims devastated by floods, earthquakes, fires, and other natural disasters in Europe, Africa, and the Middle East.

De Gaulle Decides

On 07 March 1966, French President Charles de Gaulle wrote to US President Lyndon B. Johnson asking US military forces to leave France by 01 April 1967. The letter, handwritten in French, and de Gaulle's remarks at a subsequent press conference gave his reasons for invoking the "doctrine of changed conditions."[2-5] De Gaulle wrote: "France considers that the changes which have taken place or are taking place since 1949 in Europe, in Asia, and elsewhere, as well as the evolution of her own situation and of her own forces, no longer justify where she is concerned the dispositions of a military order taken after the conclusion of the Alliance… That is why France proposes to regain on her territory the full exercise of her sovereignty, at present hampered by the permanent presence of Allied military elements or by the use of her skies, to cease her participation in integrated commands and no longer to place forces at the disposition of NATO."[6] France requested the transfer from France of SHAPE headquarters and all allied units, installations, and bases not under the control of the French government. The line of communications to Germany now would be in two halves, separated by France, neutral Switzerland, and neutral Austria.[7,8]

The Johnson administration acted surprised to receive the letter, although in May 1961 de Gaulle had advised US President John F. Kennedy that France would leave the integrated military organization of NATO after the Berlin Wall Crisis had abated. De Gaulle was uncomfortable that French forces would be commanded in wartime by an American general. He wanted his military officers to be loyal to France not to NATO.[9,10] After Kennedy had succeeded Eisenhower, de Gaulle doubted the credibility of the US nuclear retaliation, believing that the US would not sacrifice American cities to save French cities. He believed Kennedy's policy of "flexible response" would exempt the US from nuclear attack while France and Europe would be the nuclear battlefield.[11-13] Flexible response meant that NATO should proportionately respond to various levels of attack rather than solely relying on a massive nuclear response.[14] Because de Gaulle believed a nation deprived of the ability to defend itself would cease to exist as a nation, France was developing its own strategic nuclear force, called *force de frappe*.[15-17]

Gaffes by the US

In September 1954, the Pentagon instructed US Army, Europe to suspend new procurement in France and to exclude French firms from solicitation lists for bids on construction contracts. Low bids on previous solicitations were to be eliminated by awarding contracts to lowest non-French bidder.[18] The suspension, which created bad relations with the French, was lifted in January 1955.

In April 1957, Parisians reported to the Préfecture de Police that US Air Force fighter jets were buzzing Paris. The official response of the US Air Force noted that only C-119 Flying Boxcars at Évreux AB were based near Paris. The US Air Force also claimed that it was impossible to identify the offenders without their tail numbers. The likely "buzz job" culprits were F-86 Sabre pilots from Maj Charles E. Yeager's squadron while en route from Toul-Rosières AB to St.-Nazaire AD.[19]

During a September 1958 briefing on NATO forces in France, de Gaulle asked Supreme Commander Gen Lauris Norstad where nuclear weapons were located in France and the targets assigned to them. Norstad replied: "Sir, I can answer only if we are alone." "So be it," said de Gaulle. After their staffs had withdrawn, Norstad astounded de Gaulle by saying that regrettably he still could not answer.[20, 21] Norstad eventually was authorized to give information on NATO nuclear weapons to de Gaulle. However, his 21 January 1960 briefing was so sensitive that Norstad asked de Gaulle to share it with no one, not even members of his cabinet.[22, 23]

In late 1963, the French government discovered that the US had offered to share some of its depots and communication facilities in France with West Germany. Through diplomatic channels, the French reminded the US that France had sovereign rights over French soil.[24]

In June 1965, US Secretary of Defense Robert S. McNamara and his large entourage attended a dinner, hosted by Minister of the French Armed Forces Pierre Messmer, at the Hôtel de Brienne, an historic building at 14, rue Saint-Dominique in Paris.[25] During the dinner, McNamara and his party abruptly arose and departed before salad, cheese, dessert, and coffee were served. This display of bad manners was incomprehensible to the French, whose gastronomic traditions valued the pleasure of a leisurely meal of several courses. Messmer told witnesses not to tell anyone about the indignity.[26]

Basing Agreements

The French government believed the basing agreements the US had with other nations respected the sovereignty of the host country to a greater degree than the agreements with France. In Spain, the US bases were commanded by a Spaniard, with the US as a "guest" controlling base operations. The US and Spain shared responsibility for the defense of the bases and a Spanish flag flew over the bases.[27] In the UK, the bases were British, but assigned to the Americans. An RAF officer, comparable in rank to the US base commander, was assigned to the base and US and RAF officers had "dual key" control of the nuclear weapons. British Air Ministry constables were responsible for control of vehicle traffic, security of buildings, and entry to the bases. The Britishers also were fully informed on all aircraft movements and operations.[28, 29]

In France, the US installations were commanded and operated by Americans. French liaison officers had no authority at the depots and air bases. The US did not inform the French about aircraft operations, and the French had no control of the nuclear weapons. The basing agreements did not reflect the joint defense responsibilities of France and the US. Although US Ambassador Charles E. Bohlen was willing to modify the agreements so France would have authority over US installations similar to agreements with Spain and the UK, joint use was never seriously explored by McNamara. Senior military leaders, like Lt Gen Joseph M. Heiser who had served in France during the 1960s at

4th Log Command, Verdun and ComZ headquarters, Orléans, believed the complete withdrawal could have been delayed for years if the civilian leadership at the Pentagon had agreed to pursue reasonable changes to the basing agreements with France.[30]

Base Closings in 1963-64

According to Lt Gen Jack C. Fuson, who in 1962 served on the logistics staff at the Pentagon, McNamara wanted to reduce the gold flow to Europe by getting the US out of France, but "sensed that this would not be politically acceptable either in our country or in NATO." An evaluation group at the Pentagon, headed by Brig Gen Ferdinand J. Chesarek, proposed saving $32 million a year by: reducing supply levels in ComZ from 120 to 90 days, closing depots in Base Section by moving stocks to Advance Section, returning the 4th Log Cmd and 32nd Engineer Group from Verdun to the US, inactivating Petroleum Distribution Command at Fontainebleau, and reducing port activities to the single port of St.-Nazaire. McNamara approved the Chesarek plan which included the proviso that units from France would be stationed on the East Coast of the US and be ready to return to France in an emergency. McNamara honored the proviso for less than a year.[31, 32]

The Pentagon rationalized that primarily using the German port of Bremerhaven's shorter, more economical routes of supply would permit forward positioning of military stocks.[33] However, forward positioned stocks at overcrowded depots, within a thirty-mile radius of Kaiserslautern, Germany, would be a bull's-eye target for the Soviets.[34]

In fall 1963, newspapers in the US reported on Pentagon plans to reduce the number of depots in France.[35] By the end of 1964, the Pentagon had closed twenty-seven installations in France, which included most of the Base Section. The French government believed that the base closures were taken without regard for the adverse economic impact on France. The 19,000 LWRs employed by the US were about the same number employed by Simca, France's fourth largest automaker. By ordering that advanced notice not be given to the 6,200 LWRs who lost their jobs, McNamara ignored labor agreements with the French.[36] De Gaulle forcefully complained to Ambassador Bohlen about the widespread dismissals of French civilians.[37]

Base Section Installations Closed in 1963

Bassens	Bussac	Croix-Chapeau	Jeumont	la Pallice	Périgueux
Bordeaux	Chizé	Fontenet	Laleu	La Rochelle	Rochefort

McNamara Forgets War Plans

De Gaulle merely accelerated the withdrawal from France desired by McNamara. In testimony to the US Congress on 21 June 1966, McNamara denigrated the strategic importance of France by stating "neither the United States nor its allies have ever contemplated a war in which falling back upon French soil through the battlefield of Germany was an acceptable strategy for the alliance." [38-40] Actually, France was a vital element in long-standing plans to defend Europe because it was the only terrain suitable for a defense in depth. Upon receiving the Reinforced Alert, more than 5,200 medical personnel were to fall back from Germany into France to establish 18,400 hospital beds for the casualties of war. An additional 12,000 logistical troops were to relocate from Germany to France to support combat troops airlifted from the US. Combat equipment was pre-positioned in France and Germany.[41] The airlift of combat troops from the US to Europe had been practiced each year. During the first exercise in January 1962, Operation LONG THRUST, three battle groups were airlifted from Fort Lewis,

Washington.[42] Some equipment for the exercise had been stored in France at the site of the former Chenevières AB. The second exercise in 1963 was called Operation BIG LIFT by the US Army and CRESTED CAP by the US Air Force. The 2nd Armored Division was airlifted from Texas to two airbases in France and three in Germany.[43]

Rusk Confronts de Gaulle

In September 1966, the Chairman of the US House Armed Services Committee, Congressman L. Mendell Rivers of South Carolina, remarked that 60,501 Americans were buried in France. Rivers declared: "Perhaps we should make our removal from French soil complete by reinterring the bodies of these American men on American soil."[44] The US press reported that, during a Paris meeting on American withdrawal plans, US Secretary of State Dean Rusk asked de Gaulle: "Do you want us to move American cemeteries out of France as well?" According to Rusk, he had been ordered by President Johnson to make this irrelevant appeal.[45] They both knew that France had granted use of the sacred ground of the cemeteries to the US in perpetuity. The NATO basing agreements were not to be forever. De Gaulle said in 1963: "Treaties are like young girls and roses; they last as long as they last."[46]

The American Battle Monuments Commission (ABMC) maintained eleven military cemeteries in France: six for the dead and missing of World War I and five for World War II. Suresnes American Military Cemetery, located on the slopes of Mont Valérien near Paris, is the only ABMC cemetery that has burials from both world wars. Bronze plaques in the chapel honor nearly one-thousand men buried or lost at sea. During construction in the 1920s, US Gen John J. Pershing insisted that the graves of his "Doughboys" have line-of-sight to Paris.

American Military Cemetery and Memorial, Suresnes (ABMC)

Operation Fast Relocation of the Line of Communications (FRELOC)

The US Army's goal for complete withdrawal, called Operation FRELOC (acronym for "fast relocation"), was a daunting task. It was necessary to relocate the vast logistical network of installations that had matured over a period of nearly two decades and to do so without degradation of logistical support to US combat forces in Europe.[47, 48] Operation FRELOC was the largest peacetime exercise of transportation by land, sea, and air the US military had ever undertaken. The goal to move the matériel and troops by the 01 April 1967 deadline, set without negotiations by McNamara, was complicated by legal, political, and economic factors to be resolved with France and the countries receiving the matériel.

At the beginning of the withdrawal in 1966, there were more than 70,000 US military, civilian personnel, and dependents in France. In addition, there were about 2,800 personnel and dependents of the Labor Service (LS) who were Poles displaced by World War II.[49] The LS had faithfully guarded US installations for many years and now faced an uncertain future. If they returned to Poland, they likey would be sent to prison or executed by the communists. The US Army paid moving expenses from France to Germany for families of five-hundred thirty married LS personnel.[50] The US Army had more than 728,000 tons of matériel to be relocated, the US Air Force had more than 84,000 tons, and the US Navy had about 200 tons. The flagship of 6th Fleet was relocated from Villefranche-sur-Mer (near Nice) to Gaeta, Italy. There were nine US Air Force main operating bases and four former dispersed operating bases.[51] More than one-hundred ninety US military installations were to be closed. The installations, valued at $500 million, varied in size from a few buildings to major depots spread over thousands of acres.[52]

Withdrawal Plans Before Fast Relocation

Ironically, initial planning for the withdrawal of US forces from France had begun in January 1965, more than a year before de Gaulle's letter asked the US to withdraw. A US European Command study, called Project EULOC (European Line of Communications), determined that about three years would be needed to properly relocate from France.[53] The first phase of the actual fast withdrawal from France had two key elements: to dismantle and evacuate twenty-five major depots and storage sites, and to relocate and reassemble matériel, primarily in four storage depots in UK and seven major depots in Germany. War reserve stocks relocated to Germany and Italy were to provide support for about 30 to 60 days of combat. The second phase was to establish a new line of communications (LOC), including a pipeline across Benelux countries, and seven hospitals in the UK (two 25 bed expandable to 1,000 bed, and five 1,000 bed standby). The Benelux LOC would be primarily to move supplies to the battlefield.[54]

McNamara's Hands-on Oversight

McNamara insisted on numerous alternate relocation plans so he could pick and choose. It seemed to the military that McNamara was more concerned with relocating stocks to save costs than relocating ComZ to perform its mission to support combat forces in Germany. Storage of supplies for military operations involved more than selecting an inexpensive warehouse without regard to location. Stocks needed to be inspected, rotated, preserved, and delivered to combat forces when needed. In November 1966, McNamara announced that his prior written approval was required to authorize relocation of troops from France to anywhere in Europe. At the end of December 1966, nearly 250,000 tons of stock and 19,000 personnel were still in France. Because McNamara delayed major decisions, the Army had less than four winter months to move most of its stocks and personnel.[55] Northeastern France traditionally had bad winter weather—extremely low temperatures, black ice, thick fog, and mist. Road conditions would be treacherous.

Dismantling Quonset hut, April 1966 (US Army)

USAREUR Leadership

In the fall of 1966, Gen Andrew P. O'Meara, Commander-in-Chief, US Army, Europe (USAREUR), appointed Maj Gen Edward L. Rowny to direct FRELOC. Rowny, reputed to have the tenacity of a bulldog, had been Deputy Chief of Staff for Logistics for USAREUR. O'Meara was a demanding commander who expected results from his officers. He made life difficult for those who could not produce, thus earning the reputation that his initials APO stood for "Always Pissed Off." O'Meara had relieved Rowny's predecessor because planning but no significant evacuation had occurred during the first six months of FRELOC.[56]

USAREUR had to remove 90% of the supplies and matériel in France. To begin relocation of supplies, some commanders in France took initiatives that did not require Pentagon approval. In October 1966, Maj Gen Robert C. Kyser, ComZ commander, began consolidating depots. Because he was decisive, his troops called him "Rapid Robert." Stocks and personnel from Croix-Chapeau, Bussac, and Saumur were moved to Ingrandes; and from Vitry-le-François and Vassincourt to Verdun. Although the stocks would have to be moved again when Pentagon planners finally decided on replacement sites, five depots would be emptied. Whenever possible, orders for supplies to Germany were to be filled from the most distant depot in France.[57] Kyser, who was adverse to inspection itineraries, preferred to make unannounced visits to Army mess halls to eat with the troops and to Army roadway rest stops to drink coffee with the truckers.[58]

Commanders-in-Chief, USAREUR[59]

Commanding Officer	Period of Service	Commanding Officer	Period of Service
Lt Gen Manton S. Eddy*	Aug52-Apr53	GEN Clyde D. Eddleman	Apr59-Oct60
GEN Charles L. Bolté	Apr53-Sep53	GEN Bruce C. Clarke	Oct60-May62
GEN William M. Hoge	Sep53-Feb55	GEN Paul L. Freeman, Jr	May62-Mar65
GEN Anthony C. McAuliffe	Feb55-May56	GEN Andrew P. O'Meara	Mar65-Jun67
GEN Henry I. Hodes	May56-Apr59		

*European Command (EUCOM), Heidelberg, Germany, was redesignated US Army, Europe (USAREUR) on 01 Aug 1952.

Withdrawal Directives

US European Command at Camp des Loges directed its subordinate commands to turn over buildings in clean conditions, not stripped of utilities. Article 7 of the Agreement for the Châteauroux AD stipulated that all buildings and permanent improvements to the land would revert without cost to the French. Article 8 stipulated that the US could remove all supplies, equipment, and other movable property. Official policy for inactivation and turn-back of USAFE bases in France clearly stated that all facilities would be turned over to the French in good, clean condition. It recommended holding an open-house walk through with local French dignitaries shortly before vacating an installation. Insides of buildings were to be "broom clean;" electric lamps and services to be left in place; heating systems to be cleaned, pipes drained, and shut down; windows securely fastened; and doors locked and keys properly tagged. Grounds were to be policed (meaning all trash and debris picked up), grass mowed, and overall the base was to have a neat military appearance. After a joint inspection by French and US representatives, an inventory and conditions report was to be completed before keys were given to French authorities. Gen Lyman L. Lemnitzer, Supreme Commander of NATO forces, insisted the withdrawal from France be conducted in a professional manner with an attitude of regret, not revenge.[60, 61]

JAGs and GAO Advisors

Legal backgrounds were needed to cope with numerous bilateral agreements with the French government (see table on p. 161) and hundreds of individual basing agreements. Sites abandoned by the US were to be returned to the national government, local governments, or private owners. Rowny augmented his FRELOC staff with thirty Army Reserve lawyers (JAG officers) who were on active duty for six months. Rowny also invited Pentagon officials and representatives from the General Accounting Office (GAO) to Europe to give him advice on FRELOC. Rowny reasoned that it would be better to have the GAO, the fiscal investigative agency of the US Congress, on his team giving advice rather than solely functioning as a critic of FRELOC.[62, 63]

To facilitate base closure negotiations with the French, teams were sent to the Army installations to document the current value of all buildings. For each base, photos, as-built drawings and construction documents, and statistics on the cost of construction and improvements to the facilities, utilities, and roads were recorded in bound reports called "Information Brochures." The data were used to show the value of the modern warehouses, dorms (barracks), hospitals, and the like. The US Army installations had more than 3,000 permanent buildings (new and renovated) and 14,000 prefabricated structures.[64] The nine US Air Force main operating bases had hundreds of permanent buildings, trailers, and prefabs. Toul-Rosières AB dismantled sixty-four metal prefabs for shipment to US Air Forces in Europe installations in Germany, Turkey, and Libya.

Complications of Fast Relocation

The French government gave 01 April 1967 as an appropriate date to complete the withdrawal of US military forces from France. Although a longer period could be arranged for the more complicated moving operations, the Pentagon announced in September 1966 that US withdrawal from all installations would be completed by the April deadline.[65] There were many challenges to completion of fast relocation within a one-year period. Decisions by McNamara were not timely. Only nine months before the deadline, the first major decision was made authorizing 30% of stocks to be relocated from France. Less than four months remained when the second major decision was made authorizing all stocks to be relocated.⁶⁶ The Pentagon ordered everything to be moved, although it would be less costly to abandon deteriorated or obsolete equipment in place. Even piles of sand and gravel were hauled to German landfills, rather than to depots where it could be used on projects.

Matériel from France had to be superimposed on existing facilities in Germany. Ammunition, rations, clothing, and medical supplies, which required covered storage, were stored in the open. Unsorted and piled high in big heaps, most supplies from France were exposed to severe weather.⁶⁷ Although prone to water seepage, caves near Pirmasens, Germany, were used. It took years to clear up the adverse impact of overcrowding at the depots in Germany. During FRELOC, ComZ staff repeated a doggerel: "If you can, dump it in the Rhine. If you can't, stuff it into Germersheim." ⁶⁸ Germersheim was converted from a 396-acre vehicle park to a general depot for supplies removed from France. Since 1951, the US Army had used Germersheim, an old German Army training area, to store about 18,000 vehicles outdoors.⁶⁹

McNamara planned to move all ammunition from France to the US. However, O'Meara wanted the ammunition stored closer to Seventh Army in Germany. McNamara relented only after O'Meara convinced him it would cost less to move the ammunition to the UK. Ammunition could not be shipped to UK until 19 January 1967, when abandoned World War II RAF depots at Fauld, Bramshall, and Ditton Priors became operational. To obtain use of the sites, O'Meara went to London to meet with Lord Louis Mountbatten, Chief of British Defense Staff.⁷⁰ Opening of the ammunition depots was delayed because sites were close to housing estates. During World War II, 3,700 tons of ammunition stored underground at Fauld exploded leaving a 140-ft deep oval crater more than a ½ mile long and ¼ mile wide. It was the most powerful non-atomic explosion during the war. An estimated seventy-eight civilians and depot workers were killed. Villagers, not wanting to live next to tons of explosives, unsuccessfully pressured their elected representatives not to allow Americans to store ammunition nearby. However, the local government did limit the amount of ammunition passing near Fauld to 50 tons per convoy.⁷¹⁻⁷³

S&MA Supply Directives

During FRELOC, the Supply and Maintenance Agency (S&MA), commanded by Brig Gen Charles C. Case, worked three shifts a day, seven days a week, to process over one million transactions each month. In 1966, the S&MA had more than 1,500 officers, enlisted men, and DAC employees. There also were eight-hundred sixty French LWRs. Beginning in April 1966, S&MA computers were reprogrammed to search for assets in France to fill daily requisitions for Seventh Army. Because the depots in France received almost no replacements, inventories were reduced by normal use. About 100,000 tons were moved out of France using this procedure. The 70,000 tons of cargo previously shipped each month from the US to France now were sent directly to Germany.⁷⁴

The S&MA had an IBM records system that used 80-column punch cards to input data. McNamara's Pentagon planners demanded that punch cards, with the description, size, and weight of each item, be created for the millions of supplies in France. Because preparation of the cards was tedious, only 10% had been completed during the first six months of FRELOC. Plans included preparation of S&MA "supply directives" on punch cards to direct shipments from depots in France. Progress was slow because decisions by the Pentagon were not timely. As the April 1967 deadline neared, S&MA directed depots to ship, on their own initiative, the remaining stocks out of France. Vehicles were to be sent to Kaiserslautern, general supplies to Nahbollenbach, and ammunition to Miesau. Records were to be updated later. This desperate method caused S&MA to lose control of a significant portion of its stock. Some GIs believed they were part of "Operation Chaos." Compounding the confusion, an Army courier lost a box of 2,000 punch cards. In 1969, the GAO reported that $100 million in stocks supposedly moved from France could not be located.[75, 76]

The Brain Train

The S&MA Automatic Data Processing (ADP) system had two IBM 7010 computers, three IBM 1460 computers, seven magnetic tape drives, one tape library, and two Univac 1005 card processors. Because McNamara could not decide where to relocate the computers, Gen Kyser determined that railcars would provide the best interim solution. The railcars (dubbed "The Brain Train") could be moved near wherever McNamara decided to locate S&MA in Germany.[77] The computers required controlled temperature and humidity, tie downs, and an independent power supply. Eight passenger cars, owned by the US Army, were modified to house the ADP system. Two flatbed cars were used for diesel electric generators; a standard tank car for fuel. Adapting the long, narrow railcars for the computers in the limited time available was difficult. The computers on five railcars had to be connected together by cables which had a "not to exceed" length, weight had to be properly distributed, and space had to be provided for GIs to operate the equipment. The tape library was stored in a railcar that had an automatic fire suppression system. The train required eighty-four tons of cooling.[78]

When the S&MA staff, which relied on the ADP system, was relocated to Zweibrücken, Germany, the train was parked 25 miles away on a rail spur at the US Army Medical Depot at Einsiedlerhof. In the cramped space on the train, computer console operators could not easily observe tape drives. Programmers worked in a warehouse near the train. The ADP system on the train was plagued with errors. In 1968, S&MA received state-of-the-art IBM System 360 computers, which were installed in a building in Kreuzberg Kaserne at Zweibrücken.[79]

Methods of Transportation

Relocation from France involved commercial and military trucks, railcars, barges, ships, and aircraft. Nearly two-thirds of truck transport was by military vehicles. Commercial rail moved about 300,000 tons of matériel. Barges moved about 50,000 tons by inland canals. Engineer troops dismantled prefabricated metal buildings and refrigerator boxes (called "reefers"), and prepared boilers and transformers for shipment from France.[80]

US Military in France at Start of Withdrawal[81, 82]

Service	Personnel	Dependents	Installations*	Matériel (tons)
Army	17,686	15,728	358	728,791
Air Force	13,692	20,668	77	84,280
Navy and Marine Corps	318	1,153	4	196

*In addition to air bases, depots, standby hospitals, and headquarters, totals include leased property such as housing villages, microwave stations, recreation facilities, and training sites.

Nighttime Red Ball

Truck companies formed from units in France and Germany moved most of the matériel to ports in France or directly to Belgium, the Netherlands, Italy, and Germany. Rations stored at Ingrandes and Toul were moved to Livorno, Italy, near Pisa. The 37th Transportation Group, commanded by

Col John E. Murray, had 1,200 tractors and 3,000 trailers to support FRELOC.[83] Most tractors were new International Harvester diesels, which had three times the range of the Army's M52 truck tractor. Because of the drawdown of troops in Europe to support the war in Vietnam, initially the 37th was far below its authorized personnel strength.

Reveille, the traditional sunrise bugle call signaling the first formation of the day, was at dusk to recreate a "Red Ball Express" at night when civilian traffic was lowest. For safety, teams of MPs and French police strictly enforced a 40 mph speed limit.[84, 85] To catch speeders, the 64th Military Police Co used two timing wires spaced 8 ft apart on the roads. Mid-way in the twelve-hour, 350 mile drive from Ingrandes to Toul, drivers took a rest break at Fontainebleau. A "Wimpy Wagon," named for a popular hamburger restaurant on the Champs Élysées in Paris, was set up to provide soup, sandwiches, and candy to the drivers. J. Wellington Wimpy, of the popular American comic strip *Popeye*, was known for the catch phrase: "I will gladly pay you Tuesday for a hamburger today." Although Murray wanted his drivers to drive four nights straight and take the fifth night off, the task to evacuate France was so great that many drivers drove without any time off for the duration of FRELOC.[86]

Murray insisted that enlisted men be promoted based on job performance and soldierly attributes in action rather than on vocal and physical appearance before promotion boards. Miles from a source of Army spare parts, Pvt John Perkins of the 70th Trans Co fixed a disabled jeep by finding a water pump among foreign vehicles in a nearby French junk yard. Perkins received an on-the-spot promotion to private first class for his actions.[87]

Syndicated cartoonist Charles Shultz gave permission to the 37th Trans Gp drivers to use Snoopy as their "unofficial" mascot for FRELOC. The cartoon of Snoopy as a World War I pilot determined to prevail over the Red Baron was displayed on truck windows as the GIs moved out of France.[88] FRELOC truck transportation outdid the famous World War II Red Ball Express by hauling 25% more ton-miles within a similar period of time. This milestone was achieved by more than one-thousand young men who drove alone at night over poorly marked roads.[89] Typical trailer loads included 6" diameter pipe, ammunition, jeeps, transformers, and 55-gal drums. Even when hauling explosives, drivers were not escorted by MPs. Due to indecisiveness by McNamara, the weather-favorable driving months were lost and road conditions were often hazardous.

37th Transportation Group During FRELOC

28th Transportation Battalion (six companies)	106th Transportation Battalion (five companies)
53rd Transportation Battalion* (six companies)	6966th Civilian Labor Group (CLG)** (four battalions)

*On 13 March 1967, the 84th and 574th Trans Cos of the 53rd Trans Bn were sent from Toul to the US.
**Paramilitary battalion-size transportation unit formed entirely of German nationals. 6966th CLG was stationed at Kaiserslautern, West Germany.

Ships Move Cargo

Ships delivered cargo to the US, UK, Italy, and Southeast Asia. Shipments to Vietnam were "laundered" through an intermediate destination. The UK gave permission to the US Army to establish a general depot at abandoned RAF Burtonwood. Seventy-seven watercraft of the US Army marine fleet were moved from le Pellerin and Rochefort to RAF Hythe near Southampton, UK, and half of the stock of more than 1,000 pontoons was moved to Antwerp, Belgium. To reduce commercial tow charges, smaller craft were nested onto larger craft. The USNS *Marine Fiddler* cargo ship, which had two 150-

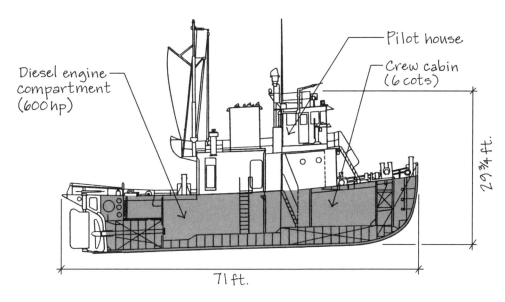

US Army Tugboat

ton capacity cranes, moved landing craft to the US for eventual use in Vietnam.[90] During the time available to move ammunition to UK, bad weather slowed cross-channel operations, French ports were closed on Sundays, SNCF railroad workers went on strike for two days, and EDF electrical workers were on strike for one day. Ammunition from Captieux, Chizé, and Rozelier was loaded at the ports of Bassens and St.-Nazaire in France and at Antwerp, Belgium. Because UK ports had a safety limit of 250 tons for ammunition in port at one time, the US only used small coastal vessels. Thirty-two commercial coastal vessels were hired to make more than two-hundred voyages. It took forty-seven days to move 60,000 tons of ammunition to ports in the UK. During a violent storm in the English Channel that delayed shipping for 48 hours, a US Army small tug sank seven miles north of Cherbourg. According to Rowny, a barge loaded with ammunition sank in bad weather.[91]

Air Force Cargo Sorties

At the beginning of FRELOC, the Air Force had more than one-hundred eighty aircraft based in France. When aircraft were moved out of France in August to October 1966, most ground support personnel were no longer needed. However, the mission to support contingency operations meant alert and refuel crews could not leave. Also to be relocated were nearly 10,000 tons of ammunition, 350 tons of chaff, 17,000 auxiliary fuel tanks, 6,500 pylons (used to support bombs and engines above the ground), and 8 million gallons of JP-4 and other aviation fuels. Nearly 3,000 vehicles were in France to support USAFE. In addition to staff cars, jeeps, and cargo trucks, the Air Force had special-purpose vehicles. Ground equipment at air bases included: refueling tank trucks, fire-rescue trucks, elevating platforms called "cherry pickers" (to de-ice aircraft), aircraft tugs (to tow aircraft), and wheeled racks and stands (to haul bombs and rockets).[92] The last airmen to leave were assigned motor pool vehicles to drive out of France.

The USAFE moved 12,000 tons of cargo in 750 sorties from France. In September 1966, maintenance support equipment at Toul-Rosières AB was moved by C-141 Starlifters and C-124 Globemasters. Évreux AB was the exit point for all cargo shipped from France by air. Beginning in January 1967, the Air Force flew two to four sorties per day, six days a week, from Évreux AB to RAF Greenham Common in the UK. Most air cargo was "classified" matériel and documents, safes, and sensitive electronic equipment. More than one million gallons of jet fuel (JP-4) were shipped from Dreux AB to the US Army petroleum tank farm at Melun, near Fontainebleau. The French government allowed Évreux AB to be used until the end of the Paris Air Show on 04 June 1967. The huge NATO depot at la Martinerie, near Châteauroux, did not close until May 1968.[93]

Like the US Army, the Air Force initially drew down supplies by shipment to Germany. Three storage sites in the UK were opened at the abandoned World War II airfields of Chelveston, Greenham Common, and Sculthorpe. Wherever possible supplies were stored in rehabilitated hangars, but almost 40% of the shipments from France had to be stored in the open.[94] Because McNamara denied a USAFE request to assign two-hundred thirty personnel to operate the three temporary storage sites, it took years to unravel the disorganized piles of matériel.[95]

US Air Force Depots in UK

RAF Air Station	USAFE Stocks from France
Chelveston	Vehicles
Greenham Common	Aircraft engines, repair parts
Sculthorpe	Aviation fuel, auxiliary fuel tanks

US Cargo to Vietnam

In April 1966, approximately 350 tons of cargo had been transported by rail from US Army depots to the port of St.-Nazaire. The *SS Newcastle Victory* was already being loaded with weapons and ammunition when the French government learned the cargo was destined for Southeast Asia. Because the French did not permit cargo for Southeast Asia to be loaded at French ports, the loading was halted. The cargo was removed from the ship, loaded onto SNCF railcars, and delivered to an Italian port where, two days later, it again was loaded onto the *Newcastle Victory*. Although the cargo was transported to Vietnam on the same ship that had been docked at St.-Nazaire, the newspaper *Presse-Ocean* reported that French honor had been saved. In December 1966, de Gaulle finally allowed cargo to be shipped from French ports directly to Vietnam.

Motorcade of French President Charles de Gaulle and US President Dwight D. Eisenhower on Pennsylvania Ave, Washington, DC, 22 April 1960 (Centre Culturel Américain)

De Gaulle and US Presidents

At the May 1960 Four Powers Summit conference in Paris, Soviet Premier Nikita Khrushchev demanded that US President Dwight D. Eisenhower apologize for the overflight of the Soviet Union by a U-2 Dragon Lady spy aircraft. Eisenhower did not apologize. Consequently, Khrushchev walked out of the meeting room and refused to attend any more conference sessions. De Gaulle came over to Eisenhower and said: "I do not know what Khrushchev is going to do, nor what is going to happen, but whatever he does I want you to know that I am with you to the end." Eisenhower, clearly moved by this unexpected expression of unconditional support, thanked de Gaulle. Unbeknownst to Eisenhower, the day before the Summit began, Khrushchev had told de Gaulle that the Soviets could destroy US bases in France at any moment.[96] De Gaulle escorted Eisenhower down the stairs to Ike's car. In the privacy of his car, Eisenhower told his interpreter, Col Vernon A. Walters, that de Gaulle was "quite a guy."[97]

President John F. Kennedy was very popular in France. His wife, Jacqueline, who had studied at the Sorbonne, charmed de Gaulle during a state visit in May 1961 to Paris. Nevertheless, relations with de Gaulle deteriorated primarily due to America's insistence that France not develop a nuclear force and de Gaulle's belief that Kennedy's response to the Cuban Missile Crisis was timid.[98, 99]

In November 1963, de Gaulle came to Washington, DC to attend the funeral of President Kennedy. At the White House, he was kept waiting for nearly 30 min for a scheduled meeting with President Lyndon B. Johnson.[100] Although warned by the FBI that there might be an assassination attempt during the funeral procession, de Gaulle declined to ride in an armor-plated vehicle, declaring: "I shall walk with Mrs. Kennedy."[101] Because of his height and bearing, de Gaulle in his brigadier general's uniform is the dominant figure in famous photos of the funeral procession.

De Gaulle and Johnson met twice more, for brief handshakes at the funerals of West German Chancellor Konrad Adenauer and President Eisenhower. De Gaulle, who disliked Johnson, told colleagues that Johnson resembled the cartoon character "Popeye the Sailor Man."[102] De Gaulle and most of the French press, which normally opposed de Gaulle, did not support Johnson's policies in Vietnam.[103, 104] De Gaulle believed the military buildup in Southeast Asia would cause the US to reduce its defense commitments to Europe. Some French military officers were still bitter that the US had not provided timely assistance when French forces were being defeated in May 1954 at Dien Bien Phu.[105] Nevertheless, because the North Vietnamese had murdered wounded French soldiers, many French officers told Maj Gen Vernon A. Walters, US Defense Attaché in Paris from 1967 to 1972, that they felt warmth in their hearts when the US was successful on the battlefields of Vietnam.[106] In addition to his routine duties as Attaché, Walters initiated secret talks between the US and North Vietnam and between the US and China.[107]

In February 1969, one month after his inauguration, President Richard M. Nixon visited Europe and met with President de Gaulle at the Élysée Palace. Unlike Johnson who never asked de Gaulle for advice on anything, Nixon asked de Gaulle for advice on Vietnam.[108] During the first Nixon administration, the US began cooperating with France's nuclear weapons program. French weapons designers were "unofficially" guided by US experts.[109] During his March 1969 visit to Washington, DC for the funeral of President Eisenhower, de Gaulle approached US Army Chief of Staff Gen William C. Westmoreland at a White House reception. Westmoreland, who had commanded all US forces in Vietnam, was surprised to receive unsolicited advice on military strategy from de Gaulle.[110]

501

Relocation of NATO Military Headquarters

SHAPE was relocated from Marly-le-Roi to rapidly built facilities at Camp de Casteau, a former Belgium infantry training post five miles north of Mons, Belgium. During the official ceremony in November 1966 to lay the foundation stone for the new headquarters, Gen Lyman L. Lemnitzer, Supreme Commander of NATO forces, snapped to attention and saluted the flags when the Casteau village band began playing. Immediately, others in the official party followed suit. Unfortunately, the band was playing Beethoven's *Ninth Symphony*, not the Belgian national anthem. The next day, a memo to all SHAPE staff officers instructed them to be able to recognize the Belgian national anthem and to familiarize themselves with the music of Beethoven.[111]

Relocation of more than 2,400 personnel was conducted in three phases: the move of a reconnaissance team to Belgium, deployment of the main staff body to Casteau during March 1967, and closure of SHAPE facilities in France by a termination group. SHAPE vehicles, augmented by commercial moving vans, transported all movable items (documents and office equipment), economically movable communications facilities, and non-NATO funded property belonging to the Allies, except France. Classified documents in safes were transported by military vehicles under MP and gendarme escort. The relocation required 890 vehicle journeys to move approximately 22,400 tons of supplies, equipment, and household goods. SHAPE support group moved from Camp Voluceau to temporary facilities at Chièvres Air Base, near Casteau.[112]

Moving vans, SHAPE Headquarters, Marly-le-Roi, 1967 (SHAPE)

The relocation of AFCENT from Fontainebleau to the Netherlands was a similar operation. AFCENT moved to buildings of the abandoned state-owned Hendrik coal mine at Brunssum and to the old army Tapijn Barracks 15 miles away, near Maastricht. The abandoned coal mine proved to be a good choice for AFCENT because communication centers had to be underground to survive an atomic blast. Officers and enlisted men lived in hotels until quarters could be built.[113, 114]

In the rush to find a replacement school for SHAPE dependents, a 14-acre apple orchard at Sterrebeck, Belgium, near Brussels, was purchased for the site of a new school. Although individuals could not sell land to a foreign government, it was mistakenly sold to the US government for $475,000. The new school was built on the only land in Europe owned by the US. At the time of the sale, SHAPE was without legal advisors because France, as host country, had supplied lawyers to SHAPE.[115, 116]

The French government agreed that SHAPE families could remain in France until the end of the 1966-67 school year, so children could complete their studies. Other dependents schools and support facilities, such as medical clinics and commissaries, could remain open. Dependent family members also could remain in France until housing and dependents schools became available in Belgium and the Netherlands. De Gaulle invited Lemnitzer to remain in Villa St.-Pierre at Marnes-la-Coquette until his quarters were completed in Belgium. Lemnitzer's family stayed in the Villa, but Lemnitzer moved to the BOQ at Casteau until the new Quarters One château was renovated.[117] By 01 April 1967, although 1,935 staff members had left Marly-le-Roi, approximately 4,000 dependents remained. By 01 July 1967, only four-hundred fifteen SHAPE staff members, overseeing closure of facilities, and approximately 2,000 dependents remained in the Paris area. Thirty families from US European Command at Camp des Loges also remained in the Paris area.[118] USEUCOM moved to Stuttgart.

The first phase of construction of a headquarters building and support facilities (barracks, mess halls, BOQs) at Casteau was completed by the deadline of 01 April 1967. It became a matter of national pride for the Belgians to meet the deadlines set for the SHAPE complex. The second phase of construction included service clubs, chapels, schools, gymnasium, and 1,700 housing units. A 50-bed hospital, supermarket, and bowling alley would be constructed in the final phase.[119]

NATO and US Military Headquarters Moved from France

Headquarters	Vacated Location	New Location
SHAPE (Supreme Headquarters, Allied Powers Europe)	Marly-le-Roi (near Paris)	Casteau, Belgium (near Mons)
AFCENT (Allied Forces Central Europe)	Fontainebleau	Brunssum and Maastricht, the Netherlands
AIRCENT (Allied Air Forces Central Europe)	Camp Guynemer (Avon)	Brunssum and Maastricht, the Netherlands
LANDCENT (Allied Land Forces Central Europe)	Fontainebleau	Brunssum and Maastricht, the Netherlands
USEUCOM (US European Command)	Camp de Loges (near Paris)	Patch Barracks (Stuttgart-Vaihingen, Germany)
SOTFE (Support Operations Task Force, Europe)	The Blockhouse (Paris)	Panzer Kaserne (Boeblingen, Germany)
USARCOMZEUR (US Army Communications Zone, Europe)	Caserne Coligny (Orléans)	Taukkunen Kaserne (Worms, Germany)
S&MA (Supply and Maintenance Agency)	Maison-Fort and Verdun	Kreuzberg Kaserne (Zweibrücken, Germany)

Withdrawal SNAFUs

Although Lemnitzer's orders were followed at many installations, there were SNAFUs (GI acronym for "situation normal, all fouled up"). Too often troops purposefully destroyed electrical services, plumbing systems, and other property due to poor unit leadership and lack of common sense. Many older officers and NCOs had witnessed, or heard of, the deplorable conditions of the buildings that the French had turned over to the US military in the early 1950s in the occupied zone of Germany. Before the Americans arrived for the inter-zonal exchange, the French military had removed sinks, toilets, and light fixtures from buildings at Bitburg, Hahn, Landstuhl, Sembach, and Spangdahlem.[120] Unlike the US, buildings in France were rented or sold stripped bare. Anything that could be moved (*mobilier*) usually was. This cultural difference created animosities that surfaced throughout FRELOC.

About one-third of the US personnel in France during the final six months of FRELOC had arrived after June 1966. These troops had little time to form friendships with the French and most did not understand why they were being asked to leave. The acronym DGCAD (don't give Charlie a dime) was chalked on walls, Army trailers, and tarps which covered the trailer loads. At one installation, hundreds of unlabeled keys to depot buildings were dumped into a metal bucket and handed over to the French. At the end of FRELOC, too few troops were available at many installations to accomplish an orderly evacuation. In 1967 at Ingrandes, one Army captain, three NCOs, and one-hundred mostly disgruntled LWRs were tasked with shipping stocks out of Braconne, Chinon, and Ingrandes. Lacking sufficient personnel, they could not properly pack and secure stocks for transport by railcars and trucks.[121] At Caserne Lariboisière in Fontainebleau, telephones were ripped from walls, light bulbs stomped on, and desks were thrown from upper floor windows because only three GIs were available to empty a four-story building in two days. At Chinon, windows and doors were removed from masonry buildings. Bulldozers were used to bury thousands of jerry cans at Melun Tank Farm in La Ferté-Alais.[122] At Phalsbourg AB, personnel damaged the stroboscopic landing lights and shot out runway lights. At Toul-Rosières AB, where 26th Tactical Reconnaissance Wing commander Col Robert L. Boardman was perturbed to be abandoning the base, personnel used axes to destroy new hangar security locks and poured bags of concrete mix into sinks and toilets.[123]

The order to remove medical equipment (X-ray units, dental chairs, steam sterilizers) from hospitals was delayed until near the end of FRELOC. ComZ planners believed the French would purchase the fully-equipped, modern hospitals.[124] If not, the hospitals could be abandoned "as is" to be a gesture of good will. When the orders were given to remove everything from the hospitals, medical staffs had been greatly reduced and packing materials (crates, hold-down bolts, lumber) for delicate equipment were unavailable. At Fontainebleau, an uncrated X-ray unit was dumped on the bed of a 2½ ton truck.[125] Because there was no security at night at Désandrouins Hospital in Verdun, locals helped themselves to abandoned supplies and equipment. At the end of July 1967, the twelve-man detachment of enlisted personnel departed for Germany, leaving behind at Verdun unsecured piles of supplies from the hospital, dependents school, and motor pool.[126]

There were no efforts to purge water and soil of contaminants. Ignored were nearly two decades of spills at air bases, motor pools, maintenance shops, and POL storage facilities. Contaminants included gasoline, diesel fuel, kerosene-base jet fuel, solvents, and battery acids.[127] Unexploded ordnance was abandoned in the ground at the 4,000-acre US Army Troop Training Area at Montmorillon, near Poitiers. At Saumur, thousands of batteries were abandoned in caves near Château des Ifs. Acres of unexploded ordnance were abandoned in the ground at USAFE Gunnery Range at Suippes. USAFE returned Suippes to the French on 23 October 1967 after persuading the French government that all ordnance had been removed.

Missing Property

After the official end of FRELOC on 01 April 1967, valuable supplies and equipment had not been removed from some of the Army installations. At Captieux Ammunition Depot, 2nd Lt Robert L. Jordan, S&MA at Zweibrücken, Germany, was sent TDY from late June through August 1967 to supervise two-dozen LWRs still working at the depot and oversee the removal of matériel that had been left behind. During two months, more than fifty tractor-trailer loads of spark-resistant brass doors and rails, pierced steel plank (PSP), and other US property were retrieved from the depot.[128]

To discourage theft of government property during FRELOC, several Air Force bases had unannounced "shakedown" inspections on all vehicles leaving the base. Shakedowns lasted at least 30 minutes, each 8-hour Air Police shift. In March 1966, an Army sergeant and two French nationals stole three-thousand sections of PSP from the Rochefort Arsenal. The perpetrators were caught by the Army's Criminal Investigation Division (CID) with help from French authorities. A local CID civilian employee, Frenchman Raymond Rohou, helped break the case.[129] To insure that the US Army did not remove the Napoléon-era canons from the Arsenal, the Mayor of Rochefort Francis Gaury emphatically told 1st Lt Thomas G. Day of the 37th Trans Gp that the canons were French property.[130]

In Luxembourg, three soldiers were caught stealing private property. Because the US had no Status of Forces Agreement with Luxembourg, their convictions were swift and sentences harsh: one year in solitary confinement; bread for breakfast and dinner, potatoes and salad for lunch; a bucket for a toilet; and no hot water. The widespread knowledge of their punishment may have motivated good behavior by other drivers of the 37th Trans Gp.[131]

The Army and Air Force had difficulties keeping accurate records. Beginning in February 1967, cargo received often was in excess of quantities ordered shipped because stocks were moved without advance notice given to the receiving depot. Significant stocks of medical supplies and ammunition from ComZ could not be located after FRELOC. In late 1968, more than 80,000 gallons of US Air Force de-icing fluid and over 200,000 rounds of small caliber ammunition still could not be located.[132]

Waste and Other Blunders

In early 1964, the USAFE sold 7,562 bombs to a West Germany company for $1.70 each. The Germans planned to use the explosives for fertilizer; the casing for scrap metal. Due to the escalation of fighting in Vietnam, the US had a shortage of 750 lb bombs. In 1965, the US bought back 5,500 of the bombs from the Germans for $21 each. US Representative Gerald R. Ford of Michigan and other members of the US Congress were outraged at the buyback price. During his testimony to Congress on 11 May 1966, McNamara asserted in Latin that the buyback was "de minimis" because it represented a small percentage of the bombs dropped in Southeast Asia that year. McNamara also claimed that the buyback was a "good bargain" because 750 lb bombs, which he sold for $1.70, now cost more than $300 each to manufacture.[133]

O'Meara ordered Rowny to move everything from France. Taking this order literally, engineer dump trucks hauled piles of sand and gravel from France to landfills in Germany.[134] At the golf courses built by the US Army and US Air Force in France, engineers rolled up putting green turf and laid it on top of existing putting greens in Germany. More than one-hundred greens were removed. Senior leaders at ComZ headquarters in Orléans learned about the missing turf from reports in French newspapers. Brig Gen Frank B. Clay, ComZ Chief of Staff, believed that if his staff had known, they would have stopped the spiteful acts.[135, 136]

Rowny also was ordered to remove the tens of thousands of 7-ft high concrete posts (canted at the top to form an overhang of multiple strands of barbed wire) used in perimeter security fences. However, believing this task to be impractical, he ignored the order. After FRELOC, it took the *Office National des Forêts* (ONF) nearly three decades to remove the posts, each firmly anchored in a buried concrete base, surrounding the perimeter of the former ammunition depot in the national forest of Trois-Fontaines. However, the US did remove most of the more than 80 miles of railroad track at the depots in France.

Chemical munitions were moved to Germany in such a hurry that the shells were stored without knowing the contents. Shell casings from France had camouflage paint that covered the standard symbols identifying contents.[137] By Army regulations, three parallel stripes were used to indicate a chemical nerve agent. Above the stripes, the specific agent was identified by letters such as GB for

Sarin. In 1990, a team of chemical munitions experts from Edgewood Arsenal, Maryland, was sent to Clausen Depot to sort through the camouflaged munitions. To disguise their work, officers of the Chemical Corps wore MP or Ordnance Corps branch insignia. Shortly thereafter, the munitions were shipped from Germany to Johnson Island in the Pacific Ocean to be destroyed.[138]

During the hectic final month of FRELOC, Army units in Germany were invited to send trucks to depots in France and take whatever supplies they needed. The goal was to eliminate shortages in Germany while helping to evacuate France. However in practice, many of the "shoppers" from Germany grabbed everything they could regardless of need. Therefore, their units acquired useless supplies which had to be destroyed because they were undocumented.[139]

The cost to dismantle three-hundred two prefab ammunition storage huts at Trois-Fontaines and move them to Karlsruhe, Germany, was twice the value of the huts.[140] Electrical transformers, essential equipment in case of power outages on air bases, were transported from Toul-Rosières AB to Germany where they were sold as scrap for less than the cost of transportation.

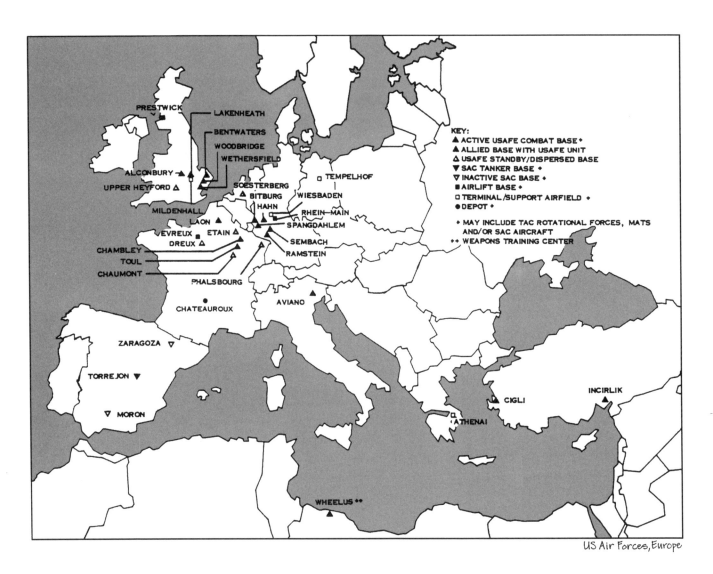

US Air Force Bases in Europe (1966)

US Air Force Redeploys

In 1965, USAFE began planning for the possible withdrawal from France by initiating "dual-basing." Although stationed in the US, squadrons were to be ready to deploy to Europe on short notice.[141] The 19th Tactical Reconnaissance Squadron (TRS) was moved from Chambley AB, France, to Shaw AFB, South Carolina. The 22nd TRS from Toul-Rosières AB was dual-based at Mountain Home AFB, Idaho. In August 1966, the 32nd TRS, which actually moved to Southeast Asia, was assigned on paper to RAF Alconbury, UK. In September 1966, the 17th TRS and 18th TRS from Laon AB were moved to RAF Upper Heyford, UK. By 10 October 1966, most of the other squadrons in France had been redeployed. The 513th Troop Carrier Wing moved its C-130 Hercules aircraft to RAF Mildenhall, UK. After FRELOC, the 19th TRS used Ramstein AB, Germany, as forward base for its RB-66 Destroyer aircraft.

US Air Force Redeployments from France (1966-67)[142, 143]

Location	Unit	Destination
Chambley AB	25th TRW	Inactivated, 15 October 1966*
	42nd TRS	Takhli, Thailand
	19th TRS	Shaw AFB, Sumter, SC
Évreux AB	513th TCW	RAF Mildenhall, UK
Laon AB	66th TRW	RAF Upper Heyford, UK
	17th TRS	RAF Upper Heyford, UK
	18th TRS	RAF Upper Heyford, UK
Toul-Rosières AB	26th TRW	Ramstein AB, Germany
	22nd TRS	Mountain Home AFB, Idaho**
	32nd TRS	RAF Alconbury, UK***
Châteauroux AD	322nd AD	High Wycombe AS, UK

*Aircraft and aircrews to Southeast Asia.
**Dual based at Sembach, Germany
***On paper only. Personnel and aircraft sent to Southeast Asia.

Abbreviations

AD	Air Depot (or Airlift Division)	TCW	Troop Carrier Wing
AS	Air Station	TRS	Tactical Reconnaissance Squadron
RAF	Royal Air Force (UK)	TRW	Tactical Reconnaissance Wing

Dependents Schools Close

De Gaulle personally made the decision to allow nine-hundred fifty dependent students to finish the 1966-67 school year at Fontainebleau, Ingrandes, Orléans, Paris, Toul, and Verdun.[144] During the withdrawal, the Army planned to abandon prefab elementary school buildings at la Chapelle St.-Mesmin, near Orléans. However, the French property owner asked that the prefabs be removed so he would not be liable to pay taxes on structures that he did not intend to use. In 1966-67, thousands of chairs, desks, textbooks, world globes, and other equipment from schools throughout France were shipped to dependents schools in Germany, Italy, Spain, and the UK. All dormitory furniture from Dreux AB was sent to Torrejon AB in Spain. C-124 Globemasters flew six sorties from Châteauroux AD to airlift all equipment and supplies from the high school at la Martinerie to RAF Upper Heyford in the UK. During the closing ceremony on 30 November 1966, the keys for the St.-Michel American Elementary School were given to the Mayor of Évreux Armand Mandle.

McNamara's Risk Taking

By most measures, the US military met the 01 April 1967 deadline. Nearly one million tons of supplies, equipment, and household goods were moved and 70,000 personnel and dependents were relocated. Forty-seven percent of US Army personnel were relocated to Germany. US Air Force wings were redeployed to UK, Germany, and the US.[145-147] However, in the event of war with the Soviets, NATO would not have the dispersed logistical infrastructure, forward-based aircraft, and significant medical support that had been available in France.[148] Former Secretary of State Dean Acheson said that, without France, nuclear weapons would have to be used at the beginning of a Soviet invasion.[149] By dismantling ComZ France, McNamara claimed that $50 to $60 million would be saved annually.[150] However, the estimated cost of FRELOC exceeded $980 million in value of facilities to be left behind in France and construction costs for new depots in the UK and expanded facilities in Germany.[151]

Lt Gen Joseph M. Heiser recalled that: "He (de Gaulle) respected America, but wanted to re-establish France. We were not cooperating at all. McNamara wanted us out of France and used the de Gaulle position on Status of Forces Agreement renewal as a way of forcing us out of France and putting blame on de Gaulle. The NATO atomic weapons could have been moved and the LOC (line of communications) remain, but McNamara wanted to be able to say he saved millions of dollars. He did, but at real strategic cost!"[152]

Top Ten Reasons Defense of Europe Was Weakened

US Army[153]
1. The new supply lines to Seventh Army from ports in West Germany and the Netherlands were too close to Soviet forces.
2. Transport of supplies stored in UK would take longer to reach combat forces in Germany. Storms in the English Channel could disrupt delivery of supplies.
3. Ports and tested Atlantic coast landing sites in France were not available to NATO forces. All US Army LCM and LCU landing craft were sent to Vietnam.
4. Essential stocks for wartime were stored in overcrowded depots in West Germany. More than three-fifths of the stocks were not dispersed. They were concentrated in depots located within a 30-mile radius of Kaiserslautern.
5. The West German railroad system serving the depots was vulnerable because it depended on electrical power generated east of the Rhine River. Initial combat with the invading Soviets likely would disable these power plants.

US Air Force[154, 155]
6. Aircraft could not be widely dispersed. Eighteen main, dispersed, and emergency air bases had been closed in France. Ability to repair NATO combat aircraft at Châteauroux AD was lost.
7. Combat aircraft sent to augment forces in Europe would be at smaller number of airbases, located closer to the Soviets.
8. Matériel needed for air combat were stored at three World War II-era airfields in the UK.

Land and air forces[156, 157]
9. Nine modern standby hospitals and two medical depots in France were closed. Medical equipment from the depots was stored in the UK.
10. More than 270,000 dependents could not be evacuated through France to safe havens in Spain and Portugal.

Goodwill Projects and Good Deeds

Public affairs officers wanted the long-standing Franco-American friendship and goodwill to continue despite the withdrawal. At Phalsbourg AB, Maj Delbert Annereau, who served three non-consecutive tours as base engineer, often helped nearby villages. During one devastating snowstorm, Air Force equipment was used to clear the streets of Phalsbourg. For his numerous acts of kindness to the French, Annereau was named *Citoyen d'honneur* of Phalsbourg.[158] During 1966-67, the US Army's 97th Engineer Battalion constructed a soccer field at Verdun, a camping ground at Charny, and extended parking at the Ossuarie de Douaumont near Verdun in preparation for France's 50th Anniversary Ceremonies commemorating the end of World War I.[159]

On 31 October 1966, ComZ was directed not to dispose of excess property by donation to French institutions or charitable organizations. Nevertheless, at some installations, soldiers ignored orders to burn excess property and supplies that were to be abandoned. In the spring of 1967, French orphanages at Étain and Châteauroux received several unauthorized bulk donations of badly needed nonperishable foods, bedding, and similar supplies.[160] At Étain AB, the base commander's family poured salt and pepper from C-rations into glass jars to give to orphanages. Mess hall chairs from Évreux AB were given to the Little Sisters of the Poor Orphanage in Évreux.[161] Medics of the 11th General Dispensary at Braconne Depot ignored orders to destroy medicine. At night, they placed boxes of medicine behind the dispensary so French civilian doctors could surreptitiously pick up the unofficial donations.[162]

Dozer work at Douaumont Ossuary, 1967 (US Army)

Humanitarian Operations

The US Army in France provided logistical support to US forces on missions to aid victims of natural disasters in the Middle East, North Africa, and Western Europe. Natural disasters to which they responded included floods, wild fires, cyclones, earthquakes, avalanches, extreme cold and winter storms, and even locust plagues.[163]

On 31 January 1953, the rampaging North Sea burst through protective dikes in the Netherlands. More than 1,000 sq miles, one-sixth of the Netherlands, was under water; one million were left homeless; and the death toll exceeded 1,800. Army troops delivered sandbags, shovels, helicopters, and amphibious trucks (DUKWs). Relief operations by USAREUR included providing food and clothing for the homeless. Army engineers demolished a World War II German bunker that caused erosion of sea walls. The 12th Air Rescue Group at Bordeaux AB, commanded by Col Robert L. Rizon, flew SA-16 Albatrosses and C-47 Skytrains to drop supplies to the flood victims and dike repair workers. USAFE airlifted 7½ tons of supplies from Périgueux QM Depot.[164, 165]

In July 1954, the Danube River flooded in Germany and Austria killing twenty-seven people and leaving 70,000 homeless. The 12th Air Rescue Group from Bordeaux AB flew C-47 Skytrains to deliver 22 tons of emergency supplies to the victims. US Army H-19 Chickasaw helicopters plucked stranded victims from roofs. An Army pilot from the 58th Medical Det, noticing that one of his rescued passengers looked familiar, asked: "Didn't I bring you out a few hours ago?" The man replied: "Yes, I enjoy riding in a helicopter so I went back by rowboat."[166]

C-119 Flying Boxcars,
Toul-Rosières AB, 1954 (US Air Force)

C-119 Flying Boxcar, Déols (NARA)

In August and September 1954, four C-119 Flying Boxcars of the 465th TCW from Toul-Rosières AB flew 21 tons of supplies to Karachi, Pakistan, and New Deli, India, when 36,000 sq mi of land were covered by flood waters.[167] In September 1954, when thousands of Algerians were homeless from earthquakes, the 465thTCW airlifted 28 tons of tents, blankets, and other needed supplies to Algeria.[168]

In late August 1955, a hailstorm struck Lyon, France. The Air Force delivered canvas tarps for temporary roof coverings at damaged factories. A Flying Boxcar delivered 40,000 sq ft of tarp, and trucks delivered another 60,000 sq ft from Air Force depots at Moulins and Châteauroux.[169]

At Dreux AB, the 60th Troop Carrier Wing, commanded by Col Clyde Box, routinely transported personnel and dependents to hospitals, delivered medicine and supplies to disaster areas, and airdropped US Army and NATO troops. During a 1955 blizzard, they delivered 350 tons of supplies to Italian villagers (Operation SNOWBOUND). In November 1955, they evacuated four-hundred eighty Allied civilians from Tel Aviv, Israel to Athens, Greece. The same month, they delivered 139 tons of Red Cross supplies for Hungarian refugees to Vienna, Austria.[170]

On 04 December 1959, after five days of very heavy rain, the Malpasset Dam, near Fréjus on the French Riviera, burst killing five-hundred and leaving thousands homeless. The Air Force delivered 2 tons of blankets, rations, fresh milk, and boots for two-hundred rescue workers.[171] GIs in ComZ contributed $10,000 to aid the homeless. To raise funds for the survivors, the Châteauroux AD Sabres basketball team played exhibition games with French teams at Tours, Châteauroux, and Montluçon.[172, 173]

Although he was not wealthy, President de Gaulle sent a personal donation of five million francs to aid survivors.[174] One young woman asked de Gaulle to allow her to marry her fiancé, who had drowned. In response to the tragedy, the French Parliament passed the "post-mortem matrimony law," which permitted marriage to a dead person.

In February 1962, North Sea tidal waves and hurricane-force winds pounded the north coast of Germany, leaving hundreds dead and over 400,000 homeless. Army installations and depots in France provided more than 50,000 blankets, 5,000 sets of winter clothing, mattresses, food, and medicine.[175] Eight C-130 Hercules aircraft from Évreux AB delivered these supplies from Army depots to Germany. Army engineers repaired roads and buildings in Hamburg.[176]

In early January 1963, floods isolated large areas of the Moroccan coastal plain. A dozen kitchen tents, sixty immersion heaters, and 2,000 blankets were airlifted by USAFE to Rabat, Morocco. Army depots at Ingrandes and Chinon supplied 1,200 tents, thirty field cooking ranges, 5,000 lbs of soap, and 35,000 "B" rations, containing no pork in deference to the Muslim population of Morocco. Two dozen Army personnel, mostly cooks, from ComZ depots were flown from Châteauroux AD.[177]

US Air Force Troop Carrier Wings (TCW) in France[178]

Wing Commander	Period of Service	Wing Commander	Period of Service
60th TCW (Dreux AB)		465th TCW (Toul-Rosières AB)*	
Col Clyde Box	Aug 55-Feb 56	Brig Gen Franklin Rose	Aug 53-May 54
Col Randolph E. Churchill	May 56-July 58	Col Earl W. Worley	May 54-July 56
Col James W. Ingram	July 58-Sep 58	Col James A. Evans	July 56-Aug 56
317th TCW (Évreux AB)		Col Robert D. Forman	Aug 56-July 57
Col Robert D. Forman	July 57-Sep 58	513th TCW (Évreux AB)	
Col John B. Wallace	Sep 58	Col Harold G. Fulmer	Apr 66-July 66
Col Arthur C. Rush	Apr 63-June 63		
Col George W. Kinney	June 63-Dec 65		

*Wing moved to Évreux AB in April 1955.

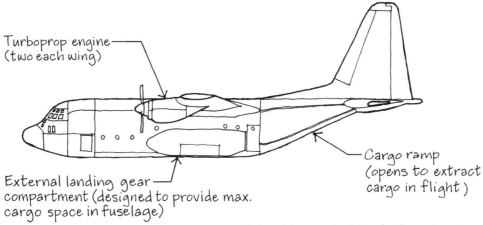

C-130E Hercules

Humanitarian Airlift Operations (USAFE in France, 1953-1966)[179]

Emergency	Location	Date	Unit (Air Base)	Delivery	Aircraft Used
Flood (>1,800 died)	The Netherlands (>1,000 sq mi)	02-17 Feb 1953	81st, 82nd, and 83rd Air Rescue Squadrons (Bordeaux AB)	Medical supplies, rations, clothing, and sandbags	C-47 Skytrain (twin-engine propeller) SA-16 Albatross (amphibious, twin-engine propeller)
Flood (70,000 homeless)	Germany and Austria (Danube River)	08-15 Jul 1954	81st, 83rd, and 84th Air Rescue Squadrons (Bordeaux AB)	Medical supplies, rations, clothing, and sandbags (22 tons)	C-47
Flood (10 million homeless)	Pakistan (Karachi) and India (New Deli)	Aug and Sep 1954	465th TCW (Toul-Rosières AB)	Red Cross supplies from Geneva, Switzerland (21 tons)	C-119 Flying Boxcar (twin-engine propeller)
Flood	Turkey	11-21 Mar 1956	465th TCW (Évreux AB) 60th TCW (Dreux AB)	Food, clothing, blankets, and tents (205 tons)	C-119
Flood (dam collapse)	France (Fréjus)	Dec 1959	322nd Airlift Div (Dreux AB)	Blankets, boots, C-rations, and fresh milk (2 tons)	C-119
Flood (and famine)	Kenya	Nov and Dec 1961	39th and 40th TCS (Évreux AB)	Corn (31½ tons)	C-130 Hercules (four-engine turboprop)
Flood	Somalia	Nov 1961-Jan 1962	40th and 41st TCS (Évreux AB)	Food and medical supplies (259 tons)	C-130
Flood, tidal waves (400,000 homeless)	Germany (Hamburg)	18-20 Feb 1962	322nd Airlift Div (Évreux AB)	Blankets, winter clothing, food, and medical supplies (117 tons)	C-130
Flood	Tunisia (Gabes)	11 Dec 1962	322nd Airlift Div (Châteauroux AD)	Blankets (2,000)	C-130
Flood	Morocco (Rharb Valley)	09-15 Jan 1963	322nd Airlift Div (Châteauroux AD)	Food (no pork), field kitchens, tents, blankets, clothing, and medical supplies (370 tons)	C-130 C-124 Globemaster II (four-engine propeller)
Flood (45,000 homeless)	Yugoslavia (Zagreb)	29 Oct-14 Nov 1964	322nd Airlift Div (Châteauroux AD and TRAB) 41st TCS (Évreux AB)	Blankets, sheets, cots, mattresses, medical supplies, and children's clothing (169 tons)	C-124 C-130
Flood (16,000 homeless)	Tunisia (Zarzis)	07 Jan 1965	322nd Airlift Div (Évreux AB)	Blankets and sleeping bags (10 tons)	C-130

Earthquake (30,000 homeless)	Algeria (Orléansville)	11-17 Sep 1954	465th TCW (Toul-Rosières AB)	Tents, blankets, and equipment (28 tons)	C-119
Earthquake	Iran (Zagros Mountains)	19 Dec 1957	322nd Airlift Div (Évreux AB)	Tents (20 tons)	C-119 C-124
Earthquake (>70,000 homeless)	Iran (west of Tehran)	03 Sep-12 Nov 1962	322nd Airlift Div (Évreux AB and Châteauroux AD)	Field hospital, tents, blankets, rations, medical supplies (901 tons)	C-130 C-124
Earthquake (>100,000 homeless)	Yugoslavia (Skopje)	27 Jul-08 Aug 1963	MATS (Châteauroux AD)	Tents, blankets, and medical supplies (84 tons)	C-124 C-135 Stratolifter (four-engine jet)
Cyclones (>100,000 homeless)	Pakistan, East	03-14 Nov 1960	40th and 41st TCS (Évreux AB)	Tents, blankets, medical supplies, vitamin pills, water purification powder (77 tons)	C-130
Hailstorm	France (Lyon)	31 Aug 1955	322nd Airlift Div (Bordeaux AB)	Canvas tarpaulins (40,000 sq ft)	C-119
Freezing Temperatures	Jordan	04-05 Feb 1961	1602nd ATW (Châteauroux AD)	Blankets (14 tons)	C-124
Locust Plague	Tunisia	27-30 Jun 1957	465th TCW (Évreux AB)	Insecticide and spraying equipment (224 tons)	C-119
Locust Plague	Morocco	22-24 Nov 1957	322nd Airlift Div and 317th TCW (Évreux AB)	Insecticide as powder and 55-gal drums of liquid (61 tons)	C-119 C-130
Cholera Epidemic	Sudan	05-06 Apr 1966	347th TCS (Évreux AB)	Cholera vaccine and medical supplies (16 tons)	C-130
Famine (700,000 starving)	Somalia	31 Dec 1964-13 Jan 1965	322nd Airlift Div (Évreux AB)	Grain sorghum (100 tons)	C-130
Drought	Ghana	29-30 Mar 1966	322nd Airlift Div (Évreux AB)	Evaporated milk (25 tons)	C-130
Hungarian Revolution Refugees	Austria, Switzerland, and West Germany (refugee centers)	Nov-Dec 1956	60th TCW (Dreux AB) 465th TCW (Évreux AB)	Medical supplies, food, blankets, and cots (189 tons)	C-119
Civil War Refugees	Congo (Leopoldville)	15 Jul-03 Oct 1960	1602nd ATW (Châteauroux AD) 322nd Airlift Div (Évreux AB)	Food (1,074 tons) and evacuated refugees (2,640)	C-124 C-130

Abbreviations:

AB	Air Base	C	Cargo Aircraft	TCS	Troop Carrier Squadron
AD	Air Depot (or Airlift Division)	MATS	Military Air Transport Service	TCW	Troop Carrier Wing
ATW	Air Transport Wing	SA	Search and rescue aircraft	TRAB	Toul-Rosières AB

Impact of Withdrawal on French Economy

The Cold War buildup in rural France linked post-World War II economic prosperity to the American presence. In addition to the huge construction program in the 1950s, which was by French contractors using French building materials, the depots and air bases employed a large workforce of French nationals (LWRs). For example, in 1958 the US military paid the French government $35 million for LWR wages.[180]

In 1958, 10% of the population of Orléans was American, 20% of Verdun.[181] In Orléans, the US Army grew to be the second largest employer in the department of the Loiret. In villages close to installations, many service jobs were generated at bars, restaurants, beauty and barber shops, auto repair garages, and small specialty food stores (*boulangeries* for bread, *boucheries* for meat). Americans living on the economy paid numerous taxes including the *contribution mobiliere* levied on occupants of dwellings to benefit municipalities and departments. By the early 1960s, it was estimated that US forces spent $150 million annually in France. At Châteauroux, nearly 60% of the local economy depended on the depot. More than 3,000 French worked at Déols and la Martinerie, many earning wages as much as 30% more than they could from comparable jobs in the French economy.[182]

In June 1966, the French government declared Châteauroux, Ingrandes, Orléans, Toul, and Verdun to be "critical employment zones," which meant that special economic advantages and support, such as government loans, would be offered to industries that would locate in these areas.[183] In March 1967, Brig Gen Charles C. Case, Chief of S&MA at Maison-Fort, sent a handwritten letter to the Préfet du Loiret Pierre Dupuch in response to his offer to do anything he could to help the departing Americans. Case's only request was that he hoped Dupuch would look after the more than eight-hundred sixty French LWRs who worked for the S&MA. Case wrote that the LWRs as a group were "loyal, diligent, and faithful" and expressed concern about their future after the Americans departed. Most were loyal to the end. By working long and hard to help the Americans leave, the LWRs would no longer have jobs.[184, 185]

It took years for some of the cadre to find employment comparable to their jobs for the Americans. A former translator for the US Army Port Area Command had to support his family by selling crêpes at the Place de Verdun in La Rochelle. In nearby Rochefort, Mme Henriette Bibaud, heroine of the NODEX aerial tramway exercises at Talmont, applied her fifteen years of experience with the French *Intendant Militaire*, serving the US Army at Rochefort and Braconne, to her job as administrator for a newly formed regional health-care organization in the Charente-Maritime.[186]

Disposal of US Installations

During 1956 to 1965, the US Army had returned to the French twenty-seven installations without asking for payment to cover the value of improvements and structures built on the properties. In 1967, US Senator Ernest Gruening of Alaska wondered why France now would negotiate payment for the installations, valued at $1 billion, to be closed during FRELOC.[187] As a small bargaining chip during FRELOC negotiations, the US Army withheld payment of $7½ million owed to French contractors.[188]

The Military Liquidation Section (MLS), attached to the American Embassy in Paris, was established in February 1967 to negotiate sales of US buildings, guard installations not yet turned over to the French, and dispose of American property remaining in France. The MLS grew to more than 1,000 personnel by June 1967.[189] Brig Gen Raymond J. Harvey was recalled from retired status to head the MLS in Paris. US European Command believed that Harvey's calm demeanor would not create waves and, hopefully, relations with France would be relatively cordial.[190]

By 01 April 1967, one-hundred nine US bases, facilities, and installations had been released to the government of France or private owners. Use of the Donges-Metz pipeline and its facilities had been negotiated by separate agreement signed with France on 24 March 1967. The US retained ownership of the pipeline system which would be operated by French commercial firms. However, during wartime its use was subject to approval by France. The MLS still had to dispose of three-hundred thirty bases, facilities, and installations.[191]

During early 1943 to May 1946, the US had rearmed the French military forces. All items delivered to the French were charged to the French lend-lease account that was to be repaid at 2% interest.[192] Sales of surplus military property to France in 1946 had been negotiated at 24¢ on the dollar of estimated original cost. The MLS would not be able to come close to this figure. For example, the US received less than 5¢ on the dollar for housing trailer sales and less than 10¢ on the dollar of the construction costs for the modern 1,000-bed standby hospitals. The US had invested $21 million at Dreux Air Base and $10 million at Chinon Depot. France offered $820 for Dreux; $3,061 for Chinon.[193] At first these offers seemed ridiculously low, but in many cases the French were being asked to pay for installations they could not use. Some Army installations, like the dependents school at St.-Cloud, could be used by the civilian sector and some air bases could be used by the French military. However, many installations were in rural areas and would require enormous expense to return them to their original condition or to renovate them for use by civilians. The French negotiators called this "negative residual value."

In August 1966, the US Foreign Excess Sales Office at 32, rue Marbeuf, Paris sold 107,631 jerry cans from Donges, Nancy, Rochefort, and Toul for 29,060 francs, about 25¢ each can. Acquisition cost to the US government was about $2.26 per can.[194] The Air Force purchased privately owned trailers for $1,800 each and sold them to the French for $90 per trailer. MLS negotiators, who settled most transactions for less than 10¢ on the dollar, may have used a target based on the 10¢ on the dollar received in World War II for disposal of matériel considered to be scrap. In the 1920s the investors Carlo Ponzi swindled out of millions did better, receiving about 30¢ on the dollar.[195]

Lemnitzer and de Gaulle

Gen Lyman L. Lemnitzer greatly admired de Gaulle and was fond of the French people. His deputy commander, Gen David A. Burchinal, also regretted leaving France. Both generals loved to play golf, but Burchinal had an advantage due to location. He was an honorary member of the St.-Cloud Golf Course, just beyond the back gate of his official quarters.[196]

Lemnitzer was instrumental in obtaining Allied agreement on the controversial Kennedy-McNamara nuclear defense policy of "flexible response" and, without rancor, oversaw the move of SHAPE from Marly-le-Roi to Casteau, Belgium.[197] Although Franco-American relations were strained during this period, Lemnitzer and de Gaulle remained good friends.[198] De Gaulle held in high esteem (*très grande estime*) Eisenhower, Norstad, and Lemnitzer, whom he believed had aided France during

Gen Lemnitzer receives Grand Cross of Legion of Honor from President de Gaulle, Les Invalides, Paris, 16 March 1967 (SHAPE)

World War II. He considered Ike to be a glorious symbol of Franco-American brotherhood in arms.[199] On the morning of 16 March 1967 in the courtyard of Les Invalides in Paris, de Gaulle presented Lemnitzer with the Grand Cross of the Legion of Honor. The award was the highest rank which could be conferred on a person who was not a head of state.[200] De Gaulle, wearing his Général de brigade uniform, gave all military commands during the presentation. After the ceremony, Lemnitzer had lunch with de Gaulle at the Élysée Palace. The meal lasted more than two hours.

Letters to Lemnitzer

During January to March 1967, Lemnitzer received hundreds of letters from French citizens expressing sorrow that the US military forces were leaving. A French woman wrote: "Permit an elderly Parisian of 73 years of age to tell you of all the pain that I feel to see you leave our country." A French man wrote: "Thinking of all the sacrifices that US families have done by giving their children to save my country, I share their pain and cry with them." Another wrote: "You must know that a French man, among so many others, sees you leaving France with a broken heart." A letter from St.-Germain-en-Laye was signed by twenty-four French with *notre affection*. It began in English, "We are several French people (among these four communists) who want here to say goodbye—a sad goodbye and thank you—never we will forget what you did for us." [201]

If Les Ricains Had Not Come

In 1967, twenty-year-old French singer Michel Sardou wrote and recorded a song of tribute to the departing Americans (called *Ricains* for short). The song, "Les Ricains," reminded French people that if Americans had not come, France would be a part of Germany and they would be speaking German and saluting Germans. Sardou sang that the French should not forget that the Americans who came were strangers to France. Sardou ends sadly with the observation that the troops asked to leave France would believe Americans who were buried in Normandy had died in vain.[202] French radio stations were unable to play "Les Ricains" because songs critical of government policy were not permitted.[203]

Sardou was not alone. At Caserne Coligny in Orléans, an anonymous Frenchman placed a mimeographed letter on the windshields of cars with 2CF plates. The letter, which was marked at the top "I am a Frenchman," expressed regret that the Americans were leaving. It said in part: "Dear American Friend, You must know that there are many Frenchmen and many citizens of Orléans who are devoted to you, who have not forgotten past comradeship in arms, or how much they owe you. Be assured that you will always be remembered." [204]

American troops had been ordered to be "neither angry nor joyful" at being evicted. They were to be "quietly regretful." Most non-communist local officials and people living near the bases were saddened their American friends were leaving.[205] On 16 August 1966 at the 22nd anniversary of the liberation of Orléans, Mayor Roger Secrétan said friendship between men remained unfailing despite vicissitudes of national politics.[206] Many cities and villages had goodbye parties where locals apologized for the policy of the French government.

In January 1967, Sp5 Johst A. Burk rode in an Army bus from Caserne Lariboisière at Fontainebleau to Orly Airport for his MATS flight home to the US. Near Orly, the bus went under an overpass that had U.S. GO HOME painted in bold letters on the side wall. Burk, who was seated near the LWR driver, could see that the elderly Frenchman was upset. The Frenchman apologized for the sign and told Burk that most French people were grateful for being liberated by the US.[207]

Ongoing Military Cooperation

Although France withdrew from the military structure of NATO, France still contributed to the defense of Europe by keeping troops in Germany. In 1967, France had more than 75,000 army and air force personnel in Germany.[208] In June 1966, the US Army 53rd Trans Bn with MP escorts moved all nuclear warheads from six French Army sites in southern Germany to three US Army depots. During icy November and snowy December 1966, the 28th Trans Bn moved all missiles, tow-away launchers, and related equipment. The relocation of nuclear warheads was nicknamed FASTDRAW; relocation of missiles was called ZIP. The French troops now would be solely conventional forces.[209]

Because de Gaulle did not renounce the North Atlantic Treaty, France still would be protected by Article 5 of the Treaty that stated an armed attack against one nation would be considered to be an attack against all NATO nations. For security from air attack, NATO granted France continuing access to the NATO Air Defense Ground Environment (NADGE) system and the Allied Command Europe communications system (ACE HIGH). ACE HIGH, which extended from Norway through central Europe to Turkey, had several long-range radio transmission stations in France.[210, 211] NADGE, installed in Europe during 1960 to 1963, was a computer-coordinated network of high-performance, early warning radar stations to identify hostile aircraft and missiles.[212] Data from the NADGE network of radar stations and its American computers were linked to French computers at the air defense center at Drachenbronn (Vosges), located about three miles from the German border at Wissembourg. Warnings of an enemy air attack automatically would be provided to France. Continuing access to NADGE was granted after de Gaulle lifted the restrictions imposed on the use of French airspace. In November 1966, France agreed to resume permitting overflights of NATO military aircraft, subject to an annual review. Before the restrictions, overflights had been virtually automatic.[213] In 1965, NATO aircraft made more than 200,000 overflights, nearly half of all air traffic over France. During the same period, French military aircraft overflew other NATO nations fewer than 3,000 times.[214]

French Chief of Staff General Charles Ailleret and NATO Supreme Commander General Lyman Lemnitzer signed a top-secret accord in 1967. The agreement included provisions that, should the Soviets use nuclear weapons, Honest John rockets and nuclear warheads would be returned to the French Army or US Army nuclear artillery units would be assigned to support French forces.[215] After 1967, the NATO allies still believed they could withdraw forces to France, after absorbing a Soviet attack in Germany.[216] The US Army quietly continued to use the Donges-Metz pipeline, an undisclosed operation not even discussed during NATO meetings on the NATO pipeline networks in France.[217]

During the early 1980s, the French designated hospitals for the US to use during wartime.[218] US Army's Medical Service Corps considered using depots at Vitry-le-François and Orléans to covertly store medical supplies in containers with French markings on the outside. Cooperation was now possible due to the friendship between US President Ronald Reagan's Secretary of Defense Caspar W. Weinberger and French Defense Minister Charles Hernu.[219]

France remained on NATOs Air Defense Committee, the Central Europe Pipeline System at Versailles, the Maintenance and Supply Agency (NAMSA), and the Hawk Missile Production and Logistics Organization at Rueil-Malmaison. In 1968, NAMSA and the NATO Supply Center at Châteauroux moved to Luxembourg.[220] France also remained in LIVE OAK, which moved to Mons, Belgium. After thirty-one years, LIVE OAK which had been formed to plan the defense of West Berlin ceased operations on 03 October 1990, the official day of the reunification of Germany.[221]

Closing Ceremonies

In January 1967, ComZ dropped two-hundred French flags from accountability. This enabled the flags to be given to French officials during closing ceremonies or be kept as souvenirs by departing commanders. The ceremony to close ComZ headquarters at Caserne Coligny in Orléans was held on 31 March 1967, when the French and American flags were lowered for the last time. The American flag was to be taken by train to Taukkunen Kaserne in Worms, Germany. The streets from Coligny to the train station at Fleury-les-Aubrais were lined six to ten deep by French citizens waving goodbye with small American flags. The special train, carrying the flag and ComZ headquarters staff who had worked seven days a week for months, was timed to cross the French-German border exactly at midnight.[222]

L to R (front row): Gen Lemnitzer, French Gen Dio, and Gen Burchinal
at closing ceremonies, Camp des Loges, 14 March 1967 (NDU Archives)

On 14 March 1967, more than 600 attended closing ceremonies at US European Command headquarters in Camp des Loges. According to US Ambassador Charles E. Bohlen, French generals attending the ceremony wept as the French and American flags were lowered for the last time.[223] The flags were huge "holiday flags" which measured 38 ft by 20 ft. At the end of the ceremony, the 76th Army Band from Orléans played "Till We Meet Again." [224] The folded French flag was given to General Louis Joseph Marie Dio, who was representing France. Dio's aides put the flag on the back seat of his Citröen. Gen David A. Burchinal took the folded American flag to his Army helicopter to symbolically fly it to Patch Barracks in Stuttgart, Germany. Actually, the helicopter circled St.-Germain-en-Laye until the crowd had departed and then landed back at the Camp des Loges helipad. Burchinal flew from Évreux AB to Germany on a T-39 Sabreliner five-passenger, turbojet aircraft.[225, 226]

On 30 March 1967, more than 2,000 attended closing ceremonies at SHAPE headquarters in Marly-le-Roi. Général d'Armée Charles Ailleret, Chief of Staff of the French Armed Forces, and Gen Lemnitzer made brief statements before the fifteen flags were lowered for the last time in France. Ailleret recalled the "dark days" when SHAPE was established in 1951 and the good feelings between French and Allied personnel during SHAPE's sixteen years in France. Lemnitzer ended by declaring that "we shall not forget this wonderful experience of living in this beautiful country." [227] As the

Flags lowered for final time, Camp des Loges, 14 March 1967 (NDU Archives)

Troops folding American flag, Camp des Loges, 14 March 1967 (NDU Archives)

Gen David A. Burchinal departs by helicopter, 14 March 1967 (NDU Archives)

crowd dispersed, the "cheeky" band of the Royal Armoured Corps (UK) played the Scottish ballad "Charlie He's My Darling."[228, 229]

Not all closings were ceremonial. On the afternoon of 31 March 1967 at S&MA computer facility at Caserne Maginot, Capt Basil J. Hobar helped his men sweep the floors and take out the trash before locking the doors for the final time. Although the storage drums, magnetic tape disks, and punch cards had been transported to Germany, Hobar's IBM mainframe computers sat idle in Verdun until they were retrieved several weeks after the officially announced withdrawal date.[230, 231]

First Lt Robert A. Hefferman, Commanding Officer of the 77th Trans Co from Ingrandes, rode "shotgun" on the last FRELOC truck out of France. Hefferman and driver Sp5 Shannon Wilson crossed the French-German border two minutes after midnight on 31 March 1967. French villagers along the route had saluted the convoy with the familiar "V for victory" sign used to greet the GI liberators of France two decades earlier.[232] The permanent presence of US military forces in France had ended.

CHRONOLOGY
US Army & US Air Force in France (1949 to 1968)

BUILDUP (Army troop levels grew from 2,100 in 1950 to more than 13,000 at end of 1951)

Year	Significant Events	Crises, Conflicts, Responses	Humanitarian Operations
1949	North Atlantic Treaty Organization (NATO) documents signed (04 Apr) Col O'Meara moves ammo and POL from Germany to France (Dec) Col Young begins negotiations on LOC (Dec)	Soviets explode atomic bomb (Aug) Berlin Airlift ends (Sep)	
1950	LOC Agreement signed by US and France (06 Nov) Tech Service troops enter France from Germany (Nov)	North Korea invades South Korea (24 June) PCF protests US forces in France	
1951	Buildup under austere conditions at French casernes and depots Status of Forces Agreement (SOFA) signed by US and France (June) Agreement signed by USAFE and French Air Force to construct sixteen US installations in France (31 Oct)	US provides military aid for French forces in Indochina (May 50 to June 54) Auriol promises ten French Army divisions to NATO (July)	
1952	Troops begin move into prefabs First supply over the beach exercise (SOB) at le Verdon-sur-Mer (June)	Aircrews from Bordeaux AB and Laon AB sent TDY to Korea (Project 7019)	
1953	Joint Construction Agency (JCA) begins operations European Command begins move from Germany to Paris area Racial integration of ComZ troops nears completion	East Berlin workers riot in protest of Soviet domination (June) Korean War armistice signed (22 July) Soviets explode thermo-nuclear device *Sloika* (Aug)	Netherlands flood (Feb) Air Rescue Squadrons from Bordeaux AB, supplies from Périgueux QM Depot
1954	Twenty ComZ depots operational ComZ to provide staging area camps for NEO evacuees First evaluation of dual-based concept, squadrons based in US and at Chaumont and Évreux ABs USAFE opens office in Paris	Indochina War ends (June) Algerian War begins (Nov) Year of maximum danger for Soviet invasion, per NSC 68 warning (estimate extended to 1957 by Gen Gruenther)	Floods in Pakistan and India (Aug-Sep) Earthquake in Algeria (Sep) Aircraft from Toul-Rosières AB
1955	Atomic-capable aircraft deploy JCA completes chain of forty microwave transmitter stations across France for USAFE	Massacre by FLN guerrillas at Phillipeville, Algeria (20 Aug)	Hailstorm at Lyon (Aug), tarps from Périgueux QM Depot
1956	NATO air bases (MOBs) completed Donges-Metz pipeline begins initial operations	Suez Crisis (US does not support France and UK, ignores Khrushchev's threat to bomb Paris) Hungarian Revolution (Oct-Nov)	Ice isolates Île de Ré (Feb), food and fuel from La Rochelle Installation Airlift of Hungarian refugees begins (Operation SAFE HAVEN)

CONSOLIDATION (more than 110,000 US military, civilians, and dependents at peak in 1961-1962)

Year	Significant Events	Crises, Conflicts, Responses	Humanitarian Operations
1957	First RORO vessel docks at St.-Nazaire (Feb) Technical Service Chiefs complete move from Heidelberg, Germany to Orléans	Soviets launch *Sputnik*, first satellite (Oct)	Locust plague in Tunisia (Jun) Aircraft from Évreux AB Earthquake in Iran (Dec) Aircraft from Évreux AB
1958	Nine standby hospitals completed De Gaulle returns to power (May) ComZ depot stocks dispersed so combat essential items of each Tech Service are stored in at least four widely separated locations Offshore discharge exercises halted, 21 emergency sites selected along coast of France	Lebanon civil war sealift and airlift (Operation BLUE BAT) Victor Alerts begin (Oct) Khrushchev threatens Allies on access to Berlin (Nov)	Flood at Nancy (Feb) Amphibious DUKWs from Nancy Depot
1959	Dispersed operating bases (DOBs) inactivated by USAFE at Brienne, Châlons, Chenevières, and Vouziers 7,300 housing units completed Atomic-capable aircraft withdrawn (Project RED RICHARD)	Norstad forms top secret LIVE OAK staff at Camp des Loges to plan defense of Berlin (Feb) De Gaulle withdraws French Mediterranean fleet from NATO (Mar)	Drought in France, ComZ troops deliver water and fight forest fires (July) Dam bursts at Fréjus (Dec) Aircraft from Dreux AB
1960	Offshore discharge exercises resume due to Berlin Crisis ComZ Tech Service staffs return from Germany to Orléans Army engineers build ten off-depot storage sites to disperse stocks	U-2 aircraft shot down over USSR (01 May) Khrushchev walks out of Paris Summit meeting (de Gaulle supports Ike)	Evacuation of refugees, Leopoldville (Jul-Oct) Aircraft from Châteauroux AD and Évreux AB
1961	Atomic blast-resistant storage structures built at Vatry, Rozelier, and Aboncourt ANG wings deploy from US to six air bases in France (Operation STAIR STEP)	France prepared to resist army *coup* from Algeria (Apr) Berlin Wall built by East Germany (Aug) Soviets break 1958 nuclear testing moratorium (Aug) Belgium Congo (Operation NEW TAPE)	SNCF train wreck near Vitry-le-François (18 June) Helicopters from Rozelier Air Field TFAD and Vitry Depot troops donate blood
1962	USAREUR combat units augmented (Operation ROUNDOUT) ComZ completes pre-positioning of supplies at Toul and Nancy for two Army divisions	Algerian War ends (Mar) Morale restored in Berlin, Gen Clay departs after eight months (May) Cuban Missile Crisis (Oct)	Tidal wave at Hamburg, Germany (Feb) Earthquake in Iran (Sep-Nov) Aircraft from Châteauroux AD and Évreux AB

DRAWDOWN AND WITHDRAWAL (from 70,000 in May 1966 to 6,000 in April 1967)

Year	Significant Events	Crises, Conflicts, Responses	Humanitarian Operations
1963	Offshore discharge exercises end McNamara orders drawdown of Base Section, fires 6,200 LWRs 2nd Armored Div airlifted from Texas to Europe (Operation BIG LIFT) ComZ forms S&MA at Orléans	South Vietnam President Diem murdered during *coup d'etat* (Nov)	Flood in Morocco (Jan) Aircraft from Châteauroux AD, supplies from Chinon and Ingrandes Depots Earthquake aid to Libya, Yugoslavia, and Iran
1964	S&MA data processing center opens at Verdun (Dec)	Air power buildup in Vietnam reduces USAFE forces (Project CLEARWATER) Khrushchev removed from power (Oct)	Famine relief supplies to Somalia (Dec 64-Jan 65) Aircraft from Évreux AB
1965	Final French nuclear test in Algerian Sahara (Feb) Phantom jet reconnaissance aircraft sent to Toul-Rosières AB (July)	Gulf of Tonkin resolution by US Congress (07 Aug) US intervention in the Dominican Republic (Operation POWER PACK)	Flood in Tunisia (Jan) Aircraft from Évreux AB
1966	Fast withdrawal of troops and base closures begin (Operation FRELOC)	Buildup of US forces in Vietnam weakens combat readiness in Europe	Drought in Ghana (Mar) Cholera epidemic in Sudan (Apr) Aircraft from Évreux AB
1967	Military Liquidation Section (MLS) locates at US Embassy in Paris Fast withdrawal completed (01 Apr) Suippes Gunnery Air Range released to MLS by USAFE (Oct)	Recovery of lost nuclear bombs ("broken arrow") near Palomares, Spain Helicopters from Chambley AB	Earthquake in Turkey (July) Medical supplies from relocated ComZ depots
1968	MLS continues return of installations to France (closes in 1970)	Secret peace talks begin in Paris between US and North Vietnam	

Abbreviations

AB	Air Base	PCF	*Parti Communiste Français* (French Communist Party)
AD	Air Depot		
ANG	Air National Guard	POL	Petroleum, oil, lubricants
ComZ	Communications Zone	RORO	Roll-on, Roll-off cargo ship
FLN	*Front de Libération Nationale* (Algeria)	S&MA	Supply and Maintenance Agency
LOC	Line of communications	SNCF	*Société nationale des chemins de fer français* (French national railroad)
LWR	Local Wage Rate (French employee)		
MOB	Main Operating Base	TDY	Temporary duty
NEO	Noncombatant evacuation order	TFAD	Trois Fontaines Ammo Depot
NSC 68	US State Dept report to President Truman (07 April 1950)	USAFE	US Air Forces in Europe
		USAREUR	US Army, Europe

REFERENCES/NOTES

Abbreviations

AD	Archives départementales, France. Archive number: Bar-le-Duc 55, Bordeaux 33, Dammarie-les-Lys 77, Évreux 27, La Rochelle 17, La Roche-sur-Yon 85, Orléans 45, and Poitiers 86
AFHRA	Air Force Historical Research Agency, Maxwell AFB, AL
AFHSO	Air Force Historical Studies Office, Bolling AFB, DC
CAC	Centre des archives contemporaines, Fontainebleau, France
CEHO	US Army Corps of Engineers History Office, Fort Belvoir, VA
CMH	US Army Center of Military History, Fort McNair, DC
Det	Detachment
Fr	French language document
MHI	US Army Military History Institute, Carlisle, PA
NARA	National Archives and Records Administration, College Park, MD
NDU	National Defense University Archives, Fort McNair, DC
SHD	Service historique de la Défense, République Française, Château de Vincennes, Vincennes, France
TC	US Army Transportation Corps School Library, Fort Lee, VA
USAFA	Clark Special Collections, McDermott Library, US Air Force Academy, Colorado Springs, CO

Troop Information Newspapers

MHI, Carlisle, PA, has eight years of The Advance; USAFA, Colorado Springs, CO, two years of Jet-48; Archives départementales de la Charente-Maritime (AD 17), La Rochelle, France, four years of Basec Mission; Médiathèque municipale de Orléans, France, three years of ComZ Cadence and six years of Orleans Item; Archives départementales du Loriet (AD 45), Orléans, France, five years of ComZ Cadence and four years of Orleans Item; and Archives départementales de l'Eure (AD 27), Évreux, France, three years of Skyliner, one year of Combat Cargo, and one year of Evreux Image.

Sources for Lineages of Commanding Officers

Troop information weekly newspapers (primarily The Advance, Basec Mission, ComZ Cadence, and The Pariscope), Panorama (monthly newspaper for French employees), The Stars and Stripes (daily), U.S. Lady (monthly), unit histories, unit rosters, installation telephone directories, Directory of Corps of Engineers Officers and Warrant Officers (yearly), The Register of Graduates (AOG, US Military Academy, West Point, NY), Official Army Register (yearly), and signature block on official documents.

Sources for Installation Tables (mid-1950s to early 1960s)

Directory and Station List of the US Army (bimonthly), The Troop Program of The Army (FY reports), USAFE unit histories (biannually), welcome brochures, troop information newspapers, USEUCOM telephone directory, US Defense Attaché reports, Mission Centrale de Liaison Pour L'Assistance aux Armées Alliées (MCLAAA) real estate lists, and real estate records of US Army Corps of Engineers and US Air Force.

CHAPTER ONE

1. D. C. McKay, <u>The United States and France</u>, Harvard University Press, Cambridge, Massachusetts (1951), p. 308.
2. N. Lambourne, <u>War Damage in Western Europe</u>, Edinburgh University Press, Edinburgh, UK (2001), pp. 63-73.
3. É. Alary et al., <u>Les Français Au Quotidien</u>, Perrin, Paris, France (2006), p. 499. (Fr)
4. M. Blumenson, <u>Breakout and Pursuit</u>, Center of Military History, Washington, DC (1960), pp. 146 and 147.
5. B. S. Gunderson, "Leaflet Dropping Operations in World War II," <u>Air Power History</u>, Spring 1998, pp. 33 and 34.
6. R. T. Wakelam, <u>The Science of Bombing: Operational Research in RAF Bomber Command</u>, University of Toronto Press, Toronto, Canada (2009), p. 23.
7. A. Knapp, <u>Les Francais Sous Les Bombes Alliées 1940-1945</u>, Éditions Tallandier, Paris, France (2014), pp. 19, 62, and 552. (Fr)
8. R. S. Ehlers, <u>Targeting the Third Reich</u>, University Press of Kansas, Lawrence, KS (2009), pp. 227 and 228.
9. S. A. Bourque, "ROUEN: Le Semaine Rouge," <u>Journal of Military and Strategic Studies</u>, Spring/Summer 2012, pp. 2 and 3. [Electronic journal of the University of Calgary, Canada.]
10. S. A. Bourque, "Operational Fires: Lisieux and Saint-Lô—The Destruction of Two Norman Towns on D-Day," <u>Canadian Military History</u>, Spring 2010, pp. 25-40.
11. É. Alary (2006), pp. 509-511. (Fr).
12. J. P. Anderson (ed), "City of Royan is Paradox, French Town That's Modern," <u>Basec Mission</u>, 30 August 1954, p. 2.
13. R. G. Davis, <u>Bombing the European Axis Powers</u>, Air University Press, Montgomery, AL (2006), pp. 8, 27-30, and 499.
14. M. R. Marrus and R. O. Paxton, <u>Vichy France and the Jews</u>, Schocken Books, New York (1983), pp. 315-321.
15. S. Fishman et al., <u>France at War: Vichy and the Historians</u>, Berg Publications, New York (2000), pp. 35-47.
16. Anon, "France Faces Up to Vichy," <u>The Economist</u>, 22 April 2000, pp. 40 and 41.
17. R. O. Paxton, <u>Vichy France</u>, Alfred A. Knopf, New York (1972), p. 183.
18. J. Bacque, <u>Just Raoul: Adventures in The French Resistance</u>, Stoddart Publishing, Toronto, Canada (1990), p. 145.
19. S. Zuccotti, <u>The Holocaust, the French, and the Jews</u>, Basic Books, New York (1993), p. 288.
20. T. J. Laub, <u>After The Fall: German Policy in Occupied France, 1940-1944</u>, Oxford University Press, Oxford, England (2010), pp. 237, 240, and 244.
21. P. W. Whitcomb, <u>France During the German Occupation 1940-1944</u>, Vols. I, II, and III, Stanford University Press, Stanford, CA (1957). M. Seal, "Haunted by History," <u>Smithsonian</u>, April 2019, pp. 46-56, 72, and 74.
22. R. Vinen, <u>The Unfree French</u>, Yale University Press, New Haven, CT (2006), pp. 5 and 368.
23. W. I. Hitchcock, <u>The Struggle for Europe</u>, Doubleday, New York (2003), p. 71.
24. T. H. White, <u>Fire in The Ashes</u>, William Sloane, New York (1953), pp. 95 and 96.
25. D. Cook, <u>Charles DeGaulle</u>, G. P. Putnam's Sons, New York (1983), p. 258.
26. R. Aron, <u>France Reborn: The History of the Liberation</u>, Charles Scribner's Sons, New York (1964), pp. 417-424. Aron gives an account of the summary executions committed after liberation, based in part on records of the Gendarmerie nationale and Ministère de l'Intérieur.
27. P. P. Hallie, <u>Lest Innocent Blood Be Shed</u>, Harper & Row, New York (1979), pp. 244-247.
28. C. Moorehead, <u>Village of Secrets: Defying the Nazis in Vichy France</u>, Chatto & Windus, London, England (2014), pp. 10 and 335-337.
29. J. Bacque (1990), pp. 60, 124, and 125.
30. P. Hellman, <u>Avenue of the Righteous</u>, Atheneum, New York (1980), pp. 109-167.
31. R. K. Smith, "Marston Mat," <u>Air Force Magazine</u>, April 1989, pp. 84-88.
32. D. C. Denfeld, "Marston Mat: American Military Mobility," <u>The Journal of America's Military Past</u>, Fall 2005, pp. 43-56.
33. R. K. Long, <u>A Cook's Tour of World War II</u>, Momentum Books, Ann Arbor, MI (1990), pp. 96-98.
34. D. C. Johnson, "U.S. Army Air Forces Continental Airfields (ETO) D-Day to V-E Day," USAF Historical Research Center, Maxwell Air Force Base, Alabama, 01 December 1988, pp. 5-7 and 9.
35. W. F. Craven and J. L. Cate (eds), <u>The Army Air Forces in World War II</u>, Vol. III, The University of Chicago Press, Chicago, IL (1951), pp. 562-572.
36. R. K. Smith (1989), p. 87.
37. M. Maurer, <u>Air Force Combat Units of World War II</u>, Office of Air Force History, Washington, DC (1961), pp. 159, 191, and 272. In the late 1940s, wings succeeded groups as the primary organizational entity.
38. W. M. Summers (ed), "French Move To Halt Plane Smugglers," <u>The Stars and Stripes</u>, 01 December 1949, p. 4.
39. J. L. Albert and B. C. Wylie, "Problems of Airfield Construction in Korea," in J. T. Stewart (ed), <u>Airpower: The Decisive Force in Korea</u>, Van Nostrand, Princeton, NJ (1957), pp. 234 and 235.
40. D. H. Tulley, "The Military Construction Program", <u>The Military Engineer</u>, November-December 1954, pp. 404-408.

References/Notes to pages 1 to 7

41. J.-B. Duroselle, France and the United States, The University of Chicago Press, Chicago, IL (1978), p. 198.
42. E. F. Ziemke, The U.S. Army in The Occupation of Germany 1944-46, Center of Military History, Washington, DC (1975), p. 327.
43. W. C. Neumann, "Operations of a Prison in PW Enclosures," The Military Police School, Carlisle Barracks, PA, 1948, pp. 1-4.
44. G. G. Lewis and J. Mewha, "History of Prisoner of War Utilization by the United States Army 1776-1945," Department of The Army, Washington, DC, DA Pamphlet No. 20-213, June 1955, p. 234.
45. R. Overmans, "German Historiography, the War Losses, and the Prisoners of War" in G. Bischof and S. E. Ambrose (eds), Eisenhower and the German POWs, Louisiana State University Press, Baton Rouge, LA (1992), p. 145.
46. B. H. Siemon and R. Wagberg, "The Employment of Local Nationals by the US Army in Europe (1945-1966)," Headquarters, US Army, Europe (USAREUR), Heidelberg, Germany, 1968, p. 57.
47. G. MacDonogh, After the Reich, Basic Books, New York (2007), pp. 416-419.
48. R. C. Baldridge, "Crossing the Atlantic on the Queen Mary in Wartime," The Journal of America's Military Past, Spring/Summer 2005, pp. 51-58.
49. J. Bykofsky and H. Larson, The Transportation Corps: Operations Overseas, Center of Military History, Washington, DC (1957), pp. 369-374.
50. J. L. Gaddis, The United States and the Origins of the Cold War 1944-1947, Columbia University Press, New York (1972), pp. 1-3.
51. J. Luns, NATO Facts and Figures, NATO Information Services, Brussels, Belgium (1976), p. 12.
52. P. D. Adler, Overseas Assignment, The Star-Courier Press, Kewanee, IL (1946), pp. 31-33.
53. R. K. Long (1990), pp. 159 and 160.
54. J. C. Sparrow, History of Personnel Demobilization in the US Army, Department of the Army, Washington, DC (1950), pp. 69 and 70.
55. P. S. Kindsvatter, "The 299th: The story of a Maintenance Company in World War II," Ordnance Magazine, Winter 2008, p. 15.
56. R. H. Ferrell, The Eisenhower Diaries, W. W. Norton & Co., New York (1981), p. 134.
57. A. Bower and E. N. Brandt, "Supply Front: The 16th Port Story," US Army Service Forces, ETO, Le Havre, France, September 1945, pp. 39-43. More than 10,000 copies of this 48-page booklet were printed by Imprimerie Industrielle et Financière (IMIFI), Brussels, Belgium as a token of good will toward the American forces. According to Ned Brandt, former 16th Port historian, the US Army gave IMIFI 24 cartons of American cigarettes. A pack of cigarettes that cost 5¢ at the PX sold for $2.50 on the black market.
58. B. W. Fowle, "Reconstruction of Le Havre," in B. W. Fowle (ed), Builders and Fighters: U.S. Army Engineers in World War II, Office of History, US Army Corps of Engineers, Fort Belvoir, VA (1992), pp. 317-326.
59. J. C. Sparrow (1950), pp. 179-181.
60. N. McGrath, "Camp Lucky Strike France," On Point, Winter 2015, pp. 44-47.
61. Anon, "Army and Air Force Installations Outside Continental U.S.," Departments of the Army and the Air Force, Washington, DC, 31 December 1953, pp. 287-289 and 291.
62. M. L. Diamond et al., The 89th Infantry Division 1942-1945, Infantry Journal Press, Washington, DC (1947), pp. 151-157.
63. G. A. Cosmas and A. E. Coudray, Medical Service in the European Theater of Operations, Center of Military History, Washington, DC (1992), p. 597.
64. M. L. Diamond et al. (1947), p. 157.
65. K. Larkins (ed), "It's Over," Smithsonian, August 2005, pp. 52-61.
66. U. Lee, The Employment of Negro Troops, Center of Military History, Washington, DC (1966), pp. 688-691.
67. J. R. Lankford, "Battling Segregation and the Nazis," Army History, Winter 2007, pp. 26-40.
68. A. L. Gropman, The Air Force Integrates, 1945-1964, Office of Air Force History, Washington, DC (1978), p. 50. Chapter 2 covers the 1945 Gillem Board recommendations for limited integration of the Army which were ignored.
69. D. P. Colley, Blood for Dignity, St. Martin's Press, New York (2003), pp. 110 and 111. Chap 8 covers Gen Eisenhower's appeal for black volunteers to the Infantry; Chap 12 covers infantry training camp for blacks in Compiègne, France.
70. J. C. Sparrow (1950), p. 186.
71. Private correspondence to author from Ellis N. Brandt (1st Lt, Public Relations Section, 16th Port, ETO, Le Havre, France, 1944-45), dated 04 February 2002, pp. 2 and 3.
72. Anon, "Army and Air Force Installations Outside Continental U.S.," Departments of the Army and the Air Force, Washington, DC, 31 December 1953, pp. 287-289 and 291.
73. P. D. Adler (1946), p. 63.
74. K. Konold, Backstage in the Big War, Brunswick Publishing, Lawrenceville, VA (1991), pp. 134 and 135. Kristine Konold served on faculty of Fine Arts section at BAU.

References/Notes to pages 7 to 12

75. C. J. Medlin (ed), BAU Beacon, Biarritz, France (1945), pp. 38 and 41. Yearbook produced by BAU students.
76. H. R. Luce (ed), "Contented G.I.s," Time, 19 November 1945, pp. 78 and 79. Article by John Dos Passos.
77. R. M. Smith and L. F. Young, "The History of Biarritz American University," US Army BAU, Biarritz, France, 1946, pp. 120-161. Capt Rhea M. Smith served as BAU historian. [Copy archived at Olin Library, Rollins College, Winter Park, FL.]
78. J. G. Umstattd, BAU in Action, The University of Texas Press, Austin, Texas (1947), pp. 1-16. Book on BAU history and educational methods, compiled by Professor James G. Umstattd and staff of BAU. Umstattd, on leave from The University of Texas, served as Dean and Academic Advisor at BAU.
79. H. J. Obermayer, Soldiering for Freedom, Texas A&M University Press, College Station, TX (2005), pp. 214 and 215.
80. E. Petrus (ed), "Patients From Hospital Entertained by Dietrich," Orleans Item, 11 December 1959, p.2.
81. J. A. Huston, The Sinews of War: Army Logistics 1775-1953, Center of Military History, Washington, DC (1988), pp. 536-538.
82. R. E. Cummings, After Action Report Third US Army, Headquarters, Third United States Army, 15 May 1945, Vol. II, Part 5, p. 43.
83. A. M. Beck et al., The Corps of Engineers: The War Against Germany, Center of Military History, Washington, DC (1985), pp. 405-413 and 455-459.
84. W. D. Trethewey, A History of the 697th Petroleum Distribution Company, self-published, Minneapolis, MN (1989). The 697th built the southern pipeline system in France.
85. J. A. Huston, Outposts and Allies, Associated University Presses, Cranbury, NJ (1988), p. 25.
86. R. A. Wells et al., "U.S. Army Lines of Communications in Europe (1945-1967)," Office of the Deputy Chief of Staff, Operations, US Army, Europe (USAREUR), Heidelberg, Germany, 1968, pp. 12 and 13.
87. E. Steere and T. M. Boardman, Final Disposition of World War II Dead, 1945-51, Historical Branch, Office of the Quartermaster General, Washington, DC (1957), pp. 689 and 690.
88. R. G. Miller, To Save a City: The Berlin Airlift 1948-1949, Air Force History and Museums Program, Washington, DC (1998), p. 17.
89. P. S. Meilinger, American Airpower Biography, Air University Press, Maxwell Air Force Base, AL (1995), pp. 45-49.
90. Interview, author with Gen (ret) Andrew P. O'Meara (Col, Deputy Director of Logistics, Headquarters, European Command, Frankfurt, Germany, 1948-51), Arlington, VA, 29 January 2005.
91. J. J. Shomon, Crosses in The Wind, Stratford House, New York (1947), p. 114.
92. C. McDermott, "The Contributions of American and European Scientists to the War Dead Identification Program in Europe," 72nd Annual Meeting of the Society for Military History, Charleston, SC, 26 February 2005.
93. E. Risch and C. L. Kieffer, The Quartermaster Corps: Organization, Supply, and Services, Vol. II, Center of Military History, Washington, DC (1955), pp. 386-404.
94. C. O. Stanley (ed), "Samec Sergeant Led Searches For Isolated WWII Graves," Orleans Item, 05 August 1955, p. 3.
95. E. Steere and T. M. Boardman (1957), pp. 339 and 356.
96. Letter from Adam Yarmolinsky (Deputy Assistant Secretary of Defense for International Security Affairs) to Ovie C. Fisher (Committee on Armed Services, US House of Representatives), Washington, DC, dated 27 July 1966. Casualty estimates prepared by General Reference Branch, US Army Center of Military History (CMH), Washington, DC. [CEHO]
97. D. W. Holt, American Military Cemeteries, McFarland, Jefferson, NC (1992), p. 447.
98. J. J. Pershing, "Our National War Memorials in Europe," The National Geographic Magazine, January 1934, pp. 1-36.
99. Interview, author with Jean Peckham Kavale (dependent of Brig Gen Howard L. Peckham, Neuilly-sur-Seine, 1948-50), Manteca, CA, 19 April 2013.
100. Interview, author with James E. Murphy (Tech Sgt, 6th Armored Cav, Straubing, Germany, 1948-50), Milton, MA, 29 July 2012. Murphy served at Île St.-Germain in 1947.
101. R. L. Gunnarsson, American Military Police in Europe, 1945-1991, McFarland, Jefferson, NC (2011), p. 220.
102. E. Steere and T. M. Boardman (1957), p. 626.
103. J. P. Kavale, A Salute to Patriotism, Cypress Publishing, Manteca, CA (2008), pp. 197 and 262. Jean Peckham Kavale, daughter of Maj Gen (ret) Howard L. Peckham, lived with her parents in Neuilly-sur-Seine, France.
104. H. P. Kelliher, "Day of Remembrance," The Albatross, 08 May 1946, p. 2. [AFHRA]
105. P. Parish (ed), Forty-five Years of Vigilance for Freedom: USAFE, 1942-1987, Office of History, Headquarters, US Air Forces in Europe (USAFE), Ramstein Air Base, Germany, 1987, p. 9.
106. Interview, author with Lt Col (ret) Charles W. Norton, USAF (Capt, EATS Pilot, Naples, Italy, 1946-47), Pendleton, SC, 26 August 2004.
107. C. E. LeMay, "Mission of the European Air Transport Service," Headquarters, United States Air Forces in Europe (USAFE), Wiesbaden, Germany, 01 December 1947. [AFHRA]

References/Notes to pages 12 to 17

108. Anon, "European Air Transport Service Guidebook," Headquarters, United States Air Forces in Europe (USAFE), Wiesbaden, Germany, 1947. [AFHRA]
109. T. A. Johanson, "Historical Record, Headquarters, EATS Terminal Orly," Paris, France, March 1946, p. 2. [AFHSO]
110. J.-P. Hoehn, "La Saga de l'US Air Force en France," Air Fan, novembre 1990, p. 34. (Fr)
111. C. L. Reynolds, "Historical Summary for the Year 1946," Headquarters, United States Air Forces in Europe (USAFE), Wiesbaden, Germany, 12 June 1947, pp. 37-39. [AFHRA]
112. L. Stallings, The Doughboys: The Story of the AEF, 1917-1918, Harper & Row, New York (1963), p. 40.
113. A. A. Durand, Stalag Luft III, Louisiana State University Press, Baton Rouge, LA (1988), p. 269.
114. E. T. Wood and S. M. Jankowski, Karski: How One Man Tried to Stop the Holocaust, Wiley, New York (1994), pp. 124-128, 197, and 201.
115. M. J. Neufeld and M. Berebaum (eds), The Bombing of Auschwitz: Should the Allies Have Attempted It?, St. Martin's Press, New York (2000), pp. 214-226.
116. R. P. Grathwol and D. M. Moorhus, Building for Peace, Center of Military History, Washington, DC (2005), p. 7.
117. M. A. Stoler, George C. Marshall: Soldier-Statesman of the American Century, Simon and Schuster, New York (1997), pp. 163-168.
118. J. B. Bonds, Bipartisan Strategy: Selling the Marshall Plan, Praeger Publishers, Westport, CT (2002), pp. 15-24.
119. W. I. Hitchcock, France Restored, The University of North Carolina Press, Chapel Hill, NC (1998), p. 207.
120. M. A. Conley, "Whatever Happened to Those Forty and Eights?," FRANCE Magazine, Fall 1987, pp. 20-22.
121. Interview, author with Robert Dawson Peckham (Cpl, U.S. Constabulary, Herzberg and Bad Windsheim, Germany, 1946-47), Kissimmee, FL, 11 April 2007.
122. E. F. Ziemke (1975), pp. 339-341.
123. W. E. Stacy, "US Army Border Operations in Germany 1945-1983," Headquarters, US Army, Europe (USAREUR), Heidelberg, Germany, 1984, pp. 14 and 18. Crime data from "History of the U.S. Constabulary 10 Jan 46-31 Dec 46," Historical Division, European Command, Frankfurt, Germany, 1947 (reproduced in the William E. Stacy 1984 historical study).
124. J. Willoughby, Remaking the Conquering Heroes, Palgrave, New York (2001), p. 151.
125. R. Cameron, "There and Back Again: Constabulary Training and Organization, 1946-1950," Conference of Army Historians, Center of Military History, 07 June 2000.
126. R. B. Bruce, "Tethered Eagle," Army History, Winter 2012, p. 9.
127. W. Markel, "The Limits of American Generalship: The JCS's Strategic Advice in Early Cold War Crises," Parameters, Spring 2008, pp. 18 and 28 (n. 3).
128. C. E. Bohlen, The Transformation of American Foreign Policy, W. W. Norton, New York (1969), pp. 41-43.
129. V. D. Hanson, "What Would Patton Say About the Present War," Imprimis, October 2004, pp. 1 and 2.
130. A. Applebaum, Iron Curtain, Doubleday, New York (2012), pp. 21 and 22.
131. D. Kagan, On the Origins of War and the Preservation of Peace, Doubleday, New York (1995), pp. 449 and 450.
132. M. J. F. Bowyer, Force for Freedom, Patrick Stephens Ltd., Somerset, England (1994), p. 38.
133. J. L. Abrahamson and P. H. Carew, Vanguard of American Atomic Deterrence, Praeger Publishers, Westport, CT (2002), pp. 116-119.
134. R. H. Campbell, The Silverplate Bombers, McFarland, Jefferson, NC (2005), pp. 1, 159, and 160.
135. R. J. Aldrich, The Hidden Hand, John Murray, London, England (2001), p. 216.
136. K. Young, "Special Weapon, Special Relationship: The Atomic Bomb Comes to Britain," The Journal of Military History, April 2013, p. 590.
137. W. R. Smyser, From Yalta to Berlin: The Cold War Struggle Over Germany, St. Martin's Press, New York (1999), p. 79.
138. Interview, author with Maj Gen (ret) Frank B. Clay (Brig Gen, Chief of Staff, US Army Communications Zone, Europe (USACOMZEUR), Orléans, France and Worms, Germany, 1966-67 and son of Gen Lucius D. Clay, Military Governor of Germany, 1947-49), Chevy Chase, MD, 27 October 2004.
139. R. Murphy, Diplomat Among Warriors, Doubleday, New York (1964), pp. 315-317.
140. F. Howley, Berlin Command, G. P. Putnam's Sons, New York (1950), p. 204.
141. D. F. Harrington, Berlin on the Brink, The University Press of Kentucky, Lexington, KY (2012), pp. 141-148.
142. J. Jansen, "An Army Engineer in Berlin During the Blockade and Airlift," Conference of Army Historians, Center of Military History, 10 June 1998.
143. D. F. Harrington, "Against All Odds," American History Illustrated, February 1982, pp. 12-15 and 30-35.
144. R. G. Miller (1998), pp. 56-58.
145. G. S. Halvorsen, The Berlin Candy Bomber, Horizon Publishers, Bountiful, Utah (2002), pp. 179-207.

146. O. Anderson, "Bonbon Bomber is Fueled for Christmas Flight," <u>The Stars and Stripes</u>, 16 December 1949, p. 11.
147. R. G. Miller (1998), pp. 62, 108, and 109.
148. G. S. Halvorsen (2002), pp. 75-77.
149. W. R. Smyser (1999), p. 86.
150. R. P. Grathwol and D. M. Moorhus, <u>American Forces in Berlin: Cold War Outpost 1945-1994</u>, US Department of Defense, Washington, DC (1994), p. 50.
151. R. Murphy (1964), p. 321.
152. P. G. Tsouras, <u>Changing Orders</u>, Facts on File, New York (1994), pp. 36-46.
153. D. Andradé, "Reflections on the Forgotten," <u>The Retired Officer</u>, June 2000, p. 61.
154. R. S. Jordan (ed), <u>Generals in International Politics</u>, The University Press of Kentucky, Lexington, KY (1987), p. 4.
155. T. B. Cochran et al., <u>Nuclear Weapons Databook</u>, Vol. I, Ballinger Publishing Co., Cambridge, MA (1984), p. 15.
156. S. T. Ross, <u>American War Plans, 1945-1950</u>, Frank Cass, London, England (1996), pp. 17-20 and 151-155.
157. J. Hoffenaar, "'Hannibal ante portus': The Soviet Military Threat and the Build-up of the Dutch Armed Forces, 1948-1958," <u>The Journal of Military History</u>, January 2002, p. 169.
158. D. H. Tulley (1954), p. 405.
159. L. S. Kaplan, <u>A Community of Interests: NATO and the Military Assistance Program, 1948-1951</u>, Historical Office, Office of the Secretary of Defense, Washington, DC (1980), pp. 101-126.
160. C. C. Crane, <u>American Airpower Strategy in Korea, 1950-1953</u>, University Press of Kansas, Lawrence, KS (2000), p. 24.
161. R. F. Futrell, <u>The United States Air Force in Korea, 1950-1953</u>, Air Force History and Museums Program, Washington, DC (2000), p. 388. Reprint of 1961 edition originally published by Duell, Sloan and Pearce, New York.
162. J. A. Engel, "The Comet Affair," <u>Air & Space</u>, August-September 2003, pp. 38 and 39.
163. R. F. Futrell (2000), p. 393.
164. W. T. Y'Blood, <u>MiG Alley: The Fight for Air Superiority</u>, Air Force History and Museums Program, Washington, DC (2000).
165. R. Wetterhahn, "The Russians of MiG Alley," <u>The Retired Officer</u>, August 2000, pp. 68-75.
166. L. H. Brune (ed), <u>The Korean War</u>, Greenwood Press, Westport, CT (1996), pp. 213-215.
167. M. J. McCarthy, "Uncertain Enemies: Soviet Pilots in the Korean War," <u>Air Power History</u>, Spring 1997, pp. 32-45.
168. T. C. Reed, <u>At The Abyss</u>, Ballantine Books, New York (2004), p. 38.
169. J. Lowry, "Lt. No," <u>Air Force Magazine</u>, July 2012, pp. 60-63.
170. J. Charmley, <u>Churchill's Grand Alliance</u>, Harcourt Brace, New York (1995), pp. 222-224.
171. P. Grose, <u>Operation Rollback</u>, Houghton Mifflin, Boston, MA (2000), pp. 167 and 168.
172. H. A. Rositzke, <u>The CIA's Secret Operations</u>, Reader's Digest Press, New York (1977), pp. 166-173.
173. D. Miller, <u>The Cold War</u>, John Murray Publishers, London, England (1998), pp. 10-13.
174. R. Dalsjö, <u>Life-line Lost</u>, Santerus Academic Press, Stockholm, Sweden (2006), p. XI.
175. J. P. Diggins, <u>The Proud Decades: America in War and Peace</u>, W. W. Norton, New York (1988), pp. 81-86. Article 5 of the pact called on all member nations to consider an attack on one of them as aggression against all.
176. G. T. Jóhannesson, "To the Edge of Nowhere?," <u>Naval War College Review</u>, Summer/Autumn 2004, pp. 115-137.
177. L. L. Lemnitzer, "Strength in NATO," <u>The Military Engineer</u>, September-October 1970, p. 302.
178. W. B. Rosson, Senior Officer Oral History Program, US Army Military History Institute, Carlisle Barracks, PA, 1981.
179. C. G. Cogan, <u>Forced To Choose: France, the Atlantic Alliance, and NATO</u>, Praeger Publishers, Westport, CT (1997), p. 106.
180. Anon, "NATO Its Development and Significance," US Department of State Publication No. 4630, August 1952, p. 38.
181. R. F. Kuisel, <u>Seducing the French</u>, University of California Press, Berkeley, CA (1993), pp. 21 and 22.
182. H. Tanner, "Position Shown by Texts," <u>New York Times</u>, 01 April 1966, p. 11.
183. D. J. Hickman, "The United States Army in Europe, 1953-1963," Headquarters, US Army, Europe (USAREUR), Heidelberg, Germany, 1964, pp. 67 and 68.
184. Anon, <u>The Military Balance</u>, The Institute for Strategic Studies, London, England (1963), pp. 15-24.
185. T. A. Hughes, "The Global Cold War 1946-90," in J. C. Bradford (ed), <u>Atlas of American Military History</u>, Oxford University Press, Oxford, England (2003), p. 218.
186. N. Avery, "Grostenquin Revisited," <u>The Roundel</u>, December 1964, pp. 23-25.
187. J. S. Hodder, "The Canadian Forces in Europe," <u>NATO Letter</u>, May 1963, pp. 14-17.
188. Anon, "Strength of the Army," Report DCSPER-46, Office of the Deputy Chief of Staff for Personnel, Department of the Army, Washington, DC, 1968.
189. Anon, "The Troop Program," Office of Assistant Chief of Staff, G-1, US Army, Washington, DC, volumes dated June 1964 through June 1968. This publication gives troop strength for Active Army Units worldwide.

References/Notes to pages 23 to 29

190. Anon, "USAF in Europe Historical Highlights," Office of History, Headquarters, US Air Forces in Europe (USAFE), Wiesbaden, Germany, 31 December 1950 through 31 December 1967.
191. V. Downs, "US Defense Activity in France," Headquarters, US European Command (USEUCOM), Secretary of the Joint Staff, Analysis & Presentation Branch, St.-Germain-en-Laye, France, 1966, p. 21. Downs lists US military population totals in France for 1954 to 1965.
192. J. R. Moenk, "Line of Communications Through France 1954-1955," Headquarters, US Army, Europe (USAREUR), Heidelberg, Germany, 1957, p. 21.
193. M. Ivanchak, "FRELOC After Action Report," Vol. II, Headquarters, US Army Communications Zone, Europe (USARCOMZEUR), 12 June 1968, p. 99.
194. O. Pottier, Les bases américaines en France (1950-1967), Éditions l'Harmattan, Paris (2003), pp. 36, 43, and 52. (Fr)
195. B. H. Siemon and R. E. Wagberg (1968), pp. 124 and 125.

CHAPTER TWO

1. J. L. Collins, "Building Strength for Western Defense," Army Information Digest, July 1954, pp. 3-8.
2. Anon, "Total Defense Expenditures of NATO Countries, 1949-1957," NATO Letter, January 1958, p. 21.
3. C. G. Cogan, Oldest Allies, Guarded Friends, Praeger Publishers, Westport, CT (1994), p. 86.
4. W. I. Hitchcock, France Restored, University of North Carolina Press, Chapel Hill, NC (1998), pp. 186 and 187.
5. Letter from Adam Yarmolinsky (Deputy Assistant Secretary of Defense for International Security Affairs) to Ovie C. Fisher (Committee on Armed Services, US House of Representatives), Washington, DC, dated 27 July 1966. [CEHO]
6. A. S. Britt, "Logistical Coordination Between Allied Forces," Military Review, September 1957, pp. 48-51.
7. Anon, "NATO and Its SHAPE Command," Armed Forces Information Bulletin, Vol. 7, US Army, Europe (USAREUR), Heidelberg, Germany, 30 October 1952, pp. 2-15.
8. A. D. Starbird, STARBIRD Remembers, self-published, Washington, DC (1982), pp. 67-73.
9. S. K. Eaton, "Origin and Development of SHAPE," Supreme Headquarters, Allied Powers Europe (SHAPE), Marly-le-Roi, 09 December 1953, pp. 65 and 69.
10. W. A. Knowlton, "Early Stages in the Organization of SHAPE," International Organization, Winter 1959, pp. 11 and 12.
11. A. J. Goodpaster, "The Development of SHAPE: 1950-1953," International Organization, May 1955, p. 257.
12. Interviews, author with Gen (ret) William A. Knowlton (Lt Col, Special Assistant to Gen Alfred M. Gruenther, SHAPE, Paris, France, 1951-54), Arlington, VA, 26 September 2003 and 10 March 2005.
13. J. M. Virden, "Ike's SHAPE Staff Makes Good," Army-Navy-Air Force Register, 11 October 1958, pp. 1 and 23.
14. Q. Reynolds, "Ike's Right Arm," The Reader's Digest, January 1952, pp. 39 and 40.
15. R. S. Jordan, An Unsung Soldier, Naval Institute Press, Annapolis, MD (2013), pp. 23 and 24.
16. W. B. Rosson, Senior Officer Oral History Program, US Army Military History Institute, Carlisle Barracks, PA, 1981, pp. 181-186.
17. H. J. Richter (ed), "Paris Calls Off Galas at Eisenhower's Request," The Stars and Stripes, 07 January 1951, p. 12.
18. D. Shear, "Eisenhower Arrives in Paris," The Stars and Stripes, 08 January 1951, pp. 1 and 12.
19. A. J. Goodpaster, "The Foundations of NATO," in J. R. Golden et al. (eds), NATO at Forty, Westview Press, Boulder, CO (1989), p. 28.
20. A. L. Jorgenson (ed), "President's Plane Flies 16 Airmen to States on Leave," The Stars and Stripes, 06 February 1954, p. 15.
21. J. L. Gilbert et al., In The Shadow of The Sphinx, History Office, US Army Intelligence and Security Command (INSCOM), Fort Belvoir, VA (2005), p. 125.
22. Interview, author with Lt Col (ret) Joseph T. Miller (PFC, 520th Military Police Co, Paris and Camp des Loges, France, 1951-52), Meridianville, AL, 07 November 2009.
23. W. H. Maehl, "Relations of the European Command with Supreme Headquarters Allied Powers Europe, December 1950-June 1952," Historical Division, US Army, Europe (USAREUR), Karlsruhe, Germany, 1953, pp. 29 and 30.
24. D. Schear, "Boxer Runs Bar at Ike's Hq," The Stars and Stripes, 28 January 1951, p. II.
25. D. Schear, "Parisians' Driving Baffle Zone Yanks at SHAPE," The Stars and Stripes, 19 January 1951, p. 11.
26. R. M. Thomas, "Marcel Bleustein-Blanchet Dies; Paris Advertising Giant Was 89," New York Times, 13 April 1996.
27. Interview, author with Maria G. Thill, formerly Maria Garcia (Cpl, WAC, 7th Signal Bn, SHAPE, Marly-le-Roi, France, 1951-53), Jordan, MN, 29 December 2009.
28. E. A. Morrow, "SHAPE's 'Pentagon' Opens Monday; 10-Year Guarantee for New Offices," New York Times, 20 July 1951, p. 5.
29. A. S. Berg, Goldwyn, Alfred A. Knopf, New York (1989), p. 458.
30. H. J. Richter (ed), "Paris Police Foil Anti-Ike Rally," The Stars and Stripes, 25 January 1951, p. 12.
31. A. Werth, France 1940-1955, Beacon Press, Boston, MA (1966), pp. 554 and 555.

32. N. Friedman, The Fifty-Year War, Naval Institute Press, Annapolis, MD (2000), p. 138.
33. P. Comert et J. Mazerette, "Réponse a 14 Questions sur la Guerre et la Paix," Paris-Match, 27 octobre 1951, pp. 16-19. (Fr)
34. R. H. Ferrell (ed), The Eisenhower Diaries, W. W. Norton & Co., New York (1981), pp. 200 and 201.
35. E. A. Morrow, "Eisenhower Takes Formal Command," New York Times, 03 April 1951, p. 8.
36. Telegram from Loren Carroll, Chief, Newsweek Paris Bureau to Newsweek, New York City, dated 17 March 1951. [SHD]
37. C. L. Robinson, When Roosevelt Planned to Govern France, University of Massachusetts Press, Amherst, MA (2011), p. 101.
38. D. Schear, "SHAPE-Its Small Staff Stresses Teamwork," The Stars and Stripes, 07 October 1951, pp. III and VI.
39. J. Hixon and B. F. Cooling, "Combined Operations in Peace and War," US Army Military History Institute, Carlisle Barracks, PA, 1982, pp. 283-285.
40. C. H. Donnelly, Autobiography, unpublished manuscript, Washington, DC, dated 10 May 1959, p. 1220. [MHI]
41. S. T. Ross and D. A. Rosenberg (eds), America's Plans for War Against the Soviet Union, 1945-1950, Vol. 12, Garland Publishing, New York (1990), pp. 141-147. Fifteen-volume set which reproduce ninety-eight war plans and studies by Joint Chiefs of Staff.
42. D. Kaiser, "US Objectives and Plans for War with the Soviet Union, 1946-54," in T. C. Imlay and M. D. Toft (eds), The Fog of Peace and War Planning, Routledge, New York (2006), pp. 209-214.
43. P. S. Meilinger, "The Early War Plans," Air Force Magazine, December 2012, p. 50.
44. P. A. Karber and A. G. Whitley, "The Operational Realm," in J. R. Golden et al. (eds), NATO at Forty, Westview Press, Boulder, CO (1989), p. 124.
45. K. Soutor, "To Stem the Red Tide," The Journal of Military History, October 1993, pp. 653-688.
46. D. A. Lane, "Annual Historical Report for 1955-1956," Headquarters, US Army, Europe (USAREUR), Heidelberg, Germany, 1957, pp. 265 and 266.
47. W. M. Summers (ed), "M'Cloy Scoffs at Blast Claim," The Stars and Stripes, 21 June 1950, pp. 1 and 12.
48. Anon, "Annual Narrative Report: Occupation Forces in Europe Series," Headquarters, US Army, Europe (USAREUR), Karlsruhe, Germany, 1950, p. 56.
49. Letter from Brig Gen Joseph J. O'Hare (US Army Attaché, Paris) to Col Simoneau (Chef du 2ᵉ Bureau EMFA, Paris, France), dated 08 March 1951. (Fr) [SHD]
50. G. R. Robertson, Engineer Memoirs, General William M. Hoge, US Army Corps of Engineers, EP 870-1-25, Alexandria, VA, January 1993, pp. 190-192.
51. J. A. Blackwell, "In the Laps of the Gods: The Origins of NATO Forward Defense," Parameters, Winter 1985, p. 69.
52. Interview, author with Daryl R. Blanchard (Capt, 555th Engineer Group, Karlsruhe, Germany, 1962-66), Toledo, OH, 07 July 2014.
53. A. Grosser, The Western Alliance, Continuum Publishing, New York (1980), pp. 157 and 158. Originally published in French as Les Occidentaux: Les pays d'Europe et les État-Unis depuis la guerre by Éditions Fayard, Paris (1978). Grosser's book covers Franco-American relations from the viewpoint of Western Europe.
54. Private email to Col (ret) Gregory W. Pedlow (SHAPE Historian, Mons, Belgium) from Peter E. W. Grey (British SHAPE Signal Squadron, Marly-le-Roi, France), 31 March 2012.
55. L. S. Kaplan, The Long Entanglement: NATOs First Fifty Years, Praeger Publishers, Westport, CT (1999), p. 62.
56. L. L. Cross, "SHAPE-Bulwark of the Free World," Army Information Digest, March 1956, pp. 26-32.
57. V. F. Caputo and J. E. Murray, Quick on the Vigor!, The Traffic Service Corp, Washington, DC (1966), pp. 159-164.
58. J. A. Hoefling, "Logistics in the Army Group," Military Review, May 1963, pp. 50-56.
59. L. Galambos (ed), The Papers of Dwight David Eisenhower, The Johns Hopkins University Press, Baltimore, MD (1989), Vol. XII, pp. 180-182.
60. S. K. Eaton (1953), p. 79.
61. C. L. Sulzberger, "SHAPE Gives Europeans Hope in Place of Fear," New York Times, 06 April 1952, p. E3.
62. S. K. Eaton (1953), pp. 82 and 83.
63. J. de Madre, "SHAPE's Fifteen Years at Rocquencourt," NATO Letter, April 1967, pp. 17-23.
64. R. J. Wood, "History of New Headquarters Building, SHAPE," Marly-le-Roi, France, 10 October 1951, 12 pp. Report prepared by Lt Col Charles E. Kabrich who served as SHAPE liaison officer to French Army Engineers during construction of headquarters building.
65. B. Welles, "Eisenhower Hails Congress' Callers," New York Times, 26 December 1951, p. 9.
66. Remarks by French President Vincent Auriol at opening of SHAPE Headquarters, Marly-le-Roi, France, 23 July 1951. [NDU]
67. Anon, The French Defense Effort, Service D'Information et de Presse, Ambassade de France, New York, October 1952, p. 8. [SHD]
68. R. S. Jordan (ed), Generals in International Politics, The University Press of Kentucky, Lexington, KY (1987), p. 32.

69. D. Middleton, <u>The Defense of Western Europe</u>, Appleton-Century-Crofts, New York (1952), p. 175.
70. D. S. Ryerson, "Language teaching in NATO," <u>Western World</u>, April 1958, pp. 63-65.
71. Anon, "U.S. Troops Under Eisenhower Learn French; Officers and Men About Equal in Proficiency," <u>New York Times</u>, 28 August 1951, p. 9.
72. L. Galambos (1989), Vol. XII, p. 365 (n. 3).
73. E. A. Morrow, "Eisenhower Takes New Headquarters," <u>New York Times</u>, 24 July 1951, pp. 1 and 3.
74. T. F. Brady, "At SHAPE, the French Must Swallow Their Pride and the English Cooking," <u>New York Times</u>, 20 March 1955, p. 20.
75. P. Braestrup, "De Gaulle Said to Oppose New NATO Headquarters," <u>New York Times</u>, 18 October 1965, p. 15.
76. E. A. Morrow, "SHAPE's 'Pentagon' Opens Monday; 10-Year Guarantee for New Offices," <u>New York Times</u>, 20 July 1951, p. 5.
77. S. Eisenhower, <u>Mrs. Ike: Memories and Reflections on the Life of Mamie Eisenhower</u>, Farrar Straus and Giroux, New York (1996), pp. 257 and 258.
78. R. S. Jordan, "Gruenther: Attempts to Retain NATO Solidarity," in R. S. Jordan (ed), <u>Generals in International Politics</u>, The University Press of Kentucky, Lexington, KY (1987), p. 56.
79. D. A. Carter, "Eisenhower Versus the Generals," <u>The Journal of Military History</u>, October 2007, p. 1173.
80. Interview, author with Francis J. Bentz (Cpl, 7th Signal Bn, SHAPE, Marly-le-Roi, France, 1951-53), East Liverpool, OH, 26 March 2010.
81. E. Behr, <u>The Good Frenchman</u>, Villard Books, New York (1993), pp. 350 and 351.
82. Interview, author with Lt Gen (ret) Edward L. Rowny (Col, Secretary of the Staff, SHAPE, Marly-le-Roi, France, 1955-58), Washington, DC, 14 August 2007.
83. Letter from Maurice Chevalier, Marnes-la-Coquette, France to Gen Lyman L. Lemnitzer, Supreme Commander, Europe (SACEUR, 1962-69), Casteau-Maisières, Belgium, dated 23 December 1967. [NDU]
84. R. J. Connolly, "SHAPE," <u>Military Police Journal</u>, September 1957, p. 17.
85. Anon, "MPs at 14-Nation Headquarters Must Measure Up, or Else," <u>Army Times</u>, 11 July 1953.
86. R. Fisher, "General Maglin Finds Europe MP's in High Gear," <u>Military Police Journal</u>, October 1954, p. 2.
87. Interview, author with David W. Brubaker (Cpl, 520th Military Police Co, SHAPE, Marly-le-Roi, 1960-62), Towanda, PA, 26 January 2010.
88. E. M. Kennedy, <u>True Compass</u>, Twelve, New York (2009), pp. 96, 101, and 102. Camp des Loges was 17 miles from "the delights of Paris," without sidewalks for most of the route. Army pants were bloused with elastic bands, not bicycle chains.
89. Interview, author with Lt Col (ret) Joseph T. Miller (PFC, 520th Military Police Co, Paris and Camp des Loges, France, 1951-52), Meridianville, AL, 25 November 2009.
90. A. L. Jorgenson (ed), "Service Women in SHAPE for Many Jobs," <u>The Stars and Stripes</u>, 06 January 1954, p. 9.
91. D. A. Bartoni (ed), "SHAPE Wires Tap Signal Amity," <u>The Stars and Stripes</u>, 04 April 1956, p. 10.
92. D. Walter, "The ComZ Pilots of the Grand Boulevards," <u>The Stars and Stripes</u>, 04 June 1959, pp. 11 and 12.
93. D. Walter, "Paris Christmas Traffic Tests Summit Chauffeurs," <u>The Stars and Stripes</u>, 22 December 1959, p.3.
94. Interview, author with Col (ret) James E. Taylor (1st Lt, Executive Officer, 22nd Transportation Co (Car), Camp Voluceau, France, 1961-63), Newport News, VA, 20 November 2014.
95. P. de Montiamont, "Le Depart du SHAPE," <u>La Revue de Deux Mondes</u>, 01 avril 1957. (Fr)
96. J. E. Kaufmann and H. W. Kaufmann, <u>Fortress France</u>, Praeger Security International, Westport, CT (2006), pp. 27 and 49.
97. C. Bartman, "France to Ask Eisenhower's Aid in Rebuilding Maginot Line," <u>The Stars and Stripes</u>, 05 February 1951, p. 4.
98. J. E. Kaufmann and H. W. Kaufmann (2006), pp. 27-30.
99. S. R. Gregory, <u>Nuclear Command and Control in NATO</u>, Macmillan Press, London, England (1996), pp. 132 and 133.
100. J. Guthrie, "Underground Command Posts," <u>International Combat Arms</u>, May 1987, p. 19.
101. G. Perrault, <u>Paris Under the Occupation</u>, The Vendome Press, New York (1989), p. 182.
102. N. Raymond, "Army's Busy Paris Switchboard," <u>The Stars and Stripes</u>, 29 March 1957, p. 11.
103. D. A. Schmidt, "Dulles Leaves for Paris," <u>New York Times</u>, 13 December 1957, p. 5.
104. Anon, "Paris Whitehouse, Signal Operations Report," Seine Area Command (SACCZ), Camp des Loges, St.-Germain-en-Laye, France, December 1959. [MHI]
105. N. Friedman (2000), p. 176.
106. J. K. Singlaub, "Special Warfare Training in 7th Army," <u>Military Review</u>, March 1964, p. 58.
107. R. J. Aldrich, <u>The Hidden Hand</u>, John Murray, London, England (2001), p. 626.
108. N. Dujmović, "Drastic Action Short of War: The Origins and Application of CIA's Covert Paramilitary Function in the Early Cold War," <u>The Journal of Military History</u>, July 2012, p. 788.

References/Notes to pages 40 to 47

109. D. Ganser, NATO's Secret Armies, Frank Cass, New York (2005), p. 93.
110. Anon, "Rock of Gilbraltar (sic)," The Groton News, 01 March 1971, p. 12.
111. S. Loof, "WWII Towers Puzzle Officials," The Philadelphia Inquirer, 19 May 2002, p. A15.
112. A. J. Mandelbaum, "NATO Signals Infrastructure in Allied Command Europe," Signal, September 1958, pp. 14, 15, and 26.
113. K. F. Zitzman, "International System Problems As Exemplified by NATO Project ACE HIGH," Signal, November 1960, p. 44.
114. M. Honick, "The New Approach, 1953-56," Supreme Headquarters, Allied Powers Europe (SHAPE), Marly-le-Roi, July 1976, pp. 253-256.
115. E. C. Page, "NATO's 'Double Jump' Network," Signal, December 1959, p. 8.
116. S. Karnow, Paris in the Fifties, Times Books, New York (1997), p. 231.
117. C. L. Sulzberger, "Variations in Pay of Armies a Poser for Atlantic Nations," New York Times, 08 August 1951, p. 7.
118. L. Galambos (1989), Vol. XII, p. 106 (n. 5).
119. Ibid, pp. 578 and 579.
120. E. A. Morrow, "Eisenhower Opens SHAPE Town Today," New York Times, 31 October, 1951, p. 9.
121. R. Q. Brown, "Regulations," Supreme Headquarters, Allied Powers Europe (SHAPE), Marly-le-Roi, France, 04 March 1952, pp. 1 and 3.
122. V. A. Walters, Silent Missions, Doubleday, Garden City, NY (1978), p. 220.
123. W. N. Thomas, "Combined Staff Leadership," Military Review, January 1965, pp. 35-42.
124. R. Sünder, "SHAPE School-An International Melting Pot," NATO Letter, June 1965, pp. 8-13.
125. C. Glass, The American Hospital of Paris During the Two World Wars, American Hospital of Paris, Neuilly-sur-Seine, France (2014), pp. 21-48.
126. G. A. Cosmas and A. E. Cowdry, Medical Service in the European Theater of Operations, Center of Military History, Washington, DC (1992), pp. 337 and 338. During the German occupation, retired French General de Chambron, a veteran of World War I, vowed to never admit "Boche" soldiers (Germans) to the American Hospital. He kept his vow until August 1944.
127. O. Gresser, "History of the American Hospital of Paris," unpublished manuscript, Neuilly-sur-Seine, France (1978), p. 8.
128. Anon, "U.S. Army Hospital, Paris," Medical Bulletin, US Army, Europe, Vol. 19, No. 3, March 1962, pp. 53 and 58.
129. A. Marx, Goldwyn, W. W. Norton & Co., New York (1976), p. 355.
130. H. J. Richter (ed), "61st Disp in Paris Treats SHAPE Yanks, Canadians," The Stars and Stripes, 05 June 1953, p. 9.
131. N. Fouché, Le Mouvement Perpétuel, Éditions Erès, Toulouse, France (1991), p. 86. (Fr)
132. J. H. Winchester, "American Medicine's Outpost in France," Today's Health, August 1969, pp. 44-47.
133. B. W. Fowle, Engineer Memoirs, Lieutenant General Edward L. Rowny, US Army Corps of Engineers, EP 870-1-49, Alexandria, VA, December 1995, p. 68.
134. A. N. Stubblebine, "NATO Defense College," The Quartermaster Review, July-August 1952, pp. 22, 23 and 124-126.
135. A. J. Lemonnier, "The NATO Defense College," Air University Quarterly Review, Fall 1952, pp. 83-88.
136. E. Taillemite, Dictionnaire des Marins Français, Éditions Maritimes & D'Outre-Mer, Paris, France (1982), p. 208. (Fr)
137. R. J. Stillman, "NATO Defense College," Military Review, January 1964, pp. 32-41.
138. A. Sington, "From the Ville Lumière to the Eternal City," NATO Letter, February 1967, pp. 18-23.
139. B. Fletcher, A History of Architecture, Charles Scribner's Sons, New York (1961), pp. 1094 and 1100. Carlu also designed the NATO air bases at Dreux and Évreux.
140. K. E. Meyer, "NATO Force Used Jargon of Its Own," The Washington Post, 05 June 1966, p. 20.
141. D. D. Eisenhower, Waging Peace, 1956-1961, Doubleday, Garden City, NY (1965), pp. 230-232.
142. D. Walter, "Enter One Landmark; Scratch One Eyesore," The Stars and Stripes, 23 September 1959, p. 11.
143. D. Walter, "Allied Ministers Meeting in New NATO Building," The Stars and Stripes, 16 December 1959, p. 3.
144. Anon, "On the Site of the Future NATO Headquarters," NATO Letter, 01 March 1956, pp. 21 and 22.
145. J. A. Huston, One For All, University of Delaware Press, Newark, DE (1984), p. 179.
146. R. Lamson, "Historical Summary: The North Atlantic Treaty Organization," Supreme Headquarters, Allied Powers Europe (SHAPE), Marly-le Roi, France, 15 September 1952, p. 3.
147. H. J. Richter (ed), "Seek Truth, Ike Urges At Fontainebleau," The Stars and Stripes, 24 May 1952, p. 2.
148. L. Galambos (1989), Vol. XIII, pp. 1026-1031, 1156 (n. 5), and 1600-1607.
149. ibid, pp. 301 and 302 and R. H. Ferrell (ed), The Eisenhower Diaries, W. W. Norton & Co., New York (1981).
150. D. Haberstam, "Command Performance," Smithsonian, November 2007, p. 59.
151. T. Fleming, "The Man Who Saved Korea," The Quarterly Journal of Military History, Winter 1993, pp. 54-61.
152. A. Grosser (1980), pp. 115 and 116.

References/Notes to pages 47 to 57

153. O. Pottier, Les Bases Américaines en France (1950-1967), Éditions l'Harmattan, Paris, France (2003), p. 282. (Fr)
154. C. C. Crane, American Airpower Strategy in Korea, 1950-1953, University Press of Kansas, Lawrence, KS (2000), pp. 143-150.
155. R. W. Daly, "The Big Lie!," Military Review, November 1962, pp. 54-60.
156. T. Méray, On Burchett, Callistemon Publications, Belgrave, Australia (2008), pp. 72-89.
157. K. W. Colegrove, The Menace of Communism, D. Van Nostrand, Princeton, NJ (1962), pp. 86 and 87.
158. M. Vandel, "Pas de Ridgway chez nous," L'Humanité, 16 mai 1952, pp. 1 and 4. (Fr) L'Humanité headlines on 17 May 1952: "Ridgway, Go Home!" and "Pas de général microbien à Paris." [CAC]
159. Anon, "The Man in the Hotchkiss," Time, 09 June 1952, pp. 28 and 29.
160. J. J. Miller and M. Molesky, Our Oldest Enemy, Doubleday, New York (2004), p. 206.
161. H. L. Katzander, "Coca-Cola--Cold War Side Show in Paris," The Stars and Stripes, 26 March 1950, p. XII.
162. G. E. Pelletier, "Ridgway: Trying to Make Good on the Promises," in R. S. Jordan (ed), Generals in International Politics, The University Press of Kentucky, Lexington, KY (1987), p. 41.
163. B. Welles, "Ridgway to Unify Vast U.S. Work For Bases in Europe to Stop Waste," New York Times, 11 January 1953, p. 1.
164. G. C. Mitchell, Matthew B. Ridgway, Stackpole Books, Mechanicsburg, PA (2002), pp. 116 and 117.
165. M. O. Wheeler, "NATO Nuclear Strategy, 1949-90," in G. Schmidt (ed), A History of NATO-The First Fifty Years, Vol. 3, Palgrave Publishers, Basingstoke, England (2001), p. 125.
166. M. B. Ridgway, Soldier: The Memoirs of Matthew B. Ridgway, Harper & Brothers, New York (1956), p. 238.
167. ibid, pp. 253 and 254.
168. A. W. Spratley (ed), "Ridgway Visits ComZ; Spends Night in BASEC Tent," ComZ Cadence, 19 June 1953, p. 1.
169. B. Welles, "'New' Gruenther Sheds Old Habits," New York Times, 16 August 1953, p. 22.
170. Interview, author with Peter J. Leofsky (PFC, 7th Signal Bn, SHAPE, Marly-le-Roi, France, 1951-53), Syracuse, NY, 12 January 2011.
171. F. Costigliola, France and the United States, Twayne Publishers, New York (1992), p. 97.
172. T. F. Brady, "NATO Chiefs End Atomic Exercise," New York Times, 01 May 1954, p. 3.
173. R. M. Leighton, Strategy, Money, and the New Look 1953-1956, Historical Office, Office of the Secretary of Defense, Washington, DC (2001), p. 511.
174. M. H. Magnussen (ed), "Atomic Annie Briefly Provided Nuclear Fire Support," Headquarters Heliogram, May-June 2010, p. 7.
175. J. P. O'Donnell, "The World's Newest Army," The Saturday Evening Post, 08 October 1955, p. 133.
176. S. J. Flanagan, NATO's Conventional Defenses, Ballinger Publishing, Cambridge, MA (1988), p. 12.
177. E. L. Rowny, It Takes One to Tango, Brassey's, McLean, VA (1992), p. 16.
178. Memo from Col Andrew J. Goodpaster (Plans and Operations, SHAPE) to Lt Gen Cortlandt Van R. Schuyler (Chief of Staff, SHAPE), Marly-le-Roi, France, dated 29 June 1954. Rowny's paper was published in August 1954 issue of The Army Combat Forces Journal, pp. 18-22.
179. R. M. Leighton (2001), pp. 152, 177, and 178.
180. I. W. Trauschweizer, "Learning with an Ally," The Journal of Military History, April 2008, p. 484.
181. A. M. Gruenther, "General Orientation: Europe," Headquarters, United States European Command (USEUCOM), St. Germain-en-Laye, France, 25 June 1954.
182. J.-B. Duroselle, France and the United States, The University of Chicago Press, Chicago, IL (1978), p. 188.
183. B. W. Fowle, Engineer Memoirs, Lieutenant General Edward L. Rowny, US Army Corps of Engineers, EP 870-1-49, Alexandria, VA, December 1995, pp. 61 and 62.
184. A. M. Gruenther, "Speech to Bonn Economic Policy Club," NATO Letter, 01 June 1956, p. 39.
185. D. D. Eisenhower (1965), p. 97.
186. D. A. Bartoni (ed), "Jet-Speed Rise Lands Norstad at Helm of SHAPE," The Stars and Stripes, 26 November 1956, p. 11.
187. J. G. Holland, "Allied Command Europe's Mobile Force," Military Review, October 1965, pp. 11-21.
188. G. W. Pedlow (ed), "NATO Strategy Documents 1949-1969," North Atlantic Treaty Organization (NATO), Bruxelles, Belgium, 1998, pp. 287-290.
189. I. W. Trauschweizer, The Cold War U.S. Army, University Press of Kansas, Lawrence, KS (2008), pp. 96 and 97.
190. M. Dyer and A. H. Hausrath, "Exercise SIDE STEP: the Problem of Civil Affairs in Europe," Operations Research Office, The Johns Hopkins University, Baltimore, MD, March 1961, pp. 1-5, 56, 57, and 73-80.
191. G. E. Miller, Stockpile, Naval Institute Press, Annapolis, MD (2010), p. 118.
192. L. S. Kaplan et al., The McNamara Ascendancy, 1961-1965, Historical Office, Office of the Secretary of Defense, Washington, DC (2006), pp. 358 and 362.
193. J. Raymond, "US Will Propose A Nuclear Force in NATO Command," New York Times, 24 November 1960, pp. 1 and 10.
194. R. S. Jordan, Norstad: Cold War NATO Supreme Commander, St. Martin's Press, New York (2000), pp. 126 and 127.

References/Notes to pages 57 to 63

195. L. L. Lemnitzer, Senior Officer Oral History Program, US Army Military History Institute, Carlisle Barracks, PA, 1972, pp. 27 and 28.
196. L. J. Binder, Lemnitzer: A Soldier for His Time, Brassey's, Washington, DC (1997), pp. 312 and 313.
197. I. W. Trauschweizer (2008), p. 136.
198. L. J. Binder (1997), pp. 327-329.
199. R. P. Smith (ed), "Greeks, Turks Back with NATO," The Stars and Stripes, 23 August 1964, p. 7
200. Letter from Gen (ret) Lyman L. Lemnitzer to Gen Andrew J. Goodpaster, Supreme Commander, Europe (SACEUR, 1969-74), dated 05 September 1969. [NDU]
201. C. Williams, The Last Great Frenchman, John Wiley & Sons, New York (1993), p. 423.
202. L. J. Binder (1997), pp. 313 and 314. UPI reported that the bomb was discovered two weeks later, not two days.
203. L. L. Lemnitzer, Senior Officer Oral History Program, US Army Military History Institute, Carlisle Barracks, PA, 1972, pp. 26 and 27.
204. S. E. Ambrose in R. S. Jordan (1987), pp. 8-30 and A. J. Goodpaster in J. R. Golden (1989), pp. 32-34. (on Eisenhower)
205. G. E. Pelletier in R. S. Jordan (1987), pp. 31-52. (on Ridgway)
206. R. S. Jordan in R. S. Jordan (1987), pp. 53-72. (on Gruenther)
207. R. S. Jordan (2000), pp. 96-212. (on Norstad)
208. L. J. Binder (1997), pp. 312-338. (on Lemnitzer)
209. J. Hackett, "NATO's Supreme Allied Commanders on Parade," Parameters, June 1988, p. 5.
210. C. R. Nelson, The Life and Work of General Andrew J. Goodpaster, Rowman & Littlefield, Lanham, MD (2016), pp. 216 and 217.

CHAPTER THREE

1. A. Brogi, A Question of Self-Esteem, Praeger Publishers, Westport, CT (2002), p. 125.
2. P. Parrish (ed), Forty-five Years of Vigilance for Freedom: USAFE, 1942-1987, Office of History, Headquarters, US Air Forces in Europe (USAFE), Ramstein Air Base, Germany, 1987, pp. 42, 48, and 53. In December 1957, Ramstein and Landstuhl became a single contiguous base.
3. D. H. Tully, "The Military Construction Program," The Military Engineer, November-December 1954, p. 405.
4. P. Drouin, "De l'Atlantique au Rhin avec l'armeé américaine," Le Monde, 22 novembre 1951, p. 4. (Fr)
5. H. A. Rositzke, The CIA's Secret Operations, Reader's Digest Press, New York (1977), pp. 84 and 85.
6. R. W. Colglazier, Senior Officer Oral History Program, US Army Military History Institute, Carlisle Barracks, PA, 1984, pp. 226 and 227.
7. L. Galambos (ed), The Papers of Dwight David Eisenhower, Vol. XII, The Johns Hopkins University Press, Baltimore, MD (1989), pp. 676 and 677.
8. Anon, "Memo from France," U.S. News & World Report, 07 November 1952, p. 45.
9. M. Valtat, "Le Général Young et ses installations font peser une lourde menace sur Orléans et sa région," L'Humanité, 18 octobre 1951, p. 2. (Fr) [AD 45]
10. M. Valtat, "Soyons amis?," L'Humanité, 19 octobre 1951, p. 2. (Fr) [AD 45]
11. M. Valtat, "On vote demain das le Loriet occupé: GO HOME!," L'Humanité, 20 octobre 1951, p. 2. (Fr) [AD 45]
12. H. J. Richter (ed), "Brest Asks Establishment of U.S. Supply Base," The Stars and Stripes, 30 November 1950, p. 3.
13. Interview, author with Col (ret) Mason J. Young, Jr. (son of Brig Gen Mason J. Young, first Commanding General, ComZ), Newport News, VA, 10 January 2003.
14. R. A. Wells et al., "U.S. Army Lines of Communications in Europe (1945-1967)," Office of the Deputy Chief of Staff, Operations, US Army, Europe (USAREUR), Heidelberg, Germany, 1968, pp. 33-35.
15. Letter from Philip W. Bonsal, Charge d'Affaires, US Embassy, Paris, France to Robert Schuman, French Foreign Minister, Paris, France, dated 13 March 1952. (Fr) [SHD]
16. J. A. Huston, Across The Face of France, Purdue University Press, Lafayette, IN (1963), p. 115.
17. D. J. Hickman, "The United States Army in Europe, 1953-63," Headquarters, US Army, Europe (USAREUR), Heidelberg, Germany, 1964, p. 112.
18. H. E. Eccles, Logistics in The National Defense, The Stackpole Company, Harrisburg, PA (1959), pp. 30-41.
19. C. R. Shrader (ed), United States Army Logistics 1775-1992, Center of Military History, Washington, DC (1997), pp. 443-445, 501-540, and 761-770.
20. J. A. Huston, The Sinews of War: Army Logistics, Center of Military History, Washington, DC (1966), pp. 591-614.
21. R. H. Scales, Certain Victory: The U.S. Army in the Gulf War, Brassey's, Dulles, VA (1994). In the Gulf War, wheeled logistical support vehicles, designed to operate on paved surfaces, often were separated from modern armored tracked vehicles by 90 miles or more.

References/Notes to pages 63 to 69

22. J. M. Heiser, Logistic Support, Department of The Army, Washington, DC (1974).
23. R. S. Allen, Lucky Forward, Vanguard Press, New York (1947), pp. 143-146.
24. C. H. Amme, NATO Without France, Hoover Institution, Stanford, CA (1967), p. 87.
25. D. J. Hickman (1964), p. 150.
26. M. J. Young, "Our New European Supply Line," Army Information Digest, October 1951, pp. 56-58.
27. J. A. Huston, One For All, University of Delaware Press, Newark, DE (1984), p. 66.
28. J. R. Moenk, "Establishment of Communications Through France, 1950-1951," Historical Division, US Army, Europe (USAREUR), Karlsruhe, Germany, 1952, p. 39.
29. C. Guy, "Aujourd'hui 'épreuve du feu' pour les bases U.S. en France," Paris Presse, 04 octobre 1951. (Fr) [SHD]
30. W. H. Maehl, "Relations of The European Command with Supreme Headquarters Allied Powers Europe, December 1950-June 1952," US Army, Europe (USAREUR), Karlsruhe, Germany, 1953, pp. 13-16.
31. Anon, "Annual Narrative Report, 01 January-31 December 1950," Headquarters, European Command (EUCOM), Karlsruhe, Germany, 1950, pp. 63 and 64.
32. Personal letter from Maj Gen Samuel D. Sturgis, Jr. to Maj Gen Lemuel Mathewson (US Commander, Berlin), dated 19 December 1952, p. 2. Letter enclosed rental agreement Young and Sturgis had with owner. [CEHO]
33. Anon, "Directory and Station List of The US Army," US Army, Washington, DC, December 1952, pp. 490-496. This bimonthly publication gives the complete listing of all Army units deployed worldwide.
34. P. Drouin, "De L'Atlantique Au Rhin avec l'armée américaine," Le Monde, 15 novembre 1951, pp. 1 and 3. (Fr) Overview of American military buildup in southwest France.
35. M. Peck, "Sturgis Says 10,000 Troops Are Living in Tents in Comm-Z," New York Herald Tribune, 04 December 1952, p. 2.
36. O. Pottier, Les Bases Américaines en France (1950-1967), Éditions l'Harmattan, Paris, France (2003), pp. 34, 36, and 90. (Fr)
37. Letter from Lt Gen Thomas B. Larkin (Acting Chief of Staff, G4, Department of the Army, Washington, DC) to Maj Gen Samuel P. Sturgis, Jr. (Commanding General, Communications Zone, France), dated 12 April 1952. [CEHO]
38. Interview, author with Jerome J. Ross (Special Agent (Sp4), 766th CIC Det Field Office, Braconne, France, 1965-66), Richfield, NJ, 14 May 2013.
39. J. A. Huston (1984), p. 71.
40. M. D. Taylor, Drill and Ceremonies, FM 22-5, Headquarters, Department of the Army, Washington, DC, August 1958.
41. W. H. McNeill, Keeping Together in Time: Dance and Drill in Human History, Harvard University Press, Cambridge, MA (1995), pp. 1-10.
42. C. Raia (ed), "New Phonetic Alphabet Due," Basec Mission, 13 January 1956, p. 2.
43. R. E. Mack, Memoir of a Cold War Soldier, The Kent State University Press, Kent, OH (2001), p. 47.
44. Interview, author with Carter J. Doering (Sgt, Tank Farm A, Metz Terminal District, St.-Baussant, France, 1965-67), Brookfield, WI, 02 November 2006.
45. M. J. Kosser, "On Getting Ahead After Getting Out," Army Information Digest, November 1967, p. 17.
46. R. Hylton, "When Are We Going?," Historical Services Division, National Guard Bureau, Arlington, VA (2000), pp. 49-61.
47. K. R. Coker, "Mobilization of the Army Reserve for the Korean War," Center of Army Reserve History, Fort McPherson, GA, May 2000, pp. 5-12.
48. R. Hylton (2000), pp. 49-61.
49. Anon, "Directory and Station List of The US Army," US Army, Washington, DC, 1951 to 1955.
50. R. Sher et al., "Integration of Negro and White Troops in the US Army, Europe, 1952-1954," Headquarters, US Army, Europe (USAREUR), Heidelberg, Germany, 1956, p. 44.
51. K. R. Coker (2000), pp. 21-34.
52. Anon, "Directory and Station List of The US Army," US Army, Washington, DC, October 1954, pp. 457-466 and December 1954, pp. 464-472. Station List may give primary location for unit such as Metz, instead of Billy-le-Grand, for 877th QM Company or omit TDY location such as St.-Hubert Sub-Depot where the 450th Ordnance Co from Trois Fontaines Ordnance Depot maintained ammo for Plan HEADRACE during three months in 1954.
53. R. Sher et al. (1956), pp. 44 and 45.
54. A. R. Sorrells, "When the balloon goes up," Part 2, Skyline, June 1955, pp. 22-31.
55. A. W. Spratley (ed), "USS Butner Calls at La Pallice, First Warship There Since 1940," ComZ Cadence, 28 November 1952, p. 1.
56. A. R. Sorrells, "When the balloon goes up," Part 1, Skyline, June 1955, pp. 17-21.
57. H. J. Whiteman, "Troop Commander's Voyage Report," 388th Fighter-Bomber Wing, Etain Air Base, France, 11 February 1955, pp. 1-4. [AFHRA]
58. Interview, author with Relon Hampton (Sp4, 76th Transportation Co (Med Tk), Maison-Fort, France, 1960-63), Premium, KY, 08 February 2013.

References/Notes to pages 69 to 78

59. Interview, author with James R. Lewis (Sp5, Braconne General Depot, France, 1964-66), Kansas City, MO, 16 February 2015.
60. Interview, author with Lee W. Stemmer (Pvt, Consolidated Supply Div, Ingrandes General Depot, France, 1958-59), Manlius, NY, 27 November 2006. Stemmer sailed to Europe on USNS *Geiger* in February 1958.
61. Interview, author with Richard K. Neeld (1st Lt, Ordnance Technical Assistance Team Leader, 565th Ordnance Co (FM), Nancy, France, 1955-57), Manahawkin, NJ, 05 November 2003.
62. Interview, author with US Air Force M/Sgt (ret) Michael A. Stone (Sp5, 275th Signal Co (Service), Maison-Fort, France, 1963-64), Colorado Springs, CO, 10 July 2009. Stone arrived on 04 December 1964 at BART on the USNS *Upshur*.
63. Interview, author with Francis J. Souza (Cpl, Headquarters Co, TFOD, Robert-Espagne, France, 1955-56), Cumberland, RI, 27 June 2012. Souza's troopship docked at BART on 02 January 1957.
64. Interview, author with Lyle A. Ross (Cpl, 529th Military Police Co, Laleu and Rochefort, France, 1952-53), Lake Havasu City, AZ, 21 April 2009.
65. F. C. Huntley (ed), "Rules and Regs on Running Your Ship or Station Newspaper," All Hands, August 1959, pp. 52 and 53.
66. H. J. Whiteman, "Now Hear This," The Eltinge Crier, 12 December 1954, p. 1.
67. Interview, author with Allen J. Kolons (Cpl, 7779th Central Medical Material Agency Det, Orléans, France, 1953), St. Louis, MO, 22 June 2007.
68. E. G. Plank, "A Guide To The USAT Gen Harry Taylor," New York Port of Embarkation, Brooklyn, NY, 1948, pp. 5-14.
69. Interview, author with Jesse Sanborn (wife of Sp3 Gerald F. Sanborn, 574th Ordnance Co (FM), Ingrandes, France, 1954-57), Monmouth, ME, 18 January 2007.
70. C. Raia (ed), "Cabin Spaces Upped for EM," Basec Mission, 21 April 1956, p. 1.
71. V. Pizer and P. H. Davis, Your Assignment Overseas, W. W. Norton, New York (1955), p. 38.
72. M. C. Day (ed), "OK Cabin Space For EM Sailing With Dependents," Orleans Item, 01 June 1956, p. 1.
73. Interview, author with Arlan I. Preblud (dependent of SFC William Preblud, Jarville-la-Malgrange, France, 1957-58), Denver, CO, 26 August 2013.
74. Interview, author with John B. Robert (PFC, Theater Special Weapons Supply Control Agency (TSWSCA), Maison-Fort, France, 1960-62), Murphy, NC, 24 January 2008.
75. Anon, "His Faithful Dog Shall Bear Him Company," Army Information Digest, November 1952, pp. 35-40.
76. L. Holt, "MSTS Puts the 'Sea' in Travel," U.S. Lady, November 1959, p. 10.
77. S. R. Mercogliano, "Sealift: The Evolution of Military Sea Transportation Service," Conference of Army Historians, Center of Military History, 08 August 2002.
78. Anon, Dictionary of American Naval Fighting Ships, Naval History Division, Navy Department, Washington, DC (1968).
79. Files of "Historical Data Card," AGAZ Form 373, Center of Military History, Washington, DC. Record of location of Army units, inclusive dates, campaigns and honors, and brief narrative of movements and exercises.
80. E. Weatherall, "Get on the Atlantic—It's the Greatest," The Stars and Stripes, 14 September 1959, pp. 11 and 12.
81. R. C. Boyd (ed), "ADSEC Sergeant Tells of 'Free' Luxury Cruise," The Advance, 30 January 1959, p. 3.
82. R. Strand, "Company Manners for GIs in France," New York Herald Tribune, Paris, 02 January 1953.
83. R. L. Parsons (ed), "Movement of 234 Passengers Hits New High Mark," The Pariscope, 15 May 1958, p. 1.
84. Anon, "Directory and Station List of the United States Army," Department of The Army, Washington, DC, volumes July 1951 through December 1953.
85. A. K. Nelson, "Anna M. Rosenberg, an Honorary Man," The Journal of Military History, January 2004, pp. 154-157.
86. M. T. Isenberg, Shield of the Republic, St. Martin's Press, New York (1993), p. 556.
87. J. L. Galloway and M. Tharp, "A General's order: Put Children first," U.S. News & World Report, 25 November 1996, pp. 43 and 44.
88. W. M. Summers (ed), "Army Plan Reported on Segregation," The Stars and Stripes, 15 January 1950, p. 4.
89. A. H. Myers, Black, White, and Olive Drab, University of Virginia Press, Charlottesville, VA (2006), pp. 74-91.
90. W. T. Bowers et al., Black Soldier, White Army, Center of Military History, Washington, DC (1996), pp. 37 and 38.
91. A. W. Spratley (ed), "Goatherders Win in Basec Battle," ComZ Cadence, 21 November 1952, p. 3.
92. M. J. MacGregor, Integration of The Armed Forces 1940-1965, Center of Military History, Washington, DC (1985), pp. 448-459.
93. R. Sher et al. (1956), pp. 11 and 41-46.
94. A. L. Jorgenson (ed), "Wilson Tells Posts to End School Segregation by '55," The Stars and Stripes, 02 February 1954, p. 6.
95. J. E. Smith, Eisenhower in War and Peace, Random House, New York (2012), p. 711.
96. A. L. Gropman, The Air Force Integrates, 1945-1964, Office of Air Force History, Washington, DC (1978), p. 151.
97. J. R. Moenk (1952), p. 27.

References/Notes to pages 78 to 85

98. Anon, "Inventory: Army and Air Force Installations Outside Continental U.S.," Departments of The Army and The Air Force, Washington, DC, 31 December 1953, pp. 68-78.
99. Statement for French Liaison Mission to Allies, signed by Jules Moch (le Ministre de la Defense Nationale), Paris, France, dated 19 février 1951. (Fr) [SHD]
100. A. Lecoeur, "Les Américains en Amérique," L'Humanité, 10 avril 1951, p. 1. (Fr) [AD 45]
101. J. Berlioz (redacteur en chef), "US Go Home," Démocratie Nouvelle, Numéro Spécial, No. 12, décembre 1951. (Fr) [CAC]
102. J. R. Moenk (1952), pp. 25 and 26. Canine was appointed by President Eisenhower to be first Director of the National Security Agency (1953-56).
103. Anon, "Memo from France," U.S. News & World Report, 07 November 1952, p. 46.
104. J. R. Moenk (1952), pp. 130-133.
105. X. H. Price (ed), American Armies and Battlefields in Europe, American Battle Monuments Commission (ABMC), Washington, DC (1938), pp. 436-447. Maj. Dwight D. Eisenhower, later 34th President of the US, was a member of the team that produced this book.
106. J. S. D. Eisenhower, Yanks, The Free Press, New York (2001), pp. 48-50.
107. B. King et al., Spearhead of Logistics, Center of Military History, Washington, DC (1994), pp. 101-115.
108. J. G. Harbord, The American Army in France, 1917-1919, Little, Brown and Co., Boston, MA (1936), pp. 602-615.
109. Anon, "Directory and Station List of The US Army," US Army, Washington, DC, 15 December 1952, pp. 490-496.
110. L. J. Eaton, "Camouflage Report on United States Forces Installations (Mainly in France)," Office of The Chief of Engineers, Department of The Army, Washington, DC, May 1953, pp. 9-32.
111. Anon, "Command Report Headquarters EUCOM/USAREUR 1952," Historical Division, Headquarters, US Army, Europe (USAREUR), Karlsruhe, Germany, 14 December 1953, pp. 421-428.
112. B. Delegue, "la 'Zone de Communications' Américaine à travers La France," Revue Militaire D'Information, mars 1952, pp. 17-20. (Fr) [SHD]
113. D. S. Sorenson, Shutting Down the Cold War, St. Martin's Press, New York (1998), pp. 8-14.
114. Anon, "Inventory: Army and Air Force Installations Outside Continental U.S.," Departments of The Army and The Air Force, Washington, DC, 31 December 1953, pp. 68-78.
115. F. Dallemagne, Les Casernes Françaises, Picard, Paris, France (1990). (Fr)
116. L. Galambos (1989), Vol. XII, pp. 355 and 356.
117. J. A. Warden, The Air Campaign, Pergamon-Brassey's, New York (1989), p. 10.
118. A. W. Tedder, Air Power in War, Hodder and Stoughton, London, England (1948).
119. B. Welles, "Atlantic Powers Speed Air Bases For Defense of Western Europe," New York Times, 19 July 1952, p. 3.
120. J. Ladoire, "L'aménagement de la base de Bordeaux-Mérignac coûte 2 milliards l'aviation américaine," Le Monde, 02 février 1952. (Fr)
121. S. W. Duke & W. Krieger, U.S. Military Forces in Europe, Westview Press, Boulder, CO (1993), p. 233.
122. Anon, "French Airfields," French Air Force-US Air Forces in Europe (USAFE) Working Party, 01 October 1951. [CEHO]
123. T. S. Matthews (ed), "Bogged Down," Time, 28 January 1952, p. 24.
124. M. S. Knaack, Post-World War II Bombers, 1945-1973, Office of Air Force History, Washington, DC (1988), p. 477.
125. J. J. McAuliffe, U.S. Air Force in France 1950-1967, Milspec Press, San Diego, CA (2005), p. 154.
126. D. Gordon, "Chaumont Memories," Air Enthusiast, November-December 2002, p 53.
127. Interview, author with Charles A. Cowell, Jr. (Capt, B-26 Navigator, 38th Bomber Wing (Light), Laon AB, 1952-54), Washington, NC, 03 September 2003.
128. M. S. Knaack (1988), p. 322.
129. M. D. Egan and J. J. McAuliffe, "USAF Bases in Cold War France," Conference of Army Historians, Center of Military History, 17 June 1996.
130. C. A. Ravenstein, Air Force Combat Wings, Office of Air Force History, Washington, DC (1984), pp. 25, 40, 66, 67, 77, 209, 210, and 260.
131. P. J. Birtles, "The South Carolina Air National Guard," Aviation News, 12 March 1993, p. 945.
132. A. R. Herzog and R. L. Scribner, "History of the 465th Troop Carrier Group," Toul-Rosières Air Base, Rosières-en-Haye, France, 15 April 1954. [AFHRA]
133. Interview, author with Lt Col (ret) Thomas D. Miller (Capt, Pilot, 50th Fighter Bomber Wing, Toul-Rosières, France, 1956-58), Lewisville, TX, 09 January 2005.
134. G. Moet, "Our Statue of Liberty," Jet-48, 01 June 1956, p. 1.
135. Interview, author with Lt Gen (ret) Albert P. Clark (Brig Gen, Wing Commander, 48th Fighter Bomber Wing, Chaumont AB, France, 1955-56), Colorado Springs, CO, 22 October 1998.

136. A. L. Jorgensen (ed), "Chaumont's 1st Sabres Placed in Operation by 48th Wing Personnel," The Stars and Stripes, 07 January 1954, p. 9.
137. J. Walters, "Supersonic Jets Give USAFE Wing New Punch," The Stars and Stripes, 26 February 1957, p. 11.
138. P. Mauffrey, Phalsbourg Air Base, Imprimerie Scheuer, Drulingen, France (1990), p. 97. (Fr)
139. Anon, "Liste des aérodromes atlantiques," OTAN, Paris, France, 1952. (Fr) [SHD]
140. D. A. Burchinal, "FRELOC Final Report," Headquarters, US European Command (USEUCOM), St.-Germain-en-Laye, France, 1967, pp. 28 and 35. Report written at Camp des Loges by Lt Col John F. McGauhey, USAF.
141. L. R. Benson, USAF Aircraft Basing in Europe, North Africa, and the Middle East, 1945-1980, Headquarters, US Air Forces in Europe (USAFE), Ramstein Air Base, Germany, 23 April 1981, pp. 99-106.
142. T. S. Snyder and S. A. Shaw, United States Airforces in Europe, Historical Highlights, 1942-1992, Headquarters, US Air Forces in Europe (USAFE), Ramstein Air Base, Germany, 23 February 1993, p. 77.
143. O. Pottier, "Les Bases Américaines en France: un outil militaire, économique et politique (1950-1967)," Revue Historique des Armées, No. 2, 1999, p. 73. (Fr)
144. F. Jarraud, Les Américains à Châteauroux 1951-1967, Chez l'auteur, Le Poinçonnet, France (1981), pp. 50 and 51. (Fr)
145. C. W. Griffith, "History of 12th Communications Construction Squadron," Moulins Vehicle Depot, Moulins, France, 30 June 1953. [AFHRA]
146. J.-P. Hoehn, "Chateauroux Air Station, 1951-1967," Air Fan, novembre 1992, pp. 30-39 and janvier 1993, pp. 36-45. (Fr)
147. J. J. McAuliffe (2005), pp. 187-217.
148. L. R. Benson (1981), pp. 142-146, 148, and 151.
149. J. J. McAuliffe (2005), pp. 140 and 141.
150. C. J. Gross, Prelude to the Total Force: The Air National Guard, 1943-1969, Office of Air Force History, Washington, DC (1985), pp. 177-190. Gross presents comprehensive data on ANG mobilizations for Korea (1950-51) and Berlin (1961).
151. C. A. Ravenstein (1984). Ravenstein compiled lineage, commanders, basing locations, aircraft flown, significant operations, and other historical information for US Air Force wings.
152. C. Zglinski, "The Rail Transportation Offices," The Pariscope, 09 January 1958, p. 3.
153. D. A. Bartoni (ed), "La Rochelle RTO Keeps 'Em Moving As Crossroads of Basec Travel Net," The Stars and Stripes, 10 April 1956, p. 9.
154. Interview, author with Melvyn Bryan Hackett (Sp4, Company D, 601st Ordnance Bn, Braconne, France, 1957-58), Grass Valley, CA, 29 January 2007.
155. J. A. Ulio, French Phrase Book, TM 30-602, War Department, Washington, DC (1943), pp. 9, 32, and 33.
156. T. D. G. Teare, The Evader, Hodder and Stoughton, London, England (1954), pp. 248-252.
157. A. Brastel, Liberation Sanglante de Quatre Villages Meusiens, Imprimerie du Barrois, Bar-le-Duc, France (1969). (Fr)
158. J. Adnet, When I See A "Forty and Eight", I Remember World War Two, Adnetech, Colorado Springs, CO (2001), pp. 107-109.
159. P. Lieb, Konventioneller Krieg oder NS-Weltanschauungskrieg? Kriegführung und Partisanenbekämpfung in Frankreich 1943/44, R. Oldenbourg Verlag, München, Germany (2007), p. 574. (Gr) Lieb includes statistics on massacres by Germans retreating from France. During the infamous 1968 My Lai massacre, several US soldiers refused to shoot non-combatants and a US Army helicopter crew intervened to rescue unarmed civilians.
160. D. C. McKay, The United States and France, Harvard University Press, Cambridge, MA (1951), pp. 295 and 307-308. Appendix I, compiled by Aaron Noland, presents statistics on the French transportation and communications networks and losses due to occupation and liberation.
161. J. L. Cooper (ed), "More Passenger Service Directed By ComZ," Basec Mission, 11 September 1953, p. 1.
162. D. Walter, "Holiday Traffic Jams French Roads," The Stars and Stripes, 30 December 1959, p. 8.
163. Interview, author with Dwight A. Brady (Sp4, Trailer Truck Driver, 89th Transportation Co, Kaiserslautern, Germany, 1966), White Pine, TN, 10 November 2015.
164. C. C. Case, "Operation FRELOC," The Review, May-June 1967, p. 134.
165. J. P. Anderson (ed), "French Bicycles Have Equal Rights With Autos, Trucks," Basec Mission, 05 November 1954, pp. 2 and 4.
166. D. Walters, "Car Accidents Killed 43 in ComZ in 1953," The Stars and Stripes, 04 February 1954, p. 9.
167. R. Brooks, "89 POV Deaths," Orleans Item, 13 September 1963, p. 1.
168. Anon, "Review of the Month," US Army Communications Zone Europe, Orléans, France, 31 January 1967, pp. 4.1 to 4.3. [MHI]
169. J. P. O'Donnell, "We're All Fouled Up In France," The Saturday Evening Post, 11 April 1953, p. 40.
170. P. H. Slaughter, "Substituting the Speed Ball for the Red Ball," National Defense Transportation Journal, May-June 1952, pp. 24-26.
171. T. Billard, "The Red Ball Express," Translog, October 1976, pp. 14, 15, and 18.
172. S. R. Waddell, United States Army Logistics: The Normandy Campaign, 1944, Greenwood Press, Westport, CT (1994), pp. 124-132.

References/Notes to pages 95 to 101

173. U. Lee, The Employment of Negro Troops, Center of Military History, Washington, DC (1966), p. 633.
174. M. Blumenson, Breakout and Pursuit, Center of Military History, Washington, DC (1960), pp. 690-692.
175. D. P. Colley, The Road to Victory, Brassey's, Washington, DC (2000), pp. 123-131.
176. R. Callaway, White Captain, Black Troops, The Lowell Press, Kansas City, MO (1993), pp. 58-66.
177. A. W. Spratley (ed), "Famed 'Red Ball Express' Rolling Again in France," ComZ Cadence, 23 January 1953, p. 4.
178. H. J. Richter (ed), "Red Ball Express Back On French Highways," The Stars and Stripes, 30 January 1953, p. 7.
179. P. J. Mahoney, "Major General Anderson, CG, USACOMZEUR, Pays First Official Visit to 37th Headquarters," The Transporter, 07 June 1963, pp. 7 and 12.
180. A. W. Spratley (ed), "FMCO Set Up To Check LOC Convoy Movements," ComZ Cadence, 17 October 1953, p. 6.
181. J. A. Huston, "The Red Ball Rolls Again," The Army Combat Forces Journal, August 1955, pp. 38-44.
182. J. T. Perkins (ed), "Trucks to Have Subtler Sound," ComZ Cadence, 28 May 1954, p. 2.
183. A. W. Spratley (ed), "US Honors Man Who Risked Life in Ammo Blaze," ComZ Cadence, 10 April 1953, p. 1.
184. E. Risch, Fuels for Global Conflict, QMC Historical Studies No. 9, Washington, DC, February 1945, pp. 60 and 61.
185. R. M. Daniel, "The Little Can That Could," Officer Review, July-August 2016, pp. 5-7.
186. R. G. Ruppenthal, Logistical Support of the Armies, Vol. II, Center of Military History, Washington, DC (1959), pp. 201-203.
187. E. R. Richardson and S. Allan, Quartermaster Supply in the European Theater of Operations in World War II, Vol. IV, The Quartermaster School, Camp Lee, Virginia, 1948, p. 33.
188. Interview, author with Lt Col (ret) Charles E. Turek (1st Lt, Platoon Leader, 877th QM Co (Petro Depot), Caserne Lariboisière, Fontainebleau, France, 1953-55), Surfside Beach, SC, 20 May 2015.
189. R. J. Crawford (ed), "Billy-le-Grand Truckers To Host French Kids For Easter," The Advance, 30 March 1956, p. 1.
190. R. J. Crawford (ed), "Santa Claus' Reality Proved Through Billy-le-Grand Soldiers," The Advance, 07 December 1956, p. 3.
191. J. R. Moenk, "Line of Communications Through France 1952-1953," Headquarters, US Army Europe (USAREUR), Karlsruhe, Germany (1955), pp. 35 and 174.
192. S. Duke, U.S. Military Forces and Installations in Europe, Oxford University Press, Oxford, England (1989), pp. 154-159.
193. H. A. Finch, "Reminiscences of an Old 'Enjine,'" The Military Engineer, May-June 1956, p. 213.
194. C. O. Stanley (ed), "Orin, Loiret Department Sign Mutual Fire Assistance Pact," Orleans Item, 11 November 1955, pp. 1 and 3.
195. A. F. Hand (ed), "83rd Engrs' Men, Equipment Help Local French Town," Basec Mission, 15 April 1955, p. 6.
196. C. Raia (ed), "Basec Rushes Food, Firewood to 400 Caught by Weather's Vise on Island," Basec Mission, 25 February 1956, p. 1.
197. Letter from M. Milon (MCLAAA, Paris, France) to Col G. B. Martin (USAFE, Paris Office), dated 10 avril 1958. (Fr) [SHD]
198. J. D. Nottingham (ed), "Army Crane Lifts Cow Out of French Well," The Stars and Stripes, 24 August 1959, p. 8.
199. A. Corbet (ed), "Lunette' sauvée de la noyade," Panorama, octobre 1959, p. 8. (Fr)
200. P. Abramovici, "Juin 1961, Le Strasbourg-Paris D'eraille L'attentat ferroviaire resté secret d'Etat," Historia, 01 mai 2004, p. 18. (Fr)
201. R. J. Weide (ed), "Added Praise Given Mercy Mission Pilots," The Lifeline Times, 26 August 1961, p. 2.
202. D. J. Hickman (1964), p. 189.
203. F. M. Achee, "No Task Too Great in France, 1951-1966," Headquarters, 97th Engineer Bn, Verdun, France, nd, p. 12. [CEHO]
204. R. P. de Malglaive, "Community Relations 1952-1967," Laon Air Base, Couvron-et-Aumencourt, France, 1967, p. 14. [AFHRA]
205. Letter from Brig Gen Charles C. Blanchard (Commanding General, Base Section) to Maj Gen Samuel D. Sturgis, Jr. (Commanding General, ComZ), dated 25 November 1952. [CEHO]
206. R. L. Bennett, "Annual Historical Report 1966," Headquarters, US Army Communications Zone, Europe (USACOMZEUR), Orléans, France, 1967, Vol. I, pp. 11-14.
207. O. Pottier (2003), pp. 161-166. (Fr)
208. Anon, "Command Report Headquarters EUCOM/USAREUR 1952," Historical Division, Headquarters, US Army, Europe (USAREUR), Karlsruhe, Germany, 14 December 1953, pp. 285 and 286.
209. J. R. Moenk, "The Line of Communications Through France, 1952-1953," Historical Division, Headquarters, US Army, Europe (USAREUR), Karlsruhe, Germany, 1955, pp. 88 and 89.
210. P. Hellman, Avenue of the Righteous, Atheneum, New York (1980), pp. 129 and 130.
211. J. P. Anderson (ed), "Braconne Raises French Flag," Basec Mission, 21 May 1954, p. 6.
212. R. J. Crawford (ed), "Tricolor Flies at Billy-le-Grand," The Advance, 27 May 1955, p. 1.
213. Interviews, author with Col (ret) John E. Hurst, Jr. (Capt, 553rd Engineer Bn, Maison-Fort, France, 1956-59), Independence, VA, 16 February and 10 March 2014.

References/Notes to pages 101 to 109

CHAPTER FOUR

1. A. W. Spratley (ed), "Engrs From Germany Rush Basec Sites for Winter Housing," ComZ Cadence, 19 September 1952, pp. 1 and 4.
2. Anon, "NATO Base Held Up By Delay on Funds," New York Times, 11 April 1952, p. 5.
3. Anon, "American General Upsets USAFE Progress After Relaxation of Curbs Imposed by French," Los Angeles Times, 14 May 1952.
4. G. R. Robertson, Engineer Memoirs, General William M. Hoge, US Army Corps of Engineers, EP 870-1-25, Alexandria, VA, January 1993, pp. 196 and 197.
5. A. L. Jorgenson (ed), "JCA to Finish Work at Saran Next Month," The Stars and Stripes, 09 December 1953, p. 8.
6. A. O. Sulzberger, "U.S. Completing Depots in France to Back Its Forces in Germany," New York Times, 12 February 1955, p. 2.
7. B. Welles, "Army Supply Line in France Snarled," New York Times, 26 May 1953, pp. 1 and 10.
8. R. Vinen, The Unfree French, Yale University Press, New Haven, CT (2006), pp. 249 and 317.
9. H. Wales, "US Waste on French Depots May Be Millions," Chicago Daily Tribune, 06 May 1952. Wales' premise that construction was slow was correct, but his allegations of scandal and waste proved to be false. According to Col Hubert E. Klemp, chief engineer at ComZ, the article contained numerous errors and exaggerations and it was likely the unnamed sources were "disgruntled bidders and barflies." [CEHO]
10. D. A. Carter, Forging The Shield: The U.S. Army in Europe, 1951-1962, Center of Military History, Washington, DC (2015), pp. 63 and 64.
11. Letter from Maj Gen Samuel D. Sturgis, Jr. to Lt Gen Lewis A. Pick (Chief of Engineers, Department of the Army, Washington, DC), dated 21 May 1952, p. 2. [CEHO]
12. Letter from Maj Gen Samuel D. Sturgis, Jr. to Brig Gen G. E. Textor (Assistant Chief of Engineers for Military Operations, Department of the Army, Washington, DC), dated 10 June 1952. [CEHO]
13. B. Welles, "Ridgway to Unify Vast U.S. Work for Bases in Europe to Stop Waste," New York Times, 11 January 1953, pp. 1 and 22.
14. B. Welles, "U.S., France Near New Bases Accord," New York Times, 14 February 1952, p. 9.
15. Anon, "Military Construction in France," Army Navy Air Force Journal, 12 February 1955, p. 11.
16. D. Walter, "JCA: It Saves the U. S. Construction Dollar," The Stars and Stripes, 20 October 1956, p. 11.
17. T. S. Matthews (ed), "Bogged Down," Time, 28 January 1952, p. 25.
18. E. Gruening, "Disposal of United States Military Installations and Supplies in France," Subcommittee on Foreign Aid Expenditures of the Committee on Government Operations, US Senate, Washington, DC, 06 April 1967, p. 11.
19. J. J. McAuliffe, U. S. Air Forces in France 1950-1967, Milspec Press, San Diego, CA (2005), pp. 429-431.
20. V. Prot, The American Forces in Châteauroux (1951-1967), Éditions Tarmeye, Mazet St.-Voy, France (1998), pp. 27-33 and 46.
21. D. Walter, "Tent City Houses SCARWAF Troops Building New Base for Air Force Near St. Nazaire," The Stars and Stripes, 11 May 1953, p. 8.
22. R. Reynolds, "Yanks to Build French Road Around Base," The Stars and Stripes, 08 February 1954, p. 9.
23. N. Raymond, "Mammoth Construction Job," The Stars and Stripes, 23 February 1957, p. 12.
24. J. L. Gilbert et al., In The Shadow of The Sphinx, History Office, US Army Intelligence and Security Command (INSCOM), Fort Belvoir, VA (2005), p. 122.
25. Anon, "Bishop Hits Laon Base Conditions," The Washington Post, 26 December 1953, p. 3.
26. Interview, author with Lt Col (ret) Thomas D. Miller (Capt, Pilot, 50th Fighter Bomber Wing, Toul-Rosières, France, 1956-58), Lewisville, TX, 09 January 2005.
27. Letter from Brig Gen James E. Whisenand (Commander, 388th Fighter Bomber Wing, Étain AB), Étain, France to Maj Gen Robert M. Lee, Commander, Twelfth Air Force, Ramstein, Germany, dated 21 February 1955. [AFHRA]
28. J.-P. Hoehn, "Il Étail Une Fois…Phalsbourg Air Base," Air Fan, avril 1980, p. 30. (Fr)
29. K. N. Gantz (ed), "Hands Across the Street," Air University Quarterly Review, Spring 1955, p. 53.
30. R. Strand, "Output Woes at Com-Z," New York Herald Tribune, Paris, 20 November 1952.
31. R. P. Grathwol and D. M. Moorhus, Building for Peace, Center of Military History, Washington, DC (2005), p. 111.
32. J. S. Arrigona and W. R. Karsteter, "History of the Joint Construction Agency in Europe," JCA, Boulogne-sur-Seine (Paris), France, 1958, p. 289. [CEHO]
33. R. J. Crawford (ed), "CBS Unit Films in ADSEC," The Advance, 11 June 1954, p. 1.
34. J. S. Arrigona and W. R. Karsteter (1958), pp. 101 and 102.
35. J. P. Anderson (ed), "Plans Made to Translate Ord Manuals," Basec Mission, 12 February 1954, p. 4.
36. J. S. Arrigona and W. R. Karsteter (1958), p. 162.
37. Interview, author with Professor Lloyd A. Leffers (1st Lt, Supply Officer, 97th Engineer Bn, Verdun, France, 1955-57), Champaign, IL, 28 January 2008.

References/Notes to pages 111 to 119

38. R. P. Grathwol and D. M. Moorhus (2005), pp. 106 and 107.
39. J. S. Arrigona and W. R. Karsteter (1958), pp. 284 and 285.
40. D. B. Grace, "Paris," <u>The Military Engineer</u>, January-February 1957, p. 73.
41. B. Welles, "U.S. Morale Low at French Bases," <u>New York Times</u>, 27 May 1953, p. 8.
42. J. S. Arrigona and W. R. Karsteter (1958), pp. 83-85.
43. R. F. Bartelmes, "Military Prefabricated Buildings," <u>The Military Engineer</u>, March-April 1957, pp. 96-99.
44. A. P. O'Meara, Jr., <u>Accidental Warrior</u>, Elderberry Press, Oakland, OR (2002), pp. 50 and 51.
45. Private correspondence to author from Harry F. Puncec (Sp4, Company Clerk, Company C, 97th Engineer Bn, Verdun and Étain, France, 1959-62), Lakewood, CO, 27 February 2002.
46. R. J. Crawford (ed), "New Quonsets to Signal Finish of Many Temporary Hutments," <u>The Advance</u>, 31 August 1956, p. 3.
47. M. C. Day (ed), "New Quonsets Constructed by 'A' Co of the 553rd EBC," <u>Orleans Item</u>, 16 November 1956, pp. 1 and 3.
48. J. P. Anderson (ed), "Saumur is First Depot to Have All US-Built Billets," <u>Basec Mission</u>, 20 August 1954, p. 1.
49. J. Anderson, "Housing in Adsec Has Come a Long, Long Way," <u>The Overseas Weekly</u>, 16 September 1956, p. 6.
50. J. P. O'Donnell, "We're All Fouled Up In France," <u>The Saturday Evening Post</u>, 11 April 1953, pp. 40 and 41.
51. D. A. Lane et al., "The US Army Deutsche Mark Construction Program 1953-1957," Headquarters, US Army, Europe (USAREUR), Heidelberg, Germany, 1958, pp. 1-4.
52. J. A. Huston, <u>Outposts and Allies</u>, Associated University Presses, Cranbury, NJ (1988), pp. 69-71.
53. R. Strand, "US Army Wives: Poor Living Facilities, High Prices, Hard Work, and Boredom Demand Pluck, Sacrifices," <u>New York Herald Tribune, Paris</u>, 12 November 1952.
54. J. R. Moenk, "Annual Historical Report 1953-54," Headquarters, US Army, Europe (USAREUR), Karlsruhe, Germany, 1955, pp. 77 and 78.
55. R. J. Dunphy, "Army, AF Act to Solve Metz Housing Problems," <u>The Stars and Stripes</u>, 02 March 1955, p. 11.
56. A. F. Head (ed), "39.6% of Basec Housing Found 'Adequate' by G-1," <u>Basec Mission</u>, 01 April 1955, p. 6.
57. K. Solem, "Verdun Signal Group Sets High Phone Service Goal," <u>The Advance</u>, 10 April 1953, p. 4.
58. R. J. Crawford (ed), "ADSEC's First Dial System Begins Operation at Metz," <u>The Advance</u>, 16 July 1954, p. 1.
59. A. Peyrefitte, <u>The Trouble with France</u>, New York University Press, New York (1986), pp. 53 and 54. Originally published in France as <u>Le Mal Français</u> (1976) by Libraire Plon.
60. Interview, author with Katherine Radosh (wife of Capt Burnett H. Radosh, Army JAG, Bussac, France, 1961-62), Lighthouse Point, FL, 24 January 2006.
61. J. Walters, "Building Operations Rushed at Chambley," <u>The Stars and Stripes</u>, 18 March 1955.
62. R. J. Dunphy, "Tough Teaching Job," <u>The Stars and Stripes</u>, 08 March 1955, p. 12.
63. Interview, author with Brig Gen (ret) Alan C. "Ace" Edmunds (Lt Col, Squadron Commander, 531st Fighter-Bomber Squadron, Chambley AB, 1954-57), Spokane, WA, 29 April 2004.
64. W. P. Riddling, "Welcome to Dreux Air Base," Pamphlet No. 190-1-1, 31 March 1966, pp. 4-6.
65. Anon, "300 logements pour l' armée américaine sont en cours de construction à Saint-Jean-de-la-Ruelle," <u>La Nouvelle République</u>, 27 mars 1956. (Fr) [AD 45]
66. D. Halberstan, <u>The Fifties</u>, Villard Books, New York (1993), pp. 131-143.
67. W. C. Baldwin, "Army Family Housing in the 1950s," Conference of Army Historians, Center of Military History, 19 June 1996.
68. Private correspondence to author from Dr. Donald A. Nitkin (Capt, 60th Station Hospital, Chinon, France, 1963-64), Clinton Township, MI, 19 August 2006.
69. J. R. Moenk, "Annual Historical Report, 1953-1954," Headquarters, US Army, Europe (USAREUR), Karlsruhe, Germany, 1955, pp. 339 and 340.
70. R. P. Grathwol and D. M. Moorhus (2005), p. 109.
71. Interview, Karl C. Dod with Maj Gen (ret) Bernard L. Robinson (Maj Gen, Director, Joint Construction Agency (JCA), Boulogne-sur-Seine, 1955-57), Manchester, MO, 08 November 1978. [CEHO]
72. Interview, author with Lt Col (ret) Edmond Ray York (1st Lt, Assistant to the CO, Ingrandes General Depot, France, 1959-62), Copperas Cove, TX, 06 March 2013.
73. Anon, "La Cité américaine des Quatre-Vents, à Olivet pred le nom de Cité Maréchal-Foch," <u>La Nouvelle République</u>, 28 novembre 1959. (Fr) [AD 45]
74. H. A. Miley, Senior Officer Oral History Program, US Army Military History Institute, Carlisle Barracks, PA, 1975, pp. 53-55.
75. Anon, "Families at Air Force Bases in France Will Get Hundreds of New Housing Units," <u>Army Navy Air Force Journal</u>, 23 March 1957, p. 8.
76. P. Mauffrey, <u>Phalsbourg Air Base</u>, Imprimerie Scheuer, Drulingen, France (1990), p. 59. (Fr)
77. N. A. Oelhafen (ed), "100th Family Moves into Chaumont Housing Project," <u>Jet-48</u>, 09 November 1956, pp. 1 and 4. [USAFA]

78. O. Pottier, "La présence militaire américaine à Chaumont (1952-1967)," Extrait d'un Mémoire de Diplôme d'Etudes Approfondies, Université de Reims Champagne-Ardenne, Reims, France, juin 1992, p. 145. (Fr)
79. Interview, author with Guy Farneau (owner of house in la Petite-Espère), St.-Jean-de-la-Ruelle, France, 09 November 2001. In 1988, Farneau hired an architect to design an attached garage and additional living space for his former RGH unit.
80. Interview, author with Ross A. Gagliano (1st Lt, Executive Officer, 228th Signal Co, Fontenet, France, 1961-62), Decatur, GA, 29 June 2006.
81. L. V. Warner, "Command Report, Headquarters, EUCOM/USAREUR 1952," Historical Division, HQ USAREUR, Karlsruhe, Germany, 14 December 1953, pp. 270 and 271.
82. J. S. Arrigona and W. R. Karsteter (1958), pp. 176-179.
83. G. H. Plankenhorn, "Installations (Bachelor Officers' Quarters)," Regulation No. 415-35, Headquarters, US Army General Depot Complex, Verdun, France, 01 May 1964, pp. 1-5.
84. J. R. Moenk (1955), p. 77.
85. Interview, author with Jerome R. Block (PFC, 39th Ordnance Co and 32nd Engineer Group, Verdun, France, 1960-63), Bolivia, NC, 10 January 2014.
86. D. Gordon, "Chaumont," Air Enthusiast, January-February 2003, p. 6.
87. H. Mackintosh, "Food Chain for the Armed Services," Army Information Digest, May 1962, p. 55.
88. D. R. Peryam, "Taste too, Is a Factor," Army Information Digest, January 1961, p. 66.
89. C. Raia (ed), "Mess Halls Improve Under 'Star' System," Basec Mission, 02 December 1955, pp. 1 and 2.
90. L. B. Sibert (ed), "833d Sig Co Mess Sgt Learns French Cooking," The Stars and Stripes, 04 March 1955, p. 9.
91. J. P. Anderson (ed), "Civilian KP's Work in Basec Mess Halls," Basec Mission, 03 December 1954, pp. 1 and 6.
92. C. Raia (ed), "Men Begin KP in Most Posts of Command," Basec Mission, 07 January 1956, pp. 1 and 2.
93. Interview, author with James L. Lepant (Sp4, 581st Engineer Co (FM), Chinon Engineer Depot, France, 1956-57), Broken Bow, NE, 31 December 2010.
94. G. Derule, "La Chapelle de la BA 136: Notre Dame de l'Assomption," Reflects, Journal de la BA 136 de Toul-Rosières, France, no. 135, janvier-mars 1993, pp. 15-18. (Fr)
95. J. P. Anderson (ed), "Americans Give Statue of Virgin To French Cathedral in La Rochelle," Basec Mission, 15 October 1954, p. 1.
96. V. F. Leaming, "No Higher Calling," Army Information Digest, July 1964, pp. 24-31.
97. F. Jarraud, Les Américains à Châteauroux 1951-1967, Chez l'auteur, Le Poinçonnet, France (1981), pp. 93-118. (Fr)
98. G. Bize, Base Aérienne de Toul-Rosières du Zénith au Nadir, Impression APRAA, Paris, France (2004), p. 29. (Fr)
99. R. Kemeling, Keepers of Freedom, CH&ER Publishing, N. Charleston. SC (2004), p. 262.
100. A. W. Spratley (ed), "Church Offers Beds for Paris Leaves," ComZ Cadence, 23 May 1952, p.1.
101. R. Dixon, A Church on the Seine, The American and Foreign Christian Union, New York (1981), pp. 34 and 35. After the 25 August 1944 liberation of Paris, US military on leave could use duckpin bowling alleys at the church.
102. M. P. Gudebrod, "Paris' American Cathedral," The Stars and Stripes, 21 January 1963, p. 14.
103. B. Weller, "U.S. Morale Low at French Bases," New York Times, 27 May 1953, p. 8.
104. C. O. Stanley (ed), "Coligny Theater Rules Announced," Orleans Item, 19 August 1955, p. 3.
105. J. C. Cougill, "Welcome to Orleans Area Command," Headquarters, OAC, Forêt d'Orléans, France, July 1961, pp. 12 and 13.
106. E. Yoder, "Military Links," Government Executive, 01 May 1997, pp. 53-56.
107. M. C. Day (ed), "Colonel Henry C. Britt Returns to CONUS," Orleans Item, 19 July 1957, pp. 1 and 2.
108. O. S. Kuwahara, "Good News for Orleans Golfers," The Stars and Stripes, 15 August 1956, pp. 12 and 13.
109. R. P. Grathwol and D. M. Moorhus (2005), pp. 116-120.
110. D. A. Lane, "Annual Historical Report for 1957-58," Headquarters, US Army, Europe (USAREUR), Heidelberg, Germany, 1958, pp. 257-265.
111. J. S. Arrigona and W. R. Karsteter (1958), pp. 112, 309, 317, and 361-363.
112. D. H. Tully, "The Military Construction Program," The Military Engineer, November-December 1954, pp. 407 and 408.
113. K. C. Dod, "Overseas Military Operations of the Corps of Engineers, 1945-1970," nd, Chap. 18. Unpublished manuscript by Karl Dod held at Office of History, US Army Corps of Engineers (CEHO), Alexandria, VA.
114. R. P. Grathwol and D. M. Moorhus (2005), pp. 101-114.

CHAPTER FIVE

1. R. W. Argo, "A Short History of EUCOM, 1947-1974," Center of Military History, Washington, DC, 23 May 1974.
2. Letter from Maj Gen Samuel D. Sturgis, Jr. (Commanding General, USACOMZEUR) to François Leduc (Chef de la Mission Centrale de Liaison pour l'Assistance aux Armées Alliées, Paris, France), dated 17 November 1952. [CAC]

3. D. A. Ruiz Palmer, "France" in J. Simon (ed), NATO-Warsaw Pact Force Mobilization, The National Defense University Press, Washington, DC (1988), pp. 273-276.
4. J. Quigley, "EUCOM Set for Shift to France," The Stars and Stripes, 27 January 1954, p. 2.
5. D. Walter, "EUCOM Hq Site Rich in Historical Lore," The Stars and Stripes, 04 May 1956, p. 11.
6. Anon, "US Army Installations France," Headquarters, US Army Communications Zone, Europe (USCOMZEUR), Orléans, France, 1966. Information Brochure on Camp des Loges. [CEHO]
7. J. R. Moenk, "Annual Historical Report for 1953-54," Headquarters, US Army, Europe (USAREUR), Karlsruhe, Germany, 1955, pp. 381-383
8. T. R. Strobridge, "History of The United States European Command," History Office, US European Command (USEUCOM), Stuttgart-Vaihingen, Germany, 1989, pp. 9 and 10.
9. C. H. Donnelly, Autobiography, unpublished manuscript, Washington, DC, dated 10 May 1959, pp. 1243 and 1244. [MHI]
10. Interview, author with Chief Petty Officer (ret) Earl L. Corbin (NCOIC, SCU 996, Headquarters, USEUCOM, Camp des Loges, France, 1954-56), Hawkins, TX, 19 March 2010.
11. R.C. Larson, "The Woman's Touch in USAREUR," Army Information Digest, March 1966, p. 62.
12. R. J. Aldrich, The Hidden Hand, John Murray, London, England (2001), pp. 544 and 545.
13. A. W. Spratley (ed), "ComZ's Seine Area Command Has Complex Mission," ComZ Cadence, 02 October 1953, p. 5.
14. D. A. Lane, "Annual Historical Report for 1954-55," Headquarters, US Army, Europe (USAREUR), Heidelberg, Germany, 1956, p. 310.
15. R. D. Donnelly, "514th Ord DAS-Army's Globe Trotters," Basec Mission, 01 May 1953, p. 4.
16. D. Miller, The Cold War, John Murray, London, England (1998), p. 337.
17. G. Menant, "Pourquoi Paques a Trahi," Paris Match, 05 octobre 1963, pp. 79-85. [Fr]
18. D. Cook, Floodtide in Europe, G. P. Putnam's Sons, New York (1965), p. 154.
19. J. Barron, KGB: The Secret Work of Soviet Secret Agents, Reader's Digest Press, New York (1974), p. 23.
20. G. W. Pedlow, "Allied Crisis Management for Berlin: The LIVE OAK Organization, 1959-1963" in W. W. Epley (ed), International Cold War Military Records and History, Office of the Secretary of Defense, Washington DC (1996), p. 95.
21. S. M. Maloney, "Berlin Contingency Planning: Prelude to Flexible Response, 1958-1963," Journal of Strategic Studies, March 2002, pp. 110-113.
22. H. Yasamee, "Britain and Berlin, 1950-1962," in W. W. Epley (ed), International Cold War Military Records and History, Office of the Secretary of Defense, Washington, DC (1996), p. 135.
23. F. Kempe, Berlin 1961, G. P. Putnam's Sons, New York (2011), pp. 347-362.
24. J. A. Fahey, Licensed To Spy, Naval Institute Press, Annapolis, MD (2002), p. 112.
25. R. P. Grathwol and D. M. Moorhus, American Forces in Berlin: Cold War Outpost 1945-1994, US Department of Defense, Washington, DC (1994), pp. 84-125.
26. L. S. Kaplan, "The Berlin Crisis, 1958-1962: Views from the Pentagon" in W. W. Epley (ed), International Cold War Military Records and History, Office of the Secretary of Defense, Washington, DC (1996), p. 73.
27. J. L. Gaddis, We Now Know, Oxford University Press, New York (1997), p. 148.
28. F. Kemp (2011), p. 418.
29. Anon, "Military taps Kubek, Yankees' first loss," The Birmingham News, 05 November 1961, p. C-10.
30. R. E. Killblane, Mentoring and Leadership, US Army Transportation Center, Fort Eustis, VA (2003), pp. 34 and 35.
31. J. E. Smith, The Defense of Berlin, The Johns Hopkins Press, Baltimore, MD (1963), pp. 339-341.
32. Anon, "Directory and Station List of The US Army," US Army, Washington, DC, 15 December 1961, pp. 470-478.
33. Historical Data Cards (Form 373), Unit History Branch, US Army Center of Military History, Washington, DC.
34. Authorized strength for officers (OFF) includes warrant officers, enlisted men (EM) includes NCOs. Data from US Army Tables of Organization (TOE) prior to Fall 1961 presented for units of: Artillery (6), Chemical (3), Engineers (5), Military Police (19), Ordnance (9), Quartermaster (10), Signal (11), and Transportation (55). Number in parentheses designates US Army branch code.
35. F. Drake and K. Drake, "The Inside Story of Stairstep," The Reader's Digest, May 1962, pp. 207-218.
36. Interview, author with Lt Col (ret) Charles W. Norton (Maj, C-124 Pilot, 31st Air Transport Squadron, Dover AFB, DE, 1958-61), Pendleton, SC, 26 August 2004.
37. M. E. Haas, Apollo's Warriors, Air University Press, Maxwell Air Force Base, AL (1997), pp. 148-161.
38. C. Steijger, A History of United States Air Forces in Europe, Airlife Publishing, Shrewsbury, England (1991), p. 100.
39. Anon, "We can't fly gripes probed," The Birmingham News, 25 November 1961, pp. 1 and 4.
40. C. J. Gross, Prelude to the Total Force: The Air National Guard, 1943-1969, Office of Air Force History, Washington, DC (1985), pp. 132-138.

References/Notes to pages 137 to 144

41. ibid, pp. 187-190.
42. K. O. Wofford, "Operating Guide," 7120th Airborne Command Control Squadron, US Air Forces in Europe, Évreux AB, France, 16 December 1966, p. 4. [AFHRA]
43. T. Vanderbilt, Survival City, Princeton Architectural Press, New York (2002), pp. 147 and 148.
44. R. R. Raines, Getting the Message Through, Center of Military History, Washington, DC (1996), p. 360.
45. Interview, author with Lawrence C. Collins (1st Lt, 257th Signal Co, Mason-Fort and Camp des Loges, 1963-65), Byron, GA, 24 January 2009.
46. Interview, author with SMSgt (ret) James E. Teal (M/Sgt, Operations Branch, J-3 Div, US European Command, Camp des Loges, St.-Germain-en-Laye, France, 1964-67), Central, SC, 14 April 2012.
47. Interview, author with SFC (ret) LaMar E. Hummel (Sgt, 175th Military Police Det, Camp des Loges, France, 1961-63), Harrisburg, PA, 28 April 2014.
48. Interview, author with Patrick H. Ryan (Sp4, 22nd Transportation Co, Camp des Loges, France, 1962-65), Lady Lake, FL, 06 August 2012. Ryan shot skeet several times with Jones.
49. D. A. Burchinal, Senior Officer Oral History Program, US Army Military History Institute, Carlisle Barracks, PA, 1975, p. 129.
50. T. North, One Soldier's Job, unpublished manuscript, nd, pp. IX-19 and 20. Maj Gen (ret) Thomas North recorded recollections of his American Battle Monuments Commission (ABMC) service during the period of 1924 to 1970.
51. J. S. Arrigona and W. R. Karsteter, "History of the Joint Construction Agency in Europe," JCA, Boulogne-sur-Seine (Paris), France, May 1958, pp. 206-215. [CEHO]
52. P. H. Symbol, "Family Housing for the Army," Army Information Digest, July 1957, pp. 20 and 21.
53. H. H. Lumpkin, From Savannah to Yorktown, Paragon House, New York (1981), pp. 234-236. Professor Henry Lumpkin served as EUCOM Historian at Camp des Loges from 1956 to 1967.
54. J. R. Moenk (1955), pp. 77 and 78.
55. M. Ivanchak, "FRELOC After Action Report 1966-67," Vol. I, Headquarters, US Army Communications Zone, Europe (USACOMZEUR), 12 June 1968, p. 321.
56. G. J. Bourg, "Military Wives' Schedules Lightened by Paris Nursery," ComZ Cadence, 19 June 1964, p. 2.
57. G. Emerson, "In France, a PX Gets a Stay of Execution," New York Times, 25 March 1967, p. 14.
58. R. P. Smith (ed), "Appropriate Dress for Movies," The Stars and Stripes, 09 March 1963, p. 14.
59. Interview, author with US Air Force M/Sgt (ret) Charles R. Timms (DAC civilian, USEUCOM, Camp des Loges, St.-Germain-en-Laye, France, 1966-67), Seneca, SC, 27 March 2003.
60. A. F. Head (ed), "Basec Milk Consumption Occupies EM at Dairy," Basec Mission, 13 May 1955, p. 2.
61. Interview, author with Brig Gen (ret) Frank A. Ramsey (1st Lt, CO, 73rd Medical Det (Vet Food Insp), la Pallice, France, 1955-57), Uvalde, TX, 31 December 2008.
62. B. Hoyer, "Milk Run," The Stars and Stripes, 16 March 1963, pp. 12 and 13.
63. C. de Gaulle, Memoirs of Hope, Simon and Schuster, New York (1971), p. 155.
64. D. Walter, "Supermarket Revolution in France," The Stars and Stripes, 30 December 1959, pp. 12 and 13.
65. D. Walter, "Paris Parking Problem Posed by Bumper Crop," The Stars and Stripes, 15 September 1959, p. 3.
66. Anon, Paris USO Information Brochure, 93, avenue Champs-Élysées, Paris, France, 1960.
67. M. Mondore, "Visit Paris," The Advance, 04 December 1959, p. 3.
68. D. Walter, "Paris' Popular USO," The Stars and Stripes, 21 February 1957, p. 12.
69. Interview, author with Col (ret) Douglass W. Donnell, USAF (student, Paris American High School (PAHS), France, 1965-66), Reston, VA, 03 June 2003.
70. O. Pottier, Les Bases Américaines en France (1950-1967), Éditions l'Harmattan, Paris, France (2003), p. 267. (Fr)
71. Private correspondence to author from Olivia de Havilland, Paris, France, dated 18 June 2009. For overview of her life in 1950s France, see O. de Havilland, Every Frenchman Has One, Crown Archetype, New York (2016).
72. S. A. Selby, The Axmann Conspiracy, Berkeley Books, New York (2012).
73. T. Boghardt, "Dirty Work? The Use of Nazi Informants by U. S. Army Intelligence in Postwar Europe," The Journal of Military History, April 2015, pp. 389 (fn 10) and 400 (fn 62). I. Sayer and D. Botting, America's Secret Army, Franklin Watts, New York (1989), pp. 342-345 and 373-382.
74. J. Prados, Safe for Democracy: The Secret Wars of the CIA, Ivan R. Dee, Chicago, IL (2006), pp. 49-52.
75. B. Klarsfeld, Wherever They May Be!, The Vanguard Press, New York (1975), pp. 215-242. Barbie's SS number was 272284.
76. H. Rousso, "De Klaus Barbie à Klaus Altmann," in G. Auda (ed), Les Chemins de la Mémoire, Ministère de la défense, Paris, France, décembre 2015, pp. 88 and 89. (Fr)
77. J. P. Finnegan and R. Danysh, Military Intelligence, Center of Military History, Washington, DC (1998), p. 106.
78. M. E. Reese, General Reinhard Gehlen: The CIA Connection, George Mason University Press, Fairfax, VA (1990), pp. 47 and 48.

References/Notes to pages 144 to 152

79. J. L. Gilbert et al., In The Shadow of The Sphinx, History Office, US Army Intelligence and Security Command (INSCOM), Fort Belvoir, VA (2005), pp. 86-94.
80. T. M. Johnson, "The Army's Spy Hunters," Blue Book Magazine, January 1952, pp. 58-62.
81. A. Jacobsen, Operation Paperclip, Little, Brown and Company, New York (2014), pp. 319-321 and 376. About five-hundred German scientists and technicians were recruited during Operation Paperclip.
82. L. C. McCaslin, Secrets of the Cold War, Helion & Co, Solihull, England (2010), pp. 75 and 180-182.
83. T. Gup, The Book of Honor, Doubleday, New York (2000), pp. 76-78.
84. W. E. Colby, Honorable Men: My Life in the CIA, Simon and Schuster, New York (1978), pp. 94 and 95. Students at CIAs Camp Peary, VA (called "The Farm") learned how to follow suspects and shake a tail. Urban exercises were at Richmond, VA.
85. R. M. Bennett, Espionage: An Encyclopedia of Spies and Secrets, Virgin Books, London, England (2002), pp. 97 and 210.
86. R. P. Feynman, Surely You're Joking, Mr. Feynman!, W. W. Norton & Co, New York (1985), p. 155.
87. Anon, "Guide to Fort Holabird," Headquarters, Fort Holabird and The Counter Intelligence Corps Center, Baltimore, MD, 1955, p. 16.
88. J. P. Finnegan and R. Danysh (1998), p. 133.
89. J. R. Moenk, "Establishment of Communications Through France, 1950-51," Headquarters, US Army, Europe (USAREUR), Karlsruhe, Germany, 1952, pp. 95 and 96.
90. Interview, author with Maj (ret) James T. Killilea, Jr. (Capt, Transportation Officer, TFAD, Robert-Espagne, France, 1963-64), Williamsburg, VA, 30 March 2011. In 1973, the American Psychiatric Association removed homosexuality from its list of metal disorders.
91. Interview, author with Patrick J. Browne (Capt, CO, 67th Military Police Co, Detachment 2, Fontainebleau, France, 1964-65), New Orleans, LA, 15 October 2011.
92. Interview, author with Professor Emeritus Gerard J. Brault (Special Agent (Cpl), 66th CIC Group, Detachment A, Orléans, Bordeaux, and Laleu, France, 1952-53), State College, PA, 22 February 2015.
93. J. Millstone (ed), "66th Captures Title," ComZ Cadence, 13 November 1953, p. 3.
94. C. Raia (ed), "Cars Go French," Basec Mission, 19 May 1956, p. 1.
95. Interview, author with Jerome J. Ross (Special Agent (Sp4), 766th CIC Det Field Office, Braconne, France, 1965-66), Richfield, NJ, 14 May 2013.
96. Interview, author with Dr. Harald Sontag (French Intern, 34th General Hospital, la Chapelle-St.-Mesmin, France, 1965-66), Paris, France, 12 December 2014.
97. Interview, author with Vincent E. Gallagher (Sp4, Classified Documents Clerk, 37th Transportation Command, St.-Pryvé-St.-Mesmin, France, 1958-60), Landsford, PA, 04 July 2012.
98. Interview, author with CWO 2 (ret) Douglas A. Brown (Special Agent-in-Charge (WO 1), 766th CIC Det Field Office, Braconne, France, 1964-66), Flower Mound, TX, 09 July 2012.
99. Private correspondence to author from Arthur M. Fell (Special Agent (1st Lt), 766th CIC Det, Orléans and La Rochelle, France, 1959-61), Montpellier, France, 09 September 2009.
100. W. Whipple, Autobiography, Self-published, Princeton, NJ, nd, pp. 209 and 210. Final draft of book by Brig Gen (ret) William Whipple, Jr. [CEHO]
101. Interview, author with Lt Col (ret) C. Miguel Duncan, III (dependent of Lt Col (ret) C. Miguel Duncan, Jr., La Rochelle, France, 1955-58), Albuquerque, NM, 10 January 2016.
102. Interview, author with Damon O. Holmes (Special Agent (Sgt), 766th CIC Det, La Rochelle, France, 1957-59), Lakeland, FL, 07 July 2013.
103. C. S. Kennedy, "Interview: Ronald D. Flack," Association for Diplomatic Studies and Training Foreign Affairs Oral History Project, Washington, DC, 1998. Flack was Special Agent (Sgt), 766th CIC Det, Saumur, France, 1958-60.
104. Interview, author with Col (ret) Robert F. Elliott (Special Agent (Sp4), 766th CIC Det, Toul, France, 1958-59), Washington, DC, 23 August 2006.
105. G. I. Zimmerman (ed), "They'll Ask You About the Air Force?," Skyliner, 23 June 1956, p. 2.
106. Interview, author with James C. Conwell (1st Lt, CO, US Army Engineer Map Depot, St.-Ay, France, 1959-62), Vancouver, BC, Canada, 19 May 2014. Conwell and three other bachelor officers rented "Moulin des Bechets." The mill had been renovated by Capt Lieto DiPrieto of the 553rd Engineers.
107. A. W. Scheflin and E. M. Opton, The Mind Manipulators, Paddington Press, London, England (1978), p. 188.
108. M. A. Lee and B. Shlain, Acid Dreams, Grove Press, New York (1985), pp. 38-40.
109. L. G. Miller, "The Use of Chemicals in Stability Operations," Military Review, December 1966, p. 45.
110. J. S. Ketchum, Chemical Warfare Secrets Almost Forgotten, ChemBooks, Santa Rosa, CA (2006), pp. 29-34 and 218-221. In 1960s, Dr. James S. Ketchum led research in effects of mind-altering drugs on volunteer test subjects at the US Army Medical Research Laboratories, Edgewood Arsenal, MD.

References/Notes to pages 152 to 158

111. A. W. Scheflin and E. M. Opton (1978), p. 189. Pvt Thornwell was evaluated by Army psychiatrist Capt (Dr) King Mendelsohn, 34th General Hospital, la Chapelle-St.-Mesmin, France.
112. Anon, "US Army Inspector General's Report," DAIG 21-75, Department of the Army, Washington, DC, 1975, pp. 142-144.
113. L. Cannon, "Army Gave Private LSD in 3-month Interrogation in 1961," The Washington Post, 08 October 1977, p. A4.
114. Interview, author with Harvey M. Kletz (attorney for James R. Thornwell), Oakland, CA, 16 July 2009.
115. E. A. Lotito, "McNair GI, Virginian Held as Red Spies," The Washington Post & Times Herald, 06 April 1965, pp. A1 and A10.
116. P. S. Diggins, "Two Given 25 Years as Spies for Russia," The Washington Post & Times Herald, 31 July 1965, p. A1.
117. J. Barron, KGB: The Secret Work of Soviet Secret Agents, Reader's Digest Press, New York (1974), pp. 199-229.
118. C. Andrew and O. Gordievsky, KGB The Inside Story, Harper Collins Publishers, New York (1990), pp. 460-462 and 714 (n. 139). Oleg Gordievsky, a KGB colonel who worked undercover in the West, escaped from Russia in 1985.
119. Interview, author with Ferdinand C. "Buzz" Meyer (Capt, CO, 202nd Military Police Co., Ingrandes and Poitiers, France, 1964-66), Bigfork, MT, 17 October 2006.
120. Interview, author with William H. McNair (Special Agent (M/Sgt), 766th CIC Det, Trois Fontaines, France, 1962-65), McLean, VA, 09 April 2011.
121. C. de Gaulle, Memoirs of Hope, Simon and Schuster, New York (1971), pp. 291-293.
122. A. Williams, "Allied Command Europe Counterintelligence Activity 25th Anniversary Commemorative Brochure," 650th Military Intelligence Det, Casteau, Belgium, 18 January 1976, 12 pp. The 450th CIC Det was re-designated the 650th MI Det on 15 October 1966.
123. Interview, author with Robert K. Strobel (Chief M/Sgt, USAF, Paris Air Passenger Center, Paris, France, 1957-60), Charleston, SC, 22 April 2009.
124. P. D. Kackley (ed), "You Can't See But They Do," The Stars and Stripes, 14 July 1959, pp. 12 and 13.
125. Interview, author with Dr. Frederick J. Shaw, Jr. (Capt, Intelligence Officer, 10th Tactical Reconnaissance Wing, RAF Alconbury, UK, 1963-67), Maxwell Air Force Base, Montgomery, AL, 25 August 2005.
126. A. L. Jorgenson (ed), "Solon Says Baron Sold U.S. House, Stole Steps," The Stars and Stripes, 03 November 1953, p. 5.
127. S. Tate (ed), Concorde: Hôtel de Talleyrand and George C. Marshall Center, University of Florida Publications Office, Gainesville, FL (2007), pp. 7, 63, and 64.
128. Anon, The American Ambassador's Residence in Paris, US Embassy, Paris, France (1997), pp. 1, 10, and 11.
129. J. Prados, Combined Fleet Decoded, Naval Institute Press, Annapolis, MD (1995), pp. 16 and 17.
130. D. A. Brugioni, Eyes in the Sky, Naval Institute Press, Annapolis, MD (2010), p. 273.
131. O. Pottier, Les Bases Américaines en France (1950-1967), Editions l'Harmattan, Paris, France (2003), pp. 135 and 136. (Fr)
132. J.-B. Duroselle, France and the United States, The University of Chicago Press, Chicago, IL (1978), p. 232.
133. J. Lacouture, DeGaulle The Ruler 1945-1970, W. W. Norton, New York (1991), p. 383.
134. H. A. Rositzke, The CIA's Secret Operations, Reader's Digest Press, New York (1977), p. 17.
135. Anon, "Strike at Orly Field Turns Evreux-Fauville Into 'Air Terminal," Skyliner, 03 December 1955, p. 1.
136. Interview, author with Col (ret) Joaquin A. Saavedra (Assistant Air Attaché, US Embassy, Paris, France, 1956-60), Silver Spring, MD, 24 August 2011.
137. J. T. Richelson, "The Grounded Spies," Air Force Magazine, December 2014, pp. 64-67.
138. D. D. Hatfield, Through the Years with the Paris Air Show, Northrop Corporation, Los Angeles, CA (1973).
139. Private correspondence to author from Col (ret) Joaquin A. Saavedra (Assistant Air Attaché, US Embassy, Paris, France, 1956-60), Silver Spring, MD, dated 19 September 2011.
140. R. S. McNamara, "Defense Attaché System," DoD Directive No. C-5105.32, Department of Defense, Washington, DC, 12 December 1964, pp. 1-6. DoD Issued Directive No. 5105.21 establishing Defense Intelligence Agency (DIA) on 01 August 1961.
141. H. K. Johnson, "Assignment to Army Attaché Duty," Army Regulation (AR) 611-60, Headquarters, Department of the Army, 20 May 1968, pp. 1 and 2.
142. R. J. Barrett, "Politico-Military Expertise: A Practical Program," Military Review, November 1966, p. 51.
143. H. J. Richter (ed), "Ike Returns to D-Day Beaches," The Stars and Stripes, 07 June 1951, pp. 1 and 12.
144. B. G. Shellum, "Vernon Walters and the Paris Peace Talks," in M. Muir and M. F. Wilkinson (eds), The Most Dangerous Years: The Cold War, 1953-1975, Virginia Military Institute, Lexington, VA (2005), pp. 234 and 235.
145. E. Petrus (ed), "ComZ Honor Guard, 76th Army Band Aid in Memorial Service," Orleans Item, 04 June 1959, p. 1.
146. C.O. Stanley (ed), "ComZ Band Plays At Paris Ceremony," Orleans Item, 08 July 1955, p. 3.
147. Letter from Gen Williston B. Palmer, Deputy Commander-in-Chief, US European Command (USEUCOM) to Gen Henry I. Hodes, Commander-in-Chief, US Army, Europe (USAREUR), St.-Germain-en-Laye, France, 08 July 1957.

References/Notes to pages 158 to 167

148. M. C. Day (ed), "Honor Guard and 76 Band Visit Paris," Orleans Item, 12 July 1957, p. 1.
149. H. Macartney, "Americans Pay Tribute at Grave of Lafayette," New York Times, 22 July 1923, p. 14.
150. T. G. Hardie, "U.S. Tourists Ignore Grave of LaFayette," The Stars and Stripes, 12 April 1951, p. 4 and J. S. Hoffman, "Furlough facts," The Stars and Stripes, 22 May 1951, p. 4.
151. Interview, author with Brig Gen (ret) Roswell E. Round (Capt, Office of Army Attaché, Paris, France, 1963-66 and DATT, US Embassy, Paris, France, 1977-80), Sarasota, FL, 24 July 2009.
152. C. J. Patch, Arming the Free World, The University of North Carolina Press, Chapel Hill, NC (1991), pp. 205-208.
153. L. Galambos (ed), The Papers of Dwight David Eisenhower, Vol. XII, The Johns Hopkins University Press, Baltimore, MD (1989), p. 353 (n. 4).
154. W. B. Palmer, "Military Assistance Program: A Progress Report," Army Information Digest, April 1962, pp. 40-46.
155. S. W. Duke and W. Krieger, U.S. Military Forces in Europe, Westview Press, Boulder, CO (1993), pp. 197 and 198.
156. R. M. Leighton, Strategy, Money, and the New Look 1953-1956, Historical Office, Office of the Secretary of Defense, Washington, DC (2001), p. 510.
157. Anon, "Military Assistance Facts," US Department of Defense, Washington, DC, March 1968, p. 15.
158. L. S. Kaplan, A Community of Interests, Historical Office, Office of the Secretary of Defense, Washington, DC (1980), pp. 61 and 62.
159. C. V. Pickell and T. C. Musgrave, "Investment in Security," Military Review, December 1960, pp. 50-59.
160. C. G. Cogan, "From the Fall of France to the Force de Frappe," in T. C. Imlay and M. D. Toft (eds), The Fog of Peace and War Planning, Routledge, New York (2006), pp. 224-248.
161. Interview, author with Lt Col (ret) Robert B. Campbell (Chief, Logistics Section, MAAG, Paris, France, 1962-63), Tacoma, WA, 14 June 2011.
162. R. F. Futrell, The Advisory Years in Southeast Asia, Office of Air Force History, US Air Force, Washington, DC (1981), p. 24.
163. G. W. McIntyre, "The Mutual Weapons Development Program," Military Review, November 1960, pp. 48-54.
164. A. F. Head (ed), "Last Medium Tank Processed," Basec Mission, 28 January 1955, p. 1.
165. D. A. Ruiz-Palmer, "France" in J. Simon (ed), NATO-Warsaw Pact Force Mobilization, National Defense University Press, Washington, DC (1988), p. 313.
166. E. F. Fisher, "USAREUR Training Assistance to the West German Army," Headquarters, US Army, Europe (USAREUR), Karlsruhe, Germany, July 1958, pp. 40-53.
167. J. R. Moenk (1955), pp. 363, 364, and 370-373.
168. C. Raia (ed), "Command Will Select Technicians To Assist in Training German Army," Basec Mission, 10 March 1956, pp. 1 and 3.
169. C. G. Cogan (2006), p. 238.
170. S. Laurent, "Les Américains à Châteauroux," Regards, 21 septembre 1951, pp. 2-4. (Fr)
171. Anon, "MDAP Air Depot," Air University Quarterly Review, Fall 1952, pp. 88-92.
172. Interview, author with Col (ret) George N. Stokes, Jr. (Capt, 7373rd Supply Services Squadron, Châteauroux AD, France, 1951-52), Austin, TX, 16 February 2004.
173. C. E. Bohlen, The Transformation of American Foreign Policy, W. W. Norton, New York (1969), p. 110.
174. V. Prot, The American Forces in Châteauroux, Editions Tarmeye, Mazet St.-Voy, France (1998), pp. 30-32.
175. Anon, "Prefabs to Replace Tents in Winter," CHAD News, 06 September 1952, p. 1.
176. H. J. Richter (ed), "Contract Awarded For 9 Barracks At Chateauroux," The Stars and Stripes, 08 February 1953, p. 10.
177. D. Walter, "There's a Round Doorknob in Chateauneuf," The Stars and Stripes, 22 September 1959, pp. 11 and 12.
178. B. E. Doherty (ed), "No Gas Problem Here," CAMA News, 14 December 1956, p. 1.
179. J. J. McAuliffe, U. S. Air Force in France 1950-1967, Milspec Press, San Diego, CA (2005), pp. 202 and 203.
180. F. Jarraud, Les Américains à Châteauroux 1951-1967, Chez l'auteur, Le Poinçonnet, France (1981), p. 50. [Fr]
181. J. D. Nottingham (ed), "Chateauroux Scheduled For Vital Future Role Under Air Force Plans," The Stars and Stripes, 23 April 1959, p. 9.
182. S. Lentz, "Adieu la France," Le Nouveau Candide, 18 avril 1966, pp. 13-15. (Fr) [CAC]
183. J. D. Nottingham (ed), "Paris Gendarmes Solve Mystery of Anti-Americans," The Stars and Stripes, 09 July 1959, p. 3.

CHAPTER SIX

1. L. Galambos (ed), The Papers of Dwight David Eisenhower, Vol. XII, The Johns Hopkins University Press, Baltimore, MD (1989), p. 335 (n. 7).
2. R. C. Richardson, "The U.S. Air Force and NATO," Air University Quarterly Review, Winter 1952-53, pp. 85-89.

3. P. S. Meilinger, "The Early War Plans," Air Force Magazine, December 2012, p. 50.
4. Letter from Gen Lauris Norstad (CINC, Allied Air Forces Central Europe, Fontainebleau, France) to Gen Matthew B. Ridgway (SACEUR, SHAPE, Marly-le-Roi, France), dated 16 December 1952, 3 pp.
5. H. Hudson, "Norstad's Stars Loom Big in AF Galaxy," New York Times, 28 December 1952, p. B2.
6. A. Bray, Le Journal de l'Occupation (1940-1944), Société des Amis et Mécènes du Château de Fontainebleau, Fontainebleau, France (2012). (Fr)
7. O. T. Outland, "Ground Force Training Center Fontainebleau, France-1945," Journal of America's Military Past, Fall 1996, pp. 33-42.
8. Anon, "Air Force of NATO Enters New Home," New York Times, 20 July 1952, p. 9.
9. H. Bordeaux, Guynemer: Knight of the Air, Yale University Press, New Haven, CT (1918).
10. P. Spiers, "Radar Teams Chart Storms For AF Crews," The Stars and Stripes, 28 November 1959, p. 9.
11. J. Gunter, "It's Peace-Full: With Cops from 7 Nations," The Stars and Stripes, 20 August 1964, p. 11.
12. C. Gardner, "European Air Defense," The Listener, 07 May 1953. (UK)
13. J. Romeyer, "Aircent dans l'O.T.A.N.," Les Ailes, 13 octobre 1961. (Fr)
14. M. T. Isenberg, Shield of The Republic, St. Martin's Press, New York (1993), p. 140.
15. L. S. Goldstein and Y. M. Zhukov, "Tale of Two Fleets," Naval War College Review, Spring 2004, pp. 34 and 35.
16. Anon, "7 Fliers Dead as NATO Ends Sham Air War," The Washington Post, 01 August 1953, p. 3.
17. D. A. Lane, "Annual Historical Report for 1955-1956," Headquarters, US Army, Europe (USAREUR), Heidelberg, Germany, 1957, p. 181.
18. R. E. Osgood, NATO The Entangling Alliance, The University of Chicago Press, Chicago, IL (1962), pp. 126 and 127.
19. M. Michel, "Exit Strategy: Pull Up, Drop, Run for It," Air & Space, April-May 2003, pp. 22-27.
20. Interview, author with Col (ret) Thomas C. Wilkinson (Capt, Pilot, 50th Tactical Fighter Wing, Toul-Rosières AB, 1956-58), Monument, CO, 04 September 2003.
21. D. Miller, The Cold War, John Murray Publishers, London, England (1998), pp. 72 and 73.
22. P. R. Checkie (ed), "NATO Deals a 7th Royal Flush," Ramstein Ramjet, 11 May 1962, pp. 1 and 2.
23. P. D. Kackley, "USAFE Men Set Sights on Gunnery Meet," The Stars and Stripes, 14 August 1959, pp. 11 and 12.
24. Anon, "RCAF's Third Victory," Flight, 30 September 1960, p. 552. (UK)
25. J. S. Hodder, "The Canadian Forces in Europe," NATO Letter, May 1963, pp. 14-17.
26. N. Avery, "Grotenquin Revisted," The Roundel, December 1964, pp. 23-25.
27. J. R. Moenk, "Annual Historical Report for 1953-1954," Headquarters, US Army, Europe (USAREUR), Karlsruhe, Germany, 1955, p. 405.
28. P. Baar et al., Marville RCAF Air Base, Michel Frères, Virton, Belgium (2003). (Fr)
29. A. Weinberg, Silver Fox, Novedi, Brussels, Belgium (1985). (Fr)
30. D. Hinton, "Stealing the Show," Air & Space, April-May 2001, pp. 16 and 17.
31. R. Kemeling, Keepers of Freedom, CH & ER Publishing, North Charleston, SC (2004), pp. 186-191.
32. E. D. Hurley (ed), "Water Survival," Toul Tiger, 13 October 1961, p. 1.
33. Lt Gen A.P. Clark Archive at US Air Force Academy, Colorado Springs, CO. Refer to Maj Felix Kozaczka's manuscript for descriptions of quick reaction alerts, toss bombing, and life in France from 1955 to 1958. [USAFA]
34. A. R. Sorrells, "Alert!," Skyline, Summer 1958, pp. 12-19.
35. R. Grant, "Victor Alert," Air Force Magazine, March 2011, p. 61.
36. G. E. Miller, Stockpile, Naval Institute Press, Annapolis, MD (2010), pp 4, 5, and 131.
37. R. C. Doty, "Basic Nuclear Dilemma," New York Times, 10 June 1959.
38. C. G. Cogan, Charles de Gaulle, Bedford Books, Boston, MA (1996), p. 126.
39. J. D. Nottingham (ed), "Shadowy 'Invader' Rouses APs to Predawn 'Manhunt," The Stars and Stripes, 28 July 1959, p. 9.
40. P. Parrish (ed), Forty-five Years of Vigilance for Freedom: USAFE, 1942-1987, Office of History, Headquarters, US Air Forces in Europe (USAFE), Ramstein Air Base, Germany, 1987, p. 95.
41. O. Pottier, Les Bases Américaines en France (1950-1967), Editions l'Harmattan, Paris, France (2003), p. 108. (Fr)
42. J. D. Nottingham (ed), "TAC Force Proves Readiness," The Stars and Stripes, 17 November 1959, p. 8.
43. S. M. Ulanoff, MATS: The Story of the Military Air Transportation Service, Franklin Watts, New York (1964), pp. 47-51.
44. J. S. Chesebro (ed), "Rapid Response, Ready Reinforcement," Army Information Digest, January 1964, p. 10.
45. J. S. Hodder, "Operation Big Lift," NATO Letter, December 1963, pp. 17-20.
46. A. R. Scholin, "Big Lift: Boon, Boondoggle, or Bust?," Air Force/Space Digest, December 1963, pp. 33-37.
47. S. Geisenheyner, "And How Did the Europeans Size up Big Lift?," Air Force/Space Digest, December 1963, pp. 38-40.
48. T. M. Kane, Military Logistics and Strategic Performance, Frank Cass, London, England (2001), p. 128.

References/Notes to pages 179 to 187

49. P. Parrish (1987), p. 249.
50. B. Welles, "Allied Air Forces Tied Together By New $9,000,000 Radio Center," New York Times, 25 July 1952, p. 3.
51. P. D. Kackley, "They Have to Do-It-Themselves," The Stars and Stripes, 22 December 1959, p. 11.
52. J. J. McAuliffe, U.S. Air Forces in France 1950-1967, Milspec Press, San Diego, CA (2005), pp. 68 and 69.
53. Interview, author with Tim Hunt (Senior Aircraftsman, British SHAPE Signal Squadron, Camp Guynemer, France, 1962-64), Fontainebleau, France, 16 September 2009.
54. Interview, author with SFC (ret) LaMar E. Hummel (Sgt, 175th Military Police Det, Camp des Loges, France, 1961-63), Harrisburg, PA, 28 April 2014.
55. D. A. Bartoni (ed), "Giant Sports Stadium Built at Fontainebleau For Airmen of AAFCE," The Stars and Stripes, 24 May 1956, p. 9.
56. D. A. Bowman, "Information Brochure," 1141st USAF Special Activities Squadron, Camp Guynemer, Avon, France, and, p. 6. [AFHRA]
57. P. Dufour, École Interarmées des Sports, Ambre Bleu, Paris, France (1997), p. 17. (Fr)
58. B. Crozier, De Gaulle, Charles Scribner's Sons, New York (1973), p. 26.
59. D. Schoenbrun, The Three Lives of Charles De Gaulle, Atheneum, New York (1968), p. 29.
60. D. A. Bartoni (ed), "AFCE Plans 9-Nation Staff Exercise," The Stars and Stripes, 18 March 1957, p. 9.
61. Anon, "Emergency Call," Time, 30 September 1957, pp. 26 and 27.
62. B. Oldfield, Never a Shot in Anger, Capra Press, Santa Barbara, CA (1989), p. XXIV.
63. B. Crozier (1973), pp. 516 and 517.
64. D. Schoenbrun (1968), p. 287.
65. O. D. Menard, The Army and The Fifth Republic, University of Nebraska Press, Lincoln, NE (1967), pp. 235-237.
66. R. Sunder, "AFCENT Leaves France for the Netherlands," NATO Letter, March 1967, pp. 12 and 13.
67. J. E. Kaufman and H. W. Kaufman, Fortress Third Reich, Da Capo Press, Cambridge, MA (2003), pp. 158-164.
68. F. W. Seidler and D. Zeigert, Hitler's Secret Headquarters, Stackpole Books, Mechanicsburg, PA (2004), pp. 124-150.
69. ibid, pp. 146-150 and 208.
70. R. Raiber, "The Führerhauptquartier," After The Battle, No. 19, August 1977, pp. 49 and 50.
71. Memo from D. G. Gilbert (US Army Center of Military History) to Chief, Public Information Division (US Army Magazine & Book Branch), dated 09 March 1960.
72. M. Séramour, "Histoire de la ligne Maginot de 1945 à nos jours," Revue Historique des Armées, No. 247, 2007, pp. 90-92. (Fr)
73. R. O'Connor, "Moselle Control-Eyes in The Sky," Toul Tiger, 13 October 1961, p. 5.
74. H. E. Klemp, "Report of Operation of Engineer Section, 1950," Headquarters, 7966 EUCOM Det, Paris, France, 28 May 1951, pp. 1-6. [CEHO]
75. J. R. Moenk, "Establishment of Communications Through France, 1950-1951," Historical Division, US Army, Europe (USAREUR), Karlsruhe, Germany, 1952, pp. 120 and 121.
76. H. J. Richter (ed), "3 Yanks, 7 Others Nabbed in Lootings at ComZ Med Depot," The Stars and Stripes, 08 August 1952, p. 3.
77. R. M. Anderson, Jr., Robert Marion Anderson 1915-1986, Self-published, Centerton, AR, 2012, pp. 18-20. In 1953-54, Maj (ret) Robert M. Anderson, Jr. attended the dependents school at Caserne Lariboisière.
78. A. L. Jorgenson (ed), "33d Medical Depot Set to Issue Supplies," The Stars and Stripes, 27 June 1953, p. 8
79. Anon, "Lariboisière: U. S. Detachment-Fontainebleau," La Liberté, 05 and 12 avril 1960. (Fr)
80. Interview, author with Terry R. Eastman (Sp5, 33rd Field Hospital, Fontainebleau, France, 1957-59), Roanoke, VA, 06 April 2012.
81. Interview, author with Robert D. Burke (Sp4, 33rd Field Hospital, Fontainebleau, France, 1957-59), Fontainebleau, France, 14 September 2012.
82. C. D. Peterson, "Orientation Pamphlet," US Army Petroleum Distribution Command, Europe, Caserne Lariboisière, Fontainebleau, France, 1961, pp. 1-4.
83. J. Walters, "They Check the Gas You Use," The Stars and Stripes, 24 July 1959, pp. 12 and 13.
84. S. L. Gillette, "Army Supply Petroleum System," The Quartermaster Review, November-December 1955, pp. 10, 11, and 151.
85. Anon, "Pipelines for NATO," The Review, September-October 1965, pp. 41, 106, 109, 110, 113, and 114.
86. J. R. Moenk (1955), pp. 335 and 336.
87. J. S. Arrigona and W. R. Karsteter, "History of the Joint Construction Agency in Europe," JCA, Boulogne-sur-Seine (Paris), France, 1958, pp. 172 and 288. [CEHO]
88. J. D. Nottingham (ed), "Shrewd Plumber Taps NATO Gasoline Line," The Stars and Stripes, 09 September 1959, p. 24.
89. Anon, "Donges-Metz and Zweibrüken-Huttenheim Pipeline Facilities Manual," Headquarters, US Army Petroleum Distribution Command Europe, Fontainebleau, France, June 1962.
90. D. A. Lane, "Annual History 1958-1959," Headquarters, US Army, Europe (USAREUR), Heidelberg, Germany, 1960, pp. 137 and 138.

References/Notes to pages 188 to 198

91. Interviews, author with Maj Gen (ret) William Timothy McLean (Capt, Chalons Terminal District, Châlons-sur-Marne, France, 1966-67), Butte, MT, 08 January 2009 and 01 August 2014.
92. Interview, author with Brig Gen (ret) Billy Jack Stalcup (1st Lt, Melun Terminal District, Fontainebleau, France, 1958-61), Alexandria, VA, 06 July 2005.
93. J. E. Walsh, "Engineers in the USAREUR Today," The Military Engineer, September-October 1958, pp. 331-333.
94. R. Wright, "A 391-mile Foot," The Stars and Stripes, 12 September 1964, pp. 12 and 13.
95. D. A. Lane (1960), p. 137.
96. Anon, "Donges-Metz and Zweibrüken-Huttenheim Pipeline Facilities Manual," Headquarters, US Army Petroleum Distribution Command Europe, Fontainebleau, France, June 1962, pp. 5, 23, 28, 31, and 35.
97. Anon, "US Army Installations France," Headquarters, US Army Communications Zone, Europe (USACOMZEUR), Orléans, France, 1966. These documents, also called "Information Brochures," recorded real estate statistics for US Army installations in France. A nearly complete set is archived at the Office of History, US Army Corps of Engineers, Fort Belvoir, VA; partial set was archived at Campbell Barracks, USAREUR, Heidelberg, Germany.
98. Interviews, author with Col (ret) Bernard R. Meisel (Capt, Chief, Tank Farm Section, Melun Terminal District, Fontainebleau, France, 1964-66), Sun City Center, FL, 23 September 2008 and 08 August 2014.
99. Anon, "Automation of Depots in the Donges-Melun-Metz System," Société des Transports Petroliers par Pipeline (TRAPIL), Paris, France, June 1987.
100. J. S. Chesebro (ed), "Heavy Storage Tank," Army Information Digest, November 1963, p. 6.
101. R. P. Smith (ed), "3rd Armd Div Tests Fuels," The Stars and Stripes, 03 January 1963, p. 9.
102. D. O. Carpenter, "Armed Forces Day Program," US Army Garrison, Seine Area Command, Fontainebleau, France, 20 May 1961, pp. 1-10.
103. N. L. Miller and W. G. Ryle, "History of the Headquarters 7495th Support Group," Fontainebleau, France, September-October 1952, p. 45. [AFHRA]
104. J. C. Moore, "Information Bulletin," Headquarters, 7495th Support Group, Fontainebleau, France, 01 May 1951, pp. 20 and 21. [AFHRA]
105. R. N. Whiting, "Nursing in the Paris Area," Medical Bulletin of the U. S. Army, Europe, Vol. 24, No.2, February 1967, pp. 53 and 54.
106. Interview, author with Forrest G. Quinn (dependent of Lt Col Thomas G. Quinn, AFCENT, Fontainebleau, France, 1966-67), Henderson, NV, 02 September 2015.
107. C. Antier, "Fontainebleau aux heures de gloire au SHAPE 1954-1966," La revue de l'histoire de Fontainebleau & de sa région, No. 5, 2013, pp. 96-98. (Fr)
108. P. D. Kackley, "The Teachers are Never Bored," The Stars and Stripes, 30 October 1959, p. 11.
109. H. Lempereur et B. Chaljub, "Les barres de la Faisanderie," École nationale supérieure d'architecture de grenoble, Grenoble, France, 2010, np. (Fr)
110. H. SchoenholzBee and C. Heliczer, MoMA Highlights, The Museum of Modern Art, New York (2004), p. 152.
111. J. D. Nottingham (ed), "Yanks Honor French Pair," The Stars and Stripes, 28 September 1959, p. 9.
112. J. Hall and R. C. Hall, "Fontainebleau," U. S. Lady, June 1964, pp. 17-21.
113. C. L. Sulzberger, The Last of the Giants, The Macmillan Company, New York (1970), pp. 393 and 394.
114. Anon, "Brochure d'Information," Etat Major, Forces Alliées Centre Europe (AFCENT), Fontainebleau, France, nd, p. 21. (Fr)
115. C. O. Stanley (ed), "Special Services Celebrated 15th Anniversary Today," Orleans Item, 22 July 1955, p. 4. By mid-1955, there were more than twenty-one service clubs in France.
116. Interview, author with Joyce Frigaard Lange (Club Director, Special Services, Fontainebleau, France, 1956), Charlotte, NC, 17 March 2011.
117. Interview, author with Gerry C. Carroll (Sp4, 507th Signal Co, Fontainebleau, France, 1958-60), Pewaukee, WI, 28 April 2014.
118. G. C. Mitchell, Matthew B. Ridgway, Stackpole Books, Mechanicsburg, PA (2002), p. 114.
119. C. de Nicolay-Mazery and J.-B. Naudin, The French Château, Thames and Hudson, London, England (1991), pp. 84-103.
120. P. Deitz, "A New Memorial Squanders a Sparkling Opportunity," Architectural Record, August 2004, p. 72.
121. H. W. Baldwin, "Western Command Rift," New York Times, 07 July 1949, p. 10.
122. G. R. Robertson, Engineer Memoirs, General William M. Hoge, US Army Corps of Engineers, EP 870-1-25, Alexandria, VA, January 1993, p. 192.
123. K. S. Morgan, Past Forgetting, Simon and Schuster, New York (1976), pp. 27 and 28.
124. B. Welles, "Eisenhower Opens 'Paper War' Today," New York Times, 07 April 1952, p. 5. The location was not secret or heavily guarded. One soldier in civilian clothes, assigned by the 16th Military Police Det (CI) to protect Ike, may have carried a concealed pistol.

References/Notes to pages 198 to 204

125. J. Briola, "L'hôtel d'Iéna transformé en QG militaire," Arts & Métiers Mag, mai 2011, p. 51. (Fr)
126. Interview, author with Francis J. Bentz (Cpl, 7th Signal Bn, SHAPE, Marly-le-Roi, France, 1951-53), East Liverpool, OH, 26 March 2010. Bentz was assigned to the US-British-French signal team that provided communications at CPX One.
127. B. L. Montgomery, "SHAPE CPX One: Final Address by DSACEUR," Marly-le-Roi, France, 11 April 1952, 12 pp.
128. B. L. Montgomery (Field Marshal The Viscount Montgomery of Alamein), "A Look at World War III," Journal of the Royal United Service Institute, November 1954. (UK)
129. R. Sunder (1967), p. 13.
130. J. Aubert, "Fontainebleau 3 ans après le départ des Americains," La Croix, Supplement A, 16-17 février 1969, pp. 1 and 4. (Fr)
131. Anon, "Séance publique, Questions orales," Assemblée Nationale, Paris, Feuilleton No. 347, 22 juin 1966, pp. 4 and 5. (Fr)

CHAPTER SEVEN

1. I. Trauschweizer, The Cold War U. S. Army, University Press of Kansas, Lawrence, KS (2008), p. 129.
2. R. B. Asprey, "Iron Curtain Patrol," Army, April 1962, pp. 42-47.
3. R. T. Hauert, "Delivering the Goods to USAREUR," Army Information Digest, January 1957, pp. 37-42.
4. J. A. Huston, The Sinews of War, Center of Military History, Washington, DC (1966), pp. 655-690. Creating and sustaining the lifeline across France utilized many of the fourteen principles of logistics proposed by Huston.
5. W. F. Craven and J. L. Cate (eds), The Army Air Forces in World War II, Vol. III, The University of Chicago Press, Chicago, IL (1951), p. 215.
6. R. G. Davis, Bombing the European Axis Powers, Air University Press, Montgomery, AL (2006), pp. 8, 27-30, and 499.
7. N. Lambourne, War Damage in Western Europe, Edinburgh University Press, Edinburgh, UK (2001), pp. 44-66 and 71.
8. A. de la Raudière, "American Liberation of Orleans On August 16, 1944, Recalled," Orleans Item, 12 August 1955, pp. 1 and 3. French Army Lieutenant Amaury de la Raudière was liaison to US Army Communications Zone at Orléans.
9. A. W. Spratley (ed), "Orleans Marks Liberation Date," ComZ Cadence, 22 August 1952, p. 1.
10. Letter from Maj Gen Samuel D. Sturgis, Jr. to Col Cary B. Hutchinson, dated 04 April 1952. [CEHO]
11. Letter from Maj Gen Samuel D. Sturgis, Jr. to Col Oliver J. Pickard (G-3, 6th Armored Div., Fort Leonard Wood, MO), dated 20 June 1952. [CEHO]
12. D. Schear, "ComZ Hq at Orleans Directs Huge Supply Setup in France," The Stars and Stripes, 04 May 1952, p. 3.
13. Letter from Maj Gen Samuel D. Sturgis, Jr. to Lt Gen Manton S. Eddy (Commander-in-Chief, US Army, Europe (USAREUR), Heidelberg, Germany), dated 27 October 1952, p. 1 and Tab A. [CEHO]
14. S. D. Sturgis, "Notes on Class II Concept," Headquarters, EUCOM Communications Zone, Orléans, France, nd, pp. 1-5. [CEHO]
15. J. R. Moenk, "Establishment of Communications Through France, 1950-51," Headquarters, US Army, Europe (USAREUR), Karlsruhe, Germany, 1952, pp. 130 and 131.
16. C. W. Borklund, "Why The Impossible is Taking A Little Longer," Armed Forces Management, August 1960, pp. 21-23.
17. Letter from Maj Gen Samuel D. Sturgis, Jr. to Lt Gen Thomas B. Larkin (G-4, Department of the Army, Washington, DC), dated 25 March 1952. [CEHO]
18. L. D. Sisk, The Dark Is All Gone, Publish America, Baltimore, MD (2002), pp. 26-28.
19. B. E. Kleber and D. Birdsell, The Chemical Warfare Service, Center of Military History, Washington, DC (1966).
20. W. M. Creasy, "CBR Attack by Invisible Invader," Army Information Digest, February 1958, pp. 46-53.
21. G. A. Cosmas and A. E. Cowdrey, Medical Services in the European Theater of Operations, Center of Military History, Washington, DC (1992), p. 592.
22. T. R. Peterson, "Training in Southwest France," The Military Engineer, May-June 1961, pp. 182 and 183.
23. B. D. Coll, The Corps of Engineers: Troops and Equipment, Office of The Chief of Military History, Washington, DC (1958), pp. 50 and 51.
24. R. V. N. Ginn, The History of the US Army Medical Service Corps, Office of The Surgeon General and Center of Military History, Washington, DC (1997), pp. 269-296.
25. A. W. Spratley (ed), "Novel OAC Unit is Medical Crew of 80th Hosp Trn," ComZ Cadence, 19 June 1953, p. 1.
26. A. L. Jorgenson (ed), "USAREUR Team Visits ComZ to Boost Ord System," The Stars and Stripes, 24 February 1954, p. 13.
27. D. A. Carter, Forging the Shield, Center of Military History, Washington, DC (2015), pp. 122 and 123.
28. E. Risch, The Quartermaster Corps: Organization, Supply, and Services, Office of The Chief of Military History, Washington, DC (1953).
29. J. R. Moenk, "Line of Communications Through France 1952-1953," Headquarters, US Army, Europe (USAREUR), Karlsruhe, Germany, 1955, p. 218.
30. A. L. Jorgenson (ed), "JCA to Finish Work at Saran Next Month," The Stars and Stripes, 09 December 1953, p. 8.
31. B. King et al., Spearhead of Logistics, Center of Military History, Washington, DC (2001), pp. 372-374.

32. F. J. Sullivan (ed), "More Tons, More Miles, Less Accidents," Orleans Item, 16 February 1961, p. 3.
33. G. J. LeFèvre de Montigny, "Logistic Problems in an Era of Wholesale Motorization," Military Review, August 1957, pp. 97 and 98.
34. D. A. Lane, "Annual Historical Report for 1956-1957," Headquarters, US Army, Europe (USAREUR), Heidelberg, Germany, 1958, pp. 208 and 209.
35. R. A. Wells et al., "U.S. Army Lines of Communications in Europe (1945-1967)," Office of the Deputy Chief of Staff, Operations, US Army, Europe, Heidelberg, Germany, 1968, p. 72.
36. B. C. Clarke, "Army Administrative Support in the Theater of Operations," Headquarters, US Army, Europe (USAREUR), Heidelberg, Germany 02 February 1962, p. 25. [MHI]
37. D. J. Hickman, "The United States Army in Europe, 1953-1963," Headquarters, US Army, Europe (USAREUR), Heidelberg, Germany, 1964, p. 159.
38. D. L. Sallee, "Outline Plan for Major Installations and Their Missions," Plans and Operations Branch, US Army Communications Zone, Europe (USACOMZEUR), Orléans, France, 24 January 1958, p. 2. [MHI]
39. J. D. Nottingham (ed), "Supply Conditions in USAREUR Criticized, but Improvements Noted," The Stars and Stripes, 01 May 1959, p. 8.
40. J. R. Moenk, "The Line of Communications Through France, 1952-53," Headquarters, US Army, Europe (USAREUR), Karlsruhe, Germany, 1955, p. 224.
41. R. R. Raines, Getting the Message Through, Center of Military History, Washington, DC (1996), p. 360.
42. R. C. Boyd (ed), "Lighthouse on Land for These Special Signalmen," The Advance, 11 July 1958, p. 3.
43. Interview, author with Ross A. Gagliano (1st Lt, Executive Officer, 228th Signal Co, Fontenet, France, 1961-62), Decatur, GA, 18 February 2006.
44. C. J. Bizet (ed), "French Employees Learn Operation of IBM Machines," ComZ Cadence, 04 February 1955, p. 4.
45. H. H. Wydom, "IBM Data Cards' Middlemen," ComZ Cadence, 07 February 1964, p. 3.
46. D. M. Polzin, "IBM Electrical Marvels for the Atomic Age," Orleans Item, 15 January 1960, p. 2.
47. P. McCormick (ed), "Dear Old UDPES," ComZ Cadence, 15 May 1964, p. 2.
48. Interview, author with Col (ret) Robert A. Atkins (Lt Col, Chief, Troop Operations Section, Engineer Division, ComZ Headquarters, Orléans, France, 1960-61), Leavenworth, KS, 02 September 2005. According to Jeffrey G. Barlow's PhD Thesis (University of South Carolina, 24 April 1981, p. 125), Gen Maxwell D. Taylor, President Kennedy's Military Representative, was astounded that ad hoc task forces "did their work….without leaving a trace or contributing to the permanent base of governmental experience."
49. J. M. Heiser, A Soldier Supporting Soldiers, Center of Military History, Washington, DC (1991), p. 117.
50. W. S. Stone, "MILSTRIP Shows the Way," Army Information Digest, January 1963, pp. 53-57.
51. Interview, author with Maj (ret) Thomas A. Spencer (Capt, 3rd Logistical Command, Orléans, France, 1964-66), Arlington, TX, 26 June 2006.
52. P. J. Mahoney (ed), "37th TC Brings MOBIDIC to Orleans," The Transporter, 15 March 1963, pp. 1 and 3.
53. Interview, author with Charles J. Lusk (Sp4, Data Processing Clerk, Headquarters Co, 8th Inf Div, Bad Kreuznach, Germany, 1967-68), Newport, OR, 08 June 2015.
54. R. J. Coakley (ed), "Fieldata Aids for the Command Post of the Future," Army Information Digest, March 1962, pp. 14-19.
55. Private correspondence to author from Col (ret) Basil J. Hobar (Capt, Documents Processing Branch, Supply & Maintenance Agency, Verdun, France, 1967), Bonita Springs, FL, 21 August 2015.
56. T. F. Donahue, "Communications Zone Asset or Liability?," Military Review, January 1956, p. 10.
57. A. W. Spratley (ed), "New Insignia Is Authorized For ComZ Use," ComZ Cadence, 22 May 1953, p. 1.
58. L. Whitman (ed), "USAREUR Slashes Logistics Overhead, Bolsters ComZ By Thousands of Spaces," Army Navy Air Force Journal, 06 October 1956, p. 5.
59. J. C. Fuson, Transportation and Logistics, Center of Military History, Washington, DC (1994), pp. 89 and 90.
60. B. Fleming, "NATO's CENTAG Hq Staff to be Expanded," The Stars and Stripes, 18 August 1959, p. 11.
61. F. J. Sullivan (ed), "TASCOM Gives Logistical Support to Troops of Seventh Army," Orleans Item, 16 February 1961, p. 9. R. A. Wells et al. (1968), pp. 85 and 86.
62. M. Ivanchak, "FRELOC After Action Report 1966-67," Vol. II, Headquarters, US Army Communications Zone, Europe (USARCOMZEUR), 12 June 1968, p. 74-78.
63. Anon, Handbook of Ordnance Materiel, ST 9-159, US Army Ordnance School, Aberdeen Proving Ground, MD, April 1959, pp. 84 and 85.
64. S. Markowitz (ed), "Complete First Command Highway Drill Since War," The Advance, 26 June 1953, p. 3.
65. D. A. Bartoni (ed), "ComZ Streamlines Overland Transport Setup," The Stars and Stripes, 28 March 1957, pp. 11 and 12.
66. D. Walter, "They Keep the Army's Supplies Rolling," The Stars and Stripes, 29 June 1959, pp. 11 and 14.

References/Notes to pages 217 to 226

67. P. C. McCormick (ed), "Four 37th TC Drivers Receive Gold Watches For 100,000 Accident-Free Miles Driven," ComZ Cadence, 15 January 1965, p. 1.
68. Interview, author with Melvyn Bryan Hackett (Sp4, Company D, 601st Ordnance Bn, Braconne, France, 1957-58), Grass Valley, CA, 29 January 2007.
69. Interview, author with John A. Bridges (Sp4, 78th Transportation Co, Croix-Chapeau, France, 1958-59), Charleston, SC, 08 October 2012.
70. P. H. Slaughter, "Substituting the 'Speed Ball' For the 'Red Ball,'" Military Review, August 1951, pp. 36-42.
71. Interview, author with Col (ret) Richard C. Rantz (Lt Col, CO, 28th Transportation Bn, Poitiers, France, 1962-63), Bellingham, WA, 08 August 2005.
72. L. S. Eden, "The Road," The Transporter, 05 July 1963, pp. 5-12.
73. A. W. Spratley (ed), "First Truck Co (Refr) Is Stationed at Saran," ComZ Cadence, 06 February 1953, p. 6.
74. M. C. Day (ed), "1st TC Refrigeration Co-Saran Is Only Unit of Kind In Europe," Orleans Item, 30 March 1956, p. 2.
75. H. J. Richter (ed), "Engineers Erecting Directional Signs Throughout ComZ," The Stars and Stripes, 08 June 1952, p. 1.
76. J. D. Nottingham (ed), "French Outlaw Dangerous Car Ornaments," The Stars and Stripes, 03 December 1959, p. 3.
77. A. L. Jorgenson (ed), "ComZ Offers Road Survey," The Stars and Stripes, 18 February 1954, p. 8.
78. R. P. Smith (ed), "36th Arty Unit Wins Roadeo Competition," The Stars and Stripes, 17 September 1964, p. 9.
79. R. P. Smith (ed), "37th Trans Comd Conducts Roadeo," The Stars and Stripes, 22 September 1964, p. 9.
80. R. P. Smith (ed), "Army Trucks Rush Coal to France," The Stars and Stripes, 30 January 1963, p. 8.
81. R. P. Smith (ed), "Coal Haul 'Keeping Home Fires Burning,'" The Stars and Stripes, 02 February 1963, p. 8.
82. B. H. Siemon and R. Wagberg, "The Employment of Local Nationals by the US Army in Europe (1945-1966)," Headquarters, US Army, Europe (USAREUR), Heidelberg, Germany, 1968, pp. 64-65 and 68.
83. W. O. Jacobson, "The Army's Built-in People-to-People Program," Army Information Digest, December 1961, pp. 17-19.
84. M. C. Day (ed), "French Personnel To Have More Supervisory Responsibilities Now," Orleans Item, 25 January 1957, p. 1.
85. B. H. Siemon and R. Wagberg (1968), pp. 68 and 69.
86. J. S. Arrigona and W. R. Karsteter, "History of the Joint Construction Agency in Europe," JCA, Boulogne-sur-Seine (Paris), France, 1958, p. 326. [CEHO]
87. M. C. Day (ed), "Hungarian Refugees Offered Employment With Army in France," Orleans Item, 14 December 1956, p. 2.
88. R. Menudier, "La presence américaine à Orléans dans le cadre de la defense atlantique 1950-1967," Université d'Orléans, Orléans, France, 1991, p. 115. (Fr) [AD 45]
89. A. W. Spratley (ed), "French Workers Win Francs," ComZ Cadence, 19 December 1952, p. 7.
90. R. C. Boyd (ed), "Incentive Award Program Offers Honors and Cash," The Advance, 06 June 1958, pp. 2 and 4.
91. R. C. Boyd (ed), "How to Get a Helicopter Ride," The Advance, 29 May 1958, p. 1.
92. J. C. Cougill, "Welcome to Orleans Area Command," Headquarters, OAC, Forêt d'Orléans, France, July 1961. Thirty page orientation pamphlet published for newly assigned personnel.
93. Interview, author with Lt Col (ret) John A. Nark (1st Lt, USEUCOM Property Account Office, Fontenet, France, 1960-61), Delran, NJ, 25 January 2006. Smoking was prevalent in France and US (> 80% males smoked).
94. H. J. Richter (ed), "ComZ Booklet Briefs Troops on France Life," The Stars and Stripes, 11 January 1953, p. 5.
95. H. J. Richter (ed), "Abide by Customs of France, Bixby Tells Basec Yanks," The Stars and Stripes, 02 February 1953, p. 6.
96. R. W. Colglazier, Senior Officer Oral History Program, Military History Institute, Carlisle Barracks, PA, 1984, pp. 216-219.
97. R. J. Coakley (ed), "Goodwill Gets Results," Army Information Digest, August 1960, pp. 42-45.
98. M. C. Day (ed), "600 French Orphans Will be Entertained," Orleans Item, 20 December 1957, p. 1.
99. J. T. Perkins (ed), "Young Riders Rock on ComZ Ponies," ComZ Cadence, 18 December 1953, p. 1.
100. R. R. Wessels, "Construction Projects," Headquarters, 553rd Engineer Bn, Maison-Fort, France, 30 September 1961. [CEHO]
101. M. C. Day, "After Hours With The Army," Orleans Item, 09 November 1956, p. 2.
102. F. H. Kohloss (ed), "Emergency Water Supply," The Military Engineer, November-December 1954, p. 428.
103. J. T. Perkins (ed), "Engineers Save Waterless French Town From Crisis," ComZ Cadence, 02 July 1954, p. 1.
104. J. Autran, "American Engineers in France, 1962," The Military Engineer, January-February 1963, p. 52.
105. D. Walter, "The Orleans Gazette," The Stars and Stripes, 29 October 1959, p. 14.
106. M. C. Day (ed), "Maison Fort Chapel Bell Symbolizes Mutual Faith," Orleans Item, 10 January 1958, pp. 1 and 6.
107. P. McCormick (ed), "Soldier Saves Drowning Woman In Flood-Swollen Loire River," ComZ Cadence, 10 April 1964, p. 1.
108. J. S. Winn, "Sp5 Hanson Awarded French Medal," The Builder, November 1964, pp. 1 and 2.
109. J. S. Winn, "Soldier's Medal for Sp5 Hanson," The Builder, March 1965, p. 1.
110. R. J. Crawford (ed), "48 Hours Saved in New Air Mail Delivery System," The Advance, 09 July 1954, p. 2.
111. B. Collins, "Bouncing Mail Has 'Stampeded' APOs Dizzy," The Stars and Stripes, 10 January 1963, p. 24.

References/Notes to pages 226 to 232

112. A. F. Head (ed), "MO Theft Brings Grief to La Rochelle Pfc," Basec Mission, 11 March 1955, p. 1.
113. Interview, author with Lt Col (ret) Ollie P. Anderson, Jr. (1st Lt, CO, 17th APU, Bussac and Braconne, France, 1961-64), Fort Washington, MD, 15 February 2006.
114. W. D. Lawrence, "The First Twenty Years," Army Information Digest, July 1960, pp. 56-61.
115. J. J. McAuliffe, U.S. Air Force in France 1950-1967, Milspec Press, San Diego, CA (2005), pp. 363 and 364.
116. Letter from Maj Gen Samuel D. Sturgis, Jr. (Commanding General, USACOMZEUR) to François Leduc (Chef de la Mission Centrale de Liaison pour l'Assistance aux Armées Alliées, Paris, France), dated 18 July 1952. [SHD]
117. A. F. Head (ed), "AF-Man Shot While Loading .45 Cal Pistol," Basec Mission, 02 September 1955, p. 1.
118. J. T. Perkins (ed), "ComZ Service Newspapers Master Publishing Problems," ComZ Cadence, 23 April 1954, p. 2.
119. A. W. Spratley (ed), "Headlines of Past Two Years Reflect ComZ, OAC's Growth," ComZ Cadence, 02 October 1953, pp. 2 and 4.
120. G. F. Locke (ed), "The ADVANCE' C'est Fini!," The Advance, 29 November 1963, pp. 1 and 4.
121. R. L. Parsons (ed), "Command Newspaper Marks 1st Anniversary," The Pariscope, 20 March 1958, p. 4.
122. N. Hamilton, "Army Information at Work," Army Information Digest, February 1959, pp. 10-16.
123. P. McCormick (ed), "Two COMZ Papers Win DoD Merit Certificates," ComZ Cadence, 27 March 1964, p. 1.
124. A. Porter, "Conversation with a Mouse," Toul Tiger, 26 January 1962, p. 8.
125. J. R. Moenk, "Annual Historical Report 1953-54," US Army, Europe (USAREUR), Karlsruhe, Germany, 1955, pp. 108 and 109.
126. H. S. Levie, "NATO Status of Forces Agreement," Army Information Digest, March 1958, pp. 12-17.
127. N. A. Oelhafen (ed), "NATO/SOFA and You," Jet-48, 28 July 1956, p. 2. [USAFA]
128. D. J. Hickman, "The United States Army in Europe, 1953-1963," Headquarters, US Army, Europe (USAREUR), Heidelberg, Germany, 1964, p. 37.
129. Interview, author with Lt Col (ret) Edwin W. Kulo (Maj, Area Provost Marshal, TFAD, Robert-Espagne, France, 1961-64), Tipp City, OH, 06 November 1999.
130. R. L. Gunnarsson, American Military Police in Europe, 1945-1991, McFarland, Jefferson, NC (2011), pp. 220-238.
131. A. W. Spratley (ed), "36 MP's Graduate From 3 Week Course," ComZ Cadence, 06 June 1952, p. 4.
132. H. B. Kraft, "Military Police School at Oberammergau," The Stars and Stripes, 03 September 1959, p. 13.
133. B. Blando, "Military Police Force Stands Ready to Safeguard OAC," Orleans Item, 06 March 1959, pp. 3 and 4.
134. R. J. Crawford (ed), "524th MP Battalion Performs Many Duties Throughout ADSEC," The Advance, 20 November 1953, p. 1.
135. C. E. Wilson, A Pocket Guide to France, US Department of Defense, DoD Pam 2-10, 23 August 1956, pp. 53-59.
136. Interview, author with Dr. John D. Chambers (PFC, Medical Corpsman, 28th General Hospital, Caserne Aufrédi, La Rochelle, France, 1955-57), Anacortes, WA, 07 December 2001.
137. J. A. Huston, Across the Face of France, Purdue University Press, Lafayette, IN (1963), pp. 152-158.
138. A. L. Jorgenson (ed), "ZI Court Kills Plea for Yank In French Jail," The Stars and Stripes, 06 January 1954, p. 16. The convicted GIs were Pvt Richard T. Keefe and Pvt Anthony R. Scaletti.
139. D. A. Lane, "Annual Historical Report for 1954-55," Headquarters, US Army, Europe (USAREUR), Heidelberg, Germany, 1956, p. 332.
140. Interview, author with Raymond A. D. Carter (Interpreter, US Army Port Command, Caserne Aufrédi, La Rochelle, France, 1956-64), La Rochelle, France, 12 October 2000.
141. A. Buchwald, I'll Always Have Paris, G. P. Putnam's Sons, New York (1996), p. 20.
142. Anon, "Stupefying Sam," Time, 31 December 1965, p. 15.
143. J. Jonnes, Hep-Cats, Narcs, and Pipe Dreams, Scribner, New York (1996), pp. 189 and 190.
144. W. W. Epley, "America's First Cold War Army 1945-1950," Land Warfare Paper No. 15, Association of the United States Army, Arlington, VA, August 1993, pp. 14 and 15.
145. J. K. Singlaub, Hazardous Duty, Summit Books, New York (1991), pp. 280 and 281.
146. I. Trauschweizer (2008), p. 242.
147. G. F. Locke (ed), "Raider Training," The Advance, 29 November 1963, p. 5.
148. M. C. Day (ed), "Ew Prove Fitness On Night Bivouac," Orleans Item, 21 September 1956, pp. 1 and 4.
149. D. A. Lane, "Annual Historical Report for 1955-1956," Headquarters, US Army, Europe (USAREUR), Heidelberg, Germany, 1957, pp. 195 and 196.
150. J. A. Nark, Memories of France 1960-1963, Self-published, Delran, NJ, 2008, pp. 10 and 11.
151. B. Blando, "Engineer Battalion Takes Army Training Test," Orleans Item, 03 April 1959, p. 2.
152. Interview, author with Robert D. Rex (Sp5, Company C, 97th Engineer Bn, Étain, France, 1965-67), Wooster, OH, 06 August 2004.
153. R. J. Crawford (ed), "ADSEC MP's End Field Training," The Advance, 26 August 1955, p. 3.
154. Interview, author with Col (ret) John F. Ferrick (1st Lt, Platoon Leader, 39th Ordnance Co, Verdun, France, 1959-62), Mims, FL, 01 February 2014.

References/Notes to pages 232 to 241

155. Interviews, author with Vincent E. Gallagher (Sp4, Headquarters Co, 37th Transportation Command, St.-Pryvé -St.-Mesmin, France, 1958-60), Lansford, PA, 04 May 2008 and 03 February 2017.
156. Private correspondence to author from James C. Conwell (1st Lt, CO, US Army Engineer Map Depot, St-Ay, France, 1959-62), Vancouver, BC, Canada, 24 September 2015.
157. Interview, author with Allison L. Lockett (Sp4, Supply Sergeant, 39th Ordnance Co, TFAD, Robert-Espagne, France, 1962-64), Enterprise, MS, 02 August 2001.
158. B. Shephard, A War of Nerves: Soldiers and Psychiatrists in the Twentieth Century, Harvard University Press, Cambridge, MA (2001), pp. 385-387.
159. L. L. Lemnitzer, "Helpful Hints for Personnel Ordered to France," DA Pamphlet 21-68, Headquarters, Department of The Army, Washington, DC, September 1960.
160. H. I. Auster, "COMZ's Communication Eyes," ComZ Cadence, 20 March 1964, p. 2.
161. Interview, author with David G. Hubby (1st Lt, Executive Officer, 103rd ASA Det, Orléans, France, 1961-63), Pittsboro, NC, 17 July 2015.
162. Interview, author with Col (ret) Robert A. Atkins (Lt Col, Chief, Plans and Programs, Engineer Division, ComZ Headquarters, Orléans, France, 1962-63), Leavenworth, KS, 15 January 2008.
163. Interview, author with Col (ret) George Stukhart, Jr. (Capt, CO, 541st Engineer Det (Terrain), Orléans, France, 1955-58), San Antonio, TX, 23 February 2007.
164. Interview, author with Keith E. Dyas (Sp4, 541st Engineer Det (Terrain), Orléans, France, 1955-56), Parker, CO, 26 February 2007.
165. D. A. Carter (2015), p. 310.
166. A. W. Knight, "Nuclear Weapons in the Cold War Army," Conference of Army Historians, Center of Military History, 08 August 2002. Brig Gen (ret) Albion W. Knight served as principal action officer for nuclear matters at Office of Deputy Chief of Staff for Operations (G3) at the Pentagon, 1959-62.
167. H. Roderick, "Crisis Management: Preventing Accidental War," Technology Review, August-September 1985, p. 43.
168. M. C. Day (ed), "Air Strip Called Smallest-Largest Air Line in World," Orleans Item, 31 August 1956, p. 1.
169. J. Freeland, "Safety Bombs Hazard in Flight Section," Orleans Item, 14 May 1959, p. 8.
170. J. Reuter, "Saran Is Home of ComZ's Own 'TWA' Air Service," Orleans Item, 21 February 1958, p. 3.
171. A. W. Spratley (ed), "Tent Unit Buys Cinders in Fight Against Mud," ComZ Cadence, 11 January 1952, p. 4.
172. Private correspondence to author from Col (ret) Robert A. Atkins (Lt Col, Chief, Plans and Programs, Engineer Division, ComZ Headquarters, Orléans, France, 1962-63), Leavenworth, KS, 15 November 1993.
173. Interview, author with Lloyd Daniel Rowell (Sgt, 29th Signal Bn, Company C, Périgueux, France, 1960-61), Coldwell, ID, 17 May 2010.
174. A. Horne, A Savage War of Peace: Algeria, 1954-1962, Viking Press, New York (1978), pp. 436-461.
175. A. Buchwald (1996), pp. 151-153.
176. F. J. Sullivan (ed), "Orleans Area Command Making Giant Strides in Fulfilling Mission," Orleans Item, 16 February 1961, p. 4.
177. M. C. Day (ed), "553rd EBC Breaks Local Record Building Prefab School Rooms," Orleans Item, 07 September 1956, p. 1.
178. M. C. Day (ed), "New ORIN Golf Links to Open June 30 at Chateau la Touche," Orleans Item, 01 June 1956, p. 3.
179. H. D. Edger, "The 819th Hospital Center," Medical Bulletin U.S. Army, Europe, Vol. 21, No. 12, December 1964, pp. 379-382.
180. A. L. Jorgenson (ed), "1st Enlisted Wacs Slated for ComZ," The Stars and Stripe, 21 February 1954, p. 8.
181. A. Holland, "1st Sig Gp Marks 44th Year in Europe," ComZ Cadence, 24 April 1964, p. 3.
182. M. C. Day (ed), "Army TC Inaugurates French Port Call Run Here To Bremerhaven," Orleans Item, 07 December 1956, pp. 1 and 4.
183. D. Walter, "Electronic Calculators Save Time for the Army," The Stars and Stripes, 04 May 1959, p. 11.
184. M. C. Day (ed), "553rd Dozers Work to Improve Quarters, Provide Community Fun," Orleans Item, 13 April 1956, pp. 1 and 2.
185. M. C. Day (ed), "553rd EBC Breaks Local Record Building Prefab School Rooms," Orleans Item, 07 September 1956, p. 1.
186. M. Katz, "553rd Engineers Take the OAC Spotlight: Battalion Tackles Problems For a Better OAC," Orleans Item, 10 October 1958, pp. 4 and 5.
187. R. R. Wessels, "Pictorial History," Headquarters, 553rd Engineer Battalion (Construction), Maison-Fort, France, 1961. Report covers construction activities from 27 March to 31 September 1961. [CEHO]
188. M. P. Gudebrod, "Tents Yes. But Concrete Moves In on Mud," The Stars and Stripes, 17 November 1961, p. 11.
189. E. Petrus, "553d Engineers Begin Floating Bridge Training," Orleans Item, 29 January 1960, p. 2.
190. R. Brooks (ed), "553rd Engineers Sponsor Courses," ComZ Cadence, 17 January 1964, p. 1.
191. M. C. Day (ed), "553rd EBC Builds A Floating Stage," Orleans Item, 06 July 1956, p. 1.
192. M. Pagan (ed), "553d Engr Bn Building Athletic Area for French Deaf and Dumb School," Orleans Item, 19 August 1960, p. 1.
193. J. Reuter, "Living in a 600-Year Old Mill," Orleans Item, 10 October 1958, p. 3.

References/Notes to pages 241 to 248

194. A. W. Spratley, "Dry Cleaning Facilities Latest QM Addition for Service to Troops," ComZ Cadence, 04 July 1952, p. 4.
195. M. C. Day (ed), "The Quartermaster's Industrial Center," Orleans Item, 19 July 1957, p. 3.
196. H. Morris, "Soldiers' Sad Soles Saved By Quartermaster Cobblers," ComZ Cadence, 24 October 1952, p. 4.
197. D. McClair (ed), "34th General's Building Dates Back to 1844," Orleans Item, 19 September 1958, p. 2.
198. R. J. Crawford (ed), "Maj Gen Gallagher Praises 'Wonderful Gesture' by French," The Advance, 16 July 1954, p. 3.
199. C. O. Stanley (ed), "American Children Learn French With Unusual Rapidity at School," Orleans Item, 03 February 1956, p. 3.
200. H. Blanquet, "Les installations américaines d'Orléans," La Republique du Centre, 26 mai 1959, p. 4; 27 mai 1959, p. 4; 28 mai 1959, p. 5; and 29 mai 1959, p. 5. (Fr) [AD 45]
201. Interview, author with James C. Conwell (1st Lt, CO, US Army Engineer Map Depot, St-Ay, France, 1959-62), Vancouver, BC, Canada, 19 May 2014.
202. D. Cardinet, "Les Programmes D'Exchange Cultural," Panorama, février 1963, pp. 4 and 5. (Fr)
203. D. McClair, "First Three Graders' Club Has Gala Debut," Orleans Item, 08 November 1957, p. 3.
204. M. Valtat, "Le Général Young et ses installations font peser une lourde menace sur Orléans et sa région," L'Humanité, 18 octobre 1951. (Fr) [AD 45]
205. B. Ivey, "The Library Grows With the Command," Orleans Item, 11 December 1959, p. 6.
206. D. Walter, "They Live in a Chateau," The Stars and Stripes, 14 June 1953, p. IV.
207. Anon, "La Cité americaine des Quatre-Vents, à Olivet prend le nom de Cité Maréchal Foch," La Nouvelle République, 28 novembre 1959, p. 1. (Fr)
208. Housing records of Préfecture du Loriet, Orléans, France, 1955-1966. [Art. 295W, Cote 68375b, Archives départementales du Loriet (AD 45), Orléans, France.]

CHAPTER EIGHT

1. Anon, "Directory and Station List of The US Army," US Army, Washington, DC, December 1952, p. 491.
2. J. R. Moenk, "Annual Historical Report for 1953-54," Headquarters, US Army, Europe (USAREUR), Karlsruhe, Germany, 1955, p. 342.
3. G. Derule, "La vie quotidienne sur la base pendant la période américaine," Reflets, Journal de la BA 136 de Toul-Rosières, France, no. 142, mai-aôut 1995, pp. 20 and 21. (Fr).
4. J. J. McAuliffe, U. S. Air Forces in France 1950-1967, Milspec Press, San Diego, CA (2005), p. 310.
5. J. H. Pruett (ed), "608th Tac Hospital Serves Over 4,000 People Monthly," Toul Tiger, 23 November 1960, pp. 4 and 5.
6. D. F. Atherton, "Semiannual Historical Report," Châteauroux Air Station, Déols, France, December 1958. [AFHRA]
7. F. Jarraud, Les Américains à Châteauroux 1951-1967, Chez l'auteur, Le Poinçonnet, France (1981), p. 31. (Fr)
8. N. Raymond, "AF Hospital's 'Extras' Make Stay More Pleasant," The Stars and Stripes, 19 March 1957, p. 11.
9. C. E. Wilson, "Protecting Your Family," DOD Pamphlet 6-3, Office of Armed Forces Information and Education, US Department of Defense, Washington, DC, 10 September 1956, pp. 9-11.
10. Interviews, author with Lance L. Barclay (1st Lt, Executive Officer, 215th General Dispensary, TFAD, Robert-Espagne, France, 1964-65), Erie, PA, 18 July and 31 August 2011.
11. H. C. Bouchelion, "Admission to Quarters," U.S. Army Hospital, Orléans, France, 12 November 1965.
12. R. L. Parsons (ed), "Appointments Advised for Routine Dispensary Visits," The Pariscope, 18 December 1958, p. 2.
13. A. W. Spratley (ed), "Converted Hydro-Diesel Train Transports Adsec Hospital Patients," ComZ Cadence, 11 July 1952, p. 4.
14. A. W. Spratley (ed), "Verdun Tries Bus Hospital To Cut Costs," ComZ Cadence, 12 September 1952, p. 4.
15. M. D. Taylor, Transportation of the Sick and Wounded, FM 8-35, Headquarters, Department of The Army, Washington, DC, December 1955.
16. K. T. Barkley, The Ambulance, Exposition Press, Hicksville, NY (1978), pp. 118-121.
17. W. R. Breyer, "Serving Servicemen Worldwide," Army Information Digest, April 1961, pp. 68-71.
18. L. Levine, "Red Cross Forges Vital Link in Emergency Leaves," The Stars and Stripes, 28 March 1963, p. 11.
19. Interview, author with Roy E. Anderson (PFC, 7831st Army Unit, TFOD, Robert-Espagne, France, 1955-56), Clemson, SC, 19 March 2013.
20. P. J. Mahoney (ed), "Red Cross Has Five Centers in France," The Transporter, 01 February 1963, p. 8.
21. R. Wright, "Mansion for the Military," The Stars and Stripes, 08 September 1964, p. 13.
22. E. Girard, "Hometown Services Overseas," Army Information Digest, February 1955, pp. 39-44.
23. E. Petrus (ed), "Capping Ceremonies of Gray Ladies Held; Two French Women Enrolled," Orleans Item, 17 April 1959, p. 2.
24. D. A. Bartoni (ed), "Europe's Only 'Gray Man' in Action," The Stars and Stripes, 28 March 1957, p. 8.
25. O. McDaniel, "High School Volunteers Become Summer 'Medics," The Stars and Stripes, 28 August, 1964, p. 11.
26. L. L. Lemnitzer, Medical Service Units Theater of Operations, FM 8-5, Headquarters, Department of The Army, Washington, DC, October 1959, pp. 57, 64, 65, 70, and 71.

References/Notes to pages 248 to 258

27. E. G. Wheeler, <u>Medical Service Theater of Operations</u>, FM 8-10, Headquarters, Department of The Army, Washington, DC, November 1959, pp. 33, 192, and 193.
28. A. W. Spratley (ed), "34th General Hospital Nearing Completion," <u>ComZ Cadence</u>, 17 April 1953, pp. 1 and 4.
29. A. L. Jorgenson (ed), "ComZ's Enlarged 34th GH Opens July 8," <u>The Stars and Stripes</u>, 27 June 1953, p. 8.
30. P. Flint, "Actress Visits, Charms Patients," <u>ComZ Cadence</u>, 11 February 1955, p. 6.
31. M. Pagan (ed), "New Outpatient, Maternity Wing Added to 34th General Hospital," <u>Orleans Item</u>, 05 August 1960, p.1.
32. J. D. Nottingham (ed), "Help for 'Halt' Embraced In Hands of ComZ Expert," <u>The Stars and Stripes</u>, 03 September 1959, p. 9.
33. Interview, author with Dr. Johst A. Burk (Sp5, Pharmacy Div, 34th General Hospital, la Chapelle-St.-Mesmin, France, 1965-66). Mohegan Lake, NY, 24 February 2016.
34. M. Pagan (ed), "French Interns Arrive at La Chapelle Hospital," <u>Orleans Item</u>, 02 September 1960, p. 2.
35. J. R. Hopkins, "Former Yale Student Is First French Intern in New Training Program," <u>Orleans Item</u>, 14 May 1959, p. 4.
36. D. Walter, "First of French Interns Start Training in ComZ," <u>The Stars and Stripes</u>, 21 April 1959, p. 9.
37. Anon, "Professional Education Program for French Interns," 34th General Hospital, la Chapelle-St.-Mesmin, France, September 1963, pp. 1-10.
38. Interview, author with Dr. Harald Sontag (French Intern, 34th General Hospital, la Chapelle-St.-Mesmin, France, 1965-66), Paris, France, 01 December 2012.
39. Private email to author from Dr. Harald Sontag (French Intern, 34th General Hospital, la Chapelle-St.-Mesmin, France, 1965-66), Strasbourg, France, 23 September 2012.
40. R. V. N. Ginn, <u>The History of the US Army Medical Service Corps</u>, Office of The Surgeon General and Center of Military History, Washington, DC (1997), pp. 120, 199, and 200. Ginn explains beefed-up echelons of medical service based on lessons learned in World War II.
41. J. S. Arrigona and W. R. Karsteter, "History of the Joint Construction Agency in Europe," JCA, Boulogne-sur-Seine (Paris), France, 1958, p. 205. [CEHO]
42. R. P. Grathwol and D. M. Moorhus, <u>Building for Peace</u>, Center of Military History, Washington, DC (2005), pp. 112 and 113.
43. Letter from Maj Gen Samuel D. Sturgis, Jr. (CG, USACOMZEUR) to François Leduc (Chef de la Mission Centrale de Liaison pour l'Assistance aux Armées Alliées), dated 27 September 1952. [CEHO]
44. M. C. Day (ed), "34th General Hospital Anniversary On September 7," <u>Orleans Item</u>, 06 September 1957, p. 3.
45. J. E. Stanton (ed), "Hospital Nursing Staff Observes Anniversary," <u>Orleans Item</u>, 31 January 1958, p. 1.
46. Interview, author with Benjamin Hicks Stone, AIA (architect and son of Edward Durell Stone, FAIA), New York, NY, 28 April 2009.
47. J. L. Amirault, "Chinon Souffle ses 10 Bougies," <u>Panorama</u>, février 1963, pp. 6 and 7. (Fr)
48. C. Raia (ed), "Hosp Nearing Finish," <u>Basec Mission</u>, 25 February 1956, p. 4.
49. C. M. Smith, <u>The Medical Department: Hospitalization and Evacuation, Zone of Interior</u>, Center of Military History, Washington, DC (1956), pp. 73-76.
50. Anon, "L'Évacuation des bases U.S. on s'interroge sur l'utilisation future de l'hôpital militaire de Chinon," <u>La Nouvelle République</u>, 05 octobre 1966. (Fr)
51. P. Labrude, "L'aérodrome de Vassincourt et Neuville-sur-Ornain (1936-1952)," <u>Anciens Aérodromes Le Magizine</u>, mai-juin 2014, pp. 2-7. (Fr)
52. F. M. Thompson, "Staff Visit to Advance Section 12-17 May 1952," Headquarters European Command Communications Zone, Orléans, France, 17 June 1952, p. 5. [CEHO]
53. R. Keating, "Yank Ingenuity Develops 'Hole' to Save Food," <u>ComZ Cadence</u>, 19 September 1952, pp. 1 and 4.
54. R. J. Crawford (ed), "Fire at Vassincourt," <u>The Advance</u>, 05 February 1954, p. 1.
55. R. R. Raines, <u>Getting the Message Through</u>, Center of Military History, Washington, DC (1996), pp. 366 and 367.
56. H. B. Kraft, "New U.S. Army Installation at Verdun," <u>The Stars and Stripes</u>, 11 October 1958, p. 11.
57. M. Perry, "Family Life With The RCAF in Europe," <u>The Roundel</u>, September 1962, pp. 20-25.
58. S. Skinner, <u>The Stand: The Final Flight of Lt. Frank Luke, Jr.</u>, Schiffer Military History, Atglen, PA (2008), pp. 216, 234, and 235.
59. R. B. Warren, "Double-Purpose Hospitals in France," <u>The Military Engineer</u>, September-October 1960, p. 402.
60. R. Sher, "Annual Historical Report for 1953-1954," Headquarters, US Army, Europe (USAREUR), Karlsruhe, Germany, 1955, p. 342.
61. A. Diggle, "Chateauroux Goes Modern," <u>The Stars and Stripes</u>, 29 August 1955, p. 12.
62. J. A. Moore, "608th Hospital Unit Takes To The Field," <u>Toul Tiger</u>, 29 September 1961, p. 5.
63. J. R. Moenk, "Establishment of Communications Through France, 1950-1951," Historical Division, US Army, Europe (USAREUR), Karlsruhe, Germany, 1952, pp. 119-121.
64. Anon, "Des Américains arrivent aux Ajones pour cinq ans," <u>La Resistance</u>, 01 avril 1953. (Fr) [AD 85]

65. D. Walter, "Basec Opens La Roche-sur-Yon Medical Depot, Staffed by Volunteers From Units in Germany," The Stars and Stripes, 30 May 1953, p. 8.
66. R. Reynolds, "Basec Med Co Diagnoses Ills of Equipment," The Stars and Stripes, 27 January 1954, p. 9.
67. D. Scarborough, "Croix Chapeau Absorbs La Roche-sur-Yon," Basec Mission, 07 January 1956, p. 4.
68. P. McCormick (ed), "Making Your Sight Just Right," ComZ Cadence, 17 April 1964, p. 2.
69. J. Renevot, "Croix-Chapeau cet inconnu…où règne l'odeur de l'éther," Panorama, mars 1962, pp. 4 and 5. (Fr)
70. Interview, author with Dr. John D. Chambers (PFC, Medical Corpsman, 28th General Hospital, Caserne Aufrédi, La Rochelle, France, 1955-57), Vancouver, BC, Canada, 16 May 2005.
71. R. J. Crawford (ed), "Vital Job of Supplying Medical Equipment for ADSEC Belongs to Vitry Medical Depot," The Advance, 06 September 1957, pp. 3 and 5.
72. R. C. Boyd (ed), "Dexion A Giant Erector Set," The Advance, 23 May 1959, p. 3.
73. D. Walter, "General Store' for USAREUR Medics," The Stars and Stripes, 18 June 1959, pp. 11 and 12.
74. R. C. Boyd (ed), "Servicemen Learn French at Vitry Medical Depot," The Advance, 03 January 1958, p. 1.
75. D. G. Francis (ed), "USAF, Army Aid Flooded Hamburg," Toul Tiger, 09 March 1962, p. 8.
76. H. R. Westphalinger, "US Army Communications Zone, Europe," Army Information Digest, December 1962, p. 16.
77. Interview, author with Sgt Maj (ret) Michael Richter (Sp4, 77th Medical Depot, Vitry-le-François, France, 1961-65), Paris, France, 17 April 2010.
78. D. A. Burchinal, "FRELOC Final Report," Headquarters, US European Command (USEUCOM), St.-Germain-en-Laye, France, 1967, p. 37. Report written at Camp de Loges by Lt Col John F. McGauhey, USAF.
79. J. Walters, "New Field Setup Speeds Hospital Care," The Stars and Stripes, 05 March 1957, p. 11.
80. C. Raia (ed), "Medics Given 24-Hour Alert Test," Basec Mission, 07 April 1956, p. 6.
81. R. J. Crawford (ed), "Real Patients Help In Field Training Problem," The Advance, 02 August 1957, pp. 3 and 5.
82. Interview, author with Danny White (Sp4, 34th General Hospital, la Chapelle-St.-Mesmin, France, 1960-62), Orting, WA, 02 May 2011.
83. M. D. Egan, "Inventory Report of Phase I Medical Kits," 39th Ordnance Co (FM), US Army Garrison, Verdun, France, 03 June 1964.
84. Anon, "Medical Disaster Control Plan," 7369th US Air Force Dispensary, Phalsbourg AB, France, 06 June 1963, pp. 18-26. [AFHRA]
85. D. A. Lane, "Annual Historical Report for 1956-1957," Headquarters, US Army, Europe (USAREUR), Heidelberg, Germany, 1958, p. 79.
86. J. B. Tucker, War of Nerves, Pantheon Books, New York (2006), pp. 111, 163, and 164.
87. M. Stubbs, "Balanced Power for a Balanced Arsenal," Army Information Digest, August 1962, pp. 53 and 54.
88. Interview, author with Lt Col (ret) John A. Nark (Capt, CO, 547th Ordnance Co, Fontenet, France, 1960-63), Delran, NJ, 06 May 2006.
89. J. K. Smart, "History of Decontamination," NBC Defense Systems, Aberdeen Proving Ground, MD, nd, pp. 14 and 20.
90. R. J. Crawford (ed), "49 Graduates from ADSEC's First CBR Course," The Advance, 19 March 1954, p. 3.
91. Interview, author with Doran A. Ditlow (Sp2, 109th Ordnance Co, Nancy, France, 1954-57), Grant, MI, 26 April 2007.
92. A. P. Head (ed), "Post's Depots Get Job Done," Basec Mission, 20 August 1955, p. 6.
93. R. J. Crawford (ed), "35 Graduate From Sampigny's RAD Defense School," The Advance, 23 March 1956, p. 1.
94. A. W. Spratley (ed), "Novel OAC Unit is Medical Crew of 80th Hosp Trn," ComZ Cadence, 19 June 1953, p. 1.
95. I. A. Nabeshima (ed), "80th Hosp Train Makes First Call," Basec Mission, 31 July 1953, p. 1.
96. E. A. Sibul, "Medical Railroading During the Korean War 1950-1953," Railroad History, Spring-Summer 2011, pp. 48-64.
97. M. Manning, "Angels of Mercy: The Army Nurse Corps on Bataan and Corregidor," Parameters, Spring 1992, p. 94.
98. G. C. Mudgett, "New-Type Hospital Train," Army Information Digest, November 1954, p. 61.
99. E. G. Wheeler, "Ambulance Train, Rail," Table of Organization and Equipment (TOE) No. 8-520E, Headquarters, Department of The Army, Washington, DC, 1964, pp. 1-3.
100. H. A. Jacobs, "Ambulances on Rails," Railway Progress, October 1954, pp. 35-39.
101. J. P. Anderson (ed), "ComZ Gets New Hospital Train For La Rochelle-La Chapelle Run," Basec Mission, 08 January 1954, p. 4.
102. A. W. Spratley (ed), "80th Hosp Train Makes First Evacuation Run After Inspection," ComZ Cadence, 24 July 1953, p. 4.
103. I. A. Nabeshima (ed), "34th GH Opening Marks First Stop for Evacuees," Basec Mission, 17 July 1953, p. 4.
104. N. Raymond, "VIP Treatment for Army's Litter Patients," The Stars and Stripes, 07 March 1957, p. 11.
105. R. P. Smith (ed), "Landstuhl Medics Hold Railroad Exercise," The Stars and Stripes, 07 January 1963, p. 9.
106. B. Quinlisk, "Medical Ambulance Train Rumbles Through Germany," Medcom Examiner, 27 September 1972, pp. 4 and 5.
107. E. B. Staats, "Use of Ambulance Trains and Assigned Personnel," Comptroller General of the United States, General Accounting Office, Washington, DC, 13 May 1971.

References/Notes to pages 265 to 272

108. R. W. Colglazier, Senior Officer Oral History Program, US Army Military History Institute, Carlisle Barracks, PA, 1984, pp. 228-230.
109. Centre des archives contemporaines (CAC), Fontainebleau, France holds documents on "NATO and US bases in France" which contain records of negotiations on reimbursement to US for improvements to real estate occupied in France during 1950 to 1967.
110. Anon, "Le scandale de l'hôpital américain de Toul," L'Est Republicain, 28 août 1967. (Fr) [AD 55]
111. Anon, "Directory and Station List of The US Army," US Army, Washington, DC, December 1951 to December 1967.
112. Historical Data Cards (Form 373), Unit History Branch, US Army Center of Military History, Washington, DC.

CHAPTER NINE

1. J. R. Moenk, "Establishment of Communications Through France, 1950-1951," Headquarters, US Army, Europe (USAREUR), Karlsruhe, Germany, 1952, pp. 126, 130, and 132.
2. V. Rowe, The Great Wall of France, G. P. Putnam's Sons, New York (1961).
3. J. J. Meehan, "Maginot Line Draws Red Propaganda Fire," The Stars and Stripes, 23 May 1952, p. 4.
4. J. W. Harris, "10,000 Local, 300 Long-Distance Calls Processed Daily Through ADSEC Switchboard," The Advance, 30 April 1954, p. 3.
5. R. J. Crawford (ed), "Dial Telephones Now Operating At Verdun; General Curtis Places First Call," The Advance, 05 November 1954, p. 1.
6. S. Markowitz (ed), "901st 'Tastes' Chow," The Advance, 29 May 1953, p. 3.
7. A. W. Spratley (ed), "Adsec Soldiers Get 'Drill' But Take it Sitting Down," ComZ Cadence, 30 May 1952, p. 4.
8. H. R. Morris, "ComZ Picks Up 'Cadence' With New Marching Bands," ComZ Cadence, 16 May 1952, p. 4.
9. R. J. Crawford (ed), "118th Army Band Covers ADSEC with Music," The Advance, 06 December 1957, p. 3.
10. Anon, "Les Américains imposeraient des architectes allemands à Verdun," L'Est République, 07 octobre 1952, p. 1. (Fr) [AD 55]
11. B. McConachy, "The Roots of Artillery Doctrine: Napoleonic Artillery Tactics Reconsidered," The Journal of Military History, July 2001, pp. 619-621.
12. Interview, author with Jesse H. Patton (Sgt, Signal Platoon, ADSEC, Verdun, France, 1959-60), Evans, GA, 08 November 2006.
13. Letter from Brig Gen W. W. Ford (Commanding General, Advance Section) to Maj Gen Samuel D. Sturgis, Jr. (Commanding General, ComZ), dated 05 May 1952. [CEHO]
14. A. W. Spratley (ed), "Traffic Trio," ComZ Cadence, 04 April 1952, p. 4.
15. Interview, author with Lyle A. Ross (Cpl, 529th Military Police Co, Laleu and Rochefort, France, 1952-53), Lake Havasu City, AZ, 21 April 2009.
16. A. W. Spratley (ed), "EM Gets Called on CGs 'Carpet' For—Compliment," ComZ Cadence, 11 April 1953, p. 4.
17. Record of telephone conference, Maj Gen Samuel D. Sturgis, Jr. (Commanding General, ComZ) with Brig Gen W. W. Ford (Commanding General, ADSEC), dated 23 September 1952. [CEHO]
18. R. J. Crawford (ed), "ADSEC-A Life Line To The Front Line' Wins First In ADSEC's Slogan Contest," The Advance, 17 December 1954, p. 1.
19. Interview, author with Frank Tisler (1st Lt, Platoon Leader, Company C, 97th Engineer Bn, Verdun, France, 1955-57), New Smyrna Beach, FL, 31 January 2008.
20. R. J. Crawford (ed), "Gen Woodward Opens Cross-France Pipeline," The Advance, 25 January 1957, p. 1.
21. R. J. Crawford (ed), "Command Change Ceremonies Formally Install New CG," The Advance, 03 January 1958, p. 3.
22. C. J. Bernardo and R. L. Bennett, History of the 4th Logistical Command, 1950-1963, US Army Communications Zone, Europe (USACOMZEUR), Orléans, France, 1965.
23. D. Walter, "Expansion Program Reflects Adsec's Importance," The Stars and Stripes, 15 April 1957, p. 11.
24. L. B. Sibert (ed), "Verdun Depot Cuts Cost on Phone Clamps," The Stars and Stripes, 11 March 1955, p. 10.
25. P. D. Kackley, "Verdun's Operation Big Splice," The Stars and Stripes, 06 November 1959, p. 11.
26. R. C. Boyd (ed), "A Fatal Dose of Lead," The Advance, 20 February 1959, p. 2.
27. R. J. Crawford (ed), "72d Ord Bn Supplies Service To 4,000 Vehicles Throughout ADSEC," The Advance, 03 February 1956, p. 3.
28. J. C. Fuson, "The Mission and General Organization of the US Army Communications Zone, Europe," Command Briefing, Headquarters, United States Army, Europe (USAREUR), Heidelberg, Germany, 08 July 1959. [MHI]
29. D. A. Lane, "Annual Historical Report for 1957-58," Headquarters, US Army, Europe (USAREUR), Heidelberg, Germany, 1958, p. 217.
30. H. A. Miley, Jr., Senior Officer Oral History Program, US Army Military History Institute, Carlisle Barracks, PA, 1975, pp. 58 and 59.

31. Interview, author with Gen (ret) Henry A. Miley, Jr. (Col, Commander, Advance Weapons Support Command, Pirmasens, Germany, 1961-63), Tampa, FL, 27 February 2006.
32. R. C. Boyd (ed), "Verdun Hospital Completes Move to Desandrouins Barracks Area," The Advance, 10 October 1958, pp. 3-5.
33. Interview, author with Renée DeLong Nixon (dependent of Maj Martin L. DeLong, USAF, Étain AB and Toul-Rosières AB, 1958-61), Danville, NY, 20 July 2016.
34. H. B. Kraft, "New U.S. Army Installation at Verdun," The Stars and Stripes, 11 October 1958, p. 11.
35. Interview, author with Nancy Peters Lynch (dependent of Maj Thomas E. Peters, Ordnance Div, 4th Logistical Command, Verdun, France, 1960-61), Locust Grove, VA, 13 April 2005.
36. J. Mewha, "The Selection of The Candidate-Unknown From the Trans-Atlantic Phase of World War II," Headquarters, United States Army, Europe (USAREUR), Heidelberg, Germany, 1958, pp. 1-31.
37. Interview, author with Jesse H. Patton (Sgt, Signal Platoon, ADSEC, Verdun, France, 1959-60), Evans, GA, 08 November 2006.
38. J. Hargrave, "Large-Scale Computer Complex Opens to Aid COMZ Logistics," ComZ Cadence, 02 October 1964, pp. 1-3.
39. Interview, author with Merwyn J. Fenner (Sp5, Supply & Maintenance Agency, Verdun, France, 1965-67), Hoopeston, IL, 09 May 2008.
40. Interview, author with Col (ret) Basil J. Hobar (Capt, Documents Processing Branch, Supply & Maintenance Agency, Verdun, France, 1967), Alexandria, VA, 30 July 2009.
41. Letter from Maj Gen Samuel D. Sturgis, Jr. (Commanding General, ComZ) to Maj Gen William H. Middleswat (Chief, Quartermaster Division, Headquarters, US Army, Europe, Heidelberg, Germany), dated 08 September 1952. [CEHO]
42. R. C. Boyd (ed), "Hollywood Guest Star Arrives In Verdun Area Next Tuesday, Oct 21st," The Advance, 17 October 1958, p. 1.
43. Interview, author with Anthony J. Zuvich (Sp4, 23rd Engineer Co (FM), Verdun, France, 1956-58), Middletown, DE, 06 January 2010.
44. W. G. Blair, "G.I. Deserter Who Chose Love In France Gets 10-Year Sentence," New York Times, 02 August 1958, pp. 1 and 4.
45. Anon, "U.S. Private, Jailed for 1944 Desertion, Is Freed to Return to His French Family," New York Times, 10 October 1958, p. 14.
46. Interview, author with Major de Garnison (4e division aéromobile, 61e division militaire territorial, l'armée de Terre Français) at 32, place Galland, Verdun, France, 11 June 1991.
47. J. Duchnowski, "Castle's origin remains matter of conjecture," Engineer Update, October 1988.
48. R. B. Buzzaird, "Insignia of The Corps of Engineers," The Military Engineer, January-February 1958, pp. 27 and 28.
49. J. T. Greenwood, "Building the Road to Alaska" in B. W. Fowle (ed), Builders and Fighters: US Army Engineers in World War II, Office of History, US Army Corps of Engineers, Fort Belvoir, VA (1992), pp. 117-135.
50. C. D. Hendricks, "Race Relations and the Contributions of African-American Troops in Alaska," The U.S. Army and World War II, Center of Military History, Washington, DC (1998), pp. 171-181.
51. U. Lee, The Employment of Negro Troops, Center of Military History, Washington, DC (1966), pp. 688-691.
52. Letter from Maj Gen Samuel D. Sturgis, Jr. (Commanding General, ComZ) to Brig Gen John B. Murphy (Chief P&A Div, HQ, EUCOM), dated 18 April 1952, pp. 1 and 2. [CEHO]
53. R. J. Crawford (ed), "Chaplain Smith to ZI; Served in France Since 1951," The Advance, 01 October 1954, p. 1.
54. J. S. Winn, "97th's Training Season," The Builder, March 1965, p. 1.
55. R. R. Connolly et al., "Aircraft Hangar at Brienne-le-Château," The Military Engineer, July-August 1965, pp. 249-252.
56. Interview, author with Lt Col (ret) Perry D. Tripp (Capt, S3, 32nd Engineer Group, Verdun, France, 1961-64), Taylors, SC, 03 March 2005.
57. A. W. Spratley (ed), "Adsec Work Overtime to Beat Jack Frost," ComZ Cadence, 05 September 1952, pp. 1 and 4.
58. R. J. Crawford (ed), "More, Better Bread Is Aim of New Verdun Garrison Bakery," The Advance, 16 August 1957, p. 3.
59. Interview, author with Lt Col (ret) Milton S. Killen (Capt, CO, 39th Ordnance Co, Verdun, France, 1960-61), Lewisville, TX, 16 February 2005.
60. C. B. Magruder, Recurring Logistic Problems As I Have Observed Them, Center of Military History, Washington, DC (1991), pp. 127 and 128.
61. P. S. Kindsvatter, "Maintenance Operations in the North African Campaign, 1942-43," Ordnance Magazine, Summer 2006, p. 14.
62. R. C. Boyd (ed), "Damaged Vehicles Fixed Like New at The 39th Ordnance Repair Shop," The Advance, 21 November 1958, p. 3.
63. G. F. Locke (ed), "4th Log Ord Shops Keep Trucks Rolling," The Advance, 19 April 1963, p. 3.
64. D. Miller, The Cold War, John Murray Publishers, London, England (1998), pp. 320-322.
65. G. F. Locke (ed), "Unit's Mission is to Provide 'Service to the Line-on the Line,'" The Advance, 05 April 1962, p. 3.

References/Notes to pages 281 to 288

66. D. A. Lane, "Annual Historical Report for 1954-55," Headquarters, US Army, Europe (USAREUR), Heidelberg, Germany, 1956, p. 57.
67. H. Godillot, "A Verdun, M. Antoine Seng établit un record difficile a battre," Panorama, février 1963, p. 1. (Fr)
68. R. S. Allen, Lucky Forward, Vanguard Press, New York (1947), pp. 143-146.
69. R. Radka (ed), "2nd Trans Safety Patrol Cuts Accident Rate," The Advance, 10 July 1959, p. 3.
70. Interview, author with Robert D. Rex (Sp5, Company C, 97th Engineer Bn, Étain, France, 1965-67), Wooster, OH, 06 August 2004. Records on American POWs are available from US Department of Defense, POW/MIA Office, Washington, DC.
71. J. H. Phillips, "Vulnerability of United States Army, Europe Line of Communication to Communist Action," Office of the Assistant Chief of Staff, Intelligence (G2), US Army, Europe (USAREUR), Heidelberg, Germany, 26 January 1954, p. 6. [MHI]
72. R. C. Boyd (ed), "BASEC Unit Helps in ADSEC Hauling Gasoline, Jet Fuel," The Advance, 11 April 1958, p. 4.
73. Interview, author with SSgt (ret) George P. Green (PFC, Quartermaster Co, Buzy, France, 1954-55), Security, CO, 03 October 2003.
74. H. J. Obermayer, Soldiering for Freedom, Texas A&M University Press, College Station, TX (2005), pp. 104 and 105.
75. Note regarding Rozelier, files of Mission Centrale de Liaison pour l'Assistance aux Armée Alliées (MCLAAA), Paris, France, dated 05 juin 1958. (Box 12Q35/8) [SHD]
76. Interview, author with Lt Col (ret) Milton S. Killen (Capt, CO, 39th Ordnance Co, Verdun, France, 1960-61), Lewisville, TX, 02 August 2013.
77. Private correspondence to author from Arthur M. Fell (Capt, Security Officer, Rozelier Ammunition Depot, France, 1961-62), Montpellier, France, dated 28 July 2013.
78. Private correspondence to author from Arthur M. Fell (Capt, Security Officer, Rozelier Ammunition Depot, France, 1961-62), Montpellier, France, dated 22 July 2007.
79. Anon, "Tragique accident à la base de Bricy," La Nouvelle République, 04 juillet 1957. (Fr) [AD 45]
80. R. J. Crawford (ed), "20 Tons of 'Duds,' Mines, Destroyed by Demolition Team in Last 18 Months," The Advance, 29 October 1954, p. 3.
81. D. Webster, Aftermath: The Remnants of War, Vintage Books, New York (1996), pp. 11-80.
82. D. A. Bartoni (ed), "Army Identifies Missing GI As Cavern Search Goes On," The Stars and Stripes, 25 April 1956, p.1.
83. R. A. Atkins, My Life in the United States Army: An Autobiography, Self-published, Leavenworth, Kansas, nd, pp. 16.11 and 16.12.
84. R. J. Crawford (ed), "Award of Soldier's Medal To Highlight Ceremony Here," The Advance, 15 February 1957, pp. 1 and 3. For photos of tunnels at Tavannes, see D. A. Bartoni (ed), The Stars and Stripes, 28 April 1956, p. 2.
85. Interview, author with WO 2 (ret) Benjamin F. Gottfried (Sp3, 249th Engineer Bn, Étain AB, France, 1961-63), Milford, DE, 19 August 2010.
86. J. F. Gallo, "Engineer Railroad Construction," The Military Engineer, January-February 1966, pp. 21 and 22.
87. C. J. Gross, Prelude to the Total Force: The Air National Guard, 1943-1969, Office of Air Force History, Washington, DC (1985), pp. 187-190.
88. Anon, "Historical Summary 1943-1967," Headquarters, 249th Engineer Bn, Karlsruhe, Germany, 1967, pp. 3-11. [MHI]
89. J. A. Hubbard, "Engineer Troop Construction in France," The Military Engineer, March-April 1964, pp. 100 and 101.
90. H. Ambrose and E. W. Link, "Taxiway and Helipad Construction," The Military Engineer, September-October 1960, pp. 373 and 374.
91. R. P. Smith (ed), "Signal Net Links U. S. Forces," The Stars and Stripes, 06 February 1963, p. 9.
92. Interview, author with Lt Col (ret) John D. Hosey (Capt, Pilot, 2nd Aviation Co, Rozelier, France, 1963-66), Woodinville, WA, 23 May 2013.
93. R. P. Smith (ed), "Eager 8th Inf Div Jumpers Back in Harness," The Stars and Stripes, 07 March 1963, p. 8.
94. Interview, author with Jerry Wayne MacDonald (Sp4, Senior Airplane Mechanic, 2nd Aviation Co, Rozelier, France, 1964-65), Spring Hill, TN, 03 October 2012.
95. S. Harding, U.S. Army Aircraft Since 1947, Schiffer Publishing, Atglen, PA (1997), pp. 35-38, 231, and 232.
96. R. C. Boyd (ed), "Flying Chaplain Serves ADSEC Troops," The Advance, 29 November 1957, p. 3.
97. R. J. Crawford (ed), "ADSEC Copter Brings Woman To Hospital Here," The Advance, 30 August 1957, pp. 1 and 3.
98. Interview, author with Col (ret) George Steven Bosan (Maj, CO, 26th Transportation Co (Lt Hel), Rozelier and Verdun, France, 1959-62), Camp Hill, PA, 19 July 2010.
99. R. J. Weide (ed), "Varied Missions Make Company Strategic Unit," The Lifeline Times, 09 September 1961, p. 3.
100. A. W. Spratley (ed), "City Theater Is Contracted For U.S. Films," ComZ Cadence, 12 December 1952, p. 1.

References/Notes to pages 288 to 296

101. Interview, author with James J. Lacey (1st Lt, Platoon Leader, Co C, 97th Engineer Bn, Jardin Fontaine, France, 1957-59), South Park, PA, 22 June 2015.
102. R. J. Crawford (ed), "Huge ComZ Const Program Underway; Over 1.2 Million Slated for ADSEC," The Advance, 25 January 1957, pp. 1 and 3.
103. J. M. Heiser, A Soldier Supporting Soldiers, Center of Military History, Washington, DC (1991), p. 116.
104. Interview, author with Lt Gen (ret) Julius W. Becton, Jr. (Maj, Chief, Operations, G3, 4th Logistical Command, Verdun, France, 1960-62), Springfield, VA, 08 December 2003.
105. W. A. McDaniel, "Welcome to Verdun," US Army Garrison, Verdun, France, 1959, pp. 8 and 9.
106. Interview, author with Dorothy S. Davis (wife of Lt Col William V. Davis, CO, 42nd Field Hospital, Verdun, France, 1960-63), Rockville, MD, 15 July 2005.
107. W. F. Spurgin, "Welcome to Verdun and to Verdun Post," Headquarters, Verdun Post, Verdun, France, 1960, p. 7.
108. Anon, Lorraine-Vosges-Alsace, Bureau National de Renseignements de Tourisme, Paris, France (1961), p. 29. (Fr)
109. G. le Hallé, Verdun ma ville, Martelle Editions, Amiens, France (1992), p. 172. (Fr)
110. D. Walter, "On the Economy' in France," The Stars and Stripes, 14 May 1959, pp. 12-14.
111. Anon, "Hier après-midi, à 'Bevaux-City' le Premier Fantassin de France a donné son nom au 'Village Louis-Best," L'Est Républicain, 11 mai 1962. (Fr) [AD 55]
112. M.-T. Bastien, "Sur Les Traces du Premier Poilu," Dépêche Meusienne, 26 mars 1994. (Fr)
113. R. P. Smith (ed), "Dependents Scramble for French Coal," The Stars and Stripes, 13 January 1963, p. 3.
114. Interview, author with Brig Gen (ret) Robert C. Hawlk (Maj, Ordnance Div, 4th Logistical Command, Verdun, France, 1962-63), Union Hall, VA, 10 March 2005.
115. N. S. Khrushchev, Khrushchev Remembers: The Last Testament, Little, Brown and Co., Boston, MA (1974), p. 425.
116. Interview, author with Harry F. Puncec (Sp4, Company Clerk, Company C, 97th Engineer Bn, Verdun and Étain, France, 1959-62), Lakewood, CO, 07 January 2010.
117. Interview, author with Gen (ret) William B. Rosson (Lt Col, Advance Planning Group, SHAPE Headquarters, Astoria Hotel, Paris, France, 1951), Salem, VA, 01 April 2002.
118. F. J. Chesarek, Senior Officer Oral History Program, US Army Military History Institute, Carlisle Barracks, PA, 1971, pp. 38 and 39.
119. D. Schoenbrun, The Three Lives of Charles de Gaulle, Atheneum, New York (1968), pp. 289 and 290.
120. J. Lanher et al., Du Sergent York a Patton Les Américains en Meuse, 1917-1919, Société des Lettres, Bar-le-Duc, France (1988). (Fr)
121. S. L. A. Marshall, World War I, Houghton Mifflin, Boston, MA (1987), pp. 244-249.
122. X. H. Price (ed), American Armies and Battlefields in Europe, American Battle Monuments Commission (ABMC), Washington, DC (1938), pp. 324 and 325.
123. P. McCormick (ed), "Accidents Plague the Unwary," ComZ Cadence, 17 April 1964, p. 1.
124. W. S. Aiton, "Unit History," 421st Ordnance Co (Ammo Depot), Trois Fontaines Ordnance Depot, Robert-Espagne, France, 03 December 1954, pp. 1 and 2. [CMH]
125. B. G. Harmon, "Unit History," Headquarters 450th Ordnance Co (Ammo Depot), Trois Fontaines Ordnance Depot, Robert-Espagne, France, 01 December 1954, pp. 1 and 2. [CMH]
126. D. Walter, "Giant Building Project Under Way at Trois Fontaines," The Stars and Stripes, 25 January 1956, p. 10.
127. F. M. Thompson, "Staff Visit to Advance Section 12-17 May 1952," Headquarters, European Command Communications Zone, Orléans, France, 17 June 1952, p. 4. [CEHO]
128. J. F. Evans, "Official Military History," 85th Ammunition Supply Squadron, St.-Mihiel Sub-Depot, France, 30 June 1953, p. 3. [AFHRA]
129. R. C. Boyd (ed), "Fire Safety Record Set By TFOD Fire Department," The Advance, 11 October 1957, p. 1.
130. L. Mayo, The Ordnance Department: On Beachhead and Battlefront, Office of The Chief of Military History, Washington, DC (1968), p. 263.
131. Anon, Care, Handling, Preservation, and Destruction of Ammunition, TM 9-1903, Departments of the Army and the Air Force, Washington, DC, October 1956, pp. 31-34.
132. A. W. Spratley (ed), "EOD Teams to Celebrate First ComZ Anniversary," ComZ Cadence, 26 June 1953, p. 4.
133. J. R. Moenk, "Line of Communications Through France 1954-1955," Headquarters, US Army, Europe (USAREUR), Karlsruhe, Germany, 1957, pp. 75 and 76.
134. R. J. Crawford (ed), "TFOD Completes 'NODEX' Ammo Job of Unloading, Storing," The Advance, 06 January 1956, pp. 1 and 3.
135. J. P. O'Donnell, "The World's Newest Army," The Saturday Evening Post, 08 October 1955, p. 134.

References/Notes to pages 296 to 305

136. D. J. Hickman, "The United States Army in Europe, 1953-63," Headquarters, US Army, Europe (USAREUR), Heidelberg, Germany, 1964, pp. 159 and 160.
137. P. Zbiorowa, Dziesieciolecie: Polskich Oddzialów Wartowniczych Przy Armii Amerykanskiej W. Europie, 1945-1955, Nakladem Funduszu Spolecznego O. W., Mannheim, Germany (1955). [Polish]
138. A. F. Head (ed), "Acquittal Won in French Trial," Basec Mission, 11 February 1955, p. 2.
139. B. J. Quinn, "USAREUR Labor Service," Army Information Digest, December 1955, pp. 19-22.
140. Letter from Brig Gen W. W. Ford (Commanding General, Advance Section) to Maj Gen Samuel D. Sturgis, Jr. (Commanding General, ComZ), dated 10 April 1952. [CEHO]
141. B. H. Siemon and R. Wagberg, "The Employment of Local Nationals by the US Army in Europe (1945-1966)," Headquarters, US Army, Europe (USAREUR), Heidelberg, Germany, 1968, pp. 60-64.
142. A. Horne, A Savage War of Peace, The Viking Press, New York (1978), pp. 118-122.
143. W. W. Ford, Wagon Soldier, Self-published, West Redding, CT (1980), p. 160.
144. H. Jordan, "The Big Steal," Argosy, November 1956, p. 17.
145. D. A. Lane, "Annual Historical Report for 1955-1956," Headquarters, US Army, Europe (USAREUR), Heidelberg, Germany, 1957, pp. 322 and 323.
146. J. H. Phillips, "Vulnerability of United States Army, Europe Line of Communication to Communist Action," Office of the Assistant Chief of Staff, Intelligence (G2), US Army, Europe (USAREUR), Heidelberg, Germany, 26 January 1954, pp. 2, 3, and 16. [MHI]
147. H. Jordan (1956), pp. 67-70.
148. R. C. Boyd (ed), "Capable Security Guard Detachment Gives TFOD Day and Night Protection," The Advance, 08 November 1957, p. 3.
149. J. F. Riddick, "Training Center for Army Dogs," Army Information Digest, June 1953, pp. 36-43.
150. R. J. Coakley (ed), "Sentry Dogs," Army Information Digest, May 1962, pp. 51-53.
151. W. Whipple, Autobiography, Self-published, Princeton, NJ, nd, pp. 329 and 330. Manuscript copy, dated 1978, archived at US Army Corps of Engineers History Office (CEHO), Fort Belvoir, VA.
152. N. A. Oelhafen (ed), "First Guard Dogs Arrive Scheduled To Begin Tonight," Jet-48, 07 December 1956, p. 1.
153. A. G. Manus, "Veterinary Mission-War Dogs," Medical Bulletin, US Army, Europe, Vol. 21, No. 6, June 1964, p. 183.
154. Interview, author with Gaston C. Jost (1st Lt, Joint Construction Agency, Vitry-le-François and Paris, France, 1956-57), Grandrupt, France, 05 March 2011.
155. Interview, author with Francis J. Souza (Cpl, Headquarters Co, TFOD, Robert-Espagne, France, 1955-56), Cumberland, RI, 08 September 2005.
156. Interview, author with Roy E. Anderson (PFC, 609th Ordnance Co, TFOD, Robert-Espagne, France, 1955-56), Dacula, GA, 15 October 2010.
157. D. Walter, "Giant Building Project Under Way at Trois Fontaines," The Stars and Stripes, 25 January 1956, p. 10.
158. M. A. Shadday, "Open House," The Fountainhead, 20 March 1964, p. 3.
159. R. J. Crawford (ed), "Move Into Permanent-Type Buildings Marks Completion of TFOD Project," The Advance, 22 November 1957, p. 5.
160. Interview, author with James A. Cicherski (1st Lt, Commissary Officer, TFAD, Robert-Espagne, France, 1963-65), Arlington, TX, 11 April 2011.
161. Interview, author with Mary Ellen Grim (widow of Capt Richard A. Grim, who rented a home at Beurey-sur-Saulx, France, 1960-63), St. Louis, MO, 19 August 2005.
162. Interviews, author with Lance L. Barclay (1st Lt, Executive Officer, 215th General Dispensary, TFAD, Robert-Espagne, France, 1964-65), Erie, PA, 18 July and 31 August 2011.
163. R. C. Boyd (ed), "Meet The Chiefs," The Advance, 20 March 1959, p. 3.
164. J. B. Tucker, War of Nerves, Pantheon Books, New York (2006), pp. 27 and 139.
165. Interview, author with Lt Col (ret) Perry D. Tripp (Capt, S3, 32nd Engineer Group, Verdun, France, 1961-64), Taylors, SC, 03 March 2005.
166. Private correspondence to author from Col (ret) George W. Johnson, Jr. (Capt, Post Engineer, TFAD, Robert-Espagne, France, 1963-64), Dallas, TX, 31 December 2003.
167. R. C. Boyd (ed), "Railhead Completed At TFOD," The Advance, 06 December 1957, p. 1.
168. G. F. Locke (ed), "Unit's Mission is to Provide 'Service to the Line-on the Line," The Advance, 05 April 1962, p. 3.
169. L. Kandel, "Directory of Key Personnel," Comptroller's Office, US Army Ammunition Depot Activity, Trois-Fontaines (TFAD), Robert-Espagne, France, 01 April 1963.
170. Interview, author with John R. Jakubik (Sp5, 582nd Transportation Co, Brienne-le-Château, France, 1962-63), Henderson, NV, 23 February 2009. In 1964-65, Col Edmund K. Ball commanded Brienne.

References/Notes to pages 305 to 312

171. P. McCormick (ed), "Avionics Detachment Serves Three Continents," ComZ Cadence, 22 May 1964, p. 3.
172. P. Richey, Fighter Pilot, B. T. Batsford, London, England (1941), p. 36.
173. R. K. Long, A Cook's Tour of World War II, Momentum Books, Ann Arbor, MI (1990), p. 126.
174. Interview, author with Col (ret) John R. Davis (1st Lt, Supply Officer, Advance Section, Verdun, France, 1951-53), Montigny-le-Bretonneux, France, 14 April 2001.
175. D. Walter, "Quarters No Problem for Families at Trois Fontaines," The Stars and Stripes, 26 January 1956, p. 10.
176. R. J. Crawford (ed), "72 Housing Units Scheduled For Sept 30th At Bar-le-Duc," The Advance, 10 August 1956, p. 1.
177. Interview, author with Joan Adrian (wife of Maj Donn R. Adrian, CO, Ordnance Co, TFAD, France, 1962-64), Frankfort, KY, 25 January 2010.
178. Interview, author with James P. Stokes (1st Lt, Deputy Chief, Maintenance Div, TFAD, Robert-Espagne, France, 1962-64), Lexington, KY, 12 January 2008.
179. J. Kemp (ed), "ADSEC Children Enjoy Life Near Chateau Jean d'Heurs," The Advance, 14 August 1953, p. 1.
180. D. Van Gorder (ed), "French Children Attend Camp Jean d'Heurs," The Advance, 28 August 1953, p. 1.
181. R. J. Crawford (ed), "AYA Summer Camp To Open June 12th," The Advance, 20 May 1955, p. 2.
182. R. Radka (ed), "TFAD's AYA Program Is in Full Operation," The Advance, 03 July 1959, p.4.
183. R. Levine (ed), "Trois-Fontaines Site of AYA Summer Camp," Orleans Item, 25 March 1966, p. 4.
184. W. P. Gardiner, "The History of the 97th Engineer Battalion (Construction)," Caserne Maginot, Verdun, France, 1966, pp. 9 and 10. [CEHO]
185. A. W. Spratley (ed), "Officers Help Poor," ComZ Cadence, 05 December 1952, p. 1.
186. R. J. Crawford (ed), "French Orphans To Get Food, Presents At Trois Fontaines," The Advance, 18 December 1953, p. 1.
187. R. Radka (ed), "Vitry (sic) Wives Present Scholarship," The Advance, 18 September 1959, p. 1.
188. L. B. Barton, "Travel Tips," The Advance, 26 November 1954, p. 2.
189. F. H. Kohloss (ed), "American Engineer Depot in France," The Military Engineer, November-December 1955, pp. 444 and 445.
190. E. E. Buegler, "Unit History," Headquarters, 698th Engineer Co (Field Maintenance), Toul, France, 09 February 1955, pp. 1 and 2. [CMH]
191. Interview, author with Col (ret) Robert A. Atkins (Maj, CO, 998th Engineer Bn, Toul, France, 1953-54), Lawrence, KS, 02 September 2005.
192. A. F. Head (ed), "Co 'B' 998th Engr, IQMD Receives CO Commendation," Basec Mission, 11 March 1955, pp. 3 and 4.
193. J. T. Farquhar, "Foundations of Air Power," Officer Review, June 2001, p. 6.
194. H. M. Mason, The Lafayette Escadrille, Smithmark, New York (1964), pp. 287-289 and 298-306.
195. E. Jablonski, Warriors With Wings: The Story of the Lafayette Escadrille, Bobbs-Merrill, Indianapolis, IN (1966), p. 200.
196. D. C. Johnson, "U.S. Army Air Forces Continental Airfields (ETO) D-Day to Y-E Day," USAF Historical Research Center, Maxwell Air Force Base, Alabama, 01 December 1988, p. 23.
197. W. F. Craven and J. L. Cate (eds), The Army Air Forces in World War II, Vol. III, The University of Chicago Press, Chicago, IL (1951), pp. 568 and 570.
198. G. J. Hauser, "Unit History, 1950-55," Headquarters, 747th Engineer Co (Heavy Equipment), Toul, France, nd, pp. 1 and 2. [CMH]
199. F. H. Kohloss (1955), p. 445.
200. A. W. Spratley (ed), "Driver Testing Course Helps Maintain Good Record," ComZ Cadence, 23 May 1952, p. 4.
201. D. R. Eastburn, "Eighteen 543d EM Get Driver Awards," ComZ Cadence, 30 November 1951, p. 4.
202. H. J. Richter (ed), "Adsec Drivers Will Compete in July 'Roadeo,'" The Stars and Stripes, 29 June 1952, p. 7.
203. H. W. Sackett, "Final Historical Report," 109th Transportation Bn (Truck), Caserne Sidi Brahim, France, 20 October 1954, pp. 1-3. [CMH]
204. R. C. Boyd (ed), "Toul Field Named After War Hero," The Advance, 11 October 1957, p. 6.
205. M. E. Meranda, "The Complete History of The 62nd Engineer Battalion," 62nd Engineer Bn, Fort Hood, TX, 1990, pp. 11 and 12. [CMH]
206. W. M. Shepherd, "Operation Roundout," The Military Engineer, November-December 1962, pp. 420 and 421.
207. J. J. McAuliffe, US Air Force in France 1950-1967, Milspec Press, San Diego, CA (2005), p. 391.
208. R. C. Boyd (ed), "Good Samaritan' Guard Rescues Tots From Snow After School-Bus Mishap," The Advance, 23 January 1959, p. 1.
209. R. C. Doty, "Basic Nuclear Dilemma," New York Times, 10 June 1959, p. 8.
210. J. J. McAuliffe (2005), p. 399.
211. P. Labrude, "Les hôpitaux construits en France pour l'US Army de 1950 à 1967," Histoire des Sciences Médicales, Vol. XLII, No. 3, 2008, pp. 307-309. (Fr)

References/Notes to pages 313 to 321

212. R. Radka (ed), "Housing Area At Toul Dedicated At Ceremonies," The Advance, 22 December 1959, p. 2.
213. J. A. Huston, Biography of a Battalion, Stackpole Books, Mechanicsburg, PA (2003), pp. 90-95.
214. H. M. Cole, The Lorraine Campaign, Center of Military History, Washington, DC (1950), pp. 94-96 and 599.
215. F. Courtot, "L'annonce du project américain a soulevé heir à Nancy, une compréhensible émotion," L'Est Républicain, 19 mai 1951. (Fr) [AD 55]
216. D. Walter, "Nancy Nears Its Day as ComZ's Choice Assignment," The Stars and Stripes, 06 November 1955, p.10.
217. R. J. Crawford (ed), "Hot 'Bomb Halts Nancy Construction," The Advance, 04 June 1954, p. 2.
218. D. Walter, "Nancy Ordnance Depot Capacity Increased Tenfold by New 7-Mile Spur Railroad Track," The Stars and Stripes, 03 June 1953, p. 9.
219. S. Markowitz (ed), "Nancy Ord Depot Rail Spur Increases Railroad Capacity," The Advance, 03 July 1953, p. 3.
220. R. J. Crawford (ed), "Over 2000 Vehicles Change Hands in NOD's 'Project Swappo," The Advance, 29 January 1954, p. 1.
221. D. Walter, "Nancy Nears Its Day as ComZ's Choice Assignment," The Stars and Stripes, 06 November 1955, p. 10.
222. R. K. Neeld, "Wheeled Vehicle Density Survey," OTA Section, 565th Ordnance Co (FM), Nancy Ordnance Depot, Nancy, France, 14 November 1955, pp. 2-7.
223. R. J. Campbell (ed), "NOD First ADSEC France Depot To Get Dial Telephone System," The Advance, 03 May 1957, p. 3.
224. R. B. Root, "4506 Labor Svc Co Leads 'Dogs Life," The Advance, 01 May 1953, p. 3.
225. R. J. Crawford (ed), "Reenactment of Great Event Nancy Highlight," The Advance, 17 September 1954, p. 1.
226. R. J. Crawford (ed) "French Spoken Here' is NOD Motto during New 'French Hour' at Depot," The Advance, 25 March 1955, p. 2.
227. R. J. Crawford (ed), "Nancy 'French Hour' Now Held Twice Weekly," The Advance, 22 April 1955, p. 1
228. Interview, author with Richard K. Neeld (1st Lt, Ordnance Technical Assistance Team Leader, 565th Ordnance Co (FM), Nancy, France, 1955-57), Manahawkin, NJ, 05 November 2003.
229. J. Kemp (ed), "ADSEC 1953: Nancy," The Advance, 15 May 1953, p. 5.
230. R. J. Crawford (ed), "Nancy Ord Men Donate Time Labor To Enlarge School," The Advance, 18 December 1953, p. 1.
231. J. R. Moenk, "The Line of Communications Through France, 1952-53," Headquarters, US Army Europe (USAREUR), Karlsruhe, Germany, 1955, p. 160.
232. B. Welles, "Army Supply Line in France Snarled," New York Times, 26 May 1953, p. 10.
233. R. C. Boyd (ed), "7 Ducks Aid Rescue Work," The Advance, 21 February 1958, p. 1.
234. D. Walter, "ComZ's Safety Patrol," The Stars and Stripes, 02 July 1959, p. 14.
235. R. Radka (ed), "94th Engineers Help Fulfill Increasing Needs," The Advance, 25 September 1959, p. 3.
236. R. J. Crawford (ed), "Nancy Still Offers Available Swimming Pool," The Advance, 08 April 1955, p. 4.
237. R. J. Crawford (ed), "Baseball Field At Nancy Named For Sgt Who Lost Life," The Advance, 13 May 1955, p. 6.
238. R. J. Crawford (ed), "14 Post Engineer, M-Pool Men Help With NOD Field," The Advance, 26 August 1955, p. 4.
239. W. C. Hall, "Engineering at Metz," The Military Engineer, January-February 1954, pp. 43-47.
240. E. Rogers, "ADSEC 1953: Metz," The Advance, 15 May 1953, p. 5.
241. R. J. Crawford (ed), "Metz's Colonel Darley Honored At Party; Achievements Lauded," The Advance, 07 January 1955, pp. 3 and 4.
242. R. J. Crawford (ed), "World War I Dud Found at St. Hubert," The Advance, 30 April 1954, p. 1.
243. J. R. Moenk (1955), pp. 163 and 164.
244. Interview, author with John T. Thorpe, Jr. (Cpl, 450th Ordnance Co, TFOD, Robert-Espagne, France, 1953-54), Troy, NY, 09 November 2011.
245. G. Learned, "The Remagen Bridge Six Years After," The Stars and Stripes, 18 March 1951, Feature Section, pp. III and IV.
246. R. J. Crawford (ed), "Former Stable is Now Sergeants' Club at Metz Quartermaster Depot," The Advance, 26 August 1955, p. 3.
247. A. W. Spratley (ed), "French Organize Franklin Club for U.S. Troops," ComZ Cadence, 20 February 1953, p. 2.
248. R. C. Boyd (ed), "Library Doors at Metz Open to LWR Personnel," The Advance, 10 October 1958, p. 2.
249. D. B. Wall, "Army's Bargain Basement Gets Many Bites," The Advance, 11 April 1958, p. 3.
250. M. Hayem, "Expropriation de Terrains sur le territoire de la commune de Woippy," 30 mars 1953. (Fr) [SHD]
251. E. Weatherall, "The Army's Rhine Route for Supplies," The Stars and Stripes, 21 August 1959, pp. 12 and 13.
252. F. M. Thompson, "Staff Visit to Advance Section 12-17 May 1952," Headquarters, European Command Communications Zone, Orléans, France, 17 June 1952, p. 2. [CEHO]
253. Anon, "Czech Guards Seize G. I.," New York Times, 07 June 1955, p. 1.
254. D. A. Lane "Annual Historical Report for 1954-1955," Headquarters, U.S. Army, Europe (USAREUR), Heidelberg, Germany, 1956, p. 337.

References/Notes to pages 322 to 330

255. Interview, author with Lt Col (ret) John W. Renn (Capt, CO, 552nd Quartermaster Co, Woippy and Toul, France, 1963-65), Anchorage, AK, 15 December 2006.
256. T. M. Kane, <u>Military Logistics and Strategic Performance</u>, Frank Cass, London, England (2001), p. 128.
257. J. S. Arrigona and W. R. Karsteter, "History of the Joint Construction Agency in Europe," JCA, Boulogne-sur-Seine (Paris), France, 1958, p. 309. [CEHO]
258. ibid, p. 189.
259. D. A. Lane, "Annual Historical Report for 1957-58," Headquarters, US Army, Europe (USAREUR), Heidelberg, Germany, 1958, p. 217.
260. D. C. Johnson (1988), p. 28.
261. S. Markowitz, "The 45th Trans Army Aviation Maint Co," <u>The Advance</u>, 20 March 1953, pp. 5 and 6.
262. P. S. Kindsvatter, "The Ordnance Corps and Army Aviation, 1949-1952," <u>Ordnance Magazine</u>, Summer 2002, pp. 14-18.
263. Interview, author with Col (ret) George N. Stokes, Jr. (Capt, CO, Det B, 73rd Warehouse Squadron, Frescaty Airfield, France, 1952-53), Austin, TX, 16 February 2004.
264. R. C. Boyd (ed), "Metz Rifle Range Near Completion for Coming ADSEC, ComZ Matches," <u>The Advance</u>, 14 March 1958, p. 5.
265. D. Van Gorder, "Trailer Park Under Construction at Metz," <u>The Advance</u>, 23 October 1953, p. 3.
266. D. Van Gorder (ed), "British Trailers Available to ADSEC Personnel," <u>The Advance</u>, 06 November 1953, p. 3.
267. E. D. Crankshaw, "Historical Report on Activation of 337th Chemical Company (Depot)," Sampigny Chemical Depot, Sampigny, France, 01 November 1954. [CMH]
268. Anon, <u>Ammunition General</u>, TM 9-1900, Departments of The Army and The Air Force, Washington, DC, June 1956.
269. Interview, author with Bobby Jack Cannon (Cpl, 7813th Army Unit, Sampigny, France, 1953-55), Shawnee, OK, 24 August 2008.
270. J. Kemp (ed), "ADSEC 1953: Sampigny," <u>The Advance</u>, 15 May 1953, p. 6.
271. M. J. Dolan, "Napalm," <u>Military Review</u>, September 1953, pp. 9-18.
272. R. J. Crawford (ed), "'Atom Blast' Featured in Sampigny Demonstration for CBR Graduates," <u>The Advance</u>, 16 April 1954, p. 1.
273. R. C. Boyd (ed), "Radiation Detection, A Phase of Defense," <u>The Advance</u>, 12 June 1959, p. 3
274. D. Cook, "How to Scrounge a Movie House," <u>New York Herald Tribune, Paris</u>, 07 August 1952.
275. S. Markowitz (ed), "French Indoor Range Loaned to Cml Depot," <u>The Advance</u>, 10 July 1953, p. 1.
276. J. Anderson, "Housing in Adsec Has Come a Long, Long Way," <u>The Overseas Weekly</u>, 16 September 1956, p. 6.
277. Anon, "Historical Report on Activation of 330th Chemical Company (Maintenance)," Sampigny Chemical Depot, Sampigny, France, 26 October 1954, p. 2. See also WD AGO Form 016, History Card, 330th Chemical Company (Maintenance). [CMH]
278. L. B. Sibert (ed), "Sampigny Constructing Prefab Metal Billets," <u>The Stars and Stripes</u>, 26 February 1955, p. 9.
279. A. L. Jorgenson (ed), "Shows Given At ComZ Base," <u>The Stars and Stripes</u>, 05 January 1954, p. 8.
280. A. L. Jorgenson (ed), "Command Changes, Housing, New Hosp Pace '53 in ComZ," <u>The Stars and Stripes</u>, 02 January 1954, p. 8.
281. R. J. Crawford (ed), "Sampigny Lanes Open New League," <u>The Advance</u>, 26 August 1955, p. 4.
282. A. W. Spratley (ed), "Sampigny School is Reminiscent of Grandma's Era," <u>ComZ Cadence</u>, 12 December 1952, p. 4.
283. J. S. Arrigona and W. R. Karsteter (1958), p. 125.
284. R. J. Crawford (ed), "Sampigny, VSD to Combine As General Depot Monday," <u>The Advance</u>, 28 June 1957, p. 1.
285. R. C. Boyd (ed), "Sampigny Mayor Thanks ADSEC for Cooperation," <u>The Advance</u>, 08 August 1958, p. 1.
286. Anon, "US Army Installations France," Headquarters, US Army Communications Zone, Europe (USACOMZEUR), Orléans, France, 1966. These documents, also called "Information Brochures," recorded real estate statistics for US Army installations in France. A nearly complete set is archived at the Office of History, US Army Corps of Engineers, Fort Belvoir, VA; partial set was archived at Campbell Barracks, USAREUR, Heidelberg, Germany.

CHAPTER TEN

1. D. Schear, "Base Hq-Supply Line Feeder," <u>The Stars and Stripes</u>, 18 May 1952, p. 7.
2. B. King et al., <u>Spearhead of Logistics</u>, Center of Military History, Washington, DC (2001), pp. 372-374. King presents an overview of military transportation in Western Europe during the early Cold War years.
3. J. A. Huston, <u>Outposts and Allies</u>, Associated University Presses, Cranbury, NJ (1988), pp. 91-94.
4. J. R. Moenk, "Establishment of Communications Through France, 1950-1951," Historical Division, Headquarters, United States Army, Europe (USAREUR), Karlsruhe, Germany, 1952, pp. 73-76.
5. Letter from Maj Gen Carter B. Magruder (Assistant Chief of Staff, G-4, Logistics, Department of the Army, Washington, DC) to Maj Gen Samuel D. Sturgis, Jr. (Commanding General, ComZ), dated 07 January 1953. [CEHO]

References/Notes to pages 330 to 339

6. C. C. Blanchard, "Base Section, LOC Across France," Army Navy Air Force Journal, 24 May 1952.
7. O. P. Newman, "European Communications," Army Navy Air Force Journal, 02 October 1954.
8. J. P. Pallud, "U-Boat Bases in France," After The Battle, No. 55, August 1987, pp. 1-46.
9. G. Williamson, U-Boat Bases and Bunkers 1941-45, Osprey Publishing, Oxford, England (2003), pp. 43-50 and 58-60.
10. N. Lambourne, War Damage in Western Europe, Edinburgh University Press, Edinburgh, England (2001), p. 61.
11. R. H. Kohn and J. P. Harahan (eds), Strategic Air Warfare, Office of Air Force History, Washington, DC (1988), pp. 34 and 35.
12. N. J. McCamley, Cold War Secret Nuclear Bunkers, Pen & Sword, South Yorkshire, England (2002), pp. 17-20.
13. Interview, author with Lt Col (ret) Edwin W. Kulo (Maj, Area Provost Marshal, TFAD, Robert-Espagne, France, 1961-64), Tipp City, OH, 06 November 1999.
14. Letter from Brig Gen Charles C. Blanchard (Commanding General, Base Section) to Maj Gen Samuel D. Sturgis, Jr. (Commanding General, ComZ), dated 25 November 1952. [CEHO]
15. D. A. Lane, "Annual Historical Report for 1955-56," Headquarters, US Army, Europe (USAREUR), Heidelberg, Germany, 1957, pp. 217 and 218.
16. C. V. Ruzek, "Map Production and Supply," Military Review, March 1954, pp. 23-40.
17. A. W. Spratley (ed), "Soldier Who Battled Mob Is Decorated," ComZ Cadence, 10 October 1952, pp. 1 and 4.
18. Notes prepared by Lt Col Monas N. Squires and Capt Alfred C. Parker, Public Information Division, USAREUR ComZ, Orléans, France, dated 05 December 1952, pp. 1-4. The UP story distorted key elements of Sturgis' remarks on 03 December 1952 to the Anglo-American Press Association in Paris, France. The UP reporter also invented quoted statements attributed to Sturgis. [CEHO]
19. D. Walter, "Airmen of Crash Rescue Flight Operate Air Force's Four-Boat European 'Fleet,'" The Stars and Stripes, 04 June 1953, p.9.
20. D. Walter, "Training Tough for Veteran Chutists of AF Para-Rescue Team at Bordeaux," The Stars and Stripes, 09 June 1953, p. 8.
21. "Cazaux Agreement," dated 01 July 1955. Agreement signed by Col René Gavoille (French Air Force Commander of BA 706) and Maj John P. Kincaid (US Air Force Commander of Detachment 1, 7413th Air Base Squadron). [AFHSO]
22. J. J. McAuliffe, U.S. Air Forces in France 1950-1967, Milspec Press, San Diego, CA (2005), pp. 158 and 159.
23. I. A. Nabeshima (ed), "Gen Bixby Dedicates Bassens Housing Site," Basec Mission, 07 August 1953, pp. 1 and 4.
24. J. P. O'Donnell, "We're All Fouled Up In France," The Saturday Evening Post, 11 April 1953, pp. 96 and 99.
25. A. F. Head (ed), "Bordeaux Inst Includes Many Different Activities," Basec Mission, 25 March 1955, pp. 2 and 3.
26. H. J. Richter (ed), "83d Engrs Start Work On Bordeaux Center," The Stars and Stripes, 27 March 1953, p. 8.
27. A. W. Spratley (ed), "Bordeaux Det Shares Cp Crespy With French," ComZ Cadence, 01 February 1952, p. 4.
28. C. Raia (ed), "Com Unit Snubs Snow," Basec Mission, 25 February 1956, p. 1.
29. R. H. Hethmon, "Here's One Old Soldier Who Won't Fade Away," ComZ Cadence, 16 January 1953, p. 4.
30. J. B. Cress, "Reconstruction of Cherbourg," The Military Engineer, July-August 1952, pp. 246-249.
31. J. R. Moenk (1952), p. 27.
32. D. J. Hickman, "The United States Army in Europe, 1953-63," Headquarters, US Army, Europe (USAREUR), Heidelberg, Germany, 1964, p. 86.
33. M. P. Gudebrod, "Tents, Yes. But Concrete Moves In on Mud," The Stars and Stripes, 17 November 1961, p. 11.
34. Interview, author with Col (ret) Linn J. Schofield (Capt, Adjutant General's Office, Headquarters, USACOMZEUR, Orléans, France, 1962-66), Falls Church, VA, 02 November 2016.
35. R. E. Killblane, Mentoring and Leading, US Army Transportation Center, Fort Eustis, VA (2003), pp. 34 and 35.
36. Letter from Col Robert A. Smoak (Commanding Officer, US Army Port Area Command, La Rochelle, France) to Claude Massol (Préfet de la Charente-Maritime), dated 30 July 1962. [AD 17]
37. C. Baldoli and A. Knapp, Forgotten Blitzes, Continnum, London, England (2012), p. 32.
38. A. Bower and E. N. Brandt, "Supply Front: The 16th Port Story," US Army Service Forces, European Theater of Operations (ETO), Le Havre, France, September 1945, pp. 12-17.
39. A. W. Spratley (ed), "74 Families are Landed At Le Havre," ComZ Cadence, 20 February 1953, p. 1.
40. O. Pottier, Les Bases Américaines en France (1950-1967), Éditions l'Harmattan, Paris, France (2003), p. 120. (Fr)
41. R. Brooks (ed), "Mail Travels Faster Through Le Havre," ComZ Cadence, 10 January 1964, p. 2.
42. R. J. Bachrodt (ed), "Le Havre Becomes Only Official POV Port," ComZ Cadence, 27 May 1966, pp. 1 and 4.
43. C. L. Sauerbier, Marine Cargo Operations, John Wiley & Sons, New York (1956), pp. 323 and 324.
44. K. Boggs, "La Rochelle Installation One Year Old Today," Basec Mission, 01 July 1955, p. 2.
45. R. Goble, "La Pallice: A Vital Port in ComZ," Basec Mission, 03 June 1959, p. 4.
46. J.-L. Labour, "Les Américains," La Rochelle, Éditions Rupella, avril 1999, p. 12. (Fr)
47. S. Stavisky, "Unions to Fight Red Sabotage of Arms Aid," The Washington Post, 30 March 1950, p. 2.

References/Notes to pages 339 to 349

48. Interview, author with Lyle A. Ross (Cpl, 529th Military Police Co, Laleu and Rochefort, France, 1952-53), Lake Havasu City, AZ, 21 April 2009.
49. Letter report from Brig Gen Charles C. Blanchard (Commander, Base Section, EUCOM ComZ, La Rochelle) to Robert Holveck (Préfet de la Charente-Maritime), dated 25 October 1951, 6 pages. [AD 17]
50. A. W. Spratley (ed), "1400 Air Force Troops Debark at La Pallice," ComZ Cadence, 21 December 1951, p. 3.
51. A. W. Spratley (ed), "Basec Major's Idea Saved Army $8000," ComZ Cadence, 05 September 1952, p. 4.
52. J.-L. Labour (1999), p. 16.
53. A. F. Head (ed), "QM Laundry Opens; 3 More are Planned," Basec Mission, 27 May 1955, pp. 1 and 4.
54. R. H. Ross, "Let's Stay Healthy," ComZ Cadence, 18 March 1955, p. 2.
55. R. J. Coakley (ed), "Dogs on Sentry Duty," Army Information Digest, May 1962, pp. 51-53.
56. B. W. Fowle, Army Medical Department Profiles, Brigadier General Frank Allen Ramsey, Office of the Surgeon General, Alexandria, VA, June 2002, pp. 5-14.
57. M. Delafosse (réd), Histoire de La Rochelle, Éditions Privat, Toulouse, France (2002), pp. 18 and 198. (Fr) The Aufrédi name is spelled three ways: Auffredy (on façade of hospital), Aufredy (street), and Aufrédi (caserne).
58. J. P. Anderson (ed), "Crumbling Old Aufredi Becomes Modern Hqs," Basec Mission, 19 March 1954, p. 2.
59. L. B. Sibert (ed), "Oyster Pickers Delay Basec Rifle Matches," The Stars and Stripes, 28 March 1955, p. 9.
60. A. W. Spratley (ed), "Basec Posts Hit By High Winds; $200,000 Damage," ComZ Cadence, 03 October 1952, pp. 1 and 8.
61. Letter from G. Hurtaud (Chef du Bureau de Liaison, La Rochelle) to Jacques Brunel (Le Préfet de la Charente-Maritime), 27 septembre 1956. (Fr) [AD 17]
62. J. M. Binno (ed), "CCMI Dogs Accused of Beastly Manners," The Medic, 01 August 1958, p. 3.
63. A. F. Head (ed), "Portable Water Supply Creates Many Problems," Basec Mission, 11 March 1955, pp. 2 and 4.
64. C. Raia (ed), "Medics Given 24-Hour Alert Test," Basec Mission, 07 April 1956, p. 6.
65. A. F. Head (ed), "Lt Hedeen Wages Fight On Malaria Mosquitoes," Basec Mission, 29 July 1955, p. 2.
66. S. Hopkins, "Exercise Tests Preparedness at Croix Chapeau," Basec Mission, 30 July 1958, p. 3.
67. D. Walter, "Medical Center Dedicated in France," The Stars and Stripes, 23 May 1959, p. 8.
68. R. P. Smith (ed), "Mercy Flight Transports Rare Blood," The Stars and Stripes, 15 February 1963, p. 9.
69. Interview, author with Lyle A. Ross (Cpl, 529th Military Police Co, Laleu and Rochefort, France, 1952-53), Lake Havasu City, AZ, 21 April 2009.
70. H. J. Richter (ed), "Rocks Injure Yank, French Cop in Jeep," The Stars and Stripes, 30 June 1952, p. 5.
71. A. F. Head (ed), "524th Services 200,000 sq mi; Men Stationed Thruout France," Basec Mission, 15 April 1955, p. 4.
72. B. Collins, "Night Patrol," The Stars and Stripes, 26 September 1964, p. 11.
73. H. J. Richter (ed), "U.S. Troops House 40 Families in Fire," The Stars and Stripes, 16 May 1952, p. 7.
74. R. C. Doty, "French are Cool to U. S. Soldiers," New York Times, 17 November 1952, p. 8.
75. C. Raia (ed), "Army Aids French In Housing Project," Basec Mission, 19 May 1956, p. 1.
76. M. Goode, "Air Unit Vital In Basec Role," Basec Mission, 22 December 1955, pp. 5 and 7.
77. A. F. Head (ed), "La R Installation One Year Old Today," Basec Mission, 01 July 1955, p. 2.
78. S. Extrade et al., La Rochelle à l'heure américaine 1950-1964, Éditions ABC Dif, Brie (Charente), France (2006), pp. 42 and 43. (Fr)
79. J. P. Anderson (ed), "Sheep Detail Saves Army Manhours at POL Depot," Basec Mission, 06 August 1954, p. 2.
80. L. Salomon, "With The Posts: La Rochelle," Basec Mission, 10 March 1956, p. 4.
81. J.-L. Labour (1999), pp. 14-15 and 19-20. (Fr) See also cote 16W435 at the archives départementales de la Charente-Maritime, La Rochelle, France. [AD 17]
82. A. F. Head (ed), "AF-Army-JCA Team Up; Improve Bord'x Billeting," Basec Mission, 11 March 1955, pp. 1 and 6.
83. Letter from Brig Gen Charles C. Blanchard (Commander, Base Section, EUCOM ComZ, La Rochelle) to Robert Holveck (Préfet de la Charente-Maritime), dated 10 September 1952. [AD 17]
84. Letter from Le Maire de Fouras (M. Bodard) to Sous-Préfet, Rochefort, 21 janvier 1953. (Fr) [AD 17]
85. J. D. Nottingham (ed), "Base Section Sp5 Discovers Mines," The Stars and Stripes, 26 September 1959, p. 9.
86. H. J. Richter (ed), "ComZ AYA Camp Opens June 15," The Stars and Stripes, 13 May 1953, p. 8.
87. A. L. Jorgenson (ed), "Basec to Start Youth Camp," The Stars and Stripes, 26 June 1953, p. 8.
88. D. A. Lane, "Annual Historical Report for 1954-1955," Headquarters, US Army, Europe (USAREUR), Heidelberg, Germany, 1956, pp. 136-138.
89. J. D. Nottingham (ed), "Amphibs Sink; 11 Yanks Safe," The Stars and Stripes, 10 June 1959, p. 9.
90. C. Ryan, The Longest Day, Simon and Schuster, New York (1959).
91. H. Bontekoe, "Zanuck Movie 'The Longest Day' to be Filmed on Beaches Here," The Sea Sider, 23 June 1961, p. 1.

References/Notes to pages 349 to 358

92. R. P. Smith (ed), "Re-enact D-Day Landings for 'The Longest Day,'" The Stars and Stripes, 08 November 1961, p. 8.
93. Interview, author with Col (ret) George Steven Bosan (Maj, CO, 26th Transportation Co (Lt Hel), Rozelier and Verdun, France, 1959-62), Camp Hill, PA, 19 July 2010.
94. C. Ryan (1959), p. 147.
95. Anon, "Soldiers Protest Use in War Movie," New York Times, 30 December 1961, p. 6.
96. J. Landauer, "Probe Asked of Troops' Role in Film," The Washington Post, 30 December 1961, p. 2.
97. R. Andersen et al., The European Roe Deer, Scandinavian University Press, Oslo, Norway (1998), pp. 259-261. Co-editor Patrick Duncan was Director, CEBC Campus located at the former US military ammunition depot at Chizé.
98. J. R. Dunlap, "Still America's All-Time Favorite Movie Star," The American Spectator, July 1997, p. 69.
99. J. P. O'Donnell (1953), p. 99.
100. L. Pacaud, Rochefort Son Combat Pour L'Arsenal, Geste Éditions, La Crèche, France (1999), p. 193. (Fr)
101. Interview, author with Maj (ret) John T. Carrig, Jr. (Capt, Post Engineer, US Army Garrison, Rochefort, France, 1954-56 and 1960-62), Arlington, VA, 08 August 2002.
102. M. P. Gudebrod, "They're Sunk—But They Like It," The Stars and Stripes, 30 April 1963, pp. 12 and 13.
103. D. Walter, "USAREUR's Unusual Underwater Soldiers," The Stars and Stripes, 13 June 1959, pp. 11 and 12.
104. M. P. Gudebrod, "They're Sunk—But They Like It," The Stars and Stripes, 30 April 1963, p. 13.
105. B. Macintyre, "New World Heroine to Sail Again," The Times, 09 January 1999, p. 17. (UK)
106. Anon, "L'Hermione refera le voyage de La Fayette," Le Figaro, 29 avril 2000. (Fr)
107. H. Bontekoe, "Maintenance Facility Completed in Rochefort Basin," The Sea Sider, 19 August 1960, p. 1.
108. Private correspondence to author from Maj (ret) John T. Carrig, Jr., Arlington, VA, 28 February 2005.
109. R. P. Smith (ed), "Shook Up' Soldiers Describe Ordeal in Gale-Tossed Atlantic," The Stars and Stripes, 23 January 1963, pp. 1 and 2.
110. N. Raymond, "Expanding Rochefort High," The Stars and Stripes, 22 February 1957, p. 13.
111. B. Coussy, La Ville de Rochefort, Ministère de l'Equipement et du Logement, Rochefort-sur-Mer, France (1998), pp. 41 and 68. (Fr)
112. S. R. Mercogliano, "Sealift: The Evolution of the Military Sea Transportation Service," Conference of Army Historians, Center of Military History, 08 August 2002.
113. J. R. Moenk, "Annual Historical Report, 1953-54," Headquarters, US Army, Europe (USAREUR), Karlsruhe, Germany, 1955, p. 242.
114. Anon, "Command Report 1952," Headquarters, European Command (EUCOM)-US Army, Europe (USAREUR), Karlsruhe, Germany, December 1953, p. 210.
115. J. R. Moenk, "Line of Communications Through France 1952-1953," Headquarters, US Army, Europe (USAREUR), Karlsruhe, Germany, 1955, pp. 192-194.
116. A. W. Spratley (ed), "EOD Teams to Celebrate First ComZ Anniversary," ComZ Cadence, 26 June 1953, p. 4.
117. H. J. Richter (ed), "U.S., French Hit Beaches in Exercise," The Stars and Stripes, 08 June 1952, p. 4.
118. A. W. Spratley (ed), "Bevy of Bovines Barge in at Beach," ComZ Cadence, 13 June 1952, p. 4.
119. Interview, author with Lyle A. Ross (Cpl, 529th Military Police Co, Laleu and Rochefort, France, 1952-53), Lake Havasu City, AZ, 18 April 2009.
120. J. Quave, "Air Alert Instructions," Headquarters, 15th Transportation Port Bn, La Rochelle, France, 26 July 1952. [TC]
121. H. J. Richter (ed), "U.S., French Hit Beaches In Exercise," The Stars and Stripes, 08 June 1952, p. 4.
122. J. E. Strahan, Andrew Jackson Higgins and the Boats that Won World War II, Louisiana State University Press, Baton Rouge, LA (1994), pp. 1-4 and 350. Higgins was the foremost designer and builder of flat-bottomed boats for the US military.
123. A. W. Spratley (ed), "Hero Receives Medal," ComZ Cadence, 06 March 1953, pp. 1 and 4.
124. A. W. Spratley (ed), "Beach Operation in Third Phase; Has New Locale," ComZ Cadence, 29 August 1952, p. 1.
125. B. R. Huetter, "Over The Beach Operations in Western France," Headquarters, 7703 Transportation Major Port, La Rochelle, France, 11 October 1952, pp. 1-5. [TC]
126. Letter from Maj Gen Samuel D. Sturgis, Jr. (CG, USACOMZEUR) to Maj Gen Carter B. Magruder (Office of the Assistance Chief of Staff, G-4, Department of the Army, Washington, DC), dated 04 December 1952. [CEHO]
127. A. W. Spratley (ed), "2 Escape Death As DUKW Sinks," ComZ Cadence, 19 December 1952, p. 3.
128. Memo for the Record, "Subject: Over-the-Beach Operations," Maj Gen S. D. Sturgis, Jr., dated 22 December 1952. [CEHO]
129. R. W. Smith, "Report on Personnel Over the Beach No. 1," Headquarters, 7703 Transportation Major Port, Rochefort, France, 30 April 1953. [TC]
130. A. W. Spratley (ed), "2 German Mines Found On Beach By Port Troops," ComZ Cadence, 09 January 1952, p. 8.

References/Notes to pages 358 to 373

131. R. W. Smith, "Report on Over-the-Beach Mission No. 8," Headquarters, 7703 Transportation Major Port, Rochefort, France, 05 February 1953, p. 3. [TC]
132. R. W. Smith, "Report on Off-shore Discharge Exercise No. 9," 7703 Transportation Major Port, Rochefort, France, 21 March 1953. [TC]
133. H. J. Richter (ed), "Basec Troops Set Cargo Record In 'Over the Beaches' Exercise," The Stars and Stripes, 31 March 1953, pp. 8 and 9.
134. J. L. Cooper (ed), "French, US Troops Complete Quiberon Bay Exercise," Basec Mission, 03 April 1953, p. 3.
135. J. L. Cooper (ed), "ODEX Completed During Port Storms," Basec Mission, 01 May 1953, p. 6.
136. J. L. Cooper (ed), "General Wins Bet," Basec Mission, 22 May 1953, p. 3.
137. J. L. Cooper (ed), "Storms Delay ODEX 12 Off Brittany Coastline," Basec Mission, 19 June 1953, p. 4.
138. E. T. Henry, "Report of Offshore Discharge Exercise No. 13," Headquarters, US Army, Europe (USAREUR), Heidelberg, Germany, 30 November 1953. [TC]
139. J. P. Anderson (ed), "7703rd Maj Port Redesignated," Basec Mission, 09 October 1953, p. 1.
140. J. P. Anderson (ed), "All Branches Participate In ODEX 14," Basec Mission, 06 November 1953, pp. 5 and 8.
141. Letter from Maj Gen Samuel D. Sturgis, Jr. (CG, USACOMZEUR) to Brig Gen Ernest A. Bixby (CG, BASEC), dated 09 December 1952, pp. 5 and 6. [CEHO]
142. J. P. Anderson (ed), "ODEX Figures Show Efficiency of Operations," Basec Mission, 04 December 1953, p. 1.
143. J. A. Masciandaro (ed), "Basec's Sea-Going Soldiers Are Commended For Their 'Seeing-Eye' Work During ODEX," Basec Mission, 18 December 1953, p. 2.
144. R. Reynolds, "Busy Boatmen Outwit Fog, Save Tanker in ODEX Test," The Stars and Stripes, 09 December 1953, p. 9.
145. G. L. Willey, "Vehicle for Land and Sea," Army Information Digest, April 1953, pp. 27-31.
146. J. P. Anderson (ed), "ODEX 16 To Start on 10 Feb," Basec Mission, 08 January 1954, pp. 1 and 4.
147. R. E. Vandenberg, "Radical Methods of Cargo Operations," Terminals Division, US Army, Washington, DC, 13 April 1954, p. 24.
148. C. A. Nebel, "Transport Without Wheels," Army Information Digest, November 1955, pp. 11-16.
149. R. E. Vandenberg (1954), p. 17.
150. C. O. Lanciano, "Military Lighterage," Military Review, August 1965, pp. 41-48.
151. L. B. Sibert (ed), "Sfc, 'Beachcomber at Heart' Taking Part in 18th NODEX," The Stars and Stripes, 04 March 1955, p. 10.
152. A. M. Beck et al., The Corps of Engineers: War Against Germany, Center of Military History, Washington, DC (1985), p. 282.
153. W. W. Whipple, "Crossing Soft Beaches," The Military Engineer, March-April 1958, pp. 104 and 105. Brig Gen (ret) William Whipple, Jr. had no middle initial (official Army abbreviation: NMI) so The Military Engineer gave him another W.
154. J. A. Ulio, "Steel-Treadway Bridge M2," TM 5-272, War Department, Washington, DC, 09 May 1944.
155. R. E. Rose, "Amphibious Operations—Where All Services Meet," Army Information Digest, September 1954, pp. 15-18.
156. R. H. Knapp, "Save--By Palletizing," Military Review, July 1951, pp. 35-43.
157. J. R. Moenk (1955), pp. 194-197.
158. L. V. Warner, "Initial Report on Supply Over the Beaches Operation," Headquarters, European Command (EUCOM), Heidelberg, Germany, 23 July 1952, p. 2.
159. R. B. Parrish, "Report of Offshore Discharge Exercise Number 12," 7703 Transportation Major Port, Rochefort, France, 13 July 1953, p. 8. [TC]
160. J. P. Anderson (ed), "Cold Weather, High Surf Slow ODEX," Basec Mission, 19 February 1954, pp. 1 and 4.
161. H. A. Jacobs, "Army Transportation--Zeroing In," Military Review, August 1955, p. 51. Nearly half of military cargo could fit in CONEX containers.
162. M. D. Losey, "CONEX: A Decade of Service," Military Review, September 1963, pp. 32-37.
163. Private correspondence to author from Brig Gen (ret) William J. Whelan (Capt, Chief, Ordnance Supply Section of COMZ Headquarters, Orléans, France, 1952-55), Tacoma, WA, dated 03 November 1993.
164. J. R. Moenk (1955), p. 294.
165. US Army 7703 Transportation Major Port, Rochefort, France, Reports for Offshore Discharge Exercises (ODEX) No. 1 through No. 16. These after-action reports are archived at the US Army Transportation Center and School Library, Fort Eustis, Virginia. In 2010, the library moved to Fort Lee, Virginia.
166. Anon, "Directory and Station List of The US Army," US Army, Washington, DC, 15 June 1953, p. 482.
167. W. Whipple, "NODEX 17 Report," Headquarters, US Army Base Section, Poitiers, France, 03 December 1957, pp. 1-4. [TC]
168. F. W. Crismon, U.S. Military Wheeled Vehicles, Cresline Publishing, Sarasota, FL (1983), pp. 457-461.
169. Anon, DUKW: Operational Procedures, Portrayal Press, Bloomfield, NJ (1987).
170. T. B. Allen, "Odd DUKW," Smithsonian, August 2002, pp. 74-77.

References/Notes to pages 373 to 382

171. N. Friedman, The Fifty-Year War, Naval Institute Press, Annapolis, MD (2000), p. 221.
172. T. C. Poulter, Over The Years, Self-published, 1977, pp. 84 and 85.
173. Anon, "The BARC, a 60 Ton Special Purpose Barge," The US Army Transportation Center, Fort Eustis, VA, 1955.
174. Anon, "Characteristics and Data of The Transportation Corps Marine Fleet and Terminal Service Equipment," ST 55-178, US Army Transportation School, Fort Eustis, VA, May 1960.
175. R. R. Bankson (ed), "BARC Tested," Military Review, February 1959, p. 64.
176. A. A. Berglund, "29th NODEX France," Headquarters, US Army Port Area Command, Caserne Aufrédi, La Rochelle, France, 06 October 1961, p. 20.
177. J. M. Heiser, Logistic Support, Department of the Army, Washington, DC (1974), p. 169.
178. A. C. Joy, "New Amphibious Trucks," Army Information Digest, March 1956, pp. 18-23.
179. C. F. London, "Joint Comparison of U.S. Army Amphibians," U.S. Army Transportation Research and Engineering Command, Fort Eustis, Virginia, November 1959.
180. D. A. Lane (1956), p. 280.
181. B. H. Sieman and R. Sher, "The Dependents' Schools Program of the U.S. Army, Europe, 1946-56," Historical Division, Headquarters, US Army, Europe (USAREUR), Heidelberg, Germany, 1958, p. 70.
182. Interview, author with Brig Gen (ret) Thomas P. O'Brien, Jr. (Capt, JAG, Port Area Command, La Rochelle, France, 1961-64), Cincinnati, OH, 11 January 2010.
183. B. Struder (ed), "Claims Office chief celebrates full decade of work in Paris," The Pariscope, 22 January 1965, p. 6.
184. Letter from Col James E. Holley (Chief of Staff, Base Section USAREUR ComZ, La Rochelle) to Capitaine de Vaisseau Bertrand (Chef de la Mission de Liaison en Zone Arrière, la Pallice), dated 27 September 1954. [AD 17]
185. A. G. Viney, "NODEX No. 1 Report," Headquarters, USAREUR Communications Zone, Orléans, France, 22 December 1954. [TC]
186. L. B. Sibert (ed), "Ft. Eustis Personnel Bring LCUs to France for NODEX Training," The Stars and Stripes, 05 March 1955, p. 9.
187. A. F. Head (ed), "NODEX Ship Sunk at Night Near La Coubre; Three Drowned," Basec Mission, 28 January 1955, pp. 1 and 4.
188. L. B. Sibert (ed), "Memorial Rites Held for Four Who Died in NODEX Exercises," The Stars and Stripes, 26 March 1955, p. 10.
189. A. F. Head (ed), "Plane Guides NODEX Craft," Basec Mission, 15 April 1955, pp. 1 and 6.
190. A. F. Head (ed), "General A. C. McAuliffe Tours Basec," Basec Mission, 08 April 1955, p. 3.
191. A. F. Head (ed), "WWII Bomb Injures EM at Le Verdon," Basec Mission, 15 April 1955, p. 1.
192. A. F. Head (ed), "Fire Damages Total $50,000 in NODEX Blaze," Basec Mission, 03 June 1955, p. 1.
193. A. F. Head (ed), "NODEX V Nears End; 3rd Ship is Discharged," Basec Mission, 14 October 1955, pp. 1 and 4.
194. C. Raia (ed), "Men Readied as Nodex Start is Set Monday," Basec Mission, 02 December 1955, p. 1.
195. C. Raia (ed), "Pier on Stilts," Basec Mission, 05 November 1955, p. 3. A. L. Mathews, "DeLong Pier Tests at Le Verdon," U.S. Army Corps of Engineers, Waterways Experiment Station, Vicksburg, MS, November 1955.
196. J. R. Moenk (1955), pp. 199 and 200.
197. J. A. Ziccarelli, "The Story of the DeLong Piers," Defense Transportation Journal, March-April 1972, pp. 26-28.
198. H. Maxton, "Self-Raising Steel Docks," The Military Engineer, September-October 1953, pp. 343-345.
199. R. R. Forsberg, "Portable Piers and Packaged Ports," Army Information Digest, September 1954, pp. 55-59.
200. D. P. Yens and J. P. Clement, "Port Construction in Vietnam," The Military Engineer, January-February 1967, pp. 20-24.
201. C. Raia (ed), "Men Readied as Nodex Start is Set Monday," Basec Mission, 02 December 1955, p. 1. "John C." (formerly USS LaSalle) was merchant ship operated by Atlantic Carriers.
202. C. Raia (ed), "Haiti Victory Arrives Mon for Nodex VII," Basec Mission, 04 February 1956, p. 1.
203. R. J. Meurn and C. L. Sauerbier, Marine Cargo Operations, Cornell Maritime Press, Centreville, MD (2004), pp. 8-19 to 8-22.
204. C. Raia (ed), "Nodex and COD, Men Defy Storm," Basec Mission, 18 February 1956, pp. 1 and 4. COD was abbreviation for Captieux Ordnance Depot.
205. G. H. McDowall, "Shipment of NODEX 7 Security Cargo," Headquarters, 11th Transportation Terminal Command B, Rochefort, France, 09 February 1956, pp. 2 and 3. [TC]
206. W. J. Murphy, "After Action Report (NODEX IX)," 11th Transportation Terminal Command, La Rochelle, France, 29 August 1956. Murphy includes two reports submitted by 117th Transportation Co (Terminal Service) and 577th Transportation Co (Aerial Tramway). [TC]
207. C. Raia (ed), "Men and Machines Dig In for Big Nodex Job," Basec Mission, 14 April 1956, p. 4.
208. J. C. Fuson, Transportation and Logistics, Center of Military History, Washington, DC (1994), pp. 80-82.
209. Anon, "Bridge Division: Products and Engineering Services," Catalog D-933, John A. Roebling's Sons, Trenton, NJ, 1957, pp. 8 and 9.

References/Notes to pages 382 to 394

210. F. Armstrong, "Ship-to-Shore Aerial Tramway," The Military Engineer, May-June 1956, pp. 178 and 179.
211. J. F. Holly, "Military Aerial Tramways," The Military Engineer, January-February 1953, pp. 40-46.
212. M. Fardet, Le Pont de Martrou, Centre International de la Mer, Rochefort, France (1988). (Fr)
213. J. M. Dixon (ed), "First urban tram opens in New York," Progressive Architecture, July 1976, p. 27.
214. S. Karnow, Paris in the Fifties, Times Books, New York (1997), p. 85.
215. R. Musel, "That American's (sic) Back in France," The Stars and Stripes, 23 September 1966, p. 11.
216. Anon, "The Use of Local French Workers During NODEX 9," 117th Transportation Co (Terminal Service), La Rochelle, France, 23 June 1956. [TC]
217. Interview, author with Henriette Bibaud, Rochefort-sur-Mer, France, 15 November 2002.
218. P. Baroux, "La petite demoiselle," Sud-Ouest, 23 juin 1994. (Fr)
219. D. A. Bartoni (ed), "Eight Aboard LCM in Gironde Estuary Rescued by Copter," The Stars and Stripes, 17 February 1957, p. 23.
220. W. W. Whipple, "Crossing Soft Beaches," The Military Engineer, March-April 1958, p. 104.
221. D. A. Lane, "Annual History, US Army, Europe, 1956-1957," Headquarters, US Army, Europe (USAREUR), Heidelberg, Germany, 1958, pp. 257-259.
222. Anon, "L'opération 'NODEX' dans la presqu'île de Rhuys," Ouest-France, 03 avril 1957, p. 7. (Fr)
223. M. C. Day (ed), "Hurricane Winds Lash NODEX Site," Orleans Item, 27 September 1957, p. 1.
224. W. Whipple, Autobiography, Self-published, Princeton, NJ, nd, pp. 330 and 331. Manuscript copy, dated 1978, archived at US Army Corps of Engineers History Office (CEHO), Fort Belvoir, VA.
225. T. L. Schleiffer, "Historical Report," 37th Ordnance Co (Park), US Army Ordnance Depot, Germersheim, Germany, 15 November 1957, p. 6. [CMH]
226. A. M. Johnson, "Report of TDY," US Army Transportation Command, Fort Eustis, VA, 05 November 1958, p. 7. [TC]
227. D. McClair (ed), "37th THTC Men to Participate in Oct. 'NODEX 18' Operation," Orleans Item, 19 September 1958, p. 2.
228. D. J. Hickman (1964), p. 162.
229. S. G. Tucker and J. L. Garrett, "Beach Stabilization Tests of Landing Mats and Prefabricated Membranes," Technical Report No. 3-592, U.S. Army Engineer Waterways Experiment Station, Corps of Engineers, Vicksburg, MS, February 1962, pp. 38 and 39.
230. J. D. Nottingham (ed), "ComZ Units Move 4,845 Tons In Cargo-Handling Exercise," The Stars and Stripes, 16 July 1959, p. 8.
231. C. F. Tank, "US Army Transportation Trailer Service-First Year of Roll-On/Roll-Off," US Army Transportation Terminal Command, Atlantic, Brooklyn, NY, 10 June 1960, p. 3.
232. B. Wistreich (ed), "Page' Arrives at Fort Eustis," The Sentinel, 24 April 1959, p. 1.
233. Interview, author with CWO 4 (ret) Carter C. James, Jr. (Chief Warrant Officer James served as master of the Page during 1966-67), Newport News, VA, 18 November 2009.
234. A. A. Berglund, "Visitor's Brochure NODEX 22," Headquarters, US Army Port Area Command, Caserne Aufrédi, La Rochelle, France, 02 May 1960, pp. 4 and 5. [AD 17]
235. J. D. Wojcik, "Engineers at NODEX," The Military Engineer, May-June 1962, pp. 170 and 171.
236. J. W. Creech and J. D. Wojcik, "Temporary Floating Pier in NODEX," The Military Engineer, July-August 1962, p. 245.
237. J. W. Creech and J. D. Wojcik, "Pile–driver Design in NODEX," The Military Engineer, September-October 1962, p. 338.
238. Interview, author with Col (ret) Peter D. Starnes (Capt, CO, 89th Engineer Co (Port Construction), Rochefort, France, 1958-60), Amherst, NH, 27 March 2006.
239. Interview, author with Joseph Daniel Wojcik (1st Lt, 89th Engineer Co (Port Construction), Rochefort, France, 1960-62), Saratoga Springs, NY, 16 July 2007.
240. Interview, author with Leon R. Tessier (Sp4, 89th Engineer Co (Port Construction), Rochefort, France, 1961-63), Bedford, NH, 12 March 2007.
241. Interview, author with Lt Col (ret) Wayne F. Alch (Capt, CO, 89th Engineer Co (Port Construction), Rochefort, France, 1960-62), Baton Rouge, LA, 30 March 2007.
242. Interview, author with James W. Reed (Sp4, 89th Engineer Co (Port Construction), Rochefort, France, 1961-62), Smith River, CA, 28 December 2011.
243. M. D. Cohen, "NODEX 30 Nears Completion, Beachsite 'A Sea of Mud," The Sea Sider, 09 February 1962, pp. 1 and 3.
244. W. W. Watson, "Annual Historical Report," Headquarters, United States Army Communications Zone, Europe, Orléans, France, 1962, p. 211.
245. J. J. Borror, "Annual Historical Summary, US Army Europe 1963," Headquarters, US Army, Europe (USAREUR), Heidelberg, Germany, 1964, pp. 243 and 244.
246. R. P. Smith (ed), "U.S. Cutting 5,400 From ComZ France," The Stars and Stripes, 29 September 1963, p. 24.

References/Notes to pages 394 to 408

247. Interview, author with Lt Col (ret) William J. Dimon (Capt, CO, 1099th Transportation Co (Med Boat), Fort Eustis, VA, 1964-66), Newport News, VA, 14 November 2008.
248. G. E. Allen, "Forward Floating Depot," Army Information Digest, June 1964, pp. 44-48.
249. US Army Port Area Command, La Rochelle, France, Reports for New Offshore Discharge Exercise (NODEX) No. 1 to 9, 11 to 15, 17, 18, 21, 23 to 30 and 32 to 34. (Four reports are missing: 19, 20, 22, and 31.) These twenty-eight after-action reports are archived at the US Army Transportation Center and School Library, Fort Eustis, Virginia. In 2010, the Library moved to Fort Lee, Virginia.
250. L. A. Sawyer and W. H. Mitchell, Victory Ships and Tankers, David & Charles, New York (1974), pp. 12-31.
251. E. Steere and T. M. Boardman, Final Disposition of World War II Dead, Historical Branch, Office of The Quartermaster General, Washington, DC (1957), p. 361.
252. A. A. Berglund (1961), pp. 1 and 2.
253. F. B. Case, "Beach Operations Under Missiles and Atomics," Military Review, May 1957, p. 25.
254. M. Van Creveld, Supplying War, Cambridge University Press, Cambridge, England (1977), p. 210.
255. Anon, "The Transportation Corps Watercraft Fleet," Headquarters, Department of the Army, Office of the Chief of Transportation (OCOFT), Washington, DC, January 1960, pp. 4 and 6.
256. M. Ivanchak, "FRELOC After Action Report 1966-67," Vol. I, Headquarters, US Army Communications Zone, Europe (USACOMZEUR), Worms, Germany, 12 June 1968, p. 170. [MHI]
257. J. F. Michel, "Planning Amphibious Operations for Atomic Warfare," The Military Engineer, March-April 1958, pp. 116-118.
258. D. A. Lane, "Annual Historical Report for 1957-1958," Headquarters, US Army, Europe (USAREUR), Heidelberg, Germany, 1958, pp. 238-240.
259. S. A. Potter, "Quiberon Bay," Military Review, September 1951, pp. 45-53.
260. R. G. Ruppenthal, Logistical Support of the Armies, Vol. I, Center of Military History, Washington, DC (1953), pp. 294-297.
261. D. A. Lane (1958), pp. 250-254.
262. J. Gunter, "The Army's Standby Fleet," The Stars and Stripes, 31 January 1965, p. 12.
263. M. Ivanchak (1968), p. 183.
264. D. Walter, "New French Subport Opens at St.-Nazaire, Will Handle 30% of Cargoes From U. S.," The Stars and Stripes, 02 May 1953, p. 9.
265. J. R. Moenk (1955), p. 176.
266. C. Raia (ed), "French Priest Aids Post," Basec Mission, 21 April 1956, p. 4.
267. Interview, author with Brig Gen (ret) Frank A. Ramsey (1st Lt, CO, 73rd Medical Det (Vet Food Insp), la Pallice, France, 1955-57), Uvalde, TX, 31 December 2008.
268. K. C. Dod, Overseas Military Operations of the Corps of Engineers, 1945-1970, Chap 18, p. 45. This unpublished manuscript is archived at US Army Corps of Engineers History Office (CEHO), Fort Belvoir, VA.
269. Interview, author with Thomas L. Simons (Sp4, Donges Terminal District, Dorieux, France, 1959-62), Humble, TX, 26 January 2009.
270. Letter from US Army Brig Gen Charles H. Hollis (Defense Attaché, Paris) to Général d'Armée Etat-Major des Armées, Division Renseignement Section Attachés Militaires, Paris, 19 octobre 1965, p. 20. (Fr) [SHD]
271. C. T. Campbell, "Rapid-Fire Answers," Army Information Digest, December 1958, pp. 54-59.
272. D. J. Hickman (1964), pp. 78 and 79.
273. R. J. Crawford (ed), "Travel Tips," The Advance, 23 April 1954, p. 2.
274. J. Bykofsky, "Terminal and Water Transport Operations, 1950-1954," Office of the Chief of Transportation, Department of the Army, Washington, DC, 01 November 1957, pp. 1-9 and 43-66.
275. R. C. Tripp, "Moving Men and Material Overseas," Army Information Digest, August 1963, pp. 30 and 31.
276. C. F. Tank (1960), p. 21.
277. ibid, pp. 20-26, and 40-43.
278. D. A. Lane (1958), p. 257.
279. M. C. Day (ed), "Ocean Trailer Crossing Launches Maiden Voyage," Orleans Item, 15 February 1957, pp. 1 and 4.
280. C. R. Shrader, United States Logistics, 1775-1992, Vol. 3, Center of Military History, Washington, DC (1997), pp. 724-726.
281. J. C. Fuson, "The Mission and General Organization of the US Army Communications Zone, Europe," Command Briefing, Headquarters, United States Army, Europe (USAREUR), Heidelberg, Germany, 08 July 1959. [MHI]
282. J. M. House, A Military History of the Cold War, 1944-1962, University of Oklahoma Press, Norman, OK (2012), p. 437.
283. N. Khrushchev, Khrushchev Remembers: The Glasnost Tapes, Little, Brown and Co., Boston, MA (1990), p. 182.
284. M. Frankel, "Learning from the Missile Crisis," Smithsonian, October 2002, p. 64.
285. L. H. Gelb, "The Lie That Screwed Up 50 Years of U.S. Foreign Policy," Foreign Policy, November 2012, pp. 24-26.

CHAPTER ELEVEN

1. D. Schear, "Base Hq-Supply Line Feeder," The Stars and Stripes, 18 May 1952, p. 7.
2. F. J. Brown, "Modern Army Supply System," Army Information Digest, April 1957, pp. 24-31.
3. W. W. Beach, "Maintenance in Procurement Planning," The Military Engineer, November-December 1966, p. 436.
4. C. C. Blanchard, "Base Section, LOF Across France," Army Navy Air Force Journal, 24 May 1952.
5. O. P. Newman, "European Communications," Army Navy Air Force Journal, 02 October 1954.
6. H. R. Westphalinger, "U.S. Army Communications Zone, Europe," Army Information Digest, December 1961, pp. 14 and 15.
7. Letter from Brig Gen Charles C. Blanchard (Commanding General, Base Section) to Maj Gen Samuel D. Sturgis, Jr. (Commanding General, ComZ), dated 25 November 1952. [CEHO]
8. Letter from Maj Gen Samuel D. Sturgis, Jr. (Commanding General, ComZ) to Brig Gen Ernest A. Bixby (Commanding General, Base Section), dated 12 December 1952, p. 4. [CEHO]
9. J. L. Cooper (ed), "Basec CG ZI-Bound," Basec Mission, 04 September 1953, pp. 4 and 7.
10. Interview, author with Keith E. Dyas (Sp4, 541st Engineer Det (Terrain), Orléans, France, 1955-56), Parker, CO, 19 January 2011.
11. Interview, author with Gen (ret) Andrew P. O'Meara (Col, Deputy Director of Logistics, Headquarters, European Command, Frankfurt, Germany, 1948-51), Arlington, VA, 29 January 2005.
12. W. Richardson, "Yanks Convert Bordeaux Area Into Vast Arsenal," The Stars and Stripes, 26 March 1951, p. 4.
13. D. Schear, "Yanks Waged War on Mud to Set Up Captieux Depot," The Stars and Stripes, 11 May 1952, p. 5.
14. R. Strand, "Two Years of Building Supply Lines," New York Herald Tribune, Paris, 19 November 1952.
15. F. Maurin and J. Lassaigne, "Voici pourquoi les Yankees transforment Le Poteau en camp de guerre," Les Nouvelles, 24 novembre 1950, pp. 1 and 6. (Fr) [AD 33]
16. J. J. Carafano, "Mobilizing Europe's Stateless," Journal of Cold War Studies, Vol. 1, No. 2, 1999, p. 66.
17. C. H. Briscoe, "America's Foreign Legionnaires," Veritas, Vol. 5, No. 1, 2009, pp. 34 and 35.
18. Interview, author with SFC (ret) Henry M. Kwiatowski (Pvt, Labor Service guard, Captieux Ordnance Depot, France, 1951), Silver Spring, MD, 26 August 2009.
19. J. A. Huston, One For All, University of Delaware Press, Newark, DE (1984), p. 66.
20. J. A. Huston, Across The Face of France, Purdue University Press, Lafayette, IN (1963), p. 122.
21. J. R. Moenk, "The Line of Communications Through France, 1952-1953," Headquarters, US Army, Europe (USAREUR), Karlsruhe, Germany, 1955, p. 142.
22. K. C. Dod, Overseas Military Operations of the Corps of Engineers, 1945-1970, Chap 17, p. 22. This unpublished manuscript is archived at US Army Corps of Engineers History Office (CEHO), Fort Belvoir, VA.
23. Letter from Lt Col William F. Kaiser (Commanding Officer, Captieux Ordnance Depot, France) to Brig Gen Earl S. Gruver (Chief of Ordnance, HQ, US Army, Europe, Heidelberg, Germany), dated 06 August 1952. [CEHO]
24. H. J. Richter (ed), "83rd Bn Cited For Work on Ammo Area," The Stars and Stripes, 12 May 1953, p. 9.
25. A. F. Head (ed), "Capt'x Battered as Storm Hits Southern Area," Basec Mission, 22 January 1955, pp. 1 and 4.
26. D. Walter, "Keeping Our Powder Dry at Captieux," The Stars and Stripes, 22 July 1959, pp. 11 and 12.
27. C. Raia (ed), "Nodex and COD, Men Defy Storm," Basec Mission, 18 February 1956, pp. 1 and 4.
28. O. L. Bell, "Captieux Installation: Ammunition Storage Igloos," Headquarters, US Army Communications Zone, Europe (USACOMZEUR), Orléans, France, 15 October 1962, pp. 1-4. Report prepared by Col Olin L. Bell (ComZ Assistant Chief of Staff, G-4). [MHI]
29. D. A. Bartoni (ed), "ComZ Col Is a Soldier-Diplomat," The Stars and Stripes, 28 February 1957, p. 9.
30. A. L. Jorgenson (ed), "83rd Engr Bn Building 27 Miles of Road in Biggest ComZ Project," The Stars and Stripes, 17 July 1953, p. 9.
31. I .A. Nabeshima (ed), "Big Haul' Passes Half Million Mark," Basec Mission, 07 August 1953, p. 1.
32. R. T. Senn, "Drainage Problem in France," The Military Engineer, May-June 1963, p. 168.
33. A. W. Spratley (ed), "Ordnance Units Supplying Ammo In 'Mudlark II," ComZ Cadence, 31 October 1952, p. 1.
34. Letter from Lt Gen Manton S. Eddy (Commander-in-Chief, US Army, Europe, Heidelberg, Germany) to Maj Gen Samuel D. Sturgis, Jr. (Commanding General, ComZ), dated 22 August 1952. [CEHO]
35. Memorandum from Maj Gen Samuel D. Sturgis, Jr. (Commanding General, ComZ) to Col LeCount H. Slocum (Chief of Staff, ComZ), 04 September 1952. [CEHO]
36. Letter from Maj Gen Samuel D. Sturgis, Jr. (Commanding General, ComZ) to Maj Gen Daniel Noce (Chief of Staff, European Command), dated 27 May 1952. [CEHO]

References/Notes to pages 423 to 428

37. D. Schear, "Yanks Waged War on Mud to Set Up Captieux Depot," The Stars and Stripes, 11 May 1952, p. 5.
38. H. J. Richter (ed), "Engrs Building Range on Stilts," The Stars and Stripes, 06 June 1953, p. 8.
39. O. L. Bell (1962), pp. 2 and 3.
40. D. Walter, "Captieux Depot Lives Down Early Reputation To Become One of ComZ's Most Modern Bases," The Stars and Stripes, 06 April 1953, p. 9.
41. J. P. Anderson (ed), "Captieux Gets Basec's Second Bowling Alley," Basec Mission, 30 April 1954, pp. 1 and 3.
42. D. A. Bartoni (ed), "Isolated Captieux Boasts Top Facilities," The Stars and Stripes, 04 April 1956, p.10.
43. A. W. Spratley (ed), "Educ Advisors Plan Program for ComZ GI's," ComZ Cadence, 05 September 1952, pp. 1 and 4.
44. H. Mann, "Captieux Ambassadors," ComZ Cadence, 25 July 1952, p. 2. In 1951, Menotti wrote the Christmas opera "Amahl and the Night Visitors" which became an annual Christmas TV-viewing tradition in the US.
45. H. R. Morris, "History Records Captieux Progress," ComZ Cadence, 21 December 1951, p. 2.
46. A. W. Spratley (ed), "Ordnance Depot in Rescue Role," ComZ Cadence, 22 February 1952, p. 1.
47. P. Grose, Operation Rollback, Houghton Mifflin, Boston, MA (2000), p. 168.
48. I. Trauschweizer, The Cold War U.S. Army, University Press of Kansas, Lawrence, KS (2008), p. 83.
49. J.-P. Mercier, Camps Américains en Aquitaine, Éditions Alan Sutton, St.-Cyr-sur-Loire, France (2009), pp. 19-74. (Fr) Mercier presents 156 photos relating to American bases in the Base Section, most of Captieux and Bussac.
50. Anon, "US Army Installations France," Headquarters, US Army Communications Zone, Europe (USACOMZEUR), Orléans, France, 1966. These documents, also called "Information Brochures," record real estate statistics for US Army installations in France. [CEHO]
51. A. W. Spratley (ed), "Engineers Finish Demolition Job On Nazi Hangar," ComZ Cadence, 25 July 1952, p. 4.
52. A. W. Spratley (ed), "Bussac's Dunnage Gets Good Use," ComZ Cadence, 15 February 1952, p. 4.
53. Interview, author with SSgt (ret) Hugh P. Cahill (Sgt, Co B, 83rd Construction Bn, Bussac, France, 1951-54), Colonial Heights, VA, 07 July 2005.
54. Interview, Richard E. Killblane (Command Historian, Fort Eustis, VA) with Albert Metts (Cpl, HQ, 2nd Transportation Truck Bn, Bussac, France, 1951-52), Ann Arbor, MI, 22 March 2002.
55. D. Schear, "Bussac Camp Biggest Truck Base in ComZ," The Stars and Stripes, 01 June 1952, p. 8.
56. A. F. Head (ed), "Camp Adds 1,500 Acres," Basec Mission, 20 August 1955, p. 3.
57. A. F. Head (ed), "Tons of Bread Made by Busy Bussac Bakery," Basec Mission, 20 August 1955, p. 5.
58. A. W. Spratley (ed), "'Jackass' Given To First 'Winner," ComZ Cadence, 26 October 1951, p. 4.
59. A. W. Spratley (ed), "595 TT Receives Safety Awards," ComZ Cadence, 11 January 1952, p. 4.
60. A. F. Head (ed), "Busy Truckers Push Supplies On Night Runs," Basec Mission, 16 July 1955, p. 2.
61. A. F. Head (ed), "Faster Van Service Now Serving Basec," Basec Mission, 08 July 1955, pp. 1 and 4.
62. R. Ivy, "106th Runs 'Shuttle' Stop at Ingrandes," Basec Mission, 04 September 1958, p. 4.
63. Anon, "583rd Trans 'Coffee Truck' Boosts Highway Safety," Basec Mission, 03 June 1959, p. 4.
64. Interview, author with Lt Col (ret) George H. Boucher (Lt Col, CO, US Army Depot Activity, Bussac, 1962-64), Anderson, SC, 07 August 2003.
65. T. L. Lyons, "106th Transportation Battalion (Truck)," Croix-Chapeau, France, 1959, np. WO Carl C. Koon served as editor for this yearbook.
66. B. F. Allen, "A-Bomb Training Aid," Army Information Digest, September 1954, pp. 31-34.
67. H. J. Richter (ed), "First Group Completed ComZ C-B-R Course," The Stars and Stripes, 18 May 1953, p. 9.
68. J. P. Anderson (ed), "Base Section CBR Defense School Opens at Camp Bussac Next Week," Basec Mission, 12 February 1954, p. 2.
69. A. L. Jorgenson (ed), "ComZ Giving 600 CBR Training," The Stars and Stripes, 21 February 1954, p. 8.
70. A. F. Head (ed), "Post's Depots Get Job Done," Basec Mission, 20 August 1955, p. 6.
71. D. Loken, "Bussac's QM POL Section Keeps Forces on the Go," Basec Mission, 04 September 1958, p. 3.
72. J. P. Anderson (ed), "Changed POL Method Saves Half-Million," Basec Mission, 19 March 1954, p. 1.
73. A. F. Head (ed), "Bussac Units Perform Varied Jobs," Basec Mission, 20 August 1955, p. 6.
74. Interview, author with Alan M. Singer (1st Lt, 7803rd Army Unit, Camp Bussac, France, 1953-54), Rockville, MD, 13 July 2016.
75. D. Meyer (ed), "Building Sights," Headquarters, 83rd Engineer Construction Bn, Camp Bussac, France, 30 June 1952, pp. 10-12. Headquarters of 83rd was located at Bussac (1951-58), Fontenet (1959-62), and Chinon (1963-67). [CEHO]
76. J. J. McAuliffe, US Air Force in France 1950-1967, Milspec Press, San Diego, CA (2005), p. 145.
77. J. P. Anderson (ed), "Assigne Accomplirons Is Latin For: 'If 83rd Can't Do It, No One Can'," Basec Mission, 06 November 1953, p. 2.

References/Notes to pages 428 to 436

78. H. J. Richter (ed), "Engineers Hurdle Bike Obstacle," The Stars and Stripes, 10 August 1952, p. 8.
79. H. J. Richter (ed), "French Honor 9 Yanks Killed in '43 Crash," The Stars and Stripes, 23 July 1951, p. 5.
80. J. P. Anderson (ed), "Bussac Officers, EM Give Orphans $1800," Basec Mission, 22 October 1954, p. 3.
81. A. F. Head (ed), "597th Engr Co Helps to Fight Fr Forest Fire," Basec Mission, 29 April 1955, p. 1.
82. C. Raia (ed), "Bussac Builds Sports Arena," Basec Mission, 10 March 1956, p. 3.
83. D. Walter, "Perigueux Group Best Reds to Win Amity Fight," The Stars and Stripes, 13 June 1953, p. 8.
84. Memo from Col Duncan Hallock (Port District Engineer, Bordeaux, France) to Maj Gen Samuel D. Sturgis, Jr. (Commanding General, ComZ), dated 12 November 1952. [CEHO]
85. J. P. Anderson (ed), "Well-Disguised C Rations Served in Mess Halls," Basec Mission, 13 August 1954, pp. 1 and 4.
86. A.F. Head (ed), "SNCF Spur Completed at Périgueux," Basec Mission, 22 April 1955, pp. 1 and 4.
87. Interview, author with Maurice P. Lewton (Sp3, Crypto Room Clerk, Périgueux Quartermaster Depot, France, 1956-58), Santa Maria, CA, 19 December 2008.
88. D. Walter, "Perigueux Group Best Reds to Win Amity Fight," The Stars and Stripes, 13 June 1953, p. 8.
89. I. A. Nabeshima (ed), "Basec Posts Celebrate Anniversaries," Basec Mission, 10 July 1953, p. 4.
90. J. P. Anderson (ed), "French Women Join with US Officers Wives," Basec Mission, 04 December 1953, p. 1.
91. A.F. Head (ed), "First Services," Basec Mission, 25 March 1955, p. 1.
92. D. Walter, "'White-Wall' Tents at Perigueux Symbolize Spirit of QM Depot," The Stars and Stripes, 19 June 1953, p. 8.
93. Interview, author with Freemont E. Reif (1st Lt, 29th Signal Bn (THQ), Périgueux, France, 1961-62), Mohegan Lake, NY, 11 August 2010.
94. A. W. Spratley (ed), "Mud Slowly Being Beaten At Braconne Ord Depot," ComZ Cadence, 29 February 1952, p. 1.
95. D. Schear, "ComZ's Ordnance Engineers," The Stars and Stripes, 25 May 1952, p. 3.
96. R. T. Blow, "Hollow Block Tilt-Up Construction," The Military Engineer, March-April 1955, pp. 103-105.
97. D. Meyer (ed), "Building Sights," Headquarters, 83rd Engineer Construction Bn, Camp Bussac, France, 30 June 1952, p. 12. [CEHO]
98. C. W. Borklund, "Why The Impossible is Taking A Little Longer," Armed Forces Management, August 1960, p. 22.
99. Interview, author with Melvyn Bryan Hackett (Sp4, Company D, 601st Ordnance Bn, Braconne, France, 1957-58), Grass Valley, CA, 17 January 2011.
100. T. R. Peterson, "Check Valve to Correct Structural Failure," The Military Engineer, March-April 1961, pp. 102 and 103.
101. O. S. Kuwahara, "No Job Too Big for ComZ 'Dragon Wagons,'" The Stars and Stripes, 24 May 1956, p. 11.
102. A. L. Jorgenson (ed), "New Braconne Rail Spur Speeds Supply Shipments," The Stars and Stripes, 15 January 1954, p. 9.
103. Interview, author with Judy Irwin (wife of 1st Lt Harry F. Irwin, Jr., 554th Ordnance Co, Braconne, France, 1963-64), West Chester, PA, 14 January 2005.
104. Interview, author with Baxter Lamar Thomas (1st Lt, 81st Transportation Co, Braconne, France, 1962-64), Charlotte, NC, 11 June 2005.
105. Private correspondence to author from James R. Lewis (Sp5, Braconne General Depot, France, 1964-66), Kansas City, MO, dated 06 March 2015.
106. J. P. Anderson (ed), "First Army Bowling Alleys Open at Braconne Ord Dep," Basec Mission, 09 April 1954, pp. 1 and 3.
107. J. S. Arrigona and W. R. Karsteter, "History of the Joint Construction Agency in Europe," JCA, Boulogne-sur-Seine (Paris), France, 1958, pp. 310 and 311. [CEHO]
108. P. McCormick (ed), "Americans Join French To Honor War Heroes," ComZ Cadence, 03 April 1964, p. 1.
109. Interview, author with CWO 2 (ret) Douglas A. Brown (Special Agent-in-Charge (WO 1), 766th CIC Det Field Office, Braconne, France, 1964-66), Flower Mound, TX, 09 July 2012.
110. M. Augeron and D. Guillemet (rads), Champlain ou les portes du Nouveau-Monde, Geste éditions, La Crèche, France (2004), p. 261. (Fr)
111. J. P. O'Donnell, "We're All Fouled Up In France," The Saturday Evening Post, 11 April 1953, p. 99.
112. A. W. Spratley (ed), "7775 Sig Svc Co Occupies Old Napoleonic Caserne," ComZ Cadence, 08 February 1952, p. 4.
113. I. A. Nabeshima (ed), "Early Pioneers Revamped All Installations," Basec Mission, 10 July 1955, pp. 3 and 4.
114. A. F. Head (ed), "Only Supply Ord School in Basec Opens at FOD," Basec Mission, 11 June 1955, pp. 1 and 4.
115. A. F. Head (ed), "French Vehicles Can Pass Thru Ordnance Depot," Basec Mission, 12 August 1955, p. 1.
116. A. F. Head (ed), "Fontenet Drops MDA for Fifth Echelon Maint," Basec Mission, 15 January 1955, pp. 1 and 2.
117. A. F. Head (ed), "First Ten Jeep Assemblies Finished by FOD Rebuild," Basec Mission, 08 July 1955, pp. 1 and 4.
118. A. L. Jorgenson (ed), "Railhead Crew Ships Vehicles," The Stars and Stripes, 19 January 1954, p. 9.
119. J. R. Moenk, "The Line of Communications Through France, 1952-1953," Headquarters, US Army, Europe (USAREUR), Karlsruhe, Germany, 1955, pp. 297, 298, and 417.

References/Notes to pages 437 to 449

120. A. F. Head (ed), "Yugoslav Army Given Vehicles from Fontenet," <u>Basec Mission</u>, 03 June 1955, p. 1.
121. T. R. Peterson, "Training in Southwest France," <u>The Military Engineer</u>, May-June 1961, p. 182.
122. L. D. Roberts, "The Bailey: The Amazing, All-Purpose Bridge" in B. W. Fowle (ed), <u>Builders and Fighters: US Army Engineers in World War II</u>, US Army Corps of Engineers, Fort Belvoir, VA (1992), pp. 181-193.
123. J. W. Johnston, "Type Field Army Signal Units," <u>Military Review</u>, December 1953, pp. 21-26.
124. E. R. Mahan, <u>Kennedy, de Gaulle, and Western Europe</u>, Palgrave Macmillan, New York (2002), pp. 90 and 91.
125. Interview, author with Lt Col (ret) John A. Nark (Capt, CO, 547th Ordnance Co, Fontenet, France, 1960-63), Delran, NJ, 25 January 2006.
126. Interview, author with Dr. Edwin J. Rennell, Jr. (Capt, 349th General Dispensary, Fontenet, France, 1961-62), Northville, MI, 13 February 2014.
127. A. F. Head (ed), "Caserne des Dunes Continues Construction for Basec Headq," <u>Basec Mission</u>, 07 May 1955, p. 2.
128. W. Whipple, <u>Autobiography</u>, Self-published, Princeton, NJ, nd, pp. 203-222. Final draft of this book by Brig Gen (ret) William Whipple, Jr. is archived at US Army Corps of Engineers History Office (CEHO), Fort Belvoir, VA.
129. G. F. Locke (ed), "A Brief History of the 4th Log Comd," <u>The Advance</u>, 29 November 1963, p. 2.
130. M. P. Gudebrod, "Command in France Introduces New Patch," <u>The Stars and Stripes</u>, 15 November 1961, p. 9.
131. Interview, author with Col (ret) George R. Cockle (Capt, 2nd Aviation Co, Poitiers, France, 1956-59), Tallahassee, FL, 28 August 2016.
132. R. E. Killblane, <u>Mentoring and Leading</u>, US Army Transportation Center, Fort Eustis, VA (2003), pp. 35-38.
133. Interview, author with Kay Gottry (wife of Lt Col Samuel M. Gottry, Medical Supply Control Agency, Poitiers, France, 1960-63), Clearwater, FL, 30 September 2005.
134. Interview, author with Dr. Donald J. Logan (Capt, Medical Officer, 42nd Field Hospital, Poitiers, France, 1962-63), Dallas, TX, 16 March 2004.
135. Anon, "Le voyage du general de Gaulle," <u>Centre-Presse</u>, 17 juin 1963. (Fr) [AD 86]
136. Interview, author with Col (ret) John R. Davis (1st Lt, Supply Officer, Advance Section, Verdun, France, 1951-53), Montigny-le-Bretonneux, France, 14 April 2001.
137. D. A. Lane, "Annual Historical Report for 1954-1955," Headquarters, US Army, Europe (USAREUR), Heidelberg, Germany, 1956, p. 211.
138. B. C. Clarke, "Army Administrative Support in the Theater of Operations," Headquarters, US Army, Europe (USAREUR), Heidelberg, Germany, 02 February 1962, pp. 23-25.
139. Anon, "Dependent's Information Booklet," Headquarters, 48th Fighter Bomber Wing, Chaumont, France, 20 August 1952, pp. 15 and 16. [USAFA]
140. D. A. Lane, "Annual Historical Report for 1956-1957," Headquarters, US Army, Europe (USAREUR), Heidelberg, Germany, 1958, pp. 125.
141. H. Fineman, "The Warrior," <u>Newsweek</u>, 09 January 1995, p. 30.
142. Interview, author with Dorothy S. Davis (volunteer nurse, 42nd Field Hospital, Verdun, France, 1960-63), Rockville, MD, 15 July 2005.
143. C. R. Petrie, "Command Report 1952," Historical Division, US Army, Europe (USAREUR), Karlsruhe, Germany, 14 December 1953, p. 170.
144. Interview, author with Lt Col (ret) Norman Eva, Jr. (Capt, Petroleum Distribution Command, Fontainebleau, France, 1960-63), Chester, VA, 04 November 2014.
145. Private correspondence to author from Lt Gen (ret) Edward L. Rowny (Maj Gen, Deputy Chief of Staff for Logistics, US Army, Europe (USAREUR), Heidelberg, Germany, 1966-68), Washington, DC, 03 January 2003.
146. D. A. Lane, "Annual Historical Report for 1957-58," Headquarters, US Army, Europe (USAREUR), Heidelberg, Germany, 1958, p. 262.
147. Interview, author with Dr. Donald J. Logan (Capt, Medical Officer, 42nd Field Hospital, Poitiers, France, 1962-63), Dallas, TX, 16 March 2004.
148. J. R. Moenk, "Annual Historical Report, 1953-1954," Headquarters, US Army, Europe (USAREUR), Karlsruhe, Germany, 1955, pp. 173 and 174.
149. D. A. Lane, "Annual Historical Report for 1957-1958," Headquarters, US Army, Europe (USAREUR), Heidelberg, Germany, 1958, p. 262.
150. D. A. Carter, <u>Forging the Shield: The U.S. Army in Europe, 1951-1962</u>, Center of Military History, Washington, DC (2015), pp. 139-142.
151. D. A. Lane, "Annual Historical Report for 1957-1958," Headquarters, US Army, Europe (USAREUR), Heidelberg, Germany, 1958, pp. 130 and 131.

References/Notes to pages 449 to 460

152. Interview, author with Col (ret) George Steven Bosan (Maj, CO, 26th Transportation Co (Lt Hel), Rozelier and Verdun, France, 1959-62), Camp Hill, PA, 18 May 2015.
153. Interview, author with Nancy Peters Lynch (dependent of Capt Thomas E. Peters, 5th Log Command, Caserne Aboville, Poitiers, France, 1957-59), Locust Grove, VA, 13 April 2005.
154. Interviews, author with Col (ret) Richard C. Rantz (Lt Col, CO, 28th Transportation Bn, Poitiers, France, 1962-63), Bellingham, WA, 15 and 21 May 2005.
155. Interview, author with Judy Grote Logan (wife of Capt Donald J. Logan, Medical Officer, 42nd Field Hospital, Poitiers, France, 1962-63), Dallas, TX, 01 June 2005.
156. Anon, "New Golf Course Slated for Opening on June 14," Basec Mission, 03 June 1959, p. 5.
157. P. McCormick (ed), "Poitiers Golf Club Begins Fulltime Summer Schedule," ComZ Cadence, 10 April 1964, p. 4.
158. W. Whipple, Autobiography, Self-published, Princeton, NJ, nd, p. 213. Final draft of this book by Brig Gen (ret) William Whipple, Jr. is archived at US Army Corps of Engineers History Office (CEHO), Fort Belvoir, VA.
159. D. A. Lane, "Annual Historical Report for 1955-56," Headquarters, US Army, Europe (USAREUR), Heidelberg, Germany, 1957, p. 297.
160. A. W. Spratley (ed), "Co A Gets 'Comfy' But Also Readies New Pre-fab Site," ComZ Cadence, 08 February 1952, p. 4.
161. Memorandum from Col Cary B. Hutchinson (Assistant Chief of Staff, G4, ComZ) to Maj Gen Samuel D. Sturgis, Jr. (Commanding General, ComZ), dated 19 August 1952. [CEHO]
162. R. Reynolds, "Electricity Still Problem, But Ingrandes QM Depot Shows Great Progress," The Stars and Stripes, 11 January 1954, p. 9.
163. Interview, author with Maj (ret) John T. Carrig, Jr. (Capt, Post Engineer, Ingrandes Quartermaster Depot, St.-Ustre, France, 1953-54), Arlington, VA, 29 October 2004.
164. C. E. Howland, "The Ingrandes QM Depot," The Quartermaster Review, September-October 1956, pp. 37, 38, and 102.
165. J. P. Anderson (ed), "New Laundry at Ingrandes Opens," Basec Mission, 05 November 1954, p. 1.
166. A. F. Head (ed), "Ingrandes Quartermaster Depot: Busy, Bustling…Growing Quickly," Basec Mission, 22 July 1955, pp. 3-5.
167. C. Raia (ed), "Combat Goods Repaired," Basec Mission, 13 January 1956, p. 1.
168. M. L. Walters (ed), "Progress: TASCOM's First Year," The TASCOM Times, 10 April 1961, p. 6.
169. Interview, author with Terrance E. Cassatt (Sp5, Stock Control Division, Ingrandes General Depot, St.-Ustre, France, 1964-66), Erie, PA, 07 February 2017.
170. A. F. Head (ed), "Ingrandes Quartermaster Depot," Basec Mission, 22 July 1955, pp. 3 and 4.
171. A. F. Head (ed), "Progress Seen In Recreation at Ingrandes," Basec Mission, 22 July 1955, p. 5.
172. R. J. Andrews, "Supply Control in Europe," The Quartermaster Review, May-June 1954, pp. 41, 86, and 91.
173. Anon, "Hawk Missile Plant Started," The Washington Post, 08 January 1960, p. 19.
174. J. P. Anderson (ed), "Ingrandes 1st Two Years Have Seen Big Changes," Basec Mission, 09 April 1954, p. 4.
175. A. L. Jorgenson (ed), "Army Kids in Central France Attend AF High School," The Stars and Stripes, 09 January 1954, p. 9.
176. Interview, author with Lee W. Stemmer (PFC, Supply Clerk, Ingrandes Quartermaster Depot, St.-Ustre, France, 1958-59), Manlius, NY, 27 November 2006.
177. A. F. Head (ed), "Unit at Ingrandes Adopts Youngsters In Fr Orphanage," Basec Mission, 05 August 1955, pp. 1 and 4.
178. F. Siegmund, "Yanks Open Hearts to French Orphans," Basec Mission, 22 December 1955, p. 2.
179. C. Raia (ed), "Homes a la U.S.," Basec Mission, 07 April 1956, p. 4.
180. Interview, author with Col (ret) Charles K. Childers (Capt, Stock Control Division, Ingrandes General Depot, St.-Ustre, France, 1965-67), Midlothian, VA, 27 April 2016.
181. J. S. Arrigona and W. R. Karsteter (1958), p. 80. [CEHO]
182. Memorandum from Maj Gen Samuel D. Sturgis, Jr. (Commanding General, ComZ) to Col Frank M. Albrecht (Chief, Engineer Division, ComZ), dated 15 August 1952. [CEHO]
183. A. V. Inge, "This is The US Army Depot Chinon," US Army Engineer Depot, Chinon, France, 1956, pp. 1 and 8. Welcome brochure for newly assigned personnel.
184. Interview, author with Lt Gen (ret) Edward L. Rowny (Maj Gen, Deputy Chief of Staff for Logistics, US Army, Europe (USAREUR), Heidelberg, Germany, 1966-68), Washington, DC, 21 March 2002.
185. R. Reynolds, "Construction of Huge Chinon Engineer Depot In French Forest Passes Half-Way Mark," The Stars and Stripes, 29 December 1953, p. 9.
186. J. D. Nottingham (ed), "Yanks Help French Fight Forest Fires," The Stars and Stripes, 03 August 1959, p. 9.
187. J. I. Gurfein, "Post Engineer Policies," Headquarters, Orleans Area Command (OAC), Orléans, France, 15 September 1960.
188. Interview, author with Marian Gurfein (widow of Col Joseph I. Gurfein, CO, Chinon General Depot, France, 1961-63), Arlington, VA, 25 January 2005.

References/Notes to pages 460 to 469

189. J. Riley, "Chinon," Basec Mission, 28 January 1956, p. 4.
190. N. Raymond, "ComZ Pipeline School Fitted for Job," The Stars and Stripes, 06 March 1957, p. 9.
191. Anon, "On s'interroge sur l'utilisation future de l'hôpital militaire de Chinon," La Nouvelle République, 05 octobre 1966. (Fr)
192. C. Raia (ed), "Parade Marks Opening of New Chinon Hospital," Basec Mission, 21 April 1956, p. 6.
193. Interview, author with Leon Ceniceros (Sp5, 56th General Hospital, Verdun, France, 1966-67), Mesa, AZ, 06 July 2009.
194. M. P. Gudebrod, "Weather Doesn't Stop Engineers," The Stars and Stripes, 16 February 1963, p. 9.
195. M. S. Brown, "Chinon Railroad Rehabilitation," The Military Engineer, May-June 1963, pp. 169 and 170.
196. P. McCormick (ed), "'Pont' Project Poses Problems," ComZ Cadence, 10 April 1964, p. 3.
197. C. D. Hendricks (ed), Bridging the Imjin, Office of History, US Army Corps of Engineers, Fort Belvoir, VA (1989).
198. D. Walter, "Life Difficult at ComZ's Chinon Engineer Depot, But Construction Program Promises Early Relief," The Stars and Stripes, 28 March 1953, p. 8.
199. Interview, author with Larry J. Randall (Sgt, Motor Pool, Chinon Engineer Depot, France, 1955-59), Springport, MI, 09 November 2005.
200. Interview, author with James L. Lepant (Sp4, 581st Engineer Co (FM), Chinon Engineer Depot, France, 1956-57), Broken Bow, NE, 21 February 2011.
201. D. A. Bartoni (ed), "Basec Signal Depot at Saumur 4 Years Old Today," The Stars and Stripes, 15 May 1956, p. 9.
202. J. L. Cooper (ed), "Rifle Range Innovations Successful," Basec Mission, 28 August 1953, p. 1.
203. J. P. Anderson (ed), "Saumur Is First Depot To Have All US-Built Billets," Basec Mission, 20 August 1954, p. 1.
204. L. D. Sisk, The Dark Is All Gone, Publish America, Baltimore, MD (2002), p. 105.
205. T. Kovalinsky, "Saumur Grows Fast," Basec Mission, 12 May 1956, p. 4.
206. Letter from Col Rolla D. Pollock (Commanding Officer, Saumur Signal Depot) to Sandra S. Calvert (wife of Pvt Larry E. Calvert), dated 29 October 1956.
207. J. P. Anderson (ed), "Saumur Helps Cut Accidents with 'Dragnet,'" Basec Mission, 19 November 1954, pp. 1 and 4.
208. R. W. Colglazier, Senior Officer Oral History Program, US Army Military History Institute, Carlisle Barracks, PA, 1984, pp. 222 and 223.
209. O. S. Kuwahara, "Saumur Underground Depot," The Stars and Stripes, 01 June 1956, p. 11.
210. A. P. Baker, American Soldiers Overseas, Praeger Publishers, Westport, CT (2004).
211. L. D. Sisk (2002), pp. 62-64.
212. A. P. Head (ed), "Preliminary Plans Completed For Multi-Million Dollar Depot," Basec Mission, 03 June 1955, p. 1.
213. O. S. Kuwahara, "Top ComZ Post? Saumur's (sic) an Entry," The Stars and Stripes, 22 April 1956, p. 9.
214. T. Meloy, "Report on U.S. Army Supply Operations in The Communications Zone in Europe," Signal, June 1960, p. 44.
215. L. R. Groves, Now It Can Be Told, Harper & Brothers, New York (1962), p. 202.
216. Interview, author with Donald G. Walker (Sp4, 510th Signal Co (Base Maint), Saumur, France, 1961-63), Galt, CA, 18 January 2011.
217. Anon, "US Army Installations France," Headquarters, US Army Communications Zone, Europe (USACOMZEUR), Orléans, France, 1966. These documents, also called "Information Brochures," recorded real estate statistics for US Army installations in France. A nearly complete set is archived at the Office of History, US Army Corps of Engineers, Fort Belvoir, VA; partial set was archived at Campbell Barracks, USAREUR, Heidelberg, Germany.
218. C. Raia (ed), "Paradrops Scheduled at New St. Andre QM Depot," Basec Mission, 18 February 1956, pp. 1 and 3.
219. Anon, "Airborne QM Supply Unit First of Kind in V Corps," Army Times, 24 March 1951.
220. J. W. Reed, "QM Operations in Holland Disaster," The Quartermaster Review, May-June 1953, pp. 18 and 118-120.
221. P. McCormick (ed), "Sp4 Saves Three Men From Burning Chopper," ComZ Cadence, 06 March 1964, p. 1.
222. B. H. Siemon, "Annual Historical Report for 1958-1959," Headquarters, US Army, Europe (USAREUR), Heidelberg, Germany, 1960, p. 72.
223. J. J. McAuliffe (2005), p. 312.
224. J. Henchel (ed), "Army Sends Trained Handlers and Police Dogs to Guard Nearby Ammunition Storage Area," Combat Cargo, 20 March 1964, pp. 1 and 6. [AD 27]
225. P. McCormick (ed), "Dog-Loving Sergeant Back Training Canines," ComZ Cadence, 03 April 1964, p. 2.
226. D. Walter, "The U.S. Army Aerial Support Center," The Stars and Stripes, 02 June 1959, pp. 12 and 13.
227. O. McDaniel, "Parachute Rigger Proves Himself," The Stars and Stripes, 18 February 1963, p. 9.
228. F. J. Sullivan, "Army Aerial Support Center Given Big Plus For Combat Readiness," Orleans Item, 16 February 1961, p. 8.
229. J. Freeland, "ComZ Aerial Unit Viewed By French Counterparts," Orleans Item, 14 May 1959, p. 7.
230. J. Henchel (ed), "French, U.S. Army and Air Force Stage First NATO Bilateral Tests," Combat Cargo, 07 February 1964, p. 6. [AD 27]

References/Notes to pages 469 to 483

231. Interview, author with Capt (ret) Ronnie D. McDorman (Sgt, 577th Quartermaster Co, St.-André-de-l'Eure, France, 1960-64), Fairland, OK, 03 May 2010.
232. D. L. Gellnicht, "Deliver It By Air," <u>Army Information Digest</u>, November 1956, pp. 30-36.
233. B. H. Roffee, "Supply from the Sky," <u>Army Information Digest</u>, March 1957, pp. 31-35.
234. J. C. Burney, "Engineer—Key to Airborne Success," <u>The Military Engineer</u>, January-February 1955, pp. 28-30.
235. M. P. Gudebrod, "AF Launches New Cargo Handling System," <u>The Stars and Stripes</u>, 06 March 1963, p. 8.
236. J. D. Nottingham (ed), "Evreux Housing Project Opens to AF Personnel," <u>The Stars and Stripes</u>, 26 July 1959, p. 9.
237. R. C. Otter (ed), <u>Anderson County Twentieth Century Memories & Reflections</u>, Friends of the Library, Anderson, SC (2006), pp. 524 and 525.
238. M. Monroe (ed), "557th Unit Drops onto Site of WWII Invasion," <u>Evreux Image</u>, 27 November 1964, pp. 1 and 4. [AD 27]
239. R. Murphy, <u>Diplomat Among Warriors</u>, Doubleday, New York (1964), p. 399.
240. G. H. Wade, "Rapid Deployment Logistics: Lebanon, 1958," Research Survey No. 3, Combat Studies Institute, Fort Leavenworth, KS, October 1984, pp. 27 and 28.
241. Anon, "The U.S. Army Task Force in Lebanon," Headquarters, US Army, Europe (USAREUR), G3 Division, Heidelberg, Germany, 1959, pp. 104-106.
242. Anon, "Directory and Station List of The US Army," US Army, Washington, DC, 15 June 1958, pp. 439-445.
243. Interview, author with Martine Dernoncourt (daughter of Jacques André Rivière, Société Navale Delmas-Vieljeux, la Pallice), La Rochelle, France, 20 September 2007
244. C. W. Borklund, "Why The Impossible is Taking a Little Longer," <u>Armed Forces Management</u>, August 1960, p. 23.
245. E. Petrus (ed), "USAG Sergeant Is Cited for Handling of Rescue Operations," <u>Orleans Item</u>, 27 February 1959, pp. 1 and 2.
246. C. R. Shrader, <u>United States Logistics, 1775-1992</u>, Vol. 3, Center of Military History, Washington, DC (1997), pp. 719-728.
247. Anon, "The U.S. Army Task Force in Lebanon," Headquarters, US Army, Europe (USAREUR), G3 Division, Heidelberg, Germany, 1959, p. 88.

CHAPTER TWELVE

1. H. R. Westphalinger, "US Army Communications Zone, Europe," <u>Army Information Digest</u>, December 1962, pp. 8-16.
2. H. A. Kissinger, <u>The Troubled Partnership</u>, McGraw-Hill, New York (1965), pp. 31-64.
3. C. H. Amme, <u>NATO Without France</u>, The Hoover Institution, Stanford, CA (1967), pp. 31-35.
4. M. M. Harrison, <u>The Reluctant Ally</u>, The Johns Hopkins University Press, Baltimore, MD (1981), pp. 134-153.
5. W. L. Kohl, "France and European Security: De Gaulle and After" in W. T. R. Fox and W. R. Schilling (eds), <u>European Security and the Atlantic System</u>, Columbia University Press, New York (1973), pp. 119-155.
6. M. Marder, "De Gaulle Qualifies His Decision on Treaty," <u>The Washington Post</u>, 25 March 1966, p. 10.
7. R. Lawrence and J. Record, <u>U.S. Force Structure in NATO</u>, The Brookings Institution, Washington, DC (1974), pp. 5-9.
8. D. S. Yost, <u>France and Conventional Defense in Central Europe</u>, Westview Press, Boulder, CO (1985), p. 60.
9. J. B. Duroselle, <u>France and the United States</u>, The University of Chicago Press, Chicago, IL (1978), pp. 229-232.
10. J. Lacourture, <u>De Gaulle The Ruler 1945-1970</u>, W. W. Norton, New York (1991), p. 373. G. J. Martin, <u>General de Gaulle's Cold War, 1963-1968</u>, Berghahn Books, New York (2013), pp. 97-122. C. Franc, "La pensée du général de Gaulle, Indépendance et solidarité," <u>Engagement</u>, No. 114, printemps 2017, pp. 85-88. (Fr)
11. H. Tanner, "France Says U.S. Atom Strategy Condemns Europe to Destruction," <u>New York Times</u>, 21 April 1966, pp. 1 and 16.
12. W. W. Kulski, <u>De Gaulle and the World</u>, Syracuse University Press, Syracuse, NY (1966), pp. 100 and 101. Kulski cites explanation by de Gaulle's Prime Minister Georges Pompidou on why France objected to a NATO policy of flexible response.
13. M. Vaïsse, "Intra-Alliance Conflict Related to Nuclear Weapons Politics: The French Case (1957-63)," in G. Schmidt (ed), <u>A History of NATO-The First Fifty Years</u>, Vol. 3, Palgrave Publishers, Basingstoke, UK (2001), p. 154. Vaïsse concludes that Franco-American conflict over nuclear weapons was part of explanation for withdrawal of France from SHAPE.
14. E. J. Drea, <u>McNamara, Clifford, and the Burden of Vietnam 1965-1969</u>, Historical Office, Office of the Secretary of Defense, Washington, DC (2011), pp. 388-391.
15. C. C. Kingseed, <u>Eisenhower and the Suez Crisis of 1956</u>, Louisiana State University Press, Baton Rouge, LA (1995), pp. 122 and 123.
16. J. L. Hess, <u>The Case for De Gaulle: An American Viewpoint</u>, William Morrow & Co., New York (1968), pp. 119-121.
17. R. C. Rantz, "De Gaulle's Force de Frappe and Defense Nationale," Research Paper, Naval Warfare Course, US Naval War College, Newport, RI, 1965.
18. D. A. Lane, "Annual Historical Report for 1954-1955," Headquarters, US Army, Europe (USAREUR), Heidelberg, Germany, 1956, p. 257.

References/Notes to pages 483 to 490

19. Interview, author with Col (ret) Thomas C. Wilkinson (Capt, Pilot, 50th Tactical Fighter Wing, Toul-Rosières AB, 1956-58), Monument, CO, 04 September 2003. Yeager, who was acknowledged to be the first pilot to break the sound barrier, did not always follow regulations.
20. M. Bundy, Danger and Survival: Choices About the Bomb in the First Fifty Years, Vintage Books, New York (1988), p. 473.
21. J. Lacouture (1991), p. 421. The account of de Gaulle's response to Norstad also was based on interviews during February 1986 with French General Alain Henry Marie Joseph de Boissieu (de Gaulle's son-in-law). The NATO minutes of the September 1958 briefing did not mention nuclear weapons. [SHD]
22. R. S. Jordan, Norstad: Cold War NATO Supreme Commander, St. Martin's Press, New York (2000), p. 127.
23. H. N. Ahmann, Oral History Interview (Gen Lauris Norstad), Air Force Historical Research Agency, Maxwell Air Force Base, Montgomery, AL, 1979.
24. S. Gruson, "U.S. Said to Offer to Let Bonn Use Bases in France," New York Times, 28 September 1963, p. 1.
25. J. Lacouture (1991), p. 5.
26. Interview, author with Xavier-Yves Ziegler, Vannes, France, 25 May 1999. Messmer did not acknowledge McNamara dinner incident until many years later.
27. T. MacAuley, "Traffic Light Setup Speeds 'Scrambles' at Torrejon," The Stars and Stripes, 25 September 1959, p. 9.
28. H. B. Kraft, "British Constabulary On Guard," The Stars and Stripes, 25 March 1957, p. 13.
29. R. L. Bennett, "Annual Historical Report 1966," Headquarters, US Army Communications Zone Europe (USACOMZEUR), Orléans, France 1967, Vol. I, pp. 11-14.
30. J. M. Heiser, A Soldier Supporting Soldiers, Center of Military History, Washington, DC (1991), p. 120.
31. J. C. Fuson, Transportation and Logistics, Center of Military History, Washington, DC (1994), pp. 99-101.
32. J. M. Heiser (1991), pp. 117-119.
33. L. Barrett, "Blow to France: U. S. Troop Shift," New York Herald Tribune, 28 September 1963, pp. 1 and 6.
34. M. S. Johnson, "Outlook for NATO if de Gaulle gets his way," U.S. News & World Report, 21 March 1966, p. 49.
35. M. M. Harrison (1981), p. 140.
36. W. Whipple, Autobiography, Self-published, Princeton, NJ, nd, p. 217. Final draft of book by Brig Gen (ret) William Whipple, Jr. is archived at US Army Corps of Engineers History Office (CEHO), Fort Belvoir, VA.
37. J. M. Heiser (1991), p. 118.
38. M. M. Harrison (1981), p. 150.
39. Anon, "Top Bases Must Go, NATO Told," The Washington Post, 13 March 1966, p. 1.
40. Anon, "Now That France is Out of NATO," U.S. News & World Report, 18 July 1966, p. 46.
41. B. C. Clarke, "Army Administrative Support in the Theater of Operations," Headquarters, US Army, Europe (USAREUR), Heidelberg, Germany, 02 February 1962, p. 18.
42. D. J. Hickman, "The United States Army in Europe, 1953-1963," Headquarters, US Army, Europe (USAREUR), Heidelberg, Germany, 1964, p. 170.
43. A. R. Scholin, "Big Lift: Boon, Boondoggle, or Bust?," Air Force/Space Digest, December 1963, pp. 33-37.
44. Anon, "Remove War Dead from French Soil," New York Times, 16 September 1966, p. 18.
45. D. Rusk, As I Saw It, I.B. Tauris & Co. Ltd., London, England (1990), p. 243.
46. D. Cook, Charles de Gaulle, G. P. Putnam's Sons, New York (1983), p. 366.
47. B. C. Clarke, "United States Army in Europe," Army Information Digest, June 1961, pp. 49-57.
48. C. W. Borklund, "What Europe's Military-Economic Leaders Think of the U.S., de Gaulle and NATO's Future," Armed Forces Management, June 1966, p. 45.
49. P. Zbiorowa, Dziesieciolecie: Polskich Oddzialow Wartowniczych Przy Armii Amerykanskiej W. Europie, 1945-1955, Nakladem Funduszu Spolecznego O. W., Mannheim, Germany (1955). [Polish]
50. Letter from Capt Frank R. Vrana (Assistant Adjutant General, Communications Zone, France) to Labor Services Agency, Schwetzingen, Germany, dated 09 August 1966.
51. A. de LaTaille, "U.S.-in France," Le Monde, 09 mars 1967, pp. 1 and 11, and 10 mars 1967, pp. 10 and 11. (Fr)
52. M. D. Egan and J. J. McAuliffe, "USAF Bases in Cold War France," Conference of Army Historians, Center of Military History, 17 June 1996.
53. O. Pottier, Les bases américaines en France (1950-1967), Éditions l'Harmattan, Paris, France (2003), pp. 130-133. (Fr)
54. Anon, "FRELOC/CRELOC Decision Papers," Headquarters, US Army Communications Zone, Europe (USACOMZEUR), Orléans, France, 1966. Vol. I (21 August 1966) through Vol. XIV (24 October 1966).
55. G. de Carmoy, The Foreign Policies of France 1944-1968, The University of Chicago Press, Chicago, IL (1970), p. 317.
56. L. J. Binder, Lemnitzer: A Soldier for His Time, Brassey's, Washington, DC (1997), p. 330.
57. Interview, author with Lt Gen (ret) Edward L. Rowny, Washington, DC, 21 March 2002.

58. T. G. Day, "Reveille at Sundown," 37th Transportation Group, US Army, Europe (USAREUR), Kapaun Barracks, Kaiserslautern, Germany, 31 March 1967, p. 100.
59. Anon, "Campbell Barracks: The Story of a Caserne," Headquarters, US Army, Europe (USAREUR) and Seventh Army, Heidelberg, Germany, December 1994, p. 10.
60. Anon, "Civil Engineering Instructions for the Inactivation and Turn-Back of USAF Facilities in France," Headquarters, USAFE, Lindsey Air Station, Wiesbaden, Germany, 1966.
61. C. Morgan, "SHAPE Farewell to France," The Christian Science Monitor, 01 April 1967, p. 14.
62. B. W. Fowle, Engineer Memoirs, Lieutenant General Edward L. Rowny, US Army Corps of Engineers, EP 870-1-49, Alexandria, VA, December 1995, pp. 103 and 104.
63. J. R. Moenk, "Line of Communications Through France 1952-1953," Headquarters, US Army, Europe (USAREUR), Karlsruhe, Germany, 1955, pp. 291-301.
64. M. D. Egan, "Withdrawal of American Forces from Cold War France: Operation FRELOC," Conference of Army Historians, Center of Military History, 11 June 1998.
65. M. M. Harrison (1981), p. 145.
66. M. Ivanchak, "FRELOC After Action Report 1966-67," Vol. I, Headquarters, US Army Communications Zone, Europe (USARCOMZEUR), Worms, Germany, 12 June 1968, p. 2. [MHI]
67. Private correspondence to author from Col (ret) Isidor J. Kirshrot (Col, Head, COMZ Supply and Maintenance Review Team (COSMART), Worms, Germany, 1967-68), University Place, WA, dated 07 November 2002. COSMART was team of experts that evaluated the impact of FRELOC on logistics in Europe.
68. Private correspondence to author from Lt Gen (ret) Edward L. Rowny (Maj Gen, Deputy Chief of Staff for Logistics, US Army, Europe (USAREUR), Heidelberg, Germany, 1966-68), Washington, DC, dated 18 July 2001.
69. Anon, "Control and Use of Excess Property and Related Foreign Assistance Problems Following U.S. Military Exclusion from France," Hearings before a Subcommittee of the Committee on Government Operations, US House of Representatives, 90th Congress, 1967, p. 124.
70. Interview, Donita M. Morrhus and Robert P. Grathwol with Gen (ret) Andrew P. O'Meara (Commander-in-Chief, US Army, Europe (USAREUR), Heidelberg, Germany, 1965-67), Arlington, VA, 18 January 1991. [CEHO]
71. J. Reed, "Largest Wartime Explosions, Fauld, Staffordshire, 1944," After The Battle, No. 18, May 1977, pp. 35-40.
72. N. J. McCamley, Disasters Underground, Pen & Sword Books, Barnsley, England (2004), pp. 77-82 and 87-139.
73. B. W. Fowle (1995), p. 103.
74. R. A. Wells et al., "U.S. Army Lines of Communications in Europe (1945-1967)," Office of the Deputy Chief of Staff, Operations, US Army, Europe (USAREUR), Heidelberg, Germany, 1968, pp. 107-118.
75. B. J. Hobar, Up From Cambria City, Self-published, Bonita Springs, FL, nd, pp. 20.29 to 20.34.
76. Anon, "Army and Air Force Controls Over Inventories in Europe," Comptroller General of the US, Washington, DC, 30 June 1969, p. 2.
77. C. C. Case, "Operation FRELOC—Pull-out from France," The Review, May-June 1967, p. 130.
78. C. D. Bakeman, "The Brain Train," The Military Engineer, July-August 1967, pp. 260-262.
79. Private correspondence to author from Col (ret) Basil J. Hobar (Maj, Supply and Maintenance Agency (S&MA), Zweibrücken, Germany, 1967-69), Bonita Springs, FL, 24 April 2017.
80. Anon, "Relocation from France of the US Army ComZ, Europe," Headquarters, US Army ComZ, Europe (USARCOMZEUR), Orléans, France, 1967.
81. G. A. Moon, "Invasion in Reverse," Army, February 1967, pp. 24-30.
82. M. Ivanchak, "FRELOC After Action Report 1966-67," Vol. I, Headquarters, US Army Communications Zone, Europe (USARCOMZEUR), Worms, Germany, 12 June 1968, pp. 1-6. [MHI]
83. D. A. Burchinal, "FRELOC Final Report," Headquarters, US European Command (USEUCOM), St.-Germain-en-Laye, France, 1967, p. 51. Report written at Camp des Loges by Lt Col John F. McGauhey, USAF.
84. R. G. Ruppenthal, Logistical Support of The Armies, Vol. I, Center of Military History, Washington, DC (1953), pp. 558-572.
85. J. A. Huston, "Normandy to the German Border: Third Army Logistics" in J. L. Bellafaire (ed), The U. S. Army and World War II, Center of Military History, Washington, DC (1998), pp. 204 and 205.
86. Interview, author with Dwight A. Brady (Sp4, Trailer Truck Driver, 89th Transportation Co, Kaiserslautern, Germany, 1966), White Pine, TN, 10 November 2015.
87. T. G. Day (1967), pp. 79, 102, and 103.
88. ibid, pp. 112 and 113.
89. C. C. Case (1967), p. 137.

References/Notes to pages 494 to 498

90. Anon, Dictionary of American Naval Fighting Ships, Vol. IV, Naval History Division, Office of the Chief of Naval Operations, Washington, DC (1969), p. 241.
91. B. W. Fowle (1995), p. 105.
92. O. McDaniel, "The Grounds for Flying High," The Stars and Stripes, 18 February 1963, pp. 12 and 13.
93. A. Rakoto, "The French Gendarmerie and the American Military in Châteauroux, 1951-1968," Conference of Army Historians, Center of Military History, 07 August 2002.
94. D. A. Burchinal (1967), p. 101.
95. J. J. McAuliffe, US Air Force in France 1950-1967, Milspec Press, San Diego, CA (2005), pp. 97 and 98.
96. C. de Gaulle, Memoirs of Hope, Simon and Schuster, New York (1971), p. 248.
97. V. A. Walters, "General De Gaulle in Action," Studies in Intelligence, Central Intelligence Agency, Washington, DC, Winter 1974, p. 125.
98. M. R. Beschloss, The Crisis Years, Kennedy and Khrushchev 1960-1963, Edward Burlingame Books, New York (1991), pp. 477 and 478.
99. J. Lacouture (1991), p. 375.
100. Anon, "Memories That Irk De Gaulle," U.S. News & World Report, 30 March 1964, p. 57.
101. S. White, De Gaulle, Harrap, London, England (1984), pp. 233 and 234.
102. C. Williams, The Last Great Frenchman, Wiley, New York (1993), pp. 434 and 436.
103. H. R. McMaster, Dereliction of Duty, Harper Collins, New York (1997), p. 164.
104. H. A. Kissinger, "The Long Shadow of Vietnam," Newsweek, 01 May 2000, p. 48.
105. R. F. Futrell, The Advisory Years in Southeast Asia, to 1965, Office of Air Force History, Washington, DC (1981), pp. 19-29. J. Jackson, De Gaulle, Haus Publishing, London, England (2003), pp. 94-109.
106. V. A. Walters, Silent Missions, Doubleday, Garden City, NY (1978), p. 457.
107. B. G. Shellum, "Vernon Walters and the Paris Peace Talks," Cold War Conference, Virginia Military Institute, Lexington, VA, 09 October 2004.
108. S. E. Ambrose, Nixon, Simon and Schuster, New York (1989), p. 254.
109. R. H. Ullman, "The Covert French Connection," Foreign Policy, Summer 1989, pp. 9 and 10.
110. Interview, author with Gen (ret) William C. Westmoreland, Charleston, SC, 02 January 1996.
111. J. de Madre (ed), "Building a New SHAPE at Casteau," NATO Letter, January 1967, pp. 14-17.
112. C. C. Case (1967), pp. 140 and 143.
113. R. Sunder, "AFCENT Leaves France for the Netherlands," NATO Letter, March 1967, pp. 12 and 13.
114. E. Rohrbach, "NATO Bases in Holland Uninviting But Capable," The Washington Post, 27 April 1967, p. 6.
115. R. P. Grathwol and D. M. Moorhus, Building for Peace, Center of Military History, Washington, DC (2005), p. 150.
116. G. S. Prugh, Senior Officer Oral History Program, US Army Military History Institute, Carlisle Barracks, PA, 11 July 1975, p. 8.
117. L. L. Lemnitzer, Senior Officer Oral History Program, US Army Military History Institute, Carlisle Barracks, PA, 1972, p. 21.
118. J. F. McGauhey, "A Historical Report of the Relocation of United States Forces from France," Master of Science Thesis, University of Vermont, April 1968, p. 118.
119. F. Felix and J. B. Newman, "The New Shape of SHAPE," The Military Engineer, July-August 1967, pp. 258-260.
120. J. M. Lucas, "Exchange of Troops and Facilities, United States and French Zones 1950-51," Historical Division, US Army, Europe (USAREUR), Heidelberg, Germany, 1952.
121. Private correspondence to author from Col (ret) Charles K. Childers (Capt, Stock Control Division, Ingrandes General Depot, St.-Ustre, France, 1965-67), Midlothian, VA, dated 30 April 2016.
122. J. R. Carey, "FRELOC: The Withdrawal of U.S. Forces from France," Research Paper, Industrial College of the Armed Forces (ICAF), Fort McNair, Washington, DC, 1979, p. 13.
123. Interview, author with French Air Force retired Colonel Pierre-Alain Antoine, Paris, France, 09 December 2015.
124. B. W. Fowle (1995), p. 105.
125. J. R. Carey (1979), p. 14.
126. Interview, author with Leon Ceniceros (Sp5, 56th General Hospital, Verdun, France, 1966-67), Mesa, AZ, 06 July 2009.
127. D. S. Sorenson, Shutting Down the Cold War, St. Martin's Press, New York (1998), pp. 80 and 81.
128. Interview, author with Robert L. "Jay" Jordan (1st Lt, Logistical Services Division (LSD), Supply and Maintenance Agency (S&MA), Zweibrücken, Germany, 1967-69), Colorado Springs, CO, 16 June 2014.
129. Interview, author with Raymond Rohou, Rochefort-sur-Mer, France, 06 October 2000.
130. Interview, author with Thomas G. Day (1st Lt, 37th Transportation Group, Orléans, France, 1967), Barnegat Light, NJ, 18 June 2007.
131. T. G. Day (1967), p. 118.

References/Notes to pages 499 to 505

132. Anon, "Movement of American Forces from France (Operation FRELOC)," US General Accounting Office (GAO), Washington, DC, 07 August 1968.
133. Anon, "U.S. is Paying $21 for $1.70 Bombs," New York Times, 17 April 1966, p. 17.
134. Private correspondence to author from Gen (ret) Andrew P. O'Meara, Arlington, VA, dated 29 November 2004.
135. B. W. Fowle (1995), p. 104.
136. Interview, author with Maj Gen (ret) Frank B. Clay (Brig Gen, Chief of Staff, US Army Communications Zone, Europe (USACOMZEUR), Orléans, France and Worms, Germany, 1966-67), Chevy Chase, MD, 27 October 2004.
137. Anon, Ammunition General, TM 9-1900, Departments of the Army and the Air Force, Washington, DC, June 1956.
138. J. B. Tucker, War of Nerves, Pantheon Books, New York (2006), pp. 295-297.
139. J. R. Carey (1979), pp. 16-18.
140. R. P. Grathwol and D. M. Moorhus (2005), p. 149.
141. B. Gros, "La querelle des bases," L'Express, 27 septembre 1965, p. 26. (Fr)
142. B. Welles, "U.S. to Pull Out Air Force Units Based in France," New York Times, 16 June 1966, pp. 1 and 6.
143. D. A. Burchinal (1967), p. 63.
144. M. Ivanchak (1968), p. 75.
145. Anon, "With Troops Pulling Out—Loss to France, to U. S.," US News & World Report, 19 September 1966, pp. 47-49.
146. Anon, "NATO Without De Gaulle," Long Island Press, 27 September 1965, p. 15.
147. B. King et al., Spearhead of Logistics, Center of Military History, Washington, DC (2001), p. 374.
148. T. M. Kane, Military Logistics and Strategic Performance, Frank Cass, London England (2001), pp. 124-148. Kane describes the highly vulnerable NATO logistics infrastructure that existed thirteen years after Operation FRELOC.
149. R. Massip, "General De Gaulle's Policy is Absurd," Le Figaro, 06 avril 1966. (English translation from French by F. Cardozo, ComZ Info Div.)
150. Anon, Government Operations Hearings, 90th Congress (1967), p. 70.
151. W. Root, "Pullout From France—Expensive Move," The Washington Post, 27 May 1966, p. 12.
152. Private correspondence to author from Lt Gen (ret) Joseph M. Heiser, Jr. (Brig Gen, Acting Commanding General, USACOMZEUR, Orléans, France, 1965), dated 03 January 1994.
153. D. A. Burchinal (1967), pp. 37 and 100.
154. P. Parrish (ed), Forty-five Years of Vigilance for Freedom: USAFE, 1942-1987, Office of History, Headquarters, US Air Forces in Europe (USAFE), Ramstein AB, Germany, 1987, pp. 133 and 137.
155. E. Drea, "The McNamara Era" in G. Schmidt (ed), A History of NATO-The First Fifty Years, Vol. 3, Palgrave Publishers, Basingstoke, UK (2001), p. 193, Drea notes that McNamara reduced reconnaissance aircraft available to NATO by nearly two-thirds.
156. Interview, author with Col (ret) Richard V. N. Ginn (Col, Deputy CO, 196th Station Hospital, SHAPE, Casteau, Belgium, 1986-89), Arlington, VA, 08 August 2002.
157. B. C. Clarke, "Army Administrative Support in the Theater of Operations," Headquarters, US Army, Europe (USAREUR), Heidelberg, Germany, 02 February 1962, p. 24.
158. P. Mauffrey, Phalsbourg Air Base: Historie de la Base de Phalsbourg, Période américaine 1953-1967, Imprimerie Scheuer, Drulingen, France (1990), p. 119. (Fr)
159. W. P. Gardiner, "The History of the 97th Engineer Battalion (Construction)," Caserne Maginot, Verdun, France, 1966, pp. 14 and 16. [CEHO]
160. Interview, author with M/Sgt (ret) Gene S. Dellinger (M/Sgt, Châteauroux AD, France, 1964-67), Déols, France, 19 September 1998.
161. L. R. Johnson, "Historical Data Record 01 January to 30 June 1967," Headquarters, 7333rd Combat Support Group, Évreux-Fauville Air Base, France, 23 June 1967. [AFHRA]
162. Interview, author with CWO 2 (ret) Douglas A. Brown (Special Agent-in-Charge (WO 1), 766th CIC Det Field Office, Braconne, France, 1964-66), Flower Mound, TX, 09 July 2012.
163. D. L. Haulman, Wings of Hope, Air Force History and Museums Program, Washington, DC (1997).
164. J. W. Reed, "QM Operations in Holland Disaster," The Quartermaster Review, May-June 1953, p. 118.
165. J. R. Moenk et al., "U.S. Military Flood Relief Operations in the Netherlands," Historical Division, US Army, Europe (USAREUR), Karlsruhe, Germany, 1953.
166. Anon, "Flood Braved for 'Copter Ride," New York Times, 14 July 1954, p. 2.
167. G. M. Foster, The Demands of Humanity: Army Medical Disaster Relief, Center of Military History, Washington, DC (1983), pp. 148-150.
168. R. W. Rhyno, "Two To Grow On," TAF Review, August 1955. TAF Review was monthly magazine published by 12th Air Force, Ramstein AB, Germany. [AFHRA]

References/Notes to pages 505 to 510

169. D. L. Haulman, The United States Air Force and Humanitarian Airlift Operations 1947-1994, Air Force History and Museums Program, Washington, DC (1998), p. 242.
170. D. Walter, "The 332d Air Division," The Stars and Stripes, 02 March 1957, p. 13.
171. P. Parish (1987), pp. 74, 81, and 100.
172. F. J. Sullivan (ed), "Entente Franco-Americaine," Orleans Item, 16 February 1961, p. 7.
173. R. J. Cookley (ed), "Goodwill Gets Results," Army Information Digest, August 1960, p. 45.
174. J. D. Nottingham (ed), "French Survivors Get Mass Inoculations," The Stars and Stripes, 06 December 1959, pp. 1 and 4.
175. D. G. Francis (ed), "USAF, Army Aid Flooded Hamburg," Toul Tiger, 09 March 1962, p. 8.
176. D. L. Haulman (1998), p. 247.
177. G. F. Locke (ed), "4th Log Sends Relief Aid to Moroccan Flood Area," The Advance, 11 January 1963, pp. 1 and 3.
178. C. A. Ravenstein, Air Force Combat Wings, 1947-1977, Office of Air Force History, Washington, DC (1984), pp. 95, 96, 168, 260, and 280.
179. D. L. Haulman (1998), pp. 236-251, 282-298, 342-348, and 404-407.
180. A. O. Stout, "The Mission and General Organization of the US Army Communications Zone, Europe," Command Briefing, Headquarters, US Army, Europe (USAREUR), Heidelberg, Germany, 08 July 1959. [MHI]
181. O. Pottier (2003), pp. 238 and 239. (Fr)
182. Anon, "With Troops Pulling Out—Loss to France, to U. S.," U.S. News & World Report, 19 September 1966, pp. 47-49.
183. R. L. Bennett, "Annual Historical Report 1966," Headquarters, USACOMZEUR, Orléans, France, Vol. II, 1967, pp. 222 and 226.
184. A. Ballet, "MM. Messmer et Jeanneney exposent les measures prises pour pallier les consequences sociales de la fermeture des bases américaines," Le Monde, 24 juin 1966, p. 9. (Fr)
185. C. Bucamp et al., "La Fermeture Prochaine des bases alliées: 16,000 Français à reclasser," Le Figaro, 14 octobre 1966, p. 5. (Fr)
186. Interview, author with Henriette Bibaud, Rochefort-sur-Mer, France, 15 November 2002.
187. E. Gruening, "Disposal of United States Military Installations and Supplies in France," Subcommittee on Foreign Aid Expenditures of the Committee on Government Operations, US Senate, Washington, DC, 06 April 1967, pp. 3-8.
188. G. S. Prugh (1975), p. 6.
189. Anon, "Control and Use of Excess Property and Related Foreign Assistance Problems Following U.S. Military Exclusion from France, 1966-67," Dawson Hearings, US House of Representatives, Washington, DC, May and June 1967, pp. 190-209.
190. Interview, author with Capt (ret) Merrill E. Kelly, USN (Commander USN, Chief, Liaison Office, Military Liquidation Section (MLS), US Embassy, Paris, France, 1967-68), Bellingham, WA, 14 July 2006.
191. D. A. Burchinal (1967), pp. 45 and 98.
192. M. Vigneras, Rearming the French, Center of Military History, Washington, DC (1957), pp. 400-404. Table 5 lists military equipment supplied by US to France.
193. Centre des archives contemporaines (CAC), Fontainebleau, France holds documents on "NATO and US bases in France" which contain records of negotiations on reimbursement to US for improvements to real estate occupied in France during 1950 to 1967.
194. Anon, "Control and Use of Excess Property and Related Foreign Assistance Problems Following U.S. Military Exclusion from France, 1966-67," Dawson Hearings, US House of Representatives, Washington, DC, May and June 1967, p. 376.
195. D. H. Dunn, Ponzi, McGraw-Hill, New York (1975), p. 338.
196. D. A. Burchinal, Senior Officer Oral History Program, US Army Military History Institute, Carlisle Barracks, PA, 1975, pp. 135 and 136.
197. B. J. Cutler, "NATO Sets Up Shop in Belgium," The Washington Daily News, 27 March 1967, p. 12.
198. L. J. Binder (1997), p. 331.
199. B. Crozier, De Gaulle, Charles Scribner's Sons, New York (1973), p. 531.
200. W. Root, "U.S. Troops Strike Colors," The Washington Post, 15 March 1967, p. 3.
201. Gen Lyman L. Lemnitzer Papers, Special Collections, Archives and History Section, National Defense University Library, Fort Lesley J. McNair, Washington, DC.
202. Michel Sardou's "Les Ricains," copyright 1967 by Éditions Warner Chappell Music France, is available on CD from Trema/Sony Music: "Les grands moments," 1999. (Fr)
203. D. Cook, Charles de Gaulle, G. P. Putnam's Sons, New York (1983), p. 379.
204. R. L. Bennett (1967), p. 340.
205. M. D. Egan, "The Rapid Withdrawal from France in 1967," Conference of Army Historians, Center of Military History, 14 July 2004.
206. R. L. Bennett (1967), p. 329.
207. Interview, author with Dr. Johst A. Burk (Sp5, Pharmacy Div, 6th General Dispensary, Fontainebleau, France, 1966-67), Mohegan Lake, NY, 24 February 2016.

208. M. M. Harrison (1981), p. 153.
209. T. G. Day (1967), pp. 35-42.
210. A. Sington, "French Link in a NATO Communications System," NATO Letter, April 1965, pp. 10-17.
211. D. A. Burchinal (1967), pp. 64-73.
212. S. Duke, United States Military Forces and Installations in Europe, Oxford University Press, Oxford, England (1989), pp. 150, 156, and 157.
213. R. S. Jordan (ed), Generals in International Politics, The University Press of Kentucky, Lexington, KY (1987), pp. 111 and 112.
214. D. A. Burchinal (1967), p. 15.
215. S. Rynning, Changing Military Doctrine: Presidents and Military Power in Fifth Republic France, 1958-2000, Praeger Publishers, Westport, CT (2002), pp. 54 and 55.
216. N. Friedman, The Fifty-year War, Naval Institute Press, Annapolis, MD (2000), p. 298.
217. Private correspondence to author from Brig Gen (ret) Albion W. Knight, Jr. (Col, Assistant Chief of Staff, Logistics, AFCENT, Maastricht, the Netherlands, 1973), dated 18 March 2003.
218. R. H. Ullman, "The Covert French Connection," Foreign Policy, Summer 1989, p. 23.
219. Interview, author with Maj Gen (ret) Christian Patte (Brig Gen, Defense Attaché, US Embassy, Paris, France, 1980-83), Charleston, SC, 05 August 2003.
220. D. A. Ruiz Palmer, "France" in J. Simon (ed), NATO-Warsaw Pact Force Mobilization, The National Defense University Press, Washington, DC (1988), pp. 269-316.
221. G. W. Pedlow, "Allied Crisis Management for Berlin: The LIVE OAK Organization, 1959-1963," in W. W. Epley (ed), International Cold War Military Records and History, Office of the Secretary of Defense, Washington, DC (1996), pp. 87-116.
222. R. C. Hipes (ed), "COMZ, From Horse and Wagon to Computer Brain," The COMZ Chronicle, 13 July 1967, p. 5.
223. C. E. Bohlen, Witness to History 1929-1969, W. W. Norton & Co., New York (1973), p. 508.
224. E. Anthérieu, "Le commandement U.S. quitte la France," Le Figaro, 15 mars 1967, p. 9. (Fr)
225. W. Root, "U.S. Troops Strike Colors," The Washington Post, 15 March 1967, p. 3.
226. M. Gordey, "Le général U.S. Lemnitzer à l'évacuation du camp des loges," France Soir, 16 mars 1967. (Fr)
227. W. Overend, "NATO Allies Haul Down Colors For Last Time on French Soil," New York International Herald Tribune, 31 March 1967, p. 1.
228. C. Morgan, "SHAPE farewell to France," The Christian Science Monitor, 01 April 1967, p. 14.
229. J. Flanner, Paris Journal 1965-1971, Vol. II, Atheneum, New York (1971), p. 176.
230. Interview, author with Col (ret) Basil J. Hobar (Maj, Supply and Maintenance Agency (S&MA), Zweibrücken, Germany, 1967-69), Arlington, VA, 24 August 2006.
231. Interview, author with Ernest D. Barrow, Jr. (Sp7, Supply and Maintenance Agency (S&MA), Verdun, France, 1966-67), Ada, OK, 16 January 2016.
232. C. C. Case (1967), p. 143.

Noncombatant Evacuation Order (NEO) Sign for Windshield of Civilian Vehicles

ACKNOWLEDGEMENTS

Listed below are interviewees who shared documents and recollections of military service in France. The list includes US Army and US Air Force veterans, dependents (wives and children), dependents school teachers, French nationals who worked at US installations, and others who provided important information, documents, photos, and contacts to help record the story of the long deployment. Starting in the 1990s, during visits to more than forty-five former US Army installations and US Air Force bases in France, the authors were graciously hosted by active-duty French military personnel and civilian occupants of the former Cold War infrastructure. They also are acknowledged below. Walter Elkins' website on US Army, Europe (usarmygermany.com) facilitated numerous contacts. The authors are grateful for the aid of Walter and everyone who contributed.

Jeffrey E. Aarnio, Jacques J. Adnet, Donn R. Adrian, Joan Adrian, Wayne F. Alch, Kenneth D. Alford, William A. Allcorn, Alan Amelinckx, Catherine Amos, Jay A. Anderson, Ollie P. Anderson, Jr., Robert M. Anderson, Jr., Roy E. Anderson, Viviane André, Stephen C. Antalics, Jr., Chantal Antier, Pierre-Alain Antoine, Michel Argence, David C. Arnold, Robert A. Atkins, Béatrice Aunier-Gauguin, Romeo Michael Baitz, Lance L. Barclay, Robert Scott Barker, Ernest D. Barrow, Jr., Philippe Baudry, Julius W. Becton, Jr., Francis J. Bentz, James A. Berry, Henriette Bibaud, L. James Binder, Daryl R. Blanchard, Jerome R. Block, Carolyn M. Blomgren, Françis "Frank" Bodry, Jon A. Boka, Lucien E. "Blackie" Bolduc, Jr., Terry J. Boote, Wesley Eugene Boothe, Rosemary Borg, Carroll R. Borland, George Steven Bosan, George H. Boucher, Warren R. Bovee, Mireille Boyd, John Boyle, Dwight A. Brady, Ellis Ned Brandt, Gerard J. "Red" Brault, John A. Bridges, Jean Briola, Douglas A. Brown, Patrick J. Browne, David W. Brubaker, Gerald N. Bryant, Voichita Bucur, Anita Burdette-Dragoo, Johst A. Burk, Robert D. Burke, Frederick M. Burr, Hugh Patrick Cahill, Robert B. Campbell, Bobby Jack Cannon, Robert Capistrano, John Ronald "Star" Carey, Frank M. Carnaggio, Shirley Carney, John T. Carrig, Jr., Shirley Gross Carrig, Gerry C. Carroll, Raymond A. D. Carter, Terrance E. Cassatt, Sophie Caussel, Leon Ceniceros, John D. Chambers, J. Pierre Chambéry, Col de la Chapelle, William Robert Chapman, Robert Chesarek, Charles K. Childers, David B. Chilson, Albert L. Christensen, James A. Cicherski, Albert P. Clark, Frank B. Clay, Calvin "Bobby" Clinkscales, George R. Cockle, William W. Coleman, Charlotte Collins, Lawrence C. Collins, James C. Conwell, Earl L. Corbin, Olivier Coucogne, Fabienne Courtot-Autran, Anthony Cousin, Charles A. Cowell, Jr., James W. Creech, David A. Crockett, Margaret L. Crosland, John E. Cross, William S. Crumlish, Vincent E. Cupit, Jane Elisabeth Currie, Robert J. Currie, Dorothy S. Davis, John R. Davis, Thomas G. Day, Edwin A. Dayton, Gene S. Dellinger, Nicholas F. Del Prete, Barry J. Dempsey, Pauline G. Dempsey, Daniel Depierre, Martine Dernoncourt, Gérard Derule, Laurent Devillers, John P. Dillon, William J. Dimon, Doran A. Ditlow, Carter J. Doering, Jeannette Doleschal, Walter Doleschal, Mary Ann Donato, Douglass W. Donnell, Nancy M. Donnell, François Doppler, Sally Letitia Britt Douglas, Normand M. Dubé, C. Miguel Duncan, III, Patrick Duncan, Louise Dunmar, Margaret H. Durand, John S. Duvall, Keith E. Dyas, Marianna Earp, Stanley P. Earp, Terry R. Eastman, Alexis Edme, Alan C. "Ace" Edmunds, Charles A. Edwards, John S. Egbert, Donald M. Elkins, Walter Elkins, Robert F. Elliott, Norman Eva, Jr., James D. Evans, Nadia Ezz-Eddine, Alain Faliguerho, Guy Farneau, Colette Faucher, M. Favrel, Arthur M. Fell, Merwyn J. Fenner, Xavier Ferrey, John F. Ferrick, William F. Ferris, Ernest F. Fisher, Jr., Roger S. Fleming, Brilsford B. Flint, Barry W. Fowle, Eugene A. Fox, Jean François, Odette François, Gary M. Frost, Dorothy Petry Gagliano, Ross A. Gagliano, Denis Galipeau, Vincent E. Gallagher, Avery Thomas Gamble, Julian J. Garcia, Manuel Garcia, Jacques Gautier, Freda Giffin, Paul F. Giguere, James W. Gilland, Richard V. N. Ginn, John J. Ginther, Jr., Richard M. Gomez, John M. Goshko, Benjamin F. Gottfried, Kay Gottry, Ruth Ellen Warrington Gray, George P. Green, Marie-Madeleine Green, Mary Ellen Grim, James A. Grimsley, Jr., Edgar A. Groelle, Franklyn W. Gross, Allen F. Grum, Robert L. Gunnarsson, Marian Gurfein, Melvyn Bryan Hackett, Edward Stephen Hager, Relon Hampton, Horst G. W. Hanak, Dale Hardy, Raymond Hardy, David I. Havelock, Olivia de Havilland, Micky Hawlk, Robert C. Hawlk, Joseph M. Heiser, Jr., Donald C. Hilbert, Basil J. Hobar, Jean-Pierre Hoehn, Damon O. Holmes, Chris R.

U.S. GO HOME

Holtorf, John D. Hosey, Sandy Hosey, Larry W. Howell, David G. Hubby, Peter A. Huchthausen, Harry William Hughes, Jr., Maureen Hughes, LaMar E. Hummel, Tim Hunt, John E. Hurst, Jr., James A. Huston, Harry F. Irwin, Jr., Judy Irwin, John R. Jakubik, Carter C. James, Jr., Emmanuel Jarry, Michael M. Jenks, George W. Johnson, Jr., James C. Johnson, Thomas E. Johnson, Carey P. Joiner, Jerry F. Jones, William H. Jones, Robert L. "Jay" Jordan, Gaston C. Jost, Jean Peckham Kavale, David W. Keating, Robert S. Keiper, Merrill E. Kelly, Reinier "Dutch" Kemeling, Richard E. Killblane, Milton S. Killen, James T. Killilea, Jr., Shirley Killilea, Isidor J. Kirshrot, Harvey M. Kletz, Daniel Noble Klinck, Joseph C. Knakal, Jr., Albion W. Knight, Jr., William A. Knowlton, James Reid Knox, Allen J. Kolons, Alice Konze, William K. Konze, John W. Kopec, Margaret D. Krisanda, Linda "Lee" Krüger, Edwin W. Kulo, Suzanne Kulo, Robert L. Kurtz, Henry M. Kwiatowski, James J. Lacey, Sebastien Lamard, Tommy J. Lampson, Joyce Frigaard Lange, Albert B. Lanier, Jr., Timothy Large, Elizabeth Larouer, Gordon E. Larsen, Viviane Laurain, Eric Law de Lauriston, Aurore de Laval, Yves LeClair, Amaury Lefébure, Lloyd A. Leffers, Alain Lemanski, Peter J. Leofsky, James L. Lepant, Isabelle Leroy, James R. Lewis, Maurice P. Lewton, Allison L. Lockett, Donald J. Logan, Judy Grote Logan, Richard K. Long, John W. Lowe, Yves Lubrano, Rosa Stoney Lumpkin, Phillip T. Lupa, Charles J. Lusk, Frank Lane Lynch, Joan Lynch, Michael Lynch, Nancy Peters Lynch, Jerry Wayne MacDonald, Jane Maher, Louis J. Maher, Luther R. Manus, Arthur A. Martin, Christian "Froggie" Martin, F. G. Mason, Jr., Thomas E. Mathisen, George T. Mauro, Jerome J. McAuliffe, Loralee McAuliffe, Walton E. McBride, Bettyann McClure, Robert D. McClure, William McCollum, Ronnie D. McDorman, Frances P. McGauhey, John F. McGauhey, William Timothy McLean, William H. McNair, Bernard R. Meisel, Jean-Pierre Mercier, Fernand Métivier, Albert "Sonny" Metts, Ferdinand C. "Buzz" Meyer, Pierre Meyer, Jean Mikaëlis, Alvin S. Milder, Henry A. Miley, Jr., Joseph T. Miller, Thomas D. Miller, Mary Ellen Millhouse, Alfred R. Moelter, Michael M. Moore, Goodwin D. Morrison, Angelo T. Munsel, James E. Murphy, Rémy Naccaro, Eugene J. Narbud, John A. Nark, Cheryl Collins Near, Richard K. Neeld, Donald A. Nitkin, Renée DeLong Nixon, Charles W. Norton, Thomas P. O'Brien, Jr., Edward J. Odachowski, Jr., Marie-Louise Oliver, Andrew P. O'Meara, Kevin J. O'Neill, Robert A. Oram, Raymond L. Parsons, Christian Patte, Rebecca Patte, Jesse H. Patton, James E. Paulhus, John C. Pease, Robert Dawson Peckham, Danielle Peters, Patricia Petit, Pierre Petit, Thomas J. Petty, James C. Pfautz, M. Pochon, Patrick G. Potter, Alain Poupineau, Patsy C. Pratte, Arlan I. Preblud, Donna Price, Valérie Prot, George S. Prugh, Jr., Harry F. Puncec, Forrest G. Quinn, Burnett H. Radosh, Katherine Radosh, André Rakoto, Howard L. Ramsdale, Frank A. Ramsey, Larry J. Randall, Erma Deanne Rantz, Richard C. Rantz, Carl W. Reddel, James W. Reed, Thomas C. Reed, Freemont E. Reif, John W. Renn, Edwin J. Rennell, Jr., Robert D. Rex, Patrick Ribayrol, Bruce E. Richards, Thomas W. Richards, Michael Richter, Paul R. Rivera, Jacques André Riviere, John B. Robert, Samuel L. Roberts, William P. Rockwood, Edmund S. "Ned" Rodriguez, Louis Rodriguez, Peter C. Roeser, Raymond Rohou, Joseph J. Roscelli, Jerome J. Ross, Lyle A. Ross, William B. Rosson, Roswell E. Round, Lloyd Daniel Rowell, Edward L. Rowny, Jean Ruaud, Leonard M. Runion, Patrick H. Ryan, William E. Ryan, Jr., Joaquin A. "Bill" Saavedra, Leon E. Salomon, Shirley Salomon, Edward K. Sampson, III, Gerald F. Sanborn, Jesse Sanborn, Robin S. Sanderson, Rebecca Binno Savage, Linn J. Schofield, Samuel A. Schotsky, Hildegard W. Schow, Gerhard W. Schulz, Jean-François Schwartz, Matthew J. Seelinger, Maryse Seraphine-Lauret, Régis Seuwin, Frederick J. Shaw, Jr., Eric A. Sibul, Bruce H. Siemon, Bennie W. Sikorski, Thomas L. Simons, Alan M. Singer, Louis D. Sisk, Robert M. Sisk, Jeffrey K. Smart, Freddie G. Smith, John F. Sobke, Kenneth C. Soderlund, Harald Sontag, Francis J. "Frank" Souza, Thomas A. Spencer, Cora Jane M. Spiller, Lynnette M. Spratley, Billy Jack Stalcup, Edward A. Starbird, Peter D. Starnes, Michael A. Stedham, Lee W. Stemmer, Larry C. Stephens, James M. Stewart, George N. Stokes, Jr., James P. Stokes, Benjamin Hicks Stone, Michael A. Stone, Laurel Silberman Stoner, Robert K. Strobel, George Stukhart, Jr., Daniel P. Sullivan, Donald R. Swygert, James E. Taylor, Robert Michael Taylor, James E. Teal, Alexander Tesich, Leon R. Tessier, Hirotaka "Grant" Tetsuka, Maria Garcia Thill, Baxter Lamar Thomas, John F. Thomas, Sally Downing Thomas, Hugh Roy Thompson, John T. Thorpe, Jr., Paul W. Tibbets, IV, Charles R. Timms, Frank Tisler, Christian Tison, Maxie Lee Trainer, Michael D. Treinen, Perry D. Tripp, Charles Edward Turek, Harris W. Tyner, Michael L. Van Cleemput, Jean-Claude Vasseur, Michel Vincent, Donald G. Walker, Annabelle Wall, William C. Westmoreland, Richard O. Westphal, Virginia Toppan Wetherill, Alden S. Whalen, Susan A. Wheeler, William J. Whelan, William Whipple, Jr., Danny White, Milton V. White, Thomas C. Wilkinson, Rodney Williams, Charles E. Wise, François Wittkowsky, Joseph Daniel Wojcik, Robert T. Wolfkill, Edmond Ray York, Mason J. Young, Jr., Ervin P. Youngstrom, Raymond Zawalski, Xavier-Yves Ziegler, Dennis L. Zoller, and Anthony J. Zuvich.

REVIEWERS

The following historians, military veterans, and subject-matter experts reviewed parts of manuscript on areas of their experience and interest. Their critiques and recommendations are gratefully acknowledged.

Bianka J. Adams, Robert M. Anderson, Jr., James C. Bradford, Elllis Ned Brandt, James C. Conwell, James M. Dorton, G. Wayne Dow, Richard V. N. Ginn, Alan L. Gropman, R. Cargill Hall, Daniel L. Haulman, Robert C. Hawlk, Charles D. Hendricks, Stuart A. Herrington, Basil J. Hobar, James A. Huston, George W. Johnson, Jr., John M. Keefe, Albion W. Knight, Jr., William A. Knowlton, Frank Layne Lynch, Bernard R. Meisel, John A. Nark, Robert Standish Norris, Thomas P. O'Brien, Jr., Andrew P. O'Meara, Burnett H. Radosh, Richard C. Rantz, William B. Rosson, and Edward L. Rowny.

ARCHIVES

The following archives, libraries, and museums in the US, Canada, and Europe provided documents and information. Some US Army museums have archival documents from early Cold War period. Archivists, historians, and staff cited below gave advice and aid which greatly facilitated research for this book.

US, Belgium, Canada, Germany
Air Force Association, Arlington VA: Chester R. Curtis, Zaur Eylanbekov. **Air Force Historical Research Agency** (AFHRA), Maxwell AFB, AL: Robert Brown, Joseph D. Caver, Archangelo "Archie" Difante, Daniel L. Haulman, Sylvester Jackson, Edward T. "Mickey" Russell, A. Timothy Warnock. **Air Force Historical Studies Office** (AFHSO), Bolling AFB, Washington, DC: Yvonne Kinkaid, Jacob Neufeld, Joaquin A. "Bill" Saavedra. **The Boeing Company Archive**, Bellevue, WA: Michael J. Lombardi. **Center of Military History** (CMH), Fort Lesley J. McNair, Washington, DC: Bianka J. Adams, Patricia A. Ames, Edward N. Bedessem, William W. Epley, John T. Greenwood, Jennifer A. Nichols, Frank R. Shirer, Gene Snyder, James A. Tobias, Adrian G. Traas, Gary A. Trogdon, Hannah M. Zeidlik. **Cooper Library**, Clemson University, Clemson, SC: Erika Anderson, Gordon M. Cochrane, Kirsten Dean, Pamela A. Draper, Priscilla G. Munson, Wesley Smith, Andrew J. Wesolek. **Corps of Engineers History Office** (CEHO), Fort Belvoir, VA: Alfred M. Beck, Michael J. Brodhead, Barry W. Fowle, Martin K. Gordon, Douglas J. Wilson. **George C. Marshall Research Library**, Virginia Military Institute, Lexington, VA: Jeffrey Kozak. **Marine Corps History Division**, Marine Corps University, Quantico, VA: Charles D. Melson. **McDermott Library**, US Air Force Academy (USAFA), Colorado Springs, CO: John S. Beardsley, Duane J. Reed, Melissa A. Robohn, Mary Elizabeth Ruwell. **Military History Institute** (MHI), Carlisle, PA: Richard Baker, Gary Johnson, Richard Sommers. **Military Police Corps Regimental Museum**, Fort Leonard Wood, MO: Nolan A. Watson. **National Archives and Records Administration** (NARA), College Park, MD: Richard Boylan. **National Defence Headquarters**, Directorate of History, Ottawa, Ontario, Canada: Stephen J. Harris. **National Defense University** (NDU), Archives, Fort Lesley J. McNair, Washington, DC: Scott Gower, Susan Lemke. **North Atlantic Treaty Organization** (NATO), SHAPE, Casteau, Belgium: Gregory W. Pedlow. **Office of the Secretary of Defense Historical Office** (OSDHO), Arlington,

VA: Edward J. Drea, Stuart I. Rochester. **Olin Library**, Rollins College, Winter Park, FL: Darla M. Moore. **US Army Engineer Museum**, Fort Leonard Wood, MO: Janet Fisher, Troy D. Morgan, Larry D. Roberts.[1] **US Army, Europe** (USAREUR),[2] History Office, Heidelberg, Germany: Thom D. Kurmel,[3] Bruce H. Siemon. **US Army Intelligence and Security Command**, Fort Belvoir, VA: Thomas N. Hauser. **US Army Medical Department Museum**, Fort Sam Houston, TX: Thomas O. McMasters. **US Army Ordnance Museum**,[4] Aberdeen Proving Ground, MD: William F. "Jack" Atwater, Keir B. Sterling.[5] **US Army Quartermaster Museum**, Fort Lee, VA: Steven E. Anders,[6] Luther D. Hanson. **US Army Transportation Center Library**[7] and **Transportation Museum**, Fort Eustis, VA: James E. Atwater, Nancy Gordon, Richard E. Killblane,[8] Tim Renick, Carolyn D. Wright. **Uniformed Services University of the Health Sciences**, Bethesda, MD: Robert J. T. Joy.

France

American Hospital of Paris (AHP), Neuilly-sur-Seine: Rebecca Allaigre. **Archives départementales** de la Charente-Maritime (AD 17), La Rochelle: Pierre-Emmanuel Augé, Marielle Chauffier, Christian Memon. **Archives départementales** de la Deux-Sévres (AD 79), Niort: Alain Paul. **Archives départementales** de l'Eure (AD 27), Évreux: Delphine Syryn. **Archives départementales** de la Gironde (AD 33), Bordeaux. **Archives départementales** du Loiret (AD 45), Orléans: Sophie LeBrun. **Archives départementales** de Seine-et-Marne (AD 77), Dammarie-les-Lys: Eliane Dufour, Isabell Rambaud, Bruno Rollet. **Archives départementales** de la Vendée (AD 85), La Roche-sur-Yon: Françoise Jaunas, Valérie Radosky. **Archives départementales** de la Vienne (AD 86), Poitiers: Pierre Carouge. **Archives municipales**, Fontainebleau: Valérie Renaud. **Archives municipales**, La Rochelle: Jacqueline Le Corre. **Bibliothèque,** Cercle National des Armées, Paris: Robert Tobal. **Bibliothèque municipale**, Fontainebleau: Marie-Dominique Ehlinger. **Centre des archives contemporaines** (CAC), Fontainebleau: Pierre Carouge, Patricia Da Costa, Alain Paul, Christine Petillat. **Délégation au patrimoine culturel de la gendarmerie,** Vincennes: Odile Jurbert. **École de gendarmerie**, Fontainebleau: Eric Bammé, Stéphane Gauffeny, Delphine Lambert. **École interarmées des sports** (EIS),[9] Avon: Marie-Noëlle Caudan, Patricia LaMotte. **Établissement de Communication et de Production Audiovisuelle de la Défense** (ECPAD), Ivry-sur-Seine: Chantal Alexis, Constance Lemans. **Médiathèque municipale de Orléans**, Salle Regine Pernoud, Orléans: Catherine Moindreau. **Mémorial de la Shoah**, Centre de documentation, Paris: Anne Huaulmé. **Musée Patrick Boyer**, Base Aérienne (BA) 120, Cazaux: Victor Igreja. **Service historique de l'Armée de l'air** (SHAA),[10] Vincennes: Agnés Beylot, Aurélie Giranton, Daniel Hary, Francine Véran. **Service historique de l'Armée de Terre** (SHAT), Vincennes: Valérie Caniart, Hervé Deborre, Gilles Krugler, Michel Roucaud. **Service historique de la Marine**, Rochefort-sur-Mer: Marc Fardet.

Notes

1. Command Historian, US Army Engineer School, Fort Leonard Wood, MO. 2. Relocated to Clay Kaserne, Wiesbaden, Germany. 3. Chief, European Health Facilities Planning Office, USAREUR, Heidelberg, Germany. 4. Relocated to Fort Lee, VA. 5. Command Historian, US Army Ordnance Center and School, Aberdeen Proving Ground, MD. 6. Corps Historian, US Army Quartermaster Center and School, Fort Lee, VA. 7. Relocated to Fort Lee, VA. 8. Command Historian, US Army Transportation Center and School, Fort Eustis, VA. 9. EIS merged with Centre sportif d'équitation militaire (CSEM) to become Centre national des sports de la Défense (CNSD). 10. SHAA and SHAT reorganized to be elements of Service historique de la Défense (SHD), Château de Vincennes, Vincennes, France.

INDEX

Listed in index under bold face headings are: *annotated maps* (France and Europe), *site plans* of US Army and Air Force bases, *tables* of NATO and Army installations (directory of facilities, units, and activities), and *lineages* of commands by general officers (dates, events, and achievements). Page numbers with lower case n indicate note or footnote. Abbreviations and acronyms are defined when first used in text and at end of *tables*.

Abandoned munitions of World Wars, 291–293, 296, 302, 389, 461
    Schü (Bouncing Betty) mines, 357, 432
    Teller mines, 373, 432
    100 lb WWII bomb, 324
    2,500 lb WWI bomb, 328
Aboncourt Depot, 134, 281, 331, 431
Acheson, Dean, 27, 508
Achilles' heel targets, 66–67, 508
Advance Section (ADSEC), 71, 275, 279
    ADSEC song, 278
Advisory Group, Aeronautical R&D (AGARD), 164
Aerial dogfights, 181
Aerial tramway, 392–396, 413, 415
    Camp Wallace tests, 394
    French workers, 393, 396
    NODEX exercises, 392–396, 399, 413, 415
Ailleret, Charles, 35, 64, 517–518
Air attachés, 163–164
Air combat with Soviets, 25–26, 91
Air Force installation site plans:
    Camp Guynemer, 180
    Châteauroux AD, 170
    Cité Touvent Apartments, 126
    Dreux AB, 483
    Étain AB, 117
    Évreux AB, 164
    Laon AB, 97
Air Force units in France, 92, 98–99
    Air base locations, 94, 506
    Depots, 96
    Hospitals, 255–256, 258, 265, 484
    La Martinerie, 170–172, 500
    Redeployments, 186, 507
Air National Guard (ANG) units, 90–92, 143–144, 294
Air Petite ComZ, 356
Air Post Offices (APO), 233–234
Air Rescue Group, 341–342, 510
    Amphibious aircraft, 341
    Helicopter rescues, 106, 388
    Rescue boats, 341–342
Airborne command post, 144–145
Aircraft:
    B–17 Flying Fortress, 17
    B–24 Liberator, 437
    B–26 Invader, 25, 91–92, 143, 181
    B–29 Superfortress, 20, 144n
    B–57 Canberra, 91
    C–47 Skytrain, 5, 16–17, 21, 163, 181, 510
        Iranian Skytrain, 107
        Shot down by Yugoslavia, 17
    C–54 Skymaster, 21, 24, 32
    C–118 Liftmaster, 144–145
    C–119 Flying Boxcar, 92n, 399, 486, 490, 510
    C–123 Provider, 398–399, 482
    C–124 Globemaster, 486, 499, 507
    C–130 Hercules, 187, 481, 483–484, 507, 511
    C–135 Stratolifter, 145
    C–141 Starlifter, 499
    F–84 Thunderjet/Thunderstreak, 25, 143–144, 171, 183
    F–86 Sabre, 78, 93, 95, 118, 144, 151, 182, 342, 490
    F–100D Super Sabre, 95, 183, 186–187, 342
    RB–66 Destroyer, 187, 507
        Shot down by Soviets, 184
    RF–101 Voodoo, 162, 184, 187
    SA–16A Albatross, 341, 510
    T–33 T–Bird, 184
        Crash near Phalsbourg, 128
    T–39 Sabreliner, 518
Airdrops, 165, 239, 479–484
Alerts, 144–145, 185–186, 221, 241, 276, 434, 451
Algerian War, 169, 229, 245, 307
Allied Air Forces Central Europe (AAFCE), 60, 179–189
    Camp Guynemer, 179–180
    Combat aircraft, 60
    Recreation at Guynemer, 189
    Training exercises, 181
    Underground communications center, 188–189
Allied Forces Central Europe (AFCENT):
    Bunker at Margival, 191, 196
    Commanders, 38, 189–191
    Exercises, 187, 190, 193
    Relocation to the Netherlands, 190, 502–503
Allied Mobile Force (AMF), 62
Ambulance trains, 216, 271–272, 320, 470
    Doodlebugs, 256
    Landstuhl hosp, Germany, 256, 272, 320
American Battle Monuments Commission (ABMC), 16, 68, 147, 492
    Unknown soldiers (WWII), 165, 283
American Cathedral, Paris, 132, 166
American Church, Paris, 132
American Graves Registration Command (AGRC), 7, 13, 15–16, 19, 51
    Caserne Lariboisière, 8, 15–16, 193
    Cherbourg, 346
American Hospital, Neuilly, 50–51, 256, 261, 264
American Red Cross, 9–10, 231, 250, 257–258, 324
    Emergency leaves to US, 257
American Youth Activities (AYA) Summer Camps:
    Boyardville, La Tremblade, Royan, 357

Château Jean d'Heurs, 314, 357
Lake Cazaux, 358
Ammunition:
    Explosions, 103, 305, 426
    Removal from France, 496, 499
    Size of ammo depots, 431
    Storage and maintenance, 291, 305, 312, 331, 358–359, 426–427, 481
    Thefts, 307
Ammunition depots, 431
    Aboncourt, 281, 331
    Captieux, 13, 424–431, 504
    Chizé, 358–360, 431
    Rozelier, 281, 291–292
    Sassey, 481
    St.–Hubert, 328–329
    St.–Mihiel, 96n, 303
    Trois–Fontaines, 103, 302–312, 431
    Vatry, 281, 312
Amphibious aircraft, 341, 510
Amphibious DUKWs, 116, 369, 381–382, 509
    Capsized near Biscarrosse, 358
    DUKW pit at Braconne, 443
    Fight fires, 325
    Personnel extraction by helicopter, 397
    Storage locations, 443, 498
    Suez Crisis (1956), 382
Anderson, Webster, 222, 231
Angoulême, 434, 442, 445, 447, 463
APC pill, 256
APOs, 232–234, 348
Arcachon, 4, 106, 108, 342, 358
Armed Forces Courier Center, Orly, 159
Armed Forces Network (AFN), 24, 69
Armstrong Field, 270, 326
Army airfields (WWII), 5–7, 90, 318, 479
Army attachés, 37, 165, 168, 417
Army aviation, 294–296
    2nd Aviation Co, 245, 294–295, 455
    19th Aviation Det, 456
    OLAM Det, 331
    26th Trans Co, 107, 296, 310, 358
    582nd Trans Co, 312–313
    87th Trans Det, 296
Army bands:
    31st Army Band, 276
    76th Army Band, 166–167, 242, 518
    118th Army Band, 276, 278
    279th Army Band, 108, 376
Army divers, 356, 361, 371, 406
    Ammo dropped in ocean, 397
    Deep water pipelines, 361, 417
    Retrieval of sunken DUKWs, 361, 389
Army dog handlers, 481
Army fixed–wing aircraft:
    L–19 Bird Dog, 277, 295, 388, 455
    L–20 Beaver, 245, 294, 455–456
    L–23 Twin Bonanza, 245, 295, 455
    U–1A Otter, 294–295, 455, 484
Army Graves Registration Service (AGRS), 13, 15
Army helicopters:
    H–13 Sioux, 269, 278, 296, 331, 356, 455
    H–19 Chickasaw, 106, 307, 341–342, 388, 396–397, 455, 510
    H–34 Choctaw, 107, 295–296, 313, 358, 397
Army hospitals, 261–262, 264
    Ambulance trains, 256, 271–272
    Damage and theft during FRELOC, 504
    French civilian hospitals, 50–51, 255
    La Chapelle, 249, 258–262
    Standby hospitals, 261–262, 264, 491
        Chanteau, 245
        Chinon, 261–262, 273, 470, 504
        Croix–Chapeau, 265–267, 353–354, 375
        Olivet, 246
        Poitiers, 273, 457
        Sales of, 273
        Toul, 273, 320–321
        Vassincourt, 262–263
        Verdun, 263–264, 278, 282, 504
        Vitry–le–François, 265, 267–268
    Station hospitals:
        32nd Sta Hosp, 255–256
        33rd Sta Hosp, 255, 345
        34th Sta Hosp, 195, 255
        60th Sta Hosp, 261–262, 265, 269, 354, 470–471
        196th Sta Hosp, 51, 261
        319th Sta Hosp, 123, 229, 255, 261, 349, 353, 433
        350th Sta Hosp, 51
    Training exercises, 269, 272, 354
    Types of, 258–259
Army installation site plans:
    Aerial tramway at Talmont, 394
    Bel Manoir, 148
    Camp Bussac, 432
    Camp des Loges, 136
    Camp Voluceau, 42
    Captieux Ordnance Depot, 424
    Caserne Aboville, 455
    Caserne Aufrédi, 352
    Caserne Coligny, 213, 243
    Caserne Lariboisière, 194
    Caserne Maginot, 276
    Chicago Area Depot, 287
    Chizé Ammunition Depot, 359
    Croix–Chapeau Medical Depot, 266
    Fontenet Ordnance Depot, 448
    Ingrandes QM Depot, 463
    Jeanne d'Arc Hospital, 321
    Laleu Installation, 355
    Louis Best Village, 128

Nancy Ordnance Depot, 323
Robert–Espagne Support Center, 309
Rochefort Arsenal, 362
SHAPE Village, 49
St.–Cloud Schools, 151
Varrains Support Center, 473
Verdun Signal Depot, 280
Vitry Medical Depot, 268
Army lawyers (JAGs), 386, 445, 456, 495
Army marine fleet, 363, 369, 413, 415, 498–499
Army National Guard (ARNG) units, 75, 141
    Engineer, 112, 286
    Medical, 75
    Ordnance, 303, 323, 442
    Quartermaster, 75
    Transportation, 290, 319, 433n
Army Post Offices (APO), 232–233
Army racial integration, 85, 286
    Bersol football team, 85
    Fifth platoons (WWII), 11
    MP prison guard units, 7
    QM graves registration units, 13
Army Reserve (USAR) units, 75–77, 141
    Chemical, 332
    Engineer, 112, 247, 317–318, 469
    Medical, 255, 262–263, 275
    Ordnance, 303, 323, 329
    Quartermaster, 104, 277, 356, 462
    Signal, 130
    Transportation, 141, 375, 433
Army Security Agency (ASA), 242
Army tugboats, 389–391, 413, 415
    Sinks in English Channel, 499
    Wet storage basin, 363
Army veterinarians:
    Care of guard dogs, 276, 351
    Commissary cold storage, 149, 310, 328
    Dairy products, 149, 275–276
    Food inspections, 149, 351, 416
Assembly area camps (WWII), 9
Athletic teams:
    Army and Air Force, 154, 297, 314, 333, 510
    Bersol, 85
    Captieux, 430
    Dependent schools, 150, 364
    Évreux, 484
Atomic Annie, 60, 205, 291, 430
Atomic blast–resistant structures (ABREST), 134, 281, 312, 331
    Rozelier, 291
Atomic bomb simulator, 435
Atropine Syrette, 270
Aufrédi Army Hospital, 351–354
Auray, 373–374, 399, 415
Auriol, Vincent, 40, 55, 58, 68, 86
Austerity program, 112

Avon, 104, 178–180, 205
Awards to French employees, 229, 288

Bacalan, 341, 343, 436
Bachelor Officer Quarters (BOQ), 48, 129, 246, 297, 314
    Alert quarters, 145
    Seine area, 147, 203
Bailey bridges, 37, 216, 389, 450
Bar–le–Duc, 307, 310, 313–315, 357
    Public bathhouse, 303
    Sacred Way, 302
Barge, amphibious, resupply, cargo (BARC), 382–384
    Experimental models, 376, 382, 384, 422
    Le Tourneau Co, 382
    Pit at ODEX, 376
    Tests at NODEX, 402, 405–406
Base Section (BASEC), 71, 353, 423, 454
Basic training, 16, 73–74, 157, 179, 190, 278
Basing agreements, 89, 115, 120, 490–492, 495
Bassens (See French ports)
Batz, 391, 399
Bayonne, 396, 406
BC and BK barges, 377, 397–399, 413
Becton, Julius W., 85, 211, 297
Bed checks, 34
Bel Manoir, 148–150, 201
Bendix City, 304, 313
Berlin Airlift, 21–24
Berlin Blockade, 19–24
Berlin Wall Crisis, 140–144, 222, 224, 247, 350, 476
    Ammo depot buildup, 291, 312, 359
    ANG units to France, 144
    Army units to France, 142–143
    Logistical commands, 454–455
    Ports in France, 346–348
Beurey–sur–Saulx, 100, 310, 314
Bevaux Trailer Court, 297
Biarritz American University (BAU), 7, 11–12
Bibaud, Henriette, 395–396, 514
Bidets, 297, 313
Big Swamp, 185, 427
Bilateral agreements with France, 28, 161
Billy–le–Grand, 104–105, 108, 296, 328
Biscarrosse Gunnery Range, 184, 342
Bixby, Ernest A., 229–230, 342, 423–424
    French customs, 230
    ODEX exercises, 374–375
    Teenage vandals, 357
Blanchard, Charles C., 71, 367–368, 374, 380
    Aid to homeless of Laleu, 356
    Base Section's slow growth, 423
    Diverts ship at ODEX, 372
    French liaison officer, 340
    Investigates attack on Army nurses, 349–350
    Rental housing oversight, 357
Blaye, 340, 389–390, 393, 438

Blériot Aircraft Factory, 33, 43, 71, 138
Blue Streak, 464
Boenderville, 124
Bohlen, Charles E., 19, 64, 161, 490–491, 518
Bois des Ognons, 240, 331
Bolos, 73, 240
Bomb destruction (WWII), 1, 9, 340, 347
 Damage at Orléans, 211–213
 Targets and accuracy, 3
Bonbon Bomber, 23
Boomers, 95
Bordeaux AB, 25, 114, 181, 350–351, 510
 Air rescue operations, 341–342
 Sheep on runways, 91
 Use during WWII, 90
Bouy, 105
Braconne Ordnance Depot, 106, 169, 442–447, 509
 Coldefy, René, 108
Brest, 3, 68, 149, 339–340, 364
Bridges:
 Bailey bridges, 216, 389, 450
 Compartments for explosives, 36–37
 Swing bridges, 37, 247
 Treadway bridges, 397–398, 405, 450
 Treadway sections at NODEXs, 378, 397–398, 450
Brienne-le-Château:
 Air Force DOB, 96, 128, 182
 Army aviation, 286, 296, 312–313
 Red Cross visits, 257
Broken Arrow, 269
Bruce, David K. E., 70, 72, 88, 161, 170
Brussels Treaty, 27–28, 204
Buchwald, Art, 151, 259
Burchinal, David A., 141, 147, 515, 518–519
Buoys, 358, 417
Bus accident at Olivet, 486–487
Buzy POL Depot, 86, 104–105, 290–291, 328
Buzz jobs, 198, 295, 490

Camp Angevilliers, 45
Camp Bussac, 86, 101, 353, 391, 397–399, 431–438
 Chemical Depot, 435
 Quartermaster POL Depot, 435
 Transportation Depot, 433–434
Camp Crespy, 343
Camp de Gron, 416–417
Camp Guynemer, 178–180, 203–204, 503
 Underground bunker, 188–189
Camp Ising, 199
Camp des Loges, 137–138, 144–146, 503
 Closing ceremony, 518
 Penetration test, 155
 Wartime evacuation, 189
Camp de Moronvilliers, 240
Camp Sougé, 340, 342
Camp Tournebride, 123, 330, 332

Camp Voluceau, 34, 42–44, 59, 205, 502
Canadian air force (See Royal Canadian Air Force, RCAF)
Captieux Ordnance Depot, 13, 424–431, 504
 Choral group, 430
 Draining the swamp, 427
 Elevated firing range, 429
 Fire due to lightning, 426
 Hutment fiasco, 426
CARE packages, 21
Caserne Aboville, 224, 423, 453–455
Caserne Aufrédi, 351–354
 BASEC headquarters, 132, 156, 423–424
 Lesbazeilles, Robert, 229
 319th Sta Hosp, 255, 267, 349
Caserne Binot, 88, 436
Caserne Carnot, 7
Caserne Coligny, 71, 212–214, 224, 241–245, 424, 516
 Bomb damage (WWII), 213
 Bus accident, 486
 Flagpoles, 109
 Intelligence units, 242, 244
 Rules for theater attendance, 133
Caserne Colin, 328–329, 334
Caserne Gribeauval, 269, 277, 288, 296–297
Caserne Harville, 89, 332–334
Caserne Jeanne d'Arc, 264, 273, 320–321
Caserne Joinville, 89, 360, 364
Caserne Lariboisière, 104, 193–196, 203–204
 AGRC, 8, 15–16, 193
 Army bus to Orly, 516
 Communications support, 196
 Damage during FRELOC, 504
 Dependents schools, 201–202
 Open house, 201
 Petroleum Distribution Command, 196–200
Caserne La Touche–Tréville, 360, 364
Caserne Limoges, 31, 34, 43, 59, 89
Caserne Luxembourg, 320, 333
Caserne Maginot, 31, 107–108, 237, 275–278, 519
 Mobile dental care, 276
 Review of troops by helicopter, 278
 Welcome to caserne, 121
Caserne Sidi Brahim, 24, 44, 289–291, 297
Caserne Thiry, 15
Caserne Voyer, 89, 447–448, 475
Caserne Xaintrailles, 343
Cave storage, 112, 244, 496, 504
 Electronic equipment, 472, 474–475
 NEO supplies, 219, 459
Cazaux air base, 90, 106, 117, 184, 342, 433
Cenon, 123, 343, 438
CF license plates, 227, 307, 416, 516
Challe, Maurice, 170, 190–191
Châlons–sur–Marne, 7, 24, 100, 198–199, 226
 Ammo railcar explosion, 103
Chambley AB, 94–95, 97, 117–118, 123, 182

Dual–based aircraft at Shaw AFB, 507
Chambon–sur–Lignon, 4
Chapels, 43, 59, 131, 193, 231, 283, 325, 440, 472
Château de Courances, 204
Château de la Fessardière, 157
Château des Ifs, 122, 472–474, 476–477, 504
Château Jean d'Heurs, 310, 314, 357
Château de la Madeleine, 203
Château de la Mothe, 129, 158, 246
Château le Petit Cormier, 154
Château de la Roche, 454
Château de Salvert, 472
Château de Suscinio (See Suscinio)
Château de la Touche, 134, 153
Château Villefallier, 250
Châteauneuf–sur–Cher, 171
Châteauroux Air Depot, 111, 170, 237, 354, 495, 510–511, 514
    Military aid to Yugoslavia, 171
    Towveyer system, 171–172
    Weather radar station, 180
Châtelaillon–Plage, 349, 353, 357
Chaumont AB, 90–96, 111–112, 117, 128–129, 171, 181, 185–187
    Statue of Liberty Wing, 93
Chemical, biological, radiological (CBR), 62, 269–270
    Camouflaged munitions, 505–506
    Chemical agents, 270, 305, 505–506
    Primary tasks of units, 216, 218
    Training schools, 270, 333, 435
Chemical Corps:
    13th Chem Bn, 332
    15th Chem Group, 435
    330th Chem Co, 332
    337th Chem Co, 332
Chenevières DOB, 96, 141, 240, 492
Cherbourg, 7–8, 85, 103, 222 (See *also* French ports)
Chesarek, Ferdinand J., 261, 287, 297–298, 454, 491
Chevalier, Maurice, 42
Chicago Area Depot (See Verdun)
Chinon Engineer Depot, 130, 389, 467–472, 504, 515
Chizé Ammo Depot, 128, 237, 351, 358–360, 431
Chronology (1948–1968), 520–522
CI (Criminal Investigation) agents, 160
CIA (Central Intelligence Agency), 27, 46–47, 162, 430
CIC (See US Army Counter Intelligence Corps)
Cigarette camps, 7–11, 67
Cimetière de Picpus, 166–167
Cité Chabasse (heroes of French resistance), 447
Cité Clemenceau, 438
Cité De Fontaine (heroes of French resistance), 203
Cité de Jean–Baptiste Rouillon (hero of French resistance), 298
Cité Lafayette, 357, 484
Cité Maréchal Foch, 127, 250
Cité Touvent Apartments, 125–126, 171

Clarke, Bruce C., 140, 212, 406, 494
Clay, Lucius D., 38, 67
    Berlin blockade, 19–24
    Berlin Wall Crisis, 140–141
Closing ceremonies, 518–519
Code pads, 145
Coffee stop trucks, 226–227, 434, 498
Cold storage plants, 287, 328
Colglazier, Robert W., 215n, 230, 272
Collapsible rubber tanks, 200–201, 334, 354, 451
Combat training, 239–240, 288, 417, 428
    Firing ranges, 200, 331, 353, 360
    Medics, 269, 354
    Military Police, 240
Command Post Exercises (CPX), 43–44, 205
    Bunkers, 191–193
    Camp Voluceau, 205
Commercial passenger ships, 8, 82–83
Computers (mainframe) on railcars, 497
ComZ license plates (See CF license plates)
ComZ Replacement Center, 417
CONEX containers, 393, 398, 404–408, 418
    Lighterage capacity, 376, 404
    Sling lifts, 379
Construction freezes, 113, 118, 135
Convoy traffic control, 102–103
Corps of Engineers, 31, 105, 216, 218, 284–285, 394
Counter Intelligence units:
    66th CIC Group, 153–154, 458
    513th Intel Group, 149–150
    450th CIC Det, 33, 153, 156, 160, 204
    766th CIC Det, 153–160, 245, 291, 309
C–rations, 106, 239, 407, 480, 509
    Humanitarian aid, 106, 479, 512–513
    Scattered cartons at ODEX, 375
    The John Wayne, 106
    Use at mess halls, 439
Criminal investigations, 160, 504–505
Croix–Chapeau Medical Depot, 265–267, 353–354, 494
Croix–de–Metz, 86, 317–318, 320, 322, 330
Cuban Missile Crisis, 144, 158, 188–189, 294, 420, 501
Curfews:
    Dependents, 125, 357
    Off–duty GIs, 236

Daily dozen, 73
Danube River flood, 510, 512
Das Boot movie, 340
Decoy aircraft, 93
Deep water pipeline, 361, 417
Defense Attaché (DATT), 165, 417
Defense Intelligence Agency (DIA), 162–163
De Gaulle, Charles:
    Annual hunts at Rambouillet, 64
    Basing agreements, 490–492
    Bomb at Toulon ceremony, 64

Cargo to Vietnam, 500
Congressman's visit to Paris, 168
Eisenhower, 36, 44, 501, 515–516
French flags, 109
French provisional government, 1, 4
Grocery stores in France, 149
JFK funeral, 501
JFK visit to Colombey, 296
Lemnitzer, 63, 515–516
Malpasset (Fréjus) dam collapse, 510–512
NATO, 36, 38, 41, 54, 489, 492
Nuclear weapons in France, 186, 281, 490
OAS ambush, 190
Pierrelatte overflights by US, 162
Pissoirs, 238
Prostate surgery, 298–299
Revolt of generals in Algeria, 245
St.–Cyr, 190
Visits to:
    Angoulême, 445
    Poitiers, 457
    St.–Dizier, 159
    Verdun, 298
Withdrawal from SHAPE, 148, 205, 489
De Grasse Village, 147
De Havilland, Olivia, 132, 151, 255, 284
    Jardin Fontaine theater, 283
    March of Dimes benefit, 259
DeLong piers, 385–386, 389–395, 408, 413
Demobilization (WWII), 8–11
Déols, 114, 125, 145, 170–172, 510, 514
Department of Army Civilians (DAC), 122–123, 256
    Housing, 122–123, 129
    Pay and allowances, 113, 123
    Workforce at 4th Log, 279
Dependents' Medical Care Act, 256
Dependents schools:
    Bus transportation, 138, 150, 201, 245, 282, 320, 364, 439, 464, 471
    Closures (1966–67), 507
    CRS–Peugeot driving circuit, 201–202
    Dormitories, 150–151, 282, 364, 439, 457, 464
    Elementary schools built by GIs, 333, 386
    High schools, 150–151, 250, 282, 364, 439, 457, 464, 471, 507
    Lycée Carnot, 179, 201
    SHAPE school, Sterrebeck, Belgium, 502
    SHAPE school, Paris, 50
Deported Jews, 3–4
    Transport to death camps, 1, 17
Depots, Air Force, 96
Désandrouins Barracks (Hospital), 263–264, 282–285, 504
Deutsche mark (DM) program, 122
Dewey, Robert K. (pulls soldiers from burning helicopter), 480
Dewey, Thomas E., 38, 85
Dietrich, Marlene, 12

Discharge and run concept, 339, 395, 413
Dispersed–operating air bases (DOB), 90, 96
Dog tags, 73, 354
Dolly trailers, 393
Donges tank farms, 417
Doodlebugs, 256
Douaumont Ossuary, 298, 509
Draftee soldiers, 72–75
Dragon wagons, 156, 445
Dreux AB, 124, 286, 398–399, 479–484, 510, 515
    Doster, George "Poppa", 143–144
    Low–level airdrops, 483
Drug smuggling, 238
Dry docks, 361–363
Dual–basing, 507
Dulles, John Foster, 31, 476
Dunnigan, Gerald H. (fatal fall at abandoned WWI fort), 293

École Militaire, 52–53
Edgewood Arsenal, 158, 506
Eisenhower, Dwight D., 31–41, 46, 54, 68, 89, 133
    Certificate of merit (WWII), 104
    Columbine, VC–121A, 32
    Construction freezes, 113, 118, 135
    Farewell to France, 55–56
    Four powers summit in Paris, 501
    Funeral of, 501
    Hôtel Astoria, 31–33, 35, 298
    Hôtel Raphaël, 32–33
    Montgomery, 36, 204–205
    NATO achievements, 65
    Nuclear policy of, 61
    Omaha Beach ceremony, 165
    Playing golf, 42, 56
    Racial integration of armed forces, 85
    Villa St.–Pierre, 41–42, 56, 64
Eisenhower, Mamie, 41–42, 56, 64, 165
Emergency aid by US military, 105–107, 509–513
Emergency ports and beaches, 414–415
Engineer Aviation Battalions (EAB), 5, 116–117, 124
Engineer Construction Battalions:
    62nd Engineers, 320
    83rd Engineers, 106, 426–427, 429, 435–437, 443, 450, 470
    84th Engineers, 471
    97th Engineers, 119, 285–286, 290, 293–294, 296, 298
    109th Engineers, 112, 286
    249th Engineers, 269, 293–294
    553rd Engineers, 109, 133, 189, 231, 240, 245–248, 269
    982nd Engineers, 112, 230–231, 247–249
    998th Engineers, 112, 317
Engineer insignia myth, 284–285
Engineer Terrain Analysis, 244, 386
Escape and evasion, 3–4, 47, 185, 322
Étain AB, 93–96, 117–118, 186–187, 298, 509
    Base construction delays, 118

Chaff, 95n
    Use during WWII, 7, 90
European Air Transport Service (EATS), 16–17, 21
European Data Gateway Station, 222
Evacuation of noncombatants (NEO):
    Evacuation routes, 458–459
    Exercises, 460, 470
    NEO kits, 458
    Supplies for NEOs, 219, 446, 459–460
    Tent camps, 460, 470
    Traffic control, 296, 457–458, 460
Évreux AB, 118, 145–146, 158, 163–164, 483–484, 490, 499–500, 509
    Boenderville trailer park, 124
    Fleet of USAF Skytrains, 163
    Iranian Skytrain visit, 107
    Mandle, Armand, 507
Excess property disposal, 329, 509, 515
Exercises:
    Carte Blanche, 182
    Coronet, 181
    Crested Cap, 492
    Indian Summer, 60
    Lion Noir, 190
    Long Haul, 225
    NEO, 460, 470
    Roadbound, 460
    Royal Flush, 184
    Side Step, 62
    Spear Head, 187
Exploding canned food, 239
Explosive ordnance disposal (EOD), 216, 291–293

Fake nuclear weapons depot, 281
Farrell rolling–wing deck, 375
Fast relocation from France (FRELOC), 434, 493–509, 514–519
    Golf course turf to Germany, 505
    Medical supplies and equipment, 51, 268, 504
    Munitions, 496, 498–499, 505–506
    Shoppers from Germany, 506
    Weakens defense of Europe, 508
Fauld (UK) explosion, 496
FAX machines, 211, 222
Fifth platoons (WWII), 11
Fillod prefabs:
    Ammo storage, 305, 426–427, 429
    Barracks, 120–121
    Chapels, 131
Firefighting platoons, 84, 303, 426
Firing–in butts, 294, 320
Flag ceremonies, 108–109, 518–519
Flame throwers, 216, 332–333
Fleming, Robert J., 224, 279, 284, 334, 454
Floating cranes, 348, 356, 363, 375, 413, 422
Floating piers, 373–374, 404–406, 415

Flying chaplain, 296
Fontainebleau:
    Château, 31, 41, 56, 179, 189
    NATO organizations, 179–184, 188–191, 204–205, 502–503
    Séramy, Paul, 205
    US Army, 71, 130, 169, 193–196, 265, 504
    Welcome booklet, 61
Fontenet Ordnance Depot, 86, 169, 230, 447–451
    Brisset, Henri, 449
Forced labor (*STO*), 1, 4, 113, 191, 340
Ford, William W., 119, 278–279
    Algerian workers camp, 307
    Trigger–happy guards, 306
    Wearing of uniforms, 278, 428
    Winterized tents, 278, 286
Forêt de la Braconne, 442
Forêt de Chinon, 467
Forêt de Chizé, 358
Forêt de Haye, 322–323
Forêt de Sommedieue, 291
Forêt de Trois–Fontaines, 302
Forêt de Villers, 328
Fort Eustis, 100, 102, 141, 380, 393, 403, 406, 408, 434
Fort Holabird, 152, 157–158, 291
Fort Leonard Wood, 75, 214, 285, 320, 471
Fort Montlouis, 47
Fort Ord, 85, 385, 471
Fort de Regret, 277
Fort Story, 337, 382, 384
Fort de Tavannes, 289, 293
Fort de Tourneville, 8
Fort du Vieux Canton, 318–319
Fort Worden, 361, 363
Forty and Eight boxcars, 17–18
Forward Floating Depot ships, 408
Fourth of July ceremonies, 166–167
Fragrant Rosy, 313
France's *force de frappe*, 159, 164, 431, 489
Fraternization policy, 81, 127, 129, 156
Fréjus dam collapse, 510–512
French airfields, 90
French–American agreements, 161
    Bruce–Parodi (1950), 70, 72, 88
    Bruce–Parodi (1951), 170
    Dillon–Bidault, 197
    Houghton–DeMurville, 28
French–American relations:
    Airfields offered to USAF, 90
    Bridge over Vienne River, 470
    Casernes used by Americans, 88–89
    Effect of withdrawal on French economy, 205, 514–515
    Engineer relations, 119
    Exchange of facilities in Germany, 67, 503
    Fiscal Liaison Office (FAFLO), 118–119

Flag ceremonies, 108–109
Franklin Club at Metz, 329
French donate chapel bell at Maison–Fort, 231
French Golf Association at Poitiers, 461
French language days, 324, 469
Gruenther pamphlet on GI behavior, 61
Joint airborne exercises, 481, 483
Letter from Frenchman at Caserne Coligny, 516
Marriages, 132, 159
Périgueux France–US Friendship Assoc, 439
Sites offered to US Army, 86
Training French B–26 crews, 91
Troop relations committee, 230
French casernes, 88–89
French Communist Party (*PCF*), 7, 43, 68, 179–180, 265
    Agricultural riots, 451
    Alleges CIA trained spies at Captieux, 430
    Disinformation, 57, 95, 349, 356, 425, 430
    Mob attacks Army warehouse, 341
    Opposition to ComZ, 85–86, 135, 159, 348, 439
    Protests, demonstrations, and riots:
        La Chapelle, 260
        La Rochelle, 352
        Paris, 57–58
        Robert–Espagne, 309
        St.–Nazaire, 416
    Sabotage at air base, 117
    Strikes at French ports, 68, 342, 349
French CRS, 166, 237, 278
    Offshore discharge exercises, 368, 386, 400
    Riot control, 260
    Student driver course, 201–202
French drivers, 100–101, 106
French economy, 205, 514–515
French hotel registration law, 159
French Interior Ministry, 86, 154, 159, 368
French Liaison Officers, 101, 107, 340, 457, 490
French orphanages:
    Bar–le–Duc and St.–Dizier, 314–315
    Châteauroux, 509
    Châtellerault (St.–Joseph's), 464
    Épernay, 105
    Étain, 509
    Évreux (Little Sisters of the Poor), 509
    La Force (Jean Bost), 437
    Mirebeau, 464
    Nancy–Toul, 326
    Olivet (Ste.–Marie's), 231
    Périgueux, 439
    Sampigny, 333
French ports:
    Bassens, 339–342, 349, 373, 433–435
    Cherbourg, 82, 141, 339–340, 346–347
    La Pallice, 78, 91, 156, 339, 348–350, 486
    Le Havre, 8–11, 18, 82–83, 141, 347–348
    St.–Nazaire, 339–340, 416–420, 486, 491

French PT&T, 47, 123, 275
French taxes, 69, 123, 205, 357, 507, 514
Frescaty Air Field, 90, 96n, 191, 331

Gaffes by US, 490
Gallagher, Philip E., 130, 424, 435
Ganeval, Jean, 24
GAO (General Accounting Office), 127, 220, 495, 497
Gazette d'Orléans, 231
Gehlen Group, 151–152
General Depots, 211, 220, 326, 334, 476
Germans in France (WWII):
    Ambush at St.–Laurent, 447
    Forced laborers sent to Germany (*STO*), 4, 113
    Jews sent to death camps, 3–4, 17
    Massacre at Robert–Espagne, 100
    Occupation zones, 2–3
    Prisons, 2–3, 50, 161, 280
    Submarine pens, 339–341
German–built prefabs, 111
German PWs in France (1944–46), 7, 10
Germersheim, 399, 496
GI gin, 256
Gigs, 74
Gingrich, Newt, 458
Girard, Georges (Medal of Freedom), 103
Go codes, 47, 145
Godfrey, Arthur, 46
Goldwyn, Samuel J., 34, 51
Golf courses, 133–134, 153, 245, 282, 296, 314, 461
    Miniature golf, 189, 429
    Turf sent to Germany, 505
Goodpaster, Andrew J., 32, 35, 61
    CPX One, 205
    Missing classified documents, 38
    NATO achievements, 65
Gradignan Army Hospital, 255, 342–343
Gray Ladies, 258, 326
Green car gang, 307, 330
Grigny, 93, 147
Grostenquin, 184–185, 264
Gruenther, Alfred M., 32–33, 41–43, 52, 57–62
    Chief of Staff to Ike, 32, 36, 59
    CPX at Camp Voluceau, 59, 205
    Gruenthergrams, 36
    NATO achievements, 65
Guynemer Trophy, 184

Hallyday, Johnny, 42
Halvorsen, Gail S. (Uncle Wiggly Wings), 23
Handy, Thomas T., 36–38
    Approves La Baule road, 117
    EUCOM, 137, 141
    Objects to French flags at US Army bases, 107
    Racial integration in Europe, 85
    Rejects prefabs for ComZ, 111–112

Hanson, Robert M. (rescues drowning woman), 231
Harbord Barracks, 231, 239, 242, 246–247, 259
Heiser, Joseph M., 215n
    Operation FRELOC, 490–491, 508
    Scuffle at Verdun, 297
    Streamlines log operations, 222
Helicopter rescues, 106–107, 296, 510
Hessian Mat, 5
Hicks, Joseph H., 170, 172
Highway transportation command, 225–228
Hitler's bunkers in France, 191
Hobart Baker Field, 320
Hoge, William M., 8, 37, 317, 494
Hollis, Charles H., 165, 168
Honest John rockets, 60, 517
Honey dipper duty, 368, 406
Hoover, Hobert H., 106, 231
Hôtel Aigle Noir, 179
Hôtel Astoria, 30–35, 160, 212, 298
    AGRC, 8, 15
    EUCOM Det, 16, 71
Hôtel d'Aube, 203
Hôtel Balmoral, 34
Hôtel Bon Repas, 340
Hôtel Cadran Bleu, 179
Hôtel Coq Hardi, 285, 297
Hôtel Littré, 83, 160
Hôtel Lutétia, 4
Hôtel Majestic, 8, 169, 190
Hôtel Queen Elizabeth, 34
Hôtel Raphaël, 32–33
Hôtel Rochester, 33
Hôtel Sainte-Catherine, 171
Hôtel Victoria Palace, 83
Hôtel West End, 113–114, 150
Houghton, Amory, 28, 161, 166
House Falls method, 392
Howitzers, 127, 141, 277, 305, 481
Howland, Chauncey E., 12, 464–465
Humanitarian aid operations, 509–513
Hungarian refugees, 82, 229, 510, 513
Hurst, John E., 109, 245, 247

IBM (mainframe) computers, 211, 222, 283, 496–497, 519
IG Farben, 111–112, 137, 216
Île-Bouchard, 240, 470
Île d'Oléron, 357, 400, 415
Île de Ré, 106, 358
Île St.-Germain, 8, 15–16, 138
Ingrandes QM Depot, 24, 127, 222, 461–465, 504
Initial supplies sent to France, 72
Insignias:
    2nd Aviation Co, 294–295
    26th Trans Co, 294
    322nd Air Div, 481
    ComZ, Europe, 223–224

    EUCOM, 223
    USAREUR, 223–224
Iron Curtain, 26–27, 72, 153

Jackson, Sumner W. (hero of French resistance), 50
Jardin Fontaine (See Verdun)
Jeanne d'Arc Hospital, 273, 320–321
Jerry cans, 102–104, 189, 196, 349, 356, 435
    Abandoned at Melun, 504
    Reserve supplies for NEO, 446, 459
    Sales (1966), 515
    Tank semi-trailers at Buzy, 290–291
Johnson, Lyndon B., 146, 408, 489, 492, 501
Johnson, Robert Lee, 159
Joint Construction Agency (JCA):
    Air base construction, 114–118
    Chapels, 131
    Construction freezes and bans, 113, 118, 135, 490
    Criteria for buildings, 119–120, 361
    Directors of JCA, 114
    Donges–Metz pipeline, 197–200
    Established by Ridgway, 113–114
    Hospitals, 118–119, 245–246, 259, 265
    Masonry buildings, 119–120, 122
    Northeast District, 114, 277
    Poor construction, 117–118
    Prefab structures, 120–121
    Recreation facilities, 132–134
    RGH and SCH housing, 124–128
    Sales of US buildings, 273, 515
    Theaters, 121, 132–133, 283, 446
    Tilt-up innovative wall construction, 442
    Why construction was slow, 135
Judicial referrals, 236
Juin, Alphonse–Pierre, 36, 38, 55, 57–58, 189–190, 205

Kennedy, Edward M., 43
Kennedy, John F.:
    Berlin Wall Crisis, 140, 347
    Cité Kennedy, 297
    Cuban Missile Crisis, 420, 501
    Flexible response to Soviets, 489, 515
    Funeral of, 501
    Selects Lemnitzer to succeed Norstad, 63
    Visit to Paris, 296
Khrushchev, Nikita, 139, 159, 298, 401, 501
King list, 458
Kitchen police (KP), 74, 79, 130
Knowlton, William A., 32, 57–58
Korean War, 24–26, 74, 241, 418
    Air war, 25–26, 117
    Ammo diverted to France, 25
    Mobilized units, 75–77, 90–91, 116
    Ridgway, 24, 57
Kyser, Robert C., 199, 224–225, 494, 497

La Baule, 117, 399, 416
La Chapelle Army Hospital (34th Gen Hosp), 12, 131, 155, 249, 258–262, 269
    BOQs, 129
    Elementary school, 249, 507
    French interns, 260
    Gray Ladies, 258
Lafayette, Marquis de:
    Grave at Picpus, 166–167
    L'Hermione, 360, 363
Lafayette Escadrille, 166, 318
Lafayette Village, 127–128, 465
Lagord, 104, 356–357, 406
Lake Cazaux, 342, 358
Laleu Installation, 237, 355–356, 368, 372, 404
Landing craft, mechanized (LCM):
    Higgins Industries, 369–370
    Jeehemys, 378
Landing craft, utility (LCU), 376–377, 388–389, 398
    CONEX load, 404
    In France, 413
    Towed by Soviets, 363
Landing ship dock (LSD), 384, 418
Laon AB, 91–97, 117, 160, 184–185, 187, 507
    Emergency deliveries of fuel oil to French hospitals, 107
    Escape and evasion exercise, 185
    Training French air crews for Indochina, 91
    Use during WWII, 7
La Pallice (See French ports)
Laporterie, Raoul (hero of French resistance), 4, 108
La Rochelle, 68, 99, 106, 348–357, 361
    St.–Louis Cathedral, 132
La Trinité–sur–Mer, 404–405
La Turballe, 375, 378, 397–398, 411, 413
    Landing mat tests, 401
Lebanon deployment (July 1958), 195–196, 419, 486–487
Le Clapet, 407, 413
Le Havre (See French ports)
Le Mans, 149, 310
LeMay, Curtis E., 13, 59, 181, 340
Lemnitzer, Lyman L., 27, 41–42, 63–64
    AFCENT, 190
    Bel Manoir, 149
    Closing ceremonies, 518–519
    EUCOM medical conference, 268
    Greece–Turkey conflict, 63
    Legion of Honor from De Gaulle, 515–516
    Letters from French citizens, 516
    Limoges china gift from De Gaulle, 64
    NATO achievements, 65
    On President Kennedy, 140
    Relocates SHAPE to Belgium, 502–503
    Signs secret accord with France, 517
    Western European Union, 27, 168
    Withdrawal from France, 205, 495, 515–516

Lemonnier, André Georges, 35, 52, 391
Le Pellerin Depot, 385, 415–416, 498
Les Demoiselles de Rochefort movie, 395
Les Ricains song, 516
Les Sables–d'Olonne, 367, 401–403
Le Verdon permanent NODEX site, 354, 360, 386
Levittowns in US, 125, 147
Lewis, James R., 78, 446
Libya, 182, 495
Lifeline the dog, 278–279
Lighter, amphibious, resupply, cargo (LARC), 377, 384–385, 408
Line haul relays, 216–217, 226–227, 434
Line of communications (LOC) agreement, 68–69
Lineages of General Officers:
    Advance Section, ComZ, Verdun, 279
    AFCENT at Fontainebleau, 191
    Army Attachés and DATTs in Paris, 165
    Base Section, ComZ, La Rochelle, 353
    Base Section, ComZ, Poitiers, 454
    Chiefs of MAAG, France, 169
    Deputy Commanders, USEUCOM, 141
    Supreme Allied Commanders, Europe (SACEUR), 65
    US Air Forces in Europe (USAFE), 188
    US Army, ComZ, Europe, 215
    US Army, Europe (USAREUR), 494
LIVE OAK, 139–140, 517
Living on economy, 122–123, 314, 357, 471
    Farm villages, 313, 451
    Rental house ratings, 48, 123
Local wage rate (LWR) employees:
    Awards and bonuses, 228–229, 288
    Background investigations, 153–154
    Hand shaking custom, 230
    Payroll at Chinon, 471
    Smoking cigarettes, 230, 446
    Urination habits, 113, 238
    US Army yearly total workforce, 29, 130, 199, 491
        Advance Section, 303
        Base Section, 423, 476
        Intermediate Section, 195, 205, 479, 496
    Wages, 228, 514
    Work at air bases, 96, 172, 186
    Work at Army depots:
        Medical, 267, 354
        Ordnance, 303, 311
        Quartermaster, 286–287, 417, 440
        Signal, 280–281
    Work in mess halls (KP), 130
Lodge Act soldiers, 425–426
Logistical commands, 223–225, 454–455
    1st Log Cmd, 224, 455
    3rd Log Cmd, 224–225
    4th Log Cmd, 224, 239, 279, 283, 454–455, 491
    5th Log Cmd, 224, 454
Louis Best Village (French hero of WWI), 128, 297–298

LSD drug, 158
Lycée Carnot, 179, 201
Lyon hailstorm, 510

Madame John, 313
Maggie's drawers, 73
Maginot, André, 275
Maginot Line forts, 44–46, 191–193, 275, 440
    Command posts, 192–193
Main–operating air bases (MOB), 90, 93–95
Maison–Fort, 103, 222, 226, 246–247, 514
    Chapel bell donation, 231
Maps:
    Advance Section, 274
    Air corridors to West Berlin, 22
    AWSCOM depots, 282
    Base Section, 422
    Bomb destruction, vi
    Bordeaux area, 344
    Braconne area, 444
    Chinon area, 467
    Cigarette camps, 10
    ComZ depots, 217
    Emergency ports and beaches, 414
    Fontainebleau area, 206
    German occupation zones, 2
    Iron Curtain, 26
    La Rochelle area, 347
    Maginot Line command posts, 192
    Metz area, 335
    NATO air bases in France, 178
    NATO at Palais de Chaillot and École Militaire, 53
    NEO evacuation routes, 459
    Occupied Berlin, 21
    Offshore discharge sites (1953), 374
    Offshore discharge sites (1954–62), 387
    Orléans area, 210
    Paris area, 173
    Poitiers area, 453
    Port area, 338
    Port at la Pallice, 349
    Relocation of matériel, 488
    Saumur area, 477
    SOB discharge site, 369
    St.–André area, 480
    Temporary burial grounds, 14
    Toul–Nancy area, 319
    Trois–Fontaines area, 304
    US Air Force bases in Europe, 506
    US Air Force installations in France, 94
    US Army airfields and pipelines (WWII), 6
    US Army Donges–Metz pipeline, 197
    US Army installations, 87
    US Army standby hospitals and medical depots, 254
    US Army supply lines through Germany, 66
    US military housing villages, 110
    US Third Army depots (WWII), 13
    USNS *Eltinge*'s Atlantic crossing, 80
    Verdun area, 299
    Verdun–Étain area, 289
Marbeuf building, 149–150, 515
Marguerites, 93, 97, 320
Marnes–le–Coquette, 41–42, 56, 62, 166, 204, 503
Marriages, 132, 159, 291, 454, 511
Marshall Plan, 18, 27, 48, 161, 168
Marville, 69, 184–185, 264, 314
Maschke Commission, 7
Massacre at Robert–Espagne (WWII), 100
Masuret, Robert R. (Soldier's Medal), 370
Mathewson, Lemuel, 103, 119
McAuliffe, Anthony C., 389, 494
McConnell, John P., 141, 145–146
McNamara, Robert S., 144, 187, 508, 515
    Air Force depots in UK, 499–500
    Ammo to UK, 496, 499
    Base Section reduces LWR workforce, 408
    Buyback of bombs for Vietnam, 505
    Drawdown of ComZ, 330, 364, 385, 491
    Forgets war plans, 491
    Golf course turf sent to Germany, 505
    Oversight of withdrawal, 415, 493, 495–498, 500
    US control of nukes, 63
    Walks out during official dinner in Paris, 490
Meaux, 80–81
Medical depots:
    Croix–Chapeau, 265–267, 353–354
    Fontainebleau, 194–195, 265, 267
    La Roche–sur–Yon, 194, 265, 354
    Vassincourt, 261–263, 265
    Vitry–le–François, 194–195, 267–268, 517
Medical Service Corps:
    Hospital units in France, 273
    Primary tasks, 216, 218
    Supply Control Agency, 455–456
    Training exercises, 269
Merci America Train, 18
Mess halls, 130, 226, 310, 439
    Food inspections, 351
    Truck terminals, 226
Metal dungeons, 78–79
Metal prefabs, 120–121, 468, 495
    Ammo storage, 426–427, 429, 481
    Barracks, 171, 200, 263, 333, 342, 346, 354, 416–417, 471
    Chapels, 131, 416
    Mess halls, 130–131
    Schools, 333, 364, 472
Metz QM Depot, 7, 83, 123, 328–329, 418
Michaelis, John H., 39, 63
Microwave sites, 47, 134, 145, 220–221
Miley, Henry A., 127
Military Air Transport Service (MATS), 83, 187, 232, 486, 516

Military Assistance Advisory Groups (MAAG), 161, 168–169
Military attachés, 161–165
Military Defense Assistance Program (MDAP), 168–172, 447, 449
Military liquidation section (MLS), 273, 386, 514–515
Military occupational specialty (MOS), 72, 74–75, 417, 486
Military police (MP), 10, 237, 355–356, 368
    382nd MP Bn, 237, 278
    524th MP Bn, 237, 240, 356
    202nd MP Co, 237, 457, 470
    520th MP Co, 33, 42–43, 59, 204
    16th MP Det (CI), 33, 160
    Stockades, 16, 79, 237, 284, 356
    Traffic patrols, 237, 278, 355
    Training schools, 237, 356
Military Sea Transportation Service (MSTS), 82–83, 374, 408, 418, 420
MILSTRIP, 222, 283
MOBIDIC computer, 223
Mobile dental units, 234, 276
Moch, Jules, 40, 85, 89
Modern Army Supply System (MASS), 423
Mont Morillon, 146
Montgomery, Bernard Law, 36, 59
    Brussels Treaty war plans, 28, 32, 36
    Château de Courances, 204
    CPX One, 204–205
Montlieu-la-Garde monument (WWII), 437
Montluçon, 459, 510
Montmorillon, 240, 504
Montreuil-Bellay Depot, 157, 448, 475–476
Moonlight requisitions, 288, 291
Moroccan floods, 511–512
Moselle Control, 193
Moulin des Bechets, 158, 247–248
Murray, Gordon W. (Soldier's Medal), 293
Murrow, Edward R., 31, 118
Mustard chemical agent, 270, 305
Mutual Weapons Development Program (MWDP), 169
MV *John U.D. Page*, 402–403, 408, 420

Nancy Ordnance Depot, 81, 169, 324–326, 418
    Nancy Staffing Plan, 228
    Red Cross Center, 257
Navy, Army, and Air Force Institute (NAAFI), 40–41
NEO (Noncombatant evacuation order), 457–460 (See *also* evacuation of noncombatants)
Netherlands flood relief, 479, 509–510
Neuilly-sur-Seine, 16, 50–51, 163, 166, 256, 261, 264
New offshore discharge exercises (NODEX), 385–412
    Ammo lost at sea, 397
    Army JAGs, 386
    Chime loads of POL drums, 389
    Combat tanks, 405–406
    Fire in medical tent at le Verdon, 389
    Floating platform under cranes, 388
    French Army participation, 400, 404, 406
    Helicopters transport cargo, 397
    Hurricane destroys floating pier, 404–405
    Innovations tested, 409–410
    Jumpers between DUKWs, 370
    Rockets transported by railcars, 392
    Ships participating, 411–412
    Trucks on lighterage receive cargo, 391
Nice, 17, 181, 344, 493
Nightclub, 44
Niort, 128, 196, 358–359, 431
Nixon, Richard M., 501
Normandy Base Section (WWII), 12
Norstad, Lauris, 36, 54, 59, 61–63, 166–167, 179–181
    AAFCE, 60, 179–189
    Briefs De Gaulle on nukes, 490
    Establishes LIVE OAK, 139–140
    Fourth of July ceremony, 167
    Hôtel Cadran Bleu, 179
    NATO achievements, 65
    Norstad Pause, 63
North Atlantic Council (NAC), 28, 31, 58, 168
    Ike at 1957 Paris meetings, 46
    Palais de Chaillot, 54
    Secure messages, 47
North Atlantic Treaty Organization (NATO), 27–29
    ACE HIGH, 47–48, 517
    AGARD, 164
    Airfields in France, 90, 178
    Central Army Group (CENTAG), 193, 224
    Closing ceremonies, 518–519
    Cost of buildup, 31, 112
    Defense College, 52–53
    Dependents schools, 150–151, 201
    Family housing, 147, 202
    Headquarters, 53–55
    LANDCENT, 203, 503
    MWDP, 169
    NADGE, 517
    Nuclear weapons, 59, 61, 281–282
    SHAPE permanent headquarters, 39–41
    SHAPE relocates to Belgium, 502–503
    SHAPE Village, 43, 48–50, 148
    Soviet spies, 138–139, 159
    Standardization program, 38–39
    Village Faisanderie, 202–203
    War plans, 36–37
    Withdrawal from France, 54, 205, 502–503
North Sea floods, 267–268, 479, 509–512
Nuclear survival kits, 269

OAS (*Organisation de l'Armée Secrète*), 106–107, 146, 190
Occupation forces in Germany, 16, 19
Offshore discharge exercises (ODEX), 371–380
    Classes, 373

Cocooned cargo, 375
PSP, 375, 377–378
Rough-terrain forklift, 373–374
Shipping containers (CONEX), 376–377, 379
O'Hare, Joseph J., 37, 165
OLAM Detachment, 331
Olivet, 127, 158, 246–250, 486–487
WACs, 231, 239, 246
O'Meara, Andrew P., 199
Berlin Airlift, 13, 424
Operation FRELOC, 494, 496, 505
O'Neill, Edward J., 215n, 224, 250, 486
Open houses, 201, 230, 334, 384, 435
Operations:
Big Lift, 187, 312, 492
Blue Bat, 195–196, 419, 486–487
Chaos, 497
Counter Punch, 190
Fadeout, 8
FRELOC, 434, 493–509, 514–519
Grand Slam, 144, 181
Killer, 57
Little Vittles, 23
Long Thrust, 190, 491–492
Mudball, 111
Mudlark II, 428
Paperclip, 152
Power Pack, 408
Red Richard, 186, 320–321, 359
Rollback, 27, 47, 426, 430
Roundout, 141–145, 224, 423, 471, 476
Sand, 368
Snowbound, 510
Stair Step, 143–144, 294
Vittles, 21–24
Ordnance Corps, 216, 218
72nd Ord Bn, 281
343rd Ord Bn, 323
39th Ord Co, 84–85, 107, 159, 241, 287–288, 312
547th Ord Co, 240, 382, 451
565th Ord Co, 281, 324
574th Ord Co, 443
586th Ord Co, 24, 245
Ordnance depots:
Braconne, 169, 442–449, 509
Captieux, 424–431
Fontenet, 169, 447–451
Nancy, 169, 228, 294, 324–326
Trois-Fontaines, 302–309, 431, 506
Orleans Area Command (OAC), 227, 230, 242, 247
Orléans, liberation of (WWII), 211–212, 249
Secrétan, Roger, 231, 516
Orly AB, 39, 83, 93, 147, 159, 163, 257, 516
Orly Field, 17, 28, 32, 245, 255
Orville the Otter, 294–295
OSI (Office of Special Investigations), 160

PAL Detachment, 244–245
Paladin van, 144
Palais de Chaillot, 53–54
Palletized cargo, 371–372, 375, 379, 386, 397
Palmer, Williston B., 62, 139, 141, 167, 334
Para-rescue airmen, 341
Paris Air Passenger Service, 83
Paris Air Show, 163, 500
Paris Blockhouse, 32, 46–47, 480
Paris train stations (*gares*), 99
Pater noster elevators, 137
Patton Athletic Field, 247
Patton combat tanks, 140, 169, 187, 325, 420, 443
Pau, 133, 481
Pauillac, 104, 196, 378, 391, 397–398
Peckham, Howard L., 15–16
Command of 7966 Det, 70–71
Perfume City, 313
Périgueux QM Depot, 106, 125, 439–440, 479
Chapel built by GIs, 440
Humanitarian aid to the Netherlands, 510
NEO staging area, 460
Revolt of generals in Algeria, 245
Pershing Hall, 150
Pershing Village, 128
Personnel over the beach exercises (POB), 116, 373, 381, 400
Pessac, 342–343, 438
Petit Beauregard, 126, 148
Petroleum Distribution Command:
Camp Bussac, 435
Caserne Lariboisière, 169, 196, 201
Donges-Metz pipeline, 197–200, 515, 517
LWR employees, 199, 417
Melun Terminal District, 197, 200, 500, 504
Pipeline schools, 169, 196, 469–470
Tank farms, 198–200, 312, 417
TRAPIL, 197–198, 200
Petroleum, oil, lubricants (POL), 104–105, 196–200
Depots, 105, 290–291, 356, 435
Pipelines (WWII), 6, 12
Storage tanks, 200
Temporary storage, 104–105, 356
Phalsbourg AB, 93–95, 128, 133, 187
Damage during FRELOC, 504
Friendliest base in France, 95, 509
German bunker, 118
Phonetic alphabet, 73
Pierced steel plank (PSP):
Ammo support expedient, 427
Cold War use, 7, 13, 140, 171, 269, 378, 436, 468
Development and use (WWII), 5–7, 17, 318
Theft of, 504–505
Use on beaches, 368, 375–378, 389, 393, 397, 401
Pissoirs, 238
Plan HEADRACE, 328–329

Pleven, René, 48, 55, 180, 197
Point system for discharge (WWII), 8
Poitiers, 107, 296, 453–457, 460–461
Poitiers Golf Association (PGA), 461
Polish Labor Service (LS), 72, 153, 423, 425
    Captieux depot, 425–426, 430
    CIC security investigations, 72, 153
    Green car gang, 307, 330
    Guard dogs, 276, 308, 324, 351
    Guards at TFAD and Rozelier, 291, 305–306
    Jardin Fontaine barracks, 122, 283
    Saumur barracks, 122, 472–473
    Units in France (1964), 306
    Withdrawal from France, 493
Pontoon cubes, 37, 373–374, 404–406
Ponzi, Carlo, 515
Poopy suits, 185
Popeye, 498, 501
Pornichet, 418
Port Haliguen, 373–374, 398–399
Porte Chaussée, 284–285
Porte Dauphine, 54–55
Pouilly POL Depot, 104–105, 328
POVs, 122, 416
    ComZ regulations, 227, 230
    License plates, 227, 307, 416, 516
    Shipment to and from US, 348, 350
    Use for NEOs, 457–458
Prisoner of war enclosures (German PWs), 7
Project CARAVAN, 124
Project EULOC, 493
Project GEORGE, 449
Project NATIVE SON, 172
Project SWAPPO, 324
Projects FASTDRAW and ZIP, 517
PTSD (Post-traumatic stress disorder), 241
Public bathhouses, 303, 320

Quartermaster (QM) Corps, 216, 218
    Aerial Support Center, 479–484
    Army's master menus, 130
    Bakery units, 248, 275, 287, 350, 433, 462
    Camp Bussac, 435
    Ingrandes QM Depot, 461–465, 504
    Laundry services, 248, 277, 329, 351, 368, 462
    Metz QM Depot, 328–329
    Périgueux QM Depot, 439–440, 510
    SAMEC at St.-Pryvé, 15, 122, 217, 225, 248
    Woippy QM Depot, 328, 330
Queuille, Henri, 86
Quiberon, 339, 373–374, 381, 386, 398–400, 415
Quonset huts, 93, 116, 325, 464, 494
    Quontown at Châteauroux, 171
    Shipped from US to St.-Nazaire, 121

Radiac sets (Geiger counters), 270, 333, 476

Radiation surveys, 269–270, 333, 435, 476
Radio relay sites, 47, 188, 220–221, 346
Rail terminals, 100
Rail Transportation Offices (RTO), 99–100, 343
RAMPS (Recovered Allied Military Personnel), 10
Randolph, A. Philip, 85
Randolph mouse, 235
Ratinaud, Mme. Adrien (rescue of cow), 106
Reagan, Ronald, 517
Recreation, 132–134, 296–297, 429–430
Red Ball Express, 101–102, 226, 375, 432
    At night, 497–498
    Hollywood movie, 102
Reefer trucks, 227, 497
Regina Village (heroine of French resistance), 322
Rental guarantee housing (RGH), 125–128
Retreat formations, 196, 242, 443
Rice, Mary Ann, 239, 246
Ridgway, Matthew B., 24, 57–58, 325
    Atomic bombs, 58, 179
    Ending segregation, 85
    Establishes JCA, 58, 113–114
    EUCOM commander, 58, 137
    Flag presentation, 132
    Inspections and farewell at Bordeaux, 58, 342–343
    Korean War, 24, 57, 85
    NATO achievements, 65
    Ridgway Go Home signs, 57, 81
Road safety patrols (TC), 103, 290, 326
Roadeos, 227–228, 319
Robert-Espagne, 60, 100, 302–306, 309–311
Robinson, Bernard L., 114, 119, 127
Rochambeau Village, 125, 472
Rochefort Arsenal, 360–364, 384, 415, 504–505
    Gaury, Francis, 505
Rochonvillers, 44–45, 192–193
Rocquencourt, 43–44, 126
Rod & Gun Clubs, 146, 297, 314
Roll on roll off ships (RORO), 402–408, 413, 418–420
    Atlantic fleet, 420
    USNS *Comet*, 402, 404–407, 419
    USNS *Taurus*, 418
Roller conveyors, 303, 389, 401, 405, 429, 484
RONTU (Relocation of non-tactical units), 219, 491
Rough-terrain forklifts, 373–374, 385, 400–401, 404, 406–408, 462
Rowny, Edward L., 42, 52, 61
    FRELOC, 494–495, 499, 505
    GAO and Army JAGs, 495
    Nuclear policy, 61
Royal Canadian Air Force (RCAF), 179, 181, 264
    Metz, 29, 193
    Station Grostenquin, 184–185
    Station Marville, 69, 184–185, 314
    Troops in France, 29
Royan, 3, 244, 357, 368, 386, 388, 393, 407

Rozelier Air Field, 107, 294–296, 310
Rozelier Ammunition Depot, 134, 291–292
Rusk, Dean, 492

SAC (Strategic Air Command), 36, 59, 117, 179, 181, 186, 188, 205
Sacred Way, 302
Safe driver awards, 102, 226, 319, 433
Sampigny Chemical Depot, 121, 270, 332–334
    Church bell, 333
    Vautrin, Mme. Georges, 334
Saran, 24, 102, 121, 154, 214, 245
    Air Field, 245
    Radio relay, 216, 220–221
    Reefer trucks, 227
Sardou, Michel, 516
Saumur Signal Depot, 157, 472–476, 494
Scissor–frame spreader for cargo slings, 379
Sea islands, 389, 393–395
Sea mules, 373
Second story job, 156
Secondary depots, 141, 220, 326, 469
Security classifications, 38
Segregated units in France, 84–85
Seine Area Command, 138–139, 147, 150, 247
Seventh Army, 19, 169, 211, 223, 428
    Chemical and nuclear weapons, 244, 281, 332
    Logistics requirements, 70, 216, 220, 280
    RONTU, 219
Shakedown inspections, 504
Shakeout towers, 481
SHAPE Command Post, 44–45
    ACE HIGH, 47–48, 517
SHAPE Village, 48–50, 148
Shaw AFB, 187, 507
Shipping containers (CONEX), 376–377, 379, 408
Shock pads, 482–484
Shoot and scoot, 60
Siberia of France, 425
Sick call, 43, 195, 256, 269, 484
Signal Corps, 216, 219
    1st Sig Group, 246
    7th Sig Bn, 42–43, 59
    29th Sig Bn (THQ), 145, 440
    102nd Sig Bn, 220–221
    228th Sig Co, 221
    256th Sig Co, 283
    269th Sig Co, 222, 242
    275th Sig Co, 196
    Caserne Lariboisière, 196
    Caserne Voyer, 447–448, 475
    Saumur Signal Depot, 472–476
    Verdun Signal Depot, 280–281
Silk Purse, 144–145
Silverplate bombers, 20
Single Integrated Operational Plan (SIOP), 186

Size of Army Installations, 337, 431, 479
Smart, Jacob E.:
    Bomb at Toulon ceremony, 64
    Camp des Loges, 155–156
    Dien Bien Phu, 169
    EUCOM Commander, 141, 146–147
    Pierrelatte overflights, 162
SNCF train service, 99, 427, 500
    Ammo explosions at Châlons, 103
    Brief stop at Poitiers, 460
    ComZ general's railcar diverted, 272
    De Gaulle's railcar at Braconne, 445
    Deliveries to Ingrandes, 462
    Depots and ports, 324, 330, 348, 363, 468
    OAS derails Strasbourg–Paris Express, 106–107
    Railcars at offshore exercises, 371, 391–392, 397, 400
Snoopy as the FRELOC mascot, 498
Snow cruiser, 384
Sommesous, 100, 104, 312
Soulac–sur–Mer, 354, 368, 397, 407
    Elementary school, 386
    Transportation units, 360, 389, 399
Special Category Personnel with Air Force (SCARWAF), 116–117, 184, 373, 381
Special Forces, 46–47, 426, 480–481
Special Services, 129, 203–204, 235–236
    Libraries, 134, 204, 250, 440
    Photo shops, 133
    Swimming pools, 189, 326
Spratley, Albert W., 234
Sprayberry, Rufus B. (flying chaplain), 296
Square–mesh matting (SMT), 5
SS *Newcastle Victory*, 500
St.–André QM Aerial Support Center, 47, 216, 479–485
St.–Ay Engineer Map Depot, 241, 249
St.–Baussant Tank Farm, 74, 198–199, 279
St.–Cloud Schools, 150–151, 515
St.–Dizier, 5, 159, 219, 303, 314
St.–Eulien, 303
St.–Georges–de–Didonne, 369, 404–405, 407
St.–Germain–en–Laye, 56, 71, 137, 150
    EUCOM closing ceremony, 518
    Letter to Lemnitzer, 516
    SHAPE Village, 48–50
    Underground bunker, 44
St.–Gilles–Croix–de–Vie, 399
St.–Jean d'Angély, 448–449, 451
St.–Jean–de–Braye, 126, 153–154, 216, 250, 272
St.–Jean–de–Luz, 12, 367, 386, 396–397, 406, 413
St.–Laurent–de–Céris, 447
St.–Mihiel, 96, 133, 303, 333
St.–Nazaire, 4, 116–117, 416 (See *also* French ports)
St.–Pryvé–St.–Mesmin, 122, 217, 225, 248
St.–Sulpice–et–Cameyrac, 86, 104–105, 433
Stalin, Joseph, 24, 26, 171
Star of David, 3

Stars and Stripes, 160, 234
Statue of Liberty Wing, 93–95
Status of Forces Agreements (SOFA), 38, 156–157, 214, 228, 236, 306, 508
Stay behinds, 27, 47, 426, 430
Ste.–Mere–Église, 7, 165, 358, 484
Stock Control Division, 246, 283
Stockades, 16, 79, 237, 284, 356
    USAFE facilities, 93, 237
Storage sites (See Technical Services)
Sturgis, Samuel D., 72, 113, 363
    Chinon inspections, 467–468
    Communist vandalism, 341
    Guards shoot at civilians, 234, 306
    Hospital locations, 262
    JCA oversees construction, 113–114
    Land for EUCOM, 137
    Living conditions in France, 214
    Mess hall at Verdun, 278
    Replaces Young at ComZ, 214
    Wearing of uniforms, 428
Suippes Gunnery Range, 182–183, 294, 504
Supplies to France (1950–51), 72
Supply Control Agencies, 81, 159, 222, 455
Supply and Maintenance Agency (S&MA), 283, 496–497, 514, 519
    Dupuch, Pierre, 514
Supply over the beach (SOB):
    Beach site preparations, 368
    First SOB, 369–370
    Permission to hold exercises, 368
    Proposed landing beaches, 367
Support Operations Task Force, Europe (SOTFE), 46–47, 480, 503
Supreme Allied Commander, Europe (SACEUR), 31
Suresnes, 33, 43, 71, 138, 166, 492
Surf deflector on cranes, 389
Surplus commodity housing (SCH), 124–128
Survival, Escape, and Evasion, 185
Suscinio, 378, 397–401, 413
    Landing mat tests, 401
Sweeney, Charles W., 95, 144n
Swimming pools, 43, 139, 146, 191, 204
    Army divers, 356
    Water survival, 185
Swing bridges, 37, 247, 470

Tables of locations for units and activities:
    Air Force bases in France, 98–99
    Army hospitals, 273
    Bordeaux, 345–346
    Braconne–Fontenet, 452
    Bussac–Captieux–Périgueux, 441–442
    Chinon–Saumur, 478
    Fontainebleau, 207–209
    La Rochelle–Rochefort, 365–366
    Metz, 336–337
    Nancy–Toul, 327–328
    Orléans, 251–253
    Paris, 174–177
    Poitiers–Ingrandes, 466–467
    St.–André, 485
    St.–Nazaire, 421
    Trois–Fontaines, 316–317
    Verdun, 300–302
Talleyrand building, 161, 169, 386, 514
Talmont, 391–396, 415, 514
Taylor, Maxwell D., 325
Technical services, 216–219
    Chiefs, 224
    Schools in US, 75
    Secondary depot sites, 220, 326, 469
    Size of installations, 337, 431, 479
Tegel airfield (Berlin), 21, 24
Telephones in France, 123, 127–128, 250, 324, 346, 451
Tempelhof airport (Berlin), 21–23
Temporary burials of Americans (WWII), 13–16
Tents:
    Concealed headquarters for EUCOM, 146
    Flying canvas, 353, 425
    Hospitals, 269, 354
    NEO tent camps, 460
    Villages (Mud City), 171, 214, 291, 303, 342–343, 368, 393, 433, 467
    Winterized, 9, 58, 111–112, 286, 317, 342, 353–354
The Longest Day movie, 358
Theater Army Support Command (TASCOM), 224, 454
Thornwell, James R., 158–159
Thumper the leak detector, 311
Tinny Weenie Airline (TWA), 245
Tito, Josip Broz, 171
Toss bombing, 144, 183
Toul Engineer Depot, 157, 285, 290, 318–322
Toul–Rosières AB, 117–118, 124, 186–187, 235, 325, 490, 504, 510
    Electronic bell in chapel, 131
    RB–66C shot down by Soviets, 184
    Use during WWII, 7, 90
Tour de France, 437
Tours, 90, 100, 133, 272, 397, 461, 470, 472, 510
Towveyer, 171–172
Trailer parks, 116, 124–125, 297, 332, 515
Training (See combat training)
Transportation Corps (TC), 216–217, 219
    9th Trans Group, 102, 225
    594th Trans Group, 99, 103, 246, 347, 386, 400
    11th Terminal Trans Command, 156, 353, 361, 375, 407
    37th Trans Command, 217, 225–228, 244, 275, 347, 400, 417, 497–498, 505
    2nd Trans Bn, 227, 290, 433
    28th Trans Bn, 226, 389, 456–457, 460, 498, 517
    106th Trans Bn, 226, 420, 434, 498

109th Trans Truck Bn, 290, 319–320
22nd Trans Co, 43–44
55th Trans Co, 104, 196, 198, 200, 291, 433, 435, 446
72nd Trans Co, 84, 227, 326, 433
Camp Bussac, 433–434
Treadway bridges, 378, 397–398, 404–406, 408, 450
Trois–Fontaines, 60, 100, 103, 302–317, 360
BOQs, 129, 310
Command Center, 310–312
Medical clinics, 310
Sarin storage, 311
St.–Hubert, 328–329
Stolen ammo, 307
Wives club, 315
Troop information newspapers, 234–236, 302
Advance, 234, 279, 283
BASEC Mission, 234
BAU Banner, 12
Bordeaux Traveler, 235
CHAD News, 235
ComZ Cadence, 154, 234
Eltinge Crier, 80–81
Goldbrick, 10
La Foret, 234
Laon Sentinel, 160
Nancy Times, 234
Orleans Item, 234
Pariscope, 234
Skyliner, 158
Sturgis Barnacle, 79
Toul Tiger, 235
Troopships, 77–82
Cabin class passengers, 81–82
Duty assignments, 79
Troop compartments, 78–79
Troopship newspapers, 79–80
Truman, Harry S., 20, 26–27, 31–32, 38, 68, 85, 152, 159, 476
Tunnels under Orléans, 109
Tunner, William H., 21, 23, 124
Two–man rule, 245, 281

Uncle Wiggly Wings, 23
Uniform Code of Military Justice (UCMJ), 129, 159, 238
UNITEX boxes, 397, 400, 402
University of Maryland Overseas, 235, 267
Unknown Soldier (WWII), 283
US Air Forces in Europe (USAFE), 24
Air attachés, 163–164
Air base construction in France, 114–118
Aircrews sent to Korea, 91
Commanders, 188
Confinement facilities, 93, 237
Depots in France, 96
Dual–basing, 507
Moselle Control, 193
Office of Special Investigations (OSI), 160

Paris liaison office, 150
Primary aircraft in France, 98–99
Quick reaction alerts, 144
RB–66C from TRAB shot down by Soviets, 184
Reconnaissance overflights in France, 162
Redeployments, 186, 507
Sites in France, 92, 94–96, 98
Vehicles, 499–500
US Ambassadors to France, 161
US Army Advance Weapons Support Command (AWSCOM), 281–282, 291, 295–296
US Army Construction Agency, France, 134–135, 263
US Army Counter Intelligence Corps (CIC), 151–160
Axmann conspiracy, 151
CIC school, 152, 157–158, 291
Classified documents, 155
Commanders in France, 160
Confinement of Thornwell, 158–159
Gehlen Group, 151–152
Penetration tests, 155–156
Polygraph exams, 154
SHAPE Unit, 33, 153, 156, 160, 204
Vehicles, 155
US Army, Europe (USAREUR), 61, 123, 137, 211
AG Publications and Records Center, 341
Berlin Wall crisis, 140–143
Commanders, 494
Deutsche mark (DM) program, 122
Engineer map depots, 249, 340–341
Nuclear response, 63
Operation BIG LIFT, 187, 312, 492
OPLAN 704–61, 222
Technical Service Chiefs, 224
Technical Services Schools in Europe, 169
Underground bunkers, 193, 246, 440
Wartime hospitals, 264–265
Woippy Depot Sergeant held prisoner by Czechs, 330
Yearly troop totals, 29
US Army Soldier's Medal, 231, 293, 370
US Constabulary in Germany, 16, 19
US Embassy Paris, 161
US European Command (EUCOM):
Camp des Loges, 137–138, 144–146, 189, 503
Closing ceremonies in France, 518
Commanders, 58, 141
Congressional visits, 358
Flag negotiations and ceremonies, 107–108
French excluded from contracts, 490
Line of communications (LOC), 85–86
LIVE OAK group, 139–140, 517
MAAGs, 168–169
Move to Germany, 503
OAS attack, 146
Prefabs rejected, 111
Property Account Office, 230
Seine Area Command, 138–139, 147, 150, 247

US Army supply classifications, 220
U.S. Go Home signs, 34, 172, 244, 341, 349, 439, 516
US Navy Sixth Fleet, 181, 493
US State Department, 27, 31, 135, 150–151, 161, 163, 363, 476, 492
Usine Bertrand, 354, 356
Usine Jeumont, 348, 350–351, 356, 404, 439
USNS *Comet*, 402, 404–407, 419–420
USNS *Marine Fiddler*, 156–157, 498–499
USNS *Taurus*, 418, 420
USO (United Service Organizations), 40, 51, 150, 344
USS *Neversail*, 408

Vassincourt, 86, 100, 261, 286, 337
    Field hospital units, 262–263, 278
    Guard dog kennels, 308
    Medical depot, 262, 265
Vatry:
    ABREST storage, 134, 281, 431
    Air Force DOB, 96
    Line haul terminal, 226–227
    Tank farm, 199, 312, 337
VD Clinics, 238
Vehicle accidents, 101, 103, 122, 302
Vélizy–Villacoublay, 5, 17, 39, 190
Verdun, 121, 129, 221, 269, 275–299, 509
    Chicago Area Depot, 286–288, 291, 293
    Jardin Fontaine, 119, 122, 283–284, 296
    Krieger, Georges, 298
    Seng, Antoine, 288
    Signal Depot, 229, 280–281
Verdun Army Hospital (See Désandrouins Barracks)
Versailles:
    Caserne Limoges, 31, 34, 43, 59, 89
    Red Ball Express, 101
    SHAPE headquarters, 33, 39–41
    450th CIC, 153–154
Veterinarian food inspections, 149, 351, 371, 416
Vichy government, 1, 3–4, 50
Victor Alerts, 185–186
Victory ships, 8, 411–413
Villa Bellune, 203
Villa les Charmes, 246
Villa Lavaurs, 201–202
Villa St.–Pierre, 41–42, 56, 61–62, 64, 503
Villa la Tourelle, 246, 250
Villa Valençay, 147
Village Faisanderie, 202–203
Villefranche-sur-Mer, 181, 493
Vitry-le-François, 153, 194–195, 257, 265, 517
    Medical depot, 267–268
    OAS derails Strasbourg–Paris Express, 106–107

WACs (Women's Army Corps), 33–34, 43, 138, 179, 246
    Field training exercises, 239
    Support of orphanages, 231, 439

Walkie–talkies, 287, 474
Walter tractors, 404, 407, 418, 420
Walters, Vernon A., 32, 165, 501
War game HOSTAGE BLEU, 62
War plans OFFTACKLE and IRONBARK, 36–37
Water supply, 356, 430, 467
    97th Eng Bn, 107, 298
    982nd Eng Bn, 231
    687th Eng Co, 343, 354
    28th Water Sup Det, 451
Water survival, 185, 341–342
Watercraft fleet in France, 413, 415
Wayne, John (Hollywood actor), 106, 358, 360
Weadock, Thomas A.:
    Establishes TC Depot at Bussac, 432
    French tourist visit, 70
    Monument at Montlieu (WWII), 437
Western Base Section (WWII), 12
Western European Union, 27, 38, 168
    Montgomery, Bernard Law, 36, 204
    War plans, 28, 36
Westmoreland, William C., 501
Westphalinger, Henry R., 224, 247, 250, 346, 471
Wet storage basins, 363, 415–416
Wheelus AB, Libya, 182, 495
Whipple, William, 156, 308
    BASEC Commander, 454
    Housing on economy, 461
    NODEX exercises, 398–400
Wimpy wagon, 498
Winch farm, 380, 408
Wives clubs, 315, 326, 439, 464
Woippy QM Depot, 307, 328, 330, 332
Woodward, William R.:
    ADSEC song, 278
    Lifeline the dog, 278–279
    Medals for rescue efforts, 293
    Security at TFAD, 307–309
Woolnough, James K., 106, 156, 397, 454
World War II deserter, 284

Yad Vashem Institute, 4
Yeager, Charles E., 490
Yorktown Village, 313–314
Young, Mason J., 16, 212–214
    Construction disguised as training, 72
    Flags at Caserne Coligny, 109
    Hôtel Astoria, 71, 212
    Negotiates logistics buildup, 68–69

Zweibrücken, 196, 200, 214, 223, 497, 503–504